APPLIED MULTIVARIATE STA
FOR THE SOCIAL SCIENCES

Now in its 6th edition, the authoritative textbook *Applied Multivariate Statistics for the Social Sciences*, continues to provide advanced students with a practical and conceptual understanding of statistical procedures through examples and data-sets from actual research studies. With the added expertise of co-author Keenan Pituch (University of Texas-Austin), this 6th edition retains many key features of the previous editions, including its breadth and depth of coverage, a review chapter on matrix algebra, applied coverage of MANOVA, and emphasis on statistical power. In this new edition, the authors continue to provide practical guidelines for checking the data, assessing assumptions, interpreting, and reporting the results to help students analyze data from their own research confidently and professionally.

Features new to this edition include:

- NEW chapter on Logistic Regression (Ch. 11) that helps readers understand and use this very flexible and widely used procedure
- NEW chapter on Multivariate Multilevel Modeling (Ch. 14) that helps readers understand the benefits of this "newer" procedure and how it can be used in conventional and multilevel settings
- NEW Example Results Section write-ups that illustrate how results should be presented in research papers and journal articles
- NEW coverage of missing data (Ch. 1) to help students understand and address problems associated with incomplete data
- Completely re-written chapters on Exploratory Factor Analysis (Ch. 9), Hierarchical Linear Modeling (Ch. 13), and Structural Equation Modeling (Ch. 16) with increased focus on understanding models and interpreting results
- NEW analysis summaries, inclusion of more syntax explanations, and reduction in the number of SPSS/SAS dialogue boxes to guide students through data analysis in a more streamlined and direct approach
- Updated syntax to reflect newest versions of IBM SPSS (21) /SAS (9.3)

- A free online resources site www.routledge.com/9780415836661 with data sets and syntax from the text, additional data sets, and instructor's resources (including PowerPoint lecture slides for select chapters, a conversion guide for 5th edition adopters, and answers to exercises).

Ideal for advanced graduate-level courses in education, psychology, and other social sciences in which multivariate statistics, advanced statistics, or quantitative techniques courses are taught, this book also appeals to practicing researchers as a valuable reference. Pre-requisites include a course on factorial ANOVA and covariance; however, a working knowledge of matrix algebra is not assumed.

Keenan Pituch is Associate Professor in the Quantitative Methods Area of the Department of Educational Psychology at the University of Texas at Austin.

James P. Stevens is Professor Emeritus at the University of Cincinnati.

APPLIED MULTIVARIATE STATISTICS FOR THE SOCIAL SCIENCES

Analyses with SAS and IBM's SPSS

Sixth edition

Keenan A. Pituch and James P. Stevens

NEW YORK AND LONDON

Sixth edition published 2016
by Routledge
711 Third Avenue, New York, NY 10017

and by Routledge
2 Park Square, Milton Park, Abingdon, Oxon, OX14 4RN

Routledge is an imprint of the Taylor & Francis Group, an informa business

Fifth edition published by Routledge 2009

Library of Congress Cataloging-in-Publication Data
Pituch, Keenan A.
   Applied multivariate statistics for the social sciences / Keenan A. Pituch and James
P. Stevens — 6th edition.
      pages cm
   Previous edition by James P. Stevens.
   Includes index.
   1. Multivariate analysis. 2. Social sciences—Statistical methods.   I. Stevens, James (James
Paul)   II. Title.
   QA278.S74 2015
   519.5'350243—dc23
   2015017536

ISBN 13: 978-0-415-83666-1(pbk)
ISBN 13: 978-0-415-83665-4(hbk)
ISBN 13: 978-1-315-81491-9(ebk)

Typeset in Times New Roman
by Apex CoVantage, LLC

Commissioning Editor: Debra Riegert
Textbook Development Manager: Rebecca Pearce
Project Manager: Sheri Sipka
Production Editor: Alf Symons
Cover Design: Nigel Turner
Companion Website Manager: Natalya Dyer
Copyeditor: Apex CoVantage, LLC

Printed and bound in the United States of America by Sheridan Books, Inc. (a Sheridan Group Company).

Keenan would like to dedicate this:
To his Wife: Elizabeth and
To his Children: Joseph and Alexis

Jim would like to dedicate this:
To his Grandsons: Henry and Killian and
To his Granddaughter: Fallon

CONTENTS

PREFACE

The first five editions of this text have been received warmly, and we are grateful for that.

This edition, like previous editions, is written for those who use, rather than develop, advanced statistical methods. The focus is on conceptual understanding rather than proving results. The narrative and many examples are there to promote understanding, and a chapter on matrix algebra is included for those who need the extra help. Throughout the book, you will find output from SPSS (version 21) and SAS (version 9.3) with interpretations. These interpretations are intended to demonstrate what analysis results mean in the context of a research example and to help you interpret analysis results properly. In addition to demonstrating how to use the statistical programs effectively, our goal is to show you the importance of examining data, assessing statistical assumptions, and attending to sample size issues so that the results are generalizable. The text also includes end-of-chapter exercises for many chapters, which are intended to promote better understanding of concepts and have you obtain additional practice in conducting analyses and interpreting results. Detailed answers to the odd-numbered exercises are included in the back of the book so you can check your work.

NEW TO THIS EDITION

Many changes were made in this edition of the text, including a new lead author of the text. In 2012, Dr. Keenan Pituch of the University of Texas at Austin, along with Dr. James Stevens, developed a plan to revise this edition and began work. The goals in revising the text were to provide more guidance on practical matters related to data analysis, update the text in terms of the statistical procedures used, and firmly align those procedures with findings from methodological research.

Key changes to this edition are:

- Inclusion of analysis summaries and example results sections
- Focus on just two software programs (SPSS version 21 and SAS version 9.3)

- New chapters on Binary Logistic Regression (Chapter 11) and Multivariate Multilevel Modeling (Chapter 14)
- Completely rewritten chapters on structural equation modeling (SEM), exploratory factor analysis, and hierarchical linear modeling.

ANALYSIS SUMMARIES AND EXAMPLE RESULTS SECTIONS

The analysis summaries provide a convenient guide for the analysis activities we generally recommend you use when conducting data analysis. Of course, to carry out these activities in a meaningful way, you have to understand the underlying statistical concepts—something that we continue to promote in this edition. The analysis summaries and example results sections will also help you tie together the analysis activities involved for a given procedure and illustrate how you may effectively communicate analysis results.

The analysis summaries and example results sections are provided for several techniques. Specifically, they are provided and applied to examples for the following procedures: one-way MANOVA (sections 6.11–6.13), two-way MANOVA (sections 7.6–7.8), one-way MANCOVA (example 8.4 and sections 8.15 and 8.17), exploratory factor analysis (sections 9.12, 9.17, and 9.18), discriminant analysis (sections 10.7.1, 10.7.2, 10.8, 10.14, and 10.15), and binary logistic regression (sections 11.19 and 11.20).

FOCUS ON SPSS AND SAS

Another change that has been implemented throughout the text is to focus the use of software on two programs: SPSS (version 21) and SAS (version 9.3). Previous editions of this text, particularly for hierarchical linear modeling (HLM) and structural equation modeling applications, have introduced additional programs for these purposes. However, in this edition, we use only SPSS and SAS because these programs have improved capability to model data from more complex designs, and reviewers of this edition expressed a preference for maintaining software continuity throughout the text. This continuity essentially eliminates the need to learn (and/or teach) additional software programs (although we note there are many other excellent programs available). Note, though, that for the structural equation modeling chapter SAS is used exclusively, as SPSS requires users to obtain a separate add on module (AMOS) for such analyses. In addition, SPSS and SAS syntax and output have also been updated as needed throughout the text.

NEW CHAPTERS

Chapter 11 on binary logistic regression is new to this edition. We included the chapter on logistic regression, a technique that Alan Agresti has called the "most important model for categorical response data," due to the widespread use of this procedure in the social sciences, given its ability to readily incorporate categorical and continuous predictors in modeling a categorical response. Logistic regression can be used for explanation and classification, with each of these uses illustrated in the chapter. With the inclusion of this new chapter, the former chapter on Categorical Data Analysis: The Log Linear Model has been moved to the website for this text.

Chapter 14 on multivariate multilevel modeling is another new chapter for this edition. This chapter is included because this modeling procedure has several advantages over the traditional MANOVA procedures that appear in Chapters 4–6 and provides another alternative to analyzing data from a design that has a grouping variable and several continuous outcomes (with discriminant analysis providing yet another alternative). The advantages of multivariate multilevel modeling are presented in Chapter 14, where we also show that the newer modeling procedure can replicate the results of traditional MANOVA. Given that we introduce this additional and flexible modeling procedure for examining multivariate group differences, we have eliminated the chapter on stepdown analysis from the text, but make it available on the web.

REWRITTEN AND IMPROVED CHAPTERS

In addition, the chapter on structural equation modeling has been completely rewritten by Dr. Tiffany Whittaker of the University of Texas at Austin. Dr. Whittaker has taught a structural equation modeling course for many years and is an active methodological researcher in this area. In this chapter, she presents the three major applications of SEM: observed variable path analysis, confirmatory factor analysis, and latent variable path analysis. Note that the placement of confirmatory factor analysis in the SEM chapter is new to this edition and was done to allow for more extensive coverage of the common factor model in Chapter 9 and because confirmatory factor analysis is inherently a SEM technique.

Chapter 9 is one of two chapters that have been extensively revised (along with Chapter 13). The major changes to Chapter 9 include the inclusion of parallel analysis to help determine the number of factors present, an updated section on sample size, sections covering an overall focus on the common factor model, a section (9.7) providing a student- and teacher-friendly introduction to factor analysis, a new section on creating factor scores, and the new example results and analysis summary sections. The research examples used here are also new for exploratory factor analysis, and recall that coverage of confirmatory analysis is now found in Chapter 16.

Major revisions have been made to Chapter 13, Hierarchical Linear Modeling. Section 13.1 has been revised to provide discussion of fixed and random factors to help you recognize when hierarchical linear modeling may be needed. Section 13.2 uses a different example than presented in the fifth edition and describes three types of widely used models. Given the use of SPSS and SAS for HLM included in this edition and a new example used in section 13.5, the remainder of the chapter is essentially new material. Section 13.7 provides updated information on sample size, and we would especially like to draw your attention to section 13.6, which is a new section on the centering of predictor variables, a critical concern for this form of modeling.

KEY CHAPTER-BY-CHAPTER REVISIONS

There are also many new sections and important revisions in this edition. Here, we discuss the major changes by chapter.

- Chapter 1 (section 1.6) now includes a discussion of issues related to missing data. Included here are missing data mechanisms, missing data treatments, and illustrative analyses showing how you can select and implement a missing data analysis treatment.
- The *post hoc* procedures have been revised for Chapters 4 and 5, which largely reflect prevailing practices in applied research.
- Chapter 6 adds more information on the use of skewness and kurtosis to evaluate the normality assumption as well as including the new example results and analysis summary sections for one-way MANOVA. In Chapter 6, we also include a new data set (which we call the SeniorWISE data set, modeled after an applied study) that appears in several chapters in the text.
- Chapter 7 has been retitled (somewhat), and in addition to including the example results and analysis summary sections for two-way MANOVA, includes a new section on factorial descriptive discriminant analysis.
- Chapter 8, in addition to the example results and analysis summary sections, includes a new section on effect size measures for group comparisons in ANCOVA/MANCOVA, revised *post hoc* procedures for MANCOVA, and a new section that briefly describes a benefit of using multivariate multilevel modeling that is particularly relevant for MANCOVA.
- The introduction to Chapter 10 is revised, and recommendations are updated in section 10.4 for the use of coefficients to interpret discriminant functions. Section 10.7 includes a new research example for discriminant analysis, and section 10.7.5 is particularly important in that we provide recommendations for selecting among traditional MANOVA, discriminant analysis, and multivariate multilevel modeling procedures. This chapter includes the new example results and analysis summary sections for descriptive discriminant analysis and applies these procedures in sections 10.7 and 10.8.
- In Chapter 12, the major changes include an update of the *post hoc* procedures (section 12.6), a new section on one-way trend analysis (section 12.8), and a revised example and a more extensive discussion of *post hoc* procedures for the one-between and one-within subjects factors design (sections 12.11 and 12.12).

ONLINE RESOURCES FOR TEXT

The book's website www.routledge.com/9780415836661 contains the data sets from the text, SPSS and SAS syntax from the text, and additional data sets (in SPSS and SAS) that can be used for assignments and extra practice. For instructors, the site hosts a conversion guide for users of the previous editions, 6 PowerPoint lecture slides providing a detailed walk-through for key examples from the text, detailed answers for all exercises from the text, and downloadable PDFs of chapters 10 and 14 from the 5th edition of the text for instructors that wish to continue assigning this content.

INTENDED AUDIENCE

As in previous editions, this book is intended for courses on multivariate statistics found in psychology, social science, education, and business departments, but the book also appeals to practicing researchers with little or no training in multivariate methods.

A word on prerequisites students should have before using this book. They should have a minimum of two quarter courses in statistics (covering factorial ANOVA and ANCOVA). A two-semester sequence of courses in statistics is preferable, as is prior exposure to multiple regression. The book does not assume a working knowledge of matrix algebra.

In closing, we hope you find that this edition is interesting to read, informative, and provides useful guidance when you analyze data for your research projects.

ACKNOWLEDGMENTS

We wish to thank Dr. Tiffany Whittaker of the University of Texas at Austin for her valuable contribution to this edition. We would also like to thank Dr. Wanchen Chang, formerly a graduate student at the University of Texas at Austin and now a faculty member at Boise State University, for assisting us with the SPSS and SAS syntax that is included in Chapter 14. Dr. Pituch would also like to thank his major professor Dr. Richard Tate for his useful advice throughout the years and his exemplary approach to teaching statistics courses.

Also, we would like to say a big thanks to the many reviewers (anonymous and otherwise) who provided many helpful suggestions for this text: Debbie Hahs-Vaughn (University of Central Florida), Dennis Jackson (University of Windsor), Karin Schermelleh-Engel (Goethe University), Robert Triscari (Florida Gulf Coast University), Dale Berger (Claremont Graduate University–Claremont McKenna College), Namok Choi (University of Louisville), Joseph Wu (City University of Hong Kong), Jorge Tendeiro (Groningen University), Ralph Rippe (Leiden University), and Philip

Schatz (Saint Joseph's University). We attended to these suggestions whenever possible.

Dr. Pituch also wishes to thank commissioning editor Debra Riegert and Dr. Stevens for inviting him to work on this edition and for their patience as he worked through the revisions. We would also like to thank development editor Rebecca Pearce for assisting us in many ways with this text. We would also like to thank the production staff at Routledge for bringing this edition to completion.

Chapter 1

INTRODUCTION

1.1 INTRODUCTION

Studies in the social sciences comparing two or more groups very often measure their participants on several criterion variables. The following are some examples:

1. A researcher is comparing two methods of teaching second-grade reading. On a posttest the researcher measures the participants on the following basic elements related to reading: syllabication, blending, sound discrimination, reading rate, and comprehension.
2. A social psychologist is testing the relative efficacy of three treatments on self-concept, and measures participants on academic, emotional, and social aspects of self-concept. Two different approaches to stress management are being compared.
3. The investigator employs a couple of paper-and-pencil measures of anxiety (say, the State-Trait Scale and the Subjective Stress Scale) and some physiological measures.
4. A researcher comparing two types of counseling (Rogerian and Adlerian) on client satisfaction and client self-acceptance.

A major part of this book involves the statistical analysis of several groups on a set of criterion measures simultaneously, that is, multivariate analysis of variance, the multivariate referring to the multiple dependent variables.

Cronbach and Snow (1977), writing on aptitude–treatment interaction research, echoed the need for multiple criterion measures:

> Learning is multivariate, however. Within any one task a person's performance at a point in time can be represented by a set of scores describing aspects of the performance . . . even in laboratory research on rote learning, performance can be assessed by multiple indices: errors, latencies and resistance to extinction, for

example. These are only moderately correlated, and do not necessarily develop at the same rate. In the paired associate's task, sub skills have to be acquired: discriminating among and becoming familiar with the stimulus terms, being able to produce the response terms, and tying response to stimulus. If these attainments were separately measured, each would generate a learning curve, and there is no reason to think that the curves would echo each other. (p. 116)

There are three good reasons that the use of multiple criterion measures in a study comparing treatments (such as teaching methods, counseling methods, types of reinforcement, diets, etc.) is very sensible:

1. Any worthwhile treatment will affect the participants in more than one way. Hence, the problem for the investigator is to determine in which specific ways the participants will be affected, and then find sensitive measurement techniques for those variables.
2. Through the use of multiple criterion measures we can obtain a more complete and detailed description of the phenomenon under investigation, whether it is teacher method effectiveness, counselor effectiveness, diet effectiveness, stress management technique effectiveness, and so on.
3. Treatments can be expensive to implement, while the cost of obtaining data on several dependent variables is relatively small and maximizes information gain.

Because we define a multivariate study as one with several dependent variables, multiple regression (where there is only one dependent variable) and principal components analysis would not be considered multivariate techniques. However, our distinction is more semantic than substantive. Therefore, because regression and component analysis are so important and frequently used in social science research, we include them in this text.

We have four major objectives for the remainder of this chapter:

1. To review some basic concepts (e.g., type I error and power) and some issues associated with univariate analysis that are equally important in multivariate analysis.
2. To discuss the importance of identifying outliers, that is, points that split off from the rest of the data, and deciding what to do about them. We give some examples to show the considerable impact outliers can have on the results in univariate analysis.
3 To discuss the issue of missing data and describe some recommended missing data treatments.
4. To give research examples of some of the multivariate analyses to be covered later in the text and to indicate how these analyses involve generalizations of what the student has previously learned.
5. To briefly introduce the Statistical Analysis System (SAS) and the IBM Statistical Package for the Social Sciences (SPSS), whose outputs are discussed throughout the text.

1.2 TYPE I ERROR, TYPE II ERROR, AND POWER

Suppose we have randomly assigned 15 participants to a treatment group and another 15 participants to a control group, and we are comparing them on a single measure of task performance (a univariate study, because there is a single dependent variable). You may recall that the *t* test for independent samples is appropriate here. We wish to determine whether the difference in the sample means is large enough, given sampling error, to suggest that the underlying population means are different. Because the sample means estimate the population means, they will generally be in error (i.e., they will not hit the population values right "on the nose"), and this is called *sampling error*. We wish to test the null hypothesis (H_0) that the population means are equal:

$$H_0 : \mu_1 = \mu_2$$

It is called the null hypothesis because saying the population means are equal is equivalent to saying that the difference in the means is 0, that is, $\mu_1 - \mu_2 = 0$, or that the difference is null.

Now, statisticians have determined that, given the assumptions of the procedure are satisfied, if we had populations with equal means and drew samples of size 15 repeatedly and computed a *t* statistic each time, then 95% of the time we would obtain *t* values in the range -2.048 to 2.048. The so-called sampling distribution of *t* under H_0 would look like this:

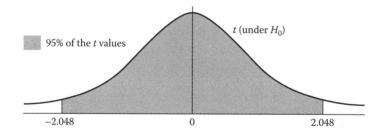

This sampling distribution is extremely important, for it gives us a frame of reference for judging what is a large value of *t*. Thus, if our *t* value was 2.56, it would be very plausible to reject the H_0, since obtaining such a large *t* value is *very unlikely* when H_0 is true. Note, however, that if we do so there is a chance we have made an error, because it is possible (although very improbable) to obtain such a large value for *t*, even when the population means are equal. In practice, one must decide how much of a risk of making this type of error (called a type I error) one wishes to take. Of course, one would want that risk to be small, and many have decided a 5% risk is small. This is formalized in hypothesis testing by saying that we set our level of significance (α) at the .05 level. That is, we are willing to take a 5% chance of making a type I error. In other words, *type I error (level of significance) is the probability of rejecting the null hypothesis when it is true.*

Recall that the formula for degrees of freedom for the t test is $(n_1 + n_2 - 2)$; hence, for this problem $df = 28$. If we had set $\alpha = .05$, then reference to Appendix A.2 of this book shows that the critical values are -2.048 and 2.048. They are called critical values because they are critical to the decision we will make on H_0. These critical values define critical regions in the sampling distribution. If the value of t falls in the critical region we reject H_0; otherwise we fail to reject:

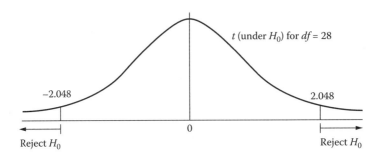

Type I error is equivalent to saying the groups differ when in fact they do not. The α level set by the investigator is a subjective decision, but is usually set at .05 or .01 by most researchers. There are situations, however, when it makes sense to use α levels other than .05 or .01. For example, if making a type I error will not have serious substantive consequences, or if sample size is small, setting $\alpha = .10$ or .15 is quite reasonable. Why this is reasonable for small sample size will be made clear shortly. On the other hand, suppose we are in a medical situation where the null hypothesis is equivalent to saying a drug is unsafe, and the alternative is that the drug is safe. Here, making a type I error could be quite serious, for we would be declaring the drug safe when it is not safe. This could cause some people to be permanently damaged or perhaps even killed. In this case it would make sense to use a very small α, perhaps .001.

Another type of error that can be made in conducting a statistical test is called a type II error. The type II error rate, denoted by β, is the probability of accepting H_0 when it is false. Thus, a type II error, in this case, is saying the groups don't differ when they do. Now, not only can either type of error occur, but in addition, they are inversely related (when other factors, e.g., sample size and effect size, affecting these probabilities are held constant). Thus, holding these factors constant, as we control on type I error, type II error increases. This is illustrated here for a two-group problem with 30 participants per group where the population effect size d (defined later) is .5:

α	β	$1 - \beta$
.10	.37	.63
.05	.52	.48
.01	.78	.22

Notice that, with sample and effect size held constant, as we exert more stringent control over α (from .10 to .01), the type II error rate increases fairly sharply (from .37 to .78). Therefore, the problem for the experimental planner is achieving an appropriate balance between the two types of errors. While we do not intend to minimize the seriousness of making a type I error, we hope to convince you throughout the course of this text that more attention should be paid to type II error. Now, the quantity in the last column of the preceding table $(1 - \beta)$ is the *power of a statistical test, which is the probability of rejecting the null hypothesis when it is false.* Thus, power is the probability of making a correct decision, or of saying the groups differ when in fact they do. Notice from the table that as the α level decreases, power also decreases (given that effect and sample size are held constant). The diagram in Figure 1.1 should help to make clear why this happens.

The power of a statistical test is dependent on three factors:

1. The α level set by the experimenter
2. Sample size
3. Effect size—How much of a difference the treatments make, or the extent to which the groups differ in the population on the dependent variable(s).

Figure 1.1 has already demonstrated that power is directly dependent on the α level. Power is *heavily* dependent on sample size. Consider a two-tailed test at the .05 level for the *t* test for independent samples. An effect size for the *t* test, as defined by Cohen (1988), is estimated as $\hat{d} = (x_1 - x_2)/s$, where s is the standard deviation. That is, effect size expresses the difference between the means in standard deviation units. Thus, if $x_1 = 6$ and $x_2 = 3$ and $s = 6$, then $\hat{d} = (6-3)/6 = .5$, or the means differ by $\frac{1}{2}$ standard deviation. Suppose for the preceding problem we have an effect size of .5 standard deviations. Holding α (.05) and effect size constant, power increases dramatically as sample size increases (power values from Cohen, 1988):

n (Participants per group)	Power
10	.18
20	.33
50	.70
100	.94

As the table suggests, given this effect size and α, when sample size is large (say, 100 or more participants per group), power is not an issue. In general, it is an issue when one is conducting a study where group sizes will be small ($n \leq 20$), or when one is evaluating a completed study that had small group size. Then, it is imperative to be very sensitive to the possibility of poor power (or conversely, a high type II error rate). Thus, in studies with small group size, it can make sense to test at a more liberal level

■ **Figure 1.1:** Graph of F distribution under H_0 and under H_0 false showing the direct relationship between type I error and power. Since type I error is the probability of rejecting H_0 when true, it is the area underneath the F distribution in critical region for H_0 true. Power is the probability of rejecting H_0 when false; therefore it is the area underneath the F distribution in critical region when H_0 is false.

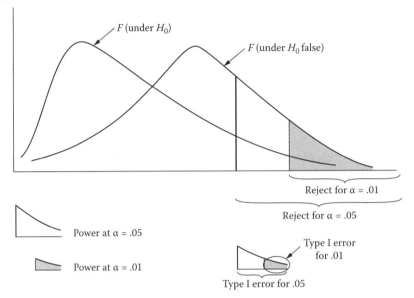

(.10 or .15) to improve power, because (as mentioned earlier) power is directly related to the α level. We explore the power issue in considerably more detail in Chapter 4.

1.3 MULTIPLE STATISTICAL TESTS AND THE PROBABILITY OF SPURIOUS RESULTS

If a researcher sets α = .05 in conducting a single statistical test (say, a *t* test), then, if statistical assumptions associated with the procedure are satisfied, the probability of rejecting falsely (a spurious result) is under control. Now consider a five-group problem in which the researcher wishes to determine whether the groups differ significantly on some dependent variable. You may recall from a previous statistics course that a one-way analysis of variance (ANOVA) is appropriate here. But suppose our researcher is unaware of ANOVA and decides to do 10 *t* tests, each at the .05 level, comparing each pair of groups. The probability of a false rejection is no longer under control for the *set* of 10 *t* tests. We define the *overall* α *for a set of tests as the probability of at least one false rejection when the null hypothesis is true*. There is an important inequality called the *Bonferroni inequality*, which gives an upper bound on overall α:

Overall $\alpha \le .05 + .05 + \cdots + .05 = .50$

Thus, the probability of a few false rejections here could easily be 30 or 35%, that is, much too high.

In general then, if we are testing k hypotheses at the $\alpha_1, \alpha_2, \ldots, \alpha_k$ levels, the Bonferroni inequality guarantees that

$$\text{Overall } \alpha \leq \alpha_1 + \alpha_2 + \cdots + \alpha_k$$

If the hypotheses are each tested at the same alpha level, say α', then the Bonferroni upper bound becomes

$$\text{Overall } \alpha \leq k\alpha'$$

This Bonferroni upper bound is conservative, and how to obtain a sharper (tighter) upper bound is discussed next.

If the tests are independent, then an *exact* calculation for overall α is available. First, $(1 - \alpha_1)$ is the probability of no type I error for the first comparison. Similarly, $(1 - \alpha_2)$ is the probability of no type I error for the second, $(1 - \alpha_3)$ the probability of no type I error for the third, and so on. If the tests are independent, then we can multiply probabilities. Therefore, $(1 - \alpha_1) (1 - \alpha_2) \ldots (1 - \alpha_k)$ is the probability of *no* type I errors for all k tests. Thus,

$$\text{Overall } \alpha = 1 - \left(1 - \alpha_1\right)\left(1 - \alpha_2\right)\cdots\left(1 - \alpha_k\right)$$

is the probability of at least one type I error. If the tests are not independent, then overall α will still be *less* than given here, although it is very difficult to calculate. If we set the alpha levels equal, say to α' for each test, then this expression becomes

$$\text{Overall } \alpha = 1 - \left(1 - \alpha'\right)\left(1 - \alpha'\right)\cdots\left(1 - \alpha'\right) = 1 - \left(1 - \alpha'\right)^k$$

No. of tests	$\alpha' = .05$		$\alpha' = .01$		$\alpha' = .001$	
	$1 - (1 - \alpha')^k$	$k\alpha'$	$1 - (1 - \alpha')^k$	$k\alpha'$	$1 - (1 - \alpha')^k$	$k\alpha'$
5	.226	.25	.049	.05	.00499	.005
10	.401	.50	.096	.10	.00990	.010
15	.537	.75	.140	.15	.0149	.015
30	.785	1.50	.260	.30	.0296	.030
50	.923	2.50	.395	.50	.0488	.050
100	.994	5.00	.634	1.00	.0952	.100

This expression, that is, $1 - (1 - \alpha')^k$, is approximately equal to $k\alpha'$ for small α'. The next table compares the two for $\alpha' = .05, .01,$ and $.001$ for number of tests ranging from 5 to 100.

First, the numbers greater than 1 in the table don't represent probabilities, because a probability can't be greater than 1. Second, note that if we are testing each of a large number of hypotheses at the .001 level, the difference between $1 - (1 - \alpha')^k$ and the Bonferroni upper bound of $k\alpha'$ is very small and of no practical consequence. Also, the differences between $1 - (1 - \alpha')^k$ and $k\alpha'$ when testing at $\alpha' = .01$ are also small for up to about 30 tests. For more than about 30 tests $1 - (1 - \alpha')^k$ provides a tighter bound and should be used. When testing at the $\alpha' = .05$ level, $k\alpha'$ is okay for up to about 10 tests, but beyond that $1 - (1 - \alpha')^k$ is much tighter and should be used.

You may have been alert to the possibility of spurious results in the preceding example with multiple t tests, because this problem is pointed out in texts on intermediate statistical methods. Another frequently occurring example of multiple t tests where overall α gets completely out of control is in comparing two groups on *each* item of a scale (test); for example, comparing males and females on each of 30 items, doing 30 t tests, each at the .05 level.

Multiple statistical tests also arise in various other contexts in which you may not readily recognize that the same problem of spurious results exists. In addition, the fact that the researcher may be using a more sophisticated design or more complex statistical tests doesn't mitigate the problem.

As our first illustration, consider a researcher who runs a four-way ANOVA ($A \times B \times C \times D$). Then 15 statistical tests are being done, one for each effect in the design: $A, B, C,$ and D main effects, and $AB, AC, AD, BC, BD, CD, ABC, ABD, ACD, BCD,$ and $ABCD$ interactions. If each of these effects is tested at the .05 level, then all we know from the Bonferroni inequality is that overall $\alpha \leq 15(.05) = .75$, which is not very reassuring. Hence, two or three significant results from such a study (if they were *not* predicted ahead of time) could very well be type I errors, that is, spurious results.

Let us take another common example. Suppose an investigator has a two-way ANOVA design ($A \times B$) with seven dependent variables. Then, there are three effects being tested for significance: A main effect, B main effect, and the $A \times B$ interaction. The investigator does separate two-way ANOVAs for each dependent variable. Therefore, the investigator has done a total of 21 statistical tests, and if each of them was conducted at the .05 level, then the overall α has gotten completely out of control. This type of thing is done *very frequently* in the literature, and you should be aware of it in interpreting the results of such studies. Little faith should be placed in scattered significant results from these studies.

A third example comes from survey research, where investigators are often interested in relating demographic characteristics of the participants (sex, age, religion, socioeconomic status, etc.) to responses to items on a questionnaire. A statistical test for relating each demographic characteristic to responses on each item is a two-way χ^2. Often in such studies 20 or 30 (or many more) two-way χ^2 tests are run (and it is so easy to run them on SPSS). The investigators often seem to be able to explain the frequent small number of significant results perfectly, although seldom have the significant results been predicted *a priori*.

A fourth fairly common example of multiple statistical tests is in examining the elements of a correlation matrix for significance. Suppose there were 10 variables in one set being related to 15 variables in another set. In this case, there are 150 between correlations, and if each of these is tested for significance at the .05 level, then $150(.05) = 7.5$, or about eight significant results could be expected by chance. Thus, if 10 or 12 of the between correlations are significant, most of them could be chance results, and it is very difficult to separate out the chance effects from the real associations. A way of circumventing this problem is to simply test each correlation for significance at a much more stringent level, say $\alpha = .001$. Then, by the Bonferroni inequality, overall $\alpha \leq 150(.001) = .15$. Naturally, this will cause a power problem (unless n is large), and only those associations that are quite strong will be declared significant. Of course, one could argue that it is only such strong associations that may be of practical importance anyway.

A fifth case of multiple statistical tests occurs when comparing the results of many studies in a given content area. Suppose, for example, that 20 studies have been reviewed in the area of programmed instruction and its effect on math achievement in the elementary grades, and that only five studies show significance. Since at least 20 statistical tests were done (there would be more if there were more than a single criterion variable in some of the studies), most of these significant results could be spurious, that is, type I errors.

A sixth case of multiple statistical tests occurs when an investigator(s) selects a small set of dependent variables from a much larger set (you don't know this has been done—this is an example of selection bias). The much smaller set is chosen because all of the significance occurs here. This is particularly insidious. Let us illustrate. Suppose the investigator has a three-way design and originally 15 dependent variables. Then $105 = 15 \times 7$ tests have been done. If each test is done at the .05 level, then the Bonferroni inequality guarantees that overall alpha is less than $105(.05) = 5.25$. So, if seven significant results are found, the Bonferroni procedure suggests that most (or all) of the results could be spurious. If all the significance is confined to three of the variables, and those are the variables selected (without your knowing this), then overall alpha $= 21(.05) = 1.05$, and this conveys a very different impression. Now, the conclusion is that perhaps a few of the significant results are spurious.

1.4 STATISTICAL SIGNIFICANCE VERSUS PRACTICAL IMPORTANCE

You have probably been exposed to the statistical significance versus practical importance issue in a previous course in statistics, but it is sufficiently important to have us review it here. Recall from our earlier discussion of power (probability of rejecting the null hypothesis when it is false) that power is heavily dependent on sample size. Thus, given very large sample size (say, group sizes > 200), most effects will be declared statistically significant at the .05 level. If significance is found, often researchers seek to determine whether the difference in means is large enough to be of practical importance. There are several ways of getting at practical importance; among them are

1. Confidence intervals
2. Effect size measures
3. Measures of association (variance accounted for).

Suppose you are comparing two teaching methods and decide ahead of time that the achievement for one method must be *at least* 5 points higher on average for practical importance. The results are significant, but the 95% confidence interval for the difference in the population means is (1.61, 9.45). You do not have practical importance, because, although the difference could be as large as 9 or slightly more, it could also be less than 2.

You can calculate an effect size measure and see if the effect is large relative to what others have found in the same area of research. As a simple example, recall that the Cohen effect size measure for two groups is $\hat{d} = (\bar{x}_1 - \bar{x}_2)/s$, that is, it indicates how many standard deviations the groups differ by. Suppose your t test was significant and the estimated effect size measure was $\hat{d} = .63$ (in the medium range according to Cohen's rough characterization). If this is large relative to what others have found, then it probably is of practical importance. As Light, Singer, and Willett indicated in their excellent text *By Design* (1990), "because practical significance depends upon the research context, only *you* can judge if an effect is large enough to be important" (p. 195).

Measures of association or strength of relationship, such as Hay's $\hat{\omega}^2$, can also be used to assess practical importance because they are essentially independent of sample size. However, there are limitations associated with these measures, as O'Grady (1982) pointed out in an excellent review on measures of explained variance. He discussed three basic reasons that such measures should be interpreted with caution: measurement, methodological, and theoretical. We limit ourselves here to a theoretical point O'Grady mentioned that should be kept in mind before casting aspersions on a "low" amount of variance accounted. The point is that most behaviors have *multiple causes*, and hence it will be difficult in these cases to account for a large amount of variance with just a single cause such as treatments. We give an example in Chapter 4 to show that treatments accounting for only 10% of the variance on the dependent variable can indeed be practically significant.

Sometimes practical importance can be judged by simply looking at the means and thinking about the range of possible values. Consider the following example.

1.4.1 Example

A survey researcher compares four geographic regions on their attitude toward education. The survey is sent out and 800 responses are obtained. Ten items, Likert scaled from 1 to 5, are used to assess attitude. The group sizes, along with the means and standard deviations for the total score scale, are given here:

	West	North	East	South
n	238	182	130	250
$\bar{x}$	32.0	33.1	34.0	31.0
S	7.09	7.62	7.80	7.49

An analysis of variance on these groups yields $F = 5.61$, which is significant at the .001 level. Examining the p value suggests that results are "highly significant," but are the results practically important? Very probably not. Look at the size of the mean differences for a scale that has a range from 10 to 50. The mean differences for all pairs of groups, except for East and South, are about 2 or less. These are trivial differences on a scale with a range of 40.

Now recall from our earlier discussion of power the problem of finding statistical significance with small sample size. That is, *results in the literature that are not significant may be simply due to poor or inadequate power, whereas results that are significant, but have been obtained with huge sample sizes, may not be practically significant.* We illustrate this statement with two examples.

First, consider a two-group study with eight participants per group and an effect size of .8 standard deviations. This is, in general, a large effect size (Cohen, 1988), and most researchers would consider this result to be practically significant. However, if testing for significance at the .05 level (two-tailed test), then the chances of finding significance are only about 1 in 3 (.31 from Cohen's power tables). The danger of not being sensitive to the power problem in such a study is that a researcher may abort a promising line of research, perhaps an effective diet or type of psychotherapy, because significance is not found. And it may also discourage other researchers.

On the other hand, now consider a two-group study with 300 participants per group and an effect size of .20 standard deviations. In this case, when testing at the .05 level, the researcher is likely to find significance (power = .70 from Cohen's tables). To use a domestic analogy, this is like using a sledgehammer to "pound out" significance. Yet the effect size here may not be considered practically significant in most cases. Based on these results, for example, a school system may decide to implement an expensive program that may yield only very small gains in achievement.

For further perspective on the practical importance issue, there is a nice article by Haase, Ellis, and Ladany (1989). Although that article is in the *Journal of Counseling Psychology*, the implications are much broader. They suggest five different ways of assessing the practical or clinical significance of findings:

1. Reference to previous research—the importance of *context* in determining whether a result is practically important.
2. Conventional definitions of magnitude of effect—Cohen's (1988) definitions of small, medium, and large effect size.
3. Normative definitions of clinical significance—here they reference a special issue of *Behavioral Assessment* (Jacobson, 1988) that should be of considerable interest to clinicians.
4. Cost-benefit analysis.
5. The good-enough principle—here the idea is to posit a form of the null hypothesis that is more difficult to reject: for example, rather than testing whether two population means are equal, testing whether the difference between them is at least 3.

Note that many of these ideas are considered in detail in Grissom and Kim (2012).

Finally, although in a somewhat different vein, with various multivariate procedures we consider in this text (such as discriminant analysis), unless sample size is large relative to the number of variables, the results will not be reliable—that is, they will not generalize. A major point of the discussion in this section is that *it is critically important to take sample size into account in interpreting results in the literature.*

1.5 OUTLIERS

Outliers are data points that split off or are very different from the rest of the data. Specific examples of outliers would be an IQ of 160, or a weight of 350 lbs. in a group for which the median weight is 180 lbs. Outliers can occur for two fundamental reasons: (1) a data recording or entry error was made, or (2) the participants are simply different from the rest. The first type of outlier can be identified by always listing the data and checking to make sure the data have been read in accurately.

The importance of listing the data was brought home to Dr. Stevens many years ago as a graduate student. A regression problem with five predictors, one of which was a set of random scores, was run without checking the data. This was a textbook problem to show students that the random number predictor would not be related to the dependent variable. However, the random number predictor was significant and accounted for a fairly large part of the variance on y. This happened simply because one of the scores for the random number predictor was incorrectly entered as a 300 rather than as a 3. In this case it was obvious that something was wrong. But with large data sets the situation will not be so transparent, and the results of an analysis could be completely thrown off by 1 or 2 errant points. The amount of time it takes to list and check the data for accuracy (even if there are 1,000 or 2,000 participants) is well worth the effort.

Statistical procedures in general can be quite sensitive to outliers. This is particularly true for the multivariate procedures that will be considered in this text. *It is very important to be able to identify such outliers and then decide what to do about them.* Why? Because we want the results of our statistical analysis to reflect most of the data, and not to be highly influenced by just 1 or 2 errant data points.

In small data sets with just one or two variables, such outliers can be relatively easy to identify. We now consider some examples.

Example 1.1
Consider the following small data set with two variables:

Case number	x_1	x_2
1	111	68
2	92	46
3	90	50
4	107	59
5	98	50
6	150	66
7	118	54
8	110	51
9	117	59
10	94	97

Cases 6 and 10 are both outliers, but for different reasons. Case 6 is an outlier because the score for case 6 on x_1 (150) is deviant, while case 10 is an outlier because the score for that subject on x_2 (97) splits off from the other scores on x_2. The graphical split-off of cases 6 and 10 is quite vivid and is given in Figure 1.2.

Example 1.2
In large data sets having many variables, some outliers are not so easy to spot and could go easily undetected unless care is taken. Here, we give an example

■ **Figure 1.2:** Plot of outliers for two-variable example.

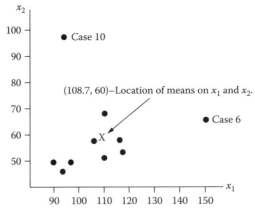

of a somewhat more subtle outlier. Consider the following data set on four variables:

Case number	x_1	x_2	x_3	x_4
1	111	68	17	81
2	92	46	28	67
3	90	50	19	83
4	107	59	25	71
5	98	50	13	92
6	150	66	20	90
7	118	54	11	101
8	110	51	26	82
9	117	59	18	87
10	94	67	12	69
11	130	*57*	16	97
12	118	51	19	*78*
13	155	40	9	58
14	118	61	20	103
15	109	66	13	88

The somewhat subtle outlier here is case 13. Notice that the scores for case 13 on none of the xs really split off dramatically from the other participants' scores. Yet the scores tend to be low on x_2, x_3, and x_4 and high on x_1, and the cumulative effect of all this is to isolate case 13 from the rest of the cases. We indicate shortly a statistic that is quite useful in detecting multivariate outliers and pursue outliers in more detail in Chapter 3.

Now let us consider three more examples, involving material learned in previous statistics courses, to show the effect outliers can have on some simple statistics.

Example 1.3

Consider the following small set of data: 2, 3, 5, 6, 44. The last number, 44, is an obvious outlier; that is, it splits off sharply from the rest of the data. If we were to use the mean of 12 as the measure of central tendency for this data, it would be quite misleading, as there are no scores around 12. That is why you were told to use the median as the measure of central tendency when there are extreme values (outliers in our terminology), because the median is unaffected by outliers. That is, it is a robust measure of central tendency.

Example 1.4

To show the dramatic effect an outlier can have on a correlation, consider the two scatterplots in Figure 1.3. Notice how the inclusion of the outlier in each case *drastically* changes the interpretation of the results. For case A there is no relationship without the outlier but there is a strong relationship with the outlier, whereas for case B the relationship changes from strong (without the outlier) to weak when the outlier is included.

Example 1.5

As our final example, consider the following data:

Group 1		Group 2		Group 3	
y1	y2	y1	y2	y1	y2
15	21	17	36	6	26
18	27	22	41	9	31
12	32	15	31	12	38
12	29	12	28	11	24
9	18	20	47	11	35
10	34	14	29	8	29
12	18	15	33	13	30
20	36	20	38	30	16
		21	25	7	23

For now, ignore variable y2, and we run a one-way ANOVA for y1. The score of 30 in group 3 is an outlier. With that case in the ANOVA we do not find significance ($F = 2.61, p < .095$) at the .05 level, while with the case deleted we do find significance well beyond the .01 level ($F = 11.18, p < .0004$). Deleting the case has the effect of producing greater separation among the three means, because the means with the case *included* are 13.5, 17.33, and 11.89, but with the case *deleted* the means are 13.5, 17.33, and 9.63. It also has the effect of reducing the within variability in group 3 substantially, and hence the pooled within variability (error term for ANOVA) will be much smaller.

■ **Figure 1.3:** The effect of an outlier on a correlation coefficient.

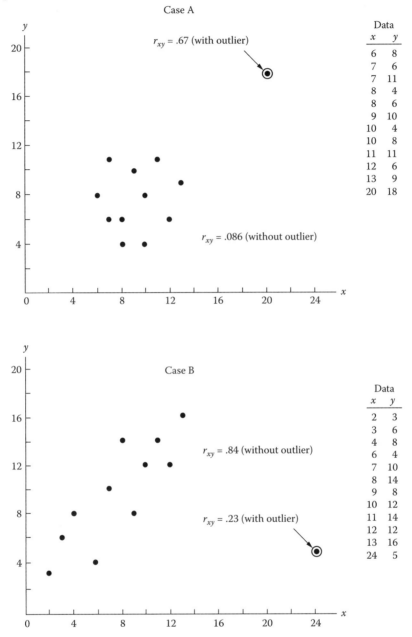

1.5.1 Detecting Outliers

If a variable is approximately normally distributed, then z scores around 3 in absolute value should be considered as potential outliers. Why? Because, in an approximate normal distribution, about 99% of the scores should lie within three standard deviations of the mean. Therefore, any z value > 3 indicates a value very unlikely to occur. Of course, if n is large, say > 100, then simply by chance we might expect a few participants to have z scores > 3 and this should be kept in mind. However, even for *any type of distribution* this rule is reasonable, although we might consider extending the rule to $z > 4$. It was shown many years ago that regardless of how the data is distributed, the percentage of observations contained within k standard deviations of the mean must be *at least* $(1 - 1/k^2) \times 100\%$. This holds only for $k > 1$ and yields the following percentages for $k = 2$ through 5:

Number of standard deviations	Percentage of observations
2	at least 75%
3	at least 88.89%
4	at least 93.75%
5	at least 96%

Shiffler (1988) showed that the largest possible z value in a data set of size n is bounded by $(n-1)/\sqrt{n}$. This means for $n = 10$ the largest possible z is 2.846 and for $n = 11$ the largest possible z is 3.015. Thus, for small sample size, any data point with a z around 2.5 should be seriously considered as a possible outlier.

After the outliers are identified, what should be done with them? The action to be taken is not to automatically drop the outlier(s) from the analysis. If one finds after further investigation of the outlying points that an outlier was due to a recording or entry error, then of course one would correct the data value and redo the analysis. Or, if it is found that the errant data value is due to an instrumentation error or that the process that generated the data for that subject was different, then it is legitimate to drop the outlier. If, however, none of these appears to be the case, then there are different schools of thought on what should be done. Some argue that such outliers should *not* be dropped from the analysis entirely, but perhaps report two analyses (one including the outlier and the other excluding it). Another school of thought is that it is reasonable to remove these outliers. Judd, McClelland, and Carey (2009) state the following:

> In fact, we would argue that it is unethical to include clearly outlying observations that "grab" a reported analysis, so that the resulting conclusions misrepresent the majority of the observations in a dataset. The task of data analysis is to build a story of what the data have to tell. If that story really derives from only a few overly influential observations, largely ignoring most of the other observations, then that story is a misrepresentation. (p. 306)

Also, outliers should not necessarily be regarded as "bad." In fact, it has been argued that outliers can provide some of the most interesting cases for further study.

1.6 MISSING DATA

It is not uncommon for researchers to have missing data, that is, incomplete responses from some participants. There are many reasons why missing data may occur. Participants, for example, may refuse to answer "sensitive" questions (e.g., questions about sexual activity, illegal drug use, income), may lose motivation in responding to questionnaire items and quit answering questions, may drop out of a longitudinal study, or may be asked not to respond to a specific item by the researcher (e.g., skip this question if you are not married). In addition, data collection or recording equipment may fail. If not handled properly, missing data may result in poor (biased) estimates of parameters as well as reduced statistical power. As such, how you treat missing data can threaten or help preserve the validity of study conclusions.

In this section, we first describe general reasons (mechanisms) for the occurrence of missing data. As we explain, the performance of different missing data treatments depends on the presumed reason for the occurrence of missing data. Second, we will briefly review various missing data treatments, illustrate how you may examine your data to determine if there appears to be a random or systematic process for the occurrence of missing data, and show that modern methods of treating missing data generally provide for improved parameter estimates compared to other methods. As this is a survey text on multivariate methods, we can only devote so much space to coverage of missing data treatments. Since the presence of missing data may require the use of fairly complex methods, we encourage you to consult in-depth treatments on missing data (e.g., Allison, 2001; Enders, 2010).

We should also point out that not all types of missing data require sophisticated treatment. For example, suppose we ask respondents whether they are employed or not, and, if so, to indicate their degree of satisfaction with their current employer. Those employed may answer both questions, but the second question is not relevant to those unemployed. In this case, it is a simple matter to discard the unemployed participants when we conduct analyses on employee satisfaction. So, if we were to use regression analysis to predict whether one is employed or not, we could use data from all respondents. However, if we then wish to use regression analysis to predict employee satisfaction, we would exclude those not employed from this analysis, instead of, for example, attempting to impute their satisfaction with their employer had they been employed, which seems like a meaningless endeavor.

This simple example highlights the challenges in missing data analysis, in that there is not one "correct" way to handle all missing data. Rather, deciding how to deal with missing data in a general sense involves a consideration of study variables and analysis goals. On the other hand, when a survey question is such that a participant is expected to respond but does not, then you need to consider whether the missing data appears to be a random event or is predictable. This concern leads us to consider what are known as missing data mechanisms.

1.6.1 Missing Data Mechanisms

There are three common missing data mechanisms discussed in the literature, two of which have similar labels but have a critical difference. The first mechanism we consider is referred to as Missing Completely at Random (or MCAR). MCAR describes the condition where data are missing for purely random reasons, which could happen, for example, if a data recording device malfunctions for no apparent reason. As such, if we were to remove all cases having any missing data, the resulting subsample can be considered a simple random sample from the larger set of cases. More specifically, data are said to be MCAR if the presence of missing data on a given variable is not related to any variable in your analysis model of interest or related to the variable itself. Note that with the last stipulation, that is, that the presence of missing data is not related to the variable itself, Allison (2001) notes that we are not able to confirm that data are MCAR, because the data we need to assess this condition are missing. As such, we are only able to determine if the presence of missing data on a given variable is or is not related to other variables in the data set. We will illustrate how one may assess this later, but note that even if you find no such associations in your data set, it is still possible that the MCAR assumption is violated.

We now consider two examples of MCAR violations. First, suppose that respondents are asked to indicate their annual income and age, and that older workers tend to leave the income question blank. In this example, missingness on income is predictable by age and the cases with complete data are not a simple random sample of the larger data set. As a result, running an analysis using just those participants with complete data would likely introduce bias because the results would be based primarily on younger workers. As a second example of a violation of MCAR, suppose that the presence of missing data on income was not related to age or other variables at hand, but that individuals with greater incomes chose not to report income. In this case, missingness on income is related to income itself, but you could not determine this because these income data are missing. If you were to use just those cases that reported income, mean income and its variance would be underestimated in this example due to nonrandom missingness, which is a form of self-censoring or selection bias. Associations between variables and income may well be attenuated due to the restriction in range in the income variable, given that the larger values for income are missing.

A second mechanism for missing data is known as Missing at Random (MAR), which is a less stringent condition than MCAR and is a frequently invoked assumption for missing data. MAR means that the presence of missing data is predictable from other study variables and after taking these associations into account, missingness for a specific variable is not related to the variable itself. Using the previous example, the MAR assumption would hold if missingness on income were predictable by age (because older participants tended not to report income) or other study variables, but was not related to income itself. If, on the other hand, missingness on income was due to those with greater (or lesser) income not reporting income, then MAR would not hold. As such, unless you have the missing data at hand (which you would not), you cannot fully verify this assumption. Note though that the most commonly recommended procedures for treating missing data—use of maximum likelihood estimation and multiple imputation—assume a MAR mechanism.

A third missing data mechanism is Missing Not at Random (MNAR). Data are MNAR when the presence of missing data for a given variable is related to that variable itself even after predicting missingness with the other variables in the data set. With our running example, if missingness on income is related to income itself (e.g., those with greater income do not report income) even after using study variables to account for missingness on income, the missing mechanism is MNAR. While this missing mechanism is the most problematic, note that methods that are used when MAR is assumed (maximum likelihood and multiple imputation) can provide for improved parameter estimates when the MNAR assumption holds. Further, by collecting data from participants on variables that may be related to missingness for variables in your study, you can potentially turn an MNAR mechanism into an MAR mechanism. Thus, in the planning stages of a study, it may helpful to consider including variables that, although may not be of substantive interest, may explain missingness for the variables in your data set. These variables are known as auxiliary variables and software programs that include the generally accepted missing data treatments can make use of such variables to provide for improved parameter estimates and perhaps greatly reduce problems associated with missing data.

1.6.2 Deletion Strategies for Missing Data

This section, focusing on deletion methods, and three sections that follow present various missing data treatments suitable for the MCAR or MAR mechanisms or both. Missing data treatments for the MNAR condition are discussed in the literature (e.g., Allison, 2001; Enders, 2010). The methods considered in these sections include traditionally used methods that may often be problematic and two generally recommended missing data treatments.

A commonly used and easily implemented deletion strategy is listwise deletion, which is not recommended for widespread use. With listwise deletion, which is the default method for treating missing data in many software programs, cases that have any missing data are removed or deleted from the analysis. The primary advantages of listwise deletion are that it is easy to implement and its use results in a single set of cases that can be used for all study analyses. A primary disadvantage of listwise deletion is that it generally requires that data are MCAR. If data are not MCAR, then parameter estimates and their standard errors using just those cases having complete data are generally biased. Further, even when data are MCAR, using listwise deletion may severely reduce statistical power if many cases are missing data on one or more variables, as such cases are removed from the analysis.

There are, however, situations where listwise deletion is sometimes recommended. When missing data are minimal and only a small percent of cases (perhaps from 5% to 10%) are removed with the use of listwise deletion, this method is recommended.

In addition, listwise deletion is a recommended missing data treatment for regression analysis under any missing mechanism (even MNAR) *if* a certain condition is satisfied. That is, if missingness for variables used in a regression analysis are missing as a function of the predictors only (and not the outcome), the use of listwise deletion can outperform the two more generally recommended missing data treatments (i.e., maximum likelihood and multiple imputation).

Another deletion strategy used is pairwise deletion. With this strategy, cases with incomplete data are not excluded entirely from the analysis. Rather, with pairwise deletion, a given case with missing data is excluded only from those analyses that involve variables for which the case has missing data. For example, if you wanted to report correlations for three variables, using the pairwise deletion method, you would compute the correlation for variables 1 and 2 using all cases having scores for these variables (even if such a case had missing data for variable 3). Similarly, the correlation for variables 1 and 3 would be computed for all cases having scores for these two variables (even if a given case had missing data for variable 2) and so on. Thus, unlike listwise deletion, pairwise deletion uses as much data as possible for cases having incomplete data. As a result, different sets of cases are used to compute, in this case, the correlation matrix.

Pairwise deletion is not generally recommended for treating missing data, as its advantages are outweighed by its disadvantages. On the positive side, pairwise deletion is easy to implement (as it is often included in software programs) and can produce approximately unbiased parameter estimates when data are MCAR. However, when the missing data mechanism is MAR or MNAR, parameter estimates are biased with the use of pairwise deletion. In addition, using different subsets of cases, as in the earlier correlation example, can result in correlation or covariance matrices that are not positive definite. Such matrices would not allow for the computation, for example, of regression coefficients or other parameters of interest. Also, computing accurate standard errors with pairwise deletion is not straightforward because a common sample size is not used for all variables in the analysis.

1.6.3 Single Imputation Strategies for Missing Data

Imputing data involves replacing missing data with score values, which are (hopefully) reasonable values to use. In general, imputation methods are attractive because once the data are imputed, analyses can proceed with a "complete" set of data. Single imputation strategies replace missing data with just a single value, whereas multiple imputation, as we will see, provides multiple replacement values. Different methods can be used to assign or impute score values. As is often the case with missing data treatments, the simpler methods are generally more problematic than more sophisticated treatments. However, use of statistical software (e.g., SAS, SPSS) greatly simplifies the task of imputing data.

A relatively easy but generally unsatisfactory method of imputing data is to replace missing values with the mean of the available scores for a given variable, referred to as *mean substitution*. This method assumes that the missing mechanism is MCAR, but even in this case, mean substitution can produce biased estimates. The main problem with this procedure is that it assumes that all cases having missing data for a given variable score only at the mean of the variable in question. This replacement strategy, then, can greatly underestimate the variance (and standard deviation) of the imputed variable. Also, given that variances are underestimated with mean substitution, covariances and correlations will also be attenuated. As such, missing data experts often suggest not using mean substitution as a missing data treatment.

Another imputation method involves using a multiple regression equation to replace missing values, a procedure known as *regression substitution* or *regression imputation*. With this procedure, a given variable with missing data serves as the dependent variable and is regressed on the other variables in the data set. Note that only those cases having complete data are typically used in this procedure. Once the regression estimates (i.e., intercept and slope values) are obtained, we can then use the equation to predict or impute scores for individuals having missing data by plugging into this equation their scores on the equation predictors. A complete set of scores is then obtained for all participants. Although regression imputation is an improvement over mean substitution, this procedure is also not recommended because it can produce attenuated estimates of variable variances and covariances, due to the lack of variability that is inherent in using the predicted scores from the regression equation as the replacement values.

An improved missing data replacement procedure uses this same regression idea, but adds random variability to the predicted scores. This procedure is known as *stochastic regression imputation*, where the term stochastic refers to the additional random component that is used in imputing scores. The procedure is similar to that described for regression imputation but now includes a residual term, scores for which are included when generating imputed values. Scores for this residual are obtained by sampling from a population having certain characteristics, such as being normally distributed with a mean of zero and a variance that is equal to the residual variance estimated from the regression equation used to impute the scores.

Stochastic single regression imputation overcomes some of the limitations of the other single imputation methods but still has one major shortcoming. On the positive side, point estimates obtained with analyses that use such imputed data are unbiased for MAR data. However, standard errors estimated when analyses are run using data imputed by stochastic regression are negatively biased, leading to inflated test statistics and an inflated type I error rate. This misestimation also occurs for the other single imputation methods mentioned earlier. Improved estimates of standard errors can be obtained by generating several such imputed data sets and incorporating variability across the imputed data sets into the standard error estimates.

The last single imputation method considered here is a maximum likelihood approach known as *expectation maximization* (EM). The EM algorithm uses two steps to estimate parameters (e.g., means, variances, and covariances) that may be of interest by themselves or can be used as input for other analyses (e.g., exploratory factor analysis). In the first step of the algorithm, the means and variance-covariance matrix for the set of variables are estimated using the available (i.e., nonmissing) data. In the second step, regression equations are obtained using these means and variances, with the regression equations used (as in stochastic regression) to then obtain estimates for the missing data. With these newly estimated values, the procedure then reestimates the variable means and covariances, which are used again to obtain the regression equations to provide new estimates for the missing data. This two-step process continues until the means and covariances are essentially the same from one iteration to the next.

Of the single imputation methods discussed here, use of the EM algorithm is considered to be superior and provides unbiased parameter estimates (i.e., the means and covariances). However, like the other single-imputation procedures, the standard errors estimated from analyses using the EM-obtained means and covariances are underestimated. As such, this procedure is not recommended for analyses where standard errors and associated statistical tests are used, as type I error rates would be inflated. For procedures that do not require statistical inference (principal component or principal axis factor analysis), use of the EM procedure is recommended. The full information maximum likelihood procedure described in section 1.6.5 is an improved maximum likelihood approach that can obtain proper estimates of standard errors.

1.6.4 Multiple Imputation

Multiple imputation (MI) is one of two procedures that are widely recommended for dealing with missing data. MI involves three main steps. In the first step, the imputation phase, missing data are imputed using a version of stochastic regression imputation, except now this procedure is done several times, so that multiple "complete" data sets are created. Given that a random procedure is included when imputing scores, the imputed score for a given case for a given variable will differ across the multiple data sets. Also, note while the default in statistical software is often to impute a total of five data sets, current thinking is that this number is generally too small, as improved standard error estimates and statistical test results are obtained with a larger number of imputed data sets. Allison (personal communication, November 8, 2013) has suggested that 100 may be regarded as the maximum number of imputed data sets needed.

The second and third steps of this procedure involve analyzing the imputed data sets and obtaining a final set of parameter estimates. In the second step, the analysis stage, the primary analysis of interest is conducted with each of the imputed data sets. So, if 100 data sets were imputed, 100 sets of parameter estimates would be obtained. In the final stage, the pooling phase, a final set of parameter estimates is obtained by combining the parameter estimates across the analyzed data sets. If the procedure is carried out properly, parameter estimates and standard errors are unbiased when the missing data mechanism is MCAR or MAR.

There are advantages and disadvantages to using MI as a missing data treatment. The main advantages are that MI provides for unbiased parameter estimates when the missing data mechanism is MCAR and MAR, and multiple imputation has great flexibility in that it can be applied to a variety of analysis models. One main disadvantage of the procedure is that it can be relatively complicated to implement. As Allison (2012) points out, users must make at least seven decisions when implementing this procedure, and it may be difficult for the user to determine the proper set of choices that should be made.

Another disadvantage of MI is that it is always possible that the imputation and analysis model differ, and such a difference may result in biased parameter estimation even when the data follow an MCAR mechanism. As an example, the analysis model may include interactions or nonlinearities among study variables. However, if such terms were excluded from the imputation model, such interactions and nonlinear associations may not be found in the analysis model. While this problem can be avoided by making sure that the imputation model matches or includes more terms than the analysis model, Allison (2012) notes that in practice it is easy to make this mistake. These latter difficulties can be overcome with the use of another widely recommended missing data treatment, full information maximum likelihood estimation.

1.6.5 Full Information Maximum Likelihood Estimation

Full information maximum likelihood, or FIML (also known as direct maximum likelihood or maximum likelihood), is another widely recommended procedure for treating missing data. When the missing mechanism is MAR, FIML provides for unbiased parameter estimation as well as accurate estimates of standard errors. When data are MCAR, FIML also provides for accurate estimation and can provide for more power than listwise deletion. For sample data, use of maximum likelihood estimation yields parameter estimates that maximize the probability for obtaining the data at hand. Or, as stated by Enders (2010), FIML tries out or "auditions" various parameter values and finds those values that are most consistent with or provide the best fit to the data. While the computational details are best left to missing data textbooks (e.g., Allison, 2001; Enders, 2010), FIML estimates model parameters, in the presence of missing data, by using all available data as well as the implied values of the missing data, given the observed data and assumed probability distribution (e.g., multivariate normal).

Unlike other missing data treatments, FIML estimates parameters directly for the analysis model of substantive interest. Thus, unlike multiple imputation, there are no separate imputation and analysis models, as model parameters are estimated in the presence of incomplete data in one step, that is, without imputing data sets. Allison (2012) regards this simultaneous missing data treatment and estimation of model parameters as a key advantage of FIML over multiple imputation. A key disadvantage of FIML is that its implementation typically requires specialized software, in particular, software used for structural equation modeling (e.g., LISREL, Mplus). SAS, however, includes such capability, and we briefly illustrate how FIML can be implemented using SAS in the illustration to which we now turn.

1.6.6 Illustrative Example: Inspecting Data for Missingness and Mechanism

This section and the next fulfill several purposes. First, using a small data set with missing data, we illustrate how you can assess, using relevant statistics, if the missing mechanism is consistent with the MCAR mechanism or not. Recall that some missing data treatments require MCAR. As such, determining that the data are not MCAR would suggest using a missing data treatment that does not require that mechanism. Second, we show the computer code needed to implement FIML using SAS (as SPSS does not offer this option) and MI in SAS and SPSS. Third, we compare the performance of different missing data treatments for our small data set. This comparison is possible because while we work with a data set having incomplete data, we have the full set of scores or parent data set, from which the data set with missing values was obtained. As such, we can determine how closely the parameters estimated by using various missing data treatments approximate the parameters estimated for the parent data set.

The hypothetical example considered here includes data collected from 300 adolescents on three variables. The outcome variable is apathy, and the researchers, we assume, intend to use multiple regression to determine if apathy is predicted by a participant's perception of family dysfunction and sense of social isolation. Note that higher scores for each variable indicate greater apathy, poorer family functioning, and greater isolation. While we generated a complete set of scores for each variable, we subsequently created a data set having missing values for some variables. In particular, there are no missing scores for the outcome, apathy, but data are missing on the predictors. These missing data were created by randomly removing some scores for dysfunction and isolation, but for only those participants whose apathy score was above the mean. Thus, the missing data mechanism is MAR as whether data are missing or not for dysfunction and isolation depends on apathy, where only those with greater apathy have missing data on the predictors.

We first show how you can examine data to determine the extent of missing data as well as assess whether the data may be consistent with the MCAR mechanism. Table 1.1 shows relevant output for some initial missing data analysis, which may obtained from the following SPSS commands:

```
[@SPSS CODE]
MVA VARIABLES=apathy dysfunction isolation
/TTEST
/TPATTERN DESCRIBE=apathy dysfunction isolation
/EM.
```

Note that some of this output can also be obtained in SAS by the commands shown in section 1.6.7.

In the top display of Table 1.1, the means, standard deviations, and the number and percent of cases with missing data are shown. There is no missing data for apathy, but 20% of the 300 cases did not report a score for dysfunction, and 30% of the sample did not provide a score for isolation. Information in the second display in Table 1.1 (Separate Variance *t* Tests) can be used to assess whether the missing data are consistent with the MCAR mechanism. This display reports separate variance *t* tests that test for a difference in means between cases with and without missing data on a given variable on other study variables. If mean differences are present, this suggests that cases with missing data differ from other cases, discrediting the MCAR mechanism as an explanation for the missing data. In this display, the second column (Apathy) compares mean apathy scores for cases with and without scores for dysfunction and then for isolation. In that column, we see that the 60 cases with missing data on dysfunction have much greater mean apathy (60.64) than the other 240 cases (50.73), and that the 90 cases with missing data on isolation have greater mean apathy (60.74) than the other 210 cases (49.27). The *t* test values, well above a magnitude of 2, also suggest that cases with missing data on dysfunction and isolation are different from cases (i.e., more apathetic) having no missing data on these predictors. Further, the standard deviation for apathy (from the EM estimate obtained via the SPSS syntax just mentioned) is about 10.2. Thus, the mean apathy differences are equivalent to about 1 standard deviation, which is generally considered to be a large difference.

▪ **Table 1.1: Statistics Used to Describe Missing Data**

	N	Mean	Std. deviation	Missing	
				Count	Percent
Apathy	300	52.7104	10.21125	0	.0
Dysfunction	240	53.7802	10.12854	60	20.0
Isolation	210	52.9647	10.10549	90	30.0

Separate Variance t Tests[a]

		Apathy	Dysfunction	Isolation
Dysfunction	*t*	–9.6	.	–2.1
	df	146.1	.	27.8
	# Present	240	240	189
	# Missing	60	0	21
	Mean (present)	50.7283	53.7802	52.5622
	Mean (missing)	60.6388	.	56.5877
Isolation	*t*	–12.0	–2.9	.
	df	239.1	91.1	.
	# Present	210	189	210
	# Missing	90	51	0
	Mean (present)	49.2673	52.8906	52.9647
	Mean (missing)	60.7442	57.0770	.

For each quantitative variable, pairs of groups are formed by indicator variables (present, missing).
[a] Indicator variables with less than 5.0% missing are not displayed.

Tabulated Patterns

Number of cases	Missing patterns[a] Apathy	Dysfunction	Isolation	Complete if . . .[b]	Apathy[c]	Dysfunction[c]	Isolation[c]
189				189	48.0361	52.8906	52.5622
51			X	240	60.7054	57.0770	.
39		X	X	300	60.7950	.	.
21		X		210	60.3486	.	56.5877

Patterns with less than 1.0% cases (3 or fewer) are not displayed.

[a] Variables are sorted on missing patterns.

[b] Number of complete cases if variables missing in that pattern (marked with X) are not used.

[c] Means at each unique pattern.

The other columns in this output table (headed by dysfunction and isolation) indicate that cases having missing data on isolation have greater mean dysfunction and those with missing data on dysfunction have greater mean isolation. Thus, these statistics suggest that the MCAR mechanism is not a reasonable explanation for the missing data. As such, missing data treatments that assume MCAR should not be used with these data, as they would be expected to produce biased parameter estimates.

Before considering the third display in Table 1.1, we discuss other procedures that can be used to assess the MCAR mechanism. First, Little's MCAR test is an omnibus test that may be used to assess whether all mean differences, like those shown in Table 1.1, are consistent with the MCAR mechanism (large p value) or not consistent with the MCAR mechanism (small p value). For the example at hand, the chi-square test statistic for Little's test, obtained with the SPSS syntax just mentioned, is 107.775 ($df = 5$) and statistically significant ($p < .001$). Given that the null hypothesis for this data is that the data are MCAR, the conclusion from this test result is that the data do not follow an MCAR mechanism. While Little's test may be helpful, Enders (2010) notes that it does not indicate which particular variables are associated with missingness and prefers examining standardized group-mean differences as discussed earlier for this purpose. Identifying such variables is important because they can be included in the missing data treatment, as auxiliary variables, to improve parameter estimates.

A third procedure that can be used to assess the MCAR mechanism is logistic regression. With this procedure, you first create a dummy-coded variable for each variable in the data set that indicates whether a given case has missing data for this variable or not. (Note that this same thing is done in the t-test procedure earlier but is entirely automated by SPSS.) Then, for each variable with missing data (perhaps with a minimum of 5% to 10% missing), you can use logistic regression with the missingness indicator for a given variable as the outcome and other study variables as predictors. By doing this, you can learn which study variables are uniquely associated with missingness.

If any are, this suggests that missing data are not MCAR and also identifies variables that need to be used, for example, in the imputation model, to provide for improved (or hopefully unbiased) parameter estimates.

For the example at hand, given that there is a substantial proportion of missing data for dysfunction and isolation, we created a missingness indicator variable first for dysfunction and ran a logistic regression equation with this indicator as the outcome and apathy and isolation as the predictors. We then created a missingness indicator for isolation and used this indicator as the outcome in a second logistic regression with predictors apathy and dysfunction. While the odds ratios obtained with the logistic regressions should be examined, we simply note here that, for each equation, the only significant predictor was apathy. This finding provides further evidence against the MCAR assumption and suggests that the only study variable responsible for missingness is apathy (which in this case is consistent with how the missing data were obtained).

To complete the description of missing data, we examine the third output selection shown in Table 1.1, labeled Tabulated Patterns. This output provides the number of cases for each missing data pattern, sorted by the number of cases in each pattern, as well as relevant group means. For the apathy data, note that there are four missing data patterns shown in the Tabulated Patterns table. The first pattern, consisting of 189 cases, consists of cases that provided complete data on all study variables. The three columns on the right side of the output show the means for each study variable for these 189 cases. The second missing data pattern includes the 51 cases that provided complete data on all variables except for isolation. Here, we can see that this group had much greater mean apathy than those who provided complete scores for all variables and somewhat higher mean dysfunction, again, discrediting the MCAR mechanism. The next group includes those cases ($n = 39$) that had missing data for both dysfunction and isolation. Note, then, that the Tabulated Pattern table provides additional information than provided by the Separate Variance t Tests table, in that now we can identify the number of cases that have missing data on more than one variable. The final group in this table ($n = 21$) consists of those who have missing data on the isolation variable only. Inspecting the means for the three groups with missing data indicates that each of these groups has much greater apathy, in particular, than do cases with complete data, again suggesting the data are not MCAR.

1.6.7 Applying FIML and MI to the Apathy Data

We now use the results from the previous section to select a missing data treatment. Given that the earlier analyses indicated that the data are not MCAR, this suggests that listwise deletion, which could be used in some situations, should not be used here. Rather, of the methods we have discussed, full information maximum likelihood estimation and multiple imputation are the best choices. If we assume that the three study variables approximately follow a multivariate normal distribution, FIML, due to its ease of use and because it provides optimal parameter estimates when data are

MAR, would be the most reasonable choice. We provide SAS and SPSS code that can be used to implement these missing data treatments for our example data set and show how these methods perform compared to the use of more conventional missing data treatments.

Although SPSS has capacity for some missing data treatments, it currently cannot implement a maximum likelihood approach (outside of the effective but limited mixed modeling procedure discussed in a Chapter 14, which cannot handle missingness in predictors, except for using listwise deletion for such cases). As such, we use SAS to implement FIML with the relevant code for our example as follows:

```
PROC CALIS DATA = apathy METHOD = fiml;
PATH apathy <- dysfunction isolation;
RUN;
```

PROC CALIS (Covariance Analysis of Linear Structural Equations) is capable of implementing FIML. Note that after indicating the data set, you simply write fiml following METHOD. Note that SAS assumes that a dot or period (like this.) represents missing data in your data set. On the second line, the dependent variable (here, apathy) for our regression equation of interest immediately follows PATH with the remaining predictors placed after the <- symbols. Assuming that we do not have auxiliary variables (which we do not here), the code is complete. We will present relevant results later in this section.

Both SAS and SPSS can implement multiple imputation, assuming that you have the Missing Values Analysis module in SPSS. Table 1.2 presents SAS and SPSS code that can be used to implement MI for the apathy data. Be aware that both sets of code, with the exception of the number of imputations, tacitly accept the default choices that are embedded in each of the software programs. You should examine SAS and SPSS documentation to see what these default options are and whether they are reasonable for your particular set of circumstances. Note that SAS code follows the three MI phases (imputation, analysis, and pooling of results). In the first line of code in Table 1.2, you write after the OUT command the name of the data set that will contain the imputed data sets (apout, here). The NIMPUTE command is used to specify the number of imputed data sets you wish to have (here, 100 such data sets). The variables used in the imputation phase appear in the second line of code. The PROC REG command, leading off the second block of code (corresponding to the analysis phase), is used because the primary analysis of interest is multiple regression. Note that regression analysis is applied to each of the 100 imputed data sets (stored in the file apout), and the resulting 100 sets of parameter estimates are output to another data file we call est. The final block of SAS code (corresponding to the pooling phase) is used to combine the parameter estimates across the imputed data sets and yields a final single set of parameter estimates, which is then used to interpret the regression results.

▨ **Table 1.2: SAS and SPSS Code for Multiple Imputation With the Apathy Data**

SAS Code

```
PROC MI DATA = apathy OUT = apout NIMPUTE = 100;
VAR apathy dysfunction isolation;
RUN;
PROC REG DATA = apout OUTEST = est COVOUT;
MODEL apathy = dysfunction isolation;
BY _Imputation_;
RUN;
PROC MIANALYZE DATA = est;
MODELEFFECTS INTERCEPT dysfunction isolation;
RUN;
```

SPSS Code

```
MULTIPLE IMPUTATION apathy dysfunction isolation
/IMPUTE METHOD=AUTO NIMPUTATIONS=100
/IMPUTATIONSUMMARIES MODELS
/OUTFILE IMPUTATIONS=impute.
REGRESSION
/STATISTICS COEFF OUTS R ANOVA
/DEPENDENT apathy
/METHOD=ENTER dysfunction isolation.
```

SPSS syntax needed to implement MI for the apathy data are shown in the lower half of Table 1.2. In the first block of commands, MULTIPLE IMPUTATION is used to create the imputed sets using the three variables appearing in that line. Note that the second line of SPSS code requests 100 such imputed data sets, and the last line in that first block outputs a data file that we named impute that has all 100 imputed data sets. With that data file active, the second block of SPSS code conducts the regression analysis of interest on each of the 100 data sets and produces a final combined set of regression estimates used for interpretation. Note that if you close the imputed data file and reopen it at some later time for analysis, you would first need to click on View (in the Data Editor) and Mark Imputed Data prior to running the regression analysis. If this step is not done, SPSS will treat the data in the imputed data file as if they were from one data set, instead of, in this case, 100 imputed data sets. Results using MI for the apathy data are very similar for SAS and SPSS, as would be expected. Thus, we report the final regression results as obtained from SPSS.

Table 1.3 provides parameter estimates obtained by applying a variety of missing data treatments to the apathy data as well as the estimates obtained from the parent data set that had no missing observations. Note that the percent bias columns in Table 1.3 are calculated as the difference between the respective regression coefficient obtained

■ **Table 1.3: Parameter Estimates for Dysfunction (β1) and Isolation (β2) Under Various Missing Data Methods**

Method	β_1	β_2	$t(\beta_1)$	$t(\beta_2)$	% Bias for β_1	% Bias for β_2
No missing data	.289 (.058)	.280 (.067)	4.98	4.18	—	—
Listwise	.245 (.067)	.202 (.067)	3.66	3.01	−15.2	−27.9
Pairwise	.307 (.076)	.226 (.076)	4.04	2.97	6.2	−19.3
Mean substitution	.334 (.067)	.199 (.072)	4.99	2.76	15.6	−28.9
FIML	.300 (.068)	.247 (.071)	4.41	3.48	3.8	−11.8
MI	.303 (.074)	.242 (.078)	4.09	3.10	4.8	−13.6

from the missing data treatment to that obtained by the complete or parent data set, divided by the latter estimate, and then multiplied by 100 to obtain the percent. For coefficient β_1, we see that FIML and MI yielded estimates that are closest to the values from the parent data set, as these estimates are less than 5% higher. Listwise deletion and mean substitution produced the worst estimates for both regression coefficients, and pairwise deletion also exhibited poorer performance than MI or FIML. In line with the literature, FIML provided the most accurate estimates and resulted in more power (exhibited by the t tests) than MI. Note, though, that with the greater amount of missing data for isolation (30%), the estimates for FIML and MI are more than 10% lower than the estimate for the parent set. Thus, although FIML and MI are the best missing data treatments for this situation (i.e., given that the data are MAR), no missing data is the best kind of missing data to have.

1.6.8 Missing Data Summary

You should always determine and report the extent of missing data for your study variables. Further, you should attempt to identify the most plausible mechanism for missing data. Section 1.6.7 provided some procedures you can use for these purposes and illustrated the selection of a missing data treatment given this preliminary analysis. The two most widely recommended procedures are full information maximum likelihood and multiple imputation, although listwise deletion can be used in some circumstances (i.e., minimal amount of missing data and data MCAR). Also, to reduce the amount of missing data, it is important to minimize the effort required by participants to provide data (e.g., use short questionnaires, provide incentives for responding). However, given that missing data are inevitable despite your best efforts, you should consider collecting data on variables that may predict missingness for the study variables of interest. Incorporating such auxiliary variables in your missing data treatment can provide for improved parameter estimates.

1.7 UNIT OR PARTICIPANT NONRESPONSE

Section 1.6 discussed the situation where data was collected from each respondent but that some cases may not have provided a complete set of responses, resulting in incomplete or missing data. A different type of missingness occurs when no data are collected from some respondents, as when a survey respondent refuses to participate in a survey. This nonparticipation, called unit or participant nonresponse, happens regularly in survey research and can be problematic because nonrespondents and respondents may differ in important ways. For example, suppose 1,000 questionnaires are sent out and only 200 are returned. Of the 200 returned, 130 are in favor of some issue at hand and 70 are opposed. As such, it appears that most of the people favor the issue. But 800 surveys were not returned. Further, suppose that 55% of the nonrespondents are opposed and 45% are in favor. Then, 440 of the nonrespondents are opposed and 360 are in favor. For all 1,000 individuals, we now have 510 opposed and 490 in favor. What looked like an overwhelming majority in favor with the 200 respondents is now evenly split among the 1,000 cases.

It is sometimes suggested, if one anticipates a low response rate and wants a certain number of questionnaires returned, that the sample size should be simply increased. For example, if one wishes 400 returned and a response rate of 20% is anticipated, send out 2,000. *This can be a dangerous and misleading practice.* Let us illustrate. Suppose 2,000 are sent out and 400 are returned. Of these, 300 are in favor and 100 are opposed. It appears there is an overwhelming majority in favor, and this is true for the respondents. But 1,600 did NOT respond. Suppose that 60% of the nonrespondents (a distinct possibility) are opposed and 40% are in favor. Then, 960 of the nonrespondents are opposed and 640 are in favor. Again, what appeared to be an overwhelming majority in favor is stacked against (1,060 vs. 940) for ALL participants.

Groves et al. (2009) discuss a variety of methods that can be used to reduce unit nonresponse. In addition, they discuss a weighting approach that can be used to adjust parameter estimates for such nonresponse when analyzing data with unit nonresponse. Note that the methods described in section 1.6 for treating missing data, such as multiple imputation, are not relevant for unit nonresponse if there is a complete absence of data from nonrespondents.

1.8 RESEARCH EXAMPLES FOR SOME ANALYSES CONSIDERED IN THIS TEXT

To give you something of a feel for several of the statistical analyses considered in succeeding chapters, we present the objectives in doing a multiple logistic regression analysis, a multivariate analysis of variance and covariance, and an exploratory factor analysis, along with illustrative studies from the literature that use each of these analyses.

1.8.1 Logistic Regression

In a previous course you have taken, simple linear regression was covered, where a dependent variable (say chemistry achievement) is predicted from just one predictor, such as IQ. It is certainly reasonable that other variables would also be related to chemistry achievement and that we could obtain better prediction by making use of these variables, such as previous average grade in science courses, attitude toward education, and math ability. In addition, in some studies, a binary outcome (success or failure) is of interest, and researchers are interested in variables that are related to this outcome. When the outcome variable is binary (i.e., pass/fail), though, standard regression analysis is not appropriate. Instead, in this case, logistic regression is often used. Thus, the objective in multiple logistic regression (called multiple because we have multiple predictors) is:

Objective: Predict a binary dependent variable from a set of independent variables.

Example

Reingle Gonzalez and Connell (2014) were interested in determining which of several predictors were related to medication continuity among a nationally representative sample of US prisoners. A prisoner was said to have experienced medication continuity if that individual had been taking prescribed medication at intake into prison and continued to take such medication after admission into prison. The logistic regression analysis indicated that, after controlling for other predictors, prisoners were more likely to experience medication continuity if they were diagnosed with schizophrenia, saw a health care professional in prison, were black, were older, and had served less time than other prisoners.

1.8.2 One-Way Multivariate Analysis of Variance

In univariate analysis of variance, several groups of participants are compared to determine whether mean differences are present for a single dependent variable. But, as was mentioned earlier in this chapter, any good treatment(s) generally affects participants in several ways. Hence, it makes sense to collect data from participants on multiple outcomes and then test whether the groups differ, on average, on the set of outcomes. This provides for a more complete assessment of the efficacy of the treatments. Thus, the objective in multivariate analysis of variance is:

Objective: Determine whether mean differences are present across several groups for a set of dependent variables.

Example

McCrudden, Schraw, and Hartley (2006) conducted an educational experiment to determine if college students exhibited improved learning relative to controls after they had received general prereading relevance instructions. The researchers were interested in determining if those receiving such instruction differed from control students for a set of various learning outcomes, as well as a measure of learning effort (reading time). The multivariate analysis indicated that the two groups had different means on the set of outcomes. Follow-up testing revealed that students who received the relevance instructions had higher mean scores on measures of factual and conceptual learning as well as the number of claims made in an essay item and the essay item score. The two groups did not differ, on average, on total reading time, suggesting that the relevance instructions facilitated learning while not requiring greater effort.

1.8.3 Multivariate Analysis of Covariance

Objective: Determine whether several groups differ on a set of dependent variables after the posttest means have been adjusted for any initial differences on the covariates (which are often pretests).

Example

Friedman, Lehrer, and Stevens (1983) examined the effect of two stress management strategies, directed lecture discussion and self-directed, and the locus of control of teachers on their scores on the State-Trait Anxiety Inventory and on the Subjective Stress Scale. Eighty-five teachers were pretested and posttested on these measures, with the treatment extending to 5 weeks. Teachers who received the stress management programs reduced their stress and anxiety more than those in a control group. However, teachers who were in a stress management program compatible with their locus of control (i.e., externals with lectures and internals with the self-directed) did not reduce stress significantly more than participants in the unmatched stress management groups.

1.8.4 Exploratory Factor Analysis

As you know, a bivariate correlation coefficient describes the degree of linear association between two variables, such as anxiety and performance. However, in many situations, researchers collect data on many variables, which are correlated, and they wish to determine if there are fewer constructs or dimensions that underlie responses to these variables. Finding support for a smaller number of constructs than observed variables provides for a more parsimonious description of results and may lead to identifying new theoretical constructs that may be the focus of future research. Exploratory factor analysis is a procedure that can be used to determine the number and nature of such constructs. Thus, the general objective in exploratory factor analysis is:

Objective: Determine the number and nature of constructs that underlie responses to a set of observed variables.

Example

Wong, Pituch, and Rochlen (2006) were interested in determining if specific emotion-related variables were predictive of men's restrictive emotionality, where this latter concept refers to having difficulty or fears about expressing or talking about one's emotions. As part of this study, the researchers wished to identify whether a smaller number of constructs underlie responses to the Restrictive Emotionality scale and eight other measures of emotion. Results from an exploratory factor analysis suggested that three factors underlie responses to the nine measures. The researchers labeled the constructs or factors as (1) Difficulty With Emotional Communication (which was related to restrictive emotionality), (2) Negative Beliefs About Emotional Expression, and (3) Fear of Emotions, and suggested that these constructs may be useful for future research on men's emotional behavior.

1.9 THE SAS AND SPSS STATISTICAL PACKAGES

As you have seen already, SAS and the SPSS are selected for use in this text for several reasons:

1. They are very widely distributed and used.
2. They are easy to use.
3. They do a very wide range of analyses—from simple descriptive statistics to various analyses of variance designs to all kinds of complex multivariate analyses (factor analysis, multivariate analysis of variance, discriminant analysis, logistic multiple regression, etc.).
4. They are well documented, having been in development for decades.

In this edition of the text, we assume that instructors are familiar with one of these two statistical programs. Thus, we do not cover the basics of working with these programs, such as reading in a data set and/or entering data. Instead, we show, throughout the text, how these programs can be used to run the analyses that are discussed in the relevant chapters. The versions of the software programs used in this text are SAS version 9.3 and SPSS version 21. Note that user's guides for SAS and SPSS are available at http://support.sas.com/documentation/cdl/en/statug/63962/HTML/default/viewer.htm #titlepage.htm and http://www-01.ibm.com/support/docview.wss?uid=swg27024972, respectively.

1.10 SAS AND SPSS SYNTAX

We nearly always use syntax, instead of dialogue boxes, to show how analyses can be conducted throughout the text. While both SAS and SPSS offer dialogue boxes to ease obtaining analysis results, we feel that providing syntax is preferred for several reasons. First, using dialogue boxes for SAS and SPSS would "clutter up" the text with pages of screenshots that would be needed to show how to conduct analyses. In contrast, using syntax is a much more efficient way to show how analysis results may be obtained. Second, with the use of the Internet, there is no longer any need for users of this text to do much if any typing of commands, which is often dreaded by students. Instead, you can simply download the syntax and related data sets and use these files to run analyses that are in the textbook. That is about as easy as it gets! If you wish to conduct analysis with your own data sets, it is a simple matter of using your own data files and, for the most part, simply changing the variable names that appear in the online syntax.

Third, instructors may not wish to devote much time to showing how analyses can be obtained via statistical software and instead focus on understanding which analysis should be used for a given situation, the specific analysis steps that should be taken (e.g., search for outliers, assess assumptions, the statistical tests and effect size measures that are to be used), and how analysis results are to be interpreted. For these instructors, then, it is a simple matter of ignoring the relatively short sections of the text that discuss and present software commands. Also, for students, if this is the case and you still you wish to know what specific sections of code are doing, we provide relevant descriptions along the way to help you out.

Fourth, there may be occasions where you wish to keep a copy of the commands that implemented your analysis. You could not easily do this if you exclusively use dialogue boxes, but your syntax file will contain the commands you used for analyses. Fifth, implementing some analysis techniques requires use of commands, as not all procedures can be obtained with the dialogue boxes. A relevant example occurs with exploratory factor analysis (Chapter 9), where parallel analysis can be implemented only with commands. Sixth, as you continue to learn more advanced techniques (such as multilevel and structural equation modeling), you will encounter other software programs (e.g., Mplus) that use only code to run analyses. Becoming familiar with using code will better prepare you for this eventuality. Finally, while we anticipate this will be not the case, if SAS or SPSS commands were to change before a subsequent edition of this text appears, we can simply update the syntax file online to handle recent updates to the programming code.

1.11 SAS AND SPSS SYNTAX AND DATA SETS ON THE INTERNET

Syntax and data files needed to replicate the analysis discussed throughout the text are available on the Internet for both SAS and SPSS (www.psypress.com/books/details/9780415836661/). You must, of course, open the SAS and SPSS programs on your computer as well as the respective syntax and data files to run the analysis. If you do not know how to do this, your instructor can help you.

1.12 SOME ISSUES UNIQUE TO MULTIVARIATE ANALYSIS

Many of the techniques discussed in this text are *mathematical maximization procedures*, and hence there is great opportunity for capitalization on chance. Often, analysis results that "look great" on a given sample may not translate well to other samples. Thus, the results are sample specific and of limited scientific utility. Reliability of results, then, is a real concern.

The notion of a *linear combination* of variables is fundamental to all the types of analysis we discuss. A general linear combination for p variables is given by:

$$y = a_1 x_1 + a_2 x_2 + a_3 x_3 + \cdots + a_p x_p,$$

where $a_1, a_2, a_3, \ldots, a_p$ are the coefficients for the variables. This definition is abstract; however, we give some simple examples of linear combinations that you are probably already familiar with.

Suppose we have a treatment versus control group design with participants pretested and posttested on some variable. Then, sometimes analysis is done on the difference scores (gain scores), that is, posttest–pretest. If we denote the pretest variable by x_1 and the posttest variable by x_2, then the difference variable $y = x_2 - x_1$ is a simple linear combination where $a_1 = -1$ and $a_2 = 1$.

As another example of a simple linear combination, suppose we wished to sum three subtest scores on a test $(x_1, x_2, \text{and } x_3)$. Then the newly created sum variable $y = x_1 + x_2 + x_3$ is a linear combination where $a_1 = a_2 = a_3 = 1$.

Still another example of linear combinations that you may have encountered in an intermediate statistics course is that of contrasts among means, as when planned comparisons are used. Consider the following four-group ANOVA, where T_3 is a combination treatment, and T_4 is a control group:

$$\frac{T_1 T_2 T_3 T_4}{\mu_1 \mu_2 \mu_3 \mu_4}$$

Then the following meaningful contrast

$$L_1 = \frac{\mu_1 + \mu_2}{2} - \mu_3$$

is a linear combination, where $a_1 = a_2 = \frac{1}{2}$ and $a_3 = -1$, while the following contrast among means,

$$L_1 = \frac{\mu_1 + \mu_2 + \mu_3}{3} - \mu_4,$$

is also a linear combination, where $a_1 = a_2 = a_3 = \frac{1}{3}$ and $a_4 = -1$. The notions of mathematical maximization and linear combinations are combined in many of the multivariate procedures. For example, in multiple regression we talk about the linear combination of the predictors that is maximally correlated with the dependent variable, and in principal components analysis the linear combinations of the variables that account for maximum portions of the total variance are considered.

1.13 DATA COLLECTION AND INTEGRITY

Although in this text we minimize discussion of issues related to data collection and measurement of variables, as this text focuses on analysis, you are forewarned that these are critical issues. No analysis, no matter how sophisticated, can compensate for poor data collection and measurement problems. Iverson and Gergen (1997) in chapter 14 of their text on statistics hit on some key issues. First, they discussed the issue of obtaining a random sample, so that one can generalize to some population of interest. They noted:

> We believe that researchers are aware of the need for randomness, but achieving it is another matter. In many studies, the condition of randomness is almost never truly satisfied. A majority of psychological studies, for example, rely on college students for their research results. (Critics have suggested that modern psychology should be called the psychology of the college sophomore.) Are college students a random sample of the adult population or even the adolescent population? Not likely. (p. 627)

Then they turned their attention to problems in survey research, and noted:

> In interview studies, for example, differences in responses have been found depending on whether the interviewer seems to be similar or different from the respondent in such aspects as gender, ethnicity, and personal preferences. . . . The place of the interview is also important. . . . Contextual effects cannot be overcome totally and must be accepted as a facet of the data collection process. (pp. 628–629)

Another point they mentioned is that what people say and what they do often do not correspond. They noted, "a study that asked about toothbrushing habits found that on the basis of what people said they did, the toothpaste consumption in this country should have been three times larger than the amount that is actually sold" (pp. 630–631).

Another problem, endemic in psychology, is using college freshmen or sophomores. This raises issues of data integrity. A student, visiting Dr. Stevens and expecting advice on multivariate analysis, had collected data from college freshmen. Dr. Stevens raised concerns about the integrity of the data, worrying that for most 18- or 19-year-olds concentration lapses after 5 or 10 minutes. As such, this would compromise the integrity of the data, which no analysis could help. Many freshmen may be thinking about the next party or social event, and filling out the questionnaire is far from the most important thing in their minds.

In ending this section, we wish to point out that many mail questionnaires and telephone interviews may be much too long. Mail questionnaires, for the most part, can be limited to two pages, and telephone interviews to 5 to 10 minutes. If you think about it, most if not all relevant questions can be asked within 5 minutes. It is always a balance between information obtained and participant fatigue, but unless participants are very motivated, they may have too many other things going in their lives to spend the time filling out a 10-page questionnaire or to spend 20 minutes on the telephone.

1.14 INTERNAL AND EXTERNAL VALIDITY

Although this is a book on statistical analysis, the design you set up is critical. In a course on research methods, you learn of internal and external validity, and of the threats to each. If you have designed an experimental study, then internal validity refers to the confidence you have that the treatment(s) are responsible for the posttest group differences. There are various threats to internal validity (e.g., history, maturation, selection, regression toward the mean). In setting up a design, you want to be confident that the treatment caused the difference, and not one of the threats. Random assignment of participants to groups controls most of the threats to internal validity, and for this reason it is often referred to as the "gold standard." It is the best way of assuring, within sampling error, that the groups are "equal" on all variables prior to treatment implementation. However, if there is a variable (we will use gender and two groups to illustrate) that is related to the dependent variable, then one should stratify on that variable and then randomly assign within each stratum. For example, if there were 36 females and 24 males, we would randomly assign 18 females and 12 males to each group. By doing this, we ensure an equal number of males and females in each group, rather than leaving this to chance. It is extremely important to understand that good research design is essential. Light, Singer, and Willett (1990), in the preface of their book, summed it up best by stating bluntly, "you can't fix by analysis what you bungled by design" (p. viii).

Treatment, as stated earlier, is generic and could refer to teaching methods, counseling methods, drugs, diets, and so on. It is dangerous to assume that the treatment(s) will be implemented as you planned, and hence it is very important to monitor the treatment to help ensure that it is implemented as intended. If the planned and implemented treatments differ, it may not be clear what is responsible for the obtained group differences. Further, posttest differences may not appear if the treatments are not implemented as intended.

Now let us turn our attention to external validity. External validity refers to the generalizability of results. That is, to what population(s) of participants, settings, and times can we generalize our results? A good book on external validity is by Shadish, Cook, and Campbell (2002).

Two excellent books on research design are the aforementioned *By Design* by Light, Singer, and Willett (which Dr. Stevens used for many years) and a book by Alan Kazdin entitled *Research Design in Clinical Psychology* (2003). Both of these books require, in our opinion, that students have at least two courses in statistics and a course on research methods.

Before leaving this section, a word of warning on ratings as the dependent variable. Often you will hear of training raters so that raters agree. This is fine. However, it does not go far enough. There is still the issue of bias with the raters, and this can be very problematic if the rater has a vested interest in the outcome. Dr. Stevens has seen too many dissertations where the person writing it is one of the raters.

1.15 CONFLICT OF INTEREST

Kazdin notes that conflict of interest can occur in many different ways (2003, p. 537). One way is through a conflict between the scientific responsibility of the investigator(s) and a vested financial interest. We illustrate this with a medical example. In the introduction to *Overdosed America* (2004), Abramson gives the following medical conflict:

> The second part, "The Commercialization of American Medicine," presents a brief history of the commercial takeover of medical knowledge and the techniques used to manipulate doctors' and the public's understanding of new developments in medical science and health care. One example of the depth of the problem was presented in a 2002 article in the *Journal of the American Medical Association*, which showed that 59% of the experts who write the clinical guidelines that define good medical care have direct financial ties to the companies whose products are being evaluated. (p. xvii)

Kazdin (2003) gives examples that hit closer to home, that is, from psychology and education:

> In psychological research and perhaps specifically in clinical, counseling and educational psychology, it is easy to envision conflict of interest. Researchers may own stock in companies that in some way are relevant to their research and their findings. Also, a researcher may serve as a consultant to a company (e.g., that develops software or psychological tests or that publishes books) and receive generous consultation fees for serving as a resource for the company. Serving as someone who gains financially from a company and who conducts research with products that the company may sell could be a conflict of interest or perceived as a conflict. (p. 539)

The example we gave earlier of someone serving as a rater for their dissertation is a potential conflict of interest. That individual has a vested interest in the results, and for him or her to remain objective in doing the ratings is definitely questionable.

1.16 SUMMARY

This chapter reviewed type I error, type II error, and power. It indicated that power is dependent on the alpha level, sample size, and effect size. The problem of multiple statistical tests appearing in various situations was discussed. The important issue of statistical versus practical importance was discussed, and some ways of assessing practical importance (confidence intervals, effect sizes, and measures of association) were mentioned. The importance of identifying outliers (e.g., participants who are 3 or more standard deviations from the mean) was emphasized. We also considered at some length issues related to missing data, discussed factors involved in selecting a missing data treatment, and illustrated with a small data set how you can select and implement a missing data treatment. We also showed that conventional missing data treatments can produce relatively poor parameter estimates with MAR data. We also briefly discussed participant or unit nonresponse. SAS and SPSS syntax files and accompanying data sets for the examples used in this text are available on the Internet, and these files allow you to easily replicate analysis results shown in this text. Regarding data integrity, what people say and what they do often do not correspond. The critical importance of a good design was also emphasized. Finally, it is important to keep in mind that conflict of interest can undermine the integrity of results.

1.17 EXERCISES

1. Consider a two-group independent-samples t test with a treatment group (treatment is generic and could be intervention, diet, drug, counseling method, etc.) and a control group. The null hypothesis is that the population means are equal. What are the consequences of making a type I error? What are the consequences of making a type II error?

2. This question is concerned with power.

   (a) Suppose a clinical study (10 participants in each of two groups) does not find significance at the .05 level, but there is a medium effect size (which is judged to be of practical importance). What should the investigator do in a future replication study?

   (b) It has been mentioned that there can be "too much power" in some studies. What is meant by this? Relate this to the "sledgehammer effect" mentioned in the chapter.

3. This question is concerned with multiple statistical tests.

   (a) Consider a two-way ANOVA ($A \times B$) with six dependent variables. If a univariate analysis is done at $\alpha = .05$ on each dependent variable, then how many tests have been done? What is the Bonferroni upper bound on overall alpha? Compute the tighter bound.

   (b) Now consider a three-way ANOVA ($A \times B \times C$) with four dependent variables. If a univariate analysis is done at $\alpha = .05$ on each dependent variable, then how many tests have been done? What is the Bonferroni upper bound on overall alpha? Compute the tighter upper bound.

4. This question is concerned with statistical versus practical importance: A survey researcher compares four regions of the country on their attitude toward education. To this survey, 800 participants respond. Ten items, Likert scaled

from 1 to 5, are used to assess attitude. A higher positive score indicates a more positive attitude. Group sizes and the means are given next.

	North	South	East	West
N	238	182	130	250
$\bar{x}$	32.0	33.1	34.0	31.0

An analysis of variance on these four groups yielded $F = 5.61$, which is significant at the .001 level. Discuss the practical importance issue.

5. This question concerns outliers: Suppose 150 participants are measured on four variables. Why could a subject not be an outlier on any of the four variables and yet be an outlier when the four variables are considered jointly?

   Suppose a Mahalanobis distance is computed for each subject (checking for multivariate outliers). Why might it be advisable to do each test at the .001 level?

6. Suppose you have a data set where some participants have missing data on income. Further, suppose you use the methods described in section 1.6.6 to assess whether the missing data appear to be MCAR and find that is missingness on income is not related to any of your study variables. Does that mean the data are MCAR? Why or why not?

7. If data are MCAR and a very small proportion of data is missing, would listwise deletion, maximum likelihood estimation, and multiple imputation all be good missing data treatments to use? Why or why not?

REFERENCES

Abramson, J. (2004). *Overdosed America: The broken promise of American medicine*. New York, NY: Harper Collins.

Allison, P.D. (2001). *Missing data*. Newbury Park, CA: Sage.

Allison, P.D. (2012). *Handling missing data by maximum likelihood*. Unpublished manuscript. Retrieved from http://www.statisticalhorizons.com/resources/unpublished-papers

Cohen, J. (1988). *Statistical power analysis for the social sciences* (2nd ed.). Hillsdale, NJ: Lawrence Erlbaum Associates.

Cronbach, L., & Snow, R. (1977). *Aptitudes and instructional methods: A handbook for research on interactions*. New York, NY: Irvington.

Enders, C.K. (2010). *Applied missing data analysis*. New York, NY: Guilford Press.

Friedman, G., Lehrer, B., & Stevens, J. (1983). The effectiveness of self-directed and lecture/discussion stress management approaches and the locus of control of teachers. *American Educational Research Journal, 20*, 563–580.

Grissom, R. J., & Kim, J. J. (2012). *Effect sizes for research: Univariate and multivariate applications* (2nd ed.). New York, NY: Routledge.

Groves, R. M., Fowler, F. J., Couper, M. P., Lepkowski, J. M., Singer, E., & Tourangeau, R. (2009). *Survey methodology* (2nd ed.). Hoboken, NJ: Wiley & Sons.

Haase, R., Ellis, M., & Ladany, N. (1989). Multiple criteria for evaluating the magnitude of experimental effects. *Journal of Consulting Psychology, 36,* 511–516.

Iverson, G., & Gergen, M. (1997). *Statistics: A conceptual approach.* New York, NY: Springer-Verlag.

Jacobson, N. S. (Ed.). (1988). Defining clinically significant change [Special issue]. *Behavioral Assessment, 10*(2).

Judd, C. M., McClelland, G. H., & Ryan, C. S. (2009). *Data analysis: A model comparison approach* (2nd ed.). New York, NY: Routledge.

Kazdin, A. (2003). *Research design in clinical psychology.* Boston, MA: Allyn & Bacon.

Light, R., Singer, J., & Willett, J. (1990). *By design.* Cambridge, MA: Harvard University Press.

McCrudden, M. T., Schraw, G., & Hartley, K. (2006). The effect of general relevance instructions on shallow and deeper learning and reading time. *Journal of Experimental Education, 74,* 291–310. doi:10.3200/JEXE.74.4.291-310

O'Grady, K. (1982). Measures of explained variation: Cautions and limitations. *Psychological Bulletin, 92,* 766–777.

Reingle Gonzalez, J. M., & Connell, N. M. (2014). Mental health of prisoners: Identifying barriers to mental health treatment and medication continuity. *American Journal of Public Health, 104,* 2328–2333. doi:10.2105/AJPH.2014.302043

Shadish, W. R., Cook, T. D., & Campbell, D. T. (2002). *Experimental and quasi-experimental designs for generalized causal inference.* Boston, MA: Houghton Mifflin.

Shiffler, R. (1988). Maximum z scores and outliers. *American Statistician, 42,* 79–80.

Wong, Y. L., Pituch, K. A., & Rochlen, A. R. (2006). Men's restrictive emotionality: An investigation of associations with other emotion-related constructs, anxiety, and underlying dimensions. *Psychology of Men and Masculinity, 7,* 113–126. doi:10.1037/1524-9220.7.2.113

Chapter 2

MATRIX ALGEBRA

2.1 INTRODUCTION

This chapter introduces matrices and vectors and covers some of the basic matrix operations used in multivariate statistics. The matrix operations included are by no means intended to be exhaustive. Instead, we present some important tools that will help you better understand multivariate analysis. Understanding matrix algebra is important, as the values of multivariate test statistics (e.g., Hotelling's T^2 and Wilks' lambda), effect size measures (D^2 and multivariate eta square), and outlier indicators (e.g., the Mahalanobis distance) are obtained with matrix algebra. We assume here that you have no previous exposure to matrix operations. Also, while it is helpful, at times, to compute matrix operations by hand (particularly for smaller matrices), we include SPSS and SAS commands that can be used to perform matrix operations.

A matrix is simply a rectangular array of elements. The following are examples of matrices:

$$\begin{bmatrix} 1 & 2 & 3 & 4 \\ 4 & 5 & 6 & 9 \end{bmatrix} \quad \begin{bmatrix} 1 & 2 & 1 \\ 2 & 3 & 5 \\ 5 & 6 & 8 \\ 1 & 4 & 10 \end{bmatrix} \quad \begin{bmatrix} 1 & 2 \\ 2 & 4 \end{bmatrix}$$
$$2 \times 4 \qquad\qquad 4 \times 3 \qquad\qquad 2 \times 2$$

The numbers underneath each matrix are the dimensions of the matrix, and indicate the size of the matrix. The first number is the number of rows and the second number the number of columns. Thus, the first matrix is a 2 × 4 since it has 2 rows and 4 columns.

A familiar matrix in educational research is the score matrix. For example, suppose we had measured six subjects on three variables. We could represent all the scores as a matrix:

$$
\text{Subjects} \quad
\begin{array}{c}
\\
\\
\\
\\
\\
1 \\
2 \\
3 \\
4 \\
5 \\
6
\end{array}
\overset{\displaystyle \begin{array}{ccc} \textit{Variables} \\ 1 \quad\ 2 \quad\ 3 \end{array}}
{\begin{bmatrix}
10 & 4 & 18 \\
12 & 6 & 21 \\
13 & 2 & 20 \\
16 & 8 & 16 \\
12 & 3 & 14 \\
15 & 9 & 13
\end{bmatrix}}
$$

This is a 6×3 matrix. More generally, we can represent the scores of N participants on p variables in an $N \times p$ matrix as follows:

$$
\text{Subjects} \quad
\begin{array}{c}
1 \\
2 \\
\\
N
\end{array}
\overset{\displaystyle \begin{array}{cccc} \textit{Variables} \\ 1 \quad\ 2 \quad\ 3 \qquad\ p \end{array}}
{\begin{bmatrix}
x_{11} & x_{12} & x_{13} & \cdots & x_{1p} \\
x_{21} & x_{22} & x_{23} & \cdots & x_{2p} \\
\vdots & \vdots & \vdots & & \vdots \\
x_{N1} & x_{N2} & x_{N3} & \cdots & x_{Np}
\end{bmatrix}}
$$

The first subscript indicates the row and the second subscript the column. Thus, x_{12} represents the score of participant 1 on variable 2 and x_{2p} represents the score of participant 2 on variable p.

The *transpose* $\mathbf{A'}$ of a matrix $\mathbf{A}$ is simply the matrix obtained by interchanging rows and columns.

Example 2.1

$$
\mathbf{A} = \begin{bmatrix} 2 & 3 & 6 \\ 5 & 4 & 8 \end{bmatrix} \qquad
\mathbf{A'} = \begin{bmatrix} 2 & 5 \\ 3 & 4 \\ 6 & 8 \end{bmatrix}
$$

The first row of $\mathbf{A}$ has become the first column of $\mathbf{A'}$ and the second row of $\mathbf{A}$ has become the second column of $\mathbf{A'}$.

$$
\mathbf{B} = \begin{bmatrix} 3 & 4 & 2 \\ 5 & 6 & 5 \\ 1 & 3 & 8 \end{bmatrix} \rightarrow
\mathbf{B'} = \begin{bmatrix} 3 & 5 & 1 \\ 4 & 6 & 3 \\ 2 & 5 & 8 \end{bmatrix}
$$

In general, if a matrix $\mathbf{A}$ has dimensions $r \times s$, then the dimensions of the transpose are $s \times r$.

A matrix with a single row is called a row vector, and a matrix with a single column is called a column vector. While matrices are written in bold uppercase letters, as we have seen, vectors are always indicated by bold lowercase letters. Also, a row vector is indicated by a transpose, for example, $\mathbf{x}'$, $\mathbf{y}'$, and so on.

Example 2.2

$$\mathbf{x}' = (1,2,3)$$
1×3 row vector

$$\mathbf{y} = \begin{bmatrix} 4 \\ 6 \\ 8 \\ 7 \end{bmatrix} 4 \times 1 \text{ column vector}$$

A row vector that is of particular interest to us later is the vector of means for a group of participants on several variables. For example, suppose we have measured 100 participants on the California Psychological Inventory and have obtained their average scores on five of the subscales. The five means would be represented as the following row vector $\mathbf{x}'$:

$$\mathbf{x}' = (24, 31, 22, 27, 30)$$

The elements on the diagonal running from upper left to lower right are said to be on the main diagonal of a matrix. A matrix $\mathbf{A}$ is said to be *symmetric* if the elements below the main diagonal are a mirror reflection of the corresponding elements above the main diagonal. This is saying $a_{12} = a_{21}$, $a_{13} = a_{31}$, and $a_{23} = a_{32}$ for a 3×3 matrix, since these are the corresponding pairs. This is illustrated by:

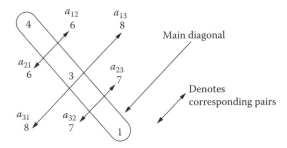

In general, a matrix $\mathbf{A}$ is symmetric if $a_{ij} = a_{ji}$, $i \neq j$, that is, if all corresponding pairs of elements above and below the main diagonal are equal.

An example of a symmetric matrix that is frequently encountered in statistical work is that of a correlation matrix. For example, here is the matrix of intercorrelations for four subtests of the Differential Aptitude Test for boys:

	VR	NA	Cler.	Mech.
Verbal reas.	1.00	.70	.19	.55
Numerical abil.	.70	1.00	.36	.50
Clerical speed	.19	.36	1.00	.16
Mechan. reas.	.55	.50	.16	1.00

This matrix is symmetric because, for example, the correlation between VR and NA is the same as the correlation between NA and VR.

Two matrices **A** and **B** are equal if and only if all corresponding elements are equal. That is to say, two matrices are equal only if they are identical.

2.2 ADDITION, SUBTRACTION, AND MULTIPLICATION OF A MATRIX BY A SCALAR

You add two matrices **A** and **B** by summing the corresponding elements.

Example 2.3

$$\mathbf{A} = \begin{bmatrix} 2 & 3 \\ 3 & 4 \end{bmatrix} \quad \mathbf{B} = \begin{bmatrix} 6 & 2 \\ 2 & 5 \end{bmatrix}$$

$$\mathbf{A} + \mathbf{B} = \begin{bmatrix} 2+6 & 3+2 \\ 3+2 & 4+5 \end{bmatrix} = \begin{bmatrix} 8 & 5 \\ 5 & 9 \end{bmatrix}$$

Notice the elements in the (1, 1) positions, that is, 2 and 6, have been added, and so on.

Only matrices of the same dimensions can be added. Thus, addition would not be defined for these matrices:

$$\begin{bmatrix} 2 & 3 & 1 \\ 1 & 4 & 6 \end{bmatrix} + \begin{bmatrix} 1 & 4 \\ 5 & 6 \end{bmatrix} \text{ not defined}$$

If two matrices are of the same dimension, you can then subtract one matrix from another by subtracting corresponding elements.

$$\begin{matrix} \mathbf{A} & & \mathbf{B} & & \mathbf{A}-\mathbf{B} \end{matrix}$$
$$\begin{bmatrix} 2 & 1 & 5 \\ 3 & 2 & 6 \end{bmatrix} - \begin{bmatrix} 1 & 4 & 2 \\ 1 & 2 & 5 \end{bmatrix} = \begin{bmatrix} 1 & -3 & 3 \\ 2 & 0 & 1 \end{bmatrix}$$

You multiply a matrix or a vector by a scalar (number) by multiplying each element of the matrix or vector by the scalar.

Example 2.4

$$2(3,1,4) = (6,2,8) \quad 1/3\begin{bmatrix} 4 \\ 3 \end{bmatrix} = \begin{bmatrix} 4/3 \\ 1 \end{bmatrix}$$

$$4\begin{bmatrix} 2 & 1 \\ 1 & 5 \end{bmatrix} = \begin{bmatrix} 8 & 4 \\ 4 & 20 \end{bmatrix}$$

2.2.1 Multiplication of Matrices

There is a restriction as to when two matrices can be multiplied. Consider the product **AB.** To multiply these matrices, *the number of columns in* **A** *must equal the number of rows in* **B**. For example, if **A** is 2 × 3, then **B** must have 3 rows, although **B** could have any number of columns. If two matrices can be multiplied they are said to be *conformable*. The dimensions of the product matrix, call it **C,** are simply the number of rows of **A** by the number of columns of **B**. In the earlier example, if **B** were 3 × 4, then **C** would be a 2 × 4 matrix. In general then, if **A** is an $r \times s$ matrix and **B** is an $s \times t$ matrix, then the dimensions of the product **AB** are $r \times t$.

Example 2.5

$$
\begin{array}{ccc}
\mathbf{A} & \mathbf{B} & \mathbf{C} \\
\begin{bmatrix} 2 & 1 & 3 \\ 4 & 5 & 6 \end{bmatrix} & \begin{bmatrix} 1 & 0 \\ 2 & 4 \\ -1 & 5 \end{bmatrix} = & \begin{bmatrix} c_{11} & c_{12} \\ c_{21} & c_{22} \end{bmatrix} \\
2 \times 3 & 3 \times 2 & 2 \times 2
\end{array}
$$

Note first that **A** and **B** can be multiplied because the number of columns in **A** is 3, which is equal to the number of rows in **B**. The product matrix **C** is a 2 × 2, that is, the outer dimensions of **A** and **B**. To obtain the element c_{11} (in the first row and first column), we multiply corresponding elements of the first row of **A** by the elements of the first column of **B**. Then, we simply sum the products. To obtain c_{12} we take the sum of products of the corresponding elements of the first row of **A** by the second column of **B**. This procedure is presented next for all four elements of **C:**

Element

$$
c_{11} \quad (2,1,3) \begin{pmatrix} 1 \\ 2 \\ -1 \end{pmatrix} = 2(1) + 1(2) + 3(-1) = 1
$$

$$
c_{12} \quad (2,1,3) \begin{pmatrix} 0 \\ 4 \\ 5 \end{pmatrix} = 2(0) + 1(4) + 3(5) = 19
$$

$$
c_{21} \quad (4,5,6) \begin{pmatrix} 1 \\ 2 \\ -1 \end{pmatrix} = 4(1) + 5(2) + 6(-1) = 8
$$

$$
c_{22} \quad (4,5,6) \begin{pmatrix} 0 \\ 4 \\ 5 \end{pmatrix} = 4(0) + 5(4) + 6(5) = 50
$$

Therefore, the product matrix **C** is:

$$\mathbf{C} = \begin{bmatrix} 1 & 19 \\ 8 & 50 \end{bmatrix}$$

We now multiply two more matrices to illustrate an important property concerning matrix multiplication.

Example 2.6

$$\overset{\mathbf{A}}{\begin{bmatrix} 2 & 1 \\ 1 & 4 \end{bmatrix}} \quad \overset{\mathbf{B}}{\begin{bmatrix} 3 & 5 \\ 5 & 6 \end{bmatrix}} = \begin{bmatrix} 2 \cdot 3 + 1 \cdot 5 & 2 \cdot 5 + 1 \cdot 6 \\ 1 \cdot 3 + 4 \cdot 5 & 1 \cdot 5 + 4 \cdot 6 \end{bmatrix} = \overset{\mathbf{AB}}{\begin{bmatrix} 11 & 16 \\ 23 & 29 \end{bmatrix}}$$

$$\overset{\mathbf{B}}{\begin{bmatrix} 3 & 5 \\ 5 & 6 \end{bmatrix}} \quad \overset{\mathbf{A}}{\begin{bmatrix} 2 & 1 \\ 1 & 4 \end{bmatrix}} = \begin{bmatrix} 3 \cdot 2 + 5 \cdot 1 & 3 \cdot 1 + 5 \cdot 4 \\ 5 \cdot 2 + 6 \cdot 1 & 5 \cdot 1 + 6 \cdot 4 \end{bmatrix} = \overset{\mathbf{BA}}{\begin{bmatrix} 11 & 23 \\ 16 & 29 \end{bmatrix}}$$

Notice that **AB** ≠ **BA**; that is, the *order* in which matrices are multiplied makes a difference. The mathematical statement of this is to say that multiplication of matrices is not commutative. Multiplying matrices in two different orders (assuming they are conformable both ways) in general yields different results.

Example 2.7

$$\overset{\mathbf{A}}{\begin{bmatrix} 3 & 1 & 2 \\ 1 & 4 & 5 \\ 2 & 5 & 2 \end{bmatrix}} \overset{\mathbf{x}}{\begin{bmatrix} 2 \\ 6 \\ 3 \end{bmatrix}} = \overset{\mathbf{Ax}}{\begin{bmatrix} 18 \\ 41 \\ 40 \end{bmatrix}}$$
$$(3 \times 3) \quad (3 \times 1) \quad (3 \times 1)$$

Note that multiplying a matrix on the right by a column vector takes the matrix into a column vector.

$$(2,5) \begin{bmatrix} 3 & 1 \\ 1 & 4 \end{bmatrix} = (11,22)$$

Multiplying a matrix on the left by a row vector results in a row vector. If we are multiplying more than two matrices, then we may *group at will*. The mathematical statement of this is that multiplication of matrices is associative. Thus, if we are considering the matrix product **ABC,** we get the same result if we multiply **A** and **B** first (and then the result of that by **C**) as if we multiply **B** and **C** first (and then the result of that by **A**), that is,

A B C = (A B) C = A (B C)

A matrix product that is of particular interest to us in Chapter 4 is of the following form:

$$\underset{1 \times p}{\mathbf{x}'} \quad \underset{p \times p}{\mathbf{S}} \quad \underset{p \times 1}{\mathbf{x}}$$

Note that this product yields a number, i.e., the product matrix is 1×1 or a number. The multivariate test statistic for two groups, Hotelling's T^2, is of this form (except for a scalar constant in front). Other multivariate statistics, for example, that are computed in a similar way are the Mahalanobis distance (section 3.14.6) and the multivariate effect size measure D^2 (section 4.11).

Example 2.8

$$\mathbf{x}' \quad \mathbf{S} \quad \mathbf{x} = (\mathbf{x}'\mathbf{S}) \quad \mathbf{x}$$

$$(4,2)\begin{bmatrix} 10 & 3 \\ 3 & 4 \end{bmatrix}\begin{bmatrix} 4 \\ 2 \end{bmatrix} = (46,20)\begin{bmatrix} 4 \\ 2 \end{bmatrix} = 184 + 40 = 224$$

2.3 OBTAINING THE MATRIX OF VARIANCES AND COVARIANCES

Now, we show how various matrix operations introduced thus far can be used to obtain two very important matrices in multivariate statistics, that is, the sums of squares and cross products (SSCP) matrix (which is computed as part of the Wilks' lambda test) and the matrix of variances and covariances for a set of variables (which is computed as part of Hotelling's T^2 test). Consider the following set of data:

x_1	x_2
1	1
3	4
2	7
$\bar{x}_1 = 2$	$\bar{x}_2 = 4$

First, we form the matrix $\mathbf{X}_d$ of deviation scores, that is, how much each score deviates from the mean on that variable:

$$\overset{\mathbf{X}}{} \qquad \overset{\bar{\mathbf{X}}}{}$$

$$\mathbf{X}_d = \begin{bmatrix} 1 & 1 \\ 3 & 4 \\ 2 & 7 \end{bmatrix} - \begin{bmatrix} 2 & 4 \\ 2 & 4 \\ 2 & 4 \end{bmatrix} = \begin{bmatrix} -1 & -3 \\ 1 & 0 \\ 0 & 3 \end{bmatrix}$$

Next we take the transpose of $\mathbf{X}_d$:

$$\mathbf{X}'_d = \begin{bmatrix} -1 & 1 & 0 \\ -3 & 0 & 3 \end{bmatrix}$$

Now we obtain the matrix of sums of squares and cross products **(SSCP)** as the product of $\mathbf{X}'_d$ and $\mathbf{X}_d$:

$$\mathbf{SSCP} = \begin{bmatrix} -1 & 1 & 0 \\ -3 & 0 & 3 \end{bmatrix} \begin{bmatrix} -1 & -3 \\ 1 & 0 \\ 0 & 3 \end{bmatrix} = \begin{bmatrix} ss_1 & ss_{12} \\ ss_{21} & ss_2 \end{bmatrix}$$

The diagonal elements are just sums of squares:

$$ss_1 = (-1)^2 + 1^2 + 0^2 = 2$$
$$ss_2 = (-3)^2 + 0^2 + 3^2 = 18$$

Notice that these deviation sums of squares are the numerators of the variances for the variables, because the variance for a variable is

$$s^2 = \sum_i \left(x_{ii} - \overline{x} \right)^2 / (n-1).$$

The sum of deviation cross products (ss_{12}) for the two variables is

$$ss_{12} = ss_{21} = (-1)(-3) + 1(0) + (0)(3) = 3.$$

This is just the numerator for the covariance for the two variables, because the definitional formula for covariance is given by:

$$s_{12} = \frac{\displaystyle\sum_{i=1}^{n} \left(x_{i1} - \overline{x}_1 \right)\left(x_{i2} - \overline{x}_2 \right)}{n-1},$$

where $\left(x_{i1} - \overline{x}_1 \right)$ is the deviation score for the ith case on x_1 and $\left(x_{i2} - \overline{x}_2 \right)$ is the deviation score for the ith case on x_2.

Finally, the matrix of variances and covariances $\mathbf{S}$ is obtained from the **SSCP** matrix by multiplying by a constant, namely, $1/(n-1)$:

$$\mathbf{S} = \frac{\mathbf{SSCP}}{n-1}$$

$$\mathbf{S} = \frac{1}{2} \begin{bmatrix} 2 & 3 \\ 3 & 18 \end{bmatrix} = \begin{bmatrix} 1 & 1.5 \\ 1.5 & 9 \end{bmatrix}$$

where 1 and 9 are the variances for variables 1 and 2, respectively, and 1.5 is the covariance.

Thus, in obtaining $\mathbf{S}$ we have done the following:

1. Represented the scores on several variables as a matrix.
2. Illustrated subtraction of matrices—to get $\mathbf{X}_d$.

3. Illustrated the transpose of a matrix—to get $\mathbf{X}'_d$.
4. Illustrated multiplication of matrices, that is, $\mathbf{X}'_d \mathbf{X}_d$, to get **SSCP**.
5. Illustrated multiplication of a matrix by a scalar, that is, by $1/(n-1)$, to obtain **S**.

2.4 DETERMINANT OF A MATRIX

The determinant of a matrix **A,** denoted by $|\mathbf{A}|$, is a unique number associated with each *square* matrix. There are two interrelated reasons that consideration of determinants is quite important for multivariate statistical analysis. First, the determinant of a covariance matrix represents the *generalized* variance for several variables. That is, it is one way to characterize in a single number how much variability remains for the set of variables after removing the shared variance among the variables. Second, because the determinant is a measure of variance for a set of variables, it is intimately involved in several multivariate test statistics. For example, in Chapter 3 on regression analysis, we use a test statistic called Wilks' Λ that involves a ratio of two determinants. Also, in k group multivariate analysis of variance (Chapter 5) the following form of Wilks' Λ $(\Lambda = |\mathbf{W}|/|\mathbf{T}|)$ is the most widely used test statistic for determining whether several groups differ on a set of variables. The **W** and **T** matrices are SSCP matrices, which are multivariate generalizations of SS_w (sum of squares within) and SS_t (sum of squares total) from univariate ANOVA, and are defined and described in detail in Chapters 4 and 5.

There is a formal definition for finding the determinant of a matrix, but it is complicated, and we do not present it. There are other ways of finding the determinant, and a convenient method for smaller matrices (4 × 4 or less) is the method of cofactors. For a 2 × 2 matrix, the determinant could be evaluated by the method of cofactors; however, it is evaluated more quickly as simply the difference in the products of the diagonal elements.

Example 2.9

$$\mathbf{A} = \begin{bmatrix} 4 & 1 \\ 1 & 2 \end{bmatrix} \quad |\mathbf{A}| = 4 \cdot 2 - 1 \cdot 1 = 7$$

In general, for a 2 × 2 matrix $\mathbf{A} = \begin{bmatrix} a & b \\ c & d \end{bmatrix}$, then $|\mathbf{A}| = ad - bc$.

To evaluate the determinant of a 3 × 3 matrix we need the method of cofactors and the following definition.

Definition: The *minor* of an element a_{ij} is the determinant of the matrix formed by deleting the ith row and the jth column.

Example 2.10
Consider the following matrix:

$$a_{12} \ a_{13}$$
$$\downarrow \ \downarrow$$

$$\mathbf{A} = \begin{bmatrix} 1 & 2 & 3 \\ 2 & 2 & 1 \\ 3 & 1 & 4 \end{bmatrix}$$

The minor of a_{12} (with this element equal to 2 in the matrix) is the determinant of the matrix $\begin{bmatrix} 2 & 1 \\ 3 & 4 \end{bmatrix}$ obtained by deleting the first row and the second column. Therefore, the minor of a_{12} is $\begin{vmatrix} 2 & 1 \\ 3 & 4 \end{vmatrix} = 8 - 3 = 5.$

The minor of a_{13} (with this element equal to 3) is the determinant of the matrix $\begin{bmatrix} 2 & 2 \\ 3 & 1 \end{bmatrix}$ obtained by deleting the first row and the third column. Thus, the minor of a_{13} is $\begin{vmatrix} 2 & 2 \\ 3 & 1 \end{vmatrix} = 2 - 6 = -4.$

Definition: The cofactor of $a_{ij} = (-1)^{i+j} \times$ minor.

Thus, the cofactor of an element will differ at most from its minor by sign. We now evaluate $(-1)^{i+j}$ for the first three elements of the **A** matrix given:

$$a_{11} : (-1)^{1+1} = 1$$

$$a_{12} : (-1)^{1+2} = -1$$

$$a_{13} : (-1)^{1+3} = 1$$

Notice that the signs for the elements in the first row alternate, and this pattern continues for all the elements in a 3 × 3 matrix. Thus, when evaluating the determinant for a 3 × 3 matrix it will be convenient to write down the pattern of signs and use it, rather than figuring out what $(-1)^{i+j}$ is for each element. That pattern of signs is:

$$\begin{bmatrix} + & - & + \\ - & + & - \\ + & - & + \end{bmatrix}$$

We denote the matrix of cofactors **C** as follows:

$$\mathbf{C} = \begin{bmatrix} c_{11} & c_{12} & c_{13} \\ c_{21} & c_{22} & c_{23} \\ c_{31} & c_{32} & c_{33} \end{bmatrix}$$

Now, *the determinant is obtained by expanding along any row or column of the matrix of cofactors*. Thus, for example, the determinant of **A** would be given by

$$|\mathbf{A}| = a_{11}c_{11} + a_{12}c_{12} + a_{13}c_{13}$$

(expanding along the first row)

or by

$$|\mathbf{A}| = a_{12}c_{12} + a_{22}c_{22} + a_{32}c_{32}$$

(expanding along the second column)

We now find the determinant of **A** by expanding along the first row:

Element	Minor	Cofactor	Element × cofactor
$a_{11} = 1$	$\begin{vmatrix} 2 & 1 \\ 1 & 4 \end{vmatrix} = 7$	7	7
$a_{12} = 2$	$\begin{vmatrix} 2 & 1 \\ 3 & 4 \end{vmatrix} = 5$	−5	−10
$a_{13} = 3$	$\begin{vmatrix} 2 & 2 \\ 3 & 1 \end{vmatrix} = -4$	−4	−12

Therefore, $|\mathbf{A}| = 7 + (-10) + (-12) = -15$.

For a 4×4 matrix the pattern of signs is given by:

$$
\begin{array}{cccc}
+ & - & + & - \\
- & + & - & + \\
+ & - & + & - \\
- & + & - & +
\end{array}
$$

and the determinant is again evaluated by expanding along any row or column. However, in this case the minors are determinants of 3×3 matrices, and the procedure becomes quite tedious. Thus, we do not pursue it any further here.

In the example in 2.3, we obtained the following covariance matrix:

$$\mathbf{S} = \begin{bmatrix} 1.0 & 1.5 \\ 1.5 & 9.0 \end{bmatrix}$$

We also indicated at the beginning of this section that the determinant of **S** can be interpreted as the generalized variance for a set of variables.

Now, the generalized variance for the two-variable example is just $|\mathbf{S}| = (1 \times 9) - (1.5 \times 1.5) = 6.75$. Because for this example there is a nonzero covariance, the generalized variance is reduced by this. That is, some of the variance of variable 2 is shared by variable 1. On the other hand, if the variables were uncorrelated (covariance = 0), then we would expect the generalized variance to be larger (because there is no shared variance between variables), and this is indeed the case:

$$|\mathbf{S}| = \begin{vmatrix} 1 & 0 \\ 0 & 9 \end{vmatrix} = 9$$

Thus, in representing the variance for a set of variables this measure takes into account all the variances and covariances.

In addition, the meaning of the generalized variance is easy to see when we consider the determinant of a 2×2 correlation matrix. Given the following correlation matrix

$$\mathbf{R} = \begin{bmatrix} 1 & r_{12} \\ r_{21} & 1 \end{bmatrix},$$

the determinant of $\mathbf{R} = |\mathbf{R}| = 1 - r^2$. Of course, since we know that r^2 can be interpreted as the proportion of variation shared, or in common, between variables, *the determinant of this matrix represents the variation remaining in this pair of variables after removing the shared variation among the variables*. This concept also applies to larger matrices where the generalized variance represents the variation remaining in the set of variables after we account for the associations among the variables. While there are other ways to describe the variance of a set of variables, this conceptualization appears in the commonly used Wilks' Λ test statistic.

2.5 INVERSE OF A MATRIX

The inverse of a square matrix $\mathbf{A}$ is a matrix $\mathbf{A}^{-1}$ that satisfies the following equation:

$$\mathbf{A}\mathbf{A}^{-1} = \mathbf{A}^{-1}\mathbf{A} = \mathbf{I}_n,$$

where $\mathbf{I}_n$ is the identity matrix of order n. The identity matrix is simply a matrix with 1s on the main diagonal and 0s elsewhere.

$$\mathbf{I}_2 = \begin{bmatrix} 1 & 0 \\ 0 & 1 \end{bmatrix} \mathbf{I}_3 = \begin{bmatrix} 1 & 0 & 0 \\ 0 & 1 & 0 \\ 0 & 0 & 1 \end{bmatrix}$$

Why is finding inverses important in statistical work? Because we do not literally have division with matrices, *multiplying one matrix by the inverse of another is the analogue of division for numbers*. This is why finding an inverse is so important. An analogy with univariate ANOVA may be helpful here. In univariate ANOVA, recall that the test statistic $F = MS_b / MS_w = MS_b \left(MS_w \right)^{-1}$, that is, a ratio of between to within variability. The analogue of this test statistic in multivariate analysis of variance is $\mathbf{BW}^{-1}$, where $\mathbf{B}$ is a matrix that is the multivariate generalization of SS_b (sum of squares between); that is, it is a measure of how differential the effects of treatments have been on the set of dependent variables. In the multivariate case, we also want to "divide" the between-variability by the within-variability, but we don't have division *per se*. However, multiplying the $\mathbf{B}$ matrix by $\mathbf{W}^{-1}$ accomplishes this for us, because, again, multiplying a matrix by an inverse of a matrix is the analogue of division. Also, as shown in the next chapter, to obtain the regression coefficients for a multiple regression analysis, it is necessary to find the inverse of a matrix product involving the predictors.

2.5.1 Procedure for Finding the Inverse of a Matrix

1. Replace each element of the matrix $\mathbf{A}$ by its minor.
2. Form the matrix of cofactors, attaching the appropriate signs as illustrated later.
3. Take the transpose of the matrix of cofactors, forming what is called the adjoint.
4. Divide each element of the adjoint by the determinant of $\mathbf{A}$.

For symmetric matrices (with which this text deals almost exclusively), taking the transpose is *not* necessary, and hence, when finding the inverse of a symmetric matrix, Step 3 is omitted.

We apply this procedure first to the simplest case, finding the inverse of a 2×2 matrix.

Example 2.11

$$\mathbf{D} = \begin{bmatrix} 4 & 2 \\ 2 & 6 \end{bmatrix}$$

The minor of 4 is the determinant of the matrix obtained by deleting the first row and the first column. What is left is simply the number 6, and the determinant of a number is that number. Thus we obtain the following matrix of minors:

$$\begin{bmatrix} 6 & 2 \\ 2 & 4 \end{bmatrix}$$

Now for a 2×2 matrix we attach the proper signs by multiplying each diagonal element by 1 and each off-diagonal element by -1, yielding the matrix of cofactors, which is

$$\begin{bmatrix} 6 & -2 \\ -2 & 4 \end{bmatrix}.$$

The determinant of $\mathbf{D} = 6(4) - (-2)(-2) = 20$.

Finally then, the inverse of $\mathbf{D}$ is obtained by dividing the matrix of cofactors by the determinant, obtaining

$$\mathbf{D}^{-1} = \begin{bmatrix} \dfrac{6}{20} & \dfrac{-2}{20} \\ \dfrac{-2}{20} & \dfrac{4}{20} \end{bmatrix}$$

To check that $\mathbf{D}^{-1}$ is indeed the inverse of $\mathbf{D}$, note that

$$
\overset{\mathbf{D}}{\begin{bmatrix} 4 & 2 \\ 2 & 6 \end{bmatrix}} \overset{\mathbf{D}^{-1}}{\begin{bmatrix} \dfrac{6}{20} & \dfrac{-2}{20} \\ \dfrac{-2}{20} & \dfrac{4}{20} \end{bmatrix}} = \overset{\mathbf{D}^{-1}}{\begin{bmatrix} \dfrac{6}{20} & \dfrac{-2}{20} \\ \dfrac{-2}{20} & \dfrac{4}{20} \end{bmatrix}} \overset{\mathbf{D}}{\begin{bmatrix} 4 & 2 \\ 2 & 6 \end{bmatrix}} = \overset{\mathbf{I}_2}{\begin{bmatrix} 1 & 0 \\ 0 & 1 \end{bmatrix}}
$$

Example 2.12

Let us find the inverse for the 3×3 **A** matrix that we found the determinant for in the previous section. Because **A** is a symmetric matrix, it is not necessary to find nine minors, but only six, since the inverse of a symmetric matrix is symmetric. Thus we just find the minors for the elements on and above the main diagonal.

$\mathbf{A} = \begin{bmatrix} 1 & 2 & 3 \\ 2 & 2 & 1 \\ 3 & 1 & 4 \end{bmatrix}$ Recall again that the minor of an element is the determinant of the matrix obtained by deleting the row and column that the element is in.

Element	Matrix	Minor
$a_{11} = 1$	$\begin{bmatrix} 2 & 1 \\ 1 & 4 \end{bmatrix}$	$2 \times 4 - 1 \times 1 = 7$
$a_{12} = 2$	$\begin{bmatrix} 2 & 1 \\ 3 & 4 \end{bmatrix}$	$2 \times 4 - 1 \times 3 = 5$
$a_{13} = 3$	$\begin{bmatrix} 2 & 2 \\ 3 & 1 \end{bmatrix}$	$2 \times 1 - 2 \times 3 = -4$
$a_{22} = 2$	$\begin{bmatrix} 1 & 3 \\ 3 & 4 \end{bmatrix}$	$1 \times 4 - 3 \times 3 = -5$
$a_{23} = 1$	$\begin{bmatrix} 1 & 2 \\ 3 & 1 \end{bmatrix}$	$1 \times 1 - 2 \times 3 = -5$
$a_{33} = 4$	$\begin{bmatrix} 1 & 2 \\ 2 & 2 \end{bmatrix}$	$1 \times 2 - 2 \times 2 = -2$

Therefore, the matrix of minors for **A** is

$$
\begin{bmatrix} 7 & 5 & -4 \\ 5 & -5 & -5 \\ -4 & -5 & -2 \end{bmatrix}.
$$

Recall that the pattern of signs is

$$\begin{bmatrix} + & - & + \\ - & + & - \\ + & - & + \end{bmatrix}.$$

Thus, attaching the appropriate sign to each element in the matrix of minors and completing Step 2 of finding the inverse we obtain:

$$\begin{bmatrix} 7 & -5 & -4 \\ -5 & -5 & 5 \\ -4 & 5 & -2 \end{bmatrix}.$$

Now the determinant of **A** was found to be -15. Therefore, to complete the final step in finding the inverse we simply divide the preceding matrix by -15, and the inverse of **A** is

$$\mathbf{A}^{-1} = \begin{bmatrix} \dfrac{-7}{15} & \dfrac{1}{3} & \dfrac{4}{15} \\ \dfrac{1}{3} & \dfrac{1}{3} & \dfrac{-1}{3} \\ \dfrac{4}{15} & \dfrac{-1}{3} & \dfrac{2}{15} \end{bmatrix}.$$

Again, we can check that this is indeed the inverse by multiplying it by **A** to see if the result is the identity matrix.

Note that for the inverse of a matrix to exist, the determinant of the matrix must *not* be equal to 0. This is because in obtaining the inverse each element is divided by the determinant, and division by 0 is not defined. If the determinant of a matrix **B** = 0, we say **B** is *singular*. If $|\mathbf{B}| \neq 0$, we say **B** is nonsingular, and its inverse does exist.

2.6 SPSS MATRIX PROCEDURE

The SPSS matrix procedure was developed at the University of Wisconsin at Madison. It is described in some detail in *SPSS Advanced Statistics 7.5*. Various matrix operations can be performed using the procedure, including multiplying matrices, finding the determinant of a matrix, finding the inverse of a matrix, and so on. To indicate a matrix you must: (1) enclose the matrix in braces, (2) separate the elements of each row by commas, and (3) separate the rows by semicolons.

The matrix procedure *must* be run from the syntax window. To get to the syntax window, click on FILE, then click on NEW, and finally click on SYNTAX. Every matrix program must begin with `MATRIX.` and end with `END MATRIX`. The periods are crucial, as each command *must* end with a period. To create a matrix **A**, use the following

```
COMPUTE A = {2, 4, 1; 3, -2, 5}.
```

Note that this is a 2 × 3 matrix. The use of the COMPUTE command to create a matrix is not intuitive. However, at present, that is the way the procedure is set up. In the next program we create matrices **A**, **B**, and **E**, multiply **A** and **B**, find the determinant and inverse for **E**, and print out all matrices.

```
MATRIX.
COMPUTE A= {2, 4, 1; 3, -2, 5}.
COMPUTE B= {1, 2; 2, 1; 3, 4}.
COMPUTE C= A*B.
COMPUTE E= {1, -1, 2; -1, 3, 1; 2, 1, 10}.
COMPUTE DETE= DET(E).
COMPUTE EINV= INV(E).
PRINT A.
PRINT B.
PRINT C.
PRINT E.
PRINT DETE.
PRINT EINV.
END MATRIX.
```

The **A**, **B**, and **E** matrices are taken from the exercises at the end of the chapter. Note in the preceding program that all commands in SPSS must end with a period. Also, note that each matrix is enclosed in braces, and rows are separated by semicolons. Finally, a separate PRINT command is required to print out each matrix.

To run (or EXECUTE) this program, click on RUN and then click on ALL from the dropdown menu. When you do, the output shown in Table 2.1 is obtained.

■ **Table 2.1: Output From SPSS Matrix Procedure**

Matrix		
Run Matrix procedure:		
A		
2	4	1
3	−2	5
B		
1	2	
2	1	
3	4	
C		
13	12	
14	24	

(Continued)

▧ **Table 2.1: (Continued)**

Matrix			
E			
	1	−1	2
	−1	3	1
	2	1	10
DETE			
3			
EINV			
9.666666667		4.000000000	−2.333333333
4.000000000		2.000000000	−1.000000000
−2.333333333		−1.000000000	.666666667
----End Matrix----			

2.7 SAS IML PROCEDURE

The SAS IML procedure replaced the older PROC MATRIX procedure that was used in version 5 of SAS. SAS IML is documented thoroughly in *SAS/IML: Usage and Reference, Version 6* (1990). There are several features that are very nice about SAS IML, and these are described on pages 2 and 3 of the manual. We mention just three features:

1. SAS/IML is a programming language.
2. SAS/IML software uses operators that apply to entire matrices.
3. SAS/IML software is interactive.

IML is an acronym for Interactive Matrix Language. You can execute a command as soon as you enter it. We do not illustrate this feature, as we wish to compare it with the SPSS Matrix procedure. So, we collect the SAS IML commands in a file and run it that way.

To indicate a matrix, you (1) enclose the matrix in braces, (2) separate the elements of each row by a blank(s), and (3) separate the rows by commas.

To illustrate use of the SAS IML procedure, we create the same matrices as we did with the SPSS matrix procedure and do the same operations and print all matrices. The syntax is shown here, and the output appears in Table 2.2.

```
proc iml;
a= {2 4 1, 3-2 5} ;
b= {1 2, 2 1, 3 4} ;
c= a*b;
e= {1-1 2, -1 3 1, 2 1 10} ;
dete= det(e);
einv= inv(e);
print a b c e dete einv;
```

▨ **Table 2.2: Output From SAS IML Procedure**

A			B		C	
2	4	1	1	2	13	12
3	−2	5	2	1	14	24
			3	4		
E			DETE	EINV		
1	−1	2	3	9.6666667	4	−2.333333
−1	3	1		4	2	−1
2	1	10		−2.333333	−1	0.6666667

2.8 SUMMARY

Matrix algebra is important in multivariate analysis for several reasons. For example, data come in the form of a matrix when N participants are measured on p variables, multivariate test statistics and effect size measures are computed using matrix operations, and statistics describing multivariate outliers also use matrix algebra. Although addition and subtraction of matrices is easy, multiplication of matrices is more difficult and nonintuitive. Finding the determinant and inverse for 3 × 3 or larger square matrices is quite tedious. Finding the determinant is important because the determinant of a covariance matrix represents the generalized variance for a set of variables, that is, the variance that remains in a set of variables after accounting for the associations among the variables. Finding the inverse of a matrix is important since multiplying a matrix by the inverse of a matrix is the analogue of division for numbers. Fortunately, SPSS MATRIX and SAS IML will do various matrix operations, including finding the determinant and inverse.

2.9 EXERCISES

1. Given:

$$A = \begin{bmatrix} 2 & 4 & 1 \\ 3 & -2 & 5 \end{bmatrix} \quad B = \begin{bmatrix} 1 & 2 \\ 2 & 1 \\ 3 & 4 \end{bmatrix} \quad C = \begin{bmatrix} 1 & 3 & 5 \\ 6 & 2 & 1 \end{bmatrix}$$

$$D = \begin{bmatrix} 4 & 2 \\ 2 & 6 \end{bmatrix} \quad E = \begin{bmatrix} 1 & -1 & 2 \\ -1 & 3 & 1 \\ 2 & 1 & 10 \end{bmatrix} \quad X = \begin{bmatrix} 1 & 2 \\ 3 & 1 \\ 4 & 6 \\ 5 & 7 \end{bmatrix}$$

$$u' = (1, 3), \quad v = \begin{bmatrix} 2 \\ 7 \end{bmatrix}$$

Find, where meaningful, each of the following:

(a) **A + C**

(b) **A + B**

(c) **AB**

(d) **AC**

(e) **u'D u**

(f) **u'v**

(g) **(A + C)'**

(h) 3 **C**

(i) |**D**|

(j) **D**$^{-1}$

(k) |**E**|

(l) **E**$^{-1}$

(m) **u'D**$^{-1}$**u**

(n) **BA** (compare this result with [c])

(o) **X'X**

2. In Chapter 3, we are interested in predicting each person's score on a dependent variable y from a linear combination of their scores on several predictors (x_i's). If there were two predictors, then the equations for N cases would look like this:

$$y_1 = e_1 + b_0 + b_1 x_{11} + b_2 x_{12}$$
$$y_2 = e_2 + b_0 + b_1 x_{21} + b_2 x_{22}$$
$$y_3 = e_3 + b_0 + b_1 x_{31} + b_2 x_{32}$$
$$\vdots \quad \vdots \quad \quad \vdots$$
$$y_N = e_N + b_0 + b_1 x_{N1} + b_2 x_{N2}$$

Note: Each e_i represents the portion of y not predicted by the xs, and each b is a regression coefficient. Express this set of prediction equations as a single matrix equation. Hint: The right hand portion of the equation will be of the form:

vector + matrix times vector

3. Using the approach detailed in section 2.3, find the matrix of variances and covariances for the following data:

x_1	x_2	x_3
4	3	10
5	2	11
8	6	15
9	6	9
10	8	5

4. Consider the following two situations:

(a) $s_1 = 10$, $s_2 = 7$, $r_{12} = .80$

(b) $s_1 = 9$, $s_2 = 6$, $r_{12} = .20$

Compute the variance-covariance matrix for (a) and (b) and compute the determinant of each variance-covariance matrix. For which situation is the generalized variance larger? Does this surprise you?

5. Calculate the determinant for

$$A = \begin{bmatrix} 9 & 2 & 1 \\ 2 & 4 & 5 \\ 1 & 5 & 3 \end{bmatrix}.$$

Could **A** be a covariance matrix for a set of variables? Explain.

6. Using SPSS MATRIX or SAS IML, find the inverse for the following 4 × 4 symmetric matrix:

```
6 8 7 6
8 9 2 3
7 2 5 2
6 3 2 1
```

7. Run the following SPSS MATRIX program and show that the output yields the matrix, determinant, and inverse.

```
MATRIX.
COMPUTE A={6, 2, 4; 2, 3, 1; 4, 1, 5}.
COMPUTE DETA=DET(A).
COMPUTE AINV=INV(A).
PRINT A.
PRINT DETA.
PRINT AINV.
END MATRIX.
```

8. Consider the following two matrices:

$$A = \begin{bmatrix} 2 & 3 \\ 3 & 6 \end{bmatrix} \quad B = \begin{bmatrix} 1 & 0 \\ 0 & 1 \end{bmatrix}$$

Calculate the following products: **AB** and **BA**.

What do you get in each case? Do you see now why **B** is called the identity matrix?

9. Consider the following covariance matrix:

$$S = \begin{bmatrix} 4 & 3 & 1 \\ 3 & 9 & 2 \\ 1 & 2 & 1 \end{bmatrix}$$

(a) Use the SPSS MATRIX procedure to print **S** and find and print the determinant.

(b) Statistically, what does the determinant represent?

REFERENCES

SAS Institute. (1990). *SAS/IML: Usage and Reference, Version 6*. Cary, NC: Author.

SPSS, Inc. (1997). *SPSS Advanced Statistics 7.5*. Chicago: Author, pp. 469–512.

Chapter 3

MULTIPLE REGRESSION FOR PREDICTION

3.1 INTRODUCTION

In multiple regression we are interested in predicting a dependent variable from a set of predictors. In a previous course in statistics, you probably studied simple regression, predicting a dependent variable from a single predictor. An example would be predicting college GPA from high school GPA. Because human behavior is complex and influenced by many factors, such single-predictor studies are necessarily limited in their predictive power. For example, in a college GPA study, we are able to improve prediction of college GPA by considering other predictors such as scores on standardized tests (verbal, quantitative), and some noncognitive variables, such as study habits and attitude toward education. That is, we look to other predictors (often test scores) that tap other aspects of criterion behavior.

Consider two other examples of multiple regression studies:

1. Feshbach, Adelman, and Fuller (1977) conducted a study of 850 middle-class children. The children were measured in kindergarten on a battery of variables: the Wechsler Preschool and Primary Scale of Intelligence (WPPSI), the deHirsch–Jansky Index (assessing various linguistic and perceptual motor skills), the Bender Motor Gestalt, and a Student Rating Scale developed by the authors that measures various cognitive and affective behaviors and skills. These measures were used to predict reading achievement for these same children in grades 1, 2, and 3.
2. Crystal (1988) attempted to predict chief executive officer (CEO) pay for the top 100 of last year's Fortune 500 and the 100 top entries from last year's Service 500. He used the following predictors: company size, company performance, company risk, government regulation, tenure, location, directors, ownership, and age. He found that only about 39% of the variance in CEO pay can be accounted for by these factors.

In modeling the relationship between y and the xs, we are assuming that a *linear* model is appropriate. Of course, it is possible that a more complex model (curvilinear) may be necessary to predict *y* accurately. Polynomial regression may be appropriate, or if there is nonlinearity in the parameters, then nonlinear procedures in SPSS (e.g., NLR) or SAS can be used to fit a model.

This is a long chapter with many sections, not all of which are equally important. The three most fundamental sections are on model selection (3.8), checking assumptions underlying the linear regression model (3.10), and model validation (3.11). The other sections should be thought of as supportive of these. We discuss several ways of selecting a "good" set of predictors, and illustrate these with two computer examples.

A theme throughout the book is determining whether the assumptions underlying a given analysis are tenable. This chapter initiates that theme, and we can see that there are various graphical plots available for assessing assumptions underlying the regression model. Another very important theme throughout this book is the mathematical maximization nature of many advanced statistical procedures, and the concomitant possibility of results looking very good on the sample on which they were derived (because of capitalization on chance), but not generalizing to a population. Thus, it becomes extremely important to validate the results on an independent sample(s) of data, or at least to obtain an estimate of the generalizability of the results. Section 3.11 illustrates both of the aforementioned ways of checking the validity of a given regression model.

A final pedagogical point on reading this chapter: Section 3.14 deals with outliers and influential data points. We already indicated in Chapter 1, with several examples, the dramatic effect an outlier(s) can have on the results of any statistical analysis. Section 3.14 is rather lengthy, however, and the applied researcher may not want to plow through all the details. Recognizing this, we begin that section with a brief overview discussion of statistics for assessing outliers and influential data points, with prescriptive advice on how to flag such cases from computer output.

We wish to emphasize that our focus in this chapter is on the use of multiple regression for prediction. Another broad related area is the use of regression for explanation. Cohen, Cohen, West, and Aiken (2003) and Pedhazur (1982) have excellent, extended discussions of the use of regression for explanation. Note that Chapter 16 in this text includes the use of structural equation models, which is a more comprehensive analysis approach for explanation.

There have been innumerable books written on regression analysis. In our opinion, books by Cohen et al. (2003), Pedhazur (1982), Myers (1990), Weisberg (1985), Belsley, Kuh, and Welsch (1980), and Draper and Smith (1981) are worthy of special attention. The first two books are written for individuals in the social sciences and have very good narrative discussions. The Myers and Weisberg books are excellent in terms of the modern approach to regression analysis, and have especially good treatments of regression diagnostics. The Draper and Smith book is one of the classic texts, generally used for a more mathematical treatment, with most of its examples geared toward the physical sciences.

We start this chapter with a brief discussion of simple regression, which most readers likely encountered in a previous statistics course.

3.2 SIMPLE REGRESSION

For one predictor, the simple linear regression model is

$$y_i = \beta_0 + \beta_1 x_1 + e_i \quad i = 1, 2, \ldots, n,$$

where β_0 and β_1 are parameters to be estimated. The e_i are the errors of prediction, and are assumed to be independent, with constant variance and normally distributed with a mean of 0. If these assumptions are valid for a given set of data, then the sample prediction errors $(\hat{e}_i)$ should have similar properties. For example, the $\hat{e}_i$ should be normally distributed, or at least approximately normally distributed. This is considered further in section 3.9. The $\hat{e}_i$ are called the residuals. How do we estimate the parameters? The *least squares* criterion is used; that is, the sum of the squared estimated errors of prediction is minimized:

$$\hat{e}_1^2 + \hat{e}_2^2 + \cdots + \hat{e}_n^2 = \sum_{i=1}^{n} \hat{e}_i^2 = \min$$

Of course, $\hat{e}_i = y_i - \hat{y}_i$, where y_i is the actual score on the dependent variable and $\hat{y}_i$ is the estimated score for the ith subject.

The scores for each subject (x_i, y_i) define a point in the plane. What the least squares criterion does is find the line that best fits the points. Geometrically, this corresponds to minimizing the sum of the squared vertical distances $(\hat{e}_i^2)$ of each person's score from their estimated y score. This is illustrated in Figure 3.1.

Example 3.1

To illustrate simple regression we use part of the Sesame Street database from Glasnapp and Poggio (1985), who present data on many variables, including 12 background variables and 8 achievement variables for 240 participants. Sesame Street was developed as a television series aimed mainly at teaching preschool skills to 3- to 5-year-old children. Data were collected on many achievement variables both before (pretest) and after (posttest) viewing of the series. We consider here only one of the achievement variables, knowledge of body parts.

SPSS syntax for running the simple regression is given in Table 3.1, along with annotation. Figure 3.2 presents a scatterplot of the variables, along with selected

▨ **Figure 3.1:** Geometrical representation of least squares criterion.

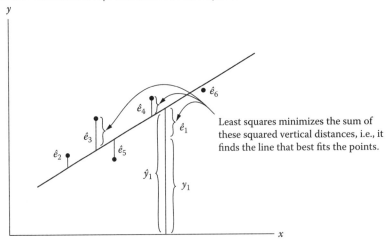

Least squares minimizes the sum of these squared vertical distances, i.e., it finds the line that best fits the points.

▨ **Table 3.1: SPSS Syntax for Simple Regression**

```
    TITLE 'SIMPLE LINEAR REGRESSION ON SESAME  DATA.'
    DATA LIST FREE/PREBODY POSTBODY.
    BEGIN DATA.
      DATA LINES
    END DATA.
    LIST.
    REGRESSION DESCRIPTIVES = DEFAULT/
     VARIABLES = PREBODY POSTBODY/
     DEPENDENT = POSTBODY/
(1) METHOD = ENTER/
(2) SCATTERPLOT (POSTBODY, PREBODY)/
(3) RESIDUALS = HISTOGRAM(ZRESID)/.
```

(1) DESCRIPTIVES = DEFAULT subcommand yields the means, standard deviations and the correlation matrix for the variables.

(2) This scatterplot subcommand yields a scatterplot for the variables.

(3) This RESIDUALS subcommand yields a histogram of the standardized residuals.

output. Inspecting the scatterplot suggests there is a positive association between the variables, reflecting a correlation of .65. Note that in the Model Summary table of Figure 3.2, the multiple correlation (R) is also .65, since there is only one predictor in the equation. In the Coefficients table of Figure 3.2, the coefficients are provided for the regression equation. The equation for the predicted outcome scores is then POSTBODY = 13.475 + .551 PEABODY. Table 3.2 shows a histogram of the standardized residuals, which suggests a fair approximation to a normal distribution.

■ **Figure 3.2:** Scatterplot and selected output for simple linear regression.

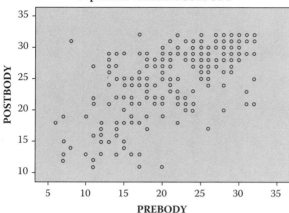

Variables Entered/Removed[a]

Model	Variables Entered	Variables Removed	Method
1	PREBODY[b]		Enter

a. Dependent Variable: POSTBODY
b. All requested variables entered.

Model Summary[b]

Model	R	R Square	Adjusted R Square	Std. Error of the Estimate
1	0.650[a]	0.423	0.421	4.119

a. Predictors: (Constant), PREBODY

Coefficients[a]

Model		Unstandardized Coefficients		Standardized Coefficients	t	Sig.
		B	Std. Error	Beta		
1	(Constant)	13.475	0.931		14.473	0.000
	PREBODY	0.551	0.042	0.650	13.211	0.000

a. Dependent Variable: POSTBODY

3.3 MULTIPLE REGRESSION FOR TWO PREDICTORS: MATRIX FORMULATION

The linear model for two predictors is a simple extension of what we had for one predictor:

$$y_i = \beta_0 + \beta_1 x_1 + \beta_2 x_2 + e_i,$$

where β_0 (the regression constant), β_1, and β_2 are the parameters to be estimated, and e is error of prediction. We consider a small data set to illustrate the estimation process.

▨ **Table 3.2: Histogram of Standardized Residuals**

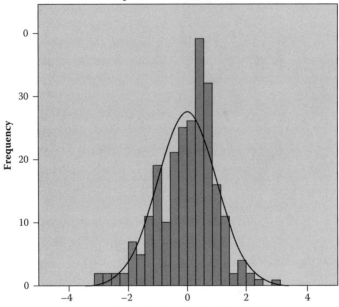

Histogram
Dependent Variable: POSTBODY

Mean = 4.16E-16
Std. Dev. = 0.996
N = 240

y	x_1	x_2
3	2	1
2	3	5
4	5	3
5	7	6
8	8	7

We model each subject's y score as a linear function of the βs:

$$
\begin{aligned}
y_1 = \quad 3 &= \quad 1 \times \beta_0 + 2 \times \beta_1 + 1 \times \beta_2 \quad + e_1 \\
y_2 = \quad 2 &= \quad 1 \times \beta_0 + 3 \times \beta_1 + 5 \times \beta_2 \quad + e_2 \\
y_3 = \quad 4 &= \quad 1 \times \beta_0 + 5 \times \beta_1 + 3 \times \beta_2 \quad + e_3 \\
y_4 = \quad 5 &= \quad 1 \times \beta_0 + 7 \times \beta_1 + 6 \times \beta_2 \quad + e_4 \\
y_5 = \quad 8 &= \quad 1 \times \beta_0 + 8 \times \beta_1 + 7 \times \beta_2 \quad + e_5
\end{aligned}
$$

This series of equations can be expressed as a single matrix equation:

$$
\mathbf{y} = \begin{bmatrix} 3 \\ 2 \\ 4 \\ 5 \\ 8 \end{bmatrix} = \overset{\mathbf{X}}{\begin{bmatrix} 1 & 2 & 1 \\ 1 & 3 & 5 \\ 1 & 5 & 3 \\ 1 & 7 & 6 \\ 1 & 8 & 7 \end{bmatrix}} \overset{\boldsymbol{\beta}}{\begin{bmatrix} \beta_0 \\ \beta_1 \\ \beta_2 \end{bmatrix}} + \overset{\mathbf{e}}{\begin{bmatrix} e_1 \\ e_2 \\ e_3 \\ e_4 \\ e_5 \end{bmatrix}}
$$

It is pretty clear that the y scores and the $\mathbf{e}$ define column vectors, while not so clear is how the boxed-in area can be represented as the product of two matrices, $\mathbf{X\beta}$.

The first column of 1s is used to obtain the regression constant. The remaining two columns contain the scores for the subjects on the two predictors. Thus, the classic matrix equation for multiple regression is:

$$\mathbf{y} = \mathbf{X\beta} + \mathbf{e} \tag{1}$$

Now, it can be shown using the calculus that the least square estimates of the βs are given by:

$$\hat{\mathbf{\beta}} = \left(\mathbf{X'X}\right)^{-1}\mathbf{X'y} \tag{2}$$

Thus, for our data the estimated regression coefficients would be:

$$\hat{\mathbf{\beta}} = \left\{ \overset{\mathbf{X'}}{\begin{bmatrix} 1 & 1 & 1 & 1 & 1 \\ 2 & 3 & 5 & 7 & 8 \\ 1 & 5 & 3 & 6 & 7 \end{bmatrix}} \overset{\mathbf{X}}{\begin{bmatrix} 1 & 2 & 1 \\ 1 & 3 & 5 \\ 1 & 5 & 3 \\ 1 & 7 & 6 \\ 1 & 8 & 7 \end{bmatrix}} \right\}^{-1} \overset{\mathbf{X'}}{\begin{bmatrix} 1 & 1 & 1 & 1 & 1 \\ 2 & 3 & 5 & 7 & 8 \\ 1 & 5 & 3 & 6 & 7 \end{bmatrix}} \overset{\mathbf{y}}{\begin{bmatrix} 3 \\ 2 \\ 4 \\ 5 \\ 8 \end{bmatrix}}$$

Let us do this in pieces. First,

$$\mathbf{X'X} = \begin{bmatrix} 5 & 25 & 22 \\ 25 & 151 & 130 \\ 22 & 130 & 120 \end{bmatrix} \text{ and } \mathbf{X'y} = \begin{bmatrix} 22 \\ 131 \\ 11 \end{bmatrix}.$$

Furthermore, you should show that

$$(\mathbf{X'X})^{-1} = \frac{1}{1016}\begin{bmatrix} 1220 & -140 & -72 \\ -140 & 116 & -100 \\ -72 & -100 & 130 \end{bmatrix},$$

where 1016 is the determinant of $\mathbf{X'X}$. Thus, the estimated regression coefficients are given by

$$\hat{\mathbf{\beta}} = \frac{1}{1016}\begin{bmatrix} 1220 & -140 & -72 \\ -140 & 116 & -100 \\ -72 & -100 & 130 \end{bmatrix}\begin{bmatrix} 22 \\ 131 \\ 111 \end{bmatrix} = \begin{bmatrix} .50 \\ 1 \\ -.25 \end{bmatrix}.$$

Therefore, the regression (prediction) equation is

$$\hat{y}_i = .50 + x_1 - .25x_2.$$

To illustrate the use of this equation, we find the predicted score for case 3 and the residual for that case:

$$\hat{y}_3 = .5 + 5 - .25(3) = 4.75$$

$$\hat{e}_3 = y_3 - \hat{y}_3 = 4 - 4.75 = -.75$$

Note that if you find yourself struggling with this matrix presentation, be assured that you can still learn to use multiple regression properly and understand regression results.

3.4 MATHEMATICAL MAXIMIZATION NATURE OF LEAST SQUARES REGRESSION

In general, then, in multiple regression the *linear combination* of the xs that is maximally correlated with y is sought. Minimizing the sum of squared errors of prediction is equivalent to *maximizing* the correlation between the observed and predicted y scores. This maximized Pearson correlation is called the multiple correlation, shown as $R = r_{y_i \hat{y}_i}$. Nunnally (1978, p. 164) characterized the procedure as "wringing out the last ounce of predictive power" (obtained from the linear combination of xs, that is, from the regression equation). Because the correlation is maximum for the sample from which it is derived, when the regression equation is applied to an independent sample from the same population (i.e., cross-validated), the predictive power drops off. If the predictive power drops off sharply, then the equation is of limited utility. That is, it has no generalizability, and hence is of limited scientific value. After all, we derive the prediction equation for the purpose of predicting with it on future (other) samples. If the equation does not predict well on other samples, then it is not fulfilling the purpose for which it was designed.

Sample size (n) and the number of predictors (k) are two crucial factors that determine how well a given equation will cross-validate (i.e., generalize). In particular, the n/k ratio is crucial. For small ratios (5:1 or less), the shrinkage in predictive power can be substantial. A study by Guttman (1941) illustrates this point. He had 136 subjects and 84 predictors, and found the multiple correlation on the original sample to be .73. However, when the prediction equation was applied to an independent sample, the new correlation was only .04. In other words, the good predictive power on the original sample was due to capitalization on chance, and the prediction equation had no generalizability.

We return to the cross-validation issue in more detail later in this chapter, where we show that *as a rough guide for social science research, about 15 subjects per predictor are needed for a reliable equation*, that is, for an equation that will cross-validate with little loss in predictive power.

3.5 BREAKDOWN OF SUM OF SQUARES AND *F* TEST FOR MULTIPLE CORRELATION

In analysis of variance we broke down variability around the grand mean into between- and within-variability. In regression analysis, variability around the mean is broken down into variability due to regression (i.e., variation of the predicted values) and variability of the observed scores around the predicted values (i.e., variation of the residuals). To get at the breakdown, we note that the variation of the residuals may be expressed as the following identity:

$$y_i - \hat{y}_i = (y_i - \bar{y}) - (\hat{y}_i - \bar{y})$$

Now we square both sides, obtaining

$$(y_i - \hat{y}_i)^2 = [(y_i - \bar{y}) - (\hat{y}_i - \bar{y})]^2.$$

Then we sum over the subjects, from 1 to *n*:

$$\sum_{i=1}^{n}(y_i - \hat{y}_i)^2 = \sum_{i=1}^{n}[(y_i - \bar{y}) - (\hat{y}_i - \bar{y})]^2.$$

By algebraic manipulation (see Draper & Smith, 1981, pp. 17–18), this can be rewritten as:

$$\sum(y_i - \bar{y})^2 \quad = \quad \sum(y_i - \hat{y}_i)^2 \quad + \quad \sum(\hat{y}_i - \bar{y})^2$$

sum of squares around the mean	=	sum of squares of the residuals	+	sum of squares due to regression	
SS_{tot}	=	SS_{res}	+	SS_{reg}	
df: $n-1$	=	$(n - k - 1)$	+	k (*df* = degrees of freedom)	(3)

This results in the following analysis of variance table and the *F* test for determining whether the population multiple correlation is different from 0.

Analysis of Variance Table for Regression

Source	SS	df	MS	F
Regression	SS_{reg}	K	SS_{reg} / k	$\dfrac{MS_{reg}}{MS_{res}}$
Residual (error)	SS_{res}	$n - k - 1$	$SS_{res} / (n - k - 1)$	

Recall that since the residual for each subject is $\hat{e}_i = y_i - \hat{y}_i$, the mean square error term can be written as $MS_{res} = \Sigma \hat{e}_i^2 / (n - k - 1)$. Now, R^2 (squared multiple correlation) is given by

$$R^2 = \frac{\text{sum of squares due to regression}}{\text{sum of squares about the mean}} = \frac{\Sigma(\hat{y} - \overline{y})^2}{\Sigma(y_i - \overline{y})^2} = \frac{SS_{reg}}{SS_{tot}}.$$

Thus, R^2 measures the proportion of total variance on y that is accounted for by the set of predictors. By simple algebra, then, we can rewrite the F test in terms of R^2 as follows:

$$F = \frac{R^2/k}{\left(1 - R^2\right)/(n - k - 1)} \text{ with } k \text{ and } (n - k - 1) df \tag{4}$$

We feel this test is of limited utility when prediction is the research goal, because it does *not necessarily* imply that the equation will cross-validate well, and this is the crucial issue in regression analysis for prediction.

Example 3.2

An investigator obtains $R^2 = .50$ on a sample of 50 participants with 10 predictors. Do we reject the null hypothesis that the population multiple correlation $= 0$?

$$F = \frac{.50/10}{(1 - .50)/(50 - 10 - 1)} = 3.9 \text{ with 10 and 39 } df$$

This is significant at the .01 level, since the critical value is 2.8.

However, because the n/k ratio is only 5/1, the prediction equation will probably not predict well on other samples and is therefore of questionable utility.

Myers' (1990) response to the question of what constitutes an acceptable value for R^2 is illuminating:

> This is a difficult question to answer, and, in truth, what is acceptable depends on the scientific field from which the data were taken. A chemist, charged with doing a linear calibration on a high precision piece of equipment, certainly expects to experience a very high R^2 value (perhaps exceeding .99), while a behavioral scientist, dealing in data reflecting human behavior, may feel fortunate to observe an R^2 as high as .70. An experienced model fitter senses when the value of R^2 is large enough, given the situation confronted. Clearly, some scientific phenomena lend themselves to modeling with considerably more accuracy then others. (p. 37)

His point is that how well one can predict depends on *context*. In the physical sciences, generally quite accurate prediction is possible. In the social sciences, where we are attempting to predict human behavior (which can be influenced by many systematic and some idiosyncratic factors), prediction is much more difficult.

3.6 RELATIONSHIP OF SIMPLE CORRELATIONS TO MULTIPLE CORRELATION

The ideal situation, in terms of obtaining a high R, would be to have each of the predictors significantly correlated with the dependent variable and for the predictors to be uncorrelated with each other, so that they measure different constructs and are able to predict different parts of the variance on y. Of course, in practice we will not find this, because almost all variables are correlated to some degree. A good situation in practice, then, would be one in which most of our predictors correlate significantly with y and the predictors have relatively low correlations among themselves. To illustrate these points further, consider the following three patterns of correlations among three predictors and an outcome.

		X_1	X_2	X_3			X_1	X_2	X_3			X_1	X_2	X_3
(1)	Y	.20	.10	.30	(2)	Y	.60	.50	.70	(3)	Y	.60	.70	.70
	X_1		.50	.40		X_1		.20	.30		X_1		.70	.60
	X_2			.60		X_2			.20		X_2			.80

In which of these cases would you expect the multiple correlation to be the largest and the smallest respectively? Here it is quite clear that R will be the smallest for 1 because the highest correlation of any of the predictors with y is .30, whereas for the other two patterns at least one of the predictors has a correlation of .70 with y. Thus, we know that R will be at least .70 for Cases 2 and 3, whereas for Case 1 we know only that R will be at least .30. Furthermore, there is no chance that R for Case 1 might become larger than that for cases 2 and 3, because the intercorrelations among the predictors for 1 are approximately as large or larger than those for the other two cases.

We would expect R to be largest for Case 2 because each of the predictors is moderately to strongly tied to y and there are low intercorrelations (i.e., little redundancy) among the predictors—exactly the kind of situation we would hope to find in practice. We would expect R to be greater in Case 2 than in Case 3, because in Case 3 there is considerable redundancy among the predictors. Although the correlations of the predictors with y are slightly higher in Case 3 (.60, .70, .70) than in Case 2 (.60, .50, .70), the much higher intercorrelations among the predictors for Case 3 will severely limit the ability of X_2 and X_3 to predict additional variance beyond that of X_1 (and hence significantly increase R), whereas this will not be true for Case 2.

3.7 MULTICOLLINEARITY

When there are moderate to high intercorrelations among the predictors, as is the case when several cognitive measures are used as predictors, the problem is referred to as *multicollinearity.* Multicollinearity poses a real problem for the researcher using multiple regression for three reasons:

1. It severely limits the size of R, because the predictors are going after much of the same variance on y. A study by Dizney and Gromen (1967) illustrates very nicely how multicollinearity among the predictors limits the size of R. They studied how well reading proficiency (x_1) and writing proficiency (x_2) would predict course grades in college German. The following correlation matrix resulted:

	x_1	x_2	y
x_1	1.00	.58	.33
x_2		1.00	.45
y			1.00

   Note the multicollinearity for x_1 and x_2 $(rx_1x_2 = .58)$, and also that x_2 has a simple correlation of .45 with y. The multiple correlation R was only .46. Thus, the relatively high correlation between reading and writing severely limited the ability of reading to add anything (only .01) to the prediction of a German grade above and beyond that of writing.

2. Multicollinearity makes determining the importance of a given predictor difficult because the effects of the predictors are confounded due to the correlations among them.

3. Multicollinearity increases the variances of the regression coefficients. The greater these variances, the more unstable the prediction equation will be.

The following are two methods for diagnosing multicollinearity:

1. Examine the simple correlations among the predictors from the correlation matrix. These should be observed, and are easy to understand, but you need to be warned that they do not always indicate the extent of multicollinearity. More subtle forms of multicollinearity may exist. One such more subtle form is discussed next.

2. Examine the variance inflation factors for the predictors.

The quantity $1/(1 - R_j^2)$ is called the jth *variance inflation factor*, where R_j^2 is the squared multiple correlation for predicting the jth predictor from all other predictors.

The variance inflation factor for a predictor indicates whether there is a strong linear association between it and all the remaining predictors. It is distinctly possible for a predictor to have only moderate or relatively weak associations with the other predictors in terms of simple correlations, and yet to have a quite high R when regressed on all the other predictors. When is the value for a variance inflation factor large enough to cause concern? Myers (1990) offered the following suggestion:

> Though no rule of thumb on numerical values is foolproof, it is generally believed that if any VIF exceeds 10, there is reason for at least some concern; then one

should consider variable deletion or an alternative to least squares estimation to combat the problem. (p. 369)

The variance inflation factors are easily obtained from SAS and SPSS (see Table 3.6 for SAS and exercise 10 for SPSS).

There are at least three ways of combating multicollinearity. One way is to combine predictors that are highly correlated. For example, if there are three measures having similar variability relating to a single construct that have intercorrelations of about .80 or larger, then add them to form a single measure.

A second way, if one has initially a fairly large set of predictors, is to consider doing a principal components or factor analysis to reduce to a much smaller set of predictors. For example, if there are 30 predictors, we are undoubtedly not measuring 30 different constructs. A factor analysis will suggest the number of constructs we are actually measuring. The factors become the new predictors, and because the factors are uncorrelated by construction, we eliminate the multicollinearity problem. Principal components and factor analysis are discussed in Chapter 9. In that chapter we also show how to use SAS and SPSS to obtain factor scores that can then be used to do subsequent analysis, such as being used as predictors for multiple regression.

A third way of combating multicollinearity is to use a technique called ridge regression. This approach is beyond the scope of this text, although Myers (1990) has a nice discussion for those who are interested.

3.8 MODEL SELECTION

Various methods are available for selecting a good set of predictors:

1. *Substantive Knowledge.* As Weisberg (1985) noted, "the single most important tool in selecting a subset of variables for use in a model is the analyst's knowledge of the substantive area under study" (p. 210). It is important for the investigator to be judicious in his or her selection of predictors. Far too many investigators have abused multiple regression by throwing everything in the hopper, often merely because the variables are available. Cohen (1990), among others, commented on the indiscriminate use of variables: There have been too many studies with prodigious numbers of dependent variables, or with what seemed to be far too many independent variables, or (heaven help us) both.

It is generally better to work with a small number of predictors because it is consistent with the scientific principle of parsimony and improves the n/k ratio, which helps cross-validation prospects. Further, note the following from Lord and Novick (1968):

Experience in psychology and in many other fields of application has shown that it is seldom worthwhile to include very many predictor variables in a regression equation, for the incremental validity of new variables, after a certain point, is usually very low. This is true because tests tend to overlap in content and consequently the addition of a fifth or sixth test may add little that is new to the battery and still relevant to the criterion. (p. 274)

Or consider the following from Ramsey and Schafer (1997):

There are two good reasons for paring down a large number of exploratory variables to a smaller set. The first reason is somewhat philosophical: simplicity is preferable to complexity. Thus, redundant and unnecessary variables should be excluded on principle. The second reason is more concrete: unnecessary terms in the model yield less precise inferences. (p. 325)

2. *Sequential Methods.* These are the forward, stepwise, and backward selection procedures that are popular with many researchers. All these procedures involve a partialing-out process; that is, they look at the contribution of a predictor with the effects of the other predictors partialed out, or held constant. Many of you may have already encountered the notion of a partial correlation in a previous statistics course, but a review is nevertheless in order.

The partial correlation between variables 1 and 2 with variable 3 partialed from both 1 and 2 is the correlation with variable 3 held constant, as you may recall. The formula for the partial correlation is given by:

$$r_{12.3} = \frac{r_{12} - r_{13}\, r_{23}}{\sqrt{1 - r_{13}^2}\,\sqrt{1 - r_{23}^2}} \qquad (5)$$

Let us put this in the context of multiple regression. Suppose we wish to know what the partial correlation of y (dependent variable) is with predictor 2 with predictor 1 partialed out. The formula would be, following what we have earlier:

$$r_{y2.1} = \frac{r_{y2} - r_{y1}\, r_{21}}{\sqrt{1 - r_{y1}^2}\,\sqrt{1 - r_{21}^2}} \qquad (6)$$

We apply this formula to show how SPSS obtains the partial correlation of .528 for INTEREST in Table 3.4 under EXCLUDED VARIABLES in the first upcoming computer example. In this example CLARITY (abbreviated as clr) entered first, having a correlation of .862 with dependent variable INSTEVAL (abbreviated as inst). The following correlations are taken from the correlation matrix, given near the beginning of Table 3.4.

$$r_{\text{inst int.clr}} = \frac{.435 - (.862)(.20)}{\sqrt{1 - .862^2}\,\sqrt{1 - .20^2}}$$

The correlation between the two predictors is .20, as shown.

We now give a brief description of the forward, stepwise, and backward selection procedures.

FORWARD—The first predictor that has an opportunity to enter the equation is the one with the largest simple correlation with *y*. If this predictor is significant, then the predictor with the largest partial correlation with *y* is considered, and so on. At some stage a given predictor will not make a significant contribution and the procedure terminates. It is important to remember that with this procedure, once a predictor gets into the equation, it stays.

STEPWISE—This is basically a variation on the forward selection procedure. However, at each stage of the procedure, a test is made of the least useful predictor. The importance of each predictor is constantly reassessed. Thus, a predictor that may have been the best entry candidate earlier may now be superfluous.

BACKWARD—The steps are as follows: (1) An equation is computed with ALL the predictors. (2) The partial *F* is calculated for every predictor, treated as though it were the last predictor to enter the equation. (3) The smallest partial *F* value, say F_1, is compared with a preselected significance, say F_0. If $F_1 < F_0$, remove that predictor and reestimate the equation with the remaining variables. Reenter stage B.

3. *Mallows' C_p.* Before we introduce Mallows' C_p, it is important to consider the consequences of under fitting (important variables are left out of the model) and over fitting (having variables in the model that make essentially no contribution or are marginal). Myers (1990, pp. 178–180) has an excellent discussion on the impact of under fitting and over fitting, and notes that "a model that is too simple may suffer from biased coefficients and biased prediction, while an overly complicated model can result in large variances, both in the coefficients and in the prediction."

This measure was introduced by C.L. Mallows (1973) as a criterion for selecting a model. It measures total squared error, and it was recommended by Mallows to choose the model(s) where $C_p \approx p$. For these models, the amount of under fitting or over fitting is minimized. Mallows' criterion may be written as

$$C_p = p + \frac{\left(s^2 - \hat{\sigma}^2\right)(N - p)}{\hat{\sigma}^2} \qquad \text{where } (p = k + 1), \tag{7}$$

where s^2 is the residual variance for the model being evaluated, and $\hat{\sigma}^2$ is an estimate of the residual variance that is usually based on the full model. Note that if the residual variance of the model being evaluated, s^2, is much larger than $\hat{\sigma}^2$, C_p increases, suggesting that important variables have been left out of the model.

4. *Use of MAXR Procedure from SAS.* There are many methods of model selection in the SAS REG program, MAXR being one of them. This procedure produces

several models; the best one-variable model, the best two-variable model, and so on. Here is the description of the procedure from the *SAS/STAT* manual:

> The MAXR method begins by finding the one variable model producing the highest R^2. Then another variable, the one that yields the greatest increase in R^2, is added. Once the two variable model is obtained, each of the variables in the model is compared to each variable not in the model. For each comparison, MAXR determines if removing one variable and replacing it with the other variable increases R^2. After comparing all possible switches, MAXR makes the switch that produces the largest increase in R^2. Comparisons begin again, and the process continues until MAXR finds that no switch could increase R^2. . . . Another variable is then added to the model, and the comparing and switching process is repeated to find the best three variable model. (p. 1398)

5. *All Possible Regressions.* If you wish to follow this route, then the SAS REG program should be considered. The number of regressions increases quite sharply as k increases, however, the program will efficiently identify good subsets. Good subsets are those that have the smallest Mallows' C value. We have illustrated this in Table 3.6. This pool of candidate models can then be examined further using regression diagnostics and cross-validity criteria to be mentioned later.

Use of one or more of these methods will often yield a number of models of roughly equal efficacy. As Myers (1990) noted:

> The successful model builder will eventually understand that with many data sets, several models can be fit that would be of nearly equal effectiveness. Thus the problem that one deals with is the selection of *one model* from a pool of *candidate models*. (p. 164)

One of the problems with the stepwise methods, which are very frequently used, is that they have led many investigators to conclude that they have found *the* best model, when in fact there may be some better models or several other models that are about as good. As Huberty (1989) noted, "and one or more of these subsets may be more interesting or relevant in a substantive sense" (p. 46).

In addition to the procedures just described, there are three other important criteria to consider when selecting a prediction equation. The criteria all relate to the generalizability of the equation, that is, how well will the equation predict on an independent sample(s) of data. The three methods of model validation, which are discussed in detail in section 3.11, are:

1. Data splitting—Randomly split the data, obtain a prediction equation on one half of the random split, and then check its predictive power (cross-validate) on the other sample.
2. Use of the PRESS statistic (R^2_{Press}), which is an external validation method particularly useful for small samples.

3. Obtain an *estimate* of the average predictive power of the equation on many other samples from the same population, using a formula due to Stein (Herzberg, 1969).

The SPSS application guides comment on over fitting and the use of several models. There is no one test to determine the dimensionality of the best submodel. Some researchers find it tempting to include too many variables in the model, which is called over fitting. Such a model will perform badly when applied to a new sample from the same population (cross-validation). Automatic stepwise procedures cannot do all the work for you. Use them as a tool to determine roughly the number of predictors needed (for example, you might find three to five variables). If you try several methods of selection, you may identify candidate predictors that are not included by any method. Ignore them, and fit models with, say, three to five variables, selecting alternative subsets from among the better candidates. You may find several subsets that perform equally as well. Then, knowledge of the subject matter, how accurately individual variables are measured, and what a variable "communicates" may guide selection of the model to report.

We don't disagree with these comments; however, we would favor the model that cross-validates best. If two models cross-validate about the same, then we would favor the model that makes most substantive sense.

3.8.1 Semipartial Correlations

We consider a procedure that, for a *given ordering* of the predictors, will enable us to determine the unique contribution each predictor is making in accounting for variance on y. This procedure, which uses semipartial correlations, will disentangle the correlations among the predictors.

The partial correlation between variables 1 and 2 with variable 3 partialed from both 1 and 2 is the correlation with variable 3 held constant, as you may recall. The formula for the partial correlation is given by

$$r_{12.3} = \frac{r_{12} - r_{13}r_{23}}{\sqrt{1 - r_{13}^2}\sqrt{1 - r_{23}^2}}.$$

We presented the partial correlation first for two reasons: (1) the semipartial correlation is a variant of the partial correlation, and (2) the partial correlation will be involved in computing more complicated semipartial correlations.

For breaking down R^2, we will want to work with the semipartial, sometimes called part, correlation. The formula for the semipartial correlation is

$$r_{12.3(s)} = \frac{r_{12} - r_{13}r_{23}}{\sqrt{1 - r_{23}^2}}.$$

The only difference between this equation and the previous one is that the denominator here doesn't contain the standard deviation of the partialed scores for variable 1.

In multiple correlation we wish to partial the independent variables (the predictors) from one another, but not from the dependent variable. We wish to leave the dependent variable intact and not partial any variance attributable to the predictors. Let $R^2_{y12\ldots k}$ denote the squared multiple correlation for the k predictors, where the predictors appear after the dot. Consider the case of one dependent variable and three predictors. It can be shown that:

$$R^2_{y.123} = r^2_{y1} + r^2_{y2.1(s)} + r^2_{y3.12(s)}, \tag{8}$$

where

$$r_{y2.1(s)} = \frac{r_{y2} - r_{y1}r_{21}}{\sqrt{1 - r^2_{21}}} \tag{9}$$

is the semipartial correlation between y and variable 2, with variable 1 partialed only from variable 2, and $r_{y3.12(s)}$ is the semipartial correlation between y and variable 3 with variables 1 and 2 partialed only from variable 3:

$$r_{y3.12(s)} = \frac{r_{y3.1(s)} - r_{y2.1(s)}r_{23.1}}{\sqrt{1 - r^2_{23.1}}} \tag{10}$$

Thus, through the use of semipartial correlations, we disentangle the correlations among the predictors and determine how much *unique* variance on each predictor is related to variance on y.

3.9 TWO COMPUTER EXAMPLES

To illustrate the use of several of the aforementioned model selection methods, we consider two computer examples. The first example illustrates the SPSS REGRESSION program, and uses data from Morrison (1983) on 32 students enrolled in an MBA course. We predict instructor course evaluation from five predictors. The second example illustrates SAS REG on quality ratings of 46 research doctorate programs in psychology, where we are attempting to predict quality ratings from factors such as number of program graduates, percentage of graduates who received fellowships or grant support, and so on (Singer & Willett, 1988).

Example 3.3: SPSS Regression on Morrison MBA Data
The data for this problem are from Morrison (1983). The dependent variable is instructor course evaluation in an MBA course, with the five predictors being clarity, stimulation, knowledge, interest, and course evaluation. We illustrate two of the sequential procedures, stepwise and backward selection, using SPSS. Syntax for running the analyses, along with the correlation matrix, are given in Table 3.3.

```
TITLE 'MORRISON MBA DATA'.
DATA LIST FREE/INSTEVAL CLARITY STIMUL KNOWLEDG INTEREST
COUEVAL.
BEGIN DATA.
1 1 2 1 1 2    1 2 2 1 1 1    1 1 1 1 1 2    1 1 2 1 1 2
2 1 3 2 2 2    2 2 4 1 1 2    2 3 3 1 1 2    2 3 4 1 2 3
2 2 3 1 3 3    2 2 2 2 2 2    2 2 3 2 1 2    2 2 2 3 3 2
2 2 2 1 1 2    2 2 4 2 2 2    2 3 3 1 1 3    2 3 4 1 1 2
2 3 2 1 1 2    3 4 4 3 2 2    3 4 3 1 1 4    3 4 3 1 2 3
3 4 3 2 2 3    3 3 4 2 3 3    3 3 4 2 3 3    3 4 3 1 1 2
3 4 5 1 1 3    3 3 5 1 2 3    3 4 4 1 2 3    3 4 4 1 1 3
3 3 3 2 1 3    3 3 5 1 1 2    4 5 5 2 3 4    4 4 5 2 3 4
END DATA.
(1) REGRESSION DESCRIPTIVES = DEFAULT/
    VARIABLES = INSTEVAL TO COUEVAL/
(2) STATISTICS = DEFAULTS TOL SELECTION/
    DEPENDENT = INSTEVAL/
(3) METHOD = STEPWISE/
(4) SAVE COOK LEVER SRESID/
(5) SCATTERPLOT(*SRESID, *ZPRED).
```

	CORRELATION MATRIX					
	Insteval	Clarity	Stimul	Knowledge	Interest	Coueval
INSTEVAL	1.000	.862	.739	.282	.435	.738
CLARITY	.862	1.000	.617	.057	.200	.651
STIMUL	.739	.617	1.000	.078	.317	.523
KNOWLEDGE	.282	.057	.078	1.000	.583	.041
INTEREST	.435	.200	.317	.583	1.000	.448
COUEVAL	.738	.651	.523	.041	.448	1.000

(1) The DESCRIPTIVES = DEFAULT subcommand yields the means, standard deviations, and the correlation matrix for the variables.

(2) The DEFAULTS part of the STATISTICS subcommand yields, among other things, the ANOVA table for each step, R, R_2, and adjusted R_2.

(3) To obtain the backward selection procedure, we would simply put METHOD = BACKWARD/.

(4) The SAVE subcommand places into the data set Cook's distance—for identifying influential data points, centered leverage values—for identifying outliers on predictors, and studentized residuals—for identifying outliers on y.

(5) This SCATTERPLOT subcommand yields the plot of the studentized residuals vs. the standardized predicted values, which is very useful for determining whether any of the assumptions underlying the linear regression model may be violated.

SPSS has "p values," denoted by `PIN` and `POUT`, which govern whether a predictor will enter the equation and whether it will be deleted. The default values are `PIN = .05` and `POUT = .10`. In other words, a predictor must be "significant" at the .05 level to enter, or must not be significant at the .10 level to be deleted.

First, we discuss the stepwise procedure results. Examination of the correlation matrix in Table 3.3 reveals that three of the predictors (CLARITY, STIMUL, and COUEVAL) are strongly related to INSTEVAL (simple correlations of .862, .739, and .738, respectively). Because clarity has the highest correlation, it will enter the equation first. Superficially, it might appear that STIMUL or COUEVAL would enter next; however we must take into account how these predictors are correlated with CLARITY, and indeed both have fairly high correlations with CLARITY (.617 and .651 respectively). Thus, they will not account for as much unique variance on INSTEVAL, above and beyond that of CLARITY, as first appeared. On the other hand, INTEREST, which has a considerably lower correlation with INSTEVAL (.44), is correlated only .20 with CLARITY. Thus, the variance on INSTEVAL it accounts for is relatively independent of the variance CLARITY accounted for. And, as seen in Table 3.4, it is INTEREST that enters the regression equation second. STIMUL is the third and final predictor to enter, because its p value (.0086) is less than the default value of .05. Finally, the other predictors (KNOWLEDGE and COUEVAL) don't enter because their p values (.0989 and .1288) are greater than .05.

■ **Table 3.4: Selected Results SPSS Stepwise Regression Run on the Morrison MBA Data**

Descriptive Statistics			
	Mean	Std. Deviation	N
INSTEVAL	2.4063	.7976	32
CLARITY	2.8438	1.0809	32
STIMUL	3.3125	1.0906	32
KNOWLEDG	1.4375	.6189	32
INTEREST	1.6563	.7874	32
COUEVAL	2.5313	.7177	32

Correlations						
		INSTEVAL	CLARITY	STIMUL	KNOWLEDG	INTEREST	COUEVAL
Pearson	INSTEVAL	1.000	.862	.739	.282	.435	.738
Correlation	CLARITY	.862	1.000	.617	.057	.200	.651
	STIMUL	.739	.617	1.000	.078	.317	.523
	KNOWLEDG	.282	.057	.078	1.000	.583	.041
	INTEREST	.435	.200	.317	.583	1.000	.448
	COUEVAL	.738	.651	.523	.041	.448	1.000

Variables Entered/Removed[a]

Model	Variables Entered	Variables Removed	Method	
1	CLARITY		Stepwise (Criteria: Probability-of-F-to-enter <= .050, Probability-of-F-to-remove >= .100).	This predictor enters the equation first, since it has the highest simple correlation (.862) with the dependent variable INSTEVAL.
2	INTEREST		Stepwise (Criteria: Probability-of-F-to-enter <= .050, Probability-of-F-to-remove >= .100).	INTEREST has the opportunity to enter the equation next since it has the largest partial correlation of .528 (see the box with EXCLUDED VARIABLES), and does enter since its p value (.002) is less than the default entry value of .05.
3	STIMUL		Stepwise (Criteria: Probability-of-F-to-enter <= .050, Probability-of-F-to-Remove >= .100).	Since STIMULUS has the strongest tie to INSTEVAL, after the effects of CLARITY and INTEREST are partialed out, it gets the opportunity to enter next. STIMULUS does enter, since its p value (.009) is less than .05.

[a] Dependent Variable: INSTEVAL

Model Summary[d]

					Selection Criteria			
Model	R	R Square	Adjusted R Square	Std. Error of the Estimate	Akaike Information Criterion	Amemiya Prediction Criterion	Mallows' Prediction Criterion	Schwarz Bayesian Criterion
1	.862[a]	.743	.734	.4112	−54.936	.292	35.297	−52.004
2	.903[b]	.815	.802	.3551	−63.405	.224	19.635	−59.008
3	.925[c]	.856	.840	.3189	−69.426	.186	11.517	−63.563

[a] Predictors: (Constant), CLARITY
[b] Predictors: (Constant), CLARITY, INTEREST
[c] Predictors: (Constant), CLARITY, INTEREST, STIMUL
[d] Dependent Variable: INSTEVAL

With just CLARITY in the equation we account for 74.3% of the variance; adding INTEREST increases the variance accounted for to 81.5%, and finally with 3 predictors (STIMUL added) we account for 85.6% of the variance in this sample.

(Continued)

ANOVA[d]

Model		Sum of Squares	df	Mean Square	F	Sig.
1	Regression	14.645	1	14.645	86.602	.000[a]
	Residual	5.073	30	.169		
	Total	19.719	31			
2	Regression	16.061	2	8.031	63.670	.000[b]
	Residual	3.658	29	.126		
	Total	19.719	31			
3	Regression	16.872	3	5.624	55.316	.000[c]
	Residual	2.847	28	.102		
	Total	19.719	31			

[a] Predictors: (Constant), CLARITY
[b] Predictors: (Constant), CLARITY, INTEREST
[c] Predictors: (Constant), CLARITY, INTEREST, STIMUL
[d] Dependent Variable: INSTEVAL

Coefficient[a]

Model		Unstandardized Coefficients		Standardized Coefficients			Collinearity Statistics	
		B	Std. Error	Beta	t	Sig.	Toler-ance	VIF
1	(Constant)	.598	.207	.862	2.882	.007	1.000	1.000
	CLARITY	.636	.068		9.306	.000		
2	(Constant)	.254	.207	.807	1.230	.229	.960	1.042
	CLARITY	.596	.060	.273	9.887	.000	.960	1.042
	INTEREST	.277	.083		3.350	.002		
3	(Constant)	.021	.203	.653	.105	.917	.619	1.616
	CLARITY	.482	.067	.220	7.158	.000	.900	1.112
	INTEREST	.223	.077	.266	2.904	.007	.580	1.724
	STIMUL	.195	.069		2.824	.009		

[a] Dependent Variable: INSTEVAL

These are the raw regression coefficients that define the prediction equation, i.e., INSTEVAL = .482 CLARITY + .223 INTEREST + .195 STIMUL + .021. The coefficient of .482 for CLARITY means that for every unit change on CLARITY there is a predicted change of .482 units on INSTEVAL, holding the other predictors constant. The coefficient of .223 for INTEREST means that for every unit change on INTEREST there is a predicted change of .223 units on INSTEVAL, holding the other predictors constant. Note that the Beta column contains the estimates of the regression coefficients when all variables are in z score form. Thus, the value of .653 for CLARITY means that for every standard deviation change in CLARITY there is a predicted change of .653 standard deviations on INSTEVAL, holding constant the other predictors.

Excluded Variables[d]

Model		Beta In	T	Sig.	Partial Correlation	Collinearity Statistics Tolerance	VIF	Minimum Tolerance
1	STIMUL	.335[a]	3.274	.003	.520	.619	1.616	.619
	KNOWLEDG	.233[a]	2.783	.009	.459	.997	1.003	.997
	INTEREST	.273[a]	3.350	.002	.528	.960	1.042	.960
	COUEVAL	.307[a]	2.784	.009	.459	.576	1.736	.576
2	STIMUL	.266[b]	2.824	.009	.471	.580	1.724	.580
	KNOWLEDG	.116[b]	1.183	.247	.218	.656	1.524	.632
	COUEVAL	.191[b]	1.692	.102	.305	.471	2.122	.471
3	KNOWLEDG	.148[c]	1.709	.099	.312	.647	1.546	.572
	COUEVAL	.161[c]	1.567	.129	.289	.466	2.148	.451

[a] Predictors in the Model: (Constant), CLARITY
[b] Predictors in the Model: (Constant), CLARITY, INTEREST
[c] Predictors in the Model: (Constant), CLARITY, INTEREST, STIMUL
[d] Dependent Variable: INSTEVAL
Since neither of these *p* values is less than .05, no other predictors can enter, and the procedure terminates.

Selected output from the backward selection procedure appears in Table 3.5. First, all of the predictors are put into the equation. Then, the procedure determines which of the predictors makes the *least* contribution when entered last in the equation. That predictor is INTEREST, and since its *p* value is .9097, it is deleted from the equation. None of the other predictors is further deleted because their *p* values are less than .10.

Interestingly, note that two *different* sets of predictors emerge from the two sequential selection procedures. The stepwise procedure yields the set (CLARITY, INTEREST, and STIMUL), where the backward procedure yields (COUEVAL, KNOWLEDGE, STIMUL, and CLARITY). However, CLARITY and STIMUL are common to both sets. On the grounds of parsimony, we might prefer the set (CLARITY, INTEREST, and STIMUL), especially because the adjusted R^2 values for the two sets are quite close (.84 and .87). Note that the adjusted R^2 is generally preferred over R^2 as a measure of the proportion of *y* variability due to the model, although we will see later that adjusted R^2 does not work particularly well in assessing the cross-validity predictive power of an equation.

Three other things should be checked out before settling on this as our chosen model:

1. We need to determine if the assumptions of the linear regression model are tenable.
2. We need an estimate of the cross-validity power of the equation.
3. We need to check for the existence of outliers and/or influential data points.

■ **Table 3.5: Selected Printout From SPSS Regression for Backward Selection on the Morrison MBA Data**

					Selection Criteria			
Model	R	R Square	Adjusted R Square	Std. Error of the Estimate	Akaike Information Criterion	Amemiya Prediction Criterion	Mallows' Prediction Criterion	Schwarz Bayesian Criterion
1	.946[a]	.894	.874	.2831	−75.407	.154	6.000	−66.613
2	.946[b]	.894	.879	.2779	−77.391	.145	4.013	−70.062

Model Summary[c]

[a] Predictors: (Constant), COUEVAL, KNOWLEDG, STIMUL, INTEREST, CLARITY
[b] Predictors: (Constant), COUEVAL, KNOWLEDG, STIMUL, CLARITY
[c] Dependent Variable: INSTEVAL

Coefficients[a]

Model		Unstandardized Coefficients		Standardized Coefficients			Collinearity Statistics	
		B	Std. Error	Beta	t	Sig.	Tolerance	VIF
1	(Constant)	−.443	.235		−1.886	.070		
	CLARITY	.386	.071	.523	5.415	.000	.436	2.293
	STIMUL	.197	.062	.269	3.186	.004	.569	1.759
	KNOWLEDG	.277	.108	.215	2.561	.017	.579	1.728
	INTEREST	.011	.097	.011	.115	.910	.441	2.266
	COUEVAL	.270	.110	.243	2.459	.021	.416	2.401
2	(Constant)	−.450	.222		−2.027	.053		
	CLARITY	.384	.067	.520	5.698	.000	.471	2.125
	STIMUL	.198	.059	.271	3.335	.002	.592	1.690
	KNOWLEDG	.285	.081	.221	3.518	.002	.994	1.006
	COUEVAL	.276	.094	.249	2.953	.006	.553	1.810

[a] Dependent Variable: INSTEVAL

Figure 3.4 shows a plot of the studentized residuals versus the predicted values from SPSS. This plot shows essentially random variation of the points about the horizontal line of 0, indicating no violations of assumptions.

The issues of cross-validity power and outliers are considered later in this chapter, and are applied to this problem in section 3.15, after both topics have been covered.

Example 3.4: SAS REG on Doctoral Programs in Psychology

The data for this example come from a National Academy of Sciences report (1982) that, among other things, provided ratings on the quality of 46 research doctoral programs in psychology. The six variables used to predict quality are:

NFACULTY—number of faculty members in the program as of December 1980

NGRADS—number of program graduates from 1975 through 1980

PCTSUPP—percentage of program graduates from 1975–1979 who received fellowships or training grant support during their graduate education

PCTGRANT—percentage of faculty members holding research grants from the Alcohol, Drug Abuse, and Mental Health Administration, the National Institutes of Health, or the National Science Foundation at any time during 1978–1980

NARTICLE—number of published articles attributed to program faculty members from 1978–1980

PCTPUB—percentage of faculty with one or more published articles from 1978–1980

Both the stepwise and the MAXR procedures were used on this data to generate several regression models. SAS syntax for doing this, along with the correlation matrix, are given in Table 3.6.

■ **Table 3.6: SAS Syntax for Stepwise and MAXR Runs on the National Academy of Sciences Data and the Correlation Matrix**

```
DATA SINGER;
INPUT QUALITY NFACUL NGRADS PCTSUPP PCTGRT NARTIC PCTPUB; LINES;
    DATA LINES
(1)  PROC REG SIMPLE CORR;
(2)  MODEL QUALITY = NFACUL NGRADS PCTSUPP PCTGRT NARTIC PCTPUB/
     SELECTION = STEPWISE VIF R INFLUENCE;
     MODEL QUALITY = NFACUL NGRADS PCTSUPP PCTGRT NARTIC PCTPUB/
     SELECTION = MAXR VIF R INFLUENCE;
RUN;
```

(1) `SIMPLE` is needed to obtain descriptive statistics (means, variances, etc.) for all variables. `CORR` is needed to obtain the correlation matrix for the variables.

(2) In this `MODEL` statement, the dependent variable goes on the left and all predictors to the right of the equals sign. `SELECTION` is where we indicate which of the procedures we wish to use. There is a wide variety of other information we can get printed out. Here we have selected `VIF` (variance inflation factors), `R` (analysis of residuals, hat elements, Cook's D), and `INFLU-ENCE` (influence diagnostics).

Note that there are two separate `MODEL` statements for the two regression procedures being requested. Although multiple procedures can be obtained in one run, you *must* have a separate `MODEL` statement for each procedure.

CORRELATION MATRIX							
		NFACUL	NCRADS	PCTSUPP	PCTCRT	NARTIC	PCTPUB	QUALITY
		2	3	4	5	6	7	1
NFACUL	2	1.000						

(Continued)

■ **Table 3.6: (Continued)**

		NFACUL	NCRADS	PCTSUPP	PCTCRT	NARTIC	PCTPUB	QUALITY
				CORRELATION MATRIX				
NCRADS	3	0.692	1.000					
PCTSUPP	4	0.395	0.337	1.000				
PCTCRT	S	0.162	0.071	0.351	1.000			
NARTIC	6	0.755	0.646	0.366	0.436	1.000		
PCTPUB	7	0.205	0.171	0.347	0.490	0.593	1.000	
QUALITY	I	0.622	0.418	0.582	0.700	0.762	0.585	1.000

One very nice feature of SAS REG is that Mallows' C_p is given for each model. The stepwise procedure terminated after four predictors entered. Here is the summary table, exactly as it appears in the output:

Summary of Stepwise Procedure for Dependent Variable QUALITY

Step	Variable Entered	Removed	Partial R**2	Model R**2	C(p)	F	Prob > F
1	NARTIC		0.5809	0.5809	55.1185	60.9861	0.0001
2	PCTGRT		0.1668	0.7477	18.4760	28.4156	0.0001
3	PCTSUPP		0.0569	0.8045	7.2970	12.2197	0.0011
4	NFACUL		0.0176	0.8221	5.2161	4.0595	0.0505

This four predictor model appears to be a reasonably good one. First, Mallows' C_p is very close to p (recall $p = k + 1$), that is, $5.216 \approx 5$, indicating that there is not much bias in the model. Second, $R^2 = .8221$, indicating that we can predict quality quite well from the four predictors. Although this R^2 is *not* adjusted, the adjusted value will not differ much because we have not selected from a large pool of predictors.

Selected output from the MAXR procedure run appears in Table 3.7. From Table 3.7 we can construct the following results:

BEST MODEL	VARIABLE(S)	MALLOWS C_p
for 1 variable	NARTIC	55.118
for 2 variables	PCTGRT, NFACUL	16.859
for 3 variables	PCTPUB, PCTGRT, NFACUL	9.147
for 4 variables	NFACUL, PCTSUPP, PCTGRT, NARTIC	5.216

In this case, the *same* four-predictor model is selected by the MAXR procedure that was selected by the stepwise procedure.

■ **Table 3.7: Selected Results From the MAXR Run on the National Academy of Sciences Data**

Maximum R-Square Improvement of Dependent Variable QUALITY

Step 1	Variable NARTIC Entered	R-square = 0.5809	C(p) = 55.1185

The above model is the best 1-variable model found.

Step 2	Variable PGTGRT Entered	R-square = 0.7477	C(p) = 18.4760
Step 3	Variable NARTIC Removed	R-square = 0.7546	C(p) = 16.8597
	Variable NFACUL Entered		

The above model is the best 2-variable model found.

Step 4	Variable PCTPUB Entered	R-square = 0.7965	C(p) = 9.1472

The above model is the best 3-variable model found.

Step 5	Variable PCTSUPP Entered	R-square = 0.8191	C(p) = 5.9230
Step 6	Variable PCTPUB Removed	R-square = 0.8221	C(p) = 5.2161
	Variable NARTIC Entered		

	DF	Sum of Squares	Mean Square	F	Prob > f
Regression	4	3752.82299	938.20575	47.38	0.0001
Error	41	811.894403	19.80230		
Total	45	4564.71739			

Variable	Parameter Estimate	Standard Error	Type II Sum of Squares	F	Prob > F
INTERCEP	9.06133	1.64473	601.05272	30.35	0.0001
NFACUL	0.13330	0.06616	80.38802	4.06	0.0505
PCTSUPP	0.094530	0.03237	168.91498	8.53	0.0057
PCTGRT	0.24645	0.04414	617.20528	31.17	0.0001
NARTIC	0.05455	0.01955	154.24692	7.79	0.0079

3.9.1 Caveat on *p* Values for the "Significance" of Predictors

The *p* values that are given by SPSS and SAS for the "significance" of each predictor at each step for stepwise or the forward selection procedures should be treated tenuously, especially if your initial pool of predictors is moderate (15) or large (30). The reason is that the ordinary F distribution is *not* appropriate here, because the largest F is being selected out of all Fs available. Thus, the appropriate critical value will be larger (and can be considerably larger) than would be obtained from the ordinary null F distribution. Draper and Smith (1981) noted, "studies have shown, for example, that in some cases where an entry F test was made at the *a* level, the appropriate probability was qa, where there were q entry candidates at that stage" (p. 311). This is saying, for example, that an experimenter may think his or her probability of erroneously including a predictor is .05, when in fact the *actual* probability of erroneously including the predictor is .50 (if there were 10 entry candidates at that point).

Thus, the F tests are positively biased, and the greater the number of predictors, the larger the bias. Hence, these *F* tests should be used only as rough guides to the usefulness of the predictors chosen. The acid test is how well the predictors do under cross-validation. It can be unwise to use *any* of the stepwise procedures with 20 or 30 predictors and only 100 subjects, because capitalization on chance is great, and the results may well not cross-validate. To find an equation that probably will have generalizability, it is best to carefully select (using substantive knowledge or any previous related literature) a small or relatively small set of predictors.

Ramsey and Schafer (1997) comment on this issue:

> The cutoff value of 4 for the *F*-statistic (or 2 for the magnitude of the t-statistic) corresponds roughly to a two-sided p-value of less than .05. The notion of "significance" cannot be taken seriously, however, because sequential variable selection is a form of data snooping.
>
> At step 1 of a forward selection, the cutoff of *F* = 4 corresponds to a hypothesis test for a single coefficient. But the actual statistic considered is the largest of several *F*-statistics, whose sampling distribution under the null hypothesis differs sharply from an *F*-distribution.
>
> To demonstrate this, suppose that a model contained ten explanatory variables and a single response, with a sample size of $n = 100$. The *F*-statistic for a single variable at step 1 would be compared to an *F*-distribution with 1 and 98 degrees of freedom, where only 4.8% of the *F*-ratios exceed 4. But suppose further that all eleven variables were generated completely at random (and independently of each other), from a standard normal distribution. What should be expected of the largest *F*-to-enter?
>
> This random generation process was simulated 500 times on a computer. The following display shows a histogram of the largest among ten *F*-to-enter values, along with the theoretical *F*-distribution. The two distributions are very different. At least one *F*-to-enter was larger than 4 in 38% of the simulated trials, even though none of the explanatory variables was associated with the response. (p. 93)

Simulated distribution of the largest of 10 F-statistics.

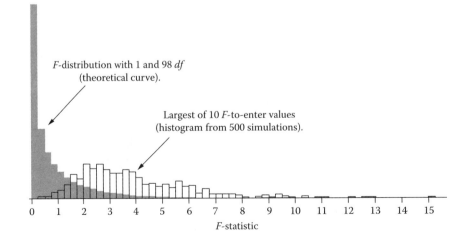

3.10 CHECKING ASSUMPTIONS FOR THE REGRESSION MODEL

Recall that in the linear regression model it is assumed that the errors are independent and follow a normal distribution with constant variance. The normality assumption can be checked through the use of the histogram of the standardized or studentized residuals, as we did in Table 3.2 for the simple regression example. The independence assumption implies that the subjects are responding independently of one another. This is an important assumption. We show in Chapter 6, in the context of analysis of variance, that if independence is violated only mildly, then the probability of a type I error may be *several* times greater than the level the experimenter thinks he or she is working at. Thus, instead of rejecting falsely 5% of the time, the experimenter may be rejecting falsely 25% or 30% of the time.

We now consider an example where this assumption was violated. Suppose researchers had asked each of 22 college freshmen to write four in-class essays in two 1-hour sessions, separated by a span of several months. Then, suppose a subsequent regression analysis were conducted to predict quality of essay response using an *n* of 88. Here, however, the responses for each subject on the four essays are obviously going to be correlated, so that there are not 88 independent observations, but only 22.

3.10.1 Residual Plots

Various types of plots are available for assessing potential problems with the regression model (Draper & Smith, 1981; Weisberg, 1985). One of the most useful graphs the studentized residuals (r) versus the predicted values ($\hat{y}_i$). If the assumptions of the linear regression model are tenable, then these residuals should scatter randomly about a horizontal line defined by $r_i = 0$, as shown in Figure 3.3a. *Any systematic pattern or clustering of the residuals suggests a model violation(s).* Three such systematic patterns are indicated in Figure 3.3. Figure 3.3b shows a systematic quadratic (second-degree equation) clustering of the residuals. For Figure 3.3c, the variability of the residuals increases systematically as the predicted values increase, suggesting a violation of the constant variance assumption.

It is important to note that the plots in Figure 3.3 are somewhat idealized, constructed to be clear violations. As Weisberg (1985) stated, "unfortunately, these idealized plots cover up one very important point; in real data sets, the true state of affairs is rarely this clear" (p. 131).

In Figure 3.4 we present residual plots for three real data sets. The first plot is for the Morrison data (the first computer example), and shows essentially random scatter of the residuals, suggesting no violations of assumptions. The remaining two plots are from a study by a statistician who analyzed the salaries of over 260 major league baseball hitters, using predictors such as career batting average, career home runs per time at bat, years in the major leagues, and so on. These plots are from Moore and McCabe (1989) and are used with permission. Figure 3.4b, which plots the residuals versus

▪ **Figure 3.3:** Residual plots of studentized residuals vs. predicted values.

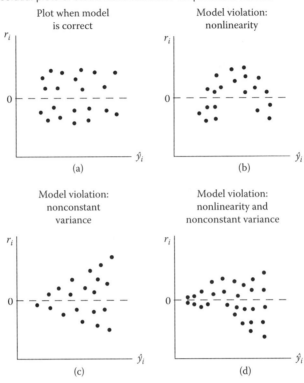

predicted salaries, shows a clear violation of the constant variance assumption. For lower predicted salaries there is little variability about 0, but for the high salaries there is considerable variability of the residuals. The implication of this is that the model will predict lower salaries quite accurately, but not so for the higher salaries.

Figure 3.4c plots the residuals versus number of years in the major leagues. This plot shows a clear curvilinear clustering, that is, quadratic. The implication of this curvilinear trend is that the regression model will tend to overestimate the salaries of players who have been in the majors only a few years or over 15 years, and it will underestimate the salaries of players who have been in the majors about five to nine years.

In concluding this section, note that if nonlinearity or nonconstant variance is found, there are various remedies. For nonlinearity, perhaps a polynomial model is needed. Or sometimes a transformation of the data will enable a nonlinear model to be approximated by a linear one. For nonconstant variance, weighted least squares is one possibility, or more commonly, a variance-stabilizing transformation (such as square root or log) may be used. We refer you to Weisberg (1985, chapter 6) for an excellent discussion of remedies for regression model violations.

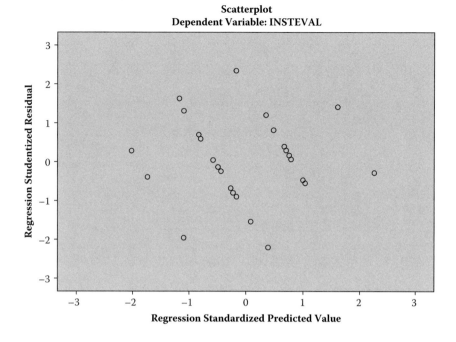

Figure 3.4: Residual plots for three real data sets suggesting no violations, heterogeneous variance, and curvilinearity.

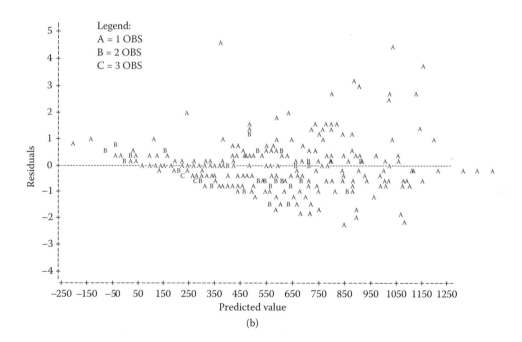

(b)

▪ **Figure 3.3: (Continued)**

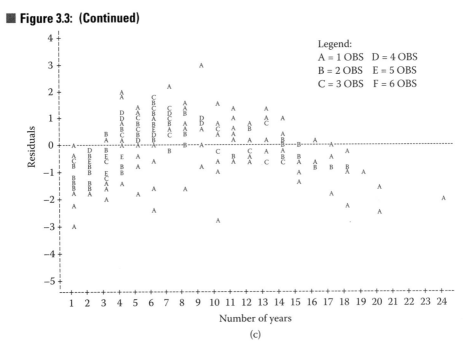

(c)

3.11 MODEL VALIDATION

We indicated earlier that it was crucial for the researcher to obtain some measure of how well the regression equation will predict on an independent sample(s) of data. That is, it was important to determine whether the equation had generalizability. We discuss here three forms of model validation, two being empirical and the other involving an *estimate* of average predictive power on other samples. First, we give a brief description of each form, and then elaborate on each form of validation.

1. *Data splitting.* Here the sample is randomly split in half. It does not have to be split evenly, but we use this for illustration. The regression equation is found on the so-called derivation sample (also called the screening sample, or the sample that "gave birth" to the prediction equation by Tukey). This prediction equation is then applied to the other sample (called validation or calibration) to see how well it predicts the *y* scores there.

2. *Compute an adjusted R^2.* There are various adjusted R^2 measures, or measures of shrinkage in predictive power, but they do not all estimate the same thing. The one most commonly used, and that which is printed out by both major statistical packages, is due to Wherry (1931). It is very important to note here that the Wherry formula estimates how much variance on *y* would be accounted for if we had derived the prediction equation in the population from which the sample was drawn. The Wherry formula does *not* indicate how well the derived equation will predict on other samples from the same population. A formula due to Stein (1960) does estimate average cross-validation predictive power. As of this writing it is not

printed out by any of the three major packages. The formulas due to Wherry and Stein are presented shortly.

3. *Use the PRESS statistic.* As pointed out by several authors, in many instances one does not have enough data to be randomly splitting it. One can obtain a good measure of *external* predictive power by use of the PRESS statistic. In this approach the *y* value for *each* subject is set aside and a prediction equation derived on the remaining data. Thus, *n* prediction equations are derived and *n* true prediction errors are found. To be very specific, the prediction error for subject 1 is computed from the equation derived on the remaining $(n - 1)$ data points, the prediction error for subject 2 is computed from the equation derived on the other $(n - 1)$ data points, and so on. As Myers (1990) put it, "PRESS is important in that one has information in the form of *n* validations in which the fitting sample for each is of size $n - 1$" (p. 171).

3.11.1 Data Splitting

Recall that the sample is randomly split. The regression equation is found on the derivation sample and then is applied to the other sample (validation) to determine how well it will predict *y* there. Next, we give a hypothetical example, randomly splitting 100 subjects.

Derivation Sample	Validation Sample		
$n = 50$	$n = 50$		
Prediction Equation	y	x_1	x_2
$\hat{y}_i = 4 + .3x_1 + .7x_2$			
	6	1	.5
	4.5	2	.3
	. . .		
	7	5	.2

Now, using this prediction equation, we predict the *y* scores in the validation sample:

$$\hat{y}_1 = 4 + .3(1) + .7(.5) = 4.65$$

$$\hat{y}_2 = 4 + .3(2) + .7(.3) = 4.81$$

. . .

$$\hat{y}_{50} = 4 + .3(5) + .7(.2) = 5.64$$

The cross-validated *R* then is the correlation for the following set of scores:

y	$\hat{y}_i$
6	4.65
4.5	4.81
. . .	
7	5.64

Random splitting and cross-validation can be easily done using SPSS and the filter case function.

3.11.2 Cross-Validation With SPSS

To illustrate cross-validation with SPSS, we use the Agresti data that appears on this book's accompanying website. Recall that the sample size here was 93. First, we randomly select a sample and do a stepwise regression on this random sample. We have selected an approximate random sample of 60%. It turns out that $n = 60$ in our random sample. This is done by clicking on DATA, choosing SELECT CASES from the dropdown menu, then choosing RANDOM SAMPLE and finally selecting a random sample of approximately 60%. When this is done a FILTER_$ variable is created, with value = 1 for those cases included in the sample and value = 0 for those cases *not* included in the sample. When the stepwise regression was done, the variables SIZE, NOBATH, and NEW were included as predictors and the coefficients, and so on, are given here for that run:

		Coefficients[a]				
		Unstandardized Coefficients		Standardized Coefficients		
Model		B	Std. Error	Beta	t	Sig.
1	(Constant)	−28.948	8.209		−3.526	.001
	SIZE	78.353	4.692	.910	16.700	.000
2	(Constant)	−62.848	10.939		−5.745	.000
	SIZE	62.156	5.701	.722	10.902	.000
	NOBATH	30.334	7.322	.274	4.143	.000
3	(Constant)	−62.519	9.976		−6.267	.000
	SIZE	59.931	5.237	.696	11.444	.000
	NOBATH	29.436	6.682	.266	4.405	.000
	NEW	17.146	4.842	.159	3.541	.001

[a] Dependent Variable: PRICE

The next step in the cross-validation is to use the COMPUTE statement to compute the predicted values for the dependent variable. This COMPUTE statement is obtained by clicking on TRANSFORM and then selecting COMPUTE from the dropdown menu. When this is done the screen in Figure 3.5 appears.

Using the coefficients obtained from the regression we have:

PRED = −62.519 + 59.931*SIZE + 29.436*NOBATH + 17.146*NEW

We wish to correlate the predicted values in the other part of the sample with the y values there to obtain the cross-validated value. We click on DATA again, and use SELECT IF FILTER_$ = 0. That is, we select those cases in the *other* part of the sample. There are 33 cases in the other part of the random sample. When this is done all

■ **Figure 3.5:** SPSS screen that can be used to compute the predicted values for cross-validation.

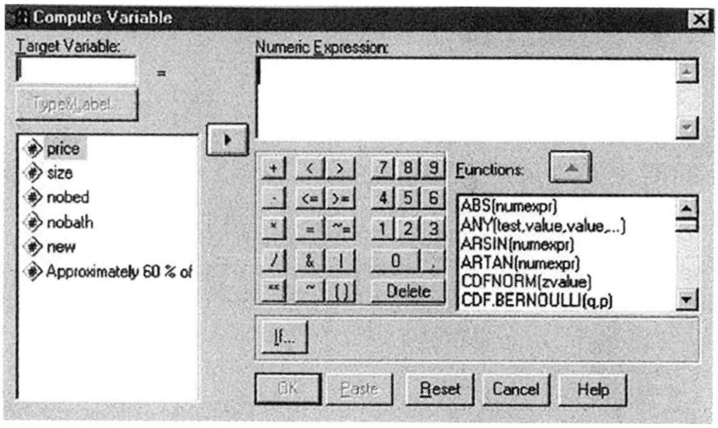

the cases with FILTER_$ = 1 are selected, and a partial listing of the data appears as follows:

	Price	Size	nobed	nobath	new	filter_$	pred
1	48.50	1.10	3.00	1.00	.00	0	32.84
2	55.00	1.01	3.00	2.00	.00	0	56.88
3	68.00	1.45	3.00	2.00	.00	1	83.25
4	137.00	2.40	3.00	3.00	.00	0	169.62
5	309.40	3.30	4.00	3.00	1.00	0	240.71
6	17.50	.40	1.00	1.00	.00	1	−9.11
7	19.60	1.28	3.00	1.00	.00	0	43.63
8	24.50	.74	3.00	1.00	.00	0	11.27

Finally, we use the CORRELATION program to obtain the bivariate correlation between PRED and PRICE (the dependent variable) in this sample of 33. That correlation is .878, which is a drop from the maximized correlation of .944 in the derivation sample.

3.11.3 Adjusted R^2

Herzberg (1969) presented a discussion of various formulas that have been used to estimate the amount of shrinkage found in R^2. As mentioned earlier, the one most commonly used, and due to Wherry, is given by

$$\hat{\rho}^2 = 1 - \frac{(n-1)}{(n-k-1)}\left(1 - R^2\right),$$

$$(11)$$

where $\hat{\rho}$ is the estimate of ρ, the population multiple correlation coefficient. This is the adjusted R^2 printed out by SAS and SPSS. Draper and Smith (1981) commented on Equation 11:

A related statistic . . . is the so called adjusted $r\left(R_a^2\right)$, the idea being that the statistic R_a^2 can be used to compare equations fitted not only to a specific set of data but also to two or more entirely different sets of data. The value of this statistic for the latter purpose is, in our opinion, not high. (p. 92)

Herzberg noted:

> In applications, the population regression function can never be known and one is more interested in how effective the *sample* regression function is in *other* samples. A measure of this effectiveness is r_c, the sample cross-validity. For any given regression function r_c will vary from validation sample to validation sample. The average value of r_c will be approximately equal to the correlation, in the *population*, of the sample regression function with the criterion. This correlation is the population cross-validity, ρ_c. Wherry's formula estimates ρ rather than ρ_c. (p. 4)

There are two possible models for the predictors: (1) regression—the values of the predictors are fixed, that is, we study y only for certain values of x, and (2) correlation—the predictors are random variables—this is a much more reasonable model for social science research. Herzberg presented the following formula for estimating $\hat{\rho}_c^2$ under the correlation model:

$$\hat{\rho}_c^2 = 1 - \frac{(n-1)}{(n-k-1)}\left(\frac{n-2}{n-k-2}\right)\left(\frac{n+1}{n}\right)(1-R^2),$$

$$(12)$$

where n is sample size and k is the number of predictors. It can be shown that $\rho_c < \rho$.

If you are interested in cross-validity predictive power, then the Stein formula (Equation 12) should be used. As an example, suppose $n = 50$, $k = 10$ and $R^2 = .50$. If you used the Wherry formula (Equation 11), then your estimate is

$$\hat{\rho}^2 = 1 - 49/39(.50) = .372,$$

whereas with the proper Stein formula you would obtain

$$\hat{\rho}_c^2 = 1 - (49/39)(48/38)(51/50)(.50) = .191.$$

In other words, use of the Wherry formula would give a misleadingly positive impression of the cross-validity predictive power of the equation. Table 3.8 shows how the estimated predictive power drops off using the Stein formula (Equation 12) for small to fairly large subject/variable ratios when $R^2 = .50$, .75, and .85.

3.11.4 PRESS Statistic

The PRESS approach is important in that one has n validations, each based on $(n - 1)$ observations. Thus, each validation is based on essentially the entire sample. This is very important when one does not have large n, for in this situation data splitting is really not practical. For example, if $n = 60$ and we have six predictors, randomly splitting the sample involves obtaining a prediction equation on only 30 subjects.

■ **Table 3.8: Estimated Cross-Validity Predictive Power for Stein Formula**[a]

	Subject/variable ratio	Stein estimate
Small (5:1)	$N = 50$, $k = 10$, $R^2 = .50$	.191[b]
	$N = 50$, $k = 10$, $R^2 = .75$	.595
	$N = 50$, $k = 10$, $R^2 = .85$	.757
Moderate (10:1)	$N = 100$, $k = 10$, $R^2 = .50$	.374
	$N = 100$, $k = 10$, $R^2 = .75$	.690
Fairly large (15:1)	$N = 150$, $k = 10$, $R^2 = .50$	.421

[a] If there is selection of predictors from a larger set, then the *median* should be used as the *k*. For example, if four predictors were selected from 30 by say stepwise regression, then the median between 4 and 30 (i.e., 17) should be the *k* used in the Stein formula.

[b] If we were to apply the prediction equation to many other samples from the same population, then on the *average* we would account for 19.1% of the variance on *y*.

Recall that in deriving the prediction (via the least squares approach), the sum of the squared errors is *minimized*. The PRESS residuals, on the other hand, are true prediction errors, because the *y* value for each subject was not simultaneously used for fit and model assessment. Let us denote the predicted value for subject *i*, where that subject was *not* used in developing the prediction equation, by $\hat{y}_{(-i)}$. Then the PRESS residual for each subject is given by

$$\hat{e}_{(-i)} = y_i - \hat{y}_{(-i)}$$

and the PRESS sum of squared residuals is given by

$$\text{PRESS} = \sum \hat{e}_{(-i)}^2. \tag{13}$$

Therefore, one might prefer the model with the smallest PRESS value. The preceding PRESS value can be used to calculate an R^2-like statistic that more accurately reflects the generalizability of the model. It is given by

$$R^2_{\text{Press}} = 1 - (\text{PRESS}) / \sum (y_i - \bar{y})^2 \tag{14}$$

Importantly, the SAS REG program routinely prints out PRESS, although it is called PREDICTED RESID SS (PRESS). Given this value, it is a simple matter to calculate the R^2 PRESS statistic, because the variance of *y* is $s_y^2 = \sum (y_i - \bar{y})^2 / (n - 1)$.

3.12 IMPORTANCE OF THE ORDER OF THE PREDICTORS

The order in which the predictors enter a regression equation can make a great deal of difference with respect to how much variance on *y* they account for, especially for moderate or highly correlated predictors. Only for uncorrelated predictors (which would rarely occur in practice) does the order not make a difference. We give two examples to illustrate.

Example 3.5

A dissertation by Crowder (1975) attempted to predict ratings of individuals having trainably mental retardation (TMs) using IQ (x_2) and scores from a Test of Social Inference (TSI). He was especially interested in showing that the TSI had incremental predictive validity. The criterion was the average ratings by two individuals in charge of the TMs. The intercorrelations among the variables were:

$$r_{x_1 x_2} = .59, r_{yx_2} - .54, r_{yx_1} = .566$$

Now, consider two orderings for the predictors, one where TSI is entered first, and the other ordering where IQ is entered first.

First ordering % of variance		Second ordering % of variance	
TSI	32.04	IQ	29.16
IQ	6.52	TSI	9.40

The first ordering conveys an overly optimistic view of the utility of the TSI scale. Because we know that IQ will predict ratings, it should be entered first in the equation (as a control variable), and then TSI to see what its incremental validity is—that is, how much it adds to predicting ratings above and beyond what IQ does. Because of the moderate correlation between IQ and TSI, the amount of variance accounted for by TSI differs considerably when entered first versus second (32.04 vs. 9.4).

The 9.4% of variance accounted for by TSI when entered second is obtained through the use of the semipartial correlation previously introduced:

$$r_{y1.2(s)} = \frac{.566 - .54(.59)}{\sqrt{1 - .59^2}} = .306 \Rightarrow r^2_{y1.2(s)} = .094$$

Example 3.6

Consider the following correlations among three predictors and an outcome:

	x_1	x_2	x_3
y	.60	.70	.70
x_1		.70	.60
x_2			.80

Notice that the predictors are strongly intercorrelated.

How much variance in y will x_3 account for if entered first? if entered last?

If x_3 is entered first, then it will account for $(.7)^2 \times 100$ or 49% of variance on y—a sizable amount.

To determine how much variance x_3 will account for if entered last, we need to compute the following second-order semipartial correlation:

$$r_{y3.12(s)} = \frac{r_{y3.1(s)} - r_{y2.1(s)} r_{23.1}}{\sqrt{1 - r_{23.1}^2}}$$

We show the details next for obtaining $r_{y3.12(s)}$:

$$r_{y2.1(s)} = \frac{r_{y2} - r_{y1} r_{21}}{\sqrt{1 - r_{21}^2}} = \frac{.70 - (.6)(.7)}{\sqrt{1 - .49}}$$

$$r_{y2.1(s)} = \frac{.28}{.714} = .392$$

$$r_{y3.1(s)} = \frac{r_{y3} - r_{y1} r_{31}}{\sqrt{1 - r_{31}^2}} = \frac{.7 - .6(6)}{\sqrt{1 - .6^2}} = .425$$

$$r_{23.1} = \frac{r_{23} - r_{21} r_{31}}{\sqrt{1 - r_{21}^2} \sqrt{1 - r_{31}^2}} = \frac{.80 - (.7)(.6)}{\sqrt{1 - .49} \sqrt{1 - .36}} = .665$$

$$r_{y3.1(s)} = \frac{.425 - .392(.665)}{\sqrt{1 - .665^2}} = \frac{.164}{.746} = .22$$

$$r_{y3.12(s)}^2 = (.22)^2 = .048$$

Thus, when x_3 enters last it accounts for only 4.8% of the variance on y. This is a tremendous drop from the 49% it accounted for when entered first. Because the three predictors are so highly correlated, most of the variance on y that x_3 could have accounted for has already been accounted for by x_1 and x_2.

3.12.1 Controlling the Order of Predictors in the Equation

With the forward and stepwise selection procedures, the order of entry of predictors into the regression equation is determined via a mathematical maximization procedure. That is, the first predictor to enter is the one with the largest (maximized) correlation with y, the second to enter is the predictor with the largest partial correlation, and so on. However, there are situations where you may not want the mathematics to determine the order of entry of predictors. For example, suppose we have a five-predictor problem, with two proven predictors from previous research. The other three predictors are included to see if they have any incremental validity. In this case we would want to enter the two proven predictors in the equation first (as control variables), and then let the remaining three predictors "fight it out" to determine whether any of them add anything significant to predicting y above and beyond the proven predictors.

With SPSS REGRESSION or SAS REG we can control the order of predictors, and in particular, we can *force* predictors into the equation. In Table 3.9 we illustrate how this is done for SPSS and SAS for the five-predictor situation.

■ **Table 3.9: Controlling the Order of Predictors and Forcing Predictors Into the Equation With SPSS Regression and SAS Reg**

SPSS REGRESSION

```
      TITLE 'FORCING X3 AND X4 & USING STEPWISE SELECTION FOR OTHERS'.
      DATA LIST FREE/Y X1 X2 X3 X4 X5.
      BEGIN DATA.
         DATA LINES
      END DATA.
      LIST.
      REGRESSION VARIABLES = Y X1 X2 X3 X4 X5
         /DEPENDENT = Y
(1)      /METHOD = ENTER X3 X4
         /METHOD = STEPWISE X1 X2 X5.
```

SAS REG

```
      DATA FORCEPR;
      INPUT Y X1 X2 X3 X4 X5;
      LINES;
         DATA LINES
      PROC REG SIMPLE CORR;
(2) MODEL Y = X3 X4 X1 X2 X5/INCLUDE = 2 SELECTION = STEPWISE;
```

(1) The METHOD = ENTER subcommand forces variables X3 and X4 into the equation, and the METHOD = STEPWISE subcommand will determine whether any of the remaining predictors (X1, X2 or X5) have semipartial correlations large enough to be "significant." If we wished to force in predictors X1, X3, and X4 and then use STEPWISE, the subcommands are /METHOD = ENTER X1 X3 X4/METH-OD = STEPWISE X2 X5.

(2) The INCLUDE = 2 forces the first 2 predictors listed in the MODEL statement into the prediction equation. Thus, if we wish to force X3 and X4 we must list them first on the = statement.

3.13 OTHER IMPORTANT ISSUES

3.13.1 Preselection of Predictors

An industrial psychologist hears about the predictive power of multiple regression and is excited. He wants to predict success on the job, and gathers data for 20 potential predictors on 70 subjects. He obtains the correlation matrix for the variables and then picks out six predictors that correlate significantly with success on the job and that have low intercorrelations among themselves. The analysis is run, and the R^2 is highly significant. Furthermore, he is able to explain 52% of the variance on y (more than other investigators have been able to do). Are these results generalizable? Probably not, since what he did involves a *double* capitalization on chance:

1. In preselecting the predictors from a larger set, he is capitalizing on chance. Some of these variables would have high correlations with y because of sampling error, and consequently their correlations would tend to be lower in another sample.
2. The mathematical maximization involved in obtaining the multiple correlation involves capitalizing on chance.

Preselection of predictors is common among many researchers who are unaware of the fact that this tends to make their results sample specific. Nunnally (1978) had a nice discussion of the preselection problem, and Wilkinson (1979) showed the considerable positive bias preselection can have on the test of significance of R^2 in forward selection. The following example from his tables illustrates. The critical value for a four-predictor problem ($n = 35$) at .05 level is .26, and the appropriate critical value for the *same n* and α level, when preselecting four predictors from a set of 20 predictors is .51. Unawareness of the positive bias has led to many results in the literature that are not replicable, for as Wilkinson noted:

> A computer assisted search for articles in psychology using stepwise regression from 1969 to 1977 located 71 articles. Out of these articles, 66 forward selections analyses reported as significant by the usual F tests were found. Of these 66 analyses, 19 were *not* significant by [his] Table 1. (p. 172)

It is important to note that both the Wherry and Stein formulas do *not* take into account preselection. Hence, the following from Cohen and Cohen (1983) should be seriously considered: "A more realistic estimate of the shrinkage is obtained by substituting for *k* the *total* number of predictors from which the selection was made" (p. 107). In other words, they are saying if four predictors were selected out of 15, use $k = 15$ in the Stein formula (Equation 12). While this may be conservative, using four will certainly lead to a positive bias. Probably a median value between 4 and 15 would be closer to the mark, although this needs further investigation.

3.13.2 Positive Bias of R^2

A study of California principals and superintendents illustrates how capitalization on chance in multiple regression (if the researcher is unaware of it) can lead to misleading conclusions. Here, the interest was in validating a contingency theory of leadership, that is, that success in administering schools calls for different personality styles depending on the social setting of the school. The theory seems plausible, and in what follows we are not criticizing the theory *per se*, but the empirical validation of it. The procedure that was used to validate the theory involved establishing a relationship between various personality attributes (24 predictors) and several measures of administrative success in heterogeneous samples with respect to social setting using multiple regression, that is, finding the multiple R for each measure of success on 24 predictors. Then, it was shown that the magnitude of the relationships was greater for subsamples homogeneous with respect to social setting. The problem was that the sample size is much too low for a reliable prediction equation. Here we present the total sample sizes and the subsamples homogeneous with respect to social setting:

	Superintendents	Principals
Total	$n = 77$	$n = 147$
Subsample(s)	$n = 29$	$n_1 = 35, n_2 = 61, n_3 = 36$

Indeed, in the homogeneous samples, the Rs were on the average .34 greater than in the total samples; however, this was an artifact of the multiple regression procedure in this case. As one proceeds from the total to the subsamples the number of predictors (k) approaches sample size (n). For this situation the multiple correlation increases to 1 *regardless* of whether there is any relationship between y and the set of predictors. And in three of four subsamples the n/k ratios are very close to 1. In particular, it is the case that $E(R^2) = k / (n - 1)$, when the population multiple correlation $= 0$ (Morrison, 1976).

To dramatize this, consider Subsample 1 for the principals. Then $E(R^2) = 24 / 34 = .706$, even when there is *no* relationship between y and the set of predictors. The F critical value required just for statistical significance of R at .05 is 2.74, which implies $R^2 = .868$, just to be confident that the population multiple correlation is different from 0.

3.13.3 Suppressor Variables

Lord and Novick (1968) stated the following two rules of thumb for the selection of predictor variables:

1. Choose variables that correlate highly with the criterion but that have low intercorrelations.
2. To these variables add other variables that have low correlations with the criterion but that have high correlations with the other predictors. (p. 271)

At first blush, the second rule of thumb may not seem to make sense, but what they are talking about is suppressor variables. To illustrate specifically why a suppressor variable can help in prediction, we consider a hypothetical example.

Example 3.7

Consider a two-predictor problem with the following correlations among the variables:

$$r_{yx_1} = .60, r_{yx_2} = 0, \text{ and } r_{x_1 x_2} = .50.$$

Note that x_1 by itself accounts for $(.6)^2 = .36$, or 36% of the variance on y. Now consider entering x_2 into the regression equation first. It will of course account for no variance on y, and it may seem like we have gained nothing. But, if we now enter x_1 into the equation (after x_2), its predictive power is enhanced. This is because there is irrelevant variance on x_1 (i.e., variance that does not relate to y), which is related to x_2. In this case that irrelevant variance is $(.5)^2 = .25$ or 25%. When this irrelevant variance is partialed out (or suppressed), the remaining variance on x_1 is more strongly tied to y. Calculation of the semipartial correlation shows this:

$$r_{y1.2(s)} = \frac{r_{yx_1} - r_{yx_2} r_{x_1 x_2}}{\sqrt{1 - r_{x_1 x_2}^2}} = \frac{.60 - 0}{\sqrt{1 - .5^2}} = .693$$

Thus, $r^2_{y1.2(s)} = .48$, and the predictive power of x_1 has increased from accounting for 36% to accounting for 48% of the variance on y.

3.14 OUTLIERS AND INFLUENTIAL DATA POINTS

Because multiple regression is a mathematical maximization procedure, it can be very sensitive to data points that "split off" or are different from the rest of the points, that is, to outliers. Just one or two such points can affect the interpretation of results, and it is certainly moot as to whether one or two points should be permitted to have such a profound influence. Therefore, it is important to be able to detect outliers and influential points. There is a distinction between the two because a point that is an outlier (either on y or for the predictors) will *not necessarily* be influential in affecting the regression equation.

The fact that a simple examination of summary statistics can result in misleading interpretations was illustrated by Anscombe (1973). He presented four data sets that yielded the same summary statistics (i.e., regression coefficients and same $r^2 = .667$). In one case, linear regression was perfectly appropriate. In the second case, however, a scatterplot showed that curvilinear regression was appropriate. In the third case, linear regression was appropriate for 10 of 11 points, but the other point was an outlier and possibly should have been excluded from the analysis. In the fourth data set, the regression line was completely determined by one observation, which if removed, would not allow for an estimate of the slope.

Two basic approaches can be used in dealing with outliers and influential points. We consider the approach of having an arsenal of tools for isolating these important points for further study, with the possibility of deleting some or all of the points from the analysis. The other approach is to develop procedures that are relatively insensitive to wild points (i.e., robust regression techniques). (Some pertinent references for robust regression are Hogg, 1979; Huber, 1977; Mosteller & Tukey, 1977). It is important to note that even robust regression may be ineffective when there are outliers in the space of the predictors (Huber, 1977). Thus, even in robust regression there is a need for case analysis. Also, a modification of robust regression (bounded-influence regression) has been developed by Krasker and Welsch (1979).

3.14.1 Data Editing

Outliers and influential cases can occur because of recording errors. Consequently, researchers should give more consideration to the data editing phase of the data analysis process (i.e., *always* listing the data and examining the list for possible errors). There are many possible sources of error from the initial data collection to the final data entry. First, some of the data may have been recorded incorrectly. Second, even if recorded correctly, when all of the data are transferred to a single sheet or a few sheets in preparation for data entry, errors may be made. Finally, even if no errors are made in these first two steps, an error(s) could be made in entering the data into the computer.

There are various statistics for identifying outliers on y and on the set of predictors, as well as for identifying influential data points. We discuss first, in brief form, a statistic for each, with advice on how to interpret that statistic. Equations for the statistics are given later in the section, along with a more extensive and somewhat technical discussion for those who are interested.

3.14.2 Measuring Outliers on y

For finding participants whose predicted scores are quite different from their actual y scores (i.e., they do not fit the model well), the *studentized residuals* (r_i) can be used. If the model is correct, then they have a normal distribution with a mean of 0 and a standard deviation of 1. Thus, about 95% of the r_i should lie within two standard deviations of the mean and about 99% within three standard deviations. Therefore, any studentized residual greater than about 3 in absolute value is unusual and should be carefully examined.

3.14.3 Measuring Outliers on Set of Predictors

The *hat elements* (h_{ii}) or leverage values can be used here. It can be shown that the hat elements lie between 0 and 1, and that the average hat element is p / n, where $p = k + 1$. Because of this, Hoaglin and Welsch (1978) suggested that $2p / n$ may be considered large. However, this can lead to more points than we really would want to examine, and you should consider using $3p / n$. For example, with six predictors and 100 subjects, any hat element, or leverage value, greater than $3(7) / 100 = .21$ should be carefully examined. This is a very simple and useful rule for quickly identifying participants who are very different from the rest of the sample on the set of predictors. Note that instead of leverage SPSS reports a centered leverage value. For this statistic, the earlier guidelines for identifying outlying values are now $2k / n$ (instead of $2p / n$) and $3k / n$ (instead of $3p / n$).

3.14.4 Measuring Influential Data Points

An influential data point is one that when deleted produces a substantial change in at least one of the regression coefficients. That is, the prediction equations with and without the influential point are quite different. *Cook's distance* (Cook, 1977) is very useful for identifying influential points. It measures the *combined* influence of the case's being an outlier on y and on the set of predictors. Cook and Weisberg (1982) indicated that a Cook's distance = 1 *would generally be considered large*. This provides a "red flag," when examining computer output for identifying influential points.

All of these diagnostic measures are easily obtained from SPSS REGRESSION (see Table 3.3) or SAS REG (see Table 3.6).

3.14.5 Measuring Outliers on *y*

The raw residuals, $\hat{e}_i = y_i - \hat{y}_i$, in linear regression are assumed to be independent, to have a mean of 0, to have constant variance, and to follow a normal distribution. However, because the n residuals have only $n - k$ degrees of freedom (k degrees of freedom were lost in estimating the regression parameters), they can't be independent. If n is large relative to k, however, then the $\hat{e}_i$ are essentially independent. Also, the residuals have different variances. It can be shown (Draper & Smith, 1981, p. 144) that the variance for the ith residual is given by:

$$s_{e_i}^2 = \hat{\sigma}^2(1 - h_{ii}), \tag{15}$$

where $\hat{\sigma}^2$ is the estimate of variance not predictable from the regression (MS_{res}), and h_{ii} is the ith diagonal element of the hat matrix $\mathbf{X(X'X)^{-1}X'}$. Recall that $\mathbf{X}$ is the score matrix for the predictors. The h_{ii} play a key role in determining the predicted values for the subjects. Recall that

$$\hat{\boldsymbol{\beta}} = (\mathbf{X'X})^{-1}\mathbf{X'Y} \text{ and } \hat{\mathbf{y}} = \mathbf{X}\hat{\boldsymbol{\beta}}.$$

Therefore, $\hat{\mathbf{y}} = \mathbf{X(X'X)^{-1}X'y}$ by simple substitution. Thus, the predicted values for y are obtained by postmultiplying the hat matrix by the column vector of observed scores on y.

Because the predicted values ($\hat{y}_i$) and the residuals are related by $\hat{e}_i = y_i - \hat{y}_i$, it should not be surprising in view of the foregoing that the variability of the $\hat{e}_i$ would be affected by the h_{ii}.

Because the residuals have different variances, we need to properly scale the residuals so that we can meaningfully compare them. This is completely analogous to what is done in comparing raw scores from distributions with different variances and different means. There, one means of standardizing was to convert to z scores, using $z_i = (x_i - x)/s$. Here we also subtract off the mean (which is 0 and hence has no effect) and then divide by the standard deviation, which is the square root of Equation 15. Thus, the studentized residual is then

$$r_i = \frac{\hat{e}_i - 0}{\hat{\sigma}\sqrt{1 - h_{ii}}} = \frac{\hat{e}_i}{\hat{\sigma}\sqrt{1 - h_{ii}}}. \tag{16}$$

Because the r_i are assumed to have a normal distribution with a mean of 0 (if the model is correct), then about 99% of the r_i should lie within three standard deviations of the mean.

3.14.6 Measuring Outliers on the Predictors

The h_{ii} are one measure of the extent to which the ith observation is an outlier for the predictors. The h_{ii} are important because they can play a key role in determining the predicted values for the subjects. Recall that

$$\hat{\beta} = (\mathbf{X}'\mathbf{X})^{-1}\mathbf{X}'\mathbf{Y} \text{ and } \hat{\mathbf{y}} = \mathbf{X}\hat{\beta}.$$

Therefore, $\mathbf{y} = \mathbf{X}(\mathbf{X}'\mathbf{X})^{-1}\mathbf{X}'\mathbf{y}$ by simple substitution.

Thus, the predicted values for y are obtained by postmultiplying the hat matrix by the column vector of observed scores on y. It can be shown that the h_{ii} lie between 0 and 1, and that the average value for $h_{ii} = k/n$. From Equation 15 it can be seen that when h_{ii} is large (i.e., near 1), then the variance for the ith residual is near 0. This means that $\hat{y}_i \approx \hat{y}_i$. In other words, an observation may fit the linear model well and yet be an influential data point. This second diagnostic, then, is "flagging" observations that need to be examined carefully because they may have an unusually large influence on the regression coefficients.

What is a significant value for the h_{ii}? Hoaglin and Welsch (1978) suggested that $2p/n$ may be considered large. Belsey et al. (1980, pp. 67–68) showed that when the set of predictors is multivariate normal, then $(n-p)[h_{ii}-1/n]/(1-h_{ii})(p-1)$ is distributed as F with $(p-1)$ and $(n-p)$ degrees of freedom.

Rather than computing F and comparing against a critical value, Hoaglin and Welsch suggested $2p/n$ as rough guide for a large h_{ii}.

An important point to remember concerning the hat elements is that the points they identify will not necessarily be influential in affecting the regression coefficients.

A second measure for identifying outliers on the predictors is Mahalanobis' (1936) distance for case i (D_i^2). This measure indicates how far a case is from the centroid of all cases for the predictors. A large distance indicates an observation that is an outlier for the predictors. The Mahalanobis distance can be written in terms of the covariance matrix $\mathbf{S}$ as

$$D_i^2 = (\mathbf{x_i} - \overline{\mathbf{x}})'\mathbf{S}^{-1}(\mathbf{x_i} - \overline{\mathbf{x}}), \tag{17}$$

where $\mathbf{x_i}$ is the vector of the data for case i and $\overline{\mathbf{x}}$ is the vector of means (centroid) for the predictors.

For a better understanding of D_i^2, consider two small data sets. The first set has two predictors. In Table 3.10, the data are presented, as well as the D_i^2 and the descriptive statistics (including $\mathbf{S}$). The D_i^2 for cases 6 and 10 are large because the score for Case 6 on x_i (150) was deviant, whereas for Case 10 the score on x_2 (97) was very deviant. The graphical split-off of Cases 6 and 10 is quite vivid and was displayed in Figure 1.2 in Chapter 1.

In the previous example, because the numbers of predictors and participants were few, it would have been fairly easy to spot the outliers even without the Mahalanobis distance. However, in practical problems with 200 or 300 cases and 10 predictors, outliers are not always easy to spot and can occur in more subtle ways. For example, a case may have a large distance because there are moderate to fairly large differences on many of the predictors. The second small data set with four predictors and $N = 15$ in Table 3.10 illustrates this latter point. The D_i^2 for case 13 is quite large (7.97) even though the scores for that subject do not split off in a striking fashion for any of the predictors. Rather, it is a cumulative effect that produces the separation.

▪ **Table 3.10: Raw Data and Mahalanobis Distances for Two Small Data Sets**

Case	Y	X_1	X_2	X_3	X_4		D_i^2
1	476	111	68	17	81		0.30
2	457	92	46	28	67		1.55
3	540	90	50	19	83		1.47
4	551	107	59	25	71		0.01
5	575	98	50	13	92		0.76
6	698	150	66	20	90	(1)	5.48
7	545	118	54	11	101		0.47
8	574	110	51	26	82		0.38
9	645	117	59	18	87		0.23
10	556	94	97	12	69		7.24
11	634	130	57	16	97		
12	637	118	51	19	78		
13	390	91	44	14	64		
14	562	118	61	20	103		
15	560	109	66	13	88		
Summary Statistics							
M	561.70000	108.70000	60.00000				
SD	70.74846	17.73289	14.84737				

$$S = \begin{bmatrix} 314.455 & 19.483 \\ 10.483 & 220.944 \end{bmatrix}$$

Note: Boxed-in entries are the first data set and corresponding D_i^2. The 10 case numbers having the largest D_i^2 for a four-predictor data set are: 10, 10.859; 13, 7.977; 6, 7.223; 2, 5.048; 14, 4.874; 7, 3.514; 5, 3.177; 3, 2.616; 8, 2.561; 4, 2.404.

(1) Calculation of D_i^2 for Case 6:

$$D_6^2 = (41.3, 6) \begin{bmatrix} 314.455 & 19.483 \\ 19.483 & 220.444 \end{bmatrix}^{-1} \begin{pmatrix} 41.3 \\ 6 \end{pmatrix}$$

$$S^{-1} = \begin{bmatrix} .00320 & -.00029 \\ -.00029 & .00456 \end{bmatrix} \rightarrow D_6^2 = 5.484$$

How large must D_i^2 be before you can say that case i is significantly separated from the rest of the data? Johnson and Wichern (2007) note that these distances, if multivariate normality holds, approximately follow a chi-square distribution with degrees of freedom equal to the number of predictors (k), with this approximation improving for larger samples. A common practice is to consider a multivariate outlier to be present when an obtained Mahalanobis distance exceeds a chi-square critical value at a conservative alpha level (e.g., .001) with k degrees of freedom. Referring back to the example with two predictors, if we assume multivariate normality, then neither case 6 ($D_i^2 = 5.48$) nor case 10 ($D_i^2 = 7.24$) would be considered as a multivariate outlier at the .001 level as the chi-square critical value is 13.815.

3.14.7 Measures for Influential Data Points

3.14.7.1 COOK'S DISTANCE

Cook's distance (CD) is a measure of the change in the regression coefficients that would occur if this case were omitted, thus revealing which cases are most influential in affecting the regression equation. It is affected by the case's being an outlier both on y and on the set of predictors. Cook's distance is given by

$$CD_i = \left(\hat{\boldsymbol{\beta}} - \hat{\boldsymbol{\beta}}_{(-i)}\right)' \mathbf{X}'\mathbf{X}\left(\hat{\boldsymbol{\beta}} - \hat{\boldsymbol{\beta}}_{(-i)}\right) \Big/ (k+1) MS_{\text{res}}, \tag{18}$$

where $\hat{\boldsymbol{\beta}}_{(-i)}$ is the vector of estimated regression coefficients with the ith data point deleted, k is the number of predictors, and MS_{res} is the residual (error) variance for the full data set.

Removing the ith data point should keep $\hat{\boldsymbol{\beta}}_{(-i)}$ close to $\hat{\boldsymbol{\beta}}$ unless the ith observation is an outlier. Cook and Weisberg (1982, p. 118) indicated that *a $CD_i > 1$ would generally be considered large*. Cook's distance can be written in an alternative revealing form:

$$CD_i = \frac{1}{(k+1)} r_i^2 \frac{h_{ii}}{1 - h_{ii}}, \tag{19}$$

where r_i is the studentized residual and h_{ii} is the hat element. Thus, *Cook's distance measures the joint (combined) influence of the case being an outlier on y and on the set of predictors*. A case may be influential because it is a significant outlier only on y, for example,

$k = 5, n = 40, r_i = 4, h_{ii} = .3: CD_i > 1,$

or because it is a significant outlier only on the set of predictors, for example,

$k = 5, n = 40, r_i = 2, h_{ii} = .7: CD_i > 1.$

Note, however, that a case may not be a significant outlier on either y or on the set of predictors, but may still be influential, as in the following:

$$k = 3, n = 20, h_{ii} = .4, r = 2.5: CD_i > 1$$

3.14.7.2 DFFITS

This statistic (Belsley et al., 1980) indicates how much the ith fitted value will change if the ith observation is deleted. It is given by

$$\text{DFFITS}_i = \frac{\hat{y}_i - \hat{y}_{i-1}}{s_{-1}\sqrt{h_{11}}}. \tag{20}$$

The numerator simply expresses the difference between the fitted values, with the ith point in and with it deleted. The denominator provides a measure of variability since $s_y^2 = \sigma^2 h_{ii}$. Therefore, *DFFITS indicates the number of estimated standard errors that the fitted value changes when the ith point is deleted.*

3.14.7.3 DFBETAS

These are very useful in detecting how much *each* regression coefficient will change if the ith observation is deleted. They are given by

$$\text{DFBETA}_i = \frac{b_j - b_{j-1}}{SE(b_{j-1})}. \tag{21}$$

Each DFBETA *therefore indicates the number of standard errors a given coefficient changes when the ith point is deleted.* DFBETAS are available on SAS and SPSS, with SPSS referring to these as standardized DFBETAS. Any DFBETA with a value $> |2|$ indicates a sizable change and should be investigated. Thus, although Cook's distance is a *composite* measure of influence, the DFBETAS indicate which specific coefficients are being most affected.

It was mentioned earlier that a data point that is an outlier either on y or on the set of predictors will not *necessarily* be an influential point. Figure 3.6 illustrates how this can happen. In this simplified example with just one predictor, both points A and B are outliers on x. Point B is influential, and to accommodate it, the least squares regression line will be pulled downward toward the point. However, Point A is not influential because this point closely follows the trend of the rest of the data.

3.14.8 Summary

In summary, then, studentized residuals can be inspected to identify y outliers, and the leverage values (or centered leverage values in SPSS) or the Mahalanobis distances can be used to detect outliers on the predictors. Such outliers will not necessarily be influential points. To determine which outliers are influential, find those whose Cook's distances are > 1. Those points that are flagged as influential by Cook's distance need to be examined carefully to determine whether they should be deleted from the analysis. If there is a reason to believe that these cases arise from a process different from

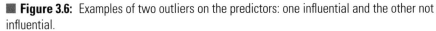

■ **Figure 3.6:** Examples of two outliers on the predictors: one influential and the other not influential.

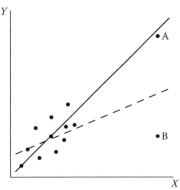

that for the rest of the data, then the cases should be deleted. For example, the failure of a measuring instrument, a power failure, or the occurrence of an unusual event (perhaps inexplicable) would be instances of a different process.

If a point is a significant outlier on y, but its Cook's distance is < 1, there is no real need to delete the point because it does not have a large effect on the regression analysis. However, one should still be interested in studying such points further to understand why they did not fit the model. After all, the purpose of any study is to understand the data. In particular, you would want to know if there are any communalities among the cases corresponding to such outliers, suggesting that perhaps these cases come from a different population. For an excellent, readable, and extended discussion of outliers, influential points, identification of and remedies for, see Weisberg (1980, chapters 5 and 6).

In concluding this summary, the following from Belsley et al. (1980) is appropriate:

> A word of warning is in order here, for it is obvious that there is room for misuse of the above procedures. High-influence data points could conceivably be removed solely to effect a desired change in a particular estimated coefficient, its *t* value, or some other regression output. While this danger exists, it is an unavoidable consequence of a procedure that successfully highlights such points . . . the benefits obtained from information on influential points far outweigh any potential danger. (pp. 15–16)

Example 3.8

We now consider the data in Table 3.10 with four predictors ($n = 15$). This data was run on SPSS REGRESSION. The regression with all four predictors is significant at the .05 level ($F = 3.94, p < .0358$). However, we wish to focus our attention on the outlier analysis, a summary of which is given in Table 3.11. Examination of the studentized residuals shows no significant outliers on *y*. To determine whether there are any significant outliers on the set of predictors, we examine the Mahalanobis distances. No cases are outliers on the xs since the estimated chi-square critical value (.001, 4) is 18.465. However, note that Cook's distances reveal that both Cases 10 and 13 are influential data points, since the distances are > 1. Note that Cases 10 and 13 are influential observations even though they were not considered as outliers on either y or on the set of predictors. We indicated that this is possible, and indeed it has occurred here. This is the more subtle type of influential point that Cook's distance brings to our attention.

In Table 3.12 we present the regression coefficients that resulted when Cases 10 and 13 were deleted. There is a fairly dramatic shift in the coefficients in each case. For Case 10 a dramatic shift occurs for x_2, where the coefficient changes from 1.27 (for all data points) to -1.48 (with Case 10 deleted). This is a shift of just over two standard errors (standard error for x_2 on the output is 1.34). For Case 13 the coefficients change in sign for three of the four predictors (x_2, x_3, and x_4).

▪ **Table 3.11: Selected Output for Sample Problem on Outliers and Influential Points**

Case Summaries[a]

	Studentized Residual	Mahalanobis Distance	Cook's Distance
1	−1.69609	.57237	.06934
2	−.72075	5.04841	.07751
3	.93397	2.61611	.05925
4	.08216	2.40401	.00042
5	1.19324	3.17728	.11837
6	.09408	7.22347	.00247
7	−.89911	3.51446	.07528
8	.21033	2.56197	.00294
9	1.09324	.17583	.02057
10	1.15951	10.85912	1.43639
11	.09041	1.89225	.00041
12	1.39104	2.02284	.10359
13	−1.73853	7.97770	1.05851
14	−1.26662	4.87493	.22751
15	−.04619	1.07926	.00007
Total N 15		15	15

[a] Limited to first 100 cases.

▪ **Table 3.12: Selected Output for Sample Problem on Outliers and Influential Points**

Model Summary

Model	R	R Square	Adjusted R Square	Std. Error of the Estimate
1	.782[a]	.612	.456	57.57994

[a] Predictors: (Constant), X4, X2, X3, X1

(Continued)

■ **Table 3.12: (Continued)**

ANOVA[a]

Model		Sum of Squares	df	Mean Square	F	Sig.
1	Regression	52231.502	4	13057.876	3.938	.036[b]
	Residual	33154.498	10	3315.450		
	Total	85386.000	14			

[a] Dependent Variable: Y
[b] Predictors: (Constant), X4, X2, X3, X1

Coefficients[a]

Model		Unstandardized Coefficients		Standardized Coefficients		
		B	Std. Error	Beta	t	Sig.
1	(Constant)	15.859	180.298		.088	.932
	X1	2.803	1.266	.586	2.215	.051
	X2	1.270	1.344	.210	.945	.367
	X3	2.017	3.559	.134	.567	.583
	X4	1.488	1.785	.232	.834	.424

[a] Dependent Variable: Y

Regression Coefficients With Case 10 Deleted		Regression Coefficients With Case 13 Deleted	
Variable	B	Variable	B
(Constant)	23.362	(Constant)	410.457
X1	3.529	X1	3.415
X2	−1.481	X2	−.708
X3	2.751	X3	−3.456
X4	2.078	X4	−1.339

3.15 FURTHER DISCUSSION OF THE TWO COMPUTER EXAMPLES

3.15.1 Morrison Data

Recall that for the Morrison data the stepwise procedure yielded the more parsimonious model involving three predictors: CLARITY, INTEREST, and STIMUL. If we were interested in an estimate of the predictive power in the population, then the Wherry estimate given by Equation 11 is appropriate. This is given under STEP NUMBER 3 on the SPSS output in Table 3.4, which shows that the ADJUSTED R SQUARE is

.840. Here the estimate is used in a descriptive sense: to describe the relationship in the population. However, if we are interested in the cross-validity predictive power, then the Stein estimate (Equation 12) should be used. The Stein adjusted R^2 in this case is

$$\rho_c^2 = 1 - (31/28)(30/27)(33/32)(1-.856) = .82.$$

This estimates that if we were to cross-validate the prediction equation on many other samples from the same population, then *on the average* we would account for about 82% of the variance on the dependent variable. In this instance the estimated drop-off in predictive power is very little from the maximized value of 85.6%. The reason is that the association between the dependent variable and the set of predictors is *very* strong. Thus, we can have confidence in the future predictive power of the equation.

It is also important to examine the regression diagnostics to check for any outliers or influential data points. Table 3.13 presents the appropriate statistics, as discussed in section 3.13, for identifying outliers on the dependent variable (studentized residuals), outliers on the set of predictors (the centered leverage values), and influential data points (Cook's distance).

First, we would expect only about 5% of the studentized residuals to be > |2| if the linear model is appropriate. From Table 3.13 we see that two of the studentized residuals are > |2|, and we would expect about 32(.05) = 1.6, so nothing seems to be awry here. Next, we check for outliers on the set of predictors. Since we have centered leverage values, the rough "critical value" here is $3k/n = 3(3)/32 = .281$. Because no centered leverage value in Table 3.13 exceeds this value, we have no outliers on the set of predictors. Finally, and perhaps most importantly, we check for the existence of influential data points using Cook's distance. Recall that Cook and Weisberg (1982) suggested if $D > 1$, then the point is influential. All the Cook's distance values in Table 3.13 are far less than 1, so we have no influential data points.

■ **Table 3.13: Regression Diagnostics (Studentized Residuals, Centered Leverage Values, and Cook's Distance) for Morrison MBA Data**

Case Summaries[a]

	Studentized Residual	Centered Leverage Value	Cook's Distance
1	−.38956	.10214	.00584
2	−1.96017	.05411	.08965
3	.27488	.15413	.00430
4	−.38956	.10214	.00584
5	1.60373	.13489	.12811
6	.04353	.12181	.00009
7	−.88786	.02794	.01240
8	−2.22576	.01798	.06413
9	−.81838	.13807	.03413

(Continued)

■ **Table 3.13:** **(Continued)**

Case Summaries[a]

	Studentized Residual	Centered Leverage Value	Cook's Distance
10	.59436	.07080	.01004
11	.67575	.04119	.00892
12	−.15444	.20318	.00183
13	1.31912	.05411	.04060
14	−.70076	.08630	.01635
15	−.88786	.02794	.01240
16	−1.53907	.05409	.05525
17	−.26796	.09531	.00260
18	−.56629	.03889	.00605
19	.82049	.10392	.02630
20	.06913	.09329	.00017
21	.06913	.09329	.00017
22	.28668	.09755	.00304
23	.28668	.09755	.00304
24	.82049	.10392	.02630
25	−.50388	.14084	.01319
26	.38362	.11157	.00613
27	−.56629	.03889	.00605
28	.16113	.07561	.00078
29	2.34549	.02794	.08652
30	1.18159	.17378	.09002
31	−.26103	.18595	.00473
32	1.39951	.13088	.09475
Total N	32	32	32

[a] Limited to first 100 cases.

In summary, then, the linear regression model is quite appropriate for the Morrison data. The estimated cross-validity power is excellent, and there are no outliers or influential data points.

3.15.2 National Academy of Sciences Data

Recall that both the stepwise procedure and the MAXR procedure yielded the same "best" four-predictor set: NFACUL, PCTSUPP, PCTGRT, and NARTIC. The maximized $R^2 = .8221$, indicating that 82.21% of the variance in quality can be accounted for by these four predictors in *this* sample. Now we obtain two measures of the cross-validity power of the equation. First, SAS REG indicated for this example the PREDICTED RESID SS (PRESS) = 1350.33. Furthermore, the sum of squares for QUALITY is 4564.71. From these numbers we can use Equation 14 to compute

$$R^2_{\text{Press}} = 1 - (1350.33) / 4564.71 = .7042.$$

This is a good measure of the external predictive power of the equation, where we have n validations, each based on $(n-1)$ observations.

The Stein *estimate* of how much variance on the average we would account for if the equation were applied to many other samples is

$$\rho^2_c = 1 - (45/41)(44/40)(47/46)(1-.822) = .7804.$$

Now we turn to the regression diagnostics from SAS REG, which are presented in Table 3.14. In terms of the studentized residuals for y (under the Student Residual column), two stand out (-2.756 and 2.376 for observations 25 and 44). These are for the University of Michigan and Virginia Polytech. In terms of outliers on the set of predictors, using $3p/n$ to identify large leverage values [$3(5)/46 = .326$] suggests that there is one unusual case: observation 25 (University of Michigan). Note that leverage is referred to as Hat Diag H in SAS.

■ **Table 3.14: Regression Diagnostics (Studentized Residuals, Cook's Distance, and Hat Elements) for National Academy of Science Data**

Obs	Student residual	Cook's D	Hat diag H
1	−0.708	0.007	0.0684
2	−0.0779	0.000	0.1064
3	0.403	0.003	0.0807
4	0.424	0.009	0.1951
5	0.800	0.012	0.0870
6	−1.447	0.034	0.0742
7	1.085	0.038	0.1386
8	−0.300	0.002	0.1057
9	−0.460	0.010	0.1865
10	1.694	0.048	0.0765
11	−0.694	0.004	0.0433
12	−0.870	0.016	0.0956
13	−0.732	0.007	0.0652
14	0.359	0.003	0.0885
15	−0.942	0.054	0.2328
16	1.282	0.063	0.1613
17	0.424	0.001	0.0297
18	0.227	0.001	0.1196
19	0.877	0.007	0.0464
20	0.643	0.004	0.0456
21	−0.417	0.002	0.0429

(Continued)

▪ **Table 3.14: (Continued)**

Obs	Student residual	Cook's D	Hat diag H
22	0.193	0.001	0.0696
23	0.490	0.002	0.0460
24	0.357	0.001	0.0503
25	−2.756	2.292	0.6014
26	−1.370	0.068	0.1533
27	−0.799	0.017	0.1186
28	0.165	0.000	0.0573
29	0.995	0.018	0.0844
30	−1.786	0.241	0.2737
31	−1.171	0.018	0.0613
32	−0.994	0.017	0.0796
33	1.394	0.037	0.0859
34	1.568	0.051	0.0937
35	−0.622	0.006	0.0714
36	0.282	0.002	0.1066
37	−0.831	0.009	0.0643
38	1.516	0.039	0.0789
39	1.492	0.081	0.1539
40	0.314	0.001	0.0638
41	−0.977	0.016	0.0793
42	−0.581	0.006	0.0847
43	0.0591	0.000	0.0877
44	2.376	0.164	0.1265
45	−0.508	0.003	0.0592
46	−1.505	0.085	0.1583

Using the criterion of Cook's $D > 1$, there is one influential data point, observation 25 (University of Michigan). Recall that whether a point will be influential is a *joint* function of being an outlier on y and on the set of predictors. In this case, the University of Michigan definitely doesn't fit the model and it differs dramatically from the other psychology departments on the set of predictors. A check of the DFBETAS reveals that it is very different in terms of number of faculty (DFBETA = −2.7653), and a scan of the raw data shows the number of faculty at 111, whereas the average number of faculty members for all the departments is only 29.5. The question needs to be raised as to whether the University of Michigan is "counting" faculty members in a different way from the rest of the schools. For example, are they including part-time and adjunct faculty, and if so, is the number of these quite large?

For comparison purposes, the analysis was also run with the University of Michigan deleted. Interestingly, the same four predictors emerge from the stepwise procedure, although the results are better in some ways. For example, Mallows' C_k is now 4.5248, whereas for the full data set it was 5.216. Also, the PRESS residual sum of squares is now only 899.92, whereas for the full data set it was 1350.33.

3.16 SAMPLE SIZE DETERMINATION FOR A RELIABLE PREDICTION EQUATION

In power analysis, you are interested in determining *a priori* how many subjects are needed per group to have, say, power = .80 at the .05 level. Thus, planning is done ahead of time to ensure that one has a good chance of detecting an effect of a given magnitude. Now, in multiple regression for prediction, the focus is different and the concern, or at least one very important concern, is development of a prediction equation that has generalizability. A study by Park and Dudycha (1974) provided several tables that, given certain input parameters, enable one to determine how many subjects will be needed for a reliable prediction equation. They considered from 3 to 25 random variable predictors, and found that with about 15 subjects per predictor the amount of shrinkage is small ($< .05$) with high probability (.90), if the squared population multiple correlation (ρ^2) is .50. In Table 3.15 we present selected results from the Park and Dudycha study for 3, 4, 8, and 15 predictors.

■ Table 3.15: Sample Size Such That the Difference Between the Squared Multiple Correlation and Squared Cross-Validated Correlation Is Arbitrarily Small With Given Probability

		Three predictors								Four predictors					
		γ								Γ					
ρ^2	ε	.99	.95	.90	.80	.60	.40	ρ^2	ε	.99	.95	.90	.80	.60	.40
.05	.01	858	554	421	290	158	81	.05	.01	1041	707	559	406	245	144
	.03	269	166	123	79	39	18		.03	312	201	152	103	54	27
	.01	825	535	410	285	160	88		.01	1006	691	550	405	253	155
.10	.03	271	174	133	91	50	27	.10	.03	326	220	173	125	74	43
	.05	159	100	75	51	27	14		.05	186	123	95	67	38	22
	.01	693	451	347	243	139	79		.01	853	587	470	348	221	140
	.03	232	151	117	81	48	27		.03	283	195	156	116	73	46
.25	.05	140	91	71	50	29	17	.25	.05	168	117	93	69	43	28
	.10	70	46	36	25	15	7		.10	84	58	46	34	20	14
	.20	34	22	17	12	8	6		.20	38	26	20	15	10	7
	.01	464	304	234	165	96	55		.01	573	396	317	236	152	97
	.03	157	104	80	57	34	21		.03	193	134	108	81	53	35
.50	.05	96	64	50	36	22	14	.50	.05	117	82	66	50	33	23
	.10	50	34	27	20	13	9		.10	60	43	35	27	19	13
	.20	27	19	15	12	9	7		.20	32	23	19	15	11	9
	.01	235	155	120	85	50	30		.01	290	201	162	121	78	52
	.03	85	55	43	31	20	13		.03	100	70	57	44	30	21

(*Continued*)

		Three predictors							Four predictors					
			γ							Γ				
ρ^2	ε	.99	.95	.90	.80	.60	.40	ρ^2	ε	.99	.95	.90	.80	.60	.40
.75	.05	51	35	28	21	14	10	.75	.05	62	44	37	28	20	15
	.10	28	20	16	13	9	7		.10	34	25	21	17	13	11
	.20	16	12	10	9	7	6		.20	19	15	13	11	9	7
	.01	23	17	14	11	9	7		.01	29	22	19	15	12	10
	.03	11	9	8	7	6	6		.03	14	11	10	9	8	7
.98	.05	9	7	7	6	6	5	.98	.05	10	9	8	8	7	7
	.10	7	6	6	6	5	5		.10	8	8	7	7	7	6
	.20	6	6	5	5	5	5		.20	7	7	7	6	6	6

		Eight predictors							Fifteen predictors					
			γ							Γ				
ρ^2	ε	.99	.95	.90	.80	.60	.40	ρ^2	ε	.99	.95	.90	.80	.60	.40
.05	.01	1640	1226	1031	821	585	418		.01	2523	2007	1760	1486	1161	918
	.03	447	313	251	187	116	71	.05	.03	640	474	398	316	222	156
	.01	1616	1220	1036	837	611	450		.01	2519	2029	1794	1532	1220	987
.10	.03	503	373	311	246	172	121	.10	.03	762	600	524	438	337	263
	.05	281	202	166	128	85	55		.05	403	309	265	216	159	119
	.01	1376	1047	893	727	538	404		.01	2163	1754	1557	1339	1079	884
	.03	453	344	292	237	174	129		.03	705	569	504	431	345	280
.25	.05	267	202	171	138	101	74	.25	.05	413	331	292	249	198	159
	.10	128	95	80	63	45	33		.10	191	151	132	111	87	69
	.20	52	37	30	24	17	12		.20	76	58	49	40	30	24
	.01	927	707	605	494	368	279		.01	1461	1188	1057	911	738	608
	.03	312	238	204	167	125	96		.03	489	399	355	306	249	205
.50	.05	188	144	124	103	77	59	.50	.05	295	261	214	185	151	125
	.10	96	74	64	53	40	31		.10	149	122	109	94	77	64
	.20	49	38	33	28	22	18		.20	75	62	55	48	40	34
	.01	470	360	308	253	190	150		.01	741	605	539	466	380	315
	.03	162	125	108	90	69	54		.03	255	210	188	164	135	113
.75	.05	100	78	68	57	44	35	.75	.05	158	131	118	103	86	73
	.10	54	43	38	32	26	22		.10	85	72	65	58	49	43
	.20	31	25	23	20	17	15		.20	49	42	39	35	31	28
	.01	47	38	34	29	24	21		.01	75	64	59	53	46	41
	.03	22	19	18	16	15	14		.03	36	33	31	29	27	25

	Eight predictors							Fifteen predictors					
	γ							Γ					
ρ^2 ε	.99	.95	.90	.80	.60	.40	ρ^2 ε	.99	.95	.90	.80	.60	.40
.98 .05	17	16	15	14	13	12	.98 .05	28	26	25	24	23	22
.10	14	13	12	12	11	11	.10	23	21	21	20	20	19
.20	12	11	11	11	11	10	.20	20	19	19	19	18	18

Note: Entries in the body of the table are the sample size such that $P(\rho^2 - \rho_c^2 < \varepsilon) = \gamma$, where ρ is population multiple correlation, ε is some tolerance, and γ is the probability.

To use Table 3.15 we need an estimate of ρ^2, that is, the squared *population* multiple correlation. Unless an investigator has a good estimate from a previous study that used similar subjects and predictors, we feel taking $\rho^2 = .50$ is a reasonable guess for social science research. In the physical sciences, estimates > .75 are quite reasonable. If we set $\rho^2 = .50$ and want the loss in predictive power to be less than .05 with probability = .90, then the required sample sizes are as follows:

	Number of predictors			
$\rho^2 = .50, \varepsilon = .05$	3	4	8	15
N	50	66	124	214
n/k ratio	16.7	16.5	15.5	14.3

The *n/k* ratios in all 4 cases are around 15/1.

We had indicated earlier that, as a rough guide, *generally* about 15 subjects per predictor are needed for a reliable regression equation in the social sciences, that is, an equation that will cross-validate well. Three converging lines of evidence support this conclusion:

1. The Stein formula for estimated shrinkage (see results in Table 3.8).
2. Personal experience.
3. The results just presented from the Park and Dudycha study.

However, the Park and Dudycha study (see Table 3.15) clearly shows that *the magnitude of* ρ (population multiple correlation) strongly affects how many subjects will be needed for a reliable regression equation. For example, if $\rho^2 = .75$, then for three predictors only 28 subjects are needed (assuming $\varepsilon = .05$, with probability = .90), whereas 50 subjects are needed for the same case when $\rho^2 = .50$. Also, from the Stein formula (Equation 12), you will see if you plug in .40 for R^2 that more than 15 subjects per predictor will be needed to keep the shrinkage fairly small, whereas if you insert .70 for R^2, significantly fewer than 15 will be needed.

3.17 OTHER TYPES OF REGRESSION ANALYSIS

Least squares regression is only one (although the most prevalent) way of conducting a regression analysis. The least squares estimator has two desirable statistical properties; that is, it is an unbiased, minimum variance estimator. Mathematically, unbiased means that $E(\hat{\beta}) = \beta$, the expected value of the vector of estimated regression coefficients, is the vector of population regression coefficients. To elaborate on this a bit, unbiased means that the estimate of the population coefficients will not be consistently high or low, but will "bounce around" the population values. And, if we were to average the estimates from many repeated samplings, the averages would be very close to the population values.

The minimum variance notion can be misleading. It does not mean that the variance of the coefficients for the least squares estimator is small per se, but that *among the class* of unbiased estimators β has the minimum variance. The fact that the variance of β can be quite large led Hoerl and Kenard (1970a, 1970b) to consider a biased estimator of β, which has considerably less variance, and the development of their ridge regression technique. Although ridge regression has been strongly endorsed by some, it has also been criticized (Draper & Smith, 1981; Morris, 1982; Smith & Campbell, 1980). Morris, for example, found that ridge regression never cross-validated better than other types of regression (least squares, equal weighting of predictors, reduced rank) for a set of data situations.

Another class of estimators are the James-Stein (1961) estimators. Regarding the utility of these, the following from Weisberg (1980) is relevant: "The improvement over least squares will be very small whenever the parameter β is well estimated, i.e., collinearity is not a problem and β is not too close to $\mathbf{O}$" (p. 258).

Since, as we have indicated earlier, least squares regression can be quite sensitive to outliers, some researchers prefer regression techniques that are relatively insensitive to outliers, that is, robust regression techniques. Since the early 1970s, the literature on these techniques has grown considerably (Hogg, 1979; Huber, 1977; Mosteller & Tukey, 1977). Although these techniques have merit, we believe that use of least squares, along with the appropriate identification of outliers and influential points, is a quite adequate procedure.

3.18 MULTIVARIATE REGRESSION

In multivariate regression we are interested in predicting several dependent variables from a set of predictors. The dependent variables might be differentiated aspects of some variable. For example, Finn (1974) broke grade point average (GPA) up into GPA required and GPA elective, and considered predicting these two dependent variables from high school GPA, a general knowledge test score, and attitude toward education. Or, one might measure "success as a professor" by considering various aspects of success such as: rank (assistant, associate, full), rating of institution working at, salary, rating by experts in the field, and number of articles published. These would constitute the multiple dependent variables.

3.18.1 Mathematical Model

In multiple regression (one dependent variable), the model was

$$\mathbf{y} = \mathbf{X}\boldsymbol{\beta} + \mathbf{e,}$$

where $\mathbf{y}$ was the vector of scores for the subjects on the dependent variable, $\mathbf{X}$ was the matrix with the scores for the subjects on the predictors, $\mathbf{e}$ was the vector of errors, and $\boldsymbol{\beta}$ was vector of regression coefficients.

In multivariate regression the $\mathbf{y}$, $\boldsymbol{\beta}$, and $\mathbf{e}$ vectors become matrices, which we denote by $\mathbf{Y}$, $\mathbf{B}$, and $\mathbf{E}$:

$$\mathbf{Y} = \mathbf{XB} + \mathbf{E}$$

$$
\underset{\mathbf{Y}}{\begin{bmatrix} y_{11} & y_{12} \cdots y_{1p} \\ y_{21} & y_{22} \cdots y_{2p} \\ \cdots\cdots \\ y_{n1} & y_{n2} & y_{np} \end{bmatrix}}
=
\underset{\mathbf{X}}{\begin{bmatrix} 1 & x_{12} \cdots x_{1k} \\ 1 & x_{22} \cdots y_{2k} \\ \cdots\cdots \\ 1 & x_{n2} & x_{nk} \end{bmatrix}}
\underset{\mathbf{B}}{\begin{bmatrix} b_{01} & b_{02} \cdots b_{1p} \\ b_{11} & b_{12} \cdots b_{1p} \\ \cdots\cdots \\ b_{k1} & b_{k2} & b_{kp} \end{bmatrix}}
+
\underset{\mathbf{E}}{\begin{bmatrix} e_{11} & e_{12} \cdots e_{1p} \\ e_{21} & e_{22} \cdots e_{2p} \\ \\ e_{n1} & e_{n2} \cdots e_{np} \end{bmatrix}}
$$

The first column of $\mathbf{Y}$ gives the scores for the subjects on the first dependent variable, the second column the scores on the second dependent variable, and so on. The first column of $\mathbf{B}$ gives the set of regression coefficients for the first dependent variable, the second column the regression coefficients for the second dependent variable, and so on.

Example 3.11

As an example of multivariate regression, we consider part of a data set from Timm (1975). The dependent variables are the Peabody Picture Vocabulary Test score and the Raven Progressive Matrices Test score. The predictors were scores from different types of paired associate learning tasks, called "named still (ns)," "named action (na)," and "sentence still (ss)." SPSS syntax for running the analysis using the SPSS MANOVA procedure are given in Table 3.16, along with annotation. Selected output from the multivariate regression analysis run is given in Table 3.17. The multivariate test determines whether there is a significant relationship between the two *sets* of variables, that is, the two dependent variables and the three predictors. At this point, you should focus on Wilks' Λ, the most commonly used multivariate test statistic. We have more to say about the other multivariate tests in Chapter 5. Wilks' Λ here is given by:

$$\Lambda = \frac{|SS_{\text{resid}}|}{|SS_{\text{tot}}|} = \frac{|SS_{\text{resid}}|}{|SS_{\text{reg}} + SS_{\text{resid}}|}, 0 \le \Lambda \le 1$$

Recall from the matrix algebra chapter that the determinant of a matrix served as a multivariate generalization for the variance of a set of variables. Thus, $|SS_{\text{resid}}|$ indicates the amount of variability for the set of two dependent variables that is not accounted for by

■ **Table 3.16: SPSS Syntax for Multivariate Regression Analysis of Timm Data—Two Dependent Variables and Three Predictors**

```
        TITLE 'MULT. REGRESS. - 2 DEP. VARS AND 3 PREDS'.
(1)     DATA LIST FREE/PEVOCAB RAVEN NS NA SS.
(3)     BEGIN DATA.
            48      8      6     12     16     76     13     14     30     27
            40     13     21     16     16     52      9      5     17      8
            63     15     11     26     17     82     14     21     34     25
            71     21     20     23     18     68      8     10     19     14
            74     11      7     16     13     70     15     21     26     25
            70     15     15     35     24     61     11      7     15     14
            54     12     13     27     21     55     13     12     20     17
            54     10     20     26     22     40     14      5     14      8
            66     13     21     35     27     54     10      6     14     16
            64     14     19     27     26     47     16     15     18     10
            48     16      9     14     18     52     14     20     26     26
            74     19     14     23     23     57     12      4     11      8
            57     10     16     15     17     80     11     18     28     21
            78     13     19     34     23     70     16      9     23     11
            47     14      7     12      8     94     19     28     32     32
            63     11      5     25     14     76     16     18     29     21
            59     11     10     23     24     55      8     14     19     12
            74     14     10     18     18     71     17     23     31     26
            54     14      6     15     14
        END DATA.
(2)     LIST.
(4)     MANOVA PEVOCAB RAVEN WITH NS NA SS/
        PRINT = CELLINFO(MEANS, COR).
```

(1) The variables are separated by blanks; they could also have been separated by commas.

(2) This LIST command is to get a listing of the data.

(3) The data is preceded by the BEGIN DATA command and followed by the END DATA command.

(4) The predictors follow the keyword WITH in the MANOVA command.

Table 3.17: Multivariate and Univariate Tests of Significance and Regression Coefficients for Timm Data

EFFECT.. WITHIN CELLS REGRESSION
MULTIVARIATE TESTS OF SIGNIFICANCE (S = 2, M = 0, N = 15)

TEST NAME	VALUE	APPROX. F	HYPOTH. DF	ERROR DF	SIG. OF F
PILLAIS	.57254	4.41203	6.00	66.00	.001
HOTELLINGS	1.00976	5.21709	6.00	62.00	.000
WILKS	.47428	4.82197	6.00	64.00	.000
ROYS	.47371				

This test indicates there is a significant (at $\alpha = .05$) regression of the set of 2 dependent variables on the three predictors.

UNIVARIATE F-TESTS WITH (3,33) D.F.

VARIABLE	SQ. MUL. R.	MUL. R	ADJ. R-SQ	F	SIG. OF F
PEVOCAB	.46345	.68077	.41467	(1) 9.50121	.000
RAVEN	.19429	.44078	.12104	2.65250	.065

These results show there is a significant regression for PEVOCAB, but RAVEN is not significantly related to the three predictors at .05, since .065 > .05.

DEPENDENT VARIABLE.. PEVOCAB

COVARIATE	B	BETA	STD. ERR.	T-VALUE	SIG. OF T.
NS	−.2056372599	−.1043054487	.40797	−.50405	.618
NA (2)	1.01272293634	.5856100072	.37685	2.68737	.011
SS	.3977340740	.2022598804	.47010	.84606	.404

DEPENDENT VARIABLE.. RAVEN

COVARIATE	B	BETA	STD. ERR.	T-VALUE	SIG. OF T.
NS	.2026184278	.4159658338	.12352	1.64038	.110
NA	.0302663367	.0708355423	.11410	.26527	.792
SS	−.0174928333	−.0360039904	.14233	−.12290	.903

(1) Using Equation 4, $F = \dfrac{R^2/k}{(1-R^2)/(n-k-1)} = \dfrac{.46345/3}{.53655/(37-3-1)} = 9.501$.

(2) These are the raw regression coefficients for predicting PEVOCAB from the three predictors, excluding the regression constant.

regression, and $|SS_{tot}|$ gives the total variability for the two dependent variables around their means. The sampling distribution of Wilks' Λ is quite complicated; however, there is an excellent F approximation (due to Rao), which is what appears in Table 3.17. Note that the multivariate $F = 4.82, p < .001$, which indicates a significant relationship between the dependent variables and the three predictors beyond the .01 level.

The univariate Fs are the tests for the significance of the regression of each dependent variable separately. They indicate that PEVOCAB is significantly related to the set of predictors at the .05 level ($F = 9.501$, $p < .000$), while RAVEN is not significantly related at the .05 level ($F = 2.652$, $p = .065$). Thus, the overall multivariate significance is primarily attributable to PEVOCAB's relationship with the three predictors.

It is important for you to realize that, although the multivariate tests take into account the correlations among the dependent variables, the regression equations that appear at the bottom of Table 3.17 are those that would be obtained if each dependent variable were regressed *separately* on the set of predictors. That is, in deriving the regression equations, the correlations among the dependent variables are ignored, or not taken into account. If you wished to take such correlations into account, multivariate multi-level modeling, described in Chapter 14, can be used. Note that taking these correlations into account is generally desired and may lead to different results than obtained by using univariate regression analysis.

We indicated earlier in this chapter that an R^2 value around .50 occurs quite often with educational and psychological data, and this is precisely what has occurred here with the PEVOCAB variable ($R^2 = .463$). Also, we can be fairly confident that the prediction equation for PEVOCAB will cross-validate, since the n/k ratio is 12.33, which is close to the ratio we indicated is necessary.

3.19 SUMMARY

1. A particularly good situation for multiple regression is where each of the predictors is correlated with y and the predictors have low intercorrelations, for then each of the predictors is accounting for a relatively distinct part of the variance on y.
2. Moderate to high correlation among the predictors (multicollinearity) creates three problems: (1) it severely limits the size of R, (2) it makes determining the importance of given predictor difficult, and (3) it increases the variance of regression coefficients, making for an unstable prediction equation. There are at least three ways of combating this problem. One way is to combine into a single measure a set of predictors that are highly correlated. A second way is to consider the use of principal components or factor analysis to reduce the number of predictors. Because such components are uncorrelated, we have eliminated multicollinearity. A third way is through the use of ridge regression. This technique is beyond the scope of this book.
3. Preselecting a small set of predictors by examining a correlation matrix from a large initial set, or by using one of the stepwise procedures (forward, stepwise, backward) to select a small set, is likely to produce an equation that is sample specific. If one insists on doing this, and we do not recommend it, then the onus is on the investigator to demonstrate that the equation has adequate predictive power beyond the derivation sample.
4. Mallows' C_p was presented as a measure that minimizes the effect of under fitting (important predictors left out of the model) and over fitting (having predictors in

the model that make essentially no contribution or are marginal). This will be the case if one chooses models for which $C_p \approx p$.

5. With many data sets, more than one model will provide a good fit to the data. Thus, one deals with selecting a model from a *pool* of candidate models.

6. There are various graphical plots for assessing how well the model fits the assumptions underlying linear regression. One of the most useful graphs plots the studentized residuals (*y*-axis) versus the predicted values (*x*-axis). If the assumptions are tenable, then you should observe that the residuals appear to be approximately normally distributed around their predicted values and have similar variance across the range of the predicted values. Any *systematic clustering* of the residuals indicates a model violation(s).

7. It is crucial to validate the model(s) by either randomly splitting the sample and cross-validating, or using the PRESS statistic, or by obtaining the Stein estimate of the *average* predictive power of the equation on other samples from the same population. Studies in the literature that have not cross-validated should be checked with the Stein estimate to assess the generalizability of the prediction equation(s) presented.

8. Results from the Park and Dudycha study indicate that the magnitude of the *population* multiple correlation strongly affects how many subjects will be needed for a reliable prediction equation. If your estimate of the squared population value is .50, then about 15 subjects per predictor are needed. On the other hand, if your estimate of the squared population value is substantially *larger* than .50, then far fewer than 15 subjects per predictor will be needed.

9. Influential data points, that is, points that strongly affect the prediction equation, can be identified by finding those cases having Cook's distances > 1. These points need to be examined very carefully. If such a point is due to a recording error, then one would simply correct it and redo the analysis. Or if it is found that the influential point is due to an instrumentation error or that the process that generated the data for that subject was different, then it is legitimate to drop the case from the analysis. If, however, none of these appears to be the case, then one strategy is to perhaps report the results of several analyses: one analysis with all the data and an additional analysis (or analyses) with the influential point(s) deleted.

3.20 EXERCISES

1. Consider this set of data:

X	Y
2	3
3	6
4	8
6	4
7	10
8	14

X	Y
9	8
10	12
11	14
12	12
13	16

(a) Run a regression analysis with these data in SPSS and request a plot of the studentized residuals (SRESID) by the standardized predicted values (ZPRED).

(b) Do you see any pattern in the plot of the residuals? What does this suggest? Does your inspection of the plot suggest that there are any outliers on Y?

(c) Interpret the slope.

(d) Interpret the adjusted R square.

2. Consider the following small set of data:

PREDX	DEP
0	1
1	4
2	6
3	8
4	9
5	10
6	10
7	8
8	7
9	6
10	5

(a) Run a regression analysis with these data in SPSS and obtain a plot of the residuals (SRESID by ZPRED).

(b) Do you see any pattern in the plot of the residuals? What does this suggest?

(c) Inspect a scatter plot of DEP by PREDX. What type of relationship exists between the two variables?

3. Consider the following correlation matrix:

	y	x_1	x_2
y	1.00	.60	.50
x_1	.60	1.00	.80
x_2	.50	.80	1.00

(a) How much variance on y will x_1 account for if entered first?

(b) How much variance on y will x_1 account for if entered second?

(c) What, if anything, do these results have to do with the multicollinearity problem?

4. A medical school admissions official has two proven predictors (x_1 and x_2) of success in medical school. There are two other predictors under consideration (x_3 and x_4), from which just one will be selected that will add the most (beyond what x_1 and x_2 already predict) to predicting success. Here are the correlations among the predictors and the outcome gathered on a sample of 100 medical students:

	x_1	x_2	x_3	x_4
y	.60	.55	.60	.46
x_1		.70	.60	.20
x_2			.80	.30
x_3				.60

(a) What procedure would be used to determine which predictor has the greater incremental validity? Do *not* go into any numerical details, just indicate the general procedure. Also, what is your educated guess as to which predictor (x_3 or x_4) will probably have the greater incremental validity?

(b) Suppose the investigator found the third predictor, runs the regression, and finds $R = .76$. Apply the Stein formula, Equation 12 (using $k = 3$), and tell exactly what the resulting number represents.

5. This exercise has you calculate an F statistic to test the proportion of variance explained by a set of predictors and also an F statistic to test the additional proportion of variance explained by adding a set of predictors to a model that already contains other predictors. Suppose we were interested in predicting the IQs of 3-year-old children from four measures of socioeconomic status (SES) and six environmental process variables (as assessed by a HOME inventory instrument) and had a total sample size of 105. Further, suppose we were interested in determining whether the prediction varied depending on sex and on race and that the following analyses were done:

To examine the relations among SES, environmental process, and IQ, two regression analyses were done for each of five samples: total group, males, females, whites, and blacks. First, four SES variables were used in the regression analysis. Then, the six environmental process variables (the six HOME inventory subscales) were added to the regression equation. For each analysis, IQ was used as the criterion variable.

The following table reports 10 multiple correlations:

Multiple Correlations Between Measures of Environmental Quality and IQ

Measure	Males $(n = 57)$	Females $(n = 48)$	Whites $(n = 37)$	Blacks $(n = 68)$	Total $(N = 105)$
SES (A)	.555	.636	.582	.346	.556
SES and HOME (A and B)	.682	.825	.683	.614	.765

(a) Suppose that all of the multiple correlations are statistically significant (.05 level) except for .346 obtained for blacks with the SES variables. Show that .346 is not significant at the .05 level. Note that F critical with (.05; 4; 63) = 2.52.

(b) For males, does the addition of the HOME inventory variables to the prediction equation significantly increase predictive power beyond that of the SES variables? Note that F critical with (.05; 6; 46) = 2.30.

Note that the following F statistic is appropriate for determining whether a set of variables B significantly adds to the prediction beyond what set A contributes:

$$F = \frac{(R^2_{y.AB} - R^2_{y.A}) / k_B}{(1 - R^2_{y.AB}) / (n - k_A - k_B - 1)}, \text{ with } k_B \text{ and } (n - k_A - k_B - 1) df,$$

where k_A and k_B represent the number of predictors in sets A and B, respectively.

6. Plante and Goldfarb (1984) predicted social adjustment from Cattell's 16 personality factors. There were 114 subjects, consisting of students and employees from two large manufacturing companies. They stated in their RESULTS section:

Stepwise multiple regression was performed. . . . The index of social adjustment significantly correlated with 6 of the primary factors of the 16 PF. . . . Multiple regression analysis resulted in a multiple correlation of $R = .41$ accounting for 17% of the variance with these 6 factors. The multiple R obtained while utilizing all 16 factors was $R = .57$, thus accounting for 33% of the variance. (p. 1217)

(a) Would you have much faith in the reliability of either of these regression equations?

(b) Apply the Stein formula (Equation 12) for random predictors to the 16-variable equation to estimate how much variance on the average we could expect to account for if the equation were cross-validated on many other random samples.

7. Consider the following data for 15 subjects with two predictors. The dependent variable, MARK, is the total score for a subject on an examination. The first predictor, COMP, is the score for the subject on a so-called compulsory paper. The other predictor, CERTIF, is the score for the subject on a previous exam.

Candidate	MARK	COMP	CERTIF	Candidate	MARK	COMP	CERTIF
1	476	111	68	9	645	117	59
2	457	92	46	10	556	94	97
3	540	90	50	11	634	130	57
4	551	107	59	12	637	118	51
5	575	98	50	13	390	91	44
6	698	150	66	14	562	118	61
7	545	118	54	15	560	109	66
8	574	110	51				

(a) Run a stepwise regression on this data.

(b) Does CERTIF add anything to predicting MARK, above and beyond that of COMP?

(c) Write out the prediction equation.

8. A statistician wishes to know the sample size needed in a multiple regression study. She has four predictors and can tolerate at most a .10 drop-off in predictive power. But she wants this to be the case with .95 probability. From previous related research the estimated squared population multiple correlation is .62. How many subjects are needed?

9. Recall in the chapter that we mentioned a study where each of 22 college freshmen wrote four essays and then a stepwise regression analysis was applied to these data to predict quality of essay response. It has already been mentioned that the n of 88 used in the study is incorrect, since there are only 22 independent responses. Now let us concentrate on a different aspect of the study. Suppose there were 17 predictors and that found 5 of them were "significant," accounting for 42.3% of the variance in quality. Using a median value between 5 and 17 and the proper sample size of 22, apply the Stein formula to estimate the cross-validity predictive power of the equation. What do you conclude?

10. A regression analysis was run on the Sesame Street ($n = 240$) data set, predicting postbody from the following five pretest measures: prebody, prelet, preform, prenumb, and prerelat. The SPSS syntax for conducting a stepwise regression is given next. Note that this analysis obtains (in addition to other output): (1) variance inflation factors, (2) a list of all cases having a studentized residual greater than 2 in magnitude, (3) the smallest and largest values for the studentized residuals, Cook's distance and centered leverage, (4) a histogram of the standardized residuals, and (5) a plot of the studentized residuals versus the standardized predicted y values.

```
regression descriptives=default/
variables = prebody to prerelat postbody/
statistics = defaults tol/
dependent = postbody/
```

```
method = stepwise/
residuals = histogram(zresid) outliers(sresid, lever, cook)/
casewise plot(zresid) outliers(2)/
scatterplot (*sresid, *zpred).
```

Selected results from SPSS appear in Table 3.18. Answer the following questions.

■ **Table 3.18: SPSS Results for Exercise 10**

Regression

	Descriptive Statistics		
	Mean	Std. Deviation	*N*
PREBODY	21.40	6.391	240
PRELET	15.94	8.536	240
PREFORM	9.92	3.737	240
PRENUMG	20.90	10.685	240
PRERELAT	9.94	3.074	240
POSTBODY	25.26	5.412	240

	Correlations					
	PREBODY	PRELET	PREFORM	PRENUMG	PRERELAT	POSTBODY
PREBODY	1.000	.453	.680	.698	.623	.650
PRELET	.453	1.000	.506	.717	.471	.371
PREFORM	.680	.506	1.000	.673	.596	.551
PRENUMG	.698	.717	.673	1.000	.718	.527
PRERELAT	.623	.471	.596	.718	1.000	.449
POSTBODY	.650	.371	.551	.527	.449	1.000

	Variables Entered/Removed[a]		
Model	Variables Entered	Variables Removed	Method
1	PREBODY	.	Stepwise (Criteria: Probability-of-F-to-enter <= .050, Probability-of-F-to-remove >= .100).
2	PREFORM	.	Stepwise (Criteria: Probability-of-F-to-enter <= .050, Probability-of-F-to-remove >= .100).

[a] Dependent Variable: POSTBODY

Model Summary[c]

Model	R	R Square	Adjusted R Square	Std. Error of the Estimate
1	.650[a]	.423	.421	4.119
2	.667[b]	.445	.440	4.049

[a] Predictors: (Constant), PREBODY
[b] Predictors: (Constant), PREBODY, PREFORM
[c] Dependent Variable: POSTBODY

ANOVA[a]

Model		Sum of Squares	df	Mean Square	F	Sig.
1	Regression	2961.602	1	2961.602	174.520	.000[b]
	Residual	4038.860	238	16.970		
	Total	7000.462	239			
2	Regression	3114.883	2	1557.441	94.996	.000[c]
	Residual	3885.580	237	16.395		
	Total	7000.462	239			

[a] Dependent Variable: POSTBODY
[b] Predictors: (Constant), PREBODY
[c] Predictors: (Constant), PREBODY, PREFORM

Coefficients[a]

Model		Unstandardized Coefficients B	Unstandardized Coefficients Std. Error	Standardized Coefficients Beta	t	Sig.	Collinearity Statistics Tolerance	Collinearity Statistics VIF
1	(Constant)	13.475	.931		14.473	.000		
	PREBODY	.551	.042	.650	13.211	.000	1.000	1.000
2	(Constant)	13.062	.925		14.120	.000		
	PREBODY	.435	.056	.513	7.777	.000	.538	1.860
	PREFORM	.292	.096	.202	3.058	.002	.538	1.860

[a] Dependent Variable: POSTBODY

Excluded Variables[a]

Model		Beta In	T	Sig.	Partial Correlation	Collinearity Statistics Tolerance	Collinearity Statistics VIF	Collinearity Statistics Minimum Tolerance
1	PRELET	.096[b]	1.742	.083	.112	.795	1.258	.795
	PREFORM	.202[b]	3.058	.002	.195	.538	1.860	.538
	PRENUMG	.143[b]	2.091	.038	.135	.513	1.950	.513
	PRERELAT	.072[b]	1.152	.250	.075	.612	1.634	.612

(*Continued*)

Excluded Variables[a]

Model		Beta In	T	Sig.	Partial Correlation	Collinearity Statistics		
						Tolerance	VIF	Minimum Tolerance
2	PRELET	.050[c]	.881	.379	.057	.722	1.385	.489
	PRENUMG	.075[c]	1.031	.304	.067	.439	2.277	.432
	PRERELAT	.017[c]	.264	.792	.017	.557	1.796	.464

[a] Dependent Variable: POSTBODY
[b] Predictors in the Model: (Constant), PREBODY
[c] Predictors in the Model: (Constant), PREBODY, PREFORM

Casewise Diagnostics[a]

Case Number	Stud. Residual	POSTBODY	Predicted Value	Residual
36	2.120	29	20.47	8.534
38	−2.115	12	20.47	−8.473
39	−2.653	21	31.65	−10.646
40	−2.322	21	30.33	−9.335
125	−2.912	11	22.63	−11.631
135	2.210	32	23.08	8.919
139	−3.068	11	23.37	−12.373
147	2.506	32	21.91	10.088
155	−2.767	17	28.16	−11.162
168	−2.106	13	21.48	−8.477
210	−2.354	13	22.50	−9.497
219	3.176	31	18.29	12.707

[a] Dependent Variable: POSTBODY

Outlier Statistics[a] (10 Cases Shown)

		Case Number	Statistic	Sig. F
Stud. Residual	1	219	3.176	
	2	139	−3.068	
	3	125	−2.912	
	4	155	−2.767	
	5	39	−2.653	
	6	147	2.506	
	7	210	−2.354	
	8	40	−2.322	
	9	135	2.210	
	10	36	2.120	

Outlier Statistics[a] (10 Cases Shown)				
		Case Number	Statistic	Sig. F
Cook's Distance	1	219	.081	.970
	2	125	.078	.972
	3	39	.042	.988
	4	38	.032	.992
	5	40	.025	.995
	6	139	.025	.995
	7	147	.025	.995
	8	177	.023	.995
	9	140	.022	.996
	10	13	.020	.996
Centered Leverage Value	1	140	.047	
	2	32	.036	
	3	23	.030	
	4	114	.028	
	5	167	.026	
	6	52	.026	
	7	233	.025	
	8	8	.025	
	9	236	.023	
	10	161	.023	

[a] Dependent Variable: POSTBODY

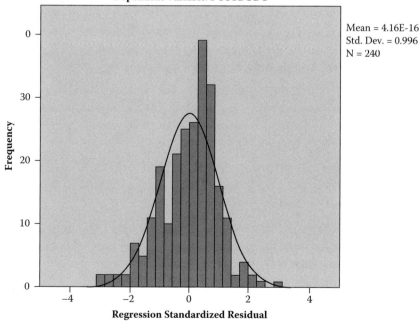

Histogram
Dependent Variable: POSTBODY

Mean = 4.16E-16
Std. Dev. = 0.996
N = 240

Frequency

Regression Standardized Residual

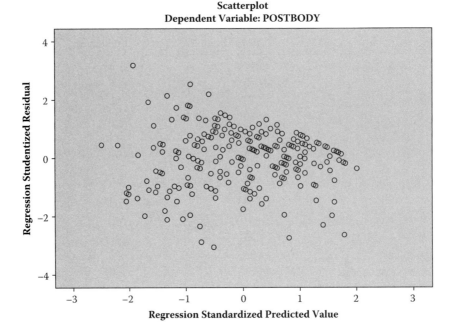

Scatterplot
Dependent Variable: POSTBODY

(a) Why did PREBODY enter the prediction equation first?

(b) Why did PREFORM enter the prediction equation second?

(c) Write the prediction equation, rounding off to three decimals.

(d) Is multicollinearity present? Explain.

(e) Compute the Stein estimate and indicate in words exactly what it represents.

(f) Show by using the appropriate correlations from the correlation matrix how the R-square change of .0219 can be calculated.

(g) Refer to the studentized residuals. Is the number of these greater than 121 about what you would expect if the model is appropriate? Why, or why not?

(h) Are there any outliers on the set of predictors?

(i) Are there any influential data points? Explain.

(j) From examination of the residual plot, does it appear there may be some model violation(s)? Why or why not?

(k) From the histogram of residuals, does it appear that the normality assumption is reasonable?

(l) Interpret the regression coefficient for PREFORM.

11. Consider the following data:

X_1	X_2
14	21
17	23
36	10
32	18
25	12

Find the Mahalanobis distance for case 4.

12. Using SPSS, run backward selection on the National Academy of Sciences data. What model is selected?

13. From one of the better journals in your content area within the last 5 years find an article that used multiple regression. Answer the following questions:

(a) Did the authors discuss checking the assumptions for regression?

(b) Did the authors report an adjusted squared multiple correlation?

(c) Did the authors discuss checking for outliers and/or influential observations?

(d) Did the authors say anything about validating their equation?

REFERENCES

Anscombe, V. (1973). Graphs in statistical analysis. *American Statistician, 27,* 13–21.

Belsley, D.A., Kuh, E., & Welsch, R. (1980). *Regression diagnostics: Identifying influential data and sources of collinearity.* NewYork, NY: Wiley.

Cohen, J. (1990). Things I have learned (so far). *American Psychologist, 45,* 1304–1312.

Cohen, J., & Cohen, P. (1983). *Applied multiple regression/correlation analysis for the behavioral sciences.* Hillsdale, NJ: Lawrence Erlbaum.

Cohen, J., Cohen, P., West, S.G., & Aiken, L.S. (2003). *Applied multiple regression/correlation for the behavioral sciences* (3rd ed.). Mahwah, NJ: Lawrence Erlbaum Associates.

Cook, R.D. (1977). Detection of influential observations in linear regression. *Technometrics, 19,* 15–18.

Cook, R.D., & Weisberg, S. (1982). *Residuals and influence in regression.* New York, NY: Chapman & Hall.

Crowder, R. (1975). *An investigation of the relationship between social I.Q. and vocational evaluation ratings with an adult trainable mental retardate work activity center population.* Unpublished doctoral dissertation, University of Cincinnati, OH.

Crystal, G. (1988). The wacky, wacky world of CEO pay. *Fortune, 117,* 68–78.

Dizney, H., & Gromen, L. (1967). Predictive validity and differential achievement on three MLA Comparative Foreign Language tests. *Educational and Psychological Measurement, 27,* 1127–1130.

Draper, N.R., & Smith, H. (1981). *Applied regression analysis.* New York, NY: Wiley.

Feshbach, S., Adelman, H., & Fuller, W. (1977). Prediction of reading and related academic problems. *Journal of Educational Psychology, 69,* 299–308.

Finn, J. (1974). *A general model for multivariate analysis.* New York, NY: Holt, Rinehart & Winston.

Glasnapp, D., & Poggio, J. (1985). *Essentials of statistical analysis for the behavioral sciences.* Columbus, OH: Charles Merrill.

Guttman, L. (1941). Mathematical and tabulation techniques. Supplementary study B. In P. Horst (Ed.), *Prediction of personnel adjustment* (pp. 251–364). New York, NY: Social Science Research Council.

Herzberg, P.A. (1969). *The parameters of cross-validation* (Psychometric Monograph No. 16). Richmond, VA: Psychometric Society. Retrieved from http://www.psychometrika.org/journal/online/MN16.pdf

Hoaglin, D., & Welsch, R. (1978). The hat matrix in regression and ANOVA. *American Statistician, 32,* 17–22.

Hoerl, A.E., & Kennard, W. (1970a). Ridge regression: Biased estimation for non-orthogonal problems. *Technometrics, 12,* 55–67.

Hoerl, A.E., & Kennard, W. (1970b). Ridge regression: Applications to non-orthogonal problems. *Technometrics, 12,* 69–82.

Hogg, R.V. (1979). Statistical robustness. One view of its use in application today. *American Statistician, 33,* 108–115.

Huber, P. (1977). *Robust statistical procedures (No. 27, Regional conference series in applied mathematics).* Philadelphia, PA: SIAM.

Huberty, C.J. (1989). Problems with stepwise methods—better alternatives. In B. Thompson (Ed.), *Advances in social science methodology* (Vol. 1, pp. 43–70). Stamford, CT: JAI.

Johnson, R.A., & Wichern, D.W. (2007). *Applied multivariate statistical analysis* (6th ed.). Upper Saddle River, NJ: Pearson Prentice Hall.

Jones, L.V., Lindzey, G., & Coggeshall, P.E. (Eds.). (1982). *An assessment of research-doctorate programs in the United States: Social & behavioral sciences.* Washington, DC: National Academies Press.

Krasker, W.S., & Welsch, R.E. (1979). *Efficient bounded-influence regression estimation using alternative definitions of sensitivity.* Technical Report #3, Center for Computational Research in Economics and Management Science, Massachusetts Institute of Technology, Cambridge, MA.

Lord, R., & Novick, M. (1968). *Statistical theories of mental test scores.* Reading, MA: Addison-Wesley.

Mahalanobis, P.C. (1936). On the generalized distance in statistics. *Proceedings of the National Institute of Science of India, 12,* 49–55.

Mallows, C.L. (1973). Some comments on Cp. *Technometrics, 15,* 661–676.

Moore, D., & McCabe, G. (1989). *Introduction to the practice of statistics.* New York, NY: Freeman.

Morris, J.D. (1982). Ridge regression and some alternative weighting techniques: A comment on Darlington. *Psychological Bulletin, 91,* 203–210.

Morrison, D. F. (1983). *Applied linear statistical methods.* Englewood Cliffs, NJ: Prentice Hall.

Mosteller, F., & Tukey, J.W. (1977). *Data analysis and regression.* Reading, MA: Addison-Wesley.

Myers, R. (1990). *Classical and modern regression with applications* (2nd ed.). Boston, MA: Duxbury.

Nunnally, J. (1978). *Psychometric theory.* New York, NY: McGraw-Hill.

Park, C., & Dudycha, A. (1974). A cross validation approach to sample size determination for regression models. *Journal of the American Statistical Association, 69,* 214–218.

Pedhazur, E. (1982). *Multiple regression in behavioral research* (2nd ed.). New York, NY: Holt, Rinehart & Winston.

Plante, T., & Goldfarb, L. (1984). Concurrent validity for an activity vector analysis index of social adjustment. *Journal of Clinical Psychology, 40,* 1215–1218.

Ramsey, F., & Schafer, D. (1997). *The statistical sleuth.* Belmont, CA: Duxbury.

SAS Institute. (1990) *SAS/STAT User's Guide* (Vol. 2). Cary, NC: Author.

Singer, J., & Willett, J. (1988, April). *Opening up the black box of recipe statistics: Putting the data back into data analysis.* Paper presented at the annual meeting of the American Educational Research Association, New Orleans, LA.

Smith, G., & Campbell, F. (1980). A critique of some ridge regression methods. *Journal of the American Statistical Association, 75,* 74–81.

Stein, C. (1960). Multiple regression. In I. Olkin (Ed.), *Contributions to probability and statistics, essays in honor of Harold Hotelling* (pp. 424–443). Stanford, CA: Stanford University Press.

Timm, N. H. (1975). *Multivariate analysis with applications in education and psychology.* Monterey, CA: Brooks-Cole.

Weisberg, S. (1980). *Applied linear regression.* New York, NY: Wiley.

Weisberg, S. (1985). *Applied linear regression* (2nd ed.). New York, NY: Wiley.

Wherry, R. J. (1931). A new formula for predicting the shrinkage of the coefficient of multiple correlation. *Annals of Mathematical Statistics, 2,* 440–457.

Wilkinson, L. (1979). Tests of significance in stepwise regression. *Psychological Bulletin, 86,* 168–174.

Chapter 4

TWO-GROUP MULTIVARIATE ANALYSIS OF VARIANCE

4.1 INTRODUCTION

In this chapter we consider the statistical analysis of two groups of participants on several dependent variables simultaneously; focusing on cases where the variables are correlated and share a common conceptual meaning. That is, the dependent variables considered together make sense as a group. For example, they may be different dimensions of self-concept (physical, social, emotional, academic), teacher effectiveness, speaker credibility, or reading (blending, syllabication, comprehension, etc.). We consider the multivariate tests along with their univariate counterparts and show that the multivariate two-group test (Hotelling's T^2) is a natural generalization of the univariate t test. We initially present the traditional analysis of variance approach for the two-group multivariate problem, and then later briefly present and compare a regression analysis of the same data. In the next chapter, studies with more than two groups are considered, where multivariate tests are employed that are generalizations of Fisher's F found in a univariate one-way ANOVA. The last part of this chapter (sections 4.9–4.12) presents a fairly extensive discussion of power, including introduction of a multivariate effect size measure and the use of SPSS MANOVA for estimating power.

There are two reasons one should be interested in using more than one dependent variable when comparing two treatments:

1. Any treatment "worth its salt" will affect participants in more than one way—hence the need for several criterion measures.
2. Through the use of several criterion measures we can obtain a more complete and detailed description of the phenomenon under investigation, whether it is reading achievement, math achievement, self-concept, physiological stress, or teacher effectiveness or counselor effectiveness.

If we were comparing two methods of teaching second-grade reading, we would obtain a more detailed and informative breakdown of the differential effects of the methods if reading achievement were split into its subcomponents: syllabication, blending, sound discrimination, vocabulary, comprehension, and reading rate. Comparing the two methods only on total reading achievement might yield no significant difference; however, the methods may be making a difference. The differences may be confined to only the more basic elements of blending and syllabication. Similarly, if two methods of teaching sixth-grade mathematics were being compared, it would be more informative to compare them on various levels of mathematics achievement (computations, concepts, and applications).

4.2 FOUR STATISTICAL REASONS FOR PREFERRING A MULTIVARIATE ANALYSIS

1. The use of fragmented univariate tests leads to a greatly inflated overall type I error rate, that is, the probability of at least one false rejection. Consider a two-group problem with 10 dependent variables. What is the probability of one or more spurious results if we do 10 t tests, each at the .05 level of significance? If we assume the tests are independent as an approximation (because the tests are not independent), then the probability of *no* type I errors is:

    $$\underbrace{(.95)(.95)\cdots(.95)}_{10 \text{ times}} \approx .60$$

    because the probability of not making a type I error for each test is .95, and with the independence assumption we can multiply probabilities. Therefore, the probability of at least one false rejection is $1 - .60 = .40$, which is unacceptably high. Thus, with the univariate approach, not only does overall α become too high, but we can't even accurately estimate it.

2. The univariate tests ignore important information, namely, the correlations among the variables. The multivariate test incorporates the correlations (via the covariance matrix) right into the test statistic, as is shown in the next section.

3. Although the groups may not be significantly different on any of the variables individually, *jointly* the set of variables may reliably differentiate the groups. That is, small differences on several of the variables may combine to produce a reliable overall difference. Thus, the multivariate test will be more powerful in this case.

4. It is sometimes argued that the groups should be compared on total test score first to see if there is a difference. If so, then compare the groups further on subtest scores to locate the sources responsible for the global difference. On the other hand, if there is no total test score difference, then stop. This procedure could definitely be misleading. Suppose, for example, that the total test scores were not significantly different, but that on subtest 1 group 1 was quite superior, on subtest 2 group 1 was somewhat superior, on subtest 3 there was no difference, and on subtest 4 group 2 was quite superior. Then it would be clear why the univariate

analysis of total test score found nothing—because of a canceling-out effect. But the two groups do differ substantially on two of the four subsets, and to some extent on a third. A multivariate analysis of the subtests reflects these differences and would show a significant difference.

Many investigators, especially when they first hear about multivariate analysis of variance (MANOVA), will lump all the dependent variables in a single analysis. This is not necessarily a good idea. If several of the variables have been included without any strong rationale (empirical or theoretical), then small or negligible differences on these variables may obscure a real difference(s) on some of the other variables. That is, the multivariate test statistic detects mainly error in the system (i.e., in the set of variables), and therefore declares no reliable overall difference. In a situation such as this, what is called for are two separate multivariate analyses, one for the variables for which there is solid support, and a separate one for the variables that are being tested on a heuristic basis.

4.3 THE MULTIVARIATE TEST STATISTIC AS A GENERALIZATION OF THE UNIVARIATE *T* TEST

For the univariate t test the null hypothesis is:

$$H_0 : \mu_1 = \mu_2 \text{ (population means are equal)}$$

In the multivariate case the null hypothesis is:

$$H_0 : \begin{pmatrix} \mu_{11} \\ \mu_{21} \\ \cdot\cdot \\ \mu_{p1} \end{pmatrix} = \begin{pmatrix} \mu_{12} \\ \mu_{22} \\ \cdot\cdot \\ \mu_{p2} \end{pmatrix} \text{ (population mean vectors are equal)}$$

Saying that the vectors are equal implies that the population means for the two groups on variable 1 are equal (i.e., $\mu_{11} = \mu_{12}$), population group means on variable 2 are equal ($\mu_{21} = \mu_{22}$), and so on for each of the p dependent variables. The first part of the subscript refers to the variable and the second part to the group. Thus, μ_{21} refers to the population mean for variable 2 in group 1.

Now, for the univariate t test, you may recall that there are three assumptions involved: (1) independence of the observations, (2) normality, and (3) equality of the population variances (homogeneity of variance). In testing the multivariate null hypothesis the corresponding assumptions are: (1) independence of the observations, (2) multivariate normality on the dependent variables in each population, and (3) equality of the covariance matrices. The latter two multivariate assumptions are much more stringent than the corresponding univariate assumptions. For example, saying that two covariance matrices are equal for four variables implies that the variances are equal for each of the variables *and* that the six covariances for each of the groups are equal. Consequences of violating the multivariate assumptions are discussed in detail in Chapter 6.

We now show how the multivariate test statistic arises naturally from the univariate t by replacing scalars (numbers) by vectors and matrices. The univariate t is given by:

$$t = \frac{\bar{y}_1 - \bar{y}_2}{\sqrt{\dfrac{(n_1 - 1)s_1^2 + (n_2 - 1)s_2^2}{n_1 + n_2 - 2}\left(\dfrac{1}{n_1} + \dfrac{1}{n_2}\right)}}, \tag{1}$$

where s_1^2 and s_2^2 are the sample variances for groups 1 and 2, respectively. The quantity under the radical, excluding the sum of the reciprocals, is the pooled estimate of the assumed common within population variance, call it s^2. Now, replacing that quantity by s^2 and squaring both sides, we obtain:

$$t^2 = \frac{(\bar{y}_1 - \bar{y}_2)^2}{s^2\left(\dfrac{1}{n_1} + \dfrac{1}{n_2}\right)}$$

$$= (\bar{y}_1 - \bar{y}_2)\left[s^2\left(\dfrac{1}{n_1} + \dfrac{1}{n_2}\right)\right]^{-1}(\bar{y}_1 - \bar{y}_2)$$

$$= (\bar{y}_1 - \bar{y}_2)\left[s^2\left(\dfrac{n_1 + n_2}{n_1 n_2}\right)\right]^{-1}(\bar{y}_1 - \bar{y}_2)$$

$$t^2 = \frac{n_1 n_2}{n_1 + n_2}(\bar{y}_1 - \bar{y}_2)(s^2)^{-1}(\bar{y}_1 - \bar{y}_2)$$

Hotelling's T^2 is obtained by replacing the means on each variable by the vectors of means in each group, and by replacing the univariate measure of within variability s^2 by its multivariate generalization $\mathbf{S}$ (the estimate of the assumed common population covariance matrix). Thus we obtain:

$$T^2 = \frac{n_1 n_2}{n_1 + n_2} \cdot (\bar{\mathbf{y}}_1 - \bar{\mathbf{y}}_2)' \mathbf{S}^{-1}(\bar{\mathbf{y}}_1 - \bar{\mathbf{y}}_2) \tag{2}$$

Recall that the matrix analogue of division is inversion; thus $(s^2)^{-1}$ is replaced by the inverse of $\mathbf{S}$.

Hotelling (1931) showed that the following transformation of T^2 yields an exact F distribution:

$$F = \frac{n_1 + n_2 - p - 1}{(n_1 + n_2 - 2)p} \cdot T^2 \tag{3}$$

with p and $(N - p - 1)$ degrees of freedom, where p is the number of dependent variables and $N = n_1 + n_2$, that is, the total number of subjects.

We can rewrite T^2 as:

$$T^2 = k\mathbf{d}'\mathbf{S}^{-1}\mathbf{d},$$

where k is a constant involving the group sizes, $\mathbf{d}$ is the vector of mean differences, and $\mathbf{S}$ is the covariance matrix. Thus, what we have reflected in T^2 is a comparison of between-variability (given by the $\mathbf{d}$ vectors) to within-variability (given by $\mathbf{S}$). This may not be obvious, because we are not literally dividing between by within as in the univariate case (i.e., $F = MS_\mathrm{h} / MS_\mathrm{w}$). However, recall that inversion is the matrix analogue of division, so that multiplying by $\mathbf{S}^{-1}$ is in effect "dividing" by the multivariate measure of within variability.

4.4 NUMERICAL CALCULATIONS FOR A TWO-GROUP PROBLEM

We now consider a small example to illustrate the calculations associated with Hotelling's T^2. The fictitious data shown next represent scores on two measures of counselor effectiveness, client satisfaction (SA) and client self-acceptance (CSA). Six participants were originally randomly assigned to counselors who used either a behavior modification or cognitive method; however, three in the behavior modification group were unable to continue for reasons unrelated to the treatment.

Behavior modification		Cognitive	
SA	CSA	SA	CSA
1	3	4	6
3	7	6	8
2	2	6	8
$\bar{y}_{11} = 2$	$\bar{y}_{21} = 4$	5	10
		5	10
		4	6
		$\bar{y}_{12} = 5$	$\bar{y}_{22} = 8$

Recall again that the first part of the subscript denotes the variable and the second part the group, that is, y_{12} is the mean for variable 1 in group 2.

In words, our multivariate null hypothesis is: "There are no mean differences between the behavior modification and cognitive groups when they are compared simultaneously on client satisfaction and client self-acceptance." Let client satisfaction be variable 1 and client self-acceptance be variable 2. Then the multivariate null hypothesis in symbols is:

$$H_0 : \begin{pmatrix} \mu_{11} \\ \mu_{21} \end{pmatrix} = \begin{pmatrix} \mu_{12} \\ \mu_{22} \end{pmatrix}$$

That is, we wish to determine whether it is tenable that the population means are equal for variable 1 ($\mu_{11} = \mu_{12}$) and that the population means for variable 2 are equal ($\mu_{21} = \mu_{22}$). To test the multivariate null hypothesis we need to calculate F in Equation 3. But to obtain this we first need T^2, and the tedious part of calculating T^2 is in obtaining S, which is our pooled estimate of within-group variability on the set of two variables, that is, our estimate of error. Before we begin calculating S it will be helpful to go back to the univariate t test (Equation 1) and recall how the estimate of error variance was obtained there. The estimate of the assumed common within-population variance (σ^2) (i.e., error variance) is given by

$$s^2 = \frac{(n_1 - 1)s_1^2 + (n_2 - 1)s_2^2}{n_1 + n_2 - 2} = \frac{ss_{g1} + ss_{g2}}{n_1 + n_2 - 2}$$

$$\downarrow \qquad\qquad\qquad\qquad \downarrow \qquad\qquad\qquad\qquad\qquad (4)$$

(cf. Equation 1)   (from the definition of variance)

where ss_{g1} and ss_{g2} are the within sums of squares for groups 1 and 2. In the multivariate case (i.e., in obtaining S) we replace the univariate measures of within-group variability (ss_{g1} and ss_{g2}) by their matrix multivariate generalizations, which we call W_1 and W_2.

W_1 will be our estimate of within variability on the two dependent variables in group 1. Because we have two variables, there is variability on each, which we denote by ss_1 and ss_2, and covariability, which we denote by ss_{12}. Thus, the matrix W_1 will look as follows:

$$W_1 = \begin{bmatrix} ss_1 & ss_{12} \\ ss_{21} & ss_2 \end{bmatrix}$$

Similarly, W_2 will be our estimate of within variability (error) on variables in group 2. After W_1 and W_2 have been calculated, we will pool them (i.e., add them) and divide by the degrees of freedom, as was done in the univariate case (see Equation 4), to obtain our multivariate error term, the covariance matrix S. Table 4.1 shows schematically the procedure for obtaining the pooled error terms for both the univariate t test and for Hotelling's T^2.

4.4.1 Calculation of the Multivariate Error Term S

First we calculate W_1, the estimate of within variability for group 1. Now, ss_1 and ss_2 are just the sum of the squared deviations about the means for variables 1 and 2, respectively. Thus,

■ **Table 4.1: Estimation of Error Term for *t* Test and Hotelling's T^2**

	t test (univariate)	T^2 (multivariate)
Assumption	Within-group population variances are equal, i.e., $\sigma_1^2 = \sigma_2^2$ Call the common value σ^2	Within-group population covariance matrices are equal, $\Sigma_1 = \Sigma_2$ Call the common value Σ
	To estimate these assumed common population values we employ the three steps indicated next:	
Calculate the within-group measures of variability.	ss_{g1} and ss_{g2}	W_1 and W_2
Pool these estimates.	$ss_{g1} + ss_{g2}$	$W_1 + W_2$
Divide by the degrees of freedom	$\dfrac{SS_{g1} + SS_{g2}}{n_1 + n_2 - 2} = \hat{\sigma}^2$	$\dfrac{W_1 + W_2}{n_1 + n_2 - 2} = \widehat{\Sigma} = S$

Note: The rationale for pooling is that if we are measuring the same variability in each group (which is the assumption), then we obtain a better estimate of this variability by combining our estimates.

$$ss_1 = \sum_{i=1}^{3}(y_{1(i)} - \bar{y}_{11})^2 = (1-2)^2 + (3-2)^2 + (2-2)^2 = 2$$

($y_{1(i)}$ denotes the score for the *i*th subject on variable 1)

and

$$ss_2 = \sum_{i=1}^{3}(y_{2(i)} - \bar{y}_{21})^2 = (3-4)^2 + (7-4)^2 + (2-4)^2 = 14$$

Finally, ss_{12} is just the sum of deviation cross-products:

$$ss_{12} = \sum_{i=1}^{3}\left(y_{1(i)} - 2\right)\left(y_{2(i)} - 4\right)$$
$$= (1-2)(3-4) + (3-2)(7-4) + (2-2)(2-4) = 4$$

Therefore, the within SSCP matrix for group 1 is

$$\mathbf{W}_1 = \begin{bmatrix} 2 & 4 \\ 4 & 14 \end{bmatrix}.$$

Similarly, as we leave for you to show, the within matrix for group 2 is

$$\mathbf{W}_2 = \begin{bmatrix} 4 & 4 \\ 4 & 16 \end{bmatrix}.$$

Thus, the multivariate error term (i.e., the pooled within covariance matrix) is calculated as:

$$\mathbf{S} = \frac{\mathbf{W_1} + \mathbf{W_2}}{n_1 + n_2 - 2} = \frac{\begin{bmatrix} 2 & 4 \\ 4 & 14 \end{bmatrix} + \begin{bmatrix} 4 & 4 \\ 4 & 16 \end{bmatrix}}{7} = \begin{bmatrix} 6/7 & 8/7 \\ 8/7 & 30/7 \end{bmatrix}.$$

Note that 6/7 is just the sample variance for variable 1, 30/7 is the sample variance for variable 2, and 8/7 is the sample covariance.

4.4.2 Calculation of the Multivariate Test Statistic

To obtain Hotelling's T^2 we need the inverse of S as follows:

$$\mathbf{S}^{-1} = \begin{bmatrix} 1.810 & -.483 \\ -.483 & .362 \end{bmatrix}.$$

From Equation 2 then, Hotelling's T^2 is

$$T^2 = \frac{n_1 n_2}{n_1 + n_2} (\bar{\mathbf{y}}_1 - \bar{\mathbf{y}}_2)' \mathbf{S}^{-1} (\bar{\mathbf{y}}_1 - \bar{\mathbf{y}}_2)$$

$$T^2 = \frac{3(6)}{3+6} (2-5, 4-8) \begin{bmatrix} 1.810 & -.483 \\ -.483 & .362 \end{bmatrix} \begin{pmatrix} 2-5 \\ 4-8 \end{pmatrix}$$

$$T^2 = (-6, -8) \begin{pmatrix} -3.501 \\ .001 \end{pmatrix} = 21$$

The exact F transformation of T^2 is then

$$F = \frac{n_1 = n_1 + n_2 - p - 1}{(n_1 + n_2 - 2)p} T^2 = \frac{9 - 2 - 1}{7(2)} (21) = 9,$$

where F has 2 and 6 degrees of freedom (cf. Equation 3).

If we were testing the multivariate null hypothesis at the .05 level, then we would reject this hypothesis (because the critical value = 5.14) and conclude that the two groups differ on the set of two variables.

After finding that the groups differ, we would like to determine which of the variables are contributing to the overall difference; that is, a *post hoc* procedure is needed. This is similar to the procedure followed in a one-way ANOVA, where first an overall F test is done. If F is significant, then a *post hoc* technique (such as Tukey's) is used to determine which specific groups differed, and thus contributed to the overall difference. Here, instead of groups, we wish to know which variables contributed to the overall multivariate significance.

Now, multivariate significance implies there is a linear combination of the dependent variables (the discriminant function) that is significantly separating the groups. We defer presentation of discriminant analysis (DA) to Chapter 10. You may see discussions in the literature where DA is preferred over the much more commonly used procedures discussed in section 4.5 because the linear combinations in DA may suggest new "constructs" that a researcher may not have expected, and that DA makes use of the correlations among outcomes throughout the analysis procedure. While we agree that discriminant analysis can be of value, there are at least three factors that can mitigate its usefulness in many instances:

1. There is no guarantee that the linear combination (the discriminant function) will be a meaningful variate, that is, that it will make substantive or conceptual sense.
2. Sample size must be considerably larger than many investigators realize in order to have the results of a discriminant analysis be reliable. More details on this later.
3. The investigator may be more interested in identifying if group differences are present for each specific variable, rather than on some combination of them.

4.5 THREE *POST HOC* PROCEDURES

We now consider three possible *post hoc* approaches. One approach is to use the Roy–Bose simultaneous confidence intervals. These are a generalization of the Scheffé intervals, and are illustrated in Morrison (1976) and in Johnson and Wichern (1982). The intervals are nice in that we not only can determine whether a pair of means is different, but in addition can obtain a range of values within which the population mean differences probably lie. Unfortunately, however, the procedure is extremely conservative (Hummel & Sligo, 1971), and this will hurt power (sensitivity for detecting differences). Thus, we cannot recommend this procedure for general use.

As Bock (1975) noted, "their [Roy–Bose intervals] use at the conventional 90% confidence level will lead the investigator to overlook many differences that should be interpreted and defeat the purposes of an exploratory comparative study" (p. 422). What Bock says applies with particularly great force to a very large number of studies in social science research where the group or effect sizes are small or moderate. In these studies, power will be poor or not adequate to begin with. To be more specific, consider the power table from Cohen (1988) for a two-tailed *t* test at the .05 level of significance. For group sizes ≤ 20 and small or medium effect sizes through .60 standard deviations, which is a quite common class of situations, the *largest* power is .45. The use of the Roy–Bose intervals will dilute the power even further to extremely low levels.

A second widely used but also potentially problematic *post hoc* procedure we consider is to follow up a significant multivariate test at the .05 level with univariate tests, each at the .05 level. On the positive side, this procedure has the greatest power of the three methods considered here for detecting differences, and provides accurate type I error control when two dependent variables are included in the design. However, the overall type I error rate increases when more than two dependent variables appear in the design. For example, this rate may be as high as .10 for three dependent variables, .15 with four dependent variables, and continues to increase with more dependent variables. As such, we cannot not recommend this procedure if more than three dependent variables are included in your design. Further, if you plan to use confidence intervals to estimate mean differences, this procedure cannot be recommended because confidence interval coverage (i.e., the proportion of intervals that are expected to capture the true mean differences) is lower than desired and becomes worse as the number of dependent variables increases.

The third and generally recommended *post hoc* procedure is to follow a significant multivariate result by univariate ts, but to do each t test at the α/p level of significance. Thus, if there were five dependent variables and we wished to have an overall α of .05, then, we would simply compare our obtained p value for the t (or F) test to α of $.05/5 = .01$. By this procedure, we are assured by the Bonferroni inequality that the overall type I error rate for the set of t tests will be less than α. In addition, this Bonferroni procedure provides for generally accurate confidence interval coverage for the set of mean differences, and so is the preferred procedure when confidence intervals are used. One weakness of the Bonferroni-adjusted procedure is that power will be severely attenuated if the number of dependent variables is even moderately large (say > 7). For example, if $p = 15$ and we wish to set overall $\alpha = .05$, then each univariate test would be done at the $.05/15 = .0033$ level of significance.

There are two things we may do to improve power for the t tests and yet provide reasonably good protection against type I errors. First, there are several reasons (which we detail in Chapter 5) for *generally* preferring to work with a relatively small number of dependent variables (say ≤ 10). Second, in many cases, it may be possible to divide the dependent variables up into two or three of the following categories: (1) those variables likely to show a difference, (2) those variables (based on past research) that may show a difference, and (3) those variables that are being tested on a heuristic basis. To illustrate, suppose we conduct a study limiting the number of variables to eight. There is fairly solid evidence from the literature that three of the variables should show a difference, while the other five are being tested on a heuristic basis. In this situation, as indicated in section 4.2, two multivariate tests should be done. If the multivariate test is significant for the fairly solid variables, then we would test each of the individual variables at the .05 level. Here we are not as concerned about type I errors in the follow-up phase, because there is prior reason to believe differences are present, and recall that there is some type I error protection provided by use of the multivariate test. Then, a separate multivariate test is done for the five heuristic variables. If this is significant, we can then use the Bonferroni-adjusted t test approach, but perhaps set overall α somewhat higher for better power (especially if sample size is small or moderate). For example, we could set overall $\alpha = .15$, and thus test each variable for significance at the $.15/5 = .03$ level of significance.

4.6 SAS AND SPSS CONTROL LINES FOR SAMPLE PROBLEM AND SELECTED OUTPUT

Table 4.2 presents SAS and SPSS commands for running the two-group sample MANOVA problem. Table 4.3 and Table 4.4 show selected SAS output, and Table 4.4 shows selected output from SPSS. Note that both SAS and SPSS give all four multivariate test statistics, although in different orders. Recall from earlier in the chapter that for two groups the various tests are equivalent, and therefore the multivariate F is the same for all four test statistics.

▪ **Table 4.2: SAS and SPSS GLM Control Lines for Two-Group MANOVA Sample Problem**

	SAS		SPSS
	TITLE 'MANOVA';		TITLE 'MANOVA'.
	DATA twogp;		DATA LIST FREE/gp y1 y2.
	INPUT gp y1 y2 @@		BEGIN DATA.
	LINES;	(6)	1 1 3 1 3 7 1 2 2
	1 1 3 1 3 7 1 2 2		2 4 6 2 6 8 2 6 8
	2 4 6 2 6 8 2 6 8		2 5 10 2 5 10 2 4 6
	2 5 10 2 5 10 2 4 6		END DATA.
		(7)	GLM y1 y2 BY gp
(1)	PROC GLM;	(8)	/PRINT=DESCRIPTIVE ETASQ
(2)	CLASS gp;		TEST(SSCP)
			/DESIGN= gp.
(3)	MODEL y1 y2 = gp;		
(4)	MANOVA H = gp/PRINTE PRINTH;		
(5)	MEANS gp; RUN;		

(1) The GENERAL LINEAR MODEL procedure is called.

(2) The CLASS statement tells SAS which variable is the grouping variable (gp, here).

(3) In the MODEL statement the dependent variables are put on the left-hand side and the grouping variable(s) on the right-hand side.

(4) You need to identify the effect to be used as the hypothesis matrix, which here by default is gp. After the slash a wide variety of optional output is available. We have selected PRINTE (prints the error SSCP matrix) and PRINTH (prints the matrix associated with the effect, which here is group).

(5) MEANS gp requests the means and standard deviations for each group.

(6) The first number for each triplet is the group identification with the remaining two numbers the scores on the dependent variables.

(7) The general form for the GLM command is dependent variables BY grouping variables.

(8) This PRINT subcommand yields descriptive statistics for the groups, that is, means and standard deviations, proportion of variance explained statistics via ETASQ, and the error and between group SSCP matrices.

■ **Table 4.3: SAS Output for the Two-Group MANOVA Showing SSCP Matrices and Multivariate Tests**

E = Error SSCP Matrix

	Y1	Y2
Y1	6	8
Y2	8	30

In 4.4, under CALCULATING THE MULIVARIATE ERROR TERM, we computed the separate $\mathbf{W_1} + \mathbf{W_2}$ matrices (the within sums of squares and cross products matrices), and then pooled or added them to obtain the covariance matrix S. What SAS is outputting here is this pooled $\mathbf{W_1} = \mathbf{W_2}$ matrix.

H = Type III SSCP Matrix for GP

	Y1	Y2
Y1	18	24
Y2	24	32

Note that the diagonal elements of this hypothesis or between-group SSCP matrix are just the between-group sum-of-squares for the univariate F tests.

MANOVA Test Criteria and Exact F Statistics for the Hypothesis of No Overall GP Effect
H = Type III SSCP Matrix for GP
E = Error SSCP Matrix

S=1 M=0 N=2

Statistic	Value	F Value	Num DF	Den DF	Pr > F
Wilks' Lambda	0.25000000	9.00	2	6	0.0156
Pillai's Trace	0.75000000	9.00	2	6	0.0156
Hotelling-Lawley Trace	3.00000000	9.00	2	6	0.0156
Roy's Greatest Root	3.00000000	9.00	2	6	0.0156

In Table 4.3, the within-group (or error) SSCP and between-group SSCP matrices are shown along with the multivariate test results. Note that the multivariate F of 9 (which is equal to the F calculated in section 4.4.2) is statistically significant ($p <$ .05), suggesting that group differences are present for at least one dependent variable. The univariate F tests, shown in Table 4.4, using an unadjusted alpha of .05, indicate that group differences are present for each outcome as each p value (.003, 029) is less than .05. Note that these Fs are equivalent to squared t values as $F = t^2$ for two groups. Given the group means shown in Table 4.4, we can then conclude that the population means for group 2 are greater than those for group 1 for both outcomes. Note that if you wished to implement the Bonferroni approach for these univariate tests (which is not necessary here for type I error control, given that we

■ **Table 4.4: SAS Output for the Two-Group MANOVA Showing Univariate Results**

Dependent Variable: Y2

Source	DF	Sum of Squares	Mean Square	F Value	Pr > F
Model	1	18.00000000	18.00000000	21.00	0.0025
Error	7	6.00000000	0.85714286		
Corrected Total	8	24.00000000			

R-Square	CoeffVar	Root MSE	Y2 Mean
0.750000	23.14550	0.925820	4.000000

Dependent Variable: Y2

Source	DF	Sum of Squares	Mean Square	F Value	Pr > F
Model	1	32.00000000	32.00000000	7.47	0.0292
Error	7	30.00000000	4.28571429		
Corrected Total	8	62.00000000			

R-Square	CoeffVar	Root MSE	Y2 Mean
0.516129	31.05295	2.070197	6.666667

Level of		Y1		Y2	
GP	N	Mean	StdDev	Mean	StdDev
1	3	2.00000000	1.00000000	4.00000000	2.64575131
2	6	5.00000000	0.89442719	8.00000000	1.78885438

have 2 dependent variables), you would simply compare the obtained p values to an alpha of .05/2 or .025. You can also see that Table 4.5, showing selected SPSS output, provides similar information, with descriptive statistics, followed by the multivariate test results, univariate test results, and then the between- and within-group SSCP matrices. Note that a multivariate effect size measure (multivariate partial eta square) appears in the Multivariate Tests output selection. This effect size measure is discussed in Chapter 5. Also, univariate partial eta squares are shown in the output table Test of Between-Subject Effects. This effect size measure is discussed is section 4.8.

Although the results indicate that group difference are present for each dependent variable, we emphasize that *because the univariate Fs ignore how a given variable is correlated with the others in the set, they do not give an indication of the relative importance of that variable to group differentiation*. A technique for determining the relative importance of each variable to group separation is discriminant analysis, which will be discussed in Chapter 10. To obtain reliable results with discriminant analysis, however, a large subject-to-variable ratio is needed; that is, about 20 subjects per variable are required.

■ Table 4.5: Selected SPSS Output for the Two-Group MANOVA

Descriptive Statistics

	GP	Mean	Std. Deviation	N
Y1	1.00	2.0000	1.00000	3
	2.00	5.0000	.89443	6
	Total	4.0000	1.73205	9
Y2	1.00	4.0000	2.64575	3
	2.00	8.0000	1.78885	6
	Total	6.6667	2.78388	9

Multivariate Tests[a]

Effect		Value	F	Hypothesis df	Error df	Sig.	Partial Eta Squared
GP	Pillai's Trace	.750	9.000[b]	2.000	6.000	.016	.750
	Wilks' Lambda	.250	9.000[b]	2.000	6.000	.016	.750
	Hotelling's Trace	3.000	9.000[b]	2.000	6.000	.016	.750
	Roy's Largest Root	3.000	9.000[b]	2.000	6.000	.016	.750

[a] Design: Intercept + GP
[b] Exact statistic

Tests of Between-Subjects Effects

Source	Dependent Variable	Type III Sum of Squares	Df	Mean Square	F	Sig.	Partial Eta Squared
GP	Y1	18.000	1	18.000	21.000	.003	.750
	Y2	32.000	1	32.000	7.467	.029	.516
Error	Y1	6.000	7	.857			
	Y2	30.000	7	4.286			
Corrected	Y1	24.000	8				
Total	Y2	62.000	8				

Between-Subjects SSCP Matrix

			Y1	Y2
Hypothesis	GP	Y1	18.000	24.000
		Y2	24.000	32.000
Error		Y1	6.000	8.000
		Y2	8.000	30.000

Based on Type III Sum of Squares

Note: Some nonessential output has been removed from the SPSS tables.

4.7 MULTIVARIATE SIGNIFICANCE BUT NO UNIVARIATE SIGNIFICANCE

If the multivariate null hypothesis is rejected, then *generally* at least one of the univariate *t*s will be significant, as in our previous example. This will not always be the case. It is possible to reject the multivariate null hypothesis and yet for none of the univariate *t*s to be significant. As Timm (1975) pointed out, "furthermore, rejection of the multivariate test does not guarantee that there exists at least one significant univariate *F* ratio. For a given set of data, the significant comparison may involve some linear combination of the variables" (p. 166). This is analogous to what happens occasionally in univariate analysis of variance.

The overall *F* is significant, but when, say, the Tukey procedure is used to determine which pairs of groups are significantly different, none is found. Again, all that significant *F* guarantees is that there is at least one comparison among the group means that is significant at or beyond the same α level: The particular comparison may be a complex one, and may or may not be a meaningful one.

One way of seeing that there will be no necessary relationship between multivariate significance and univariate significance is to observe that the tests make use of different information. For example, the multivariate test takes into account the correlations among the variables, whereas the univariate do not. Also, the multivariate test considers the differences on all variables jointly, whereas the univariate tests consider the difference on each variable separately.

4.8 MULTIVARIATE REGRESSION ANALYSIS FOR THE SAMPLE PROBLEM

This section is presented to show that ANOVA and MANOVA are special cases of regression analysis, that is, of the so-called general linear model. Cohen's (1968) seminal article was primarily responsible for bringing the general linear model to the attention of social science researchers. The regression approach to MANOVA is accomplished by dummy coding group membership. This can be done, for the two-group problem, by coding the participants in group 1 as 1, and the participants in group 2 as 0 (or vice versa). Thus, the data for our sample problem would look like this:

y_1	y_2	x	
1	3	1	
3	7	1	group 1
2	2	1	

$$
\left.\begin{array}{ccc}
4 & 6 & 0 \\
4 & 6 & 0 \\
5 & 10 & 0 \\
5 & 10 & 0 \\
6 & 8 & 0 \\
6 & 8 & 0
\end{array}\right\} \quad \text{group 2}
$$

In a typical regression problem, as considered in the previous chapters, the predictors have been continuous variables. Here, for MANOVA, the predictor is a categorical or nominal variable, and is used to determine how much of the variance in the dependent variables is accounted for by group membership.

The setup of the two-group MANOVA as a multivariate regression may seem somewhat strange since there are two dependent variables and only one predictor. In the previous chapters there has been either one dependent variable and several predictors, or several dependent variables and several predictors. However, the examination of the association is done in the same way. Recall that Wilks' Λ is the statistic for determining whether there is a significant association between the dependent variables and the predictor(s):

$$
\Lambda = \frac{|\mathbf{S}_e|}{|\mathbf{S}_e + \mathbf{S}_r|},
$$

where $\mathbf{S}_e$ is the error SSCP matrix, that is, the sum of square and cross products not due to regression (or the residual), and $\mathbf{S}_r$ is the regression SSCP matrix, that is, an index of how much variability in the dependent variables is due to regression. In this case, variability due to regression is variability in the dependent variables due to group membership, because the predictor is group membership.

Part of the output from SPSS for the two-group MANOVA, set up and run as a regression, is presented in Table 4.6. The error matrix $\mathbf{S}_e$ is called adjusted within-cells sum of squares and cross products, and the regression SSCP matrix is called adjusted hypothesis sum of squares and cross products. Using these matrices, we can form Wilks' Λ (and see how the value of .25 is obtained):

$$
\Lambda = \frac{|\mathbf{S}_e|}{|\mathbf{S}_e + \mathbf{S}_r|} = \frac{\begin{vmatrix} 6 & 8 \\ 8 & 30 \end{vmatrix}}{\begin{bmatrix} 6 & 8 \\ 8 & 30 \end{bmatrix} + \begin{bmatrix} 18 & 24 \\ 24 & 32 \end{bmatrix}}
$$

$$
\Lambda = \frac{\begin{vmatrix} 6 & 8 \\ 8 & 30 \end{vmatrix}}{\begin{vmatrix} 24 & 32 \\ 32 & 62 \end{vmatrix}} = \frac{116}{464} = .25
$$

■ **Table 4.6: Selected SPSS Output for Regression Analysis on Two-Group MANOVA with Group Membership as Predictor**

GP						
	Pillai's Trace	.750	9.000[a]	2.000	6.000	.016
	Wilks' Lambda	.250	9.000[a]	2.000	6.000	.016
	Hotelling's Trace	3.000	9.000[a]	2.000	6.000	.016
	Roy's Largest Root	3.000	9.000[a]	2.000	6.000	.016

Source	Dependent Variable	Type III Sum of Squares	df	Mean Square	F	Sig.
Corrected Model	Y1	18.000[a]	1	18.000	21.000	.003
	Y2	32.000[b]	1	32.000	7.467	.029
Intercept	Y1	98.000	1	98.000	114.333	.000
	Y2	288.000	1	288.000	67.200	.000
GP	Y1	18.000	1	18.000	21.000	.003
	Y2	32.000	1	32.000	7.467	.029
Error	Y1	6.000	7	.857		
	Y2	30.000	7	4.286		

Between-Subjects SSCP Matrix

			Y1	Y2
Hypothesis	Intercept	Y1	98.000	168.000
		Y2	168.000	288.000
	GP	Y1	18.000	24.000
		Y2	24.000	32.000
Error		Y1	6.000	8.000
		Y2	8.000	30.000
Based on Type III Sum of Squares				

Note first that the multivariate Fs are *identical* for Table 4.5 and Table 4.6; thus, significant separation of the group mean vectors is equivalent to significant association between group membership (dummy coded) and the set of dependent variables.

The univariate Fs are also the same for both analyses, although it may not be clear to you why this is so. In traditional ANOVA, the total sum of squares (ss_t) is partitioned as:

$$ss_t = ss_b + ss_w$$

whereas in regression analysis the total sum of squares is partitioned as follows:

$$ss_t = ss_{reg} + ss_{resid}$$

The corresponding F ratios, for determining whether there is significant group separation and for determining whether there is a significant regression, are:

$$F = \frac{SS_b / df_b}{SS_w / df_w} \quad \text{and} \quad F = \frac{SS_{reg} / df_{reg}}{SS_{resid} / df_{resid}}$$

To see that these F ratios are equivalent, note that because the predictor variable is group membership, ss_{reg} is just the amount of variability between groups or ss_b, and ss_{resid} is just the amount of variability not accounted for by group membership, or the variability of the scores within each group (i.e., ss_w).

The regression output also gives information that was obtained by the commands in Table 4.2 for traditional MANOVA: the squared multiple Rs for each dependent variable (labeled as partial eta square in Table 4.5). Because in this case there is just one predictor, these multiple Rs are just squared Pearson correlations. In particular, they are squared point-biserial correlations because one of the variables is dichotomous (dummy-coded group membership). The relationship between the point-biserial correlation and the F statistic is given by Welkowitz, Ewen, and Cohen (1982):

$$r_{pb} = \sqrt{\frac{F}{F + df_w}}$$

$$r_{pb}^2 = \frac{F}{F + df_w}$$

Thus, for dependent variable 1, we have

$$r_{pb}^2 = \frac{21}{21 + 7} = .75.$$

This squared correlation (also known as eta square) has a very meaningful and important interpretation. It tells us that 75% of the variance in the dependent variable is accounted for by group membership. Thus, we not only have a statistically significant relationship, as indicated by the F ratio, but in addition, the relationship is very strong. It should be recalled that it is important to have a measure of strength of relationship *along* with a test of significance, as significance resulting from large sample size might indicate a very weak relationship, and therefore one that may be of little practical importance.

Various textbook authors have recommended measures of association or strength of relationship measures (e.g., Cohen & Cohen, 1975; Grissom & Kim, 2012; Hays, 1981). We also believe that they can be useful, but you should be aware that they have limitations.

For example, simply because a strength of relationship indicates that, say, only 10% of variance is accounted for, does not *necessarily* imply that the result has no practical importance, as O'Grady (1982) indicated in an excellent review on measures of association. There are several factors that affect such measures. One very important factor is context: 10% of variance accounted for in certain research areas may indeed be practically significant.

A good example illustrating this point is provided by Rosenthal and Rosnow (1984). They consider the comparison of a treatment and control group where the dependent variable is dichotomous, whether the subjects survive or die. The following table is presented:

	Treatment outcome		
	Alive	Dead	
Treatment	66	34	100
Control	34	66	100
	100	100	

Because both variables are dichotomous, the phi coefficient—a special case of the Pearson correlation for two dichotomous variables (Glass & Hopkins, 1984)—measures the relationship between them:

$$\phi = \frac{34^2 - 66^2}{\sqrt{100(100)(100)(100)}} = -.32 \quad \phi^2 = .10$$

Thus, even though the treatment-control distinction accounts for "only" 10% of the variance in the outcome, it increases the survival rate from 34% to 66%—far from trivial. The same type of interpretation would hold if we considered some less dramatic type of outcome like improvement versus no improvement, where treatment was a type of psychotherapy. Also, the interpretation is *not* confined to a dichotomous outcome measure. Another factor to consider is the design of the study. As O'Grady (1982) noted:

> Thus, true experiments will frequently produce smaller measures of explained variance than will correlational studies. At the least this implies that consideration should be given to whether an investigation involves a true experiment or a correlational approach in deciding whether an effect is weak or strong. (p. 771)

Another point to keep in mind is that, because most behaviors have multiple causes, it will be difficult in these cases to account for a large percent of variance with just a single cause (say treatments). Still another factor is the homogeneity of the population sampled. Because measures of association are correlational-type measures, the more homogeneous the population, the smaller the correlation will tend to be, and therefore the smaller the percent of variance accounted for can potentially be (this is the restriction-of-range phenomenon).

Finally, we focus on a topic that is important in the planning phase of a study: estimation of power for the overall multivariate test. We start at a basic level, reviewing what power is, factors affecting power, and reasons that estimation of power is important. Then the notion of effect size for the univariate t test is given, followed by the multivariate effect size concept for Hotelling's T^2.

4.9 POWER ANALYSIS*

Type I error, or the level of significance (α), is familiar to all readers. This is the probability of rejecting the null hypothesis when it is true, that is, saying the groups differ when in fact they do not. The α level set by the experimenter is a subjective decision, but is usually set at .05 or .01 by most researchers to minimize the probability of making this kind of error. There is, however, another type of error that one can make in conducting a statistical test, and this is called a type II error. Type II error, denoted by β, is the probability of retaining H_0 when it is false, that is, saying the groups do not differ when they do. Now, not only can either of these errors occur, but in addition they are inversely related. That is, when we hold effect and group size constant, reducing our nominal type I rate increases our type II error rate. We illustrate this for a two-group problem with a group size of 30 and effect size $d = .5$:

A	β	$1 - \beta$
.10	.37	.63
.05	.52	.48
.01	.78	.22

Notice that as we control the type I error rate more severely (from .10 to .01), type II error increases fairly sharply (from .37 to .78), holding sample and effect size constant. Therefore, the problem for the experimental planner is achieving an appropriate balance between the two types of errors. Although we do not intend to minimize the seriousness of making a type I error, we hope to convince you that more attention should be paid to type II error. Now, the quantity in the last column is the *power* of a statistical test, which is the probability of rejecting the null hypothesis when it is false. Thus, power is the probability of making a correct decision when, for example, group mean differences are present. In the preceding example, if we are willing to take a 10% chance of rejecting H_0 falsely, then we have a 63% chance of finding a difference of a specified magnitude in the population (here, an effect size of .5 standard deviations). On the other hand, if we insist on only a 1% chance of rejecting H_0 falsely, then we have only about 2 chances out of 10 of declaring a mean difference is present. This example with small sample size suggests that in this case it might be prudent to abandon the traditional α levels of .01 or .05 to a more liberal α level to improve power sharply. Of course, one does not get something for nothing. We are taking a greater risk of rejecting falsely, but that increased risk is *more than balanced* by the increase in power.

There are two types of power estimation, *a priori* and *post hoc*, and very good reasons why each of them should be considered seriously. If a researcher is going

---

* Much of the material in this section is identical to that presented in 1.2; however, it was believed to be worth repeating in this more extensive discussion of power.

to invest a great amount of time and money in carrying out a study, then he or she would certainly want to have a 70% or 80% chance (i.e., power of .70 or .80) of finding a difference if one is there. Thus, the *a priori* estimation of power will alert the researcher to how many participants per group will be needed for adequate power. Later on we consider an example of how this is done in the multivariate case.

The *post hoc* estimation of power is important in terms of how one interprets the results of completed studies. Researchers not sufficiently sensitive to power may interpret nonsignificant results from studies as demonstrating that treatments made no difference. In fact, it may be that treatments did make a difference but that the researchers had poor power for detecting the difference. The poor power may result from small sample size or effect size. The following example shows how important an awareness of power can be. Cronbach and Snow had written a report on aptitude-treatment interaction research, not being fully cognizant of power. By the publication of their text *Aptitudes and Instructional Methods* (1977) on the same topic, they acknowledged the importance of power, stating in the preface, "[we] . . . became aware of the critical relevance of statistical power, and consequently changed our interpretations of individual studies and sometimes of whole bodies of literature" (p. ix). Why would they change their interpretation of a whole body of literature? Because, prior to being sensitive to power when they found most studies in a given body of literature had nonsignificant results, they concluded no effect existed. However, after being sensitized to power, they took into account the sample sizes in the studies, and also the magnitude of the effects. If the sample sizes were small in most of the studies with nonsignificant results, then lack of significance is due to poor power. Or, in other words, several low-power studies that report nonsignificant results of the same character *are* evidence for an effect.

The power of a statistical test is dependent on three factors:

1. The α level set by the experimenter
2. Sample size
3. Effect size—How much of a difference the treatments make, or the extent to which the groups differ in the population on the dependent variable(s).

For the univariate independent samples *t* test, Cohen (1988) defined the population effect size, as we used earlier, $d = (\mu_1 - \mu_2)/\sigma$, where σ is the assumed common population standard deviation. Thus, in this situation, the effect size measure simply indicates how many standard deviation units the group means are separated by.

Power is *heavily* dependent on sample size. Consider a two-tailed test at the .05 level for the *t* test for independent samples. Suppose we have an effect size of .5 standard deviations. The next table shows how power changes dramatically as sample size increases.

n (Subjects per group)	Power
10	.18
20	.33
50	.70
100	.94

As this example suggests, when sample size is large (say 100 or more subjects per group) power is not an issue. It is when you are conducting a study where group sizes are small ($n \leq 20$), or when you are evaluating a completed study that had a small group size, that it is imperative to be very sensitive to the possibility of poor power (or equivalently, a type II error).

We have indicated that power is also influenced by effect size. For the t test, Cohen (1988) suggested as a rough guide that an effect size around .20 is small, an effect size around .50 is medium, and an effect size > .80 is large. The difference in the mean IQs between PhDs and the typical college freshmen is an example of a large effect size (about .8 of a standard deviation).

Cohen and many others have noted that *small and medium effect sizes are very common in social science research.* Light and Pillemer (1984) commented on the fact that most evaluations find small effects in reviews of the literature on programs of various types (social, educational, etc.): "Review after review confirms it and drives it home. Its importance comes from having managers understand that they should not expect large, positive findings to emerge routinely from a single study of a new program" (pp. 153–154). Results from Becker (1987) of effect sizes for three sets of studies (on teacher expectancy, desegregation, and gender influenceability) showed only three large effect sizes out of 40. Also, Light, Singer, and Willett (1990) noted that "meta-analyses often reveal a sobering fact: Effect sizes are not nearly as large as we all might hope" (p. 195). To illustrate, they present average effect sizes from six meta-analyses in different areas that yielded .13, .25, .27, .38, .43, and .49—all in the small to medium range.

4.10 WAYS OF IMPROVING POWER

Given how poor power generally is with fewer than 20 subjects per group, the following four methods of improving power should be seriously considered:

1. Adopt a more lenient α level, perhaps $\alpha = .10$ or $\alpha = .15$.
2. Use one-tailed tests where the literature supports a directional hypothesis. This option is not available for the multivariate tests because they are inherently two-tailed.
3. Consider ways of reducing within-group variability, so that one has a more sensitive design. One way is through sample selection; more homogeneous subjects tend to vary less on the dependent variable(s). For example, use just males, rather

than males and females, or use only 6- and 7-year-old children rather than 6-through 9-year-old children. A second way is through the use of factorial designs, which we consider in Chapter 7. A third way of reducing within-group variability is through the use of analysis of covariance, which we consider in Chapter 8. Covariates that have low correlations with each other are particularly helpful because then each is removing a somewhat different part of the within-group (error) variance. A fourth means is through the use of repeated-measures designs. These designs are particularly helpful because all individual difference due to the average response of subjects is removed from the error term, and individual differences are the main reason for within-group variability.

4. Make sure there is a strong linkage between the treatments and the dependent variable(s), and that the treatments extend over a long enough period of time to produce a large—or at least fairly large—effect size.

Using these methods *in combination* can make a considerable difference in effective power. To illustrate, we consider a two-group situation with 18 participants per group and one dependent variable. Suppose a two-tailed test was done at the .05 level, and that the obtained effect size was

$$\hat{d} = (\bar{x}_1 - \bar{x}_2) / s = (8 - 4) / 10 = .40,$$

where s is pooled within standard deviation. Then, from Cohen (1988), power = .21, which is very poor.

Now, suppose that through the use of two good covariates we are able to reduce pooled within variability (s^2) by 60%, from 100 (as earlier) to 40. This is a definite realistic possibility in practice. Then our new estimated effect size would be $\hat{d} \approx 4 / \sqrt{40} = .63$. Suppose in addition that a one-tailed test was really appropriate, and that we also take a somewhat greater risk of a type I error, i.e., $\alpha = .10$. Then, our new estimated power changes dramatically to .69 (Cohen, 1988).

Before leaving this section, it needs to be emphasized that how far one "pushes" the power issue depends on the *consequences* of making a type I error. We give three examples to illustrate. First, suppose that in a medical study examining the safety of a drug we have the following null and alternative hypotheses:

H_0 : The drug is unsafe.
H_1 : The drug is safe.

Here making a type I error (rejecting H_0 when true) is concluding that the drug is safe when in fact it is unsafe. This is a situation where we would want a type I error to be very small, because making a type I error could harm or possibly kill some people.

As a second example, suppose we are comparing two teaching methods, where method A is several times more expensive than method B to implement. If we conclude that method A is more effective (when in fact it is not), this will be a very costly mistake for a school district.

Finally, a classic example of the relative consequences of type I and type II errors can be taken from our judicial system, under which a defendant is innocent until proven guilty. Thus, we could formulate the following null and alternative hypotheses:

H_0 : The defendant is innocent.
H_1 : The defendant is guilty.

If we make a type I error, we conclude that the defendant is guilty when actually innocent. Concluding that the defendant is innocent when actually guilty is a type II error. Most would probably agree that the type I error is by far the more serious here, and thus we would want a type I error to be very small.

4.11 *A PRIORI* POWER ESTIMATION FOR A TWO-GROUP MANOVA

Stevens (1980) discussed estimation of power in MANOVA at some length, and in what follows we borrow heavily from his work. Next, we present the univariate and multivariate measures of effect size for the two-group problem. Recall that the univariate measure was presented earlier.

Measures of effect size	
Univariate	**Multivariate**
$d = \dfrac{\mu_1 - \mu_2}{\sigma}$	$D^2 = (\mu_1 - \mu_2)'\Sigma^{-1}(\mu_1 - \mu_2)$
$\hat{d} = \dfrac{\overline{y}_1 - \overline{y}_2}{s}$	$\hat{D}2 = (\overline{y}_1 - \overline{y}_1)'\mathbf{S}^{-1}(\overline{y}_1 - \overline{y}_2)$

The first row gives the population measures, and the second row is used to estimate effect sizes for your study. Notice that the multivariate measure $\hat{D}2$ is Hotelling's T^2 without the sample sizes (see Equation 2); that is, it is a measure of separation of the groups that is *independent* of sample size. D^2 is called in the literature the Mahalanobis distance. Note also that the multivariate measure $\hat{D}2$ *is a natural squared generalization of the univariate measure* d, *where the means have been replaced by mean vectors and* s *(standard deviation) has been replaced by its squared multivariate generalization of within variability, the sample covariance matrix* **S**.

Table 4.7 from Stevens (1980) provides power values for two-group MANOVA for two through seven variables, with group size varying from small (15) to large (100), and with effect size varying from small ($D^2 = .25$) to very large ($D^2 = 2.25$). Earlier, we indicated that small or moderate group and effect sizes produce inadequate power for the univariate t test. Inspection of Table 4.7 shows that a similar situation exists for MANOVA. The following from Stevens (1980) provides a summary of the results in Table 4.7:

> For values of $D^2 \leq .64$ and $n \leq 25$, . . . power is generally poor ($< .45$) and never really adequate (i.e., $> .70$) for $\alpha = .05$. Adequate power (at $\alpha = .10$) for two through seven variables at a moderate overall effect size of .64 would require about 30 subjects per group. When the overall effect size is large ($D \geq 1$), then 15 or more subjects per group is sufficient to yield power values $\geq .60$ for two through seven variables at $\alpha = .10$. (p. 731)

In section 4.11.2, we show how you can use Table 4.7 to estimate the sample size needed for a simple two-group MANOVA, but first we show how this table can be used to estimate *post hoc* power.

▨ **Table 4.7: Power of Hotelling's T^2 at $\alpha = .05$ and .10 for Small Through Large Overall Effect and Group Sizes**

Number of variables	n*	D^{2**} .25		.64		1		2.25
2	15	26	(32)	44	(60)	65	(77)	95***
2	25	33	(47)	66	(80)	86		97
2	50	60	(77)	95		1		1
2	100	90		1		1		1
3	15	23	(29)	37	(55)	58	(72)	91
3	25	28	(41)	58	(74)	80		95
3	50	54	(65)	93	(98)	1		1
3	100	86		1		1		1
5	15	21	(25)	32	(47)	42	(66)	83
5	25	26	(35)	42	(68)	72		96
5	50	44	(59)	88		1		1
5	100	78		1		1		1
7	15	18	(22)	27	(42)	37	(59)	77
7	25	22	(31)	38	(62)	64	(81)	94
7	50	40	(52)	82		97		1
7	100	72		1		1		1

Note: Power values at $\alpha = .10$ are in parentheses.

* Equal group sizes are assumed.

** $D^2 = (\mu_1 - \mu_2)'\Sigma^{-1}(\mu_1 - \mu_2)$

*** Decimal points have been omitted. Thus, 95 means a power of .95. Also, a value of 1 means the power is approximately equal to 1.

4.11.1 *Post Hoc* Estimation of Power

Suppose you wish to evaluate the power of a two-group MANOVA that was completed in a journal in your content area. Here, Table 4.7 can be used, assuming the number of dependent variables in the study is between two and seven. Actually, with a slight amount of extrapolation, the table will yield a reasonable approximation for eight or nine variables. For example, for $D^2 = .64$, five variables, and $n = 25$, power $= .42$ at the .05 level. For the same situation, but with seven variables, power $= .38$. Therefore, a reasonable estimate for power for nine variables is about .34.

Now, to use Table 4.7, the value of D^2 is needed, and this almost certainly will not be reported. Very probably then, a couple of steps will be required to obtain D^2. The investigator(s) will probably report the multivariate F. From this, one obtains T^2 by reexpressing Equation 3, which we illustrate in Example 4.2. Then, D^2 is obtained using Equation 2. Because the right-hand side of Equation 2 without the sample sizes is D^2, it follows that $T^2 = [n_1 n_2/(n_1 + n_2)]D^2$, or $D^2 = [(n_1 + n_2)/n_1 n_2]T^2$.

We now consider two examples to illustrate how to use Table 4.7 to estimate power for studies in the literature when (1) the number of dependent variables is not explicitly given in Table 4.7, and (2) the group sizes are not equal.

Example 4.2

Consider a two-group study in the literature with 25 participants per group that used four dependent variables and reports a multivariate $F = 2.81$. What is the estimated power at the .05 level? First, we convert F to the corresponding T^2 value:

$$F = [(N - p - 1)/(N - 2)p]T^2 \text{ or } T^2 = (N - 2)pF/(N - p - 1)$$

Thus, $T^2 = 48(4)2.81/45 = 11.99$. Now, because $D^2 = (NT^2)/n_1 n_2$, we have $D^2 = 50(11.99)/625 = .96$. This is a large multivariate effect size. Table 4.7 does not have power for four variables, but we can interpolate between three and five variables to approximate power. Using $D^2 = 1$ in the table we find that:

Number of variables	n	$D^2 = 1$
3	25	.80
5	25	.72

Thus, a good approximation to power is .76, which is adequate power for a large effect size. Here, as in univariate analysis, with a large effect size, not many participants are needed per group to have adequate power.

Example 4.3

Now consider an article in the literature that is a two-group MANOVA with five dependent variables, having 22 participants in one group and 32 in the other. The investigators obtain a multivariate $F = 1.61$, which is not significant at the .05 level (critical value = 2.42). Calculate power at the .05 level and comment on the size of the multivariate effect measure. Here the number of dependent variables (five) is given in the table, but the group sizes are unequal. Following Cohen (1988), we use the harmonic mean as the n with which to enter the table. The harmonic mean for two groups is $\tilde{n} = 2n_1 n_2/(n_1 + n_2)$. Thus, for this case we have $\tilde{n} = 2(22)(32)/54 = 26.07$. Now, to get D^2 we first obtain T^2:

$$T^2 = (N - 2)pF/(N - p - 1) = 52(5)1.61/48 = 8.72$$

Now, $D^2 = N\, T^2/n_1 n_2 = 54(8.72)/22(32) = .67$. Using $n = 25$ and $D^2 = .64$ to enter Table 4.7, we see that power = .42. Actually, power is slightly greater than .42 because $n = 26$ and $D^2 = .67$, but it would still not reach even .50. Thus, given this effect size, power is definitely inadequate here, but a sample medium multivariate effect size was obtained that may be practically important.

4.11.2 *A Priori* Estimation of Sample Size

Suppose that from a pilot study or from a previous study that used the same kind of participants, an investigator had obtained the following pooled within-group covariance matrix for three variables:

$$\mathbf{S} = \begin{bmatrix} 16 & 6 & 1.6 \\ 6 & 9 & .9 \\ 1.6 & .9 & 1 \end{bmatrix}$$

Recall that the elements on the main diagonal of $\mathbf{S}$ are the variances for the variables: 16 is the variance for variable 1, and so on.

To complete the estimate of D^2 the difference in the mean vectors must be estimated; this amounts to estimating the mean difference expected for each variable. Suppose that on the basis of previous literature, the investigator hypothesizes that the mean differences on variables 1 and 2 will be 2 and 1.5. Thus, they will correspond to moderate effect sizes of .5 standard deviations. Why? (Use the variances on the within-group covariance matrix to check this.) The investigator further expects the mean difference on variable 3 will be .2, that is, .2 of a standard deviation, or a small effect size. What is the minimum number of participants needed, at $\alpha = .10$, to have a power of .70 for the test of the multivariate null hypothesis?

To answer this question we first need to estimate D^2:

$$\hat{D}^2 = (2, 1.5, .2) \begin{bmatrix} .0917 & -.0511 & -.1008 \\ -.0511 & .1505 & -.0538 \\ -.1008 & -.0538 & 1.2100 \end{bmatrix} \begin{pmatrix} 2.0 \\ 1.5 \\ .2 \end{pmatrix} = .3347$$

The middle matrix is the inverse of **S**. Because moderate and small univariate effect sizes produced this $\hat{D}^2$ value .3347, such a numerical value for D^2 would probably occur fairly frequently in social science research. To determine the n required for power = .70, we enter Table 4.7 for three variables and use the values in parentheses. For $n = 50$ and three variables, note that power = .65 for $D^2 = .25$ and power = .98 for $D^2 = .64$. Therefore, we have

$$\text{Power}(D^2 = .33) = \text{Power}(D^2 = .25) + [.08/.39](.33) = .72.$$

4.12 SUMMARY

In this chapter we have considered the statistical analysis of two groups on several dependent variables simultaneously. Among the reasons for preferring a MANOVA over separate univariate analyses were (1) MANOVA takes into account important information, that is, the intercorrelations among the variables, (2) MANOVA keeps the overall α level under control, and (3) MANOVA has greater sensitivity for detecting differences in certain situations. It was shown how the multivariate test (Hotelling's T^2) arises naturally from the univariate t by replacing the means with mean vectors and by replacing the pooled within-variance by the covariance matrix. An example indicated the numerical details associated with calculating T^2.

Three *post hoc* procedures for determining which of the variables contributed to the overall multivariate significance were considered. The Roy–Bose simultaneous confidence interval approach cannot be recommended because it is extremely conservative, and hence has poor power for detecting differences. The Bonferroni approach of testing each variable at the α/p level of significance is generally recommended, especially if the number of variables is not too large. Another approach we considered that does not use any alpha adjustment for the *post hoc* tests is potentially problematic because the overall type I error rate can become unacceptably high as the number of dependent variables increases. As such, we recommend this unadjusted t test procedure for analysis having two or three dependent variables. This relatively small number of variables in the analysis may arise in designs where you have collected just that number of outcomes or when you have a larger set of outcomes but where you have firm support for expecting group mean differences for two or three dependent variables.

Group membership for a sample problem was dummy coded, and it was run as a regression analysis. This yielded the same multivariate and univariate results as when the problem was run as a traditional MANOVA. This was done to show that MANOVA is a special case of regression analysis, that is, of the general linear model. In this context, we also discussed the effect size measure R^2 (equivalent to eta square and partial eta square for the one-factor design). We advised against concluding that a result is of little practical importance simply because the R^2 value is small (say .10). Several reasons were given for this, one of the most important being context. Thus, 10% variance accounted for in some research areas may indeed be of practical importance.

Power analysis was considered in some detail. It was noted that small and medium effect sizes are *very common* in social science research. The Mahalanobis D^2 was presented as a two-group multivariate effect size measure, with the following guidelines for interpretation: $D^2 = .25$ small effect, $D^2 = .50$ medium effect, and $D^2 > 1$ large effect. We showed how you can compute D^2 using data from a previous study to determine *a priori* the sample size needed for a two-group MANOVA, using a table from Stevens (1980).

4.13 EXERCISES

1. Which of the following are multivariate studies, that is, involve several correlated dependent variables?

    (a) An investigator classifies high school freshmen by sex, socioeconomic status, and teaching method, and then compares them on total test score on the Lankton algebra test.

    (b) A treatment and control group are compared on measures of reading speed and reading comprehension.

    (c) An investigator is predicting success on the job from high school GPA and a battery of personality variables.

2. An investigator has a 50-item scale and wishes to compare two groups of participants on the item scores. He has heard about MANOVA, and realizes that the items will be correlated. Therefore, he decides to do a two-group MANOVA with each item serving as a dependent variable. The scale is administered to 45 participants, and the investigator attempts to conduct the analysis. However, the computer software aborts the analysis. Why? What might the investigator consider doing before running the analysis?

3. Suppose you come across a journal article where the investigators have a three-way design and five correlated dependent variables. They report the results in five tables, having done a univariate analysis on each of the five variables. They find four significant results at the .05 level. Would you be impressed with these results? Why or why not? Would you have more confidence if the significant results had been hypothesized *a priori*? What else could they have done that would have given you more confidence in their significant results?

4. Consider the following data for a two-group, two-dependent-variable problem:

T_1		T_2	
y_1	y_2	y_1	y_2
1	9	4	8
2	3	5	6
3	4	6	7
5	4		
2	5		

(a) Compute **W**, the pooled within-SSCP matrix.

(b) Find the pooled within-covariance matrix, and indicate what each of the elements in the matrix represents.

(c) Find Hotelling's T^2.

(d) What is the multivariate null hypothesis in symbolic form?

(e) Test the null hypothesis at the .05 level. What is your decision?

5. An investigator has an estimate of $D^2 = .61$ from a previous study that used the same four dependent variables on a similar group of participants. How many subjects per group are needed to have power = .70 at = .10?

6. From a pilot study, a researcher has the following pooled within-covariance matrix for two variables:

$$\mathbf{S} = \begin{bmatrix} 8.6 & 10.4 \\ 10.4 & 21.3 \end{bmatrix}$$

From previous research a moderate effect size of .5 standard deviations on variable 1 and a small effect size of 1/3 standard deviations on variable 2 are anticipated. For the researcher's main study, how many participants per group are needed for power = .70 at the .05 level? At the .10 level?

7. Ambrose (1985) compared elementary school children who received instruction on the clarinet via programmed instruction (experimental group) versus those who received instruction via traditional classroom instruction on the following six performance aspects: interpretation (interp), tone, rhythm, intonation (inton), tempo (tem), and articulation (artic). The data, representing the average of two judges' ratings, are listed here, with GPID = 1 referring to the experimental group and GPID = 2 referring to the control group:

(a) Run the two-group MANOVA on these data using SAS or SPSS. Is the multivariate null hypothesis rejected at the .05 level?

(b) What is the value of the Mahalanobis D^2? How would you characterize the magnitude of this effect size? Given this, is it surprising that the null hypothesis was rejected?

(c) Setting overall $\alpha = .05$ and using the Bonferroni inequality approach, which of the individual variables are significant, and hence contributing to the overall multivariate significance?

GP	INT	TONE	RHY	INTON	TEM	ARTIC
1	4.2	4.1	3.2	4.2	2.8	3.5
1	4.1	4.1	3.7	3.9	3.1	3.2
1	4.9	4.7	4.7	5.0	2.9	4.5
1	4.4	4.1	4.1	3.5	2.8	4.0
1	3.7	2.0	2.4	3.4	2.8	2.3
1	3.9	3.2	2.7	3.1	2.7	3.6
1	3.8	3.5	3.4	4.0	2.7	3.2
1	4.2	4.1	4.1	4.2	3.7	2.8
1	3.6	3.8	4.2	3.4	4.2	3.0
1	2.6	3.2	1.9	3.5	3.7	3.1
1	3.0	2.5	2.9	3.2	3.3	3.1
1	2.9	3.3	3.5	3.1	3.6	3.4
2	2.1	1.8	1.7	1.7	2.8	1.5
2	4.8	4.0	3.5	1.8	3.1	2.2
2	4.2	2.9	4.0	1.8	3.1	2.2
2	3.7	1.9	1.7	1.6	3.1	1.6
2	3.7	2.1	2.2	3.1	2.8	1.7
2	3.8	2.1	3.0	3.3	3.0	1.7
2	2.1	2.0	2.2	1.8	2.6	1.5
2	2.2	1.9	2.2	3.4	4.2	2.7
2	3.3	3.6	2.3	4.3	4.0	3.8
2	2.6	1.5	1.3	2.5	3.5	1.9
2	2.5	1.7	1.7	2.8	3.3	3.1

8. We consider the Pope, Lehrer, and Stevens (1980) data. Children in kindergarten were measured on various instruments to determine whether they could be classified as low risk or high risk with respect to having reading problems later on in school. The variables considered are word identification (WI), word comprehension (WC), and passage comprehension (PC).

	GP	WI	WC	PC
1	1.00	5.80	9.70	8.90
2	1.00	10.60	10.90	11.00
3	1.00	8.60	7.20	8.70
4	1.00	4.80	4.60	6.20
5	1.00	8.30	10.60	7.80
6	1.00	4.60	3.30	4.70
7	1.00	4.80	3.70	6.40
8	1.00	6.70	6.00	7.20
9	1.00	6.90	9.70	7.20
10	1.00	5.60	4.10	4.30
11	1.00	4.80	3.80	5.30

	GP	WI	WC	PC
12	1.00	2.90	3.70	4.20
13	2.00	2.40	2.10	2.40
14	2.00	3.50	1.80	3.90
15	2.00	6.70	3.60	5.90
16	2.00	5.30	3.30	6.10
17	2.00	5.20	4.10	6.40
18	2.00	3.20	2.70	4.00
19	2.00	4.50	4.90	5.70
20	2.00	3.90	4.70	4.70
21	2.00	4.00	3.60	2.90
22	2.00	5.70	5.50	6.20
23	2.00	2.40	2.90	3.20
24	2.00	2.70	2.60	4.10

(a) Run the two group MANOVA on computer software. Is the multivariate test significant at the .05 level?

(b) Are any of the univariate Fs significant at the .05 level?

9. The correlations among the dependent variables are embedded in the covariance matrix **S**. Why is this true?

REFERENCES

Ambrose, A. (1985). *The development and experimental application of programmed materials for teaching clarinet performance skills in college woodwind techniques courses.* Unpublished doctoral dissertation, University of Cincinnati, OH.

Becker, B. (1987). Applying tests of combined significance in meta-analysis. *Psychological Bulletin, 102*, 164–171.

Bock, R. D. (1975). *Multivariate statistical methods in behavioral research.* New York, NY: McGraw-Hill.

Cohen, J. (1968). Multiple regression as a general data-analytic system. *Psychological Bulletin, 70*, 426–443.

Cohen, J. (1988). *Statistical power analysis for the social sciences* (2nd ed.). Hillsdale, NJ: Lawrence Erlbaum Associates.

Cohen, J., & Cohen, P. (1975). *Applied multiple regression/correlation analysis for the behavioral sciences.* Hillsdale, NJ: Lawrence Erlbaum.

Cronbach, L., & Snow, R. (1977). *Aptitudes and instructional methods: A handbook for research on interactions.* New York, NY: Irvington.

Glass, G. C., & Hopkins, K. (1984). *Statistical methods in education and psychology.* Englewood Cliffs, NJ: Prentice-Hall.

Grissom, R. J., & Kim, J. J. (2012). *Effect sizes for research: Univariate and multivariate applications* (2nd ed.). New York, NY: Routledge.

Hays, W. L. (1981). *Statistics* (3rd ed.). New York, NY: Holt, Rinehart & Winston.

Hotelling, H. (1931). The generalization of student's ratio. *Annals of Mathematical Statistics, 2*(3), 360–378.

Hummel, T. J., & Sligo, J. (1971). Empirical comparison of univariate and multivariate analysis of variance procedures. *Psychological Bulletin, 76,* 49–57.

Johnson, N., & Wichern, D. (1982). *Applied multivariate statistical analysis.* Englewood Cliffs, NJ: Prentice Hall.

Light, R., & Pillemer, D. (1984). *Summing up: The science of reviewing research.* Cambridge, MA: Harvard University Press.

Light, R., Singer, J., & Willett, J. (1990). *By design.* Cambridge, MA: Harvard University Press.

Morrison, D. F. (1976). *Multivariate statistical methods.* New York, NY: McGraw-Hill.

O'Grady, K. (1982). Measures of explained variation: Cautions and limitations. *Psychological Bulletin, 92,* 766–777.

Pope, J., Lehrer, B., & Stevens, J. P. (1980). A multiphasic reading screening procedure. *Journal of Learning Disabilities, 13,* 98–102.

Rosenthal, R., & Rosnow, R. (1984). *Essentials of behavioral research.* New York, NY: McGraw-Hill.

Stevens, J. P. (1980). Power of the multivariate analysis of variance tests. *Psychological Bulletin, 88,* 728–737.

Timm, N. H. (1975). Multivariate analysis with applications in education and psychology. Monterey, CA: Brooks-Cole.

Welkowitz, J., Ewen, R. B., & Cohen, J. (1982). *Introductory statistics for the behavioral sciences.* New York: Academic Press.

Chapter 5

K-GROUP MANOVA
A Priori and *Post Hoc* Procedures

5.1 INTRODUCTION

In this chapter we consider the case where more than two groups of participants are being compared on several dependent variables simultaneously. We first briefly show how the MANOVA can be done within the regression model by dummy-coding group membership for a small sample problem and using it as a nominal predictor. In doing this, we build on the multivariate regression analysis of two-group MANOVA that was presented in the last chapter. (Note that section 5.2 can be skipped if you prefer a traditional presentation of MANOVA). Then we consider traditional multivariate analysis of variance, or MANOVA, introducing the most familiar multivariate test statistic Wilks' Λ. Two fairly similar post hoc procedures for examining group differences for the dependent variables are discussed next. Each procedure employs univariate ANOVAs for each outcome and applies the Tukey procedure for pairwise comparisons. The procedures differ in that one provides for more strict type I error control and better confidence interval coverage while the other seeks to strike a balance between type I error and power. This latter approach is most suitable for designs having a small number of outcomes and groups (i.e., 2 or 3).

Next, we consider a different approach to the *k*-group problem, that of using planned comparisons rather than an omnibus *F* test. Hays (1981) gave an excellent discussion of this approach for univariate ANOVA. Our discussion of multivariate planned comparisons is extensive and is made quite concrete through the use of several examples, including two studies from the literature. The setup of multivariate contrasts on SPSS MANOVA is illustrated and selected output is discussed.

We then consider the important problem of a priori determination of sample size for 3-, 4-, 5-, and 6-group MANOVA for the number of dependent variables ranging from 2 to 15, using extensive tables developed by Lauter (1978). Finally, the chapter concludes with a discussion of some considerations that mitigate generally against the use of a large number of criterion variables in MANOVA.

5.2 MULTIVARIATE REGRESSION ANALYSIS FOR A SAMPLE PROBLEM

In the previous chapter we indicated how analysis of variance can be incorporated within the regression model by dummy-coding group membership and using it as a nominal predictor. For the two-group case, just one dummy variable (predictor) was needed, which took on a value of 1 for participants in group 1 and 0 for the participants in the other group. For our three-group example, we need two dummy variables (predictors) to identify group membership. The first dummy variable (x_1) is 1 for all subjects in Group 1 and 0 for all other subjects. The other dummy variable (x_2) is 1 for all subjects in Group 2 and 0 for all other subjects. A third dummy variable is *not* needed because the participants in Group 3 are identified by 0's on x_1 and x_2, that is, not in Group 1 or Group 2. Therefore, by default, those participants must be in Group 3. In general, for *k* groups, the number of dummy variables needed is ($k-1$), corresponding to the between degrees of freedom.

The data for our two-dependent-variable, three-group problem are presented here:

y1	y2	x_1	x_2	
2	3	1	0	Group 1
3	4	1	0	
5	4	1	0	
2	5	1	0	
4	8	0	1	Group 2
5	6	0	1	
6	7	0	1	
7	6	0	0	Group 3
8	7	0	0	
10	8	0	0	
9	5	0	0	
7	6	0	0	

Thus, cast in a regression mold, we are relating two sets of variables, the two dependent variables, and the two predictors (dummy variables). The regression analysis will then determine how much of the variance on the dependent variables is accounted for by the predictors, that is, by group membership.

In Table 5.1 we present the control lines for running the sample problem as a multivariate regression on SPSS MANOVA, and the lines for running the problem as a traditional MANOVA (using GLM). By running both analyses, you can verify that the multivariate *F*s for the regression analysis are identical to those obtained from the MANOVA run.

■ **Table 5.1: SPSS Syntax for Running Sample Problem as Multivariate Regression and as MANOVA**

```
        TITLE 'THREE GROUP MANOVA RUN AS MULTIVARIATE REGRESSION'.
        DATA LIST FREE/x1 x2 y1 y2.
        BEGIN DATA.
  (1)   1 0 2 3          1 0 3 4
        1 0 5 4          1 0 2 5
        0 1 4 8          0 1 5 6        0 1 6 7
        0 0 7 6          0 0 8 7
        0 0 10 8         0 0 9 5        0 0 7 6
        END DATA.
        LIST.
        MANOVA y1 y2 WITH x1 x2.
        TITLE 'MANOVA RUN ON SAMPLE PROBLEM'.
        DATA LIST FREE/gps y1 y2.
  (2)   BEGIN DATA.
        1 2 3            1 3 4
        1 5 4            1 2 5
        2 4 8            2 5 6          2 6 7
        3 7 6            3 8 7          3 10 8
        3 9 5            3 7 6
        END DATA.
        LIST.
        GLM y1 y2 BY gps
        /PRINT=DESCRIPTIVE
        /DESIGN= gps.
```

(1) The first two columns of data are for the dummy variables x1 and x2, which identify group membership (cf. the data display in section 5.2).

(2) The first column of data identifies group membership—again compare the data display in section 5.2.

5.3 TRADITIONAL MULTIVARIATE ANALYSIS OF VARIANCE

In the k-group MANOVA case we are comparing the groups on p dependent variables simultaneously. For the univariate case, the null hypothesis is:

$$H_0 : \mu_1 = \mu_2 = \cdots = \mu k \text{ (population means are equal)}$$

whereas for MANOVA the null hypothesis is

$$H_0 : \boldsymbol{\mu}_1 = \boldsymbol{\mu}_2 = \cdots = \boldsymbol{\mu}k \text{ (population mean vectors are equal)}$$

For univariate analysis of variance the F statistic ($F = MS_b / MS_w$) is used for testing the tenability of H_0. What statistic do we use for testing the multivariate null hypothesis? There is no single answer, as several test statistics are available. The one that is most widely known is Wilks' Λ, where Λ is given by:

$$\Lambda = \frac{|\mathbf{W}|}{|\mathbf{T}|} = \frac{|\mathbf{W}|}{|\mathbf{B} + \mathbf{W}|}, \text{ where } 0 \leq \Lambda \leq 1$$

$|\mathbf{W}|$ and $|\mathbf{T}|$ are the determinants of the within-group and total sum of squares and cross-products matrices. $\mathbf{W}$ has already been defined for the two-group case, where the observations in each group are deviated about the individual group means. Thus $\mathbf{W}$ is a measure of within-group variability and is a multivariate generalization of the univariate sum of squares within (SS_w). In $\mathbf{T}$ the observations in each group are deviated about the *grand* mean for each variable. $\mathbf{B}$ is the between-group sum of squares and cross-products matrix, and is the multivariate generalization of the univariate sum of squares between (SS_b). Thus, $\mathbf{B}$ is a measure of how differential the effect of treatments has been on a set of dependent variables. We define the elements of $\mathbf{B}$ shortly. We need matrices to define within, between, and total variability in the multivariate case because there is variability on each variable (these variabilities will appear on the main diagonals of the $\mathbf{W}$, $\mathbf{B}$, and $\mathbf{T}$ matrices) as well as covariability for each pair of variables (these will be the off diagonal elements of the matrices).

Because Wilks' Λ is defined in terms of the determinants of $\mathbf{W}$ and $\mathbf{T}$, it is important to recall from the matrix algebra chapter (Chapter 2) that the determinant of a covariance matrix is called the *generalized variance* for a set of variables. Now, because $\mathbf{W}$ and $\mathbf{T}$ differ from their corresponding covariance matrices only by a scalar, we can think of $|\mathbf{W}|$ and $|\mathbf{T}|$ in the same basic way. Thus, the determinant neatly characterizes within and total variability in terms of *single* numbers. It may also be helpful for you to recall that the generalized variance may be thought of as the variation in a set of outcomes that is unique to the set, that is, the variance that is not shared by the variables in the set. Also, for one variable, variance indicates how much scatter there is about the mean on a line, that is, in one dimension. For two variables, the scores for each participant on the variables defines a point in the plane, and thus generalized variance indicates how much the points (participants) scatter in the plane in two dimensions. For three variables, the scores for the participants define points in three-dimensional space, and hence generalized variance shows how much the subjects scatter (vary) in three dimensions. An excellent extended discussion of generalized variance for the more mathematically inclined is provided in Johnson and Wichern (1982, pp. 103–112).

For univariate ANOVA you may recall that

$$SS_t = SS_b + SS_w,$$

where SS_t is the total sum of squares.

For MANOVA the corresponding matrix analogue holds:

$$\mathbf{\mathit{T} = B + W}$$

Total SSCP = Between SSCP + Within SSCP
Matrix   Matrix   Matrix

Notice that Wilks' Λ is an inverse criterion: the smaller the value of Λ, the more evidence for treatment effects (between-group association). If there were no treatment effect, then $\mathbf{B} = 0$ and $\Lambda = \dfrac{|\mathbf{W}|}{|0 + \mathbf{W}|} = 1$, whereas if $\mathbf{B}$ were very large relative to $\mathbf{W}$ then Λ would approach 0.

The sampling distribution of Λ is somewhat complicated, and generally an approximation is necessary. Two approximations are available: (1) Bartlett's χ^2 and (2) Rao's F. Bartlett's χ^2 is given by:

$$\chi^2 = -[(N - 1) - .5(p + k)] \ln \Lambda \; p(k - 1)df,$$

where N is total sample size, p is the number of dependent variables, and k is the number of groups. Bartlett's χ^2 is a good approximation for moderate to large sample sizes. For smaller sample size, Rao's F is a better approximation (Lohnes, 1961), although generally the two statistics will lead to the same decision on H_0. The multivariate F given on SPSS is the Rao F. The formula for Rao's F is complicated and is presented later. We point out now, however, that the degrees of freedom for error with Rao's F can be *noninteger*, so that you should not be alarmed if this happens on the computer printout.

As alluded to earlier, there are certain values of p and k for which a function of Λ is exactly distributed as an F ratio (for example, $k = 2$ or 3 and any p; see Tatsuoka, 1971, p. 89).

5.4 MULTIVARIATE ANALYSIS OF VARIANCE FOR SAMPLE DATA

We now consider the MANOVA of the data given earlier. For convenience, we present the data again here, with the means for the participants on the two dependent variables in each group:

G_1		G_2		G_3	
y_1	y_2	y_1	y_2	y_1	y_2
2	3	4	8	7	6
3	4	5	6	8	7
5	4	6	7	10	8
2	5	$\overline{y}_{12} = 5$	$\overline{y}_{22} = 7$	9	5
$\overline{y}_{11} = 3$	$\overline{y}_{21} = 4$			7	6
				$\overline{y}_{13} = 8.2$	$\overline{y}_{23} = 6.4$

We wish to test the multivariate null hypothesis with the χ^2 approximation for Wilks' Λ. Recall that $\Lambda = |\mathbf{W}| / |\mathbf{T}|$, so that $\mathbf{W}$ and $\mathbf{T}$ are needed. $\mathbf{W}$ is the pooled estimate of within variability on the set of variables, that is, our multivariate error term.

5.4.1 Calculation of W

Calculation of **W** proceeds in exactly the same way as we obtained **W** for Hotelling's T^2 in the two-group MANOVA case in Chapter 4. That is, we determine how much the participants' scores vary on the dependent variables within *each* group, and then pool (add) these together. Symbolically, then,

$$\mathbf{W} = \mathbf{W}_1 + \mathbf{W}_2 + \mathbf{W}_3,$$

where $\mathbf{W}_1$, $\mathbf{W}_2$, and $\mathbf{W}_3$ are the within sums of squares and cross-products matrices for Groups 1, 2, and 3. As in Chapter 4, we denote the elements of $\mathbf{W}_1$ by ss_1 and ss_2 (measuring the variability on the variables within Group 1) and ss_{12} (measuring the covariability of the variables in Group 1).

$$\mathbf{W}_1 = \begin{bmatrix} ss_1 & ss_{12} \\ ss_{21} & ss_2 \end{bmatrix}$$

Then, for Group 1, we have

$$ss_1 = \sum_{j=1}^{4} (y_{1(j)} - \bar{y}_{11})^2$$
$$= (2-3)^2 + (3-3)^2 + (5-3)^2 + (2-3)^2 = 6$$
$$ss_2 = \sum_{j=1}^{4} (y_{2(j)} - \bar{y}_{21})^2$$
$$= (3-4)^2 + (4-4)^2 + (4-4)^2 + (5-4)^2 = 2$$
$$ss_{12} = ss_{21} \sum_{j=1}^{4} (y_{1(j)} - \bar{y}_{11})(y_{2(j)} - \bar{y}_{21})$$
$$= (2-3)(3-4) + (3-3)(4-4) + (5-3)(4-4) + (2-3)(5-4) = 0$$

Thus, the matrix that measures within variability on the two variables in Group 1 is given by:

$$\mathbf{W}_1 = \begin{bmatrix} 6 & 0 \\ 0 & 2 \end{bmatrix}$$

In exactly the same way the within SSCP matrices for groups 2 and 3 can be shown to be:

$$\mathbf{W}_2 = \begin{bmatrix} 2 & -1 \\ -1 & 2 \end{bmatrix} \quad \mathbf{W}_3 = \begin{bmatrix} 6.8 & 2.6 \\ 2.6 & 5.2 \end{bmatrix}$$

Therefore, the pooled estimate of within variability on the set of variables is given by:

$$\mathbf{W} = \mathbf{W}_1 + \mathbf{W}_2 + \mathbf{W}_3 = \begin{bmatrix} 14.8 & 1.6 \\ 1.6 & 9.2 \end{bmatrix}$$

5.4.2 Calculation of T

Recall, from earlier in this chapter, that $\mathbf{T} = \mathbf{B} + \mathbf{W}$. We find the $\mathbf{B}$ (between) matrix, and then obtain the elements of $\mathbf{T}$ by adding the elements of $\mathbf{B}$ to the elements of $\mathbf{W}$.

The diagonal elements of $\mathbf{B}$ are defined as follows:

$$b_{ii} = \sum_{j=1}^{k} n_j (\bar{y}_{ij} - \bar{\bar{y}}_i)^2,$$

where n_j is the number of subjects in group j, $\bar{y}_{ij}$ is the mean for variable i in group j, and $\bar{\bar{y}}_i$ is the grand mean for variable i. Notice that for any particular variable, say variable 1, b_{11} is simply the between-group sum of squares for a univariate analysis of variance on that variable.

The off-diagonal elements of $\mathbf{B}$ are defined as follows:

$$b_{mi} = b_{im} \sum_{j=1}^{k} n_j \left(\bar{y}_{ij} - \bar{\bar{y}}_i\right)\left(\bar{y}_{mj} - \bar{\bar{y}}_m\right)$$

To find the elements of $\mathbf{B}$ we need the grand means on the two variables. These are obtained by simply adding up all the scores on each variable and then dividing by the total number of scores. Thus $\bar{\bar{y}}_1 = 68 / 12 = 5.67$, and $\bar{\bar{y}}_2 = 69 / 12 = 5.75$.

Now we find the elements of the $\mathbf{B}$ (between) matrix:

$$b_{11} = \sum_{j=1}^{3} n_j (\bar{y}_{1j} - \bar{\bar{y}}_1)^2, \text{ where } \bar{y}_{1j} \text{ is the mean of variable 1 in group } j.$$

$$= 4(3 - 5.67)^2 + 3(5 - 5.67)^2 + 5(8.2 - 5.67)^2 = 61.87$$

$$b_{22} = \sum_{j=1}^{3} n_j (\bar{y}_{2j} - \bar{\bar{y}}_2)^2$$

$$= 4(4 - 5.75)^2 + 3(7 - 5.75)^2 + 5(6.4 - 5.75)^2 = 19.05$$

$$b_{12} = b_{21} \sum_{j=1}^{3} n_j \left(\bar{y}_{1j} - \bar{\bar{y}}_1\right)\left(\bar{y}_{2j} - \bar{\bar{y}}_2\right)$$

$$= 4(3 - 5.67)(4 - 5.75) + 3(5 - 5.67)(7 - 5.75) + 5(8.2 - 5.67)(6.4 - 5.75) = 24.4$$

Therefore, the **B** matrix is

$$B = \begin{bmatrix} 61.87 & 24.40 \\ 24.40 & 19.05 \end{bmatrix}$$

and the diagonal elements 61.87 and 19.05 represent the between-group sum of squares that would be obtained if separate univariate analyses had been done on variables 1 and 2.

Because $T = B + W$, we have

$$T = \begin{bmatrix} 61.87 & 24.40 \\ 24.40 & 19.05 \end{bmatrix} + \begin{bmatrix} 14.80 & 1.6 \\ 1.6 & 9.2 \end{bmatrix} = \begin{bmatrix} 76.72 & 26.00 \\ 26.00 & 28.25 \end{bmatrix}$$

5.4.3 Calculation of Wilks Λ and the Chi-Square Approximation

Now we can obtain Wilks' Λ:

$$\Lambda = \frac{|W|}{|T|} = \frac{\begin{vmatrix} 14.8 & 1.6 \\ 1.6 & 9.2 \end{vmatrix}}{\begin{vmatrix} 76.72 & 26 \\ 26 & 28.25 \end{vmatrix}} = \frac{14.8(9.2) - 1.6^2}{76.72(28.25) - 26^2} = .0897$$

Finally, we can compute the chi-square test statistic:

$\chi^2 = -[(N-1) - .5(p+k)] \ln \Lambda$, with $p\,(k-1)$ df
$\chi^2 = -[(12-1) - .5(2+3)] \ln (.0897)$
$\chi^2 = -8.5(-2.4116) = 20.4987$, with $2(3-1) = 4$ df

The multivariate null hypothesis here is:

$$\begin{pmatrix} \mu_{11} \\ \mu_{21} \end{pmatrix} = \begin{pmatrix} \mu_{12} \\ \mu_{22} \end{pmatrix} = \begin{pmatrix} \mu_{13} \\ \mu_{23} \end{pmatrix}$$

That is, that the population means in the three groups on variable 1 are equal, and similarly that the population means on variable 2 are equal. Because the critical value at .05 is 9.49, we reject the multivariate null hypothesis and conclude that the three groups differ overall on the set of two variables. Table 5.2 gives the multivariate *F*s and the univariate *F*s from the SPSS run on the sample problem and presents the formula for Rao's *F* approximation and also relates some of the output from the univariate *F*s to the **B** and **W** matrices that we computed. After overall multivariate significance is attained, one often would like to find out which of the outcome variables differed across groups. When such a difference is found, we would then like to describe how the groups differed on the given variable. This is considered next.

■ Table 5.2: Multivariate *F*s and Univariate *F*s for Sample Problem From SPSS MANOVA

Multivariate Tests

Effect		Value	F	Hypothesis df	Error df	Sig.
gps	Pillai's Trace	1.302	8.390	4.000	18.000	.001
	Wilks' Lambda	.090	9.358	4.000	16.000	.000
	Hotelling's Trace	5.786	10.126	4.000	14.000	.000
	Roy's Largest Root	4.894	22.024	2.000	9.000	.000

$$\frac{1-\Lambda^{1/s}}{\Lambda^{1/s}}\frac{ms-p(k-1)/2+1}{p(k-1)}, \text{where } m=N-1-(p-k)/2 \text{ and}$$

$$s=\sqrt{\frac{p^2(k-1)^2-4}{p^2+(k-1)^2-5}}$$

is approximately distributed as F with $p(k-1)$ and $ms-p(k-1)/2+1$ degrees of freedom. Here Wilks' $\Lambda=.08967$, $p=2$, $k=3$, and $N=12$. Thus, we have $m=12-1-(2+3)/2=8.5$ and

$$s=\sqrt{\{4(3-1)^2-4\}/\{4+(2)^2-5\}}=\sqrt{12/3}=2,$$

and

$$F=\frac{1-\sqrt{.08967}}{\sqrt{.08967}}\cdot\frac{8.5(2)-2(2)/2+1}{2(3-1)}=\frac{1-.29945}{.29945}\cdot\frac{16}{4}=9.357$$

as given on the printout, within rounding. The pair of degrees of freedom is $p(k-1)=2(3-1)=4$ and $ms-p(k-1)/2+1=8.5(2)-2(3-1)/2+1=16$.

Tests of Between-Subjects Effects

Source	Dependent Variable	Type III Sum of Squares	df	Mean Square	F	Sig.
gps	y1	(1) 61.867	2	30.933	18.811	.001
	y2	19.050	2	9.525	9.318	.006
Error	y1	(2) 14.800	9	1.644		
	y2	9.200	9	1.022		

(1) These are the diagonal elements of the *B* (between) matrix we computed in the example:

$$\mathbf{B}=\begin{bmatrix} 61.87 & 24.40 \\ 24.40 & 19.05 \end{bmatrix}$$

(2) Recall that the pooled within matrix computed in the example was

$$\mathbf{W}=\begin{bmatrix} 14.8 & 1.6 \\ 1.6 & 9.2 \end{bmatrix}$$

(Continued)

▨ **Table 5.2: (Continued)**

and these are the diagonal elements of **W**. The univariate F ratios are formed from the elements on the main diagonals of **B** and **W**. Dividing the elements of **B** by hypothesis degrees of freedom gives the hypothesis mean squares, while dividing the elements of **W** by error degrees of freedom gives the error mean squares. Then, dividing hypothesis mean squares by error mean squares yields the F ratios. Thus, for $Y1$ we have

$$F = \frac{30.933}{1.644} = 18.81.$$

5.5 *POST HOC* PROCEDURES

In general, when the multivariate null hypothesis is rejected, several follow-up procedures can be used. By far, the most commonly used method in practice is to conduct a series of one-way ANOVAs for each outcome to identify whether group differences are present for a given dependent variable. This analysis implies that you are interested in identifying if there are group differences present for *each* of the correlated but distinct outcomes. The purpose of using the Wilks' Λ prior to conducting these univariate tests is to provide for accurate type I error control. Note that if one were interested in learning whether linear combinations of dependent variables (instead of individual dependent variables) distinguish groups, discriminant analysis (see Chapter 10) would be used instead of these procedures.

In addition, another procedure that may be used following rejection of the overall multivariate null hypothesis is step down analysis. This analysis requires that you establish an *a priori* ordering of the dependent variables (from most important to least) based on theory, empirical evidence, and/or reasoning. In many investigations, this may be difficult to do, and study results depend on this ordering. As such, it is difficult to find applications of this procedure in the literature. Previous editions of this text contained a chapter on step down analysis. However, given its limited utility, this chapter has been removed from the text, although it is available on the web.

Another analysis procedure that may be used when the focus is on individual dependent variables (and not linear combinations) is multivariate multilevel modeling (MVMM). This technique is covered in Chapter 14, which includes a discussion of the benefits of this procedure. Most relevant for the follow-up procedures are that MVMM can be used to test whether group differences are the same or differ across multiple outcomes, when the outcomes are similarly scaled. Thus, instead of finding, as with the use of more traditional procedures, that an intervention impacts, for example, three outcomes, investigators may find that the effects of an intervention are stronger for some outcomes than others. In addition, this procedure offers improved treatment of missing data over the traditional approach discussed here.

The focus for the remainder of this section and the next is on the use of a series of ANOVAs as follow-up tests given a significant overall multivariate test result. There are different variations of this procedure that can be used, depending on the balance of the type I error rate and power desired, as well as confidence interval accuracy. We present two such procedures here. SAS and SPSS commands for the follow-up procedures are shown in section 5.6 as we work through an applied example. Note also that one may not wish to conduct pairwise comparisons as we do here, but instead focus on a more limited number of meaningful comparisons as suggested by theory and/or empirical work. Such planned comparisons are discussed in sections 5.7–5.11.

5.5.1 Procedure 1—ANOVAS and Tukey Comparisons With Alpha Adjustment

With this procedure, a significant multivariate test result is followed up with one-way ANOVAs for each outcome with a Bonferroni-adjusted alpha used for the univariate tests. So if there are p outcomes, the alpha used for each ANOVA is the experiment-wise nominal alpha divided by p, or a / p. You can implement this procedure by simply comparing the p value obtained for the ANOVA F test to this adjusted alpha level. For example, if the experiment-wise type I error rate were set at .05 and if 5 dependent variables were included, the alpha used for each one-way ANOVA would be .05 / 5 = .01. And, if the p value for an ANOVA F test were smaller than .01, this indicates that group differences are present for that dependent variable. If group differences are found for a given dependent variable and the design includes three or more groups, then pairwise comparisons can be made for that variable using the Tukey procedure, as described in the next section, with this same alpha level (e.g., .01 for the five dependent variable example). This generally recommended procedure then provides strict control of the experiment-wise type I error rate for all possible pairwise comparisons and also provides good confidence interval coverage. That is, with this procedure, we can be 95% confident that all intervals capture the true difference in means for the set of pairwise comparisons. While this procedure has good type I error control and confidence interval coverage, its potential weakness is statistical power, which may drop to low levels, particularly for the pairwise comparisons, especially when the number of dependent variables increases. One possibility, then, is to select a higher level than .05 (e.g., .10) for the experiment-wise error rate. In this case, with five dependent variables, the alpha level used for each of the ANOVAs is .10 / 5 or .02, with this same alpha level also used for the pairwise comparisons. Also, when the number of dependent variables and groups is small (i.e., two or perhaps three), procedure 2 can be considered.

5.5.2 Procedure 2—ANOVAS With No Alpha Adjustment and Tukey Comparisons

With this procedure, a significant overall multivariate test result is followed up with separate ANOVAs for each outcome with *no* alpha adjustment (e.g., $a = .05$). Again, if group differences are present for a given dependent variable, the Tukey procedure is used for pairwise comparisons using this same alpha level (i.e., .05). As such, this procedure relies more heavily on the use of Wilks' Λ as a protected test. That is, the one-way ANOVAs will be considered *only* if Wilks' Λ indicates that group differences are present on the set of outcomes. Given no alpha adjustment, this procedure is more powerful than the previous procedure but can provide for poor control of the experiment-wise type I error rate when the number of outcomes is greater than two or three and/or when the number of groups increase (thus increasing the number of pairwise comparisons). As such, we would generally not recommend this procedure with more than three outcomes and more than three groups. Similarly, this procedure does not maintain proper confidence interval coverage for the *entire set* of pairwise comparisons. Thus, if you wish to have, for example, 95% coverage for this entire set of comparisons or strict control of the family-wise error rate throughout the testing procedure, the procedure in section 5.5.1 should be used.

You may wonder why this procedure may work well when the number of outcomes and groups is small. In section 4.2, we mentioned that use of univariate ANOVAs with no alpha adjustment for each of several dependent variables is not a good idea because the experiment-wise type I error rate can increase to unacceptable levels. The same applies here, except that the use of Wilks' Λ provides us with some protection that is not present when we proceed directly to univariate ANOVAs. To illustrate, when the study design has just two dependent variables and two groups, the use of Wilks' Λ provides for strict control of the experiment-wise type I error rate even when no alpha adjustment is used for the univariate ANOVAs, as noted by Levin, Serlin, and Seaman (1994). Here is how this works. Given two outcomes, there are three possibilities that may be present for the univariate ANOVAs. One possibility is that there are no group differences for any of the two dependent variables. If that is the case, use of Wilks' Λ at an alpha of .05 provides for strict type I error control. That is, if we reject the multivariate null hypothesis when no group differences are present, we have made a type I error, and the expected rate of doing this is .05. So, for this case, use of the Wilks' Λ provides for proper control of the experiment-wise type I error rate.

We now consider a second possibility. That is, here, the overall multivariate null hypothesis is false and there is a group difference for just one of the outcomes. In this case, we cannot make a type I error with the use of Wilks' Λ since the multivariate null hypothesis is false. However, we can certainly make a type I error when we consider the univariate tests. In this case, with only one true null hypothesis, we can make a type I error for only one of the univariate F tests. Thus, if we use an unadjusted alpha for these tests (i.e., .05), then the probability of making a type I error in the set of univariate tests (i.e., the two separate ANOVAs) is .05. Again, the experiment-wise type I error rate is properly controlled for the univariate ANOVAs. The third possibility is that there are group differences present on each outcome. In this case, it is not possible to make a type I error for the multivariate test or the univariate F tests. Of course, even in this latter case, when you have more than two groups, making type I errors is possible for the pairwise comparisons, where some null group differences may be present. The use of the Tukey procedure, then, provides some type I error protection for the pairwise tests, but as noted, this protection generally weakens as the number of groups increases.

Thus, similar to our discussion in Chapter 4, we recommend use of this procedure for analysis involving up to three dependent variables and three groups. Note that with three dependent variables, the maximum type I error rate for the ANOVA F tests is expected to be .10. In addition, this situation, three or fewer outcomes and groups, may be encountered more frequently than you may at first think. It may come about because, in the most obvious case, your research design includes three variables with three groups. However, it is also possible that you collected data for eight outcome variables from participants in each of three groups. Suppose, though, as discussed in Chapter 4, that there is fairly solid evidence from the literature that group mean differences are expected for two or perhaps three of the variables, while the others are being tested on a heuristic basis. In this case, a separate multivariate test could be used for the variables that are expected to show a difference. If the multivariate test is significant, procedure 2, with no alpha adjustment for the univariate F tests, can be used. For the more exploratory set of variables, then, a separate significant multivariate test would be followed up by use of procedure 1, which uses the Bonferroni-adjusted F tests.

The point we are making here is that you may not wish to treat all dependent variables the same in the analysis. Substantive knowledge and previous empirical research suggesting group mean differences can and should be taken into account in the analysis. This may help you strike a reasonable balance between type I error control and power. As Keppel and Wickens (2004) state, the "heedless choice of the most stringent error correction can exact unacceptable costs in power" (p. 264). They advise that you need to be flexible when selecting a strategy to control type I error so that power is not sacrificed.

5.6 THE TUKEY PROCEDURE

As used in the procedures just mentioned, the Tukey procedure enables us to examine *all* pairwise group differences on a variable with experiment-wise error rate held in check. The studentized range statistic (which we denote by q) is used in the procedure, and the critical values for it are in Table A.4 of the statistical tables in Appendix A. If there are k groups and the total sample size is N, then any two means are declared significantly different at the .05 level if the following inequality holds:

$$\left| \bar{y}_i - \bar{y}_j \right| > q_{.05,k,N-k} \sqrt{\frac{MSW}{n}},$$

where MS_w is the error term for a one-way ANOVA, and n is the common group size. Alternatively, one could compute a standard t test for a pairwise difference but compare that t ratio to a Tukey-based critical value of $q / \sqrt{2}$, which allows for direct comparison to the t test. Equivalently, and somewhat more informatively, we can infer that population means for groups i and j (μ_i and μ_j) differ if the following confidence interval does *not* include 0:

$$\bar{y}_i - \bar{y}_j \pm q_{.05;k,N-k} \sqrt{\frac{MSW}{n}}$$

that is,

$$\bar{y}_i - \bar{y}_j - q_{.05;k,N-k}\sqrt{\frac{MSW}{n}} < \mu_i - \mu_j < \bar{y}_i - \bar{y}_j + q_{.05;k,N-k}\sqrt{\frac{MSW}{n}}$$

If the confidence interval includes 0, we conclude that the population means are not significantly different. Why? Because if the interval includes 0 that suggests 0 is a likely value for the true difference in means, which is to say it is reasonable to act as if $u_i = u_j$.

The Tukey procedure assumes that the variances are homogenous and it also assumes equal group sizes. If group sizes are unequal, even very sharply unequal, then various studies (e.g., Dunnett, 1980; Keselman, Murray, & Rogan, 1976) indicate that the procedure is still appropriate provided that *n* is replaced by the harmonic mean for each pair of groups *and* provided that the variances are homogenous. Thus, for groups *i* and *j* with sample sizes n_i and n_j, we replace *n* by

$$\frac{2}{\dfrac{1}{n_i} + \dfrac{1}{n_j}}$$

The studies cited earlier showed that under the conditions given, the type I error rate for the Tukey procedure is kept very close to the nominal alpha, and always less than nominal alpha (within .01 for alpha = .05 from the Dunnett study). Later we show how the Tukey procedure may be obtained via SAS and SPSS and also show a hand calculation for one of the confidence intervals.

Example 5.1 Using SAS and SPSS for *Post Hoc* Procedures

The selection and use of a *post hoc* procedure is illustrated with data collected by Novince (1977). She was interested in improving the social skills of college females and reducing their anxiety in heterosexual encounters. There were three groups in the study: control group, behavioral rehearsal, and a behavioral rehearsal + cognitive restructuring group. We consider the analysis on the following set of dependent variables: (1) anxiety—physiological anxiety in a series of heterosexual encounters, (2) a measure of social skills in social interactions, and (3) assertiveness.

Given the outcomes are considered to be conceptually distinct (i.e., not measures of an single underlying construct), use of MANOVA is a reasonable choice. Because we do not have strong support to expect group mean differences and wish to have strict control of the family-wise error rate, we use procedure 1. Thus, for the separate ANOVAs, we will use *a* / *p* or .05 / 3 = .0167 to test for group differences for each outcome. This corresponds to a confidence level of 1 − .0167 or 98.33. Use of this confidence level along with the Tukey procedure means that there is a 95% probability that all of the confidence intervals in the set will capture the respective true difference in means.

Table 5.3 shows the raw data and the SAS and SPSS commands needed to obtain the results of interest. Tables 5.4 and 5.5 show the results for the multivariate test (i.e.,

Table 5.3: SAS and SPSS Control Lines for MANOVA, Univariate *F* Tests, and Pairwise Comparisons Using the Tukey Procedure

SAS	SPSS

SAS

```
DATA novince;
INPUT gpid anx socskls assert @@;
LINES;
1 5 3 3   1 5 4 3   1 4 5 4
1 3 5 5   1 4 5 4   1 4 5 5
1 5 4 3   1 5 4 3   1 4 4 4
2 6 2 1   2 6 2 2   2 5 2 3
2 4 4 4   2 7 1 1   2 5 4 3
2 5 3 3   2 5 4 3   2 6 2 3
3 4 4 4   3 4 3 3   3 4 5 5
3 4 5 5   3 4 5 4   3 4 6 5
3 4 4 4   3 5 3 3   3 4 4 4
PROC PRINT;
PROC GLM;
CLASS gpid;
MODEL anx socskls assert=gpid;
MANOVA H = gpid;
(1) MEANS gpid/ ALPHA = .0167 CLDIFF TUKEY;
```

SPSS

```
TITLE 'SPSS with novince data'.
DATA LIST FREE/gpid anx socskls assert.
BEGIN DATA.
1 5 3 3   1 5 4 3   1 4 5 4
1 3 5 5   1 4 5 4   1 4 5 5
1 5 4 3   1 5 4 3   1 4 4 4
2 6 2 1   2 6 2 2   2 5 2 3
2 4 4 4   2 7 1 1   2 5 4 3
2 5 3 3   2 5 4 3   2 6 2 3
3 4 4 4   3 4 3 3   3 4 5 5
3 4 5 5   3 4 5 4   3 4 6 5
3 4 4 4   3 5 3 3   3 4 4 4
END DATA.
LIST.
GLM anx socskls assert BY gpid
(2) /POSTHOC=gpid(TUKEY)
    /PRINT=DESCRIPTIVE
(3) /CRITERIA=ALPHA(.0167)
    /DESIGN= gpid.
```

(1) CLDIFF requests confidence intervals for the pairwise comparisons, TUKEY requests use of the Tukey procedure, and ALPHA directs that these comparisons be made at the a / p or .05 / 3 = .0167 level. If desired, the pairwise comparisons for Procedure 2 can be implemented by specifying the desired alpha (e.g., .05).

(2) Requests the use of the Tukey procedure for the pairwise comparisons.

(3) The alpha used for the pairwise comparisons is a / p or .05 / 3 = .0167. If desired, the pairwise comparisons for Procedure 2 can be implemented by specifying the desired alpha (e.g., .05).

▨ **Table 5.4: SAS Output for Procedure 1**

SAS RESULTS

MANOVA Test Criteria and F Approximations for the Hypothesis of No Overall gpid Effect
H = Type III SSCP Matrix for gpid
E = Error SSCP Matrix
S=2 M=0 N=13

Statistic	Value	F Value	Num DF	Den DF	Pr> F
Wilks' Lambda	0.41825036	5.10	6	56	0.0003
Pillai's Trace	0.62208904	4.36	6	58	0.0011
Hotelling-Lawley Trace	1.29446446	5.94	6	35.61	0.0002
Roy's Greatest Root	1.21508924	11.75	3	29	<.0001

Note: F Statistic for Roy's Greatest Root is an upper bound.
Note: F Statistic for Wilks' Lambda is exact.

Dependent Variable: anx

Source	DF	Sum of Squares	Mean Square	F Value	Pr> F
Model	2	12.06060606	6.03030303	15.31	<.0001
Error	30	11.81818182	0.39393939		
Corrected Total	32	23.87878788			

Dependent Variable: socskls

Source	DF	Sum of Squares	Mean Square	F Value	Pr> F
Model	2	23.09090909	11.54545455	14.77	<.0001
Error	30	23.45454545	0.78181818		
Corrected Total	32	46.54545455			

Dependent Variable: assert

Source	DF	Sum of Squares	Mean Square	F Value	Pr> F
Model	2	14.96969697	7.48484848	11.65	0.0002
Error	30	19.27272727	0.64242424		
Corrected Total	32	34.24242424			

Wilks' Λ) and the follow-up ANOVAs for SAS and SPSS, respectively, but do not show the results for the pairwise comparisons (although the results are produced by the commands). To ease reading, we present results for the pairwise comparisons in Table 5.6.

The outputs in Tables 5.4 and 5.5 indicate that the overall multivariate null hypothesis of no group differences on all outcomes is to be rejected (Wilks' Λ = .418, F = 5.10,

■ Table 5.5: SPSS Output for Procedure 1

SPSS RESULTS[1]

Multivariate Tests[a]

Effect		Value	F	Hypothesis df	Error df	Sig.
Gpid	Pillai's Trace	.622	4.364	6.000	58.000	.001
	Wilks' Lambda	.418	5.098[b]	6.000	56.000	.000
	Hotelling's Trace	1.294	5.825	6.000	54.000	.000
	Roy's Largest Root	1.215	11.746[c]	3.000	29.000	.000

[a] Design: Intercept + gpid
[b] Exact statistic
[c] The statistic is an upper bound on F that yields a lower bound on the significance level.

Tests of Between-Subjects Effects

Source	Dependent Variable	Type III Sum of Squares	Df	Mean Square	F	Sig.
Gpid	Anx	12.061	2	6.030	15.308	.000
	Socskls	23.091	2	11.545	14.767	.000
	Assert	14.970	2	7.485	11.651	.000
Error	Anx	11.818	30	.394		
	Socskls	23.455	30	.782		
	Assert	19.273	30	.642		

[1] Non-essential rows were removed from the SPSS tables.

■ Table 5.6: Pairwise Comparisons for Each Outcome Using the Tukey Procedure

Contrast	Estimate	SE	98.33% confidence interval for the mean difference
Anxiety			
Rehearsal vs. Cognitive	0.18	0.27	−.61, .97
Rehearsal vs. Control	−1.18*	0.27	−1.97, −.39
Cognitive vs. Control	−1.36*	0.27	−2.15, −.58
Social Skills			
Rehearsal vs. Cognitive	0.09	0.38	−1.20, 1.02
Rehearsal vs. Control	1.82*	0.38	.71, 2.93
Cognitive vs. Control	1.73*	0.38	.62, 2.84
Assertiveness			
Rehearsal vs. Cognitive	− .27	0.34	−1.28, .73
Rehearsal vs. Control	1.27*	0.34	.27, 2.28
Cognitive vs. Control	1.55*	0.34	.54, 2.55

* Significant at the .0167 level using the Tukey HSD procedure.

$p < .05$). Further, inspection of the ANOVAs indicates that there are mean differences for anxiety ($F = 15.31$, $p < .0167$), social skills ($F = 14.77$, $p < .0167$), and assertiveness ($F = 11.65$, $p < .0167$). Table 5.6 indicates that at posttest each of the treatment groups had, on average, reduced anxiety compared to the control group (as the respective intervals do not include zero). Further, each of the treatment groups had greater mean social skills and assertiveness scores than the control group. The results in Table 5.6 do not suggest mean differences are present for the two treatment groups for any dependent variable (as each such interval includes zero). Note that in addition to using confidence intervals to merely indicate the presence or absence of a mean difference in the population, we can also use them to describe the size of the difference, which we do in the next section.

Example 5.2 Illustrating Hand Calculation of the Tukey-Based Confidence Interval

To illustrate numerically the Tukey procedure as well as an assessment of the importance of a group difference, we obtain a confidence interval for the anxiety (ANX) variable for the data shown in Table 5.3. In particular, we compute an interval with the Tukey procedure using the $1 - .05 / 3$ level or a 98.33% confidence interval for groups 1 (Behavioral Rehearsal) and 2 (Control). With this 98.33% confidence level, this procedure provides us with 95% confidence that all the intervals in the set will include the respective population mean difference. The sample mean difference, as shown in Table 5.6, is -1.18. Recall that the common group size in this study is $n = 11$. The MS_w, the mean square error, as shown in the outputs in Tables 5.4 and 5.5, is .394 for ANX. While Table A.4 provides critical values for this procedure, it does not do so for the 98.33rd ($1 - .0167$) percentile. Here, we simply indicate that the critical value for the studentized range statistic at $q_{.0167,3,30} = 4.16$. Thus, the confidence interval is given by

$$-1.18 - 4.16\sqrt{\frac{.394}{11}} < \mu_1 - \mu_2 < -1.18 + 4.16\sqrt{\frac{.394}{11}}$$
$$-1.97 < \mu_1 - \mu_2 < -.39.$$

Because this interval does not include 0, we conclude, as before, that the rehearsal group population mean for anxiety is different from (i.e., lower than) the control population mean. Why is the confidence interval approach more informative, as indicated earlier, than simply testing whether the means are different? Because the confidence interval not only tells us whether the means differ, but it also gives us a range of values within which the mean difference is likely contained. This tells us the precision with which we have captured the mean difference and can be used in judging the practical importance of the difference. For example, given this interval, it is reasonable to believe that the mean difference for the two groups in the population lies in the range from -1.97 to $-.39$. If an investigator had decided on some grounds that a difference of at least 1 point indicated a meaningful difference between groups, the investigator, while concluding that group means differ in the population (i.e., the interval does not include zero), would not be confident that an *important* difference is present (because the entire interval does not exceed a magnitude of 1).

5.7 PLANNED COMPARISONS

One approach to the analysis of data is to first demonstrate overall significance, and then follow this up to assess the subsources of variation (i.e., which dependent variables have group differences). Two procedures using ANOVAs and pairwise comparisons have been presented. That approach is appropriate in exploratory studies where the investigator first has to establish that an effect exists. However, in many instances, there is more of an empirical or theoretical base and the investigator is conducting a confirmatory study. Here the existence of an effect can be taken for granted, and the investigator has specific questions he or she wishes to ask of the data. Thus, rather than examining all 10 pairwise comparisons for a five-group problem, there may be only three or four comparisons (that may or may not be paired comparisons) of interest. It is important to use planned comparisons when the situation justifies them, because performing a small number of statistical tests cuts down on the probability of spurious results (type I errors), which can occur much more readily when a large number of tests are done.

Hays (1981) showed in univariate ANOVA that more powerful tests can be conducted when comparisons are planned. This would carry over to MANOVA. This is a very important factor weighing in favor of planned comparisons. Many studies in educational research have only 10 to 20 participants per group. With these sample sizes, power is generally going to be poor unless the treatment effect is large (Cohen, 1988). *If we plan a small or moderate number of contrasts that we wish to test, then power can be improved considerably, whereas control on overall α can be maintained through the use of the Bonferroni Inequality.* Recall this inequality states that if k hypotheses, k planned comparisons here, are tested separately with type I error rates of $\alpha_1, \alpha_2, \ldots, \alpha k$, then

$$\text{overall } \alpha \leq \alpha_1 + \alpha_2 + \cdots + \alpha k,$$

where overall α is the probability of one or more type I errors when all the hypotheses are true. Therefore, if three planned comparisons were tested each at $\alpha = .01$, then the probability of one or more spurious results can be no greater than .03 for the *set* of three tests.

Let us now consider two situations where planned comparisons would be appropriate:

1. Suppose an investigator wishes to determine whether each of two drugs produces a differential effect on three measures of task performance over a placebo. Then, if we denote the placebo as group 2, the following set of planned comparisons would answer the investigator's questions:

$$\psi_1 = \mu_1 - \mu_2 \text{ and } \psi_2 = \mu_2 - \mu_3$$

2. Second, consider the following four-group schematic design:

	Groups		
Control	T_1 & T_2 combined	T_1	T_2
μ_1	μ_2	μ_3	μ_4

Note: T_1 and T_2 represent two treatments.

As outlined, this could represent the format for a variety of studies (e.g., if T_1 and T_2 were two methods of teaching reading, or if T_1 and T_2 were two counseling approaches). Then the three most relevant questions the investigator wishes to answer are given by the following planned and so-called Helmert contrasts:

1. Do the treatments as a set make a difference?

$$\psi_1 = \mu_1 - \frac{\mu_2 + \mu_2 + \mu_4}{3}$$

2. Is the combination of treatments more effective than either treatment alone?

$$\psi_2 = \mu_2 - \frac{\mu_3 + \mu_4}{2}$$

3. Is one treatment more effective than the other treatment?

$$\psi_3 = \mu_3 - \mu_4$$

Assuming equal n per group, these two situations represent dependent versus independent planned comparisons. Two comparisons among means are *independent* if the sum of the products of the coefficients is 0. We represent the contrasts for Situation 1 as follows:

	Groups		
	1	2	3
ψ_1	1	−1	0
ψ_2	0	1	−1

These contrasts are dependent because the sum of products of the coefficients $\neq 0$ as shown:

Sum of products $= 1(0) + (-1)(1) + 0(-1) = -1$

Now consider the contrasts from Situation 2:

	Groups			
	1	2	3	4
Ψ_1	1	$-\dfrac{1}{3}$	$-\dfrac{1}{3}$	$-\dfrac{1}{3}$
Ψ_2	0	1	$-\dfrac{1}{2}$	$-\dfrac{1}{2}$
Ψ_3	0	0	1	-1

Next we show that these contrasts are pairwise independent by demonstrating that the sum of the products of the coefficients in each case $= 0$:

$$\psi_1 \text{ and } \psi_2 : 1(0) + \left(-\frac{1}{3}\right)(1) + \left(-\frac{1}{3}\right)\left(-\frac{1}{2}\right) + \left(-\frac{1}{3}\right)\left(-\frac{1}{2}\right) = 0$$

$$\psi_1 \text{ and } \psi_3 : 1(0) + \left(-\frac{1}{3}\right)(0) + \left(-\frac{1}{3}\right)(1) + \left(-\frac{1}{3}\right)(-1) = 0$$

$$\psi_2 \text{ and } \psi_3 : 0(0) + (1)(0) + \left(-\frac{1}{2}\right)(1) + \left(-\frac{1}{2}\right)(-1) = 0$$

Now consider two general contrasts for k groups:

$$\Psi_1 = c_{11}\mu_1 + c_{12}\mu_2 + \cdots + c_{1k}\mu_k$$
$$\Psi_2 = c_{21}\mu_1 + c_{22}\mu_2 + \cdots + c_{2k}\mu_k$$

The first part of the c subscript refers to the contrast number and the second part to the group. The condition for independence in symbols then is:

$$c_{11}c_{21} + c_{12}c_{22} + \cdots + c_{1k}c_{2k} = \sum_{j=1}^{k} c_{1j}c_{2j} = 0$$

If the sample sizes are not equal, then the condition for independence is more complicated and becomes:

$$\frac{c_{11}c_{21}}{n_1} + \frac{c_{12}c_{22}}{n_2} + \cdots + \frac{c_{1k}c_{2k}}{n_k} = 0$$

It is desirable, both statistically and substantively, to have orthogonal multivariate planned comparisons. Because the comparisons are uncorrelated, we obtain a nice additive partitioning of the total between-group association (Stevens, 1972). You may recall that in univariate ANOVA the between sum of squares is split into additive portions by a set of orthogonal planned comparisons (see Hays, 1981, chap. 14). Exactly the same type of thing is accomplished in the multivariate case; however, now the between matrix is split into additive portions that yield nonoverlapping pieces of information. Because the orthogonal comparisons are uncorrelated, the interpretation is clear and straightforward.

Although it is desirable to have orthogonal comparisons, the set to impose depends on the questions that are of primary interest to the investigator. The first example we gave of planned comparisons was not orthogonal, but corresponded to the important questions the investigator wanted answered. The interpretation of correlated contrasts requires some care, however, and we consider these in more detail later on in this chapter.

5.8 TEST STATISTICS FOR PLANNED COMPARISONS

5.8.1 Univariate Case

You may have been exposed to planned comparisons for a single dependent variable, the univariate case. For *k* groups, with population means μ_1, μ_2, . . ., μk, a contrast among the population means is given by

$$\Psi = c_1\mu_1 + c_2\mu_2 + \cdots + c_k\mu_k,$$

where the sum of the coefficients (c_i) must equal 0.

This contrast is estimated by replacing the population means by the sample means, yielding

$$\widehat{\Psi} = c_1\bar{x} + c_2\bar{x}_2 + \cdots + c_k\bar{x}_k$$

To test whether a given contrast is significantly different from 0, that is, to test

$$H_0 : \Psi = 0 \text{ vs. } H_1 : \Psi \neq 0,$$

we need an expression for the standard error of a contrast. It can be shown that the variance for a contrast is given by

$$\widehat{\sigma}_{\widehat{\Psi}}^2 = MS_w \cdot \sum_{i=1}^{k} \frac{c_i^2}{n_i}, \tag{1}$$

where MS_w is the error term from all the groups (the denominator of the *F* test) and n_i are the group sizes. Thus, the standard error of a contrast is simply the square root of Equation 1 and the following *t* statistic can be used to determine whether a contrast is significantly different from 0:

$$t = \frac{\widehat{\Psi}}{\sqrt{MS_w \cdot \sum_{i=1}^{k} \frac{c_i^2}{n_i}}}$$

SPSS MANOVA reports the univariate results for contrasts as F values. Recall that because $F = t^2$, the following F test with 1 and $N - k$ degrees of freedom is equivalent to a two-tailed t test at the same level of significance:

$$F = \frac{\widehat{\Psi}^2}{MS_w \cdot \sum_{i=1}^{k} \frac{c_i^2}{n_i}}$$

If we rewrite this as

$$F = \frac{\widehat{\Psi}^2 / \sum_{i=1}^{k} \frac{c_i^2}{n_i}}{MS_w}, \tag{2}$$

we can think of the numerator of Equation 2 as the sum of squares for a contrast, and this will appear as the hypothesis sum of squares (HYPOTH. *SS* specifically) on the SPSS print-out. MS_w will appear under the heading ERROR MS.

Let us consider a special case of Equation 2. Suppose the group sizes are equal and we are making a simple paired comparison. Then the coefficient for one mean will be 1 and the coefficient for the other mean will be −1, and Then the F statistic can be written as

$$F = \frac{n\widehat{\Psi}^2 / 2}{MS_w} = \frac{n}{2} \widehat{\Psi}(MS_w)^{-1}\widehat{\Psi}. \tag{3}$$

We have rewritten the test statistic in the form on the extreme right because we will be able to relate it more easily to the multivariate test statistic for a two-group planned comparison.

5.8.2 Multivariate Case

All contrasts, whether univariate or multivariate, can be thought of as fundamentally "two-group" comparisons. We are literally comparing two groups, or we are comparing one set of means versus another set of means. In the multivariate case this means that Hotelling's T^2 will be appropriate for testing the multivariate contrasts for significance.

We now have a contrast among the population mean vectors $\mu_1, \mu_2, \ldots, \mu k$, given by

$$\Psi = c_1\mu_1 + c_2\mu_2 + \cdots + c_k\mu_k.$$

This contrast is estimated by replacing the population mean vectors by the sample mean vectors:

$$\widehat{\Psi} = c_1\overline{\mathbf{x}}_1 + c_2\overline{\mathbf{x}}_2 + \cdots + c_k\overline{\mathbf{x}}_k$$

We wish to test that the contrast among the population mean vectors is the null vector:

$$H_0 : \mathbf{\Psi} = 0$$

Our estimate of error is $\mathbf{S}$, the estimate of the assumed common within-group population covariance matrix Σ, and the general test statistic is

$$T^2 = \left(\sum_{i=1}^{k} \frac{c_i^2}{n_i} \right)^{-1} \widehat{\mathbf{\Psi}}' \mathbf{S}^{-1} \widehat{\mathbf{\Psi}}, \qquad (4)$$

where, as in the univariate case, the n_i refer to the group sizes. Suppose we wish to contrast group 1 against the average of groups 2 and 3. If the group sizes are 20, 15, and 12, then the term in parentheses would be evaluated as $[1^2 / 20 + (-.5)^2 / 15 + (-.5)^2 / 12]$. Complete evaluation of a multivariate contrast is given later in Table 5.10. Note that the first part of Equation 4, involving the summation, is exactly the same as in the univariate case (see Equation 2). Now, however, there are matrices instead of scalars. For example, the univariate error term MS_w has been replaced by the matrix $\mathbf{S}$.

Again, as in the two-group MANOVA chapter, we have an exact F transformation of T^2, which is given by

$$F = \frac{(n_e - p + 1)}{n_e p} T^2 \text{ with } p \text{ and } (n_e - p + 1) \text{ degrees of freedom.}$$
$$(5)$$

In Equation 5, $n_e = N - k$, that is, the degrees of freedom for estimating the pooled within covariance matrix. Note that for $k = 2$, Equation 5 reduces to Equation 3 in Chapter 4.

For equal n per group and a simple paired comparison, observe that Equation 4 can be written as

$$T^2 = \frac{n}{2} \widehat{\mathbf{\Psi}}' \mathbf{S}^{-1} \widehat{\mathbf{\Psi}}. \qquad (6)$$

Note the analogy with the univariate case in Equation 3, except that now we have matrices instead of scalars. The estimated contrast has been replaced by the estimated mean vector contrast ($\widehat{\mathbf{\Psi}}$) and the univariate error term (MS_w) has been replaced by the corresponding multivariate error term $\mathbf{S}$.

5.9 MULTIVARIATE PLANNED COMPARISONS ON SPSS MANOVA

SPSS MANOVA is set up very nicely for running multivariate planned comparisons. The following type of contrasts are automatically generated by the program: Helmert (which we have discussed), Simple, Repeated (comparing adjacent levels of a factor), Deviation, and Polynomial. Thus, if we wish Helmert contrasts, it is not necessary to set up the coefficients, the program does this automatically. All we need do is give the following CONTRAST subcommand:

```
CONTRAST(FACTORNAME)  =  HELMERT/
```

We remind you that all subcommands are indented at least one column and begin with a keyword (in this case CONTRAST) followed by an equals sign, then the specifications, and are terminated by a slash.

An example of where Helmert contrasts are very meaningful has already been given. Simple contrasts involve comparing each group against the last group. A situation where this set of contrasts would make sense is if we were mainly interested in comparing each of several treatment groups against a control group (labeled as the last group). Repeated contrasts might be of considerable interest in a repeated measures design where a single group of subjects is measured at say five points in time (a longitudinal study). We might be particularly interested in differences at adjacent points in time. For example, a group of elementary school children is measured on a standardized achievement test in grades 1, 3, 5, 7, and 8. We wish to know the extent of change from grade 1 to grade 3, from grade 3 to grade 5, from grade 5 to grade 7, and from grade 7 to grade 8. The coefficients for the contrasts would be as follows:

		Grade		
1	3	5	7	8
1	−1	0	0	0
0	1	−1	0	0
0	0	1	−1	0
0	0	0	1	−1

Polynomial contrasts are useful in trend analysis, where we wish to determine whether there is a linear, quadratic, cubic, or other trend in the data. Again, these contrasts can be of great interest in repeated measures designs in growth curve analysis, where we wish to model the mathematical form of the growth. To reconsider the previous example, some investigators may be more interested in whether the growth in some basic skills areas such as reading and mathematics is linear (proportional) during the elementary years, or perhaps curvilinear. For example, maybe growth is linear for a while and then somewhat levels off, suggesting an overall curvilinear trend.

If none of these automatically generated contrasts answers the research questions of interest, then one can set up contrasts using SPECIAL as the code name. Special contrasts are "tailor-made" comparisons for the group comparisons suggested by your hypotheses. In setting these up, however, remember that for k groups there are only

$(k - 1)$ between degrees of freedom, so that only $(k - 1)$ nonredundant contrasts can be run. The coefficients for the contrasts are enclosed in parentheses after special:

```
CONTRAST(FACTORNAME) = SPECIAL(1, 1, . . ., 1
coefficients for contrasts)/
```

There *must* first be as many 1s as there are groups. We give an example illustrating special contrasts shortly.

Example 5.3: Helmert Contrasts

An investigator has a three-group, two-dependent variable problem with five participants per group. The first is a control group, and the remaining two groups are treatment groups. The Helmert contrasts test each level (group) against the average of the remaining levels. In this case the two single degree of freedom Helmert contrasts, corresponding to the two between degrees of freedom, are very meaningful. The first tests whether the control group differs from the average of the treatment groups on the set of variables. The second Helmert contrast tests whether the treatments are differentially effective. In Table 5.7 we present the control lines along with the data as part of the command file, for running the contrasts. Recall that when the data is part of the command file it is preceded by the BEGIN DATA command and the data is followed by the END DATA command.

The means, standard deviations, and pooled within-covariance matrix **S** are presented in Table 5.8, where we also calculate **S**$^{-1}$, which will serve as the error term for the multivariate contrasts (see Equation 4). Table 5.9 presents the output for the multivariate

■ **Table 5.7 SPSS MANOVA Control Lines for Multivariate Helmert Contrasts**

```
    TITLE 'HELMERT CONTRASTS'.
    DATA LIST FREE/gps y1 y2.
    BEGIN DATA.
    1 5 6      1 6 7      1 6 7      1 4 5      1 5 4
    2 2 2      2 3 3      2 4 4      2 3 2      2 2 1
    3 4 3      3 6 7      3 3 3      3 5 5      3 5 5
    END DATA.
    LIST.
    MANOVA y1 y2 BY gps(1,3)
        /CONTRAST(gps) = HELMERT
(1)   /PARTITION(gps)
(2)   /DESIGN = gps(1), gps(2)
        /PRINT = CELLINFO(MEANS, COV).
```

(1) In general, for *k* groups, the between degrees of freedom could be partitioned in various ways. If we wish all single degree of freedom contrasts, as here, then we could put PARTITION(gps) = (1, 1)/. Or, this can be abbreviated to PARTITION(gps)/.

(2) This DESIGN subcommand specifies the effects we are testing for significance, in this case the two single degree of freedom multivariate contrasts. The numbers in parentheses refer to the part of the partition. Thus, gps(1) refers to the first part of the partition (i.e., the first Helmert contrast) and gps(2) refers to the second part of the partition (i.e., the second Helmert contrast).

■ **Table 5.8 Means, Standard Deviations, and Pooled Within Covariance Matrix for Helmert Contrast Example**

Cell Means and Standard Deviations

Variable.. y1

FACTOR	CODE	Mean	Std. Dev.
gps	1	5.200	.837
gps	2	2.800	.837
gps	3	4.600	1.140
For entire sample		4.200	1.373

Variable.. y2

FACTOR	CODE	Mean	Std. Dev.
gps	1	5.800	1.304
gps	2	2.400	1.140
gps	3	4.600	1.673
For entire sample		4.267	1.944

Pooled within-cells Variance-Covariance matrix

	Y1	Y2
y1	.900	
y2	1.150	1.933

Determinant of pooled Covariance matrix of dependent vars. = .41750

To compute the multivariate test statistic for the contrasts we need the inverse of the above covariance matrix S, as shown in Equation 4.

The procedure for finding the inverse of a matrix was given in section 2.5. We obtain the matrix of cofactors and then divide by the determinant. Thus, here we have

$$\mathbf{S}^{-1} = \frac{1}{.4175}\begin{bmatrix} 1.933 & -1.15 \\ -1.15 & .9 \end{bmatrix} = \begin{bmatrix} 4.631 & -2.755 \\ -2.755 & 2.156 \end{bmatrix}$$

and univariate Helmert contrasts comparing the treatment groups against the control group. The multivariate contrast is significant at the .05 level ($F = 4.303$, $p < .042$), indicating that something is better than nothing. Note also that the Fs for all the multivariate tests are the *same*, since this is a single degree of freedom comparison and thus effectively a two-group comparison. The univariate results show that there are group differences on each of the two variables (i.e., $p = .014$ and .011). We also show in Table 5.9 how the hypothesis sum of squares is obtained for the first univariate Helmert contrast (i.e., for $y1$).

In Table 5.10 we present the multivariate and univariate Helmert contrasts comparing the two treatment groups. As the annotation indicates, both the multivariate and univariate contrasts are significant at the .05 level. Thus, the treatment groups differ on the set of variables, and the groups differ on each dependent variable.

■ **Table 5.9 Multivariate and Univariate Tests for Helmert Contrast Comparing the Control Group Against the Two Treatment Groups**

EFFECT.. gps (1)

Multivariate Tests of Significance (S = 1, M = 0, N = 4 1/2)

Test Name	Value	Exact F	Hypoth. DF	Error DF	Sig. of F
Pillais	.43897	4.30339	2.00	11.00	.042
Hotellings	.78244	4.30339	2.00	11.00	① .042
Wilks	.56103	4.30339	2.00	11.00	.042
Roys	.43897				

Note.. F statistics are exact.

EFFECT.. gps (1) (Cont.)

Univariate F-tests with (1, 12) D. F.

Variable	Hypoth. SS	Error SS	Hypoth. MS	Error MS	F	Sig. of F
y1	7.50000	10.80000	7.50000	.90000	8.33333	.014
y2	17.63333	23.20000	17.63333	1.93333	9.12069	.011

The univariate contrast for y1 is given by $\psi_1 = \mu_1 - (\mu_2 + \mu_3)/2$.
Using the means of Table 5.8, we obtain the following estimate for the contrast:
$\widehat{\Psi}_1 = 5.2 - (2.8 + 4.6)/2 = 1.5.$

Recall from Equation 2 that the hypothesis sum of squares is given by $\psi^2 / \sum_{i=1}^{k} \dfrac{c_i^2}{n_i}$. For equal group sizes, as

here, this becomes $n\psi^2 / \sum_{i=1}^{k} c_i^2$. Thus, HYPOTH $SS = \dfrac{5(1.5)^2}{1^2 + (-.5)^2 + (-.5)^2} = 7.5.$

The error term for the contrast, MS_w, appears under ERROR MS and is .900. Thus, the F ratio for y1 is 7.5/.90 = 8.333. Notice that both variables are significant at the .05 level.

① This indicates that the multivariate contrast $\psi_1 = \mu_1 - (\mu_2 + \mu_3)/2$ is significant at the .05 level (because .042 < .05). That is, the control group differs significantly from the average of the two treatment groups on the set of two variables.

In Table 5.10 we also show in detail how the *F* value for the multivariate Helmert contrast is arrived at.

Example 5.4: Special Contrasts

We indicated earlier that researchers can set up their own contrasts on MANOVA. We now illustrate this for a four-group, five-dependent variable example. There are two control groups, one of which is a Hawthorne control, and two treatment groups. Three very meaningful contrasts are indicated schematically:

	T_1 (control)	T_2 (Hawthorne)	T_3	T_4
ψ_1	−.5	−.5	.5	.5
ψ_2	0	1	−.5	−.5
ψ_3	0	0	1	−1

■ **Table 5.10 Multivariate and Univariate Tests for Helmert Contrast for the Two Treatment Groups**

EFFECT.. gps(2)

Multivariate Tests of Significance (S = 1, M = 0, N = 4 1/2)

Test Name	Value	Exact F	Hypoth. DF	Error DF	Sig. of F
Pillais	.43003	4.14970	2.00	11.00	.045
Hotellings	.75449	4.14970	(1) 2.00	11.00	.045
Wilks	.56997	4.14970	2.00	11.00	.045
Roys	.43003				

Note.. F statistics are exact.

Recall from Table 5.8 that the inverse of pooled within covariance matrix is

$$\mathbf{S}^{-1} = \begin{bmatrix} 4.631 & -2.755 \\ -2.755 & 2.156 \end{bmatrix}$$

Since that is a simple contrast with equal n, we can use Equation 6:

$$T^2 = \frac{n}{2}\widehat{\boldsymbol{\psi}}'\mathbf{S}^{-1}\widehat{\boldsymbol{\psi}} = \frac{n}{2}(\bar{\mathbf{x}}_2 - \bar{\mathbf{x}}_3)'\mathbf{S}^{-1}(\bar{\mathbf{x}}_2 - \bar{\mathbf{x}}_3) = \frac{5}{2}\left[\begin{pmatrix} 2.8 \\ 2.4 \end{pmatrix} - \begin{pmatrix} 4.6 \\ 4.6 \end{pmatrix}\right]'\begin{bmatrix} 4.631 & -2.755 \\ -2.755 & 2.156 \end{bmatrix}\begin{pmatrix} -1.8 \\ -2.2 \end{pmatrix} = 9.0535$$

To obtain the value of HOTELLING given on printout above we simply divide by error df, i.e., 9.0535/12 = .75446.

To obtain the F we use Equation 5:

$$F = \frac{(n_e - p + 1)}{n_e p}T^2 = \frac{(12 - 2 + 1)}{12(2)}(9.0535) = 4.1495,$$

With degrees of freedom $p = 2$ and $(n_e - p + 1) = 11$ as given above.

EFFECT.. GPS (2) (Cont.)

Univariate F-tests with (1, 12) D. F.

Variable	Hypoth. SS	Error SS	Hypoth. MS	Error MS	F	Sig. of F
y1	8.10000	10.80000	8.10000	.90000	9.00000	.011
y2	12.10000	23.20000	12.10000	(2) 1.93333	6.25862	.028

(1) This multivariate test indicates that treatment groups differ significantly at the .05 level (because .045 < .05) on the *set* of two variables.

(2) These results indicate that both univariate contrasts are significant at .05 level, i.e., the treatment groups differ on each variable.

The control lines for running these contrasts on SPSS MANOVA are presented in Table 5.11. (In this case we have just put in some data schematically and have used column input, simply to illustrate it.) As indicated earlier, note that the first four numbers in the CONTRAST subcommand are 1s, corresponding to the number of groups. The next four numbers define the first contrast, where we are comparing the control groups against the treatment groups. The following four numbers define the second contrast, and the last four numbers define the third contrast.

■ **Table 5.11 SPSS MANOVA Control Lines for Special Multivariate Contrasts**

```
TITLE 'SPECIAL MULTIVARIATE CONTRASTS'.
DATA LIST FREE/gps 1 y1 3-4 y2 6-7(1) y3 9-11(2)
   y4 13-15 y5 17-18.
BEGIN DATA.
1 28 13 476 215 74
. . . . . .
4 24 31 668 355 56
END DATA.
LIST.
MANOVA y1 TO y5 BY gps(1, 4)
   /CONTRAST(gps) = SPECIAL (1 1 1 1 -.5 -.5 .5 .5
   0 1 -.5 -.5 0 0 1 -1)
   /PARTITION(gps)
   /DESIGN = gps(1), gps(2), gps(3)
   /PRINT = CELLINFO(MEAN, COV, COR).
```

5.10 CORRELATED CONTRASTS

The Helmert contrasts we considered in Example 5.3 are, for equal n, uncorrelated. This is important in terms of clarity of interpretation because significance on one Helmert contrast implies nothing about significance on a different Helmert contrast. For correlated contrasts this is not true. To determine the unique contribution a given contrast is making we need to partial out its correlations with the other contrasts. We illustrate how this is done on MANOVA.

Correlated contrasts can arise in two ways: (1) the sum of products of the coefficients $\neq$ 0 for the contrasts, and (2) the sum of products of coefficients = 0, but the group sizes are not equal.

Example 5.5: Correlated Contrasts
We consider an example with four groups and two dependent variables. The contrasts are indicated schematically here, with the group sizes in parentheses:

	T_1 & T_2 (12) combined	Hawthorne (14) control	T_1 (11)	T_2 (8)
ψ_1	0	1	−1	0
ψ_2	0	1	−.5	−.5
ψ_3	1	0	0	−1

Notice that ψ_1 and ψ_2 as well as ψ_2 and ψ_3 are correlated because the sum of products of coefficients in each case $\neq$ 0. However, ψ_1 and ψ_3 are also correlated since group sizes are unequal. The data for this problem are given next.

GP1		GP2		GP3		GP4	
y_1	y_2	y_1	y_2	y_1	y_2	y_1	y_2
18	5	18	9	17	5	13	3
13	6	20	5	22	7	9	3
20	4	17	10	22	5	9	3
22	8	24	4	13	9	15	5
21	9	19	4	13	5	13	4
19	0	18	4	11	5	12	4
12	6	15	7	12	6	13	5
10	5	16	7	23	3	12	3
15	4	16	5	17	7		
15	5	14	3	18	7		
14	0	18	2	13	3		
12	6	14	4				
		19	6				
		23	2				

1. We used the default method (UNIQUE SUM OF SQUARES, as of Release 2.1). This gives the unique contribution of the contrast to between-group variation; that is, each contrast is adjusted for its correlations with the other contrasts.
2. We used the SEQUENTIAL sum of squares option. This is obtained by putting the following subcommand right after the MANOVA statement:

METHOD = SEQUENTIAL/

With this option each contrast is adjusted *only* for all contrasts to the *left* of it in the DESIGN subcommand. Thus, if our DESIGN subcommand is

DESIGN = gps(1), gps(2), gps(3)/

then the last contrast, denoted by gps(3), is adjusted for all other contrasts, and the value of the multivariate test statistics for gps(3) will be the *same* as we obtained for the default method (unique sum of squares). However, the value of the test statistics for gps(2) and gps(1) will differ from those obtained using unique sum of squares, since gps(2) is only adjusted for gps(1) and gps(1) is not adjusted for either of the other two contrasts.

The multivariate test statistics for the contrasts using the unique decomposition are presented in Table 5.12, whereas the statistics for the hierarchical decomposition are given in Table 5.13. As explained earlier, the results for ψ_3 are identical for both approaches, and indicate significance at the .05 level ($F = 3.499$, $p < .04$). That is, the combination of treatments differs from T_2 alone. The results for the other two contrasts, however, are quite different for the two approaches. The unique breakdown indicates that ψ_2 is significant at .05 (treatments differ from Hawthorne control) and ψ_1 is not significant (T_1 is not different from Hawthorne control). The results in Table 5.12 for the hierarchical approach yield a different conclusion for ψ_2. Obviously, the conclusions one draws in this study would depend on which approach was used to test the contrasts for significance. We express a preference in general for the unique approach.

It should be noted that the unique contribution of each contrast can be obtained using the hierarchical approach; however, in this case three DESIGN

■ **Table 5.12 Multivariate Tests for Unique Contribution of Each Correlated Contrast to Between Variation***

EFFECT.. gps (3)

Multivariate Tests of Significance (S = 1, M = 0, N = 19)

Test Name	Value	Exact F	Hypoth. DF	Error DF	Sig. of F
Pillais	.14891	3.49930	2.00	40.00	.040
Hotellings	.17496	3.49930	2.00	40.00	.040
Wilks	.85109	3.49930	2.00	40.00	.040
Roys	.14891				
Note.. F statistics are exact.					

EFFECT.. gps (2)

Multivariate Tests of Significance (S = 1, M = 0, N = 19)

Test Name	Value	Exact F	Hypoth. DF	Error DF	Sig. of F
Pillais	.18228	4.45832	2.00	40.00	.018
Hotellings	.22292	4.45832	2.00	40.00	.018
Wilks	.81772	4.45832	2.00	40.00	.018
Roys	.18228				
Note.. F statistics are exact.					

EFFECT.. gps (1)

Multivariate Tests of Significance (S = 1, M = 0, N = 19)

Test Name	Value	Exact F	Hypoth. DF	Error DF	Sig. of F
Pillais	.03233	.66813	2.00	40.00	.518
Hotellings	.03341	.66813	2.00	40.00	.518
Wilks	.96767	.66813	2.00	40.00	.518
Roys	.03233				
Note.. F statistics are exact.					

* Each contrast is adjusted for its correlations with the other contrasts.

■ **Table 5.13 Multivariate Tests of Correlated Contrasts for Hierarchical Option of SPSS MANOVA**

EFFECT.. gps (3)

Multivariate Tests of Significance (S = 1, M = 0, N = 19)

Test Name	Value	Exact F	Hypoth. DF	Error DF	Sig. of F
Pillais	.14891	3.49930	2.00	40.00	.040
Hotellings	.17496	3.49930	2.00	40.00	.040
Wilks	.85109	3.49930	2.00	40.00	.040
Roys	.14891				
Note.. F statistics are exact.					

EFFECT.. gps (2)

Multivariate Tests of Significance (S = 1, M = 0, N = 19)

Test Name	Value	Exact F	Hypoth. DF	Error DF	Sig. of F
Pillais	.10542	2.35677	2.00	40.00	.108
Hotellings	.11784	2.35677	2.00	40.00	.108
Wilks	.89458	2.35677	2.00	40.00	.108
Roys	.10542				
Note.. F statistics are exact.					

EFFECT.. gps (1)

Multivariate Tests of Significance (S = 1, M = 0, N = 19)

Test Name	Value	Exact F	Hypoth. DF	Error DF	Sig. of F
Pillais	.13641	3.15905	2.00	40.00	.053
Hotellings	.15795	3.15905	2.00	40.00	.053
Wilks	.86359	3.15905	2.00	40.00	.053
Roys	.13641				
Note.. F statistics are exact.					

Note: Each contrast is adjusted *only* for all contrasts to left of it in the DESIGN subcommand.

subcommands would be required, with each of the contrasts ordered last in one of the subcommands:

> DESIGN = gps(1), gps(2), gps(3)/
> DESIGN = gps(2), gps(3), gps(1)/
> DESIGN = gps(3), gps(1), gps(2)/

All three orderings can be done in a single run.

5.11 STUDIES USING MULTIVARIATE PLANNED COMPARISONS

Clifford (1972) was interested in the effect of competition as a motivational technique in the classroom. The participants were fifth graders, with the group about evenly divided between girls and boys. A 2-week vocabulary learning task was given under three conditions:

1. Control—a noncompetitive atmosphere in which no score comparisons among classmates were made.
2. Reward Treatment—comparisons among relatively homogeneous participants were made and accentuated by the rewarding of candy to high-scoring participants.
3. Game Treatment—again, comparisons were made among relatively homogeneous participants and accentuated in a follow-up game activity. Here high-scoring participants received an advantage in a game that was played immediately after the vocabulary task was scored.

The three dependent variables were performance, interest, and retention. The retention measure was given 2 weeks after the completion of treatments. Clifford had the following two planned comparisons:

1. Competition is more effective than noncompetition. Thus, she was testing the following contrast for significance:

$$\Psi_1 = \frac{\mu_2 - \mu_3}{2} - \mu_1$$

2. Game competition is as effective as reward with respect to performance on the dependent variables. Thus, she was predicting the following contrast would *not* be significant:

$$\Psi_2 = \mu_2 - \mu_3$$

Clifford's results are presented in Table 5.14. As predicted, competition was more effective than noncompetition for the set of three dependent variables. Estimation of the univariate results in Table 5.14 shows that the groups differed only on the interest variable. Clifford's second prediction was also confirmed, that there was no difference in the relative effectiveness of reward versus game treatments ($F = .84, p < .47$).

A second study involving multivariate planned comparisons was conducted by Stevens (1972). He was interested in studying the relationship between parents' educational level and eight personality characteristics of their National Merit Scholar children. Part of the analysis involved the following set of orthogonal comparisons (75 participants per group):

■ **Table 5.14 Means and Multivariate and Univariate Results for Two Planned Comparisons in Clifford Study**

	df	MS	F	P
1st planned comparison (control vs. reward and game)				
Multivariate test	3/61		10.04	.0001
Univariate tests				
Performance	1/63	.54	.64	.43
Interest	1/63	4.70	29.24	.0001
Retention	1/63	4.01	.18	.67
2nd planned comparison (reward vs. game)				
Multivariate test	3/61		.84	.47
Univariate tests				
Performance	1/63	.002	.003	.96
Interest	1/63	.37	2.32	.13
Retention	1/63	1.47	.07	.80

	Means for the groups		
Variable	Control	Reward	Games
Performance	5.72	5.92	5.90
Interest	2.41	2.63	2.57
Retention	30.85	31.55	31.19

1. Group 1 (parents' education eighth grade or less) versus group 2 (parents' both high school graduates).
2. Groups 1 and 2 (no college) versus groups 3 and 4 (college for both parents).
3. Group 3 (both parents attended college) versus group 4 (both parents at least one college degree).

This set of comparisons corresponds to a very meaningful set of questions: Are differences in children's personality characteristics related to differences in parental degree of education?

Another set of orthogonal contrasts that could have been of interest in this study looks like this schematically:

	Groups			
	1	2	3	4
ψ_1	1	−.33	−.33	−.33
ψ_2	0	0	1	−1
ψ_3	0	1	−.50	−.50

This would have resulted in a different meaningful, additive breakdown of the between association. However, one set of orthogonal contrasts does not have an empirical superiority over another (after all, they both additively partition the between association). In terms of choosing one set over the other, it is a matter of which set best answers your research hypotheses.

5.12 OTHER MULTIVARIATE TEST STATISTICS

In addition to Wilks' Λ, three other multivariate test statistics are in use and are printed out on the packages:

1. Roy's largest root (eigenvalue) of $\mathbf{BW}^{-1}$.
2. The Hotelling–Lawley trace, the sum of the eigenvalues of $\mathbf{BW}^{-1}$.
3. The Pillai–Bartlett trace, the sum of the eigenvalues of $\mathbf{BT}^{-1}$.

Notice that the Roy and Hotelling–Lawley multivariate statistics are natural generalizations of the univariate F statistic. In univariate ANOVA the test statistic is $F = MS_b / MS_w$, a measure of between- to within-group association. The multivariate analogue of this is $\mathbf{BW}^{-1}$, which is a "ratio" of between- to within-group association. With matrices there is no division, so we don't literally divide the between by the within as in the univariate case; however, the matrix analogue of division is inversion.

Because Wilks' Λ can be expressed as a product of eigenvalues of $\mathbf{WT}^{-1}$, *we see that all four of the multivariate test statistics are some function of an eigenvalue(s) (sum, product). Thus, eigenvalues are fundamental to the multivariate problem.* We will show in Chapter 10 on discriminant analysis that there are quantities corresponding to the eigenvalues (the discriminant functions) that are linear combinations of the dependent variables and that characterize major differences among the groups.

You might well ask at this point, "Which of these four multivariate test statistics should be used in practice?" This is a somewhat complicated question that, for full understanding, requires a knowledge of discriminant analysis and of the robustness of the four statistics to the assumptions in MANOVA. Nevertheless, the following will provide guidelines for the researcher. In terms of robustness with respect to type I error for the homogeneity of covariance matrices assumption, Stevens (1979) found that *any* of the following three can be used: Pillai–Bartlett trace, Hotelling–Lawley trace, or Wilks' Λ. For subgroup variance differences likely to be encountered in social science research, these three are equally quite robust, provided the group sizes are equal or

approximately equal $\left(\dfrac{\text{largest}}{\text{smallest}} < 1.5 \right)$. In terms of power, no one of the four statistics

is always most powerful; which depends on how the null hypothesis is false. Importantly, however, Olson (1973) found that *power differences among the four multivariate test statistics are generally quite small* ($< .06$). So as a general rule, it won't make that much of a difference which of the statistics is used. But, if the differences among the groups are concentrated on the first discriminant function, which does occur in practice, then Roy's statistic technically would be preferred since it is most powerful. However, Roy's statistic should be used in this case only if there is evidence to suggest that the homogeneity of covariance matrices assumption is tenable. Finally, when the differences among the groups involve two or more discriminant functions, the Pillai–Bartlett trace is most powerful, although its power advantage tends to be slight.

5.13 HOW MANY DEPENDENT VARIABLES FOR A MANOVA?

Of course, there is no simple answer to this question. However, the following considerations mitigate *generally* against the use of a large number of criterion variables:

1. If a large number of dependent variables are included without any strong rationale (empirical or theoretical), then small or negligible differences on most of them may obscure a real difference(s) on a few of them. That is, the multivariate test detects mainly error in the system, that is, in the set of variables, and therefore declares no reliable overall difference.
2. The power of the multivariate tests generally declines as the number of dependent variables is increased (DasGupta and Perlman, 1974).
3. The reliability of variables can be a problem in behavioral science work. Thus, given a large number of criterion variables, it probably will be wise to combine (usually add) highly similar response measures, particularly when the basic measurements tend individually to be quite unreliable (Pruzek, 1971). As Pruzek stated, one should always consider the possibility that his variables include errors of measurement that may attenuate F ratios and generally confound interpretations of experimental effects. Especially when there are several dependent variables whose reliabilities and mutual intercorrelations vary widely, inferences based on fallible data may be quite misleading (Pruzek, 1971, p. 187).
4. Based on his Monte Carlo results, Olson had some comments on the design of multivariate experiments that are worth remembering: For example, one generally will not do worse by making the dimensionality p smaller, insofar as it is under experimenter control. Variates should not be thoughtlessly included in an analysis just because the data are available. Besides aiding robustness, a small value of p is apt to facilitate interpretation (Olson, 1973, p. 906).
5. Given a large number of variables, one should always consider the possibility that there is a much smaller number of underlying constructs that will account for most of the variance on the original set of variables. Thus, the use of exploratory factor analysis as a preliminary data reduction scheme before the use of MANOVA should be contemplated.

5.14 POWER ANALYSIS—*A PRIORI* DETERMINATION OF SAMPLE SIZE

Several studies have dealt with power in MANOVA (e.g., Ito, 1962; Lauter, 1978; Olson, 1974; Pillai & Jayachandian, 1967). Olson examined power for small and moderate sample size, but expressed the noncentrality parameter (which measures the extent of deviation from the null hypothesis) in terms of eigenvalues. Also, there were many gaps in his tables: no power values for 4, 5, 7, 8, and 9 variables or 4 or 5 groups. The Lauter study is much more comprehensive, giving sample size tables for a very wide range of situations:

1. For $\alpha = .05$ or .01.
2. For 2, 3, 4, 5, 6, 8, 10, 15, 20, 30, 50, and 100 variables.

3. For 2, 3, 4, 5, 6, 8, and 10 groups.
4. For power = .70, .80, .90, and .95.

His tables are specifically for the Hotelling–Lawley trace criterion, and this might seem to limit their utility. However, as Morrison (1967) noted for large sample size, and as Olson (1974) showed for small and moderate sample size, the power differences among the four main multivariate test statistics are generally quite small. Thus, the sample size requirements for Wilks' Λ, the Pillai–Bartlett trace, and Roy's largest root will be very similar to those for the Hotelling–Lawley trace for the vast majority of situations.

Lauter's tables are set up in terms of a certain *minimum* deviation from the multivariate null hypothesis, which can be expressed in the following three forms:

1. There exists a variable i such that $\dfrac{1}{\sigma^2} \sum_{j=1}^{j} \left(\mu_{ij} - \mu_i \right) \geq q^2$, where μi is the total mean and σ^2 is variance.

2. There exists a variable i such that $1/\sigma_i \left| \mu_{ij1} - \mu_{ij2} \right| \geq d$ for two groups $j1$ and $j2$.

3. There exists a variable i such that for all pairs of groups 1 and m we have $1/\sigma_i \left| \mu_{il} - \mu_{il} \right| > c$.

In Table A.5 of Appendix A of this text we present selected situations and power values that it is believed would be of most value to social science researchers: for 2, 3, 4, 5, 6, 8, 10, and 15 variables, with 3, 4, 5, and 6 groups, and for power = .70, .80, and .90. We have also characterized the four different minimum deviation patterns as very large, large, moderate, and small effect sizes. Although the characterizations may be somewhat rough, they are reasonable in the following senses: They agree with Cohen's definitions of large, medium, and small effect sizes for one variable (Lauter included the univariate case in his tables), and with Stevens' (1980) definitions of large, medium, and small effect sizes for the two-group MANOVA case.

It is important to note that there could be several ways, other than that specified by Lauter, in which a large, moderate, or small multivariate effect size could occur. But the essential point is how many participants will be needed for a given effect size, regardless of the combination of differences on the variables that produced the specific effect size. Thus, the tables do have broad applicability. We consider shortly a few specific examples of the use of the tables, but first we present a compact table that should be of great interest to applied researchers:

		Groups			
		3	4	5	6
Effect size	Very large	12–16	14–18	15–19	16–21
	Large	25–32	28–36	31–40	33–44
	Medium	42–54	48–62	54–70	58–76
	Small	92–120	105–140	120–155	130–170

This table gives the range of sample sizes needed per group for adequate power (.70) at α = .05 when there are three to six variables.

Thus, if we expect a large effect size and have four groups, 28 participants per group are needed for power = .70 with three variables, whereas 36 participants per group are required if there were six dependent variables.

Now we consider two examples to illustrate the use of the Lauter sample size tables in the appendix.

Example 5.6
An investigator has a four-group MANOVA with five dependent variables. He wishes power = .80 at α = .05. From previous research and his knowledge of the nature of the treatments, he anticipates a moderate effect size. How many participants per group will he need? Reference to Table A.5 (for four groups) indicates that 70 participants per group are required.

Example 5.7
A team of researchers has a five-group, seven-dependent-variable MANOVA. They wish power = .70 at α = .05. From previous research they anticipate a large effect size. How many participants per group are needed? Interpolating in Table A.5 (for five groups) between six and eight variables, we see that 43 participants per group are needed, or a total of 215 participants.

5.15 SUMMARY

Cohen's (1968) seminal article showed social science researchers that univariate ANOVA could be considered as a special case of regression, by dummy-coding group membership. In this chapter we have pointed out that MANOVA can also be considered as a special case of regression analysis, except that for MANOVA it is multivariate regression because there are several dependent variables being predicted from the dummy variables. That is, separation of the mean vectors is equivalent to demonstrating that the dummy variables (predictors) significantly predict the scores on the dependent variables.

For exploratory research where the focus is on individual dependent variables (and not linear combinations of these variables), two *post hoc* procedures were given for examining group differences for the outcome variables. Each procedure followed up a significant multivariate test result with univariate ANOVAs for each outcome. If an *F* test were significant for a given outcome and more than two groups were present, pairwise comparisons were conducted using the Tukey procedure. The two procedures differ in that one procedure used a Bonferroni-adjusted alpha for the univariate *F* tests and pairwise comparisons while the other did not. Of the two procedures, the more widely recommended procedure is to use the Bonferroni-adjusted alpha for the univariate ANOVAs and the Tukey procedure, as this procedure provides for greater control of the overall type I error rate and a more accurate set of confidence intervals (in terms of coverage). The procedure that uses no such alpha adjustment should be considered only when the number of outcomes and groups is small (i.e., two or three).

For confirmatory research, planned comparisons were discussed. The setup of multivariate contrasts on SPSS MANOVA was illustrated. Although uncorrelated contrasts are desirable because of ease of interpretation and the nice additive partitioning they yield, it was noted that often the important questions an investigator has will yield correlated contrasts. The use of SPSS MANOVA to obtain the unique contribution of each correlated contrast was illustrated.

It was noted that the Roy and Hotelling–Lawley statistics are natural generalizations of the univariate F ratio. In terms of which of the four multivariate test statistics to use in practice, two criteria can be used: robustness and power. Wilks' Λ, the Pillai–Bartlett trace, and Hotelling–Lawley statistics are equally robust (for equal or approximately equal group sizes) with respect to the homogeneity of covariance matrices assumption, and therefore any one of them can be used. The power differences among the four statistics are in general quite small ($< .06$), so that there is no strong basis for preferring any one of them over the others on power considerations.

The important problem, in terms of experimental planning, of a priori determination of sample size was considered for three-, four-, five-, and six-group MANOVA for the number of dependent variables ranging from 2 to 15.

5.16 EXERCISES

1. Consider the following data for a three-group, three-dependent-variable problem:

Group 1			Group 2			Group 3		
y_1	y_2	y_3	y_1	y_2	y_3	y_1	y_2	y_3
2.0	2.5	2.5	1.5	3.5	2.5	1.0	2.0	1.0
1.5	2.0	1.5	1.0	4.5	2.5	1.0	2.0	1.5
2.0	3.0	2.5	3.0	3.0	3.0	1.5	1.0	1.0
2.5	4.0	3.0	4.5	4.5	4.5	2.0	2.5	2.0
1.0	2.0	1.0	1.5	4.5	3.5	2.0	3.0	2.5
1.5	3.5	2.5	2.5	4.0	3.0	2.5	3.0	2.5
4.0	3.0	3.0	3.0	4.0	3.5	2.0	2.5	2.5
3.0	4.0	3.5	4.0	5.0	5.0	1.0	1.0	1.0
3.5	3.5	3.5				1.0	1.5	1.5
1.0	1.0	1.0				2.0	3.5	2.5
1.0	2.5	2.0						

Use SAS or SPSS to run a one-way MANOVA. Use procedure 1 (with the adjusted Bonferroni F tests) to do the follow-up tests.

(a) What is the multivariate null hypothesis? Do you reject it at $\alpha = .05$?

(b) If you reject in part (a), then for which outcomes are there group differences at the .05 level?

(c) For any ANOVAs that are significant, use the *post hoc* tests to describe group differences. Be sure to rank order group performance based on the statistical test results.

2. Consider the following data from Wilkinson (1975):

Group A				Group B			Group C	
5	6	4	2	2	7	4	3	4
6	7	5	3	3	5	6	7	5
6	7	3	4	4	6	3	3	5
4	5	5	3	2	4	5	5	5
5	4	2	2	1	4	5	5	4

Run a one-way MANOVA on SAS or SPSS. Do the various multivariate test statistics agree in a decision on H_0?

3. This table shows analysis results for 12 separate ANOVAs. The researchers were examining differences among three groups for outpatient therapy, using symptoms reported on the Symptom Checklist 90–Revised.

SCL 90–R Group Main Effects

	Group					
	Group 1	Group 2	Group 3			
	$N = 48$	$N = 60$	$N = 57$			
Dimension	$\bar{x}$	$\bar{x}$	$\bar{x}$	F	df	Significance
Somatization	53.7	53.2	53.7	.03	2,141	*ns*
Obsessive-compulsive	48.7	53.9	52.2	2.75	2,141	*ns*
Interpersonal sensitivity	47.3	51.3	52.9	4.84	2,141	$p < .01$
Depression	47.5	53.5	53.9	5.44	2,141	$p < .01$
Anxiety	48.5	52.9	52.2	1.86	2,141	*ns*
Hostility	48.1	54.6	52.4	3.82	2,141	$p < .03$
Phobic anxiety	49.8	54.2	51.8	2.08	2,141	*ns*

(*Continued*)

Dimension	$\bar{x}$	$\bar{x}$	$\bar{x}$	F	df	Significance
Paranoid ideation	51.4	54.7	54.0	1.38	2,141	*ns*
Psychoticism	52.4	54.6	54.2	.37	2,141	*ns*
Global Severity index positive symptom	49.7	54.4	54.0	2.55	2,141	*ns*
Distress index	49.3	55.8	53.2	3.39	2,141	*p* < .04
Positive symptom total	50.2	52.9	54.4	1.96	2,141	*ns*

(a) Could we be confident that these results would replicate? Explain.

(b) In this study, the authors did not a priori hypothesize differences on the specific variables for which significance was found. Given that, what would have been a better method of analysis?

4. A researcher is testing the efficacy of four drugs in inhibiting undesirable responses in patients. Drugs A and B are similar in composition, whereas drugs C and D are distinctly different in composition from A and B, although similar in their basic ingredients. He takes 100 patients and randomly assigns them to five groups: Gp 1—control, Gp 2—drug A, Gp 3—drug B, Gp 4—drug C, and Gp 5—drug D. The following would be four very relevant planned comparisons to test:

		Control	Drug A	Drug B	Drug C	Drug D
	1	1	−.25	−.25	−.25	−.25
Contrasts	2	0	1	1	−1	−1
	3	0	1	−1	0	0
	4	0	0	0	1	−1

(a) Show that these contrasts are orthogonal.

Now, consider the following set of contrasts, which might also be of interest in the preceding study:

		Control	Drug A	Drug B	Drug C	Drug D
	1	1	−.25	−.25	−.25	−.25
Contrasts	2	1	−.5	−.5	0	0
	3	1	0	0	−.5	−.5
	4	0	1	1	−1	−1

(b) Show that these contrasts are not orthogonal.

(c) Because neither of these two sets of contrasts is one of the standard sets that come out of SPSS MANOVA, it would be necessary to use the special contrast feature to test each set. Show the control lines for doing this for each set. Assume four criterion measures.

5. Find an article in one of the better journals in your content area from within the last 5 years that used primarily MANOVA. Answer the following questions:

   (a) How many statistical tests (univariate or multivariate or both) were done? Were the authors aware of this, and did they adjust in any way?

   (b) Was power an issue in this study? Explain.

   (c) Did the authors address practical importance in ANY way? Explain.

REFERENCES

Clifford, M. M. (1972). Effects of competition as a motivational technique in the classroom. *American Educational Research Journal, 9*, 123–134.

Cohen, J. (1968). Multiple regression as a general data-analytic system. *Psychological Bulletin, 70*, 426–443.

Cohen, J. (1988). *Statistical power analysis for the social sciences* (2nd ed.). Hillsdale, NJ: Lawrence Erlbaum Associates.

DasGupta, S., & Perlman, M. D. (1974). Power of the noncentral F-test: Effect of additional variates on Hotelling's T^2-Test. *Journal of the American Statistical Association, 69*, 174–180.

Dunnett, C. W. (1980). Pairwise multiple comparisons in the homogeneous variance, unequal sample size cases. *Journal of the American Statistical Association, 75*, 789–795.

Hays, W. L. (1981). *Statistics* (3rd ed.). New York, NY: Holt, Rinehart & Winston.

Ito, K. (1962). A comparison of the powers of two MANOVA tests. *Biometrika, 49*, 455–462.

Johnson, N., & Wichern, D. (1982). *Applied multivariate statistical analysis*. Englewood Cliffs, NJ: Prentice Hall.

Keppel, G., & Wickens, T. D. (2004). *Design and analysis: A researcher's handbook* (4th ed.). Upper Saddle River, NJ: Prentice Hall.

Keselman, H. J., Murray, R., & Rogan, J. (1976). Effect of very unequal group sizes on Tukey's multiple comparison test. *Educational and Psychological Measurement, 36*, 263–270.

Lauter, J. (1978). Sample size requirements for the T2 test of MANOVA (tables for one-way classification). *Biometrical Journal, 20*, 389–406.

Levin, J. R., Serlin, R. C., & Seaman, M. A. (1994). A controlled, powerful multiple-comparison strategy for several situations. *Psychological Bulletin, 115*, 153–159.

Lohnes, P. R. (1961). Test space and discriminant space classification models and related significance tests. *Educational and Psychological Measurement, 21*, 559–574.

Morrison, D. F. (1967). *Multivariate statistical methods*. New York, NY: McGraw-Hill.

Novince, L. (1977). *The contribution of cognitive restructuring to the effectiveness of behavior rehearsal in modifying social inhibition in females*. Unpublished doctoral dissertation, University of Cincinnati, OH.

Olson, C. L. (1973). A Monte Carlo investigation of the robustness of multivariate analysis of variance. *Dissertation Abstracts International, 35*, 6106B.

Olson, C. L. (1974). Comparative robustness of six tests in multivariate analysis of variance. *Journal of the American Statistical Association, 69*, 894–908.

Pillai, K., & Jayachandian, K. (1967). Power comparisons of tests of two multivariate hypotheses based on four criteria. *Biometrika, 54*, 195–210.

Pruzek, R. M. (1971). Methods and problems in the analysis of multivariate data. *Review of Educational Research, 41*, 163–190.

Stevens, J. P. (1972). Four methods of analyzing between variation for the k-group MANOVA problem. *Multivariate Behavioral Research, 7*, 499–522.

Stevens, J. P. (1979). Comment on Olson: Choosing a test statistic in multivariate analysis of variance. *Psychological Bulletin, 86*, 355–360.

Stevens, J. P. (1980). Power of the multivariate analysis of variance tests. *Psychological Bulletin, 88*, 728–737.

Tatsuoka, M. M. (1971). *Multivariate analysis: Techniques for educational and psychological research*. New York, NY: Wiley.

Wilkinson, L. (1975). Response variable hypotheses in the multivariate analysis of variance. *Psychological Bulletin, 82*, 408–412.

Chapter 6

ASSUMPTIONS IN MANOVA

6.1 INTRODUCTION

You may recall that one of the assumptions in analysis of variance is normality; that is, the scores for the subjects in each group are normally distributed. Why should we be interested in studying assumptions in ANOVA and MANOVA? Because, in ANOVA and MANOVA, we set up a mathematical model based on these assumptions, and all mathematical models are approximations to reality. Therefore, violations of the assumptions are inevitable. The salient question becomes: How radically must a given assumption be violated before it has a serious effect on type I and type II error rates? Thus, we may set our $\alpha = .05$ and think we are rejecting falsely 5% of the time, but if a given assumption is violated, we may be rejecting falsely 10%, or if another assumption is violated, we may be rejecting falsely 40% of the time. For these kinds of situations, we would certainly want to be able to detect such violations and take some corrective action, but all violations of assumptions are not serious, and hence it is crucial to know *which* assumptions to be particularly concerned about, and under what conditions.

In this chapter, we consider in detail what effect violating assumptions has on type I error and power. There has been plenty of research on violations of assumptions in ANOVA and a fair amount of research for MANOVA on which to base our conclusions. First, we remind you of some basic terminology that is needed to discuss the results of simulation (i.e., Monte Carlo) studies, whether univariate or multivariate. The nominal α (level of significance) is the α level set by the experimenter, and is the proportion of time one is rejecting falsely when *all* assumptions are met. The *actual* α is the proportion of time one is rejecting falsely if one or more of the assumptions is violated. We say the F statistic is *robust* when the actual α is very close to the level of significance (nominal α). For example, the actual αs for some very skewed (non-normal) populations may be only .055 or .06, very minor deviations from the level of significance of .05.

6.2 ANOVA AND MANOVA ASSUMPTIONS

The three statistical assumptions for univariate ANOVA are:

1. The observations are independent. (violation very serious)
2. The observations are normally distributed on the dependent variable in each group.
   (robust with respect to type I error)
   (skewness has generally very little effect on power, while platykurtosis attenuates power)
3. The population variances for the groups are equal, often referred to as the *homogeneity of variance* assumption.
   (conditionally robust—robust if group sizes are equal or approximately equal—largest/smallest < 1.5)

The assumptions for MANOVA are as follows:

1. The observations are independent. (violation very serious)
2. The observations on the dependent variables follow a multivariate normal distribution in each group.
   (robust with respect to type I error)
   (no studies on effect of skewness on power, but platykurtosis attenuates power)
3. The population covariance matrices for the p dependent variables are equal. (conditionally robust—robust if the group sizes are equal or approximately equal—largest/smallest < 1.5)

6.3 INDEPENDENCE ASSUMPTION

Note that independence of observations is an assumption for both ANOVA and MANOVA. We have listed this assumption first and are emphasizing it for three reasons:

1. A violation of this assumption is *very* serious.
2. Dependent observations do occur fairly often in social science research.
3. Some statistics books do not mention this assumption, and in some cases where they do, misleading statements are made (e.g., that dependent observations occur only infrequently, that random assignment of subjects to groups will eliminate the problem, or that this assumption is usually satisfied by using a random sample).

Now let us consider several situations in social science research where dependence among the observations will be present. Cooperative learning has become very popular since the early 1980s. In this method, students work in small groups, interacting with each other and helping each other learn the lesson. In fact, the evaluation of the success of the group is dependent on the individual success of its members. Many studies have compared cooperative learning versus individualistic learning. It was once common that such data was not analyzed properly (Hykle, Stevens, & Markle, 1993). That is, analyses would be conducted using individual scores while not taking into account the dependence among the observations. With the increasing use of multilevel modeling, such analyses are likely not as common.

Teaching methods studies constitute another broad class of situations where dependence of observations is undoubtedly present. For example, a few troublemakers in a classroom would have a detrimental effect on the achievement of many children in the classroom. Thus, their posttest achievement would be at least partially dependent on the disruptive classroom atmosphere. On the other hand, even with a favorable classroom atmosphere, dependence is introduced, because the achievement of many of the children will be enhanced by the positive learning situation. Therefore, in either case (positive or negative classroom atmosphere), the achievement of each child is not independent of the other children in the classroom.

Another situation in which observations would be dependent is a study comparing the achievement of students working in pairs at computers versus students working in groups of three. Here, if Bill and John, say, are working at the same computer, then obviously Bill's achievement is partially influenced by John. If individual scores were to be used in the analysis, clustering effects, due to working at the same computer, need to be accounted for in the analysis.

Glass and Hopkins (1984) made the following statement concerning situations where independence may or may not be tenable: "Whenever the treatment is individually administered, observations are independent. But where treatments involve interaction among persons, such as discussion method or group counseling, the observations may influence each other" (p. 353).

6.3.1 Effect of Correlated Observations

We indicated earlier that a violation of the independence of observations assumption is very serious. We now elaborate on this assertion. Just a *small* amount of dependence among the observations causes the actual α to be several times greater than the level of significance. Dependence among the observations is measured by the intraclass correlation ICC, where:

$$ICC = MS_b - MS_w / [MS_b + (n-1)MS_w]$$

M_b and MS_w are the numerator and denominator of the F statistic and n is the number of participants in each group.

Table 6.1, from Scariano and Davenport (1987), shows precisely how dramatic an effect dependence has on type I error. For example, for the three-group case with 10 participants per group and moderate dependence ($ICC = .30$), the actual α is .54. Also, for three groups with 30 participants per group and small dependence ($ICC = .10$), the

■ **Table 6.1: Actual Type I Error Rates for Correlated Observations in a One-Way ANOVA**

Number of groups	Group size	Intraclass correlation								
		.00	.01	.10	.30	.50	.70	.90	.95	.99
2	3	.0500	.0522	.0740	.1402	.2374	.3819	.6275	.7339	.8800
	10	.0500	.0606	.1654	.3729	.5344	.6752	.8282	.8809	.9475
	30	.0500	.0848	.3402	.5928	.7205	.8131	.9036	.9335	.9708
	100	.0500	.1658	.5716	.7662	.8446	.8976	.9477	.9640	.9842
3	3	.0500	.0529	.0837	.1866	.3430	.5585	.8367	.9163	.9829
	10	.0500	.0641	.2227	.5379	.7397	.8718	.9639	.9826	.9966
	30	.0500	.0985	.4917	.7999	.9049	.9573	.9886	.9946	.9990
	100	.0500	.2236	.7791	.9333	.9705	.9872	.9966	.9984	.9997
5	3	.0500	.0540	.0997	.2684	.5149	.7808	.9704	.9923	.9997
	10	.0500	.0692	.3151	.7446	.9175	.9798	.9984	.9996	1.0000
	30	.0500	.1192	.6908	.9506	.9888	.9977	.9998	1.0000	1.0000
	100	.0500	.3147	.9397	.9945	.9989	.9998	1.0000	1.0000	1.0000
10	3	.0500	.0560	.1323	.4396	.7837	.9664	.9997	1.0000	1.0000
	10	.0500	.0783	.4945	.9439	.9957	.9998	1.0000	1.0000	1.0000
	30	.0500	.1594	.9119	.9986	1.0000	1.0000	1.0000	1.0000	1.0000
	100	.0500	.4892	.9978	1.0000	1.0000	1.0000	1.0000	1.0000	1.0000

actual α is .49, almost 10 times the level of significance. Notice, also, from the table, that for a fixed value of the intraclass correlation, the situation does not improve with larger sample size, but gets far worse.

6.4 WHAT SHOULD BE DONE WITH CORRELATED OBSERVATIONS?

Given the results in Table 6.1 for a positive intraclass correlation, one route investigators could take if they suspect that the nature of their study will lead to correlated observations is to test at a more stringent level of significance. For the three- and five-group cases in Table 6.1, with 10 observations per group and intraclass correlation = .10, the error rates are five to six times greater than the assumed level of significance of .05. Thus, for this type of situation, it would be wise to test at α = .01, realizing that the actual error rate will be about .05 or somewhat greater. For the three- and five-group cases in Table 6.1 with 30 observations per group and intraclass correlation = .10, the error rates are about 10 times greater than .05. Here, it would be advisable to either test at .01, realizing that the actual α will be about .10, or test at an even more stringent α level.

If several small groups (counseling, social interaction, etc.) are involved in each treatment, and there are clear reasons to suspect that observations will be correlated within the groups but uncorrelated across groups, then consider using the *group mean* as the unit of analysis. Of course, this will reduce the effective sample size considerably; however, this will not cause as drastic a drop in power as some have feared. The reason is that the means are much more stable than individual observations and, hence, the within-group variability will be far less.

Table 6.2, from Barcikowski (1981), shows that if the effect size is medium or large, then the number of groups needed per treatment for power .80 doesn't have to be that large. For example, at α = .10, intraclass correlation = .10, and medium effect size, 10 groups (of 10 subjects each) are needed per treatment. For power .70 (which we consider adequate) at α = .15, one probably could get by with about six groups of 10 per treatment. This is a rough estimate, because it involves double extrapolation.

A third and much more commonly used method of analysis is one that directly adjusts parameter estimates for the degree of clustering. Multilevel modeling is a procedure that accommodates various forms of clustering. Chapter 13 covers fundamental concepts and applications, while Chapter 14 covers multivariate extensions of this procedure.

■ Table 6.2: **Number of Groups per Treatment Necessary for Power > .80 in a Two-Treatment-Level Design**

		Intraclass correlation for effect size[a]					
		.10			.20		
α Level	Number of groups	.20	.50	.80	.20	.50	.80
	10	73	13	6	107	18	8
	15	62	11	5	97	17	8
	20	56	10	5	92	16	7
.05	25	53	10	5	89	16	7
	30	51	9	5	87	15	7
	35	49	9	5	86	15	7
	40	48	9	5	85	15	7
	10	57	10	5	83	14	7
	15	48	9	4	76	13	6
	20	44	8	4	72	13	6
.10	25	41	8	4	69	12	6
	30	39	7	4	68	12	6
	35	38	7	4	67	12	5
	40	37	7	4	66	12	5

[a] .20 = small effect size; .50 = medium effect size; .80 = large effect size.

Before we leave the topic of correlated observations, we wish to mention an interesting paper by Kenny and Judd (1986), who discussed how nonindependent observations can arise because of several factors, grouping being one of them. The following quote from their paper is important to keep in mind for applied researchers:

> Throughout this article we have treated nonindependence as a statistical nuisance, to be avoided because of the bias it introduces. . . . There are, however, many occasions when nonindependence is the substantive problem that we are trying to understand in psychological research. For instance, in developmental psychology, a frequently asked question concerns the development of social interaction. Developmental researchers study the content and rate of vocalization from infants for cues about the onset of interaction. Social interaction implies nonindependence between the vocalizations of interacting individuals. To study interaction developmentally, then, we should be interested in nonindependence not solely as a statistical problem, but also a substantive focus in itself. . . . In social psychology, one of the fundamental questions concerns how individual behavior is modified by group contexts. (p. 431)

6.5 NORMALITY ASSUMPTION

Recall that the second assumption for ANOVA is that the observations are normally distributed in each group. What are the consequences of violating this assumption? An excellent early review regarding violations of assumptions in ANOVA was done by Glass, Peckham, and Sanders (1972). This review concluded that the ANOVA F test is largely robust to normality violations. In particular, they found that skewness has only a slight effect (generally only a few hundredths) on the alpha level or power associated with the F test. The effects of kurtosis on level of significance, although greater, also tend to be slight.

You may be puzzled as to how this can be. The basic reason is the *Central Limit Theorem*, which states that the sum of independent observations having any distribution whatsoever approaches a normal distribution as the number of observations increases. To be somewhat more specific, Bock (1975) noted, "even for distributions which depart markedly from normality, sums of 50 or more observations approximate to normality. For moderately nonnormal distributions the approximation is good with as few as 10 to 20 observations" (p. 111). Because the sums of independent observations approach normality rapidly, so do the means, and the sampling distribution of F is based on means. Thus, the sampling distribution of F is only slightly affected, and therefore the critical values when sampling from normal and nonnormal distributions will not differ by much.

With respect to power, a platykurtic distribution (a flattened distribution with thinner tails relative to the normal distribution indicated by a negative kurtosis value) does attenuate power. Note also that more recently, Wilcox (2012) pointed that the ANOVA

F test is not robust to certain violations of normality, which if present may inflate the type I error rate to unacceptable levels. However, it appears that data have to be very nonnormal for problems to arise, and these arise primarily when group sizes are unequal. For example, in a meta analysis reported by Lix, Keselman, and Keselman (1996), when skew = 2 and kurtosis = 6, the type I error rate for the ANOVA F test remains close to its nominal value of .05 (mean alpha reported under nonnormality as .059 with a standard deviation of .026). For unequal group size with the same degree of nonnormality, type I error rates can be somewhat inflated (mean alpha = .069 with a standard deviation of .048). Thus, while the ANOVA F test appears to be largely robust under normality violations, it is important to assess normality and take some corrective steps when gross departures are found especially when group sizes are unequal.

6.6 MULTIVARIATE NORMALITY

The multivariate normality assumption is a much more stringent assumption than the corresponding assumption of normality on a single variable in ANOVA. Although it is difficult to completely characterize multivariate normality, *normality on each of the variables separately is a necessary, but not sufficient, condition for multivariate normality to hold.* That is, each of the individual variables must be normally distributed for the variables to follow a multivariate normal distribution. Two other properties of a multivariate normal distribution are: (1) any linear combination of the variables are normally distributed, and (2) all subsets of the set of variables have multivariate normal distributions. This latter property implies, among other things, that all pairs of variables must be bivariate normal. Bivariate normality, for correlated variables, implies that the scatterplots for each pair of variables will be elliptical; the higher the correlation, the thinner the ellipse. Thus, as a partial check on multivariate normality, one could obtain the scatterplots for pairs of variables from SPSS or SAS and see if they are approximately elliptical.

6.6.1 Effect of Nonmultivariate Normality on Type I Error and Power

Results from various studies that considered up to 10 variables and small or moderate sample sizes (Everitt, 1979; Hopkins & Clay, 1963; Mardia, 1971; Olson, 1973) indicate that *deviation from multivariate normality has only a small effect on type I error.* In almost all cases in these studies, the actual α was within .02 of the level of significance for levels of .05 and .10.

Olson found, however, that platykurtosis does have an effect on power, and the severity of the effect increases as platykurtosis spreads from one to all groups. For example, in one specific instance, power was close to 1 under no violation. With kurtosis present in just one group, the power dropped to about .90. When kurtosis was present in all three groups, the power dropped substantially, to .55.

You should note that what has been found in MANOVA is consistent with what was found in univariate ANOVA, in which the F statistic is often robust with respect to type I error against nonnormality, making it plausible that this robustness might extend to the multivariate case; this, indeed, is what has been found. Incidentally, there is a multivariate extension of the Central Limit Theorem, which also makes the multivariate results not entirely surprising. Second, Olson's result, that platykurtosis has a substantial effect on power, should not be surprising, given that platykurtosis had been shown in univariate ANOVA to have a substantial effect on power for small n's (Glass et al., 1972).

With respect to skewness, again the Glass et al. (1972) review suggesting that distortions of power values are rarely greater than a few hundredths for univariate ANOVA, even with considerably skewed distributions. Thus, it could well be the case that multivariate skewness also has a negligible effect on power, although we have not located any studies bearing on this issue.

6.7 ASSESSING THE NORMALITY ASSUMPTION

If a set of variables follows a multivariate normal distribution, each of the variables must be normally distributed. Therefore, it is often recommended that before other procedures are used, you check to see if the scores for each variable appear to approximate a normal distribution. If univariate normality does not appear to hold, we know then that the multivariate normality assumption is violated. There are two other reasons it makes sense to assess univariate normality:

1. As Gnanadesikan (1977) has stated, "in practice, except for rare or pathological examples, the presence of joint (multivariate) normality is likely to be detected quite often by methods directed at studying the marginal (univariate) normality of the observations on each variable" (p. 168). Johnson and Wichern (2007) made essentially the same point: "Moreover, for most practical work, one-dimensional and two-dimensional investigations are ordinarily sufficient. Fortunately, pathological data sets that are normal in lower dimensional representations but nonnormal in higher dimensions are not frequently encountered in practice" (p. 177).
2. Because the Box test for the homogeneity of covariance matrices assumption is quite sensitive to nonnormality, we wish to detect nonnormality on the individual variables and transform to normality to bring the joint distribution much closer to multivariate normality so that the Box test is not unduly affected. With respect to transformations, Figure 6.1 should be quite helpful.

6.7.1 Assessing Univariate Normality

There are several ways to assess univariate normality. First, for each group, you can examine values of skewness and kurtosis for your data. Briefly, skewness refers to lack of symmetry in a score distribution, whereas kurtosis refers to how peaked a distribution is and the degree to which the tails of the distribution are light or heavy relative

Figure 6.1: Distributional transformations (from Rummel, 1970).

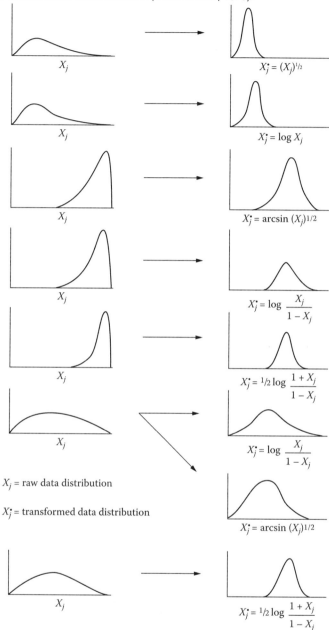

X_j = raw data distribution

X_j^* = transformed data distribution

to the normal distribution. The formulas for these indicators as used by SAS and SPSS are such that if scores are normally distributed, skewness and kurtosis will each have a value of zero.

There are two ways that skewness and kurtosis measures are used to evaluate the normality assumption. A simple rule is to compare each group's skewness and kurtosis values to a magnitude of 2 (although values of 1 or 3 are sometimes used). Then, if the values of skewness and kurtosis are each smaller in magnitude than 2, you would conclude that the distribution does not depart greatly from a normal distribution, or is reasonably consistent with the normal distribution. The second way these measures are sometimes used is to consider a score distribution to be approximately normal if the sample values of skewness and kurtosis each lie within ±2 standard errors of the respective measure. So, for example, suppose that the standard error for skewness (as obtained by SAS or SPSS) were .75 and the standard error for kurtosis were .60. Then, the scores would be considered to reasonably approximate a normal distribution if the sample skewness value were within the span of −1.5 to 1.5 (±2 × .75) and the sample kurtosis value were within the span of −1.2 to 1.2 (±2 × .60). Note that this latter procedure approximates a z test for skewness and kurtosis assuming an alpha of .05. Like any statistical test, then, this procedure will be sensitive to sample size, providing generally lower power for smaller n and greater power for larger n.

A second method of assessing univariate normality is to examine plots for each group. Commonly used plots include a histogram, stem and leaf plot, box plot, and Q-Q plot. The latter plot shows observations arranged in increasing order of magnitude and then plotted against the expected normal distribution values. This plot should resemble a straight line if normality is tenable. These plots are available on SAS and SPSS. Note that with a small or moderate group size, it may be difficult to discern whether non-normality is real or apparent, because of considerable sampling error. As such, the skewness and kurtosis values may be examined, as mentioned, and statistical tests of normality may conducted, which we consider next.

A third method of assessing univariate normality it to use omnibus statistical tests for normality. These tests includes the chi-square goodness of fit, Kolmogorov–Smirnov, Shapiro–Wilk, and the z test approximations for skewness and kurtosis discussed earlier. The chi-square test suffers from the defect of depending on the number of intervals used for the grouping, whereas the Kolmogorov–Smirnov test was shown not to be as powerful as the Shapiro–Wilk test or the combination of using the skewness and kurtosis coefficients in an extensive Monte Carlo study by Wilk, Shapiro, and Chen (1968). These investigators studied 44 different distributions, with sample sizes ranging from 10 to 50, and found that the combination of skewness and kurtosis coefficients and the Shapiro–Wilk test were the most powerful in detecting departures from normality. They also found that extreme nonnormality can be detected with sample sizes of less than 20 by using sensitive procedures (like the two just mentioned). This is important, because for many practical problems, group sizes are small. Note though that with large group sizes, these tests may be quite powerful. As such it is a good idea to use test results along with examining plots and the skewness and kurtosis descriptive statistics to get a sense of the degree of departure from normality.

For univariate tests, we prefer the Shapiro–Wilk statistic due to its superior performance for small samples. Note that the null hypothesis for this test is that the variable being tested is normally distributed. Thus, a small p value (i.e., $< .05$) indicates a violation of the normality assumption. This test statistic is easily obtained with the EXAMINE procedure in SPSS. This procedure also yields the skewness and kurtosis coefficients, along with their standard errors, and various plots. All of this information is useful in determining whether there is a significant departure from normality, and whether skewness or kurtosis is primarily responsible.

6.7.2 Assessing Multivariate Normality

Several methods can be used to assess the multivariate normality assumption. First, as noted, checking to see if univariate normality is tenable provides a check on the multivariate normality assumption because if univariate normality is not present, neither is multivariate normality. Note though that multivariate normality may not hold even if univariate normality does. As noted earlier, assessing univariate normality is often sufficient in practice to detect serious violations of the multivariate normality assumption, especially when combined with checking for bivariate normality. The latter can be done by examining all possible bivariate scatter plots (although this becomes less practical when many variables and many groups are present). Thus, for this edition of the text (as in the previous edition), we will continue to focus on the use of these methods to assess normality. We will, though, describe some multivariate methods for assessing the multivariate normality assumption as these methods are beginning to become available in general purpose software programs, such as SAS and SPSS.

Two different multivariate methods are available to assess whether the multivariate normality assumption is tenable. First, many different multivariate test statistics have been developed to assess multivariate normality, including, for example, Mardia's (1970) test of multivariate skewness and kurtosis, Small's (1980) omnibus test of multivariate normality, and the Henze–Zirkler (1990) test of multivariate normality. While there appears to be limited evaluation of the performance of these multivariate tests, Looney (1995) reports some simulation evidence suggesting that Small's test has better performance than some other tests, and Mecklin and Mundfrom (2003) found that the Henze–Zirkler test is the best performing test of multivariate normality of the methods they examined.

As of this edition of the text, SPSS does not include any tests of multivariate normality in its procedures. However, Decarlo (1997) has developed a macro that can be used with SPSS (which is freely available at http://www.columbia.edu/~ld208/). This macro implements a variety of tests for multivariate normality, including Small's omnibus test mentioned previously. SAS now includes multivariate normality tests in the PROC MODEL procedure via the fit option, which includes the Henze–Zirkler test (as well as other normality tests).

The second multivariate procedure that is available to assess multivariate normality is a graphical assessment procedure. This graph compares the squared Mahalanobis distances associated with the dependent variables to the values expected if multivariate normality holds (analogous to the univariate Q-Q plot). Often, the expected values are obtained from a chi-square distribution. Note though that Rencher and Christensen (2012) state that the chi-square approximation often used in this plot can be poor and do not recommend it for assessing multivariate normality. They discuss an alternative plot in their text.

6.7.3 Assessing Univariate Normality Using SPSS

We now show how you can use some of these procedures to assess normality. Our example comes from a study on the cost of transporting milk from farms to dairy plants.

Example 6.1

From a survey, cost data on $Y1$ = fuel, $Y2$ = repair, and $Y3$ = capital (all measures on a per mile basis) were obtained for two types of trucks, gasoline and diesel. Thus, we have a two-group MANOVA, with three dependent variables. First, we ran this data through the SPSS DESCRIPTIVES program. The complete lines for doing so are presented in Table 6.3. This was done to obtain the z scores for the variables *within each group*. Converting to z scores makes it much easier to identify potential outliers. Any variables with z values substantially greater than 2.5 or so (in absolute value) need to be examined carefully. When we examined the z scores, we found three observations with z scores greater than 2.5, all of which occurred for $Y1$. These scores were found for case 9, $z = 3.52$, case 21, $z = 2.91$ (both in group 1), and case 52, $z = 2.77$ (in group 2). These cases, then, would need to be carefully examined to make sure data entry is accurate and to make sure these score are valid.

Next, we used the SPSS EXAMINE procedure with these data to obtain, among other things, the Shapiro–Wilk test for normality for each variable in each group and the group skewness and kurtosis values. The commands for doing this appear in Table 6.4.

The test results for the three variables in each group are shown next. If we were testing for normality in each case at the .05 level, then only variable $Y1$ deviates from normality in just group 1, as the p value for the Shapiro–Wilk statistic is smaller

■ **Table 6.3: Control Lines for SPSS Descriptives for Three Variables in Two-Group MANOVA**

```
TITLE 'SPLIT FILE FOR MILK DATA'.
DATA LIST FREE/gp y1 y2 y3.
BEGIN DATA.
  DATA LINES (raw data are on-line)
END DATA.
SPLIT FILE BY gp.
DESCRIPTIVES VARIABLES=y1 y2 y3
 /SAVE
 /STATISTICS=MEAN STDDEV MIN MAX.
```

■ **Table 6.4: SPSS Commands for the EXAMINE Procedure for the Two-Group MANOVA**

```
TITLE 'TWO GROUP MANOVA — 3 DEPENDENT VARIABLES'.
DATA LIST FREE/gp y1 y2 y3.
BEGIN DATA.
 DATA LINES (data are on-line)
END DATA.
(1)  EXAMINE VARIABLES = y1 y2 y3 BY gp
(2)  /PLOT = STEMLEAF NPPLOT.
```

(1) The BY keyword will yield variety of descriptive statistics for each group: mean, median, skewness, kurtosis, etc.

(2) STEMLEAF will yield a stem-and-leaf plot for each variable in each group. NPPLOT yields normal probability plots, as well as the Shapiro–Wilk and Kolmogorov–Smirnov statistical tests for normality for each variable in each group.

than .05. In addition, while all other skewness and kurtosis values are smaller then 2, the skewness and kurtosis values for $Y1$ in group 1 are 1.87 and 4.88. Thus, both the statistical test result and the kurtosis value indicate a violation of normality for $Y1$ in group 1. Note that given the positive value for kurtosis, we would not expect this departure from normality to have much of an effect on power, and hence we would not be very concerned. We would have been concerned if we had found deviation from normality on two or more variables, and this deviation was due to platykurtosis (indicated by a negative kurtosis value). In this case, we would have applied the last transformation in Figure 6.1: [.05 log $(1 + X)$] / $(1 - X)$. Note also that the outliers found for group 1 greatly affect the assessment of normality. If these values were judged not to be valid and removed from the analysis, the resulting assessment of normality would have concluded no normality violations. This highlights the value of attending to outliers prior to engaging in other analysis activities.

		Tests of normality					
		Kolmogorov-Smirnov[a]			Shapiro-Wilk		
	Gp	Statistic	df	Sig.	Statistic	df	Sig.
y1	1.00	.157	36	.026	.837	36	.000
	2.00	.091	23	.200*	.962	23	.512
y2	1.00	.125	36	.171	.963	36	.262
	2.00	.118	23	.200*	.962	23	.500
y3	1.00	.073	36	.200*	.971	36	.453
	2.00	.111	23	.200*	.969	23	.658

* This is a lower bound of the true significance.
[a] Lilliefors Significance Correction

6.8 HOMOGENEITY OF VARIANCE ASSUMPTION

Recall that the third assumption for ANOVA is that of equal population variances. It is widely known that ANOVA F test is *not* robust when unequal group sizes are combined with unequal variances. In particular, when group sizes are sharply unequal (largest/smallest > 1.5) and the population variances differ, then if the larger groups have smaller variances the F statistic is liberal. A liberal test result means we are rejecting falsely too often; that is, actual α > nominal level of significance. Thus, you may think you are rejecting falsely 5% of the time, but the true rejection rate (actual α) may be 11%. When the larger groups have larger variances, then the F statistic is conservative. This means actual α < nominal level of significance. At first glance, this may not appear to be a problem, but note that the smaller α will cause a decrease in power, and in many studies, one can ill afford to have power further attenuated.

With group sizes are equal or approximately equal (largest/smallest < 1.5), the ANOVA F test is often robust to violations of equal group variance. In fact, early research into this issue, such as reported in Glass et al. (1972), indicated that ANOVA F test is robust to such violations provided that groups are of equal size. More recently, though, research, as described in Coombs, Algina, and Oltman (1996), has shown that the ANOVA F test, even when group sizes are equal, is not robust when group variances differ greatly. For example, as reported in Coombs et al., if the common group size is 11 and the variances are in the ratio of 16:1:1:1, then the type I error rate associated with the F test is .109. While the ANOVA F test, then, is not completely robust to unequal variances even when group sizes are the same, this research suggests that the variances must differ substantially for this problem to arise. Further, the robustness of the ANOVA F test improves in this situation when the equal group size is larger.

It is important to note that many of the frequently used tests for homogeneity of variance, such as Bartlett's, Cochran's, and Hartley's F_{max}, are quite sensitive to nonnormality. That is, with these tests, one may reject and erroneously conclude that the population variances are different when, in fact, the rejection was due to nonnormality in the underlying populations. Fortunately, Levene has a test that is more robust against nonnormality. This test is available in the EXAMINE procedure in SPSS. The test statistic is formed by deviating the scores for the subjects in each group from the group mean, and then taking the absolute values. Thus, $z_{ij} = \left| x_{ij} - \overline{x}_j \right|$, where $\overline{x}_j$ represents the mean for the jth group. An ANOVA is then done on the $\overline{z}_{ij}$s. Although the Levene test is somewhat more robust, an extensive Monte Carlo study by Conover, Johnson, and Johnson (1981) showed that if considerable skewness is present, a modification of the Levene test is necessary for it to remain robust. The mean for each group is replaced by the median, and an ANOVA is done on the deviation scores from the group medians. This modification produces a more robust test with good power. It is available on SAS and SPSS.

6.9 HOMOGENEITY OF THE COVARIANCE MATRICES*

The assumption of equal (homogeneous) covariance matrices is a very restrictive one. Recall from the matrix algebra chapter (Chapter 2) that two matrices are equal only if all corresponding elements are equal. Let us consider a two-group problem with five dependent variables. All corresponding elements in the two matrices being equal implies, first, that the corresponding diagonal elements are equal. This means that the five population variances in group 1 are equal to their counterparts in group 2. But all nondiagonal elements must also be equal for the matrices to be equal, and this implies that all covariances are equal. Because for five variables there are 10 covariances, this means that the 10 population covariances in group 1 are equal to their counterpart covariances in group 2. Thus, for only five variables, the equal covariance matrices assumption requires that 15 elements of group 1 be equal to their counterparts in group 2.

For eight variables, the assumption implies that the eight population variances in group 1 are equal to their counterparts in group 2 *and* that the 28 corresponding covariances for the two groups are equal. The restrictiveness of the assumption becomes more strikingly apparent when we realize that the corresponding assumption for the univariate t test is that the variances on only *one* variable be equal.

Hence, it is very unlikely that the equal covariance matrices assumption would ever literally be satisfied in practice. The relevant question is: Will the very plausible violations of this assumption that occur in practice have much of an effect on power?

6.9.1 Effect of Heterogeneous Covariance Matrices on Type I Error

Three major Monte Carlo studies have examined the effect of unequal covariance matrices on error rates: Holloway and Dunn (1967) and Hakstian, Roed, and Linn (1979) for the two-group case, and Olson (1974) for the k-group case. Holloway and Dunn considered both equal and unequal group sizes and modeled moderate to extreme heterogeneity. A representative sampling of their results, presented in Table 6.5, shows that *equal ns keep the actual α very close to the level of significance (within a few percentage points) for all but the extreme cases.* Sharply unequal group sizes for moderate inequality, with the larger group having smaller variability, produce a liberal test. In fact, the test can become very liberal (cf., three variables, $N_1 = 35$, $N_2 = 15$, actual α = .175). When larger groups have larger variability, this produces a conservative test.

Hakstian et al. (1979) modeled heterogeneity that was milder and, we believe, somewhat more representative of what is encountered in practice, than that considered in the Holloway and Dunn study. They also considered more disparate group sizes (up to a ratio of 5 to 1) for the 2-, 6-, and 10-variable cases. The following three heterogeneity conditions were examined:

---

* Appendix 6.2 discusses multivariate test statistics for unequal covariance matrices.

■ **Table 6.5:** Effect of Heterogeneous Covariance Matrices on Type I Error for Hotelling's T^2 (1)

| | Number of observations per group | | Degree of heterogeneity | |
| | | | D = 3 (3) | D = 10 |
Number of variables	N_1	N_2 (2)	(Moderate)	(Very large)
3	15	35	.015	0
3	20	30	.03	.02
3	25	25	.055	.07
3	30	20	.09	.15
3	35	15	.175	.28
7	15	35	.01	0
7	20	30	.03	.02
7	25	25	.06	.08
7	30	20	.13	.27
7	35	15	.24	.40
10	15	35	.01	0
10	20	30	.03	.03
10	25	25	.08	.12
10	30	20	.17	.33
10	35	15	.31	.40

(1) Nominal α = .05.

(2) Group 2 is more variable.

(3) D = 3 means that the population variances for all variables in Group 2 are 3 times as large as the population variances for those variables in Group 1.

Source: Data from Holloway and Dunn (1967).

1. The population variances for the variables in Population 2 are only 1.44 times as great as those for the variables in Population 1.
2. The Population 2 variances and covariances are 2.25 times as great as those for all variables in Population 1.
3. The Population 2 variances and covariances are 2.25 times as great as those for Population 1 for only *half* the variables.

The results in Table 6.6 for the six-variable case are representative of what Hakstian et al. found. Their results are consistent with the Holloway and Dunn findings, but they extend them in two ways. First, even for milder heterogeneity, sharply unequal group sizes can produce sizable distortions in the type I error rate (cf., 24:12, Heterogeneity 2 (negative): actual α = .127 vs. level of significance = .05). Second, *severely unequal group sizes can produce sizable distortions in type I error rates, even for very mild heterogeneity* (cf., 30:6, Heterogeneity 1 (negative): actual α = .117 vs. level of significance = .05).

Olson (1974) considered only equal *n*s and warned, on the basis of the Holloway and Dunn results and some preliminary findings of his own, that researchers would be well

■ **Table 6.6: Effect of Heterogeneous Covariance Matrices with Six Variables on Type I Error for Hotelling's T^2**

$N_1:N_2(1)$	Nominal α	Heterog. 1		Heterog. 2		Heterog. 3	
		(2) POS.	NEG.	POS.	NEG.	POS.	NEG. (3)
18:18	.01		.006		.011		.012
	.05		.048		.057		.064
	.10		.099		.109		.114
24:12	.01	.007	.020	.005	.043	.006	.018
	.05	.035	.088	.021	.127	.028	.076
	.10	.068	.155	.051	.214	.072	.158
30:6	.01	.004	.036	.000	.103	.003	.046
	.05	.018	.117	.004	.249	.022	.145
	.10	.045	.202	.012	.358	.046	.231

(1) Ratio of the group sizes.
(2) Condition in which the larger group has the larger generalized variance.
(3) Condition in which the larger group has the smaller generalized variance.

Source: Data from Hakstian, Roed, and Lind (1979).

advised to strive to attain equal group sizes in the *k*-group case. The results of Olson's study should be interpreted with care, because he modeled primarily *extreme* heterogeneity (i.e., cases where the population variances of all variables in one group were 36 times as great as the variances of those variables in all the other groups).

6.9.2 Testing Homogeneity of Covariance Matrices: The Box Test

Box (1949) developed a test that is a generalization of the Bartlett univariate homogeneity of variance test, for determining whether the covariance matrices are equal. The test uses the *generalized variances*; that is, the determinants of the within-covariance matrices. It is very sensitive to nonnormality. Thus, one may reject with the Box test because of a lack of multivariate normality, not because the covariance matrices are unequal. Therefore, before employing the Box test, it is important to see whether the multivariate normality assumption is reasonable. As suggested earlier in this chapter, a check of marginal normality for the individual variables is probably sufficient (inspecting plots, examining values for skewness and kurtosis, and using the Shapiro–Wilk test). Where there is a departure from normality, use a suitable transformation (see Figure 6.1).

Box has given an χ^2 approximation and an *F* approximation for his test statistic, both of which appear on the SPSS MANOVA output, as an upcoming example in this section shows. To decide to which of these one should pay more attention, the following rule is helpful: When all group sizes are 20 and the number of dependent variables is six, the χ^2 approximation is fine. Otherwise, the *F* approximation is more accurate and should be used.

Example 6.2

To illustrate the use of SPSS MANOVA for assessing homogeneity of the covariance matrices, we consider, again, the data from Example 1. Note that we use the SPSS MANOVA procedure instead of GLM in order to obtain the natural log of the determinants, as discussed later. Recall that this example involved two types of trucks (gasoline and diesel), with measurements on three variables: $Y1$ = fuel, $Y2$ = repair, and $Y3$ = capital. The raw data were provided in the syntax online. Recall that there were 36 gasoline trucks and 23 diesel trucks, so we have sharply unequal group sizes. Thus, a significant Box test here will produce biased multivariate statistics that we need to worry about.

The commands for running the MANOVA, along with getting the Box test and some selected output, are presented in Table 6.7. It is in the PRINT subcommand that we obtain the multivariate (Box test) and univariate tests of homogeneity of variance. Note in Table 6.7 (center) that the Box test is significant well beyond the .01 level ($F = 5.088$, $p = .000$, approximately). We wish to determine whether the multivariate test statistics will be liberal or conservative. To do this, we examine the determinants of the covariance matrices. Remember that the determinant of the covariance matrix is the generalized variance; that is, it is the multivariate measure of within-group variability for a set of variables. In this case, the larger group (group 1) has the smaller generalized variance (i.e., 3,172). The effect of this is to produce positively biased (liberal) multivariate test statistics. Also, although this is not presented in Table 6.7, the group effect is quite significant ($F = 16.375$, $p = .000$, approximately). It is possible, then, that this significant group effect may be mainly due to the positive bias present.

■ **Table 6.7: SPSS MANOVA and EXAMINE Control Lines for Milk Data and Selected Output**

```
TITLE 'MILK DATA'.
DATA LIST FREE/gp y1 y2 y3.
BEGIN DATA.
  DATA LINES (raw data are on-line)
END DATA.
MANOVA y1 y2 y3 BY gp(1,2)
  /PRINT = HOMOGENEITY(COCHRAN, BOXM).
EXAMINE VARIABLES = y1 y2 y3 BY gp
  /PLOT = SPREADLEVEL.
```

Cell Number.. 1

Determinant of Covariance matrix of dependent variables =	3172.91372
LOG (Determinant) =	8.06241

Cell Number.. 2

Determinant of Covariance matrix of dependent variables =	4860.31030
LOG (Determinant) =	8.48886

Determinant of pooled Covariance matrix of dependent vars. =		6619.49636
LOG (Determinant) =		8.79777
Multivariate test for Homogeneity of Dispersion matrices		
Boxs M =	32.53409	
F WITH (6,14625) DF =	5.08834,	P = .000 (Approx.)
Chi-Square with 6 DF =	30.54336,	P = .000 (Approx.)

		Test of Homogeneity of Variance			
		Levene Statistic	*df*1	*df*2	Sig.
y1	Based on Mean	5.071	1	57	.028
y2	Based on Mean	.961	1	57	.331
y3	Based on Mean	6.361	1	57	.014

To see whether this is the case, we look for variance-stabilizing transformations that, hopefully, will make the Box test not significant, and then check to see whether the group effect is still significant. Note, in Table 6.7, that the Levene's tests of equal variance suggest there are significant variance differences for *Y1* and *Y3*.

The EXAMINE procedure was also run, and indicated that the following new variables will have approximately equal variances: $NEWY1 = Y1 ** (-1.678)$ and $NEWY3 = Y3 ** (.395)$. When these new variables, along with *Y2*, were run in a MANOVA (see Table 6.8), the Box test was *not* significant at the .05 level ($F = 1.79, p = .097$), but the group effect was still significant well beyond the .01 level ($F = 13.785, p > .001$ approximately).

We now consider two variations of this result. In the first, a violation would not be of concern. If the Box test had been significant and the larger group had the larger generalized variance, then the multivariate statistics would be conservative. In that case, we would not be concerned, for we would have found significance at an even more stringent level had the assumption been satisfied.

A second variation on the example results that would have been of concern is if the large group had the large generalized variance and the group effect was *not* significant. Then, it wouldn't be clear whether the reason we did not find significance was because of the conservativeness of the test statistic. In this case, we could simply test at a somewhat more liberal level, once again realizing that the effective alpha level will probably be around .05. Or, we could again seek variance stabilizing transformations.

With respect to transformations, there are two possible approaches. If there is a known relationship between the means and variances, then the following two transformations are

■ **Table 6.8: SPSS MANOVA and EXAMINE Commands for Milk Data Using Two Transformed Variables and Selected Output**

```
TITLE 'MILK DATA - Y1 AND Y3 TRANSFORMED'.
DATA LIST FREE/gp y1 y2 y3.
BEGIN DATA.
  DATA LINES
END DATA.
LIST.
COMPUTE NEWy1 = y1**(-1.678).
COMPUTE NEWy3 = y3**.395.
MANOVA NEWy1 y2 NEWy3 BY gp(1,2)
  /PRINT = CELLINFO(MEANS) HOMOGENEITY(BOXM, COCHRAN).
EXAMINE VARIABLES = NEWy1 y2 NEWy3 BY gp
  /PLOT = SPREADLEVEL.
```

Multivariate test for Homogeneity of Dispersion matrices

Boxs M =	11.44292	
F WITH (6,14625) DF =	1.78967,	P = .097 (Approx.)
Chi-Square with 6 DF =	10.74274,	P = .097 (Approx.)

EFFECT .. GP

Multivariate Tests of Significance (S = 1, M = 1/2, N = 26 1/2)

Test Name	Value	Exact F	Hypoth. DF	Error DF	Sig. of F
Pillais	.42920	13.78512	3.00	55.00	.000
Hotellings	.75192	13.78512	3.00	55.00	.000
Wilks	.57080	13.78512	3.00	55.00	.000
Roys	.42920				

Note .. F statistics are exact.

Test of Homogeneity of Variance

		Levene Statistic	df1	df2	Sig.
NEWy1	Based on Mean	1.008	1	57	.320
Y2	Based on Mean	.961	1	57	.331
NEWy3	Based on Mean	.451	1	57	.505

helpful. The square root transformation, where the original scores are replaced by $\sqrt{y_{ij}}$, will stabilize the variances if the means and variances are proportional for each group. This can happen when the data are in the form of frequency counts. If the scores are proportions, then the means and variances are related as follows: $\sigma_i^2 = \mu_i(1-\mu_i)$. This is true because, with proportions, we have a binomial variable, and for a binominal variable the variance is this function of its mean. The arcsine transformation, where the original scores are replaced by arcsin $\sqrt{y_{ij}}$, will also stabilize the variances in this case.

If the relationship between the means and the variances is not known, then one can let the data decide on an appropriate transformation (as in the previous example).

We now consider an example that illustrates the first approach, that of using a *known* relationship between the means and variances to stabilize the variances.

Example 6.3

	Group 1				Group 2				Group 3			
	Y1	Y2	Y1	Y2	Y1	Y2	Y1	Y2	Y1	Y2	Y1	Y2
	.30	5	3.5	4.0	5	4	9	5	14	5	18	8
	1.1	4	4.3	7.0	5	4	11	6	9	10	21	2
	5.1	8	1.9	7.0	12	6	5	3	20	2	12	2
	1.9	6	2.7	4.0	8	3	10	4	16	6	15	4
	4.3	4	5.9	7.0	13	4	7	2	23	9	12	5
MEANS	Y1 = 3.1		Y2 = 5.6		Y1 = 8.5		Y2 = 4		Y1 = 16		Y2 = 5.3	
VARIANCES	3.31		2.49		8.94		1.66		20		8.68	

Notice that for Y1, as the means increase (from group 1 to group 3) the variances also increase. Also, the ratio of variance to mean is approximately the same for the three groups: 3.31 / 3.1 = 1.068, 8.94 / 8.5 = 1.052, and 20 / 16 = 1.25. Further, the variances for Y2 differ by a fair amount. Thus, it is likely here that the homogeneity of covariance matrices assumption is not tenable. Indeed, when the MANOVA was run on SPSS, the Box test was significant at the .05 level ($F = 2.821$, $p = .010$), and the Cochran univariate tests for both variables were also significant at the .05 level (Y1: $p = .047$; Y2: $p = .014$).

Because the means and variances for Y1 are approximately proportional, as mentioned earlier, a square-root transformation will stabilize the variances. The commands for running SPSS MANOVA, with the square-root transformation on Y1, are given in Table 6.9, along with selected output. A few comments on the commands: It is in the COMPUTE command that we do the transformation, calling the transformed variable *RTY1*. We then use the transformed variable *RTY1*, along with Y2, in the MANOVA command for the analysis. Note the stabilizing effect of the square root transformation on Y1; the standard deviations are now approximately equal (.587, .522, and .568). Also, Box's test is no longer significant ($F = 1.73$, $p = .109$).

▨ **Table 6.9: SPSS Commands for Three-Group MANOVA with Unequal Variances (Illustrating Square-Root Transformation)**

```
TITLE 'THREE GROUP MANOVA - TRANSFORMING y1'.
DATA LIST FREE/gp y1 y2.
BEGIN DATA.
   DATA LINES
END DATA.
COMPUTE RTy1 = SQRT(y1).
MANOVA RTy1 y2 BY gp(1,3)
   /PRINT = CELLINFO(MEANS) HOMOGENEITY(COCHRAN, BOXM).
```

Cell Means and Standard Deviations
 Variable .. RTy1

FACTOR	CODE	Mean	Std. Dev.
gp	1	1.670	.587
gp	2	2.873	.522
gp	3	3.964	.568
For entire sample		2.836	1.095

- -

 Variable .. y2

FACTOR	CODE	Mean	Std. Dev.
gp	1	5.600	1.578
gp	2	4.100	1.287
gp	3	5.300	2.946
For entire sample		5.000	2.101

- -

Univariate Homogeneity of Variance Tests
Variable .. RTy1
    Cochrans C(9,3) =   .36712, P = 1.000 (approx.)
    Bartlett-Box F(2,1640) =   .06176, P = .940
Variable .. y2
    Cochrans C(9,3) =   .67678, P = .014 (approx.)
    Bartlett-Box F(2,1640) =   3.35877, P = .035

- -

Multivariate test for Homogeneity of Dispersion matrices
Boxs M =   11.65338
F WITH (6,18168) DF =   1.73378, P =   .109 (Approx.)
Chi-Square with 6 DF =   10.40652, P =   .109 (Approx.)

6.10 SUMMARY

We have considered each of the assumptions in MANOVA in some detail individually. We now tie together these pieces of information into an overall strategy for assessing assumptions in a practical problem.

1. Check to determine whether it is reasonable to assume the participants are responding independently; a violation of this assumption is very serious. Logically, from the context in which the participants are receiving treatments, one should be able to make a judgment. Empirically, the intraclass correlation is a measure of the degree of dependence. Perhaps the most flexible analysis approach for correlated observations is multilevel modeling. This method is statistically correct for situations in which individual observations are correlated within clusters, and multilevel models allow for inclusion of predictors at the participant and cluster level, as discussed in Chapter 13. As a second possibility, if several groups are involved for each treatment condition, consider using the group mean as the unit of analysis, instead of the individual outcome scores.

2. Check to see whether multivariate normality is reasonable. In this regard, checking the marginal (univariate) normality for each variable should be adequate. The EXAMINE procedure from SPSS is very helpful. If departure from normality is found, consider transforming the variable(s). Figure 6.1 can be helpful. This comment from Johnson and Wichern (1982) should be kept in mind: "Deviations from normality are often due to one or more unusual observations (outliers)" (p. 163). Once again, we see the importance of screening the data initially and converting to z scores.

3. Apply Box's test to check the assumption of homogeneity of the covariance matrices. If normality has been achieved in Step 2 on all or most of the variables, then Box's test should be a fairly clean test of variance differences, although keep in mind that this test can be very powerful when sample size is large. If the Box test is not significant, then all is fine.

4. If the Box test is significant with equal ns, then, although the type I error rate will be only slightly affected, power will be attenuated to some extent. Hence, look for transformations on the variables that are causing the covariance matrices to differ.

5. If the Box test is significant with sharply unequal ns for two groups, compare the determinants of S_1 and S_2 (i.e., the generalized variances for the two groups). If the larger group has the smaller generalized variance, T^2 will be liberal. If the larger group as the larger generalized variance, T^2 will be conservative.

6. For the k-group case, if the Box test is significant, examine the $|S_i|$ for the groups. If the groups with larger sample sizes have smaller generalized variances, then the multivariate statistics will be liberal. If the groups with the larger sample sizes have larger generalized variances, then the statistics will be conservative.

It is possible for the k-group case that neither of these two conditions hold. For example, for three groups, it could happen that the two groups with the smallest and the largest sample sizes have large generalized variances, and the remaining group has a variance somewhat smaller. In this case, however, the effect of heterogeneity should not be serious, because the coexisting liberal and conservative tendencies should cancel each other out somewhat.

Finally, because there are several test statistics in the k-group MANOVA case, their relative robustness in the presence of violations of assumptions could be a criterion for preferring one over the others. In this regard, Olson (1976) argued in favor of the

Pillai–Bartlett trace, because of its presumed greater robustness against heterogeneous covariances matrices. For variance differences *likely to occur in practice*, however, Stevens (1979) found that the Pillai–Bartlett trace, Wilks' Λ, and the Hotelling–Lawley trace are essentially equally robust.

6.11 COMPLETE THREE-GROUP MANOVA EXAMPLE

In this section, we illustrate a complete set of analysis procedures for one-way MANOVA with a new data set. The data set, available online, is called SeniorWISE, because the example used is adapted from the SeniorWISE (Wisdom Is Simply Exploration) study (McDougall et al., 2010a, 2010b). In the example used here, we assume that individuals 65 or older were randomly assigned to receive (1) memory training, which was designed to help adults maintain and/or improve their memory-related abilities; (2) a health intervention condition, which did not include memory training but is included in the study to determine if those receiving memory training would have better memory performance than those receiving an active intervention, albeit unrelated to memory; or (3) a wait-list control condition. The active treatments were individually administered and posttest intervention measures were completed individually.

Further, we have data (computer generated) for three outcomes, the scores for which are expected to be approximately normally distributed. The outcomes are thought to tap distinct constructs but are expected to be positively correlated. The first outcome, self-efficacy, is a measure of the degree to which individuals feel strong and confident about performing everyday memory-related tasks. The second outcome is a measure that assesses aspects of verbal memory performance, particularly verbal recall and recognition abilities. For the final outcome measure, the investigators used a measure of daily functioning that assesses participant ability to successfully use recall to perform tasks related to, for example, communication skills, shopping, and eating. We refer to this outcome as DAFS, because it is based on the Direct Assessment of Functional Status. Higher scores on each of these measures represent a greater (and preferred) level of performance.

To summarize, we have individuals assigned to one of three treatment conditions (memory training, health training, or control) and have collected posttest data on memory self-efficacy, verbal memory performance, and daily functioning skills (or DAFS). Our research hypothesis is that individuals in the memory training condition will have higher average posttest scores on each of the outcomes compared to control participants. On the other hand, it is not clear how participants in the health training condition will do relative to the other groups, as it is possible this intervention will have no impact on memory but also possible that the act of providing an active treatment may result in improved memory self-efficacy and performance.

6.11.1 Sample Size Determination

We first illustrate *a priori* sample size determination for this study. We use Table A.5 in Appendix A, which requires us to provide a general magnitude for the effect size threshold, which we select as moderate, the number of groups (three), the number of dependent variables (three), power (.80), and alpha (.05) used for the test of the overall multivariate null hypothesis. With these values, Table A.5 indicates that 52 participants are needed for each of the groups. We assume that the study has a funding source, and investigators were able to randomly assign 100 participants to each group. Note that obtaining a larger number of participants than "required" will provide for additional power for the overall test, and will help provide for improved power and confidence interval precision (narrower limits) for the pairwise comparisons.

6.11.2 Preliminary Analysis

With the intervention and data collection completed, we screen data to identify outliers, assess assumptions, and determine if using the standard MANOVA analysis is supported. Table 6.10 shows the SPSS commands for the entire analysis. Selected results are shown in Tables 6.11 and 6.12. Examining Table 6.11 shows that there are no missing data, means for the memory training group are greater than the other groups, and that variability is fairly similar for each outcome across the three treatment groups. The bivariate pooled within-group correlations (not shown) among the outcomes support the use of MANOVA as each correlation is of moderate strength and, as expected, is positive (correlations are .342, .337, and .451).

■ **Table 6.10: SPSS Commands for the Three-Group MANOVA Example**

```
SORT CASES BY Group.
SPLIT FILE LAYERED BY Group.

FREQUENCIES VARIABLES=Self_Efficacy Verbal DAFS
 /FORMAT=NOTABLE
 /STATISTICS=STDDEV MINIMUM MAXIMUM MEAN MEDIAN SKEWNESS SESKEW
KURTOSIS SEKURT
 /HISTOGRAM NORMAL
 /ORDER=ANALYSIS.

DESCRIPTIVES VARIABLES=Self_Efficacy Verbal DAFS
 /SAVE
 /STATISTICS=MEAN STDDEV MIN MAX.

REGRESSION

 /STATISTICS COEFF
 /DEPENDENT CASE
 /METHOD=ENTER Self_Efficacy Verbal DAFS
 /SAVE MAHAL.

SPLIT FILE OFF.

EXAMINE VARIABLES = Self_Efficacy Verbal DAFS BY group
 /PLOT = STEMLEAF NPPLOT.

MANOVA Self_Efficacy Verbal DAFS BY Group(1,3)
```

(Continued)

```
/print = error (stddev cor).

DESCRIPTIVES  VARIABLES=  ZSelf_Efficacy  ZVerbal  ZDAFS  /STATIS-
TICS=MEAN STDDEV MIN MAX.

GLM Self_Efficacy Verbal DAFS BY Group
  /POSTHOC=Group(TUKEY)
  /PRINT=DESCRIPTIVE ETASQ HOMOGENEITY
  /CRITERIA =ALPHA(.0167).
```

■ **Table 6.11: Selected SPSS Output for Data Screening for the Three-Group MANOVA Example**

			Self_Efficacy	Verbal	DAFS
\multicolumn{6}{c}{Statistics}					
GROUP			Self_Efficacy	Verbal	DAFS
Memory Training	N	Valid	100	100	100
		Missing	0	0	0
	Mean		58.5053	60.2273	59.1516
	Median		58.0215	61.5921	58.9151
	Std. Deviation		9.19920	9.65827	9.74461
	Skewness		.052	−.082	.006
	Std. Error of Skewness		.241	.241	.241
	Kurtosis		−.594	.002	−.034
	Std. Error of Kurtosis		.478	.478	.478
	Minimum		35.62	32.39	36.77
	Maximum		80.13	82.27	84.17
Health Training	N	Valid	100	100	100
		Missing	0	0	0
	Mean		50.6494	50.8429	52.4093
	Median		51.3928	52.3650	53.3766
	Std. Deviation		8.33143	9.34031	10.27314
	Skewness		.186	−.412	−.187
	Std. Error of Skewness		.241	.241	.241
	Kurtosis		.037	.233	−.478
	Std. Error of Kurtosis		.478	.478	.478
	Minimum		31.74	21.84	27.20
	Maximum		75.85	70.07	75.10
Control	N	Valid	100	100	100
		Missing	0	0	0
	Mean		48.9764	52.8810	51.2481
	Median		47.7576	52.7982	51.1623
	Std. Deviation		10.42036	9.64866	8.55991
	Skewness		.107	−.211	−.371
	Std. Error of Skewness		.241	.241	.241
	Kurtosis		.245	−.138	.469

Statistics GROUP		Self_Efficacy	Verbal	DAFS
	Std. Error of Kurtosis	.478	.478	.478
	Minimum	19.37	29.89	28.44
	Maximum	73.64	76.53	69.01

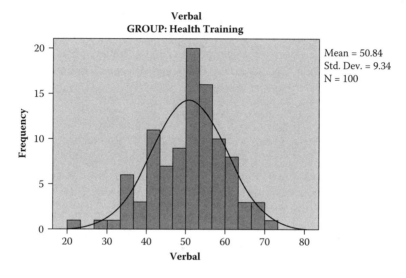

Verbal
GROUP: Health Training

Mean = 50.84
Std. Dev. = 9.34
N = 100

Inspection of the within-group histograms and z scores for each outcome suggests the presence of an outlying value in the health training group for self-efficacy ($z = 3.0$) and verbal performance ($z = -3.1$). The outlying value for verbal performance can be seen in the histogram in Table 6.11. Note though that when each of the outlying cases is temporarily removed, there is little impact on study results as the means for the health training group for self-efficacy and verbal performance change by less than 0.3 points. In addition, none of the statistical inference decisions (i.e., reject or retain the null) is changed by inclusion or exclusion of these cases. So, these two cases are retained for the entire analysis.

We also checked for the presence of multivariate outliers by obtaining the within-group Mahalanobis distance for each participant. These distances are obtained by the REGRESSION procedure shown in Table 6.10. Note here that "case id" serves as the dependent variable (which is of no consequence) and the three predictor variables in this equation are the three dependent variables appearing in the MANOVA. Johnson and Wichern (2007) note that these distances, if multivariate normality holds, approximately follow a chi-square distribution with degrees of freedom equal to, in this context, the number of dependent variables (p), with this approximation improving for larger samples. A common guide, then, is to consider a multivariate outlier to be present when an obtained Mahalanobis distance exceeds a chi-square critical value at a conservative alpha (.001) with p degrees of freedom. For this example, the chi-square critical value (.001, 3) = 16.268, as obtained from Appendix A, Table A.1. From our regression results, we ignore everything in this analysis except for the Mahalanobis distances. The largest such value obtained of 11.36 does not exceed the critical value of 16.268. Thus, no multivariate outliers are indicated.

The formal assumptions for the MANOVA procedure also seem to be satisfied. Based on the values for skewness and kurtosis, which are all close to zero as shown in Table 6.11, as well as inspection of each of the nine histograms (not shown), does not suggest substantial departures from univariate normality. We also used the Shapiro–Wilk statistic to test the normality assumption. Using a Bonferroni adjustment for the nine tests yields an alpha level of about .0056, and as each p value from these tests exceeded this alpha level, there is no reason to believe that the normality assumption is violated.

We previously noted that group variability is similar for each outcome, and the results of Box's M test ($p = .054$), as shown in Table 6.12, for equal variance-covariance matrices does not indicate a violation of this assumption. Note though that because of the relatively large sample size ($N = 300$) this test is quite powerful. As such, it is often recommended that an alpha of .01 be used for this test when large sample sizes are present. In addition, Levene's test for equal group variances for each variable considered separately does not indicate a violation for any of the outcomes (smallest p value is .118 for DAFS). Further, the study design, as described, does not suggest any violations of the independence assumption in part as treatments were individually administered to participants who also completed posttest measures individually.

6.11.3 Primary Analysis

Table 6.12 shows the SPSS GLM results for the MANOVA. The overall multivariate null hypothesis is rejected at the .05 level, F Wilks' Lambda(6, 590) = 14.79, $p < .001$, indicating the presence of group differences. The multivariate effect size measure, eta square, indicates that the proportion of variance between groups on the set of outcomes is .13. Univariate F tests for each dependent variable, conducted using an alpha level of .05 / 3, or .0167, shows that group differences are present for self-efficacy ($F[2, 297] = 29.57, p < .001$), verbal performance ($F[2, 297] = 26.71, p < .001$), and DAFS ($F[2, 297] = 19.96, p < .001$). Further, the univariate effect size measure, eta square, shown in Table 6.12, indicates the proportion of variance explained by the treatment for self-efficacy is 0.17, verbal performance is 0.15, and DAFS is 0.12.

We then use the Tukey procedure to conduct pairwise comparisons using an alpha of .0167 for each outcome. For each dependent variable, there is no statistically significant difference in means between the health training and control groups. Further, the memory training group has higher population means than each of the other groups for all outcomes. For self-efficacy, the confidence intervals for the difference in means indicate that the memory training group population mean is about 4.20 to 11.51 points greater than the mean for the health training group and about 5.87 to 13.19 points greater than the control group mean. For verbal performance, the intervals indicate that the memory training group mean is about 5.65 to 13.12 points greater than the mean

■ **Table 6.12: SPSS Selected GLM Output for the Three-Group MANOVA Example**

Box's Test of Equality of Covariance Matrices[a]

Box's M	21.047
F	1.728
df1	12
df2	427474.385
Sig.	.054

Tests the null hypothesis that the observed covariance matrices of the dependent variables are equal across groups.
[a] Design: Intercept + GROUP

Levene's Test of Equality of Error Variances[a]

	F	df1	df2	Sig.
Self_Efficacy	1.935	2	297	.146
Verbal	.115	2	297	.892
DAFS	2.148	2	297	.118

Tests the null hypothesis that the error variance of the dependent variable is equal across groups.
[a] Design: Intercept + GROUP

Multivariate Tests[a]

Effect		Value	F	Hypothesis df	Error df	Sig.	Partial Eta Squared
GROUP	Pillai's Trace	.250	14.096	6.000	592.000	.000	.125
	Wilks' Lambda	.756	14.791[b]	6.000	590.000	.000	.131
	Hotelling's Trace	.316	15.486	6.000	588.000	.000	.136
	Roy's Largest Root	.290	28.660[c]	3.000	296.000	.000	.225

[a] Design: Intercept + GROUP
[b] Exact statistic
[c] The statistic is an upper bound on F that yields a lower bound on the significance level.

Tests of Between-Subjects Effects

Source	Dependent Variable	Type III Sum of Squares	df	Mean Square	F	Sig.	Partial Eta Squared
GROUP	Self_Efficacy	5177.087	2	2588.543	29.570	.000	.166
	Verbal	4872.957	2	2436.478	26.714	.000	.152
	DAFS	3642.365	2	1821.183	19.957	.000	.118
Error	Self_Efficacy	25999.549	297	87.541			
	Verbal	27088.399	297	91.207			
	DAFS	27102.923	297	91.256			

(*Continued*)

■ **Table 6.12: (Continued)**

Multiple Comparisons

Tukey HSD

Dependent Variable	(I) GROUP	(J) GROUP	Mean Difference (I-J)	Std. Error	Sig.	98.33% Confidence Interval Lower Bound	Upper Bound
	Memory Training	Control	9.5289*	1.32318	.000	5.8727	13.1850
	Health Training	Control	1.6730	1.32318	.417	-1.9831	5.3291
Verbal	Memory Training	Health Training	9.3844*	1.35061	.000	5.6525	13.1163
	Memory Training	Control	7.3463*	1.35061	.000	3.6144	11.0782
	Health Training	Control	−2.0381	1.35061	.288	−5.7700	1.6938
DAFS	Memory Training	Health Training	6.7423*	1.35097	.000	3.0094	10.4752
	Memory Training	Control	7.9034*	1.35097	.000	4.1705	11.6363
	Health Training	Control	1.1612	1.35097	.666	−4.8940	2.5717

Based on observed means.
The error term is Mean Square(Error) = 91.256.
* The mean difference is significant at the .0167 level.

for the health training group and about 3.61 to 11.08 points greater than the control group mean. For DAFS, the intervals indicate that the memory training group mean is about 3.01 to 10.48 points greater than the mean for the health training group and about 4.17 to 11.64 points greater than the control group mean. Thus, across all outcomes, the lower limits of the confidence intervals suggest that individuals assigned to the memory training group score, on average, at least 3 points greater than the other groups in the population.

Note that if you wish to report the Cohen's d effect size measure, you need to compute these manually. Remember that the formula for Cohen's d is the raw score difference in means between two groups divided by the square root of the mean square error from the one-way ANOVA table for a given outcome. To illustrate two such calculations, consider the contrast between the memory and health training groups for self-efficacy. The Cohen's d for this difference is $7.8559/\sqrt{87.541} = 0.84$, indicating that this difference in means is .84 standard deviations (conventionally considered a large effect). For the second example, Cohen's d for the difference in verbal performance means between the memory and health training groups is $9.3844/\sqrt{91.207} = 0.98$, again indicative of a large effect by conventional standards.

Having completed this example, we now present an example results section from this analysis, followed by an analysis summary for one-way MANOVA where the focus is on examining effects for each dependent variable.

6.12 EXAMPLE RESULTS SECTION FOR ONE-WAY MANOVA

The goal of this study was to determine if at-risk older adults who were randomly assigned to receive memory training have greater mean posttest scores on memory self-efficacy, verbal memory performance, and daily functional status than individuals who were randomly assigned to receive a health intervention or a wait-list control condition. A one-way multivariate analysis of variance (MANOVA) was conducted for three dependent variables (i.e., memory self-efficacy, verbal performance, and functional status) with type of training (memory, health, and none) serving as the independent variable. Prior to conducting the formal MANOVA procedures, the data were examined for univariate and multivariate outliers. Two such observations were found, but they did not impact study results. We determined this by recomputing group means after temporarily removing each outlying observation and found small differences between these means and the means based on the entire sample (less than three-tenths of a point for each mean). Similarly, temporarily removing each outlier and rerunning the MANOVA indicated that neither observation changed study findings. Thus, we retained all 300 observations throughout the analyses.

We also assessed whether the MANOVA assumptions seemed tenable. Inspecting histograms, skewness and kurtosis values, and Shapiro–Wilk test results did not indicate any material violations of the normality assumption. Further, Box's test provided support for the equality of covariance matrices assumption (i.e., $p = .054$). Similarly, examining the results of Levene's test for equality of variance provided support that the dispersion of scores for self-efficacy ($p = .15$), verbal performance ($p = .89$), and functional status ($p = .12$) was similar across the three groups. Finally, we did not consider there to be any violations of the independence assumption because the treatments were individually administered and participants responded to the outcome measures on an individual basis.

Table 1 displays the means for each of the treatment groups, which shows that participants in the memory training group scored, on average, highest across each dependent variable, with much lower mean scores observed in the health training and control groups. Group means differed on the set of dependent variables, $\lambda = .756$, $F(6, 590) = 14.79$, $p < .001$. Given the interest in examining treatment effects for each outcome (as opposed to attempting to establish composite variables), we conducted a series of one-way ANOVAs for each outcome at the .05 / 3 (or .0167) alpha level. Group mean differences are present for self-efficacy ($F[2, 297] = 29.6, p < .001$), verbal performance ($F[2, 297] = 26.7, p < .001$), and functional status ($F[2, 297] = 20.0$, $p < .001$). Further, the values of eta square for each outcome suggest that treatment effects for self-efficacy ($\eta^2 = .17$), verbal performance ($\eta^2 = .15$), and functional status ($\eta^2 = .12$) are generally strong.

Table 2 presents information on the pairwise contrasts of interest. Comparisons of treatment means were conducted using the Tukey HSD approach, with an alpha of

■ **Table 1: Group Means (*SD*) for the Dependent Variables (*n* = 100)**

Group	Self-efficacy	Verbal performance	Functional status
Memory training	58.5 (9.2)	60.2 (9.7)	59.2 (9.7)
Health training	50.6 (8.3)	50.8 (9.3)	52.4 (10.3)
Control	49.0 (10.4)	52.9 (9.6)	51.2 (8.6)

■ **Table 2: Pairwise Contrasts for the Dependent Variables**

Dependent variable	Contrast	Differences in means (SE)	95% C.I.[a]
Self-efficacy	Memory vs. health	7.9* (1.32)	4.2, 11.5
	Memory vs. control	9.5* (1.32)	5.9, 13.2
	Health vs. control	1.7 (1.32)	−2.0, 5.3
Verbal performance	Memory vs. health	9.4* (1.35)	5.7, 13.1
	Memory vs. control	7.3* (1.35)	3.6, 11.1
	Health vs. control	−2.0 (1.35)	−5.8, 1.7
Functional status	Memory vs. health	6.7* (1.35)	3.0, 10.5
	Memory vs. control	7.9* (1.35)	4.2, 11.6
	Health vs. control	1.2 (1.35)	−2.6, 4.9

[a] C.I. represents the confidence interval for the difference in means.

Note: * indicates a statistically significant difference ($p < .0167$) using the Tukey HSD procedure.

.0167 used for these contrasts. Table 2 shows that participants in the memory training group scored significantly higher, on average, than participants in both the health training and control groups for each outcome. No statistically significant mean differences were observed between the health training and control groups. Further, given that a raw score difference of 3 points on each of the similarly scaled variables represents the threshold between negligible and important mean differences, the confidence intervals indicate that, when differences are present, population differences are meaningful as the lower bounds of all such intervals exceed 3. Thus, after receiving memory training, individuals, on average, have much greater self-efficacy, verbal performance, and daily functional status than those in the health training and control groups.

6.13 ANALYSIS SUMMARY

One-way MANOVA can be used to describe differences in means for multiple dependent variables among multiple groups. The design has one factor that represents group membership and two or more continuous dependent measures. MANOVA is used instead of multiple ANOVAs to provide better protection against the inflation of the overall type I error rate and may provide for more power than a series of ANOVAs. The primary steps in a MANOVA analysis are:

I. Preliminary Analysis
  A. Conduct an initial screening of the data.
    1) Purpose: Determine if the summary measures seem reasonable and support the use of MANOVA. Also, identify the presence and pattern (if any) of missing data.
    2) Procedure: Compute various descriptive measures for each group (e.g., means, standard deviations, medians, skewness, kurtosis, frequencies) on each of the dependent variables. Compute the bivariate correlations for the outcomes. If there is missing data, conduct missing data analysis.
    3) Decision/action: If the values of the descriptive statistics do not make sense, check data entry for accuracy. If all of the correlations are near zero, consider using a series of ANOVAs. If one or more correlations are very high (e.g., .8, .9), consider forming one or more composite variables. If there is missing data, consider strategies to address missing data.
  B. Conduct case analysis.
    1) Purpose: Identify any problematic individual observations.
    2) Procedure:
      i) Inspect the distribution of each dependent variable within each group (e.g., via histograms) and identify apparent outliers. Scatterplots may also be inspected to examine linearity and bivariate outliers.
      ii) Inspect z-scores and Mahalanobis distances for each variable within each group. For the z scores, absolute values larger than perhaps 2.5 or 3 along with a judgment that a given value is distinct from the bulk of the scores indicate an outlying value. Multivariate outliers are indicated when the Mahalanobis distance exceeds the corresponding critical value.
      iii) If any potential outliers are identified, conduct a sensitivity study to determine the impact of one or more outliers on major study results.
    3) Decision/action: If there are no outliers with excessive influence, continue with the analysis. If there are one or more observations with excessive influence, determine if there is a legitimate reason to discard the observations. If so, discard the observation(s) (documenting the reason) and continue with the analysis. If not, consider use of variable transformations to attempt to minimize the effects of one or more outliers. If necessary, discuss any ambiguous conclusions in the report.
  C. Assess the validity of the MANOVA assumptions.
    1) Purpose: Determine if the standard MANOVA procedure is valid for the analysis of the data.
    2) Some procedures:
      i) Independence: Consider the sampling design and study circumstances to identify any possible violations.
      ii) Multivariate normality: Inspect the distribution of each dependent variable in each group (via histograms) and inspect values for skewness and kurtosis for each group. The Shapiro–Wilk test statistic can also be used to test for nonnormality.

iii) Equal covariance matrices: Examine the standard deviations for each group as a preliminary assessment. Use Box's *M* test to assess if this assumption is tenable, keeping in mind that it requires the assumption of multivariate normality to be satisfied and with large samples may be an overpowered test of the assumption. If significant, examine Levene's test for equality of variance for each outcome to identify problematic dependent variables (which should also be conducted if univariate ANOVAs are the follow-up test to a significant MANOVA).

3) Decision/action:

i) Any nonnormal distributions and/or inequality of covariance matrices may be of substantive interest in their own right and should be reported and/or further investigated. If needed, consider the use of variable transformations to address these problems.

ii) Continue with the standard MANOVA analysis when there is no evidence of violations of any assumption or when there is evidence of a specific violation but the technique is known to be robust to an existing violation. If the technique is not robust to an existing violation and cannot be remedied with variable transformations, use an alternative analysis technique.

D. Test any preplanned contrasts.

1) Purpose: Test any strong *a priori* research hypotheses with maximum power.

2) Procedure: If there is rationale supporting group mean differences on two or three multiple outcomes, test the overall multivariate null hypothesis for these outcomes using Wilks' Λ. If significant, use an ANOVA *F* test for each outcome with no alpha adjustment. For any significant ANOVAs, follow up (if more than two groups are present) with tests and interval estimates for all pairwise contrasts using the Tukey procedure.

II. Primary Analysis

A. Test the overall multivariate null hypothesis.

1) Purpose: Provide "protected testing" to help control the inflation of the overall type I error rate.

2) Procedure: Examine the test result for Wilks' Λ.

3) Decision/action: If the *p*-value associated with this test is sufficiently small, continue with further tests of specific contrasts. If the *p*-value is not small, do not continue with any further testing of specific contrasts.

B. If the overall null hypothesis has been rejected, test and estimate all *post hoc* contrasts of interest.

1) Purpose: Describe the differences among the groups for each of the dependent variables, while controlling the overall error rate.

2) Procedures:

i) Test the overall ANOVA null hypothesis for each dependent variable using a Bonferroni-adjusted alpha. (A conventional unadjusted alpha can be considered when the number of outcomes is relatively small, such as two or three.)

ii) For each dependent variable for which the overall univariate null hypothesis is rejected, follow up (if more than two groups are present) with tests and interval estimates for all pairwise contrasts using the Tukey procedure.

C. Report and interpret at least one of the following effect size measures.

1) Purpose: Indicate the strength of the relationship between the dependent variable(s) and the factor (i.e., group membership).

2) Procedure: Raw score differences in means should be reported. Other possibilities include (a) the proportion of generalized total variation explained by group membership for the set of dependent variables (multivariate eta square), (b) the proportion of variation explained by group membership for each dependent variable (univariate eta square), and/or (c) Cohen's *d* for two-group contrasts.

REFERENCES

Barcikowski, R. S. (1981). Statistical power with group mean as the unit of analysis. *Journal of Educational Statistics, 6,* 267–285.

Bock, R. D. (1975). *Multivariate statistical methods in behavioral research.* New York, NY: McGraw-Hill.

Box, G.E.P. (1949). A general distribution theory for a class of likelihood criteria. *Biometrika, 36,* 317–346.

Burstein, L. (1980). The analysis of multilevel data in educational research and evaluation. *Review of Research in Education, 8,* 158–233.

Christensen, W., & Rencher, A. (1995, August). *A comparison of Type I error rates and power levels for seven solutions to the multivariate Behrens-Fisher problem.* Paper presented at the meeting of the American Statistical Association, Orlando, FL.

Conover, W.J., Johnson, M.E., & Johnson, M.M. (1981). Composite study of tests for homogeneity of variances with applications to the outer continental shelf bidding data. *Technometrics, 23,* 351–361.

Coombs, W., Algina, J., & Oltman, D. (1996). Univariate and multivariate omnibus hypothesis tests selected to control Type I error rates when population variances are not necessarily equal. *Review of Educational Research, 66,* 137–179.

DeCarlo, L.T. (1997). On the meaning and use of kurtosis. *Psychological Methods, 2,* 292–307.

Everitt, B.S. (1979). A Monte Carlo investigation of the robustness of Hotelling's one and two sample T2 tests. *Journal of the American Statistical Association, 74,* 48–51.

Glass, G.C., & Hopkins, K. (1984). *Statistical methods in education and psychology.* Englewood Cliffs, NJ: Prentice-Hall.

Glass, G., Peckham, P., & Sanders, J. (1972). Consequences of failure to meet assumptions underlying the fixed effects analysis of variance and covariance. *Review of Educational Research, 42,* 237–288.

Glass, G., & Stanley, J. (1970). *Statistical methods in education and psychology.* Englewood Cliffs, NJ: Prentice-Hall.

Gnanadesikan, R. (1977). *Methods for statistical analysis of multivariate observations*. New York, NY: Wiley.

Hakstian, A.R., Roed, J.C., & Lind, J.C. (1979). Two-sample T–2 procedure and the assumption of homogeneous covariance matrices. *Psychological Bulletin, 86*, 1255–1263.

Hays, W. (1963). *Statistics for psychologists*. New York, NY: Holt, Rinehart & Winston.

Hedges, L. (2007). Correcting a statistical test for clustering. *Journal of Educational and Behavioral Statistics, 32*, 151–179.

Henze, N., & Zirkler, B. (1990). A class of invariant consistent tests for multivariate normality. *Communication in Statistics: Theory and Methods, 19*, 3595–3618.

Holloway, L.N., & Dunn, O.J. (1967). The robustness of Hotelling's T2. *Journal of the American Statistical Association, 62*(317), 124–136.

Hopkins, J.W., & Clay, P.P.F. (1963). Some empirical distributions of bivariate T2 and homoscedasticity criterion M under unequal variance and leptokurtosis. *Journal of the American Statistical Association, 58*, 1048–1053.

Hykle, J., Stevens, J.P., & Markle, G. (1993, April). *Examining the statistical validity of studies comparing cooperative learning versus individualistic learning*. Paper presented at the annual meeting of the American Educational Research Association, Atlanta, GA.

Johnson, N., & Wichern, D. (1982). *Applied multivariate statistical analysis*. Englewood Cliffs, NJ: Prentice Hall.

Johnson, R.A., & Wichern, D.W. (2007). *Applied multivariate statistical analysis* (6th ed.). Upper Saddle River, NJ: Pearson Prentice Hall.

Kenny, D., & Judd, C. (1986). Consequences of violating the independent assumption in analysis of variance. *Psychological Bulletin, 99*, 422–431.

Kreft, I., & de Leeuw, J. (1998). *Introducing multilevel modeling*. Thousand Oaks, CA: Sage.

Lix, L.M., Keselman, C.J., & Kesleman, H.J. (1996). Consequences of assumption violations revisited: A quantitative review of alternatives to the one-way analysis of variance. *Review of Educational Research, 66*, 579–619.

Looney, S.W. (1995). How to use tests for univariate normality to assess multivariate normality. *American Statistician, 49*, 64–70.

Mardia, K.V. (1970). Measures of multivariate skewness and kurtosis with applications. *Biometrika, 57*, 519–530.

Mardia, K.V. (1971). The effect of non-normality on some multivariate tests and robustness to nonnormality in the linear model. *Biometrika, 58*, 105–121.

Maxwell, S.E., & Delaney, H.D. (2004). *Designing experiments and analyzing data: A model comparison perspective* (2nd ed.). Mahwah, NJ: Lawrence Erlbaum.

McDougall, G.J., Becker, H., Pituch, K., Acee, T.W., Vaughan, P.W., & Delville, C. (2010a). Differential benefits of memory training for minority older adults. *Gerontologist, 5*, 632–645.

McDougall, G.J., Becker, H., Pituch, K., Acee, T.W., Vaughan, P.W., & Delville, C. (2010b). The SeniorWISE study: Improving everyday memory in older adults. *Archives of Psychiatric Nursing, 24*, 291–306.

Mecklin, C.J., & Mundfrom, D.J. (2003). On using asymptotic critical values in testing for multivariate normality. *InterStat*, available online at http_interstatstatvteduInterStatARTICLES 2003articlesJ03001pdf

Nel, D.G., & van der Merwe, C.A. (1986). A solution to the multivariate Behrens-Fisher problem. *Communications in Statistics: Theory and Methods, 15*, 3719–3735.

Olson, C. L. (1973). A Monte Carlo investigation of the robustness of multivariate analysis of variance. *Dissertation Abstracts International, 35*, 6106B.

Olson, C. L. (1974). Comparative robustness of six tests in multivariate analysis of variance. *Journal of the American Statistical Association, 69*, 894–908.

Olson, C. L. (1976). On choosing a test statistic in MANOVA. *Psychological Bulletin, 83*, 579–586.

Rencher, A. C., & Christensen, W. F. (2012). *Method of multivariate analysis* (3rd ed.). Hoboken, NJ: John Wiley & Sons.

Rummel, R. J. (1970). *Applied factor analysis.* Evanston, IL: Northwestern University Press.

Scariano, S., & Davenport, J. (1987). The effects of violations of the independence assumption in the one way ANOVA. *American Statistician, 41*, 123–129.

Scheffe, H. (1959). *The analysis of variance.* New York, NY: Wiley.

Small, N. J. H. (1980). Marginal skewness and kurtosis in testing multivariate normality. *Applied Statistics, 29*, 85–87.

Snijders, T., & Bosker, R. (1999). *Multilevel analysis.* Thousand Oaks, CA: Sage.

Stevens, J. P. (1979). Comment on Olson: Choosing a test statistic in multivariate analysis of variance. *Psychological Bulletin, 86*, 355–360.

Wilcox, R. R. (2012). *Introduction to robust estimation and hypothesis testing* (3rd ed.). Waltham, MA: Elsevier.

Wilk, H. B., Shapiro, S. S., & Chen, H. J. (1968). A comparative study of various tests of normality. *Journal of the American Statistical Association, 63*, 1343–1372.

Zwick, R. (1985). Nonparametric one-way multivariate analysis of variance: A computational approach based on the Pillai-Bartlett trace. *Psychological Bulletin, 97*, 148–152.

APPENDIX 6.1

Analyzing Correlated Observations[*]

Much has been written about correlated observations, and that INDEPENDENCE of observations is an assumption for ANOVA and regression analysis. What is not apparent from reading most statistics books is how critical an assumption it is. Hays (1963) indicated over 40 years ago that violation of the independence assumption is very serious. Glass and Stanley (1970) in their textbook talked about the critical importance of this assumption. Barcikowski (1981) showed that even a SMALL violation of the independence assumption can cause the actual alpha level to be several times greater than the nominal level. Kreft and de Leeuw (1998) note: "This means that if intraclass correlation is present, as it may be when we are dealing with clustered data, the assumption of independent observations in the traditional linear model is violated" (p. 9). The Scariano and Davenport (1987) table (Table 6.1) shows the dramatic effect dependence can have on type I error rate. The problem is, as Burstein (1980) pointed out more than 25 years ago, is that "most of what goes on in education occurs within some group context" (p. 158). This gives rise to nested data and hence correlated

---

[*] The authoritative book on ANOVA (Scheffe, 1959) states that one of the assumptions in ANOVA is statistical independence of the errors. But this is equivalent to the independence of the observations (Maxwell & Delaney, 2004, p. 110).

observations. More generally, nested data occurs quite frequently in social science research. Social psychology often is focused on groups. In clinical psychology, if we are dealing with different types of psychotherapy, groups are involved. The hierarchical, or multilevel, linear model (Chapters 13 and 14) is a commonly used method for dealing with correlated observations.

Let us first turn to a simpler analysis, which makes practical sense if the effect anticipated (from previous research) or desired is at least MODERATE. With correlated data, we first compute the mean for each cluster, and then do the analysis on the means. Table 6.2, from Barcikowski (1981), shows that if the effect is moderate, then about 10 groups per treatment are necessary at the .10 alpha level for power = .80 when there are 10 participants per group. This implies that about eight or nine groups per treatment would be needed for power = .70. For a large effect size, only five groups per treatment are needed for power = .80. For a SMALL effect size, the number of groups per treatment for adequate power is much too large and impractical.

Now we consider a very important paper by Hedges (2007). The title of the paper is quite revealing: "Correcting a Significance Test for Clustering." He develops a correction for the t test in the context of randomly assigning intact groups to treatments. But the results have broader implications. Here we present modified information from his study, involving some results in the paper and some results not in the paper, but which were received from Dr. Hedges (nominal alpha = .05):

M (clusters)	n (S's per cluster)	Intraclass correlation	Actual rejection rate
2	100	.05	.511
2	100	.10	.626
2	100	.20	.732
2	100	.30	.784
2	30	.05	.214
2	30	.10	.330
2	30	.20	.470
2	30	.30	.553
5	10	.05	.104
5	10	.10	.157
5	10	.20	.246
5	10	.30	.316
10	5	.05	.074
10	5	.10	.098
10	5	.20	.145
10	5	.30	.189

In this table, we have m clusters assigned to each treatment and an assumed alpha level of .05. Note that it is the n (number of participants in each cluster), not m, that causes the alpha rate to skyrocket. Compare the actual alpha levels for intraclass correlation fixed at .10 as n varies from 100 to 5 (.626, .330, .157 and .098).

For equal cluster size (n), Hedges derives the following relationship between the t (uncorrected for the cluster effect) and t_A, corrected for the cluster effect:

$t_A = ct$, with h degrees of freedom.

The correction factor is $c = \sqrt{\left[(N-2) - 2(n-1)p\right] / (N-2)\left[1 + (n-1)p\right]}$, where p represents the intraclass correlation, and $h = (N-2) / [1 + (n-1)p]$ (good approximation).

To see the difference the correction factor and the reduced df can make, we consider an example. Suppose we have three groups of 10 participants in each of two treatment groups and that $p = .10$. A noncorrected $t = 2.72$ with $df = 58$, and this is significant at the .01 level for a two-tailed test. The corrected $t = 1.94$ with $h = 30.5$ df, and this is NOT even significant at the .05 level for a two-tailed test.

We now consider two practical situations where the results from the Hedges study can be useful. First, teaching methods is a big area of concern in education. If we are considering two teaching methods, then we will have about 30 students in each class. Obviously, just two classes per method will yield inadequate power, but the modified information from the Hedges study shows that with just two classes per method and $n = 30$, the actual type I error rate is .33 for intraclass correlation = .10. So, for more than two classes per method, the situation will just get worse in terms of type I error.

Now, suppose we wish to compare two types of counseling or psychotherapy. If we assign five groups of 10 participants each to each of the two types and intraclass correlation = .10 (and it could be larger), then actual type I error is .157, not .05 as we thought. The modified information also covers the situation where the group size is smaller and more groups are assigned to each type. Now, consider the case were 10 groups of size $n = 5$ are assigned to each type. If intraclass correlation = .10, then actual type I error = .098. If intraclass correlation = .20, then actual type I error = .145, almost three times what we want it to be.

Hedges (2007) has compared the power of clustered means analysis to the power of his adjusted t test when the effect is quite LARGE (one standard deviation). Here are some results from his comparison:

Power	n	m	Adjusted t	Cluster means
$p = .10$	10	2	.607	.265
	25	2	.765	.336
	10	3	.788	.566

(Continued)

Power	n	m	Adjusted t	Cluster means
	25	3	.909	.703
	10	4	.893	.771
	25	4	.968	.889
$p = .20$	10	2	.449	.201
	25	2	.533	.230
	10	3	.620	.424
	25	3	.710	.490
	10	4	.748	.609
	25	4	.829	.689

These results show the power of cluster means analysis does not fare well when there are three or fewer means per treatment group, and this is for a large effect size (which is NOT realistic of what one will generally encounter in practice). For a medium effect size (.5 SD) Barcikowski (1981) shows that for power > .80 you will need nine groups per treatment if group size is 30 for intraclass correlation = .10 at the .05 level.

So, the bottom line is that correlated observations occur very frequently in social science research, and researchers must take this into account in their analysis. The intraclass correlation is an index of how much the observations correlate, and an estimate of it—or at least an upper bound for it—needs to be obtained, so that the type I error rate is under control. If one is going to consider a cluster means analysis, then a table from Barcikowski (1981) indicates that one should have at least seven groups per treatment (with 30 observations per group) for power = .80 at the .10 level. One could probably get by with six or five groups for power = .70. The same table from Barcikowski shows that if group size is 10, then at least 10 groups per counseling method are needed for power = .80 at the .10 level. One could probably get by with eight groups per method for power = .70. Both of these situations assume we wish to detect at least a moderate effect size. Hedges' adjusted t has some potential advantages. For $p = .10$, his power analysis (presumably at the .05 level) shows that probably four groups of 30 in each treatment will yield adequate power (> .70). The reason we say "probably" is that power for a very large effect size is .968, and $n = 25$. The question is, for a medium effect size at the .10 level, will power be adequate? For $p = .20$, we believe we would need five groups per treatment.

Barcikowski (1981) has indicated that intraclass correlations for teaching various subjects are generally in the .10 to .15 range. It seems to us, that for counseling or psychotherapy methods, an intraclass correlation of .20 is prudent. Snidjers and Bosker (1999) indicated that in the social sciences intraclass correlations are generally in the 0 to .4 range, and often narrower bounds can be found.

In finishing this appendix, we think it is appropriate to quote from Hedges' (2007) conclusion:

> Cluster randomized trials are increasingly important in education and the social and policy sciences. However, these trials are often improperly analyzed by ignoring the effects of clustering on significance tests. . . . This article considered only *t* tests under a sampling model with one level of clustering. The generalization of the methods used in this article to more designs with additional levels of clustering and more complex analyses would be desirable. (p. 173)

APPENDIX 6.2

Multivariate Test Statistics for Unequal Covariance Matrices

The two-group test statistic that should be used when the population covariance matrices are not equal, especially with sharply unequal group sizes, is

$$T_*^2 = (\bar{\mathbf{y}}_1 - \bar{\mathbf{y}}_2)' \left[\frac{\mathbf{S}_1}{n_1} + \frac{\mathbf{S}_2}{n_2} \right]^{-1} (\bar{\mathbf{y}}_1 - \bar{\mathbf{y}}_2).$$

This statistic must be transformed, and various critical values have been proposed (see Coombs et al., 1996). An important Monte Carlo study comparing seven solutions to the multivariate Behrens–Fisher problem is by Christensen and Rencher (1995). They considered 2, 5, and 10 variables (p), and the data were generated such that the population covariance matrix for group 2 was d times the covariance matrix for group 1 (d was set at 3 and 9). The sample sizes for different p values are given here:

	$p = 2$	$p = 5$	$p = 10$
$n_1 > n_2$	10:5	20:10	30:20
$n_1 = n_2$	10:10	20:20	30:30
$n_1 < n_2$	10:20	20:40	30:60

Figure 6.2 shows important results from their study.

They recommended the Kim and Nel and van der Merwe procedures because they are conservative and have good power relative to the other procedures. To this writer, the Yao procedure is also fairly good, although slightly liberal. Importantly, however, all the highest error rates for the Yao procedure (including the three outliers) occurred when the variables were uncorrelated. This implies that the adjusted power of the Yao (which is somewhat low for $n_1 > n_2$) would be better for correlated variables. Finally, for test statistics for the k-group MANOVA case, see Coombs et al. (1996) for appropriate references.

▪ **Figure 6.2** Results from a simulation study comparing the performance of methods when unequal covariance matrices are present (from Christensen and Rencher, 1995).

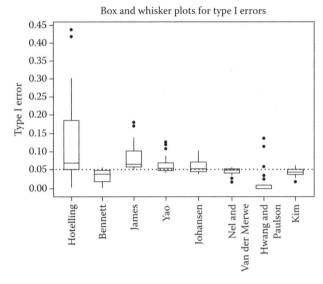

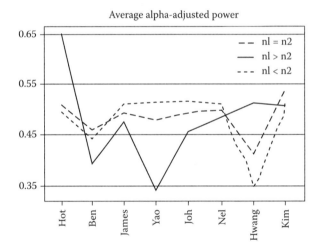

The approximate test by Nel and van der Merwe (1986) uses T_*^2, which is approximately distributed as $T_{p',v}^2$, with

$$V = \frac{\mathrm{tr}(S_e)^2 + [\mathrm{tr}(S_e)]^2}{(n_1-1)^{-1}\left\{\mathrm{tr}\left(V_1^2\right) + \left[\mathrm{tr}\left(V_1\right)\right]^2\right\} + (n_2-1)^{-1}\left\{\mathrm{tr}\left(V_2^2\right) + \left[\mathrm{tr}\left(V_2\right)\right]^2\right\}}$$

SPSS Matrix Procedure Program for Calculating Hotelling's T^2 and v (knu) for the Nel and van der Merwe Modification and Selected Output

```
MATRIX.
COMPUTE S1 = {23.013, 12.366, 2.907; 12.366, 17.544, 4.773; 2.907, 4.773, 13.963}.
COMPUTE S2 = {4.362, .760, 2.362; .760, 25.851, 7.686; 2.362, 7.686, 46.654}.
COMPUTE V1 = S1/36.
COMPUTE V2 = S2/23.
COMPUTE TRACEV1 = TRACE(V1).
COMPUTE SQTRV1 = TRACEV1*TRACEV1.
COMPUTE TRACEV2 = TRACE(V2).
COMPUTE SQTRV2 = TRACEV2*TRACEV2.
COMPUTE V1SQ = V1*V1.
COMPUTE V2SQ = V2*V2.
COMPUTE TRV1SQ = TRACE(V1SQ).
COMPUTE TRV2SQ = TRACE(V2SQ).
COMPUTE SE = V1 + V2.
COMPUTE SESQ = SE*SE.
COMPUTE TRACESE = TRACE(SE).
COMPUTE SQTRSE = TRACESE*TRACESE.
COMPUTE TRSESQ = TRACE(SESQ).
COMPUTE SEINV = INV(SE).
COMPUTE DIFFM = {2.113, -2.649, -8.578}.
COMPUTE TDIFFM = T(DIFFM).
COMPUTE HOTL = DIFFM*SEINV*TDIFFM.
COMPUTE KNU = (TRSESQ + SQTRSE)/(1/36*(TRV1SQ + SQTRV1) + 1/23*(TRV2SQ + SQTRV2)).
PRINT S1.
PRINT S2.
PRINT HOTL.
PRINT KNU.
END MATRIX.
```

Matrix

Run MATRIX procedure

S1

23.01300000	12.36600000	2.90700000
12.36600000	17.54400000	4.77300000
2.90700000	4.77300000	13.96300000

S2

4.36200000	.76000000	2.36200000
.76000000	25.85100000	7.68600000
2.36200000	7.68600000	46.65400000

HOTL

43.17860426

KNU

40.57627238

END MATRIX

6.14 EXERCISES

1. Describe a situation or class of situations where dependence of the observations would be present.

2. An investigator has a treatment versus control group design with 30 participants per group. The intraclass correlation is calculated and found to be .20. If testing for significance at .05, estimate what the actual type I error rate is.

3. Consider a four-group study with three dependent variables. What does the homogeneity of covariance matrices assumption imply in this case?

4. Consider the following three MANOVA situations. Indicate whether you would be concerned in each case with the type I error rate associated with the overall multivariate test of mean differences. Suppose that for each case the p value for the multivariate test for homogeneity of dispersion matrices is smaller than the nominal alpha of .05.

(a)	Gp 1	Gp 2	Gp 3
	$n_1 = 15$	$n_2 = 15$	$n_3 = 15$
	$|\mathbf{S}_1| = 4.4$	$|\mathbf{S}_2| = 7.6$	$|\mathbf{S}_3| = 5.9$

(b)	Gp 1	Gp 2
	$n_1 = 21$	$n_2 = 57$
	$|\mathbf{S}_1| = 14.6$	$|\mathbf{S}_2| = 2.4$

(c)	Gp 1	Gp 2	Gp 3	Gp 4
	$n_1 = 20$	$n_2 = 15$	$n_3 = 40$	$n_4 = 29$
	$|\mathbf{S}_1| = 42.8$	$|\mathbf{S}_2| = 20.1$	$|\mathbf{S}_3| = 50.2$	$|\mathbf{S}_4| = 15.6$

5. Zwick (1985) collected data on incoming clients at a mental health center who were randomly assigned to either an oriented group, which saw a videotape describing the goals and processes of psychotherapy, or a control group. She presented the following data on measures of anxiety, depression, and anger that were collected in a 1-month follow-up:

Anxiety	Depression	Anger	Anxiety	Depression	Anger
Oriented group ($n_1 = 20$)			Control group ($n_2 = 26$)		
285	325	165	168	190	160
23	45	15	277	230	63

Anxiety	Depression	Anger	Anxiety	Depression	Anger
Oriented group ($n_1 = 20$)			Control group ($n_2 = 26$)		
40	85	18	153	80	29
215	307	60	306	440	105
110	110	50	252	350	175
65	105	24	143	205	42
43	160	44	69	55	10
120	180	80	177	195	75
250	335	185	73	57	32
14	20	3	81	120	7
0	15	5	63	63	0
5	23	12	64	53	35
75	303	95	88	125	21
27	113	40	132	225	9
30	25	28	122	60	38
183	175	100	309	355	135
47	117	46	147	135	83
385	520	23	223	300	30
83	95	26	217	235	130
87	27	2	74	67	20
			258	185	115
			239	445	145
			78	40	48
			70	50	55
			188	165	87
			157	330	67

(a) Run the EXAMINE procedure on this data. Focusing on the Shapiro–Wilk test and doing each test at the .025 level, does there appear to be a problem with the normality assumption?

(b) Now, recall the statement in the chapter by Johnson and Wichern that lack of normality can be due to one or more outliers. Obtain the z scores for the variables in each group. Identify any cases having a z score greater than $|2.5|$.

(c) Which cases have z above this magnitude? For which variables do they occur? Remove any case from the Zwick data set having a z score greater than $|2.5|$ and rerun the EXAMINE procedure. Is there still a problem with lack of normality?

(d) Look at the stem-and-leaf plots for the variables. What transformation(s) from Figure 6.1 might be helpful here? Apply the transformation to the variables and rerun the EXAMINE procedure one more time. How many of the Shapiro–Wilk tests are now significant at the .025 level?

6. In Appendix 6.1 we illustrate what a difference the Hedges' correction factor, a correction for clustering, can have on t with reduced degrees of freedom. We illustrated this for $p = .10$. Show that, if $p = .20$, the effect is even more dramatic.

7. Consider Table 6.6. Show that the value of .035 for $N_1 : N_2 = 24:12$ for nominal $\alpha = .05$ for the positive condition makes sense. Also, show that the value = .076 for the negative condition makes sense.

Chapter 7

FACTORIAL ANOVA AND MANOVA

7.1 INTRODUCTION

In this chapter we consider the effect of two or more independent or classification variables (e.g., sex, social class, treatments) on a set of dependent variables. Four schematic two-way designs, where just the classification variables are shown, are given here:

Gender	Treatments				Aptitude	Teaching methods	
	1	2	3			1	2
Male					Low		
Female					Average		
					High		

Diagnosis	Drugs				Intelligence	Stimulus complexity		
	1	2	3	4		Easy	Average	Hard
Schizop.					Average			
Depressives					Super			

We first indicate what the advantages of a factorial design are over a one-way design. We also remind you what an interaction means, and distinguish between two types of interactions (ordinal and disordinal). The univariate equal cell size (balanced design) situation is discussed first, after which we tackle the much more difficult dispropor-tional (non-orthogonal or unbalanced) case. Three different ways of handling the unequal n case are considered; it is indicated why we feel one of these methods is generally superior. After this review of univariate ANOVA, we then discuss a multi-variate factorial design, provide an analysis guide for factorial MANOVA, and apply these analysis procedures to a fairly large data set (as most of the data sets provided in the chapter serve instructional purposes and have very small sample sizes). We also provide an example results section for factorial MANOVA and briefly discuss three-way MANOVA, focusing on the three-way interaction. We conclude the chapter by showing how discriminant analysis can be used in the context of a multivariate factorial design. Syntax for running various analyses is provided along the way, and selected output from SPSS is discussed.

7.2 ADVANTAGES OF A TWO-WAY DESIGN

1. A two-way design enables us to examine the *joint* effect of the independent variables on the dependent variable(s). We cannot get this information by running two separate one-way analyses, one for each of the independent variables. If one of the independent variables is treatments and the other some individual difference characteristic (sex, IQ, locus of control, age, etc.), then a significant interaction tells us that the superiority of one treatment over another depends on or is *moderated* by the individual difference characteristic. (An interaction means that the effect one independent variable has on a dependent variable is not the same for all levels of the other independent variable.) This moderating effect can take two forms:

	Teaching method		
	T_1	T_2	T_3
High ability	85	80	76
Low ability	60	63	68

(a) The degree of superiority changes, but one subgroup always does better than another. To illustrate this, consider this ability by teaching methods design: While the superiority of the high-ability students drops from 25 for T_1 (i.e., 85–60) to 8 for T_3 (76–68), high-ability students always do better than low-ability students. Because the order of superiority is maintained, in this example, *with respect to ability*, this is called an *ordinal* interaction. (Note that this does not hold for the treatment, as T_1 works better for high ability *but* T_3 is better for low ability students, leading to the next point.)

(b) The superiority reverses; that is, one treatment is best with one group, but another treatment is better for a different group. A study by Daniels and Stevens (1976) provides an illustration of a *disordinal* interaction. For a group of college undergraduates, they considered two types of instruction: (1) a traditional, teacher-controlled (lecture) type and (2) a contract for grade plan. The students were classified as internally or externally controlled, using Rotter's scale. An internal orientation means that those individuals perceive that positive events occur as a consequence of their actions (i.e., they are in control), whereas external participants feel that positive and/or negative events occur more because of powerful others, or due to chance or fate. The design and the means for the participants on an achievement posttest in psychology are given here:

		Instruction	
		Contract for grade	Teacher controlled
Locus of control	Internal	50.52	38.01
	External	36.33	46.22

The moderator variable in this case is locus of control, and it has a substantial effect on the efficacy of an instructional method. That is, the contract for grade method works better when participants have an internal locus of control, but in a reversal, the teacher controlled method works better for those with external locus of control. As such, when participant locus of control is matched to the teaching method (internals with contract for grade and externals with teacher controlled) they do quite well in terms of achievement; where there is a mismatch, achievement suffers.

This study also illustrates how a one-way design can lead to quite misleading results. Suppose Daniels and Stevens had just considered the two methods, ignoring locus of control. The means for achievement for the contract for grade plan and for teacher controlled are 43.42 and 42.11, nowhere near significance. The conclusion would have been that teaching methods do not make a difference. The factorial study shows, however, that methods definitely do make a difference—a quite positive difference if participant's locus of control is matched to teaching methods, and an undesirable effect if there is a mismatch.

The general area of matching treatments to individual difference characteristics of participants is an interesting and important one, and is called aptitude–treatment interaction research. A classic text in this area is *Aptitudes and Instructional Methods* by Cronbach and Snow (1977).

2. In addition to allowing you to detect the presence of interactions, a second advantage of factorial designs is that they can lead to more powerful tests by reducing error (within-cell) variance. If performance on the dependent variable is related to the individual difference characteristic (i.e., the blocking variable), then the reduction in error variance can be substantial. We consider a hypothetical sex × treatment design to illustrate:

	T1		T2	
Males	18, 19, 21 20, 22	(2.5)	17, 16, 16 18, 15	(1.3)
Females	11, 12, 11 13, 14	(1.7)	9, 9, 11 8, 7	(2.2)

Notice that *within* each cell there is very little variability. The within-cell variances quantify this, and are given in parentheses. The pooled within-cell error term for the factorial analysis is quite small, 1.925. On the other hand, if this had been considered as a two-group design (i.e., without gender), the variability would be much greater, as evidenced by the within-group (treatment) variances for T_1 and T_2 of 18.766 and 17.6, leading to a pooled error term for the F test of the treatment effect of 18.18.

7.3 UNIVARIATE FACTORIAL ANALYSIS

7.3.1 Equal Cell *n* (Orthogonal) Case

When there is an equal number of participants in each cell of a factorial design, then the sum of squares for the different effects (main and interactions) are uncorrelated (orthogonal). This is helpful when interpreting results, because significance for one effect implies nothing about significance for another. This provides for a clean and clear interpretation of results. It puts us in the same nice situation we had with uncorrelated planned comparisons, which we discussed in Chapter 5.

Overall and Spiegel (1969), in a classic paper on analyzing factorial designs, discussed three basic methods of analysis:

Method 1: Adjust each effect for all other effects in the design to obtain its unique contribution (regression approach), which is referred to as type III sum of squares in SAS and SPSS.

Method 2: Estimate the main effects ignoring the interaction, but estimate the interaction effect adjusting for the main effects (experimental method), which is referred to as type II sum of squares.

Method 3: Based on theory or previous research, establish an ordering for the effects, and then adjust each effect only for those effects preceding it in the ordering (hierarchical approach), which is referred to as type I sum of squares.

Note that the default method in SPSS is to provide type III (method 1) sum of squares, whereas SAS, by default, provides both type III (method 1) and type I (method 3) sum of squares.

For equal cell size designs all three of these methods yield the same results, that is, the same F tests. Therefore, it will not make any difference, in terms of the conclusions a researcher draws, as to which of these methods is used. *For unequal cell sizes, however, these methods can yield quite different results,* and this is what we consider shortly. First, however, we consider an example with equal cell size to show two things: (a) that the methods do indeed yield the same results, and (b) to demonstrate, using effect coding for the factors, that the effects are uncorrelated.

Example 7.1: Two-Way Equal Cell *n*

Consider the following 2 × 3 factorial data set:

		B		
		1	2	3
A	1	3, 5, 6	2, 4, 8	11, 7, 8
	2	9, 14, 5	6, 7, 7	9, 8, 10

In Table 7.1 we give SPSS syntax for running the analysis. In the general linear model commands, we indicate the factors after the keyword BY. Method 3, the hierarchical approach, means that a given effect is adjusted for all effects to its left in the ordering. The effects here would go in the following order: FACA (factor A), FACB (factor B), FACA by FACB. Thus, the A main effect is not adjusted for anything. The B main effect is adjusted for the A main effect, and the interaction is adjusted for both main effects.

■ Table 7.1: SPSS Syntax and Selected Output for Two-Way Equal Cell N ANOVA

```
TITLE 'TWO WAY ANOVA EQUAL N'.
DATA LIST FREE/FACA FACB DEP.
BEGIN DATA.
1 1 3    1 1 5    1 1 6
1 2 2    1 2 4    1 2 8
1 3 11   1 3 7    1 3 8
2 1 9    2 1 14   2 1 5
2 2 6    2 2 7    2 2 7
2 3 9    2 3 8    2 3 10
END DATA.
LIST.
GLM DEP BY FACA FACB
 /PRINT = DESCRIPTIVES.
```

Tests of Significance for DEP using UNIQUE sums of squares (known as Type III sum of squares)

Tests of Between-Subjects Effects

Dependent Variable: DEP

Source	Type III Sum of Squares	df	Mean Square	F	Sig.
Corrected Model	69.167[a]	5	13.833	2.204	.122
Intercept	924.500	1	924.500	147.265	.000

(Continued)

■ **Table 7.1: (Continued)**

Tests of Significance for DEP using UNIQUE sums of squares (known as Type III sum of squares)

Tests of Between-Subjects Effects

Dependent Variable: DEP

Source	Type III Sum of Squares	df	Mean Square	F	Sig.
FACA	24.500	1	24.500	3.903	.072
FACB	30.333	2	15.167	2.416	.131
FACA * FACB	14.333	2	7.167	1.142	.352
Error	75.333	12	6.278		
Total	1069.000	18			
Corrected Total	144.500	17			

[a] R Squared = .479 (Adjusted R Squared = .261)

Tests of Significance for DEP using SEQUENTIAL Sums of Squares (known as Type I sum of squares)

Tests of Between-Subjects Effects

Dependent Variable: DEP

Source	Type I Sum of Squares	df	Mean Square	F	Sig.
Corrected Model	69.167[a]	5	13.833	2.204	.122
Intercept	924.500	1	924.500	147.265	.000
FACA	24.500	1	24.500	3.903	.072
FACB	30.333	2	15.167	2.416	.131
FACA * FACB	14.333	2	7.167	1.142	.352
Error	75.333	12	6.278		
Total	1069.000	18			
Corrected Total	144.500	17			

[a] R Squared = .479 (Adjusted R Squared = .261)

The default in SPSS is to use Method 1 (type III sum of squares), which is obtained by the syntax shown in Table 7.1. Recall that this method obtains the unique contribution of each effect, adjusting for all other effects. Method 3 (type I sum of squares) is implemented in SPSS by inserting the line `/METHOD = SSTYPE(1)` immediately below the `GLM` line appearing in Table 7.1. Note, however, that the F ratios for Methods 1 and 3 are identical (see Table 7.1). Why? Because the effects are uncorrelated due to the equal cell size, and therefore no adjustment takes place. Thus, the F test for an effect "adjusted" is the same as an effect unadjusted. To show that the effects are indeed uncorrelated, we used effect coding as described in Table 7.2 and ran the problem as a regression analysis. The coding scheme is explained there.

```
TITLE 'EFFECT CODING FOR EQUAL CELL SIZE 2-WAY ANOVA'.
DATA LIST FREE/Y A1 B1 B2 A1B1 A1B2.
BEGIN DATA.
3 1 1 0 1 0     5 1 1 0 1 0     6 1 1 0 1 0
2 1 0 1 0 1     4 1 0 1 0 1     8 1 0 1 0 1
11 1 -1 -1-1 -1  7 1 -1 -1-1 -1  8 1 -1 -1-1 -1
9 -1 1 0-1 0     14 -1 1 0-1 0   5 -1 1 0 -1 0
6 -1 0 1 0 -1    7 -1 0 1 0 -1   7 -1 0 1 0 -1
9 -1 -1 -1 1 1   8 -1 -1-1 1 1   10 -1 -1 -1 1 1
END DATA.
LIST.
REGRESSION DESCRIPTIVES = DEFAULT
 /VARIABLES = Y TO A1B2
 /DEPENDENT = Y
 /METHOD = ENTER.
```

Y	A1	(1) B1	B2	A1B1	A1B2
3.00	1.00	1.00	.00	1.00	.00
5.00	1.00	1.00	.00	1.00	.00
6.00	1.00	1.00	.00	1.00	.00
2.00	1.00	.00	1.00	.00	1.00
4.00	1.00	.00	1.00	.00	1.00
8.00	1.00	.00	1.00	.00	1.00
11.00	1.00	−1.00	−1.00	−1.00	−1.00
7.00	1.00	−1.00	−1.00	−1.00	−1.00
8.00	1.00	−1.00	−1.00	−1.00	−1.00
9.00	−1.00	1.00	.00	−1.00	.00
14.00	−1.00	1.00	.00	−1.00	.00
5.00	−1.00	1.00	.00	−1.00	.00
6.00	−1.00	.00	1.00	.00	−1.00
7.00	−1.00	.00	1.00	.00	−1.00
7.00	−1.00	.00	1.00	.00	−1.00
9.00	−1.00	−1.00	−1.00	1.00	1.00
8.00	−1.00	−1.00	−1.00	1.00	1.00
10.00	−1.00	−1.00	−1.00	1.00	1.00

			Correlations			
	Y	A1	B1	B2	A1B1	A1B2
Y	1.000	−.412	−.264	−.456	−.312	−.120
A1	−.412	1.000	.000	.000	.000	.000

(*Continued*)

■ **Table 7.2: (Continued)**

	Correlations					
	Y	A1	B1	B2	A1B1	A1B2
B1	−.264	.000	1.000	.500	.000	.000
B2	−.456 (2)	.000	.500	1.000	.000	.000
A1B1	−.312	.000	.000	.000	1.000	.500
A1B2	−.120	.000	.000	.000	.500	1.000

(1) For the first effect coded variable (A1), the S's in the first level of A are coded with a 1, with the S's in the last level coded as −1. Since there are 3 levels of B, two effect coded variables are needed. The S's in the first level of B are coded as 1s for variable B1, with the S's for all other levels of B, except the last, coded as 0s. The S's in the last level of B are coded as −1s. Similarly, the S's on the second level of B are coded as 1s on the second effect-coded variable (B2 here), with the S's for all other levels of B, except the last, coded as 0's. Again, the S's in the last level of B are coded as −1s for B2. To obtain the variables needed to represent the interaction, i.e., A1B1 and A1B2, multiply the corresponding coded variables (i.e., A1 × B1, A1 × B2).

(2) Note that the correlations between variables representing *different* effects are all 0. The only nonzero correlations are for the two variables that jointly represent the B main effect (B1 and B2), and for the two variables (A1B1 and A1B2) that jointly represent the AB interaction effect.

Predictor A1 represents factor A, predictors B1 and B2 represent factor B, and predictors A1B1 and A1B2 are variables needed to represent the interaction between factors A and B. In the regression framework, we are using these predictors to explain variation on y. Note that the correlations between predictors representing *different* effects are all 0. This means that those effects are accounting for distinct parts of the variation on y, or that we have an orthogonal partitioning of the *y* variation.

In Table 7.3 we present sequential regression results that add one predictor variable at a time in the order indicated in the table. There, we explain how the sum of squares obtained for each effect is exactly the same as was obtained when the problem was run as a traditional ANOVA in Table 7.1.

Example 7.2: Two-Way Disproportional Cell Size

The data for our disproportional cell size example is given in Table 7.4, along with the effect coding for the predictors, and the correlation matrix for the effects. Here there definitely are correlations among the effects. For example, the correlations between A1 (representing the A main effect) and B1 and B2 (representing the B main effect) are −.163 and −.275. This contrasts with the equal cell n case where the correlations among the different effects were all 0 (Table 7.2). Thus, for disproportional cell sizes the sources of variation are confounded (mixed together). To determine how much unique variation on y a given effect accounts for we must adjust or partial out how

◼ Table 7.3: Sequential Regression Results for Two-Way Equal n ANOVA With Effect Coding

Model No.	1				
Variable Entered		A1			
Analysis of Variance					
		Sum of Squares	DF	Mean Square	F Ratio
Regression		24.500	1	24.500	3.267
Residual		120.000	16	7.500	
Model No.	2				
Variable Added		B2			
Analysis of Variance					
		Sum of Squares	DF	Mean Square	F Ratio
Regression		54.583	2	27.292	4.553
Residual		89.917	15	5.994	
Model No.	3				
Variable Added		B1			
Analysis of Variance					
		Sum of Squares	DF	Mean Square	F Ratio
Regression		54.833	3	18.278	2.854
Residual		89.667	14	6.405	
Model No.	4				
Variable Added		A1B1			
Analysis of Variance					
		Sum of Squares	DF	Mean Square	F Ratio
Regression		68.917	4	17.229	2.963
Residual		75.583	13	5.814	
Model No.	5				
Variable Added		A1B2			
Analysis of Variance					
		Sum of Squares	DF	Mean Square	F Ratio
Regression		69.167	5	13.833	2.204
Residual		75.333	12	6.278	

Note: The sum of squares (SS) for regression for A1, representing the A main effect, is the same as the SS for FACA in Table 7.1. Also, the additional SS for B1 and B2, representing the B main effect, is 54.833 – 24.5 = 30.333, the same as SS for FACB in Table 7.1. Finally, the additional SS for A1B1 and A1B2, representing the AB interaction, is 69.167 – 54.833 = 14.334, the same as SS for FACA by FACB in Table 7.1.

much of that variation is explainable because of the effect's correlations with the other effects in the design. Recall that in Chapter 5 the same procedure was employed to determine the unique amount of between variation a given planned comparison accounts for in a set of correlated planned comparisons.

In Table 7.5 we present the control lines for running the disproportional cell size example, along with Method 3 (type I sum of squares) and Method 1 (type III sum of squares) results. The F ratios for the interaction effect are the same, but the F ratios for the main effects are quite different. For example, if we had used Method 3 we would have declared a significant B main effect at the .05 level, but with Method 1 (unique decomposition) the B main effect is not significant at the .05 level. Therefore, with unequal n designs the method used can clearly make a difference in terms of the conclusions reached in the study. This raises the question of which of the three methods should be used for disproportional cell size factorial designs.

■ **Table 7.4: Effect Coding of the Predictors for the Disproportional Cell n ANOVA and Correlation Matrix for the Variables**

	Design		
		B	
	3, 5, 6	2, 4, 8	11, 7, 8, 6, 9
A	9, 14, 5, 11	6, 7, 7, 8, 10, 5, 6	9, 8, 10

A1	B1	B2	A1B1	A1B2	Y
1.00	1.00	.00	1.00	.00	3.00
1.00	1.00	.00	1.00	.00	5.00
1.00	1.00	.00	1.00	.00	6.00
1.00	.00	1.00	.00	1.00	2.00
1.00	.00	1.00	.00	1.00	4.00
1.00	.00	1.00	.00	1.00	8.00
1.00	−1.00	−1.00	−1.00	−1.00	11.00
1.00	−1.00	−1.00	−1.00	−1.00	7.00
1.00	−1.00	−1.00	−1.00	−1.00	8.00
1.00	−1.00	−1.00	−1.00	−1.00	6.00
1.00	−1.00	−1.00	−1.00	−1.00	9.00
−1.00	1.00	.00	−1.00	.00	9.00
−1.00	1.00	.00	−1.00	.00	14.00
−1.00	1.00	.00	−1.00	.00	5.00
−1.00	1.00	.00	−1.00	.00	11.00
−1.00	.00	1.00	.00	−1.00	6.00
−1.00	.00	1.00	.00	−1.00	7.00

		Design			
−1.00	.00	1.00	.00	−1.00	7.00
−1.00	.00	1.00	.00	−1.00	8.00
−1.00	.00	1.00	.00	−1.00	10.00
−1.00	.00	1.00	.00	−1.00	5.00
−1.00	.00	1.00	.00	−1.00	6.00
−1.00	−1.00	−1.00	1.00	1.00	9.00
−1.00	−1.00	−1.00	1.00	1.00	8.00
−1.00	−1.00	−1.00	1.00	1.00	10.00

	For A main effect	For B main effect		For AB interaction effect		
Correlation:	↓	↘	↘	↗	↘	
	A1	B1	B2	A1B1	A1B2	Y
A1	1.000	−.163	−.275	−.072	.063	−.361
B1	−.163	1.000	.495	.059	.112	−.148
B2	−.275	.495	1.000	.139	−.088	−.350
A1B1	−0.72	0.59	1.39	1.000	.468	−.332
A1B2	.063	.112	−.088	.468	1.000	−.089
Y	−.361	−.148	−.350	−.332	−.089	1.000

Note: The correlations between variables representing different effects are boxed in. Compare these correlations to those for the equal cell size situation, as presented in Table 7.2

■ **Table 7.5: SPSS Syntax for Two-Way Disproportional Cell *n* ANOVA With the Sequential and Unique Sum of Squares F Ratios**

```
TITLE 'TWO WAY UNEQUAL N'.
DATA LIST FREE/FACA FACB DEP.
BEGIN DATA.
1 1 3     1 1 5     1 1 6
1 2 2     1 2 4     1 2 8
1 3 11    1 3 7     1 3 8     1 3 6     1 3 9
2 1 9     2 1 14    2 1 5     2 1 11
2 2 6     2 2 7     2 2 7     2 2 8     2 2 10    2 2 5    2 2 6
2 3 9     2 3 8     2 3 10
END DATA
LIST.
UNIANOVA DEP BY FACA FACB
 / METHOD = SSTYPE(1)
 / PRINT = DESCRIPTIVES.
```

(*Continued*)

■ **Table 7.5: (Continued)**

Tests of Between-Subjects Effects

Dependent Variable: DEP

Source	Type I Sum of Squares	df	Mean Square	F	Sig.
Corrected Model	78.877a	5	15.775	3.031	.035
Intercept	1354.240	1	1354.240	260.211	.000
FACA	23.221	1	23.221	4.462	.048
FACB	38.878	2	19.439	3.735	.043
FACA * FACB	16.778	2	8.389	1.612	.226
Error	98.883	19	5.204		
Total	1532.000	25			
Corrected Total	177.760	24			

Tests of Between-Subjects Effects

Dependent Variable: DEP

Source	Type III Sum of Squares	df	Mean Square	F	Sig.
Corrected Model	78.877a	5	15.775	3.031	.035
Intercept	1176.155	1	1176.155	225.993	.000
FACA	42.385	1	42.385	8.144	.010
FACB	30.352	2	15.176	2.916	.079
FACA * FACB	16.778	2	8.389	1.612	.226
Error	98.883	19	5.204		
Total	1532.000	25			
Corrected Total	177.760	24			

[a] R Squared = .444 (Adjusted R Squared = .297)

7.3.2 Which Method Should Be Used?

Overall and Spiegel (1969) recommended Method 2 as generally being most appropriate. However, most believe that Method 2 is rarely be the method of choice, since it estimates the main effects ignoring the interaction. Carlson and Timm's (1974) comment is appropriate here: "We find it hard to believe that a researcher would consciously design a factorial experiment and then ignore the factorial nature of the data in testing the main effects" (p. 156).

We feel that Method 1, where we are obtaining the unique contribution of each effect, is generally more appropriate and is also widely used. This is what Carlson and Timm (1974) recommended, and what Myers (1979) recommended for experimental studies (random assignment involved), or as he put it, "whenever variations in cell frequencies can reasonably be assumed due to chance" (p. 403).

When an a priori ordering of the effects can be established (Overall & Spiegel, 1969, give a nice psychiatric example), Method 3 makes sense. This is analogous to establishing an a priori ordering of the predictors in multiple regression. To illustrate we adapt an example given in Cohen, Cohen, Aiken, and West (2003), where the research goal is to predict university faculty salary. Using 2 predictors, sex and number of publications, a presumed causal ordering is sex and then number of publications. The reasoning would be that sex can impact number of publications but number of publications cannot impact sex.

7.4 FACTORIAL MULTIVARIATE ANALYSIS OF VARIANCE

Here, we are considering the effect of two or more independent variables on a set of dependent variables. To illustrate factorial MANOVA we use an example from Barcikowski (1983). Sixth-grade students were classified as being of high, average, or low aptitude, and then within each of these aptitudes, were randomly assigned to one of five methods of teaching social studies. The dependent variables were measures of attitude and achievement. These data, with the scores for the attitude and achievement appearing in each cell, are:

			Method of instruction		
	1	2	3	4	5
High	15, 11	19, 11	14, 13	19, 14	14, 16
	9, 7	12, 9	9, 9	7, 8	14, 8
		12, 6	14, 15	6, 6	18, 16
Average	18, 13	25, 24	29, 23	11, 14	18, 17
	8, 11	24, 23	28, 26	14, 10	11, 13
	6, 6	26, 19		8, 7	
Low	11, 9	13, 11	17, 10	15, 9	17, 12
	16, 15	10, 11	7, 9	13, 13	13, 15
			7, 9	7, 7	9, 12

Of the 45 subjects who started the study, five were lost for various reasons. This resulted in a disproportional factorial design. To obtain the unique contribution of each effect, the unique sum of squares decomposition was obtained. The syntax for doing so is given in Table 7.6, along with syntax for simple effects analyses, where the latter is used to explore the interaction between method of instruction and aptitude. The results of the multivariate and univariate tests of the effects are presented in Table 7.7. All of the multivariate effects are significant at the .05 level. We use the F's associated with Wilks to illustrate (aptitude by method: $F = 2.19$, $p = .018$; method: $F = 2.46$, $p = .025$; and aptitude: $F = 5.92, p = .001$). Because the interaction is significant, we focus our interpretation on it. The univariate tests for this effect on attitude and achievement are also both significant at the .05 level. Focusing on simple treatment effects for each level of aptitude, inspection of means and simple effects testing (not shown,) indicated that treatment effects were present only for those of average aptitude. For these students, treatments 2 and 3 were generally more effective than other treatments for each dependent variable, as indicated by pairwise comparisons using a Bonferroni adjustment. This adjustment is used to provide for greater control of the family-wise type I error rate for the 10 pairwise comparisons involving method of instruction for those of average aptitude.

■ **Table 7.6: Syntax for Factorial MANOVA on SPSS and Simple Effects Analyses**

```
TITLE 'TWO WAY MANOVA'.
DATA LIST FREE/FACA FACB ATTIT ACHIEV.
BEGIN DATA.
1 1 15 11              1 1 9 7
1 2 19 11              1 2 12 9           1 2 12 6
1 3 14 13              1 3 9 9            1 3 14 15
1 4 19 14              1 4 7 8            1 4 6 6
1 5 14 16              1 5 14 8           1 5 18 16
2 1 18 13              2 1 8 11           2 1 6 6
2 2 25 24              2 2 24 23          2 2 26 19
2 3 29 23              2 3 28 26
2 4 11 14              2 4 14 10          2 4 8 7
2 5 18 17              2 5 11 13
3 1 11 9               3 1 16 15
3 2 13 11              3 2 10 11
3 3 17 10              3 3 7 9            3 3 7 9
3 4 15 9               3 4 13 13          3 4 7 7
3 5 17 12              3 5 13 15          3 5 9 12
END DATA.
LIST.
GLM ATTIT ACHIEV BY FACA FACB
 /PRINT = DESCRIPTIVES.
```

Simple Effects Analyses

```
GLM
 ATTIT BY FACA FACB
 /PLOT = PROFILE (FACA*FACB)
 /EMMEANS = TABLES(FACB) COMPARE ADJ(BONFERRONI)
 /EMMEANS = TABLES (FACA*FACB) COMPARE (FACB) ADJ(BONFERRONI).
GLM
 ACHIEV BY FACA FACB
 /PLOT = PROFILE (FACA*FACB)
 /EMMEANS = TABLES(FACB) COMPARE ADJ(BONFERRONI)
 /EMMEANS = TABLES (FACA*FACB) COMPARE (FACB) ADJ(BONFERRONI).
```

■ Table 7.7: Selected Results From Factorial MANOVA

Multivariate Tests[a]

Effect		Value	F	Hypothesis df	Error df	Sig.
Intercept	Pillai's Trace	.965	329.152[b]	2.000	24.000	.000
	Wilks' Lambda	.035	329.152[b]	2.000	24.000	.000
	Hotelling's Trace	27.429	329.152[b]	2.000	24.000	.000
	Roy's Largest Root	27.429	329.152[b]	2.000	24.000	.000
FACA	Pillai's Trace	.574	5.031	4.000	50.000	.002
	Wilks' Lambda	.449	5.917[b]	4.000	48.000	.001
	Hotelling's Trace	1.179	6.780	4.000	46.000	.000
	Roy's Largest Root	1.135	14.187[c]	2.000	25.000	.000
FACB	Pillai's Trace	.534	2.278	8.000	50.000	.037
	Wilks' Lambda	.503	2.463[b]	8.000	48.000	.025
	Hotelling's Trace	.916	2.633	8.000	46.000	.018
	Roy's Largest Root	.827	5.167[c]	4.000	25.000	.004
FACA * FACB	Pillai's Trace	.757	1.905	16.000	50.000	.042
	Wilks' Lambda	.333	2.196[b]	16.000	48.000	.018
	Hotelling's Trace	1.727	2.482	16.000	46.000	.008
	Roy's Largest Root	1.551	4.847[c]	8.000	25.000	.001

[a] Design: Intercept + FACA + FACB + FACA * FACB
[b] Exact statistic
[c] The statistic is an upper bound on F that yields a lower bound on the significance level.

Tests of Between-Subjects Effects

Source	Dependent Variable	Type III Sum of Squares	df	Mean Square	F	Sig.
Corrected Model	ATTIT	972.108[a]	14	69.436	3.768	.002
	ACHIEV	764.608[b]	14	54.615	5.757	.000
Intercept	ATTIT	7875.219	1	7875.219	427.382	.000
	ACHIEV	6156.043	1	6156.043	648.915	.000
FACA	ATTIT	256.508	2	128.254	6.960	.004
	ACHIEV	267.558	2	133.779	14.102	.000
FACB	ATTIT	237.906	4	59.477	3.228	.029
	ACHIEV	189.881	4	47.470	5.004	.004
FACA * FACB	ATTIT	503.321	8	62.915	3.414	.009
	ACHIEV	343.112	8	42.889	4.521	.002
Error	ATTIT	460.667	25	18.427		
	ACHIEV	237.167	25	9.487		
Total	ATTIT	9357.000	40			
	ACHIEV	7177.000	40			
Corrected Total	ATTIT	1432.775	39			
	ACHIEV	1001.775	39			

[a] R Squared = .678 (Adjusted R Squared = .498)
[b] R Squared = .763 (Adjusted R Squared = .631)

7.5 WEIGHTING OF THE CELL MEANS

In experimental studies that wind up with unequal cell sizes, it is reasonable to assume equal population sizes, and equal cell weighting is appropriate in estimating the grand mean. However, when sampling from intact groups (sex, age, race, socioeconomic status [SES], religions) in nonexperimental studies, the populations may well differ in size, and the sizes of the samples may reflect the different population sizes. In such cases, equally weighting the subgroup means will not provide an unbiased estimate of the combined (grand) mean, whereas weighting the means will produce an unbiased estimate. In some situations, you may wish to use both weighted and unweighted cell means in a single factorial design, that is, in a semi-experimental design. In such designs one of the factors is an attribute factor (sex, SES, ethnicity, etc.) and the other factor is treatments.

Suppose for a given situation it is reasonable to assume there are twice as many middle SES cases in a population as lower SES, and that two treatments are involved. Forty lower SES participants are sampled and randomly assigned to treatments, and 80 middle SES participants are selected and assigned to treatments. Schematically then, the setup of the weighted treatment (column) means and unweighted SES (row) means is:

		T_1	T_2	Unweighted means
SES	Lower	$n_{11} = 20$	$n_{12} = 20$	$(\mu_{11} + \mu_{12})/2$
	Middle	$n_{21} = 40$	$n_{22} = 40$	$(\mu_{21} + \mu_{22})/2$
Weighted means		$\dfrac{n_{11}\mu_{11} + n_{21}\mu_{21}}{n_{11} + n_{21}}$	$\dfrac{n_{12}\mu_{12} + n_{22}\mu_{22}}{n_{12} + n_{22}}$	

Note that Method 3 (type I sum of squares) the sequential or hierarchical approach, described in section 7.3 can be used to provide a partitioning of variance that implements a weighted means solution.

7.6 ANALYSIS PROCEDURES FOR TWO-WAY MANOVA

In this section, we summarize the analysis steps that provide a general guide for you to follow in conducting a two-way MANOVA where the focus is on examining effects for each of several outcomes. Section 7.7 applies the procedures to a fairly large data set, and section 7.8 presents an example results section. Note that preliminary analysis activities for the two-way design are the same as for the one-way MANOVA as summarized in section 6.11, except that these activities apply to the cells of the two-way design. For example, for a 2 × 2 factorial design, the scores are assumed to follow a multivariate normal distribution with equal variance-covariance matrices across each of the 4 cells. Since preliminary analysis for the two-factor design is similar to the one-factor design, we focus our summary of the analysis procedures on primary analysis.

7.6.1 Primary Analysis

1. Examine the Wilks' lambda test for the multivariate interaction.
   A. If this test is statistically significant, examine the F test of the two-way interaction for each dependent variable, using a Bonferroni correction unless the number of dependent variables is small (i.e., 2 or 3).
   B. If an interaction is present for a given dependent variable, use simple effects analyses for that variable to interpret the interaction.
2. If a given univariate interaction is not statistically significant (or sufficiently strong) OR if the Wilks' lambda test for the multivariate interaction is not statistically significant, examine the multivariate tests for the main effects.
   A. If the multivariate test of a given main effect is statistically significant, examine the F test for the corresponding main effect (i.e., factor A or factor B) for each dependent variable, using a Bonferroni adjustment (unless the number of outcomes is small). Note that the main effect for any dependent variable for which an interaction was present may not be of interest due to the qualified nature of the simple effect description.
   B. If the univariate F test is significant for a given dependent variable, use pairwise comparisons (if more than 2 groups are present) to describe the main effect. Use a Bonferroni adjustment for the pairwise comparisons to provide protection for the inflation of the type I error rate.
   C. If no multivariate main effects are significant, do not proceed to the univariate test of main effects. If a given univariate main effect is not significant, do not conduct further testing (i.e., pairwise comparisons) for that main effect.
3. Use one or more effect size measures to describe the strength of the effects and/or the differences in the means of interest. Commonly used effect size measures include multivariate partial eta square, univariate partial eta square, and/or raw score differences in means for specific comparisons of interest.

7.7 FACTORIAL MANOVA WITH SENIORWISE DATA

In this section, we illustrate application of the analysis procedures for two-way MANOVA using the SeniorWISE data set used in section 6.11, except that these data now include a second factor of gender (i.e., female, male). So, we now assume that the investigators recruited 150 females and 150 males with each being at least 65 years old. Then, within each of these groups, the participants were randomly assigned to receive (a) memory training, which was designed to help adults maintain and/or improve their memory related abilities, (b) a health intervention condition, which did not include memory training, or (c) a wait-list control condition. The active treatments were individually administered and posttest intervention measures were completed individually. The dependent variables are the same as in section 6.11 and include memory self-efficacy (self-efficacy), verbal memory performance (verbal), and daily functioning skills (DAFS). Higher scores on these measures represent a greater (and preferred) level of performance. Thus, we have a 3 (treatment levels) by 2 (gender groups) multivariate design with 50 participants in each of 6 cells.

7.7.1 Preliminary Analysis

The preliminary analysis activities for factorial MANOVA are the same as with one-way MANOVA except, of course, the relevant groups now are the six cells formed by the crossing of the two factors. As such, the scores in each cell (in the population) must be multivariate normal, have equal variance-covariance matrices, and be independent. To facilitate examining the degree to which the assumptions are satisfied and to readily enable other preliminary analysis activities, Table 7.8 shows SPSS syntax for creating a cell membership variable for this data set. Also, the syntax shows how Mahalanobis distance values may be obtained for each case within each of the 6 cells, as such values are then used to identify multivariate outliers.

For this data set, there is no missing data as each of the 300 participants has a score for each of the study variables. There are no multivariate outliers as the largest within-cell

■ **Table 7.8: SPSS Syntax for Creating a Cell Variable and Obtaining Mahalanobis Distance Values**

```
*/ Creating Cell Variable.
IF (Group = 1 and Gender = 0) Cell=1.
IF (Group = 2 and Gender = 0) Cell=2.
IF (Group = 3 and Gender = 0) Cell=3.
IF (Group = 1 and Gender = 1) Cell=4.
IF (Group = 2 and Gender = 1) Cell=5.
IF (Group = 3 and Gender = 1) Cell=6.
EXECUTE.

*/ Organizing Output By Cell.
SORT CASES BY Cell.
SPLIT FILE SEPARATE BY Cell.

*/ Requesting within-cell Mahalanobis' distances for each case.
REGRESSION
 /STATISTICS COEFF ANOVA
 /DEPENDENT Case
 /METHOD=ENTER Self_Efficacy Verbal Dafs
 /SAVE MAHAL.

*/ REMOVING SPLIT FILE.
SPLIT FILE OFF.
```

Mahalanobis distance value, 10.61, is smaller than the chi-square critical value of 16.27 (a = .001; df = 3 for the 3 dependent variables). Similarly, we did not detect any univariate outliers, as no within-cell z score exceeded a magnitude of 3. Also, inspection of the 18 histograms (6 cells by 3 outcomes) did not suggest the presence of any extreme scores. Further, examining the pooled within-cell correlations provided support for using the multivariate procedure as the three correlations ranged from .31 to .47.

In addition, there are no serious departures from the statistical assumptions associated with factorial MANOVA. Inspecting the 18 histograms did not suggest any substantial departures of univariate normality. Further, no kurtosis or skewness value in any cell for any outcome exceeded a magnitude of .97, again, suggesting no substantial departure from normality. For the assumption of equal variance-covariance matrices, we note that the cell standard deviations (not shown) were fairly similar for each outcome. Also, Box's M test (M = 30.53, p = .503), did not suggest a violation. Similarly, examining the results of Levene's test for equality of variance (not shown) provided support that the dispersion of scores for self-efficacy (p = .47), verbal performance (p = .78), and functional status (p = .33) was similar across the six cells. For the independence assumption, the study design, as described in section 6.11, does not suggest any violation in part as treatments were individually administered to participants who also completed posttest measures individually.

7.7.2 Primary Analysis

Table 7.9 shows the syntax used for the primary analysis, and Tables 7.10 and 7.11 show the overall multivariate and univariate test results. Inspecting Table 7.10 indicates that an overall group-by-gender interaction is present in the set of outcomes, Wilks' lambda = .946, F (6, 584) = 2.72, p = .013. Examining the univariate test results for the group-by-gender interaction in Table 7.11 suggests that this interaction is present for DAFS, F (2, 294) = 6.174, p = .002, but not for self-efficacy F (2, 294) = 1.603, p = .203 or verbal F (2, 294) = .369, p = .692. Thus, we will focus on examining simple effects associated with the treatment for DAFS but not for the other outcomes. Of course, main effects may be present for the set of outcomes as well. The multivariate test results in Table 7.10 indicate that a main effect in the set of outcomes is present for both group, Wilks' lambda = .748, F (6, 584) = 15.170, p < .001, and gender, Wilks' lambda = .923, F (3, 292) = 3.292, p < .001, although we will focus on describing treatment effects, not gender differences, from this point on. The univariate test results in Table 7.11 indicate that a main effect of the treatment is present for self-efficacy, F (2, 294) = 29.931, p < .001, and verbal F (2, 294) = 26.514, p < .001. Note that a main effect is present also for DAFS but the interaction just noted suggests we may not wish to describe main effects. So, for self-efficacy and verbal, we will examine pairwise comparisons to examine treatment effects pooling across the gender groups.

■ Table 7.9: SPSS Syntax for Factorial MANOVA With SeniorWISE Data

```
GLM Self_Efficacy Verbal Dafs BY Group Gender
 /SAVE=ZRESID
 /EMMEANS=TABLES(Group)
 /EMMEANS=TABLES(Gender)
 /EMMEANS=TABLES(Gender*Group)
 /PLOT=PROFILE(GROUP*GENDER GENDER*GROUP)
 /PRINT=DESCRIPTIVE ETASQ HOMOGENEITY.
```

*Follow-up univariates for Self-Efficacy and Verbal to obtain pairwise comparisons; Bonferroni method used to maintain consistency with simple effects analyses (for Dafs).

```
UNIANOVA Self_Efficacy BY Gender Group
 /EMMEANS=TABLES(Group)
 /POSTHOC=Group(BONFERRONI).

UNIANOVA Verbal BY Gender Group
 /EMMEANS=TABLES(Group)
 /POSTHOC=Group(BONFERRONI).
```

* Follow-up simple effects analyses for Dafs with Bonferroni method.

```
GLM
 Dafs BY Gender Group
 /EMMEANS = TABLES (Gender*Group) COMPARE (Group)
 ADJ(Bonferroni).
```

■ Table 7.10: SPSS Results of the Overall Multivariate Tests

Multivariate Tests[a]

Effect		Value	F	Hypothesis df	Error df	Sig.	Partial Eta Squared
Intercept	Pillai's Trace	.983	5678.271[b]	3.000	292.000	.000	.983
	Wilks' Lambda	.017	5678.271[b]	3.000	292.000	.000	.983
	Hotelling's Trace	58.338	5678.271[b]	3.000	292.000	.000	.983
	Roy's Largest Root	58.338	5678.271[b]	3.000	292.000	.000	.983
GROUP	Pillai's Trace	.258	14.441	6.000	586.000	.000	.129
	Wilks' Lambda	.748	15.170[b]	6.000	584.000	.000	.135

Multivariate Tests[a]

Effect		Value	F	Hypothesis df	Error df	Sig.	Partial Eta Squared
	Hotelling's Trace	.328	15.900	6.000	582.000	.000	.141
	Roy's Largest Root	.301	29.361[c]	3.000	293.000	.000	.231
GENDER	Pillai's Trace	.077	8.154[b]	3.000	292.000	.000	.077
	Wilks' Lambda	.923	8.154[b]	3.000	292.000	.000	.077
	Hotelling's Trace	.084	8.154[b]	3.000	292.000	.000	.077
	Roy's Largest Root	.084	8.154[b]	3.000	292.000	.000	.077
GROUP * GENDER	Pillai's Trace	.054	2.698	6.000	586.000	.014	.027
	Wilks' Lambda	.946	2.720[b]	6.000	584.000	.013	.027
	Hotelling's Trace	.057	2.743	6.000	582.000	.012	.027
	Roy's Largest Root	.054	5.290[c]	3.000	293.000	.001	.051

[a] Design: Intercept + GROUP + GENDER + GROUP * GENDER
[b] Exact statistic
[c] The statistic is an upper bound on F that yields a lower bound on the significance level.

■ **Table 7.11: SPSS Results of the Overall Univariate Tests**

Tests of Between-Subjects Effects

Source	Dependent Variable	Type III Sum of Squares	df	Mean Square	F	Sig.	Partial Eta Squared
Corrected Model	Self_Efficacy	5750.604[a]	5	1150.121	13.299	.000	.184
	Verbal	4944.027[b]	5	988.805	10.760	.000	.155
	DAFS	6120.099[c]	5	1224.020	14.614	.000	.199
Intercept	Self_Efficacy	833515.776	1	833515.776	9637.904	.000	.970
	Verbal	896000.120	1	896000.120	9750.188	.000	.971
	DAFS	883559.339	1	883559.339	10548.810	.000	.973
GROUP	Self_Efficacy	5177.087	2	2588.543	29.931	.000	.169
	Verbal	4872.957	2	2436.478	26.514	.000	.153
	DAFS	3642.365	2	1821.183	21.743	.000	.129

(*Continued*)

■ **Table 7.11: (Continued)**

Tests of Between-Subjects Effects

Source	Dependent Variable	Type III Sum of Squares	df	Mean Square	F	Sig.	Partial Eta Squared
GENDER	Self_Efficacy	296.178	1	296.178	3.425	.065	.012
	Verbal	3.229	1	3.229	.035	.851	.000
	DAFS	1443.514	1	1443.514	17.234	.000	.055
GROUP *	Self_Efficacy	277.339	2	138.669	1.603	.203	.011
GENDER	Verbal	67.842	2	33.921	.369	.692	.003
	DAFS	1034.220	2	517.110	6.174	.002	.040
Error	Self_Efficacy	25426.031	294	86.483			
	Verbal	27017.328	294	91.896			
	DAFS	24625.189	294	83.759			
Total	Self_Efficacy	864692.411	300				
	Verbal	927961.475	300				
	DAFS	914304.627	300				
Corrected	Self_Efficacy	31176.635	299				
Total	Verbal	31961.355	299				
	DAFS	30745.288	299				

[a] R Squared = .184 (Adjusted R Squared = .171)
[b] R Squared = .155 (Adjusted R Squared = .140)
[c] R Squared = .199 (Adjusted R Squared = .185)

Table 7.12 shows results for the simple effects analyses for DAFS focusing on the impact of the treatments. Examining the means suggests that group differences for females are not particularly large, but the treatment means for males appear quite different, especially for the memory training condition. This strong effect of the memory training condition for males is also evident in the plot in Table 7.12. For females, the F test for treatment mean differences, shown near the bottom of Table 7.12, suggests that no differences are present in the population, $F(2, 294) = 2.405$, $p = .092$. For males, on the other hand, treatment group mean differences are present $F(2, 294) = 25.512$, $p < .001$. Pairwise comparisons for males, using Bonferroni adjusted p values, indicate that participants in the memory training condition outscored, on average, those in the health training ($p < .001$) and control conditions ($p < .001$). The difference in means between the health training and control condition is not statistically significant ($p = 1.00$).

Table 7.13 and Table 7.14 show the results of Bonferroni-adjusted pairwise comparisons of treatment group means (pooling across gender) for the dependent variables self-efficacy and verbal performance. The results in Table 7.13 indicate that the large difference in means between the memory training and health training conditions is statistically significant ($p < .001$) as is the difference between the memory

■ Table 7.12: SPSS Results of the Simple Effects Analyses for DAFS

Estimated Marginal Means GENDER * GROUP

Estimates

Dependent Variable: DAFS

GENDER	GROUP	Mean	Std. Error	95% Confidence Interval Lower Bound	95% Confidence Interval Upper Bound
FEMALE	Memory Training	54.337	1.294	51.790	56.884
	Health Training	51.388	1.294	48.840	53.935
	Control	50.504	1.294	47.956	53.051
MALE	Memory Training	63.966	1.294	61.419	66.513
	Health Training	53.431	1.294	50.884	55.978
	Control	51.993	1.294	49.445	54.540

Pairwise Comparisons

Dependent Variable: DAFS

GENDER	(I) GROUP	(J) GROUP	Mean Difference (I-J)	Std. Error	Sig.[b]	95% Confidence Interval for ·Difference[b] Lower Bound	95% Confidence Interval for ·Difference[b] Upper Bound
FEMALE	Memory Training	Health Training	2.950	1.830	.324	−1.458	7.357
		Control	3.833	1.830	.111	−.574	8.241
	Health Training	Memory Training	−2.950	1.830	.324	−7.357	1.458
		Control	.884	1.830	1.000	−3.523	5.291
	Control	Memory Training	−3.833	1.830	.111	−8.241	.574
		Health Training	−.884	1.830	1.000	−5.291	3.523
MALE	Memory Training	Health Training	10.535*	1.830	.000	6.128	14.942
		Control	11.973*	1.830	.000	7.566	16.381
	Health Training	Memory Training	−10.535*	1.830	.000	−14.942	−6.128

(*Continued*)

Pairwise Comparisons

Dependent Variable: DAFS

GENDER	(I) GROUP	(J) GROUP	Mean Difference (I-J)	Std. Error	Sig.[b]	95% Confidence Interval for Difference[b]	
						Lower Bound	Upper Bound
	Control	Control	1.438	1.830	1.000	−2.969	5.846
		Memory Training	−11.973*	1.830	.000	−16.381	−7.566
		Health Training	−1.438	1.830	1.000	−5.846	2.969

Based on estimated marginal means
* The mean difference is significant at the .050 level.
b. Adjustment for multiple comparisons: Bonferroni.

Univariate Tests

Dependent Variable: DAFS

GENDER		Sum of Squares	Df	Mean Square	F	Sig.
FEMALE	Contrast	402.939	2	201.469	2.405	.092
	Error	24625.189	294	83.759		
MALE	Contrast	4273.646	2	2136.823	25.512	.000
	Error	24625.189	294	83.759		

Each F tests the simple effects of GROUP within each level combination of the other effects shown. These tests are based on the linearly independent pairwise comparisons among the estimated marginal means.

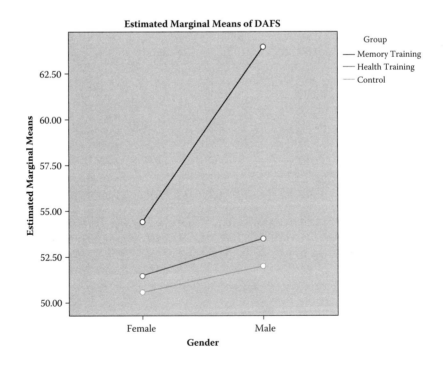

Estimated Marginal Means of DAFS

▪ Table 7.13: SPSS Results of Pairwise Comparisons for Self-Efficacy

Estimated Marginal Means
GROUP
Dependent Variable: Self_Efficacy

GROUP	Mean	Std. Error	95% Confidence Interval Lower Bound	Upper Bound
Memory Training	58.505	.930	56.675	60.336
Health Training	50.649	.930	48.819	52.480
Control	48.976	.930	47.146	50.807

Post Hoc Tests GROUP
Dependent Variable: Self_Efficacy
Bonferroni

(I) GROUP	(J) GROUP	Mean Difference (I-J)	Std. Error	Sig.	95% Confidence Interval Lower Bound	Upper Bound
Memory Training	Health Training	7.856*	1.315	.000	4.689	11.022
	Control	9.529*	1.315	.000	6.362	12.695
Health Training	Memory Training	−7.856*	1.315	.000	−11.022	−4.689
	Control	1.673	1.315	.613	−1.494	4.840
Control	Memory Training	−9.529*	1.315	.000	−12.695	−6.362
	Health Training	−1.673	1.315	.613	−4.840	1.494

Based on observed means.
The error term is Mean Square(Error) = 86.483.
* The mean difference is significant at the .050 level.

▪ Table 7.14: SPSS Results of Pairwise Comparisons for Verbal Performance

Estimated Marginal Means
GROUP
Dependent Variable: Verbal

GROUP	Mean	Std. Error	95% Confidence Interval Lower Bound	Upper Bound
Memory Training	60.227	.959	58.341	62.114
Health Training	50.843	.959	48.956	52.730
Control	52.881	.959	50.994	54.768

(Continued)

■ **Table 7.14: (Continued)**

Post Hoc Tests GROUP

Multiple Comparisons

Dependent Variable: Verbal

Bonferroni

(I) GROUP	(J) GROUP	Mean Difference (I–J)	Std. Error	Sig.	95% Confidence Interval	
					Lower Bound	Upper Bound
Memory Training	Health Training	9.384*	1.356	.000	6.120	12.649
	Control	7.346*	1.356	.000	4.082	10.610
Health Training	Memory Training	−9.384*	1.356	.000	−12.649	−6.120
	Control	−2.038	1.356	.401	−5.302	1.226
Control	Memory Training	−7.346*	1.356	.000	−10.610	−4.082
	Health Training	2.038	1.356	.401	−1.226	5.302

Based on observed means.

The error term is Mean Square(Error) = 91.896.

* The mean difference is significant at the .050 level.

training and control groups ($p < .001$). The smaller difference in means between the health intervention and control condition is not statistically significant ($p = .613$). Inspecting Table 7.14 indicates a similar pattern for verbal performance, where those receiving memory training have better average performance than participants receiving heath training ($p < .001$) and those in the control group ($p < .001$). The small difference between the latter two conditions is not statistically significant ($p = .401$).

7.8 EXAMPLE RESULTS SECTION FOR FACTORIAL MANOVA WITH SENIORWISE DATA

The goal of this study was to determine if at-risk older males and females obtain similar or different benefits of training designed to help memory functioning across a set of memory-related variables. As such, 150 males and 150 females were randomly assigned to memory training, a health intervention or a wait-list control condition. A two-way (treatment by gender) multiple analysis of variance (MANOVA) was conducted with three memory-related dependent variables—memory self-efficacy, verbal memory performance, and daily functional status (DAFS)—all of which were collected following the intervention.

Prior to conducting the factorial MANOVA, the data were examined to identify the degree of missing data, presence of outliers and influential observations, and the degree to which the outcomes were correlated. There were no missing data. No multivariate outliers were indicated as the largest within-cell Mahalanobis distance (10.61) was smaller than the chi-square critical value of 16.27 (.05, 3). Also, no univariate outliers were suggested as all within-cell univariate z scores were smaller than |3|. Further, examining the pooled within-cell correlations suggested that the outcomes are moderately and positively correlated, as these three correlations ranged from .31 to .47.

We also assessed whether the MANOVA assumptions seemed tenable. Inspecting histograms for each group for each dependent variable as well as the corresponding values for skew and kurtosis (all of which were smaller than |1|) did not indicate any material violations of the normality assumption. For the assumption of equal variance-covariance matrices, the cell standard deviations were fairly similar for each outcome, and Box's M test ($M = 30.53$, $p = .503$) did not suggest a violation. In addition, examining the results of Levene's test for equality of variance provided support that the dispersion of scores for self-efficacy ($p = .47$), verbal performance ($p = .78$), and functional status ($p = .33$) was similar across cells. For the independence assumption, the study design did not suggest any violation in part as treatments were individually administered to participants who also completed posttest measures individually.

Table 1 displays the means for each cell for each outcome. Inspecting these means suggests that participants in the memory training group generally had higher mean posttest scores than the other treatment conditions across each outcome. However, a significant multivariate test of the treatment-by-gender interaction, Wilks' lambda = .946, $F(6, 584) = 2.72$, $p = .013$, suggested that treatment effects were different for females and males. Univariate tests for each outcome indicated that the two-way interaction is present for DAFS, $F(2, 294) = 6.174$, $p = .002$, but not for self-efficacy $F(2, 294) = 1.603$, $p = .203$ or verbal $F(2, 294) = .369$, $p = .692$. Simple effects analyses for DAFS indicated that treatment group differences were present for males, $F(2, 294) = 25.512$, $p < .001$, but not females, $F(2, 294) = 2.405$, $p = .092$. Pairwise comparisons for males, using Bonferroni adjusted p values, indicate that participants in the memory training condition outscored, on average, those in the health training, $t(294) = 5.76$, $p < .001$, and control conditions $t(294) = 6.54$, $p < .001$. The difference in means between the health training and control condition is not statistically significant, $t(294) = 0.79$, $p = 1.00$.

■ **Table 1: Treatment by Gender Means (SD) For Each Dependent Variable**

	Treatment condition[a]		
Gender	Memory training	Health training	Control
	Self-efficacy		
Females	56.15 (9.01)	50.33 (7.91)	48.67 (9.93)
Males	60.86 (8.86)	50.97 (8.80)	49.29 (10.98)
	Verbal performance		
Females	60.08 (9.41)	50.53 (8.54)	53.65 (8.96)
Males	60.37 (9.99)	51.16 (10.16)	52.11 (10.32)
	Daily functional skills		
Females	54.34 (9.16)	51.39 (10.61)	50.50 (8.29)
Males	63.97 (7.78)	53.43 (9.92)	51.99 (8.84)

[a] $n = 50$ per cell.

In addition, the multivariate test for main effects indicated that main effects were present for the set of outcomes for treatment condition, Wilks' lambda = .748, $F(6, 584) = 15.170$, $p < .001$, and gender, Wilks' lambda = .923, $F(3, 292) = 3.292$, $p < .001$, although we focus here on treatment differences. The univariate F tests indicated that a main effect of the treatment was present for self-efficacy, $F(2, 294) = 29.931$, $p < .001$, and verbal $F(2, 294) = 26.514$, $p < .001$. For self-efficacy, pairwise comparisons (pooling across gender), using a Bonferroni-adjustment, indicated that participants in the memory training condition had higher posttest scores, on average, than those in the health training, $t(294) = 5.97$, $p < .001$, and control groups, $t(294) = 7.25$, $p < .001$, with no support for a mean difference between the latter two conditions ($p = .613$). A similar pattern was present for verbal performance, where those receiving memory training had better average performance than participants receiving heath training $t(294) = 6.92$, $p < .001$ and those in the control group, $t(294) = 5.42$, $p < .001$. The small difference between the latter two conditions was not statistically significant, $t(294) = -1.50$, $p = .401$.

7.9 THREE-WAY MANOVA

This section is included to show how to set up SPSS syntax for running a three-way MANOVA, and to indicate a procedure for interpreting a three-way interaction. We take the aptitude by method example presented in section 7.4 and add sex as an additional factor. Then, assuming we will use the same two dependent variables, the *only* change that is required for the syntax to run the factorial MANOVA as presented in Table 7.6 is that the GLM command becomes:

```
GLM ATTIT ACHIEV BY FACA FACB SEX
```

We wish to focus our attention on the interpretation of a three-way interaction, if it were significant in such a design. First, what does a significant three-way interaction mean in the context of a single outcome variable? If the three factors are denoted by A, B, and C, then *a significant ABC interaction implies that the two-way interaction profiles for the different levels of the third factor are different.* A nonsignificant three-way interaction means that the two-way profiles are the same; that is, the differences can be attributed to sampling error.

Example 7.3

Consider a sex, by treatment, by school grade design. Suppose that the two-way design (collapsed on grade) looked like this:

	Treatments	
	1	2
Males	60	50
Females	40	42

This profile suggests a significant sex main effect and a significant ordinal interaction with respect to sex (because the male average is greater than the female average for each treatment, and, of course, much greater under treatment 1). But it does not tell the whole story. Let us examine the profiles for grades 6 and 7 separately (assuming equal cell *n*):

	Grade 6			Grade 7	
	T_1	T_2		T_1	T_1
M	65	50	M	55	50
F	40	47	F	40	37

We see that for grade 6 that the same type of interaction is present as before, whereas for grade 7 students there appears to be no interaction effect, as the difference in means between males and females is similar across treatments (15 points vs. 13 points). The two profiles are distinctly different. The point is, school grade further moderates the sex-by-treatment interaction.

In the context of aptitude–treatment interaction (ATI) research, Cronbach (1975) had an interesting way of characterizing higher order interactions:

> When ATIs are present, a general statement about a treatment effect is misleading because the effect will come or go depending on the kind of person treated. . . . An ATI result can be taken as a general conclusion only if it is not in turn moderated by further variables. If Aptitude×Treatment×Sex interact, for example, then the Aptitude×Treatment effect does not tell the story. Once we attend to interactions, we enter a hall of mirrors that extends to infinity. (p. 119)

Thus, to examine the nature of a significant three-way multivariate interaction, one might first determine which of the individual variables are significant (by examining the univariate F's for the three-way interaction). If any three-way interactions are present for a given dependent variable, we would then consider the two-way profiles to see how they differ for those outcomes that are significant.

7.10 FACTORIAL DESCRIPTIVE DISCRIMINANT ANALYSIS

In this section, we present a discriminant analysis approach to describe multivariate effects that are statistically significant in a factorial MANOVA. Unlike the traditional MANOVA approach presented previously in this chapter, where univariate follow-up tests were used to describe statistically significant multivariate interactions and main effects, the approach described in this section uses linear combinations of variables to describe such effects. Unlike the traditional MANOVA approach, discriminant analysis uses the correlations among the discriminating variables to create composite variables that separate groups. When such composites are formed, you need to interpret the composites and use them to describe group differences. If you have not already read Chapter 10, which introduces discriminant analysis in the context of a simpler single factor design, you should read that chapter before taking on the factorial presentation presented here.

We use the same SeniorWISE data set used in section 7.7. So, for this example, the two factors are treatment having 3 levels and gender with 2 levels. The dependent variables are self-efficacy, verbal, and DAFS. Identical to traditional two-way MANOVA, there will be overall multivariate tests for the two-way interaction and for the two main effects. If the interaction is significant, you can then conduct a simple effects analyses by running separate one-way descriptive discriminant analyses for each level of a factor of interest. Given the interest in examining treatment effects with the SeniorWISE data, we would run a one-way discriminant analysis for females and then a separate one-way discriminant analysis for males with treatment as the single factor. According to Warner (2012), such an analysis, for this example, allows us to examine the composite variables that best separate treatment groups for females and that best separate treatment groups for males.

In addition to the multivariate test for the interaction, you should also examine the multivariate tests for main effects and identify the composite variables associated with such effects, since the composite variables may be different from those involved in the interaction. Also, of course, if the multivariate test for the interaction is not significant, you would also examine the multivariate tests for the main effects. If the multivariate main effect were significant, you can identify the composite variables involved in the effect by running a single-factor descriptive discriminant analysis pooling across (or ignoring) the other factor. So, for example, if there were a significant multivariate main effect for the treatment, you could run a descriptive discriminant analysis with treatment as the single factor with all cases included. Such an analysis was done in section 10.7. If a multivariate main effect for gender were significant, you could run a descriptive discriminant analysis with gender as the single factor.

We now illustrate these analyses for the SeniorWISE data. Note that the preliminary analysis for the factorial descriptive discriminant analysis is identical to that described in section 7.7.1, so we do not describe it any further here. Also, in section 7.7.2, we reported that the multivariate test for the overall group-by-gender interaction indicated that this effect was statistically significant, Wilks' lambda = .946, $F(6, 584) = 2.72$, $p = .013$. In addition, the multivariate test results indicated a statistically significant main effect for treatment group, Wilks' lambda = .748, $F(6, 584) = 15.170$, $p < .001$, and gender Wilks' lambda = .923, $F(3, 292) = 3.292$, $p < .001$. Given the interest in describing treatment effects for these data, we focus the follow-up analysis on treatment effects.

To describe the multivariate gender-by-group interaction, we ran descriptive discriminant analysis for females and a separate analysis for males. Table 7.15 provides the syntax for this simple effects analysis, and Tables 7.16 and 7.17 provide the discriminant analysis results for females and males, respectively. For females, Table 7.16 indicates that one linear combination of variables separates the treatment groups, Wilks' lambda = .776, chi-square (6) = 37.10, $p < .001$. In addition, the square of the canonical correlation ($.44^2$) for this function, when converted to a percent, indicates that about 19% of the variation for the first function is between treatment groups. Inspecting the standardized coefficients suggest that this linear combination is dominated by verbal performance and that high scores for this function correspond to high verbal performance scores. In addition, examining the group centroids suggests that, for females, the memory training group has much higher verbal performance scores, on average, than the other treatment groups, which have similar means for this composite variable.

■ **Table 7.15: SPSS Syntax for Simple Effects Analysis Using Discriminant Analysis**

* The first set of commands requests analysis results separately for each group (females, then males).

```
SORT CASES BY Gender.
SPLIT FILE SEPARATE BY Gender.
```

* The following commands are the typical discriminant analysis syntax.

```
DISCRIMINANT
 /GROUPS=Group(1 3)
 /VARIABLES=Self_Efficacy Verbal Dafs
 /ANALYSIS = ALL
 /STATISTICS=MEAN STDDEV UNIVF.
```

■ Table 7.16: SPSS Discriminant Analysis Results for Females

Summary of Canonical Discriminant Functions

		Eigenvalues[a]		
Function	Eigenvalue	% of Variance	Cumulative %	Canonical Correlation
1	.240[b]	85.9	85.9	.440
2	.040[b]	14.1	100.0	.195

[a] GENDER = FEMALE
[b] First 2 canonical discriminant functions were used in the analysis.

		Wilks' Lambda[a]		
Test of Function(s)	Wilks' Lambda	Chi-square	df	Sig.
1 through 2	.776	37.100	6	.000
2	.962	5.658	2	.059

[a] GENDER = FEMALE

Standardized Canonical Discriminant Function Coefficients[a]

	Function	
	1	2
Self_Efficacy	.452	.850
Verbal	.847	−.791
DAFS	−.218	.434

[a] GENDER = FEMALE

Structure Matrix[a]

	Function	
	1	2
Verbal	.905*	−.293
Self_Efficacy	.675	.721*
DAFS	.328	.359*

Pooled within-groups correlations between discriminating variables and standardized canonical discriminant functions.

Variables ordered by absolute size of correlation within function.

* Largest absolute correlation between each variable and any discriminant function

[a] GENDER = FEMALE

Functions at Group Centroids[a]

	Function	
GROUP	1	2
Memory Training	.673	.054
Health Training	−.452	.209
Control	−.221	−.263

Unstandardized canonical discriminant functions evaluated at group means.

[a] GENDER = FEMALE

For males, Table 7.17 indicates that one linear combination of variables separates the treatment groups, Wilks' lambda = .653, chi-square (6) = 62.251, p < .001. In addition, the square of the canonical correlation ($.583^2$) for this composite, when converted to a percent, indicates that about 34% of the composite score variation is between treatment. Inspecting the standardized coefficients indicates that self-efficacy and DAFS are the important variables that comprise the composite. Examining the group centroids indicates that, for males, the memory group has much greater self-efficacy and daily functional skills (DAFS) than the other treatment groups, which have similar means for this composite.

Summarizing the simple effects analysis following the statistically significant multivariate test of the gender-by-group interaction, we conclude that females assigned to the memory training group had much higher verbal performance than the other treatment groups, whereas males assigned to the memory training group had much higher self-efficacy and daily functioning skills. There appear to be trivial differences between the health intervention and control groups.

■ **Table 7.17: SPSS Discriminant Analysis Results for Males**

Summary of Canonical Discriminant Functions

Eigenvalues[a]

Function	Eigenvalue	% of Variance	Cumulative %	Canonical Correlation
1	.516[b]	98.0	98.0	.583
2	.011[b]	2.0	100.0	.103

[a] GENDER = MALE
[b] First 2 canonical discriminant functions were used in the analysis.

Wilks' Lambda[a]

Test of Function(s)	Wilks' Lambda	Chi-square	Df	Sig.
1 through 2	.653	62.251	6	.000
2	.989	1.546	2	.462

[a] GENDER = MALE

Standardized Canonical Discriminant Function Coefficients[a]

	Function	
	1	2
Self_Efficacy	.545	−.386
Verbal	.050	1.171
DAFS	.668	−.436

[a] GENDER = MALE

(*Continued*)

■ **Table 7.17: Continued**

Structure Matrix[a]

	Function	
	1	2
DAFS	.844[*]	.025
Self_Efficacy	.748[*]	−.107
Verbal	.561	.828[*]

Pooled within-groups correlations between discriminating variables and standardized canonical discriminant functions.
Variables ordered by absolute size of correlation within function.
[*] Largest absolute correlation between each variable and any discriminant function.
[a] GENDER = MALE

Functions at Group Centroids[a]

	Function	
GROUP	1	2
Memory Training	.999	.017
Health Training	−.400	−.133
Control	−.599	.116

Unstandardized canonical discriminant functions evaluated at group means
[a] GENDER = MALE

Also, as noted, the multivariate main effect of the treatment was also statistically significant. The follow-up analysis for this effect, which is the same as reported in Chapter 10 (section 10.7.2), indicates that the treatment groups differed on two composite variables. The first of these composites is composed of self-efficacy and verbal performance, while the second composite is primarily verbal performance. However, with the factorial analysis of the data, we learned that treatment group differences related to these composite variables are different between females and males. Thus, we would not use results involving the treatment main effects to describe treatment group differences.

7.11 SUMMARY

The advantages of a factorial over a one way design are discussed. For equal cell *n,* all three methods that Overall and Spiegel (1969) mention yield the same F tests. For unequal cell *n* (which usually occurs in practice), the three methods can yield quite different results. The reason for this is that for unequal cell *n* the effects are correlated. There is a consensus among experts that for unequal cell size the regression approach (which yields the UNIQUE contribution of each effect) is generally preferable. In SPSS and SAS, type III sum of squares is this unique sum of squares. A traditional MANOVA approach for factorial designs is provided where the focus is on examining each outcome that is involved in the main effects and interaction. In addition, a discriminant analysis approach for multivariate factorial designs is illustrated and can be used when you are interested in identifying if there are meaningful composite variables involved in the main effects and interactions.

7.12 EXERCISES

1. Consider the following 2 × 4 equal cell size MANOVA data set (two dependent variables, Y1 and Y2, and factors FACA and FACB):

	B			
	6, 10	13, 16	9, 11	21, 19
	7, 8	11, 15	8, 8	18, 15
	9, 9	17, 18	14, 9	16, 13
A	11, 8	10, 12	4, 12	11, 10
	7, 6	11, 13	10, 8	9, 8
	10, 5	14, 10	11, 13	8, 15

   (a) Run the factorial MANOVA with SPSS using the commands: GLM Y1 Y2 BY FACA FACB.

   (b) Which of the multivariate tests for the three different effects is (are) significant at the .05 level?

   (c) For the effect(s) that show multivariate significance, which of the individual variables (at .025 level) are contributing to the multivariate significance?

   (d) Run the data with SPSS using the commands:

   GLM Y1 Y2 BY FACA FACB /METHOD=SSTYPE(1).

   Recall that SSTYPE(1) requests the sequential sum of squares associated with Method 3 as described in section 7.3. Are the results different? Explain.

2. An investigator has the following 2 × 4 MANOVA data set for two dependent variables:

	B			
		13, 16	9, 11	21, 19
	7, 8	11, 15	8, 8	18, 15
		17, 18	14, 9	16, 13
			13, 11	
A	11, 8	10, 12	14, 12	11, 10
	7, 6	11, 13	10, 8	9, 8
	10, 5	14, 10	11, 13	8, 15
	6, 12			17, 12
	9, 7			13, 14
	11, 14			

(a) Run the factorial MANOVA on SPSS using the commands:

```
GLM Y1 Y2 BY FACA FACB
/EMMEANS=TABLES(FACA)
/EMMEANS=TABLES(FACB)
/EMMEANS=TABLES(FACA*FACB)
/PRINT=HOMOGENEITY.
```

(b) Which of the multivariate tests for the three effects are significant at the .05 level?

(c) For the effect(s) that show multivariate significance, which of the individual variables contribute to the multivariate significance at the .025 level?

(d) Is the homogeneity of the covariance matrices assumption for the cells tenable at the .05 level?

(e) Run the factorial MANOVA on the data set using the sequential sum of squares (Type I) option of SPSS. Are the univariate F ratios different? Explain.

REFERENCES

Barcikowski, R. S. (1983). *Computer packages and research design, Vol. 3: SPSS and SPSSX.* Washington, DC: University Press of America.

Carlson, J. E., & Timm, N. H. (1974). Analysis of non-orthogonal fixed effect designs. *Psychological Bulletin, 8,* 563–570.

Cohen, J., Cohen, P., West, S. G., & Aiken, L. S. (2003). *Applied multiple regression/correlation for the behavioral sciences* (3rd ed.). Mahwah, NJ: Lawrence Erlbaum Associates.

Cronbach, L. J. (1975). Beyond the two disciplines of scientific psychology. *American Psychologist, 30,* 116–127.

Cronbach, L., & Snow, R. (1977). *Aptitudes and instructional methods: A handbook for research on interactions.* New York, NY: Irvington.

Daniels, R. L., & Stevens, J. P. (1976). The interaction between the internal-external locus of control and two methods of college instruction. *American Educational Research Journal, 13,* 103–113.

Myers, J. L. (1979). *Fundamentals of experimental design.* Boston, MA: Allyn & Bacon.

Overall, J. E., & Spiegel, D. K. (1969). Concerning least squares analysis of experimental data. *Psychological Bulletin, 72,* 311–322.

Warner, R. M. (2012). *Applied statistics: From bivariate through multivariate techniques* (2nd ed.). Thousand Oaks, CA: Sage.

Chapter 8

ANALYSIS OF COVARIANCE

8.1 INTRODUCTION

Analysis of covariance (ANCOVA) is a statistical technique that combines regression analysis and analysis of variance. It can be helpful in nonrandomized studies in drawing more accurate conclusions. However, precautions have to be taken, otherwise analysis of covariance can be misleading in some cases. In this chapter we indicate what the purposes of ANCOVA are, when it is most effective, when the interpretation of results from ANCOVA is "cleanest," and when ANCOVA should not be used. We start with the simplest case, one dependent variable and one covariate, with which many readers may be somewhat familiar. Then we consider one dependent variable and several covariates, where our previous study of multiple regression is helpful. Multivariate analysis of covariance (MANCOVA) is then considered, where there are several dependent variables and several covariates. We show how to run MANCOVA on SAS and SPSS, interpret analysis results, and provide a guide for analysis.

8.1.1 Examples of Univariate and Multivariate Analysis of Covariance

What is a covariate? A potential covariate is any variable that is significantly correlated with the dependent variable. That is, we assume a *linear* relationship between the covariate (x) and the dependent variable (y). Consider now two typical univariate ANCOVAs with one covariate. In a two-group pretest–posttest design, the pretest is often used as a covariate, because how the participants score before treatments is generally correlated with how they score after treatments. Or, suppose three groups are compared on some measure of achievement. In this situation IQ may be used as a covariate, because IQ is usually at least moderately correlated with achievement.

You should recall that the null hypothesis being tested in ANCOVA is that the adjusted population means are equal. Since a linear relationship is assumed between the covariate and the dependent variable, the means are adjusted in a linear fashion. We consider this in detail shortly in this chapter. Thus, in interpreting output, for either univariate or MANCOVA, it is the adjusted means that need to be examined. It is important to note that SPSS and SAS do not automatically provide the adjusted means; they must be requested.

Now consider two situations where MANCOVA would be appropriate. A counselor wishes to examine the effect of two different counseling approaches on several personality variables. The subjects are pretested on these variables and then posttested 2 months later. The pretest scores are the covariates and the posttest scores are the dependent variables. Second, a teacher wishes to determine the relative efficacy of two different methods of teaching 12th-grade mathematics. He uses three subtest scores of achievement on a posttest as the dependent variables. A plausible set of covariates here would be grade in math 11, an IQ measure, and, say, attitude toward education. The null hypothesis that is tested in MANCOVA is that the adjusted population mean vectors are equal. Recall that the null hypothesis for MANOVA was that the population mean vectors are equal.

Four excellent references for further study of ANCOVA/MANCOVA are available: an elementary introduction (Huck, Cormier, & Bounds, 1974), two good classic review articles (Cochran, 1957; Elashoff, 1969), and especially a very comprehensive and thorough text by Huitema (2011).

8.2 PURPOSES OF ANCOVA

ANCOVA is linked to the following two basic objectives in experimental design:

1. Elimination of systematic bias
2. Reduction of within group or error variance.

The best way of dealing with systematic bias (e.g., intact groups that differ systematically on several variables) is through random assignment of participants to groups, thus equating the groups on all variables within sampling error. If random assignment is not possible, however, then ANCOVA can be helpful in reducing bias.

Within-group variability, which is primarily due to individual differences among the participants, can be dealt with in several ways: sample selection (participants who are more homogeneous will vary less on the criterion measure), factorial designs (blocking), repeated-measures analysis, and ANCOVA. Precisely how covariance reduces error will be considered soon. Because ANCOVA is linked to both of the basic objectives of experimental design, it certainly is a useful tool if properly used and interpreted.

In an experimental study (random assignment of participants to groups) the main purpose of covariance is to reduce error variance, because there will be no systematic bias. However, if only a small number of participants can be assigned to each group, then chance differences are more possible and covariance is useful in adjusting the posttest means for the chance differences.

In a nonexperimental study the main purpose of covariance is to adjust the posttest means for initial differences among the groups that are very likely with intact groups. It should be emphasized, however, that even the use of several covariates does *not* equate intact groups, that is, does not eliminate bias. Nevertheless, the use of two or three appropriate covariates can make for a fairer comparison.

We now give two examples to illustrate how initial differences (systematic bias) on a key variable between treatment groups can confound the interpretation of results. Suppose an experimental psychologist wished to determine the effect of three methods of extinction on some kind of learned response. There are three intact groups to which the methods are applied, and it is found that the average number of trials to extinguish the response is least for Method 2. Now, it may be that Method 2 is more effective, or it may be that the participants in Method 2 didn't have the response as thoroughly ingrained as the participants in the other two groups. In the latter case, the response would be easier to extinguish, and it wouldn't be clear whether it was the method that made the difference or the fact that the response was easier to extinguish that made Method 2 look better. The effects of the two are confounded, or mixed together. What is needed here is a measure of degree of learning at the start of the extinction trials (covariate). Then, if there are initial differences between the groups, the posttest means will be adjusted to take this into account. That is, covariance will adjust the posttest means to what they would be if all groups had started out *equally* on the covariate.

As another example, suppose we are comparing the effect of two different teaching methods on academic achievement for two different groups of students. Suppose we learn that prior to implementing the treatment methods, the groups differed on motivation to learn. Thus, if the academic performance of the group with greater initial motivation was better than the other group at posttest, we would not know if the performance differences were due to the teaching method or due to this initial difference on motivation. Use of ANCOVA may provide for a fairer comparison because it compares posttest performance assuming that the groups had the same initial motivation.

8.3 ADJUSTMENT OF POSTTEST MEANS AND REDUCTION OF ERROR VARIANCE

As mentioned earlier, ANCOVA adjusts the posttest means to what they would be if all groups started out equally on the covariate, at the grand mean. In this section we derive the general equation for linearly adjusting the posttest means for one covariate. Before we do that, however, it is important to discuss one of the assumptions underlying the analysis of covariance. That assumption for one covariate requires *equal within-group population regression slopes*. Consider a three-group situation, with 15 participants per group. Suppose that the scatterplots for the three groups looked as given in Figure 8.1.

■ **Figure 8.1:** Scatterplots of *y* and *x* for three groups.

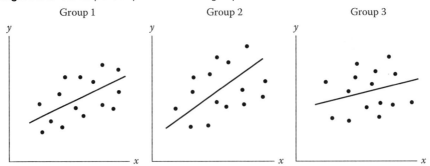

Recall from beginning statistics that the x and y scores for each participant determine a point in the plane. Requiring that the slopes be equal is equivalent to saying that the nature of the linear relationship is the *same* for all groups, or that the rate of change in y as a function of x is the same for all groups. For these scatterplots the slopes are different, with the slope being the largest for group 2 and smallest for group 3. But the issue is whether the *population* slopes are different and whether the sample slopes differ sufficiently to conclude that the population values are different. With small sample sizes as in these scatterplots, it is dangerous to rely on visual inspection to determine whether the population values are equal, because of considerable sampling error. Fortunately, there is a statistic for this, and later we indicate how to obtain it on SAS and SPSS. In deriving the equation for the adjusted means we are going to assume the slopes are equal. What if the slopes are not equal? Then ANCOVA is *not* appropriate, and we indicate alternatives later in the chapter.

The details of obtaining the adjusted mean for the ith group (i.e., any group) are given in Figure 8.2. The general equation follows from the definition for the slope of a straight line and some basic algebra. In Figure 8.3 we show the adjusted means geometrically for a hypothetical three-group data set. A positive correlation is assumed between the covariate and the dependent variable, so that a higher mean on x implies a higher mean on y. Note that because group 3 scored below the grand mean on the covariate, its mean is adjusted upward. On the other hand, because the mean for group 2 on the covariate is *above* the grand mean, covariance estimates that it would have scored lower on y if its mean on the covariate was lower (at grand mean), and therefore the mean for group 2 is adjusted downward.

8.3.1 Reduction of Error Variance

Consider a teaching methods study where the dependent variable is chemistry achievement and the covariate is IQ. Then, within each teaching method there will be considerable variability on chemistry achievement due to individual differences among the students in terms of ability, background, attitude, and so on. A sizable portion of this within-variability, we assume, is due to differences in IQ. That is, chemistry

■ **Figure 8.2:** Deriving the general equation for the adjusted means in covariance.

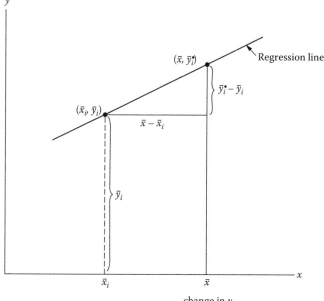

$$\text{Slope of straight line} = b = \frac{\text{change in } y}{\text{change in } x}$$

$$b = \frac{\bar{y}_i^\bullet - \bar{y}_i}{\bar{x} - \bar{x}_i}$$

$$b(\bar{x} - \bar{x}_i) = \bar{y}_i^\bullet - \bar{y}_i$$
$$\bar{y}_i^\bullet = \bar{y}_i + b(\bar{x} - \bar{x}_i)$$
$$\bar{y}_i^\bullet = \bar{y}_i - b(\bar{x}_i - \bar{x})$$

achievement scores differ partly because the students differ in IQ. If we can statistically remove this part of the within-variability, a smaller error term results, and hence a more powerful test of group posttest differences can be obtained. We denote the correlation between IQ and chemistry achievement by r_{xy}. Recall that the square of a correlation can be interpreted as "variance accounted for." Thus, for example, if $r_{xy} = .71$, then $(.71)^2 = .50$, or 50% of the within-group variability on chemistry achievement can be accounted for by variability on IQ.

We denote the within-group variability of chemistry achievement by MS_w, the usual error term for ANOVA. Now, symbolically, the part of MS_w that is accounted for by IQ is $MS_w r_{xy}^2$. Thus, the within-group variability that is left after the portion due to the covariate is removed, is

$$MS_w - MS_w r_{xy}^2 = MS_w \left(1 - r_{xy}^2\right), \tag{1}$$

and this becomes our new error term for analysis of covariance, which we denote by MS_w^*. Technically, there is an additional factor involved,

■ **Figure 8.3:** Regression lines and adjusted means for three-group analysis of covariance.

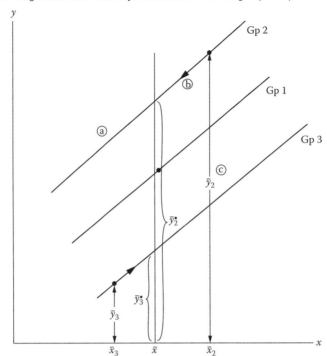

ⓐ positive correlation assumed between x and y

ⓑ The arrows on the regression lines indicate that the adjusted means can be obtained by sliding the mean up (down) the regression line until it hits the line for the grand mean.

ⓒ $\bar{y}_2$ is actual mean for Gp 2 and $\bar{y}_2^*$ represents the adjusted mean.

$$MS_w^* = MS_w\left(1 - r_{xy}^2\right)\left\{1 + 1/\left(f_e - 2\right)\right\}, \tag{2}$$

where f_e is error degrees of freedom. However, the effect of this additional factor is slight as long as $N \geq 50$.

To show how much of a difference a covariate can make in increasing the sensitivity of an experiment, we consider a hypothetical study. An investigator runs a one-way ANOVA (three groups with 20 participants per group), and obtains $F = 200/100 = 2$, which is not significant, because the critical value at .05 is 3.18. He had pretested the subjects, but did not use the pretest as a covariate because the groups didn't differ significantly on the pretest (even though the correlation between pretest and posttest was .71). This is a common mistake made by some researchers who are unaware of an important purpose of covariance, that of reducing error variance. The analysis is redone by another investigator using ANCOVA. Using the equation that we just derived for the new error term for ANCOVA she finds:

$$MS_w^* \approx 100[1 - (.71)^2] = 50$$

Thus, the error term for ANCOVA is only half as large as the error term for ANOVA! It is also necessary to obtain a new MS_b for ANCOVA; call it MS_b^*. Because the formula for MS_b^* is complicated, we do not pursue it. Let us assume the investigator obtains the following F ratio for covariance analysis:

$$F^* = 190 / 50 = 3.8$$

This is significant at the .05 level. Therefore, the use of covariance can make the difference between not finding significance and finding significance due to the reduced error term and the subsequent increase in power. Finally, we wish to note that MS_b^* can be smaller or larger than MS_b, although in a randomized study the expected values of the two are equal.

8.4 CHOICE OF COVARIATES

In general, any variables that theoretically should correlate with the dependent variable, or variables that have been shown to correlate for similar types of participants, should be considered as possible covariates. The ideal is to choose as covariates variables that of course are significantly correlated with the dependent variable *and* that have low correlations among themselves. If two covariates are highly correlated (say .80), then they are removing much of the *same* error variance from y; use of x_2 will not offer much additional power. On the other hand, if two covariates (x_1 and x_2) have a low correlation (say .20), then they are removing relatively distinct pieces of the error variance from y, and we will obtain a much greater total error reduction. This is illustrated in Figure 8.4 with Venn diagrams, where the circle represents error variance on y.

The shaded portion in each case represents the additional error reduction due to adding x_2 to the model that already contains x_1, that is, the part of error variance on y it removes that x_1 did not. Note that this shaded area is much smaller when x_1 and x_2 are highly correlated.

■ **Figure 8.4:** Venn diagrams with *solid lines* representing the part of variance on y that x_1 accounts for and *dashed lines* representing the variance on y that x_2 accounts for.

x_1 and x_2 Low correl. x_1 and x_2 High correl.

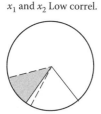 

Solid lines—part of variance on y that x_1 accounts for.

Dashed lines—part of variance on y that x_2 accounts for.

If the dependent variable is achievement in some content area, then one should always consider the possibility of at least three covariates:

1. A measure of ability in that specific content area
2. A measure of general ability (IQ measure)
3. One or two relevant noncognitive measures (e.g., attitude toward education, study habits, etc.).

An example of this was given earlier, where we considered the effect of two different teaching methods on 12th-grade mathematics achievement. We indicated that a plausible set of covariates would be grade in math 11 (a previous measure of ability in mathematics), an IQ measure, and attitude toward education (a noncognitive measure).

In studies with small or relatively small group sizes, it is particularly imperative to consider the use of two or three covariates. Why? Because for small or medium effect sizes, which are *very common* in social science research, power for the test of a treatment will be poor for small group size. Thus, one should attempt to reduce the error variance as much as possible to obtain a more sensitive (powerful) test.

Huitema (2011, p. 231) recommended limiting the number of covariates to the extent that the ratio

$$\frac{C+(J-1)}{N} < .10, \quad (3)$$

where C is the number of covariates, J is the number of groups, and N is total sample size. Thus, if we had a three-group problem with a total of 60 participants, then $(C+2)/60 < .10$ or $C < 4$. We should use fewer than four covariates. If this ratio is $> .10$, then the estimates of the adjusted means are likely to be unstable. That is, if the study were replicated, it could be expected that the equation used to estimate the adjusted means in the original study would yield very different estimates for another sample from the same population.

8.4.1 Importance of Covariates Being Measured Before Treatments

To avoid confounding (mixing together) of the treatment effect with a change on the covariate, one should use information from only those covariates gathered before treatments are administered. If a covariate that was measured after treatments is used and that variable was affected by treatments, then the change on the covariate may be correlated with change on the dependent variable. Thus, when the covariate adjustment is made, you will remove part of the treatment effect.

8.5 ASSUMPTIONS IN ANALYSIS OF COVARIANCE

Analysis of covariance rests on the same assumptions as analysis of variance. Note that when assessing assumptions, you should obtain the model residuals, as we show later, and not the within-group outcome scores (where the latter may be used in ANOVA). Three additional assumptions are a part of ANCOVA. That is, ANCOVA also assumes:

1. A linear relationship between the dependent variable and the covariate(s).[*]
2. Homogeneity of the regression slopes (for one covariate), that is, that the slope of the regression line is the same in each group. For two covariates the assumption is parallelism of the regression planes, and for more than two covariates the assumption is known as homogeneity of the regression hyperplanes.
3. The covariate is measured without error.

Because covariance rests partly on the same assumptions as ANOVA, any violations that are serious in ANOVA (such as the independence assumption) are also serious in ANCOVA. Violation of *all three* of the remaining assumptions of covariance may be serious. For example, if the relationship between the covariate and the dependent variable is curvilinear, then the adjustment of the means will be improper. In this case, two possible courses of action are:

1. Seek a transformation of the data that is linear. This is possible if the relationship between the covariate and the dependent variable is monotonic.
2. Fit a polynomial ANCOVA model to the data.

There is always measurement error for the variables that are typically used as covariates in social science research, and measurement error causes problems in both randomized and nonrandomized designs, but is more serious in nonrandomized designs. As Huitema (2011) notes, in randomized experimental designs, the power of ANCOVA is reduced when measurement error is present but treatment effect estimates are not biased, provided that the treatment does not impact the covariate.

When measurement error is present on the covariate, then treatment effects can be seriously biased in nonrandomized designs. In Figure 8.5 we illustrate the effect measurement error can have when comparing two *different* populations with analysis of covariance. In the hypothetical example, with no measurement error we would conclude that group 1 is superior to group 2, whereas with considerable measurement error the opposite conclusion is drawn. This example shows that if the covariate means are not equal, then the difference between the adjusted means is partly a function of the reliability of the covariate. Now, this problem would not be of particular concern if we had a very reliable covariate such as IQ or other cognitive variables from a good standardized test. If, on the other hand, the covariate is a noncognitive variable, or a variable derived from a nonstandardized instrument (which might well be of questionable reliability), then concern would definitely be justified.

A violation of the homogeneity of regression slopes can also yield misleading results if ANCOVA is used. To illustrate this, we present in Figure 8.6 a situation where the

---

[*] Nonlinear analysis of covariance is possible (cf., Huitema, 2011, chap. 12), but is rarely done.

■ Figure 8.5: Effect of measurement error on covariance results when comparing subjects from two different populations.

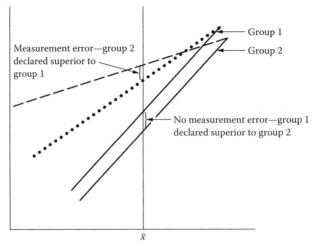

——— Regression lines for the groups with no measurement error
•••• Regression line for group 1 with considerable measurement error
– – – Regression line for group 2 with considerable measurement error

■ Figure 8.6: Effect of heterogeneous slopes on interpretation in ANCOVA.

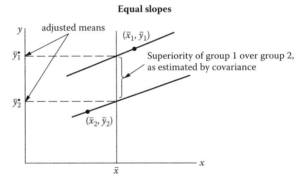

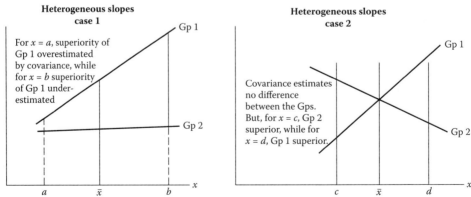

assumption is met and two situations where the assumption is violated. Notice that with homogeneous slopes the estimated superiority of group 1 at the grand mean is an accurate estimate of group 1's superiority for all levels of the covariate, since the lines are parallel. On the other hand, for case 1 of heterogeneous slopes, the superiority of group 1 (as estimated by ANCOVA) is *not* an accurate estimate of group 1's superiority for other values of the covariate. For $x = a$, group 1 is only slightly better than group 2, whereas for $x = b$, the superiority of group 1 is seriously underestimated by covariance. The point is, *when the slopes are unequal there is a covariate by treatment interaction.* That is, how much better group 1 is depends on which value of the covariate we specify.

For case 2 of heterogeneous slopes, the use of covariance would be totally misleading. Covariance estimates no difference between the groups, while for $x = c$, group 2 is quite superior to group 1. For $x = d$, group 1 is superior to group 2. We indicate later in the chapter, in detail, how the assumption of equal slopes is tested on SPSS.

8.6 USE OF ANCOVA WITH INTACT GROUPS

It should be noted that some researchers (Anderson, 1963; Lord, 1969) have argued strongly against using ANCOVA with intact groups. Although we do not take this position, it is important that you be aware of the several limitations or possible dangers when using ANCOVA with intact groups. First, even the use of several covariates will *not* equate intact groups, and one should never be deluded into thinking it can. The groups may still differ on some unknown important variable(s). Also, note that equating groups on one variable may result in accentuating their differences on other variables.

Second, recall that ANCOVA adjusts the posttest means to what they would be if all the groups had started out equal on the covariate(s). You then need to consider whether groups that are equal on the covariate would ever exist in the real world. Elashoff (1969) gave the following example:

> Teaching methods A and B are being compared. The class using A is composed of high-ability students, whereas the class using B is composed of low-ability students. A covariance analysis can be done on the posttest achievement scores holding ability constant, as if A and B had been used on classes of equal and average ability. . . . It may make no sense to think about comparing methods A and B for students of average ability, perhaps each has been designed specifically for the ability level it was used with, or neither method will, in the future, be used for students of average ability. (p. 387)

Third, the assumptions of linearity and homogeneity of regression slopes need to be satisfied for ANCOVA to be appropriate.

A fourth issue that can confound the interpretation of results is differential growth of participants in intact or self-selected groups on some dependent variable. If the natural growth is much greater in one group (treatment) than for the control group and covariance finds a significance difference after adjusting for any pretest differences, then it is not clear whether the difference is due to treatment, differential growth, or part of each. Bryk and Weisberg (1977) discussed this issue in detail and propose an alternative approach for such growth models.

A fifth problem is that of measurement error. Of course, this same problem is present in randomized studies. But there the effect is merely to attenuate power. In nonrandomized studies measurement error can seriously bias the treatment effect. Reichardt (1979), in an extended discussion on measurement error in ANCOVA, stated:

> Measurement error in the pretest can therefore produce spurious treatment effects when none exist. But it can also result in a finding of no intercept difference when a true treatment effect exists, or it can produce an estimate of the treatment effect which is in the opposite direction of the true effect. (p. 164)

It is no wonder then that Pedhazur (1982), in discussing the effect of measurement error when comparing intact groups, said:

> The purpose of the discussion here was only to alert you to the problem in the hope that you will reach two obvious conclusions: (1) that efforts should be directed to construct measures of the covariates that have very high reliabilities and (2) that ignoring the problem, as is unfortunately done in most applications of ANCOVA, will not make it disappear. (p. 524)

Huitema (2011) discusses various strategies that can be used for nonrandomized designs having covariates.

Given all of these problems, you may well wonder whether we should abandon the use of ANCOVA when comparing intact groups. But other statistical methods for analyzing this kind of data (such as matched samples, gain score ANOVA) suffer from many of the same problems, such as seriously biased treatment effects. The fact is that inferring cause–effect from intact groups is treacherous, regardless of the type of statistical analysis. Therefore, the task is to do the best we can and exercise considerable caution, or as Pedhazur (1982) put it, "the conduct of such research, indeed all scientific research, requires sound theoretical thinking, constant vigilance, and a thorough understanding of the potential and limitations of the methods being used" (p. 525).

8.7 ALTERNATIVE ANALYSES FOR PRETEST–POSTTEST DESIGNS

When comparing two or more groups with pretest and posttest data, the following three other modes of analysis are possible:

1. An ANOVA is done on the difference or gain scores (posttest–pretest).
2. A two-way repeated-measures ANOVA (this will be covered in Chapter 12) is done. This is called a one between (the grouping variable) and one within (pretest–posttest part) factor ANOVA.
3. An ANOVA is done on residual scores. That is, the dependent variable is regressed on the covariate. Predicted scores are then subtracted from observed dependent scores, yielding residual scores ($\hat{e}_i$). An ordinary one-way ANOVA is then performed on these residual scores. Although some individuals feel this approach is equivalent to ANCOVA, Maxwell, Delaney, and Manheimer (1985) showed the two methods are not the same and that analysis on residuals should be avoided.

The first two methods are used quite frequently. Huck and McLean (1975) and Jennings (1988) compared the first two methods just mentioned, along with the use of ANCOVA for the pretest–posttest control group design, and concluded that ANCOVA is the preferred method of analysis. Several comments from the Huck and McLean article are worth mentioning. First, they noted that with the repeated-measures approach it is the *interaction F* that is indicating whether the treatments had a differential effect, and not the treatment main effect. We consider two patterns of means to illustrate the interaction of interest.

	Situation 1			Situation 2	
	Pretest	Posttest		Pretest	Posttest
Treatment	70	80	Treatment	65	80
Control	60	70	Control	60	68

In Situation 1 the treatment main effect would probably be significant, because there is a difference of 10 in the row means. However, the difference of 10 on the posttest just transferred from an initial difference of 10 on the pretest. The interaction would not be significant here, as there is no differential change in the treatment and control groups here. Of course, in a randomized study, we should not observe such between-group differences on the pretest. On the other hand, in Situation 2, even though the treatment group scored somewhat higher on the pretest, it increased 15 points from pretest to posttest, whereas the control group increased just 8 points. That is, there was a *differential* change in performance in the two groups, and this differential change is the interaction that is being tested in repeated measures ANOVA. One way of thinking of an interaction effect is as a "difference in the differences." This is exactly what we have in Situation 2, hence a significant interaction effect.

Second, Huck and McLean (1975) noted that the interaction F from the repeated-measures ANOVA is *identical* to the F ratio one would obtain from an ANOVA on the gain (difference) scores. Finally, whenever the regression coefficient is not equal to 1 (generally the case), the error term for ANCOVA will be smaller than for the gain score analysis and hence the ANCOVA will be a more sensitive or powerful analysis.

Although not discussed in the Huck and McLean paper, we would like to add a caution concerning the use of gain scores. It is a fairly well-known measurement fact that the reliability of gain (difference) scores is generally not good. To be more specific, *as the correlation between the pretest and posttest scores approaches the reliability of the test, the reliability of the difference scores goes to 0.* The following table from Thorndike and Hagen (1977) quantifies things:

Correlation between tests	Average reliability of two tests					
	.50	.60	.70	.80	.90	.95
.00	.50	.60	.70	.80	.90	.95
.40	.17	.33	.50	.67	.83	.92
.50	.00	.20	.40	.60	.80	.90
.60		.00	.25	.50	.75	.88
.70			.00	.33	.67	.83
.80				.00	.50	.75
.90					.00	.50
.95						.00

If our dependent variable is some noncognitive measure, or a variable derived from a nonstandardized test (which could well be of questionable reliability), then a reliability of about .60 or so is a definite possibility. In this case, if the correlation between pretest and posttest is .50 (a realistic possibility), the reliability of the difference scores is only .20. On the other hand, this table also shows that if our measure is quite reliable (say .90), then the difference scores will be reliable provided that the correlation is not too high. For example, for reliability = .90 and pre–post correlation = .50, the reliability of the differences scores is .80.

8.8 ERROR REDUCTION AND ADJUSTMENT OF POSTTEST MEANS FOR SEVERAL COVARIATES

What is the rationale for using several covariates? First, the use of several covariates may result in greater error reduction than can be obtained with just one covariate. The error reduction will be substantially greater if the covariates have relatively low intercorrelations among themselves (say < .40). Second, with several covariates, we can make a better adjustment for initial differences between intact groups.

For one covariate, the amount of error reduction is governed primarily by the magnitude of the correlation between the covariate and the dependent variable (see Equation 2). For several covariates, the amount of error reduction is determined by the magnitude of the multiple correlation between the dependent variable and the set of covariates (predictors). This is why we indicated earlier that it is desirable to have covariates with low intercorrelations among themselves, for then the multiple correlation will be larger, and we will achieve greater error reduction. Also, because R^2 has a variance accounted for interpretation, we can speak of the percentage of *within* variability on the dependent variable that is accounted for by the set of covariates.

Recall that the equation for the adjusted posttest mean for one covariate was given by:

$$y_i^* = \bar{y}_i - b(\bar{x}_i - \bar{x}), \tag{4}$$

where b is the estimated common regression slope.

With several covariates $(x_1, x_2, \ldots, x_k)$, we are simply regressing y on the set of xs, and the adjusted equation becomes an extension:

$$\bar{y}_j^* = \bar{y}_j - b_1\left(\bar{x}_{1j} - \bar{x}_1\right) - b_2\left(\bar{x}_{2j} - \bar{x}_2\right) - \cdots - b_k\left(\bar{x}_{kj} - \bar{x}_k\right), \tag{5}$$

where the b_i are the regression coefficients, $\bar{x}_{1j}$ is the mean for the covariate 1 in group j, $\bar{x}_{2j}$ is the mean for covariate 2 in group j, and so on, and the $\bar{x}_i$ are the grand means for the covariates. We next illustrate the use of this equation on a sample MANCOVA problem.

8.9 MANCOVA—SEVERAL DEPENDENT VARIABLES AND SEVERAL COVARIATES

In MANCOVA we are assuming there is a significant relationship between the set of dependent variables and the set of covariates, or that there is a significant regression of the ys on the xs. This is tested through the use of Wilks' Λ. We are also assuming, for more than two covariates, homogeneity of the regression hyperplanes. The null hypothesis that is being tested in MANCOVA is that the adjusted population mean vectors are equal:

$$H_0 : \boldsymbol{\mu}_{1_{adj}} = \boldsymbol{\mu}_{2_{adj}} = \boldsymbol{\mu}_{3_{adj}} = \cdots = \boldsymbol{\mu}_{j_{adj}}$$

In testing the null hypothesis in MANCOVA, adjusted W and T matrices are needed; we denote these by **W*** and **T***. In MANOVA, recall that the null hypothesis was tested using Wilks' Λ. Thus, we have:

$$\begin{array}{cc} \text{MANOVA} & \text{MANCOVA} \\[6pt] \begin{array}{c}\text{Test} \\ \text{Statistic}\end{array} \quad \Lambda = \dfrac{|\mathbf{W}|}{|\mathbf{T}|} & \Lambda^* = \dfrac{\left|\mathbf{W}^*\right|}{\left|\mathbf{T}^*\right|} \end{array}$$

The calculation of **W*** and **T*** involves considerable matrix algebra, which we wish to avoid. For those who are interested in the details, however, Finn (1974) has a nicely worked out example.

In examining the output from statistical packages it is important to *first* make two checks to determine whether MANCOVA is appropriate:

1. Check to see that there is a significant relationship between the dependent variables and the covariates.
2. Check to determine that the homogeneity of the regression hyperplanes is satisfied.

If either of these is not satisfied, then covariance is not appropriate. In particular, if condition 2 is not met, then one should consider using the Johnson–Neyman technique, which determines a region of nonsignificance, that is, a set of *x* values for which the groups do not differ, and hence for values of *x* outside this region one group is superior to the other. The Johnson–Neyman technique is described by Huitema (2011), and extended discussion is provided in Rogosa (1977, 1980).

Incidentally, if the homogeneity of regression slopes is rejected for several groups, it does not automatically follow that the slopes for all groups differ. In this case, one might follow up the overall test with additional homogeneity tests on all combinations of pairs of slopes. Often, the slopes will be homogeneous for many of the groups. In this case one can apply ANCOVA to the groups that have homogeneous slopes, and apply the Johnson–Neyman technique to the groups with heterogeneous slopes. At present, neither SAS nor SPSS offers the Johnson–Neyman technique.

8.10 TESTING THE ASSUMPTION OF HOMOGENEOUS HYPERPLANES ON SPSS

Neither SAS nor SPSS automatically provides the test of the homogeneity of the regression hyperplanes. Recall that, for one covariate, this is the assumption of equal regression slopes in the groups, and that for two covariates it is the assumption of parallel regression planes. To set up the syntax to test this assumption, it is necessary to understand what a violation of the assumption means. As we indicated earlier (and displayed in Figure 8.4), a violation means there is a covariate-by-treatment interaction. Evidence that the assumption is met means the interaction is not present, which is consistent with the use of MANCOVA.

Thus, what is done on SPSS is to set up an effect involving the interaction (for a given covariate), and then test whether this effect is significant. If so, this means the assumption is *not* tenable. This is one of those cases where researchers typically do not want significance, for then the assumption is tenable and covariance is appropriate. With the SPSS GLM procedure, the interaction can be tested for each covariate across the multiple outcomes simultaneously.

Example 8.1: Two Dependent Variables and One Covariate
We call the grouping variable TREATS, and denote the dependent variables by $Y1$ and $Y2$, and the covariate by $X1$. Then, the key parts of the GLM syntax that

produce a test of the assumption of no treatment-covariate interaction for any of the outcomes are

```
GLM Y1 Y2 BY TREATS WITH X1
/DESIGN=TREATS X1 TREATS*X1.
```

Example 8.2: Three Dependent Variables and Two Covariates

We denote the dependent variables by $Y1$, $Y2$, and $Y3$, and the covariates by $X1$ and $X2$. Then, the relevant syntax is

```
GLM Y1 Y2 Y3 BY TREATS WITH X1 X2
/DESIGN=TREATS X1 X2 TREATS*X1 TREATS*X2.
```

These two syntax lines will be embedded in others when running a MANCOVA on SPSS, as you can see in a computer example we consider later. With the previous two examples and the computer examples, you should be able to generalize the setup of the control lines for testing homogeneity of regression hyperplanes for any combination of dependent variables and covariates.

8.11 EFFECT SIZE MEASURES FOR GROUP COMPARISONS IN MANCOVA/ANCOVA

A variety of effect size measures are available to describe the differences in adjusted means. A raw score (unstandardized) difference in adjusted means should be reported and may be sufficient if the scale of the dependent variable is well known and easily understood. In addition, as discussed in Olejnik and Algina (2000) a standardized difference in adjusted means between two groups (essentially a Cohen's d measure) may be computed as

$$d = \frac{\overline{y}_{adj1} - \overline{y}_{adj2}}{MSW^{1/2}},$$

where MSW is the pooled mean squared error from a one-way ANOVA that includes the treatment as the only explanatory variable (thus excluding any covariates). This effect size measure, among other things, assumes that (1) the covariates are participant attribute variables (or more properly variables whose variability is intrinsic to the population of interest, as explained in Olejnik and Algina, 2000) and (2) the homogeneity of variance assumption for the outcome is satisfied.

In addition, one may also use proportion of variance explained effect size measures for treatment group differences in MANOVA/ANCOVA. For example, for a given outcome, the proportion of variance explained by treatment group differences may be computed as

$$\eta^2 = \frac{SS_{effect}}{SS_{total}},$$

where SS_{effect} is the sum of squares due to the treatment from the ANCOVA and SS_{total} is the total sum of squares for a given dependent variable. Note that computer software commonly reports partial η^2, which is *not* the effect size discussed here and which removes variation due to the covariate from SS_{total}. Conceptually, η^2 describes the strength of the treatment effect for the general population, whereas partial η^2 describes the strength of the treatment for participants having the same values on the covariates (i.e., holding scores constant on all covariates). In addition, an overall multivariate strength of association, multivariate eta square (also called tau square), can be computed and is

$$\eta^2_{multivariate} = 1 - \Lambda^{1/r},$$

where Λ is Wilk's lambda and r is the smaller of (p, q), where p is the number of dependent variables and q is the degrees of freedom for the treatment effect. This effect size is interpreted as the proportion of generalized variance in the set of outcomes that is due the treatment. Use of these effect size measures is illustrated in Example 8.4.

8.12 TWO COMPUTER EXAMPLES

We now consider two examples to illustrate (1) how to set up syntax to run MANCOVA on SAS GLM and then SPSS GLM, and (2) how to interpret the output, including determining whether use of covariates is appropriate. The first example uses artificial data and is simpler, having just two dependent variables and one covariate, whereas the second example uses data from an actual study and is a bit more complex, involving two dependent variables and two covariates. We also conduct some preliminary analysis activities (checking for outliers, assessing assumptions) with the second example.

Example 8.3: MANCOVA on SAS GLM

This example has two groups, with 15 participants in group 1 and 14 participants in group 2. There are two dependent variables, denoted by POSTCOMP and POSTHIOR in the SAS GLM syntax and on the printout, and one covariate (denoted by PRECOMP). The syntax for running the MANCOVA analysis is given in Table 8.1, along with annotation.

Table 8.2 presents two multivariate tests for determining whether MANCOVA is appropriate, that is, whether there is a significant relationship between the two dependent variables and the covariate, and whether there is no covariate by group interaction. The multivariate test at the top of Table 8.2 indicates there is a significant relationship between the covariate and the set of outcomes ($F = 21.46$, $p = .0001$). Also, the multivariate test in the middle of the table shows there is *not* a covariate-by-group interaction effect ($F = 1.90$, $p < .1707$). This supports the decision to use MANCOVA.

■ **Table 8.1: SAS GLM Syntax for Two-Group MANCOVA: Two Dependent Variables and One Covariate**

```
        TITLE 'MULTIVARIATE ANALYSIS OF COVARIANCE'; DATA COMP;
        INPUT GPID PRECOMP POSTCOMP POSTHIOR @@;
        LINES;
        1 15 17 3 1 10 6 3 1 13 13 1 1 14 14 8
        1 12 12 3 1 10 9 9 1 12 12 3 1 8 9 12
        1 12 15 3 1 8 10 8 1 12 13 1 1 7 11 10
        1 12 16 1 1 9 12 2 1 12 14 8
        2 9 9 3 2 13 19 5 2 13 16 11 2 6 7 18
        2 10 11 15 2 6 9 9 2 16 20 8 2 9 15 6
        2 10 8 9 2 8 10 3 2 13 16 12 2 12 17 20
        2 11 18 12 2 14 18 16
        PROC PRINT;
        PROC REG;
①      MODEL POSTCOMP POSTHIOR = PRECOMP;
        MTEST;
②      PROC GLM;
        CLASS GPID;
        MODEL POSTCOMP POSTHIOR = PRECOMP GPID PRECOMP*GPID;
        MANOVA H = PRECOMP*GPID;
③      PROC GLM;
        CLASS GPID;
        MODEL POSTCOMP POSTHIOR = PRECOMP GPID;
        MANOVA H = GPID;
④      LSMEANS GPID/PDIFF;
        RUN;
```

① PROC REG is used to examine the relationship between the two dependent variables and the covariate. The MTEST is needed to obtain the multivariate test.

② Here GLM is used with the MANOVA statement to obtain the multivariate test of no overall PRECOMP BY GPID interaction effect.

③ GLM is used again, along with the MANOVA statement, to test whether the adjusted population mean vectors are equal.

④ This statement is needed to obtain the adjusted means.

The multivariate null hypothesis tested in MANCOVA is that the adjusted population mean vectors are equal, that is,

$$H_0 : \begin{pmatrix} \mu_{11}^* \\ \mu_{21}^* \end{pmatrix} = \begin{pmatrix} \mu_{12}^* \\ \mu_{22}^* \end{pmatrix}.$$

▨ **Table 8.2: Multivariate Tests for Significant Regression, Covariate-by-Treatment Interaction, and Group Differences**

Multivariate Test:

<table>
<tr><td colspan="6" align="center">Multivariate Statistics and Exact F Statistics</td></tr>
<tr><td></td><td colspan="5" align="center">S = 1   M = 0   N = 12</td></tr>
<tr><td>Statistic</td><td>Value</td><td>F</td><td>Num DF</td><td>Den DF</td><td>Pr > F</td></tr>
<tr><td>Wilks' Lambda</td><td>0.37722383</td><td>21.46</td><td>2</td><td>26</td><td>0.0001</td></tr>
<tr><td>Pillar's Trace</td><td>0.62277617</td><td>21.46</td><td>2</td><td>26</td><td>0.0001</td></tr>
<tr><td>Hotelling-Lawley Trace</td><td>1.65094597</td><td>21.46</td><td>2</td><td>26</td><td>0.0001</td></tr>
<tr><td>Roy's Greatest Root</td><td>1.65094597</td><td>21.46</td><td>2</td><td>26</td><td>0.0001</td></tr>
</table>

MANOVA Test Criteria and Exact F Statistics for the Hypothesis
of no Overall PRECOMP*GPID Effect

<table>
<tr><td colspan="3">H = Type III SS&CP Matrix for PRECOMP*GPID</td><td colspan="3" align="center">E = Error SS&CPMatrix</td></tr>
<tr><td></td><td colspan="5" align="center">S = 1   M = 0   N = 11</td></tr>
<tr><td>Statistic</td><td>Value</td><td>F</td><td>Num DF</td><td>Den DF</td><td>Pr > F</td></tr>
<tr><td>Wilks' Lambda</td><td>0.86301048</td><td>1.90</td><td>2</td><td>24</td><td>0.1707</td></tr>
<tr><td>Pillar's Trace</td><td>0.13698952</td><td>1.90</td><td>2</td><td>24</td><td>0.1707</td></tr>
<tr><td>Hotelling-Lawley Trace</td><td>0.15873448</td><td>1.90</td><td>2</td><td>24</td><td>0.1707</td></tr>
<tr><td>Roy's Greatest Root</td><td>0.15873448</td><td>1.90</td><td>2</td><td>24</td><td>0.1707</td></tr>
</table>

MANOVA Test Criteria and Exact F Statistics for the Hypothesis of no Overall GPID Effect

<table>
<tr><td colspan="3" align="center">H = Type III SS&CP Matrix for GPID</td><td colspan="3" align="center">E = Error SS&CP Matrix</td></tr>
<tr><td></td><td colspan="5" align="center">S = 1   M = 0   N = 11.5</td></tr>
<tr><td>Statistic</td><td>Value</td><td>F</td><td>Num DF</td><td>Den DF</td><td>Pr > F</td></tr>
<tr><td>Wilks' Lambda</td><td>0.64891393</td><td>6.76</td><td>2</td><td>25</td><td>0.0045</td></tr>
<tr><td>Pillar's Trace</td><td>0.35108107</td><td>6.76</td><td>2</td><td>25</td><td>0.0045</td></tr>
<tr><td>Hotelling-Lawley Trace</td><td>0.54102455</td><td>6.76</td><td>2</td><td>25</td><td>0.0045</td></tr>
<tr><td>Roy's Greatest Root</td><td>0.54102455</td><td>6.76</td><td>2</td><td>25</td><td>0.0045</td></tr>
</table>

The multivariate test at the bottom of Table 8.2 ($F = 6.76$, $p = .0045$) shows that we reject the multivariate null hypothesis at the .05 level, and hence conclude that the groups differ on the *set* of adjusted means. The univariate ANCOVA follow-up F tests in Table 8.3 ($F = 5.26$ for POSTCOMP, $p = .03$, and $F = 9.84$ for POSTHIOR, $p = .004$) indicate that adjusted means differ for each of the dependent variables. The adjusted means for the variables are also given in Table 8.3.

Can we have confidence in the reliability of the adjusted means? From Huitema's inequality we need $C + (J - 1) / N < .10$. Because here $J = 2$ and $N = 29$, we obtain

■ **Table 8.3: Univariate Tests for Group Differences and Adjusted Means**

Source	DF	Type I SS	Mean Square	F Value	Pr > F
PRECOMP	1	237.6895679	237.6895679	43.90	<0.001
GPID	1	28.4986009	28.4986009	5.26	0.0301

Source	DF	Type III SS	Mean Square	F Value	Pr > F
PRECOMP	1	247.9797944	247.9797944	45.80	<0.001
GPID	1	28.4986009	28.4986009	5.26	0.0301

Source	DF	Type I SS	Mean Square	F Value	Pr > F
PRECOMP	1	17.6622124	17.6622124	0.82	0.3732
GPID	1	211.5902344	211.5902344	9.84	0.0042

Source	DF	Type III SS	Mean Square	F Value	Pr > F
PRECOMP	1	10.2007226	10.2007226	0.47	0.4972
GPID	1	211.5902344	211.5902344	9.84	0.0042

General Linear Models Procedure Least Squares Means

GPID	POSTCOMP LSMEAN	Pr > |T| H0: LSMEAN1 = LSMEAN2
1	12.0055476	0.0301
2	13.9940562	
GPID	POSTHIOR LSMEAN	Pr > |T| H0: LSMEAN1 = LSMEAN2
1	5.0394385	0.0042
2	10.4577444	

$(C + 1) / 29 < .10$ or $C < 1.9$. Thus, we should use fewer than two covariates for reliable results, and we have used just one covariate.

Example 8.4: MANCOVA on SPSS MANOVA

Next, we consider a social psychological study by Novince (1977) that examined the effect of behavioral rehearsal (group 1) and of behavioral rehearsal plus cognitive restructuring (combination treatment, group 3) on reducing anxiety (NEGEVAL) and facilitating social skills (AVOID) for female college freshmen. There was also a control group (group 2), with 11 participants in each group. The participants were pretested and posttested on four measures, thus the pretests were the covariates.

For this example we use only two of the measures: avoidance and negative evaluation. In Table 8.4 we present syntax for running the MANCOVA, along with annotation explaining what some key subcommands are doing. Table 8.5 presents syntax for obtaining within-group Mahalanobis distance values that can be used to identify multivariate outliers among the variables. Tables 8.6, 8.7, 8.8, 8.9, and 8.10 present selected analysis results. Specifically, Table 8.6 presents descriptive statistics for the study variables, Table 8.7 presents results for tests of the homogeneity of the regression planes, and Table 8.8 shows tests for homogeneity of variance. Table 8.9 provides the overall multivariate tests as well as follow-up univariate tests for the MANCOVA, and Table 8.10 presents the adjusted means and Bonferroni-adjusted comparisons for adjusted mean differences. As in one-way MANOVA, the Bonferroni adjustments guard against type I error inflation due to the number of pairwise comparisons.

Before we use the MANCOVA procedure, we examine the data for potential outliers, examine the shape of the distributions of the covariates and outcomes, and inspect descriptive statistics. Using the syntax in Table 8.5, we obtain the Mahalanobis distances for each case to identify if multivariate outliers are present on the set of dependent variables and covariates. The largest obtained distance is 7.79, which does not exceed the chi-square critical value (.001, 4) of 18.47. Thus, no multivariate outliers

■ **Table 8.4: SPSS MANOVA Syntax for Three-Group Example: Two Dependent Variables and Two Covariates**

```
TITLE 'NOVINCE DATA — 3 GP ANCOVA-2 DEP VARS AND 2 COVS'.
DATA LIST FREE/GPID AVOID NEGEVAL PREAVOID PRENEG.
BEGIN DATA.
1 91 81 70 102      1 107 132 121 71   1 121 97 89 76     1 86 88 80 85
1 137 119 123 117   1 138 132 112 106  1 133 116 126 97
1 127 101 121 85    1 114 138 80 105   1 118 121 101 113  1 114 72 112 76
2 107 88 116 97     2 76 95 77 64      2 116 87 111 86    2 126 112 121 106
2 104 107 105 113   2 96 84 97 92      2 127 88 132 104   2 99 101 98 81
2 94 87 85 96       2 92 80 82 88      2 128 109 112 118
3 121 134 96 96     3 140 130 120 110  3 148 123 130 111  3 147 155 145 118
3 139 124 122 105   3 121 123 119 122  3 141 155 104 139  3 143 131 121 103
3 120 123 80 77     3 140 140 121 121  3 95 103 92 94
END DATA.
LIST.
GLM AVOID NEGEVAL BY GPID WITH PREAVOID PRENEG
/PRINT=DESCRIPTIVE ETASQ
① /DESIGN=GPID PREAVOID PRENEG GPID*PREAVOID GPID*PRENEG.
② GLM AVOID NEGEVAL BY GPID WITH PREAVOID PRENEG
/EMMEANS=TABLES(GPID) COMPARE ADJ(BONFERRONI)
  /PLOT=RESIDUALS
  /SAVE=RESID ZRESID
  /PRINT=DESCRIPTIVE ETASQ HOMOGENEITY
  /DESIGN=PREAVOID PRENEG GPID.
```

① With the first set of GLM commands, the design subcommand requests a test of the equality of regression planes assumption for each outcome. In particular, GPID*PREAVOID GPID*PRENEG creates the product variables needed to test the interactions of interest.

② This second set of GLM commands produces the standard MANCOVA results. The EMMEANS subcommand requests comparisons of adjusted means using the Bonferroni procedure.

■ **Table 8.5: SPSS Syntax for Obtaining Within-Group Mahalanobis Distance Values**

```
①  SORT CASES BY gpid(A).
SPLIT FILE by gpid.
②  REGRESSION
/STATISTICS COEFF OUTS R ANOVA
/DEPENDENT case
/METHOD=ENTER avoid negeval preavoid preneg
/SAVE MAHAL.
EXECUTE.
SPLIT FILE OFF.
```

① To obtain the Mahalanobis' distances within groups, cases must first be sorted by the grouping variable. The `SPLIT FILE` command is needed to obtain the distances for each group separately.

② The regression procedure obtains the distances. Note that case (which is the case ID) is the dependent variable, which is irrelevant here because the procedure uses information from the "predictors" only in computing the distance values. The "predictor" variables here are the dependent variables and covariates used in the MANCOVA, which are entered with the `METHOD` subcommand.

are indicated. We also computed within-group z scores for each of the variables separately and did not find any observation lying more than 2.5 standard deviations from the respective group mean, suggesting no univariate outliers are present. In addition, examining histograms of each of the variables as well as scatterplots of each outcome and each covariate for each group did not suggest any unusual values and suggested that the distributions of each variable appear to be roughly symmetrical. Further, examining the scatterplots suggested that each covariate is linearly related to each of the outcome variables, supporting the linearity assumption.

Table 8.6 shows the means and standard deviations for each of the study variables by treatment group (GPID). Examining the group means for the outcomes (AVOID, NEGEVAL) indicates that Group 3 has the highest means for each outcome and Group 2 has the lowest. For the covariates, Group 3 has the highest mean and the means for Groups 2 and 1 are fairly similar. Given that random assignment has been properly done, use of MANCOVA (or ANCOVA) is preferable to MANOVA (or ANOVA) for the situation where covariate means appear to differ across groups because use of the covariates properly adjusts for the differences in the covariates across groups. See Huitema (2011, pp. 202–208) for a discussion of this issue.

Having some assurance that there are no outliers present, the shapes of the distributions are fairly symmetrical, and linear relationships are present between the covariates and the outcomes, we now examine the formal assumptions associated with the procedure. (Note though that the linearity assumption has already been assessed.) First, Table 8.7 provides the results for the test of the assumption that there is no treatment-covariate interaction for the set of outcomes, which the GLM procedure performs separately for

■ **Table 8.6: Descriptive Statistics for the Study Variables by Group**

			Report		
GPID		AVOID	NEGEVAL	PREAVOID	PRENEG
1.00	Mean	116.9091	108.8182	103.1818	93.9091
	N	11	11	11	11
	Std. deviation	17.23052	22.34645	20.21296	16.02158
2.00	Mean	105.9091	94.3636	103.2727	95.0000
	N	11	11	11	11
	Std. deviation	16.78961	11.10201	17.27478	15.34927
3.00	Mean	132.2727	131.0000	113.6364	108.7273
	N	11	11	11	11
	Std. deviation	16.16843	15.05988	18.71509	16.63785

each covariate. The results suggest that there is no interaction between the treatment and PREAVOID for any outcome, multivariate $F = .277$, $p = .892$ (corresponding to Wilks' Λ) and no interaction between the treatment and PRENEG for any outcome, multivariate $F = .275$, $p = .892$. In addition, Box's M test, $M = 6.689$, $p = .418$, does not indicate the variance-covariance matrices of the dependent variables differs across groups. Note that Box's M does not test the assumption that the variance-covariance matrices of the *residuals* are similar across groups. However, Levene's test assesses whether the *residuals* for a given outcome have the same variance across groups. The results of these tests, shown in Table 8.8, provide support that this assumption is not violated for the AVOID outcome, $F = 1.184$, $p = .320$ and for the NEGEVAL outcome, $F = 1.620$, $p = .215$. Further, Table 8.9 shows that PREAVOID is related to the set of outcomes, multivariate $F = 17.659$, $p < .001$, as is PRENEG, multivariate $F = 4.379$, $p = .023$.

Having now learned that there is no interaction between the treatment and covariates for any outcome, that the residual variance is similar across groups for each outcome, and that the each covariate is related to the set of outcomes, we attend to the assumption that the residuals from the MANCOVA procedure are independently distributed and follow a multivariate normal distribution in each of the treatment populations. Given that the treatments were individually administered and individuals completed the assessments on an individual basis, we have no reason to suspect that the independence assumption is violated. To assess normality, we examine graphs and compute skewness and kurtosis of the residuals. The syntax in Table 8.4 obtains the residuals from the MANCOVA procedure for the two outcomes for each group. Inspecting the histograms does not suggest a serious departure from normality, which is supported by the skewness and kurtosis values, none of which exceeds a magnitude of 1.5.

Table 8.7: Multivariate Tests for No Treatment-Covariate Interactions

Multivariate Tests[a]

Effect		Value	F	Hypothesis df	Error df	Sig.	Partial eta squared
Intercept	Pillai's Trace	.200	2.866[b]	2.000	23.000	.077	.200
	Wilks' Lambda	.800	2.866[b]	2.000	23.000	.077	.200
	Hotelling's Trace	.249	2.866[b]	2.000	23.000	.077	.200
	Roy's Largest Root	.249	2.866[b]	2.000	23.000	.077	.200
GPID	Pillai's Trace	.143	.922	4.000	48.000	.459	.071
	Wilks' Lambda	.862	.889[b]	4.000	46.000	.478	.072
	Hotelling's Trace	.156	.856	4.000	44.000	.498	.072
	Roy's Largest Root	.111	1.334[c]	2.000	24.000	.282	.100
PREAVOID	Pillai's Trace	.553	14.248[b]	2.000	23.000	.000	.553
	Wilks' Lambda	.447	14.248[b]	2.000	23.000	.000	.553
	Hotelling's Trace	1.239	14.248[b]	2.000	23.000	.000	.553
	Roy's Largest Root	1.239	14.248[b]	2.000	23.000	.000	.553
PRENEG	Pillai's Trace	.235	3.529[b]	2.000	23.000	.046	.235
	Wilks' Lambda	.765	3.529[b]	2.000	23.000	.046	.235
	Hotelling's Trace	.307	3.529[b]	2.000	23.000	.046	.235
	Roy's Largest Root	.307	3.529[b]	2.000	23.000	.046	.235
GPID * PREAVOID	Pillai's Trace	.047	.287	4.000	48.000	.885	.023
	Wilks' Lambda	.954	.277[b]	4.000	46.000	.892	.023
	Hotelling's Trace	.048	.266	4.000	44.000	.898	.024
	Roy's Largest Root	.040	.485[c]	2.000	24.000	.622	.039
GPID * PRENEG	Pillai's Trace	.047	.287	4.000	48.000	.885	.023
	Wilks' Lambda	.954	.275[b]	4.000	46.000	.892	.023
	Hotelling's Trace	.048	.264	4.000	44.000	.900	.023
	Roy's Largest Root	.035	.415[c]	2.000	24.000	.665	.033

[a] Design: Intercept + GPID + PREAVOID + PRENEG + GPID * PREAVOID + GPID * PRENEG
[b] Exact statistic
[c] The statistic is an upper bound on F that yields a lower bound on the significance level.

Table 8.8: Homogeneity of Variance Tests for MANCOVA

Box's test of equality of covariance matrices[a]

Box's M	6.689
F	1.007
df1	6
df2	22430.769
Sig.	.418

Tests the null hypothesis that the observed covariance matrices of the dependent variables are equal across groups.
[a] Design: Intercept + PREAVOID + PRENEG + GPID

Levene's test of equality of error variances[a]				
	F	df1	df2	Sig.
AVOID	1.184	2	30	.320
NEGEVAL	1.620	2	30	.215

Tests the null hypothesis that the error variance of the dependent variable is equal across groups.

[a] Design: Intercept + PREAVOID + PRENEG + GPID

■ Table 8.9: MANCOVA and ANCOVA Test Results

Multivariate tests[a]							
Effect		Value	F	Hypothesis df	Error df	Sig.	Partial eta squared
Intercept	Pillai's Trace	.219	3.783[b]	2.000	27.000	.036	.219
	Wilks' Lambda	.781	3.783[b]	2.000	27.000	.036	.219
	Hotelling's Trace	.280	3.783[b]	2.000	27.000	.036	.219
	Roy's Largest Root	.280	3.783[b]	2.000	27.000	.036	.219
PREAVOID	Pillai's Trace	.567	17.659[b]	2.000	27.000	.000	.567
	Wilks' Lambda	.433	17.659[b]	2.000	27.000	.000	.567
	Hotelling's Trace	1.308	17.659[b]	2.000	27.000	.000	.567
	Roy's Largest Root	1.308	17.659[b]	2.000	27.000	.000	.567
PRENEG	Pillai's Trace	.245	4.379[b]	2.000	27.000	.023	.245
	Wilks' Lambda	.755	4.379[b]	2.000	27.000	.023	.245
	Hotelling's Trace	.324	4.379[b]	2.000	27.000	.023	.245
	Roy's Largest Root	.324	4.379[b]	2.000	27.000	.023	.245
GPID	Pillai's Trace	.491	4.555	4.000	56.000	.003	.246
	Wilks' Lambda	.519	5.246[b]	4.000	54.000	.001	.280
	Hotelling's Trace	.910	5.913	4.000	52.000	.001	.313
	Roy's Largest Root	.889	12.443[c]	2.000	28.000	.000	.471

[a] Design: Intercept + PREAVOID + PRENEG + GPID

[b] Exact statistic

[c] The statistic is an upper bound on F that yields a lower bound on the significance level.

Tests of between-subjects effects							
Source	Dependent variable	Type III sum of squares	df	Mean square	F	Sig.	Partial eta squared
Corrected model	AVOID	9620.404[a]	4	2405.101	25.516	.000	.785
	NEGEVAL	9648.883[b]	4	2412.221	10.658	.000	.604

Tests of between-subjects effects

Source	Dependent variable	Type III sum of squares	df	Mean square	F	Sig.	Partial eta squared
Intercept	AVOID	321.661	1	321.661	3.413	.075	.109
	NEGEVAL	1479.664	1	1479.664	6.538	.016	.189
PREAVOID	AVOID	3402.401	1	3402.401	36.097	.000	.563
	NEGEVAL	262.041	1	262.041	1.158	.291	.040
PRENEG	AVOID	600.646	1	600.646	6.372	.018	.185
	NEGEVAL	1215.510	1	1215.510	5.371	.028	.161
GPID	AVOID	1365.612	2	682.806	7.244	.003	.341
	NEGEVAL	4088.115	2	2044.057	9.032	.001	.392
Error	AVOID	2639.232	28	94.258			
	NEGEVAL	6336.995	28	226.321			
Total	AVOID	474588.000	33				
	NEGEVAL	425470.000	33				
Corrected Total	AVOID	12259.636	32				
	NEGEVAL	15985.879	32				

[a] R Squared = .785 (Adjusted R Squared = .754)

[b] R Squared = .604 (Adjusted R Squared = .547)

Having found sufficient support for using MANCOVA, we now focus on the primary test of interest, which assesses whether or not there is a difference in adjusted means for the set of outcomes. The multivariate $F = 5.246$ ($p = .001$), shown in first output selection of Table 8.9, indicates that the adjusted means differ in the population for the set of outcomes, with $\eta^2_{multivariate} = 1 - .519^{1/2} = .28$. The univariate ANCOVAs on the bottom part of Table 8.9 suggest that the adjusted means differ across groups for AVOID, $F = 7.24$, $p = .003$, with $\eta^2 = 1365.61 / 12259.64 = .11$, and NEGEVAL $F = 9.02$, $p = .001$, with $\eta^2 = 4088.12 / 15985.88 = .26$. Note that we ignore the partial eta squares that are in the table.

Since group differences on the adjusted means are present for both outcomes, we consider the adjusted means and associated pairwise comparisons for each outcome, which are shown in Table 8.10. Considering the social skills measure first (AVOID), examining the adjusted means indicates that the combination treatment (Group 3) has the greatest mean social skills, after adjusting for the covariates, compared to the other groups, and that the control group (Group 2) has the lowest social skills. The results of the pairwise comparisons, using a Bonferroni adjusted alpha (i.e., .05 / 3), indicates that the two treatment groups (Groups 1 and 3) have similar adjusted mean social skills and that each of the treatment groups has greater adjusted mean social skills than the control group. Thus, for this outcome, behavioral rehearsal seems to be an effective way to improve social skills, but the addition of cognitive restructuring does not seem to further improve these skills. The d effect size measure, using MSW of 280.067 ($MSW^{1/2} = 16.74$) with no covariates in the analysis model, is 0.27 for Group 3 versus Group 1, 0.68 for Group 1 versus Group 2, and 0.95 for Group 3 versus Group 2.

For the anxiety outcome (NEGEVAL), where higher scores indicate less anxiety, inspecting the adjusted means at the top part of Table 8.10 suggests a similar pattern. However, the error variance is much greater for this outcome, as evidenced by the larger standard errors shown in Table 8.10. As such, the only difference in adjusted means present in the population for NEGEVAL is between Group 3 and the control, where $d = 29.045 / 16.83 = 1.73$ (with $MSW = 283.14$). Here, then the behavioral rehearsal and cognitive restructuring treatment shows promise as this

■ Table 8.10: Adjusted Means and Bonferroni-Adjusted Pairwise Comparisons

		Estimates			
				95% Confidence interval	
Dependent variable	GPID	Mean	Std. error	Lower bound	Upper bound
AVOID	1.00	120.631[a]	2.988	114.510	126.753
	2.00	109.250[a]	2.969	103.168	115.331
	3.00	125.210[a]	3.125	118.808	131.612
NEGEVAL	1.00	111.668[a]	4.631	102.183	121.154
	2.00	96.734[a]	4.600	87.310	106.158
	3.00	125.779[a]	4.843	115.860	135.699

[a] Covariates appearing in the model are evaluated at the following values: PREAVOID = 106.6970, PRENEG = 99.2121.

			Pairwise comparisons				
						95% Confidence interval for difference[b]	
Dependent variable	(I) GPID	(J) GPID	Mean difference (I-J)	Std. error	Sig.[b]	Lower bound	Upper bound
AVOID	1.00	2.00	11.382*	4.142	.031	.835	21.928
		3.00	−4.578	4.474	.945	−15.970	6.813
	2.00	1.00	−11.382*	4.142	.031	−21.928	−.835
		3.00	−15.960*	4.434	.004	−27.252	−4.668
	3.00	1.00	4.578	4.474	.945	−6.813	15.970
		2.00	15.960*	4.434	.004	4.668	27.252

						95% Confidence interval for difference[b]	
Dependent variable	(I) GPID	(J) GPID	Mean difference (I-J)	Std. error	Sig.[b]	Lower bound	Upper bound
NEGEVAL	1.00	2.00	14.934	6.418	.082	−1.408	31.277
		3.00	−14.111	6.932	.154	−31.763	3.541
	2.00	1.00	−14.934	6.418	.082	−31.277	1.408
		3.00	−29.045*	6.871	.001	−46.543	−11.548
	3.00	1.00	14.111	6.932	.154	−3.541	31.763
		2.00	29.045*	6.871	.001	11.548	46.543

Pairwise comparisons

Based on estimated marginal means

* The mean difference is significant at the .050 level.

[b] Adjustment for multiple comparisons: Bonferroni.

group had much less mean anxiety, after adjusting for the covariates, than the control group.

Can we have confidence in the reliability of the adjusted means for this study? Huitema's inequality suggests we should be somewhat cautious, because the inequality suggests we should just use one covariate, as the ratio $\dfrac{C+(J-1)}{N}$ in this example is $\dfrac{2+(3-1)}{33} = .12$, which is larger than the recommended value of .10. Thus, replication of this study using a larger sample size would provide for more confidence in the results.

8.13 NOTE ON *POST HOC* PROCEDURES

Note that in previous editions of this text, the Bryant-Paulson (1976) procedure was used to conduct inferences for pairwise differences among groups in MANCOVA (or ANCOVA). This procedure was used, instead of the Tukey (or Tukey–Kramer) procedure because the covariate(s) used in social science research are essentially always random, and it was thought to be important that this information be incorporated into the *post hoc* procedures, which the Tukey procedure does not. Huitema (2011), however, notes that Hochberg and Varon-Salomon (1984) found that the Tukey procedure adequately controls for the inflation of the family-wise type I error rate for pairwise comparisons when a covariate is random and has greater power (and provides narrower intervals) than other methods. As such, Huitema (2011, chaps. 9–10) recommends use of the procedure to obtain simultaneous confidence intervals for pairwise comparisons. However, at present, SPSS does not incorporate this procedure for MANCOVA (or ANCOVA). Readers interested in using the Tukey procedure may consult Huitema. We used the Bonferroni procedure because it can be readily obtained with SAS and SPSS, but note that this procedure is somewhat less powerful than the Tukey approach.

8.14 NOTE ON THE USE OF MVMM

An alternative to traditional MANCOVA is available with multivariate multilevel modeling (MVMM; see Chapter 14). In addition to the advantages associated with MVMM discussed there, MVMM also allows for different covariates to be used for each outcome. The more traditional general linear model (GLM) procedure, as implemented in this chapter with SPSS and SAS, requires that any covariate that appears in the model be included as an explanatory variable for *every* dependent variable, even if a given covariate were not related to a given outcome. Thus, MVMM, in addition to other benefits, allows for more flexible use of covariates for multiple analysis of covariance models.

8.15 EXAMPLE RESULTS SECTION FOR MANCOVA

For the example results section, we use the study discussed in Example 8.4.

The goal of this study was to determine whether female college freshmen randomly assigned to either behavioral rehearsal or behavioral rehearsal plus cognitive restructuring (called combined treatment) have better social skills and reduced anxiety after treatment compared to participants in a control condition. A one-way multivariate analysis of covariance (MANCOVA) was conducted with two dependent variables, social skills and anxiety, where higher scores on these variables reflect greater social skills and *less* anxiety. Given the small group size available ($n = 11$), we administered pretest measures of each outcome, which we call pre-skills and pre-anxiety, to allow for greater power in the analysis. Each participant reported complete data for all measures.

Prior to conducting MANCOVA, the data were examined for univariate and multivariate outliers, with no such observations found. We also assessed whether the MANCOVA assumptions seemed tenable. First, tests of the homogeneity of regression assumption indicated that there was no interaction between treatment and pre-skills, $\Lambda = .954$, $F(4, 46) = .277$, $p = .892$, and between treatment and pre-anxiety, $\Lambda = .954$, $F(4, 46) = .275$, $p = .892$, for any outcome. In addition, no violation of the variance-covariance matrices assumption was indicated (Box's $M = 6.689, p = .418$), and the variance of the residuals was not different across groups for social skills, Levene's $F(2, 30) = 1.184$, $p = .320$, and anxiety, $F(2, 30) = 1.620$, $p = .215$. Further, there were no substantial departures from normality, as suggested by inspection of histograms of the residuals for each group and that all values for skewness and kurtosis of the residuals were smaller than $|1.5|$. Further, examining scatterplots suggested that each covariate is positively and linearly related to each of the outcome variables. Test results from the MANCOVA indicated that pre-skills is related to the set of outcomes, $\Lambda = .433$, $F(2, 27) = 17.66$, $p < .001$, as is pre-anxiety, $\Lambda = .755$, $F(2, 27) = 4.38$, $p = .023$. Finally, we did not consider there to be any violations of the independence assumption because the treatments were individually administered and participants responded to the measures on an individual basis.

Table 1 displays the group means, which show that participants in the combined treatment had greater posttest mean scores for social skills and anxiety (less anxiety) than those in the other groups, and performance in the control condition was worst. Note that while sample pretest means differ somewhat, use of covariance analysis provides proper adjustments for these preexisting differences, with these adjusted means shown in Table 1. MANCOVA results indicated that the adjusted group means differ on the set of outcomes, $\lambda = .519$, $F(4, 54) = 5.23$, $p = .001$. Univariate ANCOVAs indicated that group adjusted mean differences are present for social skills, $F(2, 28) = 7.24$, $p = .003$, and anxiety, $F(2, 28) = 9.03$, $p = .001$.

■ **Table 1: Observed *(SD)* and Adjusted Means for the Analysis Variables (*n* = 11)**

Group	Pre-skills	Social skills	Social skills[1]	Pre-anxiety	Anxiety	Anxiety[1]
Combined	113.6 (18.7)	132.3 (16.2)	125.2	108.7 (16.6)	131.0 (15.1)	125.8
Behavioral Rehearsal	103.2 (20.2)	116.9 (17.2)	120.6	93.9 (16.0)	108.8 (22.2)	111.7
Control	103.3 (17.3)	105.9 (16.8)	109.3	95.0 (15.3)	94.4 (11.1)	96.7

[1] This column shows the adjusted group means.

Table 2 presents information on the pairwise contrasts. Comparisons of adjusted means were conducted using the Bonferroni approach to provide type I error control for the number of pairwise comparisons. Table 2 shows that adjusted mean social skills are greater in the combined treatment and behavioral rehearsal group compared to the control group. The contrast between the two intervention groups is not statistically significant. For social skills, Cohen's *d* values indicate the presence of fairly large effects associated with the interventions, relative to the control group.

For anxiety, the only difference in adjusted means present in the population is between the combined treatment and control condition. Cohen's *d* for this contrast indicates that this mean difference is quite large relative to the other effects in this study.

■ **Table 2: Pairwise Contrasts for the Adjusted Means**

Outcome	Contrast	Contrast (*SE*)	Cohen's *d*
Social skills	Combined vs. control	15.96* (4.43)	0.95
	Behavioral rehearsal vs. control	11.38* (4.14)	0.68
	Combined vs. behavioral rehearsal	4.58 (4.47)	0.27
Anxiety	Combined vs. control	29.05* (6.87)	1.73
	Behavioral rehearsal vs. control	14.93 (6.42)	0.89
	Combined vs. behavioral rehearsal	14.11 (6.93)	0.84

Note: * indicates a statistically significant contrast ($p < .05$) using the Bonferroni procedure.

8.16 SUMMARY

The numbered list below highlights the main points of the chapter.

1. In analysis of covariance a linear relationship is assumed between the dependent variable(s) and the covariate(s).

2. Analysis of covariance is directly related to the two basic objectives in experimental design of (1) eliminating systematic bias and (2) reduction of error variance. Although ANCOVA does not eliminate bias, it can reduce bias. This can be helpful in nonexperimental studies comparing intact groups. The bias is reduced by adjusting the posttest means to what they would be if all groups had started out equally on the covariate(s), that is, at the grand mean(s). There is disagreement among statisticians about the use of ANCOVA with intact groups, and several precautions were mentioned in section 8.6.

3. The main reason for using ANCOVA in an experimental study (random assignment of participants to groups) is to reduce error variance, yielding a more powerful test of group differences. When using several covariates, greater error reduction may occur when the covariates have low intercorrelations among themselves.

4. Limit the number of covariates (C) so that

$$\frac{C + (J - 1)}{N} < .10,$$

where J is the number of groups and N is total sample size, so that stable estimates of the adjusted means are obtained.

5. In examining output from the statistical packages, make two checks to determine whether MANCOVA is appropriate: (1) Check that there is a significant relationship between the dependent variables and the covariates, and (2) check that the homogeneity of the regression hyperplanes assumption is tenable. If either of these is not satisfied, then MANCOVA is not appropriate. In particular, if (2) is not satisfied, then the Johnson–Neyman technique may provide for a better analysis.

6. Measurement error for covariates causes loss of power in randomized designs, and can lead to seriously biased treatment effects in nonrandomized designs. Thus, if

one has a covariate of low or questionable reliability, then true score ANCOVA should be considered.

7. With three or more groups, use the Tukey or Bonferroni procedure to obtain confidence intervals for pairwise differences.

8.17 ANALYSIS SUMMARY

The key analysis procedures for one-way MANCOVA are:

I. Preliminary Analysis
   A. Conduct an initial screening of the data.
      1) Purpose: Determine if the summary measures seem reasonable and support the use of MANCOVA. Also, identify the presence and pattern (if any) of missing data.
      2) Procedure: Compute various descriptive measures for each group (e.g., means, standard deviations, medians, skewness, kurtosis, frequencies) for the covariate(s) and dependent variables. If there is missing data, conduct missing data analysis.
   B. Conduct a case analysis.
      1) Purpose: Identify any problematic individual observations that may change important study results.
      2) Procedure:
         i) Inspect bivariate scatterplots of each covariate and outcome for each group to identify apparent outliers. Compute and inspect within-group Mahalanobis distances for the covariate(s) and outcome(s) and within-group z-scores for each variable. From the final analysis model, obtain standardized residuals. Note that absolute values larger than 2.5 or 3 for these residuals indicate outlying values.
         ii) If any potential outliers are identified, consider doing a sensitivity study to determine the impact of one or more outliers on major study results.
   C. Assess the validity of the statistical assumptions.
      1) Purpose: Determine if the standard MANCOVA procedure is valid for the analysis of the data.
      2) Some procedures:
         i) Homogeneity of regression: Test treatment-covariate interactions. A nonsignificant test result supports the use of MANCOVA.
         ii) Linearity of regression: Inspect the scatterplot of each covariate and each outcome within each group to assess linearity. If the association appears to be linear, test the association between the covariate(s) and the set of outcomes to assess if the covariates should be included in the final analysis model.
         iii) Independence assumption: Consider study circumstances to identify possible violations.

iv) Equality of covariance matrices assumption of the residuals: Levene's test can be used to identify if the residual variation is the same across groups for each outcome. Note that Box's M test assesses if the covariance matrices of outcome scores (not residuals) are equal across groups.

v) Multivariate normality: Inspect the distribution of the residuals for each group. Compute within-group skewness and kurtosis values, with values exceeding $|2|$ indicative of nonnormality.

vi) Each covariate is measured with perfect reliability: Report a measure of reliability for the covariate scores (e.g., Cronbach's alpha). Consider using an alternate technique (e.g., structural equation modeling) when low reliability is combined with a decision to retain the null hypothesis of no treatment effects.

3) Decision/action: Continue with the standard MANCOVA when there is (a) no evidence of violations of any assumptions or (b) there is evidence of a specific violation but the technique is known to be robust to an existing violation. If the technique is not robust to an existing violation, use an alternative analysis technique.

II. Primary Analysis

A. Test the overall multivariate null hypothesis of no difference in adjusted means for the set of outcomes.

1) Purpose: Provide "protected testing" to help control the inflation of the overall type I error rate.

2) Procedure: Examine the results of the Wilks' lambda test associated with the treatment.

3) Decision/action: If the p-value associated with this test is sufficiently small, continue with further testing as described later. If the p-value is not small, do not continue with any further testing.

B. If the multivariate null hypothesis has been rejected, test for group differences on each dependent variable.

1) Purpose: Describe the adjusted mean outcome differences among the groups for each of the dependent variables.

2) Procedures:

i) Test the overall ANCOVA null hypothesis for each dependent variable using a conventional alpha (e.g., .05) that provides for greater power when the number of outcomes is relatively small (i.e., two or three) or with a Bonferroni adjustment for a larger number of outcomes or whenever there is great concern about committing type I errors.

ii) For each dependent variable for which the overall univariate null hypothesis is rejected, follow up (if more than two groups are present) with tests and interval estimates for all pairwise contrasts using a Bonferroni adjustment for the number of pairwise comparisons.

C. Report and interpret at least one of the following effect size measures.
   1) Purpose: Indicate the strength of the relationship between the dependent variable(s) and the factor (i.e., group membership).
   2) Procedure: Adjusted means and their differences should be reported. Other possibilities include (a) the proportion of generalized total variation explained by group membership for the set of dependent variables (multivariate eta square), (b) the proportion of variation explained by group membership for each dependent variable (univariate eta square), and/or (c) Cohen's d for two-group contrasts.

8.18 EXERCISES

1. Consider the following data from a two-group MANCOVA with two dependent variables (Y1 and Y2) and one covariate (X):

GPID	X	Y1	Y2
1.00	12.00	13.00	3.00
1.00	10.00	6.00	5.00
1.00	11.00	17.00	2.00
1.00	14.00	14.00	8.00
1.00	13.00	12.00	6.00
1.00	10.00	6.00	8.00
1.00	8.00	12.00	3.00
1.00	8.00	6.00	12.00
1.00	12.00	12.00	7.00
1.00	10.00	12.00	8.00
1.00	12.00	13.00	2.00
1.00	7.00	14.00	10.00
1.00	12.00	16.00	1.00
1.00	9.00	9.00	2.00
1.00	12.00	14.00	10.00
2.00	9.00	10.00	6.00
2.00	16.00	16.00	8.00
2.00	11.00	17.00	8.00
2.00	8.00	16.00	21.00
2.00	10.00	14.00	15.00
2.00	7.00	18.00	12.00
2.00	16.00	20.00	7.00
2.00	9.00	12.00	9.00
2.00	10.00	11.00	7.00
2.00	8.00	13.00	4.00
2.00	16.00	19.00	6.00
2.00	12.00	15.00	20.00
2.00	15.00	17.00	7.00
2.00	12.00	21.00	14.00

Run a MANCOVA using SAS or SPSS.

(a) Is MANCOVA appropriate? Explain.

(b) If MANCOVA is appropriate, then are the adjusted mean vectors significantly different at the .05 level?

(c) Are adjusted group mean differences present for both variables?

(d) What are the adjusted means? Which group has better performance?

(e) Compute Cohen's *d* for the two contrasts (which requires a MANOVA to obtain the relevant *MSW* for each outcome).

2. Consider a three-group study (randomized) with 24 participants per group. The correlation between the covariate and the dependent variable is .25, which is statistically significant at the .05 level. Is ANCOVA going to be *very* useful in this study? Explain.

3. Suppose we were comparing two different teaching methods and that the covariate was IQ. The homogeneity of regression slopes is tested and rejected, implying a covariate-by-treatment interaction. Relate this to what we would have found had we blocked (or formed groups) on IQ and ran a factorial ANOVA (IQ by methods) on achievement.

4. In this example, three tasks were employed to ascertain differences between good and poor undergraduate writers on recall and manipulation of information: an ordered letters task, an iconic memory task, and a letter reordering task. In the following table are means and standard deviations for the percentage of correct letters recalled on the three dependent variables. There were 15 participants in each group.

Task	Good writers		Poor writers	
	M	*SD*	*M*	*SD*
Ordered letters	57.79	12.96	49.71	21.79
Iconic memory	49.78	14.59	45.63	13.09
Letter reordering	71.00	4.80	63.18	7.03

Consider this results section:

The data were analyzed via a multivariate analysis of covariance using the background variables (English usage ACT subtest, composite ACT, and grade point average) as covariates, writing ability as the independent variable, and task scores (correct recall in the ordered letters task, correct recall in the iconic memory task, and correct recall in the letter reordering task) as the dependent variables. The global test was significant, $F(3, 23) = 5.43$, $p < .001$. To control for experiment-wise type I error rate at .05, each of the three univariate analyses was conducted at a per comparison rate of .017. No significant difference was observed between groups on the ordered letters task, univariate $F(1, 25) = 1.92$, $p > .10$. Similarly, no significant difference was observed between groups on the iconic memory task, univariate $F < 1$. However, good writers obtained significantly higher scores on the letter reordering task than the poor writers, univariate $F(1, 25) = 15.02$, $p < .001$.

(a) From what was said here, can we be confident that covariance is appropriate here?

(b) The "global" multivariate test referred to is not identified as to whether it is Wilks' Λ, Roy's largest root, and so on. Would it make a difference as to which multivariate test was employed in this case?

(c) The results mention controlling the experiment-wise error rate at .05 by conducting each test at the .017 level of significance. Which *post hoc* procedure is being used here?

(d) Is there a sufficient number of participants for us to have confidence in the reliability of the adjusted means?

5. What is the main reason for using covariance analysis in a randomized study?

REFERENCES

Anderson, N.H. (1963). Comparison of different populations: Resistance to extinction and transfer. *Psychological Bulletin, 70*, 162–179.

Bryant, J.L., & Paulson, A.S. (1976). An extension of Tukey's method of multiple comparisons to experimental design with random concomitant variables. *Biometrika, 63*(3), 631–638.

Bryk, A.D., & Weisberg, H.I. (1977). Use of the nonequivalent control group design when subjects are growing. *Psychological Bulletin, 85*, 950–962.

Cochran, W.G. (1957). Analysis of covariance: Its nature and uses. *Biometrics, 13*, 261–281.

Elashoff, J.D. (1969). Analysis of covariance: A delicate instrument. *American Educational Research Journal, 6*, 383–401.

Finn, J. (1974). *A general model for multivariate analysis*. New York, NY: Holt, Rinehart & Winston.

Hochberg, Y., & Varon-Salomon, Y. (1984). On simultaneous pairwise comparisons in analysis of covariance. *Journal of the American Statistical Association, 79*, 863–866.

Huck, S., Cormier, W., & Bounds, W. (1974). *Reading statistics and research*. New York, NY: Harper & Row.

Huck, S., & McLean, R. (1975). Using a repeated measures ANOVA to analyze the data from a pretest–posttest design: A potentially confusing task. *Psychological Bulletin, 82*, 511–518.

Huitema, B.E. (2011). *The analysis of covariance and alternatives: Statistical methods for experiments* (2nd ed.). Hoboken, NJ: Wiley.

Jennings, E. (1988). Models for pretest-posttest data: Repeated measures ANOVA revisited. *Journal of Educational Statistics, 13*, 273–280.

Lord, F. (1969). Statistical adjustments when comparing pre-existing groups. *Psychological Bulletin, 70*, 162–179.

Maxwell, S., Delaney, H.D., & Manheimer, J. (1985). ANOVA of residuals and ANCOVA: Correcting an illusion by using model comparisons and graphs. *Journal of Educational Statistics, 95*, 136–147.

Novince, L. (1977). *The contribution of cognitive restructuring to the effectiveness of behavior rehearsal in modifying social inhibition in females*. Unpublished doctoral dissertation, University of Cincinnati, OH.

Olejnik, S., & Algina, J. (2000). Measures of effect size for comparative studies: Applications, interpretations, and limitations. *Contemporary Educational Psychology 25*, 241–286.

Pedhazur, E. (1982). *Multiple regression in behavioral research* (2nd ed.). New York, NY: Holt, Rinehart & Winston.

Reichardt, C. (1979). The statistical analysis of data from nonequivalent group designs. In T. Cook & D. Campbell (Eds.), *Quasi-experimentation: Design and analysis issues for field settings* (pp. 147–206). Chicago, IL: Rand McNally.

Rogosa, D. (1977). *Some results for the Johnson-Neyman technique*. Unpublished doctoral dissertation, Stanford University, CA.

Rogosa, D. (1980). Comparing non-parallel regression lines. *Psychological Bulletin, 88*, 307–321.

Thorndike, R., & Hagen, E. (1977). *Measurement and evaluation in psychology and education*. New York, NY: Wiley.

Chapter 9

EXPLORATORY FACTOR ANALYSIS

9.1 INTRODUCTION

Consider the following two common classes of research situations:

1. Exploratory regression analysis: An experimenter has gathered a moderate to large number of predictors (say 15 to 40) to predict some dependent variable.
2. Scale development: An investigator has assembled a set of items (say 20 to 50) designed to measure some construct(s) (e.g., attitude toward education, anxiety, sociability). Here we think of the items as the variables.

In both of these situations the number of simple correlations among the variables is very large, and it is quite difficult to summarize by inspection precisely what the pattern of correlations represents. For example, with 30 items, there are 435 simple correlations. Some way is needed to determine if there is a small number of underlying constructs that might account for the main sources of variation in such a complex set of correlations.

Furthermore, if there are 30 items, we are undoubtedly not measuring 30 different constructs; hence, it makes sense to use a variable reduction procedure that will indicate how the variables cluster or hang together. Now, if sample size is not large enough (how large N needs to be is discussed in section 9.6), then we need to resort to a logical clustering (grouping) based on theoretical or substantive grounds. On the other hand, with adequate sample size an empirical approach is preferable. Two basic empirical approaches are (1) principal components analysis for variable reduction, and (2) factor analysis for identifying underlying factors or constructs. In both approaches, the basic idea is to find a smaller number of entities (components or factors) that account for most of the variation or the pattern of correlations. In factor analysis a mathematical model is set up and factor scores may be estimated, whereas in components analysis we are simply transforming the original variables into a new set of linear combinations (the principal components).

In this edition of the text, we focus this chapter on exploratory factor analysis (not principal components analysis) because researchers in psychology, education, and the social sciences in general are much more likely to use exploratory factor analysis, particularly as it used to develop and help validate measuring instruments. We do, though, begin the chapter with the principal components method. This method has been commonly used to extract factors in factor analysis (and remains the default method in SPSS and SAS). Even when different extraction methods, such as principal axis factoring, are used in factor analysis, the principal components method is often used in the initial stages of exploratory factor analysis. Thus, having an initial exposure to principal components will allow you to make an easy transition to principal axis factoring, which is presented later in the chapter, and will also allow you to readily see some underlying differences between these two procedures. Note that confirmatory factor analysis, covered in this chapter in previous editions of the text, is now covered in Chapter 16.

9.2 THE PRINCIPAL COMPONENTS METHOD

If we have a single group of participants measured on a set of variables, then principal components partitions the total variance (i.e., the sum of the variances for the original variables) by first finding the linear combination of the variables that accounts for the maximum amount of variance:

$$y_1 = a_{11}x_1 + a_{12}x_2 + \cdots + a_{1p}x_p,$$

where y_1 is called the first principal component, and if the coefficients are scaled such that $\mathbf{a}_1'\mathbf{a}_1 = 1$ [where $\mathbf{a}_1' = (a_{11}, a_{12}, \ldots, a_{1p})$] then the variance of y_1 is equal to the *largest* eigenvalue of the sample covariance matrix (Morrison, 1967, p. 224). The coefficients of the principal component are the elements of the eigenvector corresponding to the largest eigenvalue.

Then the procedure finds a second linear combination, *uncorrelated* with the first component, such that it accounts for the next largest amount of variance (after the variance attributable to the first component has been removed) in the system. This second component, y_2, is

$$y_2 = a_{21}x_1 + a_{22}x_2 + \cdots + a_{2p}x_p,$$

and the coefficients are scaled so that $\mathbf{a}_2'\mathbf{a}_2 = 1$, as for the first component. The fact that the two components are constructed to be uncorrelated means that the Pearson correlation between y_1 and y_2 is 0. The coefficients of the second component are the elements of the eigenvector associated with the second largest eigenvalue of the covariance matrix, and the sample variance of y_2 is equal to the second largest eigenvalue.

The third principal component is constructed to be uncorrelated with the first two, and accounts for the third largest amount of variance in the system, and so on. The principal components method is therefore still another example of a mathematical maximization procedure, where each successive component accounts for the maximum amount of the variance in the original variables that is left.

Thus, through the use of principal components, a set of correlated variables is transformed into a set of uncorrelated variables (the components). The goal of such an analysis is to obtain a relatively small number of components that account for a significant proportion of variance in the original set of variables. When this method is used to extract factors in factor analysis, you may also wish to make sense of or interpret the factors.

The factors are interpreted by using coefficients that describe the association between a given factor and observed variable (called *factor or component loadings*) that are sufficiently large in absolute magnitude. For example, if the first factor loaded high and positive on variables 1, 3, 5, and 6, then we could interpret that factor by attempting to determine what those four variables have in common. *The analysis procedure has empirically clustered the four variables, and the psychologist may then wish to give a name to the factor to make sense of the composite variable.*

In the preceding example we assumed that the loadings were all in the same direction (all positive for a given component). Of course, it is possible to have a mixture of high positive and negative loadings on a particular component. In this case we have what is called a *bipolar* component. For example, in factor analyses of IQ tests, the second factor may be bipolar contrasting verbal abilities against spatial-perceptual abilities.

Social science researchers often extract factors from a correlation matrix. The reason for this standardization is that scales for tests used in educational, sociological, and psychological research are usually arbitrary. If, however, the scales are reasonably commensurable, performing a factor analysis on the *covariance* matrix is preferable for statistical reasons (Morrison, 1967, p. 222). The components obtained from the correlation and covariance matrices are, in general, *not* the same. The option of doing factor analysis on either the correlation or covariance matrix is available on SAS and SPSS. Note though that it is common practice to conduct factor analysis using a correlation matrix, which software programs will compute behind the scenes from raw data prior to conducting the analysis.

A precaution that researchers contemplating a factor analysis with a small sample size (certainly any N less than 100) should take, especially if most of the elements in the sample correlation matrix are small ($< |.30|$), is to apply Bartlett's sphericity test (Cooley & Lohnes, 1971, p. 103). This procedure tests the null hypothesis that the variables in the *population* correlation matrix are uncorrelated. If one fails to reject with this test, then there is no reason to do the factor analysis because we cannot conclude that the variables are correlated. Logically speaking, if observed variables do not "hang together," an analysis that attempts to cluster variables based on their associations does not make sense. The sphericity test is available on both the SAS and SPSS packages.

Also, when using principal components extraction in factor analysis, the composite variables are sometimes referred to as components. However, since we are using principal components simply as a factor extraction method, we will refer to the entities obtained as factors. Note that when principal axis factoring is used, as it is later in the chapter, the entities extracted in that procedure are, by convention, referred to as factors.

9.3 CRITERIA FOR DETERMINING HOW MANY FACTORS TO RETAIN USING PRINCIPAL COMPONENTS EXTRACTION

Perhaps the most difficult decision in factor analysis is to determine the number of factors that should be retained. When the principal components method is used to extract factors, several methods can be used to decide how many factors to retain.

1. A widely used criterion is that of Kaiser (1960): Retain only those factors having eigenvalues are greater than 1. Although using this rule generally will result in retention of only the most important factors, blind use could lead to retaining factors that may have no practical importance (in terms of percent of variance accounted for).

    Studies by Cattell and Jaspers (1967), Browne (1968), and Linn (1968) evaluated the accuracy of the eigenvalue > 1 criterion. In all three studies, the authors determined how often the criterion would identify the correct number of factors from matrices with a known number of factors. The number of variables in the studies ranged from 10 to 40. Generally, the criterion was accurate to fairly accurate, with gross overestimation occurring only with a large number of variables (40) *and* low communalities (around .40). Note that the communality of a variable is the amount of variance for a variable accounted for by the set of factors. The criterion is more accurate when the number of variables is small (10 to 15) or moderate (20 to 30) and the communalities are high (> .70). Subsequent studies (e.g., Zwick & Velicer, 1982, 1986) have shown that while use of this rule can lead to uncovering too many factors, it may also lead to identifying too few factors.

2. A graphical method called the *scree test* has been proposed by Cattell (1966). In this method the magnitude of the eigenvalues (vertical axis) is plotted against their ordinal numbers (whether it was the first eigenvalue, the second, etc.). Generally what happens is that the magnitude of successive eigenvalues drops off sharply (steep descent) and then tends to level off. The recommendation is to retain all eigenvalues (and hence factors) in the sharp descent *before* the first one on the line where they start to level off. This method will generally retain factors that account for large or fairly large and distinct amounts of variances (e.g., 31%, 20%, 13%, and 9%). However, blind use might lead to not retaining factors that, although they account for a smaller amount of variance, might be meaningful. Several studies (Cattell & Jaspers, 1967; Hakstian, Rogers, & Cattell, 1982; Tucker, Koopman, & Linn, 1969) support the general accuracy of the scree procedure. Hakstian et al. note that for $N > 250$ and a mean communality $> .60$, either the Kaiser or scree

rules will yield an accurate estimate for the number of true factors. They add that such an estimate will be just that much more credible if the Q/P ratio is < .30 (P is the number of variables and Q is the number of factors). With mean communality .30 or $Q/P > .3$, the Kaiser rule is less accurate and the scree rule much less accurate. A primary concern associated with the use of the scree plot is that it requires subjective judgment in determining the number of factors present, unlike the numerical criterion provided by Kaiser's rule and parallel analysis, discussed next.

3. A procedure that is becoming more widely used is parallel analysis (Horn, 1965), where a "parallel" set of eigenvalues is created from random data and compared to eigenvalues from the original data set. Specifically, a random data set having the same number of cases and variables is generated by computer. Then, factor analysis is applied to these data and eigenvalues are obtained. This process of generating random data and factor analyzing them is repeated many times. Traditionally, you then compare the average of the "random" eigenvalues (for a given factor across these replicated data sets) to the eigenvalue obtained from the original data set for the corresponding factor. The rule for retaining factors is to retain a factor in the original data set only if its eigenvalue is greater than the average eigenvalue for its random counterpart. Alternatively, instead of using the average of the eigenvalues for a given factor, the 95th percentile of these replicated values can be used as the comparison value, which provides a somewhat more stringent test of factor importance.

    Fabrigar and Wegener (2012, p. 60) note that while the performance of parallel process analysis has not been investigated exhaustively, studies to date have shown it to perform fairly well in detecting the proper number of factors, although the procedure may suggest the presence of too many factors at times. Nevertheless, given that none of these methods performs perfectly under all conditions, the use of parallel process analysis has been widely recommended for factor analysis. While not available at present in SAS or SPSS, parallel analysis can be implemented using syntax available at the website of the publisher of Fabrigar and Wegener's text. We illustrate the use of this procedure in section 9.12.

4. There is a statistical significance test for the number of factors to retain that was developed by Lawley (1940). However, as with all statistical tests, it is influenced by sample size, and large sample size may lead to the retention of too many factors.

5. Retain as many factors as will account for a specified amount of total variance. Generally, one would want to account for a large proportion of the total variance. In some cases, the investigator may not be satisfied unless 80–85% of the variance is accounted for. Extracting factors using this method, though, may lead to the retention of factors that are essentially variable specific, that is, load highly on only a single variable, which is not desirable in factor analysis. Note also that in some applications, the actual amount of variance accounted for by meaningful factors may be 50% or lower.

6. Factor meaningfulness is an important consideration in deciding on the number of factors that should be retained in the model. The other criteria are generally mathematical, and their use may not always yield meaningful or interpretable factors. In exploratory factor analysis, your knowledge of the research area plays an important role in interpreting factors and deciding if a factor solution is worthwhile. Also, it is

not uncommon that use of the different methods shown will suggest different numbers of factors present. In this case, the meaningfulness of different factor solutions takes precedence in deciding among solutions with empirical support.

So what criterion should be used in deciding how many factors to retain? Since the methods look at the issue from different perspectives and have certain strengths and limitations, multiple criteria should be used. *Since the Kaiser criterion has been shown to be reasonably accurate when the number of variables is < 30 and the communalities are > .70, or when* N *> 250 and the mean communality is > .60, we would use it under these circumstances.* For other situations, use of the scree test with an *N* > 200 will probably not lead us too far astray, provided that most of the communalities are reasonably large. We also recommend general use of parallel analysis as it has performed well in simulation studies. Note that these methods can be relied upon to a lesser extent when researchers have some sense of the number of factors that may be present. In addition, when the methods conflict in the number of factors that should be retained, you can conduct multiple factor analyses directing your software program to retain different numbers of factors. Given that the goal is to arrive at a coherent final model, the solution that seems most interpretable (most meaningful) can be reported.

9.4 INCREASING INTERPRETABILITY OF FACTORS BY ROTATION

Although a few factors may, as desired, account for most of the variance in a large set of variables, often the factors are not easily interpretable. The factors are derived not to provide interpretability but to maximize variance accounted for. Transformation of the factors, typically referred to as rotation, often provides for much improved interpretability. Also, as noted by Fabrigar and Wegener (2012, p. 79), it is important to know that rotation does not change key statistics associated with model fit, including (1) the total amount (and proportion) of variance explained by all factors and (2) the values of the communalities. In other words, unrotated and rotated factor solutions have the same mathematical fit to the data, regardless of rotation method used. As such, it makes sense to use analysis results based on those factor loadings that facilitate factor interpretation.

Two major classes of rotations are available:

1. Orthogonal (rigid) rotations—Here the new factors obtained by rotation are still uncorrelated, as were the initially obtained factors.
2. Oblique rotations—Here the new factors are allowed to be correlated.

9.4.1 Orthogonal Rotations

We discuss two such rotations:

1. Quartimax—Here the idea is to clean up the variables. That is, the rotation is done so that each variable loads mainly on one factor. Then that variable can be

considered to be a relatively pure measure of the factor. The problem with this approach is that most of the variables tend to load on a single factor (producing the "g factor" in analyses of IQ tests), making interpretation of the factor difficult.

2. Varimax—Kaiser (1960) took a different tack. He designed a rotation to clean up the factors. That is, with his rotation, each factor has high correlations with a smaller number of variables and low or very low correlations with the other variables. This will generally make interpretation of the resulting factors easier. The varimax rotation is available in SPSS and SAS.

It should be mentioned that when rotation is done, the *maximum variance property* of the originally obtained factors is destroyed. The rotation essentially reallocates the loadings. Thus, the first rotated factor will no longer *necessarily* account for the maximum amount of variance. The amount of variance accounted for by each rotated factor has to be recalculated.

9.4.2 Oblique Rotations

Numerous oblique rotations have been proposed: for example, oblimax, quartimin, maxplane, orthoblique (Harris–Kaiser), promax, and oblimin. Promax and oblimin are available on SPSS and SAS.

Many have argued that correlated factors are much more reasonable to assume in most cases (Cliff, 1987; Fabrigar & Wegener, 2012; Pedhazur & Schmelkin, 1991; Preacher & MacCallum, 2003), and therefore oblique rotations are generally preferred. The following from Pedhazur and Schmelkin (1991) is interesting:

> From the perspective of construct validation, the decision whether to rotate factors orthogonally or obliquely reflects one's conception regarding the structure of the construct under consideration. It boils down to the question: Are aspects of a postulated multidimensional construct intercorrelated? The answer to this question is relegated to the status of an assumption when an orthogonal rotation is employed. . . . The preferred course of action is, in our opinion, to rotate both orthogonally and obliquely. When, on the basis of the latter, it is concluded that the correlations among the factors are negligible, the interpretation of the simpler orthogonal solution becomes tenable. (p. 615)

You should know, though, that when using an oblique solution, interpretation of the factors becomes somewhat more complicated, as the associations between variables and factors are provided in two matrices:

1. Factor pattern matrix—The elements here, called pattern coefficients, are analogous to standardized partial regression coefficients from a multiple regression analysis. From a factor analysis perspective, a given coefficient indicates the unique importance of a factor to a variable, holding constant the other factors in the model.
2. Factor structure matrix—The elements here, known as structure coefficients, are the simple correlations of the variables with the factors.

For orthogonal rotations or completely orthogonal factors these two matrices are identical.

9.5 WHAT COEFFICIENTS SHOULD BE USED FOR INTERPRETATION?

Two issues arise in deciding which coefficients are to be used to interpret factors. The first issue has to do with the type of rotation used: orthogonal or oblique. When an orthogonal rotation is used, interpretations are based on the structure coefficients (as the structure and pattern coefficients are identical). When using an oblique rotation, as mentioned, two sets of coefficients are obtained. While it is reasonable to examine structure coefficients, Fabrigar and Wegener (2012) argue that using pattern coefficients is more consistent with the use of oblique rotation because the pattern coefficients take into account the correlation between factors *and* are parameters of a correlated-factor model, whereas the structure coefficients are not. As such, they state that focusing exclusively on the structure coefficients in the presence of an oblique rotation is "inherently inconsistent with the primary goals of oblique rotation" (p. 81).

Given that we have selected the type of coefficient (structure or pattern), the second issue pertains to which observed variables should be used to interpret a given factor. While there is no universal standard available to make this decision, the idea is to use only those variables that have a strong association with the factor. A threshold value that can be used for a structure or pattern coefficient is one that is equal to or greater than a magnitude of .40. For structure coefficients, using a value of |.40| would imply that an observed variable shares more than 15% of its variance ($.4^2 = .16$) with the factor that it is going to be used to help name. Other threshold values that are used are .32 (because it corresponds to approximately 10% variance explained) and .50, which is a stricter standard corresponding to 25% variance explained. This more stringent value seems sensible to use when sample size is relatively small and may also be used if it improves factor interpretability. For pattern coefficients, although a given coefficient cannot be squared to obtain the proportion of shared variance between an observed variable and factor, these different threshold values are generally considered to represent a reasonably strong association for standardized partial regression coefficients in general (e.g., Kline, 2005, p. 122). To interpret what the variables with high loadings have in common, that is, to name the component, a researcher with expertise in the content area is typically needed.

Also, we should point out that standard errors associated with factor loadings are not available for some commonly used factor analysis methods, including principal component and principal axis factoring. As such, statistical tests for the loadings are not available with these methods. One exception involves the use of maximum likelihood estimation to extract factors. This method, however, assumes the observed variables follow a multivariate normal distribution in the population and would require a user to rely on the procedure to be robust to this violation. We do not cover maximum likelihood factor extraction in this chapter, but interested readers can consult Fabrigar and Wegener (2012), who recommend use of this procedure.

9.6 SAMPLE SIZE AND RELIABLE FACTORS

Various rules have been suggested in terms of the sample size required for reliable factors. Many of the popular rules suggest that sample size be determined as a function of the number of variables being analyzed, ranging anywhere from two participants per variable to 20 participants per variable. And indeed, in a previous edition of this text, five participants per variable as the minimum needed were suggested. However, a Monte Carlo study by Guadagnoli and Velicer (1988) indicated, contrary to the popular rules, that the most important factors are factor saturation (the absolute magnitude of the loadings) and absolute sample size. Also, the number of variables per factor is somewhat important. Subsequent research (MacCallum, Widaman, Zhang, & Hong, 1999; MacCallum, Widaman, Preacher, & Hong, 2001; Velicer & Fava, 1998) has highlighted the importance of communalities along with the number and size of loadings.

Fabrigar and Wegener (2012) discuss this research and minimal sample size requirements as related to communalities and the number of strong factor loadings. We summarize the minimal sample size requirements they suggest as follows:

1. When the average communality is .70 or greater, good estimates can be obtained with sample sizes as low as 100 (and possibly lower) provided that there are at least three substantial loadings per factor.
2. When communalities range from .40 to .70 and there are at least three strong loadings per factor, good estimates may be obtained with a sample size of about 200.
3. When communalities are small (< .40) and when there are only two substantial loadings on some factors, sample sizes of 400 or greater may be needed.

These suggestions are useful in establishing at least some empirical basis, rather than a seat-of-the-pants judgment, for assessing what factors we can have confidence in. Note though that they cover only a certain set of situations, and it may be difficult in the planning stages of a study to have a good idea of what communalities and loadings may actually be obtained. If that is the case, Fabrigar and Wegener (2012) suggest planning on "moderate" conditions to hold in your study, as described by the earlier second point, which implies a minimal sample size of 200.

9.7 SOME SIMPLE FACTOR ANALYSES USING PRINCIPAL COMPONENTS EXTRACTION

We provide a simple hypothetical factor analysis example with a small number of observed variables (items) to help you get a better handle on the basics of factor analysis. We use a small number of variables in this section to enable better understanding of key concepts. Section 9.12 provides an example using real data where a larger number of observed variables are involved. That section also includes extraction of factors with principal axis factoring.

For the example in this section, we assume investigators are developing a scale to measure the construct of meaningful professional work, have written six items related to meaningful professional work, and would like to identify the number of constructs underlying these items. Further, we suppose that the researchers have carefully reviewed relevant literature and have decided that the concept of meaningful professional work involves two interrelated constructs: work that one personally finds engaging and work that one feels is valued by one's workplace. As such, they have written three items intended to reflect engagement with work and another three items designed to reflect the idea of feeling valued in the workplace. The engagement items, we suppose, ask workers to indicate the degree to which they find work stimulating (item 1), challenging (item 2), and interesting (item 3). The "feeling valued" concept is thought to be adequately indicated by responses to items asking workers to indicate the degree to which they feel recognized for effort (item 4), appreciated for good work (item 5), and fairly compensated (item 6). Responses to these six items—stimulate, challenge, interest, recognize, appreciate, and compensate—have been collected, we suppose from a sample of 300 employees who each provided responses for all six items. Also, higher scores for each item reflect greater properties of the attribute being measured (e.g., more stimulating, more challenging work, and so on).

9.7.1 Principal Component Extraction With Three Items

For instructional purposes, we initially use responses from just three items: stimulate, challenge, and interest. The correlations between these items are shown in Table 9.1. Note each correlation is positive and indicates a fairly strong relationship between variables. Thus, the items seem to share something in common, lending support for a factor analysis.

In conducting this analysis, the researchers wish to answer the following research questions:

1. How many factors account for meaningful variation in the item scores?
2. Which items are strongly related to any resultant factors?
3. What is the meaning of any resultant factor(s)?

To address the first research question about the number of factors that are present, we apply multiple criteria including, for the time being, inspecting eigenvalues, examining a scree plot, and considering the meaningfulness of any obtained factors. Note that we add to this list the use of parallel analysis in section 9.12. An eigenvalue indicates the strength of relationship between a given factor and the set of observed variables. As we know, the strength of relationship between two variables is often summarized by a correlation coefficient, with values larger in magnitude reflecting a stronger association.

■ **Table 9.1: Bivariate Correlations for Three Work-Related Items**

Correlation matrix

	1	2	3
Stimulate	1.000	.659	.596
Challenge	.659	1.000	.628
Interest	.596	.628	1.000

Another way to describe the strength of association between two variables is to square the value of the correlation coefficient. When the correlation is squared, this measure may be interpreted as the proportion of variance in one variable that is explained by another. For example, if the correlation between a factor and an observed variable is .5, the proportion of variance in the variable that is explained by the factor is .25. In factor analysis, we are looking for factors that are not just associated with one variable but are strongly related to, or explain the variance of, a set of variables (here, items). With principal components extraction, an eigenvalue is the *amount* of variance in the set of observed variables that is explained by a given factor and is also the variance of the factor. As you will see, this amount of variance can be converted to a proportion of explained variance. In brief, larger eigenvalues for a factor means that it explains more variance in the set of variables and is indicative of important factors.

Table 9.2 shows selected summary results using principal components extraction with the three work-related items. In the Component column of the first table, note that three factors (equal to the number of variables) are formed in the initial solution. In the Total column, the eigenvalue for the first factor is 2.256, which represents the total amount of variance in the three items that is explained by this factor. Recall that the total maximum variance in a set of variables is equal to the number of variables. So, the total amount of variance that could have been explained is three. Therefore, the *proportion* of the total variance that is accounted for by the first factor is 2.256 / 3, which is about .75 or 75%, and is shown in the third (and fourth column) for the initial solution. The remaining factors have eigenvalues well below 1, and using Kaiser's rule would not be considered as important in explaining the remaining item variance. Therefore, applying Kaiser's rule suggests that one factor explains important variation in the set of items.

Further, examining the scree plot shown in Table 9.2 provides support for the single-factor solution. Recall that the scree plot displays the eigenvalues as a function of the factor number. Notice that the plot levels off or is horizontal at factor two. Since the procedure is to retain only those factors that appear *before* the leveling off occurs, only one factor is to be retained for this solution. Thus, applying Kaiser's rule and inspecting the scree plot provides empirical support for a single-factor solution.

To address the second research question—which items are related to the factor—we examine the factor loadings. When one factor has been extracted (as in this example), a factor loading is the correlation between a given factor and variable (also called a structure coefficient). Here, in determining if a given item is related to the factor, we use a loading of .40 in magnitude or greater. The loadings for each item are displayed in the component matrix of Table 9.2, with each loading exceeding .80. Thus, each item is related to the single factor and should be used for interpretation.

Now that we have determined that each item is important in defining the factor, we can attempt to label the factor to address the final research question. Generally, since the factor loadings are all positive, we can say that employees with high scores on the factor also have high scores on stimulate, challenge, and interest (with an analogous statement holding for low scores on the factor). Of course, in this example,

■ Table 9.2: Selected Results Using Principal Components Extraction for Three Items

Total variance explained

Component	Initial eigenvalues			Extraction sums of squared loadings		
	Total	% of Variance	Cumulative %	Total	% of Variance	Cumulative %
1	2.256	75.189	75.189	2.256	75.189	75.189
2	.409	13.618	88.807			
3	.336	11.193	100.000			

Extraction Method: Principal Component Analysis.

Component matrix[a]

	Component
	1
Stimulate	.867
Challenge	.881
Interest	.852

Extraction Method: Principal Component Analysis.

Scree Plot

the researchers have deliberately constructed the items so that they reflect the idea of engaging professional work. This analysis, then, provides empirical support for referring to this construct as engagement with work.

9.7.2 A Two-Factor Orthogonal Model Using Principal Components Extraction

A second illustrative factor analysis using principal components extraction includes all six work-related variables and will produce uncorrelated factors (due to an orthogonal rotation selected). The reason we will present an analysis that constrains the factors to be uncorrelated is that it is sometimes used in factor analysis. In section 9.7.4, we present an analysis that allows the factors to be correlated. We will also examine how the results of the orthogonal and oblique factor solutions differ.

For this example, factor analysis with principal components extraction is used to address the following research questions:

1. How many factors account for substantial variation in the set of items?
2. Is each item strongly related to factors that are obtained?
3. What is the meaning of any resultant factor(s)?

When the number of observed variables is fairly small and/or the pattern of their correlations is revealing, inspecting the bivariate correlations may provide an initial indication of the number of factors that are present. Table 9.3 shows the correlations among the six items. Note that the first three items are strongly correlated with each other and last three items are strongly correlated with each other. However, the correlations between these two apparent sets of items are, perhaps, only moderately correlated. Thus, this "eyeball" analysis suggests that two distinct factors are associated with the six items.

Selected results of a factor analysis using principal components extraction for these data are shown in Table 9.4. Inspecting the initial eigenvalues suggests, applying Kaiser's rule, that two factors are related to the set of items, as the eigenvalues for the first two factors are greater than 1. In addition, the scree plot provides additional support for the two-factor solution, as the plot levels off after the second factor. Note that the two factors account for 76% of the variance in the six items.

■ Table 9.3: Bivariate Correlations for Six Work-Related Items

Variable	1	2	3	4	5	6
Stimulate	1.000	–	–	–	–	–
Challenge	.659	1.000	–	–	–	–
Interest	.596	.628	1.000	–	–	–
Recognize	.177	.111	.107	1.000	–	–
Appreciate	.112	.109	.116	.701	1.000	–
Compensate	.140	.104	.096	.619	.673	1.000

Table 9.4: Selected Results from a Principal Components Extraction Using an Orthogonal Rotation

Total variance explained

Component	Initial eigenvalues			Extraction sums of squared loadings			Rotation sums of squared loadings		
	Total	% of Variance	Cumulative %	Total	% of Variance	Cumulative %	Total	% of Variance	Cumulative %
1	2.652	44.205	44.205	2.652	44.205	44.205	2.330	38.838	38.838
2	1.934	32.239	76.445	1.934	32.239	76.445	2.256	37.607	76.445
3	.417	6.954	83.398						
4	.384	6.408	89.806						
5	.341	5.683	95.489						
6	.271	4.511	100.000						

Extraction Method: Principal Component Analysis.

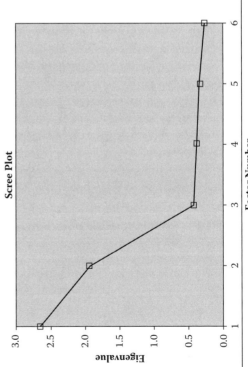

Scree Plot

Component matrix[a]

	Component	
	1	2
Stimulate	.651	.572
Challenge	.628	.619
Interest	.609	.598
Recognize	.706	−.521
Appreciate	.706	−.559
Compensate	.682	−.532

Extraction Method: Principal Component Analysis.

[a] 2 components extracted.

Rotated component matrix[a]

	Component	
	1	2
Stimulate	.100	.861
Challenge	.052	.880
Interest	.052	.851
Recognize	.874	.086
Appreciate	.899	.058
Compensate	.863	.062

Extraction Method: Principal Component Analysis.

Rotation Method: Varimax with Kaiser Normalization.

[a] Rotation converged in 3 iterations.

With a multifactor solution, factor interpretability is often more readily accomplished with factor rotation. This analysis was conducted with varimax rotation, an orthogonal rotation that assumes factors are uncorrelated (and keeps them that way). When factors are extracted and rotated, the variance accounted for by a given factor is referred to as the sum of squared loadings. These sums, following rotation, are shown in Table 9.4, under the heading Rotation Sums of Squared Loadings. Note that the sums of squared loadings for each factor are more alike following rotation. Also, while the sums of squared loadings (after rotation) are numerically different from the original eigenvalues, the *total* amount and percent of variance accounted for by the set of factors is the same pre- and post-rotation. Note in this example that after rotation, each factor accounts for about the same percent of item variance (e.g., 39%, 38%). Note, then, that if you want to compare the relative importance of the factors, it makes more sense to use the sum of squared loadings following rotation, because the factor extraction procedure is designed to yield initial (unrotated) factors that have descending values for the amount of variance explained (i.e., the first factor will have the largest eigenvalue and so on).

Further, following rotation, the factor loadings will generally be quite different from the unrotated loadings. The unrotated factor loadings (corresponding to the initially extracted factors) are shown in the component matrix in Table 9.4. Note that these structure coefficients are difficult to interpret as the loadings for the first factor are all positive and fairly strong whereas the loadings for the second factor are positive and negative. This pattern is fairly common in multifactor solutions.

A much more interpretable solution, consistent in this case with the item correlations, is achieved after factor rotation. The Rotated Component Matrix displays the rotated loadings, and with an orthogonal rotation, the loadings still represent the correlation between a component and given item. Thus, using the criteria in the previous section (loadings greater than .40 represent a strong association), we see that the variables stimulate, challenge, and interest load highly only on factor two and that variables recognize, appreciate, and compensate load highly only on the other factor. As such, it is clear that factor two represents the engagement factor, as labeled previously. Factor one is composed of items where high scores on the factor, given the positive load-ings on the important items, are indicative of employees who have high scores on the items recognize, appreciate, and compensate. Therefore, there is empirical support for believing that these items tap the degree to which employees feel valued at the work-place. Thus, answering the research questions posed at the beginning of this section, two factors (an engagement and a valued factor) are strongly related to the set of items, and each item is related to only one of the factors.

Note also that the values of the structure coefficients in the Rotated Component Matrix of Table 9.4 are characteristic of a specific form of what is called simple structure. Simple structure is characterized by (1) each observed variable having high loadings on only some components and (2) each component having multiple high loadings and the rest of the loadings near zero. Thus, in a multifactor model each factor is defined by a subset of variables, and each observed variable is related to at least one factor. With these data, using rotation achieves a very interpretable pattern where each item loads on only one factor. Note that while this is often desired because it eases interpretation, simple structure does not require that a given variable load on only one factor. For example, consider a math problem-solving item on a standardized test. Performance on such an item may be related to examinee reading and math ability. Such cross-loading associations may be expected in a factor analysis and may represent a reasonable and interpretable finding. Often, though, in instrument development, such items are considered to be undesirable and removed from the measuring instrument.

9.7.3 Calculating the Sum of the Squared Loadings and Communalities From Factor Loadings

Before we consider results from the use of an oblique rotation, we show how the sum of squared loadings and communalities can be calculated given the item-factor correlations. The sum of squared loadings can be computed by squaring the item-factor correlations for a given factor and summing these squared values for that factor (column). Table 9.5 shows the rotated loadings from the two-factor solution with an orthogonal (varimax) rotation from the previous section with the squares to be taken for each value. As shown in the bottom of the factor column, this value is the sum of squared loadings for the factor and represents the amount of variance explained by a factor for the set of items. As such, it is an aggregate measure of the strength of association between a given factor and set of observed variables. Here it is useful to think of a given factor as an independent variable explaining variation in a set of responses. Thus, a low value for the sum of squared loadings suggests that a factor is not strongly related to the set of observed variables. Recall that such factors (factors 3–6) have already been removed from this analysis because their eigenvalues were each smaller than 1.

The communalities, on the other hand, as shown in Table 9.5, are computed by summing the squared loadings *across* each of the factors for a given observed variable and represent the proportion of variance in a variable that is due to the factors. Thus,

■ **Table 9.5: Variance Calculations from the Two-Factor Orthogonal Model**

Items	Value factor	Engagement factor	Sum across the row	Communality
Stimulate	$.100^2$	$.861^2$	$.100^2 + .861^2$	$= .75$
Challenge	$.052^2$	$.880^2$	$.052^2 + .880^2$	$= .78$
Interest	$.052^2$	$.851^2$	$.052^2 + .851^2$	$= .73$
Recognize	$.874^2$	$.086^2$	$.874^2 + .086^2$	$= .77$
Appreciate	$.899^2$	$.058^2$	$.899^2 + .058^2$	$= .81$
Compensate	$.863^2$	$.062^2$	$.863^2 + .062^2$	$= .75$
Sum down the column	$.100^2 + .052^2 + .052^2 + .874^2 + .899^2 + .863^2$	$.861^2 + .880^2 + .851^2 + .086^2 + .058^2 + .062^2$		
Amount of variance (sum of squared loadings)	$= 2.33$	$= 2.25$		

a communality is an aggregate measure of the strength of association between a given variable and a set of factors. Here, it is useful to think of a given observed variable as a dependent variable and the factors as independent variables, with the communality representing the r-square (or squared multiple correlation) from a regression equation with the factors as predictors. Thus, a low communality value suggests that an observed variable is not related to any of the factors. Here, all variables are strongly related to the factors, as the factors account for (minimally) 73% of the variance in the Interest variable and up to 81% of the variance in the Appreciate variable.

Variables with low communalities would likely not be related to any factor (which would also then be evident in the loading matrix), and on that basis would not be used to interpret a factor. In instrument development, such items would likely be dropped from the instrument and/or undergo subsequent revision. Note also that communalities do not change with rotation, that is, these values are the same pre- and post-rotation. Thus, while rotation changes the values of factor loadings (to improve interpretability) and the amount of variance that is due to a given factor, rotation does not change the values of the communalities and the *total* amount of variance explained by both factors.

9.7.4 A Two-Factor Correlated Model Using Principal Components Extraction

The final illustrative analysis we consider with the work-related variables presents results for a two-factor model that allows factors to be correlated. By using a varimax rotation, as we did in section 9.7.2, the factors were constrained to be completely uncorrelated. However, assuming the labels we have given to the factors (engagement and feeling valued in the workplace) are reasonable, you might believe that these factors are positively related. If you wish to estimate the correlation among factors, an oblique type of rotation must be used. Note that using an oblique rotation does not force the factors to be correlated but rather allows this correlation to be nonzero. The oblique rotation used here is direct quartimin, which is also known as direct oblimin when the parameter that controls the degree of correlation (called delta or tau) is at its recommended default value of zero. This oblique rotation method is commonly used. For this example, the same three research questions that appeared in section 9.7.2 are of interest, but we are now interested in an additional research question: What is the direction and magnitude of the factor correlation?

Selected analysis results for these data are shown in Table 9.6. As in section 9.7.2, examining the initial eigenvalues suggests, applying Kaiser's rule, that two factors are strongly related to the set of items, and inspecting the scree plot provides support for this solution. Note though the values in Table 9.6 under the headings Initial Eigenvalues and Extraction Sums of Squared Loadings are *identical* to those provided in Table 9.4 even though we have requested an oblique rotation. The reason for these identical results is that the values shown under these headings are from a model where the factors have not been rotated. Thus, using various rotation methods does not affect the eigenvalues that are used to determine the number of important factors present in the data. After the factors have been rotated, the sums of squared loadings associated with each factor are located under the heading Rotation Sums of Squared Loadings. Like the loadings for the orthogonal solution, these sums of squared loadings are more similar for the two factors than before rotation. However, unlike the values for the orthogonal rotation, these post-rotation values cannot be meaningfully summed to provide a total amount of variance explained by the two factors, as such total variance obtained by this sum would now include the overlapping (shared) variance between factors. (Note that the total amount of variance explained by the two factors remains $2.652 + 1.934 = 4.586$.) The post-rotation sum of squared loadings can be used, though,

■ **Table 9.6: Selected Analysis Results Using Oblique Rotation and Principal Components Extraction**

Total variance explained

Component	Initial eigenvalues			Extraction sums of squared loadings			Rotation sums of squared loadings[a]
	Total	% of Variance	Cumulative %	Total	% of Variance	Cumulative %	Total
1	2.652	44.205	44.205	2.652	44.205	44.205	2.385
2	1.934	32.239	76.445	1.934	32.239	76.445	2.312
3	.417	6.954	83.398				
4	.384	6.408	89.806				
5	.341	5.683	95.489				
6	.271	4.511	100.000				

Extraction Method: Principal Component Analysis.

[a] When components are correlated, sums of squared loadings cannot be added to obtain a total variance.

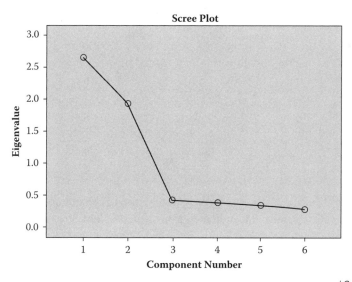

Scree Plot

(Eigenvalue vs. Component Number)

(Continued)

■ **Table 9.6: (Continued)**

Pattern matrix			Structure matrix		
	Component			Component	
	1	2		1	2
Stimulate	.033	.861	Stimulate	.167	.867
Challenge	−.017	.884	Challenge	.120	.882
Interest	−.015	.855	Interest	.118	.853
Recognize	.875	.018	Recognize	.878	.154
Appreciate	.902	−.012	Appreciate	.900	.128
Compensate	.866	−.005	Compensate	.865	.129

Extraction Method: Principal Component Analysis. Rotation Method: Oblimin with Kaiser Normalization.

Extraction Method: Principal Component Analysis. Rotation Method: Oblimin with Kaiser Normalization.

Component correlation matrix		
Component	1	2
1	1.000	.155
2	.155	1.000

to make a rough comparison of the relative importance of each factor. Here, given that three items load on each factor, and that the each factor has similarly large and similarly small loadings, each factor is about the same in importance.

As noted in section 9.4.2, with an oblique rotation, two types of matrices are provided. Table 9.6 shows the pattern matrix, containing values analogous to standardized partial regression coefficients, and the structure matrix, containing the correlation between the factors and each observed variable. As noted, using pattern coefficients to interpret factors is more consistent with an oblique rotation. Further, using the pattern coefficients often provides for a clearer picture of the factors (enhanced simple structure). In this case, using either matrix leads to the same conclusion as the items stimulate, challenge, and interest are related strongly (pattern coefficient $> .40$) to only one factor and the items recognize, appreciate, and compensate are related strongly only to the other factor.

Another new piece of information provided by use of the oblique rotation is the factor correlation. Here, Table 9.6 indicates a positive but not strong association of .155. Given that the factors are not highly correlated, the orthogonal solution would not be unreasonable to use here, although a correlation of this magnitude (i.e., $> |.10|$) can be considered as small but meaningful (Cohen, 1988).

Thus, addressing the research questions for this example, two factors are important in explaining variation in the set of items. Further, inspecting the values of the pattern coefficients suggested that each item is related to only its hypothesized factor. Using an oblique rotation to estimate the correlation between factors, we found that the two factors—engagement and feeling valued in the workplace—are positively but modestly correlated at 0.16.

Before proceeding to the next section, we wish to make a few additional points. Nunnally (1978, pp. 433–436) indicated several ways in which one can be fooled by factor analysis. One point he made that we wish to comment on is that of ignoring the simple correlations among the variables after the factors have been derived—that is, not checking the correlations among the variables that have been used to define a factor—to see if there is communality among them in the simple sense. As Nunnally noted, in some cases, variables used to define a factor may have simple correlations near zero. For our example this is not the case. Examination of the simple correlations in Table 9.3 for the three variables used to define factor 1 shows that the correlations are fairly strong. The same is true for the observed variables used to define factor 2.

9.8 THE COMMUNALITY ISSUE

With principal components extraction, we simply transform the original variables into linear combinations of these variables, and often a limited number of these combinations (i.e., the components or factors) account for most of the total variance. Also, we use 1s in the diagonal of the correlation matrix. Factor analysis using other extraction methods differs from principal components extraction in two ways: (1) the hypothetical factors that are derived in pure or common factor analysis can only be *estimated* from the original variables whereas with principal components extraction, because the components are specific linear combinations, no estimate is involved; and (2) numbers less than 1, the communalities, are put in the main diagonal of the correlation matrix in common factor analysis. A relevant question is: Will different factors emerge if communalities (e.g., the squared multiple correlation of each variable with all the others) are placed in the main diagonal?

The following quotes from five different sources give a pretty good sense of what might be expected in practice under some conditions. Cliff (1987) noted that "the choice of common factors or components methods often makes virtually no difference to the conclusions of a study" (p. 349). Guadagnoli and Velicer (1988) cited several studies by Velicer et al. that "have demonstrated that principal components solutions differ little from the solutions generated from factor analysis methods" (p. 266). Harman (1967) stated, "as a saving grace, there is much evidence in the literature that for all but very small data sets of variables, the resulting factorial solutions are little affected by the particular choice of communalities in the principal diagonal of the correlation matrix" (p. 83). Nunnally (1978) noted, "it is very safe to say that if there are as many as 20 variables in the analysis, as there are in nearly all exploratory factor analysis, then it does not matter what one puts in the diagonal spaces" (p. 418). Gorsuch (1983) took a somewhat more conservative position: "If communalities are reasonably high (e.g., .7 and up), even unities are probably adequate communality estimates in a problem with more than 35 variables" (p. 108). A general, somewhat conservative conclusion from these is that when the number of variables is moderately large (say > 30), and the analysis contains virtually no variables expected to have low communalities (e.g., .4), then practically any of the factor procedures will lead to the same interpretations.

On the other hand, principal components and common factor analysis may provide different results when the number of variables is fairly small (< 20), and some communalities are low. Further, Fabrigar and Wegener (2012) state, despite the Nunnally assertion described earlier, that these conditions (relatively low communalities and a small number of observed variables or loadings on a factor) are not that unusual for social science research. For this reason alone, you may wish to use a common factor analysis method instead of, or along with, principal components extraction. Further, as we discuss later, the common factor analysis method is conceptually more appropriate when you hypothesize that latent variables are present. As such, we now consider the common factor analysis model.

9.9 THE FACTOR ANALYSIS MODEL

As mentioned, factor analysis using principal components extraction may provide similar results to other factor extraction methods. However, the principal components and common factor model, discussed later, have some fundamental differences and may at times lead to different results. We briefly highlight the key differences between the principal component and common factor models and point out general conditions where use of the common factor model may have greater appeal. A key difference between the two models has to do with the goal of the analysis. The goal of principal component analysis is to obtain a relatively small number of variates (linear combinations of variables) that account for as much variance in the set of variables as possible. In contrast, the goal of common factor analysis is to obtain a relatively small number of *latent* variables that account for the maximum amount of *covariation* in a set of observed variables. The classic example of this latter situation is when you are developing an instrument to measure a psychological attribute (e.g., motivation) and you write items that are intended to tap the unobservable latent variable (motivation). The common factor analysis model assumes that respondents with an underlying high level of motivation will respond similarly across the set of motivation items (e.g., have high scores across such items) because these items are caused by a common factor (here motivation). Similarly, respondents who have low motivation will provide generally low responses across the same set of items, again due to the common underlying factor. Thus, if you assume that unobserved latent variables are causing individuals to respond in predictable ways across a set of items (or observed variables), then the common factor model is conceptually better suited than use of principal components for this purpose.

A visual display of the key elements of a factor analysis model helps further highlight differences between the common factor and principal component models. Figure 9.1 is a hypothesized factor analysis model using the previous example involving the work-related variables. The ovals at the bottom of Figure 9.1 represent the hypothesized "engagement" and "valued" constructs or latent variables. As shown by the single-headed arrows, these constructs, which are unobservable, are hypothesized to cause responses in the indicators (the engagement items, E1–E3, and the value items, V1–V3). Contrary to that shown in Figure 9.1, note that in *exploratory* factor analysis, each construct is assumed to linearly impact *each* of the observed variables. That is, arrows would appear from the engagement oval to each of the value variables (V1–V3) and from the valued oval to variables E1–E3. In exploratory factor analysis such cross-loadings cannot be set *a priori* to zero. So, the depiction in Figure 9.1 represents the researcher's hypothesis of interest. If this hypothesis is correct, these undepicted cross-loadings would be essentially zero. Note also that the double-headed curved arrow linking the two constructs at the bottom of Figure 9.1 means that the constructs are assumed to be correlated. As such, an oblique rotation that allows for such a correlation would be used. Further, the ovals at the top of Figure 9.1 represent unique variance that affects each observed variable. This unique variance, according to the factor analysis model, is composed of two entities: systematic variance that is inherent or specific to a given indicator (e.g., due to the way an item is presented or written) and variance due to random measurement error. Note that in the factor analysis model this unique variance (composed of these two entities) is removed from the observed variables (i.e., removed from E1, E2, and so on).

■ **Figure 9.1:** A hypothesized factor analysis model with three engagement (E1–E3) and three value items (V1–V3).

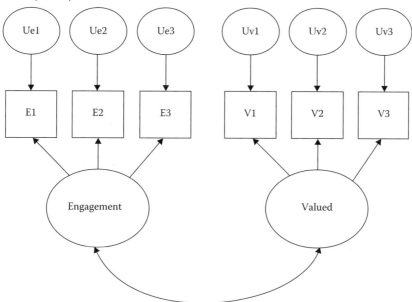

So, how does this depiction compare to the principal components model? First, the principal components model does not acknowledge the presence of the unique variances associated with the items as shown in the top of Figure 9.1. Thus, the principal components model assumes that there is no random measurement error and no specific variance associated with each indicator. As such, in the principal components model, all variation associated with a given variable is included in the analysis. In contrast, in common factor analysis, only the variation that is shared or is in common among the indicators (assumed to be in common or shared because of underlying factors) can be impacted by the latent variables. This common variance is referred to as the communality, which is often measured initially by the proportion of variance in an observed variable that is common to all of the other observed variables. When the unique variance is small (or the communalities are high), as noted, factor analysis and the principal components method may well lead to the same analysis results because they are both analyzing essentially the same variance (i.e., the common variance and total variable variance are almost the same).

Another primary difference between factor and principal components analysis is the assumed presence of latent variables in the factor analysis model. In principal components, the composite variables (the components) are linear combinations of observed variables and are not considered to be latent variables, but instead are weighted sums of the observed variables. In contrast, the factor analysis model, with the removal of the unique variance, assumes that latent variables are present and underlie (as depicted in Figure 9.1) responses to the indicators. Thus, if you are attempting to identify whether latent variables underlie responses to observed variables and explain why observed variables are associated (as when developing a measuring instrument or attempting to develop theoretical constructs from a set of observed variables), the exploratory factor analysis model is consistent with the latent variable hypothesis and is, theoretically, a more suitable analysis model.

Also, a practical difference between principal components and common factor analysis is the possibility that in common factor analysis unreasonable parameter estimates may be obtained (such as communalities estimated to be one or greater). Such occurrences, called Heywood cases, may be indicative of a grossly misspecified factor analysis model (too many or too few factors), an overly small sample size, or data that are inconsistent with the assumptions of exploratory factor analysis. On the positive side, then, Heywood cases could have value in alerting you to potential problems with the model or data.

9.10 ASSUMPTIONS FOR COMMON FACTOR ANALYSIS

Now that we have discussed the factor analysis model, we should make apparent the assumptions underlying the use of common factor analysis. First, as suggested by Figure 9.1, the factors are presumed to underlie or cause responses among the observed variables. The observed variables are then said to be "effect" or "reflective" indicators.

This presumed causal direction is the reason why observed variables that are caused by a common factor should be fairly highly correlated. While this causal direction may be reasonable for many situations, indicators are sometimes thought to cause changes in the factors. For example, it may be reasonable to assume indicators of socioeconomic status (SES, such as income or salary) are causally related to an SES factor, with increases in the observed indicators (e.g., inheriting a fortune) causing an increase in the SES construct. Common factor analysis is not intended for such causal or formative-indicator models. Having a good conceptual understanding of the variables being studied will help you determine if it is believable that observed variables are effect indicators. Further discussion of causal indicator and other related models can be found in, for example, Bollen and Bauldry (2011).

A second assumption of the factor analysis model is that the factors and observed variables are linearly related. Given that factors are unobservable, this assumption is difficult to assess. However, there are two things worth keeping in mind regarding the linearity assumption. First, factor analysis results that are not meaningful (i.e., uninterpretable factors) may be due to nonlinearity. In such a case, if other potential causes are ruled out, such as obtaining too few factors, it may be possible to use data transformations on the observed variables to obtain more sensible results. Second, considering the measurement properties of the observed variables can help us determine if linearity is reasonable to assume. For example, observed variables that are categorical or strictly ordinal in nature are generally problematic for standard factor analysis because linearity presumes an approximate equal interval between scale values. That is, the interpretation of a factor loading—a 1-unit change in the factor producing a certain unit change in a given observed variable—is not meaningful without, at least, an approximate equal interval. With such data, factor analysis is often implemented with structural equation modeling or other specialized software to take into account these measurement properties. Note that Likert-scaled items are, perhaps, often considered to operate in the gray area between the ordinal and interval property and are sometimes said to have a quasi-interval like property. Floyd and Widamen (1995) state that standard factor analysis often performs well with such scales, especially those having five to seven response options.

Another assumption for common factor analysis is that there is no perfect multicollinearity present among the observed variables. This situation is fairly straightforward to diagnose with the collinearity diagnostics discussed in this book. Note that this assumption implies that a given observed variable is not a linear sum or composite of other variables involved in the factor analysis. If a composite variable (i.e., $y_3 = y_1 + y_2$) and its determinants (i.e., y_1, y_2) were included in the analysis, software programs would typically provide an error message indicating the correlation matrix is not positive definite, with no further results being provided.

An assumption that is NOT made when principal components or principal axis factoring is used is multivariate or univariate normality. Given that these two procedures are almost always implemented without estimating standard errors or using statistical inference, there is no assumption that the observed variables follow a multivariate or univariate normal distribution. Note though that related to the quasi-interval measurement property just discussed, more replicable factor analysis results are generally obtained when scores do not deviate grossly from a normal distribution.

One important nonstatistical consideration has to do with the variables included in the factor analysis. The variables selected should be driven by the constructs one is hypothesizing to be present. If constructs are poorly defined or if the observed variables poorly represent a construct of interest, then factor analysis results may not be meaningful. As such, hypothesized factors may not emerge or may only be defined by a single indicator.

9.11 DETERMINING HOW MANY FACTORS ARE PRESENT WITH PRINCIPAL AXIS FACTORING

In this section, we discuss criteria for determining the number of factors in exploratory factor analysis given the use of principal axis factoring. Principal axis factoring is a factor extraction method suitable for the common factor model. While there are several methods that can be used to extract factors in exploratory factor analysis, some of which are somewhat better at approximating the observed variable correlations, principal axis factoring is a readily understood and commonly used method. Further, principal axis factoring has some advantages relative to other extraction methods, as it does not assume multivariate normality and is not as likely to run into estimation problems as is, for example, maximum likelihood extraction (Fabrigar & Wegener, 2012). As mentioned, mathematically, the key difference between principal components and principal axis factoring is that in the latter estimates of communalities replace the 1s used in the diagonal of the correlation matrix. This altered correlation matrix, with estimated communalities in the diagonal, is often referred to as the *reduced* correlation matrix.

While the analysis procedures associated with principal axis factoring are very similar to those used with principal components extraction, the use of the reduced correlation matrix complicates somewhat the issue of using empirical indicators to determine the number of factors present. Recall that with principal components extraction, the use of Kaiser's rule (eigenvalues > 1) to identify the number of factors is based on the idea that a given factor, if important, ought to account for at least as much as the variance of a given observed variable. However, in common factor analysis, the variance of the observed variables that is used in the analysis excludes variance unique to each variable. As such, the observed variable variance included in the analysis is smaller when principal axis factoring is used. Kaiser's rule, then, as applied to the reduced correlation matrix is overly stringent and may lead to overlooking important factors. Further, no similar rule (eigenvalues > 1) is generally used for the eigenvalues from the reduced correlation matrix.

Thus, the multiple criteria used in factor analysis to identify the number of important factors are somewhat different from those used with the principal components method. Following the suggestion in Preacher and MacCallum (2003), we will still rely on Kaiser's rule except that this rule will be applied to the matrix used with principal components extraction, the *unreduced* correlation matrix—that is, the unaltered or conventional correlation matrix of the observed variables with 1s on the diagonal. Even though this correlation matrix is not used in common factor analysis, Preacher and MacCallum note that this procedure may identify the proper number of factors (especially when communalities are high) and is reasonable to use provided other criteria are used to identify the number of factors. Second, although the application of Kaiser's rule is not appropriate for the *reduced* correlation matrix, you can still examine the scree plot of the eigenvalues obtained from use of the *reduced* correlation matrix to identify the number of factors. Third, parallel analysis based on the *reduced* correlation matrix can be used to identify the number of factors. Note that the eigenvalues from the reduced correlation matrix are readily obtained with the use of SAS software, but SPSS does not, at present, provide these eigenvalues. Further, neither software program provides the eigenvalues for the parallel analysis procedure. The eigenvalues from the reduced correlation matrix as well as the eigenvalues produced via the parallel analysis procedure can be obtained using syntax found in Fabrigar and Wegener (2012). Further, the publisher's website for that text currently provides the needed syntax in electronic form, which makes it easier to implement these procedures. Also, as before, we will consider the meaningfulness of any retained factors as an important criterion. This interpretation depends on the pattern of factor loadings as well as, for an oblique rotation, the correlation among the factors.

9.12 EXPLORATORY FACTOR ANALYSIS EXAMPLE WITH PRINCIPAL AXIS FACTORING

We now present an example using exploratory factor analysis with principal axis factoring. In this example, the observed variables are items from a measure of test anxiety known as the Reactions to Tests (RTT) scale. The RTT questionnaire was developed by Sarason (1984) to measure the four hypothesized dimensions of worry, tension, test-irrelevant thinking, and bodily symptoms. The summary data (i.e., correlations) used here are drawn from a study of the scale by Benson and Bandalos (1992), who used confirmatory factor analysis procedures. Here, we suppose that there has been no prior factor analytic work with this scale (as when the scale is initially developed), which makes exploratory factor analysis a sensible choice. For simplicity, only three items from each scale are used. Each item has the same four Likert-type response options, with larger score values indicating greater tension, worry, and so on. In this example, data are collected from 318 participants, which, assuming at least moderate communalities, is a sufficiently large sample size.

The hypothesized factor model is shown in Figure 9.2. As can be seen from the figure, each of the three items for each scale is hypothesized to load only on the scale it was written to measure (which is typical for an instrument development context), and the factors are hypothesized to correlate with each other. The 12 ovals in the top of the figure (denoted by U1, U2, and so on) represent the unique variance associated with each indicator, that is, the variance in a given item that is not due to the presumed underlying latent variable. Given the interest in determining if latent variables underlie responses to the 12 items (i.e., account for correlations across items), a common factor analysis is suitable.

9.12.1 Preliminary Analysis

Table 9.7 shows the correlations for the 12 items. Examining these correlations suggests that the associations are fairly strong within each set and weaker across the sets (e.g., strong correlations among the tension items, among the worry items, and so on, but not across the different sets). The exception occurs with the body items, which have reasonably strong correlations with other body items but appear to be somewhat similarly correlated with the tension items. The correlation matrix suggests multiple factors are present but it is not clear if four distinct factors are present. Also, note that correlations are positive as expected, and several correlations exceed a magnitude of .30, which supports the use of factor analysis.

We do not have the raw data and cannot perform other preliminary analysis activities, but we can describe the key activities. Histograms (or other plots) of the scores of each item and associated z-scores should be examined to search for outlying values. Item means and standard deviations should also be computed and examined to see if they are reasonable values. All possible bivariate scatterplots could also be examined to check for bivariate outliers, although this becomes less practical as the number of item increases. Further, the data set should be inspected for missing data. Note that if it were reasonable to assume that data are missing at random, use of the Expectation Maximization (EM) algorithm can be an effective missing data analysis strategy, given that no hypothesis testing is conducted (i.e., no standard errors need to be estimated). Further, multicollinearity diagnostics should be

▪ **Figure 9.2:** Four-factor test anxiety model with three indicators per factor.

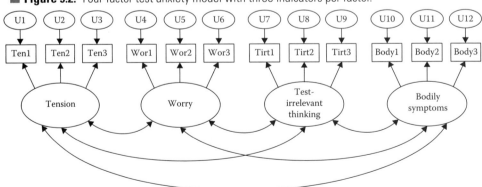

■ **Table 9.7: Item Correlations for the Reactions-to-Tests Scale**

	1	2	3	4	5	6	7	8	9	10	11	12
Ten1	1.000											
Ten2	.657	1.000										
Ten3	.652	.660	1.000									
Wor1	.279	.338	.300	1.000								
Wor2	.290	.330	.350	.644	1.000							
Wor3	.358	.462	.440	.659	.566	1.000						
Tirt1	.076	.093	.120	.317	.313	.367	1.000					
Tirt2	.003	.035	.097	.308	.305	.329	.612	1.000				
Tirt3	.026	.100	.097	.305	.339	.313	.674	.695	1.000			
Body1	.287	.312	.459	.271	.307	.351	.122	.137	.185	1.000		
Body2	.355	.377	.489	.261	.277	.369	.196	.191	.197	.367	1.000	
Body3	.441	.414	.522	.320	.275	.383	.170	.156	.101	.460	.476	1.000

examined, as estimation with principal axis factoring will fail if there is perfect multicollinearity.

Note also that you can readily obtain values for the Mahalanobis distance (to identify potential multivariate outliers) and variance inflation factors (to determine if excessive multicollinearity is present) from SPSS and SAS. To do this, use the regression package of the respective software program and regress ID or case number (a meaningless dependent variable) on the variables used in the factor analysis. Be sure to request values for the Mahalanobis distance and variance inflation factors, as these values will then appear in your data set and/or output. See sections 3.7 and 3.14.6 for a discussion of the Mahalanobis distance and variance inflation factors, respectively. Sections 9.14 and 9.15 present SPSS and SAS instructions for factor analysis.

9.12.2 Primary Analysis

Given that a four-factor model is hypothesized, we begin by requesting a four-factor solution from SPSS (and SAS) using principal axis factoring with an oblique rotation, which allows us to estimate the correlations among the factors. The oblique rotation we selected is the commonly used direct quartimin. The software output shown next is mostly from SPSS, which we present here because of the somewhat more complicated nature of results obtained with the use of this program. Table 9.8 presents the eigenvalues SPSS provides when running this factor analysis. The initial eigenvalues on the left side of Table 9.8 are those obtained with a principal components solution (because that is what SPSS reports), that is, from the correlation matrix with 1s in the diagonal. While this is not the most desirable matrix to use when using principal axis factoring (which uses communalities on the diagonal), we noted previously that Kaiser's rule, which should not be applied to the reduced matrix, can at times identify the correct number of factors when applied to the standard correlation matrix. Here, applying Kaiser's rule suggests the presence of three factors, as the eigenvalues associated with factors 1–3 are each larger than 1. Note though that under the heading Extraction Sums of Squared Loadings four factors are extracted, as we asked SPSS to disregard Kaiser's rule and simply extract four factors. Note that the values under the extracted heading are the sum of squared loadings obtained via principal axis factoring prior to rotation, while those in the final column are the sum of squared loadings after factor rotation. Neither of these latter estimates are the initial or preliminary eigenvalues from the reduced correlation matrix that are used to identify (or help validate) the number of factors present.

In addition to Kaiser's rule, a second criterion we use to identify if the hypothesized four-factor model is empirically supported is to obtain the initial eigenvalues from the reduced matrix and examine a scree plot associated with these values. In SAS, these values would be obtained when you request extraction with principal axis factoring. With SPSS, these initial eigenvalues are currently not part of the standard output, as we have just seen, but can be obtained by using syntax mentioned previously and provided in Fabrigar and Wegener (2012). These eigenvalues are shown on the left side of Table 9.9. Note that, as discussed previously, it is not appropriate to apply Kaiser's

■ **Table 9.8: Eigenvalues and Sum-of-Squared Loadings Obtained from SPSS for the Four-Factor Model**

	Total variance explained						
	Initial eigenvalues			Extraction sums of squared loadings			Rotation sums of squared loadings[a]
Factor	Total	% of Variance	Cumulative %	Total	% of Variance	Cumulative %	Total
1	4.698	39.149	39.149	4.317	35.972	35.972	3.169
2	2.241	18.674	57.823	1.905	15.875	51.848	2.610
3	1.066	8.886	66.709	.720	5.997	57.845	3.175
4	.850	7.083	73.792	.399	3.322	61.168	3.079
5	.620	5.167	78.959				
6	.526	4.381	83.339				
7	.436	3.636	86.975				
8	.385	3.210	90.186				
9	.331	2.762	92.947				
10	.326	2.715	95.662				
11	.278	2.314	97.976				
12	.243	2.024	100.000				

Extraction Method: Principal Axis Factoring.

[a] When factors are correlated, sums of squared loadings cannot be added to obtain a total variance.

rule to these eigenvalues, but it is appropriate to inspect a scree plot of these values, which is shown in Table 9.9. Note that this scree plot of initial eigenvalues from the reduced correlation matrix would not be produced by SPSS, as it produces a scree plot of the eigenvalues associated with the standard or unreduced correlation matrix. So, with SPSS, you need to request a scatterplot (i.e., outside of the factor analysis procedure) with the initial eigenvalues from the reduced correlation matrix appearing on the vertical axis and the factor number on the horizontal axis. This scatterplot, shown in Table 9.9, appears to indicate the presence of at least two factors and possibly up to

■ Table 9.9: Eigenvalues From Principal Axis Extraction and Parallel Process Analysis

Raw Data Eigenvalues From Reduced Correlation Matrix		Random Data Eigenvalues From Parallel Analysis		
Root	Eigen.	Root	Means	Prcntyle
1.000000	4.208154	1.000000	.377128	.464317
2.000000	1.790534	2.000000	.288660	.356453
3.000000	.577539	3.000000	.212321	.260249
4.000000	.295796	4.000000	.150293	.188854
5.000000	.014010	5.000000	.098706	.138206
6.000000	-.043518	6.000000	.046678	.082671
7.000000	-.064631	7.000000	-.006177	.031410
8.000000	-.087582	8.000000	-.050018	-.015718
9.000000	-.095449	9.000000	-.099865	-.064311
10.000000	-.156846	10.000000	-.143988	-.112703
11.000000	-.169946	11.000000	-.194469	-.160554
12.000000	-.215252	12.000000	-.249398	-.207357

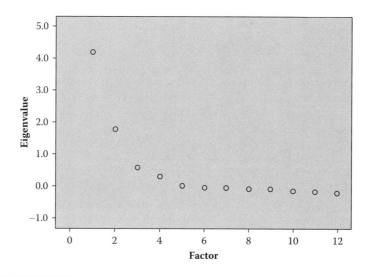

four factors, as there is a bit of a drop after the fourth factor, with the plot essentially leveling off completely after the fourth factor. As mentioned previously, use of this plot can be somewhat subjective.

A third criterion that we use to help us assess if the four-factor model is reasonable involves parallel analysis. Recall that with use of parallel analysis a set of eigenvalues is obtained from replicated random datasets (100 used in this example), and these values are compared to the eigenvalues from the data set being analyzed (here, the initial eigenvalues from the reduced matrix). Table 9.9 shows the eigenvalues from the reduced matrix on the left side. The right side of the table shows the mean eigenvalue as well as the value at the 95th percentile for each factor from the 100 replicated random data sets. Note that the first eigenvalue from the analyzed factor model (4.21) is greater than the mean eigenvalue (.377), as well as the value at the 95th percentile (.464) for the corresponding factor from parallel analysis. The same holds for factors two through four but not for factor five. Thus, use of parallel analysis supports a four-factor solution, as the variation associated with the first four factors is greater than variation expected by chance. (Note that is common to obtain negative eigenvalues when the *reduced* correlation matrix is analyzed. The factors associated with such eigenvalues are obviously not important.)

Before we consider the factor loadings and correlations to see if the four factors are interpreted as hypothesized, we consider the estimated communalities, which are shown in Table 9.10, and indicate the percent of item variance explained by the four extracted factors. An initial communality (a best guess) is the squared multiple correlation between a given item and all other items, whereas the values in the extraction column represent the proportion of variance in each item that is due to the four extracted factors obtained from the factor model. Inspecting the extracted communalities suggests that each item is at least moderately related to the set of factors. As such, we would expect that each item will have reasonably high loadings on at least one factor. Although we do not show the communalities as obtained via SAS, note that SPSS and SAS provide identical values for the communalities. Note also, as shown in the seventh column of Table 9.8, that the four factors explain 61% of the variance in the items.

Table 9.11 shows the pattern coefficients, structure coefficients, and the estimated correlations among the four factors. Recall that the pattern coefficients are preferred over the structure coefficients for making factor interpretations given the use of an oblique rotation. Inspecting the pattern coefficients and applying a value of $|.40|$ to identify important item-factor associations lends support to the hypothesized four-factor solution. That is, factor 1 is defined by the body items, factor 2 by the test-irrelevant thinking items, factor 3 by the worry items, and factor 4 by the tension items. Note the inverse association among the items and factors for factors 3 and 4. For example, for factor 3, participants scoring higher on the worry items (greater worry) have lower scores on the factor. Thus, higher scores on factor three reflect reduced anxiety (less worry) related to tests whereas higher scores on factor 2 are suggestive of greater anxiety (greater test-irrelevant thinking).

■ Table 9.10: Item Communalities for the Four-Factor Model

Communalities

	Initial	Extraction
TEN1	.532	.636
TEN2	.561	.693
TEN3	.615	.721
WOR1	.552	.795
WOR2	.482	.537
WOR3	.565	.620
IRTHK1	.520	.597
IRTHK2	.542	.638
IRTHK3	.606	.767
BODY1	.322	.389
BODY2	.337	.405
BODY3	.418	.543

Extraction Method: Principal Axis Factoring.

■ Table 9.11: Pattern, Structure, and Correlation Matrices From the Four-Factor Model

Pattern matrix[a]

	Factor			
	1	2	3	4
TEN1	.022	−.027	−.003	−.783
TEN2	−.053	.005	−.090	−.824
TEN3	.361	.005	.041	−.588
WOR1	−.028	−.056	−.951	.052
WOR2	.028	.071	−.659	−.049
WOR3	.110	.087	−.605	−.137
IRTHK1	−.025	.757	−.039	−.033
IRTHK2	.066	.776	−.021	.094
IRTHK3	−.038	.897	.030	−.027
BODY1	.630	−.014	−.068	.061
BODY2	.549	.094	.027	−.102
BODY3	.710	−.034	−.014	−.042

Extraction Method: Principal Axis Factoring.
Rotation Method: Oblimin with Kaiser Normalization.
[a] Rotation converged in 8 iterations.

(*Continued*)

■ **Table 9.11: (Continued)**

Structure matrix

	Factor			
	1	2	3	4
TEN1	.529	.047	−.345	−.797
TEN2	.532	.102	−.426	−.829
TEN3	.727	.135	−.400	−.806
WOR1	.400	.376	−.888	−.341
WOR2	.411	.390	−.728	−.362
WOR3	.527	.411	−.761	−.481
IRTHK1	.227	.771	−.394	−.097
IRTHK2	.230	.796	−.375	−.023
IRTHK3	.214	.875	−.381	−.064
BODY1	.621	.187	−.351	−.380
BODY2	.628	.242	−.337	−.457
BODY3	.735	.173	−.373	−.510

Extraction Method: Principal Axis Factoring.
Rotation Method: Oblimin with Kaiser Normalization.

Factor correlation matrix

Factor	1	2	3	4
1	1.000	.278	−.502	−.654
2	.278	1.000	−.466	−.084
3	−.502	−.466	1.000	.437
4	−.654	−.084	.437	1.000

Extraction Method: Principal Axis Factoring.
Rotation Method: Oblimin with Kaiser Normalization.

These factor interpretations are important when you examine factor correlations, which are shown in Table 9.11. Given these interpretations, the factor correlations seem sensible and indicate that factors are in general moderately correlated. One exception to this pattern is the correlation between factors 2 (test irrelevant thinking) and 4 (tension), where the correlation is near zero. We note that the near-zero correlation between test-irrelevant thinking and tension is not surprising, as other studies have found the test-irrelevant thinking factor to be the most distinct of the four factors. A second possible exception to the moderate correlation pattern is the fairly strong association between factors 1 (body) and 4 (tension). This fairly high correlation might suggest to some that these factors may not be that distinct. Recall that we made a similar observation when we examined the correlations among the observed variables, and that applying Kaiser's rule supported the presence of three factors.

Thus, to explore this issue further, you could estimate a factor model requesting software to extract three factors. You can then inspect the pattern coefficients and factor correlations to determine if the three-factor solution seems meaningful. When we did this, we found that the body and tensions items loaded only on one factor, the worry items loaded only on a second factor, and the test-irrelevant thinking items loaded only on a third factor. Further, the factor correlations were reasonable. Thus, assuming that it is reasonable to consider that the tension and body items reflect a single factor, there is support for both the three- and four-factor models. In such a case, a researcher might present both sets of results and/or offer arguments for why one solution would be preferred over another. For example, Sarason (1984, p. 937) preferred the four-factor model stating that it allowed for a more fine-grained analysis of test anxiety. Alternatively, such a finding, especially in the initial stages of instrument development, might compel researchers to reexamine the tension and body items and possibly rewrite them to make them more distinct. It is also possible that this finding is sample specific and would not appear in a subsequent study. Further research with this scale may then be needed to resolve this issue.

Before proceeding to the next section, we show some selected output for this same example that is obtained from SAS software. The top part of Table 9.12 shows the preliminary eigenvalues for the four-factor model. These values are the same as those shown in Table 9.9, which were obtained with SPSS by use of a specialized macro. A scree plot of these values, which can readily be obtained in SAS, would essentially be the same plot as shown in Table 9.9. Note that inspecting the eigenvalues in Table 9.12 indicates a large drop off after factor 2 and somewhat of a drop off after factor 4, possibly then supporting the four-factor solution. The middle part of Table 9.12 shows the pattern coefficients for this solution. These values have the same magnitude as those shown in Table 9.11, but note that the signs for the defining coefficients (i.e., pattern coefficients > |.40|) here are all positive, suggesting that the signs of the coefficients are somewhat arbitrary and indeed are done for computational convenience by software. (In fact, within a given column of pattern or structure coefficients, you can reverse all of the signs if that eases interpretation.) In this case, the positive signs ease factor interpretation because higher scores on each of the four anxiety components reflect greater anxiety (i.e., greater tension, worrying, test-irrelevant thinking, and bodily symptoms). Accordingly, all factor correlations, as shown in Table 9.12, are positive.

9.13 FACTOR SCORES

In some research situations, you may, after you have achieved a meaningful factor solution, wish to estimate factor scores, which are considered as *estimates* of the true underlying factor scores, to use for subsequent analyses. Factor scores can be used as predictors in a regression analysis, dependent variables in a MANOVA or ANOVA, and so on. For example, after arriving at the four-factor model, Sarason (1984) obtained scale scores and computed correlations for each of the four subscales of the RTT questionnaire (discussed in section 9.12) and a measure of "cognitive interference" in order

■ Table 9.12: Selected SAS Output for the Four-Factor Model

Preliminary Eigenvalues: Total = 6.0528105 Average = 0.50440088

	Eigenvalue	Difference	Proportion	Cumulative
1	4.20815429	2.41762010	0.6952	0.6952
2	1.79053420	1.21299481	0.2958	0.9911
3	0.57753939	0.28174300	0.0954	1.0865
4	0.29579639	0.28178614	0.0489	1.1353
5	0.01401025	0.05752851	0.0023	1.1377
6	−.04351826	0.02111277	−0.0072	1.1305
7	−.06463103	0.02295100	−0.0107	1.1198
8	−.08758203	0.00786743	−0.0145	1.1053
9	−.09544946	0.06139632	−0.0158	1.0896
10	−.15684578	0.01309984	−0.0259	1.0636
11	−.16994562	0.04530621	−0.0281	1.0356
12	−.21525183		−0.0356	1.0000

Rotated Factor Pattern (Standardized Regression Coefficients)

	Factor1	Factor2	Factor3	Factor4
TEN1	−0.02649	0.00338	0.78325	0.02214
TEN2	0.00510	0.09039	0.82371	−0.05340
TEN3	0.00509	−0.04110	0.58802	0.36089
WOR1	−0.05582	0.95101	−0.05231	−0.02737
WOR2	0.07103	0.65931	0.04864	0.02843
WOR3	0.08702	0.60490	0.13716	0.10978
TIRT1	0.75715	0.03878	0.03331	−0.02514
TIRT2	0.77575	0.02069	−0.09425	0.06618
TIRT3	0.89694	−0.02998	0.02734	−0.03847
BODY1	−0.01432	0.06826	−0.06017	0.62960
BODY2	0.09430	−0.02697	0.10260	0.54821
BODY3	−0.03364	0.01416	0.04294	0.70957

Inter-Factor Correlations

	Factor1	Factor2	Factor3	Factor4
Factor1	1.00000	0.46647	0.08405	0.27760
Factor2	0.46647	1.00000	0.43746	0.50162
Factor3	0.08405	0.43746	1.00000	0.65411
Factor4	0.27760	0.50162	0.65411	1.00000

to obtain additional evidence for the validity of the scales. Sarason hypothesized (and found) that the worry subscale of the RTT is most highly correlated with cognitive interference.

While several different methods of estimating factor scores are available, two are commonly used. One method is to estimate factor scores using a regression method. In this method, regression weights (not the factor loadings) are obtained and factor scores are created by multiplying each weight by the respective observed variable, which is in z-score form. For example, for the six work-related variables that appeared in section 9.7, Table 9.13 shows the regression weights that are obtained when you use principal axis factoring (weights can also be obtained for the principal components method). With these weights, scores for the first factor (engagement) are formed as follows: Engagement = $.028 \times z_{stimulate} + .000 \times z_{challenge} + .001 \times z_{interest} + .329 \times z_{recognize} + .463 \times z_{appreciate} + .251 \times z_{compensate}$. Scores for the second factor are computed in a similar way by using the weights in the next column of that table. Note that SPSS and SAS can do these calculations for you and place the factor scores in your data set (so no manual calculation is required).

A second, and simpler, method to estimate factor scores especially relevant for scale construction is to sum or average scores across the observed variables that load highly on a given factor as observed in the pattern matrix. This method is known as unit weighting because values of 1 are used to weight important variables as opposed to the exact regression weights used in the foregoing procedure. To illustrate, consider estimating factor or scale scores for the RTT example in section 9.12. For the first factor, inspecting the pattern coefficients in Table 9.11 indicated that only the bodily symptom items (Body1, Body2, Body3) are strongly related to that factor. Thus, scores for this factor can be estimated as Bodily Symptoms = 1 × Body1 + 1 × Body2 + 1 × Body3, which, of course, is the same thing as summing across the three items. When variables

■ Table 9.13: **Factor Score Regression Weights for the Six Work-Related Variables**

Factor score coefficient matrix

	Factor	
	1	2
Stimulate	.028	.338
Challenge	.000	.431
Interest	.001	.278
Recognize	.329	.021
Appreciate	.463	.006
Compensate	.251	.005

Extraction Method: Principal Axis Factoring.
Rotation Method: Oblimin with Kaiser Normalization.
Factor Scores Method: Regression.

are on the same scale, as they often are in an instrument development context, averaging the scores can be used here as well, which provides for greater meaning because the score scale of the observed scores and factor scores are the same, making averaging an appealing option. Note that if the observed variables are not on the same scale, the observed variables could first be placed in z-score form and then summed (or averaged).

Note that for some factors the defining coefficients may all be negative. In this case, negative signs can be used to obtain factor scores. For example, scores for factor 4 in the RTT example, given the signs of the pattern coefficients in Table 9.11, can be computed as Tension $= -1 \times$ Ten1 $- 1 \times$ Ten2 $- 1 \times$ Ten3. However, scale scores in this case will be negative, which is probably not desired. Given that the coefficients are each negative, here, a more sensible alternative is to simply sum scores across the tension items ignoring the negative signs. (Remember that it is appropriate to change signs of the factor loadings within a given column provided that all signs are changed within that column.) When that is done, higher scale scores reflect greater tension, which is consistent with the item scores (and with the output produced by SAS in Table 9.12). Be aware that the signs of the correlations between this factor and all other factors will be reversed. For example, in Table 9.11, the correlation between factors 1 (body) and 4 (tension) is negative. If scores for the tension items were simply summed or averaged (as recommended here), this correlation of scale scores would then be positive, indicating that those reporting greater bodily symptoms also report greater tension. For this example, then, summing or averaging raw scores across items for each subscale would produce all positive correlations between factors, as likely desired.

You should know that use of different methods to estimate factor scores, including these two methods, will not produce the same factor scores (which is referred to as factor score indeterminacy), although such scores may be highly correlated. Also, when factor scores are estimated, the magnitude of the factor correlations as obtained in the factor analysis (i.e., like those in Table 9.11) will not be the same as those obtained if you were to compute factor scores and then compute correlations associated with these estimated scores. One advantage with regression weighting is that its use maximizes the correlation between the underlying factors and the estimated factor scores. However, use of regression weights to produce factor scores, while optimal for the sample at hand, do not tend to hold up well in independent samples. As such, simple unit weighting is often recommended, and studies examining the performance of unit weighting support its use in estimating factor scores (Fava & Velicer, 1992; Grice, 2001; Nunnally, 1978). Note also that this issue does not arise with the principal components method. That is, with principal components extraction and when the regression method is used to obtain factor (or component) scores, the obtained factor score correlations will match those found via the use of principal components extraction.

9.14 USING SPSS IN FACTOR ANALYSIS

This section presents SPSS syntax that can be used to conduct a factor analysis with principal axis extraction. Note that SPSS can use raw data or just the correlations obtained from raw data to implement a factor analysis. Typically, you will have raw data available and will use that in conducting a factor analysis. Table 9.14 shows syntax needed assuming you are using raw data, and Table 9.15 shows syntax that can be used when you only have a correlation matrix available. Syntax in Table 9.15 will allow you to duplicate analysis results presented in section 9.12. Section 9.15 presents the corresponding SAS syntax.

The left side of Table 9.14 shows syntax that can be used when you wish to apply Kaiser's rule to help determine the number of factors present. Note that in the second line of the syntax, where the VARIABLES subcommand appears, you simply list the observed variables from your study (generically listed here as var1, var2, and so on). For the ANALYSIS subcommand in the next line, you can list the same variables again or, as shown here, list the first variable name followed by the word "to" and then the last variable name, assuming that the variables 1–6 appear in that order in your data set. Further, SPSS will apply Kaiser's rule to eigenvalues obtained from the unreduced correlation matrix when you specify MINEIGEN(1) after the CRITERIA subcommand in line 5 of the code. As discussed in sections 9.11 and 9.12, you must use supplemental syntax to obtain eigenvalues from the reduced correlation matrix, which is desirable when using principal axis factoring.

In the next line, following the EXTRACTION subcommand, PAF requests SPSS to use principal axis factoring. (If PC were used instead of PAF, all analysis results would be based on the use of principal components extraction). After the ROTATION command, OBLIMIN requests SPSS to use the oblique rotation procedure known as direct quartimin. Note that replacing OBLIMIN with VARIMAX would direct SPSS to use the orthogonal rotation varimax. The SAVE subcommand is an optional line that requests the estimation of factor scores using the regression procedure discussed in

■ **Table 9.14: SPSS Syntax for Factor Analysis With Principal Axis Extraction Using Raw Data**

Using Kaiser's Rule	Requesting Specific Number of Factors
FACTOR	FACTOR
/VARIABLES var1 var2 var3 var4 var5 var6	/VARIABLES var1 var2 var3 var4 var5 var6
/ANALYSIS var1 to var6	/ANALYSIS var1 to var6
/PRINT INITIAL EXTRACTION ROTATION	/PRINT INITIAL EXTRACTION ROTATION
/CRITERIA MINEIGEN(1) ITERATE(25)	/CRITERIA FACTORS(2) ITERATE(25)
/EXTRACTION PAF	/EXTRACTION PAF
/CRITERIA ITERATE(25)	/CRITERIA ITERATE(25)
/ROTATION OBLIMIN	/ROTATION OBLIMIN
/SAVE REG(ALL)	/SAVE REG(ALL)
/METHOD=CORRELATION.	/METHOD=CORRELATION.

section 9.13. The last line directs SPSS to use correlations (as opposed to covariances) in conducting the factor analysis.

The right side of the Table 9.14 shows syntax that can be used when you wish to extract a specific number of factors (as done in section 9.12) instead of relying, for example, on Kaiser's rule to determine the number of factors to be extracted. Note that the syntax on the right side of the table is identical to that listed on the left except for line 5 of the syntax. Here, the previously used MINEIGEN(1) has been replaced with the statement FACTORS(2). The FACTORS(2) statement in line 5 directs SPSS to extract two factors, regardless of their eigenvalues. FACTORS(3) would direct SPSS to extract three factors and so on. Note that neither set of syntax requests a scree plot of eigenvalues. As described, with SPSS, such a plot would use eigenvalues from the unreduced correlation matrix. When principal axis factoring is used, it is generally preferred to obtain a plot of the eigenvalues from the reduced correlation matrix.

Table 9.15 shows SPSS syntax that was used to obtain the four-factor solution presented in section 9.12.2. The first line is an optional title line. The second line, following the required phrase MATRIX DATA VARIABLES=, lists the 12 observed variables used in the analysis. The phrase N_SCALER CORR, after the CONTENTS subcommand, informs SPSS that a correlation matrix is used as entry and that sample size (N) will be specified prior to the correlation matrix. After the BEGIN DATA command, you must indicate the sample size for your data (here, 318), and then input the correlation matrix. After the END DATA code just below the correlation matrix, the FACTOR MATRIX IN(COR=*) informs SPSS that the factor analysis will use as data the correlation matrix entered earlier. Note that PAF is the extraction method requested, and that SPSS will extract four factors no matter what the size of the eigenvalues are. Also, note that the direct quartimin rotation procedure is requested, given that the factors are hypothesized to be correlated.

9.15 USING SAS IN FACTOR ANALYSIS

This section presents SAS syntax that can be used to conduct factor analysis using principal axis extraction. Like SPSS, SAS can implement a factor analysis with raw data or using just the correlations obtained from raw data. Table 9.16 shows syntax assuming you are using raw data, and Table 9.17 shows syntax that can be used when you only have a correlation matrix available. Syntax in Table 9.17 will allow you to duplicate analysis results presented in section 9.12.

The left side of Table 9.16 shows syntax that can be used when you wish to apply Kaiser's rule to help determine the number of factors present. The syntax assumes that the data set named my_data is the active data set in SAS. The first line initiates the factor analysis procedure in SAS where you must indicate the data set that is being used (simply called my_data here). The second line of the syntax directs SAS to apply Kaiser's rule to extract factors having an eigenvalue larger than 1, and the code METHOD=prin

■ Table 9.15: SPSS Syntax for Factor Analysis With Principal Axis Extraction Using Correlation Input

```
TITLE PAF WITH REACTIONS-TO-TEST DATA.
MATRIX DATA VARIABLES=TEN1 TEN2 TEN3 WOR1 WOR2 WOR3 IRTHK1 IRTHK2 IRTHK3 BODY1 BODY2 BODY3
  /CONTENTS=N_SCALER CORR.
BEGIN DATA.
318
1.0
.6568918 1.0
.6521357 .6596083 1.0
.2793569 .3381683 .3001235 1.0
.2904172 .3298699 .3498588 .6440856 1.0
.3582053 .4621011 .4395827 .6592054 .5655221 1.0
.0759346 .0926851 .1199888 .3173348 .3125095 .3670677 1.0
.0033904 .0347001 .0969222 .3080404 .3054771 .3286743 .6118786 1.0
.0261352 .1002678 .0967460 .3048249 .3388673 .3130671 .6735513 .6951704 1.0
.2866741 .3120085 .4591803 .2706903 .3068059 .3512327 .1221421 .1374586 .1854188 1.0
.3547974 .3772598 .4888384 .2609631 .2767733 .3692361 .1955429 .1913100 .1966969 .3665290 1.0
.4409109 .4144444 .5217488 .3203353 .2749568 .3834183 .1703754 .1557804 .1011165 .4602662 .4760684 1.0
END DATA.
FACTOR MATRIX IN (COR=*)
  /PRINT INITIAL EXTRACTION CORRELATION ROTATION
  /CRITERIA FACTORS (4) ITERATE (25)
  /EXTRACTION PAF
  /CRITERIA ITERATE (25)
  /ROTATION OBLIMIN.
```

■ **Table 9.16: SAS Syntax for Factor Analysis Using Raw Data**

Using Kaiser's Rule With PC	Requesting Specific Number of Factors With PAF
`PROC FACTOR DATA = my_data`	`PROC FACTOR DATA = my_data`
`MINEIGEN = 1.0 METHOD=prin` `PRIOR=one ROTATE=oblimin;`	`PRIORS=smc NFACTORS=2 METHOD=prinit` `ROTATE=oblimin SCREE SCORE OUTSTAT=fact;`
`VAR var1 var2 var3 var4 var5 var6;`	`VAR var1 var2 var3 var4 var5 var6;`
`RUN;`	`PROC SCORE DATA = my_data SCORE = fact` `OUT=scores;`
	`RUN;`

PRIOR=one directs SAS to use principal components extraction with values of 1 on the diagonal of the correlation matrix. Thus, this line requests SAS to use the unreduced correlation matrix and extract any factors whose corresponding eigenvalue is greater than 1. If you wanted to use principal components extraction only for the purpose of applying Kaiser's rule (as is done in section 9.12), you would disregard output from this analysis except for the initial eigenvalues.

To complete the explanation of the syntax, ROTATE=oblimin directs SAS to use the oblique rotation method direct quartimin. The orthogonal rotation method varimax can be implemented by replacing the ROTATE=oblimin with ROTATE=varimax. After the VAR command on the fourth line, you must indicate the variables being used in the analysis, which are generically named here var1, var2, and so on. RUN requests the procedure to be implemented.

The right side of the Table 9.16 shows syntax that uses principal axis factoring, requests a specific number of factors be extracted (as done in section 9.12), and obtains factor scores (which are optional). The code also requests a scree plot of the eigenvalues using the reduced correlation matrix. The second line of the code directs SAS to use, initially, squared multiple correlations (smc) as estimates of variable communalities (instead of the 1s used in principal components extraction). Also, NFACTORS=2 in this same line directs SAS to extract two factors while METHOD=prinit directs SAS to use an iterative method to obtain parameter estimates (which is done by default in SPSS). Thus, use of the code PRIORS=smc and METHOD=prinit requests an iterative principal axis factoring solution (identical to that used by SPSS earlier). Again, the ROTATE=oblimin directs SAS to employ the direct quartimin rotation, and SCREE instructs SAS to produce a scree plot of the eigenvalues from the reduced correlation matrix (unlike SPSS, which would provide a SCREE plot of the eigenvalues associated with the unreduced correlation matrix). The SCORE OUTSTAT code is optional

■ Table 9.17 SAS Syntax for Factor Analysis With Principal Axis Extraction Using Correlation Input

```
TITLE 'paf with reaction to tests scale';
DATA rtsitems (TYPE=CORR);
   INFILE CARDS MISSOVER;
   _TYPE_ = 'CORR';
   INPUT _NAME_ $ ten1 ten2 ten3 wor1 wor2 wor3 tirtt1 tirtt2 tirt3 body1 body2 body3;
   DATALINES;
ten1 1.0
ten2 .6568918 1.0
ten3 .6521357 .6596083 1.0
wor1 .2793569 .3381683 .3001235 1.0
wor2 .2904172 .3298699 .3498588 .6440856 1.0
wor3 .3582053 .4621011 .4395827 .6592054 .565522 1 .0
tirt1 .0759346 .0926851 .1199888 .3173348 .3125095 .3670677 1.0
tirt2 .0033904 .0347001 .0969222 .3080404 .3054771 .3286743 .6118786 1.0
tirt3 .0261352 .1002678 .0967460 .3048249 .3388673 .3130671 .6735513 .6951704 1.0
body1 .2866741 .312008 5 .4591803 .2706903 .3068059 .3512327 .1221421 .1374586 .1854188 1.0
body2 .3547974 .3772598 .4888384 .2609631 .2767733 .3692361 .1955429 .1913100 .3665290 1.0
body3 .4409109 .414444 .5217488 .3203353 .2749568 .3834183 .1703754 .1557804 .1011165 .4602662 .4760684  1.0
PROC FACTOR PRIORS=smc NFACTORS=4 METHOD=prinit ROTATE=oblimin NOBS=318 SCREE;
RUN;
```

and requests that the factor score coefficients, used in creating factor scores (as well as other output), be placed in a file called here fact. Following the variable line, the next couple of lines is optional and is used to create factor scores using the regression method and have these scores placed in a data file called here scores. RUN executes the code.

Table 9.17 shows SAS syntax that was used to obtain the four-factor solution presented in section 9.12.2. Line 1 is an optional title line. In lines 2–4, all of the code shown is required when you are using a correlation matrix as input; the only user option is to name the dataset (here called rtsitems). In line 5, the required elements include everything up to and including the dollar sign ($). The remainder of that line includes the variable names that appear in the study. After the DATALINES command, which is required, you then provide the correlation matrix with the variable names placed in the first column. After the correlation matrix is entered, the rest of the code is similar to that used when raw data are input. The exception is NOBS=318, which you use to tell SAS how large the sample size is; for this example, the number of observations (NOBS) is 318.

9.16 EXPLORATORY AND CONFIRMATORY FACTOR ANALYSIS

This chapter has focused on exploratory factor analysis (EFA). The purpose of EFA is to identify the factor structure for a set of variables. This often involves determining how many factors exist, as well as the pattern of the factor loadings. Although most EFA programs allow for the number of factors to be specified in advance, it is not possible in these programs to force variables to load only on certain factors. EFA is generally considered to be more of a theory-generating than a theory-testing procedure. In contrast, *confirmatory factor analysis* (CFA), which is covered in Chapter 16, is generally based on a strong theoretical or empirical foundation that allows you to specify an exact factor model in advance. This model usually specifies which variables will load on which factors, as well as such things as which factors are correlated. It is more of a theory-testing procedure than is EFA. Although, in practice, studies may contain aspects of both exploratory and confirmatory analyses, it is useful to distinguish between the two techniques in terms of the situations in which they are commonly used. Table 9.18 displays some of the general differences between the two approaches.

Let us consider an example of an EFA. Suppose a researcher is developing a scale to measure self-concept. The researcher does not conceptualize specific self-concept factors in advance and simply writes a variety of items designed to tap into various aspects of self-concept. An EFA of these items may yield three factors that the researcher then identifies as physical, social, and academic self-concept. The researcher notes that items with large loadings on one of the three factors tend to have very small loadings on the other two, and interprets this as further support for the presence of three distinct factors or dimensions of underlying self-concept. In scale development, EFA is often considered to be a better choice.

▪ **Table 9.18 Comparison of Exploratory and Confirmatory Factor Analysis**

Exploratory—theory generating	Confirmatory—theory testing
Heuristic—weak literature base	Strong theory or strong empirical base
Determine the number of factors	Number of factors fixed *a priori*
Determine whether the factors are correlated or uncorrelated	Factors fixed *a priori* as correlated or uncorrelated
Variables free to load on all factors	Variables fixed to load on a specific factor or factors

Continuing the scale development example, as researchers continue to work with this scale in future research, CFA becomes a viable option. With CFA, you can specify both the number of factors hypothesized to be present (e.g., the three self-concept factors) but also specify which items belong to a given dimension. This latter option is not possible in EFA. In addition, CFA is part of broader modeling framework known as structural equation modeling (SEM), which allows for the estimation of more sophisticated models. For example, the self-concept dimensions in SEM could serve as predictors, dependent variables, or intervening variables in a larger analysis model. As noted in Fabrigar and Wegener (2012), the associations between these dimensions and other variables can then be obtained in SEM without computing factor scores.

9.17 EXAMPLE RESULTS SECTION FOR EFA OF REACTIONS-TO-TESTS SCALE

The following results section is based on the example that appeared in section 9.12. In that analysis, 12 items measuring text anxiety were administered to college students at a major research university, with 318 respondents completing all items. Note that most of the next paragraph would probably appear in a method section of a paper.

The goal of this study was to identify the dimensions of text anxiety, as measured by the newly developed RTT measure. EFA using principal axis factoring (PAF) was used for this purpose with the oblique rotation method direct quartimin. To determine the number of factors present, we considered several criteria. These include the number of factors that (1) had eigenvalues greater than 1 when the unreduced correlation matrix was used (i.e., with 1s on the diagonal of the matrix), (2) were suggested by inspecting a scree plot of eigenvalues from the reduced correlation matrix (with estimates of communalities in the diagonal of correlation matrix), which is consistent with PAF, (3) had eigenvalues larger than expected by random as obtained via parallel analysis, and (4) were conceptually coherent when all factor analysis results were examined. The 12 items on the scale represented possible dimensions of anxiety as suggested in the relevant literature. Three items were written for each of the hypothesized dimensions, which represented tension, worry, test-irrelevant thinking, and bodily symptoms. For each item, a 4-point response scale was used (from "not typical of me" to "very typical of me").

Table 1 reports the correlations among the 12 items. (Note that we list generic item names here. You should provide some descriptive information about the content of the items or perhaps list each of the items, if possible.) In general, inspecting the correlations appears to provide support for the four hypothesized dimensions, as correlations are mostly greater within each dimension than across the assumed dimensions. Examination of Mahalanobis distance values, variance inflation factors, and histograms associated with the items did not suggest the presence of outlying values or excessive multicollinearity. Also, scores for most items were roughly symmetrically distributed.

■ **Table 1: Item Correlations (N = 318)**

	1	2	3	4	5	6	7	8	9	10	11	12
Ten1	1.000											
Ten2	.657	1.000										
Ten3	.652	.660	1.000									
Wor1	.279	.338	.300	1.000								
Wor2	.290	.330	.350	.644	1.000							
Wor3	.358	.462	.440	.659	.566	1.000						
Tirt1	.076	.093	.120	.317	.313	.367	1.000					
Tirt2	.003	.035	.097	.308	.305	.329	.612	1.000				
Tirt3	.026	.100	.097	.305	.339	.313	.674	.695	1.000			
Body1	.287	.312	.459	.271	.307	.351	.122	.137	.185	1.000		
Body2	.355	.377	.489	.261	.277	.369	.196	.191	.197	.367	1.000	
Body3	.441	.414	.522	.320	.275	.383	.170	.156	.101	.460	.476	1.000

To initiate the exploratory factor analysis, we requested a four-factor solution, given we selected items from four possibly distinct dimensions. While application of Kaiser's rule (to eigenvalues from the unreduced correlation matrix) suggested the presence of three factors, parallel analysis indicated four factors, and inspecting the scree plot suggested the possibility of four factors. Given that these criteria differed on the number of possible factors present, we also examined the results from a three-factor solution, but found that the four-factor solution was more meaningful.

Table 2 shows the communalities, pattern coefficients, and sum of squared loadings for each factor, all of which are shown after factor rotation. The communalities range from .39 to .80, suggesting that each item is at least moderately and in some cases strongly related to the set of factors. Inspecting the pattern coefficients shown in Table 2 and using a magnitude of least .4 to indicate a nontrivial pattern coefficient, we found that the test-irrelevant thinking items load only on factor 1, the worry items load only on factor 2, the tension items load only on factor 3, and the bodily symptom items load only on factor 4. Thus, there is support that the items thought to be reflective of the same factor are related only to the hypothesized factor. The sums of squared loadings suggest that the factors are fairly similar in importance. As a whole, the four factors explained 61% of the variation of the item scores. Further, the factors, as expected, are positively and mostly moderately correlated, as indicated in Table 3. In sum, the factor analysis provides support for the four hypothesized dimensions underlying text anxiety.

■ **Table 2: Selected Factor Analysis Results for the Reaction-to-Tests Scale**

Item	Factors				Communality
	Test-irrelevant thinking	Worry	Tension	Bodily symptoms	
Tension1	−0.03	0.00	0.78	0.02	0.64
Tension2	0.01	0.09	0.82	−0.05	0.69
Tension3	0.01	−0.04	0.59	0.36	0.72
Worry1	−0.06	0.95	−0.05	−0.03	0.80
Worry2	0.07	0.66	0.05	0.03	0.54
Worry3	0.09	0.60	0.14	0.11	0.62
TIRT1[1]	0.76	0.04	0.03	−0.03	0.60
TIRT2	0.78	0.02	−0.09	0.07	0.64
TIRT3	0.90	−0.03	0.03	−0.04	0.77
Body1	−0.01	0.07	−0.06	0.63	0.39
Body2	0.09	−0.03	0.10	0.55	0.41
Body3	−0.03	0.01	0.04	0.71	0.54
Sum of squared loadings	2.61	3.17	3.08	3.17	

[1] TIRT = test irrelevant thinking.

■ **Table 3: Factor Correlations**

	1	2	3	4
Test-irrelevant thinking	1.00			
Worry	0.47	1.00		
Tension	0.08	0.44	1.00	
Bodily symptoms	0.28	0.50	0.65	1.00

9.18 SUMMARY

Exploratory factor analysis can be used when you assume that latent variables underlie responses to observed variables and you wish to find a relatively small number of underlying factors that account for relationships among the larger set of variables. The procedure can help obtain new theoretical constructs and/or provide initial validation for the items on a measuring instrument. Scores for the observed variables should be at least moderately correlated and have an approximate interval level of measurement. Further, unless communalities are expected to be generally high ($> .7$), a minimal sample size of 200 should be used. The key analysis steps are highlighted next.

I. Preliminary Analysis
    A. Conduct case analysis.
        1) Purpose: Identify any problematic individual observations and determine if scores appear to be reasonable.

2) Procedure:
   i) Inspect the distribution of each observed variable (e.g., via histograms) and identify apparent outliers. Scatterplots may also be inspected to examine linearity and bivariate outliers. Examine descriptive statistics (e.g., means, standard deviations) for each variable to assess if the scores appear to be reasonable for the sample at hand.
   ii) Inspect the z-scores for each variable, with absolute values larger than perhaps 2.5 or 3 along with a judgment that a given value is distinct from the bulk of the scores indicating an outlying value. Examine Mahalanobis distance values to identify multivariate outliers.
   iii) If any potential outliers or score abnormalities are identified, check for data entry errors. If needed, conduct a sensitivity study to determine the impact of one or more outliers on major study results. Consider use of variable transformations or case removal to attempt to minimize the effects of one or more outliers.
B. Check to see that data are suitable for factor analysis.
   1) Purpose: Determine if the data support the use of exploratory factor analysis. Also, identify the presence and pattern (if any) of missing data.
   2) Procedure: Compute and inspect the correlation matrix for the observed variables to make sure that correlations (especially among variables thought to represent a given factor) are at least moderately correlated ($> |.3|$). If not, consider an alternate analysis strategy (e.g., a causal indicator model) and/or check accuracy of data entry. If there is missing data, conduct missing data analysis. Check variance inflation factors to make sure that no excessive multicollinearity is present.

II. Primary Analysis
   A. Determine how many factors underlie the data.
      1) Purpose: Determine the number of factors needed in the factor model.
      2) Procedure: Select a factor extraction method (e.g., principal axis factoring) and use several criteria to identify the number of factors. Assuming principal axis factoring is implemented, we suggest use of the following criteria to identify the number of factors:
         i)   Retain factors having eigenvalues from the unreduced correlation matrix (with 1s on the diagonals) that are greater than 1 (Kaiser's rule);
         ii) Examine a scree plot of the eigenvalues from the reduced correlation matrix (with communalities on the diagonals) and retain factors appearing before the plot appears to level off;
         iii) Retain factors having eigenvalues that are larger than those obtained from random data (as obtained from parallel analysis);
         iv) Retain only those factors that make sense conceptually (as evidenced particularly by factor loadings and correlations); and
         v)   Consider results from models having different numbers of factors (e.g., two, three, or four factors) to avoid under- and over-factoring and assess which factor model is most meaningful.

   B. Rotate factors and attempt to identify the meaning of each factor.
      1) Purpose: Determine the degree to which factors are correlated (assuming multiple factors are present) and label or interpret factors so that they are useful for future research.
      2) Procedure:
         i) Select an oblique rotation method (e.g., direct quartimin) to estimate factor correlations. If factor correlations are near zero, an orthogonal rotation (e.g., varimax) can be used.
        ii) Determine which variables are related to a given factor by using a factor loading that reflects a reasonably strong association (e.g., $> |.40|$). Label or interpret a given factor based on the nature of the observed variables that load on it. Consider whether the factor correlations are reasonable given the interpretation of the factors.
        iii) Summarize the strength of association between the factors and observed variables with the communalities, the sum of squared loadings for each factor, and the percent of total variance explained in the observed scores.
   C. (Optional) If needed for subsequent analyses, compute factor scores using a suitable method for estimating such scores.

9.19 EXERCISES

1. Consider the following principal components solution with five variables using no rotation and then a varimax rotation. Only the first two components are given, because the eigenvalues corresponding to the remaining components were very small ($< .3$).

Variables	Unrotated solution		Varimax solution	
	Comp 1	Comp 2	Comp 1	Comp 2
1	.581	.806	.016	.994
2	.767	−.545	.941	−.009
3	.672	.726	.137	.980
4	.932	−.104	.825	.447
5	.791	−.558	.968	−.006

  (a) Find the amount and percent of variance accounted for by each unrotated component.
  (b) Find the amount and percent of variance accounted for by each varimax rotated component.
  (c) Compare the variance accounted for by each unrotated component with the variance accounted for by each corresponding rotated component.
  (d) Compare (to 2 decimal places) the total amount and percent of variance accounted for by the two unrotated components with the total amount and

percent of variance accounted for by the two rotated components. Does rotation change the variance accounted for by the two components?

(e) Compute the communality (to two decimal places) for the first observed variable using the loadings from the (i) unrotated loadings and (ii) loadings following rotation. Do communalities change with rotation?

2. Using the correlation matrix shown in Table 9.3, run an exploratory factor analysis (as illustrated in section 9.12) using principal axis extraction with direct quartimin rotation.

(a) Confirm that the use of Kaiser's rule (using the unreduced correlation matrix) and the use of parallel analysis as discussed in sections 9.11 and 9.12 (using the reduced correlation matrix) provide support for a two factor solution.

(b) Do the values in the pattern matrix provide support for the two-factor solution that was obtained in section 9.7?

(c) Are the factors correlated?

3. For additional practice in conducting an exploratory factor analysis, run an exploratory factor analysis using principal axis extraction using the correlations shown in Table 9.7 but do not include the bodily symptom items. Run a two- and three-factor solution for the remaining nine items.

(a) Which solution(s) have empirical support?

(b) Which solution seems more conceptually meaningful?

4. Bolton (1971) measured 159 deaf rehabilitation candidates on 10 communication skills, of which six were reception skills in unaided hearing, aided hearing, speech reading, reading, manual signs, and finger spellings. The other four communication skills were expression skills: oral speech, writing, manual signs, and finger-spelling. Bolton conducted an exploratory factor analysis using principal axis extraction with a varimax rotation. He obtained the following correlation matrix and varimax factor solution:

	Correlation Matrix of Communication Variables for 159 Deaf Persons											
	C_1	C_2	C_3	C_4	C_5	C_6	C_7	C_8	C_9	C_{10}	M	S
C_1	*39*										1.10	0.45
C_2	59	*55*									1.49	1.06
C_3	30	34	*61*								2.56	1.17
C_4	16	24	62	*81*							2.63	1.11
C_5	−02	−13	28	37	*92*						3.30	1.50
C_6	00	−05	42	51	90	*94*					2.90	1.44
C_7	39	61	70	59	05	20	*71*				2.14	1.31
C_8	17	29	57	88	30	46	60	*78*			2.42	1.04
C_9	−04	−14	28	33	93	86	04	28	*92*		3.25	1.49
C_{10}	−04	−08	42	50	87	94	17	45	90	*94*	2.89	1.41

Note: The italicized diagonal values are squared multiple correlations.

	Varimax Factor Solution for 10 Communication Variables for 159 Deaf Persons	I	II
C_1	Hearing (unaided)		49
C_2	Hearing (aided)		66
C_3	Speech reading	32	70
C_4	Reading	45	71
C_5	Manual signs	94	
C_6	Finger-spelling	94	
C_7	Speech		86
C_8	Writing	38	72
C_9	Manual signs	94	
C_{10}	Fingerspelling	96	
Percent of common variance		53.8	39.3

Note: Factor loadings less than .30 are omitted.

(a) Interpret the varimax factors. What does each of them represent?

(b) Does the way the variables that define factor 1 correspond to the way they are correlated? That is, is the empirical clustering of the variables by the principal axis technique consistent with the way those variables go together in the original correlation matrix?

5. Consider the following part of the quote from Pedhazur and Schmelkin (1991): "It boils down to the question: Are aspects of a postulated multidimensional construct intercorrelated? The answer to this question is relegated to the status of an assumption when an orthogonal rotation is employed" (p. 615). What did they mean by the last part of this statement?

REFERENCES

Benson, J., & Bandalos, D. L. (1992). Second-order confirmatory factor analysts of the Reactions to Tests scale with cross-validation. *Multivariate Behavioral Research, 27*, 459–487.

Bollen, K.A., & Bauldry, S. (2011). Three Cs in measurement models: Causal indicators, composite indicators, and covariates. *Psychological Methods, 16*, 265–284.

Bolton, B. (1971). A factor analytical study of communication skills and nonverbal abilities of deaf rehabilitation clients. *Multivariate Behavioral Research, 6*, 485–501.

Browne, M.W. (1968). A comparison of factor analytic techniques. *Psychometrika, 33*, 267–334.

Cattell, R.B. (1966). The meaning and strategic use of factor analysis. In R.B. Cattell (Ed.), *Handbook of multivariate experimental psychology* (pp. 174–243). Chicago, IL: Rand McNally.

Cattell, R.B., & Jaspers, J.A. (1967). A general plasmode for factor analytic exercises and research. *Multivariate Behavior Research Monographs, 3*, 1–212.

Cliff, N. (1987). *Analyzing multivariate data*. New York, NY: Harcourt Brace Jovanovich.

Cohen, J. (1988). *Statistical power analysis for the social sciences* (2nd ed.). Hillsdale, NJ: Lawrence Erlbaum Associates.

Cooley, W.W., & Lohnes, P.R. (1971). *Multivariate data analysis*. New York, NY: Wiley.

Fabrigar, L.R., & Wegener, D.T. (2012). *Factor analysis*. New York, NY: Oxford University Press.

Floyd, F.J., & Widamen, K.F. (1995). Factor analysis in the development and refinement of clinical assessment instruments. *Psychological Assessment, 7*, 286–299.

Grice, J.W. (2001). A comparison of factor scores under conditions of factor obliquity. *Psychological Methods, 6*, 67–83.

Gorsuch, R.L. (1983). *Factor analysis* (2nd ed.). Hillsdale, NJ: Lawrence Erlbaum Associates.

Guadagnoli, E., & Velicer, W. (1988). Relation of sample size to the stability of component patterns. *Psychological Bulletin, 103*, 265–275.

Hakstian, A.R., Rogers, W.D., & Cattell, R.B. (1982). The behavior of numbers factors rules with simulated data. *Multivariate Behavioral Research, 17*, 193–219.

Harman, H. (1967). *Modern factor analysis* (2nd ed.). Chicago, IL: University of Chicago Press.

Horn, J.L. (1965). A rationale and test for the number of factors in factor analysis. *Psychometrika, 30*, 179–185.

Kaiser, H.F. (1960). The application of electronic computers to factor analysis. *Educational and Psychological Measurement, 20*, 141–151.

Kline, R.B. (2005). *Principles and Practice of Structural Equation Modeling* (2nd ed.) New York, NY: Guilford Press.

Lawley, D.N. (1940). The estimation of factor loadings by the method of maximum likelihood. *Proceedings of the Royal Society of Edinburgh, 60*, 64.

Linn, R.L. (1968). A Monte Carlo approach to the number of factors problem. *Psychometrika, 33*, 37–71.

MacCallum, R.C., Widaman, K.F., Zhang, S., & Hong, S. (1999). Sample size in factor analysis. *Psychological Methods, 4*, 84–89.

MacCallum, R.C., Widaman, K.F., Preacher, K.J., & Hong, S. (2001). Sample size in factor analysis: The role of model error. *Multivariate Behavioral Research, 36*, 611–637.

Morrison, D.F. (1967). *Multivariate statistical methods*. New York, NY: McGraw-Hill.

Nunnally, J. (1978). *Psychometric theory*. New York, NY: McGraw-Hill.

Pedhazur, E., & Schmelkin, L. (1991). *Measurement, design, and analysis*. Hillsdale, NJ: Lawrence Erlbaum.

Preacher, K.J., & MacCallum, R.C. (2003). Repairing Tom Swift's electric factor analysis machine. *Understanding Statistics, 2*(1), 13–43.

Sarason, I.G. (1984). Stress, anxiety, and cognitive interference: Reactions to tests. *Journal of Personality and Social Psychology, 46*, 929–938.

Tucker, L.R., Koopman, R.E, & Linn, R.L. (1969). Evaluation of factor analytic research procedures by means of simulated correlation matrices. *Psychometrika, 34*, 421–459.

Velicer, W.F., & Fava, J.L. (1998). Effects of variable and subject sampling on factor pattern recovery. *Psychological Methods, 3*, 231–251.

Zwick, W.R., & Velicer, W.F. (1982). Factors influencing four rules for determining the number of components to retain. *Multivariate Behavioral Research, 17*, 253–269.

Zwick, W.R., & Velicer, W.F. (1986). Comparison of five rules for determining the number of components to retain. *Psychological Bulletin, 99*, 432–442.

Chapter 10

DISCRIMINANT ANALYSIS

10.1 INTRODUCTION

Discriminant analysis is used for two purposes: (1) to describe mean differences among the groups in MANOVA; and (2) to classify participants into groups on the basis of a battery of measurements. Since this text is primarily focused on multivariate tests of group differences, more space is devoted in this chapter to what is often called descriptive discriminant analysis. We also discuss the use of discriminant analysis for classifying participants, limiting our attention to the two-group case. We show the use of SPSS for descriptive discriminant analysis and SAS for classification.

Loosely speaking, descriptive discriminant analysis can be viewed conceptually as a combination of exploratory factor analysis and traditional MANOVA. Similar to factor analysis, where an initial concern is to identify how many linear combinations of variables are important, in discriminant analysis an initial task is to identify how many discriminant functions (composite variables or linear combinations) are present (i.e., give rise to group mean differences). Also, as in factor analysis, once we determine that a discriminant function or composite variable is important, we attempt to name or label it by examining coefficients that indicate the strength of association between a given observed variable and the composite. These coefficients are similar to pattern coefficients (but will now be called standardized discriminant function coefficients). Assuming we can meaningfully label the composites, we turn our attention to examining group differences, as in MANOVA. However, note that a primary difference between MANOVA, as it was presented in Chapters 4–5 and discriminant analysis, is that in discriminant analysis we are interested in identifying if groups differ not on the observed variables (as was the case previously), but on the *composites* (formally, discriminant functions) that are formed in the procedure. The success of the procedure then depends on whether such meaningful composite variables can be obtained. If not, the traditional MANOVA procedures of Chapters 4–5 can be used (or multivariate multilevel modeling as described in Chapter 14, or perhaps logistic regression). Note that the statistical assumptions for descriptive discriminant analysis, as well as all preliminary analysis activities, are exactly the same as for MANOVA. (See Chapter 6 for these assumptions as well as preliminary analysis activities.)

10.2 DESCRIPTIVE DISCRIMINANT ANALYSIS

Discriminant analysis is used here to break down the total between association in MANOVA into *additive* pieces, through the use of uncorrelated linear combinations of the original variables (these are the discriminant functions or composites). An additive breakdown is obtained because the composite variables are derived to be uncorrelated.

Discriminant analysis has two very nice features: (1) parsimony of description; and (2) clarity of interpretation. It can be quite parsimonious in that when comparing five groups on say 10 variables, we may find that the groups differ mainly on only two major composite variables, that is, the discriminant functions. It has clarity of interpretation in the sense that separation of the groups along one function is unrelated to separation along a different function. This is all fine, *provided* we can meaningfully name the composites and that there is adequate sample size so that the results are generalizable.

Recall that in multiple regression we found the linear combination of the predictors that was maximally correlated with the dependent variable. Here, in discriminant analysis, linear combinations are again used, in this case that best distinguish the groups. As throughout the text, linear combinations are central to many forms of multivariate analysis.

An example of the use of discriminant analysis, which is discussed later in this chapter, involves National Merit Scholars who are classified in terms of their parents' education, from eighth grade or less up to one or more college degrees, yielding four groups. The discriminating or observed variables are eight vocational personality variables (realistic, conventional, enterprising, sociability, etc.). The major personality differences among the scholars are captured by one composite variable (the first discriminant function), and show that the two groups of scholars whose parents had more education are less conventional and more enterprising than scholars whose parents have less education.

Before we begin a detailed discussion of discriminant analysis, it is important to note that discriminant analysis is a *mathematical maximization* procedure. What is being maximized will be made clear shortly. The important thing to keep in mind is that any time this type of procedure is employed there is a tremendous opportunity for capitalization on chance, especially if the number of participants is *not large* relative to the number of variables. That is, the results found on one sample may well not replicate on another independent sample. Multiple regression, it will be recalled, was another example of a mathematical maximization procedure. Because discriminant analysis is formally equivalent to multiple regression for two groups (Stevens, 1972), we might expect a similar problem with replicability of results. And indeed, as we see later, this is the case.

If the discriminating variables are denoted by $x_1, x_2, \ldots, x_p$, then in discriminant analysis the row vector of coefficients $\mathbf{a}_1'$ is sought, which maximizes $\mathbf{a}_1'\mathbf{B}\mathbf{a}_1 / \mathbf{a}_1'\mathbf{W}\mathbf{a}_1$, where $\mathbf{B}$ and $\mathbf{W}$ are the between and the within sum of squares and cross-products matrices. The linear combination of the discriminating variables involving the elements of $\mathbf{a}_1'$ as coefficients is the best discriminant function, in that it provides for maximum separation on the groups. Note that both the numerator and denominator in the quotient are scalars (numbers). *Thus, the procedure finds the linear combination of the discriminating variables, which maximizes between to within association.* The quotient shown corresponds to the largest eigenvalue (φ_1) of the $\mathbf{B}\mathbf{W}^{-1}$ matrix. The next best discriminant function, corresponding to the second largest eigenvalue of $\mathbf{B}\mathbf{W}^{-1}$, call it φ_2, involves the elements of $\mathbf{a}_2'$ in the ratio $\mathbf{a}_2'\mathbf{B}\mathbf{a}_2 / \mathbf{a}_2'\mathbf{W}\mathbf{a}_2$, as coefficients. This function is derived to be *uncorrelated* with the first discriminant function. It is the next best discriminator among the groups, in terms of separating them. The third discriminant function would be a linear combination of the discriminating variables, derived to be uncorrelated from both the first and second functions, which provides the next maximum amount of separation, and so on. The ith discriminant function (d_i) then is given by $d_i = \mathbf{a}_i'\mathbf{x}$, where $\mathbf{x}$ is the column vector of the discriminating variables.

If k is the number of groups and p is the number of observed or discriminating variables, then the number of possible discriminant functions is the minimum of p and $(k-1)$. Thus, if there were four groups and 10 discriminating variables, three composite variables would be formed in the procedure. For two groups, no matter how many discriminating variables, there will be only one composite variable. Finally, in obtaining the discriminant functions, the coefficients (the a_{ij}) are scaled so that $\mathbf{a}_i'\mathbf{a}_i = 1$ for each composite (the so-called unit norm condition). This is done so that there is a unique solution for each discriminant function.

10.3 DIMENSION REDUCTION ANALYSIS

Statistical tests, along with effect size measures described later, are typically used to determine the number of linear composites for which there are between-group mean differences. First, it can be shown that Wilks' Λ can be expressed as the following function of eigenvalues (φ_i) of $\mathbf{B}\mathbf{W}^{-1}$ (Tatsuoka, 1971, p. 164):

$$\Lambda = \frac{1}{1+\phi_1} \frac{1}{1+\phi_2} \cdots \frac{1}{1+\phi_r},$$

where r is the number of possible composite variables. Now, Bartlett showed that the following V statistic can be used for testing the significance of Λ:

$$V = \left[N - 1 - (p+k)/2 \right] \cdot \sum_{i=1}^{r} \ln(1 + \phi_i),$$

where V is approximately distributed as a χ^2 with $p(k-1)$ degrees of freedom.

The test procedure for determining how many of the composites are significant is a residual procedure. The procedure is sometimes referred to as dimension reduction analysis because significant composites are removed or peeled away during the testing process, allowing for additional tests of group differences of the remaining composites (i.e., the residual or leftover composites). The procedure begins by testing all of the composites together, using the V statistic. The null hypothesis for this test is that there are no group mean differences on any of the linear composites. Note that the values for Wilks' lambda obtained for this test statistic is mathematically equivalent to the Wilks' lambda used in section 5.4 to determine if groups differ for any of the observed variables for MANOVA. If this omnibus test for all composite variables is significant, then the largest eigenvalue (corresponding to the first composite) is removed and a test made of the remaining eigenvalues (the first residual) to determine if there are group differences on any of the remaining composites. If the first residual (V_1) is not significant, then we conclude that only the first composite is significant. If the first residual is significant, we conclude that the second composite is also significant, remove this composite from the testing process, and test any remaining eigenvalues to determine if group mean differences are present on any of the remaining composites. We do this by examining the second residual, that is, the V statistic with the largest two eigenvalues removed. If the second residual is not significant, then we conclude that only the first two composite variables are significant, and so on. In general then, when the residual after removing the first s eigenvalues is not significant, we conclude that only the first s composite variables are significant. Sections 10.7 and 10.8 illustrate dimension reduction analysis.

Table 10.1 gives the expressions for the test statistics and degrees of freedom used in dimension reduction analysis, here for the case where four composite variables are formed. The constant term, in brackets, is denoted by C for the sake of conciseness and is $[N - 1 - (p + k) / 2]$. The general formula for the degrees of freedom for the rth residual is $(p - r)[k - (r + 1)]$.

■ **Table 10.1: Residual Test Procedure for Four Possible Composite Variables**

Name	Test statistic	df
V	$C \sum_{i=1}^{4} \ln(1 + \phi_i)$	$p(k-1)$
V_1	$C[\ln(1 + \phi_2) + \ln(1 + \phi_3) + \ln(1 + \phi_4)]$	$(p-1)(k-2)$
V_2	$C[\ln(1 + \phi_3) + \ln(1 + \phi_4)]$	$(p-2)(k-3)$
V_3	$C[\ln(1 + \phi_4)]$	$(p-3)(k-4)$

10.4 INTERPRETING THE DISCRIMINANT FUNCTIONS

Once important composites are found, we then seek to interpret or label them. An important step in interpreting a composite variable is to identify which of the observed variables are related to it. The approach is similar to factor analysis where, after you have identified the number of factors present, you then identify which observed variables are related to the factor.

To identify which observed variables are related to a given composite, two types of coefficients are available:

1. Standardized (canonical) discriminant function coefficients—These are obtained by multiplying the raw (or unstandardized) discriminant function coefficient for each variable by the standard deviation of that variable. Similar to standardized regression coefficients, they represent the unique association between a given observed variable and composite, controlling for or holding constant the effects of the other observed variables.
2. The structure coefficients, which are the bivariate correlations between each composite variable and each of the original variables.

There are opposing views in the literature on which of these coefficient types should be used. For example, Meredith (1964), Porebski (1966), and Darlington, Weinberg, and Walberg (1973) argue in favor of using structure coefficients for two reasons: (1) the assumed greater stability of the correlations in small- or medium-sized samples, especially when there are high or fairly high intercorrelations among the variables; and (2) the correlations give a direct indication of which variables are most closely aligned with the unobserved trait that the canonical variate (discriminant function) represents.

On the other hand, Rencher (1992) showed that using structure coefficients is analogous to using univariate tests for each observed variable to determine which variables discriminate between groups. Thus, he concluded that using structure coefficients is not useful "because they yield only univariate information on how well the variables individually separate the means" (p. 225). As such, he recommends use of the standardized discriminant function coefficients, which take into account information on the set of discriminating variables. We note, in support of this view, that the composite scores that are used to compare groups are obtained from a raw score form of the standardized equation that uses a variable's unique effect to obtain the composite score. Therefore, it makes sense to interpret a function by using the same weights (now, in standardized form) that are used in forming its scores.

In addition, as a practical matter, simulation research conducted by Finch and Laking (2008) and Finch (2010) indicate that more accurate identification of the discriminating variables that are related to a linear composite is obtained by use of standardized rather than structural coefficients. In particular, Finch found that use of structural coefficients too often resulted in finding that a discriminating variable is related to the composite when it is in fact not related. He concluded that using structural coefficients to identify important discriminating variables "seems to be overly simplistic, frequently leading to incorrect decisions regarding the nature of the group differences" (p. 48). Note though that one weakness identified with the use of standardized coefficients by Finch and Laking occurs when a composite variable is related to only one discriminating variable (as opposed to multiple discriminating variables). In this univariate type of situation, they found that use of standardized coefficients too often suggests that the composite is (erroneously) related to another discriminating variable. Section 10.7.5 discusses alternatives to discriminant analysis that can be used in this situation.

Given that the standardized coefficients are preferred for interpreting the composite variables, how do you identify which of the observed variables is strongly related to a composite? While there are various schools of thought, we propose using the largest (in absolute value) coefficients to select which variables to use to interpret the function, a procedure that is also supported by simulation research conducted by Finch and Laking (2008). When we interpret the composite itself, of course, we also consider the signs (positive or negative) of these coefficients. We also note that standard errors associated with these coefficients are not available with the use of traditional methods. Although Finch (2010) found some support for using a bootstrapping procedure to provide inference for structure coefficients, there has been very little research on the performance of bootstrapping in the context of discriminant analysis. Further, we are not aware of any research that has examined the performance of bootstrap methods for standardized coefficients. Future research may shed additional light on the effectiveness of bootstrapping for discriminant analysis.

10.5 MINIMUM SAMPLE SIZE

Two Monte Carlo (computer simulation) studies (Barcikowski & Stevens, 1975; Huberty, 1975) *indicate that unless sample size is large relative to the number of variables, both the standardized coefficients and the correlations are very unstable.* That is, the results obtained in one sample (e.g., interpreting the first composite variable using variables 3 and 5) will very likely not hold up in another sample from the same population. *The clear implication of both studies is that unless the* N (*total sample size*) / p (*number of variables*) *ratio is quite large, say 20 to 1, one should be very cautious in interpreting the results.* This is saying, for example, that if there are 10 variables in a discriminant analysis, at least 200 participants are needed for the investigator to have confidence that the variables selected as most important in interpreting a composite variable would again show up as most important in another sample. In addition, while the procedure does not require equal group sizes, it is generally recommended that, at bare minimum, the number of participants in the smallest group should be at or larger than 20 (and larger than the number of observed variables).

10.6 GRAPHING THE GROUPS IN THE DISCRIMINANT PLANE

If there are two or more significant composite variables, then a useful device for assessing group differences is to graph them in the discriminant plane. The horizontal direction corresponds to the first composite variable, and thus lateral separation among the groups indicates how much they have been distinguished on this composite. The vertical dimension corresponds to the second composite, and thus vertical separation tells us which groups are being distinguished in a way unrelated to the way they were separated on the first composite (because the composites are uncorrelated).

Given that each composite variable is a linear combination of the original varia-bles, group means of each composite can be easily obtained because the mean of the linear combination is equal to the linear combination of the means on the original variables. That is,

$$\bar{d}_1 = a_{11}\bar{x}_1 + a_{12}\bar{x}_2 + \cdots + a_{1p}\bar{x}_p,$$

where d_1 is the composite variable (or discriminant function) and the x_i are the original variables. Note that this is analogous to multiple regression, where if you insert the mean of each predictor into a regression equation the mean of the outcome is obtained.

The matrix equation for obtaining the coordinates of the groups on the composite var-iables is given by:

$$\mathbf{D} = \bar{\mathbf{X}}\mathbf{V},$$

where $\bar{\mathbf{X}}$ is the matrix of means for the original variables in the various groups and $\mathbf{V}$ is a matrix whose *columns* are the raw coefficients for the discriminant functions (the first column for the first function, etc.). To make this more concrete we consider the case of three groups and four variables. Then the matrix equation becomes:

$$\mathbf{D} = \bar{\mathbf{X}} \quad \mathbf{V}$$
$$(3 \times 2) = (3 \times 4)(4 \times 2)$$

The specific elements of the matrices would be as follows:

$$\begin{bmatrix} d_{11} & d_{12} \\ d_{21} & d_{22} \\ d_{31} & d_{32} \end{bmatrix} = \begin{bmatrix} \bar{x}_{11} & \bar{x}_{12} & \bar{x}_{13} & \bar{x}_{14} \\ \bar{x}_{21} & \bar{x}_{22} & \bar{x}_{23} & \bar{x}_{24} \\ \bar{x}_{31} & \bar{x}_{32} & \bar{x}_{33} & \bar{x}_{34} \end{bmatrix} \begin{bmatrix} a_{11} & a_{12} \\ a_{21} & a_{22} \\ a_{31} & a_{32} \\ a_{41} & a_{42} \end{bmatrix}$$

In this equation $\bar{x}_{11}$ gives the mean for variable 1 in group 1, $\bar{x}_{12}$ the mean for variable 2 in group 1, and so on. The first row of $\mathbf{D}$ gives the x and y Cartesian coordinates of group 1 on the two discriminant functions; the second row gives the location of group 2 in the discriminant plane, and so on. Sections 10.7.2 and 10.8.2 show a plot of group centroids.

10.7 EXAMPLE WITH SENIORWISE DATA

The first example used here is from the SeniorWISE data set that was used in section 6.11. We use this example having relatively few observed variables to facilitate understanding of discriminant analysis. Recall for that example participants aged 65 and older were randomly assigned to receive one of three treatments: memory training, a health intervention, or a control condition. The treatments were administered and posttest measures were completed on an individual basis. The posttest or discriminating variables (as called in discriminant analysis) are measures of self-efficacy, verbal memory performance (or verbal), and daily functioning (or DAFS). In the analysis in section 6.11 (MANOVA with follow-up ANOVAs), the focus was to describe treatment effects for each of the outcomes (because the treatment was hypothesized to impact each variable, and researchers were interested in reporting effects for each of the three outcomes). For discriminant analysis, we seek parsimony in describing such treatment effects and are now interested in determining if there are linear combinations of these variables (composites) that separate the three groups. Specifically, we will address the following research questions:

1. Are there group mean differences for any of the composite variables? If so, how many composites differ across groups?
2. Assuming there are important group differences for one or more composites, what does each of these composite variables mean?
3. What is the nature of the group differences? That is, which groups have higher/lower mean scores on the composites?

10.7.1 Preliminary Analysis

Before we begin the primary analysis, we consider some preliminary analysis activities and examine some relevant results provided by SPSS for discriminant analysis. As mentioned previously, the same preliminary analysis activities are used for discriminant analysis and MANOVA. Table 10.2 presents some of these results as obtained by the SPSS discriminant analysis procedure. Table 10.2 shows that the memory training group had higher mean scores across each variable, while the other two groups had relatively similar performance across each of the variables. Note that there are 100 participants in each group. The F tests for mean differences indicate that such differences are present for each of the observed variables. Note though that these differences in means reflect strictly univariate differences and do not take into account the correlations among these variables, which we will do shortly. Also, given that an initial multivariate test of overall mean differences has not been used here, these univariate tests do not offer any protection against the inflation of the overall Type I error rate. So, to interpret these test results, you should apply a Bonferroni-adjusted alpha for these tests, which can be done by comparing the p value for each test to alpha divided by the number of tests being performed (i.e., $.05 / 3 = .0167$). Given that each p value is smaller than this adjusted alpha allows us to conclude that there are mean differences present for each observed variable in the population. Note that while univariate differences are not the focus in discriminant analysis, they are useful to consider because they give us a sense of the variables that *might* be important when we take the correlations among variables into account. These correlations, pooled across each of the three groups, are shown at the bottom of Table 10.2. The observed variables are positively and moderately correlated, the latter of which supports the use of discriminant analysis. Also, note that the associations are not overly strong, suggesting that multicollinearity is not an issue.

■ **Table 10.2: Descriptive Statistics for the SeniorWISE Study**

Group Statistics

GROUP		Mean	Std. deviation	Valid N (listwise) Unweighted	Weighted
Memory training	Self_Efficacy	58.5053	9.19920	100	100.000
	Verbal	60.2273	9.65827	100	100.000
	DAFS	59.1516	9.74461	100	100.000
Health training	Self_Efficacy	50.6494	8.33143	100	100.000
	Verbal	50.8429	9.34031	100	100.000
	DAFS	52.4093	10.27314	100	100.000
Control	Self_Efficacy	48.9764	10.42036	100	100.000
	Verbal	52.8810	9.64866	100	100.000
	DAFS	51.2481	8.55991	100	100.000
Total	Self_Efficacy	52.7104	10.21125	300	300.000
	Verbal	54.6504	10.33896	300	300.000
	DAFS	54.2697	10.14037	300	300.000

Tests of Equality of Group Means

	Wilks' Lambda	F	df1	df2	Sig.
Self_Efficacy	.834	29.570	2	297	.000
Verbal	.848	26.714	2	297	.000
DAFS	.882	19.957	2	297	.000

Pooled Within-Groups Matrices

		Self_Efficacy	Verbal	DAFS
Correlation	Self_Efficacy	1.000	.342	.337
	Verbal	.342	1.000	.451
	DAFS	.337	.451	1.000

The statistical assumptions for discriminant analysis are the same as for MANOVA and are assessed in the same manner. Table 10.3 reports Box's M test for the equality of variance-covariance matrices as provided by the discriminant analysis procedure. These results are exactly the same as those reported in section 6.11 and suggest that the assumption of equal variance-covariance matrices is tenable. Also, as reported in section 6.11, for this example there are no apparent violations of the multivariate normality or independence assumptions. Further, for the MANOVA of these data as reported in section 6.11, we found that no influential observations were present. Note though that since discriminant analysis uses a somewhat different testing procedure (i.e., dimension reduction analysis) than MANOVA and has a different procedure to assess the importance of individual variables, the impact of these outliers can be assessed here as well. We leave this task to interested readers.

10.7.2 Primary Analysis

Given that the data support the use of discriminant analysis, we can proceed to address each of the research questions of interest. The first primary analysis step is to determine the number of composite variables that separate groups. Recall that the number of such discriminant functions formed by the procedure is equal to the smaller of the number of groups -1 (here, $3 - 1 = 2$) or the number of discriminating variables (here, $p = 3$). Thus, two composites will be formed, but we do not know if any will be statistically significant.

To find out how many composite variables we should consider as meaningfully separating groups, we first examine the results of the dimension reduction analysis, which are shown in Table 10.4. The first statistical test is an omnibus test for group differences for all of the composites, two here. The value for Wilks' lambda, as shown in the lower table, is .756, which when converted to a chi-square test is 82.955 ($p < .001$). This result indicates that there are between group mean differences on, at least, one linear composite variable (i.e., the first discriminant function). This composite is then removed from the testing process, and we now test whether there are group differences on the second (and final) composite. The lower part of Table 10.4 reports the relevant

■ **Table 10.3: Test Results for the Equality of Covariance Matrices Assumption**

Box's Test of Equality of Covariance Matrices

Test Results

Box's M		21.047
F	Approx.	1.728
	df1	12
	df2	427474.385
	Sig.	.054

Tests null hypothesis of equal population covariance matrices.

information for this test, for which the Wilks' lambda is .975, the chi-square test is 7.472 with $p = .024$. These test results suggest that there are group differences on both composites. However, we do not know at this point if these composite variables are meaningful or if the group differences that are present can be considered as nontrivial. Recall that our sample size is 300, so it is possible that the tests are detecting small group differences.

So, in addition to examining test results for the dimension reduction analysis, we also consider measures of effect size to determine the number of composite variables that separate groups. Here, we focus on two effect size measures: the proportion of variance that is between groups and the proportion of between-group variance that is due to each variate. The proportion of variance that is between groups is not directly provided by SPSS but can be easily calculated from canonical correlations. The canonical correlation is the correlation between scores on a composite and group membership and is reported for each function in Table 10.4 (i.e., .474 and .158). If we square the canonical correlation, we obtain the proportion of variance in composite scores that is between groups, analogous to eta square in ANOVA. For this first composite, this proportion of variance is $.474^2 = .225$. This value indicates that about 23% of the score variation for the first composite is between groups, which most investigators would likely regard as indicative of substantial group differences. For the second composite, the proportion of variation between groups is much smaller at $.158^2 = .025$.

The second measure of effect size we consider is the percent of between-group variation that is due to each of the linear composites, that is, the functions. This measure compares the composites in terms of the total between-group variance that is present in the analysis. To better understand this measure, it is helpful to calculate the sum of squares between groups for each of the composites as would be obtained if a one-way ANOVA were conducted with the composite scores as the dependent variable. This can

■ Table 10.4: Dimension Reduction Analysis Results for the SeniorWISE Study

Summary of Canonical Discriminant Functions

Eigenvalues

Function	Eigenvalue	% of Variance	Cumulative %	Canonical Correlation
1	.290[a]	91.9	91.9	.474
2	.026[a]	8.1	100.0	.158

[a] First 2 canonical discriminant functions were used in the analysis.

Wilks' Lambda

Test of Function(s)	Wilks' Lambda	Chi-square	Df	Sig.
1 through 2	.756	82.955	6	.000
2	.975	7.472	2	.024

be done by multiplying the value of $N - k$, where N is the total sample size and k is the number of groups, by the eigenvalues for each function. The eigenvalues are shown in Table 10.4 (i.e., .290 and .026), although here we use more decimal places for accuracy. Thus, for the first composite, the amount of variance that is between groups is $(300 - 3)(.290472) = 86.27018$, and for the second composite is $(297)(.025566) = 7.593102$. The total variance that is between groups for the set of composite variables is then $86.27018 + 7.593102 = 93.86329$.

Now, it is a simple matter to compute the proportion of the total between-group variance that is due to each composite. For the first composite, this is $86.27018 / 93.86329 = .919$, or that 92% of the total between-group variance is due to this composite. For the second composite, the total between-group variation due to it is $7.593102 / 93.86329 = .081$, or about 8%. Note that these percents do not need to be calculated as they are provided by SPSS and shown in Table 10.4 under the "% of Variance" column.

Summarizing our findings thus far, there are group mean differences on two composites. Further, there are substantial group differences on the first composite, as it accounts for 92% of the total between-group variance. In addition, about 23% of the variance for this composite is between groups. The second composite is not as strongly related to group membership as about 2.5% of the variance is between groups, and this composite accounts for about 8% of the total between-group variance. Given the relatively weak association between the second composite and group membership, you could focus attention primarily on the first composite. However, we assume that you would like to describe group differences for each composite.

We now focus on the second research question that involves interpreting or naming the composite variables. To interpret the composites, we use the values reported for the standardized canonical discriminant function coefficients, as shown in Table 10.5, which also shows the structure coefficients. Examining Table 10.5, we see that the observed variables are listed in the first column of each output table and the coefficients are shown under the respective composite or function number (1 or 2). For the first composite, the standardized coefficients are 0.575, 0.439, and 0.285 for self-efficacy, verbal, and DAFS, respectively. It is a judgment call, but the coefficients seem to be fairly similar in magnitude, although the unique contribution of DAFS is somewhat weaker. However, given that a standardized regression coefficient near 0.3 is often regarded as indicative of a sufficiently strong association, we will use all three variables to interpret the first composite. While a specialist in the research topic might be able to apply a more meaningful label here, we can say that higher scores on the first composite correspond to individuals having (given positive coefficients for each variable) higher scores on memory self-efficacy, verbal performance, and daily functioning. (Note that using the structure coefficients, which are simple bivariate correlations, would in this case lead to the same conclusion about observed variable importance.) For the second composite, inspection of the standardized coefficients suggests that verbal performance is *the* dominant variable for that function (which also happens to be the same conclusion that would be reached by use of the structure coefficients). For that composite variable, then, we can say that higher scores are indicative of participants who have low scores (given the negative sign) on verbal performance.

We now turn our attention to the third research question, which focuses on describing group differences. Table 10.6 shows the group centroids for each of the composites. In Chapters 4–5, we focused on estimating group differences for each of the observed variables. With discriminant function analysis, we no longer do that. Instead, the statistical procedure forms linear combinations of the observed variables, which are the composites or functions. We have created two such composites in this example, and the group means for these functions, known as centroids, are shown in Table 10.6. Further, each composite variable is formed in such a way so that the scores have a grand mean of zero and a standard deviation of 1. This scaling facilitates interpretation, as we will see. Note also that there are no statistical tests provided for these contrasts, so our description of the differences between groups is based on the point estimates of the centroids. However, a plot of the group centroids is useful in assessing which groups are different from others. Figure 10.1 presents a plot of the group centroids (and discriminant function scores). Note that a given square in the figure appearing next to each labeled group is the respective group's centroid.

First, examining the values of the group centroids in Table 10.6 for the first composite indicates that the typical (i.e., mean) score for those in the memory training group is about three-quarters of a standard deviation above the grand mean for this composite variable. Thus, a typical individual in this group has relatively high scores on self-efficacy, verbal performance, and daily functioning. In contrast, the means for the other groups indicate that the typical person in these groups has below average scores for this composite variable. Further, the difference in means between the memory training and other groups is about 1 standard deviation ($.758 - [-.357] = 1.12$ and $.758 - [-.401] = 1.16$). In contrast, the health training and control groups have similar

▨ **Table 10.5: Structure and Standardized Discriminant Function Coefficients**

Structure matrix			Standardized canonical discriminant function coefficients		
	Function			Function	
	1	2		1	2
Self_Efficacy	.821*	.367	Self_Efficacy	.575	.552
Verbal	.764*	−.634	Verbal	.439	−1.061
DAFS	.677*	.236	DAFS	.285	.529

Pooled within-groups correlations between discriminating variables and standardized canonical discriminant functions

Variables ordered by absolute size of correlation within function.

* Largest absolute correlation between each variable and any discriminant function

■ **Table 10.6: Group Means (Centroids) for the Discriminant Functions**

Functions at Group Centroids

	Function	
GROUP	1	2
Memory Training	.758	−.007
Health Training	−.357	.198
Control	−.401	−.191

■ **Figure 10.1: Group centroids (represented by squares) and discriminant function scores (represented by circles).**

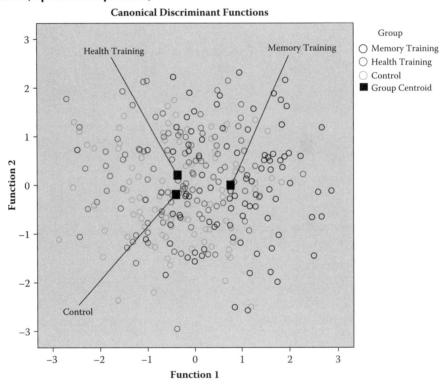

means on this composite. For the second composite, although group differences are much smaller, it appears that the health training and control groups have a noticeable mean difference on this composite, suggesting that participants in the health training group score lower on average than those in the control group on verbal performance.

Inspecting Figure 10.1 also suggests that mean scores for function (or composite) 1 are much higher for the memory training group than the other groups. The means for function 1 are displayed along the horizontal axis of Figure 10.1. We can see that the mean for the memory training group is much further to the right (i.e., much larger) than the other means. Note that the means for the other groups essentially overlap one another on the left side of the plot. The vertical distances among group means represents mean differences for the scores of the second composite. These differences are much smaller but the health intervention and control group means seem distinct.

In sum, we found that there were fairly large between-group differences on one composite variable (the first function) and smaller differences on the second. With this analysis, we conclude that the memory training group had much higher mean scores on a composite variable reflecting memory self-efficacy, verbal performance, and daily functioning than the other groups, which had similar means on this function. For the second function, which was defined by verbal performance, participants in the health training group had somewhat lower mean verbal performance than those in the control group.

10.7.3 SPSS Syntax for Descriptive Discriminant Analysis

Table 10.7 shows SPSS syntax used for this example. The first line invokes the discriminant analysis procedure. In the next line, after the required GROUP subcommand, you provide the name of the grouping variable (here, Group) and list the first and last numerical values used to designate the groups in your data set (groups 1–3, here). After the required VARIABLES subcommand, you list the observed variables. The ANALYSIS ALL subcommand, though not needed here to produce the proper results, avoids obtaining a warning message that would otherwise appear in the output. After the STATISTICS subcommand in the next to last line, MEAN and STDEV request group means and standard deviations for each observed variable, UNIVF provides univariate F tests of group mean differences for each observed variable, and CORR requests the pooled within-group correlation, output for which appears in Table 10.2. BOXM requests the Box's M test for the equal variance-covariance matrices assumption, the output for which was shown in Table 10.3. The last line requests a plot of the group centroids, as was shown in Figure 10.1. In general, SPSS will plot just the first two discriminant functions, regardless of the number of composites in the analysis.

10.7.4 Computing Scores for the Discriminant Functions

It has been our experience that students often find discriminant analysis initially, at least, somewhat confusing. This section, not needed for results interpretation, attempts

■ **Table 10.7: SPSS Commands for Discriminant Analysis for the SeniorWISE Study**

```
DISCRIMINANT
 /GROUPS=Group(1 3)
 /VARIABLES=Self_Efficacy Verbal Dafs
 /ANALYSIS ALL
 /STATISTICS=MEAN STDDEV UNIVF BOXM CORR
 /PLOT=COMBINED.
```

to clarify the nature of discriminant analysis by focusing on the scores for the composites, or discriminant functions. As stated previously, scores for composite variables are obtained using a linear combination of variables (which are weighted in such a way as to produce maximum group separation). We can compute scores for the composites obtained with the example at hand using the raw score discriminant function coefficients, which are shown in Table 10.8. (Note that we interpret composite variables by using standardized coefficients, which are obtained from the raw score coefficients.)

For example, using the raw score coefficients for function 1, we can compute scores for this composite for each person in the data set with the expression

$$d_1 = -7.369 + .061(Self\_Efficacy) + .046(Verbal) + .030(DAFS),$$

where d_1 represents scores for the first discriminant function. Table 10.9 shows the raw scores for these discriminating variables as well as for the discriminant functions (d_1 and d_2) for the first 10 cases in the data set. To illustrate, to compute scores for the first composite variable for the first case in the data set, we would simply insert the scores for the observed variables into the equation and obtain

$$d_1 = -7.369 + .061(71.12) + .046(68.78) + .030(84.17) = 2.67.$$

Such scores would then be computed for each person simply by placing their raw scores for the observed variables into the expression. Scores for the second discriminant function would then be computed by the same process, except that we would use the coefficients shown in Table 10.8 for the second composite variable.

It is helpful, then, to remember that when using discriminant analysis, you are simply creating outcome variables (the composites), each of which is a weighted sum of the observed scores. Once obtained, if you were to average the scores within each group for d_1 in Table 10.9 (for all 300 cases) and then for d_2, you would obtain the group centroids that are shown in Table 10.6 and in Figure 10.1 (which also shows the individual

■ **Table 10.8: Raw Score Discriminant Function Coefficients**

Canonical Discriminant Function Coefficients

	Function	
	1	2
Self_Efficacy	.061	.059
Verbal	.046	−.111
DAFS	.030	.055
(Constant)	−7.369	−.042
Unstandardized coefficients		

■ **Table 10.9: Scores for the First 10 Cases Including Discriminant Function Scores**

	Self_Efficacy	Verbal	DAFS	GROUP	CASE	D1	D2
1	71.12	68.78	84.17	1.00	1.00	2.67249	1.17202
2	52.79	65.93	61.80	1.00	2.00	.74815	-.83122
3	48.48	47.47	38.94	1.00	3.00	-1.04741	-.30143
4	44.68	53.71	77.72	1.00	4.00	.16354	.92961
5	63.27	62.74	60.50	1.00	5.00	1.20672	.06957
6	57.46	61.66	58.31	1.00	6.00	.73471	-.27450
7	63.45	61.41	47.59	1.00	7.00	.77093	-.48837
8	55.29	44.32	52.05	1.00	8.00	-.38224	1.17767
9	52.78	67.72	61.08	1.00	9.00	.80802	-1.07156
10	46.04	52.51	36.77	1.00	10.00	-1.03078	-1.12454

function scores). Thus, with discriminant analysis you create composite variables, which, if meaningful, are used to assess group differences.

10.7.5 Univariate or Composite Variable Comparisons?

Since the data used in the illustration were also used in section 6.11, we can compare results obtained in section 6.11 to those obtained with discriminant analysis. While both procedures use at least one omnibus multivariate test to determine if groups differ, traditional MANOVA (as exemplified by the procedures used in section 6.11) uses univariate procedures only to describe specific group differences, whereas discriminant analysis focuses on describing differences in means for composite variables. Although this is not always the case, with the preceding example the results obtained from traditional MANOVA and discriminant analysis results were fairly similar, in that use of each procedure found that the memory training group scored higher on average on self-efficacy, verbal performance, and DAFS. Note though that use of discriminant analysis suggested a group difference for verbal performance (between the health and control conditions), which was not indicated by traditional MANOVA. Given different analysis results may be obtained by use of these two procedures, is one approach preferred over the other?

There are different opinions about which technique is preferred, and often a preference is stated for discriminant analysis, primarily because it takes associations among variables into account throughout the analysis procedure (provided that standardized discriminant function coefficients are used). However, the central issue in selecting an analysis approach is whether you are interested in investigating group differences (1) for each of the observed variables or (2) in linear composites of the observed variables. If you are interested in forming composite variables or believe that the observed variables at hand may measure one or more underlying constructs, discriminant analysis is the method to use for that purpose. For this latter reason, use of discriminant analysis, in general, becomes more appealing as the number of dependent (or discriminating variables) increases as it becomes more difficult to believe that each observed variable represents a distinct stand-alone construct of interest. In addition, the greater parsimony potentially offered by discriminant analysis is also appealing when the number of dependent variables is large.

A limitation of discriminant analysis is that meaningful composite variables may not be obtained. Also, in discriminant analysis, there seems to be less agreement on how you should determine which discriminating variables are related to the composites. While we favor use of standardized coefficients, researchers often use structure coefficients, which we pointed out is essentially adopting a univariate approach. Further, there are no standard errors associated with either of these coefficients, so determining which variables separate groups seems more tentative when compared to the traditional MANOVA approach. Although further research needs to be done, Finch and Laking (2008), as discussed earlier, found that when only one discriminating variable is related to a function, use of standardized weights too often results (erroneously) in another discriminating variable being identified as the important variable. This suggests that when you believe that group differences will be due to only one variable in the set, MANOVA or another alternative mentioned shortly should be used. All things being equal, use of a larger number of variables again tends to support use of discriminant analysis, as it seems more likely in this case that meaningful composite variables will separate groups.

For its part, MANOVA is sensible to use when you are interested in describing group differences for each of the observed variables and not in forming composites. Often, in such situations, methodologists will recommend use of a series of Bonferroni-corrected ANOVAs without use of any multivariate procedure. We noted in Chapter 5 that use of MANOVA has some advantages over using a series of Bonferroni-adjusted ANOVAs. First, use of MANOVA as an omnibus test of group differences provides for a more exact type I rate in testing for any group differences on the set of outcomes. Second, and perhaps more important, *when the number of observed dependent variables is relatively small*, you can use the protected test provided by MANOVA to obtain greater power for the F tests of group differences on the observed variables. As mentioned in Chapter 5, with two outcomes and no Bonferroni-correction for the follow-up univariate F tests that are each, let's assume, tested using a standard .05 alpha, the maximum risk of making a type I error for the set of such F tests, following the use of Wilks' Λ as a protected test, is .05, as desired. However, an overcorrected alpha of .025 would be used in the ANOVA-only approach, resulting in unnecessarily lower power. With three outcomes, this type I error rate, at worst, is .10 with use of the traditional MANOVA approach. Note that with more dependent variables, this approach will not properly control the inflation of the type I error rate. So, in this case, Bonferroni-adjusted alphas would be preferred, or perhaps the use of discriminant analysis as meaningful composites might be formed from the larger number of observed variables.

We also wish to point out an alternative approach that has much to offer when you are interested in group differences on a set of outcome variables. A common criticism of the traditional MANOVA approach is that the follow-up univariate procedures ignore associations among variables, while discriminant analysis does not. While this is true, you can focus on tests for specific observed variables *while also* taking correlations among the outcomes into account. That is, multivariate multilevel modeling (MVMM) procedures described in Chapter 14, while perhaps more difficult to implement, allow you to test for group differences for given observed variables (without forming composites) while taking into account correlations among the outcomes. In addition, if you are interested in examining group differences on each of several outcomes and were to adopt the often recommended procedure of using only a series of univariate tests (without any multivariate analysis), you would miss out on some critical advantages offered by MVMM. One such benefit involves missing data on the outcomes, with such cases typically being deleted when a univariate procedure is used, possibly resulting in biased parameter estimates. On the other hand, if there were missing data on one or more outcomes and missingness were related to these outcomes, use of MVMM as described in Chapter 14 would provide for optimal parameter estimates due to using information on the associations among the dependent variables. The main point we wish to make here is that you can, with use of MVMM, test for group differences on a given dependent variable while taking associations among the outcomes into account.

10.8. NATIONAL MERIT SCHOLAR EXAMPLE

We present a second example of descriptive discriminant analysis that is based on a study by Stevens (1972), which involves National Merit Scholars. Since the original data are no longer available, we simulated data so that the main findings match those reported by Stevens. In this example, the grouping variable is the educational level of both parents of the National Merit Scholars. Four groups were formed: (1) those students for whom at least one parent had an eighth-grade education or less ($n = 90$); (2) those students both of whose parents were high school graduates ($n = 104$); (3) those students both of whose parents had gone to college, with at most one graduating ($n = 115$); and (4) those students both of whose parents had at least one college degree ($n = 75$). The discriminating variables are a subset of the Vocational Personality Inventory (VPI): realistic, intellectual, social, conventional, enterprising, artistic, status, and aggression.

This example is likely more typical of discriminant analysis applications than the previous example in that there are eight discriminating variables instead of three, and that a nonexperimental design is used. With eight variables, you would likely not be interested in describing group differences for each variable but instead would prefer a more parsimonious description of group differences. Also, with eight variables, it is much less likely that you are dealing with eight distinct constructs. Instead, there may be combinations of variables (discriminant functions), analogous to constructs in factor analysis, that may meaningfully distinguish the groups. For the primary analysis of these data, the same syntax used in Table 10.7 is used here, except that the names of the observed and grouping variables are different. For preliminary analysis, we follow the outline provided in section 6.13. Note that complete SPSS syntax for this example is available online.

10.8.1 Preliminary Analysis

Inspection of the Mahalanobis distance for each group did not suggest the presence of any multivariate outliers, as the largest value (18.9) was smaller than the corresponding chi-square critical value (.001, 8) of 26.125. However, four cases had within-group z-scores greater than 3 in magnitude. When we removed these cases temporarily, study results were unchanged. Therefore, we used all cases for the analysis. There are no missing values in the data set, and no evidence of multicollinearity as all variance inflation factors were smaller than 2.2. The variance inflation factors were obtained by running a regression analysis using all cases with case ID regressed on all discriminating variables and collinearity diagnostics requested. Also, the within-group pooled correlations, not shown, range from near zero to about .50, and indicate that the variables are, in general, moderately correlated, supporting the use of discriminant analysis.

In addition, the formal assumptions for discriminant analysis seem to be satisfied. None of the skewness and kurtosis values for each variable within each group were larger than a magnitude of 1, suggesting no serious departures of the normality assumption. For the equality of variance-covariance matrices assumption, we examined the group standard deviations, the log determinants of the variance-covariance matrices, and Box's M test. The group standard deviations were similar across groups for each variable, as an examination of Table 10.10 would suggest. The log determinants, shown in Table 10.11, are also very similar. Recall that the determinant of the covariance matrix is a measure of the generalized variance. Similar values for the log of the determinant for each group covariance matrix support the assumption being satisfied. Third, as shown in Table 10.11, Box's M test is not significant ($p = .249$), suggesting no serious departures from the assumption of equal group variance-covariance matrices. Further, the study design does not suggest any violations of the independence assumption, as participants were randomly sampled. Further, there is no reason to believe that a clustering effect or any other type of nonindependence is present.

10.8.2 Primary Analysis

Before we present results from the dimension reduction analysis, we consider the group means and univariate F tests for between-group differences for each discriminating variable. Examining the univariate F tests, shown in Table 10.12, indicates the presence of group differences for the conventional and enterprising variables. The group means for these variables, shown in Table 10.10, suggest that the groups having a college education have lower mean values for the conventional variable but higher means for the enterprising variable. Keep in mind though that these are univariate differences, and the multivariate procedure that focuses on group differences for composite variables may yield somewhat different results.

■ Table 10.10: Group Means and Standard Deviations for the National Merit Scholar Example

Report

Group		Real	Intell	Social	Conven	Enterp	Artis	Status	Aggress
Eighth grade	Mean	52.9284	55.6887	56.0231	55.7774	54.0273	55.0320	58.6137	56.1801
	N	90	90	90	90	90	90	90	90
	Std. deviation	11.01032	10.67135	9.29340	9.90840	8.88914	10.56371	11.05943	10.35341
High school diploma	Mean	52.6900	55.4460	54.9282	55.2867	53.9990	54.2293	57.7603	55.4509
	N	104	104	104	104	104	104	104	104
	Std. deviation	9.59393	9.51507	11.10255	10.24910	10.05422	11.65962	11.22663	11.00961
Some college	Mean	51.9323	56.1798	56.5980	50.1635	63.7137	56.0942	59.1374	56.8192
	N	115	115	115	115	115	115	115	115
	Std. deviation	9.82378	8.87025	10.19737	9.24970	9.80477	10.37180	10.27787	9.95956
College degree	Mean	50.4033	55.5278	56.8009	49.4474	63.5549	57.4365	59.0436	55.8459
	N	75	75	75	75	75	75	75	75
	Std. deviation	9.71628	9.83051	8.79044	9.33980	8.35383	8.68600	8.91861	8.88810
Total	Mean	52.0724	55.7386	56.0507	52.7269	58.7814	55.6024	58.6234	56.1087
	N	384	384	384	384	384	384	384	384
	Std. deviation	10.03575	9.64327	9.98216	10.07118	10.53246	10.50751	10.46155	10.12810

■ **Table 10.11: Statistics for Assessing the Equality of the Variance-Covariance Matrices Assumption**

Log Determinants

Group	Rank	Log determinant
Eighth grade	8	34.656
High school diploma	8	34.330
Some college	8	33.586
College degree	8	33.415
Pooled within-groups	8	34.327

The ranks and natural logarithms of determinants printed are those of the group covariance matrices.

Test Results

Box's M		122.245
F	Approx.	1.089
	$df1$	108
	$df2$	269612.277
	Sig.	.249

Tests null hypothesis of equal population covariance matrices.

■ **Table 10.12: Univariate F Tests for Group Mean Differences**

Tests of Equality of Group Means

	Wilks' Lambda	F	$df1$	$df2$	Sig.
Real	.992	1.049	3	380	.371
Intell	.999	.124	3	380	.946
Social	.995	.693	3	380	.557
Conven	.921	10.912	3	380	.000
Enterp	.790	33.656	3	380	.000
Artis	.988	1.532	3	380	.206
Status	.997	.367	3	380	.777
Aggress	.997	.351	3	380	.788

The results of the dimension reduction analysis are shown in Table 10.13. With four groups and eight discriminating variables in the analysis, three discriminant functions will be formed. Table 10.13 shows that only the test with all functions included is statistically significant (Wilks' lambda = .564, chi-square = 215.959, $p < .001$). Thus, we conclude that only one composite variable distinguishes between groups in the population. In addition, the square of the canonical correlation ($.656^2$) for this composite, when converted to a percent, indicates that about 43% of the score variation for the first function is between groups. As noted, the test results do not provide support for the presence of group differences for the remaining functions, and the proportion of variance between groups associated with these composites is much smaller at .007 ($.085^2$) and .002 ($.049^2$) for the second and third functions, respectively. In addition, about 99% of the between-group variation is due to the first composite variable. Thus, we drop functions 2 and 3 from further consideration.

We now use the standardized discriminant function coefficients to identify which variables are uniquely associated with the first function and to interpret this function. Inspecting the values for the coefficients, as shown in Table 10.14, suggests that the conventional and enterprising variables are the only variables strongly related to this function. (Note that we do not pay attention to the coefficients for functions 2 and 3 as there are no group differences for these functions.) Interpreting function 1, then, we can say that a participant who has high scores for this function is characterized by having high scores on the conventional variable but low scores (given the negative coefficient) on the enterprising variable. Conversely, if you have a low score on the first function, you are expected to have high scores on the enterprising variable and low scores on the conventional variable.

To describe the nature of group differences for the first function, we consider the group means for this function (i.e., the group centroids) and examine a plot of the group centroids. Table 10.15 shows the group centroids, and Figure 10.2 plots the means for the first two functions and shows the individual function scores. The means in Table 10.15 for the first function show that children whose parents have had exposure to college (some college or a college degree) have much lower mean scores on this function than children whose parents did not attend college (high school diploma or eighth-grade education). Given our interpretation of this function, we conclude that Merit Scholars

■ **Table 10.13: Dimension Reduction Analysis Results**

Eigenvalues

Function	Eigenvalue	% of Variance	Cumulative %	Canonical correlation
1	.756[a]	98.7	98.7	.656
2	.007[a]	.9	99.7	.085
3	.002[a]	.3	100.0	.049

[a] First 3 canonical discriminant functions were used in the analysis.

Wilks' Lambda

Test of function(s)	Wilks' Lambda	Chi-square	df	Sig.
1 through 3	.564	215.959	24	.000
2 through 3	.990	3.608	14	.997
3	.998	.905	6	.989

▪ **Table 10.14: Standardized Discriminant Function Coefficients**

Standardized Canonical Discriminant Function Coefficients

	Function		
	1	2	3
Real	.248	.560	.564
Intell	−.208	.023	−.319
Social	.023	−.056	.751
Conven	.785	−.122	−.157
Enterp	−1.240	.127	−.175
Artis	.079	−.880	.253
Status	.067	.341	.538
Aggress	.306	.504	−.067

▪ **Figure 10.2:** Group centroids and discriminant function scores for the first two functions.

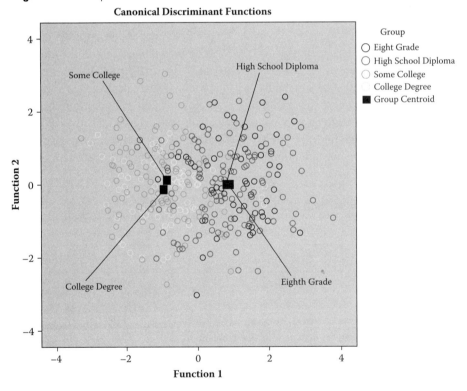

whose parents have at least some college education tend to be much less conventional and much more enterprising than scholars of other parents. Inspection of Figure 10.2 also provides support for large group differences between those with college education

■ **Table 10.15: Group Means for the Discriminant Functions (Group Centroids)**

Functions at Group Centroids

Group	Function		
	1	2	3
Eighth grade	.894	−.003	.072
High school diploma	.822	−.002	−.065
Some college	−.842	.100	.002
College degree	−.922	−.146	.001

Unstandardized canonical discriminant functions evaluated at group means

and those without and very small differences within these two sets of groups. Finally, we can have confidence in the reliability of the results from this study since the participant/variable ratio is very large, about 50 to 1. Section 10.15 provides an example write-up of these results.

10.9 ROTATION OF THE DISCRIMINANT FUNCTIONS

In factor analysis, rotation of the factors often facilitates interpretation. The discriminant functions can also be rotated (varimax) to help interpret them, which can be accomplished with SPSS. However, rotation of functions is not recommended, as the meaning of the composite variables that were obtained to maximize group differences can change with rotation.

Up to this point, we have used all the variables in forming the discriminant functions. There is a procedure, called stepwise discriminant analysis, for selecting the best set of discriminators, just as one would select the best set of predictors in a regression analysis. It is to this procedure that we turn next.

10.10 STEPWISE DISCRIMINANT ANALYSIS

A popular procedure with the SPSS package is stepwise discriminant analysis. In this procedure the first variable to enter is the one that maximizes separation among the groups. The next variable to enter is the one that adds the most to further separating the groups, and so on. It should be obvious that this procedure capitalizes on chance in the same way stepwise regression analysis does, where the first predictor to enter is the one that has the maximum correlation with the dependent variable, the second predictor to enter is the one that adds the next largest amount to prediction, and so on.

The Fs to enter and the corresponding significance tests in stepwise discriminant analysis must be interpreted with caution, especially if the participant/variable ratio is small (say ≤ 5). The Wilks' Λ for the best set of discriminators is positively biased, and this bias can lead to the following problem (Rencher & Larson, 1980):

> Inclusion of too many variables in the subset. If the significance level shown on a computer output is used as an informal stopping rule, some variables will likely be included which do not contribute to the separation of the groups. A subset chosen with significance levels as guidelines will not likely be stable, i.e., a different subset would emerge from a repetition of the study. (p. 350)

Hawkins (1976) suggested that a variable be entered only if it is significant at the $a / (k - p)$ level, where a is the desired level of significance, p is the number of variables already included, and $(k - p)$ is the number of variables available for inclusion. Although this probably is a good idea if the N / p ratio is small, it probably is conservative if $N / p > 10$.

10.11 THE CLASSIFICATION PROBLEM

The classification problem involves classifying participants (entities in general) into the one of several groups that they most closely resemble on the basis of a set of measurements. We say that a participant most closely resembles group i if the vector of scores for that participant is closest to the vector of means (centroid) for group i. Geometrically, the participant is closest in a distance sense (Mahalanobis distance) to the centroid for that group. Recall that in Chapter 3 we used the Mahalanobis distance to measure outliers on the set of predictors, and that the distance for participant i is given as:

$$D_i^2 = \left(\mathbf{x}_i - \overline{\mathbf{x}}\right)' \mathbf{S}^{-1} \left(\mathbf{x}_i - \overline{\mathbf{x}}\right),$$

where $\mathbf{x}_i$ is the vector of scores for participant i, $\overline{\mathbf{x}}$ is the vector of means, and $\mathbf{S}$ is the covariance matrix. It may be helpful to review the section on the Mahalanobis distance in Chapter 3, and in particular a worked-out example of calculating it in Table 3.10.

Our discussion of classification is brief, and focuses on the two-group problem. For a thorough discussion see Johnson and Wichern (2007), and for a good review of discriminant analysis see Huberty (1984).

Let us now consider several examples from different content areas where classifying participants into groups is of practical interest:

1. A bank wants a reliable means, on the basis of a set of variables, to identify low-risk versus high-risk credit customers.
2. A reading diagnostic specialist wishes a means of identifying in kindergarten those children who are likely to encounter reading difficulties in the early elementary grades from those not likely to have difficulty.

3. A special educator wants to classify children with disabilities as either having a learning disability or an emotional disability.

4. A dean of a law school wants a means of identifying those likely to succeed in law school from those not likely to succeed.

5. A vocational guidance counselor, on the basis of a battery of interest variables, wishes to classify high school students into occupational groups (artists, lawyers, scientists, accountants, etc.) whose interests are similar.

10.11.1 The Two-Group Situation

Let $\mathbf{x'} = (x_1, x_2, \ldots, x_p)$ denote the vector of measurements on the basis of which we wish to classify a participant into one of two groups, G_1 or G_2. Fisher's (1936) idea was to transform the multivariate problem into a univariate one, in the sense of finding the linear combination of the xs (a single composite variable) that will maximally discriminant the groups. This is, of course, the single discriminant function. It is assumed that the two populations are multivariate normal and have the same covariance matrix. Let $\mathbf{d} = (a_1 x_1 + a_2 x_2 + \ldots + a_p x_p)$ denote the discriminant function, where $\mathbf{a'} = (a_1, a_2, \ldots, a_p)$ is the vector of coefficients. Let $\bar{\mathbf{x}}_1$ and $\bar{\mathbf{x}}_2$ denote the vectors of means for the participants on the p variables in groups 1 and 2. The location of group 1 on the discriminant function is then given by $\bar{d}_1 = \mathbf{a'} \cdot \bar{\mathbf{x}}_1$ and the location of group 2 by $\bar{d}_2 = \mathbf{a'} \cdot \bar{\mathbf{x}}_2$. The midpoint between the two groups on the discriminant function is then given by $m = \left(\bar{d}_1 + \bar{d}_2\right)\big/2$.

If we let d_i denote the score for the ith participant on the discriminant function, then the *decision rule* is as follows:

If $d_i \geq m$, then classify the participant in group 1.
If $d_i < m$, then classify the participant in group 2.

As we have already seen, software programs can be used to obtain scores for the discriminant functions as well as the group means (i.e., centroids) on the functions (so that we can easily determine the midpoint m). Thus, applying the preceding decision rule, we are easily able to determine why the program classified a participant in a given group. In this decision rule, we assume the group that has the higher mean is designated as group 1.

This midpoint rule makes intuitive sense and is easiest to see for the single-variable case. Suppose there are two normal distributions with equal variances and means 55 (group 1) and 45. The midpoint is 50. If we consider classifying a participant with a score of 52, it makes sense to put the person into group 1. Why? Because the score puts the participant much closer to what is typical for group 1 (i.e., only 3 points away from the mean), whereas this score is nowhere near as typical for a participant from group 2 (7 points from the mean). On the other hand, a participant with a score of 48.5 is more appropriately placed in group 2 because that person's score is closer to what is typical for group 2 (3.5 points from the mean) than what is typical for group 1 (6.5 points from the mean). In the following example, we illustrate the percentages of participants that would be misclassified in the univariate case and when using the discriminant function scores.

10.11.2 A Two-Group Classification Example

We consider the Pope, Lehrer, and Stevens (1980) data used in Chapter 4. Children in kindergarten were measured with various instruments to determine whether they could be classified as low risk (group 1) or high risk (group 2) with respect to having reading problems later on in school. The observed group sizes for these data are 26 for the low-risk group and 12 for the high-risk group. The discriminating variables considered here are word identification (WI), word comprehension (WC), and passage comprehension (PC). The group sizes are sharply unequal and the homogeneity of covariance matrices assumption here was not tenable, so that in general a quadratic rule (see section 10.12) could be implemented. We use this example just for illustrative purposes.

Table 10.16 shows the raw data and the SAS syntax for obtaining classification results with the SAS DISCRIM procedure using ordinary linear discriminant analysis. Table 10.17 provides resulting classification-related statistics for the 38 cases in the data. Note in Table 10.17 that the observed group membership for each case is displayed in the second column, and the third column shows the predicted group membership based on the results of the classification procedure. The last two columns show estimated probabilities of group membership. The bottom of Table 10.17 provides a summary of the classification results. Thus, of the 26 low-risk cases, 17 were classified

■ **Table 10.16: SAS DISCRIM Code and Raw Data for the Two-Group Example**

```
data pope;
input gprisk wi wc pc @@;
lines;
1   5.8   9.7   8.9   1   10.6  10.9  11    1   8.6   7.2   8.7
1   4.8   4.6   6.2   1   8.3   10.6  7.8   1   4.6   3.3   4.7
1   4.8   3.7   6.4   1   6.7   6.0   7.2   1   7.1   8.4   8.4
1   6.2   3.0   4.3   1   4.2   5.3   4.2   1   6.9   9.7   7.2
1   5.6   4.1   4.3   1   4.8   3.8   5.3   1   2.9   3.7   4.2
1   6.1   7.1   8.1   1   12.5  11.2  8.9   1   5.2   9.3   6.2
1   5.7   10.3  5.5   1   6.0   5.7   5.4   1   5.2   7.7   6.9
1   7.2   5.8   6.7   1   8.1   7.1   8.1   1   3.3   3.0   4.9
1   7.6   7.7   6.2   1   7.7   9.7   8.9
2   2.4   2.1   2.4   2   3.5   1.8   3.9   2   6.7   3.6   5.9
2   5.3   3.3   6.1   2   5.2   4.1   6.4   2   3.2   2.7   4.0
2   4.5   4.9   5.7   2   3.9   4.7   4.7   2   4.0   3.6   2.9
2   5.7   5.5   6.2   2   2.4   2.9   3.2   2   2.7   2.6   4.1
proc discrim data = pope testdata = pope testlist;
class gprisk;
var wi wc pc;
run;
```

■ Table 10.17: Classification Related Statistics for Low-Risk and High-Risk Participants

Obs	From GPRISK	CLASSIFIED into GPRISK	Posterior probability of membership in GPRISK	
			1	2
1	1	1	0.9317	0.0683
2	1	1	0.9840	0.0160
3	1	1	0.8600	0.1400
4	1	2[a]	0.4365	0.5635
5	1	1	0.9615	0.0385
6	1	2[a]	0.2511	0.7489
7	1	2[a]	0.3446	0.6554
8	1	1	0.6880	0.3120
9	1	1	0.8930	0.1070
10	1	2[a]	0.2557	0.7443
11	1	2[a]	0.4269	0.5731
12	1	1	0.9260	0.0740
13	1	2[a]	0.3446	0.6554
14	1	2[a]	0.3207	0.6793
15	1	2[a]	0.2295	0.7705
16	1	1	0.7929	0.2071
17	1	1	0.9856	0.0144
18	1	1	0.8775	0.1225
19	1	1	0.9169	0.0831
20	1	1	0.5756	0.4244
21	1	1	0.7906	0.2094
22	1	1	0.6675	0.3325
23	1	1	0.8343	0.1657
24	1	2[a]	0.2008	0.7992
25	1	1	0.8262	0.1738
26	1	1	0.9465	0.0535
27	2	2	0.0936	0.9064
28	2	2	0.1143	0.8857
29	2	2	0.3778	0.6222
30	2	2	0.3098	0.6902
31	2	2	0.4005	0.5995
32	2	2	0.1598	0.8402
33	2	2	0.4432	0.5568
34	2	2	0.3676	0.6324
35	2	2	0.2161	0.7839
36	2	1[a]	0.5703	0.4297
37	2	2	0.1432	0.8568
38	2	2	0.1468	0.8532

(*Continued*)

■ **Table 10.17: (Continued)**

Number of Observations and Percent: into GPRISK:

From GPRISK			1	2	Total	
1	low-risk		17	9	26	We have 9 low-risk
			65.38	34.62	100.00	participants misclassified as high-risk.
2	high-risk		1	11	12	There is only 1 high-risk
			8.33	91.67	100.00	participant misclassified as low-risk.

[a] Misclassified observation.

correctly into this group (group 1) by the procedure. For the high-risk group, 11 of the 12 cases were correctly classified.

We can see how these classifications were made by using the information in Table 10.18. This table shows the means for the groups on the discriminant function (.46 for low risk and −1.01 for high risk), along with the scores for the participants on the discriminant function (these are listed under CAN.V, an abbreviation for canonical variate). The midpoint, as calculated after Table 10.18, is −.275. Given the discriminant function scores and means, it is a simple matter to classify cases into groups. That is, if the discriminant function score for a case is larger than −.275, this case will be classified into the low-risk group, as the function score is closer to the low risk mean of .46. On the other hand, if a case has a discriminant function score less than −.275, this case will be classified into the high-risk group. To illustrate, consider case 1. This case, observed as being low risk, has a discriminant function score obtained from the procedure of 1.50. This value is larger than the midpoint of −.275 and so is classified as being low risk. This classification matches the observed group membership for this case and is thus correctly classified. In contrast, case 4, also in the low-risk group, has a discriminant function score of −.44, which is below the midpoint. Thus, this case is classified (incorrectly) into the high-risk group by the classification procedure. At the bottom of Table 10.19, the histogram of the discriminant function scores shows that we have a fairly good separation of the two groups, although there are several (nine) misclassifications of low-risk participants' being classified as high risk, as their discriminant function scores fell below −.275.

10.11.3 Assessing the Accuracy of the Maximized Hit Rates

The classification procedure is set up to maximize the hit rates, that is, the number of correct classifications. This is analogous to the maximization procedure in multiple regression, where the regression equation was designed to maximize predictive power. With regression, we saw how misleading the prediction on the derivation sample could be. There is the same need here to obtain a more realistic estimate of the hit rate through use of an external classification analysis. That is, an analysis is needed in which the data to be classified are *not* used in constructing the classification function. There are two ways of accomplishing this:

■ Table 10.18: Means for Groups on Discriminant Function, Scores for Cases on Discriminant Function, and Histogram of Discriminant Scores

Group	Mean Coordinates		Symbol for cases	Symbol for mean
Low risk (1)	0.46	0	L	1
High risk	−1.01	0	H	2

Low risk group (2)

Case	CAN.V	Case	CAN.V	Case	CAN.V
1	1.50	11	−0.47	21	0.63
2	2.53	12	1.44	22	0.20
3	0.96	13	−0.71	23	0.83
4	−0.44	14	−0.78	24	−1.21
5	1.91	15	−1.09	25	0.79
6	−1.01	16	0.64	26	1.68
7	−0.71	17	2.60		
8	0.27	18	1.07		
9	1.17	19	1.36		
10	−1.00	20	−0.06		

High risk group

Case	CAN.V	Case	CAN.V
27	−1.81	37	−1.49
28	−1.66	38	−1.47
29	−0.81		
30	−0.82		
31	−0.55		
32	−1.40		
33	−0.43		
34	−0.64		
35	−1.15		
36	−0.08		

Histogram for discriminant function scores   Only misclassification for high risk subjects (case 36)

```
                              H
                  L   H   L   L                   L
H   H    HHH LHL  L   L   L HHH  L      HL  LL  L  LL  L  L   L   L  LL   L  L  LL
      -1.50      -1.00        -.500   0.00    .500   1.00            1.50   2.00  2.50 3.00
 -1.75      -1.25       -.750      |-.250       .750         1.25      1.75   2.25  2.75
     ◄── Score on discriminant function < −.275         Score on discriminant function > −.275 ──►
         (classify as high risk)                         (classify as high risk)
 Note there are 9 Ls (low risk) subjects above with values < −.275, which will be misclassified as high risk (cf. Classification Matrix)
```

(1) These are the means for the groups on the discriminant function. Thus, the midpoint is

$$\frac{.46 + (-1.01)}{2} = -.275$$

(2) The scores listed under CAN.V (for canonical variate) are the scores for the participants on the discriminant function.

1. We can use the *jackknife* procedure of Lachenbruch (1967). Here, each participant is classified based on a classification statistic derived from the remaining $(n - 1)$ participants. This is the procedure of choice for small or moderate sample sizes, and is obtained by specifying CROSSLIST as an option in the SAS DISCRIM program (see Table 10.19). The jackknifed probabilities, not shown, for the Pope data are somewhat different from those obtained with standard discriminant function analysis (as given in Table 10.17), but the classification results are identical.

2. If the sample size is large, then we can randomly split the sample and cross-validate. That is, we compute the classification function on one sample and then check its hit rate on the other random sample. This provides a good check on the external validity of the classification function.

10.11.4 Using Prior Probabilities

Ordinarily, we would assume that any given participant has *a priori* an equal probability of being in any of the groups to which we wish to classify, and SPSS and SAS have equal prior probabilities as the default option. Different *a priori* group probabilities can have a substantial effect on the classification function. The pertinent question is, "How often are we justified in using unequal *a priori* probabilities for group membership?" If indeed, based on content knowledge, one can be confident that the different sample sizes result *because* of differences in population sizes, then prior probabilities are justified. However, several researchers have urged caution in using anything but equal priors (Lindeman, Merenda, & Gold, 1980; Tatsuoka, 1971). Prior probabilities may be specified in SPSS or SAS (see Huberty & Olejnik, 2006).

▨ **Table 10.19: SAS DISCRIM Syntax for Classifying the Pope Data With the Jackknife Procedure**

```
data pope;
input gprisk wi wc pc @@;
lines;
1    5.8    9.7    8.9    1    10.6   10.9   11     1    8.6    7.2    8.7
1    4.8    4.6    6.2    1    8.3    10.6   7.8    1    4.6    3.3    4.7
1    4.8    3.7    6.4    1    6.7    6.0    7.2    1    7.1    8.4    8.4
1    6.2    3.0    4.3    1    4.2    5.3    4.2    1    6.9    9.7    7.2
1    5.6    4.1    4.3    1    4.8    3.8    5.3    1    2.9    3.7    4.2
1    6.1    7.1    8.1    1    12.5   11.2   8.9    1    5.2    9.3    6.2
1    5.7    10.3   5.5    1    6.0    5.7    5.4    1    5.2    7.7    6.9
1    7.2    5.8    6.7    1    8.1    7.1    8.1    1    3.3    3.0    4.9
1    7.6    7.7    6.2    1    7.7    9.7    8.9
2    2.4    2.1    2.4    2    3.5    1.8    3.9    2    6.7    3.6    5.9
2    5.3    3.3    6.1    2    5.2    4.1    6.4    2    3.2    2.7    4.0
2    4.5    4.9    5.7    2    3.9    4.7    4.7    2    4.0    3.6    2.9
2    5.7    5.5    6.2    2    2.4    2.9    3.2    2    2.7    2.6    4.1
proc discrim data = pope testdata = pope crosslist;
class gprisk;
var wi wc pc;
```

When the CROSSLIST option is listed, the program prints the cross validation classification results for each observation. Listing this option invokes the jackknife procedure.

10.11.5 Illustration of Cross-Validation With National Merit Data

We consider an additional example to illustrate randomly splitting a sample (a few times) and cross-validating the classification function with SPSS. This procedure estimates a classification function for the randomly selected cases (the developmental sample), applies this function to the remaining or unselected cases (the cross-validation sample), and then summarizes the percent correctly classified for the developmental and cross-validation samples. To illustrate the procedure, we have selected two groups from the National Merit Scholar example presented in section 10.8. The two groups selected here are (1) those students for whom at least one parent had an eighth-grade education or less ($n = 90$) and (2) those students both of whose parents had at least one college degree ($n = 75$). The same discriminating variables are used here as before.

We begin the procedure by randomly selecting 100 cases from the National Merit data three times (labeled Select1, Select2, and Select3). Figure 10.3 shows 10 cases from this data set (which is named Merit Cross). We then cross-validated the classification function for each of these three randomly selected samples on the remaining 65 participants. SPSS syntax for conducting the cross-validation procedure is shown in Table 10.20. The first three lines of Table 10.20, as well as line 5, are essentially the same commands as shown in Table 10.7. Line 4 selects cases from the first random sample (via Select1). When you wish to cross-validate the second sample, you need to replace Select1 with Select2, and then replacing that with Select3 will cross-validate the third sample. Line 6 of Table 10.20 specifies the use of equal prior probabilities, and the last line requests a summary table of results.

The results of each of the cross-validations are shown in Table 10.21. Note that the percent correctly classified in the second random sample is actually higher in the cross-validation sample (87.7%) than in the developmental sample (80.0%), which is unusual but can happen. This also happens in the third sample (82.0% to 84.6%). With

■ **Figure 10.3:** Selected cases appearing in the cross validation data file (i.e., Merit Cross).

	Real	Intell	Social	Conven	Enterp	Artis	Status	Aggress	id	Group	Select1	Select2	Select3
1	53.90	48.38	45.31	42.48	40.31	48.75	40.53	41.37	1	1.00	0	0	1
2	36.07	32.87	61.69	53.85	58.66	63.91	69.65	57.82	2	1.00	1	1	1
3	45.81	66.16	50.55	50.45	51.76	74.53	47.32	41.37	3	1.00	0	1	0
4	45.45	45.83	69.69	46.36	54.97	62.85	68.77	56.85	4	1.00	0	1	1
5	57.63	54.23	48.68	50.12	49.46	44.25	56.81	64.92	5	1.00	1	1	0
6	57.76	89.77	68.12	60.61	58.44	67.47	65.33	65.64	6	1.00	1	1	0
7	42.03	43.92	53.25	53.73	52.87	50.54	64.33	50.53	7	1.00	1	0	0
8	40.21	39.83	48.97	51.75	64.71	62.02	67.19	56.28	8	1.00	0	1	1
9	51.30	43.87	49.32	60.96	65.09	59.74	47.20	38.16	9	1.00	1	1	0
10	55.66	41.23	51.75	46.97	45.23	47.71	36.57	36.56	10	1.00	1	1	1

■ **Table 10.20: SPSS Commands for Cross-Validation**

```
DISCRIMINANT
 /GROUPS=Group(1 2)
 /VARIABLES=Real Intell Social Conven Enterp Artis Status Aggress
 /SELECT=Select1(1)
 /ANALYSIS ALL
 /PRIORS EQUAL
 /STATISTICS=TABLE.
```

Table 10.21: Cross-Validation Results for the Three Random Splits of National Merit Data

				Classification Results First Sample[a,b]		
				Predicted group membership		
			Group	Eighth grade	College degree	Total
Cases selected	Original	Count	Eighth grade	51	7	58
			College degree	6	36	42
		%	Eighth grade	87.9	12.1	100.0
			College degree	14.3	85.7	100.0
Cases not selected	Original	Count	Eighth grade	23	9	32
			College degree	7	26	33
		%	Eighth grade	71.9	28.1	100.0
			College degree	21.2	78.8	100.0

[a] 87.0% of selected original grouped cases correctly classified.
[b] 75.4% of unselected original grouped cases correctly classified.

				Classification Results Second Sample[a,b]		
				Predicted group membership		
			Group	Eighth grade	College degree	Total
Cases selected	Original	Count	Eighth grade	47	11	58
			College degree	9	33	42
		%	Eighth grade	81.0	19.0	100.0
			College degree	21.4	78.6	100.0
Cases not selected	Original	Count	Eighth grade	29	3	32
			College degree	5	28	33
		%	Eighth grade	90.6	9.4	100.0
			College degree	15.2	84.8	100.0

[a] 80.0% of selected original grouped cases correctly classified.
[b] 87.7% of unselected original grouped cases correctly classified.

				Classification Results Third Sample[a,b]		
				Predicted group membership		
			Group	Eighth grade	College degree	Total
Cases selected	Original	Count	Eighth grade	45	8	53
			College degree	10	37	47
		%	Eighth grade	84.9	15.1	100.0
			College degree	21.3	78.7	100.0
Cases not selected	Original	Count	Eighth grade	28	9	37
			College degree	1	27	28
		%	Eighth grade	75.7	24.3	100.0
			College degree	3.6	96.4	100.0

[a] 82.0% of selected original grouped cases correctly classified.
[b] 84.6% of unselected original grouped cases correctly classified.

the first sample, the more typical case occurs where the percent correctly classified in the unselected or cross-validation cases drops off quite a bit (from 87.0% to 75.4%).

10.12 LINEAR VERSUS QUADRATIC CLASSIFICATION RULE

A more complicated quadratic classification rule is available that is sometimes used by investigators when the equality of variance-covariances matrices assumption is violated. However, Huberty and Olejnik (2006, pp. 280–281) state that when sample size is small or moderate the standard linear function should be used. They explain that classification results obtained by use of the linear function are more stable from sample to sample even when covariance matrices are unequal and when normality is met or not. For larger samples, they note that the quadratic rule is preferred when covariance matrices are clearly unequal.

Note that when normality and constant variance assumptions are not satisfied, an alternative to discriminant analysis (and traditional MANOVA) is logistic regression, as logistic regression does not require that scores meet the two assumptions. Huberty and Olejnik (2006, p. 386) summarize research comparing the use of logistic regression and discriminant analysis for classification purposes and note that these procedures do not appear to have markedly different performance in terms of classification accuracy. Note though that logistic regression is often regarded as a preferred procedure because its assumptions are considered to be more realistic, as noted by Menard (2010). Logistic regression is also a more suitable procedure when there is a mix of continuous and categorical variables, although Huberty and Olejnik indicate that a dichotomous discriminating variable (coded 0 and 1) can be used for the discriminant analysis classification procedure. Note that Chapter 11 provides coverage of binary logistic regression.

10.13 CHARACTERISTICS OF A GOOD CLASSIFICATION PROCEDURE

One obvious characteristic of a good classification procedure is that the hit rate be high; we should have mainly correct classifications. But another important consideration, which is sometimes overlooked, is the cost of misclassification (financial or otherwise). The cost of misclassifying a participant from group A in group B may be greater than misclassifying a participant from group B in group A. We give three examples to illustrate:

1. A medical researcher wishes to classify participants as low risk or high risk in terms of developing cancer on the basis of family history, personal health habits, and environmental factors. Here, saying a participant is low risk when in fact he is high risk is more serious than classifying a participant as high risk when he is low risk.
2. A bank wishes to classify low- and high-risk credit customers. Certainly, for the bank, misclassifying high-risk customers as low risk is going to be more costly than misclassifying low-risk as high-risk customers.

3. This example was illustrated previously, of identifying low-risk versus high-risk kindergarten children with respect to possible reading problems in the early elementary grades. Once again, misclassifying a high-risk child as low risk is more serious than misclassifying a low-risk child as high risk. In the former case, the child who needs help (intervention) doesn't receive it.

10.14 ANALYSIS SUMMARY OF DESCRIPTIVE DISCRIMINANT ANALYSIS

Given that the chapter has focused primarily on descriptive discriminant analysis, we provide an analysis summary here for this procedure and a corresponding results write-up in the next section. Descriptive discriminant analysis provides for greater parsimony in describing between-group differences compared to traditional MANOVA because discriminant analysis focuses on group differences for composite variables. Further, the results of traditional MANOVA and discriminant analysis may differ because discriminant analysis, a fully multivariate procedure, takes associations between variables into account throughout the analysis procedure.

Note that section 6.13 provides the preliminary analysis activities for this procedure (as they are the same as one-way MANOVA). Thus, we present just the primary analysis activities here for descriptive discriminant analysis having one grouping variable.

10.14.1 Primary Analysis

A. Determine the number of discriminant functions (i.e., composite variables) that separate groups.

1) Use dimension reduction analysis to identify the number of composite variables for which there are statistically significant mean differences. Retain, initially, any functions for which the Wilks' lambda test is statistically significant.

2) Assess the strength of association between each statistically significant composite variable and group membership. Use (a) the square of the canonical correlation and (b) the proportion of the total between-group variation due to a given function for this purpose. Retain any composite variables that are statistically significant and that appear to be strongly (i.e., nontrivially) related to the grouping variable.

B. For any composite variable retained from the previous step, determine the meaning of the composite and label it, if possible.

1) Inspect the standardized discriminant function coefficients to identify which of the discriminating variables are related to a given function. Observed variables having greater absolute values should be used to interpret the function. After identifying the important observed variables, use the signs of each of the corresponding coefficients to identify what high and low scores on the composite variable represent. Consider what the observed variables have in common when attempting to label a composite.

2) Though standardized coefficients should be used to identify important variables and determine the meaning of a composite variable, it may be helpful initially to examine univariate F tests for group differences for each observed variable and inspect group means and standard deviations for the significant variables.

C. Describe differences in means on meaningful discriminant functions as identified in steps A and B.

1) Examine group centroids and identify groups that seem distinct from others. Remember that each composite variable has a grand mean of 0 and a pooled within-group standard deviation of 1.

2) Examine a plot of group centroids to help you determine which groups seem distinct from others.

10.15 EXAMPLE RESULTS SECTION FOR DISCRIMINANT ANALYSIS OF THE NATIONAL MERIT SCHOLAR EXAMPLE

Discriminant analysis was used to identify how National Merit Scholar groups differed on a subset of variables from the Vocational Personality Inventory (VPI): realistic, intellectual, social, conventional, enterprising, artistic, status, and aggression. The four groups for this study were (1) those students for whom at least one parent had an eighth-grade education or less ($n = 90$); (2) those students both of whose parents were high school graduates ($n = 104$); (3) those students both of whose parents had gone to college, with at most one graduating ($n = 115$); and (4) those students both of whose parents had at least one college degree ($n = 75$).

No multivariate outliers were indicated as the Mahalanobis distance for each case was smaller than the corresponding critical value. However, univariate outliers were indicated as four cases had z scores greater than $|3|$ for the observed variables. When we removed these cases temporarily, study results were unchanged. The analysis reported shortly, then, includes all cases. Also, there were no missing values in the data set, and no evidence of multicollinearity as all variance inflation factors associated with the discriminating variables were smaller than 2.2. Inspection of the within-group pooled correlations, which ranged from near zero to about .50, indicate that the variables were, in general, moderately correlated.

In addition, there did not appear to be any serious departures from the statistical assumptions associated with discriminant analysis. For example, none of the skewness and kurtosis values for each variable within each group were larger than a magnitude of 1, suggesting no serious departures of the normality assumption. For the equality of variance-covariance matrices assumption, the log determinants of the within group covariance matrices were similar, as were the group standard deviations, and the results of Box's M test ($p = .249$) did not suggest a violation. In addition, the study design did not suggest any violations of the independence assumption as participants were randomly sampled.

While the discriminant analysis procedure formed three functions (due to four groups being present), only the test with all functions included was statistically significant (Wilks' Λ = .564, $\chi^2(24)$ = 215.96, $p < .001$). As such, the first function separated the groups. Further, using the square of the canonical correlation, we computed that 43% of the score variation for the first function was between groups. Also, virtually all (99%) of the total between-group variation was due to the first function. As such, we dropped functions 2 and 3 from further consideration.

Table 1 shows the standardized discriminant function coefficients for this first function, as well as univariate test results. Inspecting the standardized coefficients suggested that the conventional and enterprising variables were the only variables strongly related to this function. Note that the univariate test results, although not taking the variable correlations into account, also suggested that groups differ on the conventional and enterprising variables. Using the standardized coefficients to interpret the function, or composite variable, we concluded that participants having higher scores on the function are characterized by having relatively high scores on the conventional variable but low scores on the enterprising variable. Conversely, participants having below average scores on the first function are considered to have relatively high scores on the enterprising variable and low scores on the conventional variable.

The group centroids for the first function as well as means and standard deviations for the relevant observed variables are shown in Table 2. Although the results from the multivariate discriminant analysis procedure do not always correspond to univariate results, results here were similar. Specifically, inspecting the group centroids in Table 2 indicates that children whose parents have had exposure to college (some college or a college degree) have much lower mean scores on this function than children whose parents did not attend college (high school diploma or eighth-grade education). Given our interpretation of this function, we conclude that Merit Scholars whose parents have at least some college education tend to be much less conventional and much more enterprising than students of other parents. Note that inspecting the group means for the conventional and enterprising variables also supports this conclusion.

■ Table 1: **Standardized Discriminant Function Coefficients and Univariate Test Results**

Variable	Standardized coefficients	Univariate F tests	p Values for F tests
Realistic	.248	1.049	.371
Intellectual	−.208	.124	.946
Social	.023	.693	.557
Conventional	.785	10.912	< .001
Enterprising	−1.240	33.656	< .001
Artistic	.079	1.532	.206
Status	.067	.367	.777
Aggression	.306	.351	.788

■ Table 2: Group Centroids and Means (SD)

	Centroids	Means (SD)	
Education level	Function	Conventional	Enterprising
Eighth grade or less	.894	55.77 (9.91)	54.03 (8.89)
High school graduate	.822	55.29 (10.25)	54.00 (10.05)
Some college	−.842	50.16 (9.25)	63.71 (9.80)
College degree	−.922	49.45 (9.34)	63.56 (8.35)

10.16 SUMMARY

1. Discriminant analysis is used for two purposes: (a) for describing mean composite variable differences among groups, and (b) for classifying cases into groups on the basis of a battery of measurements.
2. The major differences among the groups are revealed through the use of uncorrelated linear combinations of the original variables, that is, the discriminant functions. Because the discriminant functions are uncorrelated, they yield an additive partitioning of the between association.
3. About 20 cases per variable are needed for reliable results, to have confidence that the variables selected for interpreting the discriminant functions would again show up in an independent sample from the same population.
4. Stepwise discriminant analysis should be used with caution.
5. For the classification problem, it is assumed that the two populations are multivariate normal and have the same covariance matrix.
6. The hit rate is the number of correct classifications, and is an optimistic value, because we are using a mathematical maximization procedure. To obtain a more realistic estimate of how good the classification function is, use the jackknife procedure for small or moderate samples, and randomly split the sample and cross-validate with large samples.
7. If discriminant analysis is used for classification, consider use of a quadratic classification procedure if the covariance matrices are unequal and sample size is large.
8. There is evidence that linear classification is more reliable when small and moderate samples are used.
9. The cost of misclassifying must be considered in judging the worth of a classification rule. Of procedures A and B, with the same overall hit rate, A would be considered better if it resulted in less costly misclassifications.

10.17 EXERCISES

1. Although the sample size is small in this problem, obtain practice in conducting a discriminant analysis and interpreting results by running a discriminant analysis using the SPSS syntax shown in Table 10.7 (modifying variable names as needed, of course) with the data from Exercise 1 in Chapter 5.

(a) Given there are three groups and three discriminating variables, how many discriminant functions are obtained?

(b) Which of the discriminant functions are significant at the .05 level?

(c) Calculate and interpret the square of the canonical correlations.

(d) Interpret the "% of Variance Explained" column in the eigenvalues table.

(e) Which discriminating variables should be used to interpret the first function? Using the observed variable names given (i.e., Y1, Y2, Y3), what do high and low scores represent on the first function?

(f) Examine the group centroids and plot. Describe differences in group means for the first discriminant function.

(g) Does this description seem consistent or conflict with the univariate results shown in the output?

(h) What is the recommended *minimum* sample size for this example?

2. This exercise shows that some of the key descriptive measures used in discriminant analysis can computed (and then interpreted) fairly easily using the scores for the discriminant functions. In section 10.7.4, we computed scores for the discriminant function using the raw score discriminant function coefficients. SPSS can compute these for you and place them in the data set. This can be done by placing this subcommand /SAVE=SCORES after the subcommand /ANALYSIS ALL in Table 10.7.

(a) Use the SeniorWISE data set (as used in section 10.7) and run a discriminant analysis placing this new subcommand in the syntax. Note that the scores for the discriminant functions (Dis1_1, Dis2_1), now appearing in your data set, match those reported in Table 10.10.

(b) Using the scores for the first discriminant function, conduct a one-ANOVA with group as the factor, making sure to obtain the ANOVA summary table results and the group means. Note that the group means obtained here match the group centroids reported in Table 10.6. Note also that the grand mean for this function is zero, and the pooled within-group standard deviation is 1. (The ANOVA table shows that the pooled within-group mean square is 1. The square root of this value is then the pooled within-group standard deviation.)

(c) Recall that an eigenvalue in discriminant analysis is a ratio of the between-group to within-group sum-of-squares for a given function. Use the results from the one-way ANOVA table obtained in (b) and calculate this ratio, which matches the eigenvalue reported in Table 10.4.

(d) Use the relevant sum-of-squares shown in this same ANOVA table and compute eta-square. Note this value is equivalent to the square of the canonical correlation for this function that was obtained by the discriminant analysis in section 10.7.2.

3. Press and Wilson (1978) examined population change data for the 50 states. The percent change in population from the 1960 census to the 1970 census for each state was coded as 0 or 1, according to whether the change was below or above the median change for all states. This is the grouping variable. The following demographic variables are to be used to predict the population changes: (a) per capita income (in $1,000), (b) percent birth rate, (c) presence or absence of a coastline, and (d) percent death rate.

(a) Run the discriminant analysis, forcing in all predictors, to see how well the states can be classified (as below or above the median). What is the hit rate?

(b) Run the jackknife classification. Does the hit rate drop off appreciably?

Data for Exercise 3

State	Population change	Income	Births	Coast	Deaths
Arkansas	0.00	2.88	1.80	0.00	1.10
Colorado	1.00	3.86	1.90	0.00	0.80
Delaware	1.00	4.52	1.90	1.00	0.90
Georgia	1.00	3.35	2.10	1.00	0.90
Idaho	0.00	3.29	1.90	0.00	0.80
Iowa	0.00	3.75	1.70	0.00	1.00
Mississippi	0.00	2.63	3.30	1.00	1.00
New Jersey	1.00	4.70	1.60	1.00	0.90
Vermont	1.00	3.47	1.80	0.00	1.00
Washington	1.00	4.05	1.80	1.00	0.90
Kentucky	0.00	3.11	1.90	0.00	1.00
Louisiana	1.00	3.09	2.70	1.00	1.30
Minnesota	1.00	3.86	1.80	0.00	0.90
New Hampshire	1.00	3.74	1.70	1.00	1.00
North Dakota	0.00	3.09	1.90	0.00	0.90
Ohio	0.00	4.02	1.90	0.00	1.00
Oklahoma	0.00	3.39	1.70	0.00	1.00
Rhode Island	0.00	3.96	1.70	1.00	1.00
South Carolina	0.00	2.99	2.00	1.00	0.90
West Virginia	0.00	3.06	1.70	0.00	1.20
Connecticut	1.00	4.92	1.60	1.00	0.80
Maine	0.00	3.30	1.80	1.00	1.10
Maryland	1.00	4.31	1.50	1.00	0.80
Massachusetts	0.00	4.34	1.70	1.00	1.00
Michigan	1.00	4.18	1.90	0.00	0.90
Missouri	0.00	3.78	1.80	0.00	1.10
Oregon	1.00	3.72	1.70	1.00	0.90
Pennsylvania	0.00	3.97	1.60	1.00	1.10

(*Continued*)

State	Population change	Income	Births	Coast	Deaths
Texas	1.00	3.61	2.00	1.00	0.80
Utah	1.00	3.23	2.60	0.00	0.70
Alabama	0.00	2.95	2.00	1.00	1.00
Alaska	1.00	4.64	2.50	1.00	1.00
Arizona	1.00	3.66	2.10	0.00	0.90
California	1.00	4.49	1.80	1.00	0.80
Florida	1.00	3.74	1.70	1.00	1.10
Nevada	1.00	4.56	1.80	0.00	0.80
New York	0.00	4.71	1.70	1.00	1.00
South Dakota	0.00	3.12	1.70	0.00	2.40
Wisconsin	1.00	3.81	1.70	0.00	0.90
Wyoming	0.00	3.82	1.90	0.00	0.90
Hawaii	1.00	4.62	2.20	1.00	0.50
Illinois	0.00	4.51	1.80	0.00	1.00
Indiana	1.00	3.77	1.90	0.00	0.90
Kansas	0.00	3.85	1.60	0.00	1.00
Montana	0.00	3.50	1.80	0.00	1.00
Nebraska	0.00	3.79	1.80	0.00	1.10
New Mexico	0.00	3.08	2.20	0.00	0.90
North Carolina	1.00	3.25	1.90	1.00	0.90
Tennessee	0.00	3.12	1.90	0.00	1.00
Virginia	1.00	3.71	1.80	1.00	0.80

REFERENCES

Barcikowski, R., & Stevens, J.P. (1975). A Monte Carlo study of the stability of canonical correlations, canonical weights and canonical variate-variable correlations. *Multivariate Behavioral Research, 10*, 353–364.

Bartlett, M.S. (1939). A note on tests of significance in multivariate analysis. *Proceedings of the Cambridge Philosophical Society*,180–185.

Darlington, R.B., Weinberg, S., & Walberg, H. (1973). Canonical variate analysis and related techniques. *Review of Educational Research, 43*, 433–454.

Finch, H. (2010). Identification of variables associated with group separation in descriptive discriminant analysis: Comparison of methods for interpreting structure coefficients. *Journal of Experimental Education, 78*, 26–52.

Finch, H., & Laking, T. (2008). Evaluation of the use of standardized weights for interpreting results from a descriptive discriminant analysis. *Multiple Linear Regression Viewpoints, 34*(1), 19–34.

Fisher, R.A. (1936). The use of multiple measurement in taxonomic problems. *Annals of Eugenics, 7*, 179–188.

Hawkins, D.M. (1976). The subset problem in multivariate analysis of variance. *Journal of the Royal Statistical Society, 38*, 132–139.

Huberty, C.J. (1975). The stability of three indices of relative variable contribution in discriminant analysis. *Journal of Experimental Education, 44*(2), 59–64.

Huberty, C.J. (1984). Issues in the use and interpretation of discriminant analysis. *Psychological Bulletin, 95*, 156–171.

Huberty, C.J., & Olejnik, S. (2006). *Applied MANOVA and discriminant analysis.* Hoboken, NJ: John Wiley & Sons.

Johnson, R.A., & Wichern, D.W. (2007). *Applied multivariate statistical analysis* (6th ed.). Upper Saddle River, NJ: Pearson Prentice Hall.

Lachenbruch, P.A. (1967). An almost unbiased method of obtaining confidence intervals for the probability of misclassification in discriminant analysis. *Biometrics, 23*, 639–645.

Lindeman, R.H., Merenda, P.F., & Gold, R.Z. (1980). *Introduction to bivariate and multivariate analysis.* Glenview, IL: Scott Foresman.

Menard, S. (2010). *Logistic regression: From introductory to advanced concepts and applications.* Thousand Oaks, CA: Sage.

Meredith, W. (1964). Canonical correlation with fallible data. *Psychometrika, 29*, 55–65.

Pope, J., Lehrer, B., & Stevens, J.P. (1980). A multiphasic reading screening procedure. *Journal of Learning Disabilities, 13*, 98–102.

Porebski, O.R. (1966). Discriminatory and canonical analysis of technical college data. *British Journal of Mathematical and Statistical Psychology, 19*, 215–236.

Press, S.J., & Wilson, S. (1978). Choosing between logistic regression and discriminant analysis. *Journal of the American Statistical Association, 7*, 699–705.

Rencher, A.C. (1992). Interpretation of canonical discriminant functions, canonical variates, and principal components. *American Statistician, 46*, 217–225.

Rencher, A.C., & Larson, S.F. (1980). Bias in Wilks' in stepwise discriminant analysis. *Technometrics, 22*, 349–356.

Stevens, J.P. (1972). Four methods of analyzing between variation for the k-group MANOVA problem. *Multivariate Behavioral Research, 7*, 499–522.

Stevens, J.P. (1980). Power of the multivariate analysis of variance tests. *Psychological Bulletin, 88*, 728–737.

Tatsuoka, M.M. (1971). *Multivariate analysis: Techniques for educational and psychological research.* New York, NY: Wiley.

Chapter 11

BINARY LOGISTIC REGRESSION

11.1 INTRODUCTION

While researchers often collect continuous response data, binary (or dichotomous) response data are also frequently collected. Examples of such data include whether an individual is abstinent from alcohol or drugs, has experienced a "clinically significant change" following treatment, enlists in the military, is diagnosed as having type 2 diabetes, reports a satisfactory retail shopping experience, and so on. Such either/or responses are often analyzed with logistic regression.

The widespread use of logistic regression is likely due to its similarity with standard regression analyses. That is, in logistic regression, a predicted outcome is regressed on an explanatory variable or more commonly a set of such variables. Like standard regression analysis, the predictors included in the logistic regression model can be continuous or categorical. Interactions among these variables can be tested by including relevant product terms, and statistical tests of the association among a set of explanatory variables and the outcome are handled in a way similar to standard multiple regression.

Further, like standard regression, logistic regression can be used in a confirmatory type of approach to test the association between explanatory variables and a binary outcome in an attempt to obtain a better understanding of factors that affect the outcome. For example, Berkowitz, Stover, and Marans (2011) used logistic regression to determine if an intervention resulted in reduced diagnosis of posttraumatic stress disorder in youth compared to a control condition. Dion et al. (2011) used logistic regression to identify if teaching strategies that included peer tutoring produced more proficient readers relative to a control condition among first-grade students. In addition, logistic regression can be used as more of an exploratory approach where the goal is to make predictions about (or classify) individuals. For example, Le Jan et al. (2011) used logistic regression to develop a model to predict dyslexia among children.

While there are many similarities between logistic and standard regression, there are key differences, all of which are essentially due to the inclusion of a binary outcome.

Perhaps the most noticeable difference between logistic and standard regression is the use of the odds of an event occurring (i.e., the odds of $Y = 1$) in logistic regression. The use of these odds is most evident in the odds ratio, which is often used to describe the effect a predictor has on the binary outcome. In addition, the natural log of the odds of $Y = 1$ is used as the predicted dependent variable in logistic regression. The use of the natural log of the odds may seem anything but natural for those who are encountering logistic regression for the first time. For that reason, we place a great deal of focus on the odds of $Y = 1$ and the transformations that are used in logistic regression.

Specifically, the outline of the chapter is as follows. We introduce a research example that will be used throughout the chapter and then discuss problems that arise with the use of traditional regression analysis when the outcome is binary. After that, we focus on the odds and odds ratio that are a necessary part of the logistic regression procedure. After briefly casting logistic regression as a part of the generalized linear model, we discuss parameter estimation, statistical inference, and a general measure of association. Next, several sections cover issues related to preliminary analysis and the use of logistic regression as a classification procedure. The chapter closes with sections on the use of SAS and SPSS, an example results section, and a logistic regression analysis summary. Also, to limit the scope of the chapter, we do not consider extensions to logistic regression (e.g., multinomial logistic regression), which can be used when more than two outcome categories are present.

11.2 THE RESEARCH EXAMPLE

The research example used throughout the chapter involves an intervention designed to improve the health status of adults who have been diagnosed with prediabetes. Individuals with prediabetes have elevated blood glucose (or sugar), but this glucose level is not high enough to receive a diagnosis of full-blown type 2 diabetes. Often, individuals with prediabetes develop type 2 diabetes, which can have serious health consequences. So, in the attempt to stop the progression from prediabetes to full-blown type 2 diabetes, we suppose that the researchers have identified 200 adults who have been diagnosed with prediabetes. Then, they randomly assigned the patients to receive treatment as normal or the same treatment plus the services of a diabetes educator. This educator meets with patients on an individual basis and develops a proper diet and exercise plan, both of which are important to preventing type 2 diabetes.

For this hypothetical study, the dependent variable is diagnosis of type 2 diabetes, which is obtained 3 months after random assignment to the intervention groups. We will refer to this variable as *health*, with a value of 0 indicating diagnosis of type 2 diabetes, or poor health, and a value of 1 indicating no such diagnosis, or good health. The predictors used for the chapter are:

- *treatment*, as described earlier, with the treatment-as-normal group (or the control group) and the diabetes educator group (or educator group), and

- a measure of motivation collected from patients shortly after diagnosis indicating the degree to which they are willing to change their lifestyle to improve their health.

Our research hypotheses is that, at the 3-month follow-up, the educator treatment will result in improved health status relative to the control condition and that those with greater motivation will also have better health status. For the 200 participants in the sample, 84 or 42% were healthy (no diabetes) at the 3-month follow-up. The mean and standard deviation for motivation for the entire sample were 49.46 and 9.86, respectively.

11.3 PROBLEMS WITH LINEAR REGRESSION ANALYSIS

The use of traditional regression analysis with a binary response has several limitations that motivate the use of logistic regression. To illustrate these limitations, consider Figure 11.1, which is a scatterplot of the predicted and observed values for a binary response variable as a linear function of a continuous predictor. First, given an outcome with two values (0 and 1), the mean of Y for a given X score (i.e., a conditional mean or predicted value on the regression line in Figure 11.1) can be interpreted as the probability of $Y = 1$. However, with the use of traditional regression, predicted probabilities may assume negative values or exceed 1, the latter of which is evident in the plot. While these invalid probabilities may not always occur with a given data set, there is nothing inherent in the linear regression procedure to prevent such predicted values.

▨ **Figure 11.1:** Scatterplot of binary Y across the range of a continuous predictor.

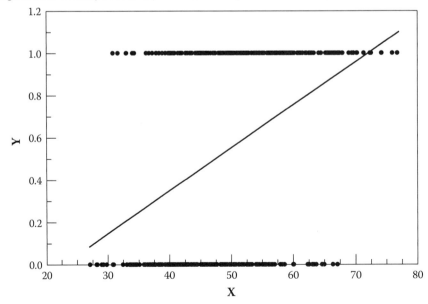

A second problem associated with the use of linear regression when the response is binary is that the distributional assumptions associated with this analysis procedure do not hold. In particular, the outcome scores for a given X score cannot be normally distributed around the predicted value as there are only two possible outcome scores (i.e., 0 and 1). Also, as suggested in Figure 11.1, the variance of the outcome scores is not constant across the range of the predicted values, as this variance is relatively large near the center of X (where the observed outcome values of 0 and 1 are both present) but is much smaller at the minimum and maximum values of X where only values of 0 and 1 occur for the outcome.

A third problem with the use of standard linear regression is the assumed *linear* functional form of the relationship between Y and X. When the response is binary, the predicted probabilities are often considered to follow a nonlinear pattern across the range of a continuous predictor, such that these probabilities may change very little for those near the minimum and maximum values of a predictor but more rapidly for individuals having scores near the middle of the predictor distribution. For example, Figure 11.2 shows the estimated probabilities obtained from a logistic regression analysis of the data shown in Figure 11.1. Note the nonlinear association between Y and X, such that the probability of $Y = 1$ increases more rapidly as X increases near the middle of the distribution but that the increase nearly flattens out for high X scores. The S-shaped nonlinear function for the probability of $Y = 1$ is a defining characteristic of logistic regression with continuous predictors, as it represents the assumed functional form of the probabilities.

In addition to functional form, note that the use of logistic regression addresses other problems that were apparent with the use of standard linear regression. That is, with logistic regression, the probabilities of $Y = 1$ cannot be outside of the 0 to 1 range. The

■ **Figure 11.2:** Predicted probabilities of $Y = 1$ from a logistic regression equation.

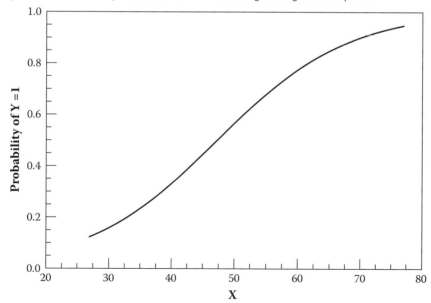

logit transformation, discussed in the next section, restricts the predicted probabilities to the 0 to 1 range. Also, values for the binary response will not be assumed to follow a normal distribution, as assumed in linear regression, but are assumed to follow a binomial (or, more specifically, Bernoulli) distribution. Also, neither normality nor constant variance will be assumed.

11.4 TRANSFORMATIONS AND THE ODDS RATIO WITH A DICHOTOMOUS EXPLANATORY VARIABLE

This section presents the transformations that occur with the use of logistic regression. You are encouraged to replicate the calculations here to get a better feel for the odds and, in particular, the odds ratio that is at the heart of logistic regression analysis. Note also that the natural log of the odds, or the logits, serve as the predicted dependent variable in logistic regression. We will discuss why that is the case as we work through the transformations. We first present the transformations and odds ratio for the case where the explanatory variable is dichotomous.

To illustrate the transformations, we begin with a simple case where, using our example, *health* is a function of the binary *treatment* indicator variable. Table 11.1 presents a cross-tabulation with our data for these variables. As is evident in Table 11.1, adults in the educator group have better health. Specifically, 54% of adults in the educator group have good health (no diabetes diagnosis), whereas 30% of the adults in the control group do. Of course, if *health* and *treatment* were the only variables included in the analysis, a chi-square test of independence could be used to test the association between the two variables and may be sufficient for these data. However, we use these data to illustrate the transformations and the odds ratio used in logistic regression.

11.4.1 Probability and Odds of $Y = 1$

We mimic the interpretations of effects in logistic regression by focusing on only one of the two outcome possibilities—here, good health status (coded as $Y = 1$)—and calculate the probability of being healthy for each of the treatment groups. For the 100 adults in the educator group, 54 exhibited good health. Thus, the probability of being

■ **Table 11.1: Cross-Tabulation of Health and Treatment**

Health	Treatment group		Total
	Educator	Control	
Good	54 (54%)	30 (30%)	84
Poor	46 (46%)	70 (70%)	116
Total	100	100	200

Note: Percentages are calculated within treatment groups.

healthy for those in this group is 54 / 100 = .54. For those in the control group, the probability of being healthy is 30 / 100 or .30. You are much more likely, then, to demonstrate good health if you are in the educator group.

Using these probabilities, we can then calculate the odds of $Y = 1$ (being of good health) for each of the treatment groups. The odds are calculated by taking the probability of $Y = 1$ over 1 minus that probability, or

$$\text{Odds}(Y = 1) = \frac{P(Y = 1)}{1 - P(Y = 1)}, \tag{1}$$

where P is the probability of $Y = 1$. Thus, the odds of $Y = 1$ is the probability of $Y = 1$ over the probability of $Y = 0$. To illustrate, for those in the educator group, the odds of being healthy are .54 / (1 − .54) = 1.17. To interpret these odds, we can say that for adults in the educator group, the probability of being healthy is 1.17 times the probability of being unhealthy. Thus, the odds is a ratio contrasting the size of the probability of $Y = 1$ to the size of the probability of $Y = 0$. For those in the control group, the odds of $Y = 1$ are .30 / .70 or 0.43. Thus, for this group, the probability of being healthy is .43 times the probability of being unhealthy.

Table 11.2 presents some probabilities and corresponding odds, as well as the natural logs of the odds that are discussed later. While probabilities range from 0 to 1, the odds, range from 0 to, theoretically, infinity. Note that an odds of 1 corresponds to a probability of .5, odds smaller than 1 correspond to probabilities smaller than .5, and odds larger than 1 correspond to probabilities greater than .5. In addition, if you know the odds of $Y = 1$, the probability of $Y = 1$, can be computed using

$$P(Y = 1) = \frac{\text{Odds}(Y = 1)}{1 + \text{Odds}(Y = 1)}. \tag{2}$$

For example, if your odds are 4, then the probability of $Y = 1$ is 4 / (4 + 1) = .8, which can be observed in Table 11.2.

■ **Table 11.2: Comparisons Between the Probability, the Odds, and the Natural Log of the Odds**

Probability	Odds	Natural log of the odds
.1	.11	−2.20
.2	.25	−1.39
.3	.43	−0.85
.4	.67	−0.41
.5	1.00	0.00
.6	1.50	0.41
.7	2.33	0.85
.8	4.00	1.39
.9	9.00	2.20

Those learning logistic regression often ask why the odds are needed, since probabilities seem very natural to understand and explain. As Allison (2012) points out, the odds provide a much better measure for making multiplicative comparisons. For example, if your probability of being healthy is .8 and another person has a probability of .4, it is meaningful to say that your probability is twice as great as the other's. However, since probabilities cannot exceed 1, it does not make sense to consider a probability that is twice as large as .8. However, this kind of statement does not present a problem for the odds. For example, when transformed to odds, the probability of .8 is .8 / .2 = 4. An odds twice as large as that is 8, which, when transformed back to a probability, is 8 / (1 + 8) = .89. Thus, the odds lend themselves to making multiplicative comparisons and can be readily converted to probabilities to further ease interpretations in logistic regression.

11.4.2 The Odds Ratio

The multiplicative comparison idea leads directly into the odds ratio, which is used to capture the effect of a predictor in logistic regression. For a dichotomous predictor, the odds ratio is literally the ratio of odds for two different groups. For the example in this section, the odds ratio, or O.R.,

$$\text{O.R.} = \frac{\text{Odds of } Y = 1 \text{ for the Educator Group}}{\text{Odds of } Y = 1 \text{ for the Control Group}}. \tag{3}$$

Note that if the odds of $Y = 1$ were the same for each group, indicating no association between variables, the odds ratio would equal 1. For this expression, an odds ratio greater than 1 indicates that those in the educator group have greater odds (and thus a greater probability) of $Y = 1$ than those in the control group, whereas an odds ratio smaller than 1 indicates that those in the educator group have smaller odds (and thus a smaller probability) of $Y = 1$ than those in the control group. With our data and using the odds calculated previously, the odds ratio is 1.17 / .43 = 2.72 or 2.7.

To interpret the odds ratio of 2.7, we can say that the odds of being in good health for those in the educator group are about 2.7 times the odds of being healthy for those in the control group. Thus, whereas the odds multiplicatively compares two probabilities, the odds ratio provides this comparison in terms of the *odds*. To help ensure accurate interpretation of the odds ratio (as a ratio of odds and not probabilities), you may find it helpful to begin with the statement "the odds of $Y = 1$" (describing what $Y = 1$ represents, of course). Then, it seems relatively easy to fill out the statement with "the odds of $Y = 1$ for the first group" (i.e., the group in the numerator) "are x times the odds of $Y = 1$ for the reference group" (i.e., the group in the denominator). That is the generic and standard interpretation of the odds ratio for a dichotomous predictor.

But, what if the odds for those in the control group had been placed in the numerator of the odds ratio and the odds for those in the educator group had been placed in the denominator? Then, the odds ratio would have been .43 / 1.17 = .37, which is, of course, a valid odds ratio. This odds ratio can then be interpreted as the odds of being healthy for adults in the control group are .37 times (or roughly one third the size of) the odds of those in the educator group. Again, the odds of the first group (here the control group) are compared to the odds of the group in the denominator (the educator group). You may find it more natural to interpret odds ratios that are greater than 1. If an odds ratio is smaller than 1, you only need to take the reciprocal of the odds ratio to obtain an odds ratio larger than 1. Taking the reciprocal switches the groups in the numerator and denominator of the odds ratio, which here returns the educator group back to the numerator of the odds ratio. When taking a reciprocal of the odds ratio, be sure that your interpretation of the odds ratio reflects this switch in groups. For this example, the reciprocal of .37 yields an odds ratio of 1 / .37 = 2.7, as before.

11.4.3 The Natural Log of the Odds

Recapping the transformations, we have shown how the following can be calculated and interpreted: the probability of $Y = 1$, the odds of $Y = 1$, and the odds ratio. We now turn to the natural log of the odds of $Y = 1$, which is also called the log of the odds, or the logits. As mentioned, one problem associated with the use of linear regression when the outcome is binary is that the predicted probabilities may lie outside the 0 to 1 range. Linear regression could be used, however, if we can find a transformation that produces values like those found in a normal distribution, that is, values that are symmetrically distributed around some center value and that range to, theoretically, minus and plus infinity. In our discussion of the odds, we noted that the odds have a minimum of zero but have an upper limit, like the upper limit in a normal distribution, in the sense that these values extend toward infinity. Thus, the odds do not represent an adequate transformation of the predicted probabilities but gets us halfway there to the needed transformation.

The natural log of the odds effectively removes this lower bound that the odds have and can produce a distribution of scores that appear much like a normal distribution. To some extent, this can be seen in Table 11.2 where the natural log of the odds is symmetrically distributed around the value of zero, which corresponds to a probability of 0.5. Further, as probabilities approach either 0 or 1, the natural log of the odds approaches negative or positive infinity, respectively.

Mathematically speaking, the natural log of a value, say X, is the power to which the natural number e (which can be approximated by 2.718) must be raised to obtain X. Using the first entry in Table 11.2 as an example, the natural log of the odds of .11 is −2.20, or the power that e (or 2.718) must be raised to obtain a value of .11 is −2.20. For those wishing to calculate the natural log of the odds, this can be done on the calculator typically by using the "ln" button. The natural log of the odds can also be transformed to the odds by exponentiating the natural log. That is,

$$e^{\ln(\text{odds})} = \text{Odds}, \tag{4}$$

where ln(odds) is the natural log of the odds. To illustrate, to return the value of -2.20 to the odds metric, simply exponentiate this value. So, $e^{-2.20} = 0.11$. The odds can then be transformed to a probability by using Equation 2. Thus, the corresponding probability for an odds of .11 is $.11 / (1 + .11) = .1$.

Thus, the natural log of the odds is the final transformation needed in logistic regression. In the context of logistic regression, the logit transformation of the *predicted* values transforms a distribution of predicted probabilities into a distribution of scores that approximate a normal distribution. As a result, with the logit as the dependent variable for the response, linear regression analyses can proceed, where the logit is expressed as a linear function of the predictors. Note also that this transformation used in logistic regression is fundamentally different from the types of transformations mentioned previously in the text. Those transformations (e.g., square root, logarithmic) are applied to the observed outcome scores. Here, the transformations are applied to the *predicted* probabilities. The fact that the 0 and 1 outcome scores themselves are not transformed in logistic regression is apparent when you attempt to find the natural log of 0 (which is undefined). In logistic regression, then, the transformations are an inherent part of the modeling procedure. We have also seen that the natural log of the odds can be transformed into the odds, which can then be transformed into a probability of $Y = 1$.

11.5 THE LOGISTIC REGRESSION EQUATION WITH A SINGLE DICHOTOMOUS EXPLANATORY VARIABLE

Now that we know that the predicted response in logistic regression is the natural log (abbreviated ln) of the odds and that this variate is expressed as a function of explanatory variables, we can present a logistic regression equation and begin to interpret model parameters. Continuing the example with the single dichotomous explanatory variable, the equation is

$$\ln(\text{odds } Y = 1) = \beta_0 + \beta_1 \text{ treat}, \tag{5}$$

where *treat* is a dummy-coded indicator variable with 1 indicating educator group and 0 the control group. Thus, β_0 represents the predicted log of the odds of being healthy for those in the control group and β_1 is the regression coefficient describing the association between *treat* and *health* in terms of the natural log of the odds. We show later how to run logistic regression analysis with SAS and SPSS but for now note that the estimated values for β_0 and β_1 with the chapter data are $-.85$ and 1.01, respectively.

Using Equation 5, we can now calculate the natural log of the odds, the odds, the odds ratio, and the predicted probabilities for the two groups given that we have the regression coefficients. Inserting a value of 1 for *treat* in Equation 5 yields a value for the log of the odds for the educator group of $-.847 + 1.008(1) = .161$. Their odds (using Equation 4) is then $e^{(.161)} = 1.175$, and their probability of demonstrating good health (using Equation 2) is $1.175 / (1 + 1.175) = .54$, the same as reported in Table 11.1. You can verify the values for the control group, which has a natural log of $-.847$, an odds of $.429$, and a probability of $.30$. We can also compute the odds ratio by using Equation 3, which is $1.175 / .429 = 2.739$.

There is a second and more commonly used way to compute the odds ratio for explanatory variables in logistic regression. Instead of working through the calculations in the preceding paragraph, you simply need to exponentiate β_1 of Equation 5. That is, e^{β_1} = the odds ratio, so $e^{1.008} = 2.74$. Both SAS and SPSS provide odds ratios for explanatory variables in logistic regression and can compute predicted probabilities for values of the predictors in your data set. The calculations performed in this section are intended to help you get a better understanding of some of the key statistics used in logistic regression.

Before we consider including a continuous explanatory variable in logistic regression, we now show why exponentiating the regression coefficient associated with an explanatory variable produces the odds ratio for that variable. Perhaps the key piece of knowledge needed here is to know that $e^{(a + b)}$, where a and b represent two numerical values, equals $(e^a)(e^b)$. So, inserting a value of 1 for *treat* in Equation 5 yields $\ln = \beta_0 + \beta_1$, and inserting a value of zero for this predictor returns $\ln = \beta_0$. Since the right side of these expressions is equal to the natural log of the odds, we can find the odds for both groups by using Equation 4, which for the educator group is then $e^{(\beta_0 + \beta_1)} = e^{\beta_0} e^{\beta_1}$ given the equality mentioned in this paragraph, and then for the control group is e^{β_0}. Using these expressions to form the odds ratio (treatment to control) yields $\text{O.R.} = \dfrac{e^{\beta_0} e^{\beta_1}}{\beta_0}$, which by division is equal to $\text{O.R.} = e^{\beta_1}$. Thus, exponentiating the regression coefficient associated with the explanatory variable returns the odds ratio. This is also true for continuous explanatory variables, to which we now turn.

11.6 THE LOGISTIC REGRESSION EQUATION WITH A SINGLE CONTINUOUS EXPLANATORY VARIABLE

When a continuous explanatory variable is included in a logistic regression equation, in terms of what has been presented thus far, very little changes from what we saw for a dichotomous predictor. Recall for this data set that *motivation* is a continuous predictor that has mean of 49.46 and standard deviation of 9.86. The logistic regression equation now expresses the natural log of the odds of *health* as a function of *motivation* as

$$\ln(\text{odds } Y = 1) = \beta_0 + \beta_1 motiv, \tag{6}$$

where *motiv* is motivation. The estimates for the intercept and slope, as obtained by software, are -2.318 and 0.040, respectively for these data. The positive value for the slope indicates that the odds and probability of being healthy increase as motivation increases. Specifically, as *motivation* increases by 1 point, the odds of being healthy increase by a factor of $e^{(.04)} = 1.041$. Thus, for a continuous predictor, the interpretation of the odds ratio is the factor or multiplicative change in the odds for a one point increase in the predictor. For a model that is linear in the logits (as Equation 6), the change in the odds is constant across the range of the predictor.

As in the case when the predictor is dichotomous, the odds and probability of $Y = 1$ can be computed for any values of the predictor of interest. For example, inserting a value of 49.46 into Equation 6 results in a natural log of $-.340$ (i.e., $-2.318 + .04 \times 49.46$), an odds of 0.712 ($e^{-.34}$), and a probability of .42 (0.712 / 1.712). To illustrate once more the meaning of the odds ratio, we can compute the same values for students with a score of 50.46 on *motivation* (an increase of 1 point over the value of 49.46). For these adults, the log of the odds is -0.300. Note that the change in the log of the odds for the 1 point increase in *motivation* is equal to the slope of $-.14$. While this is a valid measure to describe the association between variables, the natural log of the odds is not a metric that is familiar to a wide audience. So, continuing on to compute the odds ratio, for those having a *motivation* score of 50.46, the odds is then 0.741 (e^{-3}), and the probability is .43. Forming an odds ratio (comparing adults having a *motivation* score of 50.46 to those with a score of 49.46) yields 0.741 / 0.712 = 1.041, equal to, of course $e^{(.04)}$.

In addition to describing the impact of a 1-point change for the predictor on the odds of exhibiting good health, we can obtain the impact for an increase of greater than 1 point on the predictor. The expression that can be used to do this is $e^{\beta \times c}$, where c is the increase of interest in the predictor (by default a value of 1 is used by computer software). Here, we choose an increment of 9.86 points on *motivation*, which is about a 1 standard deviation change. Thus, for a 9.86 point increase in *motivation*, the odds of having good health increase by a factor of $e^{(.04)(9.86)} = e^{(.394)} = 1.48$. Comparing adults whose *motivation* score differs by 1 standard deviation, those with the higher score are predicted to have odds of good health that are about 1.5 times the odds of adults with the lower *motivation* score. Note that the odds ratio for an increase of 1 standard deviation in the predictor can be readily obtained from SAS and SPSS by using z-scores for the predictor.

11.7 LOGISTIC REGRESSION AS A GENERALIZED LINEAR MODEL

Formally, logistic regression can be cast in terms of a generalized linear model, which has three parts. First, there is a random component or sampling model that describes the assumed population distribution of the dependent variable. For logistic regression, the dependent variable is assumed to follow a Bernoulli distribution (a special form of the binomial distribution), with an expected value or mean of p (i.e., the probability of $Y = 1$) and variance that is a function of this probability. Here, the variance of the binary outcome is equal to $p(1 - p)$. The second component of the generalized linear model is the link function. The link function transforms the expected value of the outcome so that it may be expressed as a linear function of predictors. With logistic regression, the link function is the natural log of the odds, which converts the predicted probabilities to logits. As mentioned earlier this link function also constrains the predicted probabilities to be within the range of 0 to 1.

The final component of the generalized linear model is the systematic component, which directly expresses the transformed predicted value of the response as a function of predictors. This systematic component then includes information from predictors to allow you to gain an understanding of the association between the predictors and the binary response. Thus, a general expression for the logistic regression model is

$$\ln(\text{odds } Y = 1) = \beta_0 + \beta_1 X_1 + \beta_2 X_2 + \ldots \beta_m X_m, \tag{7}$$

where m represents the final predictor in the model. Note that there is an inverse of the natural log of the odds (which we have used), which transforms the predicted log of the odds to the expected values or probabilities. This transformation, called the logistic transformation, is

$$p = \frac{e^{(\beta_0 + \beta_1 X_1 + \beta_2 X_2 + \cdots + \beta_m X_m)}}{1 + e^{(\beta_0 + \beta_1 X_1 + \beta_2 X_2 + \cdots + \beta_m X_m)}},$$

and where you may recognize, from earlier, that the numerator is the odds of $Y = 1$. Thus, another way to express Equation 7 is

$$p = \text{logistic} \left(\beta_0 + \beta_1 X_1 + \beta_2 X_2 + \cdots + \beta_m X_m \right),$$

where it is now clear that we are modeling probabilities in this procedure and that the transformation of the predicted outcome is an inherent part of the modeling procedure.

The primary reason for presenting logistic regression as a generalized linear model is that it provides you with a broad framework for viewing other analysis techniques. For example, standard multiple regression can also be cast as a type of generalized linear model as its sampling model specifies that the outcomes scores, given the predicted values, are assumed to follow a normal distribution with constant variance around each predicted value. The link function used is linear regression is called the identity link function because the expected or predicted values are multiplied by a value of 1 (indicating, of course, no transformation). The structural model is exactly like Equation 7 except that the predicted Y values replace the predicted logits. A variety of analysis models can also be subsumed under the generalized linear modeling framework.

11.8 PARAMETER ESTIMATION

As with other statistical models that appear in this text, parameters in logistic regression are typically estimated by a maximum likelihood estimation (MLE) procedure. MLE obtains estimates of the model parameters (the βs in Equation 7 and their standard errors) that maximize the likelihood of the data for the entire sample. Specifically, in logistic regression, parameter estimates are obtained by minimizing a fit function where smaller values reflect smaller differences between the observed Y values and the model estimated probabilities. This function, called here $-2LL$ or "negative 2 times the log likelihood" and also known as the model deviance, may be expressed as

$$-2LL = -2 \times \sum \left[\left(Y_i \times \ln \hat{p}_i \right) + \left(1 - Y_i \right) \times \ln \left(1 - \hat{p}_i \right) \right], \tag{8}$$

where $\hat{p}_i$ represents the probability of $Y = 1$ obtained from the logistic regression model and the expression to the right of the summation symbol is the log likelihood.

The expression for $-2LL$ can be better understood by inserting some values for Y and the predicted probabilities for a given individual and computing the log likelihood and $-2LL$. Suppose that for an individual whose obtained Y score is 1, the predicted probability is also a value of 1. In that case, the log likelihood becomes $1 \times \ln(1) = 0$, as the far right-hand side of the log likelihood vanishes when $Y = 1$. A value of zero for the log likelihood, of course, represents no prediction error and is the smallest value possible for an individual. Note that if all cases were perfectly predicted, $-2LL$ would also equal zero. Also, as the difference between an observed Y score (i.e., group membership) and the predicted probability increase, the log likelihood becomes greater (in absolute value), indicating poorer fit or poorer prediction. You can verify that for $Y = 1$, the log likelihood equals $-.105$ for a predicted probability of .9 and $-.51$ for a predicted probability of .6. You can also verify that with these three cases $-2LL$ equals 1.23. Thus, $-2LL$ is always positive and larger values reflect poorer prediction.

There are some similarities between ordinary least squares (OLS) and maximum likelihood estimation that are worth mentioning here. First, OLS and MLE are similar in that they produce parameter estimates that minimize prediction error. For OLS, the quantity that is minimized is the sum of the squared residuals, and for MLE it is $-2LL$. Also, larger values for each of these quantities for a given sample reflect poorer prediction. For practical purposes, an important difference between OLS and MLE is that the latter is an iterative process, where the estimation process proceeds in cycles until (with any luck) a solution (or convergence) is reached. Thus, unlike OLS, MLE estimates may not converge. Allison (2012) notes that in his experience if convergence has not been attained in 25 iterations, MLE for logistic regression will not converge. Lack of convergence may be due to excessive multicollinearity or to complete or nearly completion separation. These issues are discussed in section 11.15.

Further, like OLS, the parameter estimates produced via MLE have desirable properties. That is, when assumptions are satisfied, the regression coefficient estimates obtained with MLE are consistent, asymptotically efficient, and asymptotically normal. In addition, as in OLS where the improvement in model fit (increment in R^2) can be statistically tested when predictors are added to a model, a statistical test for the improvement in model fit in logistic regression, as reflected in a decrease in $-2LL$, is often used to assess the contribution of predictors. We now turn to this topic.

11.9 SIGNIFICANCE TEST FOR THE ENTIRE MODEL AND SETS OF VARIABLES

When there is more than one predictor in a logistic regression model, you will generally wish to test whether a set of variables is associated with a binary outcome of interest. One common application of this is when you wish to use an omnibus test to determine if any predictors in the entire set are associated with the outcome. A second application occurs when you want to test whether a subset of predictors (e.g., the coded variables associated with a categorical explanatory variable) is associated with the outcome. Another application involves testing an interaction when multiple product terms represent an interaction of interest. We illustrate two of these applications later.

For testing whether a set of variables is related to a binary outcome, a likelihood ratio test is typically used. The likelihood ratio test works by comparing the fit between two statistical models: a reduced model that excludes the variable(s) being tested and a full model that adds the variable(s) to the reduced model. The fit statistic that is used for this purpose is $-2LL$, as the difference between this fit statistic for the two models being compared has a chi-square distribution with degrees of freedom equal to the number of predictors added in the full model. A significant test result supports the use of the full model, as it suggests that the fit of the model is improved by inclusion of the variables in the full model. Conversely, an insignificant test result suggests that the inclusion of the new variables in the full model does not improve the model fit and thus supports the use of the reduced model as the added predictors are not related to the outcome. Note that the proper use of this test requires that one model is nested in the other, which means that the same cases appear in each model and that the full model simply adds one or more predictors to those already in the reduced model.

The likelihood ratio test is often initially used to test the omnibus null hypothesis that the impact of all predictor is zero, or that $\beta_1 = \beta_2 = \ldots \beta_m = 0$ in Equation 7. This test is analogous to the overall test of predictors in standard multiple regression, which is often used as a "protected" testing approach before the impact of individual predictors is considered. To illustrate, we return to the chapter data where the logistic regression equation that includes both predictors is

$$\ln(\text{odds } Y = 1) = \beta_0 + \beta_1 treat + \beta_2 motiv, \tag{9}$$

where $Y = 1$ represents good health status, *treat* is the dummy-coded treatment variable (1 = educator group and 0 = control), and *motiv* is the continuous motivation variable.

To obtain the likelihood test result associated with this model, you first estimate a reduced model that excludes all of the variables being tested. The reduced model in this case, then, contains just the outcome and the intercept of Equation 9, or $\ln(\text{odds } Y = 1) = \beta_0$. The fit of this reduced model, as obtained via computer software, is 272.117 (*i.e.*, $-2LL_{reduced}$). The fit of the full model, which contains the two predictors in Equation 9 (i.e., the set of variables that are to be tested), is 253.145 (i.e., $-2LL_{full}$). The difference in these model fit values ($-2LL_{reduced} - 2LL_{full}$) *is* the chi-square test statistic for the overall model and is $272.117 - 253.145 = 18.972$. A chi-square critical value using an alpha of .05 and degrees of freedom equal to the number of predictors that the full model adds to the restricted model (here, 2) is 5.99. Given that the chi-square test statistic exceeds the critical value, this suggests that at least one of the explanatory variables is related to the outcome, as the model fit is improved by adding this set of predictors.

As a second illustration of this test, suppose we are interested in testing whether the *treatment* interacts with *motivation*, thinking perhaps that the educator treatment will be more effective for adults having lower motivation. In this case, the reduced model is Equation 9, which contains no interaction terms, and the full model adds to that an interaction term, which is the product of *treat* and *motiv*. The full model is then

$$\ln(\text{odds } Y = 1) = \beta_0 + \beta_1 treat + \beta_2 motiv + \beta_3 treat \times motiv. \tag{10}$$

As we have seen, the fit of the reduced model (Equation 9) is 253.145, and the fit of this new full model (Equation 10) is 253.132. The difference in fit chi-square statistic is then $253.145 - 253.132 = 0.013$. Given a chi-square critical value ($\alpha = .05$, $df = 1$) of 3.84, the improvement in fit due to adding the interaction term to a model that assumes no interaction is present is not statistically significant. Thus, we conclude that there is no interaction between the *treatment* and *motivation*.

11.10 MCFADDEN'S PSEUDO *R*-SQUARE FOR STRENGTH OF ASSOCIATION

Just as with traditional regression analysis, you may wish to complement tests of association between a set of variables and an outcome with an explained variance measure of association. However, in logistic regression, the variance of the observed outcome scores depends on the predicted probability of $Y = 1$. Specifically, this variance is equal to $p_i(1 - p_i)$, where p_i is the probability of $Y = 1$ that is obtained from the logistic regression model. As such, the error variance of the outcome is not constant across the range of predicted values, as is often assumed in traditional regression or analysis of variance. When the error variance is constant across the range of predicted values, it makes sense to consider the part of the outcome variance that is explained by the model and the part that is error (or unexplained), which would then apply across the range of predicted outcomes (due to the assumed constant variance). Due to variance heterogeneity, this notion of explained variance does not apply to logistic regression. Further, while there are those who do not support use of proportion of variance explained measures in logistic regression, such pseudo *R*-square measures may be useful in summarizing the strength of association between a set of variables and the outcome. While many different pseudo *R*-square measures have been developed, and there is certainly no consensus on which is preferred, we follow Menard's (2010) recommendation and illustrate use of McFadden's pseudo *R*-square.

McFadden's (1974) pseudo R-square, denoted R_L^2, is based on the improvement in model fit as predictors are added to a model. An expression that can be used for R_L^2 is

$$R_L^2 = \frac{\chi^2}{-2LL_{baseline}}, \tag{11}$$

where the numerator is the χ^2 test for the difference in fit between a reduced and full model and the denominator is the measure of fit for the model that contains only the intercept, or the baseline model with no predictors. The numerator then reflects the *amount* that the model fit, as measured by the difference in the quantity $-2LL$ for a reduced model and its full model counterpart, is reduced by or improved due to a set of predictors, analogous to the amount of variation reduced by a set of predictors in traditional regression. When this amount (i.e., χ^2) is divided by $-2LL_{baseline}$, the resulting proportion can be interpreted as the proportional reduction in the lack of fit associated with the baseline model due to the inclusion of the predictors, or the proportional improvement in model fit, analogous to R^2 in traditional regression. In addition to the close correspondence to R^2, R_L^2 also has lower and upper bounds of 0 and 1, which is not shared by other pseudo R^2 measures. Further, R_L^2 can be used when the dependent variable has more than two categories (i.e., for multinomial logistic regression).

We first illustrate use of R_L^2 to assess the contribution of *treatment* and *motivation* in predicting health status. Recall that the fit of the model with no predictors, or $-2LL_{baseline}$, is 272.117. After adding *treatment* and *motivation*, the fit is 253.145, which is a reduction or improvement in fit of 18.972 (which is the χ^2 test statistic) and the numerator of Equation 11. Thus, R_L^2 is 18.972/272.117 or .07, indicating a 7% improvement in model fit due to *treatment* and *motivation*. Note that R_L^2 indicates the *degree* that fit improves when the predictors are added while the use of the χ^2 test statistic is done to determine *whether* an improvement in fit is present or different from zero in the population.

The R_L^2 statistic can also be used to assess the contribution of subsets of variables while controlling for other predictors. In section 11.9, we tested for the improvement in fit that is obtained by adding an interaction between *treatment* and *motivation* to a model that assumed this interaction was not present. Relative to the main effects model, the amount that the model fit improved after including the interaction is 0.013 and the proportional improvement in model fit due to adding the interaction to the model, or the strength of association between the interaction and outcome, is then 0.013 / 272.117, which is near zero.

McFadden (1979) cautioned that values for R_L^2 are typically smaller than R-square values observed in standard regression analysis. As a result, researchers cannot rely on values, for example, as given in Cohen (1988) to indicate weak, moderate, or strong associations. McFadden (1979) noted that for the entire model values of .2 to .4 represent a strong improvement in fit, but these values of course cannot reasonably be applied in every situation as they may represent a weak association in some contexts and may be unobtainably high in others. Note also that, at present, neither SAS nor SPSS provides this measure of association for binary outcomes.

11.11 SIGNIFICANCE TESTS AND CONFIDENCE INTERVALS FOR SINGLE VARIABLES

When you are interested in testing the association between an individual predictor and outcome, controlling for other predictors, several options are available. Of those introduced here, the most powerful approach is the likelihood ratio test described in section 11.9. The reduced model would exclude the variable of interest, and the full model would include that variable. The main disadvantage of this approach is practical, in that multiple analyses would need to be done in order to test each predictor. In this example, with a limited number of predictors, the likelihood ratio test would be easy to implement.

A more convenient and commonly used approach to test the effects of individual predictors is to use a z test, which provides results equivalent to the Wald test that is often reported by software programs. The z test of the null hypothesis that a given regression coefficient is zero (i.e., $\beta_j = 0$) is

$$z = \frac{\beta_j}{S_{\beta_j}}, \tag{12}$$

where S_{β_j} is the standard error for the regression coefficient. To test for significance, you compare this test statistic to a critical value from the standard normal distribution. So, if alpha were .05, the corresponding critical value for a two-tailed test would be ±1.96. The Wald test, which is the square of the z test, follows a chi-square distribution with 1 degree of freedom. The main disadvantage associated with this procedure is that when β_j becomes large, the standard error of Equation 12 becomes inflated, which makes this test less powerful than the likelihood ratio test (Hauck & Donner, 1977).

A third option to test the effect of a predictor is to obtain a confidence interval for the odds ratio. A general expression for the confidence interval for the odds ratio, denoted CI(OR), is given by

$$\text{CI(OR)} = e\left(c_{\beta_j} \pm z(a)\left(cS_\beta\right)\right), \tag{13}$$

where c is the increment of interest in the predictor (relevant only for a continuous variable) and $z(a)$ represents the z value from the standard normal distribution for the associated confidence level of interest (often 95%). If a value of 1 is not contained in the interval, then the null hypothesis of no effect is rejected. In addition, the use of confidence intervals allows for a specific statement about the population value of the odds ratio, which may be of interest.

11.11.1 Impact of the Treatment

We illustrate the use of these procedures to assess the impact of the *treatment* on *health*. When Equation 9 is estimated, the coefficient reflecting the impact of the *treatment*, β_1, is 1.014 ($SE = .302$). The z test for the null hypothesis that $\beta_1 = 0$ is then 1.014 / .302 = 3.36 ($p = .001$), indicating that the treatment effect is statistically significant. The odds ratio of about 3 ($e^{1.014} = 2.76$) means that the odds of good health for adults in the educator group are about 3 times the odds of those in the control group, controlling for *motivation*. The 95% confidence interval is computed as $e^{(1.014 \pm 1.96 \times .302)}$ and is 1.53 to 4.98. The interval suggests that the odds of being diabetes free for those in the educator group may be as small as 1.5 times and as large as about 5 times the odds of those in the control group.

11.12 PRELIMINARY ANALYSIS

In the next few sections, measures of residuals and influence are presented along with the statistical assumptions associated with logistic regression. In addition, other problems that may arise with data for logistic regression are discussed. Note that formulas presented for the following residuals assume that continuous predictors are used in the logistic regression model. When categorical predictors only are used, where many cases are present for each possible combination of the levels of these variables (sometimes referred to as aggregate data), different formulas are used to calculate residuals (see Menard, 2010). We present formulas here for individual (and not aggregate) data because this situation is more common in social science research. As throughout the text, the goal of preliminary analysis is to help ensure that the results obtained by the primary analysis are valid.

11.13 RESIDUALS AND INFLUENCE

Observations that are not fit well by the model may be detected by the Pearson residual. The Pearson residual is given by

$$r_i = \frac{Y_i - \hat{p}_i}{\sqrt{\hat{p}_i(1 - \hat{p}_i)}}, \tag{14}$$

where $\hat{p}_i$ is the probability (of $Y = 1$) as predicted by the logistic regression equation for a given individual i. The numerator is the difference (i.e., the raw residual) between an observed Y score and the probability predicted by the equation, and the denominator is the standard deviation of the Y scores according to the binomial distribution. In large samples, this residual may approximate a normal distribution with a mean of 0 and a standard deviation of 1. Thus, a case with a residual value that is quite distinct from the others and that has a value of r_i greater than $|2.5|$ or $|3.0|$ suggest a case that is not fit well by the model. It would be important to check any such cases to see if data are entered correctly and, if so, to learn more about the kind of cases that are not fit well by the model.

An alternative or supplemental index for outliers is the deviance residual. The deviance residual reflects the contribution an individual observation makes to the model deviance, with larger absolute values reflecting more poorly fit observations. This residual may be computed for a given case by calculating the log likelihood in Equation 8 (the expression to the right of the summation symbol), multiplying this value by -2, and then taking the square root of this value. The sign of this residual (i.e., positive or negative) is determined by whether the numerator in Equation 14 is positive or negative. Some have expressed preference for use of the deviance residual over the Pearson residual because the Pearson residual is relatively unstable when the predicted probably of $Y = 1$ is close to 0 or 1. However, Menard (2010) notes an advantage of the Pearson residual is that it has larger values and so outlying cases are more greatly emphasized with this residual. As such, we limit our discussion here to the Pearson residual.

In addition to identifying outlying cases, a related concern is to determine if any cases are influential or unduly impact key analysis results. There are several measures of influence that are analogous to those used in traditional regression, including, for example, leverage, a Cook's influence measure, and delta beta. Here, we focus on delta beta because it is directed at the influence a given observation has on the impact of a specific explanatory variable, which is often of interest and is here in this example with the impact of the intervention being a primary concern. As with traditional regression, delta beta indicates the change in a given logistic regression coefficient if a case were deleted. Note that the sign of the index ($+$ or $-$) refers to whether the slope increases or decreases when the case is *included* in the data set. Thus, the sign of the delta beta needs to be reversed if you wish to interpret the index as the impact of specific case on a given regression coefficient when the case is deleted. For SAS users, note that raw delta beta values are not provided by the program. Instead, SAS provides standardized delta beta values, obtained by dividing a delta beta value by its standard error. There is some agreement that standardized values larger than a magnitude of 1 may exert influence on analysis. To be on the safe side, though, you can examine further any cases having outlying values that are less than this magnitude.

We now illustrate examining residuals and delta beta values to identify unusual and influential cases with the chapter data. We estimated Equation 9 and found no cases had a Pearson residual value greater than 2 in magnitude. We then inspected histograms of the delta betas for β_1 and β_2. Two outlying delta beta values appear to be present for *motivation* (β_2), the histogram for which is shown in Figure 11.3. The value of delta beta for each of these cases is about $-.004$. Given the negative value, the value for β_2 will increase if these cases were removed from the analysis. We can assess the impact of both of these cases on analysis results by temporarily removing the observations and reestimating Equation 9. With all 200 cases, the value for β_2 is 0.040 and $e^{(.04)} = 1.041$, and with the two cases removed β_2 is 0.048 and $e^{(.048)} = 1.049$. The change, then, obtained by removing these two cases seems small both for the coefficient and

■ **Figure 11.3:** Histogram of delta beta values for coefficient β_2.

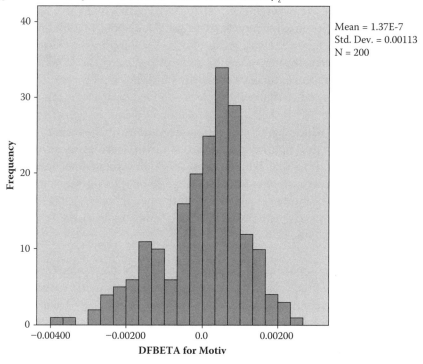

the odds ratio. We also note that with the removal of these two cases, all of the con-clusions associated with the statistical tests are unchanged. Thus, these two discrepant cases are not judged to exert excessive influence on key study results.

11.14 ASSUMPTIONS

Three formal assumptions are associated with logistic regression. First, the logistic regression model is assumed to be correctly specified. Second, cases are assumed to be independent. Third, each explanatory variable is assumed to be measured without error. You can also consider there to be a fourth assumption for logistic regression. That is, the statistical inference procedures discussed earlier (based on asymptotic the-ory) assume that a large sample size is used. These assumptions are described in more detail later. Note that while many of these assumptions are analogous to those used in traditional regression, logistic regression does not assume that the residuals follow a normal distribution or that the residuals have constant variance across the range of pre-dicted values. Also, other practical data-related issues are discussed in section 11.15.

11.14.1 Correct Specification

Correct specification is a critical assumption. For logistic regression, correct specifi-cation means that (1) the correct link function (e.g., the logistic link function) is used, and (2) that the model includes explanatory variables that are nontrivially related to the outcome and excludes irrelevant predictors. For the link function, there appears to be consensus that choice of link function (e.g., use of a logistic vs. probit link function) has no real consequence on analysis results. Also, including predictors in the model that are trivially related to the outcome (i.e., irrelevant predictors) is known to increase the standard errors of the coefficients (thus reducing statistical power) but does not result in biased regression coefficient estimates. On the other hand, excluding important determinants introduces bias into the estimation of the regression coefficients and their standard errors, which can cast doubt on the validity of the results. You should rely on theory, previous empirical work, and common sense to identify important explanatory variables. If there is little direction to guide variable selection, you could use exploratory methods as used in traditional regression (i.e., the sequential methods discussed in section 3.8) to begin the theory development process. The conclusions drawn from the use of such methods are generally much more tentative than studies where a specific theory guides model specification.

The need to include important predictors in order to avoid biased estimates also extends to the inclusion of important nonlinear terms and interactions in the statistical model, similar to traditional regression. Although the probabilities of $Y = 1$ are nonlinearly related to explanatory variables in logistic regression, the log of the odds or the logit, given no transformation of the predictors, is assumed to be linearly related to the predictors, as in Equation 7. Of course, this functional form may not be correct.

The Box–Tidwell procedure can be used to test the linear aspect of this assumption. To implement this procedure, you create new variables in the data set, which are the natural logs of each continuous predictor. Then, you multiply this transformed variable by the original predictor, essentially creating a product variable that is the original continuous variable times its natural log. Any such product variables are then added to the logistic regression equation. If any are statistically significant, this suggests that the logit has a nonlinear association with the given continuous predictor. You could then search for an appropriate transformation of the continuous explanatory variable, as suggested in Menard (2010).

The Box–Tidwell procedure to test for nonlinearity in the logit is illustrated here with the chapter data. For these data, only one predictor, *motivation*, is continuous. Thus, we computed the natural log of the scores for this variable and multiplied them by *motivation*. This new product variable is named *xlnx*. When this predictor is added to those included in Equation 9, the *p* value associated with the coefficient of *xlnx* is .909, suggesting no violation of the linearity assumption. Section 11.18 provides the SAS and SPSS commands needed to implement this procedure as well as selected output.

In addition to linearity, the correct specification assumption also implies that important interactions have been included in the model. In principle, you could include all possible interaction terms in the model in an attempt to determine if important interaction terms have been omitted. However, as more explanatory variables appear in the model, the number of interaction terms increases sharply with perhaps many of these interactions being essentially uninterpretable (e.g., four- and five-way interactions). As with traditional regression models, the best advice may be to include interactions as suggested by theory or that are of interest. For the chapter data, recall that in section 11.9 we tested the interaction between *treatment* and *motivation* and found no support for the interaction.

11.14.2 Hosmer–Lemeshow Goodness-of-Fit Test

In addition to these procedures, the Hosmer–Lemeshow (HL) test offers a global goodness-of-fit test that compares the estimated model to one that has perfect fit. Note that this test does not assess, as was the case with the likelihood ratio test in section 11.9, whether model fit is improved when a set of predictors is added to a reduced model. Instead, the HL test assesses whether the fit of a given model deviates from the perfect fitting model, given all relevant explanatory variables are included. Alternatively, as Allison (2012) points out, the HL test can be interpreted as a test of the null hypothesis that no additional interaction or nonlinear terms are needed in the model. Note, however, that the HL test does not assess whether other predictors that are entirely excluded from the estimated model could improve model fit.

Before highlighting some limitations associated with the procedure, we discuss how it works. The procedure compares the observed frequencies of $Y = 1$ to the frequencies predicted by the logistic regression equation. To obtain these values, the sample is divided, by convention, into 10 groups referred to as the deciles of risk. Each group is formed based on the probabilities of $Y = 1$, with individuals in the first group consisting of those cases that have the lowest predicted probabilities, those in the second group are cases that have next lowest predicted probabilities, and so on. The predicted, or expected, frequencies are then obtained by summing these probabilities over the cases in each of the 10 groups. The observed frequencies are obtained by summing the number of cases actually having $Y = 1$ in each of the 10 groups.

The probabilities obtained from estimating Equation 9 are now used to illustrate this procedure. Table 11.3 shows the observed and expected frequencies for each of the 10 deciles. When the probabilities of $Y = 1$ are summed for the 20 cases in group 1, this sum or expected frequency is 3.995. Note that under the Observed column of Table 11.3, 4 of these 20 cases actually exhibited good health. For this first decile, then, there is a very small difference between the observed and expected frequencies, suggesting that the probabilities produced by the logistic regression equation, for this group, approximate reality quite well. Note that Hosmer and Lemeshow (2013) suggest computing the quantity $\dfrac{\text{Observed} - \text{Expected}}{\sqrt{\text{Expected}}}$ for a given decile with values larger than 2 in magnitude indicating a problem in fit for a particular decile. The largest such value here is 0.92 for decile 2, i.e., $(7 - 4.958)/\sqrt{4.958} = 0.92$. This suggests that there are small differences between the observed and expected frequencies, supporting the goodness-of-fit of the estimated model.

▪ **Table 11.3: Deciles of Risk Table Associated With the Hosmer–Lemeshow Goodness-of-Fit Test**

| Number of groups | Health = 1 | | Number of cases |
	Observed	Expected	
1	4	3.995	20
2	7	4.958	20
3	6	5.680	20
4	3	6.606	20
5	9	7.866	20
6	8	8.848	20
7	10	9.739	20
8	9	10.777	20
9	15	12.156	20
10	13	13.375	20

In addition to this information, this procedure offers an overall goodness-of-fit statistical test for the differences between the observed and expected frequencies. The null hypothesis is that these differences reflect sampling error, or that the model has perfect fit. A decision to retain the null hypothesis (i.e., $p > a$) supports the adequacy of the model, whereas a reject decision signals that the model is misspecified (i.e., has omitted nonlinear and/or interaction terms). The HL test statistic approximates a chi-square distribution with degrees of freedom equal to the number of groups formed (10, here) − 2. Here, we simply report that the χ^2 test value is 6.88 ($df = 8$), and the corresponding p value is .55. As such, the goodness-of-fit of the model is supported (suggesting that adding nonlinear and interaction terms to the model will not improve its fit).

There are some limitations associated with the Hosmer–Lemeshow goodness-of-fit test. Allison (2012) and Menard (2010) note that this test may be underpowered and tends to return a result of correct fit of the model, especially when fewer than six groups are formed and when sample size is not large (i.e., less than 500). Further, Allison (2012) notes that even when more than six groups are formed, test results are sensitive to the number of groups formed in the procedure. He further discusses erratic behavior with the performance of the test, for example, that including a statistically significant interaction in the model can produce HL test results that indicate worse model fit (the opposite of what is intended). Research continues on ways to improve the HL test (Prabasaj, Pennell, & Lemeshow, 2012). In the meantime, a sensible approach may be to examine the observed and expected frequencies produced by this procedure to identify possible areas of misfit (as suggested by Hosmer & Lemeshow, 2013) use the Box–Tidwell procedure to assess the assumption of linearity, and include interactions in the model that are based on theory or those that are of interest.

11.14.3 Independence

Another important assumption is that the observations are obtained from independent cases. Dependency in observations may arise from repeatedly measuring the outcome and in study designs where observations are clustered in settings (e.g., students in schools) or cases are paired or matched on some variable(s), as in a matched case-control study. Note that when this assumption is violated and standard analysis is used, type I error rates associated with tests of the regression coefficients may be inflated. In addition, dependence can introduce other problems, such as over- and underdispersion (i.e., where the assumed binomial variance of the outcome does not hold for the data). Extensions of the standard logistic regression procedure have been developed for these situations. Interested readers may consult texts by Allison (2012), Hosmer and Lemeshow (2013), or Menard (2010), that cover these and other extensions of the standard logistic regression model.

11.14.4 No Measurement Error for the Predictors

As with traditional regression, the predictors are assumed to be measured with perfect reliability. Increasing degrees of violation of this assumption lead to greater bias in the estimates of the logistic regression coefficients and their standard errors. Good advice here obviously is to select measures of constructs that are known to have the greatest reliability. Options you may consider when reliability is lower than desired is to exclude such explanatory variables from the model, when it makes sense to do that, or use structural equation modeling to obtain parameter estimates that take measurement error into account.

11.14.5 Sufficiently Large Sample Size

Also, as mentioned, use of inferential procedures in logistic regression assume large sample sizes are being used. How large a sample size needs to be for these properties to hold for a given model is unknown. Long (1997) reluctantly offers some advice and suggests that samples smaller than 100 are likely problematic, but that samples larger than 500 should mostly be adequate. He also advises that there be at least 10 observations per predictor. Note also that the sample sizes mentioned here do not, of course, guarantee sufficient statistical power. The software program NCSS PASS (Hintze, 2002) may be useful to help you obtain an estimate of the sample size needed to achieve reasonable power, although it requires you to make *a priori* selections about certain summary measures, which may require a good deal of speculation.

11.15 OTHER DATA ISSUES

There are other issues associated with the data that may present problems for logistic regression analysis. First, as with traditional regression analysis, excessive multicollinearity may be present. If so, standard errors of regression coefficients may be inflated or the estimation process may not converge. Section 3.7 presented methods to detect multicollinearity and suggested possible remedies, which also apply to logistic regression.

Another issue that may arise in logistic regression is known as perfect or complete separation. Such separation occurs when the outcome is perfectly predicted by an explanatory variable. For example, for the chapter data, if all adults in the educator group exhibited good health status ($Y = 1$) and all in the control group did not ($Y = 0$), perfect separation would be present. A similar problem is known as quasi-complete or nearly complete separation. In this case, the separation is nearly complete (e.g., $Y = 1$ for nearly all cases in a given group and $Y = 0$ for nearly all cases in another group). If complete or quasi-complete separation is present, maximum likelihood estimation may not converge or, if it does, the estimated coefficient for the explanatory variable associated with the separation and its standard error may be extremely large. In practice, these separation issues may be due to having nearly as many variables in the analysis as there are cases. Remedies here include increasing sample size or removing predictors from the model.

A related issue and another possible cause of quasi-complete separation is known as zero cell count. This situation occurs when a level of a categorical variable has only one outcome score (i.e., $Y = 1$ or $Y = 0$). Zero cell count can be detected during the initial data screening. There are several options for dealing with zero cell count. Potential remedies include collapsing the levels of the categorical variable to eliminate the zero count problem, dropping the categorical variable entirely from the analysis, or dropping cases associated with the level of the "offending" categorical variable. You may also decide to retain the categorical variable as is, as other parameters in the model should not be affected, other than those involving the contrasts among the levels of the categorical variable with that specific level. Allison (2012) also discusses alternative estimation options that may be useful.

11.16 CLASSIFICATION

Often in logistic regression, as in the earlier example, investigators are interested in quantifying the degree to which an explanatory variable, or a set of such variables, is related to the probability of some event, that is, the probability of $Y = 1$. Given that the residual term in logistic regression is defined as difference between observed group membership and the predicted probability of $Y = 1$, a common analysis goal is to determine if this error is reduced after including one or more predictors in the model. McFadden's R_L^2 is an effect size measure that reflects improved prediction (i.e., smaller error term), and the likelihood ratio test is used to assess if this improvement is due to sampling error or reflects real improvement in the population. Menard (2010) labels this type of prediction as *quantitative* prediction, reflecting the degree to which the predicted probabilities of $Y = 1$ more closely approximate observed group membership after predictors are included.

In addition to the goal of assessing the improvement in quantitative prediction, investigators may be interested or primarily interested in using logistic regression results to classify participants into groups. Using the outcome from this chapter, you may be interested in classifying adults as having a diabetes-free diagnosis or of being at risk of being diagnosed with type 2 diabetes. Accurately classifying adults as being at risk of developing type 2 diabetes may be helpful because adults can then change their lifestyle to prevent its onset. In assessing how well the results of logistic regression can effectively classify individuals, a key measure used is the number of errors made by the classification. That is, for cases that are *predicted* to be of good health, how many actually are and how many errors are there? Similarly, for those cases predicted to be of poor health, how many actually are?

When results from a logistic regression equation are used for classification purposes, the interest turns to minimizing the number of classification errors. In this context, the interest is to find out if a set of variables reduces the number of classification errors, or improves *qualitative* prediction (Menard, 2010). When classification is a study goal, a new set of statistics then is needed to describe the reduction in the number of classification errors. This section presents statistics that can be used to address the accuracy of classifications made by use of a logistic regression equation.

11.16.1 Percent Correctly Classified

A measure that is often used to assess the accuracy of prediction is the percent of cases correctly classified by the model. To classify cases into one of two groups, the probabilities of $Y = 1$ are obtained from a logistic regression equation. With these probabilities, you can classify a given individual after selecting a *cut point*. A cut point is a probability of $Y = 1$ that you select, with a commonly used value being .50, at or above which results in a case being classified into one of two groups (e.g., success) and below which results in a case being classified into the other group (e.g., failure). Of course to assess the accuracy of classification in this way, the outcome data must already be collected. Given that actual group membership is already known, it is a simple matter to count the number of cases correctly and incorrectly classified. The percent of cases classified correctly can be readily determined, with of course higher values reflecting greater accuracy. Note that if the logistic regression equation is judged to be useful in classifying cases, the equation could then be applied to future samples without having the outcome data collected for these samples. Cross-validation of the results with an independent sample would provide additional support for using the classification procedure in this way.

We use the chapter data to obtain the percent of cases correctly classified by the full model. Table 11.4 uses probabilities obtained from estimating Equation 9 to classify cases into one of two groups: (1) of good health, a classification made when the probability of being of good health is estimated by the equation to be 0.5 or greater; or (2) of poor health, a classification made when this probability is estimated at values less than 0.5. In the Total column, Table 11.4 shows that the number of observed cases that did not exhibit good health was 116, whereas 84 cases exhibited good health. Of the

116 adults diagnosed with type 2 diabetes, 92 were predicted to have this diagnosis. Of those who were of good health, 37 were predicted to be diabetes free by the equation (i.e., the probability of $Y = 1$ was greater than .5 for these 37 cases). The total number of cases correctly classified is then $92 + 37 = 129$. The percent of cases correctly classified is then the number of cases correctly classified over the sample size times 100. As such, $(129 / 200) \times 100 = 64.5\%$ of the cases are correctly classified by the equation. Note that SAS provides a value, not shown here, for the percent of cases correctly classified that is adjusted for bias due to using information from a given case to also classify it.

11.16.2 Proportion Reduction in Classification Errors

While the percent correctly classified is a useful summary statistic, you cannot determine from this statistic alone the degree to which the predictor variables are responsible for this success rate. When the improvement in *quantitative* prediction was assessed, we examined $-2LL$, a measure of lack of fit obtained from the baseline model, and found the amount this quantity was reduced (or fit improved) after predictors were added to the model. We then computed the ratio of these 2 values (i.e., R_L^2) to describe the proportional improvement in fit. A similar notion can be applied to classification errors to obtain the degree to which more accurate classifications are due to the predictors in the model.

To assess the improvement in classification due to the set of predictors, we compare the amount of classification errors made with no predictors in the model (i.e., the null model) and determine the amount of classification errors made after including the predictors. This amount is then divided by the number of classification errors made by the null model. Thus, an equation that can be used to determine the proportional reduction in classification errors is

$$\text{Proportional error reduction} = \frac{PErrors_{null} - PErrors_{full}}{PErrors_{null}}, \tag{15}$$

where $PErrors_{null}$ and $PErrors_{full}$ are the proportions of classification errors for the null and full models, respectively. For the null model, the proportion of classification errors can be computed as the proportion of the sample that is in the smaller of the two outcome categories (i.e., $Y = 0$ or 1). The error rate may be calculated this way because the probability of $Y = 1$ that is used to classify all cases in the null model (where this probability is a constant) is simply the proportion of cases in the larger outcome category, leaving the classification error rate for the null model to be 1 minus this probability.

▪ **Table 11.4: Classification Results for the Chapter Data**

Observed	Predicted Unhealthy	Predicted Healthy	Total	Percent correct
Unhealthy	92	24	116	79.3
Healthy	47	37	84	44.0
Total				64.5

For the full model, the proportion of cases classified incorrectly is 1 minus the proportion of cases correctly classified.

We illustrate the calculation and interpretation of Equation 15 with the chapter data. Since there are 116 cases in the unhealthy group and 84 cases in the healthy group, the proportion of classification errors in the null model is 84 / 200 = .42. As can be obtained from Table 11.4, the proportion of cases incorrectly classified by use of the full model is (24 + 47) / 200 = .355.

Therefore, the proportional reduction in the number of classification errors that is due to the inclusion of the predictors in the full model is

(.42 − .355) / .42 = .155.

Inclusion of the predictors, then, results in a 16% reduction in the number of classification errors compared to the null model.

In addition to this descriptive statistic on the improvement in prediction, Menard (2010) notes that you can test whether the degree of prediction improvement is different from zero in the population. The binomial statistic d can be used for this purpose and is computed as

$$d = \frac{PErrors_{null} - PErrors_{full}}{\sqrt{PErrors_{null}(1 - PErrors_{null}) / N}}. \tag{16}$$

In large samples, this statistic approximates a normal distribution. Further, if you are interested in testing if classification accuracy improves due to the inclusion of predictors (instead of changes, as the proportional reduction in error may be negative), a one-tailed test is used.

Illustrating the use of the binomial d statistic with the chapter data,

$$d = \frac{.42 - .355}{\sqrt{.42(1 - .42) / 200}}$$
$$= .065 / .035$$
$$= 1.86.$$

For a one-tailed test at .05 alpha, the critical value from the standard normal distribution is 1.65. Since 1.86 > 1.65, a reduction in the number of classification errors due to the predictors in the full model is present in the population.

11.17 USING SAS AND SPSS FOR MULTIPLE LOGISTIC REGRESSION

Table 11.5 shows SAS and SPSS commands that can be used to estimate Equation 9 and obtain other useful statistics. Since SAS and SPSS provide similar output, we show only SPSS output in Table 11.6. Although not shown in the output, the commands in Table 11.5 also produce logistic regression classification tables as well as a table showing the deciles of risk used in the Hosmer–Lemeshow procedure.

Table 11.5 shows selected output from SPSS. With SPSS, results are provided in blocks. Block 0, not shown, provides results for a model with the outcome and intercept only. In Block 1, the results are provided for the full model having the predictors *treatment* and *motivation*. The first output in Table 11.5 provides the chi-square test for the improvement in fit due to the variables added in Block 1 (i.e., 18.972), which is an omnibus test of two predictors. The Model Summary output provides the overall

■ **Table 11.5: SAS and SPSS Control Lines for Multiple Logistic Regression**

SAS
(1) PROC LOGISTIC DATA = Dataset;
(2) MODEL health (EVENT = '1') = treat motiv
/LACKFIT CL CTABLE PPROB = .5 IPLOTS;
(3) OUTPUT OUT = Results PREDICTED = Prob DFBETAS = _All_
RESCHI = Pearson;
RUN;

SPSS
(4) LOGISTIC REGRESSION VARIABLES health
(5) /METHOD=ENTER treat motiv
(6) /SAVE=PRED DFBETA ZRESID
(7) /CASEWISE OUTLIER(2)
(8) /PRINT=GOODFIT CI(95)
(9) /CRITERIA=PIN(0.05) POUT(0.10) ITERATE(20) CUT(0.5).

(1) Invokes the logistic regression procedure and indicates the name of the data set to be analyzed, which has been previously read into SAS.

(2) Indicates that health is the outcome and that the value coded 1 for this outcome (here, good health) is the event being modeled. The predictors appear after the equals sign. After the slash, LACKFIT requests the Hosmer-Lemeshow test, CL requests confidence limits for the odds ratios, CTABLE and PPROB = .5 produces a classification table using a cut value of .5, and IPLOTS is used to request plots of various diagnostics.

(3) OUTPUT OUT saves the following requested diagnostics in a data set called Results. PREDICTED requests the probabilities of Y = 1 and names the corresponding column prob. DFBETAS requests the delta betas for all coefficients and uses a default naming convention, and RESCHI requests the standardized residuals and names the associated column Pearson.

(4) Invokes the logistic regression procedure and specifies that the outcome is health.

(5) Adds predictors treat and motiv.

(6) Saves to the active data set the predicted probabilities of Y = 1, delta betas, and standardized residuals from the full model.

(7) Requests information on cases having standardized residuals larger than 2 in magnitude.

(8) Requests output for the Hosmer-Lemeshow goodness-of-fit test and confidence intervals.

(9) Lists the default criteria; relevant here are the number of iterations and the cut value used for the classification table.

■ **Table 11.6: Selected Output From SPSS**

Omnibus Tests of Model Coefficients

		Chi-square	df	Sig.
Step 1	Step	18.972	2	.000
	Block	18.972	2	.000
	Model	18.972	2	.000

Model Summary

Step	−2 Log likelihood	Cox & Snell R Square	Nagelkerke R Square
1	253.145[a]	.090	.122

[a] Estimation terminated at iteration number 4 because parameter estimates changed by less than .001.

Variables in the Equation

		B	S.E.	Wald	df	Sig.	Exp(B)	95% C.I.for EXP(B) Lower	Upper
Step 1[a]	Treat	1.014	.302	11.262	1	.001	2.756	1.525	4.983
	Motiv	.040	.015	6.780	1	.009	1.041	1.010	1.073
	Constant	−2.855	.812	12.348	1	.000	.058		

[a] Variable(s) entered on step 1: Treat, Motiv.

Hosmer and Lemeshow Test

Step	Chi-square	Df	Sig.
1	6.876	8	.550

model fit ($-2LL$) along with other pseudo R-square statistics. The Variables in the Equation section provides the point estimate, the standard error, test statistic information, odds ratio, and the 95% confidence interval for the odds ratio for the predictors. Note that the odds ratios are given in the column Exp(B). Test statistic information for the HL test is provided at the bottom of Table 11.6.

11.18 USING SAS AND SPSS TO IMPLEMENT THE BOX–TIDWELL PROCEDURE

Section 11.14.1 presented the Box–Tidwell procedure to assess the specification of the model, particularly to identify if nonlinear terms are needed to improve the fit of the model. Table 11.7 provides SAS and SPSS commands that can be used to implement this procedure using the chapter data set. Further, selected output is provided and shows support for the linear form of Equation 9 as the coefficient associated with the product term *xlnx* is not statistically significant (i.e., $p = .909$).

Now that we have presented the analysis of the chapter data, we present an example results section that summarizes analysis results in a form similar to that needed for a journal article. We close the chapter by presenting a summary of the key analysis procedures that is intended to help guide you through important data analysis activities for binary logistic regression.

■ **Table 11.7: SAS and SPSS Commands for Implementing the Box-Tidwell Procedure and Selected Output**

SAS	SPSS
Commands	

(1) `xlnx = motiv*LOG(motiv);`
(2) `PROC LOGISTIC DATA = Data-`
`set; MODEL health`
`(EVENT = '1') = treat`
`motiv xlnx;`
`RUN;`
	(1) `COMPUTE`
	`xlnx=motiv*LN(motiv).`
	(2) `LOGISTIC REGRESSION VARIA-`
	`BLES health`
	`/METHOD=ENTER treat motiv`
	`xlnx`
	`/CRITERIA=PIN(0.05)`
	`POUT(0.10) ITERATE(20)`
	`CUT(0.5).`

Selected SAS Output

Analysis of Maximum Likelihood Estimates

Parameter	DF	Estimate	Standard Error	Wald Chi-Square	Pr > ChiSq
Intercept	1	−2.1018	6.6609	0.0996	0.7523
treat	1	1.0136	0.3022	11.2520	0.0008
motiv	1	−0.0357	0.6671	0.0029	0.9574
xlnx	1	0.0155	0.1360	0.0130	0.9093

Selected SPSS Output

Variables in the Equation

		B	S.E.	Wald	df	Sig.	Exp(B)
Step 1[a]	Treat	1.014	.302	11.252	1	.001	2.755
	Motiv	−.036	.667	.003	1	.957	.965
	xlnx	.015	.136	.013	1	.909	1.016
	Constant	−2.102	6.661	.100	1	.752	.122

[a] Variable(s) entered on step 1: Treat, Motiv, xlnx.
(1) Creates a variable named `xlnx` that is the product of the variable *motivation* and its natural log.
(2) Estimates Equation 9 but also includes this new product variable.

11.19 EXAMPLE RESULTS SECTION FOR LOGISTIC REGRESSION WITH DIABETES PREVENTION STUDY

A binary logistic regression analysis was conducted to determine the impact of an intervention where adults who have been diagnosed with prediabetes were randomly assigned to receive a treatment as usual (control condition) or this same treatment but also including the services of a diabetes educator (educator condition). The outcome was health status 3 months after the intervention began with a value of 1 indicating healthy status (no type 2 diabetes diagnosis) and 0 indicating poor health status (type 2 diabetes diagnosis). The analysis also includes a measure of perceived motivation collected from patients shortly after diagnosis indicating the degree to which they are willing to change their lifestyle to improve their health. Of the 200 adults participating in the study, 100 were randomly assigned to each treatment.

Table 1 shows descriptive statistics for each treatment condition as well as statistical test results for between-treatment differences. The two groups had similar mean motivation, but a larger proportion of those in the educator group had a diabetes-free diagnosis at posttest. Inspection of the data did not suggest any specific concerns, as there were no missing data, no outliers for the observed variables, and no multicollinearity among the predictors.

For the final fitted logistic regression model, we examined model residuals and delta beta values to determine if potential outlying observations influenced analysis results, and we also assessed the degree to which statistical assumptions were violated. No cases had outlying residual values, but two cases had delta beta values that were somewhat discrepant from the rest of the sample. However, a sensitivity analysis showed that these observations did not materially change study conclusions. In addition, use of the Hosmer–Lemeshow procedure did not suggest any problems with the functional form of the model, as there were small differences between the observed and expected frequencies for each of the 10 deciles formed in the procedure. Further, use of the Box–Tidwell procedure did not suggest there was a nonlinear association between *motivation* and the natural log of the odds for *health* ($p = .909$) and a test of the interaction between the *treatment* and *motivation* was not significant ($p = .68$). As adults received the treatment

▩ **Table 1: Comparisons Between Treatments for Study Variables**

Variable	Educator n = 100	Control n = 100	p Value[a]
Motivation, mean (SD)	49.83 (9.98)	49.10 (9.78)	0.606
Dichotomous variable	n (%)	n (%)	
Diabetes-free diagnosis	54 (54.0)	30 (30.0)	0.001

[a] *P* values from independent samples *t* test for *motivation* and Pearson chi-square test for the diagnosis.

■ **Table 2: Logistic Regression Estimates**

			Odds ratio	
Variable	β(SE)	Wald test	Estimate	95% CI
Treatment	1.014 (.302)	11.262	2.756	[1.53, 4.98]
Motivation[a]	0.397 (.153)	6.780	1.488	[1.10, 2.01]
Constant	−0.862 (.222)	15.022	0.422	

Note: CI = confidence interval.
[a] *Z* scores are used for *motivation*.
* $p < .05$.

on a individual basis, we have no reason to believe that the independence assumption is violated.

Table 2 shows the results of the logistic regression model, where *z*-scores are used for *motivation*. The likelihood ratio test of the model was statistically significant ($\chi^2 = 18.97$, $df = 2$, $p < .01$). As Table 2 shows, the treatment effect and the association between *motivation* and *health* was statistically significant. The odds ratio for the treatment effect indicates that for those in the educator group, the odds of being diabetes free at posttest are 2.76 times the odds of those in the control condition, controlling for *motivation*. For *motivation*, adults with greater motivation to improve their heath were more likely to have a diabetes-free diagnosis. Specifically, as *motivation* increases by 1 standard deviation, the odds of a healthy diagnosis increase by a factor of 1.5, controlling for *treatment*.

11.20 ANALYSIS SUMMARY

Logistic regression is a flexible statistical modeling technique with relatively few statistical assumptions that can be used when the outcome variable is dichotomous, with predictor variables allowed to be of any type (continuous, dichotomous, and/or categorical). Logistic regression can be used to test the impact of variables hypothesized to be related to the outcome and/or to classify individuals into one of two groups. The primary steps in a logistic regression analysis are summarized next.

I. Preliminary analysis
    A. Conduct an initial screening of the data.
        1) Purpose: Determine if summary measures seem reasonable and support the use of logistic regression. Also, identify the presence and pattern (if any) of missing data.
        2) Procedure: Conduct univariate and bivariate data screening of study variables. Examine collinearity diagnostics to identify if extreme multicollinearity appears to be present.

3) Decision/action: If inspection of the descriptive measures does not suggest problems, continue with the analysis. Otherwise, take action needed to address such problems (e.g., conduct missing data analysis, check data entry scores for accuracy, consider data transformations). Consider alternative data analysis strategies if problems cannot be resolved.

B. Identify if there are any observations that are poorly fit by the model and/or influence analysis results.
1) Inspect Pearson residuals to identity observations poorly fit by the model.
2) Inspect delta beta and/or Cook's distance values to determine if any observations may influence analysis results.
3) If needed, conduct sensitivity analysis to determine the impact of individual observations on study results.

C. Assess the statistical assumptions.
1) Use the Box–Tidwell procedure to check for nonlinear associations and consider if any interactions should be tested to assess the assumption of correct model specification. Inspect deciles obtained from the Hosmer–Lemeshow procedure and consider using the HL goodness-of-fit test results if sample size is large (e.g., > 500).
2) Consider the research design and study circumstances to determine if the independence assumption is satisfied.
3) If any assumption is violated, seek an appropriate remedy as needed.

II. Primary analysis
A. Test the association between the entire set of explanatory variables and the outcome with the likelihood ratio test. If it is of interest, report the McFadden pseudo R-square to describe the strength of association for the entire model.

B. Describe the unique association of each explanatory variable on the outcome.
1) For continuous and dichotomous predictors, use the odds ratio and its statistical test (as well as associated confidence interval, if desired) to assess each association.
2) For variables involving 2 or more degrees of freedom (e.g., categorical variables and some interactions), test the presence of an association with the likelihood ratio test and, for any follow-up comparisons of interest, estimate and test odds ratios (and consider use of confidence intervals).

C. Consider reporting selected probabilities of $Y = 1$ obtained from the model to describe the association of a key variable or variables of interest.

D. If classification of cases is an important study goal, do the following:
1) Report the classification table as well as the percent of cases correctly classified given the cut value used.
2) Report the reduction in the proportion of classification errors due to the model and test whether this reduction is statistically significant.
3) If possible, obtain an independent sample and cross validate the classification procedure.

11.21 EXERCISES

1. Consider the following research example and answer the questions.

A researcher has obtained data from a random sample of adults who have recently been diagnosed with coronary heart disease. The researchers are interested in whether such patients comply with their physician's recommendations about managing the disease (e.g., exercise, diet, take needed medications) or not. The dependent variable is coded as $Y = 1$ indicating compliance and $Y = 0$ indicating noncompliance.

The predictor variables of interest are:

X1 patient gender (1 = female; 0 = male)

X2 motivation (continuously measured)

(a) Why would logistic regression likely be used to analyze the data?

(b) Use the following table to answer the questions.

Logistic Regression Results

Variable	Coefficient	p Value for the Wald test
X1	0.01	0.97
X2	0.2	0.03
Constant	–5.0	

(c) Write the logistic regression equation.

(d) Compute and interpret the odds ratio for each of the variables in the table. For the motivation variable, compute the odds ratio for a 10-point increase in motivation.

2. The results shown here are based on an example that appears in Tate (1998). Researchers are interested in identifying if completion of a summer individualized remedial program for 160 eighth graders (coded 1 for completion, 0 if not), which is the outcome, is related to several predictor variables. The predictor variables include student aptitude, an award for good behavior given by teachers during the school year (coded 1 if received, 0 if not), and age. Use these results to address the questions that appear at the end of the output.

For the model with the Intercept only: $-2LL = 219.300$

For the model with predictors: $-2LL = 160.278$

Logistic Regression Estimates

Variable (coefficient)	$\beta(SE)$	Wald chi-square test	p Value	Odds ratio Estimate	Odds ratio 95% CI
Aptitude (β_1)	.138(.028)	23.376	.000	1.148	[1.085, 1.213]
Award (β_2)	3.062(.573)	28.583	.000	21.364	[6.954, 65.639]
Age (β_3)	1.307(.793)	2.717	.099	3.694	[.781, 17.471]
Constant	−22.457(8.931)	6.323	.012	.000	

Cases Having Standardized Residuals > |2|

Case	Observed Outcome	Predicted Probability	Residual	Pearson
22	0	.951	−.951	−4.386
33	1	.873	−.873	−2.623
90	1	.128	.872	2.605
105	0	.966	−.966	−5.306

Classification Results (With Cut Value of .05)

Observed	Predicted Dropped out	Predicted Completed	Total	Percent correct
Dropped out	50	20	70	71.4
Completed	11	79	90	87.8
Total				80.6

(a) Report and interpret the test result for the overall null hypothesis.

(b) Compute and interpret the odds ratio for a 10-point increase in aptitude.

(c) Interpret the odds ratio for the award variable.

(d) Determine the number of outliers that appear to be present.

(e) Describe how you would implement the Box–Tidwell procedure with these data.

(f) Assuming that classification is a study goal, list the percent of cases correctly classified by the model, compute and interpret the proportional reduction in classification errors due to the model, and compute the binomial d test to determine if a reduction in classification errors is present in the population.

REFERENCES

Allison, P.D. (2012). *Logistic regression using SAS: Theory and applications.* (2nd ed.). Cary, NC: SAS Institute, Inc.

Berkowitz, S., Stover, C., & Marans, S. (2011). The Child and Family Traumatic Stress Intervention: Secondary prevention for youth at risk of developing PTSD. *Journal of Child Psychology & Psychiatry, 52*(6), 676–685.

Cohen, J. (1988). *Statistical power analysis for the social sciences* (2nd ed.). Hillsdale, NJ: Lawrence Erlbaum Associates.

Dion, E., Roux, C., Landry, D., Fuchs, D., Wehby, J., & Dupéré, V. (2011). Improving attention and preventing reading difficulties among low-income first-graders: A randomized study. *Prevention Science, 12*, 70–79.

Hauck, W.W., & Donner, A. (1977). Wald's test as applied to hypotheses in logit analysis. *Journal of the American Statistical Association, 72*, 851–853; with correction in W.W. Hauck & Donner (1980), *Journal of the American Statistical Association, 75*, 482.

Hintze, J. (2002). PASS 2002 [Computer software]. Kaysville, UT: NCSS.

Hosmer, D.W., & Lemeshow, S. (2013). *Applied logistic regression* (3rd ed.). Hoboken, NJ: John Wiley & Sons.

Le Jan, G., Le Bouquin-Jeannès, R., Costet, N., Trolès, N., Scalart, P., Pichancourt, D., & Gombert, J. (2011). Multivariate predictive model for dyslexia diagnosis. *Annals of Dyslexia, 61*(1), 1–20.

Long, J.S. (1997). *Regression models for categorical and limited dependent variables.* Thousand Oaks, CA: Sage.

McFadden, D. (1974). Conditional logit analysis of qualitative choice behavior. In P. Zarembka (Ed.), *Frontiers in econometrics* (pp. 105–142). New York, NY: Academic Press.

McFadden, D. (1979). Quantitative methods for analysing travel behaviour of individuals: Some recent developments. In D.A. Hensher & P.R. Stopher (Eds.), *Behavioural travel modelling* (pp. 279–318). London: Croom Helm.

Menard, S. (2010). *Logistic regression: From introductory to advanced concepts and applications.* Thousand Oaks, CA: Sage.

Prabasaj, P., Pennell, M.L., & Lemeshow, S. (2012). Standardizing the power of the Hosmer–Lemeshow goodness of fit test in large data sets. *Statistics in Medicine, 32*, 67–80.

Tate, R.L. (1998). *An introduction to modeling outcomes in the behavioral and social sciences.* Edina, MN: Burgess International Group.

Chapter 12

REPEATED-MEASURES ANALYSIS

12.1 INTRODUCTION

Recall that the two basic objectives in experimental design are the elimination of systematic bias and the reduction of error (within group or cell) variance. The main reason for within-group variability is individual differences among the subjects. Thus, even though the subjects receive the same treatment, their scores on the dependent variable can differ considerably because of differences on IQ, motivation, socioeconomic status (SES), and so on. One statistical way of reducing error variance is through analysis of covariance, which was discussed in Chapter 8.

Another way of reducing error variance is through blocking on a variable such as IQ. Here, the subjects are first blocked into more homogeneous subgroups, and then randomly assigned to treatments. For example, participants may be in blocks with only 9-point IQ ranges: 91–100, 101–110, 111–120, 121–130, and 131–140. The subjects within each block may score similarly on the dependent variable, and the average scores for the subjects may differ substantially between blocks. But all of this variability between blocks is removed from the within-variability, yielding a much more sensitive (powerful) test.

In *repeated-measures designs*, blocking is carried to its extreme. That is, *we are blocking on each subject. Thus, variability among the subjects due to individual differences is completely removed from the error term.* This makes these designs much more powerful than completely randomized designs, where different subjects are randomly assigned to the different treatments. Given the emphasis in this text on power, one should seriously consider the use of repeated-measures designs where appropriate and practical. And there are many situations where such designs are appropriate. The simplest example of a repeated-measures design you may have encountered in a beginning statistics course involves the correlated or dependent samples *t* test. Here, the same participants are pretested and posttested (measured repeatedly) on a dependent variable with an intervening treatment. The subjects are used as their own controls. Another class of repeated measures situations occurs when we are comparing the *same* participants under several different treatments (drugs, stimulus displays of different complexity, etc.).

Repeated measures is also the natural design to use when the concern is with performance trends over time. For example, Bock (1975) presented an example comparing boys' and girls' performance on vocabulary over grades 8 through 11. Here we may be concerned with the mathematical form of the trend, that is, whether it is linear, quadratic, cubic, and so on.

Another distinct advantage of repeated-measures designs, because the same subjects are being used repeatedly, is that far fewer subjects are required for the study. For example, if three treatments are involved in a completely randomized design, we may require 45 subjects (15 subjects per treatment). With a repeated-measures design we would need only 15 subjects. This can be a very important practical advantage in many cases, since numerous subjects are not easy to come by in areas such as counseling, school psychology, clinical psychology, and nursing.

In this chapter, consideration is given to repeated-measures designs of varying complexity. We start with the simplest design: a single group of subjects measured under various treatments (conditions), or at different points in time. Schematically, it would look like this:

		Treatments				
		1	2	3	...	k
	1					
	2					
Subjects	:					
	N					

We then consider a similar design except that time, instead of treatment, is the within-subjects factor. When time is the within-subjects factor, trend analysis may be of interest. With trend analysis, the investigator is interested in assessing the *form* or pattern of change across time. This pattern may linear or nonlinear.

We then consider a one-between and one-within design. Many texts use the terms *between* and *within* in referring to repeated measures factors. A between variable is simply a grouping or classification variable such as sex, age, or social class. A within variable is one on which the subjects have been measured repeatedly (such as time). Some authors even refer to a repeated-measure design as a within-subjects design (Keppel & Wickens, 2004). An example of a one-between and one-within design would be as follows, where the same males and females are measured under all three treatments:

	Treatments		
	1	2	3
Males			
Females			

Another useful application of repeated measures occurs in combination with a one-way ANOVA design. In a one-way design involving treatments, participants are posttested to determine which treatment is best. If we are interested in the lasting or residual effects of treatments, then we need to measure the subjects at least a few more times. Huck, Cormier, and Bounds (1974) presented an example in which three teaching methods are compared, but in addition the subjects are again measured 6 weeks and 12 weeks later to determine the residual effect of the methods on achievement. A repeated-measures analysis of such data *could* yield a quite different conclusion as to which method might be preferred. Suppose the pattern of means looked as follows:

	POSTTEST	SIX WEEKS	12 WEEKS
METHOD 1	66	64	63
METHOD 2	69	65	59
METHOD 3	62	56	52

Just looking at a one-way ANOVA on posttest scores (if significant) could lead one to conclude that method 2 is best. Examination of the pattern of achievement over time, however, shows that, for lasting effect, method 1 is to be preferred, because after 12 weeks the achievement for method 1 is superior to method 2 (63 vs. 59). What we have here is an example of a method-by-time interaction.

In the previous example, teaching method is the between variable and time is the within, or repeated measures factor. You should be aware that other names are used to describe a one-between and one-within design, such as split plot, Lindquist Type I, and two-way ANOVA with repeated measures on one factor. Our computer example in this chapter involves weight loss after 2, 4, and 6 months for three treatment groups.

Next, we consider a one-between and two-within repeated-measures design, using the following example. Two groups of subjects are administered two types of drugs at each of three doses. The study aims to estimate the relative potency of the drugs in inhibiting a response to a stimulus. Schematically, the design is as follows:

	Drug 1			Drug 2		
Dose	1	2	3	1	2	3
Gp 1						
Gp 2						

Each participant is measured six times, for each dose of each drug. The two within variables are dose and drug.

Then, we consider a two-between and a one-within design. The study we use here is the same as with the split plot design except that we add age as a second between-subjects factor. The study compares the relative efficacy of a behavior modification approach to dieting versus a behavior modification approach + exercise on weight loss for a group of overweight women across three time points. The design is:

GROUP	AGE	WGTLOSS1	WGTLOSS2	WGTLOSS3
CONTROL	20–30 YRS			
CONTROL	30–40 YRS			
BEH. MOD.	20–40 YRS			
BEH. MOD.	30–40 YRS			
BEH. MOD. + EXER.	20–30 YRS			
BEH. MOD. + EXER.	30–40 YRS			

This is a two between-factor design, because we are subdividing the subjects on the basis of both treatment and age; that is, we have two grouping variables.

For each of these designs we provide software commands for running both the univariate and multivariate approaches to repeated-measures analysis on SAS and SPSS. We also interpret the primary results of interest, which focus on testing for group differences and change across time. To keep the chapter length manageable, though, we largely dispense with conducting preliminary analysis (e.g., searching for outliers, assessing statistical assumptions). Instead, we focus on the primary tests of interest for about 10 different repeated measures designs. We also discuss and illustrate *post hoc* testing for some of the designs.

Additionally, we consider profile analysis, in which two or more groups of subjects are compared on a battery of tests. The analysis determines whether the profiles for the groups are parallel. If the profiles are parallel, then the analysis will determine whether the profiles are coincident.

Although increased precision and economy of subjects are two distinct advantages of repeated-measures designs, such designs also have potentially serious disadvantages unless care is taken. When several treatments are involved, the order in which treatments are administered might make a difference in the subjects' performance. Thus, it is important to *counterbalance* the order of treatments.

For two treatments, this would involve randomly assigning half of the subjects to get treatment *A* first, and the other half to get treatment *B* first, which would look like this schematically:

Order of administration	
1	2
A	*B*
B	*A*

It is balanced because an equal number of subjects have received each treatment in each position.

For three treatments, counterbalancing involves randomly assigning one third of the subjects to each of the following sequences:

Order of administration of treatments		
A	*B*	*C*
B	*C*	*A*
C	*A*	*B*

This is balanced because an equal number of subjects have received each treatment in each position. This type of design is called a Latin Square.

Also, it is important to allow sufficient time between treatments to minimize carryover effects, which certainly could occur if treatments, for example, were drugs. How much time is necessary is, of course, a substantive rather than a statistical question. A nice discussion of these two problems is found in Keppel and Wickens (2004) and Myers (1979).

12.2 SINGLE-GROUP REPEATED MEASURES

Suppose we wish to study the effect of four drugs on reaction time to a series of tasks. Sufficient time is allowed to minimize the effect that one drug may have on the subject's response to the next drug. The following data is from Winer (1971):

Ss	Drugs				Means
	1	2	3	4	
1	30	28	16	34	27
2	14	18	10	22	16
3	24	20	18	30	23
4	38	34	20	44	34
5	26	28	14	30	24.5
M	26.4	25.6	15.6	32	24.9 (grand mean)
SD	8.8	6.5	3.8	8.0	

We will analyze this set of data in three different ways: (1) as a completely randomized design (pretending there are different subjects for the different drugs), (2) as a univariate repeated-measures analysis, and (3) as a multivariate repeated-measures analysis. The purpose of including the completely randomized approach is to contrast the error variance that results against the markedly smaller error variance that results in the repeated measures approach. The multivariate approach to repeated-measures analysis may be new to our readers, and a specific numerical example will help in understanding how some of the printouts on the packages are arrived at.

12.2.1 Completely Randomized Analysis of the Drug Data

This simply involves doing a one-way ANOVA. Thus, we compute the sum of squares between (SS_b) and the sum of squares within (SS_w):

$$SS_b = n \sum_{j=1}^{4} (\bar{y}_j - \bar{y})^2 = 5[(26.4 - 24.9)^2 + (25.6 - 24.9)^2 + (15.6 - 24.9)^2 +$$

$$(32 - 24.9)^2]$$

$$SS_b = 698.2$$

$$SS_w = (30 - 26.4)^2 + (14 - 26.4)^2 + \cdots + (26 - 26.4)^2 + \cdots$$

$$+ (34 - 32)^2 + \cdots + (30 - 32)^2 = 793.6$$

Thus, $MS_b = 698.2 / 3 = 232.73$ and $MS_w = 793.6 / 16 = 49.6$, and our $F = 232.73 / 49.6 = 4.7$, with 3 and 16 degrees of freedom. This is not significant at the .01 level, because the critical value is 5.29.

12.2.2 Univariate Repeated-Measures Analysis of the Drug Data

Note from the column of means for the drug data that the participants' average responses to the four drugs differ considerably (ranging from 16 to 34). We quantify this variability through the so-called sum of squares for blocks (SS_{bl}), where we are blocking on the subjects. The error variability that we calculated is split up into two parts, $SS_w = SS_{bl} + SS_{res}$, where SS_{res} stands for sum of squares residual. Denote the number of repeated measures by k.

Now we calculate the sum of squares for blocks:

$$SS_{bl} = k \sum_{i=1}^{5} (\bar{y}_i - \bar{y})^2$$

$$= 4[(27 - 24.9)^2 + (16 - 24.9) + \cdots + (24.5 - 24.9)^2]$$

$$SS_{bl} = 680.8$$

Our error term for the repeated-measures analysis is formed from $SS_{res} = SS_w - SS_{bl} = 793.6 - 680.8 = 112.8$. Note that the vast portion of the within variability is due to individual differences (680.8 out of 793.6), and that we have removed all of this from our error term for the repeated-measures analysis. Now,

$$MS_{res} = SS_{res} / (n - 1)(k - 1) = 112.8 / 4(3) = 9.4,$$

and $F = MS_b / MS_{res} = 232.73 / 9.4 = 24.76$, with $(k-1) = 3$ and $(n-1)(k-1) = 12$ degrees of freedom. This is significant well beyond the .01 level, and is approximately five times as large as the F obtained under the completely randomized design.

12.3 THE MULTIVARIATE TEST STATISTIC FOR REPEATED MEASURES

Before we consider the multivariate approach, it is instructive to go back to the t test for correlated (dependent) samples. Here, we suppose participants are pretested and posttested, and we form a set of difference (d_1) scores.

Ss	Pretest	Posttest	d_i
1	7	10	3
2	5	4	−1
3	6	8	2
N	3	7	4

The null hypothesis here is

$$H_0 : \mu_1 = \mu_2 \text{ or equivalently that } \mu_1 - \mu_2 = 0$$

The t test for determining the tenability of H_0 is

$$t = \frac{\bar{d}}{s_d / \sqrt{n}},$$

where $\bar{d}$ is the average difference score and s_d is the standard deviation of the difference scores. It is important to note that the analysis is done on the difference variable d_i.

In the multivariate case for repeated measures the test statistic for k *repeated measures is formed from the* (k − 1) *difference variables and their variances and covariances.* The transition here from univariate to multivariate parallels that for the two-group independent samples case:

Independent samples	Dependent samples
$t^2 = \dfrac{(\bar{y}_1 - \bar{y}_2)^2}{s^2 (1/n_1 + 1/n_2)}$	$t^2 = \dfrac{\bar{d}^2}{s_d^2 / n}$
$t^2 = \dfrac{n_1 n_2}{n_1 + n_2} (\bar{y}_1 - \bar{y}_2)(s^2)^{-1}(\bar{y}_1 - \bar{y}_2)$	$t^2 = n\bar{d}(s_d^2)^{-1}\bar{d}$

(Continued)

Independent samples	Dependent samples
To obtain the multivariate statistic we replace the means by mean vectors and the pooled within-variance (s^2) by the pooled within-covariance matrix.	To obtain the multivariate statistic we replace the mean difference by a vector of mean differences and the variance of difference scores by the matrix of variances and covariances on the $(k-1)$ created difference variables.
$$T^2 = \frac{n_1 n_2}{n_1 + n_2}(\bar{\mathbf{y}}_1 - \bar{\mathbf{y}}_2)'\mathbf{S}^{-1}(\bar{\mathbf{y}}_1 - \bar{\mathbf{y}}_2)$$	$$T^2 = n\mathbf{y}_d'\mathbf{S}_d^{-1}\mathbf{y}_d$$
$\mathbf{S}$ is the pooled within covariance matrix, i.e., the measure of error variability.	$\mathbf{y}_d'$ is the row vector of mean differences on the $(k-1)$ difference variables, i.e., $\mathbf{y}_d' = (\bar{y}_1 - \bar{y}_2, \ \bar{y}_2 - \bar{y}_3, \cdots \bar{y}_{k-1} - \bar{y}_k)$ and $\mathbf{S}d$ is the matrix of variances and covariances on the $(k-1)$ difference variables, i.e., the measure of error variability.

We now calculate the preceding multivariate test statistic for dependent samples (repeated measures) on the drug data. This should help to clarify the somewhat abstract development thus far.

12.3.1 Multivariate Analysis of the Drug Data

The null hypothesis we are testing for the drug data is that the drug population means are equal, or in symbols:

$$H_0 : \mu_1 = \mu_2 = \mu_3 = \mu_4$$

But this is equivalent to saying that $\mu_1 - \mu_2 = 0$, $\mu_2 - \mu_3 = 0$, and $\mu_3 - \mu_4 = 0$. (You are asked to show this in one of the exercises.) We create three difference variables on the adjacent repeated measures ($y_1 - y_2$, $y_2 - y_3$, and $y_3 - y_4$) and test H_0 by determining whether the means on all three of these difference variables are simultaneously 0. Here we display the scores on the difference variables:

	$y_1 - y_2$	$y_2 - y_3$	$y_3 - y_4$	
	2	12	−18	
	−4	8	−12	
	4	2	−12	
	4	14	−24	Thus, the row vector of mean differences here is $\mathbf{y}_d' =$
	−2	14	−16	(.8, 10, −16.4)
Means	.8	10	−16.4	
Variances	13.2	26	24.8	

We need to create $\mathbf{S}_d$, the matrix of variances and covariances on the difference variables. We already have the variances, but need to compute the covariances. The calculation for the covariance for the first two difference variables is given next and calculation of the other two is left as an exercise.

$$S_{y1-y2,y2-y3} = \frac{(2-.8)(12-10)+(-4-.8)(8-10)+\cdots+(-2-.8)(14-10)}{4} = -3$$

Recall that in computing the covariance for two variables the scores for the subjects are simply deviated about the means for the variables. The matrix of variances and covariances is

$$
\begin{array}{ccc}
y_1 - y_2 & y_2 - y_3 & y_3 - y_4
\end{array}
$$

$$
S_d = \begin{bmatrix} 13.2 & -3 & -8.6 \\ -3 & 26 & -19 \\ -8.6 & -19 & 24.8 \end{bmatrix}
$$

Therefore,

$$
T^2 = 5(.8,10,-16.4)\overbrace{\begin{bmatrix} .458 & .384 & .453 \\ .384 & .409 & .446 \\ .453 & .446 & .539 \end{bmatrix}}^{\mathbf{S}_d^{-1}} \overbrace{\begin{pmatrix} .8 \\ 10 \\ -16.4 \end{pmatrix}}^{\mathbf{y}_d}
$$

$$
T^2 = (-16.114,-14.586,-20.086)\begin{pmatrix} .8 \\ 10 \\ -16.4 \end{pmatrix} = 170.659
$$

There is an exact F transformation of T^2, which is

$$
F = \frac{n-k+1}{(n-1)(k-1)}T^2, \text{with}(k-1)\text{ and}(n-k+1)df.
$$

Thus,

$$
F = \frac{5-4+1}{4(3)}(170.659) = 28.443, \text{with 3 and 2 } df.
$$

This F value is significant at the .05 level, exceeding the critical value of 19.16. The critical value is very large here, because the error degrees of freedom is extremely small (2). We conclude that the drugs are different in effectiveness.

12.4 ASSUMPTIONS IN REPEATED-MEASURES ANALYSIS

The three assumptions for a single-group univariate repeated-measures analysis are:

1. Independence of the observations
2. Multivariate normality
3. Sphericity (sometimes called circularity).*

The first two assumptions are also required for the multivariate approach, but the sphericity assumption is not necessary. You should recall from Chapter 6 that a violation of the independence assumption is very serious in independent samples ANOVA and MANOVA, and it is also serious here. Just as ANOVA and MANOVA are fairly robust against violation of multivariate normality, so that also carries over here.

What is the sphericity condition? Recall that in testing the null hypothesis for the previous numerical example, we transformed the original four repeated measures to three new variables, which were then used jointly in the multivariate approach. In general, if there are k repeated measures, then we transform to $(k - 1)$ new variables. There are other choices for the $(k - 1)$ variables than the adjacent differences used in the drug example, which will yield the *same* multivariate test statistic. This follows from the invariance property of the multivariate test statistic (Morrison, 1976, p. 145).

Suppose that the $(k - 1)$ new variates selected are orthogonal (uncorrelated) and are scaled such that the sum of squares of the coefficients for each variate is 1. Then we have what is called an *orthonormal* set of variates. If the transformation matrix is denoted by $\mathbf{C}$ and the population covariance matrix for the original repeated measures by $\mathbf{\Sigma}$, then the sphericity assumption says that the covariance matrix for the new (transformed) variables is a diagonal matrix, with equal variances on the diagonal:

$$
\text{Transformed Variables}
$$

$$
\mathbf{C'\Sigma C} = \sigma^2 \mathbf{I} = \begin{array}{c} 1 \\ 2 \\ 3 \\ \vdots \\ k-1 \end{array}
\begin{array}{cccccc}
1 & 2 & 3 & \cdots & k-1 \\
\end{array}
\left[\begin{array}{ccccc}
\sigma^2 & 0 & 0 & \cdots & 0 \\
0 & \sigma^2 & 0 & \cdots & 0 \\
0 & 0 & \sigma^2 & & \\
\vdots & \vdots & \vdots & \ddots & \\
0 & 0 & & & \sigma^2
\end{array}\right]
$$

---

* For many years it was thought that a stronger condition, called uniformity (compound symmetry) was necessary. The uniformity condition required that the population variances for all treatments be equal and also that all population covariances are equal. However, Huynh and Feldt (1970) and Rouanet and Lepine (1970) showed that sphericity is an exact condition for the F test to be valid. Sphericity requires only that the variances of the differences for *all* pairs of repeated measures be equal.

Saying that the off-diagonal elements are 0 means that the covariances for all trans-formed variables are 0, which implies that the correlations are 0.

Box (1954) showed that if the sphericity assumption is not met, then the F ratio is posi-tively biased (we are rejecting falsely too often). In other words, we may set our α level at .05, but may be rejecting falsely 8% or 10% of the time. The extent to which the covariance matrix deviates from sphericity is reflected in a parameter called ϵ (Green-house & Geisser, 1959). We give the formula for $\hat{\epsilon}$ in one of the exercises. If sphericity is met, then $\epsilon = 1$, while for the worst possible violation the value of $\epsilon = 1 / (k - 1)$, where k is the number of levels of the repeated measures factor (e.g., treatment or time). To adjust for the positive bias, a lower bound estimate of ϵ can be used, although this makes the test *very* conservative. This approach alters the degrees of freedom from

$(k - 1)$ and $(k - 1)(n - 1)$ to 1 and $(n - 1)$.

Using the modified degrees of freedom then effectively increases the critical value to which the F test is compared to determine statistical significance. This adjustment of the degrees of freedom (and thus the F critical value) is intended to reduce the inflation of the type I error rate that occurs when the sphericity assumption is violated.

However, this lower bound estimate of ϵ provides too much of an adjustment, making an adjustment for the worst possible case. Because this procedure is too conservative, we don't recommend it. A more reasonable approach is to estimate ϵ. SPSS and SAS GLM both print out the Greenhouse–Geisser estimate of ϵ. Then, the degrees of free-dom are adjusted from

$(k - 1)$ and $(k - 1)(n - 1)$ to $\hat{\epsilon}(k - 1)$ and $\hat{\epsilon}(k - 1)(n - 1)$.

Results from Collier, Baker, Mandeville, and Hayes (1967) and Stoloff (1967) show that this approach keeps the actual alpha very close to the level of significance. Huynh and Feldt (1976) found that even multiplying the degrees of freedom by $\hat{\epsilon}$ is somewhat conservative when the true value of ϵ is above about .70. They recommended an alter-native measure of ϵ, which is printed out by both SPSS and SAS GLM.

The Greenhouse–Geisser estimator tends to *underestimate* ϵ, especially when ϵ is close to 1, while the Huynh–Feldt estimator tends to *overestimate* ϵ (Maxwell & Delaney, 2004). One possibility then is to use the average of the estimators as the estimate of ϵ. At present, neither SAS nor SPSS provide p values for this average method. A rea-sonable, though perhaps somewhat conservative, approach then is to use the Green-house–Geisser estimate. Maxwell and Delaney (p. 545) recommend this method when the univariate approach is used, noting that it properly controls the type I error rate whereas the Huynh and Feldt approach may not.

In addition, there are various statistical tests for sphericity, with the Mauchley test (Kirk, 1982, p. 259) being widely available in various software. However, based on the results of Monte Carlo studies (Keselman, Rogan, Mendoza, & Breen, 1980; Rogan, Keselman, & Mendoza, 1979), we don't recommend using these tests. The studies just described showed that the tests are highly sensitive to departures from multivariate normality and from their respective null hypotheses. Not using the Mauchley test does not cause a serious problem, though. Instead, one can use the Greenhouse–Geisser adjustment procedure without using the Mauchley test because it takes the degree of the violation into account. That is, minimal adjustments are made for minor violations of the sphericity assumption and greater adjustments are made when violations are more severe (as indicated by the estimate of ϵ). Note also that another option is to use the multivariate approach, which does not invoke the sphericity assumption. Keppel and Wickens (2004) recommend yet another option. In this approach, one does not use the overall test results. Instead, one proceeds directly to *post hoc* tests or contrasts of interest that control the overall alpha, by, for example, using the Bonferroni method.

12.5 COMPUTER ANALYSIS OF THE DRUG DATA

We now consider the univariate and multivariate repeated-measures analyses of the drug data that was worked out in numerical detail earlier in the chapter. Table 12.1 shows the control lines for SAS and SPSS. Tables 12.2 and 12.5 present selected results from SAS, and Tables 12.3 and 12.4 present selected output from SPSS. In Table 12.2, the first output selection shows the multivariate results. Note that the multivariate test is significant at the .05 level ($F = 28.41$, $p = .034$), and that the F value agrees, within rounding error, with the F calculated in section 12.3.1 ($F = 28.44$). Given that p is smaller than alpha (i.e., .05), we conclude that the reaction means differ across the four drugs. We wish to note that this example is not a good situation, particularly for the multivariate approach, because the small sample size makes this procedure less powerful than the univariate approach (although a significant effect was obtained here). We discuss this situation later on in the chapter.

The next output selection in Table 12.2 provides the univariate test results for these data. Note that to the right of the F value of 24.76 (as was also calculated in section 12.2.2), there are three columns of p values. The first column makes no adjustments for possible violations of the sphericity assumption, and we ignore this column. The second p value (.0006) is obtained by use of the Greenhouse–Geisser procedure (labeled G-G), which indicates mean differences are present. The final column in that output selection is the p value from the Huynh–Feldt procedure. The last output selection in Table 12.2 provides the estimates of ϵ as obtained by the two procedures shown. These estimates, as explained earlier, are used to adjust the degrees of freedom for the univariate F test (i.e., 24.76).

Table 12.3 presents the analogous output from SPSS, although it is presented in a different format. The first output selection provides the multivariate test result, which is the same as obtained in SAS. The second output selection provides results from the Mauchley test of the sphericity assumption, which we ignore, and also shows estimates

SAS	SPSS

DATA Oneway;
INPUT y1 y2 y3 y4;
LINES;
30.00 28.00 16.00 34.00
14.00 18.00 10.00 22.00
24.00 20.00 18.00 30.00
38.00 34.00 20.00 44.00
26.00 28.00 14.00 30.00
(1) PROC GLM;
(2) MODEL y1 y2 y3 y4 = /
     NOUNI;
(3) REPEATED drug 4
     CONTRAST(1) /SUMMARY MEAN;
RUN;
	DATA LIST FREE/ y1 y2 y3 y4.
	BEGIN DATA.
	30.00 28.00 16.00 34.00
	14.00 18.00 10.00 22.00
	24.00 20.00 18.00 30.00
	38.00 34.00 20.00 44.00
	26.00 28.00 14.00 30.00
	END DATA.
	(4) GLM y1 y2 y3 y4
	(5) /WSFACTOR=drug 4
	(6) /EMMEANS=TABLES(drug)
	     COMPARE ADJ(BONFERRONI)
	     /PRINT=DESCRIPTIVE
	(7) /WSDESIGN=drug.

(1) PROC GLM invokes the general linear modeling procedure.

(2) MODEL specifies the dependent variables and NOUNI suppresses display of univariate statistics that are not relevant for this analysis.

(3) REPEATED names drug as a repeated measure factor with four levels; SUMMARY and MEANS request statistical test results and means and standard deviations for each treatment level. CONTRAST(1) requests comparisons of mean differences between group 1 and each of the remaining groups. The complete set of pairwise comparisons for this example can be obtained by rerunning the analysis and replacing CONTRAST(1) with CONTRAST(2), which would obtain contrasts between group 2 and each of the other groups, and then conducting a third run using CONTRAST(3). In general, the number of times this procedure needs to be run with the CONTRAST statements is one less than the number of levels of the repeated measures factor.

(4) GLM invokes the general linear modeling procedure.

(5) WSFACTOR indicates that the within-subjects factor is named drug, and it has four levels.

(6) EMMEANS requests the expected marginal means and COMPARE requests pairwise comparisons among the four means with a Bonferroni adjusted alpha.

(7) WSDESIGN requests statistical testing of the drug factor.

■ Table 12.2: Selected SAS Results for Single-Group Repeated Measures

MANOVA Test Criteria and Exact F Statistics for the Hypothesis of No Drug Effect
H = Type III SSCP Matrix for drug
E = Error SSCP Matrix
S=1 M=0.5 N=0

Statistic	Value	F Value	Num DF	Den DF	Pr > F
Wilks' Lambda	0.02292607	28.41	3	2	0.0342
Pillai's Trace	0.97707393	28.41	3	2	0.0342
Hotelling- Lawley Trace	42.61846352	28.41	3	2	0.0342
Roy's Greatest Root	42.61846352	28.41	3	2	0.0342

(Continued)

■ **Table 12.2: (Continued)**

The GLM Procedure
Repeated Measures Analysis of Variance
Univariate Tests of Hypotheses for Within Subject Effects

Source	DF	Type III SS	Mean Square	F Value	Pr > F	Adj Pr > F G – G	Adj Pr > F H – F
Drug	3	698.2000000	232.7333333	24.76	.0001	0.0006	<.0001
Error(drug)	12	112.8000000	9.4000000				

Greenhouse-Geisser Epsilon	0.6049
Huynh-Feldt Epsilon	1.0789

■ **Table 12.3 Selected SPSS Results for Single-Group Repeated Measures**

Multivariate Tests[a]

Effect		Value	F	Hypothesis df	Error df	Sig.
Drug	Pillai's Trace	.977	28.412[b]	3.000	2.000	.034
	Wilks' Lambda	.023	28.412[b]	3.000	2.000	.034
	Hotelling's Trace	42.618	28.412[b]	3.000	2.000	.034
	Roy's Largest Root	42.618	28.412[b]	3.000	2.000	.034

[a] Design: Intercept
 Within Subjects Design: drug
[b] Exact statistic

Mauchly's Test of Sphericity[a]

Measure: MEASURE_1

Within Subjects Effect	Mauchly's W	Approx. Chi-Square	df	Sig.	Epsilon[b] Greenhouse-Geisser	Epsilon[b] Huynh-Feldt	Epsilon[b] Lower-bound
Drug	.186	4.572	5	.495	.605	1.000	.333

Tests the null hypothesis that the error covariance matrix of the orthonormalized transformed dependent variables is proportional to an identity matrix.

[a] Design: Intercept
 Within Subjects Design: drug
[b] May be used to adjust the degrees of freedom for the averaged tests of significance. Corrected tests are displayed in the Tests of Within-Subjects Effects table.

Tests of Within-Subjects Effects

Measure: MEASURE_1

Source		Type III Sum of Squares	df	Mean Square	F	Sig.
Drug	Sphericity Assumed	698.200	3	232.733	24.759	.000
	Greenhouse-Geisser	698.200	1.815	384.763	24.759	.001
	Huynh-Feldt	698.200	3.000	232.733	24.759	.000
	Lower-bound	698.200	1.000	698.200	24.759	.008
Error(drug)	Sphericity Assumed	112.800	12	9.400		
	Greenhouse-Geisser	112.800	7.258	15.540		
	Huynh-Feldt	112.800	12.000	9.400		
	Lower-bound	112.800	4.000	28.200		

of ϵ using the Greenhouse–Geisser, Huynh–Feldt, and lower-bound procedures. The last output selection shows the univariate test results. We focus our attention on the Greenhouse–Geisser row, where the p value is rounded to $p = .001$, again indicating differences in the reaction means across the drug types. Note that the adjusted degrees of freedom for this procedure are 1.815 and 7.258, whereas the unadjusted degrees of freedom, as used in section 12.2.2, are 3 and 12. These unadjusted degrees of freedom appear in the sphericity assumed rows, where inference is conducted assuming no violation of the sphericity assumption and with no corresponding adjustment to the inference for the F test (which again we ignore).

Table 12.4 shows the estimated marginal means and provides Bonferroni adjusted multiple comparisons for the four reaction means from SPSS. The comparisons that are statistically significant involve drug 4, which indicates that average reaction time is greater for drug 4 than for drugs 3 and 1. Table 12.5 shows the results from the multiple comparisons as can be obtained from SAS. (The output titles have been edited to ease comprehension.) To obtain pairwise comparisons using SAS, you can simply rerun the analysis the needed number of times (here, 3) and use the CONTRAST commands as described under Table 12.1.

Instead of using multiple dependent samples t tests, as SPSS does, SAS uses corresponding F tests that produce p values that are equivalent to that provided by the t tests. Note though that the p values obtained by SAS here, and, as displayed in Table 12.5, are *not* Bonferroni adjusted. Thus, if you wish to use a Bonferroni adjustment, you can

■ **Table 12.4: Multiple Comparisons from SPSS for Single-Group Repeated Measures**

Estimates

Measure: MEASURE_1

| Drug | Mean | Std. Error | 95% Confidence Interval | |
			Lower Bound	Upper Bound
1	26.400	3.919	15.519	37.281
2	25.600	2.926	17.477	33.723
3	15.600	1.720	10.823	20.377
4	32.000	3.578	22.067	41.933

Pairwise Comparisons

Measure: MEASURE_1

| (I) drug | (J) drug | Mean Difference (I-J) | Std. Error | Sig.[b] | 95% Confidence Interval for Difference[b] | |
					Lower Bound	Upper Bound
1	2	.800	1.625	1.000	−7.082	8.682
	3	10.800	2.577	.083	−1.700	23.300
	4	−5.600*	.748	.010	−9.230	−1.970
2	1	−.800	1.625	1.000	−8.682	7.082
	3	10.000	2.280	.071	−1.062	21.062
	4	−6.400	1.600	.097	−14.162	1.362
3	1	−10.800	2.577	.083	−23.300	1.700
	2	−10.000	2.280	.071	−21.062	1.062
	4	−16.400*	2.227	.011	−27.204	−5.596
4	1	5.600*	.748	.010	1.970	9.230
	2	6.400	1.600	.097	−1.362	14.162
	3	16.400*	2.227	.011	5.596	27.204

Based on estimated marginal means
* The mean difference is significant at the .050 level.
[b] Adjustment for multiple comparisons: Bonferroni.

■ **Table 12.5: Multiple Comparisons from SAS for Single-Group Repeated Measures**

Drug 1 vs. Drug 2

Source	DF	Type III SS	Mean Square	F Value	Pr > F
Mean	1	3.20000000	3.20000000	0.24	0.6483
Error	4	52.80000000	13.20000000		

Drug 1 vs. Drug 3

Source	DF	Type III SS	Mean Square	F Value	Pr > F
Mean	1	583.2000000	583.2000000	17.57	0.0138
Error	4	132.8000000	33.2000000		

Drug 1 vs. Drug 4

Source	DF	Type III SS	Mean Square	F Value	Pr > F
Mean	1	156.8000000	156.8000000	56.00	0.0017
Error	4	11.2000000	2.8000000		

Drug 2 vs. Drug 3

Source	DF	Type III SS	Mean Square	F Value	Pr > F
Mean	1	500.0000000	500.0000000	19.23	0.0118
Error	4	104.0000000	26.0000000		

Drug 2 vs. Drug 4

Source	DF	Type III SS	Mean Square	F Value	Pr > F
Mean	1	204.8000000	204.8000000	16.00	0.0161
Error	4	51.2000000	12.8000000		

Drug 3 vs. Drug 4

Source	DF	Type III SS	Mean Square	F Value	Pr > F
Mean	1	1344.800000	1344.800000	54.23	0.0018
Error	4	99.200000	24.800000		

do this by multiplying the obtained p value by the number of tests conducted (here, 6). So, for example, for the group 2 versus group 3 comparison, the Bonferroni-adjusted p value, using SAS results, is, $6 \times .0118 = .071$, which is the same p value shown in Table 12.4, as obtained with SPSS, as SPSS and SAS provide identical results.

12.6 *POST HOC* PROCEDURES IN REPEATED-MEASURES ANALYSIS

As in a one-way independent samples ANOVA, if an overall difference is found, you would almost always want to determine which specific treatments or conditions differed, as we did in the previous section. This entails a *post hoc* procedure. Pairwise comparisons are easily interpreted and implemented and are quite meaningful. If the assumption of sphericity is satisfied, a Tukey procedure, which uses a pooled error term from the within-subjects ANOVA, could be used. However, Maxwell and Delaney (2004) note that the sphericity assumption is likely to be violated in most within-subjects designs. If so, Maxwell (1980) found that use of the Tukey approach does not always provide adequate control of the overall type I error. Instead, Maxwell and Delaney recommend a Bonferroni approach (as does Keppel & Wickens, 2004) that uses separate error terms from just those groups involved in a given comparison. In this case, the assumption of sphericity cannot be violated as the error term used in each comparison is based only on the two groups being compared (as in the two-group dependent samples *t* test).

The Bonferroni procedure is easy to use, and, as we have seen, is readily available from SPSS and can be easily applied to the contrasts obtained from SAS. As we saw in the previous section, this approach uses multiple *dependent sample t* (or *F*) tests, and uses the Bonferroni inequality to keep overall α under control. For example, if there are five treatments, then there will be 10 paired comparisons. If we wish overall α to equal .05, then we simply do each dependent *t* test at the .05 / 10 = .005 level of significance. In general, if there are *k* treatments, then to keep overall α at .05, do each test at the .05 / [$k(k-1) / 2$] level of significance (because for *k* treatments there are $k(k-1) / 2$ paired comparisons). Note that with the SPSS results in Table 12.4, the *p* values for the pairwise comparisons have already been adjusted (as have the confidence intervals). So, to test for significance, you simply compare a given *p* value to the overall alpha used for the analysis (here, .05). With the SAS results in Table 12.5, you need to do the adjustment manually (e.g., multiply each *p* value by the number of comparisons tested).

12.7 SHOULD WE USE THE UNIVARIATE OR MULTIVARIATE APPROACH?

In terms of controlling type I error, there is no strong basis for preferring the multivariate approach, because use of the modified test (i.e., multiplying the degrees of freedom by ε̂) yields an "honest" error rate. Another consideration is power. If sphericity holds, then the univariate approach is more powerful. When sphericity is violated, however, then the situation is much more complex. Davidson (1972) stated, "when small but reliable effects are present with the effects being highly variable . . . the multivariate test is far more powerful than the univariate test" (p. 452). And O'Brien and Kaiser (1985), after mentioning several studies that compared the power of the multivariate and modified univariate tests, state, "*Even though a limited number of situations have been investigated, this work found that no procedure is uniformly more powerful or even usually the most powerful*" (p. 319). More recently, Algina and Keselman (1997), based on their simulation study, recommend the multivariate approach over the univariate approach when ε ≤ .90 given that the number of levels of the repeated measures factor (*a*) is 4 or less, provided that $n \geq a + 15$ or when $5 \leq a \leq 8$, ε ≤ .85, and $n \geq a + 30$.

Maxwell and Delaney (2004, pp. 671–676) present a thoughtful discussion of the univariate and multivariate approaches. In discussing the recommendations of Algina and Keselman (1997), they note that even when these guidelines hold, "there is no guarantee that the multivariate approach is more powerful" (p. 674) Also, when these conditions are not met, which suggests use of univariate approach, they note that even in these situations, the multivariate approach may be more powerful. They do, though, recommend the multivariate approach if n is not too small, that is, if n is chosen appropriately. Keppel and Wickens (2004) also favor this approach, noting that it avoids issues associated with the sphericity assumption and is "more frequently used than other possibilities" (p. 379).

These remarks then generally support the use of the multivariate approach, unless one has only a handful of observations more than the number of repeated measures, because of power considerations. However, given that there is no guarantee that one approach will be more powerful than the other, even when guidelines suggest its use, we still tend to agree with Barcikowski and Robey (1984) that, given an exploratory study, *both* the adjusted univariate and multivariate tests be routinely used because they may differ in the treatment effects they will discern. In such a study, the overall level of significance might be set for each test. Thus, if you wish overall alpha to be .05, do each test at the .025 level of significance.

12.8 ONE-WAY REPEATED MEASURES—A TREND ANALYSIS

We now consider a similar design, but focus on the pattern of change across time, where time is the within-subjects variable. In general, trend analysis is appropriate whenever a factor is a quantitative (not qualitative) variable. Perhaps the most common such quantitative factor in repeated measures studies involves time, where participants are assessed on an outcome variable at each of several points across time (e.g., days, weeks, months). With a trend analysis, we are not so much interested in comparing means from one time point to another, but instead are interested in describing the form of the expected change across time.

In our example here, an investigator, interested in verbal learning, has obtained recall scores after exposing participants to verbal material after 1, 2, 3, 4, and 5 days. She expects a decline in recall across the 5-day time period and is interested in modeling the form of the decline in verbal recall. For this, trend analysis is appropriate and in particular orthogonal (uncorrelated) polynomials are in order. If the decline in recall is essentially constant over the days, then a significant linear (straight-line) trend, or first-degree polynomial, will be found. On the other hand, if the decline in recall is slow over the first 2 days and then drops sharply over the remaining 3 days, a quadratic trend (part of a parabola), or second-degree polynomial, will be found. Finally, if the decline is slow at first, then drops off sharply for the next few days and finally levels off, we will find a cubic trend, or third-degree polynomial. Figure 12.1 shows each of these cases.

The fact that the polynomials are uncorrelated means that the linear, quadratic, cubic, and quartic components are partitioning distinct (different) parts of the variation in the data.

▨ **Figure 12.1:** Linear, quadratic, and cubic trends across time.

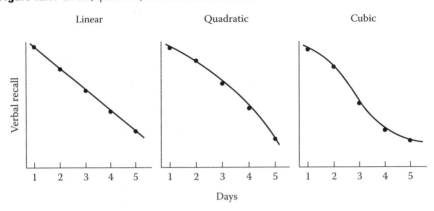

In Table 12.6 we present the SAS and SPSS control lines for running the trend analysis on the verbal recall data. Both SAS and SPSS provide trend analysis in the form of polynomial contrasts. In fact, these contrasts are built into the programs. So, all we need to do is request them, which is what has been done in the following commands.

Table 12.7 provides the SPSS results for the trend analysis. Inspecting the means for each day (y1 through y5) indicates that mean recall is relatively high on day 1 but drops off substantially as time passes. The multivariate test result, $F(4, 12) = 65.43$,

▨ **Table 12.6: SAS and SPSS Control Lines for the Single-Group Trend Analysis**

SAS	SPSS
DATA TREND;	DATA LIST FREE/ y1 y2 y3 y4 y5.
INPUT y1 y2 y3 y4 y5;	BEGIN DATA.
LINES;	26 20 18 11 10
26 20 18 11 10	34 35 29 22 23
34 35 29 22 23	41 37 25 18 15
41 37 25 18 15	29 28 22 15 13
29 28 22 15 13	35 34 27 21 17
35 34 27 21 17	28 22 17 14 10
28 22 17 14 10	38 34 28 25 22
38 34 28 25 22	43 37 30 27 25
43 37 30 27 25	42 38 26 20 15
42 38 26 20 15	31 27 21 18 13
31 27 21 18 13	45 40 33 25 18
45 40 33 25 18	29 25 17 13 8
29 25 17 13 8	39 32 28 22 18
39 32 28 22 18	33 30 24 18 7
33 30 24 18 7	34 30 25 24 23
34 30 25 24 23	37 31 25 22 20
37 31 25 22 20	END DATA.

SAS	SPSS
| ```
PROC GLM;
(1) MODEL y1 y2 y3 y4 y5 = /
    NOUNI;
(2) REPEATED Days 5 (1 2 3
    4 5)
(3) POLYNOMIAL/SUMMARY MEAN;
RUN;
``` | ```
(1) GLM y1 y2 y3 y4 y5
(4) /WSFACTOR=Day 5 Polynomial
    /PRINT=DESCRIPTIVE
(5) /WSDESIGN=day.
``` |

(1) MODEL (in SAS) and GLM (in SPSS) specifies the outcome variables used.

(2) REPEATED labels Days as the within-subjects factor, having five levels, which are provided in the parenthesis.

(3) POLYNOMIAL requests the trend analysis and SUMMARY and MEAN request statistical test results and means and standard deviations for the days factor.

(4) WSFACTOR labels Day as the within-subjects factor with five levels, Polynomial requests the trend analysis.

(5) WSDESIGN requests statistical testing for the day factor.

■ Table 12.7: Selected SPSS Results for the Single-Group Trend Analysis

Descriptive Statistics

	Mean	Std. Deviation	N
y1	35.2500	5.77927	16
y2	31.2500	5.77927	16
y3	24.6875	4.68642	16
y4	19.6875	4.68642	16
y5	16.0625	5.63878	16

Multivariate Tests[a]

Effect		Value	F	Hypothesis df	Error df	Sig.
Day	Pillai's Trace	.956	65.426[b]	4.000	12.000	.000
	Wilks' Lambda	.044	65.426[b]	4.000	12.000	.000
	Hotelling's Trace	21.809	65.426[b]	4.000	12.000	.000
	Roy's Largest Root	21.809	65.426[b]	4.000	12.000	.000

[a] Design: Intercept
 Within Subjects Design: Day
[b] Exact statistic

(*Continued*)

▇ **Table 12.7: (Continued)**

Tests of Within-Subjects Effects

Measure: MEASURE_1

Source		Type III Sum of Squares	Df	Mean Square	F	Sig.
Day	Sphericity Assumed	4025.175	4	1006.294	164.237	.000
	Greenhouse-Geisser	4025.175	1.821	2210.222	164.237	.000
	Huynh-Feldt	4025.175	2.059	1954.673	164.237	.000
	Lower-bound	4025.175	1.000	4025.175	164.237	.000
Error(Day)	Sphericity Assumed	367.625	60	6.127		
	Greenhouse-Geisser	367.625	27.317	13.458		
	Huynh-Feldt	367.625	30.889	11.902		
	Lower-bound	367.625	15.000	24.508		

Tests of Within-Subjects Contrasts

Measure: MEASURE_1

Source	Day	Type III Sum of Squares	Df	Mean Square	F	Sig.
Day	Linear	3990.006	1	3990.006	237.036	.000
	Quadratic	6.112	1	6.112	1.672	.216
	Cubic	24.806	1	24.806	9.144	.009
	Order 4	4.251	1	4.251	3.250	.092
Error(Day)	Linear	252.494	15	16.833		
	Quadratic	54.817	15	3.654		
	Cubic	40.694	15	2.713		
	Order 4	19.621	15	1.308		

$p < .001$, indicates recall means change across time (as does the Greenhouse–Geisser adjusted univariate F test). The final output selection in Table 12.7 displays the results from the polynomial contrasts. Note that for these data four patterns of change are tested, a linear, quadratic (or second order), a cubic (or third order), and a fourth-order pattern. The number of such terms that will be fit to the data are one less than the number of levels of the within-subjects factor (e.g., days with 5 levels here, so 4 patterns tested). As indicated in the table, the linear trend is statistically significant at the .05 level ($F = 237.04$, $p < .001$), as is the cubic component ($F = 9.14$, $p = .009$). The linear trend is by far the most pronounced, and a graph of the means for the data in Figure 12.2 shows this, although a cubic curve (with a few bends) fits the data slightly better.

Analysis results obtained from SAS are in a similar format to what we have seen previously from SAS, so we do not report these here. However, the format of the results from the polynomial contrasts is quite different than that reported by SPSS. Table 12.8 displays the results for the polynomial contrasts obtained from SAS. The test for the linear trend is shown under the output selection Contrast Variable: Days_1. The test for the quadratic change is shown under the output selection Contrast Variable: Days_2, and so on. Of course, the results obtained by SAS match those obtained by SPSS.

■ **Figure 12.2:** Linear and cubic plots for verbal recall data.

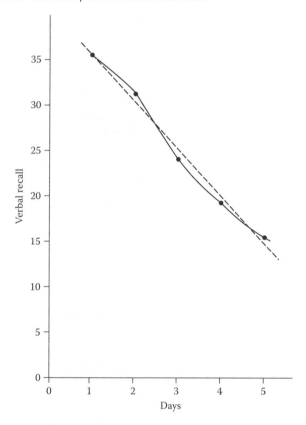

■ **Table 12.8: Selected SAS Results for the Single-Group Trend Analysis**

Contrast Variable: Days_1

Source	DF	Type III SS	Mean Square	F Value	Pr > F
Mean	1	3990.006250	3990.006250	237.04	<.0001
Error	15	252.493750	16.832917		

(Continued)

■ **Table 12.8: (Continued)**

Contrast Variable: Days_2

Source	DF	Type III SS	Mean Square	F Value	Pr > F
Mean	1	6.11160714	6.11160714	1.67	0.2155
Error	15	54.81696429	3.65446429		

Contrast Variable: Days_3

Source	DF	Type III SS	Mean Square	F Value	Pr > F
Mean	1	24.80625000	24.80625000	9.14	0.0085
Error	15	40.69375000	2.71291667		

Contrast Variable: Days_4

Source	DF	Type III SS	Mean Square	F Value	Pr > F
Mean	1	4.25089286	4.25089286	3.25	0.0916
Error	15	19.62053571	1.30803571		

In concluding this example, the following from Myers (1979) is important:

> Trend or orthogonal polynomial analyses should never be routinely applied whenever one or more independent variables are quantitative. . . . *It is dangerous to identify statistical components freely with psychological processes.* It is one thing to postulate a cubic component of *A*, to test for it, and to find it significant, thus substantiating the theory. It is another matter to assign psychological meaning to a significant component that has not been postulated on a priori grounds. (p. 456)

12.9 SAMPLE SIZE FOR POWER = .80 IN SINGLE-SAMPLE CASE

Although the classic text on power analysis by Cohen (1977) has power tables for a variety of situations (*t* tests, correlation, chi-square tests, differences between correlations, differences between proportions, one-way and factorial ANOVA, etc.), it does *not* provide tables for repeated-measures designs. Some work has been done in this area, most of it confined to the single sample case. The PASS program (2002) does calculate power for more complex repeated-measures designs. The following is taken from the PASS 2002 User's Guide—II:

> This module calculates power for repeated-measures designs having up to three within factors and three between factors. It computes power for various test statistics including the F test with the Greenhouse-Geisser correction, Wilks' lambda, Pillai-Bartlett trace, and Hotelling-Lawley trace. (p. 1127)

Robey and Barcikowski (1984) have given power tables for various alpha levels for the single group repeated-measures design. Their tables assume a common correlation for the repeated measures, which generally will not be tenable (especially in longitudinal studies); however, a later paper by Green (1990) indicated that use of an estimated *average* correlation (from all the correlations among the repeated measures) is fine. Selected results from their work are presented in Table 12.9, which indicates sample size needed for power = .80 for small, medium, and large effect sizes at alpha = .01, .05, .10, and .20 for two through seven repeated measures. We give two examples to show how to use the table.

■ **Table 12.9: Sample Sizes Needed for Power = .80 in Single-Group Repeated Measures**

Average corr.	Effect size[a]	Number of repeated measures					
		2	3	4	5	6	7
		$\alpha = .01$					
.30	.12	404	324	273	238	214	195
	.30	68	56	49	44	41	39
	.49	28	24	22	21	21	21
.50	.14	298	239	202	177	159	146
	.35	51	43	38	35	33	31
	.57	22	19	18	18	18	18
.80	.22	123	100	86	76	69	65
	.56	22	20	19	18	18	18
	.89	11	11	11	12	12	13
		$\alpha = .05$					
.30	.12	268	223	192	170	154	141
	.30	45	39	35	32	30	29
	.49	19	17	16	16	16	16
.50	.14	199	165	142	126	114	106
	.35	34	30	27	25	24	23
	.57	14	14	13	13	13	14
.80	.22	82	69	60	54	50	47
	.56	15	14	13	13	14	14
	.89	8	8	8	9	10	10
		$\alpha = .10$					
.30	.12	209	178	154	137	125	116
	.30	35	31	28	26	25	24
	.49	14	14	13	13	13	13
.50	.14	154	131	114	102	93	87
	.35	26	24	22	20	20	19
	.57	11	11	11	11	11	12
.80	.22	64	55	49	44	41	39
	.56	12	11	11	11	12	12
	.89	6	7	7	8	9	9

(Continued)

■ **Table 12.9: (Continued)**

Average corr.	Effect size[a]	Number of repeated measures					
		2	3	4	5	6	7
		$\alpha = .20$					
.30	.12	149	130	114	103	94	87
	.30	25	23	21	20	19	19
	.49	10	10	10	10	11	11
.50	.14	110	96	85	76	70	65
	.35	19	17	16	16	15	15
	.57	8	8	8	9	9	10
.80	.22	45	40	36	33	31	30
	.56	8	8	9	9	10	10
	.89	4	5	6	7	8	8

[a] These are small, medium, and large effect sizes, and are obtained from the corresponding effect size measures for independent samples ANOVA (i.e., .10, .25, and .40) by dividing by $\sqrt{1 - \text{correl}}$. Thus, for example,

$$.14 = \frac{.10}{\sqrt{1 - .50}}, \text{ and } .57 = \frac{.40}{\sqrt{1 - .50}}$$

Example 12.1

An investigator has a three treatment design: That is, each of the subjects is exposed to three treatments. He uses $r = .80$ as his estimate of the average correlation of the subjects' responses to the three treatments. How many subjects will he need for power = .80 at the .05 level, if he anticipates a medium effect size?

Reference to Table 12.9 with correl = .80, effect size = .56, $k = 3$, and $\alpha = .05$, shows that only 14 subjects are needed.

Example 12.2

An investigator will be carrying out a longitudinal study, measuring the subjects at five points in time. She wishes to detect a large effect size at the .10 level of significance, and estimates that the average correlation among the five measures will be about .50. How many subjects will she need?

Reference to Table 12.9 with correl = .50, effect size = .57, $k = 5$, and $\alpha = .10$, shows that 11 subjects are needed.

12.10 MULTIVARIATE MATCHED-PAIRS ANALYSIS

It was mentioned in Chapter 4 that often in comparing intact groups the subjects are matched or paired on variables known or presumed to be related to performance on the dependent variable(s). This is done so that if a significant difference is found, the investigator can be more confident it was the treatment(s) that "caused" the difference. In Chapter 4 we gave a univariate example, where kindergarteners were compared against nonkindergarteners on first-grade readiness, after they were matched on IQ, SES, and number of children in the family.

Now consider a multivariate example, that is, where there are several dependent variables. Kvet (1982) was interested in determining whether excusing elementary school children from regular classroom instruction for the study of instrumental music affected sixth-grade reading, language, and mathematics achievement. These were the three dependent variables. Instrumental and noninstrumental students from four public school districts were used in the study. We consider the analysis from just one of the districts. The instrumental and noninstrumental students were matched on the following variables: sex, race, IQ, cumulative achievement in fifth grade, elementary school attended, sixth-grade classroom teacher, and instrumental music outside the school.

Table 12.10 shows the control lines for running the analysis on SAS and SPSS. Note that we compute three difference variables, on which the multivariate analysis is done, and that it is these difference variables that are used in the MODEL (SAS) and GLM (SPSS) statements. We are testing whether these three difference variables (considered jointly) differ significantly from the 0 vector, that is, whether the group mean differences on all three variables are jointly 0.

Again we obtain a T^2 value, as for the single sample multivariate repeated-measures analysis; however, the exact F transformation is somewhat different:

$$F = \frac{N - p}{(N - 1)p} T^2, \text{ with } p \text{ and } (N - p) df,$$

where N is the number of matched pairs and p is the number of difference variables.

The multivariate test results shown in Table 12.11 indicate that the instrumental group does not differ from the noninstrumental group on the set of three difference variables ($F = .9115$, $p < .46$). Thus, the classroom time taken by the instrumental group does not appear to adversely affect their achievement in these three basic academic areas.

12.11 ONE-BETWEEN AND ONE-WITHIN DESIGN

We now add a grouping (between) variable to the one-way repeated measures design. This design, having one-between and one-within subjects factor, is often called a split plot design. For this design, we consider hypothetical data from a study comparing the relative efficacy of a behavior modification approach to dieting versus a

Table 12.10: SAS and SPSS Control Lines for Multivariate Matched-Pairs Analysis

SAS

```
DATA MatchedPairs;
INPUT read1 read2 lang1 lang2 math1 math2;
LINES;
62 67 72 66 67 35
66 66 96 87 74 63
70 74 69 73 85 63
85 99 99 71 91 60
82 83 69 99 63 66
55 61 52 74 55 67
91 99 99 99 99 87
78 62 79 69 54 65
85 99 99 75 66 61
95 87 99 96 82 82
87 91 87 82 98 85
96 99 96 76 74 61
54 60 69 80 66 71
69 60 87 80 69 71
87 87 88 99 95 82
78 72 66 76 52 74
72 58 74 69 59 58
PROC PRINT DATA = MatchedPairs;
RUN;
DATA MatchedPairs; SET MatchedPairs;
Readdiff = read1-read2;
Langdiff = lang1-lang2;
Mathdiff = math1-math2;
RUN;
PROC GLM;
MODEL Readdiff Langdiff Mathdiff = /;
MANOVA H =INTERCEPT;
RUN;
```

SPSS

```
DATA LIST FREE/read1 read2 lang1 lang2 math1 math2.
BEGIN DATA.
62 67 72 66 67 35 95 87 99 96 82 82
66 66 96 87 74 63 87 91 87 82 98 85
70 74 69 73 85 63 96 99 96 76 74 61
85 99 99 71 91 60 54 60 69 80 66 71
82 83 69 99 63 66 69 60 87 80 69 71
55 61 52 74 55 67 87 87 88 99 95 82
91 99 99 99 99 87 78 72 66 76 52 74
78 62 79 69 54 65 72 58 74 69 59 58
85 99 99 75 66 61
END DATA.
COMPUTE Readdiff = read1-read2.
COMPUTE Langdiff = lang1-lang2.
COMPUTE Mathdiff = math1-math2.
LIST.
GLM Readdiff Langdiff Mathdiff
    /INTERCEPT=INCLUDE
    /EMMEANS=TABLES(OVERALL)
    /PRINT=DESCRIPTIVE.
```

■ **Table 12.11: Multivariate Test Results for Matched Pairs Example**

SAS Output

MANOVA Test Criteria and Exact F Statistics for the Hypothesis of No Overall Intercept Effect
H = Type III SSCP Matrix for Intercept
E = Error SSCP Matrix
S=1 M=0.5 N=6

Statistic	Value	F Value	Num DF	Den DF	Pr > F
Wilks' Lambda	0.83658794	0.91	3	14	0.4604
Pillai's Trace	0.16341206	0.91	3	14	0.4604
Hotelling-Lawley Trace	0.19533160	0.91	3	14	0.4604
Roy's Greatest Root	0.19533160	0.91	3	14	0.4604

SPSS Output

Multivariate Tests[a]

Effect		Value	F	Hypothesis df	Error df	Sig.
Intercept	Pillai's Trace	.163	.912[b]	3.000	14.000	.460
	Wilks' Lambda	.837	.912[b]	3.000	14.000	.460
	Hotelling's Trace	.195	.912[b]	3.000	14.000	.460
	Roy's Largest Root	.195	.912[b]	3.000	14.000	.460

[a] Design: Intercept
[b] Exact statistic

behavior modification plus exercise approach (combination treatment) on weight loss for a group of overweight women. There is also a control group in this study. In this experimental design, 12 women are randomly assigned to one of the three treatment conditions, and weight loss is measured 2 months, 4 months, and 6 months after the program begins. Note that weight loss is relative to the weight measured at the previous occasion.

When a between-subjects variable is included in this design, there are two *additional* assumptions. One new assumption is the homogeneity of the covariance matrices on the repeated measures for the groups. That is, the population variances and covariances for the repeated measures are assumed to be the same for all groups. In our example, the group sizes are equal, and in this case a violation of the equal covariance matrices assumption is not serious. That is, the within-subjects tests (for the within-subject main effect and the interaction) are robust (with respect to type I error) against a violation of this assumption (see Stevens, 1986, chap. 6). However, if the group sizes are substantially unequal, then a violation is serious, and Stevens (1986) indicated in Table 6.5 what should be added to test this assumption. A key assumption for the validity of the within-subjects tests that was also in place for the single-group repeated measures is the assumption of sphericity that now applies to the repeated measures within each of the groups. It is still the case here that the unadjusted univariate F tests for the within-subjects effects are not robust to a violation of sphericity. Note that the combination of the sphericity *and* homogeneity of the covariance matrices assumption has been called multisample sphericity. The second new assumption is homogeneity of variance for the between-subjects main effect test. This assumption applies not to the raw scores but to the average of the outcome scores across the repeated measures for each subject. As with the typical between-subjects homogeneity assumption, the procedure is robust when the between-subjects group sizes are similar, but a liberal or conservative F test may result if group sizes are quite discrepant and these variances are not the same.

Table 12.12 provides the SAS and SPSS commands for the overall tests associated with this analysis. Table 12.13 provides selected SAS and SPSS results. Note that this analysis can be considered as a two-way ANOVA. As such, we will test main effects for diet and time, as well as the interaction between these two factors. The time main effect and the time-by-diet interaction are within-subjects effects because they involve change in means or change in treatment effects across time. The uni-variate tests for these effects appear in the first output selections for SAS and SPSS in Table 12.13. Using the Greenhouse–Geisser procedure, the main effect of time is statistically significant ($p < .001$) as is the time-by-diet interaction ($p = .003$). (Note that these effects are also significant using the multivariate approach, which is not shown to conserve space.) The last output selections for SAS and SPSS in Table 12.13 indicate that the main effect of diet is also statistically significant, $F(2, 33) = 4.69, p = .016$.

To interpret the significant effects, we display in Table 12.14 the means involved in the main effects and interaction as well as a plot of the cell means for the two factors. Recall that graphically an interaction is evidenced by nonparallel lines. In this graph you can see that the profiles for diets 1 and 2 are essentially parallel; however, the profile for diet 3 is definitely not parallel with the profiles for diets 1 and 2. And, in particular, it is the relatively greater weight loss at time 2 for diet 3 (i.e., 5.9 pounds) that is making the profile distinctly nonparallel. The main effect of diet, evident in Table 12.14, indicates that the population row means are not equal. The sample means suggest that, weight loss averaging across time, is greatest for diet 3. The main effect of time indicates that the population column means differ. The sample column means suggest that weight loss is greater after month 2 and 4, than after month 6. In addition to the graph, the cell means in Table 12.14 can also be used to describe the interaction. Note that weight loss for each treatment was relatively large at 2 months, but only those in the diet 3 condition experienced essentially the same weight loss at 2 and 4 months, whereas the weight loss for the other two treatments tapered off at the 4-month period. This created much larger differences between the diet groups at 4 months relative to the other months.

Table 12.12: SAS and SPSS Control Lines for One-Between and One-Within Repeated Measures Analysis

SAS	SPSS

```
SAS

DATA weight;
INPUT diet wgtloss1 wgtloss2 wgtloss3;
LINES;
1 4 3 3
1 4 4 3
1 4 3 1
1 3 2 1
1 5 3 2
1 6 5 4
1 6 5 4
1 5 4 1
1 3 3 2
1 5 4 1
1 4 2 2
1 5 2 1
2 6 3 2
2 5 4 1
2 7 6 3
2 6 4 2
2 3 2 1
2 5 5 4
2 4 3 1
2 4 2 1
2 6 5 3
2 7 6 4
```

```
SPSS

DATA LIST FREE/diet wgtloss1 wgtloss2 wgtloss3.
BEGIN DATA.
1 4 3 3    1 4 3 1    4 3 1
1 3 2 1    1 5 3 2    6 5 4
1 6 5 4    1 5 4 1    3 3 2
1 5 4 1    1 4 2 2    5 2 1
2 6 3 2    2 5 4 1    2 7 6 3
2 6 4 2    2 3 2 1    2 5 5 4
2 4 3 1    2 4 2 1    2 6 5 3
3 8 4 2    3 3 6 3    7 7 4
3 4 7 1    3 9 7 3    2 4 1
3 3 5 1    3 6 5 2    6 6 3
3 9 5 2    3 7 9 4    3 8 6 1
END DATA.
(2) GLM wgtloss1 wgtloss2 wgtloss3 BY diet
       /WSFACTOR=time 3
(3)    /PLOT=PROFILE(time*diet)
(4)    /EMMEANS=TABLES(time) COMPARE ADJ(BONFERRONI)
       /PRINT=DESCRIPTIVE
(5)    /WSDESIGN=time
       /DESIGN=diet.
```

(Continued)

SAS	SPSS
2 4 3 2	
2 7 4 3	
3 8 4 2	
3 3 6 3	
3 7 7 4	
3 4 7 1	
3 9 7 3	
3 2 4 1	
3 3 5 1	
3 6 5 2	
3 6 6 3	
3 9 5 2	
3 7 9 4	
3 8 6 1	

```
PROC GLM;
(1) CLASS diet;
(2) MODEL wgtloss1 wgtloss2 wgtloss3 = diet/
NOUNI;
REPEATED time 3 /SUMMARY MEAN;
RUN;
```

(1) CLASS indicates diet is a grouping (or classification) variable.

(2) MODEL (in SAS) and GLM (in SPSS) indicates that the weight scores are function of diet.

(3) PLOT requests a profile plot.

(4) The EMMEANS statement requests the marginal means (pooling over diet) and Bonferroni-adjusted multiple comparisons associated with the within-subjects factor (time).

(5) WSDESIGN requests statistical testing associated with the within-subjects time factor, and the DESIGN command requests testing results for the between-subjects diet factor.

■ Table 12.13: Selected Output for One-Between One-Within Design

SAS Results

The GLM Procedure

Repeated Measures Analysis of Variance

Univariate Tests of Hypotheses for Within Subject Effects

Source	DF	Type III SS	Mean Square	F Value	Pr > F	G – G	H-F-L
						Adj Pr > F	
Time	2	181.3518519	90.6759259	88.37	<.0001	<.0001	<.0001
time*diet	4	20.9259259	5.2314815	5.10	0.0012	0.0033	0.0029
Error(time)	66	67.7222222	1.0260943				

The GLM Procedure

Repeated Measures Analysis of Variance

Tests of Hypotheses for Between Subjects Effects

Source	DF	Type III SS	Mean Square	F Value	Pr > F
diet	2	36.9074074	18.4537037	4.69	0.0161
Error	33	129.8611111	3.9351852		

SPSS Results

Tests of Within-Subjects Effects

Measure: MEASURE_1

Source		Type III Sum of Squares	Df	Mean Square	F	Sig.
Time	Sphericity Assumed	181.352	2	90.676	88.370	.000
	Greenhouse-Geisser	181.352	1.556	116.574	88.370	.000
	Huynh-Feldt	181.352	1.717	105.593	88.370	.000
	Lower-bound	181.352	1.000	181.352	88.370	.000

(Continued)

■ Table 12.13: (Continued)

Source		Type III Sum of Squares	Df	Mean Square	F	Sig.
time * diet	Sphericity Assumed	20.926	4	5.231	5.098	.001
	Greenhouse-Geisser	20.926	3.111	6.726	5.098	.003
	Huynh-Feldt	20.926	3.435	6.092	5.098	.002
	Lower-bound	20.926	2.000	10.463	5.098	.012
Error(time)	Sphericity Assumed	67.722	66	1.026		
	Greenhouse-Geisser	67.722	51.337	1.319		
	Huynh-Feldt	67.722	56.676	1.195		
	Lower-bound	67.722	33.000	2.052		

Tests of Between-Subjects Effects

Measure: MEASURE_1
Transformed Variable: Average

Source	Type III Sum of Squares	Df	Mean Square	F	Sig.
Intercept	1688.231	1	1688.231	429.009	.000
Diet	36.907	2	18.454	4.689	.016
Error	129.861	33	3.935		

■ **Table 12.14:   Cell and Marginal Means for the One-Between One-Within Design**

		TIME			
		1	2	3	ROW MEANS
	1	4.50	3.33	2.083	3.304
DIETS	2	5.33	3.917	2.250	3.832
	3	6.00	5.917	2.250	4.722
COLUMN MEANS		5.278	4.389	2.194	

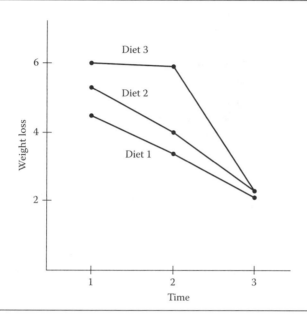

12.12 *POST HOC* PROCEDURES FOR THE ONE-BETWEEN AND ONE-WITHIN DESIGN

In the previous section, we presented and discussed statistical test results for the main effects and interaction. We also used cell and marginal means and a graph to describe results. When three or more levels of a factor are present in a design, researchers may also wish to conduct follow-up tests for specific effects of interest. In our example, an investigator would likely focus on simple effects given the interaction between diet and time. We will provide testing procedures for such simple effects, but for completeness, we briefly discuss pairwise comparisons associated with the diet and time main effects. Note that for the follow-up procedures discussed in this section, there is more than one way to obtain results via SAS and SPSS. In this section, we use procedures, while not always the most efficient, are intended to help you better understand the comparisons you are making.

12.12.1 Comparisons Involving Main Effects

As an example of this, to conduct pairwise comparisons for the means involved in a statistically significant main effect of the between-subjects factor (here, diet), you can simply compute the average of each participant's scores across the time points of the study and run a one-way ANOVA with these average values, requesting pairwise comparisons. As such, this is nothing more than a one-way ANOVA, except that average scores for an individual are used as the dependent variable in the analysis. When you conduct this ANOVA, the error term used is the pooled term from the ANOVA you are conducting. So, it would be important to check the homogeneity of variance assumption. Also, you may also wish to use the Bonferroni procedure to control the inflation of the type I error rate for the set of comparisons. These comparisons would involve the row means shown in Table 12.14.

For the within-subjects factor (here, time), pairwise comparisons may also be conducted, which could be considered when the main effect of this factor is significant. Here, it is best to use the built-in functions provided by SAS and SPSS to obtain these comparisons. For SPSS, these comparisons are obtained using the syntax in Table 12.11. For SAS, the CONTRAST command shown in and discussed under Table 12.1 can be used to obtain these comparisons. Note that with three levels of the within-subject factor in this example (i.e., the three time points), two such computer runs with SAS would be needed to obtain the three pairwise comparisons. The Bonferroni procedure may also be used here. These comparisons would involve the column means of Table 12.14.

12.12.2 Simple Effects Analyses

When an interaction is present (here, time by diet), you may wish to focus on the analysis of simple effects. With this split plot design, two types of simple effects are often of interest. One simple effects analysis compares the effect of the treatment at each time point to identify when treatment differences are present. The means involved here are those shown for the groups in Table 12.14 for each time point of the study (i.e., 4.5, 5.33, and 6.00 for time 1; 3.33, 3.917, and 5.917 for time 2; and so on). The second type of simple effects analysis is to compare the time means for each treatment group separately to describe the change across time for each group. In Table 12.14, these comparisons involve the means across time for each of the given groups (i.e., 4.5, 3.33, and 2.083 for diet 1; 5.55, 3.917, and 2.25 for diet 2; and so on). Note that polynomial contrasts could be used instead of pairwise comparisons to describe growth or decay across time. We illustrate pairwise comparisons later.

12.12.3 Simple Effects Analyses for the Within-Subjects Factor

A simple and intuitive way to describe the change across time for each group is to conduct a one-way repeated measures ANOVA for each group separately, here with time as the within-subjects factor. Multiple comparisons are then typically of interest when the change across time is significant. The top part of Table 12.15 shows the control lines for this analysis using the data shown in Table 12.12. Note that for SAS, an additional analysis would need to be conducted replacing CONTRAST(1) with CON-TRAST(2) to obtain all the needed pairwise comparisons.

■ **Table 12.15:　SAS and SPSS Control Lines for Simple Effects Analyses**

SAS	SPSS
One-Way Repeated Measures ANOVAs for Each Treatment	

`PROC GLM;`
`(1) BY diet;`
`MODEL wgtloss1 wgtloss2 wgt-`
`loss3 = / NOUNI;`
`(2) REPEATED time 3 CONTRAST(1)`
`/SUMMARY MEAN;`
`RUN;`
	`(1) SPLIT FILE SEPARATE BY`
	`diet.`
	`GLM wgtloss1 wgtloss2 wgtloss3`
	`/WSFACTOR=time 3`
	`(3) /EMMEANS=TABLES(time)`
	`COMPARE ADJ(BONFERRONI)`
	`/PRINT=DESCRIPTIVE`
	`/WSDESIGN=time.`

One-Way Between Subjects ANOVAs at Each Time Point	

`PROC GLM;`
`CLASS diet;`
`(4) MODEL wgtloss1 wgtloss2`
`wgtloss3 = diet /;`
`(5) LSMEANS diet / ADJ=BON;`
`RUN;`
	`(6) UNIANOVA wgtloss1 BY diet`
	`(7) /EMMEANS=TABLES(diet)`
	`COMPARE ADJ(BONFERRONI)`
	`/PRINT=HOMOGENEITY`
	`DESCRIPTIVE`
	`/DESIGN=diet.`

(1) These commands are used so that separate analyses are conducted for each diet group.
(2) `CONTRAST(1)` will obtain contrasts in means for time 1 vs. time 2 and then time 1 vs. time 3. Re-running the analysis using `CONTRAST(2)` instead of `CONTRAST(1)` will provide the time 2 vs. time 3 contrast to complete the pairwise comparisons. Note these comparisons are not Bonferroni adjusted.
(3) `EMMEANS` requests Bonferroni-adjusted pairwise comparisons for the effect of time within each group.
(4) The `MODEL` statement requests three separate ANOVAS for weight at each time point.
(5) The `LSMEANS` line requests Bonferroni-adjusted pairwise comparisons among the diet group means.
(6) This command requests a single ANOVA for the weight loss scores at time 1. To obtain separate ANOVAs for times 2 and 3, this analysis needs to be rerun replacing `wgtloss1` with `wgtloss2`, and then with `wgtloss3`.
(7) `EMMEANS` requests Bonferroni-adjusted pairwise comparisons for the diet groups.

Table 12.16 provides selected analysis results for the simple effects of time. The top three output selections (univariate results from SAS) indicate that within each treatment, mean weight loss changed across time. Note that the same conclusion is reached by the multivariate procedure. To conserve space, and because it is of interest, we present only the pairwise comparisons from the third treatment group. These results, shown in the last output selection in Table 12.16 (from SPSS) indicate that in this treatment group, there is no difference in means between time 1 and time 2 ($p = 1.0$), suggesting that a similar average amount of weight was lost from 0 to 2 months, and from 2 to 4 months (about a 6-pound drop each time as shown in Table 12.14). At month 6, though, this degree of weight loss is not maintained, as the 3.67-pound difference in weight loss between the last two time

■ Table 12.16: Selected Results from Separate One-Way Repeated Measures ANOVAs

Univariate Tests of Hypotheses for Within Subject Effects
diet=1

Source	DF	Type III SS	Mean Square	F Value	Pr > F	Adj Pr > F G – G	H – F
Time	2	35.05555556	17.52777778	35.23	<.0001	<.0001	<.0001
Error(time)	22	10.94444444	0.49747475				

Univariate Tests of Hypotheses for Within Subject Effects
diet=2

Source	DF	Type III SS	Mean Square	F Value	Pr > F	Adj Pr > F G – G	H – F
Time	2	57.16666667	28.58333333	71.19	<.0001	<.0001	<.0001
Error(time)	22	8.83333333	0.40151515				

Univariate Tests of Hypotheses for Within Subject Effects
diet=3

Source	DF	Type III SS	Mean Square	F Value	Pr > F	Adj Pr > F G – G	H – F
Time	2	110.0555556	55.0277778	25.25	<.0001	<.0001	<.0001
Error(time)	22	47.9444444	2.1792929				

Pairwise Comparisons[a]

Measure: MEASURE_1

(I) time	(J) time	Mean Difference (I-J)	Std. Error	Sig.[c]	95% Confidence Interval for Difference[c] Lower Bound	Upper Bound
1	2	.083	.733	1.000	−1.984	2.150
	3	3.750*	.664	.000	1.877	5.623
2	1	−.083	.733	1.000	−2.150	1.984
	3	3.667*	.333	.000	2.727	4.607
3	1	−3.750*	.664	.000	−5.623	−1.877
	2	−3.667*	.333	.000	−4.607	−2.727

Based on estimated marginal means

* The mean difference is significant at the .050 level.

[a] diet = 3.00

[c] Adjustment for multiple comparisons: Bonferroni.

points is statistically significant. This pattern for diet 3 is in contrast to each of the other groups, where the amount of average weight loss decreased across each of the time points.

Note that with these within-subject simple effect tests, there are different options available. With the procedure we just used, for the test of time within each treatment condition, the error term we used involved only those scores in a given diet group. If the assumption of multiple sample sphericity holds, a more powerful test can be obtained by pooling the separate error terms across groups. However, if this assumption is not satisfied, the pooled error term is not appropriate. Further, as we did in the one-way repeated measures design, the error term used for a pairwise comparison involved only those scores in a given comparison. Keppel and Wickens (2004, p. 458) note that it is possible to use an error term for a given comparison that pools error terms across the treatment groups. Such a pooled error term requires that the assumption of equal population variance and covariances is satisfied, which, if the case, would provide for a more powerful test. However, if this assumption were violated, the inferences made using this pooled error approach would not be appropriate. Thus, the procedure we illustrated is safer than using a pooled error approach but less powerful, the latter of which is applicable only if the relevant assumptions are satisfied.

Another choice we made involved control of the type I error rate. For the test of the simple effect of time in each group, we used an alpha of .05 that was not adjusted for the number of treatment conditions in the study (here, the three groups). So here, we are assuming that each simple effect test of time within a given diet group represents a distinct family of interest, for which an alpha of .05 would likely be used. A more conservative, but less powerful approach, would be to regard the set of tests here to represent a single family, for which the nominal overall type I error rate may be set at .05 / 3. Note though that for the pairwise comparisons of cell means, (as shown in the last output selection in Table 12.16), we used a Bonferroni adjustment to provide for more strict control of the type I error rate for each family. A less conservative approach here would be to rely on the test for the effect of time in each group to provide for type I error protection when comparing cell means, where no alpha adjustment would be used. The logic for this latter approach depends on conducting tests for cell means only if the test of time for the group at hand is statistically significant.

12.12.4 Simple Effects Analyses for the Between-Subjects Factor

Given the presence of the time-by-diet interaction, the second type of simple effect that is often of interest is to compare treatment group differences at each time point. Again, a simple and useful procedure is to select just those scores at a given time point and conduct separate one-way between-subjects ANOVAs with treatment as the factor at each time point. If group differences are present at a given time point, pairwise comparisons can be requested to pinpoint group differences. Like the procedure for the within-subjects simple effects, this procedure does not use a pooled error term involving all of the scores. However, the procedure does use a pooled error term (from the ANOVA) at each time point, so it is important to determine if the homogeneity assumption is reasonable for each ANOVA. Note that while it is possible to use a pooled error term for this analysis based on all scores (i.e., across the three time points), Maxwell and Delaney (2004, p. 604) note that the homogeneity assumption for this pooled error term (involving all scores) is likely violated when time is the within-subjects factor. So, again, the procedure we illustrate here is safer but less powerful than a testing procedure that, in this case, pools the error term across all cells. Also, the procedure we illustrate assumes that the tests of treatment group differences at each time point are regarded as separate families. As such, for each ANOVA the nominal alpha level we use is .05. If we find that group differences are present at a given time point, we use the Bonferroni method to provide for strict control of this family-wise error rate when conducting pairwise comparisons of cell means.

Table 12.15, in the lower half, provides the control lines for conducting the simple effect analyses associated with diet. Note that with SPSS, that syntax needs to be run as described after Table 12.15 for as many levels of the repeated measures factor are present, here, three for the three measurement occasions. Selected results of this analysis that focus on diet group differences at the second time point (month 4) are displayed in Table 12.17. The reason for displaying just these results is that the one-way ANOVA F test for group differences at the first time point is not statistically significant, $F(2,$

■ **Table 12.17: Selected Results From the One-Way Between-Subjects ANOVA at Month Four**

Estimates

Dependent Variable: wgtloss2

Diet	Mean	Std. Error	95% Confidence Interval	
			Lower Bound	Upper Bound
1.00	3.333	.378	2.565	4.102
2.00	3.917	.378	3.148	4.685
3.00	5.917	.378	5.148	6.685

Tests of Between-Subjects Effects

Dependent Variable: wgtloss2

Source	Type III Sum of Squares	Df	Mean Square	F	Sig.
Corrected Model	44.056[a]	2	22.028	12.866	.000
Intercept	693.444	1	693.444	405.021	.000
Diet	44.056	2	22.028	12.866	.000
Error	56.500	33	1.712		
Total	794.000	36			
Corrected Total	100.556	35			

[a] R Squared = .438 (Adjusted R Squared = .404)

Pairwise Comparisons

Dependent Variable: wgtloss2

| (I) diet | (J) diet | Mean Difference (I-J) | Std. Error | Sig.[b] | 95% Confidence Interval for Difference[b] | |
					Lower Bound	Upper Bound
1.00	2.00	−.583	.534	.848	−1.931	.764
	3.00	−2.583*	.534	.000	−3.931	−1.236
2.00	1.00	.583	.534	.848	−.764	1.931
	3.00	−2.000*	.534	.002	−3.347	−.653
3.00	1.00	2.583*	.534	.000	1.236	3.931
	2.00	2.000*	.534	.002	.653	3.347

Based on estimated marginal means

* The mean difference is significant at the .05 level.

[b] Adjustment for multiple comparisons: Bonferroni.

33) = 2.29, p = .12, with the same finding holding for diet group differences at the last time point, $F(2, 33) = 0.08$, $p = .92$. However, as Table 12.17 shows, group differences are present at the second time point, $F(2, 33) = 12.87$, $p < .001$. In addition, the Bonferroni-adjusted pairwise comparisons as shown in Table 12.17 indicate the weight loss, at time 2, was greater for diet group 3 compared to the other groups. As noted, it is this greater weight loss for diet group 3 at time 2 that led to the time-by-diet interaction.

12.13 ONE-BETWEEN AND TWO-WITHIN FACTORS

We consider both the univariate and multivariate analyses of a one-between and two-within repeated measures data set from Elashoff (1981). Two groups of subjects were given three different doses of two drugs. There are several different questions of interest in this study: Will the drugs be differentially effective for different groups? Is the effectiveness of the drugs dependent on dose level? Is the effectiveness of the drugs dependent both on dose level and on the group?

Table 12.18 shows the SAS and SPSS commands for this analysis. For the data lines, note that the first score is group ID; the second score is for drug 1, dose 1; the third

| | DRUG | | | | | |
| | 1 | | | 2 | | |
DOSE	1	2	3	1	2	3
GROUP 1	17.50	22.50	27.0	19.0	21.88	26.50
GROUP 2	19.63	22.38	24.0	26.88	28.63	33.0

■ **Table 12.18:   SAS and SPSS Control Lines for the One-Between and Two-Within Example**

SAS	SPSS
DATA ELAS;	DATA LIST FREE/ gpid y1 y2 y3 y4 y5 y6.
INPUT gp y1 y2 y3 y4 y5 y6;	BEGIN DATA.
LINES;	1 19 22 28 16 26 22 2 16 20 24 30 34 36
1 19 22 28 16 26 22	1 11 19 30 12 18 28 2 26 26 26 24 30 32
1 11 19 30 12 18 28	1 20 24 24 24 22 29 2 22 27 23 33 36 45
1 20 24 24 24 22 29	1 21 25 25 15 10 26 2 16 18 29 27 26 34
1 21 25 25 15 10 26	1 18 24 29 19 26 28 2 19 21 20 22 22 21
1 18 24 29 19 26 28	1 17 23 28 15 23 22 2 20 25 25 29 29 33
1 17 23 28 15 23 22	1 20 23 23 26 21 28 2 21 22 23 27 26 35
1 20 23 23 26 21 28	1 14 20 29 25 29 29 2 17 20 22 23 26 28
1 14 20 29 25 29 29	END DATA.
2 16 20 24 30 34 36	GLM y1 y2 y3 y4 y5 y6 BY gpid
2 26 26 26 24 30 32	(1) /WSFACTOR=drug 2 dose 3
2 22 27 23 33 36 45	/EMMEANS=TABLES(gpid)
2 16 18 29 27 26 34	/EMMEANS=TABLES(drug)
2 19 21 20 22 22 21	/EMMEANS=TABLES(dose)
2 20 25 25 29 29 33	/EMMEANS=TABLES(gpid*drug)
2 21 22 23 27 26 35	/EMMEANS=TABLES(gpid*dose)
2 17 20 22 23 26 28	/EMMEANS=TABLES(drug*dose)
PROC GLM;	/EMMEANS=TABLES(gpid*drug*dose)
CLASS gp;	/PRINT=DESCRIPTIVE HOMOGENEITY
MODEL y1 y2 y3 y4 y5 y6 = gp /NOUNI;	/WSDESIGN=drug dose drug*dose
(1) REPEATED drug 2, dose 3;	/DESIGN=gpid.
RUN;	

(1) Note that in these lines the drug factor is indicated to have two levels and the dose factor is indicated to have three levels. Note that the REPEATED command in SAS is sufficient to request test results for the main effects of the within subjects factors and their interaction. With SPSS, these effects are specified in the WSDESIGN command.

score is for drug 1, dose 2; and so on. Table 12.19 provides some descriptive statistics for the 12 cells in the design. In Table 12.20 are the univariate test results for all seven effects in the study (i.e., three main effects, three 2-way interactions, and one 3-way interaction). Note also that use of the multivariate tests, not shown in Table 12.20, reach the same conclusion. In particular, the results indicate statistically significant main effects of group, drug, and dose, and a group-by-drug interaction. Let us examine why the GROUP, DRUG, DRUG*GP and DOSE effects are significant. We take the means from Table 12.19 and insert them into the design, yielding:

	DRUG					
	1			**2**		
DOSE	1	2	3	1	2	3
GROUP 1	17.50	22.50	27.0	19.0	21.88	26.50
GROUP 2	19.63	22.38	24.0	26.88	28.63	33.0

■ Table 12.19: Means, Standard Deviations, and Cell Sizes for the One-Between and Two-Within Example

Descriptive Statistics

	Gpid	Mean	Std. deviation	N
y1	1.00	17.5000	3.42261	8
	2.00	19.6250	3.42000	8
	Total	18.5625	3.48270	16
y2	1.00	22.5000	2.07020	8
	2.00	22.3750	3.24863	8
	Total	22.4375	2.63233	16
y3	1.00	27.0000	2.61861	8
	2.00	24.0000	2.72554	8
	Total	25.5000	3.01109	16
y4	1.00	19.0000	5.34522	8
	2.00	26.8750	3.75832	8
	Total	22.9375	6.03842	16
y5	1.00	21.8750	5.89037	8
	2.00	28.6250	4.62717	8
	Total	25.2500	6.19139	16
y6	1.00	26.5000	2.92770	8
	2.00	33.0000	6.84523	8
	Total	29.7500	6.09371	16

■ Table 12.20: Univariate Analyses from SAS GLM for One-Between and Two-Within Example

The GLM Procedure
Repeated Measures Analysis of Variance
Univariate Tests of Hypotheses for Within Subject Effects

Source	DF	Type III SS	Mean Square	F Value	Pr > F
Drug	1	348.8437500	348.8437500	13.00	(2) 0.0029
drug*gp	1	326.3437500	326.3437500	12.16	(2) 0.0036
Error(drug)	14	375.6458333	(4) 26.8318452		

						Adj Pr > F	
Source	DF	Type III SS	Mean Square	F Value	Pr > F	G – G	H–F–L
Dose	2	758.7708333	379.3854167	36.51	<.0001	(3) <.0001	<.0001
dose*gp	2	42.2708333	21.1354167	2.03	0.1497	0.1565	0.1500
Error(dose)	28	290.9583333	(4) 10.3913690				

| Greenhouse-Geisser Epsilon | 0.8787 |
| Huynh-Feldt-Lecoutre Epsilon | 0.9949 |

(Continued)

■ **Table 12.20: (Continued)**

							Adj Pr > F	
Source	DF	Type III SS		Mean Square	F Value	Pr > F	G – G	H–F–L
drug*dose	2	12.0625000		6.0312500	0.68	0.5140	0.4724	0.4834
drug*dose*gp	2	14.8125000		7.4062500	0.84	0.4436	0.4134	0.4215
Error(drug*dose)	28	247.7916667	(4)	8.8497024				

Greenhouse-Geisser Epsilon	0.7297
Huynh-Feldt-Lecoutre Epsilon	0.7931

The GLM Procedure
Repeated Measures Analysis of Variance
Tests of Hypotheses for Between Subjects Effects

Source	DF	Type III SS		Mean Square	F Value		Pr > F
gp	1	270.0104167		270.0104167	7.09	(1)	0.0185
Error	14	532.9791667	(4)	38.0699405			

(1) Groups differ significantly at the .05 level, since .0185 < .05.
(2) & (3) The drug main effect and drug by group interaction are significant at the .05 level, while the dose main effect is also significant at the .05 level.
(4) Note that four different error terms are involved in this design, an additional complication with complex repeated-measures designs. The error terms are boxed.

The dose main effect is apparent in that the increases in the outcome as dose increases are similar for each group and for each drug type. Now, collapsing on dose, the group × drug means are obtained which reveal the reason for the other significant effects. This table is:

	DRUG	
	1	2
GROUP 1	22.33	22.46
GROUP 2	22.00	29.50

Note that the mean in cell 11 (22.33) is simply the average of 17.5, 22.5, and 27, while the mean in cell 12 (22.46) is the average of 19, 21.88, and 26.5, and so on. It is now apparent that the outlier cell mean of 29.5 is what "caused" the significance for the drug and group effects. For some reason drug 2 was not as effective with group 2 in inhibiting the response. As such, the small difference in outcome means between the two groups for drug 1 (averaging over dose) becomes a much larger group difference for drug 2. Thus, group differences depend on drug. The nonsignificant 3-way interaction indicates that this pattern is present for each dosage level. We mentioned previously, especially in connection with multiple regression, how influential an individual subject's score can be in affecting the results. This example shows the same type of thing, only now the outlier is a mean.

12.14 TWO-BETWEEN AND ONE-WITHIN FACTORS

To illustrate how to run a two-between and one-within factor repeated-measures design we return to the example used in sections 12.11 and 12.12, where we compared the relative efficacy of a behavior modification approach to dieting versus a behavior modification plus exercise approach (combination treatment) on weight loss for a group of overweight women. There is also a control group in this study. However, we now add age as a between-subjects factor. One purpose for adding this variable may be to learn if the diet-by-time interaction obtained previously holds for (or differs across) the age groups. That is, the investigator wishes to determine whether age further moderates the effectiveness of the diet approach. In this example, we have 18 women between 20 and 30 years old who have been randomly assigned to one of the three groups. Then, 18 women between 30 to 40 years old have been randomly assigned to one of the three groups. As before, weight loss is measured 2 months, 4 months, and 6 months after the program begins. Schematically, the design is as follows:

GROUP	AGE	WGTLOSS1	WGTLOSS2	WGTLOSS3
CONTROL	20–30 YRS			
CONTROL	30–40 YRS			
BEH. MOD.	20–30 YRS			
BEH. MOD.	30–40 YRS			
BEH. MOD. + EXER.	20–30 YRS			
BEH. MOD. + EXER.	30–40 YRS			

Treatment and age are the two grouping or between-subjects variables and time (over which weight loss is measured) is the within-subjects variable. Table 12.21 shows the SAS and SPSS control lines for this example. Table 12.22 shows the tests for the between-subjects effects and the univariate tests for the within-subjects effects. (Again, use of the multivariate tests reaches the same conclusions.) The first output selection in Table 12.22, showing the tests for between-subjects effects, indicates that only the diet main effect is significant at the .05 level ($F = 4.30, p < .023$). The next output selection in Table 12.22 shows the univariate test results for the within-subjects effects. Using the Greenhouse–Geisser (G-G) results, we find that both time ($F = 84.57, p \leq .0001$) and the diet-by-time interaction ($F = 4.88, p = .0045$) are significant.

To interpret the significant effects, we can obtain the means for diet by time, collapsing over the two age groups. These means are identical to those shown in Table 12.14. There, we saw that the diet-by-time interaction was due to the weight loss of group 3 at the second time point. That is, diet group 3 lost, on average, a similar amount of weight at time 1 and time 2, whereas the other diet groups experienced diminished weight loss at time 2. Note that the three-way time × diet × age interaction is not statistically significant at the .05 level, indicating that this two-way diet-by-time interaction holds across the two age groups. Thus, age does not further moderate the impact of diet group on weight loss.

■ Table 12.21: SAS and SPSS Control Lines for the Two-Between and One-Within Example

SAS	SPSS
DATA weight2;	DATA LIST FREE / diet age y1 y2
INPUT diet age y1 y2 y3;	y3.
LINES;	BEGIN DATA.
1 1 4 3 3	1 1 4 3 3 1 1 4 4 3 1 1 4 3 1
1 1 4 4 3	11 3 2 1 1 1 5 3 2 1 1 6 5 4
1 1 4 3 1	1 2 6 5 4 1 2 5 4 1 1 2 3 3 2
1 1 3 2 1	1 2 5 4 1 1 2 4 2 2 1 2 5 2 1
1 1 5 3 2	2 1 6 3 2 2 1 5 4 1 2 1 7 6 3
1 1 6 5 4	2 1 6 4 2 1 2 3 2 1 2 1 5 5 4
1 2 6 5 4	2 2 4 3 1 2 2 4 2 1 2 2 6 5 3
1 2 5 4 1	2 2 7 6 4 2 2 4 3 2 2 2 7 4 3
1 2 3 3 2	3 1 8 4 2 3 1 3 6 3 3 1 7 7 4
1 2 5 4 1	3 1 4 7 1 31 9 7 3 3 1 2 4 1
1 2 4 2 2	3 2 3 5 1 3 2 6 5 2 3 2 6 6 3
1 2 5 2 1	3 2 9 5 2 3 2 7 9 4 3 2 8 6 1
2 1 6 3 2	END DATA.
2 1 5 4 1	GLM y1 y2 y3 BY diet age
2 1 7 6 3	/WSFACTOR=time 3
2 1 6 4 2	/PRINT=DESCRIPTIVE
2 1 3 2 1	/CRITERIA=ALPHA(.05)
2 1 5 5 4	(2)/WSDESIGN=time
2 2 4 3 1	(1) /DESIGN=diet age diet*age.
2 2 4 2 1	
2 2 6 5 3	
2 2 7 6 4	
2 2 4 3 2	
2 2 7 4 3	
3 1 8 4 2	
3 1 3 6 3	
3 1 7 7 4	
3 1 4 7 1	
3 1 9 7 3	
3 1 2 4 1	
3 2 3 5 1	
3 2 6 5 2	
3 2 6 6 3	
3 2 9 5 2	
3 2 7 9 4	
3 2 8 6 1	
PROC GLM;	
CLASS diet age;	

SAS	SPSS

```
(1) MODEL y1 y2 y3 = diet age
diet*age /NOUNI;
(2)REPEATED time 3;
RUN;
```

(1) The MODEL (SAS) and DESIGN (SPSS) statements specify that weight loss is a function of the two between-subjects factors and their interaction.

(2) The REPEATED (SAS) and WSDESIGN (SPSS) statements incorporate the effect of time into the model as well as its associated interactions.

■ **Table 12.22:　Selected SAS Output for the Two-Between and One-Within Example**

The GLM Procedure
Repeated Measures Analysis of Variance
Tests of Hypotheses for Between Subjects Effects

Source	DF	Type III SS	Mean Square	F Value	Pr > F
diet	2	36.9074074	18.4537037	4.30	0.0229
age	1	0.2314815	0.2314815	0.05	0.8180
diet*age	2	0.7962963	0.3981481	0.09	0.9117
Error	30	128.8333333	4.2944444		

The GLM Procedure
Repeated Measures Analysis of Variance
Univariate Tests of Hypotheses for Within Subject Effects

Source	DF	Type III SS	Mean Square	F Value	Pr > F	Adj Pr > F G – G	Adj Pr > F H–F–L
Time	2	181.3518519	90.6759259	84.57	<.0001	<.0001	<.0001
time*diet	4	20.9259259	5.2314815	4.88	0.0018	0.0045	0.0039
time*age	2	1.7962963	0.8981481	0.84	0.4377	0.4128	0.4172
time*diet*age	4	1.5925926	0.3981481	0.37	0.8282	0.7810	0.7894
Error(time)	60	64.3333333	1.0722222				

Greenhouse-Geisser Epsilon	0.7775
Huynh-Feldt-Lecoutre Epsilon	0.8122

12.15 TWO-BETWEEN AND TWO-WITHIN FACTORS

This is a very complex design, an example of which appears in Bock (1975, pp. 483–484). The data was from a study by Morter, who was concerned about the comparability of the first and second responses on the form definiteness and form appropriateness variables of the Holtzman Inkblot procedure for a preadolescent group of subjects. The

■ **Table 12.23:   Control Lines for the Two-Between and Two-Within Repeated Measures Example on SPSS**

```
TITLE 'Two Between and Two Within'.
DATA LIST FREE/grade iq fd1 fd2 fa1 fa2.
BEGIN DATA.
1  1   2   1   0   2       1  1  -7  -2  -2  -5       1  1  -3  -1  -3  -1
1  1   1   1   0  -3       1  1   1  -1  -4  -2       1  1  -7   1  -4  -3
1  2   0  -4  -9  -7       1  2  -1  -9  -9  -4       1  2  -6  -6   3  -4
1  2  -2  -4  -4  -5       1  2  -2  -1  -3  -3       1  2  -9  -9  -3   1
2  1   3   4   2  -3       2  1  -1  -1  -3  -3       2  1   2   2   2   0
2  1   2   0  -2   0       2  1   0  -1   2   2       2  1   3   3  -4  -2
2  1  -1   2   2  -1       2  1  -3  -2   3  -2
2  2  -3  -2   5   2       2  2   2   3  -2  -3       2  2   2   4   1   3
2  2   3   2  -5  -5       2  2  -4  -3  -3  -3       2  2   6   4  -9  -9
2  2   2   1  -3   0       2  2  -1  -4  -2   0       2  2  -2  -1   2  -2
2  2  -2   4  -1   0
END DATA.
```

```
LIST.
(1) GLM fd1 fd2 fa1 fa2 BY grade iq
 /WSFACTOR = form 2 time 2
(2) /WSDESIGN = form time form*time
 /PRINT DESCRIPTIVE HOMOGENEITY
 /DESIGN = grade iq grade*iq.
```

(1)		FORM	FD		FA	
		TIME	1	2	1	2
GRADE 4	HI IQ					
	LOW IQ					
GRADE 7	HI IQ					
	LOW IQ					

(2) As seen in the other examples, WSDESIGN specifies the within-subjects effects to be tested and DESIGN specifies the between-subjects effects to be tested.

two between factors are grade level (4 and 7) and IQ (high and low), with these two factors being crossed. The two within-subjects factors are form and time, where each subject completed both forms at each of the two times. The schematic layout for the design is given at the bottom of Table 12.23, which also gives the syntax for running the analysis with SPSS, along with the data.

It may be quite helpful for you to compare the control lines for this example with those for the one-between and two-within example in Table 12.18, as they are quite similar. The main difference here is that there is an additional between variable, hence an additional factor after the keyword BY in the GLM command and three between-subjects effects in the DESIGN subcommand. You are referred to Bock (1975) for an interpretation of the results.

12.16 TOTALLY WITHIN DESIGNS

There are research situations where the *same* subjects are measured under various treatment combinations, that is, where the same subjects are in each cell of the design.

This may be particularly the case when few subjects are available. We consider three examples to illustrate.

Example 12.3

A researcher in child development is interested in observing the same group of preschool children (all 4 years of age) in two situations at two different times (morning and afternoon) of the day. She is concerned with the extent of their social interaction, and will measure this by having two observers independently rate the amount of social interaction. The average of the two ratings will serve as the dependent variable. The within-subjects factors here are situation and time of day. There are four scores for each child: social interaction in Situation 1 in the morning and afternoon, and social interaction in Situation 2 in the morning and afternoon. We denote the four scores by Y1, Y2, Y3, and Y4.

Such a totally within repeated-measures design is easily set up with SPSS GLM. The control lines are given here:

```
TITLE 'Two Within Design'.
DATA LIST FREE/y1 y2 y3 y4.
BEGIN DATA.
DATA LINES
END DATA.
GLM y1 y2 y3 y4
/WSFACTOR = sit 2 time 2
/WSDESIGN = sit time sit*time
/PRINT DESCRIPTIVE.
```

Note in this example that *only univariate* tests will be printed out by SPSS for all three effects. This is because there is only 1 degree of freedom for each effect, and hence only one transformed variable for each effect.

Example 12.4

Suppose in an ergonomic study we are interested in the effects of day of the work week and time of the day (AM or PM) on various measures of posture. We select 30 computer operators, and for this example we consider just one measure of posture called shoulder flexion. We then have a two-factor totally within design that looks as follows:

	Monday		Wednesday		Friday	
	AM	PM	AM	PM	AM	PM
1						
2						
3						
.						
.						
.						
30						

Example 12.5

A social psychologist is interested in determining how self-reported anxiety level for 35- to 45-year-old men varies as a function of situation, who the men are with, and how many people are involved. A questionnaire will be administered to 20 such men, asking them to rate their anxiety level (on a Likert scale from 1 to 7) in three situations (going to the theater, going to a football game, and going to a dinner party), with primarily friends and primarily strangers, and with a total of 6 people and with 12 people. Thus, the men will be reporting anxiety for 12 different contexts. This is a three-within, crossed repeated-measures design, where situation (three levels) is crossed with the nature of the group (two levels) and with the number in the group (two levels).

12.17 PLANNED COMPARISONS IN REPEATED-MEASURES DESIGNS

Planned orthogonal comparisons can also be easily set up in SPSS for repeated-measures designs. To illustrate, we consider the setup of Helmert contrasts for a single group repeated-measures design with data again from Bock (1975). The study involved the effect of three drugs on the duration of sleep of 10 mental patients. The drugs were given orally on alternate evenings, and the hours of sleep were compared with an intervening control night. Each of the drugs was tested a number of times with each patient. Thus, there are four levels for treatment: the control condition and the three drugs. The first drug (Level 2) was of a different type from the other two, which were of a similar type. Therefore, Helmert contrasts are appropriate. SPSS syntax for this analysis is shown in Table 12.24 and selected results appear in Table 12.25. The top output selection in Table 12.25 indicates that the first two Helmert contrasts are significant at the .05 level (which would

▨ **Table 12.24: SPSS Syntax for Helmert Contrasts in a Single-Group Repeated-Measures Design**

```
TITLE 'Helmert Contrasts For Repeated Measures'.
DATA LIST FREE/y1 y2 y3 y4.
BEGIN DATA.
.6 1.3 2.5 2.1          3 1.4 3.8 4.4          4.7 4.5 5.8 4.7
6.2 6.1 6.1 6.7         3.2 6.6 7.6 8.3         2.5 6.2 8 8.2
2.8 3.6 4.4 4.3         1.1 1.1 5.7 5.8         2.9 4.9 6.3 6.4
5.5 4.3 5.6 4.8
END DATA.
LIST.
GLM y1 y2 y3 y4
(1) /WSFACTOR=Drug 4 Helmert
    /METHOD=SSTYPE(3)
(2) /PRINT=DESCRIPTIVE TEST(MMATRIX)
    /WSDESIGN=Drug.
```

(1) Helmert requests the Helmert contrasts.

(2) TEST (MMATRIX) will output the contrast coefficients.

■ **Table 12.25: Selected Results for the Helmert Contrasts**

Tests of Within-Subjects Contrasts

Measure: MEASURE_1

Source	Drug	Type III Sum of Squares	df	Mean Square	F	Sig.
Drug	Level 1 vs. Later	32.400	1	32.400	8.776	.016
	Level 2 vs. Later	24.806	1	24.806	15.222	.004
	Level 3 vs. Level 4	.001	1	.001	.003	.959
Error(Drug)	Level 1 vs. Later	33.227	9	3.692		
	Level 2 vs. Later	14.666	9	1.630		
	Level 3 vs. Level 4	3.289	9	.365		

also hold if a Bonferroni-adjusted alpha were applied to the analysis). The second output selection shows the contrast coefficients for this analysis that can be used to test the grand mean (which is not of interest), and the last output selection shows the Helmert contrast coefficients. For readers of previous editions of this text, the coefficients here are not orthonormalized by SPSS so they are not the same as the coefficients shown in previous editions, although the test results are not affected by this transformation.

Average
Measure: MEASURE_1
Transformed Variable: AVERAGE

Y1	.250
Y2	.250
Y3	.250
Y4	.250

Drug[a]

Measure: MEASURE_1

Dependent Variable	Drug		
	Level 1 vs. Later	Level 2 vs. Later	Level 3 vs. Level 4
Y1	1.000	.000	.000
Y2	−.333	1.000	.000
Y3	−.333	−.500	1.000
Y4	−.333	−.500	−1.000

[a] The contrasts for the within subjects factors are:
Drug: Helmert contrast

There is an important additional point to be made regarding planned comparisons with repeated-measures designs. If SPSS GLM syntax were used to set up *nonorthogonal contrasts, SPSS will orthogonalize them, which is not desirable.* This leads us to consider nonorthogonal contrasts in SPSS, which require the use of the SPSS MANOVA procedure, along with a TRANSFORM statement, as we will see.

12.17.1 Nonorthogonal Contrasts in SPSS

In previous editions of this text we simply referred readers to Appendix B, which provides additional information about these contrasts and is directly from SPSS. However, it is helpful to provide some elaboration here. It is important to note, as SPSS points out, that SPSS is structured so that orthogonal contrasts are needed in repeated measures to obtain proper overall test results. However, for nonorthogonal contrasts, the contrasts obtained by the repeated measures commands do not obtain the correct results. Let us consider an example to illustrate. This example, which involves *nonorthogonal* contrasts, will be run as repeated measures AND in a way that preserves the nonorthogonality of the contrasts. The control lines for each analysis are given in Table 12.26.

When nonorthogonal contrasts are run using repeated measures syntax, as on the left side of Table 12.26, they are transformed into orthogonal contrasts so that the multivariate test is correct. To see what contrasts the program is actually testing one MUST refer to the transformation matrix. SPSS warns of this:

> MANOVA automatically orthonormalizes contrast matrices for WSFACTORS. If the special contrasts that were requested are nonorthogonal, the contrasts actually fitted are not the contrasts requested. See the transformation matrix for the actual contrasts fitted. (Nichols, 1993, n.p.)

Note that in the correct syntax, any reference to repeated measures is removed, such as `WSFACTOR`, `WSDESIGN`, and `ANALYSIS (REPEATED)`. In addition, the `TRANS-FORM=SPECIAL` replaces the `CONTRAST(drugs)=SPECIAL` statement that is used in the incorrect syntax. In the incorrect syntax, the contrasts we requested are transformed into an orthogonal set, as this matrix of contrast coefficients suggests:

	T1	T2	T3	T4
Y1	.500	.254	.828	.000
Y2	.500	−.085	−.276	.816
Y3	.500	.592	−.483	−.408
Y4	.500	−.761	−.069	−.408

In contrast, with the correct syntax, SPSS uses the coefficients we input, as shown:

	T1	T2	T3	T4
Y1	1.000	1.000	1.000	.000
Y2	1.000	1.000	−.500	1.000
Y3	1.000	−1.000	−.500	−.500
Y4	1.000	−1.000	.000	−.500

■ Table 12.26: Incorrect and Correct Syntax for Obtaining Nonorthogonal Contrasts for the Single-Group Repeated Measures Design

Incorrect Syntax	Correct Syntax
TITLE 'Non-Orthogonal Contrasts'.	TITLE 'Non-Orthogonal Contrasts'.
DATA LIST FREE /y1 y2 y3 y4	DATA LIST FREE/y1 y2 y3 y4.
BEGIN Data.	BEGIN DATA.
.6 1.3 2.5 2.1 3 1.4 3.8 4.4 4.7 4.5 5.8 4.7	.6 1.3 2.5 2.1 3 1.4 3.8 4.4 4.7 4.5 5.8 4.7
6.2 6.1 6.7 3.2 6.6 7.6 8.3 2.5 6.2 8 8.2	6.2 6.1 6.7 3.2 6.6 7.6 8.3 2.5 6.2 8 8.2
2.8 3.6 4.4 4.3 1.1 1.1 5.7 5.8 2.9 4.9 6.3 6.4	2.8 3.6 4.4 4.3 1.1 1.1 5.7 5.8 2.9 4.9 6.3 6.4
5.5 4.3 5.6 4.8	5.5 4.3 5.6 4.8
END DATA.	END DATA.
MANOVA y1 TO y4	MANOVA y1 TO y4
/WSFACTOR=Drugs(4)	/TRANSFORM=SPECIAL (1 1 1 1 1 1 1-1 1-1 -1 1 -.5 - .5 0
/CONTRAST (Drugs)=SPECIAL (1 1 1 1 1 1	0 1 -.5 -.5)
-1-1 1 -.5 0 0 1 -.5 -.5)	/PRINT=TRANSFORM
/PRINT=TRANSFORM	/ANALYSIS=(T1/T2 T3 T4).
/WSDESIGN=Drugs	
/ANALYSIS (REPEATED).	

With either syntax, the multivariate test is the SAME in both cases ($F = 5.53737$, $p = .029$). However, the univariate tests for the three contrasts, T2, T3, and T4 (i.e., the transformed variables), using the proper syntax are respectively $F = 16.86253$, 7.35025, and 15.22245, each of which is significant at the .05 level. The test statistics (t tests) for the contrasts obtained by use of the incorrect syntax are not proper and in this case lead to different conclusions.

Also, it is *very important* that *separate* error terms are used for testing each of the planned comparisons for significance. Boik (1981) showed that for even a very slight deviation from sphericity ($\epsilon = .90$), the use of a pooled error term can result in a type I error rate quite different from the level of significance. For $\epsilon = .90$ Boik showed, if testing at $\alpha = .05$, that the actual alpha for single degree of freedom contrasts ranged from .012 to .097. In some cases, the pooled error term will underestimate the amount of error and for other contrasts the error will be overestimated, resulting in a conservative test. Fortunately, SPSS provides separate error terms for the contrasts (for example, see the mean square errors in the first output selection of Table 12.25). Thus, the SPSS syntax presented here uses proper error terms for contrasts, whether the contrasts are orthogonal or nonorthogonal.

12.18 PROFILE ANALYSIS

In profile analysis the interest is in comparing the performance of two or more groups on a battery of test scores (interest, achievement, personality). It is assumed that the tests are scaled similarly or that they are commensurable. In profile analysis there are three questions that may be asked of the data in the following order:

1. Are the profiles parallel? If the answer to this is yes for two groups, it would imply that one group scored uniformly better than the other on all variables, assuming group differences are present, which leads to the next question.
2. If the profiles are parallel, then are they coincident? In other words, did the groups score the same on each variable?
3. If the profiles are coincident, then is the profile level or what is also called flat? In other words, are the means on all variables equal to the same constant?

Next, Figure 12.3 shows *hypothetical* examples of parallel and nonparallel profiles, with the variables representing achievement in different content areas.

If the profiles are not parallel, then there is a group-by-variable interaction. That is, how much better one group does than another depends on the variable.

Why is it necessary that the tests be scaled similarly in order to have the results of a profile analysis meaningfully interpreted? To illustrate, suppose we compared two groups on three variables, A, B, and C, two of which were on a 1 to 5 scale and the

■ **Figure 12.3:** Examples of parallel and nonparallel profiles.

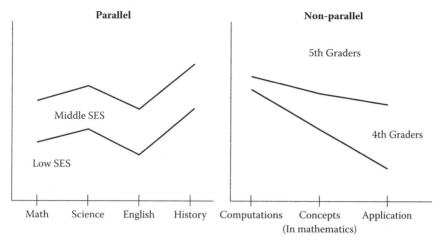

■ **Figure 12.4:** Nonparallel profiles resulting from different scales used for variables *A*, *B*, and *C*.

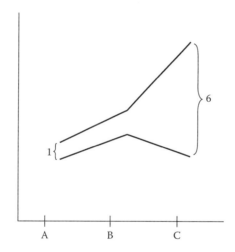

other on a 1 to 30 scale, that is, not scaled similarly. Suppose the graph in Figure 12.4 resulted, suggesting nonparallel profiles.

But the nonparallelism is a scaling artifact. The magnitude of superiority of group 1 for Test *A* is 1/5, which is exactly the same order of superiority on Test *C*, $6/30 = 1/5$. A way of dealing with this problem if the tests are scaled differently is to first convert to some type of standard score (e.g., z or T) before proceeding with the profile analysis.

We now consider the running and interpretation of a profile analysis using SPSS, with some data from Johnson and Wichern (1988), which is available online.

Example 12.6

In a study of love and marriage, a sample of married men and women (not from the same couple) were asked to respond to the following questions:

1. What is the level of passionate love you feel for your partner?
2. What is the level of passionate love that your partner feels for you?
3. What is the level of companionate love that you feel for your partner?
4. What is the level of companionate love that your partner feels for you?

The responses to all four questions were on a Likert-type scale from 1 (none at all) to 5 (a tremendous amount). We wish to determine whether the profiles for the men and women are parallel. There were 30 men and 30 women who responded. The control lines for running the analysis on SPSS are given in Table 12.27.

The multivariate test of parallelism appears in Table 12.28 and is the test for the dv-by-sex interaction. Here, we see that this test shows that parallelism is tenable at the .01 level, because the probability of .057 is greater than .01. Now, it is meaningful to proceed to the second question in profile analysis, and ask whether the profiles are coincident. The test for this is provided in the second output selection of Table 12.28 and shows that the profiles can be considered coincident, that is, the same, as $p = .196$. Given that we have concluded that the profiles are the same, it is reasonable to ask whether the participants scored the same on all four tests, that is, the question of equal scale means. The multivariate test for equal scale means, appearing in the first output selection of Table 12.28, which is the test for dv pooling across groups, indicates this is not tenable ($p < .001$). The relevant

---

■ **Table 12.27: Control Lines for Profile Analysis of Participant Ratings**

```
TITLE 'Profile Analysis On Participant Ratings'.
DATA LIST FREE/sex passyou passpart compyou comppart.
BEGIN DATA.
        DATA LINES
END DATA.
GLM passyou passpart compyou comppart BY sex
(1) /WSFACTOR=dv 4 Repeated
    /PLOT=PROFILE(dv*sex)
    /EMMEANS=TABLES(sex)
    /EMMEANS=TABLES(dv)
    /EMMEANS=TABLES(sex*dv)
    PRINT=DESCRIPTIVE
    /WSDESIGN=DV
    /DESIGN=sex.
```

(1) The `Repeated` statement sets up contrasts between the first and second dependent variables, then the second and third dependent variables, and then the third and fourth dependent variables.

means, shown in the third output selection, suggest that the participants generally scored higher on the latter two variables. The contrasts for dv shown in the last output selection of Table 12.28 support this judgment as the contrast between the second and third variables (passpart and compyou) is statistically significant ($p = .001$).

■ **Table 12.28: Selected Output From Profile Analysis**

Multivariate Tests[a]						
Effect		Value	F	Hypothesis df	Error df	Sig.
Dv	Pillai's Trace	.303	8.115[b]	3.000	56.000	.000
	Wilks' Lambda	.697	8.115[b]	3.000	56.000	.000
	Hotelling's Trace	.435	8.115[b]	3.000	56.000	.000
	Roy's Largest Root	.435	8.115[b]	3.000	56.000	.000
dv * sex	Pillai's Trace	.125	2.660[b]	3.000	56.000	.057
	Wilks' Lambda	.875	2.660[b]	3.000	56.000	.057
	Hotelling's Trace	.143	2.660[b]	3.000	56.000	.057
	Roy's Largest Root	.143	2.660[b]	3.000	56.000	.057

[a] Design: Intercept + sex
Within Subjects Design: dv
[b] Exact statistic

Tests of Between-Subjects Effects					

Measure: MEASURE_1
Transformed Variable: Average

Source	Type III Sum of Squares	Df	Mean Square	F	Sig.
Intercept	1066.817	1	1066.817	6843.359	.000
Sex	.267	1	.267	1.711	.196
Error	9.042	58	.156		

Measure: MEASURE_1

Dv	Mean	Std. Error	95% Confidence Interval	
			Lower Bound	Upper Bound
1	3.867	.094	3.678	4.055
2	4.050	.094	3.863	4.237
3	4.483	.075	4.333	4.634
4	4.467	.077	4.312	4.621

Tests of Within-Subjects Contrasts

Measure: MEASURE_1

Source	Dv	Type III Sum of Squares	df	Mean Square	F	Sig.
Dv	Level 1 vs. Level 2	2.017	1	2.017	2.912	.093
	Level 2 vs. Level 3	11.267	1	11.267	12.948	.001
	Level 3 vs. Level 4	.017	1	.017	.212	.647
dv * sex	Level 1 vs. Level 2	.817	1	.817	1.179	.282
	Level 2 vs. Level 3	.267	1	.267	.306	.582
	Level 3 vs. Level 4	.417	1	.417	5.292	.025
Error(dv)	Level 1 vs. Level 2	40.167	58	.693		
	Level 2 vs. Level 3	50.467	58	.870		
	Level 3 vs. Level 4	4.567	58	.079		

12.19 DOUBLY MULTIVARIATE REPEATED-MEASURES DESIGNS

In this section we consider a complex, but, not unusual in practice, repeated-measures design, in which the same subjects are measured on several variables at each point in time, or on several variables for each treatment or condition, when treatment is a within-subjects factor. The following are three examples:

1. We are interested in tracking elementary school children's achievement in math and reading, and we have their standardized test scores obtained in grades 2, 4, 6, and 8. Here we have data for two variables, each measured at four points in time.
2. As a second example of a doubly multivariate problem, suppose we have 53 subjects measured on five types of tests on three occasions. In this example, there are also two between variables (group and gender).
3. A study by Wynd (1992) investigated the effect of stress reduction in preventing smoking relapse. Subjects were randomly assigned to an experimental group or control group. They were then invited to three abstinence-booster sessions (three-part treatment) provided at 1-, 2-, and 3-month intervals. After each of these sessions, they were measured on three variables: imagery, stress, and smoking rate.

Why are the data from the three situations considered to be *doubly* multivariate? Recall from Chapter 4 that we defined a multivariate problem as one involving several correlated dependent variables. In these cases, the problem is doubly multivariate because there is a correlational structure *within* each measure and a different correlational structure *across* the measures. For item 1, the children's scores on math ability will be correlated across the grades, as will their verbal scores, but, in addition, there will be some correlation between their math and verbal scores.

12.20 SUMMARY

1. Repeated-measures designs are much more powerful than completely randomized designs, because the variability due to individual differences is removed from the error term, and individual differences are the major reason for error variance.

2. Two major advantages of repeated-measures designs are increased precision (because of the smaller error term), and the fact that many fewer subjects are needed than in a completely randomized design. Two potential disadvantages are that the order of treatments may make a difference (this can be dealt with by counterbalancing) and carryover effects.

3. Either a univariate or a multivariate approach can be used for repeated-measures analysis. The assumptions for a single-group univariate repeated-measures analysis are (a) independence of the observations, (b) multivariate normality, and (c) sphericity (also called circularity). For the multivariate approach, the first two assumptions are still needed, but the sphericity assumption is *not* needed. Sphericity requires that the variances of the differences for *all pairs* of repeated measures be equal. Although statistical tests of sphericity exist, they are not recommended.

4. Under a violation of sphericity the type I error rate for the univariate approach is inflated. However, a modified (adjusted) univariate approach, obtained by multiplying each of the degrees of freedom by $\hat{\varepsilon}$, yields an honest type I error rate.

5. Because both the modified (Greenhouse–Geisser adjusted) univariate approach and the multivariate approach control the type I error rate, the choice between them can be made on the basis of the power of the tests. The multivariate test probably should be avoided when $n < k + 10$, because under this condition its power will tend to be low. When sphericity is violated, research suggests that when N is moderately large the multivariate approach may generally provide more power. It is difficult to know, though, at what point N becomes sufficiently large. So, if power is the criterion you are using to make this decision, it seems reasonable to consider both tests, because they may differ in the effects they will detect.

6. If the sphericity assumption is tenable, then a Tukey procedure is a good *post hoc* technique for locating significant pairwise differences. If the sphericity assumption is violated, as may often be the case, the Bonferroni approach should be used. That is, do multiple *correlated t* tests, but use the Bonferroni inequality to keep the overall alpha level under control.

7. When several groups are involved, then an additional assumption is multisample sphericity, which states that the sphericity assumption is satisfied for each level of the between-subjects factor *and* that the population variance-covariance matrix of the

repeated measures is the same across the groups. The overall tests are robust to violations of this second assumption provided that group sizes are similar. Violations of the first assumption are generally more problematic, which is the basis for recommending use of the Greenhouse–Geisser and/or multivariate tests for the within-subjects effects.

8. Designs with only within-subject factors are fairly common in certain areas of research. These are designs where the *same* subjects are involved in every treatment combination or in each situation. Totally within designs are easily set up on SPSS.

9. In testing contrasts with repeated-measures designs it is imperative that *separate* error terms be used for each contrast, because Boik (1981) showed that if a pooled error term is used the actual alpha will be quite different from the presumed level of significance.

10. In profile analysis we are comparing two or more groups of subjects on a battery of tests. It is assumed that the tests are scaled similarly. If they are not, then the scores must be converted to some type of standard score (e.g., z or T) for the analysis to be meaningful. Nonparallel profiles means there is a group-by-variable interaction; that is, how much better one group does than another depends on the variable.

12.21 EXERCISES

1. In the multivariate analysis of the drug data we stated that $H_0 : \mu_1 = \mu_2 = \mu_3 = \mu_4$ is equivalent to saying that $\mu_1 - \mu_2 = 0$ and $\mu_2 - \mu_3 = 0$ and $\mu_3 - \mu_4 = 0$. Show this is true.

2. Consider the following data set from a single-sample repeated-measures design with three repeated measures:

	Treatments		
Ss	1	2	3
1	5	6	1
2	3	4	2
3	3	7	1
4	6	8	3
5	6	9	3
6	4	7	2
7	5	9	2

(a) Do a univariate repeated-measures analysis by hand (i.e., using a calculator), using the procedure employed in the text. Do you reject at the .05 level?

(b) Do a multivariate repeated-measures analysis by hand with the following difference variables: $y_1 - y_2$ and $y_2 - y_3$.

(c) Run the data on SAS or SPSS, obtaining both the univariate and multivariate results, to check the answers you obtained in (a) and (b).

(d) Note the SAS and SPSS uses polynomial transformations as the default for this analysis, whereas you used a difference score transformation in letter (b). Yet, the same multivariate F is obtained in each case. What point that we mentioned in the text does this illustrate?

(e) Use the Bonferroni procedure at the .05 level to determine which pairs of treatments differ.

3. A school psychologist is testing the effectiveness of a stress management approach in reducing the state and trait anxiety for college students. The subjects are pretested and matched on these variables and then randomly assigned within each pair to either the stress management approach or to a control group. The following data are obtained:

	Stress management		Control	
Pairs	State	Trait	State	Trait
1	41	38	46	35
2	48	41	47	50
3	34	33	39	36
4	31	40	28	38
5	26	23	35	19
6	37	31	40	30
7	44	32	46	45
8	53	47	58	53
9	46	41	47	48
10	34	38	39	39
11	33	39	36	41
12	50	45	54	40

(a) Test at the .05 level, using the multivariate matched pairs analysis, whether the stress management approach was successful.

(b) Which of the variables are contributing to multivariate significance?

4. Suppose that in the Elashoff drug example the two groups of subjects had been given the three different doses of two drugs under two different conditions. Then we would have a one-between and three-within design. Set up schematically the appropriate repeated measures design. What modifications in the control lines from Table 12.18 would be necessary to run this analysis? (SPSS users can ignore the EMMEANS lines.)

5. The extent of the departure from the sphericity assumption can be measured by

$$\hat{\varepsilon} = \frac{k^2 \left(\bar{s}_{ii} - \bar{s} \right)^2}{(k-1)\left(\sum\sum s_{ij}^2 - 2k \sum_i \bar{s}_i^2 + k^2 \bar{s}^2 \right)},$$

where

$\bar{s}$　is the mean of all entries in the covariance matrix **S**

$\bar{s}_{ii}$　is the mean of entries on main diagonal of **S**

$\bar{s}_i$　is the mean of all entries in row i of **S**

s_{ij} is the ijth entry of $\mathbf{S}$

Find $\hat{\varepsilon}$ for the following covariance matrix:

$$\mathbf{S} = \begin{bmatrix} 4 & 3 & 2 \\ 3 & 5 & 2 \\ 2 & 2 & 6 \end{bmatrix} \left(answer\ \hat{\varepsilon} = .82 \right)$$

6. Trend analysis was run using data from Potthoff and Roy (1964). It consists of growth measurements for 11 girls (coded as 1) and 16 boys at ages 8, 10, 12, and 14. Since some of the data is suspect (as the SAS manual notes), we have deleted observations 19 and 20 before running the analysis. Following is part of the SPSS printout that seeks to identify if there are any trend differences between girls and boys as well as any significant overall trends:

Descriptive Statistics

	Gp	Mean	Std. deviation	N
y1	1.00	21.1818	2.12453	11
	2.00	22.7857	2.61441	14
	Total	22.0800	2.49867	25
y2	1.00	22.2273	1.90215	11
	2.00	24.2143	1.95836	14
	Total	23.3400	2.14437	25
y3	1.00	23.0909	2.36451	11
	2.00	25.4286	2.40078	14
	Total	24.4000	2.61805	25
y4	1.00	24.0909	2.43740	11
	2.00	27.7143	2.11873	14
	Total	26.1200	2.87692	25

Tests of Within-Subjects Contrasts

Measure: MEASURE_1

Source	Year	Type III sum of squares	df	Mean square	F	Sig.
year	Linear	201.708	1	201.708	84.319	.000
	Quadratic	1.015	1	1.015	1.086	.308
	Cubic	.792	1	.792	.942	.342
year × gp	Linear	12.652	1	12.652	5.289	.031
	Quadratic	1.255	1	1.255	1.343	.258
	Cubic	.288	1	.288	.343	.564
Error(year)	Linear	55.020	23	2.392		
	Quadratic	21.485	23	.934		
	Cubic	19.350	23	.841		

(a) Are there any significant (at the .05 level) interactions (linear by gender, etc.)?

(b) Are there any significant (at .05) year effects?

7. Consider the following covariance matrix:

$$
\begin{array}{c c c c}
 & y_1 & y_2 & y_3 \\
S = \begin{array}{c} y_1 \\ y_2 \\ y_3 \end{array} & \left[\begin{array}{c c c} 1.0 & .5 & 1.5 \\ .5 & 3.0 & 2.5 \\ 1.5 & 2.5 & 5.0 \end{array}\right]
\end{array}
$$

Calculate the variances of the three difference variables: $y_1 - y_2$, $y_1 - y_3$, and $y_2 - y_3$. Note that the formula for the variance of the difference scores for the ith and jth repeated measures is $S^2_{i-j} = S^2_i + S^2_j - 2S_{ij}$, where S^2_i is the variance for variable i and S^2_j is the variance for variable j and s_{ij} is their covariance. What do you think $\hat{\varepsilon}$ will be equal to in this case?

8. Consider the following real data, where the dependent variable is the Beck depression score:

	WINTER	SPRING	SUMMER	FALL
1	7.50	11.55	1.00	1.21
2	7.00	9.00	5.00	15.00
3	1.00	1.00	.00	.00
4	.00	.00	.00	.00
5	1.06	.00	1.10	4.00
6	1.00	2.50	.00	2.00
7	2.50	.00	.00	2.00
8	4.50	1.06	2.00	2.00
9	5.00	2.00	3.00	5.00
10	2.00	3.00	4.21	3.00
11	7.00	7.35	5.88	9.00
12	2.50	2.00	.01	2.00
13	11.00	16.00	13.00	13.00
14	8.00	10.50	1.00	11.00

(a) Run this on SPSS or SAS as a single group repeated measures. Is it significant at the .05 level, assuming sphericity?

(b) Is the adjusted univariate test significant at the .05 level?

(c) Is the multivariate test significant at the .05 level?

9. Marketing researchers are conducting a study to evaluate both consumer beliefs and the stability of those beliefs about the following three brands of toothpaste: Crest, Colgate, and Arm & Hammer. The beliefs to be assessed are (1) good taste and (2) cavity prevention. They also wish to determine the extent to which the beliefs are moderated by sex and by age (20–35, 36–50, and 51 and up). The subjects will be asked their beliefs at two points in time separated by a 2-month interval.

(a) Set up schematically the appropriate repeated-measures design.

(b) Show the syntax needed to run the analysis using SPSS GLM (including the DATA step) and/or SAS PROC GLM (including the INPUT lines).

10. Consider the following data for a single group repeated-measures design:

$$k = 4, n = 8, \varepsilon = .70, \alpha = .05$$

(a) Find the degrees of freedom for the unadjusted univariate test, the Greenhouse–Geisser test, and the conservative test.

(b) Suppose there were no true differences in means and that an investigator had obtained $F = 3.29$ for this case and used the unadjusted test. What type of error would he make?

(c) Suppose there are real mean differences and a different investigator in a replication study had obtained $F = 4.03$ and applied the conservative test. What type of error would he make?

11. A researcher is interested in the smoking behavior of a group of 30 professional men, 10 of whom are 30–40 years of age, 10 are 41–50, and the remaining 10 are 51–60. She wishes to determine whether how much they smoke is influenced by the time of day (morning or afternoon) and by context (at home or in the office). The men are observed in each of the four situations and the number of cigarettes smoked is recorded. She also wishes to determine whether the age of the men influences their smoking behavior.

(a) What type of repeated-measures design is this?

(b) Show the SPSS and/or SAS syntax needed to obtain the overall test results (including the DATA step in SPSS and the INPUT step in SAS).

12. Find an article from one of the better journals in your content area from within the last 5 years that used a repeated-measures design. Answer the following questions:

(a) What type (in terms of between and within factors) of design was used?

(b) Did the authors do a multivariate analysis?

(c) Did the authors do a univariate analysis? Was it the unadjusted or adjusted univariate test?

(d) Was any mention made of the relative power of the adjusted univariate versus multivariate approach?

REFERENCES

Algina, J., & Keselman, H. J. (1997). Detecting repeated measures effects with univariate and multivariate statistics. *Psychological Methods, 2*, 208–218.

Barcikowski, R. S., & Robey, R. R. (1984). Decisions in a single group repeated measures analysis: Statistical tests and three computer packages. *American Statistician, 38*, 248–250.

Bock, R. D. (1975). *Multivariate statistical methods in behavioral research.* New York, NY: McGraw-Hill.

Boik, R. J. (1981). A priori tests in repeated measures design: Effects of nonsphericity. *Psychometrika, 46*, 241–255.

Box, G.E.P. (1954). Some theorems on quadratic forms applied in the study of analysis of variance problems: II. Effect of inequality of variance and of correlation between errors in the two-way classification. *Annals of Mathematical Statistics, 25*, 484–498.

Cohen, J. (1977). *Statistical power analysis for the behavioral sciences.* New York, NY: Academic Press.

Collier, R. O., Baker, F. B., Mandeville, C. K., & Hayes, T. F. (1967). Estimates of test size for several test procedures on conventional variance ratios in the repeated measures design. *Psychometrika, 32*, 339–353.

Davidson, M. L. (1972). Univariate versus multivariate tests in repeated measures experiments. *Psychological Bulletin, 77*, 446–452.

Elashoff, J. D. (1981). Data for the panel session in software for repeated measures analysis of variance. *Proceedings of the Statistical Computing Section of the American Statistical Association.*

Green, S. (1990, April). *Power analysis in repeated measures analysis of variance with heterogeneity correlated trials.* Paper presented at the annual meeting of the American Educational Research Association, Boston, MA.

Greenhouse, S. W., & Geisser, S. (1959). On methods in the analysis of profile data. *Psychometrika, 24*, 95–112.

Huck, S., Cormier, W., & Bounds, W. (1974). *Reading statistics and research.* New York, NY: Harper & Row.

Huynh, H., & Feldt, L. S. (1970). Conditions under which mean square ratios in repeated measurement designs have exact F distributions. *Journal of the American Statistical Association, 65*, 1582–1589.

Huynh, H., & Feldt, L. (1976). Estimation of the Box collection for degrees of freedom from sample data in the randomized block and split plot designs. *Journal of Educational Statistics, 1*, 69–82.

Johnson, N., & Wichern, D. (1988). *Applied multivariate statistical analysis* (2nd ed.). Englewood Cliffs, NJ: Prentice-Hall.

Keppel, G., & Wickens, T. D. (2004). *Design and analysis: A researcher's handbook* (4th ed.). Upper Saddle River, NJ: Prentice Hall.

Keselman, H. J., Rogan, J. C., Mendoza, J. L., & Breen, L. L. (1980). Testing the validity conditions of repeated measures F tests. *Psychological Bulletin, 87*, 479–481.

Kirk, R. E. (1982). *Experimental design: Procedures for the behavioral sciences.* Belmont, CA: Brooks-Cole.

Kvet, E. (1982). *Excusing elementary students from regular classroom activities for the study of instrumental music: The effect of sixth grade reading, language and mathematics achievement.* Unpublished doctoral dissertation, University of Cincinnati, OH.

Maxwell, S. E. (1980). Pairwise multiple comparisons in repeated measures designs. *Journal of Educational Statistics, 5,* 269–287.

Maxwell, S. E., & Delaney, H. D. (2004). *Designing experiments and analyzing data: A model comparison perspective* (2nd ed.). Mahwah, NJ: Lawrence Erlbaum.

Morrison, D. F. (1976). *Multivariate statistical methods.* New York, NY: McGraw-Hill.

Myers, J. L. (1979). *Fundamentals of experimental design.* Boston, MA: Allyn & Bacon.

Nichols. D. P. (1993). Obtaining nonorthogonal contrasts in repeated measures designs. *Keywords,* number 52. Chicago, SPSS, Inc. Retrieved from SPSS website: ftp://public.dhe.ibm.com/software/analytics/spss/support/Stats/Docs/Statistics/Articles/nonortho.htm

O'Brien, R., & Kaiser, M. (1985). MANOVA method for analyzing repeated measures designs: An extensive primer. *Psychological Bulletin, 97*(2), 316–333.

Potthoff, R. F., & Roy, S. N. (1964). A generalized multivariate analysis of variance model useful especially for growth curve problems. *Biometrika, 51,* 313–326.

Robey, R. R., & Barcikowski, R. S. (1984). Calculating the statistical power of the univariate and multivariate repeated measures analyses of variance for the single group case under various conditions. *Educational and Psychological Measurement, 44,* 137–143.

Rogan, J. C., Keselman, H. J., & Mendoza, J. L. (1979). Analysis of repeated measurements. *British Journal of Mathematical and Statistical Psychology, 32,* 269–286.

Rouanet, H., & Lepine, D. (1970). Comparisons between treatments in a repeated measures design: ANOVA and multivariate methods. *British Journal of Mathematical and Statistical Psychology, 23,* 147–163.

Stevens, J. P. (1986). *Applied multivariate statistics for the social sciences.* Hillsdale, NJ: Lawrence Erlbaum Associates.

Stoloff, P. H. (1967). *An empirical evaluation of the effects of violating the assumption of homogeneity of covariance for the repeated measures design of the analysis of variance* (Tech. Rep.). College Park: University of Maryland.

Winer, B. J. (1971). *Statistical principles in experimental design* (2nd ed.). New York, NY: McGraw-Hill.

Wynd, C. A. (1992). Relaxation imagery used for stress reduction in the prevention of smoking relapse. *Journal of Advanced Nursing, 17,* 294–302.

Chapter 13

HIERARCHICAL LINEAR MODELING

13.1 INTRODUCTION

In the social sciences, nested data structures are very common. As Burstein (1980) noted, "much of what goes on in education occurs within some group context" (p. 158). Nested data (which can yield correlated observations) occurs whenever participants are clustered together in groups, as is frequently found in social science research. For example, students in the same school will typically be more alike than students from different schools. Responses of clients to counseling for those clients clustered together in therapy groups will depend to some extent on the group dynamics, resulting in a within-therapy group dependency (Kreft & de Leeuw, 1998). *Yet, a key inferential assumption made in virtually any statistical technique (including regression, ANOVA, etc.) used in the social sciences (and covered in this text) is that the observations are independent.*

Kenny and Judd (1986) noted that while nonindependence is commonly treated as a nuisance, there are still "many occasions when nonindependence is the substantive problem that we are trying to understand in psychological research" (p. 431). These authors refer to researchers interested in studying social interaction. Kenny and Judd note that social interaction by definition implies nonindependence. If a researcher is interested in studying social interaction, or behavior that occurs in various settings or contexts, the inherent nonindependence is not so much a statistical problem to be surmounted as a focus of interest.

Figure 13.1 provides a general depiction of a two-level nested design, where such dependence is often present. The lower or first level comprises the participants, each of which is a member of or belongs to only one cluster. Within each cluster are n participants (which may vary across clusters), and N refers to the number of clusters in the design. Examples of such two level designs include employees within workplaces, soldiers within military units, households within neighborhoods, and even citizens within nations. These scenarios, as well as students nested within schools and clients within therapy groups, are examples of two-level designs.

■ **Figure 13.1:** General depiction of a two-level design, with participants nested in clusters.

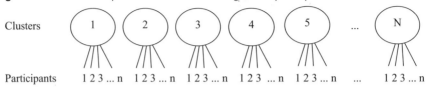

Such clustering or nestedness does not always involve just two levels. A commonly encountered three-level design found in educational research involves students (level one) nested within classrooms (level two), clustered within schools (level three). Individuals (level one) are nested within families (level two) that are clustered in neighborhoods (level three). Clients (level one) are frequently counseled in groups (level two) that are clustered within counseling centers (level three). There is an endless list of such groupings. When data are clustered in these ways, the use of multilevel modeling is often needed to provide accurate statistical inference.

Although nested data may suggest use of multilevel modeling, a key consideration is the nature of the clustering or grouping variable. If participants are nested or grouped in what is considered to be a fixed factor, then traditional analysis may be appropriate. A fixed factor may be thought of as one where if a replication study were to be done, the same levels of that factor would be included in the study. A classic example is a two-group or multiple-group experimental design, where traditional analysis of variance (ANOVA) may be used. In this case, treatment group membership is almost always considered to be a fixed factor, so that if the study were replicated, the same set of treatment conditions would be implemented. Note that there is no consideration that the treatment conditions represent a sample from a population of conditions that could have been included in the study. Rather, all the conditions of interest are included in the study.

Consider, however the nature of the participants included in the standard experimental design. If a replication study were conducted, a different set of participants would likely be included in the study. That is, the participants are thought to represent a sample from a larger population of interest. Participants, thus, are considered to be a random factor. In the traditional experimental design, then, one random factor is included (often individuals), and one or more fixed factors of interest (e.g., treatment conditions, gender) are included.

The key for recognizing the need for multilevel analysis is that such analysis is often needed when two or more factors in the design are considered to be random factors. For example, with students nested in schools, both students and schools are likely to be considered as random factors, so that if the study were replicated, a different set of students and schools would be included (or sampled) in the study. Stated in another way, both students and schools may be considered as representing a larger population of students and schools, respectively. For clients nested within each of many therapists, both clients and therapists may be considered as random factors, as would employees and workplaces in a study involving, for example, factors affecting worker productivity. Thus, it is the inclusion of multiple random factors in a research design that signals the need for multilevel analysis.

13.2 PROBLEMS USING SINGLE-LEVEL ANALYSES OF MULTILEVEL DATA

Sophisticated estimation techniques, developed mostly in the late 1970s, led to the creation of multilevel software programs that greatly facilitated use of multilevel modeling (Arnold, 1992; Raudenbush & Bryk, 2002). Before this time, researchers typically used single-level regression models to examine relationships between variables at different levels (e.g., student and school), despite the expected violation of the independence assumption. This mismatch between design characteristics and analysis model may be problematic for a variety of reasons.

First, suppose a researcher is interested in the relationship between students' test scores and characteristics of the schools they attend. A design of such a study may involve a random selection of schools, followed by a random selection of students within each of the schools. Note that schools and students would be considered as random factors, as each represents a sample from a larger population of interest, suggesting a need for multilevel analysis. When investigating the question of interest, a researcher who chose to ignore dependency in the data would have two analytical choices using single-level modeling. The researcher could aggregate the student outcome data to the school level and use resultant school-level data in a single-level regression analysis. In this case, the outcome would often be the school's average student score, with predictors consisting of school descriptors and average school characteristics summarized across students within each school. One of the primary problems with such an analysis is that valuable information is lost concerning variability of students' scores *within* schools, statistical power may be decreased, and the ecological validity of the inferences has been compromised (Hox, 2010; Kreft & de Leeuw, 1998).

Alternatively, the researcher could disaggregate the student- and school-level data. This generally undesirable form of modeling would involve using students as the unit of analysis and ignoring the nonindependence of students' scores within each school. In the single-level regression that would be used with disaggregated data, the outcome would be the student's test score, with predictors including student and school characteristics. The problem in this analysis is that variation across students and schools is, most likely, improperly combined in the model residual term and does not properly reflect variation at the student and school levels. An important consequence here is that the standard errors associated with the estimate of the effects of school predictors may be substantially underestimated. Such misestimated standard errors then lead to inflated type I error rates and poor confidence interval estimates. This problem worsens when there is greater dependency among the observations.

A commonly used measure of the degree of dependence between individuals is called the intra-class correlation (ICC), or residual ICC when explanatory variables are included in the model. The more that characteristics of the context (say, school) are related to the individual (student) outcome of interest, the greater will be the ICC. And, as the ICC is larger, the greater the need is for multilevel analysis. For two-level data-sets (where there is only one level of clustering), the ICC (when numerically positive, which is generally the case) can be interpreted as the proportion of the total variance in the outcome that occurs between the clusters (as opposed to within the clusters). Hedges and Hedberg (2007) note that ICCs in educational research typically range from .05 to .20, although, of course, smaller or larger values may be obtained.

However, it is important to realize that even an ICC that is slightly larger than zero can have a dramatic effect on type I error rates, as can be seen in Table 6.1, which is taken from Scariano and Davenport (1987). Note from the table that for an ICC of only .01, with three clusters (or groups) and 30 participants per cluster, the actual alpha is inflated to .0985 for a one-way ANOVA F test that does not take into account the positive ICC. With a three-cluster $n = 30$ scenario and an ICC of .10, the actual alpha is .4917, which means that a researcher has about a 50% chance of declaring that group mean differences are present, when none truly are.

Fortunately, researchers do not have to choose between the loss of information associated with aggregation of dependent data or the inflated type I error rates associated with disaggregated data. Thus, instead of choosing a single level at which to conduct analyses of clustered or hierarchical data, researchers can instead use the technique called multilevel or hierarchical linear modeling. This chapter will provide an introduction to some basic multilevel models. Several excellent multilevel modeling texts are available (e.g., Heck, Thomas, & Tabata, 2014; Hox, 2010; Kreft & de Leeuw, 1998; Raudenbush & Bryk, 2002; Snijders & Bosker, 2012) that will provide the interested reader additional details as well as discussion of more advanced topics in multilevel modeling.

Several terms are used to describe essentially the same family of multilevel models including multilevel modeling, hierarchical linear modeling (HLM), (co)variance component models, multilevel regression models, and linear mixed effects models. The terms multilevel modeling and hierarchical linear modeling will be used here.

In this chapter, formulation of a two-level model will be presented first. This will be followed with a two-level example where students are nested within schools. In this example, we will begin with what is called an unconditional model (no predictors at either level). Then, we add a predictor at level 1 and then predictors at level 2. This model building approach (from simple to more complex models) is a common practice in multilevel modeling. We also consider the centering of explanatory variables in some detail, which is an important yet sometimes confusing aspect of multilevel modeling. We then consider a second example where the study goal is to evaluate the efficacy of treatments on a dependent variable in the context of a cluster randomized trial. For each example, we show how multilevel analysis can be conducted using SAS and SPSS and interpret analysis results.

13.3 FORMULATION OF THE MULTILEVEL MODEL

There are two common ways to display the analysis models for multilevel modeling. Multilevel models may be expressed as a set of equations at each level separately, or each level's equations can be combined to provide a single expression. The multiple levels formulation is often easier to comprehend especially when you are first learning HLM but the combined equation also has advantages. With the multilevel expression, the level-1 or lower-level model contains variables measured at the micro level (e.g., student level) while the level-2 or upper-level model contains variables at the cluster or macro level (e.g., the school level). We will use both the multilevel and combined equations here.

13.4 TWO-LEVEL MODEL—GENERAL FORMULATION

Before presenting the general formulation of the two-level model, some terminology will be explained. First, Raudenbush and Bryk (2002) distinguish between unconditional and conditional models. An unconditional model is one in which no predictors (at any of the levels) are included. A conditional model includes at least one predictor at any of the levels. A commonly used model in HLM is one that is conditional at level-1 and unconditional at level-2. We will see later that such a model, when it has variable intercepts and slopes, is referred to as a random-coefficient model.

Second, output obtained from multilevel modeling software is often separated into what are called fixed and random effects, which are related to the fixed and random factors described previously. In brief, the effects of a random factor (e.g., student, school) are summarized with variances (and sometimes covariances), whereas the effect of a fixed factor is summarized (as they are in single-level regression) with a regression coefficient. We will also see that it is possible that a fixed factor may have both fixed and random effects. In the following example, students are nested in schools, and the dependent variable is math achievement. There is one explanatory variable at the student level, student *ses* (a continuous variable), and the primary variable of interest at the school level (*public*) is a dummy-coded variable indicating whether a school is public (coded as 1) or private (coded as 0).

First, we consider the random effects. Similar to analysis of variance, the effect of a student is captured initially as a deviation of given student's *math* score around the predicted value for the school attended by that student. The deviations for a set of students within a school are then summarized by a variance term, reflecting within-school variance in the *math* scores (often modeled as constant across schools). Similarly, the effect of school is captured initially as a deviation of a given school's *math* mean around the grand mean, and the deviations for the sample of schools are then summarized by a school-level variance term, reflecting between-school variance in the math scores.

In contrast, the impact of school type (public vs. private), a fixed factor, is summarized by a regression coefficient (i.e., a fixed effect) capturing the difference in predicted *math* scores between these two school types. Also, the impact of student *ses* is summarized by a regression coefficient (fixed effect). However, note that the impact of student *ses* on *math* achievement could be different across schools. These varying effects can be considered as an interaction between a fixed factor (student *ses*) and a random factor (school), with the interaction interpreted in the usual way, that is, the effect of one variable (*ses*) depends on school. Such an interaction is considered to be a random factor and thus is represented by a variance term, describing the degree to which the within-school *ses-math* slopes vary across schools. If these terms are not yet clear, working through the multilevel regression models, to which we now turn, should help you better understand these effects.

The two-level example with students nested in schools involves estimating the association between *math* test scores and a measure of student *ses* at the student level. With the multilevel formulation of the model, the level-1 or student-level model is

$$Y_{ij} = \beta_{0j} + \beta_{1j}(X_{ij} - \overline{X}_j) + r_{ij}, \tag{1}$$

where Y_{ij} is student i's *math* score in a given school j, X_{ij} is student i's *ses* score, and $\overline{X}_j$ is the mean *ses* score for the sample of students at the given school j. The expression $X_{ij} - \overline{X}_j$ is referred to as group-mean centering because the group, or school *ses* mean, is subtracted from each student's *ses* score. We discuss centering in more detail in section 13.6 but note for now that a primary advantage of using group-mean centering is that the regression coefficient, β_{1j}, represents the pure within-school association between student *ses* and *math* scores. As such, β_{1j} represents the expected change in student *math* as student *ses* increases by 1 point in that school. Note that other forms of centering for *ses* or use of raw or uncentered *ses* scores may result in β_{1j} representing an undesirable blend of the within-and between-school associations of *math* and *ses*, associations that may be different. Further, when group-mean centering is used in Equation 1, β_{0j} is the school mean *math* score (or $\overline{Y}_j$). A simple way to understand why this is so is to recall that the regression line in a simple linear regression equation runs through $\overline{Y}$ and $\overline{X}$. Thus, when $\overline{X}_j$ is inserted into Equation 1 for X_{ij} to obtain the expected Y_{ij} score, the expected Y_{ij} score is $\overline{Y}_j$ (due to $\overline{Y}_j$ and $\overline{X}_j$ lying on the regression line), and all terms on the right hand side of Equation 1 disappear except for β_{0j}, which then must be equal to $\overline{Y}_j$. The r_{ij} represents the residual or the deviation of student i's *math* score from the Y value predicted from the equation. It is assumed that r_{ij} is normally distributed with a mean of zero and variance σ^2, or $r_{ij} \sim N(0, \sigma^2)$.

As mentioned earlier, a commonly used model is the random-coefficient model, which includes predictors at level 1 but has no predictors at level 2 and allows both the level-1 intercept (i.e., β_{0j}) and slope (i.e., β_{1j}) to vary. Why is this model used? First, the model will provide us with the overall averages of the regression coefficients in Equation 1. Given that these coefficients are readily interpretable (as a given school's *math* mean and the within-school *ses-math* slope), the average of these quantities would provide the overall *math* average across students and schools and the overall *ses-math* slope, with the latter indicating the degree to which, averaging across schools, student *ses* and *math* are related. In addition to these averages, it is perhaps natural to think that schools have different *math* means and that the association between *ses* and *math* may also differ across schools. We can estimate a school-level model that will provide for us the mean value of each of these coefficients across the sample and estimate the extent to which each coefficient varies (and covaries) across schools. Further, in subsequent models, it is a common research focus to attempt to account for such variation with school-level, or more generally cluster-level, variables.

Note that in the upper- or school-level model, *the regression coefficients,* β_{0j} and β_{1j}, in Equation 1 become outcome variables at the school level. This school-level model is

$$\beta_{0j} = \gamma_{00} = u_{0j} \tag{2}$$

and

$$\beta_{1j} = \gamma_{10} + u_{1j}. \tag{3}$$

In Equation 2, β_{0j} is the intercept or school *math m*ean, due to the use of group-mean centering in Equation 1, and, thus, γ_{00} *is the average of the individual school intercepts across schools, or the overall math mean,* and u_{0j} is a deviation of a given school's math mean from this overall average. Note that we previously labeled these deviations as random effects. These effects or residuals are assumed to be normally distributed with a mean of zero and a variance denoted by τ_{00}, or $u_{0j} \sim N(0, \tau_{00})$. The regression coefficient, γ_{00}, is regarded as a fixed effect.

Similarly, in Equation 3, β_{1j} represents the *ses-math* achievement slope for a given school. As such, γ_{10}, the fixed effect, *is the average of the student-level ses-math slopes across schools* (or, in other words, the average measure of the association between student *math* and *ses*), and u_{1j} is deviation of a given school's slope around this average slope value, where these residuals (or random effects) are assumed to be normally distributed with a mean of zero and a variance of τ_{11}, or $u_{1j} \sim N(0, \tau_{11})$. In addition to the assumptions given, it is commonly assumed that the intercept and slope (β_{0j} and β_{1j}, or equivalently u_{0j} and u_{1j}) are bivariately normally distributed with covariance τ_{01}, or equivalently τ_{10} (Raudenbush & Bryk, 2002). If so, the school-level random effects would be summarized by the variance-covariance matrix

$$\begin{bmatrix} \tau_{00} & \tau_{10} \\ \tau_{01} & \tau_{11} \end{bmatrix}. \tag{4}$$

Note that variances and covariances, as well as fixed effects, can be tested for significance to guide model specification.

A combined equation can be formed by replacing β_{0j} and β_{1j} in Equation 1 with the right sides of Equations 2 and 3, respectively. This combined model is

$$Y_{ij} = \gamma_{00} + \gamma_{10}(X_{ij} - \bar{X}_j) + u_{0j} + u_{1j}(X_{ij} - \bar{X}_j) + r_{ij}. \tag{5}$$

Note that the number and nature of the effects can be determined perhaps more easily with this model formulation than the multilevel one. Here, there are two fixed effects (γ_{00} and γ_{10}) and three random effects (u_{0j}, u_{1j}, r_{ij}). Further, note that the error variation of the outcome involves between- and within-school components and includes the variation in the *ses-math* slopes across schools, reflected by the term $u_{1j}(X_{ij} - \bar{X}_j)$. This latter term allows the variation in Y_{ij}, particularly the between-school variation, to depend on values of the student predictor. The heterogeneous variance can be understood by imagining a situation where high *ses* students perform similarly high on *math*, no matter which school they attend. For high *ses* students, then, variation across schools in *math* would be small. On the other hand, suppose some schools are much more effective than other schools in educating low *ses* students. Thus, for low *ses* students, there would be great differences in *math* achievement *across* schools. Accounting for such between-school differences by introducing school-level predictors is often a substantive research goal. In addition, while there are five effects in the model, six parameters would be estimated here: the two fixed effects, the student-level variance (σ^2), and the three variance-covariance terms for the school effects as depicted in Equation 4.

Given Equation 1, there is another fairly common model specification for the random effects besides that given in Equation 4. This model allows only the intercept of Equation 1 to vary across schools and is thus called a random intercept model. The student-level equation is the same as Equation 1, but the school-level equations, presented more succinctly than previously, are now,

$$\begin{cases} \beta_{0j} = \gamma_{00} + u_{0j} \\ \beta_{1j} = \gamma_{10} \end{cases}. \tag{6}$$

In this model, all of the parameters are interpreted the same as before but the *ses-math* slopes are specified to be the same across schools, as no residual term appears in Equation 6 for β_{1j}. This specification is sometimes used when a nonsignificant test result is obtained for τ_{11} in Equation 4 or when parameters cannot be estimated due to nonconvergence. This latter issue may arise when the population variance (τ_{11}) is at or near zero.

Table 13.1 provides a summary of the multilevel models described in this section. These models are commonly used in multilevel modeling. Note that the interpretations of the parameters for the random-coefficient and random intercept models

■ **Table 13.1: Multilevel Models and Parameters Estimated**

Level	Equation	Parameters estimated
	Unconditional model	
1 2	$Y_{ij} = \beta_{0j} + r_{ij}$ $\beta_{0j} = \gamma_{00} + u_{0j}$	The overall outcome average (γ_{00}), within-cluster variance of Y_{ij} (σ^2), and the variance of the cluster means (i.e., the variance of β_{0j}, or τ_{00})
	Random coefficient model	
1 2 2	$Y_{ij} = \beta_{0j} + \beta_{1j}(X_{ij} - \bar{X}_j) + r_{ij}$ $\beta_{0j} = \gamma_{00} + u_{0j}$ $\beta_{1j} = \gamma_{10} + u_{1j}$	The overall outcome average (γ_{00}), the variance of the level-1 residuals (σ^2), the overall association between X_{ij} and Y_{ij} (γ_{10}), the variance of the cluster means (τ_{00}), the variance of the slopes (i.e., the variance of β_{1j}, or τ_{11}), and the covariance of the means and slopes (τ_{01})
	Random intercept model	
1 2 2	$Y_{ij} = \beta_{0j} + \beta_{1j}(X_{ij} - \bar{X}_j) + r_{ij}$ $\beta_{0j} = \gamma_{00} + u_{0j}$ $\beta_{1j} = \gamma_{10}$	The overall outcome average (γ_{00}), the variance of the level-1 residuals (σ^2), the overall association between X_{ij} and Y_{ij} (γ_{10}), and the variance of the cluster means (τ_{00})

depend on the centering used for the predictor variable (X_{ij}). Centering is discussed in section 13.6. Of course, more predictors can be used at level 1, and researchers almost always include predictors at level 2, none of which appears in the equations in Table 13.1. The next section includes predictors at level 2.

Having discussed the general formulation of some two-level models, in the next section we work through a series of models that are often used in multilevel modeling. We first describe the data set and data file layout for a two-level design and provide some descriptive statistics for the data set we are using. When we work through the models, we interpret model parameters and discuss statistical tests that can be used to test various null hypotheses. We also show how such models can be estimated with SAS and SPSS.

13.5 EXAMPLE 1: EXAMINING SCHOOL DIFFERENCES IN MATHEMATICS

The data we are using here, with some modification, appears in Heck et al. (2014) and reflects a two-level design where a random sample of schools ($N = 419$) is selected followed by a random selection of students within the schools ($n = 6,871$).[1] Table 13.2

---

[1] Copyright (2014) from *Multilevel and Longitudinal Modeling with IBM SPSS* by Heck, Thomas, and Tabata. Reproduced by permission of Taylor and Francis Group, LLC, a division of Informa plc.

shows the first 15 cases for the data set used here, and Table 13.3 shows descriptive statistics. In Table 13.2, schcode is the school ID (sorted from 1 to 419), and id is the student ID variable. The student outcome is *math*, and *ses* is the student-level predictor. Note that some of the *ses* scores are negative, which is due to these scores being centered around their respective school *ses* mean. At the school level, the focal variable of interest is the dichotomous *public*, with 73% of the schools in the sample being public. The other school-level variable *meanses*, is included as a control variable, and was formed by computing the mean of the uncentered (raw) student *ses* scores for the students included in the sample from each of the given schools. Scores for mean *ses* were then subsequently centered. Note that the student-level variables in Table 13.2 vary within a school but the school-level variables are constant for each person within a school. Also, note that even though we have variables at two different levels (student and school), all of the variables appear in one data file.

In addition, you might wonder why mean *ses* is needed in the analysis model, given that we have a student *ses* variable. There are two primary reasons for this. First, when student *ses* is group-mean centered, it cannot serve as a control variable for any school-level predictor, because this form of centering makes the student predictor uncorrelated with school predictors. As such, if we wish to use group-mean centering for student *ses* and also control for *ses* differences between schools when we compare public and private schools' *math* performance, mean *ses* must be included as a predictor variable. Second, sometimes, the association between a predictor and an outcome at level 1 (e.g., student *ses* and *math*) may differ from the association of these variables at the school level (e.g., school mean *ses* and school mean *math*). When these associations differ, school mean *ses* is said to have contextual effect on math performance.

■ **Table 13.2: Data Set Showing First 15 Cases**

	schcode	id	math	ses	public	Meanses
1	1	6701	47.14	8.58	0	-2.92
2	1	6702	63.61	5.58	0	-2.92
3	1	6703	57.71	-2.42	0	-2.92
4	1	6704	53.90	-5.42	0	-2.92
5	1	6705	58.01	2.58	0	-2.92
6	1	6706	59.87	1.58	0	-2.92
7	1	6707	62.56	-.42	0	-2.92
8	1	6708	47.01	-6.42	0	-2.92
9	1	6709	72.42	4.58	0	-2.92
10	1	6710	65.84	-.42	0	-2.92
11	1	6711	57.34	.58	0	-2.92
12	1	6712	62.56	-8.42	0	-2.92
13	2	3703	61.95	-7.85	0	6.51
14	2	3704	70.22	6.15	0	6.51
15	2	3705	58.78	4.15	0	6.51

■ Table 13.3: Variables and Descriptive Statistics for HLM Analysis

Variable	Variable name	Values	Mean	SD
		Student-level		
Math achievement	Math	27.42 to 99.98	57.73	8.78
Socioeconomic status	Ses	−21.71 to 24.10	0.00	6.07
		School-level		
School type	Public	1 = public, 0 = other	0.73	0.44
School ses	Meanses	−13.34 to 14.20	0.00	4.94

These within- and between-school associations, sometimes of intrinsic interest, are estimated by including student *ses* and mean *ses* in the same analysis model. Section 13.6.1 discusses contextual effects in more detail.

In the analysis that follows, we assume that the researchers are interested primarily in examining differences between public and private schools in *math* achievement. With these data, researchers can not only examine whether public or private schools have, on average, greater math achievement, but may also examine whether the association between student *ses* and *math* is different for the two school types. What is desired, perhaps, is to determine if there are schools where *math* performance is generally high but that the *ses-math* slope is relatively small. Such a co-occurrence would indicate that there are schools where students of varying *ses* values are all performing relatively high in mathematics and that math performance does not depend in a great way on student *ses*. If such schools are present, the analysis can then determine whether such schools tend to be public or private.

13.5.1 The Unconditional Model

Researchers often begin multilevel analysis with a completely unconditional model. This model provides for us an estimate of the overall average across all students and schools for the outcome (i.e., *math*), as well as an estimate of the variation that is within and between schools for *math*. This model is:

$$\text{math}_{ij} = \beta_{0j} + r_{ij}, \tag{7}$$

where the outcome *math* for student i in school j is modeled as a function of school j's intercept (β_{0j}) and a residual term r_{ij}. Note that when no explanatory variables are included on the right side of the model, the intercept becomes the average of the quantity on the left side. Thus, β_{0j} represents a given school's math mean.

At level 2, school j's intercept (or *math* mean) is modeled as function of a school-level intercept and residual:

$$\beta_{0j} = \gamma_{00} + u_{0j} \tag{8}$$

Again, with no predictors on the right side of the model, γ_{00} represents the average of the school *math* means, or is sometimes referred to as the overall average. The school random effect (i.e., u_{0j}) represents the deviation of a given school's *math* mean from the overall math average. Note that the residual terms in Equations 7 and 8 are assumed to be normally distributed, with a mean of zero, and have constant variance, with the student- or within-school variance denoted by σ^2 and the school-level variance denoted by τ_{00}. The student and school random effects (r_{ij}, u_{0j}) are assumed to be uncorrelated. As before, the combined model is formed by replacing the regression coefficients in Equation 7 with the right-hand side of Equation 8. This model is

$$\text{math}_{ij} = \gamma_{00} + u_{0j} + r_{ij}, \tag{9}$$

where there is one fixed effect (γ_{00}), a school-level random effect (u_{0j}), and a student random effect (r_{ij}), the latter of which is referred to as a residual (not random effect) by SAS and SPSS.

Table 13.4 shows the SAS and SPSS commands needed to estimate Equation 9, and Table 13.5 shows selected analysis results. In Table 13.5, the results from SAS and SPSS are virtually identical with a couple of differences (i.e., degrees of freedom for tests of fixed effects and p values reported for tests of variances). First, in the Fit Statistics table in SAS and in the Information Criteria table of SPSS, −2 Restricted Log Likelihood is a measure of lack of fit (sometimes referred to as model deviance), estimated here to be 48,877.3. This value can be used to conduct a statistical test for the intercept variance (τ_{00}), which we will illustrate shortly. In the Fixed Effect output tables, the intercept (γ_{00}) is estimated to be 57.67, which is the overall *math* average. Typically, the intercept would not be tested for significance, unless zero is a value of interest as the null hypothesis is that $\gamma_{00} = 0$. Note that the degrees of freedom associated with the test of the fixed effect differs between SAS (418) and SPSS (416.066). West, Welch, and Galecki (2014) explain that t tests with multilevel models do not exactly follow a t distribution. As a result, different methods are available to estimate a degrees of freedom for this test. The MIXED procedure in SPSS uses the Satterthwaite method (by default and exclusively) to estimate the degrees of freedom, with this method intended to provide more accurate inferences when small sample sizes are present. SAS PROC MIXED has a variety of methods available to estimate this degrees of freedom. While the Satterthwaite method can be requested in SAS, the syntax in Table 13.3 uses the default method (called containment), which estimates the degrees of freedom based on the model specified for the random effects (West et al., 2014, p. 131).

In the Covariance Parameters table of Table 13.5, the student-level variance in *math* is estimated to be 66.55, and the school-level *math* variance is estimated to be 10.64. The Wald z tests associated with these variances suggest that *math* variation is present in the population within and between schools (the null hypothesis for each variance is that it is zero in the population). Note that when using these z tests

■ **Table 13.4: SAS and SPSS Control Lines for Estimating the Completely Unconditional Model**

SAS	SPSS
(1) PROC MIXED METHOD = REML NOCLPRINT COVTEST NOITPRINT;	(5) MIXED math
	(6) /FIXED=| SSTYPE(3)
(2) CLASS schcode;	(7) /METHOD=REML
(3) MODEL math = / SOLUTION;	(8) /PRINT=G SOLUTION TESTCOV
(4) RANDOM intercept / SUBJECT=schcode; RUN;	(9) /RANDOM=INTERCEPT | SUBJECT(schcode)COVTYPE(VC).

(1) PROC MIXED invokes the mixed modeling procedure; METHOD = REML requests restricted maximum likelihood estimation, NOCLPRINT suppresses printing of the number of schools, COVTEST requests z tests for variance-covariance elements, and NOITPRINT suppresses printing of information on iteration history.

(2) CLASS defines the cluster-level variable and must precede the MODEL statement.

(3) MODEL specifies that math is the dependent variable and no predictors are included, although the intercept (γ_{00}) is included by default, SOLUTION displays fixed effects estimates in the output.

(4) RANDOM specifies random effects for the intercept and the identifier (schcode) indicates that students are nested in schools. This line is omitted when a deviance test is used for τ_{00}.

(5) MIXED invokes the mixed modeling procedure and math is then indicated as the dependent variable.

(6) FIXED indicates that no fixed effects are included in the model although the intercept (γ_{00}) is included by default. SSTYPE(3) requests the type 3 sum of squares.

(7) METHOD requests restricted maximum likelihood estimation.

(8) PRINT requests school-level variance components, the fixed effect estimates and tests, and statistical test results for the variance parameters.

(9) RANDOM specifies random effects for the intercept and the identifier (schcode) indicates that students are nested in schools, COVTYPE(VC) requests the estimation of the intercept variance (τ_{00}). This line is omitted when a deviance test is used for τ_{00}.

for variances, Hox (2010) recommends that the obtained p values be divided by 2 because while this z test is a two-tailed test, variances must be zero or greater. It is important to note that SAS provides these recommended p values, whereas SPSS does not. So, p values obtained from SPSS for variances should be divided by 2 when assessing statistical significance. Given the small p values here, the results indicate, then, that within school, student *math* scores vary and between schools *math* means vary. Note though that these z tests provide approximate p values as variances are not normally distributed. More accurate inference for variances can be obtained by testing model deviances, which are generally preferred over the z tests and is discussed next.

As is the case with other statistical techniques discussed in this book, statistical tests that compare model deviances may often be conducted when maximum likelihood estimation is used. With multilevel modeling, two forms of maximum likelihood estimation are generally available in software programs: Full Maximum Likelihood

■ Table 13.5: Results From the Unconditional Model

SAS

Fit Statistics

-2 Res Log Likelihood	48877.3
AIC (smaller is better)	48881.3
AICC (smaller is better)	48881.3
BIC (smaller is better)	48889.3

Solution for Fixed Effects

Effect	Estimate	Standard Error DF		t Value	Pr > |t|
Intercept	57.6742	0.1883	418	306.34	<.0001

Covariance Parameter Estimates

Cov Parm	Subject	Estimate	Standard Error	Z Value	Pr > Z
Intercept	Schcode	10.6422	1.0287	10.35	<.0001
Residual		66.5507	1.1716	56.80	<.0001

SPSS

Information Criteria[a]

-2 Restricted Log Likelihood	48877.256
Akaike's Information Criterion (AIC)	48881.256
Hurvich and Tsai's Criterion (AICC)	48881.257
Bozdogan's Criterion (CAIC)	48896.925
Schwarz's Bayesian Criterion (BIC)	48894.925

The information criteria are displayed in smaller-is-better forms.

[a] Dependent Variable: math.

Fixed Effects

Estimates of Fixed Effects[a]

Parameter	Estimate	Std. Error	Df	T	Sig.	95% Confidence Interval Lower Bound	Lower Bound
Intercept	57.674234	.188266	416.066	306.344	.000	57.304162	58.044306

[a] Dependent Variable: math.

Covariance Parameters

Estimates of Covariance Parameters[a]

Parameter		Estimate	Std. Error	Wald Z	Sig.	95% Confidence Interval Lower Bound	Lower Bound
Residual		66.550655	1.171618	56.802	.000	64.293492	68.887062
Intercept [subject = schcode]	Variance	10.642209	1.028666	10.346	.000	8.805529	12.861989

[a] Dependent Variable: math.

(FML) and Restricted Maximum Likelihood (RML), with the latter preferred when the number of clusters is relatively small because it provides for unbiased estimates of variance and covariances. However, when RML is used, only variances and covariances (not fixed effects) may be properly tested with the deviance method. When FML is used, both fixed effects and variance-covariance elements may be tested using model deviances, although West et al. (2014, p. 36) recommend deviance tests of variance-covariances be done with RML only and tests of fixed effects be conducted with FML. In this example, RML, which is the default estimation procedure for SAS and SPSS, is used for estimation.

To conduct a test using deviances to determine if the intercept varies across schools, two models, one nested in the other, need to be estimated. Then, one obtains an overall measure of model fit, the deviance, and computes the difference between the nested and full model deviances. This difference, in effect, follows a chi-square distribution with a given alpha level (i.e., .05) and degrees of freedom, where the latter is equal to the difference in the number of parameters estimated between the full and nested model. Note that since the intercept variance cannot be negative, Snijders and Bosker (2012, p. 98) recommend halving the p values, which is the same as doubling the alpha level used for the test (i.e., .10.)

To test the variance of the intercept ($H_0 : \tau_{00} = 0$) using deviances, the two comparison models must be identical in terms of the fixed effects and can only differ in the variances estimated. Thus, to estimate an appropriate comparison model here, Equation 7 is the level-1 model. The level-2 model is the same as Equation 8 except there is no u_{0j} term in the model for β_{0j}, as each u_{0j} is constrained to be zero. As such, the variance of β_{0j} (i.e., τ_{00}) in this new model is constrained to be zero. This new model, then, is nested in the three-parameter model, represented by Equation 9, and estimates two parameters: one fixed effect (like the previous model) but just one variance component, the student-level variance (σ^2). Note that to obtain the results for this nested model, you use the same syntax as shown in Table 13.4, except that the RANDOM subcommand line is removed, which constrains τ_{00} to zero.

To complete the statistical test, we estimated this reduced two-parameter model and found that the deviance, or the quantity -2 times the log likelihood, is 49,361.120, whereas the original unconditional model deviance is 48,877.256 (as shown in Table 13.5). The difference between these deviances is 483.864, which is greater than the corresponding chi-square value of 2.706 (.10, $df = 1$). Therefore, we conclude that the school *math* means vary in the population.

Summarizing the results obtained from this unconditional model, performance on the *math* test is, on average, 57.7. *Math* scores vary both within and between schools. Inspecting the variance estimates indicates that a majority of *math* variance is within schools. In this two-level design, the intraclass correlation provides a measure of the proportion of variability in the outcome that exists between clusters. For the example here, the intraclass correlation provides a measure of the proportion of variability in *math* that is *between* schools. The formula for the intraclass correlation for a two-level model is:

$$\rho_{ICC} = \frac{\tau_{00}}{\tau_{00} + \sigma^2} \tag{10}$$

For the current data set, the intraclass correlation estimate then is

$$\rho_{ICC} = \frac{\tau_{00}}{\tau_{00} + \sigma^2} = \frac{10.642}{10.642 + 66.551} = .138. \tag{11}$$

Thus, about 14% of the variation in *math* scores is between schools. According to Spybrook and Raudenbush (2009, p. 304), the intraclass correlation for academic outcomes in two-level educational research with students nested in schools is often in the range from 0.1 to 0.2, which is consistent with the data here and suggests that an important part of the math variation is present across schools.

13.5.2 Random-Coefficient Model

A second model often used in multilevel analysis is the random-coefficient model. In this model, one or more predictors are added to the level-1 model, and the lower-level intercept and slope for at least one of the predictors are specified to vary across clusters. In this example, student *ses* will be included as a predictor variable and we will determine if the association between *ses* and *math* varies across schools. The level-1 or student-level model is

$$math_{ij} = \beta_{0j} + \beta_{1j}\left(ses_{ij} - \overline{ses}_j\right) + r_{ij}, \tag{12}$$

where group-mean centered *ses* is now included as a predictor at level 1. As discussed in section 13.4, with group-mean centering, β_{0j} represents a given school *j*'s math mean, and β_{1j} represents the within-school association between *ses* and *math*. The student-level residual term represents the part of the student-level *math* score that is not predictable by *ses*, and $r_{ij} \sim N(0, \sigma^2)$.

In the school-level model, the regression coefficients of Equation 12 serve as outcome variables and no school-level predictors are included. This model is

$$\begin{cases} \beta_{0j} = \gamma_{00} + u_{0j} \\ \beta_{1j} = \gamma_{10} + u_{1j} \end{cases}, \tag{13}$$

where the two fixed effects (i.e.,γ_{00} and γ_{10}) represent the overall *math* average and overall average of the student-level slopes relating *ses* to *math*. We allow the residual terms to vary and covary, as in Equation 4. The combined expression for the multilevel model is then

$$math_{ij} = \gamma_{00} + \gamma_{10}\left(ses_{ij} - \overline{ses}_j\right) + u_{0j} + u_{1j}\left(ses_{ij} - \overline{ses}_j\right) + r_{ij}. \tag{14}$$

Table 13.6 shows the syntax that can be used to estimate Equation 14 using SAS and SPSS. Table 13.7 shows selected SPSS results, as results from SAS, as we have seen, are very similar. In Table 13.7, the deviance for the random-coefficient model is 48,479.875. Recall that since RML was used, we cannot use this deviance to test any hypotheses associated with the fixed effects. However, we will use this deviance to test the slope variance (i.e., τ_{11}). The estimates of the fixed effects are that the mean *math* score is 57.7, and the average of the within-school *ses-math* slopes is .313, indicating that student *math* scores increase by about .3 points as student *ses* increases by 1 point. The corresponding t test ($t = 18.759$) and p value ($< .001$) for this association indicates a positive association is present in the population.

For the variance and covariance estimates, we begin with the student-level residual variance in Table 13.7, which is 62.18 ($p < .001$), indicating that significant student-level variance in *math* remains after adding *ses*. The estimates for the school variance-covariance components are readily seen in the last output table in Table 13.7, which is the variance-covariance matrix for the school random effects. This table shows that the variance in *math* means between schools is 10.91, the variance in slopes is .01, and the covariance between the school *math* means and *ses-math* slopes

■ **Table 13.6: SAS and SPSS Control Lines for Estimating the Random-Coefficient Model**

SAS	SPSS
``` PROC MIXED METHOD = REML NOCLPRINT COVTEST NOITPRINT; CLASS schcode; (1) MODEL math = ses / SOLUTION; (2) RANDOM intercept ses / type = un SUBJECT=schcode; RUN; ```	``` (3) MIXED math WITH ses (4) /FIXED= ses	SSTYPE(3) /METHOD=REML /PRINT=G SOLUTION TESTCOV (5) /RANDOM=INTERCEPT ses	SUBJECT(schcode) COVTYPE(UN). ```

(1) The MODEL statement adds ses as a predictor variable.
(2) The RANDOM statement specifies that random effects appear in the model for the school math means and the ses-math slopes; type = un specifies that a variance-covariance matrix be estimated for the school random effects. Note that removing ses from this statement would specify a random intercept model, which constrains τ_{11} and τ_{01} to zero.
(3) The MIXED statement indicates that ses is included as a covariate.
(4) The FIXED statement requests that a fixed effect be estimated for ses.
(5) The RANDOM statement specifies that random effects appear in the model for the school math means and the ses-math slopes; COVTYPE (UN) specifies that a variance-covariance matrix be estimated for the school random effects. Note that removing ses from this statement would specify a random intercept model, which constrains τ_{11} and τ_{01} to zero.

■ Table 13.7: SPSS Results From the Random-Coefficient Model

Information Criteria[a]	
-2 Restricted Log Likelihood	48479.875
Akaike's Information Criterion (AIC)	48487.875
Hurvich and Tsai's Criterion (AICC)	48487.881
Bozdogan's Criterion (CAIC)	48519.215
Schwarz's Bayesian Criterion (BIC)	48515.215

The information criteria are displayed in smaller-is-better forms.

[a] Dependent Variable: math.

Fixed Effects

Estimates of Fixed Effects[a]

Parameter	Estimate	Std. Error	Df	t	Sig.	95% Confidence Interval	
						Lower Bound	Upper Bound
Intercept	57.675771	.188222	416.090	306.425	.000	57.305787	58.045755
Sesgrpcen	.312781	.016674	384.194	18.759	.000	.279998	.345565

[a] Dependent Variable: math.

Covariance Parameters

Estimates of Covariance Parameters[a]

Parameter		Estimate	Std. Error	Wald Z	Sig.	95% Confidence Interval	
						Lower Bound	Upper Bound
Residual		62.176171	1.122366	55.397	.000	60.014834	64.415345
Intercept + sesgrpcen [subject = schcode]	UN (1,1)	10.909371	1.028421	10.608	.000	9.068958	13.123270
	UN (2,1)	−.162162	.067697	−2.395	.017	−.294846	−.029477
	UN (2,2)	.011194	.007102	1.576	.115	.003228	.038814

[a] Dependent Variable: math.

Random Effect Covariance Structure (G)[a]

	Intercept | schcode	sesgrpcen | schcode
Intercept | schcode	10.909371	−.162162
sesgrpcen | schcode	−.162162	.011194

Unstructured

[a] Dependent Variable: math.

is −.16. The correlation, then, between school *math* means and *ses-math* slopes is −.16/$\sqrt{10.91 \times .01}$ = −.48. This negative correlation indicates that schools with higher *math* means tend to have flatter *ses-math* slopes, suggesting that math performance in some schools is relatively high *and* more equitable for students having various *ses* values. Note that the value of the slope variance (.01) is not, perhaps, readily interpretable and in an absolute sense seems small. To render the slope variance more meaningful, we can compute the expression $\gamma_{10} \pm 2 \times \sqrt{\tau_{11}}$, which obtains values of β_{1j} that are 2 standard deviations above and below the mean slope value. For these data, these slope values are .113 and .513. Thus, this suggests that there are schools in the sample where the *ses-math* slope is fairly small (about a .11 increase in *math* for a point change in *ses*), whereas this association in other schools is stronger (about a .51 increase in *math* for a point change in *ses*). Further, using the *z* tests, the *p* values provided in the Covariance Parameters table indicate that the variance in the *math* means (*p* < .001) and the covariance of the *math* means and *ses-math* slopes (*p* = .017) is significant at the .05 level but that the variance in *ses-math* slopes is not (*p* / 2 = .115 / 2 = .058). As discussed, these *z* tests do not provide as accurate inference as deviance tests, so in the next section we consider using a deviance test to assess the variance-covariance terms associated with the slope.

Figure 13.2 provides a visual depiction of these results. This plot shows predicted *math* scores for each of 50 schools as a function of student *ses* (with 50 schools selected instead of all schools to ease viewing). Given that *ses* is group-mean centered, the mean *math* score for a given school is located on the regression line above an *ses* score

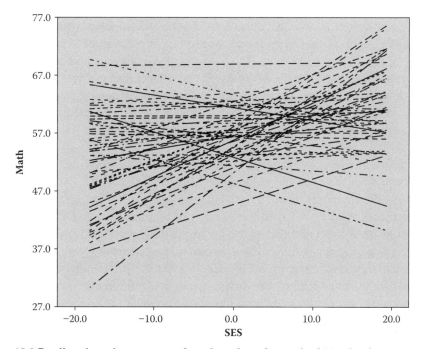

Figure 13.2 Predicted *math* scores as a function of *ses* for each of 50 schools.

of zero. Examining the plot suggests that these mean *math* scores vary greatly across schools. In addition, the plot also suggests that the *math-ses* slopes vary across schools as some slopes are near zero, while others are mostly positive. Also, the negative correlation between the *math* means and *math-ses* slopes is evident in that schools having predicted math scores greater than 57 when *ses* is zero tend to have slopes near zero (flat slopes), whereas other schools (with lower mean *math* scores) tend to have positive *math-ses* slopes.

13.5.3 Deviance Test for a Within-School Slope Variance and Covariance

Previously, we showed how model deviances can be used to test a single variance (e.g., τ_{00}). We now show how model deviances can be used to test the variance and covariance associated with adding a random effect for a within-school slope. As before, we compare the deviance from two models, where one model is nested in the other. The random-coefficient model (i.e., the full model) has already been estimated, and this model includes six parameters: two fixed effects (γ_{00} and γ_{01}) and four variance-covariance terms, that is, the student-level variance (σ^2), the variance of the math means (τ_{00}), the slope variance (τ_{11}), and the covariance between the *math* means and *ses-math* slopes (τ_{01}). The nested model that we will estimate will constrain the slope variance (τ_{11}) to zero and by doing so will also constrain the covariance (τ_{01}) to zero.

Recall that when testing variance-covariance terms, the two comparison models must have the same fixed effects. Thus, for this reduced model, Equation 12 remains the student-level model. In addition, Equation 13 is the school-level model, except that there is no u_{1j} term in the model for β_{1j}, as each u_{1j} is constrained to be zero (which then constrains τ_{11} and τ_{01} to zero). Thus, the reduced model has four parameters: the same two fixed effects as the random-coefficient model, but just two variances: the student-level variance (σ^2) and the variance of the *math* means (τ_{00}). Note that this random intercept model can be estimated with SAS and SPSS by removing *ses* from the respective RANDOM statement from the syntax in Table 13.6.

We estimated the random intercept model to conduct this deviance test. The estimate of the deviance from the random intercept model is 48,488.846, whereas the random-coefficient model returned a deviance of 48,479.875. The difference between these deviances is 8.971. A key difference between the deviance test of a single variance (as illustrated in section 13.5.1) and the test of the variance and covariance here is that this test statistic is not distributed as a standard chi-square test (Snijders & Bosker, 2012, p. 99; West et al. 2014, p. 36). Instead, this test statistic follows a chi-bar distribution, which is a mix of chi-square distributions having different degrees of freedom. Snijders and Bosker (2012, p. 99) provide selected critical values for such a distribution, and we use a critical value from their text given an alpha of .05 and when the slope variance and covariance for a *single* predictor (here, *ses*) is being tested, with this critical value being 5.14. Given in our example that the test statistic of 8.971 exceeds this critical value of 5.14, we conclude that there is sufficient variation-covariation in the *ses-math* slopes to treat these slopes as randomly varying. We will then add school-level predictors to the model for β_{1j}.

Although the deviance test used here provides more accurate inference for variance-covariance terms than the z test, we caution that it may not always be wise to require a significant test result for the variance of a random slope (e.g., τ_{11}) before adding school predictors to the model for the corresponding coefficient (e.g., β_{1j}). As Snijders and Bosker (2012) note, there may be theoretical reasons to test the impact of a school-level predictor on a within-school slope, and the power for the test of a school predictor is greater (perhaps much greater) than the power for the test of the variance of a random slope. Note that while more than one random slope may be tested simultaneously (with different critical values needed when more than one random slope is tested), Hox (2010, p. 58) and Heck et al. (2014, p. 14) recommend testing random slopes one variable at a time to avoid convergence problems. Multilevel modeling texts (e.g., Hox, 2010; Raudenbush & Bryk, 2002; Snijders & Bosker, 2012; West et al., 2014) provide more information about these test procedures, as well as deviance testing for fixed effects.

13.5.4 Model Including Student and School Predictors

By using the random-coefficient model, we learned that there is a positive association between *ses* and *math* achievement, and that school *math* means and *ses-math* slopes vary across schools. We now test the primary question of interest: Do public and private schools differ in mean *math* achievement and *ses-math* slopes? In the previous section, the correlation between the *math* means and *ses-math* slopes, as well as the plot in Figure 13.2, indicated that there are schools in the sample that have relatively high *math* scores and relatively low *ses-math* slopes, suggesting that some schools exhibit what is sometimes called excellence and equity. The question now is whether these particular schools tend to be public or private. In addressing this question, we will also control for between-school *ses* differences.

A key purpose of the random-coefficient model presented previously is to determine how level-1 predictors should be modeled. In our example, we learned that student *ses* is related to math performance and that the *ses-math* slopes should be modeled as varying across schools. Thus, both fixed and random effects associated with *ses* should be included in the model. Also, since we are adding no additional predictors to the level-1 model, the student-level model as specified in Equation 12, which was supported by the data, remains the student-level model for this analysis. The school-level models, however, are now modified to include the predictors of interest. These models for the school *math* means (β_{0j}) and the *ses-math* slopes (β_{1j}) are now

$$\begin{cases} \beta_{0j} = \gamma_{00} + \gamma_{01}\text{public} + \gamma_{02}\overline{\text{SES}}_j + u_{0j}, \\ \beta_{1j} = \gamma_{10} + \gamma_{11}\text{public} + \gamma_{12}\overline{\text{SES}}_j + u_{1j} \end{cases} \tag{15}$$

where public (coded 1 for public, 0 otherwise) and mean *ses* (i.e., $\overline{SES}_j$), centered across schools, have been added as predictors. The combined model is then

$$math_{ij} = \gamma_{00} + \gamma_{01}\text{public} + \gamma_{02}\overline{SES}_j + \gamma_{10}\left(ses_{ij} - \overline{ses}_j\right) + \gamma_{11}\left(\text{public}\right)$$
$$\left(ses_{ij} - \overline{ses}_j\right) + \gamma_{12}\left(\overline{SES}_j\right)\left(ses_{ij} - \overline{ses}_j\right) + u_{0j} + u_{1j}\left(ses_{ij} - \overline{ses}_j\right) + r_{ij}. \tag{16}$$

As Equation 16 shows, there are six fixed effects and three random effects in the model. Although nine effects are present, a total of 10 parameters are estimated because we also estimate the covariance among the school random effects (u_{0j}, u_{1j}), which is not evident in Equation 16.

Inspecting Equation 16 reveals the nature of the fixed effects that are estimated. The coefficients in the model, γ_{01}, γ_{02}, and γ_{10}, may be viewed as analogous to main effects, here of school type, mean *ses* and student *ses*, respectively, as there are no product variables associated with these terms. In contrast, γ_{11} and γ_{12} represent what are called cross-level interactions because each coefficient is associated with a product variable involving school- and student-level predictors. If you look back at Equation 15, you can see then that whenever predictor variables are added to the model for a slope (here, β_{1j}), cross-level interactions will appear in the model. This makes sense because if γ_{11} and/or γ_{12} are nonzero, this implies that β_{1j} (which carries the association between *ses* and *math*) depends on one or both school-level predictors, consistent with an interaction interpretation (i.e., the effect of one variable depends on another).

The cross-level interactions are interpreted in the usual manner. That is, a nonzero value for γ_{11} indicates that the association between *public* and *math* depends on or varies across student *ses* or that the association between student *ses* and *math* depends on or is different for the two school types. Also, a nonzero value for γ_{12} indicates that the association between mean *ses* and *math* depends on student *ses* or that the association between student *ses* and *math* depends on or varies across mean *ses* levels. Inspecting Equation 16 also reveals that the model does not allow for an interaction between *public* and mean *ses*, which could be included in the model but we assume is not hypothesized by the researchers. Inspecting the combined equation, then, is useful for determining the types of effects, particularly, interactions that are included in the model.

To interpret the fixed effects, one may focus on Equation 15 or Equation 16. Equation 16 casts the effects in terms of a single student response (*math*). As such, researchers wishing to describe how each predictor impacts this single response would focus on Equation 16. Another way to describe the effects would be to focus on Equation 15. Note that this equation sets up two response variables: school mean *math* and the within-school *ses-math* slopes, where these outcomes are correlated. Researchers interested in describing the associations between the school predictors and these two school-level responses would focus on Equation 15. Here, we assume that the researchers are interested in comparing the performance of public and private schools on the two school outcomes (as appears to be commonly done). As such, we focus on Equation 15 to interpret the fixed effects.

Table 13.8 provides SAS and SPSS syntax that can be used to estimate the model. Using Equation 15 and the selected results shown in Table 13.9, we now interpret the effects. First, by examining Equation 15 for β_{0j}, we see that γ_{00} represents the school mean *math* score for a private school (given the coding for *public*) that has the sample average *ses* (given the centering of mean *ses*). Table 13.9 indicates that this mean *math* score for private schools having the sample average *ses* is expected to be 57.86. The difference in mean *math* scores between public and private schools, controlling for mean *ses*, is represented by γ_{01}, which is estimated to be $-.17$ points, favoring private schools, but is not statistically significant ($p = .55$). The last fixed effect in the equation for the school *math* means is γ_{02}, which represents the association between mean *ses* and mean *math*, controlling for school type. This estimate is .59 ($p < .05$), indicating that mean *math* scores are expected to increase by more than a half point as mean *ses* increases, holding school type constant. Thus, mean *math* performance is greater in schools having higher mean *ses*.

We now focus on Equation 15 where the outcome variable is the *ses-math* slopes. In this model, γ_{10} represents the *ses-math* slope for a private school that has the sample mean *ses*. Table 13.9 shows that this association is .36 ($p < .05$), indicating that student *math* scores are expected to increase by .36 points as *ses* increases by 1 point in private schools having the mean *ses*. The difference in predicted *ses-math* slopes between public and private schools, controlling for mean *ses*, is represented by γ_{11} and

■ **Table 13.8: SAS and SPSS Control Lines for Estimating the Model With Student and School Predictors**

SAS	SPSS
PROC MIXED METHOD = REML NOCLPRINT COVTEST NOITPRINT; CLASS schcode; (1) MODEL math = public Meanses ses public*ses Meanses*ses / SOLUTION; RANDOM intercept ses / type = un SUBJECT=schcode; RUN;	(2) MIXED math WITH public Meanses ses (3) /FIXED= public Meanses ses public*ses Meanses*ses | SSTYPE(3) /METHOD=REML /PRINT=G SOLUTION TESTCOV /RANDOM=INTERCEPT ses | SUBJECT (schcode) COVTYPE(UN).

(1) The MODEL statement specifies the predictor variables for math are now public, meanses, ses, public*ses, and meanses*ses.

(2) The MIXED statement indicates that math is the outcome and the covariates are public, meanses, and ses.

(3) The FIXED statement requests that fixed effects be estimated for public, meanses, ses, public*ses, and meanses*ses.

■ **Table 13.9: SPSS Output for the Model With Student and School Predictors**

Fixed Effects

Estimates of Fixed Effects[a]

Parameter	Estimate	Std. Error	Df	T	Sig.	95% Confidence Interval Lower Bound	Upper Bound
Intercept	57.859078	.238468	406.989	242.628	.000	57.390295	58.327861
Public	−.165129	.278869	411.097	−.592	.554	−.713316	.383058
Meanses	.588304	.025359	385.305	23.199	.000	.538445	.638164
Ses	.363018	.031978	409.267	11.352	.000	.300156	.425880
public * ses	−.065590	.037286	399.665	−1.759	.079	−.138891	.007710
Meanses * ses	−.002633	.003734	491.439	−.705	.481	−.009968	.004703

[a] Dependent Variable: math.

Covariance Parameters

Estimates of Covariance Parameters[a]

Parameter		Estimate	Std. Error	Wald Z	Sig.	95% Confidence Interval Lower Bound	Upper Bound
Residual		62.203595	1.122733	55.404	.000	60.041548	64.443497
Intercept +	UN (1,1)	2.565643	.453243	5.661	.000	1.814780	3.627175
ses [sub-	UN (2,1)	−.109477	.043315	−2.527	.011	−.194373	−.024581
ject = schcode]	UN (2,2)	.010668	.007014	1.521	.128	.002940	.038701

[a] Dependent Variable: math.

Random Effect Covariance Structure (G)[a]

	Intercept | schcode	sesgrpcen | schcode
Intercept | schcode	2.565643	−.109477
ses| schcode	−.109477	.010668

Unstructured
[a] Dependent Variable: math.

is estimated to be −.07, with public schools having flatter *ses-math* slopes, although this public-private school difference in *ses-math* slopes is not statistically significant ($p = .08$). The last fixed effect in the equation for the within-school *ses-math* slopes is γ_{12}, which represents the association between mean *ses* and the *ses-math* slopes, controlling for school type. This estimate is −.002 ($p = .48$), indicating that the within-school *ses-math* associations are not related to mean *ses*.

Estimates for the variance-covariance elements appear in the last two output selections of Table 13.9. The student-residual variance is 62.20 ($p < .001$). The variance that remains in school *math* means is 2.57 ($p < .001$), the residual covariance between the *math* means and the *ses-math* slopes is $-.11$ ($p = .011$), and the variance remaining in the *math* slopes is .01 ($p = .128 / 2 = .064$). Note that deviance testing is generally preferred for variance components as illustrated in previous sections.

In addition to the numerical results, it is also possible to obtain various graphs of predicted outcomes. Figure 13.3 shows predicted math scores across student *ses* (range of -20 to 20 displayed) for public and private schools holding mean *ses* at its average value (zero). This graph was obtained by using the compute statement in SPSS into which was placed the parameter estimates for the fixed effects in Equation 16 along with the values of student *ses* and *public* in the data set. The equation for the graph is then

$$math_{ij} = 57.86 - .17\left(public\right) + .36\left(ses_{ij} - \overline{ses}_j\right) - .07(public)\left(ses_{ij} - \overline{ses}_j\right). \qquad (17)$$

Two key findings are evident in the graph. First, note there are very small differences between the predicted *math* values for public and private schools across student *ses*. In addition, although the slope of the lines are somewhat different (with public schools having flatter slopes), this difference appears to be negligible and, of course, was not statistically significant, as we observed in the results (i.e., $\gamma_{11} = -.07, p = .08$). Second, for each school type, student *ses* is positively, and by appearance, strongly related to *math* achievement. Although not shown here, it is also possible to display the impact of mean *ses* in such a plot by obtaining predicted values for schools having different mean *ses* values.

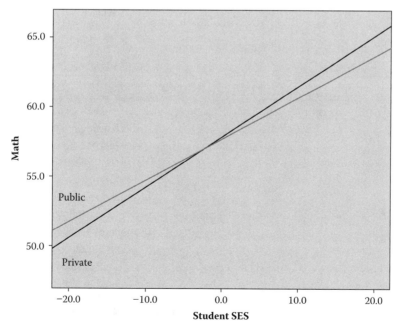

Figure 13.3 Predicted math scores for public and private schools across student *ses* holding mean *ses* constant at its average.

We now summarize the key results from the analysis. First, *math* achievement, for the population of schools, varied across students and schools, with most of the *math* variation occurring at the student level. In addition, while a positive association was found between student *ses* and *math* achievement, this association varied across schools with *ses* being more strongly related to *math* achievement in some schools than others. However, after controlling for between-school *ses* differences, public and private schools did not differ in *math* achievement. In addition, the association between student *ses* and *math* did not differ for public and private schools. As such, neither school type had greater *math* achievement or a more equitable association between *ses* and *math*. *Math* achievement was, though, positively related to student and school *ses*.

13.5.5 Summary of Commonly Used Statistical Tests in SPSS and SAS

Section 13.5 introduced a variety of statistical tests that can be used in multilevel modeling. Table 13.10 provides a summary of commonly used tests available in SPSS and SAS to test parameters of interest, along with relevant remarks. As noted previously, the *z* tests shown in the table for variance-covariance terms provide approximate significance values. When possible, deviance tests should be used for variance-covariances.

▪ **Table 13.10: Statistical Tests Commonly Used in SPSS and SAS for Multilevel Modeling**

Parameter	Test	Remarks
Fixed effects (regression coefficients)		
Single effect (e.g., γ_{10})	*t* test, or chi-square deviance test	Deviance test requires use of FML
Multiple effects[1] (e.g., γ_{01}, γ_{11})	Chi-square deviance test	Deviance test requires use of FML
Random effects (variances-covariances)		
A single variance (e.g., σ^2, τ_{00}, or τ_{11})	*z* test, or chi-square deviance test	For *z* test, SPSS users should compare $p / 2$ to α; deviance test can be used with RML or FML (RML preferred) and the chi-square critical value should be obtained using $2 \times \alpha$
A single covariance (e.g., τ_{01})	*z* test or chi-square deviance test	No adjustments are needed for the *p* value (for the *z* test) or α (for the chi-square critical value)
Variance and covariance (e.g., τ_{01} and τ_{11})	Deviance test	The test statistic should be compared to a chi-bar critical value

Note: Deviance test requires estimation of full and reduced models. FML is full maximum likelihood and RML is restricted maximum likelihood.

(1) We illustrate use of this test in section 14.6.2.

13.6 CENTERING PREDICTOR VARIABLES

Predictor variables in multilevel modeling will often need to be centered to produce meaningful results, particularly for predictors at the lower levels of the data (i.e., level 1 in a two-level design). The discussion and recommendations provided later are limited to two-level designs (although the key concepts apply to three-level designs) where repeated measures have *not* been collected. That is, this discussion is not intended for so-called growth curve modeling applications.

In multilevel modeling, centering of predictors is generally done with one of two methods: grand- or group-mean centering. We limit our discussion to these two methods. While it is important to consider the substantive research questions in selecting a centering method, it is often the case that group-mean centering will generally provide for more meaningful parameter estimates. The reasons for this have to do with the presence of contextual effects as well as a problem that may arise when level-1 predictors have slopes that vary across clusters (e.g., schools).

13.6.1 Contextual Effects and Centering

There are different ways to think about contextual effects, but a contextual effect is present when the association between a predictor and outcome (*ses* and *math*) is different at level 1 and level 2. To explore this idea, let's return to our data set and set up a basic multilevel model that will estimate within-school and between-school associations of *ses* on *math*. This model is

$$math_{ij} = \beta_{0j} + \beta_{1j}\left(ses_{ij} - \overline{ses}_j\right) + r_{ij}, \tag{18}$$

where group-mean centered *ses* is now included as a predictor at level 1. A simple school-level model that includes mean *ses* is

$$\begin{cases} \beta_{0j} = \gamma_{00} + \gamma_{01}meanses_j + u_{0j} \\ \beta_{1j} = \gamma_{10} \end{cases}, \tag{19}$$

where only the intercept from the student-level equation is allowed to vary across schools.

The parameters from Equations 18 and 19 are readily interpretable. We have seen that with group-mean centering at the student level, β_{0j} represents school *j*'s *math* mean, and β_{1j} represents the within-school association, or slope, for *math* and *ses*. Since no school random effect is included in the model for β_{1j} in Equation 19, γ_{10} represents the within-school association between *ses* and *math* (which is assumed to be constant across schools). This within-school association is often referred to as β_w and is interpreted as the expected within-school change in student *math* achievement as student *ses* increases by 1 point. Further, in Equation 19, the school *math* means (β_{0j}) are regressed on *mean ses*. As such, γ_{01} represents the expected change in school *math* means for a unit change in *mean ses*. Parameter γ_{01} is often referred as β_b as it captures the between-school association for *ses* and *math*. If the within- and between-school associations are the same (i.e., $\beta_b = \beta_w$), then no contextual effect is present. However, if these associations differ (i.e., $\beta_b \neq \beta_w$), then a contextual effect is present for *ses*.

We estimated Equations 18 and 19 with our *math* data and found that β_b was estimated to be .59 ($p < .001$), and β_w was estimated to be .32 ($p < .001$). Thus, there seems to be a large difference in these associations. In this model, the contextual effect is equal to this difference and is $\beta_c = \beta_b - \beta_w$, which is .59 − .32 = .27. This contextual effect, although not yet tested for significance, is nearly as large as the within-school association, suggesting that it represents an important association.

Let's now consider the same model but replace group-mean centered *ses* within grand-mean *centered* ses. Grand-mean centering involves subtracting the grand mean for the predictor from each person's score for that predictor, which simply then subtracts a constant value from each person's predictor score. Note, in contrast, that with group-mean centering, from school to school, a potentially different value is subtracted from each person's raw score, as school *ses* means are likely to be different. With grand-mean centering, the student-level model is

$$math_{ij} = \beta_{0j} + \beta_{1j}\left(ses_{ij} - \overline{ses}\right) + r_{ij}, \tag{20}$$

where $\overline{ses}$ is the average student *ses* score across all schools. The school-level model is unchanged and is

$$\begin{cases} \beta_{0j} = \gamma_{00} + \gamma_{01}meanses_j + u_{0j} \\ \beta_{1j} = \gamma_{10} \end{cases}. \tag{21}$$

While these equations are similar to Equations 18 and 19, not every parameter is interpreted in the same way. In Equation 20, β_{0j} is no longer the school *math* mean. Instead, it is the *math* mean for school *j* that is adjusted for between-school differences on *mean ses*, or may be thought of as the expected *math* score for a student in school *j* who has the overall average *ses* score. Further, γ_{01} does not represent β_b, but instead represents the contextual effect β_c. According to Raudenbush and Bryk (2002), a contextual effect can be interpreted as "the expected difference in the outcomes between two students who have the same individual *ses*, but who attend schools differing by one unit in *mean ses*" (p. 141). That is, holding constant student *ses*, to what degree is a student's math score expected to change if a given student were to attend a higher *ses* school? (This effect of school context is the reason it is called the contextual effect.) Note though that by virtue of including mean *ses* parameter γ_{10} represents the within-school association between *ses* and *math*, or is equal to β_w, the same result as obtained with group-mean centering. To illustrate this, we estimated Equations 20 and 21 with our example data. The estimate of γ_{10} (β_w) is .32, as previously, and the estimate of γ_{01} is .27 ($p < .001$), which is the contextual effect (as $\beta_b - \beta_w = .27$).

Note, then, that when a random intercept model is estimated, and a level-1 predictor and its mean are included as predictors, either group-mean or grand-mean centering of the level-1 predictor may be used. Group-mean centering can be used to obtain point estimates and statistical tests for β_w and β_b, and grand-mean centering provides an easy way to obtain a point estimate and statistical test of β_c. In this particular case, the models, for which different forms of centering were used, provide identical fit and are considered equivalent models, in the sense that parameter values from one model are a simple expression of the parameter values in the other model (i.e., $\beta_c = \beta_b - \beta_w$). *However, this case is atypical, and use of different centering methods for level-1 predictors generally does not result in equivalent models.* We now consider potential problems that may arise with grand- and then group-mean centering. After that, we make our centering recommendations.

13.6.2 Problems With Grand-Mean Centering

One problem that may arise with grand-mean centering occurs when the random-coefficient model is estimated. Recall that this model is often used to determine if fixed and random effects are present for a level-1 predictor. With grand-mean centering of the level-1 predictor, this model, using our running example, is

$$math_{ij} = \beta_{0j} + \beta_{1j}\left(ses_{ij} - \overline{ses}\right) + r_{ij} \tag{22}$$

and the school-level model, including no predictors, is

$$\begin{cases} \beta_{0j} = \gamma_{00} + u_{0j} \\ \beta_{1j} = \gamma_{10} + u_{1j} \end{cases}. \tag{23}$$

In the group-mean centered version of this model (Equations 12 and 13), and focusing on the parameter of interest, γ_{10} represents the within-school association between *ses* and *math*. Unfortunately, when a contextual effect is present ($\beta_b \neq \beta_w$) and when grand-mean centering is used for the level-1 predictor, γ_{10} becomes a *weighted average* of β_w and β_b and does not have a clear interpretation. As such, Raudenbush and Bryk (2002) state that in this case γ_{10} is an "inappropriate estimator of the person-level effect" and is an "uninterpretable blend" of effects (p. 139). With our running example, estimating Equations 22 and 23 produces an estimate of γ_{10} of .40, which is lies between the estimates obtained earlier of β_w (.32) and β_b (.59). In this case, γ_{10} is not a meaningful parameter and use of grand-mean centering in random-coefficient models should generally be avoided. Note that with group-mean centering, estimating these same equations yields an estimate of γ_{10} that is .32 (consistent with β_w as obtained previously).

The reason that grand-mean centering fails to produce a meaningful parameter estimate for the random-coefficient model when a contextual effect is present is as follows. A grand-mean centered predictor may be expressed as $\left(X_{ij} - \overline{X}\right) = \left(X_{ij} - \overline{X}_j\right) + \left(\overline{X}_j - \overline{X}\right)$. On the right hand side of the equation, note that terms in the first parenthesis represent within-cluster variability while the expression in the second parenthesis represents between-cluster, or between-school, variability. In Equation 23, though, only one fixed effect for the predictor is estimated, and if β_w and β_b differ, the resultant coefficient (γ_{10}) is, as mentioned, a weighted average of these coefficients. Note when group-mean centering is used, each cluster, or school, has a mean of zero for this predictor, due to the centering. Therefore, there is no between-cluster variation in a group-mean centered level-1 predictor. As a result, when group-mean centering is used for a predictor at level 1, the fixed effect associated with this variable reflects only the within-cluster, or within-school, variation (i.e., β_w). Note that if there is no contextual effect, (i.e., $\beta_b = \beta_w$), this problem with grand-mean centering does not arise. It will also not arise when all of the clusters have the same mean on the predictor (i.e., all $\overline{X}_j$ are the same). This situation will be present, for example, if participants are randomly assigned to treatments within clusters, and each cluster has the same proportion (e.g., .50) of participants in each treatment condition. In this case, there would be no variability across clusters in, for example, a dummy-coded level-1 treatment variable.

Further, problems with grand-mean centering are not necessarily corrected when the mean of the predictor (i.e., $\overline{X}_j$) is added to Equation 23 for β_{0j}. While including the mean of the predictor worked great for Equations 20 and 21, note that Equation 21 is a random intercept model, as the slope β_{1j} was not allowed to vary. If Equation 21 were modified to allow both the intercept and slope to vary, as in Equation 23, the use of grand-mean centering can provide attenuated estimates of slope variance when the mean of the predictor (i.e., $\overline{X}_j$) varies across clusters. That is, τ_{11} may be underestimated when grand-mean centering is used in variable slope models. Interested readers may consult Raudenbush and Bryk (2002, pp. 143–149) for an explanation. Thus, when a slope of a level-1 predictor is modeled as varying across clusters, group-mean centering is preferred. Raudenbush and Bryk state this about multilevel models in general, not just contextual effect models, by recommending group-mean centering for level-1 predictors "to detect and estimate properly the slope heterogeneity" (p. 143) when $\overline{X}_j$ varies across clusters.

13.6.3 Problems With Group-Mean Centering

While group-mean centering may often be less problematic than grand-mean centering for level-1 predictors, there is a problem that arises when group-mean centering is used. Specifically, when group-mean centering is used and the raw score mean of that predictor (i.e., $\overline{X}_j$) is *not* included in the model, this level-1 predictor does not provide for statistical control for predictors at level 2 of the model (e.g., the school level). Again, the use of group-mean centering removes cluster variability from this predictor, rendering it useless as a control variable at the cluster level (although it works fine as a control variable for other level-1 predictors). A simple way to address this problem, as illustrated section 13.5.4, is to include the mean of the predictor in the model for β_{0j} (and β_{1j} if an interaction with the level-1 predictor is hypothesized).

In addition, Enders and Tofighi (2007), in an informative discussion of centering, note that study goals drive the selection of centering choices. They recommend the use of grand-mean centering for level-1 predictors when one wishes to control for differences across clusters and when the focal variable of interest is a level-2 predictor (again assuming that a random intercept model is appropriate). The cluster randomized trial is the leading example here, where clusters or organizations are randomly assigned to treatment conditions, and the treatment variable is a level-2 predictor. In this situation, the level-1 variables are not of interest except as potential control variables. In this case, use of grand-mean centering would provide for statistical adjustments for the impact of the level-2 predictor variable, although the regression coefficients associated with the control variables may still be a blend of β_b and β_w. In this case, another way of providing statistical control is to use group-mean centering for the level-1 control variables and then include the means of these variables (i.e., $\bar{X}_j$) as predictors, where the latter variables then provide the statistical control. This recommendation appears in Raudenbush and Bryk (2002, p. 258), who note that this method is preferable to the first option when a contextual effect is present.

13.6.4 Centering Recommendations

Our centering recommendations follow from the discussion of problems associated with grand- and group-mean centering of level-1 predictors. First, grand-mean centering of level-1 predictors is perhaps best used in contextual effect models where only the intercept varies at the cluster level (as in Equations 20 and 21). Note also that the mean of the same predictor variable appears as a predictor in the model. Use of grand-mean centering in Equation 20 facilitates the testing of contextual effects while also providing a proper estimate of the within-cluster association (β_w). Second, if the association between level-1 predictors and the outcome is not of primary interest (and no slope variability is present for these variables), grand-mean centering could be used for the level-1 predictors to provide statistical control for situations where the focal variable(s) of interest is at the second level, as in the cluster randomized trial. Note though that use of group-mean centering of the level-1 predictors while also including the cluster mean of these variables as predictors in the model may be a better option when contextual effects are present.

Group-mean centering can be more widely used than grand-mean centering of level-1 predictors. First, since grand-mean centering may be problematic when slopes associated with a level-1 variable vary across clusters (e.g., schools), group-mean centering should be used for level-1 predictors having variable slopes or when one is interested in determining if slopes vary (as in the random-coefficient model). More generally, group-mean centering is preferred when the association between a level-1 predictor and the outcome is of primary interest, as such centering will provide for a pure (unconfounded) estimate of the within-cluster association (i.e., β_w), which may not be the case when grand-mean centering is used. Estimating within-cluster associations (β_w) is commonly of interest in multilevel modeling applications. As such, group-mean centering will likely be relevant for your study. Note that group-mean centering should also be used in situations where interactions with level-1 variables are of interest (both within- and cross-level interactions). In these cases, obtaining estimates of pure within-group associations is an important goal, which is accomplished by group-mean centering.

We offer some final comments related to centering. First, for each centering method, the mean value of the level-1 predictor should generally be included as a predictor variable at the second level of the model (i.e., for β_{0j}) to assess the presence of contextual effects, which is also recommended in the literature (Raudenbush & Bryk, 2002, p. 258; Snijders & Bosker, 2012, p. 102). Of course, for grand-mean centering, this assumes that only the intercept varies at level 2. Second, the same recommendations and comments hold for binary predictors at level 1. If a binary predictor variable has between-cluster variability (which may not always be the case), the use of group-mean centering at level-1 for this variable will provide for a proper estimate of the within-school group difference. Finally, we have not discussed centering for level-2 predictors, as centering versus not centering these predictors is generally of little consequence. Of course, group-mean centering cannot be used here (as it would have no effect on the predictor scores), but grand-mean centering of level-2 predictors is possible, which Raudenbush and Bryk (2002, p. 35) note is often convenient. We used this centering in section 13.5.4 so that the cluster-level intercepts (i.e., γ_{00}, γ_{10}) had a meaningful interpretation, although such centering is generally not necessary.

13.7 SAMPLE SIZE

In example 1, sample sizes were quite large at level 1 (i.e., 6,871 students) and level 2 (419 schools). Applied researchers do not always have ready access to such large sample sizes at each level, so it is natural to wonder about sample size needs for multilevel modeling. In the literature, sample sizes needed for multilevel models have been examined in two different ways. First, researchers have established rules of thumb for sample sizes needed at various levels to ensure that parameter estimates are accurate or unbiased. Software programs have also been developed to help researchers estimate needed sample sizes to ensure adequate power (e.g., .80) to test effects of interest.

Hox (2010) presents a summary of various rules of thumb that are generally considered to be necessary to provide good parameter estimates. An important point is that sample size requirements depend on the type of effects (e.g., fixed, random) that are of interest in one's study and also are generally different from level 1 to level 2. For two-level designs, Kreft (1996) offered a 30/30 rule, which means that 30 clusters with 30 persons per cluster are needed to provide for proper estimates. Hox (2010) notes that while these values may be reasonable to provide valid estimates of certain fixed effects they are not generally applicable for estimating cross-level interactions or variance-covariances. If one were estimating cross-level interactions, Hox suggests a 50/20 rule, with 50 clusters and 20 participants per cluster needed. Hox also suggests a 100/10 rule if estimating variance-covariance parameters are of great interest, with 100 clusters having 10 participants per cluster.

More recently, though, Bell, Morgan, Schoeneberger, Kromery, and Ferron (2014) examined how well fixed effects and their standard errors (though not random effects) were estimated for a variety of different effects (e.g., main effects of level-1 and level-2 predictors, various interactions among these) and for different numbers and types of predictor variables (binary and continuous predictors) when sample sizes at each level are fairly small. They found that when the number of clusters is 20 or greater (even when within-cluster sample sizes are as small as 5 to 10), fixed effects estimates and their standard errors are accurate. Further, even when the number of clusters was as small as 10, these estimates were generally accurate. Note that, in their study, RML was used along with the Kenward–Roger method of estimating the denominator degrees of freedom for the tests of the effects, which is intended to provide for improved inference for small sample sizes. We will use this method to estimate the degrees of freedom in Example 2. Note though that while Bell et al. found that estimation was accurate when cluster and sample size were small, statistical power to detect the presence of effects was often too low given the sample, effect sizes, and other factors included in their study.

Statistical power programs are available for multilevel models to enable *a priori* estimates of statistical power, given various sample sizes, effect sizes, intraclass correlations, and other factors affecting power in multilevel designs. Van Breukelen and Moorbeek (2013) describe various power-related programs, including, for example, Optimal Design, PINT, and MLPowSim. As described by van Breukelen and Moorbeek, Optimal Design can be used to estimate power for various multilevel experimental designs, including longitudinal designs, for a specific set of models. PINT provides *a priori* estimates of standard errors for fixed effects in two level designs, and MLPowSim can be used for various random effects models. In addition, Mathieu, Aguinis, Culpepper, and Chen (2012) developed software that can be used specifically to estimate sample sizes needed to detect the presence of cross-level interactions.

13.8 EXAMPLE 2: EVALUATING THE EFFICACY OF A TREATMENT

Multilevel models can also be used to analyze data arising from multilevel experimental designs, such as determining whether two or more counseling (or, say teaching) methods impact an outcome. The example used here compares mean performance on client empathy for two counseling methods, referred to as "new treatment" and "control" conditions. It should be noted that for this example a smaller sample size is used than is typically recommended for HLM analyses. This is done to facilitate the presentation. Note though as suggested by the research of Bell et al. (2014) mentioned in the previous section, we will use RML estimation combined with methods to compute the denominator degrees of freedom for tests of fixed effects (i.e., Kenward–Roger for SAS and Satterthwaite for SPSS), both of which are intended to provide for accurate inferences in the presence of small sample sizes. For our example, five groups (which we will refer to as clusters) of clients are treated with each counseling method, and each cluster has four clients. Thus, the design involves clients nested within clusters that have been randomly assigned to one of two treatment conditions. Thus, this is a small-scale cluster-randomized trial where clusters or groups (not individuals) have been randomly assigned to experimental conditions and scores for an outcome and covariate have been collected from participants. Note that the two counseling methods do not constitute a separate level as method is a fixed factor that describes the clusters, as the counseling method conditions do not represent a sample from some larger population of possible counseling methods. Even if they did, two levels would be much too small to serve as the upper level of a multilevel model. Thus, this cluster randomized trial is a two-level nested design, with clients (level 1) nested within clusters (level 2). Counseling method is a fixed level-2 (cluster-level) variable.

Given the relatively small number of observations in the data set, we present the following data set. Shown are the client id, the cluster id, client *empathy* (which is the outcome of interest), client scores on a measure of *contentment* (which is intended to serve as a covariate), and counseling method (*method*) employed in the relevant clusters coded either as 0 for the new treatment or 1 for control.

Note that in the online data set, group- and grand-mean centered forms of *contentment* are present, labeled respectively, *groupcontent* and *grandcontent*, as well as *meancontent*, which was obtained by computing the cluster means for the *contentment* variable.

ClientId	Cluid	Empathy	Contentment	Method
1	1	23	33	0
2	1	22	33	0
3	1	20	27	0
4	1	19	25	0
5	2	16	22	0
6	2	17	21	0
7	2	18	28	0
8	2	19	31	0
9	3	25	28	0
10	3	28	38	0
11	3	29	35	0
12	3	31	34	0
13	4	27	38	0
14	4	23	27	0
15	4	22	28	0
16	4	21	25	0
17	5	32	28	0
18	5	31	37	0
19	5	28	33	0
20	5	26	30	0
21	6	13	27	1
22	6	12	22	1
23	6	14	34	1

ClientId	Cluid	Empathy	Contentment	Method
24	6	15	28	1
25	7	16	30	1
26	7	17	37	1
27	7	14	27	1
28	7	12	25	1
29	8	11	28	1
30	8	10	23	1
31	8	20	34	1
32	8	15	33	1
33	9	21	29	1
34	9	18	31	1
35	9	19	30	1
36	9	23	39	1
37	10	18	27	1
38	10	17	36	1
39	10	16	36	1
40	10	23	32	1

Table 13.11 shows some basic descriptive statistics for each counseling method based on the client scores (without regard to cluster, as will be considered in the multilevel analysis). Inspecting Table 13.11 indicates that mean *empathy* is greater by about 6.5 points for the new treatment condition, the two treatment groups have similar mean scores on *contentment* (which is expected due to the random assignment of clusters), and that variability for each variable is similar across the two methods.

Due to the limited number of clusters and participants in this example, statistical power to detect treatment effects will, in general, not be sufficient unless there are large treatment effects. So, while we will include *contentment* as a covariate shortly, we first estimate a multilevel model with only *method* included. Note that a null model (i.e., with no predictors) could also be estimated but our presentation here focuses on treatment effects. The client- or level-1 model is

$$empathy_{ij} = \beta_{0j} + r_{ij}, \tag{24}$$

where the outcome *empathy* is modeled as a function of a cluster intercept and residual term r_{ij} where $r_{ij} \sim N(0, \sigma^2)$. With no predictor in Equation 24, β_{0j} represents a given cluster j's *empathy* mean. The cluster-level model, which includes the dummy-coded method predictor, is

$$\beta_{0j} = \gamma_{00} + \gamma_{01}(method) + u_{0j}, \tag{25}$$

■ **Table 13.11: Descriptive Statistics for the Study Variables**

Method	Empathy		Contentment	
	M	SD	M	SD
New treatment (n = 20)	23.85	4.96	30.05	5.00
Control (n = 20)	17.40	4.95	30.40	4.69

where γ_{00}, given the coding for *method*, represents the *empathy* mean for the new treatment condition, and γ_{01} represents the difference in *empathy* means for the two treatment conditions. The residuals are assumed to be normally distributed, with a mean of zero, and have homogeneous variance, or $u_{0j} \sim N(0, \tau_{00})$. When we estimated this model, we found that γ_{00} is estimated to be 23.85 (which is the same as in Table 13.11 due to the design being completely balanced) and that the estimate for γ_{01} is −6.45 ($SE = 3.02, p = .065$). Thus, using an alpha of .05, we could not conclude that the difference of about 6.5 points, which favors the new treatment condition, is statistically significant. The nonsignificance is somewhat expected given the small sample size in this study.

To improve statistical power, we now consider the covariate *contentment*. This predictor is at the client level and so it is possible that the within-cluster and between-cluster associations between *contentment* and *empathy* differ. If so, including both the client and mean form of this covariate may provide for greater power than may be obtained by just adding the client-level predictor alone. So, for now, we include client *contentment* and cluster mean *contentment*. With group-mean centered *contentment,* the client-level model becomes

$$empathy_{ij} = \beta_{0j} + \beta_{1j}contentment_{ij} + r_{ij}. \tag{26}$$

With group mean centering, β_{0j} remains a given clusters *j*'s *empathy* mean and β_{1j} captures the within-cluster association between *empathy* and *contentment*. Since adding the group-mean centered *contentment* will not explain any variance at the cluster level, we now include mean *contentment* (uncentered) in the cluster-level model, which is now

$$\begin{cases} \beta_{0j} = \gamma_{00} + \gamma_{01}\left(method_j\right) + \gamma_{02}meancontent_j + u_{0j} \\ \beta_{1j} = \gamma_{10} \end{cases}. \tag{27}$$

Note that the within-cluster slope (β_{1j}) is specified as a fixed effect at the cluster level, as its variance (τ_{11}) is assumed to be zero, an assumption we will check shortly. The combined equation is then

$$empathy_{ij} = \gamma_{00} + \gamma_{01}method_j + \gamma_{02}meancontent_j + \gamma_{10}contentment_j + u_{0j} + r_{ij} \tag{28}$$

Thus, the fixed effects of interest are γ_{01}, which represents the difference in *empathy* means between the two treatment conditions, controlling for mean *contentment*, γ_{02}, which represents the change in mean *empathy* given a unit increase in mean *contentment*, holding treatment condition constant, and γ_{10} is the within-cluster association between *empathy* and *contentment*.

Table 13.12 presents SAS and SPSS syntax that was used to estimate Equation 28, and Table 13.13 reports the SAS results (as results obtained using SPSS were similar). Focusing on the parameter of interest, the treatment effect estimate of -7.03 ($p < .001$) indicates that after adjusting for differences in mean *contentment*, the new treatment mean is about 7 points greater than the control mean, with this difference being statistically significant. Note that by including the *contentment* variables, the standard error of the treatment effect is now 1.25, compared to 3.02 in the model without any covariates, with this power increase due to adding these covariates. Note that both client *contentment* and mean *contentment* are positively related to *empathy*. Also, the difference in these latter coefficients, $\gamma_{02} - \gamma_{10} = 1.66 - .33 = 1.33$, is indicative of a contextual effect (which can be tested for significance if desired).

If desired, we can compute adjusted means for the two counseling conditions by combining parameter estimates, covariate means (zero for *contentment* and 30.23 for mean *contentment*) and the dummy codes for *method* using Equation 28, while inserting means (zeros) for the random effects. So, to compute the adjusted mean *empathy* for the control group, the computation is $-26.15 - 7.03(1) + 1.66(30.23) = 17.00$. For the new treatment, the adjusted *empathy* mean is $-26.15 - 7.03(0) + 1.66(30.23) = 24.03$. This difference, $17.0 - 24.3 = -7.03$, is the treatment effect estimate, of course, and has already been found to be statistically significant.

Although the analysis is largely concluded, we estimate a couple of models, the first to check for the possibility of variable within-cluster slopes and the second to compare the results of the previous model with those obtained by using grand-mean centering for client *contentment* (without inclusion of mean *contentment*). Testing for variable slopes (β_{1j} of Equation 26) is of interest for two reasons. First, finding such variation would be of interest for those who hypothesize that the treatment may interact with client *contentment*, as it may be hypothesized that clients experiencing the new treatment will have relatively high *empathy* regardless of their prior level of *contentment*. As such, within-cluster slopes in the new treatment condition may be much flatter or smaller than the positive association obtained in the previous analysis (i.e., $\gamma_{10} = .33$). Observing variation in these slopes, although not a prerequisite for testing such an interaction, suggests the possibility of such an interaction. In addition, the standard error of the treatment effect, as previously estimated, may be misestimated if slope variation were present, so including such variation may provide for more accurate inference for the treatment effect. To test for the possibility that the within-cluster or client-level association between *empathy* and *contentment* varies across clusters, we estimated Equations 26 and 27, except that we modified the cluster-level equation, keeping Equation 27 as is for β_{0j} but including a residual term for the slope that so the slope equation is $\beta_{1j} = \gamma_{10} + u_{1j}$.

■ **Table 13.12: SAS and SPSS Control Lines for Estimating Equation 28**

SAS	SPSS

PROC MIXED METHOD = REML NOCLPRINT
COVTEST NOITPRINT;
CLASS cluid;
(1) MODEL empathy = method groupcontent
    meancontent / ddfm=kenwardroger
    SOLUTION;
RANDOM intercept / type = vc SUBJECT
=cluid;
RUN;
	(1) MIXED empathy WITH method groupcon-
	    tent meancontent
	    /FIXED= method groupcontent mean-
	    content | SSTYPE(3)
	    /METHOD=REML
	    /PRINT=G SOLUTION TESTCOV
	    /RANDOM=INTERCEPT | SUBJECT(cluid)
	    COVTYPE(VC).

(1) In the MODEL (SAS) and MIXED (SPSS) statements, the variable groupcontent is the within-cluster centered client *contentment* variable and meancontent is the cluster mean *contentment* variable. Also for SAS, the ddfm = kenwardroger option requests that the denominator degrees of freedom for fixed effect tests be calculated using the Kenward-Roger method. SPSS MIXED does not offer this option but by default uses the Satterthwaite method to compute these degrees of freedom. Each of these methods is intended to provide for better inference when sample size is small.

When we estimated Equations 26 and 27 but now allowing for variable slopes, we initially requested estimates for a full variance-covariance matrix for the cluster random effects, which includes estimates of the intercept variance (τ_{00}), slope variance (τ_{11}), and the covariance (τ_{01}) of the random effects. However, the estimated model did not converge (for both SAS and SPSS), which is often indicative of variance-covariance components that are near zero. We then estimated the same model but constrained the covariance (τ_{01}) to zero. This can be done in SAS by replacing the RANDOM line that appears in Table 13.12 with the statement RANDOM intercept groupcontent / type = vc SUBJECT=cluid; and in SPSS by replacing the RANDOM statement with /RANDOM = INTERCEPT groupcontent| SUBJECT(cluid) COVTYPE(VC).

When this was done, convergence was attained, and the estimate of the slope variance τ_{11} is .002 ($SE = .04$, $p = .48$), suggesting no variation in slopes. Of course, this p value is obtained from the z test, and we know that deviance testing is preferred over the z test for variances. Note that Equations 26 and 27 are nested in the current equations because Equations 26 and 27 are identical to the current equations except that the slope variance is constrained to be zero. The deviance associated with Equations 26 and 27, as shown in Table 13.13, is 183.000 and the deviance for the variable slope model is also 183.000. We can readily see that there is no improvement in fit by allowing for slope variation. Formally, we would compare this difference in fit (here, zero) to a corresponding chi-square critical value of 2.706, again doubling the alpha of .05 given we are testing a single variance with 1 degree of freedom. So, there is no support for variable slopes. Note that a conventional chi-square critical value can be used here

■ **Table 13.13: SAS Output for Equation 28 (or Equivalently Equations 26 and 27)**

Fit Statistics	
-2 Res Log Likelihood	183.0
AIC (smaller is better)	187.0
AICC (smaller is better)	187.3
BIC (smaller is better)	187.6

Solution for Fixed Effects					
Effect	Estimate	Standard Error	DF	t Value	Pr > |t|
Intercept	−26.1484	7.9531	7	−3.29	0.0133
METHOD	−7.0323	1.2483	7	−5.63	0.0008
groupCONTENT	0.3274	0.08212	29	3.99	0.0004
MEANCONTENT	1.6638	0.2630	7	6.33	0.0004

Covariance Parameter Estimates					
Cov Parm	Subject	Estimate	Standard Error	Z Value	Pr > Z
Intercept	CLUID	2.7454	2.0921	1.31	0.0947
Residual		4.5164	1.1861	3.81	<.0001

Note: Predictor variable groupCONTENT is the group-mean centered client *contentment* variable and MEAN-CONTENT is the cluster mean *contentment* variable.

because we are testing one parameter (i.e., τ_{11}), as opposed to the two parameters (i.e., τ_{11} and τ_{01}) that were tested in section 13.5.3.

Finally, we might wonder whether using grand-mean centering and excluding mean *content* would provide for a more powerful analysis than obtained by Equation 28. To test this idea, we replaced the group-mean centered client *contentment* in Equation 28 with grand-mean centered *contentment* (referred to as grandcontent in the online data set) and removed mean *contentment* from the model. Recall that a grand-mean centered level-1 variable can explain variation in an outcome at level 2, while a group-mean centered level-1 predictor cannot. Further, by not including the mean of the predictor in the grand-mean centered model, we could potentially increase the power for the test of the treatment effect because the degrees of freedom for this effect are larger (providing a lower critical value) with the omission of the variable. When we estimated this new grand-mean centered model, the treatment effect estimate (−6.6) was somewhat different than that obtained with Equation 28, and the standard error was larger (2.48). Given this larger standard error, there is no advantage to using this grand-mean centered model. Also, Equation 28 is arguably a better model because it provides for valid estimates of the within- and between-cluster associations of *empathy* and *contentment* when a contextual effect is present, whereas the grand-mean centered model just described blends these effects.

13.9 SUMMARY

In this chapter, we provided an introduction to multilevel modeling as well as the use of SAS and SPSS to estimate model parameters for a two-level cross-sectional design. It should be noted that while it is relatively easy to use software to estimate model parameters, it is more challenging to understand the model being estimated, which is necessary, of course, to properly interpret the resulting parameter estimates and associated significance tests. Examining the equations for multilevel models in both forms, that is, equations expressed separately for each level and the combined equation, is helpful for understanding the effects that are being estimated. In addition, graphical displays of results, particularly for interactions, helps you achieve and convey understanding of study findings. It is also helpful to recognize that the fixed effects in such models are essentially regression coefficients. It is the random effects and their associated variance-covariance components that may be initially challenging to understand. Further, while not demonstrated in this chapter, because this is an introductory treatment, residuals can be estimated to allow for an examination of statistical assumptions. As in any analysis, one should attempt to determine if the assumptions of the procedure are reasonably satisfied, whether outlying and influential observation are present, and whether important interactions or nonlinear associations have been left out of the model.

Consulting multilevel modeling texts, many of which were cited in this chapter, will help you learn how to assess statistical assumptions. In addition, these texts will provide you with additional worked examples, fuller descriptions of the estimation processes used, as well as other important multilevel modeling techniques. These include models for growth across time, dichotomous or ordinal outcomes, multivariate outcomes, meta-analysis, and use with more complicated data structures, such as those with three or more levels, cross-classification, and multiple membership, each involving multiple random effects. You should also be aware that in addition to SAS and SPSS, several other software programs can be used to estimate multilevel models including, for example, HLM (Raudenbush, Bryk, Cheong, Congdon Jr., & du Toit, 2011), MLwiN (Rasbash, Browne, Healy, Cameron, & Charlton, 2012), Mplus (Muthén & Muthén, 1998–2013), and R (R Development Core Team, 2014).

We hope that you continue learning about multilevel modeling, as this technique is being increasingly applied to a wide variety of research designs.

REFERENCES

Arnold, C. L. (1992). An introduction to hierarchical linear models. *Measurement and Evaluation in Counseling and Development, 25,* 58–90.

Bell, B. A., Morgan, G. B., Schoeneberger, J. A., Kromrey, J. D., & Ferron, J. M. (2014). How low can you go? An investigation of the influence of sample size and model complexity on point and interval estimates in two-level linear models. *Methodology, 10,* 1–11.

Burstein, L. (1980). The analysis of multilevel data in educational research and evaluation. *Review of Research in Education, 8,* 158–233.

Enders, C. K., & Tofighi, D. (2007). Centering predictor variables in cross-sectional multilevel models: A new look at an old issue. *Psychological Methods, 12*, 121–138.

Heck, R. H., Thomas, S. L., & Tabata, L. N. (2014). *Multilevel and longitudinal modeling with IBM SPSS* (2nd ed.). New York, NY: Routledge.

Hedges, L. V., & Hedberg, E. C. (2007). Intraclass correlation values for planning group-randomized trials in education. *Educational Evaluation and Policy Analysis, 29*, 60–87.

Hox, J. J. (2010). *Multilevel analysis: Techniques and applications* (2nd ed.). New York, NY: Routledge.

Kenny, D., & Judd, C. (1986). Consequences of violating the independent assumption in analysis of variance. *Psychological Bulletin, 99*, 422–431.

Kreft, I.G.G. (1996). *Are multilevel techniques necessary? An overview, including simulation studies.* Unpublished report, California State University, Los Angeles. Available at http://www.eric.ed.gov

Kreft, I., & de Leeuw, J. (1998). *Introducing multilevel modeling.* Thousand Oaks, CA: Sage.

Mathieu, J. E., Aguinis, H., Culpepper, S. A., & Chen, G. (2012). Understanding and estimating the power to detect cross-level interaction effects in multilevel modeling. *Journal of Applied Psychology, 97*, 951–966.

Muthén, L. K., & Muthén, B. O. (1998–2013). *Mplus user's guide* (7th ed.). Los Angeles, CA: Author.

Rasbash, J., Browne, W. J., Healy, M., Cameron, B., & Charlton, C. (2012). *MLwiN Version 2.25.* Bristol, England: Centre for Multilevel Modelling, University of Bristol.

Raudenbush, S., & Bryk, A. S. (2002). *Hierarchical linear models: Applications and data analysis methods* (2nd ed.). Thousand Oaks, CA: Sage.

Raudenbush, S. W., Bryk, A. S., Cheong, Y. F., Congdon, R. T., Jr., & du Toit, M. (2011). *HLM 7: Hierarchical linear and nonlinear modeling.* Lincolnwood, IL: Scientific Software International.

R Development Core Team. (2014). *R: A language and environment for statistical computing.* R Foundation for Statistical Computing, Vienna, Austria. Retrieved from http://www.R-project.org/

Scariano, S., & Davenport, J. (1987). The effects of violations of the independence assumption in the one way ANOVA. *American Statistician, 41*, 123–129.

Snijders, T.A.B., & Bosker, R. J. (2012). *Multilevel analysis: An introduction to basic and advanced multilevel modeling* (2nd ed.). Los Angeles, CA: Sage.

Spybrook, J., & Raudenbush, S. W. (2009). An examination of the precision and technical accuracy of the first wave of group-randomized trials funded by the Institute of Education Sciences. *Educational Evaluation and Policy Analysis, 31*, 298–318.

Van Breukelen, G., & Moorbeek, M. (2013). Design considerations in multilevel studies. In M. A. Scott, J. S. Simonoff, & B. D. Marx (Eds.), *The SAGE handbook of multilevel modeling* (pp. 183–199). Thousand Oaks, CA: Sage.

West, B.T., Welch, K. B., & Galecki, A.T. (2014). *Linear mixed models: A practical guide using statistical software* (2nd ed.). New York, NY: CRC Press.

Chapter 14

MULTIVARIATE MULTILEVEL MODELING

14.1 INTRODUCTION

Previous chapters in this text have addressed the use of multivariate analysis of variance (MANOVA) and hierarchical linear modeling or, more generally, multilevel modeling. Traditional applications of these procedures have limitations that restrict their use. In particular, standard use of MANOVA assumes that responses of individuals are independently distributed, an assumption that may be violated when participants are nested in organizations or settings (such as students nested in schools, clients nested in therapists, workers nested in workplaces). When such dependence is present, use of MANOVA may result in unacceptably high type I error rates associated with the effects of explanatory variables, as detailed in Chapter 6. For its part, multilevel modeling accommodates the dependence arising from such clustered data that MANOVA does not. However, standard multilevel modeling is able to incorporate only one dependent variable from units, often participants, at the lower level. Thus, such use of multilevel modeling is not able to take advantage of the benefits associated with multivariate analysis that have been described previously in this book.

An extension of traditional MANOVA and multilevel analysis, multivariate multilevel modeling (MVMM) can accommodate dependence of responses that results from the nesting of participants in settings while simultaneously modeling multiple outcomes. More generally, MVMM may be employed in a variety of research designs that involve repeated measures analysis, multivariate growth curve modeling, multilevel structural equation modeling, and multilevel mediation analysis. MVMM also shares key features of models where items comprise the lowest level of the data structure, such as with applications of multilevel item response theory and those where researchers wish to form an overall scale using responses, for example, from several survey items. As such, MVMM can be viewed as a gateway technique to other advanced applications that enable investigators to address a wide range of research questions.

This chapter focuses on some basic applications of multivariate multilevel modeling where multiple outcomes have been collected from individuals. After presenting motivation for using this multivariate procedure, we explain the format of the data required to conduct MVMM and show how the SAS and SPSS software programs can reorganize data into the needed format. We then show how standard multilevel models can be modified to include multiple outcome variables, where scores for these variables have been collected from individuals. We then present a research example with simulated data that we use to illustrate two sets of analyses. The first set of analyses, with two-level models, is designed to ease you into MVMM but also to show that MVMM can replicate the results produced by standard MANOVA when no organizational nesting is present. This is important because an investigator may wish to use MVMM instead of MANOVA in such a design because of the ability of MVMM to include individuals in the analysis who have some missing data on the outcomes and to readily test for the equivalence of effects. In the second set, various three-level analyses using MVMM are conducted, with multiple outcomes nested within students who are nested in schools. In these analyses, we show how covariates and interactions can be modeled when multiple outcomes are present in a multilevel design.

14.2 BENEFITS OF CONDUCTING A MULTIVARIATE MULTILEVEL ANALYSIS

When data are collected on multiple outcomes, researchers have a choice to conduct univariate or multivariate analysis. As stated earlier in the text, one reason for considering a multivariate analysis is to help guard against the inflation of the overall type I error rate by using an initial global multivariate test as a protected testing approach. A second reason is that instead of examining univariate group differences using a total score, obtained by summing or averaging scores across multiple subtests, investigators can compare group differences on the multiple subtests, which may provide more insight into the nature of group differences.

These advantages for multivariate analysis are also applicable to MVMM. However, there are some additional advantages associated with the use of MVMM:

1. The MVMM approach does not require that a participant provide scores for each dependent variable. Rather, if a participant provides a score for at least one of the dependent variables, that participant may be included in the analysis. Thus, compared to the standard MANOVA approach, MVMM makes greater use of available data, which may provide for increased power. Further, SAS and SPSS provide maximum likelihood treatment of missing data for MVMM, which we noted in Chapter 1, provides for optimal estimates of parameters when the missing data mechanism is Missing Completely at Random (MCAR) or Missing at Random (MAR).

2. Snijders and Bosker (2012) note that use of MVMM may result in smaller standard errors for the tests of predictors on a given outcome compared to a univariate analysis. They note that the additional precision and increase in power for the multivariate approach may be substantial when the dependent variables are

more highly correlated and participants have missing data on some of the outcome variables.

3. When the dependent variables are similarly scaled, MVMM can be used to test whether the effects of an explanatory variable are the same or differ across the multiple outcomes. In an experimental setting, for example, an investigator may learn if treatment effects are stronger for some outcomes than others, which may suggest revising the nature and/or implementation of the intervention.

4. When participants are clustered in organizations, MVMM can be used to describe the associations between the outcome variables at the participant and cluster levels due to the partitioning of variability that is obtained with multilevel modeling. Instead of learning about how scores for a single outcome vary across participants and clusters, as with traditional multilevel modeling, MVMM can inform investigators of the *associations* between outcome variables that are within and between clusters.

Of course, MVMM is a more complicated analysis procedure compared to univariate analysis. As such, instead of proceeding immediately into an analysis with MVMM, an investigator may wish to conduct preliminary analysis using one outcome at a time in order to obtain an initial understanding of how a given outcome is related to the explanatory variables of interest. Once that is attained, MVMM could be conducted to make use potentially of a greater number of observations, provide the formal significance testing needed for the study, and decompose the correlations among outcomes at the participant and cluster (or other) levels.

14.3 RESEARCH EXAMPLE

This chapter presents two sets of illustrative analyses involving MVMM that each use the same hypothetical research example. In this example, we suppose a study is being conducted to assess the effectiveness of a new component of an existing health curriculum that is being introduced to fifth graders in a large school district. The new component, delivered by a computer-based type of game, focuses on nutrition education. The program is intended to complement the regular health curriculum but, due to its perhaps more engaging delivery, is expected to impart greater knowledge of proper nutrition and motivation for adhering to a healthier diet. Ultimately, the goal of the intervention is that students will begin (or continue) a lifetime habit of proper nutrition. Each set of analyses will focus on estimating and testing treatment effects for the multiple outcome variables.

In order to minimize potential contamination between students in the same school, the researchers have selected a cluster randomized trial where schools are randomly assigned to the new computer-based instruction or regular nutrition education as provided in the existing curriculum. The researchers, we suppose, were able to recruit 40 elementary schools and randomly assigned 20 schools to each condition. To simplify the presentation, only one class per school was selected to be included in the study.

Note that if multiple classes were selected, the design would have a student, class, and school level, instead of just the student and school level used in this example. Such a design would be a better choice if a broader within-school type of intervention were expected to lead to improved students norms and outcomes regarding proper nutrition. We also simplified the simulation of data by using a common class size of 20. However, such a perfectly balanced design is not required.

In such a design, the research team would likely select several dependent variables of interest. For the purposes of this chapter, we use two outcomes, each of which is continuous. These dependent variables are measures of intention to eat a healthy diet (called *intention*) and knowledge of proper nutrition (or *knowledge*). Some analyses in this chapter include a student pretest score measuring knowledge of proper nutrition, which is called *pretest*. Table 14.1 shows means and standard deviations for the student-level variables averaged across all schools for each treatment condition.

14.4 PREPARING A DATA SET FOR MVMM USING SAS AND SPSS

Three general steps can be taken to conduct analyses with SAS and SPSS. First, a data file is created with a long or vertical format. Second, preliminary analysis is done to assess the nature of any missing data, determine if outlying values are present, and help ensure that assumptions associated with the procedure are reasonably satisfied. Third, analysis models are specified and parameters are estimated. We illustrate the first and third steps below, but not preliminary analysis. While such analysis activities are beyond the scope of this chapter, other resources are available to assist in these activities and assess more generally the adequacy of the model (e.g., Goldstein, 2011; Raudenbush & Bryk, 2002; Snijders & Bosker, 2012).

In this section, we show how a data set that is organized in wide or horizontal format can be reformatted into the long or vertical format required for MVMM using SAS and SPSS. A two-level MVMM is used for this purpose with our two outcomes (labeled here as $Y1$ and $Y2$) considered to be nested within students. Table 14.2 shows data in the wide format for five cases of the chapter data set. This truncated data set contains a record number, a student id variable, a column of scores for $Y1$, a separate column of scores for $Y2$, and a treatment indicator variable, coded as $-.5$ for the control group and $.5$ for the treatment group.11 Dummy-coding can also be used here. It will become clear

■ Table 14.1: Means and (Standard Deviations) for Each Treatment Condition

Treatment	Intention	Knowledge	Pretest
Experimental	54.42 (10.27)	54.61 (10.39)	50.14 (10.29)
Control	45.69 (9.85)	45.98 (10.54)	49.73 (10.16)

Note: Means are based on 800 students (400 experimental and 400 control).

▪ **Table 14.2: Selected Cases Showing Variables in Wide Format**

Record	Student	Y1	Y2	Treat
1	1	29	47	−.50
2	2	52	50	−.50
3	3	42	36	−.50
4	4	47	64	−.50
.	.	.	.	.
.	.	.	.	.
800	800	66	50	.5

later in the chapter why we used this coding for the treatment groups. The wide format depicted in Table 14.2 means that each student has one record, and all of the variables for that student, particularly $Y1$ and $Y2$, appear on that same record in different columns. Thus, given that there are 800 students in the data set, the data set contains 800 records.

However, for MVMM, data need to be in the long format. That is, instead of having the scores for the dependent variables appear in separate columns, scores for all dependent variables must be placed in a single column, which creates multiple records for each individual. Thus, in the reformatted data set, an individual will have multiple records, equal to the number of outcome scores obtained from that individual. So, if there are 1,000 students in the sample and data have been collected on three outcomes for each student, the data set needed for MVMM will have 3,000 records. In the example for this chapter, each of the 800 individuals has two outcome scores, so the data will be organized into the long format containing 1,600 records.

Table 14.3 presents data from the same cases shown in Table 14.2 except that data are now in the long or vertical format, with the number of records equal to 1,600. Note that scores for each student appear on two separate lines or rows. Further, the columns containing variables $Y1$ and $Y2$ have been dropped. In their place are two new variables, Index1 and Response, both of which can be created by computer, as shown below. The Response variable contains the scores for $Y1$ and $Y2$ in single column. Index1 indicates the sequence of outcome variables in the Response column (i.e., $Y1$ followed by $Y2$). Also, the Student ID and Treatment variables are in the long format, with the values for a given case repeated across records. The far right-hand side of Table 14.3 shows two dummy-coded indicator variables, a_1 and a_2. These variables are used in the statistical model as shown in the next section. Note that a_1 is coded 1 when a given record contains a score for $Y1$ and zero otherwise. Similarly, a_2 is coded 1 when a given record contains a score for $Y2$ and zero otherwise.

The SAS and SPSS programs can reorganize a data set in the wide format to one in the long format. Table 14.4 provides the commands that can be used to convert a data set from wide to long format and to create the dummy-coded indicator variables a_1 and a_2. These commands assume the dataset is already open in the respective software programs.

Table 14.3: Selected Cases Showing Variables in Long Format

Record	Student	Index1	Response	Treat	a_1	a_2
1	1	1	29	−.50	1	0
2	1	2	47	−.50	0	1
3	2	1	52	−.50	1	0
4	2	2	50	−.50	0	1
5	3	1	42	−.50	1	0
6	3	2	36	−.50	0	1
7	4	1	47	−.50	1	0
8	4	2	64	−.50	0	1
.	.	.	.	.	.	.
.	.	.	.	.	.	.
1599	800	1	66	.5	1	0
1600	800	2	50	.5	0	1

Table 14.4: SAS and SPSS Control Lines for Reorganizing Data From the Wide to Long Format and for Creating Dummy-Coded Indicator Variables

SAS	SPSS

REORGANIZING DATA

SAS	SPSS
`DATA LONG; SET WIDE;`	`(4)  VARSTOCASES/`
`(1) INDEX1=1; IF Y1 NE. THEN RESPONSE=Y1;`	`(5)  MAKE Response FROM Y1 Y2/`
`    ELSE DELETE; OUTPUT;`	`(6)  INDEX=Index1(2)/`
`    INDEX1=2; IF Y2 NE. THEN RESPONSE=Y2;`	`(7)  KEEP=School Student Treat/`
`    ELSE DELETE; OUTPUT;`	`(8)  NULL=DROP.`
`(2) KEEP SCHOOL STUDENT TREAT INDEX1`	
`    RESPONSE;`	

CREATING DUMMY-CODED INDICATOR VARIABLES

SAS	SPSS
`DATA LONG; SET LONG;`	`(9)  RECODE INDEX1 (1=1) (ELSE=0)`
`(3) IF INDEX1=1 THEN DO; A1=1; A2=0; END;`	`     INTO A1.`
`IF INDEX1=2 THEN DO; A1=0; A2=1; END;`	`(10) EXECUTE.`
	`     RECODE INDEX1 (2=1) (ELSE=0)`
	`     INTO A2.`
	`     EXECUTE.`

(1) This creates the index and response variables shown in Table 14.3. In addition, any missing responses in the wide format will be dropped in the long data set.

(2) The KEEP statement lists all the variables to be included in the long data set.

(3) The general form for the IF-THEN statement to execute more than one action is IF condition THEN DO; action; action; END;

(4) The VARSTOCASES command restructures the wide data set into the long format.

(5) The MAKE subcommand combines the FROM variables (here Y1 and Y2) into a single column with Response as the variable name.

(Continued)

■ **Table 14.4: (Continued)**

(6) The number in parenthesis indicates the number of values for the index variable and corresponds to the number of dependent variables in the wide data set.

(7) This KEEP subcommand indicates which variables from the wide data set to retain in the long data set. The KEEP variables are a subset of all the variables in the long data set.

(8) This drops missing responses from the long data set.

(9) This RECODE command changes the values of an existing variable (here Index1) and displays the new values under a new variable (here A1). Within each parenthesis, the equals sign is preceded by the original value and followed by the new value.

(10) The EXECUTE command reads the data and executes the RECODE command.

14.5 INCORPORATING MULTIPLE OUTCOMES IN THE LEVEL-1 MODEL

For MVMM, organizing the data set in the long format and using dummy-coded variables are keys to converting a standard univariate multilevel model into a multivariate model. For this chapter, the notation used for the equations follows that used in Raudenbush and Bryk (2002). For the two-level MVMM with two outcomes, the level-1 model can be displayed as:

$$Y_{ij} = \pi_{1j} a_{1j} + \pi_{2j} a_{2j}, \tag{1}$$

where Y_{ij} in this example is the single column labeled Response in Table 14.3 that contains the scores for each outcome i ($Y1$ and $Y2$), for a given student j. The variables a_{1j} and a_{2j} are dummy-coded variables for a given outcome i of student j, as shown in Table 14.3. Note that Equation 1 has no intercept and no error term.

It is important to understand what parameters π_{1j} and π_{2j} in Equation 1 represent. Note that when $a_{1j} = 1$, a_{2j}, due to the coding that is used, is always equal to zero. In this case, Equation 1 becomes $Y_{ij} = \pi_{1j}$ (1) or simply π_{1j}, which must equal $Y1$ due to the structure of the response column and dummy-coded variables. That is, when $a_{1j} = 1$, the response variable in Equation 1 draws observations from only those records having a score for $Y1$ in the response column, which in this data set also corresponds to selecting the odd numbered records only (given no missing data for the outcomes). Similarly, when $a_{2j} = 1$, $Y_{ij} = \pi_{2j}$, which must equal $Y2$ (*knowledge*), as $a_{1j} = 0$ in this case. So, when $a_{2j} = 1$, the response in Equation 1 uses only those scores from the even numbered records in the data set, which correspond to $Y2$. As a result, π_{1j} and π_{2j} represent the dependent variables $Y1$ and $Y2$ in this analysis due to the data and model set up.

Equation 1, or a slightly modified form of it, is used for all analyses in this chapter, and these level-1 parameters are the dependent variables at the student-level (level 2) of the analysis. Note, however, that SAS and SPSS software, as shown in the next section, simplify the modeling process by having the user express the response as a function of the Index1 variable, shown in Table 14.5. Thus, with these software programs, the a variables in Equation 1 generally do not need to be created by the user or specified as explanatory variables in the modeling process. However, we show later in the chapter that the a variables are useful in certain situations.

14.6 EXAMPLE 1: USING SAS AND SPSS TO CONDUCT TWO-LEVEL MULTIVARIATE ANALYSES

For the first example, three different analyses will be conducted, all of which include the measure and student levels, but ignore the school level. Note that you would generally want to include the school level in the analysis model, given the nested design, as omitting this level may result in an inflated type I error rate for the test of a given

■ Table 14.5: SAS and SPSS Control Lines for Estimating the Two-Level Empty Model

SAS	SPSS
(1) PROC MIXED DATA=LONG METHOD=ML COVTEST;	(5) MIXED RESPONSE BY INDEX1/
(2) CLASS INDEX1 STUDENT;	(6) FIXED=INDEX1 | NOINT/
(3) MODEL RESPONSE = INDEX1 / NOINT SOLUTION;	(7) METHOD=ML/
(4) REPEATED INDEX1 / SUBJECT = STUDENT TYPE=UN R;	(8) PRINT=R SOLUTION TESTCOV/
	(9) REPEATED=INDEX1 | SUBJECT STUDENT) COVTYPE(UN).

(1) We fit the MVMM using the `MIXED` procedure and specify full maximum likelihood (ML) as the estimation method. We also request hypothesis test results for the variance and covariance components with the `COVTEST` option.

(2) The CLASS statement defines the grouping variable(s) and must precede the `MODEL` statement.

(3) The MODEL statement specifies the dependent variable and the fixed effects. `INDEX1` is listed as a fixed effect to estimate separate intercepts for Y1 and Y2, and the `NOINT` option is included to suppress the default intercept at level 1. The `SOLUTION` option displays the fixed effects estimates in the output.

(4) This `REPEATED` statement specifies an unstructured covariance structure (`UN`) for the residual covariance or **R** matrix with the `TYPE=` option and displays the matrix in the output with the **R** option. The level-2 unit identifier (`STUDENT`) appears after the SUBJECT=option, indicating that outcomes are nested in students.

(5) The general form for the `MIXED` command is `MIXED dependent variables BY factors WITH covariates`. There are no covariates in this model, so the `WITH` part is not included.

(6) This FIXED subcommand estimates separate intercepts for Y1 and Y2 by specifying INDEX1 as a fixed effect and suppresses the default intercept term at level 1 with the `NOINT` option.

(7) The estimation method is full maximum likelihood (ML).

(8) This `PRINT` subcommand displays the residual covariance matrix (R), the fixed and random effects estimates (`SOLUTION`), and the statistical tests results for the variance and covariance parameters (`TESTCOV`).

(9) This `REPEATED` subcommand identifies the level-2 unit as `SUBJECT` and an unstructured covariance structure (`UN`) for the residual covariance matrix.

predictor. We include the school level in the analysis model in section 14.7. The first analysis for our two-level model will include the outcomes, but will have no predictors. The goal of this analysis is to obtain some descriptive statistics and the model deviance, which will be used to test the effect of the treatment. In the second analysis, a coded treatment variable will be included as an explanatory variable for each outcome. The goal of this analysis is to determine if students in the intervention group score significantly greater, on average, than those in the control group for any of the outcomes. If a significant overall treatment effect is present, then the treatment effect for each outcome will be estimated and tested for significance. In the third analysis, we presume that the outcome scores are measured on the same scale (which they are for the simulated data set). We then test whether the impact of the treatment is the same for each outcome.

14.6.1 Estimating the Empty or Null Model

The first analysis of the data does not include any explanatory variables and is called an unconditional or empty model. For this model, Equation 1 is the level-1 model. At the second level of the model, the parameters, π_{1j} and π_{2j}, which represent the variables *intention* ($Y1$) and *knowledge* ($Y2$), are allowed to vary across students. This level-2 model is

$$\pi_{1j} = \beta_{10} + r_{1j} \tag{2}$$

$$\pi_{2j} = \beta_{20} + r_{2j}, \tag{3}$$

where β_{10} and β_{20} represent the mean for *intention* and *knowledge*, respectively. The residual terms (r_{1j} and r_{2j}) are assumed to follow a bivariate normal distribution, with an expected mean of zero, some variance and covariance.

The five parameters to be estimated for this empty model are two fixed effects (i.e., β_{10}, β_{20}), which are the means of $Y1$ and $Y2$, the variance of r_{1j}, or $Y1$ ($\tau_{\pi 11}$), the variance of r_{2j}, or $Y2$ ($\tau_{\pi 22}$), and their covariance ($\tau_{\pi 12}$). Note that 1,600 cases are being used in the analysis. The SAS and SPSS commands for estimating these parameters are given in Table 14.5 and selected results are presented in Table 14.6.

In Table 14.6, the SAS and SPSS outputs show that the means for *intention* ($Y1$) and *knowledge* ($Y2$), as shown in the tables of fixed effects, are respectively, 50.05 and 50.29, with variances 119.95 and 127.90, and covariance 60.87, as shown in the covariance parameter tables and also in the R or residual covariance matrices. Given the covariance matrix, the standard deviations for *intention* and *knowledge* are, respectively, 10.95 and 11.31, and the correlation of the residuals is .491, indicating that *intention* and *knowledge* are positively and moderately correlated. The model deviance for the five parameters is 12,030.2, as shown in the outputs. This deviance value, as previously indicated in this text, reflects the fit of the model. This model deviance (i.e., $-2LL$) will be compared to the deviance obtained when the treatment variable is added the model to determine whether the fit of the model improves with the addition of the treatment indicator variable. Note that the full maximum likelihood estimation procedure (as implemented throughout the chapter), not restricted maximum likelihood, needs to be used when one wishes to test the effects of explanatory variables using deviances.

Note that although we do not place much focus on testing variances in this chapter, each variance and covariance element can be tested for significance with a z test, as described in Chapter 13. This test is provided by SAS and SPSS through the COV-TEST and TESTCOV options, respectively, and is shown in the covariance parameters tables in Table 14.6. However, the z test for variances should be used as a rough guide for determining statistical significance as the sampling distribution of the variance is *approximately* normal. A chi-square test using model deviances is preferred for testing variances, with such a test illustrated in section 14.7.3.

14.6.2 Including an Explanatory Variable in the Model

We now include the treatment variable in this multivariate analysis. The goal of the analysis is to determine if there are treatment effects for any outcome, which will be accomplished by a global test of the null hypothesis that no treatment effects are present for any outcome. If treatment effects are present, then the effects and statistical test results for the treatment will be examined for each outcome. For this two-level model, Equation 1 is the level-1 model. At the student level, Equations 2 and 3 are modified so that the treatment variable (Treat) is added to each of the equations. Although dummy coding can be used for the treatment variable, the coding employed here uses values of $-.5$ and $.5$ representing membership in the control and treatment conditions, respectively. The level-2 model that is used now is

$$\pi_{1j} = \beta_{10} + \beta_{11}X_j + r_{1j} \tag{4}$$

$$\pi_{2j} = \beta_{20} + \beta_{21}X_j + r_{2j}, \tag{5}$$

where X_j represents the treatment variable. Due to the coding used for the treatment variable, β_{10} and β_{20} represent the mean for *intention* and *knowledge*, respectively. More importantly, β_{11} and β_{21} represent the mean difference between students in the experimental and control conditions for *intention* and *knowledge*, respectively. The residual terms are assumed to follow a bivariate normal distribution, with an equal variance-covariance matrix across treatment groups. Note that the multivariate null hypothesis for the test of the treatment is $H_0 : \beta_{11} = \beta_{21} = 0$, which will be tested by using deviances from this and the empty model of Equations 1–3.

For this model, four fixed effects (the four βs in Equations 4 and 5) and the three variance-covariance elements are to be estimated. Note that to include an explanatory variable in the model so that separate effects of that variable are estimated for each outcome, SAS and SPSS require that a given explanatory variable be multiplied by the

Table 14.6 Selected Output for the Two-Level Empty Model

	SAS	

Estimated R Matrix for Student 1

Row	Col1	Col2
1	119.95	60.8689
2	60.8689	127.9

Fit Statistics

-2 Log Likelihood	12030.2
AIC (smaller is better)	12040.2
AICC (smaller is better)	12040.2
BIC (smaller is better)	12063.6

Solution for Fixed Effects

Effect	Index1	Estimate	Standard Error	DF	t Value	Pr > |t|
Index1	1	50.0548	0.3872	800	129.27	<.0001
Index1	2	50.2909	0.3998	800	125.78	<.0001

Covariance Parameter Estimates

Cov Parm	Subject	Estimate	Standard Error	Z Value	Pr Z
UN(1,1)	Student	119.95	5.9976	20	<.0001
UN(2,1)	Student	60.8689	4.8794	12.47	<.0001
UN(2,2)	Student	127.9	6.3951	20	<.0001

	SPSS	

Estimates of Fixed Effects[a]

Parameter	Estimate	Std. Error	Df	t	Sig.	95% Confidence Interval	
						Lower Bound	Upper Bound
[Index1=1]	50.054814	0.38722	800	129.267		49.294726	50.814902
[Index1=2]	50.290916	0.399847	800	125.775		49.506042	51.075789

[a] Dependent Variable: Response.

(*Continued*)

▨ **Table 14.6: (Continued)**

Estimates of Covariance Parameters[a]

Parameter		Estimate	Std. Error	Wald Z	Sig.	95% Confidence Interval Lower Bound	95% Confidence Interval Upper Bound
Repeated	UN (1,1)	119.95174	5.997587	20	0	108.754309	132.302067
Measures	UN (2,1)	60.868913	4.879436	12.475	0	51.305394	70.432431
	UN (2,2)	127.902203	6.39511	20	0	115.962601	141.071116

[a] Dependent Variable: Response.

Information Criteria[a]

-2 Log Likelihood	12030.164
Akaike's Information Criterion (AIC)	12040.164
Hurvich and Tsai's Criterion (AICC)	12040.202
Bozdogan's Criterion (CAIC)	12072.053
Schwarz's Bayesian Criterion (BIC)	12067.053

The information criteria are displayed in smaller-is-better forms.

[a] Dependent Variable: Response.

Residual Covariance (R) Matrix[a]

	[Index1 = 1]	[Index1 = 2]
[Index1 = 1]	119.95174	60.868913
[Index1 = 2]	60.868913	127.902203

Unstructured

[a] Dependent Variable: Response.

Index1 variable. So, to estimate β_{11} and β_{21} in SAS, the term TREAT*INDEX1 must be added to the MODEL statement shown in Table 14.5. In SPSS, we add the statements WITH TREAT to the MIXED command and TREAT*INDEX1 to the FIXED subcommand. The complete SAS and SPSS control lines for estimating all models in this chapter are shown in section 14.9. Table 14.7 shows selected results for this model.

As shown in the outputs, the deviance for this current model is 11,847.6, with seven parameters estimated. Recall that the deviance for the empty model was 12,030.2 with five parameters estimated. The global test for the null hypothesis that no treatment effects are present for any of the outcomes (H_0: $\beta_{11} = \beta_{21} = 0$) can be tested by computing the difference in these deviances, which is distributed as a chi-square value having degrees of freedom equal to the difference in the number of parameters estimated for

■ Table 14.7: Selected Output for the Two-Level Model With Treatment Effects

SAS

Solution for Fixed Effects

Effect	Index1	Estimate	Standard Error	DF	t Value	Pr > |t|
Index1	1	50.0548	0.3552	800	140.92	<.0001
Index1	2	50.2909	0.3696	800	136.06	<.0001
Treat*Index1	1	8.7233	0.7104	800	12.28	<.0001
Treat*Index1	2	8.6257	0.7393	800	11.67	<.0001

Estimated R Matrix for Student 1

Row	Col1	Col2
1	100.93	42.0579
2	42.0579	109.3

Covariance Parameter Estimates

Cov Parm	Subject	Estimate	Standard Error	Z Value	Pr Z
UN(1,1)	Student	100.93	5.0464	20	<.0001
UN(2,1)	Student	42.0579	4.0001	10.51	<.0001
UN(2,2)	Student	109.3	5.4651	20	<.0001

Fit Statistics

-2 Log Likelihood	11847.6
AIC (smaller is better)	11861.6
AICC (smaller is better)	11861.7
BIC (smaller is better)	11894.4

SPSS

Estimates of Fixed Effects[a]

Parameter	Estimate	Std. Error	Df	t	Sig.	95% Confidence Interval	
						Lower Bound	Upper Bound
[Index1=1]	50.054814	0.35519	800	140.924		49.3576	50.752029
[Index1=2]	50.290916	0.369631	800	136.057		49.565355	51.016477
[Index1=1] * Treat	8.723254	0.71038	800	12.28		7.328825	10.117683
[Index1=2] * Treat	8.625689	0.739262	800	11.668		7.174567	10.07681

[a] Dependent Variable: Response.

(*Continued*)

■ **Table 14.7: (Continued)**

Estimates of Covariance Parameters[a]

Parameter		Estimate	Std. Error	Wald Z	Sig.	95% Confidence Interval Lower Bound	95% Confidence Interval Upper Bound
Repeated	UN (1,1)	100.92795	5.046398	20		91.50638	111.319573
Measures	UN (2,1)	42.057895	4.00007	10.514		34.217901	49.897889
	UN (2,2)	109.301577	5.465079	20		99.098334	120.555355

[a] Dependent Variable: Response.

Information Criteria[a]

-2 Log Likelihood	11847.606
Akaike's Information Criterion (AIC)	11861.606
Hurvich and Tsai's Criterion (AICC)	11861.676
Bozdogan's Criterion (CAIC)	11906.25
Schwarz's Bayesian Criterion (BIC)	11899.25

The information criteria are displayed in smaller-is-better forms.
[a] Dependent Variable: Response.

Residual Covariance (R) Matrix[a]

	[Index1 = 1]	[Index1 = 2]
[Index1 = 1]	100.92795	42.057895
[Index1 = 2]	42.057895	109.301577

Unstructured
[a] Dependent Variable: Response.

these models, i.e., $7 - 5 = 2$. This deviance test can be used here because the empty model can be obtained from this current model by constraining the treatment effects to be zero. Computing the difference in model deviances results in a chi-square value of $12,030.2 - 11,847.6 = 182.6$, which is statistically significant, as this value exceeds the chi-square critical value of 5.99 ($\alpha = .05$, $df = 2$).

Since rejection of the overall multivariate null hypothesis suggests that treatment effects are present for at least one of the outcomes, we now consider the estimates and statistical test results of the treatment effect for each outcome. Here, the two null hypotheses being tested are $H_0 : \beta_{11} = 0$ and $H_0 : \beta_{21} = 0$. As shown in the outputs, the treatment effects are 8.72 ($SE = .710$) for *intention* and 8.63 ($SE = .739$) for *knowledge*. The t ratios of about 12.28 ($p < .05$) and 11.67 ($p < .05$), respectively, for *intention* and *knowledge*, suggest that treatment effects are present for each outcome in the population. To obtain the group means for each outcome, values of $-.5$ and $.5$ for the control and experimental group can be inserted into Equations 4 and 5, along with the parameter estimates. Thus, for *intention*, the control group mean is $50.055 - .5(8.723) = 45.693$, and the experimental group mean is $50.055 + .5(8.723) = 54.417$. For *knowledge*, you can confirm that the control group mean is 45.978 and the experimental group mean is 54.604. The residual variances are also shown in the outputs, and they are 100.93 ($SD =10.05$) for *intention* and 109.30 ($SD = 10.45$) for *knowledge*. The correlation between the residuals can be calculated in the usual manner and is .400.

14.6.3 Comparison to Traditional MANOVA Results

For comparison purposes, we provide and briefly discuss selected SPSS results from a traditional multivariate analysis of these same data with the treatment as the explanatory variable. Table 14.8 shows that the *p* value associated with Wilks' lambda is quite small, leading to the decision to reject the overall multivariate null hypothesis for the treatment effects, the same decision as obtained with MVMM. In the parameter estimates table in Table 14.8, SPSS automatically dummy codes the treatment variable, coding the value for the experimental and control groups, in this example, as 0 and 1, respectively. Thus, in that table, the intercept represents the experimental group average for a given outcome, and the treatment effect is computed by subtracting the experimental mean from the control mean (thus obtaining negative differences). Other than that, the SPSS results in this table are virtually the same as those obtained with the MVMM approach, with the difference in means estimated to be 8.72 ($SE =.711$) for *intentions* and 8.63 ($SE =.740$) for *knowledge*. Thus, if desired, MVMM can be used in place of traditional multivariate analysis. The remaining analyses in this chapter illustrate some extensions of the traditional MANOVA approach that can be more effectively handled by MVMM.

14.6.4 Testing Whether the Effect of a Predictor Differs Across Outcomes

The final analysis conducted with the two-level example tests whether the effect of the treatment is of the same magnitude for each outcome. Given that the outcomes are measured on or placed on the same scale, investigators may wish to learn if a new intervention has stronger effects for some outcomes than others. This can be done by first constraining the fixed effects—in this case treatment effects—to be equal, and then testing the difference in fit using the deviances between this constrained model and one where the effects are freely estimated. In Equations 4 and 5, the effects of the treatment are freely estimated (i.e., without constraints) for *intention* (β_{11}) and *knowledge* (β_{21}). In this analysis, we test whether these treatment effects are the same or different for the two outcomes. The model used now is essentially the same as with the previous analysis except that an assumed common treatment effect will be estimated. As such, the number of parameters estimated is now six, consisting of three fixed effects (i.e., only one treatment effect estimate) and the three elements in the variance-covariance matrix.

■ **Table 14.8: Selected Output From a Traditional MANOVA**

	Multivariate Tests[b]					
Effect		Value	F	Hypothesis df	Error df	Sig.
Intercept	Pillai's Trace	.972	13654.003[a]	2.000	797.000	.000
	Wilks' Lambda	.028	13654.003[a]	2.000	797.000	.000
	Hotelling's Trace	34.263	13654.003[a]	2.000	797.000	.000
	Roy's Largest Root	34.263	13654.003[a]	2.000	797.000	.000
Treat	Pillai's Trace	.204	102.149[a]	2.000	797.000	.000
	Wilks' Lambda	.796	102.149[a]	2.000	797.000	.000
	Hotelling's Trace	.256	102.149[a]	2.000	797.000	.000
	Roy's Largest Root	.256	102.149[a]	2.000	797.000	.000

[a] Exact statistic
[a] Design: Intercept + Treat

	Parameter Estimates						
						95% Confidence Interval	
Dependent Variable	Parameter	B	Std. Error	t	Sig.	Lower Bound	Upper Bound
Y1	Intercept	54.416	.503	108.196	.000	53.429	55.404
	[Treat=-.50]	-8.723	.711	-12.264	.000	-10.119	-7.327
	[Treat=.50]	0[a]	.	.	.	.	.
Y2	Intercept	54.604	.523	104.327	.000	53.576	55.631
	[Treat=-.50]	-8.626	.740	-11.653	.000	-10.079	-7.173
	[Treat=.50]	0[a]	.	.	.	.	.

[a] This parameter is set to zero because it is redundant.

To estimate this model in SAS and SPSS, we replace the TREAT*INDEX1 term in the previous model with TREAT. Complete control lines for this model can be found in section 14.9. Selected outputs are presented in Table 14.9.

As shown in the outputs, the deviance associated with this constrained treatment-effects model is 11,847.621, which is only slightly larger (i.e., reflecting worse fitting) than the previous model that provided separate estimates of treatment effects. Specifically, the difference in model deviances, which is distributed as a chi-square value is $11{,}847.621 - 11{,}847.606 = 0.015$, which does not exceed the chi-square critical value of 3.84 ($\alpha = .05$, $df = 1$). Thus, this test does not suggest that these two models have different fit. As such, there is evidence supporting the hypothesis that the effect of the intervention is similar for *intention* and *knowledge*. Note that in the SAS and SPSS outputs, shown in the fixed effects tables of Table 14.9, the common treatment effect is estimated to be 8.678 ($SE = .606$) and is statistically significant ($p < .05$).

■ Table 14.9: Selected Output for the Two-Level Model With Treatment Effects Constrained to Be Equal

SAS

Solution for Fixed Effects

Effect	Index1	Estimate	Standard Error	DF	t Value	Pr > |t|
Index1	1	50.0548	0.3552	799	140.92	<.0001
Index1	2	50.2909	0.3696	799	136.06	<.0001
Treat		8.6777	0.606	799	14.32	<.0001

Estimated R Matrix for Student 1

Row	Col1	Col2
1	100.93	42.0573
2	42.0573	109.3

Covariance Parameter Estimates

Cov Parm	Subject	Estimate	Standard Error	Z Value	Pr Z
UN(1,1)	Student	100.93	5.0464	20	<.0001
UN(2,1)	Student	42.0573	4.0001	10.51	<.0001
UN(2,2)	Student	109.3	5.4651	20	<.0001

Fit Statistics

-2 Log Likelihood	11847.6
AIC (smaller is better)	11859.6
AICC (smaller is better)	11859.7
BIC (smaller is better)	11887.7

SPSS

Estimates of Fixed Effects[a]

Parameter	Estimate	Std. Error	Df	T	Sig.	95% Confidence Interval Lower Bound	Upper Bound
[Index1=1]	50.054814	0.355191	799.994	140.924		49.357598	50.75203
[Index1=2]	50.290916	0.369632	799.993	136.057		49.565353	51.016479
Treat	8.67771	0.606001	800	14.32		7.488171	9.867249

[a] Dependent Variable: Response.

(*Continued*)

■ **Table 14.9: (Continued)**

Estimates of Covariance Parameters[a]

Parameter		Estimate	Std. Error	Wald Z	Sig.	95% Confidence Interval Lower Bound	Upper Bound
Repeated	UN (1,1)	100.928469	5.046442	20		91.506817	111.320185
Measures	UN (2,1)	42.057303	4.000082	10.514		34.217285	49.89732
	UN (2,2)	109.302254	5.465135	20		99.098907	120.556151

[a] Dependent Variable: Response.

Information Criteria[a]

-2 Log Likelihood	11847.621
Akaike's Information Criterion (AIC)	11859.621
Hurvich and Tsai's Criterion (AICC)	11859.673
Bozdogan's Criterion (CAIC)	11897.887
Schwarz's Bayesian Criterion (BIC)	11891.887

The information criteria are displayed in smaller-is-better forms.

[a] Dependent Variable: Response.

Residual Covariance (R) Matrix[a]

	[Index1 = 1]	[Index1 = 2]
[Index1 = 1]	100.928469	42.057303
[Index1 = 2]	42.057303	109.302254

Unstructured

[a] Dependent Variable: Response.

14.7 EXAMPLE 2: USING SAS AND SPSS TO CONDUCT THREE-LEVEL MULTIVARIATE ANALYSES

The previous examples illustrated two-level multivariate analyses, but did not include the school level in the statistical model. In the research design used in this chapter, students are nested in one of 40 schools. Often, such nesting needs to be accounted for in the analysis because the responses of students within treatment groups are not independent, as is assumed in the previous analysis. Instead, these responses are likely related because the students share a similar environment. As discussed previously, such dependence, if not accounted for statistically, can increase type I error rates associated with fixed effects and may lead to false claims of, in this case, the presence of treatment effects. The analyses in this section take the within-school dependence into account by adding a third level—the school level—to the multilevel model. Further, instead of including only the treatment variable in the model, we include other explanatory variables, including student gender, student pretest knowledge, a school average of these pretest scores, and a treatment-gender product term.

There is one primary hypothesis underlying these analyses. That is, while treatment effects are expected to be present for *intention* and *knowledge* for both boys and girls, boys are expected to derive greater benefit from the computer-based instruction. The reason for this extra impact of the intervention, we assume, is that fifth-grade boys will enjoy playing the instructional video game more than girls. As a result, the impact that the experimental program has for *intention* and *knowledge* will be greater for boys than girls. Thus, the investigators hypothesize the presence of a treatment-by-gender interaction for both outcomes, where the intervention will have stronger effects on *intention* and *knowledge* for boys than for girls.

In addition, because the cluster randomized trial with this limited number of schools (i.e., 40) does not generally provide for great statistical power, knowledge pretest scores were collected from all students. These scores are expected to be fairly strongly associated with both outcomes. Further, because associations may be stronger at the school level than at the student level, the researchers computed school averages of the knowledge pretest scores and plan to include this variable in the model to provide for increased power.

Three MVMM analyses are illustrated next. The first analysis includes the treatment variable as the sole explanatory variable. The purpose of this analysis is to obtain a preliminary estimate of the treatment effect for each outcome. The second analysis includes all of the explanatory variables as well as the treatment-by-gender interaction. The primary purpose of this analysis is to test the hypothesized interactions. If the multivariate test for the interaction is significant, the analysis will focus on examining the treatment-by-gender interaction for each outcome, and if significant, describing the nature of any interactions obtained. The third analysis will illustrate a multivariate test for multiple variance and covariance elements. Often, in practice, it is not clear if, for example, the association between a student explanatory variable and outcome is the same or varies across schools. Researchers may then rely on empirical evidence (e.g., a statistical test result) to address this issue.

14.7.1 A Three-Level Model for Treatment Effects

For this first analysis, Equation 1, which had previously been the level-1 model, needs to be modified slightly in order to acknowledge the inclusion of the school level. The level-1 model now is:

$$Y_{ijk} = \pi_{1jk} a_{1jk} + \pi_{2jk} a_{2jk}, \tag{6}$$

which is identical to Equation 1 except that subscript k has been added. Thus, π_{1jk} and π_{2jk} represent the *intention* and *knowledge* posttest scores, respectively, for a given student j who is attending a given school k. The second- or student-level of the model, with no explanatory variables included, is then

$$\pi_{1jk} = \beta_{10k} + r_{1jk} \tag{7}$$

$$\pi_{2jk} = \beta_{20k} + r_{2jk}, \tag{8}$$

where β_{10k} and β_{20k} represent the mean for a given school k for *intention* and *knowledge*, respectively. The student-level or within-school residual terms (r_{1jk} and r_{2jk}) are assumed to follow a bivariate normal distribution, with an expected mean of zero, variances ($\tau_{\pi1}$ and $\tau_{\pi2}$), and covariance ($\tau_{\pi12}$). Since treatment assignment varies across and not within schools, the treatment indicator variable (coded $-.5$ and $.5$ for control and experimental schools, respectively) appears in the school-level model. This third- or school-level model is

$$\beta_{10k} = \gamma_{100} + \gamma_{101}Treat_k + u_{10k} \tag{9}$$

$$\beta_{20k} = \gamma_{200} + \gamma_{201}Treat_k + u_{20k}, \tag{10}$$

where γ_{100} and γ_{200} represent the overall average for *intention* and *knowledge*, respectively. The key parameters are γ_{101} and γ_{201}, which represent the differences in means between the experimental and control groups for *intention* and *knowledge*. The school-level residual terms are u_{10k} and u_{20k}, which are assumed to follow a bivariate normal distribution with an expected mean of zero and constant variances ($\tau_{\beta11}$ and $\tau_{\beta22}$), and covariance ($\tau_{\beta12}$).

The software commands for reorganizing a data set given in Table 14.4 can be used here to change the data set from the wide to the needed long format. Note that the Keep commands in Table 14.4 should be modified to also include variables *gender*, *pretest*, *meanpretest*, and *TXG*, which are used in subsequent analyses. Table 14.10 shows some cases for the reorganized data set that is needed for this section.

The variables in this data set include a school and student id, the index variable identifying the response as *Y1* or *Y2*, *response* containing the scores for the outcomes, *treatment* (with $-.5$ for the control group and $.5$ for the experimental group), *gender* (with $-.5$ indicating female and $.5$ male), *pretest* knowledge, *meanpretest*, and a treatment-by-gender product variable (denoted *TXG*), which is needed to model the interaction of interest. To ensure that the output you obtain will correspond to that in the text, all variables except the index and id variables should appear as continuous variables in the data set.

The model described in Equations 6–10 has four fixed effects (the four γs) and six variance-covariance elements, for a total of 10 parameters. As shown in Table 14.11, we build upon the SAS and SPSS commands for the two-level models to estimate these parameters and present selected results in Table 14.12. Note that the R matrix is

▨ **Table 14.10: Selected Cases Showing Variables in Long Format for Three-Level Models**

Record	School	Student	Index1	Response	Treat	Gender	Pretest	Mean Pretest	TXG
1	1	1	1	29	−.50	−.50	48	46	.25
2	1	1	2	47	−.50	−.50	48	46	.25
3	1	2	1	52	−.50	.50	52	46	−.25
4	1	2	2	50	−.50	.50	52	46	−.25
5	1	3	1	42	−.50	−.50	41	46	.25
6	1	3	2	36	−.50	−.50	41	46	.25
7	1	4	1	47	−.50	.50	63	46	−.25
8	1	4	2	64	−.50	.50	63	46	−.25
.	.	.	.	.	.	.	.	.	.
.	.	.	.	.	.	.	.	.	.
1599	40	800	1	66	.50	.50	41	53	.25
1600	40	800	2	50	.50	.50	41	53	.25

the variance-covariate matrix for the student-level residuals, and the G matrix is the variance-covariance matrix for the school-level residuals.

In Table 14.12, the outputs (in the fixed effects tables) show that students scored higher, on average, for both *intentions* ($\gamma_{101} = 8.72$, $p < .05$) and *knowledge* ($\gamma_{201} = 8.63$, $p < .05$) when they were exposed to the experimental nutritional educational program. In addition, after taking treatment membership into account, most of the posttest score variability is within schools, as the proportion of remaining variability that is between schools for *intention* is about .03 (i.e., 3.31 / (3.31 + 97.62)) and .08 (i.e., 8.74 / (8.74 + 100.56)) for *knowledge*. Note that estimates for the variances and covariances appear in the covariance parameter tables and in the R and G matrices of Table 14.12. The correlation among the residuals, which can be calculated manually, at the student level is .40 and at the school level is .38. Note that if desired, an empty model omitting the treatment variable from Equations 9 and 10 could be estimated prior to this model. If that were done, model deviances could be compared as in sections 14.6.1 and 14.6.2 to test the overall multivariate null hypothesis of no treatment effect. A test of model deviances will be used to provide a multivariate test of the interaction of interest.

14.7.2 A Three-Level Model With Multiple Predictors

In the second analysis, all explanatory variables are included and the multivariate null hypothesis of no treatment-by-gender interaction for any of the outcomes is tested. For this analysis, Equation 6 remains the level-1 model. The student-level model is modified to include *gender* (coded −.5 for females and .5 for males) and *pretest*, which is group-mean centered. For the remaining models in this chapter, variable names, instead of symbols, are used to ease understanding of the models. Thus, the student-level model is

■ Table 14.11: SAS and SPSS Control Lines for Estimating the Three-Level Model With Treatment Effects

SAS	SPSS
PROC MIXED DATA=LONG METHOD=ML COVTEST;	MIXED RESPONSE BY INDEX1 WITH TREAT/
(1) CLASS INDEX1 STUDENT SCHOOL; MODEL RESPONSE = INDEX1 TREAT*INDEX1 / NOINT SOLUTION;	FIXED=INDEX1 TREAT*INDEX1 | NOINT/ METHOD=ML/
(2) RANDOM INDEX1 / SUBJECT=SCHOOL TYPE=UN G;	PRINT=G R SOLUTION TESTCOV/ (4) RANDOM=INDEX1 | SUBJECT
(3) REPEATED INDEX1 / SUBJECT = STUDENT(SCHOOL) TYPE=UN R;	(SCHOOL) COVTYPE(UN)/ (5) REPEATED=INDEX1 | SUBJECT (SCHOOL*STUDENT) COVTYPE(UN).

(1) We add the level-3 unit identifier (SCHOOL) as a CLASS variable.

(2) The RANDOM statement estimates separate random effects for INDEX1 (i.e., Y1 and Y2) at the SCHOOL level and displays the corresponding variance-covariance matrix, G matrix.

(3) The nesting of level-2 units within level-3 units appears as STUDENT(SCHOOL). The R matrix is the person-level variance covariance matrix.

(4) The RANDOM subcommand specifies random effects for Y1 and Y2 at the school level and requests an unstructured school-level variance-covariance matrix, G matrix.

(5) SCHOOL*STUDENT refers to the nesting of level-2 units within level-3 units and specifies an unstructured matrix for the student-level variance-covariance matrix, which is the R matrix.

■ Table 14.12: Selected Output for the Three-Level Model With Treatment Effects

SAS						

Solution for Fixed Effects

Effect	Index1	Estimate	Standard Error	DF	t Value	Pr > |t|
Index1	1	50.0548	0.4525	76	110.62	<.0001
Index1	2	50.2909	0.5867	76	85.72	<.0001
Treat*Index1	1	8.7233	0.905	1520	9.64	<.0001
Treat*Index1	2	8.6257	1.1734	1520	7.35	<.0001

Estimated R Matrix for Student (School)

Row	Col1	Col2
1	97.6186	40.0357
2	40.0357	100.56

(Continued)

Covariance Parameter Estimates

Cov Parm	Subject	Estimate	Standard Error	Z Value	Pr Z
UN(1,1)	School	3.3094	1.8484	1.79	0.0367
UN(2,1)	School	2.0222	1.806	1.12	0.2629
UN(2,2)	School	8.7416	3.0898	2.83	0.0023
UN(1,1)	Student(School)	97.6186	5.0077	19.49	<.0001
UN(2,1)	Student(School)	40.0357	3.8763	10.33	<.0001
UN(2,2)	Student(School)	100.56	5.1586	19.49	<.0001

Fit Statistics

-2 Log Likelihood	11813.4
AIC (smaller is better)	11833.4
AICC (smaller is better)	11833.5
BIC (smaller is better)	11850.3

Estimated G Matrix

Row	Effect	Index1	School	Col1	Col2
1	Index1	1	1	3.3094	2.0222
2	Index1	2	1	2.0222	8.7416

SPSS

Estimates of Fixed Effects[a]

Parameter	Estimate	Std. Error	Df	t	Sig.	95% Confidence Interval	
						Lower Bound	Upper Bound
[Index1=1]	50.054814	0.452502	40	110.618		49.140274	50.969355
[Index1=2]	50.290916	0.58672	40	85.715		49.105111	51.476721
[Index1=1] * Treat	8.723254	0.905004	40	9.639		6.894173	10.552335
[Index1=2] * Treat	8.625689	1.17344	40	7.351		6.254078	10.997299

[a] Dependent Variable: Response.

Estimates of Covariance Parameters[a]

Parameter		Estimate	Std. Error	Wald Z	Sig.	95% Confidence Interval	
						Lower Bound	Upper Bound
Repeated	UN (1,1)	97.618558	5.007726	19.494		88.280884	107.943901
Measures	UN (2,1)	40.035727	3.876274	10.328		32.438371	47.633084

Estimates of Covariance Parameters[a]

Parameter		Estimate	Std. Error	Wald Z	Sig.	95% Confidence Interval Lower Bound	Upper Bound
	UN (2,2)	100.55996	5.158614	19.494		90.940926	111.196421
Index1	UN (1,1)	3.309392	1.848448	1.79	0.073	1.107421	9.889709
[subject =	UN (2,1)	2.022168	1.806048	1.12	0.263	-1.517621	5.561956
School]	UN (2,2)	8.741618	3.089764	2.829	0.005	4.37251	17.476435

[a] Dependent Variable: Response.

Random Effect Covariance Structure (G)[a]

	[Index1=1]	School	[Index1=2]	School
[Index1=1]	School	3.309392	2.022168
[Index1=2]	School	2.022168	8.741618

Unstructured
[a] Dependent Variable: Response.

Information Criteria[a]

-2 Log Likelihood	11813.380
Akaike's Information Criterion (AIC)	11833.38
Hurvich and Tsai's Criterion (AICC)	11833.518
Bozdogan's Criterion (CAIC)	11897.157
Schwarz's Bayesian Criterion (BIC)	11887.157

The information criteria are displayed in smaller-is-better forms.
[a] Dependent Variable: Response.

Residual Covariance (R) Matrix[a]

	[Index1 = 1]	[Index1 = 2]
[Index1 = 1]	97.618558	40.035727
[Index1 = 2]	40.035727	100.55996

Unstructured
[a] Dependent Variable: Response.

$$\pi_{1jk} = \beta_{10k} + \beta_{11k}Gender_{jk} + \beta_{12k}Pretest_{jk} + r_{1jk} \tag{11}$$

$$\pi_{2jk} = \beta_{20k} + \beta_{21k}Gender_{jk} + \beta_{22k}Pretest_{jk} + r_{2jk}. \tag{12}$$

The student-level or within-school residual terms (r_{1jk} and r_{2jk}) are assumed to follow a bivariate normal distribution, with an expected mean of zero, some variance, and a covariance.

At the school level, each of the regression coefficients in Equations 11 and 12 may be considered as outcomes to be modeled. However, the investigators assume that the association between the pretest and each of the outcomes is the same across schools, so β_{12k} and β_{22k} are modeled as fixed effects in the school-level model. Also, in order to model the treatment-by-gender interaction, the treatment variable needs to be added in the model for β_{11k} and β_{21k}. Further, *meanpretest*, which is grand-mean centered, is included in the model for β_{10k} and β_{20k} so that it may serve as a covariate for each outcome. This school-level model is

$$\beta_{10k} = \gamma_{100} + \gamma_{101}Treat_k + \gamma_{102}MeanPretest_k + u_{10k} \tag{13}$$

$$\beta_{11k} = \gamma_{110} + \gamma_{111}Treat_k \tag{14}$$

$$\beta_{12k} = \gamma_{120} \tag{15}$$

$$\beta_{20k} = \gamma_{200} + \gamma_{201}Treat_k + \gamma_{202}MeanPretest_k + u_{20k} \tag{16}$$

$$\beta_{21k} = \gamma_{210} + \gamma_{211}Treat_k \tag{17}$$

$$\beta_{22k} = \gamma_{220}. \tag{18}$$

Note that there are no residual terms included in the Equations 14 and 17, which suggests that any systematic between-school variability in male-female performance is due to the treatment. This assumption is tested in the third analysis. Thus, Equations 13–18 have two residual terms, u_{10k} and u_{20k}, which are assumed to follow a bivariate normal distribution with an expected mean of zero and constant variance and covariance.

The focus of this analysis is on the interaction between *treatment* and *gender*. Perhaps the best way to recognize which coefficients represent this interaction is to form equations for Y1 (*intention*) and Y2 (*knowledge*), separately. Recall that Y1 is the same as π_{1jk} in Equation 11, and Y2 is the same as π_{2jk} in Equation 12. Therefore, separate equations for the outcomes can be formed by replacing each of the β terms on the right hand side of Equations 11 and 12 with the expressions for these coefficients found in Equations 13–18. Thus, the equations for Y1 and Y2 may be expressed as

$$Y1 = \gamma_{100} + \gamma_{101}Treat_k + \gamma_{102}MeanPretest_k + \gamma_{110}Gender_{jk} + \gamma_{111}TXG_{jk}$$
$$+ \gamma_{120}Pretest_k + u_{10k} + r_{1jk} \tag{19}$$

$$Y2 = \gamma_{200} + \gamma_{201}Treat_k + \gamma_{202}MeanPretest_k + \gamma_{210}Gender_{jk} + \gamma_{211}TXG_{jk}$$

$$+\gamma_{220}Pretest_k + u_{20k} + r_{2jk}. \tag{20}$$

From Equations 19 and 20, the treatment-by-gender product variable (TXG) is readily recognizable, and the absence of other product terms indicates that no other interactions are included in the model. Thus, γ_{111} and γ_{211} represent the treatment-by-gender interactions (cross-level interactions) for *intention* and *knowledge*. Note that while some software programs (e.g., HLM) would include these cross-level interaction terms without a user needing to enter the specific product variable, the SAS and SPSS programs require a user to enter this product term.

Note that in this data set, the number of girls and boys is the same in each of the 40 schools (which is not a requirement of the model). As a result, the use of the coding $-.5$ and .5 for females and males effectively makes *gender* a centered variable (centered within schools). Such centering is useful here because it (1) results in parameters β_{11k} and β_{21k} of Equations 11 and 12 reflecting only within-school gender differences on the outcomes and (2) reduces multicollinearity, given that the product of *gender* and *treatment* appears in the model. Similarly, *pretest* is also centered within-schools, so that (1) parameters β_{12k} and β_{22k} of Equations 11 and 12 represent the within-school associations of *pretest* and each of the outcomes and (2) parameters γ_{102} and γ_{202} of Equations 13 and 16 represent the between-school associations between *meanpretest* and each of the outcomes. We also center *meanpretest* in Equations 13 and 16, which while not necessary, is done here so that the intercepts of these equations continue to represent the means for *Y*1 and *Y*2. Table 14.13 shows the SAS and SPSS commands that can be used to create a group-mean centered student pretest variable, called *pretest_cen*, and a centered school pretest variable, called *meanpretest_cen*.

Note that in this model, there are 12 fixed effects, six γs in each of the equations for *Y*1 and *Y*2 and six variance-covariance elements, with three such terms at each of the student and school levels. To estimate these parameters, we insert additional terms into the SAS and SPSS commands from Table 14.11. These additions are shown in Table 14.14, and selected results are presented in Table 14.15.

The multivariate hypothesis of no interaction for the two outcomes can be conducted by comparing the deviance from the current model to the deviance from the model that omits the *TXG* variable from Equations 19 and 20. Although the results from the model where both interactions are constrained to be zero (i.e., $\gamma_{111} = \gamma_{211} = 0$) are not shown here, we estimated that model, and its deviance is 11,358.5. Note that this no interaction model has 16 parameters estimated (i.e., two fewer than the current model with the removal of *TXG* from Equations 19 and 20). As shown in the SAS and SPSS outputs in Table 14.15, the deviance from the current model is 11,338.9, and there are 18 parameters estimated. The difference in model fit, as reflected by the difference in model deviances, is then $11,358.5 - 11,338.9 = 19.6$, which is statistically significant as it exceeds the chi-square critical value of 5.99 ($\alpha = .05$, $df = 2$). Thus, the statistically

▪ **Table 14.13: SAS and SPSS Control Lines for Creating Centered Student Pretest and School Pretest Variables**

SAS	SPSS
CREATING CENTERED PRETEST VARIABLE	

DATA LONG; SET LONG;
 (1) PRETEST_CEN=PRETEST-
     MEANPRETEST;
	(1) COMPUTE PRETEST_CEN=PRETEST
	     − MEANPRETEST.
	     EXECUTE.

CREATING CENTERED MEANPRETEST VARIABLE	

(2) PROC SQL;
 (3) CREATE TABLE LONG2 AS
 (4) SELECT *, MEAN
     (MEANPRETEST),
 (5) MEANPRETEST − MEAN
     MEANPRETEST) as
     MEANPRETEST_CEN
 (6) FROM LONG
 (7) QUIT;
	(8) AGGREGATE/ MEANPRETEST_
	     MEAN=MEAN(MEANPRETEST).
	 (5) COMPUTE MEANPRETEST_
	     CEN=MEANPRETEST − MEANPRE-
	     TEST_MEAN.
	     EXECUTE.

(1) We create the group-mean centered variable (PRETEST_CEN) by subtracting the respective school's mean (MEANPRETEST) from each student's pretest score (PRETEST).

(2) The SQL procedure is just one way to center data.

(3) The general form for the CREATE statement is CREATE TABLE name of new dataset AS.

(4) The SELECT statement includes a SELECT clause and a FROM clause. The * selects all the columns from the dataset specified in (6) below. The MEAN function calculates the mean of the scores for the variable within the parentheses (here, school pretest scores or MEANPRETEST).

(5) We create a centered variable (MEANPRETEST_CEN) by subtracting the grand mean from each school's mean.

(6) The name of the original dataset appears in the FROM clause.

(7) QUIT terminates PROC SQL.

(8) We use the AGGREGATE and following subcommand to create a MEANPRETEST score (MEANPRETEST_MEAN) created for each record.

significant improvement in fit obtained by allowing for treatment-by-gender interactions for both outcomes suggests the presence of a treatment-by-gender interaction for at least one of the dependent variables.

Examining the outputs for the estimates of the treatment-by-gender interaction for each outcome in Table 14.15 (in the fixed effects tables) shows that the point estimates of the interaction for *intention* is 4.791 ($SE = 1.247$) and for *knowledge* is 3.293 ($SE = 1.116$). The corresponding t ratios, 3.84 and 2.95, and p values (each smaller than .05) suggest that the treatment-by-gender interaction is significant for each outcome. To better understand these interactions, we use the LSMEANS statement in

■ **Table 14.14: SAS and SPSS Control Lines for Estimating the Three-Level Model With All Explanatory Variables and a Treatment-by-Gender Interaction**

SAS	SPSS

PROC MIXED DATA=LONG METHOD=ML COVTEST;
    CLASS INDEX1 STUDENT
    SCHOOL;
(1) MODEL RESPONSE = INDEX1
    TREAT*INDEX1 GENDER*INDEX1
    PRETEST_CEN*INDEX1
    MEANPRETEST_CEN*INDEX1 TX-
    G*INDEX1 / NOINT SOLUTION;
    RANDOM INDEX1 / SUBJECT=-
    SCHOOL TYPE=UN G;
    REPEATED INDEX1 /
    SUBJECT = STUDENT(SCHOOL)
    TYPE=UN R;
	(2) MIXED RESPONSE BY
	    INDEX1 WITH TREAT GENDER
	    PRETEST_CEN
	    MEANPRETEST_CEN TXG /
	(1) FIXED=INDEX1 TREAT*INDEX1
	    GENDER*INDEX1 PRETEST_
	    CEN*INDEX1
	    MEANPRETEST_CEN*INDEX1
	    TXG*INDEX1 | NOINT/
	    METHOD=ML/
	    PRINT=G R SOLUTION
	    TESTCOV/
	    RANDOM=INDEX1 | SUBJECT
	    (SCHOOL) COVTYPE(UN)/
	    REPEATED=INDEX1 |
	    SUBJECT(SCHOOL*
	    STUDENT) COVTYPE(UN).

(1) We add GENDER*INDEX1, PRETEST_CEN*INDEX1, MEANPRETEST_CEN*INDEX1, and TXG*INDEX1 as fixed effects.
(2) We include GENDER, PRETEST_CEN, MEANPRETEST_CEN, and TXG as covariates.

SAS and the EMMEANS subcommand in SPSS to obtain the experimental and control group means for males and females, holding constant the values of the other explanatory variables at their means, as well as tests of the simple effects of the treatment. Table 14.16 shows the commands from Table 14.14 along with the changes required for the LSMEANS and EMMEANS commands. Selected output is summarized in Table 14.17.

For *intention*, the differences in means between the experimental and control groups shown in Table 14.17 suggest that the intervention has positive effects for both males and females, but that this impact is greater for males. Specifically, the treatment effect for males is 11.00 points and for females is 6.21 points. The extra impact the treatment provides to males then is $11.00 - 6.21$ or 4.79, which is equal to γ_{111} in Equation 19, with this additional impact being statistically significant as shown in Table 14.15. As described earlier, while the computer-based intervention is hypothesized to have greater effects for boys than girls, the investigators also hypothesized that the intervention will have positive effects for both boys and girls. The p-values for the tests of these simple effects, shown in Table 14.17, suggest that the intervention has a positive impact on *intention* for both groups. Note that SAS also provides the associated

■ Table 14.15: Selected Output for the Three-Level Model With a Treatment-By-Gender Interaction

			SAS			

Solution for Fixed Effects

Effect	Index1	Estimate	Standard Error	DF	t Value	Pr > |t|
Index1	1	50.0548	0.4269	74	117.24	<.0001
Index1	2	50.2909	0.3409	74	147.51	<.0001
Treat*Index1	1	8.6057	0.8555	1514	10.06	<.0001
Treat*Index1	2	8.2513	0.6832	1514	12.08	<.0001
Gender* Index1	1	3.6551	0.6243	1514	5.85	<.0001
Gender* Index1	2	2.3247	0.5589	1514	4.16	<.0001
Pretest_ cen*Index1	1	0.3981	0.03232	1514	12.32	<.0001
Pretest_ cen*Index1	2	0.6123	0.02893	1514	21.16	<.0001
MeanPretest_ c*Index1	1	0.2854	0.1285	1514	2.22	0.0265
MeanPretest_ c*Index1	2	0.9091	0.1026	1514	8.86	<.0001
TXG*Index1	1	4.7911	1.247	1514	3.84	0.0001
TXG*Index1	2	3.2932	1.1163	1514	2.95	0.0032

Covariance Parameter Estimates

Cov Parm	Subject	Estimate	Standard Error	Z Value	Pr Z
UN(1,1)	School	3.4041	1.6425	2.07	0.0191
UN(2,1)	School	0.4806	0.9475	0.51	0.612
UN(2,2)	School	1.5342	1.0518	1.46	0.0723
UN(1,1)	Student(School)	77.7445	3.9882	19.49	<.0001
UN(2,1)	Student(School)	13.6003	2.5723	5.29	<.0001
UN(2,2)	Student(School)	62.3026	3.1961	19.49	<.0001

Estimated G Matrix

Row	Effect	Index1	School	Col1	Col2
1	Index1	1	1	3.4041	0.4806
2	Index1	2	1	0.4806	1.5342

(Continued)

■ Table 14.15: (Continued)

Fit Statistics	
-2 Log Likelihood	11338.9
AIC (smaller is better)	11374.9
AICC (smaller is better)	11375.3
BIC (smaller is better)	11405.3

Estimated R Matrix for Student(School)		
Row	Col1	Col2
1	77.7445	13.6003
2	13.6003	62.3026

SPSS

Estimates of Fixed Effects[a]

Parameter	Estimate	Std. Error	Df	t	Sig.	95% Confidence Interval	
						Lower Bound	Upper Bound
[Index1=1]	50.054814	0.426947	40	117.239		49.191922	50.917707
[Index1=2]	50.290916	0.340931	40	147.511		49.601869	50.979963
[Index1=1] * Treat	8.605723	0.855533	40	10.059		6.876627	10.33482
[Index1=2] * Treat	8.251335	0.68317	40	12.078		6.870597	9.632073
[Index1=1] * Gender	3.655092	0.624344	760	5.854		2.429448	4.880735
[Index1=2] * Gender	2.324697	0.55891	760	4.159		1.227506	3.421888
[Index1=1] * Pretest_cen	0.398114	0.032318	760	12.319		0.334672	0.461557
[Index1=2] * Pretest_cen	0.612272	0.028931	760	21.163		0.555478	0.669065
[Index1=1] * MeanPretest_cen	0.285419	0.128524	40	2.221	0.032	0.025662	0.545177
[Index1=2] * MeanPretest_cen	0.909107	0.102631	40	8.858		0.701683	1.116532
[Index1=1] * TXG	4.791081	1.246977	760	3.842		2.343153	7.239009
[Index1=2] * TXG	3.293155	1.116289	760	2.95	0.003	1.10178	5.484531

[a] Dependent Variable: Response.

Estimates of Covariance Parameters[a]

Parameter		Estimate	Std. Error	Wald Z	Sig.	Lower Bound	Upper Bound
Repeated Measures	UN (1,1)	77.744543	3.988211	19.494		70.307912	85.967765
	UN (2,1)	13.600348	2.572286	5.287		8.558761	18.641935
	UN (2,2)	62.302597	3.196056	19.494		56.343061	68.892488
Index1 [subject = School]	UN (1,1)	3.404127	1.642546	2.072	0.038	1.32217	8.76444
	UN (2,1)	0.480581	0.94748	0.507	0.612	-1.376445	2.337608
	UN (2,2)	1.534221	1.051837	1.459	0.145	0.400238	5.881087

[a] Dependent Variable: Response.

Random Effect Covariance Structure (G)[a]

	[Index1=1] | School	[Index1=2] | School
[Index1=1] | School	3.404127	0.480581
[Index1=2] | School	0.480581	1.534221

Unstructured
[a] Dependent Variable: Response.

Information Criteria[a]

-2 Log Likelihood	11338.913
Akaike's Information Criterion (AIC)	11374.913
Hurvich and Tsai's Criterion (AICC)	11375.346
Bozdogan's Criterion (CAIC)	11489.713
Schwarz's Bayesian Criterion (BIC)	11471.713

The information criteria are displayed in smaller-is-better forms.
[a] Dependent Variable: Response.

Residual Covariance (R) Matrix[a]

	[Index1 = 1]	[Index1 = 2]
[Index1 = 1]	77.744543	13.600348
[Index1 = 2]	13.600348	62.302597

Unstructured
[a] Dependent Variable: Response.

■ **Table 14.16: SAS and SPSS Control Lines for Estimating and Testing Simple Treatment Effects**

SAS	SPSS
PROC MIXED DATA=LONG2 METHOD=ML COVTEST;	(4) MIXED RESPONSE BY INDEX1 TREAT GENDER TXG WITH PRETEST_CEN
(1) CLASS INDEX1 STUDENT SCHOOL TREAT GENDER TXG; MODEL RESPONSE = INDEX1 TREAT*INDEX1 GENDER*INDEX1 PRETEST_CEN*INDEX1 MEAN- PRETEST_CEN*INDEX1 TXG* INDEX1	MEANPRETEST_CEN/ FIXED=INDEX1 TREAT*INDEX1 GENDER^INDEX1 PRETEST_ CEN*INDEX1
(2) INDEX1*TREAT*GENDER*TXG / NOINT SOLUTION; RANDOM INDEX1 / SUBJECT =SCHOOL TYPE=UN G; REPEATED INDEX1 / SUBJECT = STUDENT(SCHOOL) TYPE=UN R;	(2) MEANPRETEST_CEN*INDEX1 TXG*INDEX1 INDEX1* TREAT*GENDER*TXG | NOINT/ METHOD=ML/ RANDOM=INDEX1 | SUBJECT (SCHOOL) COVTYPE(UN) REPEATED=INDEX1 | SUBJECT (SCHOOL*STUDENT)
(3) LSMEANS INDEX1*TREAT* GENDER*TXG / DIFF;	COVTYPE (UN) (5) EMMEANS TABLES(INDEX1* TREAT*GENDER) COMPARE(TREAT).

(1) We add TREAT, GENDER, and TXG as CLASS variables in order to include them in the LSMEANS statement in (3) below.

(2) We add INDEX1*TREAT*GENDER*TXG as a fixed effect.

(3) LSMEANS calculates means associated with the treatment-by-gender interactions. The DIFF option calculates the pairwise differences of cell means and corresponding *t*-values.

(4) We change TREAT, GENDER, and TXG from WITH variables to BY variables as needed for this procedure.

(5) EMMEANS estimates the marginal means associated with the treatment-by-gender interactions specified in the TABLES keyword (INDEX1*TREAT*GENDER). COMPARE calculates and tests simple effects associated with the treatment as requested by listing the factor (TREAT).

t- values for these tests. SPSS users, however, will need to manually compute the *t* ratios by dividing the mean differences by their corresponding standard errors.

For *knowledge*, Table 14.17 again suggests that the impact of the treatment is stronger for males than females. For males, the treatment effect is 9.90 points, which is statistically significant ($t = 11.22, p < .05$). For females, the impact of the treatment is about 6.60 points with this effect also being statistically significant ($t = 7.49, p < .05$). The extra impact the intervention has on *knowledge* for males is then $9.90 - 6.60$ or about 3.30, which is equivalent to γ_{211} in Equation 20, and which the results in Table 14.15 (shown there as 3.2932) indicate is statistically significant.

■ Table 14.17: Estimated Experimental and Control Means and Tests of Simple Treatment Effects

Group	Experimental	Control	Mean Difference	Standard Error	t Value*	p value
			Intention			
Male	57.38	46.38	11.00	1.06	10.39	.
Female	51.33	45.12	6.21	1.06	5.87	.000
			Knowledge			
Male	56.40	46.50	9.90	0.88	11.22	.000
Female	52.43	45.83	6.60	0.88	7.49	.000

* Not provided in SPSS output.

■ Table 14.18: SAS and SPSS Control Lines With Gender as a Random Effect for Knowledge

SAS	SPSS
PROC MIXED DATA=LONG METHOD=ML COVTEST; CLASS INDEX1 STUDENT SCHOOL; MODEL RESPONSE = INDEX1 TREAT*INDEX1 GENDER*INDEX1 PRETEST_CEN*INDEX1 MEANPRE-TEST_CEN*INDEX1 TXG*INDEX1 / NOINT SOLUTION; (1) RANDOM INDEX1 GENDER*A2 / SUBJECT=SCHOOL TYPE=UN G; REPEATED INDEX1 / SUBJECT = STUDENT(SCHOOL) TYPE=UN R;	MIXED RESPONSE BY INDEX1 WITH TREAT GENDER PRETEST_CEN (2) MEANPRETEST_CEN TXG A2/ FIXED=INDEX1 TREAT* INDEX1 GENDER*INDEX1 PRETEST_CEN*INDEX1 MEANPRETEST_CEN* INDEX1 TXG*INDEX1	NOINT SSTYPE(3)/ METHOD=ML/ PRINT=G R SOLUTION TESTCOV/ (1) RANDOM=INDEX1 GENDER*A2	SUBJECT(SCHOOL) COV-TYPE(UN) REPEATED=INDEX1	SUBJECT(SCHOOL*STUDENT) COVTYPE(UN) .

(1) We cross GENDER with the dummy-coded indicator variable A2 and include this term as a random effect. Note that we would specify GENDER*INDEX1 as a random effect to test whether the effect of GENDER varies across schools for both outcomes. Attempts to estimate this model resulted in convergence failure as the between-school variance associated with the gender difference for intention is essentially equal to zero.

(2) We add A2 as a covariate.

Table 14.19: Selected Output for the Model With Gender as a Random Effect for Knowledge

SAS

Covariance Parameter Estimates

Cov Parm	Subject	Estimate	Standard Error	Z Value	Pr Z
UN(1,1)	School	3.4044	1.6427	2.07	0.0191
UN(2,1)	School	0.4824	0.9476	0.51	0.6107
UN(2,2)	School	1.5466	1.0526	1.47	0.0709
UN(3,1)	School	0.7638	1.5399	0.50	0.6199
UN(3,2)	School	0.9222	1.2335	0.75	0.4547
UN(3,3)	School	0.8685	2.9360	0.30	0.3837
UN(1,1)	Student(School)	77.7445	3.9882	19.49	<.0001
UN(2,1)	Student(School)	13.5723	2.5719	5.28	<.0001
UN(2,2)	Student(School)	62.0642	3.2725	18.97	<.0001

Estimated R Matrix for Student(School)

Row	Col1	Col2
1	77.7445	13.5723
2	13.5723	62.0642

Fit Statistics

-2 Log Likelihood	11338.1
AIC (smaller is better)	11380.1
AICC (smaller is better)	11380.7
BIC (smaller is better)	11415.6

Estimated G Matrix

Row	Effect	Index1	School	Col1	Col2	Col3
1	Index1	1	1	3.4044	0.4824	0.7638
2	Index1	2	1	0.4824	1.5466	0.9222
3	Gender*a2		1	0.7638	0.9222	0.8685

SPSS

Estimates of Covariance Parameters[a]

Parameter		Estimate	Std. Error	Wald Z	Sig.	95% Confidence Interval	
						Lower Bound	Upper Bound
Repeated Measures	UN (1,1)	77.744543	3.988211	19.494		70.307912	85.967765
	UN (2,1)	13.572284	2.571881	5.277		8.53149	18.613079

SPSS

Estimates of Covariance Parameters[a]

Parameter		Estimate	Std. Error	Wald Z	Sig.	95% Confidence Interval	
						Lower Bound	Upper Bound
	UN (2,2)	62.064233	3.272486	18.965		55.970572	68.821327
Index1 +	UN (1,1)	3.40445	1.642689	2.072	0.038	1.322305	8.765207
Gender * A2	UN (2,1)	0.482374	0.947619	0.509	0.611	-1.374925	2.339673
[subject =	UN (2,2)	1.546609	1.052627	1.469	0.142	0.407428	5.870982
School]	UN (3,1)	0.763736	1.539926	0.496	0.62	-2.254465	3.781936
	UN (3,2)	0.922211	1.233522	0.748	0.455	-1.495447	3.339869
	UN (3,3)	0.868756	2.936166	0.296	0.767	0.001154	654.235886

[a] Dependent Variable: Response.

Random Effect Covariance Structure (G)[a]

	[Index1=1] | School	[Index1=2] | School	Gender * A2 | School
[Index1=1] | School	3.40445	0.482374	0.763736
[Index1=2] | School	0.482374	1.546609	0.922211
Gender * A2 | School	0.763736	0.922211	0.868756

Unstructured
[a] Dependent Variable: Response.

Information Criteria[a]

-2 Log Likelihood	11338.119
Akaike's Information Criterion (AIC)	11380.119
Hurvich and Tsai's Criterion (AICC)	11380.705
Bozdogan's Criterion (CAIC)	11514.052
Schwarz's Bayesian Criterion (BIC)	11493.052

The information criteria are displayed in smaller-is-better forms.
[a] Dependent Variable: Response.

Residual Covariance (R) Matrix[a]

	[Index1 = 1]	[Index1 = 2]
[Index1 = 1]	77.744543	13.572284
[Index1 = 2]	13.572284	62.064233

Unstructured
[a] Dependent Variable: Response.

Although the main focus of this analysis is on the treatment effects, we note that the student and school pretest variables are positively related to each of the outcome variables, as shown in Table 14.15 (in the fixed effects tables). Further, the variances and covariances are generally smaller in this model than in the previous model, indicating that including the additional explanatory variables accounted for more variation and covariation of *intention* and *knowledge*. Also, the residual correlation (not shown in the output) at the student level is now .195 and at the school level is .210.

14.7.3 A Multivariate Test for Multiple Variance-Covariances

The final analysis for the three-level MVMM tests whether the within-school difference between males and females on *knowledge* varies across schools. In Equation 12, β_{21k} represents the expected difference between males and females on *knowledge* that is within a given school k, controlling for the other variables in the model. In Equation 17, this gender difference was assumed to be constant from school to school. It may often be the case that investigators do not have strong *a priori* hypothesis for specifying whether such effects are fixed or vary across schools. While it may often be prudent to model such effects as fixed across schools, because including trivial variation can cause estimation problems, true variation, if present, should be included in the analysis since exclusion of this variation can result in an increased type I error rate for the test of the fixed effects.

To use an empirical basis for modeling the gender difference as fixed or varying, we illustrate a multivariate test to determine if this difference on *knowledge* varies across schools, after controlling for the other variables in the model. To implement this test, a random term associated with this gender difference needs to be added to Equation 17. To do this in SAS and SPSS, we reproduce the commands from Table 14.14 and then utilize the dummy-coded indicator variable a_2 that was created at the beginning of the chapter (see Table 14.3). Table 14.18 shows the needed commands, and Table 14.19 presents the variance-covariance matrices and model fit statistics estimated for this model.

By adding a residual to Equation 17 (u_{21k}), three total parameters are added to this model compared to the previous model. The three parameters and their estimates (appearing in the G matrices and tables of covariance parameters in Table 14.19) are the school-level residual variance for u_{21k} for the gender effects (i.e., .87) and two new covariances for the school-level residuals, the covariance of (1) u_{10k} and u_{21k} (i.e., .76) and (2) u_{20k} and u_{21k} (i.e., .92). The multivariate null hypothesis assumes that the parameter values for all of the new terms are zero in the population. This can be tested by comparing the deviance from this model to the deviance in the previous model. Note that the previous model is nested in the current model because the previous model can be obtained from this one by constraining each of these three terms to a value of zero. The deviance for the previous model was 11,338.9 (with 18 parameters) and for this model, as shown in the output, is 11,338.1 (with 21 parameters). Thus, the improvement in fit obtained by adding these three terms is negligible, as the chi-square test statistic is $11,338.9 - 11,338.1 = 0.8$, which does not exceed the critical value of 7.815 ($\alpha = .05$ and $df = 3$). Thus, there is no empirical support to include these additional random effects. Table 14.19 Selected Output for the Model With Gender as a Random Effect for Knowledge

14.8 SUMMARY

The primary goals of this chapter were to provide an introduction to MVMM and help readers implement such analyses. The initial hurdles for MVMM are to understand how the data need to be formatted, with multiple outcomes appearing in a single column and sequenced within individuals, and how the level-1 model can be specified to include multiple outcomes in a conventional multilevel model. This level-1 model differs from standard models because it does not include an intercept, has no residual term, and makes use of dummy-coded indicator variables so that model parameters become specific dependent variables. However, once these hurdles are cleared, including explanatory variables and random effects is similar to multilevel modeling in general. We also provided analysis examples with increasing complexity to enable understanding of MVMM and to provide more realistic examples. Note also that while SAS and SPSS were used throughout the chapter to reorganize data from the wide to long format and conduct analyses, MVMM analyses can also be carried out by other software programs, such as MLwiN, HLM, and Mplus.

Further, we pointed out that MVMM is an important analysis tool for several reasons. First, MVMM can be used in the place of traditional MANOVA (where multiple outcomes are nested in individuals). If missing data on some outcomes are present, MVMM makes use of more observations than would a traditional application of MANOVA (using listwise deletion), which allows for greater power in testing for group differences (e.g., treatment effects). In addition, SAS and SPSS provide for maximum likelihood estimation for treating missing data, which provides for optimal parameter estimates when data are missing completely at random or missing at random. Also, as illustrated in the chapter, it is straightforward in MVMM to test for the equality of the effects of an explanatory variable across multiple outcomes. These features alone could in the future make MVMM a routine modeling procedure for multivariate data. Second, if individuals are nested in settings, such as schools, clinics, or workplaces, the use of MVMM is generally preferred over traditional MANOVA because MVMM can properly model the dependence of observations such shared contexts produces while also incorporating multiple dependent variables. Third, like traditional MANOVA and as implemented in this chapter, you can use MVMM to provide for global tests of multiple parameters to help control for the inflation of the type I error rate associated with more numerous testing of individual parameters.

Finally, there are useful extensions of MVMM applications, such as parallel growth curve modeling, where growth in multiple outcomes, as well as explanatory variables that predict such growth, can be investigated, or multilevel mediation analysis where the multiple outcomes incorporated at level 1 are mediators and outcomes. Thus, having exposure to the basic ideas of MVMM can be helpful for readers who wish to tackle these and many other extensions of MVMM. Such extensions will likely grow as investigators find new ways to model phenomena of interest.

14.9 SAS AND SPSS COMMANDS USED TO ESTIMATE ALL MODELS IN THE CHAPTER

SAS Control Lines

Two-Level Empty Model

```
PROC MIXED DATA=LONG METHOD=ML COVTEST;
CLASS INDEX1 STUDENT;
MODEL RESPONSE = INDEX1 / NOINT SOLUTION;
REPEATED INDEX1 / SUBJECT = STUDENT TYPE=UN R;
```

Two-Level Model with Treatment Effects

```
PROC MIXED DATA=LONG METHOD=ML COVTEST;
CLASS INDEX1 STUDENT;
MODEL RESPONSE = INDEX1 TREAT*INDEX1 / NOINT SOLUTION;
REPEATED INDEX1 / SUBJECT = STUDENT TYPE=UN R;
```

Two-Level Model with Treatment Effects Constrained to be Equal

```
PROC MIXED DATA=LONG METHOD=ML COVTEST;
CLASS INDEX1 STUDENT;
MODEL RESPONSE = INDEX1 TREAT / NOINT SOLUTION;
REPEATED INDEX1 / SUBJECT = STUDENT TYPE=UN R;
```

Three-Level Model with Treatment Effects

```
PROC MIXED DATA=LONG METHOD=ML COVTEST;
CLASS INDEX1 STUDENT SCHOOL;
MODEL RESPONSE = INDEX1 TREAT*INDEX1 / NOINT SOLUTION;
RANDOM INDEX1 / SUBJECT=SCHOOL TYPE=UN G;
REPEATED INDEX1 / SUBJECT = STUDENT(SCHOOL) TYPE=UN R;
```

Three-Level Model with Multiple Predictors

```
PROC MIXED DATA=LONG METHOD=ML COVTEST;
CLASS INDEX1 STUDENT SCHOOL;
MODEL RESPONSE = INDEX1 TREAT*INDEX1 GENDER*INDEX1
PRETEST_CEN*INDEX1 MEANPRETEST_CEN*INDEX1 TXG*INDEX1 / NOINT
SOLUTION;
RANDOM INDEX1 / SUBJECT=SCHOOL TYPE=UN G;
REPEATED INDEX1 / SUBJECT = STUDENT(SCHOOL) TYPE=UN R;
```

Three-Level Model with Estimates of Cell Means for Treatment-by-Gender Interaction

```
PROC MIXED DATA=LONG2 METHOD=ML COVTEST;
```

(Continued)

■ **Table 14.19: (Continued)**

```
CLASS INDEX1 STUDENT SCHOOL TREAT GENDER TXG;
MODEL RESPONSE = INDEX1 TREAT*INDEX1 GENDER*INDEX1
PRETEST_CEN*INDEX1 MEANPRETEST_CEN*INDEX1 TXG*INDEX1
INDEX1*TREAT*GENDER*TXG / NOINT SOLUTION;
RANDOM INDEX1 / SUBJECT=SCHOOL TYPE=UN G;
REPEATED INDEX1 / SUBJECT = STUDENT(SCHOOL) TYPE=UN R;
LSMEANS INDEX1*TREAT*GENDER*TXG / DIFF;
```

Three-Level Model with Multivariate Test of Multiple Variance-Covariances

```
PROC MIXED DATA=LONG METHOD=ML COVTEST;
CLASS INDEX1 STUDENT SCHOOL;
MODEL RESPONSE = INDEX1 TREAT*INDEX1 GENDER*INDEX1
PRETEST_CEN*INDEX1 MEANPRETEST_CEN*INDEX1 TXG*INDEX1 / NOINT
SOLUTION;
RANDOM INDEX1 GENDER*A2 / SUBJECT=SCHOOL TYPE=UN G;
REPEATED INDEX1 / SUBJECT = STUDENT(SCHOOL) TYPE=UN R;
```

SPSS Control Lines

Two-Level Empty Model

```
MIXED RESPONSE BY INDEX1/
FIXED=INDEX1 | NOINT/
METHOD=ML/
PRINT=R SOLUTION TESTCOV/
REPEATED=INDEX1 | SUBJECT(STUDENT) COVTYPE(UN).
```

Two-Level Model with Treatment Effects

```
MIXED RESPONSE BY INDEX1 WITH TREAT/
FIXED=INDEX1 TREAT*INDEX1 | NOINT/
METHOD=ML/
PRINT=R SOLUTION TESTCOV/
REPEATED=Index1 | SUBJECT(STUDENT) COVTYPE(UN).
```

Two-Level Model with Treatment Effects Constrained to be Equal

```
MIXED RESPONSE BY INDEX1 WITH TREAT/
FIXED=INDEX1 TREAT | NOINT/
METHOD=ML/
PRINT=R SOLUTION TESTCOV/
REPEATED=Index1 | SUBJECT(STUDENT) COVTYPE(UN).
```

Three-Level Model with Treatment Effects

```
MIXED RESPONSE BY INDEX1 WITH TREAT/
FIXED=INDEX1 TREAT*INDEX1 | NOINT/
METHOD=ML/
PRINT=G R SOLUTION TESTCOV/
RANDOM=INDEX1 | SUBJECT(SCHOOL) COVTYPE(UN)/
REPEATED=INDEX1 | SUBJECT(SCHOOL*STUDENT) COVTYPE(UN).
```

Three-Level Model with Multiple Predictors

```
MIXED RESPONSE BY INDEX1 WITH TREAT GENDER PRETEST_CEN
MEANPRETEST_CEN TXG /
FIXED=INDEX1 TREAT*INDEX1 GENDER*INDEX1 PRETEST_CEN*INDEX1
MEANPRETEST_CEN*INDEX1 TXG*INDEX1 | NOINT/
METHOD=ML/
PRINT=G R SOLUTION TESTCOV/
RANDOM=INDEX1 | SUBJECT(SCHOOL) COVTYPE(UN)/
REPEATED=INDEX1 | SUBJECT(SCHOOL*STUDENT) COVTYPE(UN).
```

Three-Level Model with Estimates of Cell Means for Treatment-by-Gender Interaction

```
MIXED RESPONSE BY INDEX1 TREAT GENDER TXG WITH PRETEST_CEN
MEANPRETEST_CEN/
FIXED=INDEX1 TREAT*INDEX1 GENDER*INDEX1 PRETEST_CEN*INDEX1
MEANPRETEST_CEN*INDEX1 TXG*INDEX1 INDEX1*TREAT*GENDER*TXG
NOINT/
METHOD=ML/
RANDOM=INDEX1 | SUBJECT(SCHOOL) COVTYPE(UN)
REPEATED=INDEX1 | SUBJECT(SCHOOL*STUDENT) COVTYPE(UN)
EMMEANS TABLES(INDEX1*TREAT*GENDER) COMPARE(TREAT ).
```

Three-Level Model with Multivariate Test of Multiple Variance-Covariances

```
MIXED RESPONSE BY INDEX1 WITH TREAT GENDER PRETEST_CEN
MEANPRETEST_CEN TXG A2/
FIXED=INDEX1 TREAT*INDEX1 GENDER*INDEX1 PRETEST_CEN*INDEX1
MEANPRETEST_CEN*INDEX1 TXG*INDEX1 | NOINT SSTYPE(3)/
METHOD=ML/
PRINT=G R SOLUTION TESTCOV/
RANDOM=INDEX1 GENDER*A2 | SUBJECT(SCHOOL) COVTYPE(UN)
REPEATED=INDEX1 | SUBJECT(SCHOOL*STUDENT) COVTYPE(UN).
```

REFERENCES

Goldstein, H. (2011). *Multilevel statistical models* (4th ed.). Chichester, UK: John Wiley & Sons.

Raudenbush, S., & Bryk, A. S. (2002). *Hierarchical linear models: Applications and data analysis methods* (2nd ed.). Thousand Oaks, CA: Sage.

Snijders, T.A.B., & Bosker, R.J. (2012). *Multilevel analysis: An introduction to basic and advanced multilevel modeling* (2nd ed.). Los Angeles, CA: Sage.

Chapter 15

CANONICAL CORRELATION

15.1 INTRODUCTION

In Chapter 3, we examined breaking down the association between two sets of variables using multivariate regression analysis. This is the appropriate technique if our interest is in prediction, and if we wish to focus our attention primarily on the individual variables (both predictors and dependent) rather than on linear combinations of the variables. *Canonical correlation* is another means of breaking down the association for two sets of variables, and *is appropriate if the wish is to parsimoniously describe the number and nature of mutually independent relationships existing between the two sets*. This is accomplished through the use of pairs of linear combinations that are uncorrelated.

Because the combinations are uncorrelated, we will obtain a very nice additive partitioning of the total between association. Thus, there are several similarities to principal components analysis (discussed in Chapter 9). Both are variable reduction schemes that use uncorrelated linear combinations. In components analysis, generally the first few linear combinations (the components) account for most of the total variance in the original set of variables, whereas in canonical correlation the first few pairs of linear combinations (the so-called canonical variates) generally account for most of the between association. Also, in interpreting the principal components, we used the associations between the original variables and the components. In canonical correlation, the associations between the original variables and the canonical variates will again be used to name the canonical variates.

One could consider doing canonical regression. However, as Darlington, Weinberg, and Walberg (1973) stated, investigators are generally not interested in predicting linear combinations of the dependent variables.

Let us now consider a couple of situations where canonical correlation would be useful. An investigator wishes to explore the relationship between a set of personality variables (say, as measured by the Cattell 16 PF scale or by the California Psychological

Inventory) and a battery of achievement test scores for a group of high school students. The first pair of canonical variates will tell us what type of personality profile (as revealed by the linear combination and named by determining which of the original variables associate most highly with this linear combination) is maximally associated with a given profile of achievement (as revealed by the linear combination for the achievement scores). The second pair of canonical variates will yield an uncorrelated personality profile that is associated with a different pattern of achievement, and so on.

As a second example, consider the case where a single group of subjects is measured on the *same* set of variables at two different points in time. We wish to investigate the stability of the personality profiles of female college subjects from their freshman to their senior years. Canonical correlation analysis will reveal which dimension of personality is most stable or reliable. This dimension would be named by determining which of the original variables associate most highly with the canonical variates corresponding to the largest canonical correlation. Then the analysis will find an uncorrelated dimension of personality that is next most reliable. This dimension is named by determining which of the original variables has the highest association with the second pair of canonical variates, and so on. This type of *multivariate reliability analysis* using canonical correlation has been in existence for some time. Merenda, Novack, and Bonaventure (1976) did such an analysis on the subtest scores of the California Test of Mental Maturity for a group of elementary school children.

15.2 THE NATURE OF CANONICAL CORRELATION

To focus more specifically on what canonical correlation does, consider the following hypothetical situation. A researcher is interested in the relationship between job success and academic achievement. He has two measures of job success: (1) the amount of money the individual is making, and (2) the status of the individual's position. He has four measures of academic achievement: (1) high school GPA, (2) college GPA, (3) number of degrees, and (4) ranking of the college where the last degree was obtained. We denote the first set of variables by xs and the second set of variables (academic achievement) by ys.

The canonical correlation procedure first finds two linear combinations (one from the job success measures and one from the academic achievement measures) that have the maximum possible Pearson correlation. That is,

$$u_1 = a_{11}x_1 + a_{12}x_2 \text{ and } v_1 = b_{11}y_1 + b_{12}y_2 + b_{13}y_3 + b_{14}y_4$$

are found such that $r_{u_1 v_1}$ is maximum. Note that if this were done with data, the as and bs would be known numerical values, and a single score for each subject on each linear composite could be obtained. These two sets of scores for the subjects are then correlated just as we would perform the calculations for the scores on two individual variables, say x and y. The maximized correlation for the scores on two linear composites ($r_{u_1 v_1}$) is called the *largest canonical correlation*, and we denote it by R_1.

Now, the procedure searches for a second pair of linear combinations, *uncorrelated* with the first pair, such that the Pearson correlation between this pair is the next largest possible. That is,

$$u_2 = a_{21}x_1 + a_{22}x_2 \quad \text{and} \quad v_2 = b_{21}y_1 + b_{22}y_2 + b_{23}y_3 + b_{24}y_4$$

are found such that $r_{u_2 v_2}$ is maximum. This correlation, because of the way the procedure is set up, will be less than $r_{u_1 v_1}$. For example, $r_{u_1 v_1}$ might be .73 and $r_{u_2 v_2}$ might be .51. We denote the second largest canonical correlation by R_2.

When we say that this second pair of canonical variates is uncorrelated with the first pair we mean that (1) the canonical variates *within* each set are uncorrelated, that is, $r_{u_1 u_2} = 0$, and (2) the canonical variates are uncorrelated *across* sets, that is, $r_{u_1 v_2} = r_{v_1 u_2} = 0$.

For this example, there are just two possible canonical correlations and hence only two pairs of canonical variates. In general, if one has p variables in one set and q in the other set, the number of possible canonical correlations is min $(p,q) = m$ (see Tatsuoka, 1971, p. 186, for the reason). Therefore, for our example, there are only min $(2,4) = 2$ canonical correlations. To determine how many of the possible canonical correlations indicate statistically significant relationships, a residual test procedure identical in form to that for discriminant analysis is used. Thus, canonical correlation is still another example of a mathematical maximization procedure (as were multiple regression and principal components), which partitions the total between association through the use of uncorrelated pairs of linear combinations.

15.3 SIGNIFICANCE TESTS

First, we determine whether there is *any* association between the two sets with the following test statistic:

$$V = -\{(N - 1.5) - (p - q)/2\} \sum_{i=1}^{m} \ln(1 - R_i^2),$$

where N is sample size and R_i denotes the ith canonical correlation. V is approximately distributed as a χ^2 statistic with pq degrees of freedom. If this overall test is significant, then the largest canonical correlation is removed and the residual is tested for significance. If we denote the term in braces by k, then the first residual test statistic (V_1) is given by

$$V_1 = -k \cdot \sum_{i=2}^{m} \ln(1 - R_i^2).$$

V_1 is distributed as a χ^2 with $(p - 1)(q - 1)$ degrees of freedom. If V_1 is not significant, then we conclude that only the largest canonical correlation is significant. If V_1 is significant, then we continue and examine the next residual (which has the two largest roots removed), V_2, where

$$V_1 = -k \cdot \sum_{i=3}^{m} \ln(1 - R_i^2).$$

V_2 is distributed as a χ^2 with $(p - 2)(q - 2)$ degrees of freedom. If V_2 is not significant, then we conclude that only the two largest canonical correlations are significant.

If V_2 is significant, we examine the next residual, and so on. In general, then, when the residual after removing the first s canonical correlations is not significant, we conclude that only the first s canonical correlations are significant. The degree of freedom for the ith residual is $(p - i)(q - i)$.

When we introduced canonical correlation, it was indicated that the canonical variates additively partition the association. The reason they do is because the variates are uncorrelated both within and across sets. As an analogy, recall that when the predictors are uncorrelated in multiple regression, we obtain an additive partitioning of the variance on the dependent variable.

The sequential testing procedure has been criticized by Harris (1976). However, a Monte Carlo study by Mendoza, Markos, and Gonter (1978) has refuted Harris's criticism. Mendoza et al. considered the case of a total of 12 variables, six variables in each set, and chose six population situations. The situations varied from three strong population canonical correlations (η_i), .9, .8, and .7, to three weak population canonical correlations (.3, .2, and .1), to a null condition (all population canonical correlations = 0). The last condition was inserted to check on the accuracy of their generation procedure. One thousand sample matrices, varying in size from 25 to 100, were generated from each population, and the number of significant canonical correlations declared by Bartlett's test (the one we have described) and three other tests were recorded.

Strong population canonical correlations (.9, .8, and .7) will be detected more than 90% of the time with as small a sample size as 50. For a more moderate population canonical correlation (.50), a sample size of 100 is needed to detect it about 67% of the time. A weak population canonical correlation (.30), which is probably *not* worth detecting because it would be of little practical value, requires a sample size of 200 to be detected about 60% of the time. It is fortunate that the tests are conservative in detecting weaker canonical correlations, given the tenuous nature of trying to accurately interpret the canonical variates associated with smaller canonical correlations (Barcikowski & Stevens, 1975), as we show in the next section.

15.4 INTERPRETING THE CANONICAL VARIATES

The two methods in use for interpreting the canonical variates are the same as those used for interpreting the discriminant functions:

1. Examine the standardized coefficients.
2. Examine the canonical variate–variable correlations.

For both of these methods, it is the largest (in absolute value) coefficients or correlations that are used. We now refer you back to the corresponding section in the chapter on discriminant analysis, because all of the discussion there is relevant here and will not be repeated.

We do add, however, some detail from the Barcikowski and Stevens (1975) Monte Carlo study on the stability of the coefficients and the correlations, since it was for canonical correlation. They sampled eight correlation matrices from the literature and found that *the number of subjects per variable necessary to achieve reliability in determining the most important variables for the two largest canonical correlations was very large, ranging from 42/1 to 68/1. This is a somewhat conservative estimate, and if we were just interpreting the largest canonical correlation, then a ratio of about 20/1 is sufficient for accurate interpretation.* However, it doesn't seem likely, in general, that in practice there will be just one significant canonical correlation. The association between two sets of variables is likely to be more complex than that.

To impress on you the danger of misinterpretation if the subject to variable ratio is not large, we consider the *second* largest canonical correlation for a 31-variable example from our study. Suppose we were to interpret the left canonical variate using the canonical variate–variable correlations for 400 subjects. This yields a subject to variable ratio of about 13 to 1, a ratio many readers might feel is large enough. However, the frequency rank table (i.e., a ranking of how often each variable was ranked from most to least important) that resulted is presented here:

Var.	Total number of times less than third	Rank			Population value
		1	2	3	
1	76	4	11	9	.43
2	43	34	7	16	.64
3	86	1	4	9	.10
4	74	6	12	8	.16
5	60	19	16	5	.07
6	92	2	4	2	.09
7	78	1	5	16	.34
8	64	11	13	12	.40
9	72	6	13	9	.27
10	55	16	15	14	.62

Variables 2 and 10 are clearly the most important. Yet, with an *n* of 400, about 50% of the time each of them is *not* identified as being one of the three most important variables for interpreting the canonical variate. Furthermore, variable 5, which is clearly not an important variable in the population, is identified 40% of the time as one of the three most important variables.

In view of these reliability results, an investigator considering a canonical analysis on a fairly large number of variables (say 20 in one set and 15 in the other set) should consider doing a components analysis on *each* set to reduce the total number of variables dramatically, and then relate the two sets of components via canonical correlation. This should be done even if the investigator has 300 subjects, for this yields a subject to variable ratio less than 10 to 1 with the *original* set of variables. The practical implementation of this procedure, as seen in section 15.7, can be accomplished efficiently and elegantly with the SAS package.

15.5 COMPUTER EXAMPLE USING SAS CANCORR

To illustrate how to run canonical correlation on SAS CANCORR and how to interpret the output, we consider data from a study by Lehrer and Schimoler (1975). This study examined the cognitive skills underlying an inductive problem-solving method that has been used to develop critical reasoning skills for educable mentally retarded (EMR) children. A total of 112 EMR children were given the Cognitive Abilities Test, which consists of four subtests measuring the following skills: oral vocabulary (CAT1), relational concepts (CAT2), multimental concepts (one that doesn't belong) CAT3, and quantitative concepts (CAT4). We relate these skills via canonical correlation to seven subtest scores from the Children's Analysis of Social Situations (CASS), a test that is a modification of the Test of Social Inference. The CASS was developed as a means of assessing inductive reasoning processes. For the CASS, the children respond to a sample picture and various pictorial stimuli at various levels: CASS1—labeling, or identification of a relevant object; CASS2—detail, which represents a further elaboration of an object; CASS3—low-level inference, or a guess concerning a picture based on obvious clues; CASS4—high-level inference; CASS5—prediction, or a statement concerning future outcomes of a situation; CASS6—low-level generalization, or a rule derived from the context of a picture, but that is specific to the situation in that picture; and CASS7—high-level inference, or deriving a rule that extends beyond the specific situation.

In Table 15.1 we present the correlation matrix for the 11 variables, and in Table 15.2 give the control lines from SAS CANCORR for running the canonical correlation analysis, along with the significance tests.

Table 15.3 has the standardized coefficients and canonical variate–variable correlations that we use jointly to interpret the pair of canonical variates corresponding to the only significant canonical correlation. These coefficients and loadings are boxed in on Table 15.3. For the cognitive ability variables (CAT), note that all four variables have uniformly strong loadings, although the loading for CAT1 is extremely high (.953). Using the standardized coefficients, we see that CAT2 through CAT4 are redundant, because their coefficients are considerably lower than that for CAT1. For the CASS

■ **Table 15.1: Correlation Matrix for Cognitive Ability Variables and Inductive Reasoning Variables**

CAT1	1.000									
CAT2	.662	1.000								
CAT3	.661	.697	1.000							
CAT4	.641	.730	.703	1.000						
CASS1	.131	−.112	.033	.040	1.000					
CASS2	.253	.031	.185	.149	.641	1.000				
CASS3	.332	.133	.197	.132	.574	.630	1.000			
CASS4	.381	.304	.304	.382	.312	.509	.583	1.000		
CASS5	.413	.313	.276	.382	.254	.491	.491	.731	1.000	
CASS6	.520	.485	.450	.466	.034	.117	.294	.595	.534	1.000
CASS7	.434	.392	.380	.390	.065	.100	.203	.328	.355	.508	1.000

■ **Table 15.2: SAS CANCORR Control Lines for Canonical Correlation Relating Cognitive Abilities Subtests to Subtests From Children's Analysis of Social Situations**

```
TITLE 'CANONICAL CORRELATION';
DATA CANCORR (TYPE = CORR);
  INFILE CARDS MISSOVER;
  _TYPE_ = 'CORR';
  INPUT_NAME_$ CAT1  CAT2 CAT3 CAT4 CASS1 CASS2 CASS3 CASS4 CASS5
CASS6 CASS7;
  DATALINES;
CAT1  1.00
CAT2   .662 1.00
CAT3   .661   .697 1.00
CAT4   .641   .730 .703 1.00
CASS1  .131   .112 .033  .040 1.00
CASS2  .253   .031 .185  .149  .641 1.00
CASS3  .332   .133 .197  .132  .574  .630  1.00
CASS4  .381   .304 .304  .382  .312  .509   .583 1.00
CASS5  .413   .313 .276  .382  .254  .491   .491  .731 1.00
CASS6  .520   .485 .450  .466  .034  .117   .294  .595 .534 1.00
CASS7  .434   .392 .380  .390  .065  .100   .203  .328 .355   508 1.00
PROC CANCORR EDF = 111 CORR;
VAR CAT1 CAT2 CAT3 CAT4;
WITH CASS1 CASS2 CASS3 CASS4 CASS5 CASS6 CASS7;
RUN;
```

variables, the loadings on CASS4 through CASS7 are clearly the strongest and of uniform magnitude. Turning to the coefficients for those variables, we see that CASS4 and CASS5 are redundant, because they clearly have the smallest coefficients. Thus, the only significant linkage between the two sets of variables relates oral vocabulary (CAT1) to the children's ability to generalize in social situations, particularly low-level

■ **Table 15.3: Standardized Coefficients and Canonical Variate–Variable Loadings**

Standardized Canonical Coefficients for the 'VAR' Variables

	V1	V2	V3	V4
CAT1	0.6335	-0.9443	-0.0323	-0.9203
CAT2	0.1667	1.1608	-1.0872	-0.3546
CAT3	0.1379	-0.5733	-0.3969	1.4165
CAT4	0.1844	0.5093	1.5292	0.0373

Standardized Canonical Coefficients for the 'WITH' Variables

	W1	W2	W3	W4
CASS1	-0.1514	-0.3489	0.8569	-0.3278
CASS2	0.2442	-0.5986	-0.0074	1.0501
CASS3	0.1147	-0.4960	-1.0745	-0.7008
CASS4	-0.0955	0.6283	0.6701	0.4818
CASS5	0.1417	0.2634	0.4085	-1.1733
CASS6	0.6355	-0.1528	-0.3615	0.3456
CASS7	0.3681	0.0392	-0.0006	0.2203

Correlations Between the VAR Variables and Their Canonical Variables

	V1	V2	V3	V4
CAT1	0.9533	-0.2284	-0.0341	-0.1948
CAT2	0.8169	0.5078	-0.2688	0.0507
CAT3	0.8025	-0.0304	-0.1009	0.5872
CAT4	0.8091	0.3483	0.4359	0.1843

Correlations Between the WITH Variables and Their Canonical Variables

	W1	W2	W3	W4
CASS1	0.1227	-0.7570	0.5359	-0.1785
CASS2	0.3515	-0.6995	0.3642	0.1302
CASS3	0.4571	-0.6147	-0.1024	-0.3762
CASS4	0.6508	0.0401	0.3906	-0.0743
CASS5	0.6797	0.0289	0.3916	-0.4701
CASS6	0.8984	0.1539	-0.0325	0.0233
CASS7	0.7477	0.0779	0.0174	0.0788

generalization. We now consider a study from the literature that used canonical correlation analysis.

15.6 A STUDY THAT USED CANONICAL CORRELATION

A study by Tetenbaum (1975) addressed the issue of the validity of student ratings of teachers. She noted that current instruments generally list several teaching behaviors and ask the student to rate the instructor on each of them. The assumption is made that all students focus on the same teaching behavior, and furthermore, that when focusing on the same behavior, students perceive it in the same way. Tetenbaum noted that principles from social perception theory (Warr and Knapper, 1968) make both of these assumptions questionable. She argued that the social psychological needs of the students would influence their ratings, stating, "it was reasoned that in the process of rating a teacher the student focuses on the need-related aspects of the perceptual situation and bases his judgment on those areas of the teacher's performance most relevant to his own needs" (p. 418).

To assess student needs, the *Personality Research Form* was administered to 405 graduate students. The entire scale was not administered because some of the needs were not relevant to an academic setting. The part administered was then factor analyzed and a four-factor solution was obtained. For each factor, the three subscales having the highest loadings (.50) were selected to represent that factor, with the exception of one subscale (dominance), which had a high loading on more than one factor, and one subscale (harm avoidance), which was not felt to be relevant to the classroom setting. The final instrument consisted of 12 scales, three scales representing each of the four obtained factors: Factor I, Cognitive Structure (CS), Impulsivity (IM), Order (OR); Factor II, Endurance (EN), Achievement (AC), Understanding (UN); Factor III, Affiliation (AF), Autonomy (AU), Succorance (SU); Factor IV, Aggression (AG), Defendance (DE), Abasement (AB). These factors were named Need for Control, Need for Intellectual Striving, Need for Gregariousness-Defendance, and Need for Ascendancy, respectively.

Student ratings of teachers were obtained on an instrument constructed by Tetenbaum that consisted of 12 vignettes, each describing a college classroom in which the teacher was engaged in a particular set of behaviors. The particular behaviors were designed to correspond to the four need factors; that is, within the 12 vignettes, there were three replications for each of the four teacher orientations. For example, in three teacher vignettes, the orientation was aimed at meeting control needs. In these vignettes, the teachers attempted to control the classroom environment by organizing and structuring all lessons and assignments by stressing order, neatness, clarity, and logic, and by encouraging deliberation of thought and moderation of emotion so that the students would know what was expected of them.

Tetenbaum hypothesized that specific student needs (e.g., control needs) would be related to teacher orientations that met those needs. The 12 need variables (Set 1) were related to the 12 rating variables (Set 2) via canonical correlation. Three significant canonical correlations were obtained: $R_1 = .486$, $R_2 = .389$, and $R_3 = .323$ ($p < .01$ in all cases). Tetenbaum chose to use the canonical variate–variable correlations to interpret the variates. These are presented in Table 15.4. Examining the underlined correlations for the first pair (i.e., for the largest canonical correlation), we see that it clearly reflects the congruence between the intellectual striving needs and ratings on the corresponding vignettes, as well as the congruence between the ascendancy needs and ratings. The second pair of canonical variates (corresponding to the second largest canonical correlation) reflects the congruence between the control needs and the ratings. Note that the correlation for impulsivity is negative, because a low score on this variable would imply a high rating for a teacher who exhibits order and moderation of emotion. The interpretation of the third pair of canonical variates is not as clean as it was for the first two pairs. Nevertheless, the correspondence between gregariousness–dependency needs and ratings is revealed, a correspondence that did *not* appear for the first two pairs. However, there are high loadings on other needs and ratings as well. The interested reader is referred to Tetenbaum's article for a discussion of why this may have happened.

In summary, then, the correspondence that Tetenbaum hypothesized between student needs and ratings was clearly revealed by canonical correlation. Two of the need-rating correspondences were revealed by the first canonical correlation, a third correspondence (for control needs) was established by the second canonical correlation, and finally the gregariousness need-rating correspondence was revealed by the third canonical correlation.

Through the use of factor analysis, the author in this study was able to reduce the number of variables to 24 and achieve a fairly large subject to variable ratio (about 17/1). Based on our Monte Carlo results, one could interpret the largest canonical correlation with confidence; however, the second and third canonical correlations should be interpreted with some caution.

■ **Table 15.4: Canonical Variate–Variable Correlations for Tetenbaum Study**

Canonical variables						
First pair		Second pair		Third pair		
Needs	Ratings	Needs	Ratings	Needs	Ratings	
.111	.028	.614	.453	−.018	−.325	⎫
−.099	−.051	−.785	.491	.078	−.397	⎬ Control
.065	.292	.774	.597	−.050	.059	⎭
−.537	−.337	.210	.263	.439	.177	⎫
−.477	−.294	.252	.125	.500	.102	⎬ Intellectual Striving
−.484	−.520	−.005	.154	.452	.497	⎭
−.134	−.233	−.343	−.210	−.354	−.335	⎫
.270	−.141	.016	.114	.657	−.468	⎬ Gregarious
−.271	−.072	−.155	−.175	−.414	−.579	⎭
−.150	.395	.205	.265	.452	.211	⎫
.535	.507	−.254	.034	.421	.361	⎬ Ascendancy
.333	.673	−.312	−.110	.289	.207	⎭

Note: Correlations >|.3| are underlined.

15.7 USING SAS FOR CANONICAL CORRELATION ON TWO SETS OF FACTOR SCORES

As indicated previously, if there is a large or fairly large number of variables in each of two sets, it is desirable to do a factor analysis on each set of variables for two reasons:

1. To obtain a more parsimonious description of what each set of variables is really measuring.
2. To reduce the total number of variables that will appear in the eventual canonical correlation analysis so that a much larger subject/variable ratio is obtained, making for more reliable results.

The practical implementation of doing the component analyses and then passing the factor scores for a canonical correlation can be accomplished quite efficiently and elegantly with the SAS package. To illustrate, we use the National Academy of Science data from Chapter 3. Those data were based on 46 observations and involved the following seven variables: QUALITY, NFACUL, NGRADS, PCTSUPP, PCTGRT, NARTIC, and PCTPUB. We use SAS to do a components analysis on NFACUL, NGRADS, and PCTSUPP and then do a separate component analysis on PCTGRT, NARTIC, and

▪ **Table 15.5: SAS Control Lines for a Components Analysis on Each of Two Sets of Variables and Then a Canonical Correlation Analysis on the Two Sets of Factor Scores**

```
     DATA NATACAD;
     INPUT QUALITY NFACUL NGRADS PCTSUPP PCTGRT NARTIC PCTPUB;
     LINES;
(1)  PROC PRINCOMP N = 2 OUT = FSCORE1;
     VAR NFACUL NGRADS PCTSUPP;
(2)  PROC PRINCOMP N = 3 PREFIX = PCTSET2 OUT = FSCORE2;
     VAR PCTGRT NARTIC PCTPUB;
(3)  PROC PRINT DATA = FSCORE2;
(4)  PROC CANCORR CORR;
     VAR PRIN1 PRIN2;
     WITH PCTSET21 PCTSET22 PCTSET23;
     RUN;
```

(1) The principal components procedure is called and a components analysis is done on only the three variables indicated.

(2) The components procedure is called again, this time to do a components analysis on the PCTGRT, NARTIC, and PCTPUB variables. To distinguish the names for the components retained for this second analysis, we use the PREFIX option.

(3) This statement is to obtain a listing of the data for all the variables, that is, the original variables, the factor scores for the two components for the first analysis, and the factor scores for the three components from the second analysis.

(4) The canonical correlation procedure is called to determine the relationship between the two components from the first analysis and the three components from the second analysis.

PCTPUB. Obviously, with such a small number of variables in each set, a factor analysis is really not needed, but this example is for pedagogical purposes only. Then we use the SAS canonical correlation program (CANCORR) to relate the two sets of factor scores. The complete SAS control lines for doing both component analyses and the canonical correlation analysis on the factor scores are given in Table 15.5.

Now, let us consider a more realistic example, that is, where factor analysis is really needed. Suppose an investigator has 15 variables in set X and 20 variables in set Y. With 250 subjects, she wishes to run a canonical correlation analysis to determine the relationship between the two sets of variables. Recall from section 15.4 that at least 20 subjects per variable are needed for reliable results, and the investigator is not near that ratio. Thus, a components analysis is run on each set of variables to achieve a more adequate ratio and to determine more parsimoniously the main constructs involved for each set of variables. The components analysis and varimax rotation are done for each set. On examining the output for the two component analyses, using Kaiser's rule and the scree test in combination, she decides to retain three factors for set X and four factors for set Y. In addition, from examination of the output, the investigator finds that the communalities for variables 2 and 7 are low. That is, these variables are relatively independent of what the three factors are measuring, and thus she decides to retain these original variables for the eventual canonical analysis. Similarly, the communality for variable 12 in set Y is low, and that variable will also be retained for the canonical analysis.

We denote the variables for set X by X1, X2, X3, . . ., X15 and the variables for set Y by Y1, Y2, Y3, . . ., Y20. The complete control lines in this case are:

```
DATA REAL;
INPUT X1 X2 X3 X4 X5 X6 X7 X8 X9 X10 X11 X12 X13 X14 X15
Y1 Y2 Y3 Y4 Y5 Y6 Y7 Y8 Y9 Y10 Y11 Y12 Y13 Y14 Y15 Y16 Y17
Y18 Y19 Y20;
LINES;
DATA
PROC FACTOR ROTATE = VARIMAX N = 3 SCREE OUT = FSCORES1;
VAR X1 - X15;
PROC DATASETS;
MODIFY FSCORES1;
RENAME FACTOR1 = SET1FAC1 FACTOR2 = SET1FAC2 FACTOR3 = SET1FAC3;
PROC FACTOR ROTATE = VARIMAX N = 4 SCREE OUT = FSCORES2;
VAR Y1 - Y20;
PROC PRINT DATA = FSCORES2;
PROC CANCORR CORR;
VAR SET1FAC1 SET1FAC2 SET1FAC3 X2 X7;
WITH FACTOR1 FACTOR2 FACTOR3 FACTOR4 Y12;
RUN;
```

15.8 THE REDUNDANCY INDEX OF STEWART AND LOVE

In multiple regression, the squared multiple correlation represents the proportion of criterion variance accounted for by the optimal linear combination of the predictors. In canonical correlation, however, a squared canonical correlation tells us only the amount of variance that the two canonical variates share, and does not necessarily indicate considerable variance overlap between the two sets of variables. The canonical variates are derived to maximize the correlation between them, and thus, we can't necessarily expect each canonical variate will extract much variance from its set. For example, the third canonical variable from set X may be close to a last principle component and thus extract negligible variance from set X, that is, it may not be an important factor for battery X. Stewart and Love (1968) realized that interpreting squared canonical correlations as indicating the amount of informational overlap between two batteries (sets of variables) was not appropriate and developed their own index of redundancy.

The essence of the Stewart and Love idea is quite simple. First, determine how much variance in Y the first canonical variate (C_1) accounts for. How this is done will be indicated shortly. Then multiply the extracted variance (we denote this by VC_1) by the square of the canonical correlation between C_1 and the corresponding canonical variate (P_1) from set X. This product then gives the amount of variance in set Y that is predictable from the first canonical variate for set X. Next, the amount of variance in Y that the second canonical variate (C_2) for Y accounts for is determined, and is multiplied by the square of the canonical correlation between C_2 and the corresponding canonical variate (P_2) from set X. This product gives the amount of variance in set Y predictable from the second canonical variate for set X. This process is repeated for all possible canonical correlations. Then the products are added (since the respective pairs of canonical variates are uncorrelated) to determine the redundancy in set Y, given set X, which we denote by $R_{Y/X}$. If the square of the ith canonical correlation is denoted by λ_i, then $R_{Y/X}$ is given by:

$$R_{Y/X} = \sum_{i=1}^{h} \lambda_i \; VC_i,$$

where h is the number of possible canonical correlations.

The amount of variance canonical variate i extracts from set Y is given by:

$$VC_1 = \frac{\Sigma \text{ squared canonical variate } - \text{ variable correlations}}{q \text{ (number of variables in set } Y)}$$

There is an important point we wish to make concerning the redundancy index. It is equal to the average squared multiple correlation for predicting the variables in one set from the variables in the other set. To illustrate, suppose we had four variables in set X and three variables in set Y, and we computed the multiple correlation for each y variable *separately* with the four predictors. Then, if these multiple correlations are squared and the sum of squares divided by 3, this number is equal to $R_{Y/X}$. This fact hints at a problem with the redundancy index, as Cramer and Nicewander (1979) noted:

> Moreover, the redundancy index is not multivariate in the strict sense because it is unaffected by the intercorrelations of the variables being predicted. The redundancy index is only multivariate in the sense that it involves several criterion variables. (p. 43)

This is saying we would obtain the same amount of variance accounted for with the redundancy index for three y variables that are highly correlated as we would for three y variables that have low intercorrelations (other factors being held constant). This is very undesirable in the same sense as it would be undesirable if, in a multiple regression context, the multiple correlation were unaffected by the magnitude of the intercorrelations among the predictors.

This defect can be eliminated by first orthogonalizing the y variables (e.g., obtaining a set of uncorrelated variables, such as principal components or varimax rotated factors), and then computing the average squared multiple correlation between the uncorrelated y variables and the x variables. In this case we could, of course, compute the redundancy index, but it is unnecessary since it is equal to the average squared multiple correlation.

Cramer and Nicewander recommended using the *average squared canonical correlation* as the measure of variance accounted for. Thus, for example, if there were two canonical correlations, simply square each of them and then divide by 2.

15.9 ROTATION OF CANONICAL VARIATES

In Chapter 9 on principal components, it was stated that often the interpretation of the components can be difficult, and that a rotation (e.g., varimax) can be quite helpful in obtaining factors that tend to load high on only a small number of variables and therefore are considerably easier to interpret. In canonical correlations, the same rotation idea can be employed to increase interpretability. The situation, however, is much more complex, since two sets of factors (the successive pairs of canonical variates) are being simultaneously rotated. Cliff and Krus (1976) showed mathematically that such a procedure is sound, and the practical implementation of the procedure is possible in multivariance (Finn, 1978). Cliff and Krus also demonstrated, through an example, how interpretation is made clearer through rotation.

When such a rotation is done, the variance will be spread more evenly across the pairs of canonical variates; that is, the maximization property is lost. Recall that this is what happened when the components were rotated. But we were willing to sacrifice this property for increased interpretability. Of course, only the canonical variates corresponding to *significant* canonical correlations should be rotated, in order to ensure that the rotated variates still correspond to significant association (Cliff & Krus, 1976).

15.10 OBTAINING MORE RELIABLE CANONICAL VARIATES

In concluding this chapter, we mention five approaches that will increase the probability of accurately interpreting the canonical variates, that is, the probability that the interpretation made in the given sample will hold up in another sample from the same population. The first two points have already been made, but are repeated as a means of summarizing:

1. Have a very large (1,000 or more) number of subjects, or a large subject to variable ratio.
2. If there is a large or fairly large number of variables in each set, then perform a components analysis on each set. Use only the components (or rotated factors) from each set that account for most of the variance in the canonical correlation analysis. In this way, an investigator, rather than doing a canonical analysis on a total of, say, 35 variables with 300 subjects, may be able to account for most of the variance in each of the sets with a total of 10 components, and thus achieve a much more favorable subject to variable ratio (30/1). The components analysis approach is one means of attacking the multicollinearity problem, which makes accurate interpretation difficult.
3. Ensure at least a moderate to large subject to variable ratio by judiciously selecting *a priori* a small number of variables for each of the two sets that will be related.
4. Another way of dealing with multicollinearity is to use canonical ridge regression. With this approach the coefficients are biased, but their variance will be much less, leading to more accurate interpretation. Monte Carlo studies (Anderson & Carney, 1974; Barcikowski & Stevens, 1975) of the effectiveness of ridge canonical regression show that it can yield more stable canonical variate coefficients and canonical variate–variable correlations. Barcikowski and Stevens examined 11 different correlation matrices that exhibited varying degrees of within and between multicollinearity. They found that, in general, ridge became more effective as the degree of multicollinearity increased. Second, ridge canonical regression was particularly effective with small subject to variable ratios. These are precisely the situations where the greater stability is desperately needed.
5. Still another approach to more accurate interpretation of canonical variates was presented by Weinberg and Darlington (1976), who used biased coefficients of 0 and 1 to form the canonical variates. This approach makes interpretation of the most important variables, those receiving 1s in the canonical variates, relatively easy.

15.11 SUMMARY

Canonical correlation is a parsimonious way of breaking down the association between two sets of variables through the use of linear combinations. In this way, because the combinations are uncorrelated, we can describe the number and nature of independent relationships existing between two sets of variables. That canonical correlation does indeed give a parsimonious description of association that can be seen by considering the case of five variables in set X and 10 variables in set Y. To obtain an overall picture of the association using simple correlations would be very difficult, because we would have to deal with 50 fragmented between correlations. Canonical correlation, on the other hand, consolidates or channels all the association into five uncorrelated big pieces, that is, the canonical correlations.

Two devices are available for interpreting the canonical variates: (1) standardized coefficients, and (2) canonical variate–variable correlations. Both of these are quite unreliable unless the n/total number of variables ratio is very large: at least 42/1 if interpreting the largest two canonical correlations, and about 20/1 if interpreting only the largest canonical correlation. The correlations should be used for substantive interpretation of the canonical variates, that is, for naming the constructs, and the coefficients are used for determining which of the variables are redundant. Because of the probably unattainably large n required for reliable results (especially if there are a fairly large or large number of variables in each set), several suggestions were given for obtaining reliable results with the n available, or perhaps just a somewhat larger n. The first suggestion involved doing a components analysis and varimax rotation on each set of variables and then relating the components or rotated factors via canonical correlation. An efficient, practical implementation of this procedure, using the SAS package, was illustrated.

Some other means of obtaining more reliable canonical variates were:

1. Selecting *a priori* a small number of variables from each of the sets, and then relating these. This would be an option to consider if the n was not judged to be large enough to do a reliable components analysis—for example, if there were 20 variables in set X and 30 variables in set Y and $n = 120$.
2. The use of canonical ridge regression.
3. The use of the technique developed by Weinberg and Darlington.

A study from the literature that used canonical correlation was discussed in detail.

The redundancy index, for determining the variance overlap between two sets of variables, was considered. It was indicated that this index suffers from the defect of being unaffected by the intercorrelations of the variables being predicted. This is undesirable in the same sense as it would be undesirable if the multiple correlation were unaffected by the intercorrelations of the predictors.

Finally, in evaluating studies from the literature that have used canonical correlation, remember it isn't just the n in a vacuum that is important. The n/total number of variables ratio, along with the degree of multicollinearity, must be examined to determine how much confidence can be placed in the results. Thus, not a great deal of confidence can be placed in the results of a study involving a total of 25 variables (say 10 in set X and 15 in set Y) based on 200 subjects. Even if a study had 400 subjects, but did the canonical analysis on a total of 60 variables, it is probably of little scientific value because the results are unlikely to replicate.

15.12 EXERCISES

1. Name four features that canonical correlation and principal components analysis have in common.

2. Suppose that a canonical correlation analysis on two sets of variables yielded r canonical correlations. Indicate schematically what the matrix of intercorrelations for the canonical variates would look like.

3. Shin (1971) examined the relationship between creativity and achievement. He used Guilford's battery to obtain the following six creativity scores: ideational fluency, spontaneous flexibility, associational fluency, expressional fluency, originality, and elaboration. The Kropp test was used to obtain the following six achievement variables: knowledge, comprehension, application, analysis, synthesis, and evaluation. Data from 116 11th-grade suburban high school students yielded the following correlation matrix.

   Examine the association between the creativity and achievement variables via canonical correlation, and from the printout answer the following questions:

   (a) How would you characterize the strength of the relationship between the two sets of variables from the simple correlations?

   (b) How many of the canonical correlations are significant at the .05 level?

   (c) Use the canonical variable loadings to interpret the canonical variates corresponding to the largest canonical correlation.

   (d) How large an n is needed for reliable interpretation of the canonical variates in (c)?

   (e) Considering all the canonical correlations, what is the value of the redundancy index for the creativity variables given the achievement variables? Express in words what this number tells us.

   (f) Cramer and Nicewander (1979) argued that the *average* squared canonical correlation should be used as the measure of association for two sets of variables, stating, "this index has a clear interpretation, being an arithmetic mean, and gives the proportion of variance of the average of the canonical variates of the y variables predictable from the x variables" (p. 53). Obtain the Cramer–Nicewander measure for the present problem, and compare its magnitude to that obtained for the measure in (e). Explain the reason for the difference and, in particular, the direction of the difference.

	IDEAFLU	FLEXIB	ASSOCFLU	EXPRFLU	ORIG	ELAB	KNOW	COMPRE	APPLIC	ANAL	SYNTH	EVAL
IDEAFLU	1.000											
FLEXIB	0.710	1.000										
ASSOCFLU	0.120	0.120	1.000									
EXPRFLU	0.340	0.450	0.430	1.000								
ORIG	0.270	0.330	0.240	0.330	1.000							
ELAB	0.210	0.110	0.420	0.460	0.320	1.000						
KNOW	0.130	0.270	0.210	0.390	0.270	0.380	1.000					
COMPRE	0.180	0.240	0.150	0.360	0.330	0.260	0.620	1.000				
APPLIC	0.080	0.140	0.090	0.250	0.130	0.230	0.440	0.660	1.000			
ANAL	0.100	0.160	0.090	0.250	0.120	0.280	0.580	0.660	0.640	1.000		
SYNTH	0.130	0.230	0.420	0.500	0.410	0.470	0.460	0.470	0.370	0.530	1.000	
EVAL	0.080	0.150	0.360	0.280	0.210	0.260	0.300	0.240	0.190	0.290	0.580	1.000

4. Shanahan (1984) examined the nature of the reading–writing relationship through canonical correlation analysis. Measures of writing ability (*t* unit, vocabulary diversity, episodes, categories, information units, spelling, phonemic accuracy, and visual accuracy) were related to reading measures of vocabulary, word recognition, sentence comprehension, and passage comprehension. Separate canonical correlation analyses were done for 256 second graders and 251 fifth graders.

(a) How many canonical correlations will there be for each analysis?

(b) Shanahan found that for second graders there were only two significant canonical correlations, and he only interpreted the largest one. Given his sample size, was he wise in doing this?

(c) For fifth graders there was only one significant canonical correlation. Given his sample size, can we have confidence in the reliability of the results?

(d) Shanahan presents the following canonical variate–variable correlations for the largest canonical correlation for both the second- and fifth-grade samples. If you have an appropriate content background, interpret the results and then compare your interpretation with his.

Canonical Factor Structures for the Grade 2 and Grade 5 Samples: Correlations of Reading and Writing Variables with Canonical Variables

| | Canonical variable | | | |
| | 2nd grade | | 5th grade | |
	Reading	Writing	Reading	Writing
Writing				
t-Unit	.32	.41	.19	.25
Vocabulary diversity	.46	.59	.47	.60
Episodes	.25	.32	.20	.26
Categories	.37	.48	.33	.43
Information units	.36	.46	.24	.30
Spelling	.74	.95	.71	.92
Phonemic accuracy	.60	.77	.67	.86
Visual accuracy	.69	.89	.68	.88
Reading				
Comprehension	.81	.63	.79	.61
Cloze	.86	.66	.80	.62
Vocabulary	.65	.51	.89	.69
Phonics	.88	.68	.85	.66

5. Estabrook (1984) examined the relationship among the 11 subtests on the Wechsler Intelligence Scale for Children–Revised (WISC–R) and the 12 subtests on the Woodcock–Johnson Tests of Cognitive Ability for 152 learning disabled children. He seemed to acknowledge sample size as a problem in his study, stating, "the primary limitation of this study is the size of the sample. . . . However, a more conservative criterion of $100(p + q) + 50$ (where p and q refer to the number of variables in each set) has been suggested by Thorndike" (p. 1176). Is this really a conservative criterion according to the results of Barcikowski and Stevens (1975)?

REFERENCES

Anderson, D.A., & Carney, E.S. (1974). *Ridge regression estimation procedures applied to canonical correlation analysis*. Unpublished manuscript, Cornell University, Ithaca, NY.

Barcikowski, R., & Stevens, J.P. (1975). A Monte Carlo study of the stability of canonical correlations, canonical weights and canonical variate-variable correlations. *Multivariate Behavioral Research, 10*, 353–364.

Cliff, N., & Krus, D.J. (1976). Interpretation of canonical analysis: Rotated vs. unrotated solutions. *Psychometrika, 41*, 35–42.

Cramer, E., & Nicewander, W.A. (1979). Some symmetric, invariant measures of multivariate association. *Psychometrika, 44*, 43–54.

Darlington, R.B., Weinberg, S., & Walberg, H. (1973). Canonical variate analysis and related techniques. *Review of Educational Research, 43*, 433–454.

Estabrook, G.E. (1984). A canonical correlation analysis of the Wechsler Intelligence Scale for Children—Revised and the Woodcock-Johnson Tests of Cognitive Ability in a sample referred for suspected learning disabilities. *Journal of Educational Psychology, 76*, 1170–1177.

Finn, J. (1978). *Multivariance: Univariate and multivariate analysis of variance, covariance and regression*. Chicago, IL: National Educational Resources.

Harris, R.J. (1976). The invalidity of partitioned U tests in canonical correlation and multivariate analysis of variance. *Multivariate Behavioral Research, 11*, 353–365.

Lehrer, B., & Schimoler, G. (1975). Cognitive skills underlying an inductive problem-solving strategy. *Journal of Experimental Education, 43*, 13–21.

Mendoza, J.L., Markos, V.H., & Gonter, R. (1978). A new perspective on sequential testing procedures in canonical analysis: A Monte Carlo evaluation. *Multivariate Behavioral Research, 13*, 371–382.

Merenda, P., Novack, H., & Bonaventure, E. (1976). Multivariate analysis of the California Test of Mental Maturity, primary forms. *Psychological Reports, 38*, 487–493.

Shanahan, T. (1984). Nature of the reading-writing relation: An exploratory multivariate analysis. *Journal of Educational Psychology, 76*, 466–477.

Shin, S.H. (1971). *Creativity, intelligence and achievement: A study of the relationship between creativity and intelligence, and their effects on achievement*. Unpublished doctoral dissertation, University of Pittsburgh, PA.

Stewart, D., & Love, W. (1968). A general canonical correlation index. *Psychological Bulletin, 70*, 160–163.

Tatsuoka, M.M. (1971). *Multivariate analysis: Techniques for educational and psychological research*. New York, NY: Wiley.

Tetenbaum, T. (1975). The role of student needs and teacher orientations in student ratings of teachers. *American Educational Research Journal, 12*, 417–433.

Weinberg, S.L., & Darlington, R.B. (1976). Canonical analysis when the number of variables is large relative to sample size. *Journal of Educational Statistics, 1*, 313–332.

Warr, P.B., & Knapper, C. (1968). *The perception of people and events.* London: Wiley.

Chapter 16

STRUCTURAL EQUATION MODELING

Tiffany A. Whittaker
University of Texas at Austin

16.1 INTRODUCTION

Structural equation modeling (SEM) is a broad designation that encompasses a number of different techniques with which researchers may model the relationships among different variables that are observed (e.g., IQ score, GPA, years in school) and/or unobserved (e.g., motivation, need for achievement, academic self-concept). SEM may also be referred to as covariance structure analysis, latent variable analysis, causal modeling, and simultaneous equation modeling. This chapter will introduce three SEM techniques, including observed variable path analysis, confirmatory factor analysis (CFA), and latent variable path analysis. The presentations in this chapter will be more conceptual than statistical and, thus, will not include the respective system of equations for the models presented. Readers interested in learning more about the equations associated with each SEM technique are encouraged to consult Bollen's (1989) text.

16.2 NOTATION, TERMINOLOGY, AND SOFTWARE

Structural equation models are typically illustrated visually and include various symbols that represent variables and their interrelationships, such as squares, circles, one-headed arrows, and two-headed arrows. Table 16.1 provides a summary of the conventional symbols and terminology used in SEM.

In SEM, squares denote observed variables whereas circles signify unobserved or latent variables. One-headed arrows correspond to direct effects while two-headed arrows signify that two variables are simply related. For instance, Figure 16.1 illustrates an observed variable path model.

As seen in Figure 16.1, X1 and X2 are modeled to directly affect Y1 (represented by paths *a* and *c*, respectively) and Y2 (represented by paths *b* and *d*, respectively). Y1 is

▨ **Table 16.1: Conventional Symbols and Terminology**

Diagram	Description	Conventional notation	Chapter notation
⬭	A latent variable that is not directly measured (may also be called a factor or construct)	η (eta) represents latent endogenous variables	F
		ξ (ksi) represents latent exogenous variables	
⬜	Observed variable (may also be called measured or manifest variable)	Y represents observed endogenous variables (also indicators of η)	Y
		X represents observed exogenous variables (also indicators of ξ)	X
⬭	Errors or disturbances for latent endogenous variables	ζ (zeta) represents errors for latent endogenous variables	D
⬭	Errors or residuals for observed endogenous variables	ε (epsilon) represents errors for Y variables	E
		δ (delta) represents errors for X variables	E

▨ **Figure 16.1** Observed variable path model example.

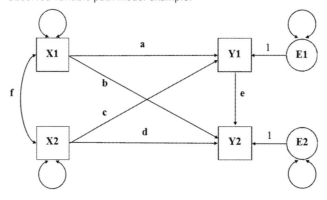

also modeled to directly affect Y2 (represented by path *e*). Because these variables are illustrated pictorially with squares, they represent observed variables that are directly measured (e.g., annual income, math score). In this example, X1 and X2 are exogenous or independent variables and Y1 and Y2 are endogenous or dependent variables. In general, variables (observed or latent) that have arrows pointing toward them are endogenous whereas variables (observed or latent) that are directly affecting other variables and have no arrows pointing toward them are exogenous variables. Additionally, X1 and X2 are modeled to covary because they are connected with a double-headed arrow (represented by the covariance f).

Another concept that is important to introduce is error. As in standard regression analysis, when a variable is endogenous, it will have explained variance (e.g., R square) as well as unexplained variance. Thus, endogenous variables in SEM have error terms associated with them. These are oftentimes represented via circles because they are also unobserved or latent and have direct effects on their respective endogenous variables. Errors are generally exogenous variables since they have direct effects on endogenous variables. In Figure 16.1, both Y1 and Y2 have errors associated with them (E1 and E2, respectively) since they are endogenous variables. You may also notice double-headed arrows associated with exogenous variables in Figure 16.1. This reflects the fact that these variables are free to vary and that their variances will be estimated because they are not directly affected by other variables in the model. Table 16.2 provides a summary of directional symbols used in SEM.

If the observed variables in Figure 16.1 were instead unobserved constructs or latent factors (e.g., self-efficacy, perceived social support), they would be pictorially illustrated with circles instead of squares. This is demonstrated in the structural equation model or latent variable path model in Figure 16.2.

■ Table 16.2: Additional Symbols in SEM

Diagram	Description
X ⟶ Y	Represents a direct effect from X to Y
X ⟷ Y	Represents a covariance between X and Y
⟲	Variances associated with exogenous variables, including errors or disturbances associated with endogenous variables

■ **Figure 16.2** Latent variable path model example.

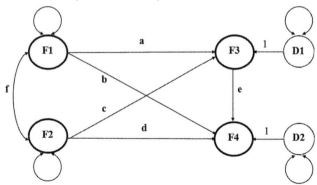

F1 and F2 are exogenous or independent latent variables, and F3 and F4 are endogenous or dependent latent variables. In Figure 16.2, the endogenous factors (F3 and F4) still have errors associated with them, but they are typically differentiated from the errors associated with observed variables and commonly called disturbances (e.g., D1 and D2, respectively).

Various software programs exist that are capable of analyzing structural equation models. Some of the programs are stand-alone software, such as LISREL, EQS, AMOS, Mx, and M*plus*. Other procedures that estimate parameters for structural equation models are available and are subsumed within larger software platforms, such as the CALIS procedure in SAS, the SEPATH procedure in STATISTICA, the RAMONA procedure in SYSTAT, and add-on packages in R (lavaan and sem). A review of the capabilities of these software programs is beyond the scope of this chapter. A fairly comprehensive discussion of available SEM software programs is provided in Kline (2011) as well as the available syntax for examples using LISREL, EQS, and M*plus*. Further, Barbara Byrne has written a chapter describing popular SEM software (Byrne, 2012b) in addition to several books describing the analysis of structural equation models using different software, including LISREL (Byrne, 1998), EQS (Byrne, 2006), AMOS (Byrne, 2010), and M*plus* (Byrne, 2012a). To be consistent with the software used in this textbook, software application examples in this chapter will be done using the CALIS procedure in SAS (SPSS does not include a structural equation modeling procedure). Hence, basic knowledge of SAS will be assumed when presenting these examples.

16.3 CAUSAL INFERENCE

Given the various types of relationships that may exist in path models, it is important to briefly discuss the issue of causal inference. By no means is this discussion exhaustive. As such, readers should refer to seminal readings in the area (Davis, 1985; Mulaik, 2009; Pearl, 2000; Pearl, 2012; Sobel, 1995).

As is evident in the models previously presented in this chapter, one-headed arrows represent hypotheses concerning causal directions. For instance, in Figure 16.1, X1 is hypothesized to directly affect both Y1 and Y2. Based on theoretical bases, the implication is that X1 causes Y1 and Y2. In SEM, three conditions are generally necessary to infer causality: association, isolation, and temporal precedence. Association simply means that the cause and effect are observed to covary with one another. Isolation signifies that the cause and effect continue to covary when they are isolated from other influential variables. This condition is generally the most difficult to meet in its entirety, but it may be closer to realization if data are collected for the variables that may influence the relationship between the cause and effect (e.g., SES) and controlled for statistically and/or with respect to design considerations (e.g., collecting data only on females to avoid the influence of sex differences). Temporal precedence indicates that the hypothesized cause occurs prior to the hypothesized effect in time. Temporal precedence may be accomplished by way of collecting data using methods incorporated in experimental (e.g., random assignment) or quasi-experimental designs (e.g., manipulation of treatment exposure) or collecting data for the causal variables prior to collecting data for the outcome variables on which they are hypothesized to affect.

16.4 FUNDAMENTAL TOPICS IN SEM

Before introducing the models associated with the three SEM techniques mentioned in the opening paragraph (i.e., observed variable path analysis, CFA, and latent variable path analysis), there are some fundamental topics in SEM that must first be outlined because they generally apply to all of the models in the SEM arena. These topics include model identification, model estimation, model fit, and model modification and selection. Some of these fundamentals will be discussed again in the context of the model being introduced for more clarity.

16.4.1 Identification

Model identification is a fundamental requirement for parameters to be estimated in a model. Before elaborating upon this important issue, it is first necessary to introduce some relevant information concerning the data input and the parameters to be estimated in a model. Figure 16.3 will be used to demonstrate these issues.

The model in Figure 16.3 is a basic multiple regression model with two predictor variables (X1 and X2) and one outcome variable (Y). In SEM, procedures are performed on the covariances among the observed variables. Thus, the input data used in SEM analyses consists of a sample covariance matrix, which is simply the unstandardized version of a correlation matrix. The sample covariance matrix (**S**) is given here for the variables used in Figure 16.3:

$$\mathbf{S} = \begin{bmatrix} 200 & 110 & 115 \\ 110 & 220 & 130 \\ 115 & 130 & 175 \end{bmatrix}$$

■ **Figure 16.3** Multiple regression model with two predictors.

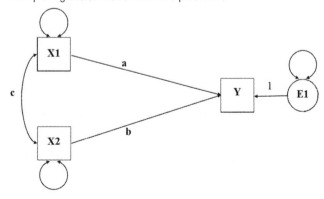

As you know, the variances of X1, X2, and Y appear in the main diagonal of the sample covariance matrix (noted in the covariance matrix with bold font). Here, the variances of X1, X2, and Y are equal to 200, 220, and 175, respectively. Further, the covariances between all possible pairs of variables appear in the off-diagonal elements of the sample covariance matrix (noted in the covariance matrix with italics). For instance, the covariance between X1 and X2 is 110; the covariance between X1 and Y is 115; and the covariance between X2 and Y is 130. This is what SEM software then uses during the estimation process which will be discussed in more detail subsequently.

You can determine if a given model is identified by calculating the difference between the number of nonredundant observations in the sample covariance matrix ($p*$) and the number of model parameters that must be estimated (q; for a more detailed explanation of the various rules of model identification, see Bollen, 1989 and Kenny & Milan, 2012). Nonredundant observations do *not* pertain to the number of participants for which data were collected. Rather, the nonredundant observations in a sample covariance matrix include the variance elements in the main diagonal of the sample covariance matrix and the upper or lower triangle of covariance elements in the sample covariance matrix. In the sample covariance matrix for the model in Figure 16.3, there are three variances and three covariances. Thus, there are six nonredundant observations. The number of nonredundant observations in a sample covariance matrix can more easily be calculated with the following formula:

$$p* = \frac{p(p+1)}{2} = \frac{3(3+1)}{2} = 6,$$

where $p*$ is the number of nonredundant observations and p is the number of observed variables in the model. The second quantity needed to determine if a model is identified is the number of model parameters (q) requiring estimation in SEM. This number consists of the variances of exogenous variables (which include error and/or disturbance variances), direct effects (represented with one-headed arrows), and covariances (represented with double-headed arrows).

Three different scenarios may occur when subtracting the number of model parameters that are to be estimated from the number of nonredundant observations, resulting in three different types of models: 1) just-identified; 2) over-identified; and 3) under-identified. A just-identified model has the same number of nonredundant observations in the sample covariance matrix as model parameters to estimate and is sometimes referred to as a saturated model. An over-identified model contains more nonredundant observations in the sample covariance matrix than model parameters to estimate. Models that are just- and over-identified allow model parameters to be estimated. However, an under-identified model, having fewer nonredundant observations in the sample covariance matrix than parameters to estimate, does not allow for parameters to be estimated. Thus, prior to collecting data, you should determine if your hypothesized model is identified, thus allowing you to obtain parameter estimates.

To illustrate, consider the multiple regression model in Figure 16.3. To obtain the number of parameters that will be estimated, we first observe that the variances of X1, X2, and E1 (exogenous variables) will be estimated. In addition, the direct effect from X1 to Y and the direct effect from X2 to Y will be estimated. Lastly, the covariance between X1 and X2 will be estimated. As a result, we have six parameters to be estimated, and recall that there are six nonredundant observations in the sample covariance matrix. The difference between nonredundant observations and parameters to estimate ($p^* - q$), in this case, is $6 - 6 = 0$. This value is referred to as the degrees of freedom associated with the theoretical model (df_T). Thus, there are zero df_T associated with our multiple regression model presented in Figure 16.3, which means that it is a just-identified model. Over-identified models will be associated with more than zero (positive) df_T whereas under-identified models will result in negative (less than zero) df_T.

Under-identified models are mathematically impossible to analyze because there are an infinite set of solutions that will satisfy the structural model, which makes estimation of a unique set of model parameters unattainable. To help illustrate the notion of under-identification, we borrow an example from Kline (2011, chap. 6) because it nicely clarifies the concept. Consider the following equation in which we have one known value (6) and two unknown values (a and b):

$$a + b = 6$$

Note that you would not be able to uniquely solve for a and b in this equation because they could take on numerous sets of corresponding values that satisfy the equation (i.e., that sum to 6).

Further, while models that are just- and over-identified allow for parameters to be estimated, there is an important difference between these models. That is, just-identified models reproduce the data exactly whereas there may be multiple solutions when estimating over-identified models. Just-identified models reproduce the data perfectly because there is only one solution for the parameter estimates. Further, because just-identified models simply reproduce the data, the model fits the data perfectly. Thus, you *cannot* test the model fit of just-identified models (which is often desired) whereas you can test the model fit of over-identified models (more to come later about model fit). To help illustrate this point, consider the following set of equations in which we have three known values (17, 13, and 5) and three unknown values (a, b, and c):

$$a + bc = 17$$
$$b + ac = 13$$
$$c = 5$$

Solving for c was easy enough (because it was given). To solve for the remaining unknown values, however, you will have to revisit the algebra course you took during your high school days. Here are the solved values:

$a = 2$
$b = 3$
$c = 5$

Note that there is only one solution for a, b, and c values that will satisfy the three equations (as in a just-identified model).

When estimating parameters in over-identified models, you will not be able to solve the equations so easily. For instance, suppose that you instead hypothesized that X1 directly affected X2, which in turn directly affected Y (as opposed to the multiple regression model). This would render the model illustrated in Figure 16.4.

Again, there are six non-redundant observations in the sample covariance matrix:

$$p^* = \frac{p(p+1)}{2} = \frac{3(3+1)}{2} = 6$$

Note that the number of nonredundant observations is the same as before because we have three observed variables. Although you are hypothesizing a different causal relationship between the three variables, you are using the same sample covariance matrix. What does change, however, is the number of parameters to estimate given that the hypothesized model differs from the previous one. With this model, there are now five parameters to estimate, including the variances of X1, E1, and E2 in addition to the two direct effects, one from X1 to X2 and the other from X2 to Y. Thus, the df_T associated with this model is $6 - 5 = 1$, resulting in an over-identified model.

To help illustrate the difficulty with solving for unknown values in over-identified models, consider the following set of equations with three known values (5, 4, and 18) and two unknown values (a and b):

$a = 5$
$b = 4$
$ab = 18$

As seen from this example, you would not be able to solve for values of a and b that would reproduce the data perfectly (i.e., $ab = 4 \times 5 \neq 18$). Consequently, a criterion is

■ **Figure 16.4:** Over-identified observed variable path model.

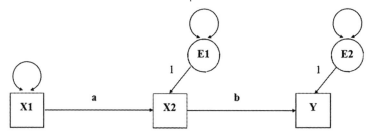

necessary to determine which estimates are the most optimal estimates for the model. When thinking about this, think back to linear regression in which the difference between observed and predicted Y values are minimized when solving for the intercept and slope values. A similar concept is implemented in SEM. The underlying principle in SEM analysis is to minimize the discrepancy between the elements in the sample covariance matrix and the corresponding elements in the covariance matrix that is implied (or reproduced) by the hypothesized model. More specifically, structural equation models are tested to determine how well they account for the variances and covariances among the observed variables.

16.4.2 Estimation

Consider the basic equation used in structural equation procedures:

$$\Sigma = \Sigma(\theta),$$

where Σ is the population covariance matrix for p observed variables, θ is the vector containing model parameters, and $\Sigma(\theta)$ is the covariance matrix implied by the function of model parameters (θ) (Bollen, 1989). In applications of structural equation modeling, the population covariance matrix (Σ) is unknown and is estimated by the sample covariance matrix (**S**). The unknown model parameters (θ) are also estimated $(\hat{\theta})$ by minimizing a discrepancy function between the sample covariance matrix (**S**) and the implied covariance matrix $\Sigma(\theta)$:

$$F\left[\mathbf{S}, \Sigma(\theta)\right].$$

Substituting the estimates of the unknown model parameters in $\Sigma(\theta)$ results in the implied covariance matrix, $\hat{\Sigma} = \Sigma(\hat{\theta})$. The unknown model parameters are estimated to reduce the discrepancy between the implied covariance matrix and the sample covariance matrix. An indication of the discrepancy between the sample covariance matrix and the implied covariance matrix may be deduced from the residual matrix:

$$\left(\mathbf{S} - \hat{\Sigma}\right),$$

with values closer to zero indicating better fit of the structural model to the data (Bollen, 1989).

Estimation of model parameters in SEM is an iterative process that begins with initial structural model parameter estimates, or starting values, which are either generated by the model fitting software package or provided by the user. Depending upon these values, the model fitting program will iterate through sequential cycles that calculate improved estimates. That is, the elements of the implied covariance matrix that are based on the parameter estimates from each iteration will become closer to the elements of the observed covariance matrix (Kline, 2011). The discrepancy function is fundamentally the sum of squared differences between respective elements in the sample covariance matrix (**S**) and the implied covariance matrix $\left(\widehat{\mathbf{\Sigma}}\right)$ and will result in a single value.

If the structural model is just-identified, the discrepancy function will equal zero because the elements in the sample covariance matrix will exactly equal the elements in the implied covariance matrix, $\mathbf{S} = \widehat{\mathbf{\Sigma}}$ (Bollen, 1989). For instance, the residual matrix associated with the just-identified model in Figure 16.3 would be calculated as follows:

$$\left(\mathbf{S} - \widehat{\mathbf{\Sigma}}\right) = \begin{bmatrix} 200 & 110 & 115 \\ 110 & 220 & 130 \\ 115 & 130 & 175 \end{bmatrix} - \begin{bmatrix} 200 & 110 & 115 \\ 110 & 220 & 130 \\ 115 & 130 & 175 \end{bmatrix} = \begin{bmatrix} 0 & 0 & 0 \\ 0 & 0 & 0 \\ 0 & 0 & 0 \end{bmatrix}$$

For over-identified structural models, the sample covariance matrix will not equal the implied covariance matrix, but the estimation iterations will proceed until the difference between the discrepancy function in one iteration to the next falls below a specified default value used in the software program (e.g., < .00005 in M*plus*) or until the maximum number of iterations has been reached (Kline, 2011). For instance, after estimating parameters for the over-identified model in Figure 16.4, the residual matrix would be calculated as follows:

$$\left(\mathbf{S} - \widehat{\mathbf{\Sigma}}\right) = \begin{bmatrix} 200 & 110 & 115 \\ 110 & 220 & 130 \\ 115 & 130 & 175 \end{bmatrix} - \begin{bmatrix} 200 & 110 & 65 \\ 110 & 220 & 130 \\ 65 & 130 & 175 \end{bmatrix} = \begin{bmatrix} 0 & 0 & 50 \\ 0 & 0 & 0 \\ 50 & 0 & 0 \end{bmatrix}$$

Notice how all of the values in the implied covariance matrix $\left(\widehat{\mathbf{\Sigma}}\right)$ equal their respective values in the sample covariance matrix (**S**) with the exception of the covariance between X1 and Y. Specifically, the relationship (or covariance) between X1 and Y was not fully explained by the hypothesized model as compared to the remaining relationships (or variances and covariances). This is a consequence of not modeling X1 as directly affecting Y in the model. Accordingly, the difference between respective elements will not equal zero for this relationship in the residual matrix.

SEM software programs have default settings for the maximum number of iterations allowed during the estimation process. When the number of iterations necessary to obtain parameter estimates exceeds the maximum number of iterations without reaching the specified minimum difference between the discrepancy function from one iteration to the next, the estimates have failed to converge on the parameters. That is, the estimation process failed to reach a solution for the parameter estimates. Nonconvergent solutions may provide unstable parameter estimates that should not be considered reliable. Nonconvergence may be corrected by increasing the maximum number of iterations allowed in the SEM software, changing the minimum difference stopping criteria (e.g., < .0005) between iterations, or providing start values that are closer to the initial estimates of the model parameter estimates. If these corrections do not result in a convergent solution, other issues may need to be addressed, such as sample size and model complexity (Bollen, 1989).

Recall that the unknown model parameters $(\mathbf{\theta})$ are estimated $\left(\hat{\mathbf{\theta}}\right)$ by minimizing a discrepancy function. Different types of discrepancy functions may be used during the estimation process. Again, a discrepancy function, sometimes referred to as a loss or fit function, basically reflects the sum of squared differences between respective elements in the sample covariance matrix $(\mathbf{S})$ and the implied covariance matrix $\left(\hat{\mathbf{\Sigma}}\right)$. However, the various estimators currently available implement different matrix weighting procedures while calculating these differences (see Bollen, 1989, and Lei & Wu, 2012, for more detailed explanations concerning estimation procedures).

The most widely employed discrepancy function in structural equation modeling, and usually the default discrepancy function in structural equation modeling software (e.g., LISREL, EQS, AMOS, and M*plus*), is the maximum likelihood (ML) discrepancy function (see Ferron & Hess, 2007 for a detailed example using ML estimation). ML estimation is based on the assumption of multivariate normality among the observed variables and is often referred to as normal theory ML. The popularity of the ML discrepancy function is evident when considering the following strengths of the estimators' properties. Under small sample size conditions, ML estimators may be biased, although they are asymptotically unbiased. Thus, as sample size increases, the expected values of the ML estimates represent the true values in the population. The ML estimator is also consistent, meaning that as sample size approaches infinity, the probability that the estimate is close to the true value becomes larger (approaches 1.0). Another essential property of ML estimators is asymptotic efficiency. That is, the ML estimator has the lowest asymptotic variance among a class of consistent estimators. Further, the ML estimator is scale invariant in that the values of the ML discrepancy function will be the same for any change in the scale of the observed variables (Bollen, 1989).

Another normal theory estimator is generalized least squares (GLS; for a review of GLS, see Bollen, 1989). When the assumption of multivariate normality is met, ML and GLS estimates are asymptotically equal. Thus, as sample size increases, the estimates produced by GLS are approximately equal to the estimates produced by ML. However, ML estimation has been shown to outperform GLS estimation under model misspecification conditions (Olsson, Foss, Troye, & Howell, 2000).

Under violations of the assumption associated with multivariate normality, the parameters estimated by ML are generally robust and produce consistent estimates (Beauducel & Herzberg, 2006; DiStefano, 2002; Dolan, 1994). However, skewed and kurtotic distributions may sometimes render an incorrect asymptotic covariance matrix of parameter estimates (Bollen, 1989). Further, increased levels of skewness (e.g., greater than 3.0) and/or kurtosis (e.g., greater than 8.0) largely invalidates the property of asymptotic efficiency associated with the estimated parameters, producing inaccurate model test statistics (Kline, 2011). Consequently, observed variables with nonnormal distributions may affect statistical significance tests of overall model fit as well as the consistency and efficiency of the estimated parameters.

Other discrepancy functions that produce asymptotically efficient estimators have been proposed that do not require multivariate normality among the observed variables. One of these discrepancy functions is the weighted least squares (WLS) function (Browne, 1984), also referred to as asymptotically distribution free (ADF) estimation (see Browne, 1984, and Muthén & Kaplan, 1985, for more information concerning WLS estimation). WLS was proposed as an efficient estimator for any arbitrary distribution of observed variables, including ordered categorical variables (Browne, 1984). Although WLS estimation has been shown to be efficient and more consistent than ML estimation under the presence of nonnormality among categorical variables (Muthén & Kaplan, 1985), the performance of WLS estimation in other studies has been questionable under certain conditions. For instance, model fit tests associated with WLS have been shown to reject the correct factor model too frequently, even under normal distributions at small sample sizes (Hu, Bentler, & Kano, 1992), and increasingly overestimate the expected value of the model fit test statistic as nonnormality and model misspecification increase (Curran, West, & Finch, 1996). Although WLS has demonstrated better efficiency under nonnormal distributions than ML (Chou, Bentler, & Satorra, 1991; Muthén & Kaplan, 1985), WLS efficiency is adversely affected under conditions of increasing nonnormality, small sample sizes, and large model size (Muthén & Kaplan, 1992). Thus, WLS estimation requires very large (and possibly inaccessible) sample sizes (approximately 2,500 to 5,000) for accurate model fit tests and parameter estimates (Finney & DiStefano, 2006; Hu et al., 1992; Loehlin, 2004). In addition, WLS estimation is more computationally intensive than other estimation procedures due to taking the inverse of a full weighting matrix, which increases in size as the number of observed variables increases (Loehlin, 2004).

Robust WLS approaches were subsequently developed in order to correct for the difficulties inherent with full WLS estimation (see Muthén, du Toit, & Spisic, 1997, and Jöreskog & Sörbom, 1996, for more information concerning robust WLS). Generally, these approaches use a diagonal weight matrix instead of a full weight matrix. Robust WLS has been shown to outperform full WLS with respect to chi-square test and parameter estimate accuracy (Flora & Curran, 2004; Forero & Maydeu-Olivares, 2009).

As discussed earlier, model test statistics and the standard errors of the parameter estimates may become biased under increased conditions of nonnormality when using normal theory estimators, such as ML estimation (Hoogland & Boomsma, 1998; Hu et al., 1992). While nonnormal theory estimators (e.g., WLS) and their robust counterparts may be implemented, another alternative is to implement the Satorra and Bentler (1994) scaling correction that adjusts the model test statistic (i.e., a chi-square test statistic, χ^2) to provide a chi-square test statistic that more closely approximates the chi-square distribution and adjusts the standard errors to be more robust when assumptions of normality are violated using ML estimation. The Satorra–Bentler scaled χ^2 test statistic $\left(\chi^2_{SB}\right)$ has been shown to perform more accurately than ML or WLS chi-square tests (Chou et al., 1991) under increasing nonnormality conditions. The χ^2_{SB} has also performed more accurately than ML or WLS chi-square tests under model misspecification conditions (Curran et al., 1996). The Satorra–Bentler scaled standard errors for the model parameters have also been shown to be more robust than ML and WLS under increasing nonnormality conditions, demonstrating less bias (Chou et al., 1991).

We conclude this section by noting that under conditions of normality and mild conditions of nonnormality, ML estimation is generally recommended and will perform well with respect to the resulting chi-square test of model fit and the standard errors associated with the model parameters. As the variables deviate more from normality, however, the Satorra–Bentler scaling correction is recommended for more appropriate chi-square tests of model fit and standard errors associated with the model parameters. When estimating models that incorporate ordered categorical data as outcomes (e.g., Likert scale responses), particularly with less than four response categories, a robust WLS approach is advised.

16.4.3 Model Fit

Assessing the fit of structural equation models is multifaceted. It entails not only examining model fit at a global level, but also involves assessing the fit in terms of the plausibility of the parameter estimates. The following subsections of model fit provide information concerning each of these facets of model fit.

16.4.3.1 CHI-SQUARE TESTS OF MODEL FIT

The fundamental hypothesis in covariance structure analysis is that the population covariance matrix of p observed variables, Σ, is equal to the reproduced implied covariance matrix, $\Sigma(\theta)$, based on the hypothesized structural model: $\Sigma = \Sigma(\theta)$. For over-identified structural models, each estimation procedure previously discussed is able to provide a test associated with this fundamental hypothesis for the theoretical model. Once a discrepancy or fit function (e.g., ML) has been minimized, resulting in a single value (F), this value is multiplied by $(N-1)$, yielding an approximately chi-square distributed statistic (Bollen, 1989):

$$\chi^2_T = F(N-1).$$

This chi-square test of model fit is a test of the overall fit of the theoretical model to the data with $p^* - q$ (i.e., number of non-redundant observations − number of parameters) degrees of freedom (df_T). The theoretical model is rejected if

$$\chi^2_T > c_a,$$

where c_α is the critical value of the chi-square test and α is the significance level of the chi-square test (e.g., $\alpha = .05$). It is important to note that the χ^2_T will equal a value of zero (with $df_T = 0$) when the model is just-identified because the value of the minimized fit function will equal zero. It is also important to note that the Satorra–Bentler scaled chi-square statistic $\left(\chi^2_{SB}\right)$ involves dividing the chi-square statistic obtained using a normal-theory estimator (e.g., ML) by a scaling correction in order to adjust for nonnormality (Satorra & Bentler, 1994).

The chi-square test for the theoretical model is testing the null hypothesis that the population covariance matrix, $\boldsymbol{\Sigma}$ (estimated using our sample covariance matrix, $\mathbf{S}$), is equal to the implied covariance matrix in the population, $\boldsymbol{\Sigma}(\boldsymbol{\theta})$ (after estimating the parameters using our sample data, $\hat{\boldsymbol{\Sigma}}$). Thus, the more consistent the relationships are in our theoretical model with the observed data, the more likely the sample covariance matrix will be similar to the implied covariance matrix. Given that the null hypothesis signifies that our hypothesized model explains the observed relationships well, we do not want to reject the null hypothesis. Thus, we would like the chi-square test of the theoretical model $\left(\chi^2_T\right)$ to be nonsignificant, statistically speaking, to provide support for our hypothesized relationships.

Another chi-square test is available in SEM, which is the chi-square test of the baseline or null model, χ^2_B. The baseline or null model is a model in which all of the observed variables in the model are treated as exogenous (independent) and are not correlated with any of the other variables in the model. For instance, the baseline model for the multiple regression model initially presented in Figure 16.3 would look like the model illustrated in Figure 16.5.

Notice that only the variances of the p variables in the baseline model are estimated (in this case, three variances) given that they are treated as exogenous and the lack of interrelationships hypothesized in this model. The degrees of freedom associated with this model (df_B) are calculated similarly to that previously described in which

■ **Figure 16.5** Baseline model for the multiple regression model with two predictors.

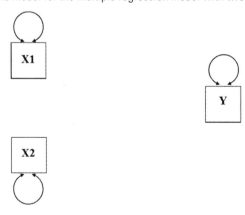

the number of parameters to estimate is subtracted from the number of nonredundant observations ($p* - q = 6 - 3 = 3\ df_B$). The df_B may also be calculated as:

$$df_B = \frac{p(p-1)}{2} = \frac{3(3-1)}{2} = 3.$$

The null hypothesis is the same for the test of the baseline model $\left[\text{i.e., } \boldsymbol{\Sigma} = \boldsymbol{\Sigma}(\boldsymbol{\theta})\right]$. It is in our best interest to fail to reject the null hypothesis when testing the fit of the theoretical model in order to provide support for our theoretically driven hypothesized relationships among the variables. However, consider the implication of failing to reject the null hypothesis in the case with the baseline model. That is, if our observed sample covariance matrix is similar to an implied covariance matrix for a baseline model in which no relationships among the variables are hypothesized, this would suggest that our variables do not covary (or correlate) with one another. Consequently, rejecting the null hypothesis for the baseline model would provide support for the presence of interrelationships among our variables of interest. Otherwise, modeling relationships among variables that do not covary at the outset is a moot point.

The chi-square test statistic has been criticized for its sensitivity to sample size, which is evident from the formula

$$\chi_T^2 = F(N-1).$$

Thus, as sample size increases, the χ_T^2 test statistic is more likely to identify small differences between the observed and implied covariance matrices as being significant. Consequently, the null hypothesis, $\boldsymbol{\Sigma} = \boldsymbol{\Sigma}(\boldsymbol{\theta})$, is more likely to be rejected, indicating poor fit of the hypothesized structural model. A method that may be used to determine if a chi-square statistic is sensitive to sample size when assessing model fit is to continue adding parameters to a model until the chi-square is no longer statistically significant. Adding parameters to estimate in a model will generally improve model fit.

16.4.3.2 FIT INDICES

This sample size dependency of the chi-square statistic has led to the proposal of numerous alternative fit indices that evaluate model fit and supplement the χ_T^2 test statistic (Bentler & Bonett, 1980; Hu & Bentler, 1999; Kline, 2011). While different classifications of these fit indices exist (e.g., see Kline, 2011), Hu and Bentler (1998; 1999) classified model fit indices as either incremental or absolute fit indices. Table 16.3 provides the formulas, properties, and associated cutoff values for the more commonly used fit indices in SEM.

Commonly used incremental fit indices include the Normed Fit Index (NFI; Bentler & Bonnett, 1980), Bollen's (1986) Incremental Fit Index (IFI), the Non-normed Fit Index (NNFI), which is also called the Tucker-Lewis Index (TLI; Tucker & Lewis, 1973), and the Comparative Fit Index (CFI; Bentler, 1990). Incremental fit indices measure

▇ Table 16.3: Commonly Used Model Fit Indices in SEM

Fit index	Properties	Recommended cutoff
Incremental fit indices		
Normed Fit Index (NFI) $$\frac{\chi_B^2 - \chi_T^2}{\chi_B^2}$$	Ranges from 0–1	.90 or greater
Incremental Fit Index (IFI) $$\frac{\chi_B^2 - \chi_T^2}{\chi_B^2 - df_T}$$	Theoretical range is from 0–1 (can be outside theoretical range)	.90 or greater
Non-normed Fit Index (NNFI)/ Tucker-Lewis Index (TLI) $$\frac{(\chi_B^2 / df_B) - (\chi_T^2 / df_T)}{(\chi_B^2 / df_B) - 1}$$	Theoretical range is from 0–1 (can be outside of theoretical range)	.90 and greater
Comparative Fit Index (CFI) $$1 - \frac{\max(\chi_T^2 - df_T, 0)}{\max(\chi_B^2 - df_B, \chi_T^2 - df_T, 0)}$$	Ranges from 0–1	.90 and greater
Absolute fit indices		
Goodness-of-Fit Index $$1 - \left[\frac{\sum_{i=1}^{p(p+1)/2} (sr_i)^2}{\sum_{i=1}^{p(p+1)/2} (\text{stand var/cov}_i)^2} \right]$$ sr = standardized residual stand var/cov = standardized variance/covariance	Theoretical range is from 0–1 (maximum value is 1 but can be lower than 0)	.90 or greater
Adjusted Goodness-of-Fit Index $$1 - [p(p+1)/2df_T](1 - GFI)$$	Theoretical range is from 0–1 (maximum value is 1 but can be lower than 0)	.90 or greater
McDonald's Fit Index (MFI) $$\exp\left[\frac{-.5(\chi_T^2 - df_T)}{N-1} \right]$$	Theoretical range is from 0–1 (can exceed a value of 1)	.90 or greater
Standardized Root Mean-Square Residual (SRMR) $$\sqrt{\frac{\sum_{i=1}^{p(p+1)/2} (sr_i)^2}{p(p+1)/2}}$$ sr = standardized residual		0 = perfect fit .05 or less = good fit .05–.10 = acceptable fit
Root Mean-Square Error of Approximation (RMSEA) $$\sqrt{\frac{\chi_T^2 - df_T}{df_T(N-1)}}$$	Accompanied by 90% Confidence Interval and p-value for test of close fit	.05 or less = close fit .05–.08 = adequate fit

the proportionate improvement in a model's fit to the data by comparing a specific structural equation model k to a baseline structural equation model. The typical baseline comparison model is the null model in which all of the variables in the model are independent of each other or uncorrelated (Kline, 2011). This can easily be seen in the formulas for these indices in Table 16.3. You may also notice that some of these fit indices include degrees of freedom (df_T) in their calculation (e.g., CFI, IFI, NNFI/ TLI). This is done in order to counter the impact of model complexity. Specifically, models tend to fit better when estimating more parameters than when estimating fewer parameters. Thus, as the number of parameters being estimated in a model increases, the smaller the df_T becomes (remember: $p* - q$). The weight of the df_T is most easily seen for the IFI formula in Table 16.3. Notice in this formula that as the df_T becomes smaller, the IFI value becomes larger (all other things remaining constant). Thus, a subclassification of model fit indices exists with respect to model complexity adjustments. Traditionally, models with values of .90 and above associated with these indices have been considered to fit the data acceptably.

Absolute fit indices measure how well a structural equation model reproduces the data. Commonly used absolute fit indices include the Goodness-of-Fit Index (GFI) and its adjusted version, the Adjusted Goodness-of-Fit Index (AGFI; Jöreskog & Sörbom, 1984), McDonald's (1989) Fit Index (MFI), the Standardized Root Mean-Square Residual (SRMR; Bentler, 1995), and the Root Mean-Square Error of Approximation (RMSEA; Steiger & Lind, 1980). Conventionally, models with values of .90 or above associated with the GFI, the AGFI, and MFI have been deemed as acceptably fitting the data. Hu and Bentler (1995) suggested that SRMR values of .05 and less indicate "good fit" and values between .05 and .10 indicate "acceptable fit." Browne and Cudeck (1993) proposed that RMSEA values of .05 and less indicate "close fit" and values between .05 and .08 indicate "adequate fit." The RMSEA is the only fit index of those mentioned that is supplemented with a confidence interval and associated p-value. It is important to note that if a value of .05 is contained within the 90% confidence interval associated with the RMSEA and is accompanied by a p-value greater than .05, this is recognized as evidence of acceptable model fit. A p-value greater than .05 would indicate a failure to reject the null that the RMSEA is equal to or less than .05 and that the model is "close fitting." In contrast, a p-value less than .05 would indicate that the null be rejected that the RMSEA is equal to or less than .05 and that the model is not "close fitting." It is also noteworthy to point out that some of the absolute fit indices also adjust for model complexity (e.g., see formulas for the AGFI, MFI, and RMSEA in Table 16.3).

Given the various types of model fit indices available in SEM, some recommendations concerning the evaluation of model fit as well as the reporting of model fit information is necessary. Given that incremental and absolute fit indices indicate different aspects of model fit, it is largely recommended to report values of several fit indices. According to Kline (2011), a minimum collection of fit indices to report would consist of the χ_T^2 test statistic with corresponding degrees of freedom and level of significance, the CFI, the GFI, the RMSEA (with associated 90% CI and p-value), and the SRMR.

In a large-scale simulation study, Hu and Bentler (1999) examined the performance of a number of model fit indices in SEM under varied conditions of model misspecification, sample size, and model complexity. Ultimately, they recommended using joint criteria when assessing model fit. This was proposed in order to reduce the potential of rejecting the "correct" model (paralleling a type II error) and failing to reject the "incorrect" (or misspecified) model (paralleling a type I error). For instance, they suggested a cutoff value for the SRMR of .10 or less along with a supplemental fit index cutoff value of .96 or less for the NNFI/TLI, IFI, RNI, MFI, or CFI to support acceptable model fit. They also advocated using a cutoff value for the SRMR of .10 or less along with an RMSEA value of .06 or less to support adequate fit of a model to the data.

In reaction to this article, more stringent fit index cutoff values, particularly for the NNFI/TLI, IFI, RNI, MFI, and CFI, began to be promoted as well as reported in applications of SEM while citing Hu and Bentler (1999). Although use of their joint criteria helps reduce the potential of both type I and II errors with respect to model retention, use of these criteria may also result in higher than expected type I and type II errors in some circumstances. In fact, Hu and Bentler (1989; 1999) noted limitations concerning the use of their recommendations in all scenarios because additional research is needed and the joint criteria may not be generalizable to all conditions (Fan & Sivo, 2005; Yuan, 2005). Marsh, Hau, and Wen (2004) nicely summarized and called into question some issues surrounding the current state of model fit evaluation in SEM applications. While some are still proponents of using the joint criteria and the increased cutoff values associated with some of the fit indices, others are content with using the originally proposed cutoff values associated with the model fit indices in SEM.

16.4.3.3 PARAMETER ESTIMATES

Of course, even if a model exhibits good fit (based on the obtained model fit indices), the model parameter estimates should also be examined to ensure that they are appropriate. For example, if it has been consistently demonstrated in the relevant literature that the relationship between motivation and achievement is a positive and moderate association, the standardized regression coefficient or correlation estimated in a structural equation model should correspond with this past evidence. If an expected association is not obtained, other problems may be occurring in the hypothesized model that warrant attention. As in multiple regression analysis, these problems could be the result of multicollinearity and/or suppressor relationships as well as measurement issues (e.g., poor reliability of measures used).

If unstandardized parameter estimates are presented in a model, the direct paths may be interpreted as unstandardized partial regression coefficients. The two-headed arrow represents something that is implicit in multiple regression models, which is that predictors (or covariates) covary with each other. Standardized estimates may be presented in models instead of unstandardized estimates. The choice depends on how meaningful the interpretations are when using the original data's metric. For example, interpreting total scores comprised of Likert or other response scale options may not be as meaningful as interpreting data concerning age, GPA, education in years, or IQ. Another consideration for the presentation of estimates in path models is to report findings consistently with past literature in the area. That is, if similar studies in which similar scales or measures have been used reported their findings in a certain metric (unstandardized or standardized), it would be practical to report findings in the same metric for comparison purposes. Applied researchers in the social and behavioral sciences regularly report standardized results because of the prevalent use of total scores from questionnaires and for ease of interpretation across studies.

Regardless of the metric in which the data are reported, the sample covariance matrix, which is an unstandardized version of a correlation matrix, is used as input in SEM analyses. The unstandardized data are used because of statistical testing purposes. That is, information concerning the distributional properties of the variables (particularly variability information) is necessary in order to compute standard errors associated with parameter estimates. Parameter estimates are divided by their respective standard errors in order to calculate a z statistic (or t statistic, depending upon the software), which may be compared to the critical z value to determine if it is statistically significantly different from zero. If parameters are estimated using a correlation matrix with a normal theory estimator (e.g., ML) instead of a covariance matrix, the parameter estimates and their respective standard errors as well as model fit values may be erroneous. Some software programs will allow for the estimation of a correlation matrix with some minor modifications to the command or input file (e.g., LISREL and M*plus*, PROC CALIS in SAS). Other methods exist that also allow the estimation of parameters using a correlation matrix, but they generally require that the user set up complicated nonlinear constraints that are challenging. See Browne (1982) and Steiger (2002) for more information concerning this issue.

16.4.3.4 RECOMMENDATIONS

All in all, it is not clear whether there will ever be overarching consensus concerning model fit in SEM, which is a complicated and sizeable topic of research. Model fit is affected by various components, including the actual fit index calculation, sample size, estimation procedure, and model complexity (to name a few). Accordingly, it is proposed that model fit be evaluated not only globally using model fit indices, but it should also be evaluated in terms of the appropriateness of the model parameter estimates associated with the hypothesized relationships.

At the global level, we recommend that the χ^2_T with respective df_T and significance level be reported. We also recommend that two incremental fit indices and two absolute fit indices be reported. Thus, it is suggested that the TLI and the CFI be reported given that they are comparatively unaffected by sample size (Hu & Bentler, 1995; West, Taylor, & Wu, 2012). Further, the RMSEA (with 90% CI and p-value) and the SRMR are recommended for use during model fit assessment given previous findings concerning their relative performance to other fit indices (Hu & Bentler, 1999; West et al., 2012). We also recommend using the originally proposed (or traditional) cutoff values when assessing overall model fit. The reason for this is because when working with real data, the true model in the population will not be known. Accordingly, we prefer to err on the side of failing to reject misspecified models as compared to rejecting the "correct" model should it be attainable.

16.4.4 Model Modification and Selection

When structural equation models do not demonstrate adequate fit through the use of the χ_T^2 test statistic and/or fit indices, researchers may modify or respecify their model and subsequently retest the model fit to the data (MacCallum, Roznowski, & Necowitz, 1992). Given that models in SEM are *a priori* models based on theoretically driven hypotheses concerning the relationships among the variables, inadequate fit of the model may be viewed by some as an indication that the hypothetical model is not credible and, as a result, modification of the model is not advised. On the other hand, some may consider inadequate fit of a model as an indication that specification errors exist in the model, meaning that there is disagreement between the hypothesized model and the correct or true model in the population. Specification errors refer to the inclusion of extraneous associations in the model and/or the exclusion of pertinent associations in the model (MacCallum, 1986). Inadequate model fit is more commonly attributed to the exclusion of pertinent associations, which is regarded by some to result in more severe consequences than the alternative (Saris, Satorra, & van der Veld, 2009). Consequently, applied researchers will most likely add associations (additional parameters to estimate) to the originally proposed model for model fit improvement. In practice, "true" structural equation models are not known to the researcher and the resulting hypothesized models symbolize approximations of the true model in the population (Cudeck & Browne, 1983). Accordingly, some consider model modification indispensable for attaining a model that suitably explains the relationships among the variables of interest in the model (Saris et al., 2009).

Notwithstanding these different viewpoints concerning model modification, it is universally accepted that once modifications of a model begin, it becomes an exploratory model in practice. As with model selection in multiple regression analyses, modifications followed by the retesting of models in SEM on the basis of model fit evaluations capitalizes on the chance occurrences in the sample in which the models are being assessed. Therefore, modifications should be justified by theoretical bases and the resulting model should be cross-validated in a subsequent sample in order to provide support for the model's predictive validity (MacCallum et al., 1992). The following subsections introduce different approaches that may be used by applied researchers when modifying and/or selecting models in SEM.

16.4.4.1 MODIFICATION INDICES AND THE EPC

During model modification or model respecification, different statistics may be used to help you determine which parameters may be added to a model in order to improve its fit to the data. The most widely used statistic for this purpose is the Modification Index (MI) or Lagrange Multiplier (LM), which provides an estimated value of the decrease in the model χ^2_T if a specific association (covariance or direct effect) were added and its respective parameter were then estimated. See Satorra (1989) and Sörbom (1989) for more information concerning the MI or LM. Specific parameters associated with a large MI or LM (e.g., greater than a χ^2 critical value of 3.84 that corresponds with 1 degree of freedom at an alpha level of .05) would be assessed as to whether it would be theoretically reasonable to incorporate into the model and estimated. In general, specification searches employing the MI or LM would be conducted by first checking whether adding any associations (or parameters) to the model would significantly decrease the model's χ^2_T (by at least 3.84 points). If this is the case, researchers would judge the set of possible parameters or respecifications to decide which would result in the largest reduction in the χ^2_T. If the parameter or respecification resulting in the largest reduction in χ^2_T is theoretically conceivable, it could be added to the model and estimated. This procedure would be repeated until the addition of parameters would no longer result in a significant reduction in the model's χ^2_T, or until none of the possible parameters or respecifications that would reduce the χ^2_T significantly is theoretically justifiable to add to the model (Bollen, 1989).

Research in this area concerning the accuracy of the MI or LM with respect to arriving at the correct model has demonstrated less than satisfactory results. For instance, MacCallum's (1986) simulation study examined the performance of the MI/LM with respect to arriving at the correct model under varied conditions, including model misspecification, sample sizes, and type of search (restricted to include only parameters in the correct model versus unrestricted to include any parameter suggested by the MI/LM to include in the model). The findings were largely disappointing, and MacCallum (1986) cautioned applied researchers about the confidence placed on the MI/LM during the model modification process. While two studies have demonstrated more promising results concerning the accuracy of the MI/LM (Chou & Bentler, 1990; Hutchinson, 1993), the findings from other studies echoed MacCallum's (1986) discouraging findings (Kaplan,1988; MacCallum et al., 1992; Silvia & MacCallum, 1988).

An additional statistic that researchers may consult to aid in the identification of parameters that may be added to a model in order to improve fit is the expected parameter change (EPC). The unstandardized EPC was first introduced by Saris, Satorra, and Sörbom (1987). The EPC provides the estimated value of a parameter if it were added and estimated in the respecified model. See Saris, Satorra, & Sörbom (1987) for more information concerning the EPC. Similar to the model modification process using the MI/LM, parameters associated with the largest relative EPC would be assessed with respect to theoretical credibility and could be added to the model and freely estimated. Again, this procedure would be repeated until the parameters are not associated with sizeable EPC values relative to others in the set of potential parameters to add or until none of the parameters associated with sizeable EPC values relative to others in the set is theoretically reasonable to include in the model. There are also standardized versions of the EPC available (Chou & Bentler, 1993; Kaplan, 1989; Luijben, 1989).

Saris et al. (1987) delineated four scenarios in which the EPC could notably contribute to the model modification process (in accordance with theory, of course). First, a sizeable, statistically significant MI/LM corresponding with a sizeable EPC value for a certain parameter would suggest the inclusion of the parameter in the model to be freely estimated. Second, a sizeable, statistically significant MI/LM corresponding with a small EPC value would suggest not including the parameter in the model to be freely estimated because this may be a function of the MI's/LM's sensitivity to sample size. Third, a small, nonsignificant MI/LM corresponding with a sizeable EPC value would, regrettably, be inconclusive and a power analysis is recommended for the MI/LM. Fourth, a small, nonsignificant MI/LM corresponding with a small EPC value associated with a certain parameter would suggest not including the parameter in the model to be freely estimated. It is important to note that Saris et al. (1987) did not provide cutoff criteria with respect to how sizeable an EPC value should be when determining whether or not to add a particular parameter to model. Studies examining the accuracy of the EPC during the model modification process have found promising results (Kaplan, 1989; Luijben & Boomsma, 1988; Whittaker, 2012).

16.4.4.2 RESIDUALS

Another useful tool that may help identify potential model misspecification is the residual covariance matrix. Remember that the residual covariance matrix is the matrix resulting from taking the difference between the observed sample covariance matrix and the model-implied covariance matrix. The elements in a residual covariance matrix for over-identified models will not equal zero, but the estimation of parameter estimates will yield values in the residual covariance matrix as close to zero as is possible given the hypothesized relationships. Relatively large nonzero values in the off-diagonal of the residual covariance matrix would suggest that the relationship between two variables is not explained well by the theoretical model. Thus, this could represent a possible model misspecification (omission of an association) that the researcher could examine and evaluate in light of theoretical explanations. The elements in the residual covariance matrix are presented in unstandardized units (i.e., in the raw data metric) and in standardized units. Thus, the standardized residuals may be examined to see if a nonzero residual value is significantly different than zero (if greater than $|1.96|$).

16.4.4.3 WALD TEST

While model modification more commonly occurs in order to improve model fit by way of adding parameters to estimate in a model, the model modification process can also involve eliminating associations from a model to reach a more parsimonious model. Adding parameters to a model is referred to as model building whereas eliminating parameters from a model is referred to as model trimming. Similar to the MI/LM, the Wald statistic estimates the increase in the χ_T^2 test statistic that would occur if a parameter were fixed to zero (not freely estimated in the model). Thus, the Wald statistic estimates whether a parameter may be dropped from the model without significantly increasing the χ_T^2 test statistic.

16.4.4.4 CHI-SQUARE DIFFERENCE TEST

The two models being compared in the procedures using the MI/LM and the Wald statistic are considered as nested models. In other words, one of these models is a subset of the model to which it is compared. For instance, if the MI/LM indicated that the $\boldsymbol{\chi}_T^2$ test statistic would significantly decrease by adding a parameter to Model 1, Model 1 would be nested in the model with the new parameter estimated (Model 2). Moreover, if the Wald statistic indicated that the $\boldsymbol{\chi}_T^2$ test statistic would not significantly increase by eliminating a parameter from Model 1, the model formed by eliminating the parameter (Model 2) would be nested in Model 1.

These two test statistics ultimately determine if a statistically significant difference exists between two models' χ^2 test statistics when adding or eliminating a model parameter and is given by the chi-square difference test ($\Delta\chi^2$):

$$\Delta\chi^2 = \chi^2_{\text{restricted}} - \chi^2_{\text{unrestricted}},$$

where $\chi^2_{\text{restricted}}$ is the chi-square value associated with the nested, less parameterized (restricted) model and $\chi^2_{\text{unrestricted}}$ is the chi-square value associated with the more parameterized, less restricted (unrestricted) model, with corresponding degrees of freedom for the $\Delta\chi^2$ test:

$$\Delta df = df_{\text{restricted}} - df_{\text{unrestricted}}.$$

When the $\Delta\chi^2$ test indicates a significant difference between two nested models ($\Delta\chi^2 > c_a$), the nested model with less parameters has been oversimplified. That is, the less parameterized (nested) model has significantly decreased the overall fit of the model when compared to the model with more parameters. In this situation, then, the more parameterized model would be selected over the less parameterized model. On the other hand, when the $\Delta\chi^2$ test is not significant ($\Delta\chi^2 > c_a$), the two models are comparable in terms of overall model fit. In this situation, the less parameterized would most likely be selected over the more parameterized model in support of parsimony. It is important to note here that the $\Delta\chi^2$ test is possible because it uses likelihood ratio χ^2 statistics as opposed to Pearson χ^2 statistics. It is also important to note that when the fit of nested models is being compared the $\Delta\chi^2$ test must be modified if you use a scaled Satorra–Bentler chi-square or a chi-square obtained from using a variance-adjusted estimator (see http://www.statmodel.com/chidiff.shtml; www.uoguelph.ca/~scolwell/difftest.html; Satorra & Bentler, 2001).

16.4.4.5 INFORMATION-BASED CRITERIA

When structural equation models are not related in a nested classification but involve the same variables of interest and it is desired to compare them for model selection purposes, the $\Delta\chi^2$ test is an inappropriate method to assess significant model fit differences because neither of the two models can serve as a baseline comparison model. A comparison of chi-square test statistics associated with nonnested models could be conducted, but this is not highly recommended because models with more parameters tend to have smaller χ^2 values, indicating better fit than less parameterized models. Another instinct might also be to compare the model fit indices of competing nonnested models. This also would not be recommended because models with more parameters tend to fit the data better than models with fewer parameters. Thus, this would not necessarily be a fair comparison. Also, if comparing competing nonnested models, the objective would be to compare adequately fitting models at the outset. As such, information-based criteria, which have also been referred to as cross-validation indices (Cudeck & Browne, 1983), have been advocated as tools that may be used to compare nonnested structural equation models. These information-based model selection indices are different from the model fit indices previously discussed in that they do not have cutoff values to which models may be gauged in terms of overall model fit. Instead, these information criteria are used comparatively among at least two competing models. Specifically, the model associated with the smallest information criteria value in a set of competing models would be selected as the model demonstrating more predictive validity (or would be generalizable in subsequent samples from the same population) than the comparison models. It is important to note that these information criteria may actually be used to compare nested or non-nested models. They are simply more popular for nonnested model comparisons given that a statistical significance test can be conducted with nested models ($\Delta\chi^2$).

While various information-based criteria exist, the most popular information-based criterion is Akaike's (1987) Information Criterion (AIC),

$$AIC = \chi_T^2 + 2q,$$

where q is the number of parameters estimated in the model. Additional information-based criteria that are widely used include Schwarz's Bayesian information criterion (BIC; Schwarz, 1978),

$$BIC = \chi_T^2 + q\left[\ln(N)\right],$$

where ln is the natural log and N is the sample size; and Bozdogan's (1987) consistent AIC (CAIC),

$$CAIC = \chi_T^2 + q\left[\ln(N)+1\right].$$

It must be noted that you may see variations in the presentation of the formulas associated with these criteria in assorted sources. Regardless of their calculation, the model associated with the smallest information-based criterion value would be selected as the model demonstrating better predictive accuracy than the comparison models.

Research in this area has demonstrated that the AIC has a propensity toward selecting more complex (more parameterized) models (Bozdogan, 1987; Browne & Cudeck, 1989; Shibata, 1976), whereas the BIC and CAIC have a propensity toward selecting less complex (less parameterized) models (Whittaker & Stapleton, 2006). Further, the BIC and the CAIC tend to perform more accurately than the AIC in terms of selecting the "correct" model from a set of misspecified competing models (Haughton, Oud, & Jansen, 1997; Whittaker & Stapleton, 2006). Still, these information-based criteria begin to behave more comparably (and accurately) as conditions associated with the data become more favorable (e.g., larger sample sizes and stronger associations among variables; Bandalos, 1993; Cudeck & Browne, 1983; Whittaker & Stapleton, 2006). Readers are encouraged to consult West et al. (2012) and Whittaker and Stapleton (2006) for more information concerning these and additional model selection indices.

16.5 THREE PRINCIPAL SEM TECHNIQUES

The following sections cover three principal applications of SEM, including observed variable path analysis, confirmatory factor analysis, and latent variable path analysis. For each of these sections, we describe and provide examples of each application. We also present and describe the SAS code needed to estimate these models and display the analysis results with interpretations.

16.6 OBSERVED VARIABLE PATH ANALYSIS

Observed variable path analysis is an extension of multiple regression analysis in which the relationships among measured variables may be modeled. Figures 16.1, 16.3, and 16.4 all represent observed variable path models in which squares represent variables that are directly measured (as opposed to constructs). Indirect effects are commonly examined and tested in observed variable path models. The following sub-sections present an observed variable path model with hypothesized indirect effects.

16.6.1 Indirect Effects

Path models, whether observed or latent, include interesting types of relationships among variables. For instance, researchers are commonly interested in hypotheses concerning whether or not a certain variable intervenes or mediates the relationship between two or more variables. Mediation models are popular in the SEM arena because of the capability of estimating direct and indirect effects in a model simultaneously. Indirect or mediated effects are comprised of two (or more) one-headed arrows aiming in the same direction wherein one arrow is pointed toward the mediator and the other arrow is stemming from the mediator.

Consider the model in Figure 16.6 posited by Howard and Maxwell (1982), in which they examined the relationships between motivation, student progress, expected grade in class, and student satisfaction in the class (measured using two separate questions, one regarding the instructor and the other regarding the subject matter) in an undergraduate sample at two time points during a semester (mid-semester and end of semester).

■ **Figure 16.6** Course satisfaction model hypothesized by Howard and Maxwell (1982).

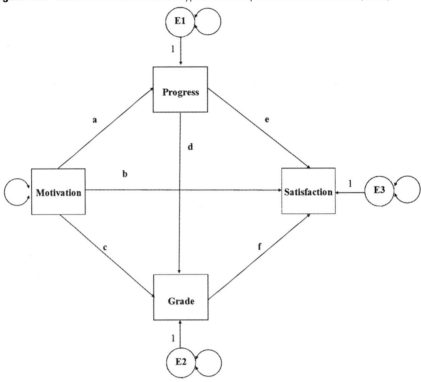

In terms of identification, there are 10 nonredundant observations in the sample covariance matrix:

$$p^* = \frac{p(p+1)}{2} = \frac{4(4+1)}{2} = 10.$$

Four variances require estimation, including the variance of motivation and the three error variances associated with progress, grade, and satisfaction; and six direct effects require estimation, totaling 10 parameters to estimate. Thus, this model is a just-identified model with 0 df_T.

In this model, motivation has direct effects on progress, satisfaction, and grade (paths a, b, and c, respectively). Progress and grade both have direct effects on satisfaction (paths e and f, respectively). Further, progress has a direct effect on grade (path d). While the direct effects (paths a through f) were of theoretical interest to the authors, the indirect effects in this model were more interesting given their hypothesis of mediation. In this model, there are three channels through which motivation indirectly affects satisfaction. That is, motivation is hypothesized to indirectly affect satisfaction via progress, via grade, and via progress then via grade. The indirect effects of motivation on satisfaction via these three channels correspond to the products of the path coefficients associated with their direct effects, namely *ae*, *cf*, and *adf*, respectively. Progress also indirectly affects satisfaction via grade (represented by the product *df*). Typically, researchers present the results from a mediation model in effects decomposition tables in which the direct, indirect, and total effects within a model are summarized. For instance, a table for this model would look similar to Table 16.4 with estimated values in place of the path letters corresponding to direct and indirect effects.

The path model for satisfaction regarding the instructor at the second measurement occasion (end of semester) with standardized results is presented in Figure 16.7. Using the standardized estimates from this model, the resulting effects decomposition table with standardized direct, indirect, and total effects is presented in Table 16.5. You can see that none of the indirect effects are statistically significant in this example. To conclude, Howard and Maxwell (1982) argued that motivation and progress were more influential than expected grade that had previously been thought to heavily impact course satisfaction ratings.

■ **Figure 16.7** Satisfaction with instructor model with standardized results from Howard and Maxwell's (1982) study.

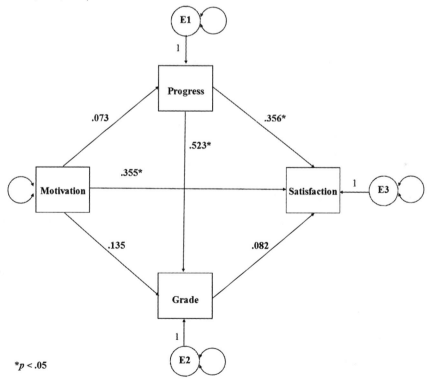

*p < .05

■ **Table 16.4: Effects Decomposition Table Example for Path Model in Howard and Maxwell (1982)**

Association	Direct	Indirect	Total
Motivation, Progress	a	—	a
Motivation, Satisfaction	b	ae + cf + adf	b + ae + cf + adf
Motivation → Progress → Satisfaction		ae	
Motivation → Grade → Satisfaction		cf	
Motivation → Progress → Grade → Satisfaction		adf	
Motivation, Grade	c	—	c
Progress, Grade	d	—	d
Progress, Satisfaction	e	df	e + df
Grade, Satisfaction	f	—	f

■ **Table 16.5: Standardized Direct, Indirect, and Total Effects for Satisfaction With Instructor at Time 2 in Howard and Maxwell (1982)**

Association	Direct	Indirect	Total
Motivation, Progress	.073	–	.073
Motivation, Satisfaction	.355*	TI = .04	.395
Motivation → Progress → Satisfaction		.026	
Motivation → Grade → Satisfaction		.011	
Motivation → Progress → Grade → Satisfaction		.003	
Motivation, Grade	.135	–	.135
Progress, Grade	.523*	–	.523
Progress, Satisfaction	.356*	.043	.399
Grade, Satisfaction	.082	–	.082

Note: TI = Total indirect. *p < .05.

16.6.2 Tests of Indirect Effects

There are numerous approaches available to estimate the statistical significance of indirect effects. A full-length discussion of all the available approaches to test mediation is beyond the scope of this chapter. You should consult MacKinnon, Fairchild, and Fritz (2007), MacKinnon, Lockwood, Hoffman, West, and Sheets (2002), and Shrout and Bolger (2002) for more information concerning mediational methods. A brief presentation of the more commonly used approaches in the SEM arena will, however, be presented next.

One of the simplest procedures that may be used to test the significance of an indirect effect is a modified version of the causal steps method originally proposed by Baron and Kenny (1986). This modified approach was proposed by Cohen and Cohen (1983) and has been referred to as the joint test of statistical significance (MacKinnon et al., 2002). As the name implies, the indirect effect is deemed statistically significant if each of the direct effects that comprise the indirect effect is statistically significant. For instance, a significant indirect effect would exist between motivation and satisfaction via progress in Howard and Maxwell's (1982) study if both the direct effect of motivation on progress and the direct effect from progress to satisfaction were statistically significant (see Table 16.5).

Another approach is to calculate a standard error associated with the indirect effect and conduct a statistical significance test of the indirect effect. Using a simple mediation model as an example, consider Figure 16.8 in which X directly affects Y and indirectly affects Y via the mediator variable M.

The product of paths a and b would comprise the indirect effect of X on Y via M. There are various formulas available that may be used to calculate standard errors for indirect effects. The most widely used calculation for the standard error associated with an indirect effect $\left(\sigma_{\hat{a}\hat{b}}\right)$, derived by Sobel (1982), is:

$$\sigma_{\hat{a}\hat{b}} = \sqrt{\hat{a}^2 s_{\hat{b}}^2 + \hat{b}^2 s_{\hat{a}}^2},$$

where $\hat{a}$ is the unstandardized path value from X to M; $s_{\hat{b}}$ is the standard error associated with the path from M to Y (b); $\hat{b}$ is the unstandardized path value from M to Y; and $s_{\hat{a}}$ is the standard error associated with the path from X to M (a). Dividing the indirect effect, ab, by its associated standard error, $\sigma_{\hat{a}\hat{b}}$, yields a z test. If this value is greater than ±1.96, this would indicate that the unstandardized indirect effect is significantly different from zero at $\alpha = .05$. The majority of SEM software includes these tests (or variants of these tests) for indirect effects (e.g., LISREL, EQS, and M*plus*). We note that this standard error can also be used to create a 95% confidence interval around the indirect effect point estimate:

$$\hat{a}\hat{b} \pm \left(\sigma_{\hat{a}\hat{b}}\right)\left(z_{\alpha/2}\right),$$

where $z_{\alpha/2}$ is the z critical that cuts off the middle 95% of scores (i.e., 1.96). If a zero falls in the confidence interval, the indirect effect would not be considered statistically significant.

A criticism of using the Sobel test (and similar variants) when testing indirect effects is that the distribution of the product of direct effects (e.g., ab) is not approximately

■ **Figure 16.8** Simple mediation model.

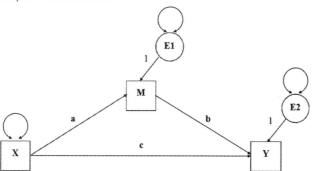

normally distributed unless the sample size is quite large. Thus, calculating standard errors for these indirect effects and assuming an underlying normal distribution when testing their statistical significance may lead to erroneous conclusions (Preacher & Hayes, 2008). Methodological researchers have derived alternative tests that attempt to correct for this drawback. One option gaining in popularity involves the use of bootstrapping estimation techniques to obtain the standard errors associated with indirect effects. Some SEM software programs (e.g., AMOS and M*plus*) can implement bootstrapping techniques when calculating standard errors and, thus, provide more appropriate standard errors, statistical significance tests, and confidence intervals.

Other tools are available for applied researchers when calculating indirect effects. For instance, Kristopher Preacher's webpage has an entire section dedicated to conducting mediational analyses. See his page at http://www.quantpsy.org/medn.htm for various tools to help calculate statistical significance tests, including the Sobel test and bootstrapping, for indirect effects. MacKinnon, Fritz, Williams, and Lockwood (2007) wrote programs in SAS, SPSS, and R that calculate confidence intervals for the product of two paths comprising an indirect effect called PRODCLIN. Tofighi and MacKinnon (2011) created a more advanced program in R called RMediation that calculates confidence intervals for the product of two paths comprising an indirect effect using several different methods and produces plots of the distribution of the indirect effect.

Research in this area has suggested that bootstrapping techniques are recommended when sample sizes are small in order to increase the power to detect significant indirect effects (Shrout & Bolger, 2002). In addition, the modified causal steps approach, or the joint test of statistical significance, while performing more conservatively than some methods, demonstrated adequate performance across various conditions examined in MacKinnon et al.'s (2002) simulation study with respect to maintaining adequate power and effectively controlling for type I error. In the same study, the Sobel test, and its variants, performed fairly conservatively and had very low type I error rates. See MacKinnon et al. (2002) for information concerning other techniques that may be used to optimize the power associated with the test of indirect effects while still maintaining appropriate type I error control.

16.7 OBSERVED VARIABLE PATH ANALYSIS WITH THE MUELLER STUDY

In this section, an example of an observed variable path analysis with analyses of indirect effects is illustrated using PROC CALIS in SAS. Data for this illustration were taken from a study conducted by Mueller (1988) in which he examined the impact of the selective nature of a college on future income among college graduates with a 4-year bachelor's degree using observed variable path analysis. The model that will be used in the subsequent example is not the same as the model originally proposed and tested by Mueller (1988). Instead, the model in Figure 16.9, which includes a subset of the fifteen variables originally analyzed in Mueller (1988), will be examined for simplicity.

These data were taken from various national data sets collected through surveys contracted by the American Council on Education (ACE; see Mueller, 1988, for a description of the variables). In this model, academic ability, drive to achieve, and degree aspirations are exogenous variables hypothesized to covary and to directly impact highest degree earned and selectivity. Highest degree earned and selectivity, in turn, are hypothesized to directly influence current salary. Three indirect effects are modeled as originating from academic ability, drive to achieve, and degree aspirations to current income by way of highest degree earned that are represented by the following products: *ag*, *cg*, and *eg*, respectively. Three additional indirect effects are modeled as originating from academic ability, drive to achieve, and degree aspirations to current income by way of college selectivity, which are represented by the following products: *bh*, *dh*, and *fh*, respectively.

Before discussing the SAS code for this model using PROC CALIS, let us first determine the df_T associated with this model. There are six observed variables in this model. Accordingly, we have:

$$p^* = \frac{p(p+1)}{2} = \frac{6(6+1)}{2} = 21.$$

Thus, there are 21 nonredundant observations in the sample covariance matrix. From examining the model, there are six variances to estimate (the variances of the three exogenous variables and the three error variances associated with the three endogenous variables, highest degree, selectivity, and current income); eight direct effects to estimate (paths *a* through *h*); and three covariances among the exogenous variables, totaling 17 parameters. Consequently, this is an over-identified model with 4 df_T.

■ **Figure 16.9** Observed variable path analysis model from the Mueller (1988) study.

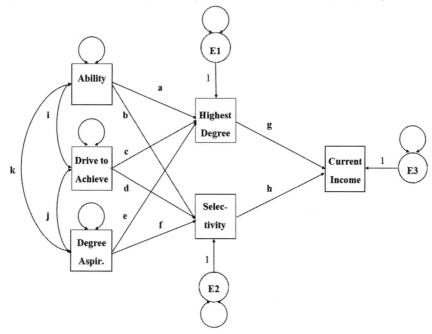

Mueller's (1988) article presented the intercorrelations among all variables as well as their corresponding standard deviations separately for men and for women. The data for the women were used in this example. This type of summary information can be used to calculate the covariance matrix that can then be used as input in SAS. The SAS code presented in Table 16.6 creates a correlation matrix with standard deviations in a temporary SAS data set so that the covariance matrix can be used during the analyses. Although the correlation matrix is being used as input, the raw data may also be used as input in PROC CALIS.

16.7.1 SAS Code for the Mueller Study

In the temporary data set called COLLEGE, a correlation matrix (TYPE=CORR) is being created. The INFILE CARDS statement allows you to use the file reference CARDS, which allows us to use options associated with the INFILE statement (DATA-LINES could also be used in place of CARDS). Specifically, this is used so that we may use the MISSOVER option with the INFILE statement. MISSOVER prevents SAS from going to a new line of data when inputting the instream data if any of the values are missing. This is important since we are using the lower triangle of the correlation matrix and, thus, it is not a complete symmetric matrix.

The input statement assigns variable names to the columns in the data file work. COLLEGE. TYPE is the variable type (e.g., STD for standard deviation and CORR for correlation value) and NAME is the name of the observed variables. The variable names are then written to be input in that particular order that follows the arrangement of the correlation matrix. Following the CARDS statement is the information

■ **Table 16.6: SAS Code to Create a Temporary Data Set Containing a Correlation Matrix and Standard Deviations**

```
DATA COLLEGE(TYPE=CORR);
   INFILE CARDS MISSOVER;
   INPUT _TYPE_ $ _NAME_ $ ABILITY ACHIEVE DEG_ASP HI_DEG
                           SELECTIV INCOME;

CARDS;
STD         .     .71  .75  .90  .69 1.84 1.37
CORR ABILITY 1.00
CORR ACHIEVE  .28 1.00
CORR DEG_ASP  .19  .21 1.00
CORR HI_DEG   .15  .15  .23 1.00
CORR SELECTIV .35  .09  .20  .20 1.00
CORR INCOME   .08  .11  .09  .11  .23 1.00
;
```

necessary to create the correlation matrix in SAS with standard deviations and sample size information. STD is the standard deviation for each respective variable (in the same order as in the INPUT statement). Following that is the standard form of entering the lower triangle of the correlation matrix. This should align directly with the corresponding relationships for each of the variables. The entire correlation matrix may also be entered in the SAS code instead of the upper or lower triangle to create the data set with a correlation matrix.

The SAS code to analyze the observed variable path model in Figure 16.9 using PROC CALIS is presented in Table 16.7. PROC CALIS invokes the CALIS procedure. The options following the PROC CALIS statement do the following: DATA=COLLEGE indicates the input data set (created previously using the correlation matrix with standard deviations); COVARIANCE requests that the covariance matrix be used when estimating parameters; RESIDUAL requests that the residual matrices (unstandardized and standardized) be included in the output; MODIFICATION requests modification indices (MI) or Lagrange Multiplier (LM) tests to be provided in the output; TOTEFF requests that the direct, indirect, and total effects be provided in the output; and NOBS indicates the sample size.

■ **Table 16.7: SAS Code to Analyze the Observed Variable Path Model for the Mueller Study Using PROC CALIS**

```
PROC CALIS DATA=COLLEGE COVARIANCE RESIDUAL MODIFICATION TOTEFF
NOBS=3094;
    LINEQS
        HI_DEG = B14 ABILITY + B24 ACHIEVE + B34 DEG_ASP + E1,
        SELECTIV = B15 ABILITY + B25 ACHIEVE + B35 DEG_ASP + E2,
        INCOME = B46 HI_DEG + B56 SELECTIV + E3;
    VARIANCE
        E1 = VARE1,
        E2 = VARE2,
        E3 = VARE3,
        ABILITY = VARV1,
        ACHIEVE = VARV2,
        DEG_ASP = VARV3;
    COV
        ABILITY ACHIEVE = COV_12,
        ABILITY DEG_ASP = COV_13,
        ACHIEVE DEG_ASP = COV_23;
RUN;
```

The linear equations relating the variables in the model are specified in the LINEQS statement. The form specifies that the endogenous variable is a function of the variables directly affecting it as well as error. For instance, in the following equation:

```
HI_DEG = B14 ABILITY + B24 ACHIEVE + B34 DEG_ASP + E1
```

the variable highest degree earned is a function of the direct effect of ability (which is associated with the partial regression slope parameter B14), the direct effect of achieve (which is associated with the partial regression slope parameter B24), the direct effect of degree aspirations (which is associated with the partial regression slope parameter B34), and the direct effect of error (E1). Selectivity is directly affected by ability, drive to achieve, degree aspirations, and error (E2). Income is directly affected in the model by highest degree earned, college selectivity, and error (E3). These equations are separated by commas.

The VARIANCE statement indicates which variance parameters to estimate in the hypothesized model. These include variances of exogenous variables (including error variances). Thus, three error variances will be estimated, E1, E2, and E3, which will be labeled as VARE1, VARE2, and VARE3, respectively, in the output. The variances of the three observed exogenous variables (ability, achieve, and degree aspirations) will be estimated and labeled as VARV1, VARV2, and VARV3, respectively, in the output. It is important to note that these variances will be calculated by default if not included in the CALIS procedure code. These statements are separated by commas.

The COV statement indicates which variables you hypothesize to covary in the model. For instance, covariances between all of the exogenous variables were hypothesized. As such, the covariance between ability and achieve will be estimated and labeled as COV_12 in the output; the covariance between ability and degree aspirations will be estimated and labeled as COV_13 in the output; and the covariance between achieve and degree aspirations will be estimated and labeled as COV_23 in the output. It must be noted that the default is to estimate covariances among all exogenous observed variables in the CALIS procedure. Thus, the covariances between ability, achieve, and degree aspirations would be estimated by default if omitted from the code. If you hypothesize no covariance among exogenous observed variables, you can set them equal to zero. For example, the following statement would set the covariance between ability and achieve equal to zero and, hence, would not be freely estimated in the model:

```
ABILITY ACHIEVE = 0
```

These statements are separated by commas.

16.7.2 Analysis Results: Model Fit and Residuals

There is an abundance of output provided in SAS when using PROC CALIS, including model specification information, descriptive statistics, and optimization information (to name a few). The following discussion of abbreviated SAS output will focus on the most relevant output when conducting path analyses. The Fit Summary table is presented in two separate tables given its length. Table 16.8 presents the top half of the Fit Summary table.

In the Modeling Information section, you can see the number of nonredundant observations (21) labeled as the number of moments and the number of parameters (17) estimated. In the Absolute Index section of the table, the model chi-square is presented, $\chi^2(4) = 84.36$, $p < .05$, which indicates that the test of overall model fit is significant. Again, this is opposite of the desired result. Remember, the hypothesis is that the observed sample covariance matrix is equal to the implied covariance matrix. Also in the Absolute Index section of the table, the SRMR is .03, which is below both the "good fit" (.05) and the "acceptable fit" (.10) cutoff values. The remaining fit indices of interested are presented in Table 16.9, which is the bottom half of the Fit Summary table.

The Parsimony Index section provides the value of the RMSEA estimate, corresponding 90% confidence interval, and the p-value associated with the test of "close fit." The RMSEA estimate is equal to .08 (90% CI: .07, .10) with $p < .05$. Thus, the RMSEA estimate suggests inadequate model fit because .08 falls at the top of the "adequate fit" cutoff range (.05–.08), a value of .05 is not contained in the 90% CI, and the p-value is less than .05, suggesting a not "close-fitting" model. The Incremental Index section provides values associated with the CFI (.94) and the TLI (.79; Bentler–Bonnett

■ **Table 16.8: Top Half of Fit Summary Table From PROC CALIS for the Mueller Study**

Fit Summary		
Modeling Info	Number of Observations	3094
	Number of Variables	6
	Number of Moments	21
	Number of Parameters	17
	Number of Active Constraints	0
	Baseline Model Function Value	0.4593
	Baseline Model Chi-Square	1420.6759
	Baseline Model Chi-Square DF	15
	Pr > Baseline Model Chi-Square	<.0001
Absolute Index	Fit Function	0.0273
	Chi-Square	84.3579
	Chi-Square DF	4
	Pr > Chi-Square	<.0001
	Z-Test of Wilson & Hilferty	7.7148
	Hoelter Critical N	348
	Root Mean Square Residual (RMR)	0.0399
	Standardized RMR (SRMR)	0.0332
	Goodness of Fit Index (GFI)	0.9911

■ **Table 16.9: Bottom Half of Fit Summary Table from PROC CALIS for the Mueller Study**

Parsimony Index	Adjusted GFI (AGFI)	0.9531
	Parsimonious GFI	0.2643
	RMSEA Estimate	0.0806
	RMSEA Lower 90% Confidence Limit	0.0661
	RMSEA Upper 90% Confidence Limit	0.0960
	Probability of Close Fit	0.0003
	ECVI Estimate	0.0383
	ECVI Lower 90% Confidence Limit	0.0298
	ECVI Upper 90% Confidence Limit	0.0492
	Akaike Information Criterion	118.3579
	Bozdogan CAIC	237.9906
	Schwarz Bayesian Criterion	220.9906
	McDonald Centrality	0.9871
Incremental Index	Bentler Comparative Fit Index	0.9428
	Bentler-Bonett NFI	0.9406
	Bentler-Bonett Non-normed Index	0.7856
	Bollen Normed Index Rho1	0.7773
	Bollen Non-normed Index Delta2	0.9433
	James et al. Parsimonious NFI	0.2508

Non-normed Index in SAS). Hence, the CFI meets the original proposed cutoff value of .90 or greater whereas the TLI (NNFI) does not meet this criteria.

The unstandardized (or raw) residual matrix is presented in Table 16.10. Remember that the residual matrix is the difference between the sample covariance matrix and the implied covariance matrix. Values closer to zero in the residual matrix indicate that the relationship (variance or covariance) is explained well by the hypothesized model. As seen in the unstandardized (raw) residual matrix, there are seven variances/covariances with nonzero residual values. The relationship explained the least well given the hypothesized model is the relationship between highest degree earned and college selectivity because it has the largest residual value (.155). SAS also provides the ranking of these seven residual values in descending order. These values, however, are in the original metric, so it is difficult to gauge if these are substantially different from zero. Consequently, the standardized residual matrix is also provided when including RESIDUAL in the CALIS procedure options list. The standardized residual matrix is presented in Table 16.11.

The standardized residual values may be interpreted as z scores. Thus, a value greater than ± 1.96 would indicate that the residual is significantly different from zero. Five of the seven nonzero residual values, according to the matrix, are greater than $|1.96|$ or significantly different than zero. The largest residual is now associated with the relationship between income and selectivity.

■ Table 16.10: Unstandardized Residual Matrix from PROC CALIS for the Mueller Study

	ABILITY	ACHIEVE	DEG_ASP	HI_DEG	SELECTIV	INCOME
			Raw Residual Matrix			
ABILITY	0.00000	0.00000	0.00000	0.00000	0.00000	−0.00567
ACHIEVE	0.00000	0.00000	0.00000	0.00000	0.00000	0.08271
DEG_ASP	0.00000	0.00000	0.00000	0.00000	0.00000	0.03863
HI_DEG	0.00000	0.00000	0.00000	0.00000	0.15500	0.02500
SELECTIV	0.00000	0.00000	0.00000	0.15500	0.00000	0.02052
INCOME	−0.00567	0.08271	0.03863	0.02500	0.02052	0.00662

Rank Order of the 7 Largest Raw Residuals		
Var1	Var2	Residual
SELECTIV	HI_DEG	0.15500
INCOME	ACHIEVE	0.08271
INCOME	DEG_ASP	0.03863
INCOME	HI_DEG	0.02500
INCOME	SELECTIV	0.02052
INCOME	INCOME	0.00662
INCOME	ABILITY	−0.00567

■ Table 16.11: Standardized Residual Matrix From PROC CALIS for the Mueller Study

	ABILITY	ACHIEVE	DEG_ASP	HI_DEG	SELECTIV	INCOME
			Asymptotically Standardized Residual Matrix			
ABILITY	0.00000	0.00000	0.00000	0.00000	0.00000	−0.35977
ACHIEVE	0.00000	0.00000	0.00000	0.00000	0.00000	4.67826
DEG_ASP	0.00000	0.00000	0.00000	0.00000	0.00000	1.87743
HI_DEG	0.00000	0.00000	0.00000	0.00000	7.60477	7.60428
SELECTIV	0.00000	0.00000	0.00000	7.60477	0.00000	7.60591
INCOME	−0.35977	4.67826	1.87743	7.60428	7.60591	7.60542

Rank Order of the 7 Largest Asymptotically Standardized Residuals		
Var1	Var2	Residual
INCOME	SELECTIV	7.60591
INCOME	INCOME	7.60542
SELECTIV	HI_DEG	7.60477
INCOME	HI_DEG	7.60428
INCOME	ACHIEVE	4.67826
INCOME	DEG_ASP	1.87743
INCOME	ABILITY	−0.35977

16.7.3 Analysis Results: Unstandardized Parameter Estimates

The unstandardized parameter estimates for the model are presented in Table 16.12. The unstandardized partial regression coefficients, corresponding standard errors, and significance tests are presented in the Linear Equations section. The unstandardized partial regression coefficient associated with regressing college selectivity on ability indicates that as academic ability increases by 1 point, selectivity is estimated to increase by .86 points, controlling for everything else. This estimate (.8603) is divided by its respective standard error (.0454), which can be found in the row beneath the estimated value. This results in what SAS labels a t test (18.95); however, to interpret statistical significance, you compare the t value to a critical value of ± 1.96 (a critical z value with

■ **Table 16.12: Unstandardized Parameter Estimates From PROC CALIS for the Mueller Study**

Linear Equations									
HI_DEG	=	0.0869	* ABILITY +	0.0772	* ACHIEVE +	0.1498	* DEG_ASP +	1.0000	E1
Std Err		0.0177	B14	0.0168	B24	0.0137	B34		
t Value		4.9018		4.5849		10.9142			
SELECTIV	=	0.8603	* ABILITY +	-0.0814	* ACHIEVE +	0.2942	* DEG_ASP +	1.0000	E2
Std Err		0.0454	B15	0.0432	B25	0.0352	B35		
t Value		18.9449		-1.8848		8.3638			
INCOME	=	0.1324	* HI_DEG +	0.1613	* SELECTIV +	1.0000	E3		
Std Err		0.0348	B46	0.0130	B56				
t Value		3.8069		12.3720					

Estimates for Variances of Exogenous Variables					
Variable Type	Variable	Parameter	Estimate	Standard Error	t Value
Error	E1	VARE1	0.44233	0.01125	39.32556
	E2	VARE2	2.90493	0.07387	39.32556
	E3	VARE3	1.76960	0.04500	39.32556
Observed	ABILITY	VARV1	0.50410	0.01282	39.32556
	ACHIEVE	VARV2	0.56250	0.01430	39.32556
	DEG_ASP	VARV3	0.81000	0.02060	39.32556

Covariances Among Exogenous Variables					
Var1	Var2	Parameter	Estimate	Standard Error	t Value
ABILITY	ACHIEVE	COV_12	0.14910	0.00994	14.99540
ABILITY	DEG_ASP	COV_13	0.12141	0.01170	10.38108
ACHIEVE	DEG_ASP	COV_23	0.14175	0.01240	11.42979

Squared Multiple Correlations			
Variable	Error Variance	Total Variance	R-Square
HI_DEG	0.44233	0.47610	0.0709
SELECTIV	2.90493	3.38560	0.1420
INCOME	1.76960	1.87028	0.0538

alpha = .05) because SEM is considered a population technique. This coefficient is statistically significant (18.94 > 1.96). The unstandardized partial regression coefficient associated with regressing college selectivity on drive to achieve indicates that as drive to achieve increases by 1 point, selectivity is estimated to decrease by .08 points, holding everything else constant. Yet, this estimate is not statistically significant ($-1.88 < -1.96$). All of the remaining direct effects in the model are statistically significant.

The variance estimates and the covariances are also presented in Table 16.12 in the Estimates for Variances of Exogenous Variables and Covariances Among Exogenous Variables sections, respectively. The error variances associated with highest degree earned (E1), selectivity (E2), and income (E3) are significantly different from zero as seen from their associated t statistics, which are greater than 1.96. Accordingly, there is significant unexplained variability in highest degree earned, selectivity, and income. It is important to note that the t statistics associated with all of these error variances (as well as for the variances of observed exogenous variables) are identical (see Table 16.12). The reason for this is due to the calculation of the variance associated with each of these estimates in which a constant value is included (i.e., $N - 1 - q$) in the denominator. As a result, the t statistics will be the same (see Jöreskog, n.d., for more information concerning the calculation of variances for error variances and resulting t statistics in LISREL).

The covariances among the three exogenous variables (ability, drive to achieve, and degree aspirations) are all statistically significant. Information concerning unexplained and explained variance in the endogenous variables is presented in the Squared Multiple Correlations section in Table 16.12. For instance, the error variance associated with highest degree earned (.44233) can be divided by the total variance of highest degree earned (.47610) to obtain the proportion of unexplained variability in highest degree earned, which is equal to .929. Thus, approximately 93% of the variance in highest degree earned is unexplained by the model. For college selectivity, approximately 86% of the variance in selectivity is unexplained (2.90493 / 3.3856 = .858). Subtracting these values from a value of one results in the R square value of .07 for highest degree earned and .14 for selectivity, respectively. These are also provided in the output (see Table 16.12). As such, approximately 7% of the variability in highest degree earned and 14% of the variability in selectivity is explained by the model. There is even less variability in income that is explained by the model (approximately 5%).

The TOTEFF options in the CALIS procedure invoked information concerning Total Effects, Direct Effects, and Indirect Effects to be included in the output and the unstandardized estimates for these effects are presented in Table 16.13.

■ **Table 16.13: Unstandardized Total, Direct, and Indirect Effects From PROC CALIS for the Mueller Study**

	Total Effects				
	Effect / Std Error / t Value / p Value				
	HI_DEG	SELECTIV	ABILITY	ACHIEVE	DEG_ASP
HI_DEG	0	0	0.0869	0.0772	0.1498
			0.0177	0.0168	0.0137
			4.9018	4.5849	10.9142
			<.0001	<.0001	<.0001
INCOME	0.1324	0.1613	0.1503	−0.002902	0.0673
	0.0348	0.0130	0.0137	0.007889	0.008616
	3.8069	12.3720	10.9359	−0.3678	7.8099
	0.000141	<.0001	<.0001	0.7130	<.0001
SELECTIV	0	0	0.8603	−0.0814	0.2942
			0.0454	0.0432	0.0352
			18.9449	−1.8848	8.3638
			<.0001	0.0595	<.0001

	Direct Effects				
	Effect / Std Error / t Value / p Value				
	HI_DEG	SELECTIV	ABILITY	ACHIEVE	DEG_ASP
HI_DEG	0	0	0.0869	0.0772	0.1498
			0.0177	0.0168	0.0137
			4.9018	4.5849	10.9142
			<.0001	<.0001	<.0001
INCOME	0.1324	0.1613	0	0	0
	0.0348	0.0130			
	3.8069	12.3720			
	0.000141	<.0001			
SELECTIV	0	0	0.8603	−0.0814	0.2942
			0.0454	0.0432	0.0352
			18.9449	−1.8848	8.3638
			<.0001	0.0595	<.0001

	Indirect Effects				
	Effect / Std Error / t Value / p Value				
	HI_DEG	SELECTIV	ABILITY	ACHIEVE	DEG_ASP
HI_DEG	0	0	0	0	0
INCOME	0	0	0.1503	−0.002902	0.0673
			0.0137	0.007889	0.008616
			10.9359	−0.3678	7.8099
			<.0001	0.7130	<.0001
SELECTIV	0	0	0	0	0

Total effects are comprised of both direct and indirect effects. Because highest degree earned and selectivity were hypothesized to affect income directly, and not indirectly, their total effects are equal to their direct effects. Below the unstandardized coefficient is its respective standard error. Again, the coefficient is divided by its respective standard error to obtain the t test, which indicates if the coefficient is statistically significantly different from zero and is listed below the standard error in each of these cells. Recall that t statistics greater than ± 1.96 indicate statistical significance of the coefficient. The p-value associated with the t test is listed below the t statistic value. As seen previously in Table 16.12 with the unstandardized results, the direct effect of highest degree earned (.13) on income and the direct effect of selectivity on income (.16) are statistically significant ($ps < .001$ as indicated in Table 16.13).

There were six indirect effects hypothesized in the example model. These effects were hypothesized to originate from ability, drive to achieve, and degree aspirations and indirectly affect income via highest degree earned and via college selectivity. Notice, however, that in the Indirect Effects section in Table 16.13, only three indirect effects are listed from ability, drive to achieve, and degree aspirations to income. These represent the *total indirect effects*, of which two are statistically significant using the Sobel test. Specifically, the total indirect effects from ability and from degree aspirations to income are statistically significant. For instance, the total indirect effect from ability to income is the sum of (1) the specific indirect effect from ability to income via highest degree earned and (2) the specific indirect effect from ability to income via college selectivity. Specific indirect effects are comprised of the product of the corresponding unstandardized direct effect paths involved in the relationship (see the Direct Effects section in Table 16.13). As such, the specific indirect effect from ability to income via highest degree earned (.0869 × .1324 = .0115) and the specific indirect effect from ability to income via college selectivity (.8603 × .1613 = .1388) sums to the total indirect effect (.1503) shown in the Indirect Effects section in Table 16.13. Likewise, the total indirect effect of degree aspirations on income (.0673) is the sum of the specific indirect effect from degree aspirations to income via highest degree (.1498 × .1324 = .0198) earned and the specific indirect effect from degree aspirations to income via college selectivity (.2942 × .1613 = .0475).

Although the Sobel test is not provided for the specific indirect effects, these could easily be calculated by hand or by using the Sobel test calculator on Kristopher Preacher's webpage (http://www.quantpsy.org/sobel/sobel.htm). Alternatively, the joint test of statistical significance method could be used to infer statistical significance associated with these specific indirect effects. Congruent with the joint test of statistical significance, because all of the direct effect paths involved in the specific indirect effects from ability and from degree aspirations to income via highest degree earned and via college selectivity are statistically significant (see the Direct Effects section in Table 16.13), the specific indirect effects may also be inferred to be statistically significant. Although the total indirect effect from drive to achieve to income is not statistically significant (see the Indirect Effects section in Table 16.13), the specific indirect effect from drive to achieve to income via highest degree earned may be inferred to be statistically significant because the direct paths that comprise this indirect effect are statistically significant (.0772 × .1324 = .0102; see the Direct Effects section in Table 16.12).

16.7.4 Analysis Results: Standardized Parameter Estimates

The standardized estimates are printed in SAS output following the unstandardized parameter estimates and are presented in Table 16.14.

■ **Table 16.14: Standardized Parameter Estimates From PROC CALIS for the Mueller Study**

Standardized Results for Linear Equations

```
HI_DEG   =  0.0894 * ABILITY +  0.0839 * ACHIEVE +  0.1954 * DEG_ASP + 1.0000  E1
Std Err     0.0182   B14        0.0183   B24        0.0176   B34
t Value     4.9186              4.5987             11.1109


SELECTIV =  0.3319 * ABILITY + −0.0332 * ACHIEVE +  0.1439 * DEG_ASP + 1.0000  E2
Std Err     0.0166   B15        0.0176   B25        0.0171   B35
t Value    19.9399             −1.8856              8.4363


INCOME   =  0.0668 * HI_DEG +  0.2170 * SELECTIV + 1.0000  E3
Std Err     0.0175   B46       0.0171   B56
t Value     3.8150            12.6708
```

Standardized Results for Variances of Exogenous Variables					
Variable Type	Variable	Parameter	Estimate	Standard Error	t Value
Error	E1	VARE1	0.92906	0.00890	104.40535
	E2	VARE2	0.85802	0.01163	73.79955
	E3	VARE3	0.94617	0.00788	120.04049
Observed	ABILITY	VARV1	1.00000		
	ACHIEVE	VARV2	1.00000		
	DEG_ASP	VARV3	1.00000		

Standardized Results for Covariances Among Exogenous Variables					
Var1	Var2	Parameter	Estimate	Standard Error	t Value
ABILITY	ACHIEVE	COV_12	0.28000	0.01657	16.89684
ABILITY	DEG_ASP	COV_13	0.19000	0.01733	10.96255
ACHIEVE	DEG_ASP	COV_23	0.21000	0.01719	12.21791

The standardized partial regression coefficients, corresponding standard errors, and significance tests are presented in the Standardized Results for Linear Equations section. The standardized partial regression coefficient associated with regressing college selectivity on ability indicates that as academic ability increases by 1 standard deviation, college selectivity is estimated to increase by .33 standard deviations, controlling for drive to achieve and degree aspirations. Standard errors are also computed for the standardized estimates (.0166). The standardized estimate (.3319) is divided by its respective standard error (.0166), which results in a t test (19.9399). This t test indicates a statistically significant standardized coefficient because it is greater than 1.96. The standardized partial regression coefficient associated with regressing college selectivity on drive to achieve indicates that as drive to achieve increases by 1 standard deviation, college selectivity is estimated to decrease by .03 standard deviations, holding all else constant. According to the t test, this estimate is not statistically significant $(-1.89 < -1.96)$. The remaining standardized direct effects are statistically significant.

The variance estimates and the covariances are also presented in Table 16.14 in the Standardized Results for Estimates for Variances of Exogenous Variables and Standardized Results for Covariances Among Exogenous Variables sections, respectively. The standardized error variances associated with highest degree earned (E1), selectivity (E2), and income (E3) are significantly different from zero as seen from their associated t statistics, which are greater than 1.96. These standardized estimates indicate the proportion of unexplained variance in highest degree earned, selectivity, and income. That is, approximately 93% of the variance in highest degree earned is unexplained by the model. Likewise, approximately 86% of the variance in college selectivity is unexplained and approximately 95% of the variance in income is unexplained. Subtracting the standardized variance estimates from a value of one results in the R square value of .07 for highest degree earned, .14 for college selectivity, and .05 for income. These results match those in Table 16.12. The correlations (Standardized Results for Covariances Among Exogenous Variables) among all three exogenous variables (i.e., ability, drive to achieve, and degree aspirations) range from .19 to .28 and are all statistically significant.

The standardized results for the total effects, direct effects, and the indirect effects are presented in Table 16.15. These tables mimic those for the unstandardized total, direct, and indirect effects tables presented in Table 16.13. The difference is that these results are computed using the standardized results as illustrated in Table 16.14. For instance, using values from the Standardized Direct Effects section in Table 16.14, the specific indirect effect from degree aspirations to income via highest degree (.1954 × .0668 = .0131) earned and the specific indirect effect from degree aspirations to income via college selectivity (.1439 × .2170 = .0312) sum to equal the total indirect effect from degree aspirations to income (.0443), which is statistically significant (see the Standardized Indirect Effects section in Table 16.14). The total indirect effect from ability to income is also statistically significant whereas the total indirect effect from drive to achieve to income is not statistically significant. The joint statistical significance method indicates that the specific indirect effects from ability to income via highest degree earned and via college selectivity are statistically significant; the

■ Table 16.15: Standardized Total, Direct, and Indirect Effects From PROC CALIS for the Mueller Study

	HI_DEG	SELECTIV	ABILITY	ACHIEVE	DEG_ASP
Standardized Total Effects					
Effect / Std Error / t Value / p Value					
HI_DEG	0	0	0.0894	0.0839	0.1954
			0.0182	0.0183	0.0176
			4.9186	4.5987	11.1109
			<.0001	<.0001	<.0001
INCOME	0.0668	0.2170	0.0780	−0.001592	0.0443
	0.0175	0.0171	0.006996	0.004327	0.005615
	3.8150	12.6708	11.1512	−0.3679	7.8869
	0.000136	<.0001	<.0001	0.7130	<.0001
SELECTIV	0	0	0.3319	−0.0332	0.1439
			0.0166	0.0176	0.0171
			19.9399	−1.8856	8.4363
			<.0001	0.0594	<.0001
Standardized Direct Effects					
Effect / Std Error / t Value / p Value					
HI_DEG	0	0	0.0894	0.0839	0.1954
			0.0182	0.0183	0.0176
			4.9186	4.5987	11.1109
			<.0001	<.0001	<.0001
INCOME	0.0668	0.2170	0	0	0
	0.0175	0.0171			
	3.8150	12.6708			
	0.000136	<.0001			
SELECTIV	0	0	0.3319	−0.0332	0.1439
			0.0166	0.0176	0.0171
			19.9399	−1.8856	8.4363
			<.0001	0.0594	<.0001
Standardized Indirect Effects					
Effect / Std Error / t Value / p Value					
HI_DEG	0	0	0	0	0
INCOME	0	0	0.0780	−0.001592	0.0443
			0.006996	0.004327	0.005615
			11.1512	−0.3679	7.8869
			<.0001	0.7130	<.0001
SELECTIV	0	0	0	0	0

specific indirect effects from degree aspirations to income via highest degree earned and via college selectivity are statistically significant; and the specific indirect effect from drive to achieve to income via highest degree earned is statistically significant. The specific indirect effect from drive to achieve to income via college selectivity is not statistically significant because the direct path from drive to achieve to college selectivity is not statistically significant.

16.7.5 Analysis Results: Model Modification

Output concerning model modification is subsequently printed in SAS. For instance, the Wald test associated with this example observed variable path model is presented in Table 16.16.

Remember, the Wald test indicates which parameter may be eliminated (i.e., not estimated or set equal to zero) in the model without increasing the chi-square test of model fit statistic significantly. SAS provides a multivariate (cumulative) test and a univariate (incremental) test. The multivariate test indicates the cumulative increase in chi-square when dropping the set of suggested parameters from the model whereas the univariate test indicates the increase in chi-square when dropping one parameter at a time. In this example, the Wald test indicates that parameter B25 may be dropped from the model, which would increase the chi-square test of model fit by 3.55 points, which is not a significant increase as indicated in the PR > ChiSq column (i.e., $p > .05$). The B25 parameter is associated with the direct effect of drive to achieve on selectivity, which is not statistically significant in the model (see Table 16.12).

The results for the Lagrange Multiplier [LM; also called modification indices (MI)] tests are presented subsequently in Table 16.17.

■ **Table 16.16: Wald Test From PROC CALIS for the Mueller Study**

	Stepwise Multivariate Wald Test				
	Cumulative Statistics			Univariate Increment	
Parm	Chi-Square	DF	Pr > ChiSq	Chi-Square	Pr > ChiSq
B25	3.55247	1	0.0595	3.55247	0.0595

■ **Table 16.17: LM Tests From PROC CALIS for the Mueller Study**

	Rank Order of the 4 Largest LM Stat for Paths from Endogenous Variables			
To	From	LM Stat	Pr > ChiSq	Parm Change
HI_DEG	SELECTIV	57.83259	<.0001	0.05336
SELECTIV	HI_DEG	57.83259	<.0001	0.35042
HI_DEG	INCOME	6.49345	0.0108	0.06971
SELECTIV	INCOME	1.83862	0.1751	0.08316

(Continued)

■ **Table 16.17: Continued**

| Rank Order of the 3 Largest LM Stat for Paths from Exogenous Variables | | | | |
To	From	LM Stat	Pr > ChiSq	Parm Change
INCOME	ACHIEVE	21.88610	<.0001	0.15139
INCOME	DEG_ASP	3.52476	0.0605	0.05220
INCOME	ABILITY	0.12944	0.7190	−0.01305

| Rank Order of the 7 Largest LM Stat for Paths with New Endogenous Variables | | | | |
To	From	LM Stat	Pr > ChiSq	Parm Change
ABILITY	ACHIEVE	57.83259	<.0001	6.11099
DEG_ASP	ACHIEVE	57.83259	<.0001	3.18465
ACHIEVE	DEG_ASP	57.83259	<.0001	10.08094
ABILITY	DEG_ASP	57.83259	<.0001	−3.18231
ACHIEVE	INCOME	21.79302	<.0001	0.04497
ABILITY	INCOME	3.72997	0.0534	−0.01860
DEG_ASP	INCOME	1.25843	0.2619	0.01356

| Rank Order of the 3 Largest LM Stat for Error Variances and Covariances | | | | |
Var1	Var2	LM Stat	Pr > ChiSq	Parm Change
E2	E1	57.83259	<.0001	0.15500
E3	E1	8.26566	0.0040	−0.17903
E2	E3	0.0002707	0.9869	0.00181

Note: There is no parameter to free in the default LM tests for the covariances of exogenous variables. Ranking is not displayed.

Remember, LM tests indicate which parameters, if added and freely estimated in the model, would result in a significant decrease in the chi-square test of model fit. The "Largest LM Stat for Paths from Endogenous Variables" is presented first. Thus, these indicate paths that could be estimated that originate from and terminate to endogenous or dependent variables. This table suggests that either the direct effect from college selectivity to highest degree earned or the direct effect from highest degree earned to college selectivity would decrease the chi-square test statistic by approximately 57.83 points, which is a significant reduction in chi-square ($p < .05$). The "Parm Change" is the expected parameter change (EPC), which is the estimated value of the parameter if it were added and estimated in the model. The direct effect from college selectivity to highest degree earned would result in an estimated partial regression coefficient of approximately .05 whereas the direct effect from highest degree earned to college selectivity would result in an estimated partial regression coefficient of approximately .35.

The "Rank Order of the 3 Largest LM Stat for Paths from Exogenous Variables" are displayed next, which indicate paths that could be estimated that originate from exogenous or independent variables. Consequently, adding the path from drive to achieve to income in the model (estimated to be .15 according to the EPC) would decrease the chi-square statistic by approximately 21.89 points ($p < .05$). Adding the path from degree aspirations to income (estimated to be .05) would decrease the chi-square statistic by approximately 3.52 points ($p > .05$) and adding the path from ability to income (estimated to be $-.01$) would decrease the chi-square by approximately .13 point ($p > .05$). Thus, adding drive to achieve to income would result in a statistically significant improvement in fit whereas adding either of the other two suggested paths would not significantly improve model fit in terms of the chi-square statistic.

The "Rank Order of the 7 Largest LM Stat for Paths with New Endogenous Variables" are subsequently displayed in the output. These indicate which paths may be estimated that originate from endogenous variables and terminate with exogenous variables in the model. The first four paths listed would reduce the chi-square statistic similarly (by approximately 58 points; $p < .05$) and involve estimating direct effects among the three exogenous variables (ability, drive to achieve, and degree aspirations). The fifth path listed would reduce the chi-square by approximately 22 points ($p < .05$) and involves adding a direct effect from income to drive to achieve. The remaining two paths involve direct effects from income to ability and from income to degree aspirations, but these would not result in a significant reduction in the chi-square statistic ($ps > .05$).

The "Rank Order of the 3 Largest LM Stat for Error Variances and Covariances" are also printed in the output. These suggest which error covariances may be estimated to help improve model fit. For instance, adding the covariance between the error associated with highest degree earned (E1) and the error associated with college selectivity (E2) would result in a decrease in chi-square of approximately 58 points ($p < .05$). Adding the covariance between the errors associated with highest degree earned (E1) and income (E3) would decrease the chi-square by approximately 8 points ($p < .05$). Adding the covariance between the errors associated with college selectivity (E2) and income (E3) would not reduce the chi-square significantly (by .0003 points; $p > .05$). Covariances among errors associated with two variables indicate that the two respective variables systematically covary for reasons above and beyond those hypothesized to explain the relationship between the two variables in the model.

16.7.6 Model Respecification

Given that the model fit of this model was not adequate, the LM tests were consulted to help improve fit. Of the largest LM tests, the suggested direct effect from college selectivity to highest degree earned made theoretical sense in that the less selective the college is, the less likely one would obtain a higher degree at the institution. Along similar lines, the more selective the college is, the more likely one would obtain a higher degree at the institution. This direct effect was added to the model and freely estimated. Model fit improved with the addition of this direct effect in the respecified model. The model chi-square is still statistically significant, $\chi^2(3) = 25.98$, $p < .05$, which indicates that the test of overall model fit is significant. The SRMR (.02), the RMSEA [.05 (90% CI: .03, .07) with $p > .05$], the CFI (.98), and the NNFI/TLI (.91) all suggest good model fit. The path from college selectivity to highest degree earned is statistically significant. The standardized results suggested that as college selectivity increased by 1 standard deviation, highest degree was estimated to increase by .14 standard deviations, holding all else constant. It is important to note that the endogenous variables included in this model are coded on ordinal scales. For example, highest degree earned ranged from 1 (high school diploma or equivalent) to 7 (advanced professional); selectivity (average SAT score) ranged from 1 (less than 775) to 9 (1300 or greater); and current income ranged from 1 (none) to 10 ($40,000 or greater). As previously discussed, nonnormality of the endogenous variables may result in inaccurate chi-square tests of model fit and standard errors. As such, robust estimators that provide scaled chi-square statistics and standard errors would be recommended in this situation. Because the raw data were not readily available, however, these variables were treated as interval in the demonstration.

The Wald test still suggested dropping the direct effect from drive to achieve to college selectivity. In addition, adding the path from drive to achieve to income in the model would result in the largest statistically significant decrease in the chi-square statistic according to the LM tests. Adding this direct effect would make theoretical sense in that stronger drives to achieve could result in a person making higher income subsequently in life. Consequently, this direct path was added to the model and was freely estimated in a respecified model.

Model fit also improved with the addition of this direct effect in the respecified model. The model chi-square is not statistically significant as it was before, $\chi^2(2) = 4.07$, $p > .05$. The SRMR (.01), the RMSEA [.02 (90% CI: .00, .04) with $p > .05$], the CFI (1.00), and the NNFI/TLI (.99) all suggest good model fit. The path from drive to achieve to income is statistically significant and indicates that as drive to achieve increases by 1 standard deviation, current income is estimated to increase by .08 standard deviations, controlling for everything else. Again, the Wald test still indicated that the direct effect from drive to achieve to selectivity could be dropped without significantly increasing the model chi-square statistic. Accordingly, this path was dropped from the respecified model. This respecified model fit the data well [$\chi^2(3) = 7.62$, $p > .05$; SRMR = .01; RMSEA = .02 (90% CI: .00, .04) with $p > .05$; CFI = 1.00; and NNFI/TLI = .98].

16.7.7 Results for the Final Model

The abbreviated SAS output for this final model is presented in Appendix 16.1. When reporting the results for this model, the model fit information could be summarized similarly to that in Table 16.18 and the effects decomposition table would look similar to that shown in Table 16.19. The final model is illustrated pictorially in Figure 16.10.

It must be noted that there is some rounding error involved with some of the values presented in Table 16.19 due to hand calculating the specific indirect effects using the values in the output for direct effects. Nonetheless, the values are fairly close to those reported in the SAS output (see Appendix 16.1). In Figure 16.10, the standardized results are reported with asterisks indicating statistical significance. When interpreting results in SEM, some readers would like to see the corresponding standard errors associated with the parameter estimates. These can easily be incorporated into figures in parentheses next to their respective parameter estimates or they could be presented in table form. Also, notice that the error variance estimates are presented in Figure 16.10. An alternative to presenting the findings this way could be to report the R square associated with each of the endogenous variables either in the figure illustrating the model or they could be described in the results section of a paper. Another alternative is to include the path value from the error to the endogenous variable in the figure. These paths are calculated by taking the square root of the error variance estimate. For instance, the direct effect from E1 to highest degree earned is $\sqrt{.91} = .95$. This value would then be included as the path value from E1 to highest degree earned to represent the direct effect of the error on highest degree earned. When reporting the unstandardized results in a figure, the unstandardized direct effects, covariances, and error variances would simply replace the standardized results in Figure 16.10.

▨ **Table 16.18: Model Fit Information for Observed Variable Path Model Example From Mueller (1988)**

Model	χ^2	df	SRMR	RMSEA (90% CI) p-value	CFI	NNFI/TLI
Original Model	84.36*	4	.03	.08 (.07, .10) $p < .05$	.94	.79
Respecified Model – Added Selectivity → Highest Degree	25.98*	3	.02	.05 (.03, .07) $p > .05$	.98	.91
Respecified Model – Added Achieve → Income	4.07	2	.01	.02 (.00, .04) $p > .05$	1.00	.99
Respecified Model – Dropped Achieve → Selectivity	7.62	3	.01	.02 (.00, .04) $p > .05$	1.00	.98

Note: *$p < .05$.

■ Table 16.19: Standardized Direct, Indirect, and Total Effects for Observed Variable Path Model Example From Mueller (1988)

Association	Direct	Indirect	Total
Ability, Highest Degree Earned	.0421*	.0460*	.0881
Ability → Selectivity → Highest Degree			
Ability, College Selectivity	.3237*	—	.3237
Ability, Current Income	—	TI = .0707*	.0707
Ability → Highest Degree → Income		.0023*	
Ability → Selectivity → Income		.0684*	
Achieve, Highest Degree Earned	.0886*	—	.0886
Achieve, College Selectivity	—	—	—
Achieve, Current Income	.0826*	.0049*	.0875
Achieve → Highest Degree → Income			
Degree Aspirations, Highest Degree Earned	.1749*	.0197*	.1946
Degree Aspirations → Selectivity → Highest Degree			
Degree Aspirations, College Selectivity	.1385*	—	.1385
Degree Aspirations, Current Income	—	TI = .0390*	.0390
Degree Aspirations → Highest Degree → Income		.0097*	
Degree Aspirations → Selectivity → Income		.0293*	
Highest Degree Earned, Current Income	.0553*	—	.0553
Selectivity, Highest Degree Earned	.1422*	—	.1422
Selectivity, Income	.2114*	.0079*	.2193
Selectivity → Highest Degree → Income			

Note: TI = Total indirect. *$p < .05$.

■ Figure 16.10 Results for the final model from the Mueller (1988) study with standardized estimates.

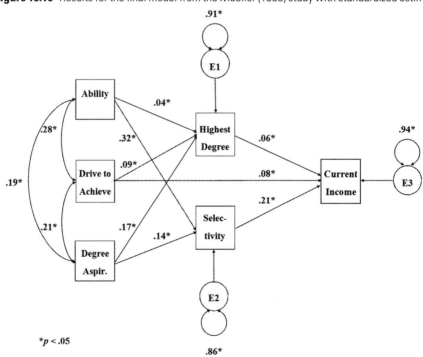

*$p < .05$

16.8 CONFIRMATORY FACTOR ANALYSIS

The path models previously discussed have modeled the relationships among variables that are observed or directly measured. Frequently in the social and behavioral sciences, the variables of interest are unobservable or represent latent constructs that cannot be directly measured (e.g., motivation, self-efficacy, depression, aptitude). Confirmatory factor analysis (CFA) models, also called measurement models, allow researchers to test the construct validity of latent variables of interest. In contrast to exploratory factor analysis (EFA), CFA models are *a priori*, meaning that the number of factors in the model must be specified by the user in addition to which items will load on which factors, and whether the factors will covary with one another. CFA is commonly used during the scale development process following the item development and initial administration process, which is accompanied by an EFA that explores the possible factor structure underlying the responses to the items. Thus, after an EFA or multiple EFAs (which is recommended by some), a subsequent sample is administered the items retained during the EFA and a CFA may be conducted on the newly collected data to provide further support of the factor structure uncovered by the EFA.

16.8.1 Identification in CFA

Figure 16.11 illustrates a one-factor CFA model in which the latent factor, F1, underlies four measured or indicator variables (Y1–Y4).

■ **Figure 16.11** One-factor confirmatory factor analysis model with four indicator variables.

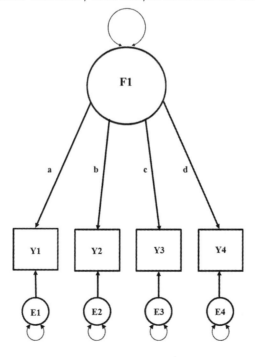

In this model, the factor is an independent or exogenous variable and has direct effects on each of the four measured indicator variables. Paths a through d are called factor loadings and can be interpreted similarly to traditional regression coefficients given that it is a one-factor model. For instance, for every 1-unit increase in F1, each of the indicators (observed variables) is estimated to change by their factor loading value and direction as denoted by their respective sign (assuming the factor loadings are in unstandardized units). Thus, CFA models hypothesize that the factor directly affects the responses to (or scores on) each of the indicator variables. Because of this, it is inherent in CFA models that the factor is the reason that its respective indicators covary. Indicator variables for a factor are endogenous variables in CFA models and, thus, they will have error variances associated with them (E1–E4 in Figure 16.11). Accordingly, the factor will explain variability in the item responses (or scores) as well as also will the unobservable construct of error.

The method of determining whether or not a CFA model is identified is similar to that used for determining the identification of path models, with some slight distinctions. Nonredundant observations are computed using the same formula with CFA models. For the model presented in Figure 16.11, there are 10 nonredundant observations ($p* = 10$) in the sample covariance matrix with $p = 4$ observed variables:

$$p* = \frac{p(p+1)}{2} = \frac{4(4+1)}{2} = 10.$$

Although a factor structure will be imposed on the data, we are still working with observed variables as the indicators for the factor. Again, the sample covariance matrix is what is analyzed in SEM analyses, including CFA. As indicated before, the model parameters that must be estimated include the variances and covariances of exogenous variables and direct paths to endogenous variables. For the model in Figure 16.11, then, it appears that 9 parameters ($q = 9$) must be estimated, including the four error variances associated with the observed indicators Y1–Y4, the variance of the exogenous factor F1, and the four direct paths from the factor to each of the observed indicators. Subtracting the nine parameters to (9) estimate from the number of nonredundant observations (10) results in a model with $df_T = 1$, which signifies an over-identified model.

Because the exogenous factor is unmeasured (or latent), however, its scale of measurement is unknown, which would actually prohibit the estimation of all of the model parameters in the model, even though our calculation indicates that it is over-identified. To set the scale of the factor, two options are available. One option is to fix the factor variance to a specific value, which is typically a value of one. When using this option, the factor is standardized, but the observed variable indicators are not standardized. The second option is to scale the factor via one of the indicator variable's variance. This is done by fixing one of the direct paths from the factor to an indicator variable (a factor loading) to a specific value, which again is typically a value of 1.0. Indicators for which loadings are set equal to 1.0 to scale the factor are referred to as reference indicators. You may have noticed in most of the figures previously presented that values of 1.0 are inserted in the direct paths from the errors to their respective endogenous variable. Because errors are latent, their scale of measurement is also unknown. Thus, they are scaled by setting the direct paths to their corresponding endogenous variable to values of 1.0. This is done by default in SEM software and does not need to be specified by the user.

For the model in Figure 16.11, then, setting the latent factor variance to a value of one will result in eight model parameters ($q = 8$) that must be estimated, resulting in an over-identified model with $df_T = 2$. It must be noted that a single-factor CFA model with three indicator variables is a just-identified model. Although you be able to get by with fewer than three indicators per factor in a multiple-factor solution, three indicators per factor are recommended to avoid identification problems. Readers interested in more detail concerning CFA models are encouraged to read Brown's (2015) book.

Another important aside deals with the selection of the reference indicator. While the variable selected to serve as the reference indicator is generally arbitrary in the context of CFA models, it has serious implications for other techniques in the SEM arena, particularly in multiple-group modeling (Cheung & Rensvold, 1999; Yoon & Millsap, 2007). If a reference indicator is used for CFA models, it is best to pick one that is at least positively correlated with the factor if set to a value of +1.0. Otherwise, estimation problems may be encountered because you are fixing its relationship with the factor (and, in turn, its relationship with the other variables loading on the same factor) to a relationship that contradicts the original data. Readers interested in more discussion of reference indicator selection methods in SEM when used in other techniques may refer to Hancock, Stapleton, and Arnold-Berkovits (2009).

The standardized solution is unaffected by the scaling of the factor. Standardized loadings represent the correlations between items and their respective factor and may be interpreted similarly to traditional standardized regression coefficients given that it is a one-factor model. For instance, as the factor increases by 1 standard deviation, the indicator is estimated to change by their standardized factor loading value in standard deviation units in the direction of that signified by its corresponding sign.

16.9 CFA WITH REACTIONS-TO-TESTS DATA

The data used in Chapter 9 for the EFA illustration will be used to demonstrate a CFA conducted in SAS. As a reminder, these data were taken from the Reactions to Tests (RTT) scale developed by Sarason (1984) to measure four factors of test anxiety. These four factors include Tension, Worry, Test-irrelevant Thinking, and Bodily Symptoms. Three items were used to measure each of the four underlying factors. Thus, a four-factor, correlated structure on which their three respective items loaded was analyzed in SAS. This factor model is represented in Figure 16.12.

■ **Figure 16.12** CFA model for the reactions to tests scale developed by Sarason (1984).

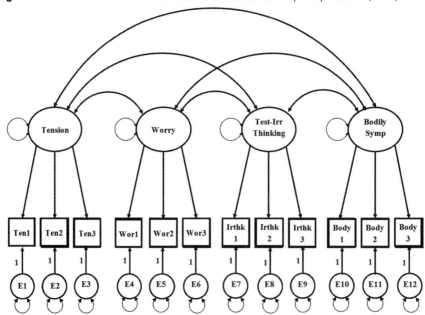

There are 78 non-redundant observations in the sample covariance matrix associated with the model in Figure 16.12:

$$p* = \frac{p(p+1)}{2} = \frac{12(12+1)}{2} = 78.$$

To set the scale of the four factors, the factor variances will be set equal to values of 1.0 and, thus, will not require estimation. There are 12 error variances, 12 factor loadings, and six factor covariances to estimate, resulting in 30 total parameters. This is an over-identified model with $df_T = 48$.

16.9.1 SAS Code for RTT CFA

The SAS code presented in Table 16.20 creates a covariance matrix in a temporary SAS data set so that it can be used during the analysis. Although the covariance matrix is being used in this example, the raw data may also be used in PROC CALIS when analyzing CFA models.

In the temporary data set called ANXIETY, a covariance matrix (TYPE=COV) is being created. The INFILE CARDS statement allows you to use the file reference CARDS, which allows you to use options associated with the INFILE statement (DATALINES could also be used in place of CARDS). Specifically, this is used so that we may use the MISSOVER option with the INFILE statement. MISSOVER prevents SAS from going to a new line of data when inputting the instream data if any of the values are missing. This is important since we are using the lower triangle of the covariance matrix and, thus,

■ Table 16.20: **SAS Code to Create a Temporary Data Set Containing the Covariance Matrix for the RTT CFA Model**

```
DATA ANXIETY (TYPE=COV);
  INFILE CARDS MISSOVER;
  INPUT _TYPE_ $ _NAME_ $ TEN1 TEN2 TEN3 WOR1 WOR2 WOR3
                          IRTHK1 IRTHK2 IRTHK3 BODY1 BODY2 BODY3;

CARDS;
COV TEN1   .7821
COV TEN2   .5602 .9299
COV TEN3   .5695 .6281 .9751
COV WOR1   .1969 .2599 .2362 .6352
COV WOR2   .2289 .2835 .3079 .4575 .7943
COV WOR3   .2609 .3670 .3575 .4327 .4151 .6783
COV IRTHK1 .0556 .0740 .0981 .2094 .2306 .2503 .6855
COV IRTHK2 .0025 .0279 .0798 .2047 .2270 .2257 .4224 .6952
COV IRTHK3 .0180 .0753 .0744 .1892 .2352 .2008 .4343 .4514 .6065
COV BODY1  .1617 .1919 .2892 .1376 .1744 .1845 .0645 .0731 .0921 .4068
COV BODY2  .2628 .3047 .4043 .1742 .2066 .2547 .1356 .1336 .1283 .1958 .7015
COV BODY3  .2966 .3040 .3919 .1942 .1864 .2402 .1073 .0988 .0599 .2233 .3033 .5786
```

it is not a complete symmetric matrix. The INPUT statement assigns variable names to the columns in the data file work.ANXIETY. TYPE is the variable type (i.e., COV for covariance value) and NAME is the name of the observed variables. The variable names are then written to be input in that particular order, which follows the arrangement of the covariance matrix. Following the CARDS statement is the information necessary to create the covariance matrix in SAS (DATALINES may also be used in place of CARDS). Following that is the standard form of entering the lower triangle of the covariance matrix. This should align directly with the corresponding relationships for each of the variables. The entire symmetric covariance matrix may also be entered in the SAS code instead of the upper or lower triangle to create the data set with a covariance matrix.

The SAS code to analyze the four-factor correlated CFA model in Figure 16.12 using PROC CALIS is presented in Table 16.21.

■ **Table 16.21: SAS Code to Analyze the CFA Model for the RTT Scale in Figure 16.13 Using PROC CALIS**

```
PROC CALIS DATA=ANXIETY COVARIANCE RESIDUAL MODIFICATION
NOBS=318;
    LINEQS
        TEN1    = L11 F1 + E1,
        TEN2    = L21 F1 + E2,
        TEN3    = L31 F1 + E3,
        WOR1    = L12 F2 + E4,
        WOR2    = L22 F2 + E5,
        WOR3    = L32 F2 + E6,
        IRTHK1  = L13 F3 + E7,
        IRTHK2  = L23 F3 + E8,
        IRTHK3  = L33 F3 + E9,
        BODY1   = L14 F4 + E10,
        BODY2   = L24 F4 + E11,
        BODY3   = L34 F4 + E12;
    VARIANCE
        E1 - E12 = VARE1-VARE12,
        F1 = 1.0,
        F2 = 1.0,
        F3 = 1.0,
        F4 = 1.0;
    COV
        F1 F2 = COV12,
        F1 F3 = COV13,
        F1 F4 = COV14,
        F2 F3 = COV23,
        F2 F4 = COV24,
        F3 F4 = COV34;
RUN;
```

PROC CALIS invokes the CALIS procedure. The options following the PROC CALIS statement do the following: DATA=ANXIETY indicates the input data set; COVARIANCE requests that the covariance matrix be used when estimating parameters; RESIDUAL requests that the residual matrices (unstandardized and standardized) be included in the output; MODIFICATION requests modification indices (MI) or Lagrange Multiplier (LM) tests to be provided in the output; and NOBS indicates the number of participants on which the data are based (in this case, 318 participants completed the RTT scale).

The linear equations relating the variables in the model are specified in the LINEQS statement. As in the observed variable path analysis example, the form specifies that the endogenous variable is a function of the variables directly affecting it as well as error. Thus, in the following equation:

```
TEN1 = L11 F1 + E1
```

the variable tension1 is a function of the direct effect of F1 (which is associated with the factor loading L11) and the direct effect of error (E1). You can see that all twelve items are a function of their respective factor (labeled F1 through F4) and error (labeled E1 through E12). The assignment of parameter labels in this example adopts a convention used in LISREL in which lambdas (L) are factor loadings and the numbers refer to the item number on its respective factor (e.g., 24 indicates it is the second indicator variable for factor 4). Again, these equations are separated by commas.

The VARIANCE statement indicates which variance parameters to estimate in the hypothesized model. These include variances of exogenous variables (including error variances and factor variance). Thus, 12 error variances will be estimated (E1 – E12), which will be labeled as VARE1–VARE12, respectively, in the output. The four factors must be scaled for identification purposes. In this example, all four of the factor variances have been set to a value of one (e.g., F1 = 1.0). It must be noted that these variances will be estimated by default if not included in the CALIS procedure code. Thus, if the statements setting the factor variances equal to 1.0 are excluded, one reference indicator per factor should be designated. This can be done, for example, as follows for F1 by fixing the loading of tension1 on F1 equal to a value of 1.0:

```
TEN1 = 1 F1 + E1
```

Thus, every factor would require this specification with one of their respective indicators.

The COV statement indicates which variables you hypothesize to covary in the model. In this model, covariances between all of the exogenous factors were hypothesized. For instance, the covariance between tension (F1) and worry (F2) will be estimated and labeled as COV_12. The default is to estimate covariances among all exogenous latent variables (with the exception of errors and disturbances) in the CALIS procedure. Consequently, the covariances among all four factors would be estimated by default if not included in the code. If you hypothesize no covariance among the exogenous latent variables, you can set them equal to zero. For example, the following statement would set the covariance between F1 (tension) and F2 (worry) equal to zero and, hence, would not be freely estimated in the model:

```
F1 F2 = 0
```

Again, these statements are separated by commas.

16.9.2 Analysis Results: Model Fit

The Fit Summary table is presented in Tables 16.22 (top half) and 16.23 (bottom half).

Using the cutoff values previously discussed, the fit indices (with the exception of the model chi-square statistic) indicate that the four-factor correlated model fits the data well [$\chi^2(48) = 88.40$, $p < .05$; SRMR = .04; RMSEA = .05 (90% CI: .03, .07) with $p > .05$; CFI = .98; and NNFI/TLI = .97]. The unstandardized factor loadings (with

▪ **Table 16.22: Top Half of Fit Summary Table From PROC CALIS for RTT CFA Example**

	Fit Summary	
Modeling Info	Number of Observations	318
	Number of Variables	12
	Number of Moments	78
	Number of Parameters	30
	Number of Active Constraints	0
	Baseline Model Function Value	5.5711
	Baseline Model Chi-Square	1766.0539
	Baseline Model Chi-Square DF	66
	Pr > Baseline Model Chi-Square	<.0001
Absolute Index	Fit Function	0.2789
	Chi-Square	88.3955
	Chi-Square DF	48
	Pr > Chi-Square	0.0003
	Z-Test of Wilson & Hilferty	3.3856
	Hoelter Critical N	234
	Root Mean Square Residual (RMR)	0.0256
	Standardized RMR (SRMR)	0.0364
	Goodness of Fit Index (GFI)	0.9565

■ **Table 16.23: Bottom Half of Fit Summary Table From PROC CALIS for RTT CFA Example**

Parsimony Index	Adjusted GFI (AGFI)	0.9294
	Parsimonious GFI	0.6957
	RMSEA Estimate	0.0515
	RMSEA Lower 90% Confidence Limit	0.0342
	RMSEA Upper 90% Confidence Limit	0.0682
	Probability of Close Fit	0.4194
	ECVI Estimate	0.4762
	ECVI Lower 90% Confidence Limit	0.4045
	ECVI Upper 90% Confidence Limit	0.5738
	Akaike Information Criterion	148.3955
	Bozdogan CAIC	291.2571
	Schwarz Bayesian Criterion	261.2571
	McDonald Centrality	0.9385
Incremental Index	Bentler Comparative Fit Index	0.9762
	Bentler-Bonett NFI	0.9499
	Bentler-Bonett Non-normed Index	0.9673
	Bollen Normed Index Rho1	0.9312
	Bollen Non-normed Index Delta2	0.9765
	James et al. Parsimonious NFI	0.6909

corresponding standard errors and t test statistics) are presented in Tables 16.24 (for Tension and Worry factors) and 16.25 (for Test-Irrelevant Thinking and Bodily Symptoms factors).

16.9.3 Analysis Results: Parameter Estimates

All of the unstandardized factor loadings are statistically significant (t statistics are greater than |1.96|). The variance estimates of the error variances associated with each of the indicators (though not presented) indicate that a significant amount of variance is unexplained by their respective factor. The Covariances Among Exogenous Variables and the Squared Multiple Correlations are shown in Table 16.26.

As demonstrated by the t statistics for the covariances among the exogenous factors, all covariances among the factors are statistically significant, with the exception of the covariance between F1 (Tension) and F3 (Test-Irrelevant Thinking). Because all of the factor variances were set to equal 1.0, these covariances are actually the correlations among factors. The R square values suggested that the explained variance in the indicators ranged from 36% to 74%. Thus, the factors explained at least 36% of the variance in their respective indicator.

■ Table 16.24: Unstandardized Factor Loadings for RTT CFA Example (Tension and Worry Factor Loadings)

		Linear Equations				
TEN1	=	0.6881	*	F1	+ 1.0000	E1
Std Err		0.0441		L11		
t Value		15.5878				
TEN2	=	0.7649	*	F1	+ 1.0000	E2
Std Err		0.0478		L21		
t Value		16.0087				
TEN3	=	0.8408	*	F1	+ 1.0000	E3
Std Err		0.0475		L31		
t Value		17.6955				
WOR1	=	0.6449	*	F2	+ 1.0000	E4
Std Err		0.0398		L12		
t Value		16.1838				
WOR2	=	0.6649	*	F2	+ 1.0000	E5
Std Err		0.0458		L22		
t Value		14.5134				
WOR3	=	0.6698	*	F2	+ 1.0000	E6
Std Err		0.0411		L32		
t Value		16.2961				

■ Table 16.25: Unstandardized Factor Loadings for RTT CFA Example (Test-Irrelevant Thinking and Bodily Symptoms Factors)

IRTHK1	=	0.6445*	F3	+ 1.0000	E7
Std Err		0.0417	L13		
t Value		15.4664			
IRTHK2	=	0.6688*	F3	+ 1.0000	E8
Std Err		0.0416	L23		
t Value		16.0851			
IRTHK3	=	0.6705*	F3	+ 1.0000	E9
Std Err		0.0379	L33		
t Value		17.6880			

BODY1 =	0.3837*	F4	+	1.0000	E10
Std Err	0.0365	L14			
t Value	10.5115				
BODY2 =	0.5443*	F4	+	1.0000	E11
Std Err	0.0472	L24			
t Value	11.5246				
BODY3 =	0.5585*	F4	+	1.0000	E12
Std Err	0.0420	L34			
t Value	13.2939				

■ **Table 16.26: Covariances Among Factors and Squared Multiple Correlations of Indicators in RRT CFA Example**

Covariances Among Exogenous Variables					
Var1	Var2	Parameter	Estimate	Standard Error	t Value
F1	F2	COV12	0.55015	0.04996	11.01069
F1	F3	COV13	0.11423	0.06476	1.76399
F1	F4	COV14	0.77837	0.04156	18.72978
F2	F3	COV23	0.49176	0.05298	9.28262
F2	F4	COV24	0.59452	0.05458	10.89274
F3	F4	COV34	0.28632	0.06742	4.24701

Squared Multiple Correlations			
Variable	Error Variance	Total Variance	R-Square
TEN1	0.30857	0.78210	0.6055
TEN2	0.34486	0.92990	0.6291
TEN3	0.26822	0.97510	0.7249
WOR1	0.21936	0.63520	0.6547
WOR2	0.35224	0.79430	0.5565
WOR3	0.22970	0.67830	0.6614
IRTHK1	0.27009	0.68550	0.6060
IRTHK2	0.24793	0.69520	0.6434
IRTHK3	0.15688	0.60650	0.7413
BODY1	0.25957	0.40680	0.3619
BODY2	0.40523	0.70150	0.4223
BODY3	0.26669	0.57860	0.5391

The standardized factor loadings (with corresponding standard errors and *t* test statistics) are presented in Tables 16.27 (for Tension and Worry factors) and 16.28 (for Test-Irrelevant Thinking and Bodily Symptoms factors).

As seen with the unstandardized factor loadings, all of the standardized factor loadings are statistically significant (*t* statistics are greater than |1.96|). Further, all of the standardized factor loading values are .60 or greater. The standardized variance estimates for the exogenous variables (including the error variances associated with each of the

▪ **Table 16.27: Standardized Factor Loadings for RTT CFA Example (Tension and Worry Factor Loadings)**

Standardized Results for Linear Equations						
TEN1	=	0.7781	*	F1	+	1.0000	E1
Std Err		0.0280		L11		
t Value		27.8027				
TEN2	=	0.7932	*	F1	+	1.0000	E2
Std Err		0.0270		L21		
t Value		29.4269				
TEN3	=	0.8514	*	F1	+	1.0000	E3
Std Err		0.0233		L31		
t Value		36.5504				
WOR1	=	0.8091	*	F2	+	1.0000	E4
Std Err		0.0275		L12		
t Value		29.4711				
WOR2	=	0.7460	*	F2	+	1.0000	E5
Std Err		0.0314		L22		
t Value		23.7608				
WOR3	=	0.8132	*	F2	+	1.0000	E6
Std Err		0.0272		L32		
t Value		29.8801				

▪ **Table 16.28: Standardized Factor Loadings for RTT CFA Example (Test-Irrelevant Thinking and Bodily Symptoms Factors)**

IRTHK1	=	0.7785	*	F3	+	1.0000	E7
Std Err		0.0287		L13		
t Value		27.1137				

```
IRTHK2   =   0.8021   *   F3   +   1.0000   E8
Std Err      0.0274       L23
t Value      29.3261


IRTHK3   =   0.8610   *   F3   +   1.0000   E9
Std Err      0.0244       L33
t Value      35.2893


BODY1    =   0.6016   *   F4   +   1.0000   E10
Std Err      0.0445       L14
t Value      13.5328


BODY2    =   0.6499   *   F4   +   1.0000   E11
Std Err      0.0418       L24
t Value      15.5613


BODY3    =   0.7342   *   F4   +   1.0000   E12
Std Err      0.0376       L34
t Value      19.5101
```

■ Table 16.29: Standardized Variances of and Covariances Among Exogenous Variables for RTT CFA Example

Standardized Results for Variances of Exogenous Variables					
Variable Type	Variable	Parameter	Estimate	Standard Error	t Value
Error	E1	VARE1	0.39454	0.04355	9.05879
	E2	VARE2	0.37086	0.04276	8.67297
	E3	VARE3	0.27507	0.03967	6.93427
	E4	VARE4	0.34534	0.04443	7.77329
	E5	VARE5	0.44346	0.04685	9.46657
	E6	VARE6	0.33864	0.04427	7.64981
	E7	VARE7	0.39400	0.04470	8.81421
	E8	VARE8	0.35662	0.04388	8.12775
	E9	VARE9	0.25866	0.04202	6.15637
	E10	VARE10	0.63807	0.05349	11.92876
	E11	VARE11	0.57766	0.05428	10.64226
	E12	VARE12	0.46092	0.05526	8.34070
Latent	F1		1.00000		
	F2		1.00000		
	F3		1.00000		
	F4		1.00000		

(Continued)

■ **Table 16.29: Continued**

Standardized Results for Covariances Among Exogenous Variables					
Var1	Var2	Parameter	Estimate	Standard Error	t Value
F1	F2	COV12	0.55015	0.04996	11.01069
F1	F3	COV13	0.11423	0.06476	1.76399
F1	F4	COV14	0.77837	0.04156	18.72978
F2	F3	COV23	0.49176	0.05298	9.28262
F2	F4	COV24	0.59452	0.05458	10.89274
F3	F4	COV34	0.28632	0.06742	4.24701

indicators) and the correlations among exogenous variables (i.e., all of the factors) are presented in Table 16.29.

The smallest correlation among the factors is between the Tension factor and the Test-Irrelevant Thinking factor, which is equal to .11 and is not statistically significant according to its associated t test (1.76 < 1.96). The statistically significant correlations among factors range from .29 to .78. You may have noticed that these correlations are identical to the covariances among factors presented in Table 16.26. Again, these values match because the factor variances were set equal to 1.0, resulting in the standardization of the factors. The standardized error variance estimates associated with the indicators specify the proportion of unexplained variance in each of the indicators. The most unexplained variance estimated (approximately 64%) is demonstrated for the item associated with E10, which is the first bodily symptoms item (body1). Subtracting these values from a value of one results in the R square values presented previously in Table 16.26 (e.g., $1 - .64 = .36$ for the bodily symptoms1 indicator).

16.9.4 Analysis Results: Model Modification

The Wald test and LM tests were printed in the SAS output because we used the MODIFICATION option in PROC CALIS. The Wald test is presented in Table 16.30. The Wald test agrees with the output regarding the covariance between F1 (Tension) and F3 (Test-Irrelevant Thinking). Hence, the Wald test is suggesting that this covariance (parameter COV12) can be dropped from the model without significantly increasing chi-square ($p > .05$). If theory supports this decision, you could justify dropping this covariance from the model. In contrast, if theory supports this covariance between the two factors, it should be retained, regardless of statistical significance.

The LM tests are presented in Tables 16.31 and 16.32. The LM Tests for Paths from Endogenous Variables shown in Table 16.31 indicate which direct paths originating from endogenous variables (in this case, the indicator variables) may be added to the model to significantly decrease the chi-square statistic. The top three LM suggestions include adding a direct path from worry3 to worry2, a direct path from worry2 to worry3, and a direct path from worry3 to tension2. The LM Tests for Paths from

Exogenous Variables suggest which direct paths from exogenous variables (in this case, the factors) may be added to significantly decrease the chi-square. Hence, these suggest the addition of cross-loadings. For instance, allowing tension3 to load on the Bodily Symptoms factor in addition to the Tension factor would reduce the chi-square

■ **Table 16.30: The Wald Test for the RTT CFA Example**

| | Stepwise Multivariate Wald Test | | | | |
| | Cumulative Statistics | | | Univariate Increment | |
Parm	Chi-Square	DF	Pr > ChiSq	Chi-Square	Pr > ChiSq
COV13	3.11166	1	0.0777	3.11166	0.0777

■ **Table 16.31: LM Tests for the RTT CFA Example**

| | Rank Order of the 10 Largest LM Stat for Paths from Endogenous Variables | | | |
To	From	LM Stat	Pr > ChiSq	Parm Change
WOR3	WOR2	14.16120	0.0002	-0.33957
WOR2	WOR3	14.16075	0.0002	-0.52072
WOR3	TEN2	13.25134	0.0003	0.14798
WOR2	WOR1	12.99412	0.0003	0.50217
WOR1	WOR2	12.99366	0.0003	0.31273
TEN3	BODY1	12.97464	0.0003	0.25305
WOR1	TEN3	12.60477	0.0004	-0.14216
TEN2	TEN1	10.57540	0.0011	0.33976
TEN1	TEN2	10.57540	0.0011	0.30402
TEN3	BODY2	9.14647	0.0025	0.16979

| | Rank Order of the 10 Largest LM Stat for Paths from Exogenous Variables | | | |
To	From	LM Stat	Pr > ChiSq	Parm Change
TEN3	F4	18.32723	<.0001	0.45216
WOR3	F4	12.36214	0.0004	0.20495
WOR3	F1	11.94309	0.0005	0.17102
WOR1	F1	9.58317	0.0020	-0.14815
WOR1	F4	8.71089	0.0032	-0.16626
TEN1	F4	5.75662	0.0164	-0.22028
TEN2	F4	4.45498	0.0348	-0.21171
BODY3	F3	2.61711	0.1057	-0.07448
TEN1	F3	2.60138	0.1068	-0.06366
TEN2	F2	2.41395	0.1203	0.08676

■ **Table 16.32: LM Tests for the RTT CFA Model Example**

	Rank Order of the 10 Largest LM Stat for Paths with New Endogenous Variables			
To	From	LM Stat	Pr > ChiSq	Parm Change
F4	TEN3	18.56890	<.0001	0.63971
F2	WOR1	14.16250	0.0002	0.78963
F2	WOR3	12.99261	0.0003	−0.74913
F1	TEN3	10.57557	0.0011	−0.62440
F4	TEN2	8.58264	0.0034	−0.32532
F1	WOR1	6.50164	0.0108	−0.32712
F1	WOR3	5.40273	0.0201	0.29429
F2	TEN2	4.58009	0.0323	0.21502
F1	TEN1	4.37550	0.0365	0.29548
F4	TEN1	2.75440	0.0970	−0.18916

Note: No LM statistic in the default test set for the covariances of exogenous variables is nonsingular. Ranking is not displayed.

	Rank Order of the 10 Largest LM Stat for Error Variances and Covariances			
Var1	Var2	LM Stat	Pr > ChiSq	Parm Change
E6	E5	14.16122	0.0002	−0.11961
E5	E4	12.99369	0.0003	0.11016
E2	E1	10.57543	0.0011	0.10484
E9	E12	7.97824	0.0047	−0.04842
E3	E10	7.69945	0.0055	0.05595
E4	E3	6.54831	0.0105	−0.05123
E1	E10	5.13997	0.0234	−0.04368
E6	E2	4.99702	0.0254	0.04769
E3	E2	4.37546	0.0365	−0.08521
E3	E11	4.16317	0.0413	0.05304

by approximately 18.33 points. Other top LM suggested cross-loadings include worry3 cross-loading both on the Bodily Symptoms factor and on the Tension factor. Again, theoretical justifications would need to be considered when deciding whether or not to allow cross-loadings. If you did want to allow tension3 to cross-load on the Bodily Symptoms factor, for instance, the equation in PROC CALIS would look similar to the following in the LINEQS section:

```
TEN3 = L31 F1 + L31_4 F4 + E3
```

in which the parameter L31_4 represents the factor loading of tension3 on the Bodily Functions factor (F4).

The LM Tests for Paths with New Endogenous Variables in Table 16.32 recommend paths originating from endogenous to exogenous variables. For instance, the chi-square would decrease by approximately 18.57 points if the direct effect from tension3 to the Bodily Symptoms factor (F4) was added to the model. The chi-square would decrease by approximately 14.16 points if the direct effect from worry1 to the Worry factor (F2) was added to the model, representing a bidirectional relationship. The last LM tests in Table 16.32 are for Error Variances and Covariances. Thus, the chi-square would decrease by approximately 14.16 points if the covariance between the errors associated with worry2 (E5) and worry3 (E6) was added to the model. Similarly, the chi-square would decrease more than 12 points if the covariance between the errors associated with worry2 (E5) and worry1 (E4) was added to the model. Again, these error covariances indicate the possibility that something above and beyond the explanation by the Worry factor (F2) is influencing the relationship between the variables. Of course, the choice to add any of these parameters in the model would depend upon theoretical validations. If you did want to add an error covariance, for instance, between worry2 (E5) and worry3 (E6), it would look like the following in the COV section of PROC CALIS:

```
E5 E6 = COV_E56
```

16.9.5 Results for the Final Model

The results of CFA models, depending upon their complexity, may be presented in a figure or they could be tabled. For instance, the RTT CFA model could be presented similarly to the model illustrated in Figure 16.13.

■ **Figure 16.13** CFA model for the reactions to tests scale with standardized estimates.

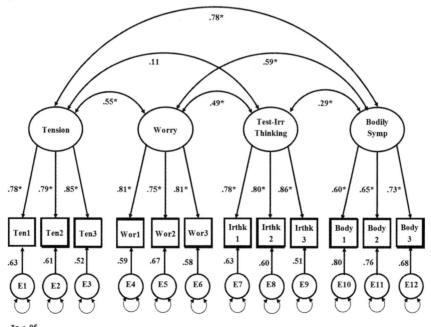

*p < .05

In this model, the standardized factor loadings are reported and the standardized paths from the errors to each respective indicator is presented. This could be presented differently, for instance, by including the standardized residual variance at the top of the arrow from the error to its respective indicator:

or the R square associated with each indicator could instead be presented:

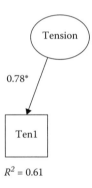

If you also want to report standard errors in the figures, those can easily be incorporated in parenthesis next to their respective parameter estimate. If the model is highly complex, you may want to present the results in tables instead of in figures. Tables 16.33 and 16.34 provide examples of how you could present these results in table form. Kline (2011) also presents example tables when reporting the findings from CFA in

■ **Table 16.33: Unstandardized Loadings, Standard Errors, Standardized Factors Loadings, and R Square Values for the RTT CFA Model**

Item	Unstandardized loadings	S.E.	Standardized loadings	R square
Tension1	.69*	.04	.78	.61
Tension2	.76*	.05	.79	.63
Tension3	.84*	.05	.85	.72

Item	Unstandardized loadings	S.E.	Standardized loadings	R square
Worry1	.64*	.04	.81	.65
Worry2	.66*	.05	.75	.56
Worry3	.67*	.04	.81	.66
Test-Irrelevant Thinking1	.64*	.04	.78	.61
Test-Irrelevant Thinking1	.67*	.04	.80	.64
Test-Irrelevant Thinking1	.67*	.04	.86	.74
Bodily Symptoms1	.38*	.04	.60	.36
Bodily Sypmtoms2	.54*	.05	.65	.42
Bodily Symptoms3	.56*	.04	.73	.54

Note: *$p < .05$.

▨ **Table 16.34: Factor Intercorrelations for the RTT CFA Model**

Factor	Tension	Worry	Test-Irrelevant Thinking	Bodily Symptoms
Tension	—			
Worry	.55*	—		
Test-Irrelevant Thinking	.11	.49*	—	
Bodily Symptoms	.78*	.59*	.29*	—

Note: *$p < .05$.

which the unstandardized measurement errors are reported with respective standard errors and standardized estimates.

CFA is a valuable tool that may be used to provide support for theoretically meaningful factor structures underlying observed scores. It can aid in the detection of the nature of the dimensionality of the factor structure by way of comparing nested and nonnested CFA models (e.g., Galassi, Schanberg, & Ware, 1992). CFA models are also the foundation of latent variable path models.

16.10 LATENT VARIABLE PATH ANALYSIS

The causal links previously modeled among observed variables in observed variable path analysis models may also be modeled among unobserved or latent variables (see Figure 16.2). Latent variable path analysis allows relationships among latent factors, which are indicated by observed variables, to be modeled. In observed variable path analysis models, the observed variables may be a measureable single score (e.g., GRE scores) or an aggregate of responses to items from a questionnaire (e.g., total or averaged score), which may then be used to "represent" a construct of interest (e.g., student motivation). In observed variable path analysis models, an assumption is that each exogenous variable and aggregate variable (endogenous or exogenous) has no measurement error and, hence, has perfect reliability. If this assumption is not supported, which is often the case with measures used in the social sciences and in educational settings, the results of the observed variable path analysis may result in biased estimates (Bollen, 1989). Since applied researchers are essentially interested in examining the relationships among constructs, latent variable path analysis incorporates the latent or unobserved factors that underlie the observed variables. Consequently, latent variable path analysis counters the undesirable effects associated with measurement error seen in observed variable path models by modeling the unobservable error that accompanies measured variables (as was seen in CFA models).

16.10.1 Specification and Identification of Latent Variable Path Models

Latent variable path models, which are also called structural models, are basically extensions of observed variable path models. For instance, consider the latent variable path model in Figure 16.14 from a study conducted by Duncan and Stoolmiller (1993) in which they investigated the determinants (i.e., social support and self-efficacy) of maintaining an exercise program across time.

■ **Figure 16.14 Latent variable path model for exercise behavior proposed by Duncan and Stoolmiller (1993).**

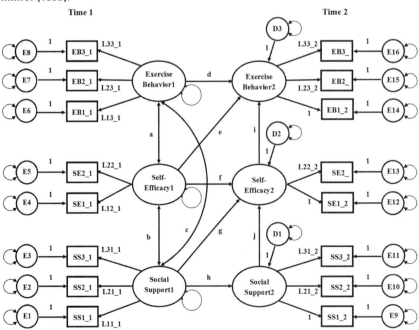

In this example, each factor that is modeled at both measurement occasions are indicated by the same three indicator variables. That is, the same three questions per factor are asked at the two different time points and serve as indicators for their respective factor at time 1 and at time 2. You should notice similarities between this model and an observed variable path model. The one-headed arrows represent direct effects (*d* through *j*) among the factors that are analogous to partial regression coefficients. For instance, the self-efficacy factor at time 1 is hypothesized to directly impact the self-efficacy factor at time 2 (path *f*), which in turn is hypothesized to directly affect the exercise behavior factor at time 2 (path *i*). The two-headed arrows connecting the three factors at time 1 represent hypothesized covariances (*a*, *b*, and *c*) among these factors instead of causal relationships.

In latent variable path models, factors may be exogenous or endogenous. For example, all of the time 1 factors are exogenous factors that directly affect other factors at time 2. Social support, self-efficacy, and exercise behavior at time 2 all represent endogenous factors in the model because they are receiving causal inputs from other factors in model. As in previously discussed models, errors will be associated with the endogenous factors, which in turn directly affect their respective endogenous factor. However, in latent variable path analysis, these errors are typically termed disturbances to make a distinction between unexplained variance associated with an endogenous latent variable as compared to the unexplained variance associated with an endogenous observed variable. Disturbances are unobserved variables and are, thus, denoted with circles in which a "D" is contained (see Figure 16.14).

You may also notice that indirect effects are modeled at the structural level. For example, the social support and self-efficacy factors at time 2 are modeled as mediating the relationships between the social support and self-efficacy factors at time 1 and the exercise behavior factor at time 2 via three channels (corresponding to the products *hji*, *gi*, and *fi*, respectively). Similar to the analyses of indirect effects in observed variable path analysis, mediational relationships among latent variables can also be tested for their statistical significance.

As illustrated in the model in Figure 16.14, each of the latent constructs symbolizes a measurement or a CFA model in which the latent factor underlies their corresponding indicator variables. Determining model identification is similar to that described for CFA models with another distinction concerning the scaling of endogenous factors. Before discussing this issue more, let us first determine the number of nonredundant observations in the sample covariance matrix:

$$p^* = \frac{p(p+1)}{2} = \frac{16(16+1)}{2} = 136.$$

with 16 observed variables.

Recall that the variances of and covariances among exogenous variables, direct effects, and covariances require estimation in SEM. As with CFA models, the scale of the factors in structural models are unknown and must be set. In CFA, we could either set the scale of the factor by setting its variance equal to a value of 1.0 or setting the factor loading of a reference indicator equal to a value of 1.0. These methods were acceptable because the factors were exogenous. When factors become endogenous variables in structural models, because they are directly affected by another factor in the model, the only option available to set its scale is by way of using a reference indicator. The reason for this is because we do not estimate the variances of endogenous variables. Instead, the variances of disturbances associated with endogenous factors are estimated. Thus, to set the scale of an endogenous factor, the reference indicator method of scaling must be used. The model in Figure 16.14 portrays which loadings will be set to a value of 1.0 to serve as the reference indicator for its corresponding factor. All of the other loadings will be estimated and are designated as such with lambdas and associated parameter coefficient numbers.

The parameters to estimate in this model include 16 error variances (one per indicator); three disturbance variances (one per endogenous factor); 13 factor loadings; seven direct effects among the factors; and three covariances among the factors at time 1, resulting in 42 total parameters to estimate in this hypothesized model. Thus, the df_T for this model is 94 ($136 - 42 = 94$). It is important to note that two of the factors in the model, if estimated independently of this structural model, would be under-identified because they only have two indicators (i.e., self-efficacy factors at time 1 and at time 2). The social support and exercise behavior factors at times 1 and 2, if estimated independently of this structural model, would be just-identified because they have three indicators. As mentioned previously, three indicators per factor is recommended for the identification of CFA models. Nonetheless, under-identified CFA models can be estimated if included in a larger model, as in this case.

16.10.2 Two-Step Model Testing Procedure in Latent Variable Path Analysis

This brings us to a discussion of model testing with latent variable path models. When working with latent variable path models, the structural model (i.e., the relationships among the factors) introduces a new tier in the analysis in addition to the measurement model. More specifically, if the model presented in Figure 16.14 did not fit the data acceptably after running the initial analysis, the location of unacceptable fit within the model may be difficult to decode because the structural and measurement models are being estimated simultaneously. Consequently, a two-step model fitting sequence, suggested by Anderson and Gerbing (1988), is a popular method used when analyzing latent variable path models in order to identify the source of poor fit in the model. The first step of the two-step modeling approach involves specifying a model in which all of the factors covary with all of the other factors in the model. This model is referred to as the initial measurement model. As a result of allowing all of the factors to covary with one another, the structural part of the model is a just-identified or saturated model. Because no additional parameters may be estimated at the structural level, it fits the data perfectly. Accordingly, if this model fits the data unacceptably, the poor model fit is due to the measurement model. That is, the relationships among the indicator variables are not explained well by the measurement model. As such, the LM/MI tests may be consulted to identify possible parameters to add and the model may be respecified to help improve fit to the data. These parameters typically consist of error covariances or cross-loadings. If the initial measurement model fits the data well or once the respecified model fits acceptably after adding parameters, you can continue to the second step of the two-step modeling approach, which involves assessing the fit of the latent variable path model. The resulting model (the initial measurement model or the respecified measurement model) in this step is referred to as the final measurement model.

The second step of the two-step modeling approach consists of imposing the structural model on the final measurement model. Thus, all of the covariances among factors are released and the structural parameters (i.e., the relationships among the factors) are specified in the model. This is referred to as the initial structural model and is nested in the final measurement model. When assessing the fit of the model in the second step of the two-step modeling process, it is important to realize that it will not fit as well as the final measurement model. Remember that the structural or latent variable path model is just-identified in the first step. Thus, the latent variable path model fits the data perfectly. The fit of the hypothesized structural model is assessed during the second step. Because structural models will commonly be over-identified models, the fit will tend to become worse during the second step of the two-step modeling process. The hope is that the fit will not become significantly worse. This is why it is important that the measurement model fit well before imposing the structural relationships.

If the initial structural model fits the data acceptably, a chi-square difference test ($\Delta\chi^2$) may be conducted to see if a significant decline in model fit occurred when imposing the structural relationships. If the $\Delta\chi^2$ is not significant, the structural model did not decrease model fit and can be retained. If there is a significant difference in fit between the two models, model modifications may be considered for the structural part of the model. If the initial structural model does not fit the data well, again, LM/MI tests can be assessed for potential respecifications. Once the model fits adequately, the $\Delta\chi^2$ may then be conducted between the final structural model and the final measurement model. Again, a significant test would indicate a significant loss of fit when specifying the structural model on the measurement model. An important consideration is that the sample size sensitivity of the chi-square extends to the $\Delta\chi^2$ test statistic. Others have suggested using differences between fit indices associated with comparison models instead of the $\Delta\chi^2$, such as the CFI (e.g., Cheung & Rensvold, 2002, and Meade, Johnson, & Braddy, 2008). A four-step modeling approach has also been suggested (see Mulaik & Millsap, 2000, for more information about the four-step modeling approach).

16.11 LATENT VARIABLE PATH ANALYSIS WITH EXERCISE BEHAVIOR STUDY

The latent variable path model illustrated in Figure 16.14 that was examined by Duncan and Stoolmiller (1993) will be used to demonstrate a latent variable path analysis using SAS. The SAS code for the initial measurement model in which all of the factors covary with all of the other factors is presented in Table 16.35. All of the options in the PROC CALIS statement in this example have been previously described. The number of participants for this study is fairly small ($N = 84$).

▨ **Table 16.35: SAS Code for Initial Measurement Model for the Latent Variable Path Model of Exercise Behavior**

```
PROC CALIS DATA=EXERCISE COVARIANCE RESIDUAL MODIFICATION
NOBS=84;
   LINEQS
      SS1_1 = L11_1 FSS1 + E1,
      SS2_1 = L21_1 FSS1 + E2,
      SS3_1 = L31_1 FSS1 + E3,
      SE1_1 = L12_1 FSE1 + E4,
      SE2_1 = L22_1 FSE1 + E5,
      EB1_1 = L13_1 FEB1 + E6,
      EB2_1 = L23_1 FEB1 + E7,
      EB3_1 = L33_1 FEB1 + E8,
      SS1_2 = 1     FSS2 + E9,
      SS2_2 = L21_2 FSS2 + E10,
      SS3_2 = L31_2 FSS2 + E11,
      SE1_2 = 1     FSE2 + E12,
      SE2_2 = L22_2 FSE2 + E13,
      EB1_2 = 1     FEB2 + E14,
      EB2_2 = L23_2 FEB2 + E15,
      EB3_2 = L33_2 FEB2 + E16;
   VARIANCE
      E1 - E16 = VARE1-VARE16,
      FSS1 = 1.0,
      FSE1 = 1.0,
      FEB1 = 1.0,
      FSS2 = VARFSS2,
      FSE2 = VARFSE2,
      FEB2 = VARFEB2;
   COV
      FSS1 FSE1 = COV1,
      FSS1 FEB1 = COV2,
      FSS1 FSS2 = COV3,
      FSS1 FSE2 = COV4,
      FSS1 FEB2 = COV5,
      FSE1 FEB1 = COV6,
      FSE1 FSS2 = COV7,
      FSE1 FSE2 = COV8,
      FSE1 FEB2 = COV9,
```

```
      FEB1  FSS2  =  COV10,
      FEB1  FSE2  =  COV11,
      FEB1  FEB2  =  COV12,
      FSS2  FSE2  =  COV13,
      FSS2  FEB2  =  COV14,
      FSE2  FEB2  =  COV15;
RUN;
```

The linear equations relating the variables in the model are specified in the LINEQS statement. As in the CFA example, all of the equations in the initial measurement model relate the observed indicator variables to their corresponding factor. For instance, in the following equation:

```
   SS1_1  =  L11_1  FSS1  +  E1
```

the variable SS1_1 (social support item 1 at time 1) is a function of the direct effect of FSS1 (the social support factor at time 1), which is associated with the factor loading L11_1 and the direct effect of error (E1). The _1 and _2 specify the relevant measurement occasion associated with the indicator. Because social support, self-efficacy, and exercise behavior factors at time 2 are endogenous, their scale must be set by way of a reference indicator. Thus, each of these factors has one of its respective item's factor loading set equal to value of 1.0. For instance, the following statement sets the factor loading for the first item (SS1) loading on the social support factor at time 2 equal to a value of 1 instead of allowing it to be freely estimated:

```
   SS1_2  =  1  FSS2  +  E9
```

In the VARIANCE statement, all of the error variances associated with the sixteen indicators will be estimated (E1 – E16) and labeled in the output as VARE1–VARE16, respectively. The variances of the three exogenous factors at time 1 were set to a value of one (e.g., FSS1 = 1.0), and the variances of the three factors at time 2 (which will ultimately be endogenous in the structural model) will be estimated (e.g., FSS2 = VARFSS2). Again, these variances will be estimated by default unless otherwise specified. The COV statement is where all of the factors are modeled to covary in the initial measurement model and will be labeled as COV1 through COV15 in the output. Again, these would be modeled by default in the CALIS procedure if omitted from the code.

16.11.1 Two-Step Modeling With the Exercise Behavior Study

The initial measurement model did not fit the data adequately [$\chi^2(89) = 180.38$, $p < .05$; SRMR = .09; RMSEA = .11 (90% CI: .09, .13) with $p < .05$; CFI = .88; and NNFI/TLI = .84]. As such, the LM/MI tests were examined to evaluate potential model respecifications. Although the various output for the LM/MI tests were printed, only the LM/MI tests associated with error covariances were examined in order to be consistent with the original study. As such cross-loadings were not considered. The LM/MI tests for Error Variances and Covariances are shown in Table 16.36.

The largest decrease in the chi-square statistic (by approximately 25.18 points) would result if the covariance between E14 and E6 were added to the model. These errors are associated with the first item for the exercise behavior factor at time 1 (EB1_1) and at time 2 (EB1_2). The addition of this error covariance is theoretically reasonable given that these indicators are the same item measured at different occasions. Thus, the way in which a person responds to an item at one measurement occasion is likely to be similar to the way they respond to the same item at a subsequent measurement occasion. This error covariance was added to the model (E14 E6 = COV14_6 was included in the COV statement in PROC CALIS) and the model was reanalyzed. While the model fit of this respecified model did improve [$\chi^2(88) = 156.62, p < .05$; SRMR = .08; RMSEA = .10 (90% CI: .07, .12) with $p < .05$; CFI = .91; and NNFI/TLI = .88], it was still unacceptable. LM/MI tests associated with the error covariances were again examined for those that would decrease the chi-square significantly if added to the model and would be theoretically justified. This process was repeated sequentially until the model fit was acceptable. In the end, four additional covariances between errors associated with the same item measured at time 1 and at time 2 were added to the model, including pairs 13–5, 11–3, 10–2, and 16–18. The final measurement model fit the data acceptably well [$\chi^2(84) = 92.48, p > .05$; SRMR = .07; RMSEA = .03 (90% CI: .00, .07) with $p > .05$; CFI = .99; and NNFI/TLI = .98]. As such, this is the final measurement model.

Now that the measurement model fits the date adequately, the initial structural model can be analyzed. The SAS code for this model is presented in Table 16.37.

■ **Table 16.36: LM Tests for Error Variances and Covariances From PROC CALIS for the Initial Measurement Model of Exercise Behavior**

Rank Order of the 10 Largest LM Stat for Error Variances and Covariances				
Var1	Var2	LM Stat	Pr > ChiSq	Parm Change
E14	E6	25.17856	<.0001	8.76739
E13	E5	20.99473	<.0001	2.55923
E5	E12	20.28727	<.0001	−2.11353
E11	E3	12.44762	0.0004	0.85090
E9	E1	11.75956	0.0006	0.66092
E8	E14	11.05086	0.0009	−2.17658
E10	E2	10.92726	0.0009	0.46800
E16	E8	10.05405	0.0015	1.22001
E13	E4	9.78739	0.0018	−1.43268
E7	E14	9.00517	0.0027	−2.11006

■ **Table 16.37: SAS Code for Initial Structural Model for the Latent Variable Path Model of Exercise Behavior**

```
PROC CALIS DATA=EXERCISE COVARIANCE RESIDUAL MODIFICATION TOTEFF
NOBS=84;
   LINEQS
      SS1_1 = L11_1 FSS1 + E1,
      SS2_1 = L21_1 FSS1 + E2,
      SS3_1 = L31_1 FSS1 + E3,
      SE1_1 = L12_1 FSE1 + E4,
      SE2_1 = L22_1 FSE1 + E5,
      EB1_1 = L13_1 FEB1 + E6,
      EB2_1 = L23_1 FEB1 + E7,
      EB3_1 = L33_1 FEB1 + E8,
      SS1_2 = 1      FSS2 + E9,
      SS2_2 = L21_2 FSS2 + E10,
      SS3_2 = L31_2 FSS2 + E11,
      SE1_2 = 1      FSE2 + E12,
      SE2_2 = L22_2 FSE2 + E13,
      EB1_2 = 1      FEB2 + E14,
      EB2_2 = L23_2 FEB2 + E15,
      EB3_2 = L33_2 FEB2 + E16,
      FSS2  = SS1_SS2 FSS1 + D1,
      FSE2  = SS1_SE2 FSS1 + SS2_SE2 FSS2 + SE1_SE2 FSE1 + D2,
      FEB2  = SE1_EB1 FSE1 + SE2_EB2 FSE2 + EB1_EB2 FEB1 + D3;
   VARIANCE
      E1 - E16 = VARE1-VARE16,
      FSS1 = 1.0,
      FSE1 = 1.0,
      FEB1 = 1.0,
      D1-D3 = VARD1-VARD3;
   COV
      FSS1 FSE1 = COV1,
      FSS1 FEB1 = COV2,
      FSE1 FEB1 = COV3,
      E14  E6   = COV14_6,
      E13  E5   = COV13_5,
      E11  E3   = COV11_3,
      E10  E2   = COV10_2,
      E16  E8   = COV16_8;
RUN;
```

Because indirect effects are hypothesized at the structural level in this model, the TOTEFF option was listed in order to request output for the total, direct, and indirect effects among the factors at the structural level. Three new equations are included in the LINEQS statement to specify the relationships among the factors at the structural model. For instance, the following equation for the exercise behavior factor at time 2 (FEB2):

```
FEB2 = SE1_EB1 FSE1 + SE2_EB2 FSE2 + EB1_EB2 FEB1 + D3
```

denotes that it is directly affected by the self-efficacy factor at time 1 (FSE1), the self-efficacy factor at time 2 (FSE2), and the exercise behavior factor at time 1 (FEB1) with associated parameter coefficients (SE1_EB1, SE2_EB2, and EB1_EB2, respectively). It is also affected by a disturbance (D3). In the VARIANCE statement, the errors associated with the indicators will be estimated and the variances of the three exogenous factors at time 1 will be set equal to 1. The variances of the disturbances associated with the three endogenous factors at time 2 (D1-D3) will now be estimated and be labeled as VARD1-VARD3 in the output, respectively. In the COV statement, the only remaining factor covariances are between the three exogenous factors at time 1. Also specified in the COV statement are the five error covariances suggested by the LM/MI tests when respecifying the initial measurement model.

The abbreviated output for the initial structural model is presented in Appendix 16.2. The initial structural model fit the data well according to the fit criteria [$\chi^2(89) = 105.12$, $p > .05$; SRMR = .10; RMSEA = .05 (90% CI: .00, .08) with $p > .05$; CFI = .98; and NNFI/TLI = .97]. You could present the model fit information in a summary table similar to that in Table 16.38.

The $\Delta\chi^2$ between the final measurement model and the structural model [$\Delta\chi^2(5) = 12.64$, $p < .05$] is statistically significant. Thus, imposing our structural model on our measurement model resulted in a significant loss of fit. Although this is not the desired outcome, the final structural model fits the data well.

In the Squared Multiple Correlations table in Appendix 16.2, you can see the R square values not only associated with each indicator variable, but also those associated with the endogenous factors. For instance, approximately 58% of the variance in the social support factor at time 2 (FSS2) is explained by the model; approximately 59% of the

■ **Table 16.38: Model Fit Summary Table for Latent Variable Path Model for Exercise Behavior**

Model	χ^2	df	SRMR	RMSEA (90% CI) p-value	CFI	NNFI/TLI
Initial measurement model	180.38*	89	.09	.11 (.09, .13) p < .05	.88	.84
Final measurement model	92.48	84	.07	.03 (.00, .07) p > .05	.99	.98
Initial/final structural model	105.12	89	.11	.05 (.00, .08) p > .05	.98	.97

Note: *p < .05.

variance in the self-efficacy factor at time 2 (FSE2) is explained by the model; and approximately 90% of the variance in exercise behavior at time 2 (FEB2) is explained by the model.

All of the standardized factor loadings are statistically significant because all of the *t* statistics associated with these loadings are greater than |1.96| (see the Standardized Results for Linear Equations output in Appendix 16.2). With the exception of the direct effect of the social support factor at time 1 on the self-efficacy factor at time 2, the standardized direct effects among factors are all statistically significant. For example, as social support at time 1 increases by one standard deviation, social support at time 2 is estimated to increase by approximately .76 standard deviation units, controlling for everything else.

16.11.2 Results of the Final Model

When presenting these results, you may include the standardized values in the model as seen in Figure 16.15. It must be noted that the five error covariances between the same items measured at times 1 and 2 (i.e., 14–6; 13–15; 11–3, 10–2; and 16–18) are not illustrated in the figure for simplicity. Or, you could only present the picture of the structural model with standardized values and present a table similar to that in Table 16.33 for the measurement model.

Of particular interest in this model are the indirect effects among the factors at the structural level. The TOTEFF option in the PROC CALIS statement invoked the test of

▨ **Figure 16.15** Latent variable path model for exercise behavior with standardized estimates.

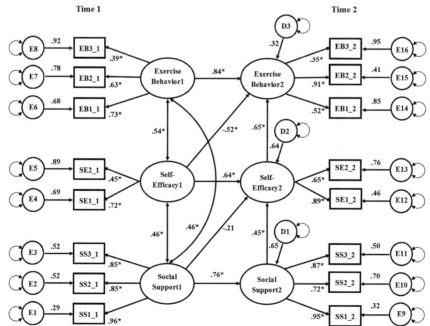

total, direct, and indirect effects. The standardized results for these effects are included in Appendix 16.2. Similar to the effects decomposition table for the observed variable path model with indirect effects, Table 16.39 presents the direct and indirect effects for this structural model. Specific indirect effects can again be tested for statistical significance using the joint statistical significance test. Thus, indirect effects comprised of significant direct effects would be deemed as statistically significant.

To illustrate, the indirect effect of social support at time 1 on self-efficacy at time 2 (via social support at time 2) and the indirect effect of social support at time 1 on exercise behavior at time 2 (via both social support and self-efficacy at time 2) are statistically significant. Using the values from the Standardized Direct Effects section in Appendix 16.2, the indirect effect from social support at time 1 to self-efficacy at time 2 via social support at time 2 is equal to .3408 ($.7583 \times .4494 = .3408$). The indirect effect of social support at time 1 on exercise behavior at time 2 via social support at time 2 and self-efficacy at time 2 is equal to .2222 ($.7583 \times .4494 \times .6521 = .2222$). In contrast, the indirect effect of social support at time 1 on exercise behavior at time 2 via self-efficacy at time 2 is not statistically significant because the direct effect

■ **Table 16.39: Standardized Direct, Indirect, and Total Effects for Latent Variable Path Model of Exercise**

Association	Direct	Indirect	Total
Social Support1, Self-Efficacy1	–	–	–
Social Support1, Exercise Behavior1	–	–	–
Social Support1, Social Support2	.7583*	–	.7583
Social Support1, Self-Efficacy2 SS1 → SS2 → SE2	–.2141	.3408*	.1267
Social Support1, Exercise Behavior2 SS1 → SE2 → EB2 SS1 → SS2 → SE2 → EB2	–	TI = .0826 –.1396 .2222*	.0826
Self-Efficacy1, Exercise Behavior1	–	–	–
Self-Efficacy1, Social Support2	–	–	–
Self-Efficacy1, Self-Efficacy2	.6416*	–	.6416
Self-Efficacy1, Exercise Behavior2 SE1 → SE2 → EB2	–.5226	.4184*	–.1042
Exercise Behavior1, Social Support2	–	–	–
Exercise Behavior1, Self-Efficacy2	–	–	–
Exercise Behavior1, Exercise Behavior2	.8405*	–	.8405
Social Support2, Self-Efficacy2	.4494*	–	.4494
Social Support2, Exercise Behavior2 SS2 → SE2 → EB2	–	.2931*	.2931
Self-Efficacy2, Exercise Behavior2	.6521*	–	.6521

Note: SS = Social Support; SE = Self-Efficacy; EB = Exercise Behavior; TI = Total indirect.
*$p < .05$.

of social support at time 1 on self-efficacy at time 2 is not statistically significant ($-.2141 \times .6521 = -.1396$). The indirect effect of self-efficacy at time 1 on exercise behavior at time 2 via self-efficacy at time 2 is statistically significant ($.6416 \times .6521 = .4184$). Finally, the indirect effect of social support at time 2 on exercise behavior at time 2 via self-efficacy at time 2 is statistically significant ($.4494 \times .6521 = .2931$; see Table 16.39).

16.12 SEM CONSIDERATIONS

As with any statistical technique, satisfying assumptions related to the properties of the data and/or the parameterization of a model in SEM is necessary for making appropriate inferences. In this section, some of these issues will be presented. Because a thorough discussion of these issues is beyond the scope of this chapter, you will be provided with relevant references for further reading (see Kaplan, 2009, and Kline, 2011, for more information concerning these issues as well).

16.12.1 Assumptions and Properties of the Data in SEM

One of the main assumptions in SEM analyses is that the scores for endogenous variables follow a multivariate normal distribution. When using ML estimation or other normal theory estimators, the assumption of normality is necessary to obtain accurate model fit statistics and parameter estimates with their associated standard errors. As previously discussed, when endogenous variables are extremely nonnormal and/or categorical in nature, alternative estimators must be implemented to ensure appropriate conclusions concerning the findings. Methods to assessing normality were described in Chapter 6 of this text.

As in multiple regression analyses, the models in SEM are assumed to be correctly specified. As mentioned previously, model misspecification may occur because of omitted relationships that should be included in the model or relationships included in the model are irrelevant and should be excluded from the model. Specification searches using the LM/MI tests and/or the EPC may lead to the identification of an omitted relevant relationship in the model (Saris et al., 2009) whereas the Wald test may lead to the identification of irrelevant relationships in the model. Nevertheless, studies have shown that specification searches do not always correctly lead a researcher to the true model in the population (MacCallum, 1986). Omitted relationships may also be due to not measuring variables that may be relevant. Although omitted relationships are generally considered more serious than the alternative of including an irrelevant relationship, both misspecification errors can result in biased parameter estimates (Kaplan, 2009). This assumption is difficult to confidently satisfy in practice because researchers may not be aware of all germane predictors to include in a model. Accordingly, understanding the relationships among germane predictors based on the relevant theory is crucial in order to reduce potential misspecification errors.

Missing data is an unfortunate byproduct of needing humans to participate in research studies in the social and behavioral studies. There are texts and courses dedicated solely to this topic, and Chapter 1 of this text provides an introduction to missing data analysis. Needless to say, it is a researcher's responsibility to try to understand the missing data mechanisms. Little (1988) proposed a test that can detect whether data are missing completely at random (MCAR; see Craig Ender's webpage for a SAS macro that will conduct this test: https://webapp4.asu.edu/directory/person/839490). A procedure to detect whether or not data are missing at random (MAR) in models with latent variables incorporated has been suggested by Falcaro, Pendleton, & Pickles, 2013). Methods that deal with data that are MCAR or MAR are available (e.g., full information maximum likelihood and multiple imputation methods) that work well when recovering parameter estimates. When data are not missing at random (NMAR), however, other advanced methods developed that account for the missing data trigger may be implemented (Enders, 2011; Little, 1994; Little & Rubin, 1987; Schafer & Graham, 2002). Longitudinal data will most likely result in missing data across measurement times for various expected reasons, such as fatigue, illness, or other human factors (moving, time constraints). However, missing data could be a function of the outcome of interest in longitudinal studies (e.g., when collecting data on health outcomes for a sample of participants with cancer). At a minimum, researchers should examine potential sources of missing data and implement a missing data treatment that has been shown to perform well under MAR conditions (e.g., FIML). Of course, researchers should also mention the limitations associated with the uncertainty of the missing data mechanism.

A frequently asked question by students and researchers of SEM is one that deals with sample size requirements when analyzing different models. The answer is not as straightforward as they would like. This is because the answer depends upon the complexity of the model being analyzed, the relationships among variables in the model, and the estimator being used (Worthington & Whittaker, 2006). SEM is based on large sample theory and large samples are necessary to avoid convergence problems and unstable parameter estimates. Generally, it is recommended that a sample size of at least 200 be used for SEM analyses (Kline, 2011). Further, given the relationship between sample size and model complexity, it is recommended that sample size be decided using the $N{:}q$ or number of participants (N) to number of parameters to estimate (q) ratio. Bentler and Chou (1987) recommended that this ratio be at a minimum 5:1 and more optimally 10:1. Jackson (2003) recommended an optimal ratio of 20:1 for increased confidence in the results. Thus, researchers should strive to meet the 20:1 ratio if feasible without falling below the 5:1 ratio of sample size to parameters to estimate.

16.12.2 Model Typology

It is important to briefly discuss a general model typology used in SEM in case you run across the terms. This typology can apply to both observed and latent variable path models. Two different types of models exist in the SEM arena: recursive and nonrecursive

models. Recursive models are less complicated than nonrecursive models and generally do not include error/disturbance covariances or what are called feedback loops. In
contrast, nonrecursive models may include error/disturbance covariances or feedback
loops. For instance, the models in Figures 16.1–16.4 and in Figures 16.6–16.10 are
all examples of recursive models. Another example of a recursive model is shown in
Figure 16.16 in which the errors of two endogenous variables are allowed to covary.
Although the errors covary in this model, it is recursive because neither endogenous
variable has a direct effect on the other. Some refer to this type of model as partially
recursive. In contrast, the model illustrated in Figure 16.17 is a nonrecursive model
because a direct effect from Y1 to Y2 is also modeled, which results in a reciprocal
pattern of causation between Y1 and Y2 (i.e., Y1 → Y2 ↔ Y1).

▪ **Figure 16.16** Recursive observed variable path model.

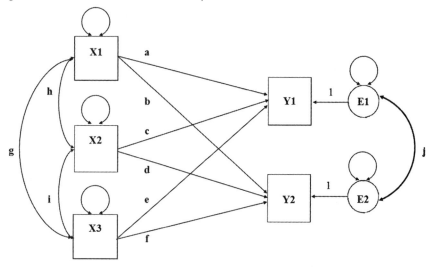

▪ **Figure 16.17** Nonrecursive observed variable path model.

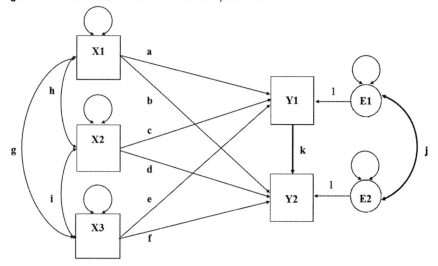

Another example of a nonrecursive model with a direct feedback loop is shown in Figure 16.18. In Figure 16.18, Y1 is hypothesized to directly affect Y2, which in turn is hypothesized to directly affect Y1. When direct feedback loops are considered, they appear in studies having cross-sectional data or data collected at a single time point. This is because you are specifying that the two variables involved are reciprocally related or that both variables are the cause of and affected by the other variable. As such, temporal precedence is not a consideration for these relationships. An example of an indirect feedback loop is demonstrated in Figure 16.19.

■ **Figure 16.18** Nonrecursive observed variable path model with a direct feedback loop.

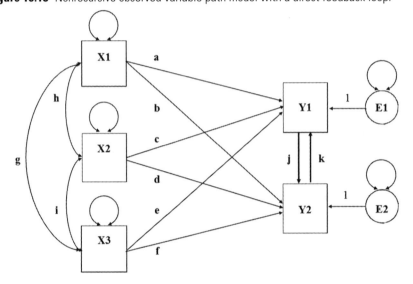

■ **Figure 16.19** Nonrecursive observed variable path model with an indirect feedback loop.

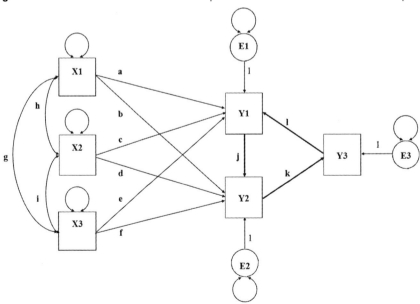

These feedback loops include three or more variables and create a reciprocal pattern of causation among the variables involved. In this example, Y1 directly affects Y2, which in turn directly affects Y3, which, in turn directly affects Y1. The major implications with respect to the differentiation between these two types of models deals with identification and estimation. As a general rule, a recursive model is an identified model and, thus, its parameters are able to be estimated. On the other hand, identification of a nonrecursive model may prove more difficult, and, thus, estimation of its parameters may not be possible (if under-identified) or the estimation process may encounter problems. For instance, correlations greater than 1.0 or negative variances may result from modeling relationships in nonrecursive models. In the end, theory should guide the specification of these models and you should determine if the model will be identified prior to estimation. See Bollen (1989) and Kline (2011) for more information concerning nonrecursive models.

16.12.3 Equivalent Models

Another consideration in SEM is the issue of equivalent models. Equivalent models are those in which the causal relationships among variables are specified differently, yet mathematically, they result in identical implied covariance matrices. Consequently, equivalent models are indistinguishable with respect to fit criteria because they fit the data identically. These types of models may occur with observed variable path models, CFA models, and latent variable path models. For instance, the four models in Figure 16.20 are equivalent observed variable path models. The variances of exogenous variables, errors, and path letters are excluded for illustrative simplicity. It is important to note that because errors are omitted from these diagrams, the covariance between X1 and X2 in Figure 16.20c is actually the covariance between the errors for X1 and X2.

■ **Figure 16.20** Four equivalent observed variable path models.

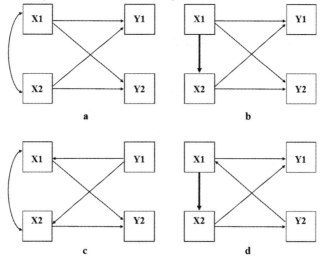

Notice that the four models portray quite different theoretical connections between some of the variables. For instance, the covariance between X1 and X2 in Figure 16.20a and 16.20c symbolizes a different relationship between these two variables as compared to the direct effect of X1 on X2 as in Figure 16.20b and 16.20d. The direct effects linking X1 and Y2 as well as X2 and Y1 also change causal direction in these equivalent models. The implications of equivalent models are that they cannot be distinguished based on model fit because of the mathematical equivalencies of models. Thus, knowledge of the relevant theory is necessary to make more appropriate decisions concerning the direction of causal relationships in a model. Further, you should also evaluate the parameter estimates in equivalent models to ensure their plausibility.

Equivalent models are often not considered by researchers but warrant some consideration in studies in which causal directions among the variables of interest are not clearly prescribed. For instance, MacCallum, Wegener, Uchino, and Fabrigar (1993) conducted a study concerning equivalent models and included the following in their discussion:

> A tempting way to manage the problem with equivalent models is to argue that the original model is more compelling and defensible than the equivalent models because of its a priori status. That is, because the original model was developed from theory or prior research or both and was found to yield an interpretable solution and adequate fit to the data, it is inherently more justifiable as a meaningful explanation of the data than the alternative equivalent models. We believe, however, that such a defense would often be the product of wishful thinking. This argument implies that no other equally good explanation of the data is plausible as the researcher's a priori model simply because the researcher did not generate the alternatives a priori. Such a position ignores the possibilities that prior research and theoretical development might not have been adequate or complete, that the researcher might not have been aware of alternative theoretical views, or that the researcher simply did not think of reasonable alternative models of the relationships among the variables under study. (p. 197)

16.13 ADDITIONAL MODELS IN SEM

While space is not available to offer detailed explanations of additional modeling techniques in the SEM arena, a brief synopsis of techniques available in SEM will be provided. All of the models discussed in this chapter have involved using data collected from a single group of participants. SEM is a popular tool with which models may be compared for multiple groups. All of the models described in this chapter can be used in a multiple-group analysis context. Briefly, multiple-group in SEM allows tests of whether certain model parameters of interest (e.g., causal paths, factor loadings, covariances) are the same or unequal across groups. This technique is a common method to test for invariance or equivalence in models at various levels (measurement and structural) across groups. Invariance testing is a vast area of study in SEM and a thorough explanation of this topic is beyond the scope of this chapter (see Vandenberg & Lance, 2000, for more information concerning this topic).

Just as in multiple regression, models in SEM may include interaction terms among the variables. These variables may be observed and/or unobserved. With observed variables, products of two variables may be created to represent their interaction. Latent variable interactions may also be analyzed using SEM techniques. Various methods are available when creating interaction terms among latent factors (see, e.g., Marsh, Wen, & Hau, 2006).

Two SEM techniques allow comparisons of the mean of factors across groups. For instance, a researcher may be interested in whether differences exist between males and females on a factor used to represent math anxiety. One of the techniques that can assess this difference involves regressing a factor (e.g., math anxiety) on a dummy coded predictor (e.g., sex) or a set of dummy-coded predictors (e.g., undergraduate major). The direct path from the dummy-coded sex variable to the math anxiety factor would indicate the difference, on average, between males and females on math anxiety. This model is commonly referred to as a multiple indicator multiple cause or MIMIC model (Jöreskog & Goldberger, 1975). The second technique that can assess mean differences on factors across groups is structured means modeling (SMM; Sörbom, 1974), which actually incorporates a mean structure in a multiple group model. Factor mean difference estimates can then be estimated by way of regressing the factor on a constant. Effect sizes associated with these factor mean differences can also be calculated for aid in interpretation (Hancock, 2001).

In addition, longitudinal data may be analyzed in SEM using various techniques, particularly using what is called latent growth curve modeling (LGCM). LGCM allows individual growth in outcomes of interest to be modeled across three or more measurement occasions (three is necessary for identification purposes). A latent growth curve model is similar to a CFA model in which each indicator is an outcome measured at each measurement occasion. A basic latent growth curve model includes two factors that are used to characterize two dimensions of growth or change across time. One factor is the Intercept factor, which indicates the standing of the participants on the measured outcome (e.g., reading score) at a specified time-based reference point. The second factor is the Slope factor, which captures the participants' linear growth trajectory on the measured outcome across time. Observed and/or unobserved predictors of the intercept and slope factors may be modeled to explain their variability. The flexibility of LGCM allows equally spaced or unequally spaced measurement occasions to be modeled as well as nonlinear trajectories (Hancock & Lawrence, 2006). In addition, multivariate extensions of the basic LGCM may be easily modeled (McArdle, 1988; Sayer & Cumsille, 2001).

Further, in the social and behavioral sciences, data commonly exhibit dependencies in the form of clustering or nested groups. For instance, data may be collected from participants who attend the same class or attend the same therapy group. The data for the participants that share a common teacher or therapist cannot be assumed to be independent. That is, outcomes for participants in the same cluster (e.g., class or therapy group) will share similarities in their outcomes due to the influence of a common source (e.g., same teacher or same therapist). This dependency, if not accounted for in statistical analyses, including SEM, may result in standard error estimates that are smaller than they would be if this dependency did not exist. Consequently, type I error rates associated with significance tests of parameter estimates may be inflated (Snijders & Bosker, 1999). Multilevel modeling methods (as presented in Chapters 13 and 14 in this text) are available to appropriately account for the variability in outcomes due to the clustering or nesting structure and adjust the standard errors associated with parameter estimates for these dependencies among the data. These methods are also available in the SEM arena and may be applied to any of the techniques introduced in this chapter and beyond. Multilevel SEM is a flexible tool that allows structural equation models to be analyzed while incorporating the appropriate statistical adjustments when dependencies due to nesting or clustering exist in the data responses (Rabe-Hesketh, Skrondal, & Zheng, 2012; Stapleton, 2006).

A technique growing in popularity in the SEM arena is mixture modeling. Mixture modeling provides model parameter estimates from different populations that are not directly identifiable by observed classifications, which is the case when using multiple group SEM analyses. Mixture models may be comprised of observed and latent variable path models, CFA models, latent growth models, and variants of these models (see Gagné, 2006, for an introduction to mixture models in SEM). Mixture modeling allows researchers to examine the differences or heterogeneity in a model's parameters as a function of a grouping variable that is unobserved or latent. For instance, a researcher may postulate that measures of academic self-concept are more reliable for certain groups of high school kids, but an explicit measure that agrees with the grouping (e.g., low vs. high need for achievement in school) may not be available. In consequence, the researcher first uses the data to inform whether or not heterogeneity exists in a model's parameter estimates. The number of latent classes or unobserved groups hypothesized to produce these differences must be specified by the researcher. The parameter estimates from the mixture model and the characteristics observed in the data are then used to help with the interpretation of the results. For instance, the researcher examining academic self-concept may find support for a three latent-class factor model. After considering the results and information concerning the high school kids in the dataset, the researcher may be able to discover what characterizes membership in each of the three latent classes (e.g., low, moderate, and high involvement in school).

16.14 FINAL THOUGHTS

SEM is a popular and flexible tool that may be used to answer a number of research questions in the social and behavioral sciences. Nonetheless, it is a mathematical tool that is often used in the context of nonexperimental studies. As such, it is the user's responsibility to ensure that the appropriate assumptions are supported and the inferences are soundly based on theory and the proper causal stipulations. When we find support for a model using model fit information, there are alternative models and/ or equivalent models that may fit just as well or identically. Model fit and specification searches lend themselves to minimizing errors within specific samples. Thus, cross-validation, which is commonly neglected, is highly suggested when conducting SEM analyses, particularly if any model modifications have been performed. See Breckler (1990) and Cliff (1983) for a review of mistakes commonly made in SEM and recommendations for best practices in SEM.

Once again, the importance of theory in SEM cannot be overstated. It is what guides model building and respecification and it informs us of the plausibility of parameter estimates. To end, we would like to conclude with a statement written by Wolfe (1985) when considering what is easy and what is difficult when analyzing causal models. He wrote that "the easy part is mathematical. The hard part is constructing causal models that are consistent with sound theory. In short, causal models are no better than the ideas that go with them" (p. 385).

REFERENCES

Akaike, H. (1973). Information theory and an extension of the maximum likelihood principle. In B. N. Petrov and F. Csaki (Eds.), *Second international symposium on information theory.* Budapest: Akademiai Kiado.

Anderson, J.C., & Gerbing, D.W. (1988). Structural equation modeling in practice: A review and recommended two-step approach. *Psychological Bulletin, 103*(3), 411–423.

Bandalos, D.L. (1993). Factors influencing cross-validation of confirmatory factor analysis models. *Multivariate Behavioral Research, 28*(3), 351–374.

Baron, R.M., & Kenny, D.A. (1986). The moderator-mediator variable distinction in social psychology research: Conceptual, strategic, and statistical considerations. *Journal of Personality and Social Psychology, 51*(6), 1173–1182.

Beauducel, A., & Herzberg, P.Y. (2006). On the performance of maximum likelihood versus means and variance adjusted weighted least square estimation in confirmatory factor analysis. *Structural Equation Modeling, 13*(2), 186–203.

Bentler, P.M. (1990). Comparative fit indexes in structural models. *Psychological Bulletin, 107*(2), 238–246.

Bentler, P.M. (1995). *EQS structural equations program manual.* Los Angeles, CA: BMDP Statistical Software.

Bentler, P.M., & Bonett, D.G. (1980). Significance tests and goodness of fit in the analysis of covariance structures. *Psychological Bulletin, 88*(3), 588–606.

Bentler, P.M., & Chou, C-P. (1987). Practical issues in structural modeling. *Sociological Methods & Research, 16*(1), 78–117.

Bollen, K.A. (1986). Sample size and Bentler and Bonnett's nonnormed fit index. *Psychometrika, 51*(3), 375–377.

Bollen, K.A. (1989). *Structural equations with latent variables.* New York: John Wiley & Sons.

Bozdogan, H. (1987). Model selection and Akaike's information criterion (AIC): The general theory and its analytical extensions. *Psychometrika, 52*(3), 345–370.

Breckler, S. J. (1990). Applications of covariance structure modeling in psychology: Cause for concern? *Psychological Bulletin, 107*(2), 260–273.

Brown, T.A. (2015). *Confirmatory factor analysis for applied research* (2nd ed.). New York: Guilford Press.

Browne, M.W. (1984). Asymptotic distribution free methods in the analysis of covariance structures. *British Journal of Mathematical and Statistical Psychology, 37*(1), 62–83.

Browne, M.W., & Cudeck, R. (1989). Single sample cross-validation indices for covariance structures. *Multivariate Behavioral Research, 24*(4), 445–455.

Browne, M.W., & Cudeck, R. (1993). Alternative ways of assessing model fit. In K.A. Bollen & J.S. Long (Eds.), *Testing structural equation models* (pp. 136–162). Newbury Park, CA: Sage.

Byrne, B.M. (1998). *Structural equation modeling with LISREL, PRELIS, and SIMPLIS: Basic concepts, applications, and programming.* Mahwah, NJ: Erlbaum.

Byrne, B.M. (2006). *Structural equation modeling with EQS: Basic concepts, applications, and programming* (2nd ed.). Mahwah, NJ: Erlbaum.

Byrne, B.M. (2010). *Structural equation modeling with Amos: Basic concepts, applications, and Programming* (2nd ed.). Mahwah, NJ: Erlbaum.

Byrne, B.M. (2012a). *Structural equation modeling with Mplus: Basic concepts, applications, and programming.* New York, NY: Taylor & Francis Group.

Byrne, B.M. (2012b). Choosing structural equation modeling computer software: Snapshots of LISREL, EQS, Amos, and Mplus. In R.H. Hoyle (Ed.), *Handbook of structural equation modeling* (pp. 307–324). New York, NY: Guilford Press.

Cheung, G.W., & Rensvold, R.B. (1999). Testing factorial invariance across groups: A reconceptualization and proposed new method. *Journal of Management, 25*(1), 1–27.

Cheung, G.W., & Rensvold, R.B. (2002). Evaluating goodness-of-fit indexes for testing measurement invariance. *Structural Equation Modeling, 9*(2), 233–255.

Chou, C-P., & Bentler, P.M. (1990). Model modification in covariance structure modeling: A comparison among likelihood ratio, Lagrange multiplier, and Wald tests. *Multivariate Behavioral Research, 25*(1), 115–136.

Chou, C-P., & Bentler, P.M. (1993). Invariant standardized estimated parameter change for model modification in covariance structure analysis. *Multivariate Behavioral Research, 28*(1), 97–110.

Chou, C-P., Bentler, P.M., & Satorra, A. (1991). Scaled test statistics and robust standard errors for non-normal data in covariance structure analysis: A Monte Carlo study. *British Journal of Mathematical and Statistical Psychology, 44*(2), 347–357.

Cliff, N. (1983). Some cautions concerning the application of causal modeling methods. *Multivariate Behavioral Research, 18*(1), 115–126.

Cohen, J., & Cohen, P. (1983). *Applied multiple regression/correlation analysis for the behavioral sciences.* Hillsdale, NJ: Erlbaum.

Cudeck, R., & Browne, M.W. (1983). Cross-validation of covariance structures. *Multivariate Behavioral Research, 18*(2), 147–167.

Curran, P. J., West, S. G., & Finch, J. F. (1996). The robustness of test statistics to nonnormality and specification error in confirmatory factor analysis. *Psychological Methods, 1*(1), 16–29.

Davis, J. A. (1985). *The logic of causal order*. Beverly Hills, CA: Sage.

DiStefano, C. (2002). The impact of categorization with confirmatory factor analysis. *Structural Equation Modeling, 9*(3), 327–346.

Dolan, C. V. (1994). Factor analysis of variables with 2, 3, 5 and 7 response categories: A comparison of categorical variable estimators using simulated data. *British Journal of Mathematical and Statistical Psychology, 47*(2), 309–326.

Duncan, T. E., & Stoolmiller, M. (1993). Modeling social and psychological determinants of exercise behaviors via structural equation systems. *Research Quarterly for Exercise and Sport, 64*(1), 1–16.

Enders, C. (2011). Missing not at random models for latent growth curve analyses. *Structural Equation Modeling, 16*(1), 1–16.

Falcaro, M., Pendleton, N., & Pickles, A. (2013). Analysing censored longitudinal data with non-ignorable missing values: Depression in older age. *Journal of the Royal Statistical Society: Series A (Statistics in Society), 176*(2), 415–430.

Fan, X., & Sivo, S. A. (1995). Sensitivity of fit indexes to misspecified structural or measurement model components: Rationale of two-index strategy revisited. *Structural Equation Modeling, 12*(3), 343–367.

Ferron, J. M., & Hess, M. R. (2007). Estimation in SEM: A concrete example. *Journal of Educational and Behavioral Statistics, 32*(1), 110–120.

Finney, S. J., & DiStefano, C. (2006). Non-normal and categorical data in structural equation modeling. In G. R. Hancock & R. O. Mueller (Eds.), *Structural equation modeling: A second course* (pp. 269–314). Greenwich, CT: Information Age.

Flora, D. B., & Curran, P. J. (2004). An empirical evaluation of alternative methods of estimation for confirmatory factor analysis with ordinal data. *Psychological Methods, 9*(4), 466–491.

Forero, C. G., & Maydeu-Olivares, A. (2009). Estimation of IRT graded response models: Limited versus full information methods. *Psychological Methods, 14*(3), 275–299.

Gagné, P. (2006). Mean and covariance structure mixture models. In G. R. Hancock & R. O. Mueller (Eds.), *Structural equation modeling: A second course* (pp. 197–224). Greenwich, CT: Information Age.

Galassi, J. P., Schanberg, R., & Ware, W. B. (1992). The Patient Reactions Assessment: A brief measure of the quality of the patient-provider relationship. *Psychological Assessment, 4*(3), 346–351.

Hancock, G. R. (2001). Effect size, power, and sample size determination for structured means modeling and MIMIC approaches to between-groups hypothesis testing of means on a single latent construct. *Psychometrika, 66*(3), 373–388.

Hancock, G. R., & Lawrence, F. R. (2006). Using latent growth models to evaluate longitudinal change. In G. R. Hancock & R. O. Mueller (Eds.), *Structural equation modeling: A second course* (pp. 171–196). Greenwich, CT: Information Age.

Hancock, G. R., Stapleton, L. M., & Arnold-Berkovits, I. (2009). The tenuousness of invariance tests within multisample covariance and mean structure models. In T. Teo & M. S. Khine

(Eds.), *Structural equation modeling: Concepts and applications in educational research* (pp. 137–174). Rotterdam, Netherlands: Sense.

Haughton, D.M.A., Oud, J.H.L., & Jansen, R.A.R.G. (1997). Information and other criteria in structural equation model selection. *Communication in Statistics. Part B: Simulation & Computation, 26*(4), 1477–1516.

Hoogland, J.J., & Boomsma, A. (1998). Robustness studies in covariance structure modeling: An overview and meta-analysis. *Sociological Methods & Research, 26*(3), 329–367.

Howard, G.S., & Maxwell, S.E. (1982). Do grades contaminate student evaluations of instruction? *Research in Higher Education, 16*(2), 175–188.

Hu, L., & Bentler, P. (1995). Evaluating model fit. In R.H. Hoyle (Ed.), *Structural equation modeling. Concepts, issues, and applications* (pp. 76–99). London: Sage.

Hu, L., & Bentler, P.M. (1998). Fit indices in covariance structure modeling: Sensitivity to underparameterized model misspecification. *Psychological Methods, 3*(4), 424–453.

Hu, L., & Bentler, P.M. (1999). Cutoff criteria for fit indexes in covariance structure analysis: Conventional criteria versus new alternatives. *Structural Equation Modeling, 6*(1), 1–55.

Hu, L., Bentler, P.M., & Kano, Y. (1992). Can test statistics in covariance structure analysis be trusted? *Psychological Bulletin, 112*(2), 351–362.

Hutchinson, S.R. (1993). Univariate and multivariate specification search indices in covariance structure modeling. *Journal of Experimental Education, 61*(2), 171–181.

Jackson, D.L. (2003). Revisiting sample size and number of parameter estimates: Some support for the N:q hypothesis. *Structural Equation Modeling, 10*(1), 128–141.

Jöreskog, K.G. (n.d.). Why are *t*-values for error variances equal? A paradox in path models for observed variables. Retrieved from http://www.ssicentral.com/lisrel/resources.html#t

Jöreskog, K.G., & Goldberger, A.S. (1975). Estimation of a model with multiple indicators and multiple causes of a single latent variable. *Journal of the American Statistical Association, 70*(351), 631–639.

Jöreskog, K.G., & Sörbom, D. (1984). *LISREL VI user's guide* (3rd ed.). Mooresville, IN: Scientific Software.

Jöreskog, K.G., & Sörbom, D. (1996). *LISREL 8: User's reference guide*. Chicago, IL: Scientific Software International.

Kaplan, D. (1988). The impact of specification error on the estimation, testing, and improvement of structural equation models. *Multivariate Behavioral Research, 23*(1), 69–86.

Kaplan, D. (1989). Model modification in covariance structure analysis: Application of the expected parameter change statistic. *Multivariate Behavioral Research, 24*(3), 285–305.

Kaplan, D. (2009). *Structural equation modeling: Foundations and extensions* (2nd ed.). Thousand Oaks, CA: Sage.

Kenny, D.A., & Milan, S. (2012). Identification: A nontechnical discussion of a technical issue. In R.H. Hoyle (Ed.), *Handbook of structural equation modeling* (pp. 145–163). New York, NY: Guilford Press.

Kline, R. (2011). *Principles and practice of structural equation modeling* (3rd ed.). New York, NY: Guilford Press.

Lei, P.-W., & Wu, Q. (2012). Estimation in structural equation modeling. In R.H. Hoyle (Ed.), *Handbook of structural equation modeling* (pp. 164–180). New York, NY: Guilford Press.

Little, R.J.A. (1988). A test of missing completely at random for multivariate data with missing values. *Journal of the American Statistical Association, 83*(404), 1198–1202.

Little, R.J.A. (1994). A class of pattern-mixture models for normal incomplete data. *Biometrika, 81*(3), 471–483.

Little, R.J.A., & Rubin, D.B. (1987). *Statistical analysis with missing data.* New York, NY: Wiley.

Loehlin, J.C. (2004). *Latent variable models* (4th ed.). Mahwah, NJ: Erlbaum.

Luijben, T.C.W. (1989). *Statistical guidance for model modification in covariance structure analysis.* Amsterdam: Sociometric Research Foundation.

Luijben, T.C., & Boomsma, A. (1988). Statistical guidance for model modification in covariance structure analysis. *Compstat 1988*, 335–340.

MacCallum, R.C. (1986). Specification searches in covariance structure analysis. *Psychological Bulletin, 100*(1), 107–120.

MacCallum, R.C., Roznowski, M., & Necowitz, L.B. (1992). Model modifications in covariance structure analysis: The problem of capitalization on chance. *Psychological Bulletin, 111*(3), 490–504.

MacCallum, R.C., Wegener, D.T., Uchino, B.N., & Fabrigar, L.R. (1993). The problem of equivalent models in applications of covariance structure analysis. *Psychological Bulletin, 114*(1), 185–199.

MacKinnon, D.P., Fairchild, A.J., & Fritz, M.S. (2007). Mediation analysis. *Annual Review of Psychology, 58*(1), 593–614.

MacKinnon, D.P., Fritz, M.S., Williams, J., & Lockwood, C.M. (2007). Distribution of the product confidence limits for the indirect effect: Program PRODCLIN. *Behavior Research Methods, 39*(3), 384–389.

MacKinnon, D.P., Lockwood, C.M., Hoffman, J.M., West, S.G., & Sheets, V. (2002). A comparison of methods to test mediated and other intervening variable effects. *Psychological Methods, 7*(1), 83–104.

Marsh, H.W., Hau, K.-T., & Wen, Z. (2004). In search of golden rules: Comment on hypothesis-testing approaches to setting cutoff values for fit indexes and dangers in overgeneralizing Hu and Bentler's findings. *Structural Equation Modeling, 11*(3), 320–341.

Marsh, H.W., Wen, Z., & Hau, K.-T. (2006). Structural equation models of latent interaction and quadratic effects. In G.R. Hancock & R.O. Mueller (Eds.), *Structural equation modeling: A second course* (pp. 225–265). Greenwich, CT: Information Age.

McArdle, J.J. (1988). Dynamic but structural equation modeling of repeated measures data. In J.R. Nesselroade & R.B. Cattell (Eds.), *Handbook of multivariate experimental psychology* (Vol. 2, pp. 561–614). New York, NY: Plenum Press.

McDonald, R.P. (1989). An index of goodness-of-fit based on noncentrality. *Journal of Classification, 6*(1), 97–103.

Meade, A.W., Johnson, E.C., & Braddy, P.W. (2008). Power and sensitivity of alternative fit indices in tests of measurement invariance. *Journal of Applied Psychology, 93*(3), 568–592.

Mueller, R.O. (1988). The impact of college selectivity on income for men and women. *Research in Higher Education, 29*(2), 175–191.

Mulaik, S.A. (2009). *Linear causal modeling with structural equations.* Boca Raton, FL: Chapman & Hall/CRC.

Mulaik, S.A., & Millsap, R.E. (2000). Doing the four-step right. *Structural Equation Modeling, 7*(1), 36–73.

Muthén, B., du Toit, S.H.C., & Spisic, D. (1997). *Robust inference using weighted least squares and quadratic estimating equations in latent variable modeling with categorical and continuous outcomes.* Retrieved from http://pages.gseis.ucla.edu/ faculty/ muthen/ articles/Article_075.pdf

Muthén, B., & Kaplan, D. (1985). A comparison of some methodologies for the factor analysis of non-normal Likert variables. *British Journal of Mathematical and Statistical Psychology, 38*(2), 171–189.

Muthén, B., & Kaplan, D. (1992). A comparison of some methodologies for the factor analysis of non-normal Likert variables: A note on the size of the model. *British Journal of Mathematical and Statistical Psychology, 45*(1), 19–30.

Olsson, U.H., Foss, T., Troye, S.V., & Howell, R.D. (2000). The performance of ML, GLS, and WLS estimation in structural equation modeling under conditions of misspecification and nonnormality. *Structural Equation Modeling, 7*(4), 557–595.

Pearl, J. (2000). *Causality: Models, reasoning, and inference.* New York, NY: Cambridge University Press.

Pearl, J. (2012). The causal foundations of structural equation modeling. In R.H. Hoyle (Ed.), *Handbook of structural equation modeling* (pp. 68–91). New York, NY: Guilford Press.

Preacher, K.J., & Hayes, A.F. (2008). Asymptotic and resampling strategies for assessing and comparing indirect effects in multiple mediator models. *Behavior Research Methods, 40*(3), 879–891.

Rabe-Hesketh, S., Skrondal, A., & Zheng, X. (2012). Multilevel structural equation modeling. In R.H. Hoyle (Ed.), *Handbook of structural equation modeling* (pp. 512–531). New York, NY: Guilford Press.

Sarason, I.G. (1984). Stress, anxiety, and cognitive interference: Reactions to tests. *Journal of Personality and Social Psychology, 46*(4), 929–938.

Saris, W.E., Satorra, A., & Sörbom, D. (1987). The detection and correction of specification errors in structural equation models. In C.C. Clogg (Ed.), *Sociological Methodology* (pp. 105–129). San Francisco, CA: Jossey-Bass.

Saris, W.E., Satorra, A., & van der Veld, W.M. (2009). Testing structural equation models or detection of misspecifications? *Structural Equation Modeling, 16*(4), 561–582.

Satorra, A. (1989). Alternative test criteria in covariance structure analysis: A unified approach. *Psychometrika, 54*(1), 131–151.

Satorra, A., & Bentler, P.M. (1994). Corrections to test statistics and standard errors in covariance structure analysis. In A. von Eye & C.C. Clogg (Eds.), *Latent variables analysis: Applications for developmental research* (pp. 399–419). Thousand Oaks, CA: Sage.

Satorra, A., & Bentler, P.M. (2001). A scaled difference chi-square test statistic for moment structure analysis. *Psychometrika, 66*(4), 507–514.

Sayer, A.G., & Cumsille, P.E. (2001). Second-order latent growth models. In L.M. Collins & A.G. Sayer (Eds.), *New methods for the analysis of change* (pp. 179–200). Washington, DC: American Psychological Association.

Schafer, J.L., & Graham, J.W. (2002). Missing data: Our view of the state of the art. *Psychological Methods, 7*(2), 147–177.

Shrout, P.E., & Bolger, N. (2002). Mediation in experimental and nonexperimental studies: New procedures and recommendations. *Psychological Methods, 7*(2), 422–445.

Silvia, E.M., & MacCallum, R.C. (1988). Some factors affecting the success of specification searches in covariance structure modeling. *Multivariate Behavioral Research, 23*(3), 297–326.

Snijders, T.A.B., & Bosker, R.J. (1999). Multilevel analysis: An introduction to basic and advanced multilevel modeling. London: Sage.

Sobel, M.E. (1995). Causal inference in the social and behavioral sciences. In G. Arminger, C.C. Clogg, & M.E. Sobel (Eds.), *Handbook of statistical modeling for the social and behavioral sciences* (pp. 1–35). New York, NY: Plenum.

Schwarz, G. (1978). Estimating the dimension of a model. *Annals of Statistics, 6*(2), 461–464.

Shibata, R. (1976). Selection of the order of an autoregressive model by Akaike's information criterion. *Biometrika, 63*(1), 117–126.

Sobel, M.E. (1982). Asymptotic intervals for indirect effects in structural equations models. In S. Leinhart (Ed.), *Sociological methodology 1982* (pp. 290–312). San Francisco, CA: Jossey-Bass.

Sörbom, D. (1974). A general method for studying differences in factor means and factor structure between groups. *British Journal of Mathematical and Statistical Psychology, 27*(2), 229–239.

Sörbom, D. (1989). Model modification. *Psychometrika, 54*(3), 371–384.

Stapleton, L.M. (2006). Using multilevel structural equation modeling techniques with complex sample data. In G.R. Hancock & R.O. Mueller (Eds.), *Structural equation modeling: A second course* (pp. 345–383). Greenwich, CT: Information Age.

Steiger, J.H., & Lind, J.C. (1980, May). *Statistically based tests for the number of common factors*. Paper presented at the annual meeting of the Psychometric Society, Iowa City, IA.

Tofighi, D., & MacKinnon, D.P. (2011). Rmediation: An R package for mediation analysis confidence limits. *Behavior Research Methods, 43*(3), 692–700.

Tucker, L.R., & Lewis, C. (1973). A reliability coefficient for maximum likelihood factor analysis. *Psychometrika, 38*(1), 1–10.

Vandenberg, R.J., & Lance, C.E. (2000). A review and synthesis of the measurement invariance literature: Suggestions, practices, and recommendations for organizational research. *Organizational Research Methods, 3*(1), 4–69.

West, S.G., Taylor, A.B., & Wu, W. (2012). Model fit and model selection in structural equation modeling. In R.H. Hoyle (Ed.), *Handbook of structural equation modeling* (pp. 209–231). New York, NY: Guilford Press.

Whittaker, T.A. (2012). Using the modification index and standardized expected parameter change for model modification. *Journal of Experimental Education, 80*(1), 26–44.

Whittaker, T.A., & Stapleton, L.M. (2006). The performance of cross-validation indices used to select among competing covariance structure models under multivariate nonnormality conditions. *Multivariate Behavioral Research, 41*(3), 295–335.

Wolfe, L.M. (1985). Applications of causal models in higher education. In J.C. Smart (Ed.), *Higher education: Handbook of theory and research* (Vol. 1, pp. 381–413). New York, NY: Agathon.

Worthington, R.L., & Whittaker, T.A. (2006). Scale development research: A content analysis and recommendations for best practices. *Counseling Psychologist, 34*(6), 806–838.

Yoon, M., & Millsap, R.E. (2007). Detecting violations of factorial invariance using data-based specification searches: A Monte Carlo study. *Structural Equation Modeling, 14*(3), 435–463.

Yuan, K.-H. (2005). Fit indices versus test statistics. *Multivariate Behavioral Research, 40*(1), 115–148.

APPENDIX 16.1

Abbreviated SAS Output for Final Observed Variable Path Model

Fit Summary		
Modeling Info	Number of Observations	3094
	Number of Variables	6
	Number of Moments	21
	Number of Parameters	18
	Number of Active Constraints	0
	Baseline Model Function Value	0.4593
	Baseline Model Chi-Square	1420.6759
	Baseline Model Chi-Square DF	15
	Pr > Baseline Model Chi-Square	<.0001
Absolute Index	Fit Function	0.0025
	Chi-Square	7.6190
	Chi-Square DF	3
	Pr > Chi-Square	0.0546
	Z-Test of Wilson & Hilferty	1.6109
	Hoelter Critical N	3173
	Root Mean Square Residual (RMR)	0.0117
	Standardized RMR (SRMR)	0.0096
	Goodness of Fit Index (GFI)	0.9992
Parsimony Index	Adjusted GFI (AGFI)	0.9943
	Parsimonious GFI	0.1998
	RMSEA Estimate	0.0223
	RMSEA Lower 90% Confidence Limit	0.0000
	RMSEA Upper 90% Confidence Limit	0.0426
	Probability of Close Fit	0.9901
	ECVI Estimate	0.0141
	ECVI Lower 90% Confidence Limit	0.0126
	ECVI Upper 90% Confidence Limit	0.0181
	Akaike Information Criterion	43.6190
	Bozdogan CAIC	170.2889
	Schwarz Bayesian Criterion	152.2889
	McDonald Centrality	0.9993
Incremental Index	Bentler Comparative Fit Index	0.9967
	Bentler-Bonett NFI	0.9946
	Bentler-Bonett Non-normed Index	0.9836
	Bollen Normed Index Rho1	0.9732
	Bollen Non-normed Index Delta2	0.9967
	James et al. Parsimonious NFI	0.1989

Asymptotically Standardized Residual Matrix

	ABILITY	ACHIEVE	DEG_ASP	HI_DEG	SELECTIV	INCOME
ABILITY	0.00000	0.00000	0.00000	0.00000	0.00000	−1.61891
ACHIEVE	0.00000	0.00000	0.00000	−1.88372	−1.88372	−1.88274
DEG_ASP	0.00000	0.00000	0.00000	0.00000	0.00000	1.06999
HI_DEG	0.00000	−1.88372	0.00000	−1.88372	−1.88372	−1.88337
SELECTIV	0.00000	−1.88372	0.00000	−1.88372	0.00000	−1.88435
INCOME	−1.61891	−1.88274	1.06999	−1.88337	−1.88435	−1.88339

Standardized Results for Linear Equations

HI_DEG   = 0.0421*ABILITY+ 0.0886*ACHIEVE +0.1749*DEG_ASP+0.1422*SELECTIV+1.0000 E1
Std Err   0.0190 B14   0.0181 B24   0.0177 B34   0.0184 B54
t Value   2.2158   4.9046   9.8959   7.7453

SELECTIV= 0.3237*ABILITY+ 0.1385*DEG_ASP+1.0000 E2
Std Err   0.0161 B15   0.0168 B35
t Value   20.0873   8.2267

INCOME = 0.0553*HI_DEG+ 0.2114*SELECTIV+0.0826*ACHIEVE +1.0000 E3
Std Err   0.0179 B46   0.0175 B56   0.0176 B26
t Value   3.0901   12.1121   4.6898

Standardized Results for Variances of Exogenous Variables

Variable Type	Variable	Parameter	Estimate	Standard Error	t Value
Error	E1	VARE1	0.91101	0.00977	93.27893
	E2	VARE2	0.85901	0.01160	74.05702
	E3	VARE3	0.93511	0.00855	109.40187
Observed	ABILITY	VARV1	1.00000		
	ACHIEVE	VARV2	1.00000		
	DEG_ASP	VARV3	1.00000		

Standardized Results for Covariances Among Exogenous Variables

Var1	Var2	Parameter	Estimate	Standard Error	t Value
ABILITY	ACHIEVE	COV_12	0.28000	0.01657	16.89684
ABILITY	DEG_ASP	COV_13	0.19000	0.01733	10.96255
ACHIEVE	DEG_ASP	COV_23	0.21000	0.01719	12.21791

(*Continued*)

Standardized Total Effects					
Effect / Std Error / t Value / p Value					
	HI_DEG	SELECTIV	ABILITY	ACHIEVE	DEG_ASP
HI_DEG	0	0.1422	0.0882	0.0886	0.1946
		0.0184	0.0182	0.0181	0.0176
		7.7453	4.8564	4.9046	11.0688
		<.0001	<.0001	<.0001	<.0001
INCOME	0.0553	0.2192	0.0733	0.0875	0.0400
	0.0179	0.0171	0.006746	0.0175	0.005414
	3.0901	12.7875	10.8657	5.0021	7.3941
	0.002001	<.0001	<.0001	<.0001	<.0001
SELECTIV	0	0	0.3237	0	0.1385
			0.0161		0.0168
			20.0873		8.2267
			<.0001		<.0001

APPENDIX 16.2

Abbreviated SAS Output for the Final Latent Variable Path Model for Exercise Behavior

Fit Summary		
Modeling Info	Number of Observations	84
	Number of Variables	16
	Number of Moments	136
	Number of Parameters	47
	Number of Active Constraints	0
	Baseline Model Function Value	10.7621
	Baseline Model Chi-Square	893.2570
	Baseline Model Chi-Square DF	120
	Pr > Baseline Model Chi-Square	<.0001
Absolute Index	Fit Function	1.2665
	Chi-Square	105.1160
	Chi-Square DF	89
	Pr > Chi-Square	0.1168
	Z-Test of Wilson & Hilferty	1.1916
	Hoelter Critical N	89
	Root Mean Square Residual (RMR)	0.9104
	Standardized RMR (SRMR)	0.0970
	Goodness of Fit Index (GFI)	0.8733

Parsimony Index	Adjusted GFI (AGFI)	0.8064
	Parsimonious GFI	0.6477
	RMSEA Estimate	0.0467
	RMSEA Lower 90% Confidence Limit	0.0000
	RMSEA Upper 90% Confidence Limit	0.0788
	Probability of Close Fit	0.5402
	ECVI Estimate	2.6907
	ECVI Lower 90% Confidence Limit	2.7727
	ECVI Upper 90% Confidence Limit	3.0687
	Akaike Information Criterion	199.1160
	Bozdogan CAIC	360.3644
	Schwarz Bayesian Criterion	313.3644
	McDonald Centrality	0.9085
Incremental Index	Bentler Comparative Fit Index	0.9792
	Bentler-Bonett NFI	0.8823
	Bentler-Bonett Non-normed Index	0.9719
	Bollen Normed Index Rho1	0.8413
	Bollen Non-normed Index Delta2	0.9800
	James et al. Parsimonious NFI	0.6544

Squared Multiple Correlations

Variable	Error Variance	Total Variance	R-Square
SS1_1	0.50862	6.05200	0.9160
SS2_1	0.85011	3.12930	0.7283
SS3_1	1.99287	7.39512	0.7305
SE1_1	1.99482	4.16200	0.5207
SE2_1	3.60724	4.53175	0.2040
EB1_1	8.24764	17.83037	0.5374
EB2_1	2.18553	3.61000	0.3946
EB3_1	3.06846	3.61997	0.1524
SS1_2	0.71810	6.91700	0.8962
SS2_2	1.70380	3.51067	0.5147
SS3_2	1.95256	7.89840	0.7528
SE1_2	1.12159	5.37838	0.7915
SE2_2	2.89953	5.05542	0.4265
EB1_2	15.54943	21.31787	0.2706
EB2_2	1.10344	6.46395	0.8293
EB3_2	3.27431	3.72164	0.1202
FSS2	2.63415	6.19890	0.5751
FSE2	1.75357	4.25679	0.5881
FEB2	0.59540	5.76844	0.8968

(Continued)

Standardized Results for Linear Equations

SS1_1	=	0.9571	*	FSS1	+ 1.0000	E1
Std Err		0.0198		L11_1		
t Value		48.3838				
SS2_1	=	0.8534	*	FSS1	+ 1.0000	E2
Std Err		0.0342		L21_1		
t Value		24.9685				
SS3_1	=	0.8547	*	FSS1	+ 1.0000	E3
Std Err		0.0340		L31_1		
t Value		25.1536				
SE1_1	=	0.7216	*	FSE1	+ 1.0000	E4
Std Err		0.1009		L12_1		
t Value		7.1543				
SE2_1	=	0.4517	*	FSE1	+ 1.0000	E5
Std Err		0.1017		L22_1		
t Value		4.4417				
EB1_1	=	0.7331	*	FEB1	+ 1.0000	E6
Std Err		0.0711		L13_1		
t Value		10.3153				
EB2_1	=	0.6282	*	FEB1	+ 1.0000	E7
Std Err		0.0818		L23_1		
t Value		7.6794				
EB3_1	=	0.3903	*	FEB1	+ 1.0000	E8
Std Err		0.1041		L33_1		
t Value		3.7485				
SS1_2	=	0.9467		FSS2	+ 1.0000	E9
Std Err		0.0250				
t Value		37.8737				
SS2_2	=	0.7174	*	FSS2	+ 1.0000	E10
Std Err		0.0568		L21_2		
t Value		12.6365				
SS3_2	=	0.8676	*	FSS2	+ 1.0000	E11
Std Err		0.0345		L31_2		
t Value		25.1259				

```
SE1_2   =   0.8896      FSE2    + 1.0000   E12
Std Err     0.0586
t Value    15.1765


SE2_2   =   0.6530   *  FSE2    + 1.0000   E13
Std Err     0.0728      L22_2
t Value     8.9693


EB1_2   =   0.5202      FEB2    + 1.0000   E14
```

Standardized Results for Variances of Exogenous Variables

Variable Type	Variable	Parameter	Estimate	Standard Error	t Value
Error	E1	VARE1	0.08404	0.03786	2.21969
	E2	VARE2	0.27166	0.05834	4.65648
	E3	VARE3	0.26949	0.05808	4.63955
	E4	VARE4	0.47929	0.14556	3.29265
	E5	VARE5	0.79599	0.09186	8.66537
	E6	VARE6	0.46256	0.10420	4.43906
	E7	VARE7	0.60541	0.10277	5.89115
	E8	VARE8	0.84765	0.08129	10.42782
	E9	VARE9	0.10382	0.04732	2.19370
	E10	VARE10	0.48532	0.08146	5.95786
	E11	VARE11	0.24721	0.05992	4.12556
	E12	VARE12	0.20854	0.10430	1.99937
	E13	VARE13	0.57355	0.09509	6.03157
	E14	VARE14	0.72941	0.09115	8.00238
	E15	VARE15	0.17071	0.13342	1.27948
	E16	VARE16	0.87980	0.07224	12.17958
Latent	FSS1		1.00000		
	FSE1		1.00000		
	FEB1		1.00000		
Disturbance	D1	VARD1	0.42494	0.08139	5.22116
	D2	VARD2	0.41195	0.12325	3.34239
	D3	VARD3	0.10322	0.12983	0.79501

(Continued)

Standardized Results for Covariances Among Exogenous Variables

Var1	Var2	Parameter	Estimate	Standard Error	t Value
FSS1	FSE1	COV1	0.45828	0.12066	3.79815
FSS1	FEB1	COV2	0.46192	0.10410	4.43735
FSE1	FEB1	COV3	0.54355	0.12855	4.22836
E14	E6	COV14_6	0.43611	0.08332	5.23441
E13	E5	COV13_5	0.45709	0.07705	5.93238
E11	E3	COV11_3	0.13442	0.03889	3.45626
E10	E2	COV10_2	0.15816	0.04755	3.32651
E16	E8	COV16_8	0.29152	0.09095	3.20529

Standardized Total Effects

Effect / Std Error / t Value / p Value

	FEB2	FSE2	FSS2	FEB1	FSE1	FSS1
EB1_1	0	0	0	0.7331	0	0
				0.0711		
				10.3153		
				<.0001		
EB1_2	0.5202	0.3392	0.1525	0.4372	-0.0542	0.0430
	0.0876	0.0992	0.0626	0.1080	0.0825	0.0415
	5.9374	3.4184	2.4345	4.0464	-0.6572	1.0347
	<.0001	0.000630	0.0149	<.0001	0.5111	0.3008
EB2_1	0	0	0	0.6282	0	0
				0.0818		
				7.6794		
				<.0001		
EB2_2	0.9107	0.5938	0.2669	0.7654	-0.0949	0.0752
	0.0733	0.1445	0.1014	0.1203	0.1443	0.0720
	12.4315	4.1101	2.6322	6.3609	-0.6578	1.0451
	<.0001	<.0001	0.008483	<.0001	0.5107	0.2960
EB3_1	0	0	0	0.3903	0	0
				0.1041		
				3.7485		
				0.000178		
EB3_2	0.3467	0.2261	0.1016	0.2914	-0.0361	0.0286
	0.1042	0.0887	0.0496	0.1013	0.0559	0.0288
	3.3279	2.5501	2.0475	2.8775	-0.6466	0.9948
	0.000875	0.0108	0.0406	0.004008	0.5179	0.3198

Standardized Total Effects

Effect / Std Error / t Value / p Value

	FEB2	FSE2	FSS2	FEB1	FSE1	FSS1
SE1_1	0	0	0	0	0.7216 0.1009 7.1543 <.0001	0
SE1_2	0	0.8896 0.0586 15.1765 <.0001	0.3998 0.1337 2.9910 0.002780	0	0.5708 0.1234 4.6263 <.0001	0.1127 0.1107 1.0187 0.3083
SE2_1	0	0	0	0	0.4517 0.1017 4.4417 <.0001	0
SE2_2	0	0.6530 0.0728 8.9693 <.0001	0.2935 0.1014 2.8935 0.003810	0	0.4190 0.1053 3.9787 <.0001	0.0827 0.0816 1.0137 0.3107
SS1_1	0	0	0	0	0	0.9571 0.0198 48.3838 <.0001
SS1_2	0	0	0.9467 0.0250 37.8737 <.0001	0	0	0.7179 0.0552 13.0124 <.0001
SS2_1	0	0	0	0	0	0.8534 0.0342 24.9685 <.0001
SS2_2	0	0	0.7174 0.0568 12.6365 <.0001	0	0	0.5440 0.0649 8.3814 <.0001
SS3_1	0	0	0	0	0	0.8547 0.0340 25.1536 <.0001
SS3_2	0	0	0.8676 0.0345 25.1259 <.0001	0	0	0.6580 0.0595 11.0542 <.0001

(Continued)

Standardized Total Effects

Effect / Std Error / t Value / p Value

	FEB2	FSE2	FSS2	FEB1	FSE1	FSS1
FEB2	0	0.6521	0.2931	0.8405	-0.1042	0.0826
		0.1601	0.1115	0.1276	0.1580	0.0790
		4.0733	2.6293	6.5877	-0.6597	1.0454
		<.0001	0.008556	<.0001	0.5094	0.2959
FSE2	0	0	0.4494	0	0.6416	0.1267
			0.1479		0.1300	0.1248
			3.0390		4.9340	1.0151
			0.002374		<.0001	0.3101
FSS2	0	0	0	0	0	0.7583
						0.0537
						14.1314
						<.0001

Standardized Direct Effects

Effect / Std Error / t Value / p Value

	FEB2	FSE2	FSS2	FEB1	FSE1	FSS1
EB1_1	0	0	0	0.7331	0	0
				0.0711		
				10.3153		
				<.0001		
EB1_2	0.5202	0	0	0	0	0
	0.0876					
	5.9374					
	<.0001					
EB2_1	0	0	0	0.6282	0	0
				0.0818		
				7.6794		
				<.0001		
EB2_2	0.9107	0	0	0	0	0
	0.0733					
	12.4315					
	<.0001					
EB3_1	0	0	0	0.3903	0	0
				0.1041		
				3.7485		
				0.000178		

Standardized Direct Effects

Effect / Std Error / t Value / p Value

	FEB2	FSE2	FSS2	FEB1	FSE1	FSS1
EB3_2	0.3467 0.1042 3.3279 0.000875	0	0	0	0	0
SE1_1	0	0	0	0	0.7216 0.1009 7.1543 <.0001	0
SE1_2	0	0.8896 0.0586 15.1765 <.0001	0	0	0	0
SE2_1	0	0	0	0	0.4517 0.1017 4.4417 <.0001	0
SE2_2	0	0.6530 0.0728 8.9693 <.0001	0	0	0	0
SS1_1	0	0	0	0	0	0.9571 0.0198 48.3838 <.0001
SS1_2	0	0	0.9467 0.0250 37.8737 <.0001	0	0	0
SS2_1	0	0	0	0	0	0.8534 0.0342 24.9685 <.0001
SS2_2	0	0	0.7174 0.0568 12.6365 <.0001	0	0	0
SS3_1	0	0	0	0	0	0.8547 0.0340 25.1536 <.0001

(*Continued*)

Standardized Direct Effects

Effect / Std Error / t Value / p Value

	FEB2	FSE2	FSS2	FEB1	FSE1	FSS1
SS3_2	0	0	0.8676 0.0345 25.1259 <.0001	0	0	0
FEB2	0	0.6521 0.1601 4.0733 <.0001	0	0.8405 0.1276 6.5877 <.0001	−0.5226 0.2110 −2.4768 0.0133	0
FSE2	0	0	0.4494 0.1479 3.0390 0.002374	0	0.6416 0.1300 4.9340 <.0001	-0.2141 0.1649 -1.2986 0.1941
FSS2	0	0	0	0	0	0.7583 0.0537 14.1314 <.0001

Standardized Indirect Effects

Effect / Std Error / t Value / p Value

	FEB2	FSE2	FSS2	FEB1	FSE1	FSS1
EB1_1	0	0	0	0	0	0
EB1_2	0	0.3392 0.0992 3.4184 0.000630	0.1525 0.0626 2.4345 0.0149	0.4372 0.1080 4.0464 <.0001	−0.0542 0.0825 −0.6572 0.5111	0.0430 0.0415 1.0347 0.3008
EB2_1	0	0	0	0	0	0
EB2_2	0	0.5938 0.1445 4.1101 <.0001	0.2669 0.1014 2.6322 0.008483	0.7654 0.1203 6.3609 <.0001	−0.0949 0.1443 −0.6578 0.5107	0.0752 0.0720 1.0451 0.2960
EB3_1	0	0	0	0	0	0
EB3_2	0	0.2261 0.0887 2.5501 0.0108	0.1016 0.0496 2.0475 0.0406	0.2914 0.1013 2.8775 0.004008	−0.0361 0.0559 −0.6466 0.5179	0.0286 0.0288 0.9948 0.3198

Standardized Indirect Effects

Effect / Std Error / t Value / p Value

	FEB2	FSE2	FSS2	FEB1	FSE1	FSS1
SE1_1	0	0	0	0	0	0
SE1_2	0	0	0.3998	0	0.5708	0.1127
			0.1337		0.1234	0.1107
			2.9910		4.6263	1.0187
			0.002780		<.0001	0.3083
SE2_1	0	0	0	0	0	0
SE2_2	0	0	0.2935	0	0.4190	0.0827
			0.1014		0.1053	0.0816
			2.8935		3.9787	1.0137
			0.003810		<.0001	0.3107
SS1_1	0	0	0	0	0	0
SS1_2	0	0	0	0	0	0.7179
						0.0552
						13.0124
						<.0001
SS2_1	0	0	0	0	0	0
SS2_2	0	0	0	0	0	0.5440
						0.0649
						8.3814
						<.0001
SS3_1	0	0	0	0	0	0
SS3_2	0	0	0	0	0	0.6580
						0.0595
						11.0542
						<.0001
FEB2	0	0	0.2931	0	0.4184	0.0826
			0.1115		0.1623	0.0790
			2.6293		2.5774	1.0454
			0.008556		0.009955	0.2959
FSE2	0	0	0	0	0	0.3408
						0.1179
						2.8901
						0.003852
FSS2	0	0	0	0	0	0

(Continued)

Standardized Direct Effects

Effect / Std Error / t Value / p Value

	HI_DEG	SELECTIV	ABILITY	ACHIEVE	DEG_ASP
HI_DEG	0	0.1422	0.0421	0.0886	0.1749
		0.0184	0.0190	0.0181	0.0177
		7.7453	2.2158	4.9046	9.8959
		<.0001	0.0267	<.0001	<.0001
INCOME	0.0553	0.2114	0	0.0826	0
	0.0179	0.0175		0.0176	
	3.0901	12.1121		4.6898	
	0.002001	<.0001		<.0001	
SELECTIV	0	0	0.3237	0	0.1385
			0.0161		0.0168
			20.0873		8.2267
			<.0001		<.0001

Standardized Indirect Effects

Effect / Std Error / t Value / p Value

	HI_DEG	SELECTIV	ABILITY	ACHIEVE	DEG_ASP
HI_DEG	0	0	0.0460	0	0.0197
			0.006412		0.003500
			7.1798		5.6284
			<.0001		<.0001
INCOME	0	0.007864	0.0733	0.004900	0.0400
		0.002742	0.006746	0.001876	0.005414
		2.8676	10.8657	2.6123	7.3941
		0.004136	<.0001	0.008993	<.0001
SELECTIV	0	0	0	0	0

Appendix A

STATISTICAL TABLES

Contents

Table A.1: Percentile Points for χ^2 Distribution

df							Probability							
	.99	.98	.95	.90	.80	.70	.50	.30	.20	.10	.05	.02	.01	.001
1	.03157	.03628	.00393	.0158	.0642	.148	.455	1.074	1.642	2.706	3.841	5.412	6.635	10.827
2	.0201	.0404	.103	.211	.446	.713	1.386	2.408	3.219	4.605	5.991	7.824	9.210	13.815
3	.115	.185	.352	.584	1.005	1.424	2.366	3.665	4.642	6.251	7.815	9.837	11.345	16.268
4	.297	.429	.711	1.064	1.649	2.195	3.357	4.878	5.989	7.779	9.488	11.668	13.277	18.465
5	.554	.752	1.145	1.610	2.343	3.000	4.351	6.064	7.289	9.236	11.070	13.388	15.086	20.517
6	.872	1.134	1.635	2.204	3.070	3.828	5.348	7.231	8.558	10.645	12.592	15.033	16.812	22.457
7	1.239	1.564	2.167	2.833	3.822	4.671	6.346	8.383	9.803	12.017	14.067	16.622	18.475	24.322
8	1.646	2.032	2.733	3.490	4.594	5.527	7.344	9.524	11.030	13.362	15.507	18.168	20.090	26.125
9	2.088	2.532	3.325	4.168	5.380	6.393	8.343	10.656	12.242	14.684	16.919	19.679	21.666	27.877
10	2.558	3.059	3.940	4.865	6.179	7.267	9.342	11.781	13.442	15.987	18.307	21.161	23.209	29.588
11	3.053	3.609	4.575	5.578	6.989	8.148	10.341	12.899	14.631	17.275	19.675	22.618	24.725	31.264
12	3.571	4.178	5.226	6.304	7.807	9.034	11.340	14.011	15.812	18.549	21.026	24.054	26.217	32.909
13	4.107	4.765	5.892	7.042	8.634	9.926	12.340	15.119	16.985	19.812	22.362	25.472	27.688	34.528
14	4.660	5.368	6.571	7.790	9.467	10.821	13.339	16.222	18.151	21.064	23.685	26.873	29.141	36.123
15	5.229	5.985	7.261	8.547	10.307	11.721	14.339	17.322	19.311	22.307	24.996	28.259	30.578	37.697
16	5.812	6.614	7.962	9.312	11.152	12.624	15.338	18.418	20.465	23.542	26.296	29.633	32.000	39.252
17	6.408	7.255	8.672	10.085	12.002	13.531	16.338	19.511	21.615	24.769	27.587	30.995	33.409	40.790
18	7.015	7.906	9.390	10.865	12.857	14.440	17.338	20.601	22.760	25.989	28.869	32.346	34.805	42.312
19	7.633	8.567	10.117	11.651	13.716	15.352	18.338	21.689	23.900	27.204	30.144	33.687	36.191	43.820
20	8.260	9.237	10.851	12.443	14.578	16.266	19.337	22.775	25.038	28.412	31.410	35.020	37.566	45.315
21	8.897	9.915	11.591	13.240	15.445	17.182	20.337	23.858	26.171	29.615	32.671	36.343	38.932	46.797
22	9.542	10.600	12.338	13.041	16.314	18.101	21.337	24.939	27.301	30.813	33.924	37.659	40.289	48.268
23	10.196	11.293	13.091	14.848	17.187	19.021	22.337	26.018	28.429	32.007	35.172	38.968	41.638	49.728

24	10.856	11.992	13.848	15.659	18.062	19.943	23.337	27.096	29.553	33.196	36.415	40.270	42.980	51.179
25	11.524	12.697	14.611	16.473	18.940	20.867	24.337	28.172	30.675	34.382	37.652	41.566	44.314	52.620
26	12.198	13.409	15.379	17.292	19.820	21.792	25.336	29.246	31.795	35.563	38.885	42.856	45.642	54.052
27	12.879	14.125	16.151	18.114	20.703	22.719	26.336	30.319	32.912	36.741	40.113	44.140	46.963	55.476
28	13.565	14.847	16.928	18.939	21.588	23.647	27.336	31.391	34.027	37.916	41.337	45.419	48.278	56.893
29	14.256	15.574	17.708	19.768	22.475	24.577	28.336	32.461	35.139	39.087	42.557	46.693	49.588	58.302
30	14.953	16.306	18.493	20.599	23.364	25.508	29.336	33.530	36.250	40.256	43.773	47.962	50.892	59.703

Note: For larger values of df, the expression $\sqrt{2\chi^2} - \sqrt{2df - 1}$ may be used as a normal deviate with unit variance, remembering that the probability for χ^2 corresponds with that of a single tail of the normal curve.

Source: Reproduced from E.F. Lindquist, *Design and Analysis of Experiments in Psychology and Education*, Boston, MA: Houghton Mifflin, 1953, p. 29, with permission.

■ Table A.2: Critical Values for *t*

	Level of Significance for One-Tailed Test					
	.10	.05	.025	.01	.005	.0005
	Level of Significance for Two-Tailed Test					
df	.20	.10	.05	.02	.01	.001
1	3.078	6.314	12.706	31.821	63.657	636.619
2	1.886	2.920	4.303	6.965	9.925	31.598
3	1.638	2.353	3.182	4.541	5.841	12.941
4	1.533	2.132	2.776	3.747	4.604	8.610
5	1.476	2.015	2.571	3.365	4.032	6.859
6	1.440	1.943	2.447	3.143	3.707	5.959
7	1.415	1.895	2.365	2.998	3.449	5.405
8	1.397	1.860	2.306	2.896	3.355	5.041
9	1.383	1.833	2.262	2.821	3.250	4.781
10	1.372	1.812	2.228	2.764	3.169	4.587
11	1.363	1.796	2.201	2.718	3.106	4.437
12	1.356	1.782	2.179	2.681	3.055	4.318
13	1.350	1.771	2.160	2.650	3.012	4.221
14	1.345	1.761	2.145	2.624	2.977	4.140
15	1.341	1.753	2.131	2.602	2.947	4.073
16	1.337	1.746	2.120	2.583	2.921	4.015
17	1.333	1.740	2.110	2.567	2.898	3.965
18	1.330	1.734	2.101	2.552	2.878	3.922
19	1.328	1.729	2.093	2.539	2.861	3.883
20	1.325	1.725	2.086	2.528	2.845	3.850
21	1.323	1.721	2.080	2.518	2.831	3.819
22	1.321	1.717	2.074	2.508	2.819	3.792
23	1.319	1.714	2.069	2.500	2.807	3.767
24	1.318	1.711	2.064	2.492	2.797	3.745
25	1.316	1.708	2.060	2.485	2.787	3.725
26	1.315	1.706	2.056	2.479	2.779	3.707
27	1.314	1.703	2.052	2.473	2.771	3.690
28	1.313	1.701	2.048	2.467	2.763	3.674
29	1.311	1.699	2.045	2.462	2.756	3.659
30	1.310	1.697	2.042	2.457	2.750	3.646
40	1.303	1.684	2.021	2.423	2.704	3.551
60	1.296	1.671	2.000	2.390	2.660	3.460
120	1.289	1.658	1.980	2.358	2.617	3.373
∞	1.282	1.645	1.960	2.326	2.576	3.291

Source: Reproduced from E. F. Lindquist, *Design and Analysis of Experiments in Psychology and Education*, Boston, MA: Houghton Mifflin, 1953, p. 37, with permission.

◼ Table A.3: Critical Values for *F*

		df for Numerator							
df Error	α	1	2	3	4	5	6	8	12
1	.01	4052	4999	5403	5625	5764	5859	5981	6106
	.05	161.45	199.50	215.71	224.58	230.16	233.99	238.88	243.91
	.10	39.86	49.50	53.59	55.83	57.24	58.20	59.44	60.70
	.20	9.47	12.00	13.06	13.73	14.01	14.26	14.59	14.90
2	.01	98.49	99.00	99.17	99.25	99.30	99.33	99.36	99.42
	.05	18.51	19.00	19.16	19.25	19.30	19.33	19.37	19.41
	.10	8.53	9.00	9.16	9.24	9.29	9.33	9.37	9.41
	.20	3.56	4.00	4.16	4.24	4.28	4.32	4.36	4.40
3	.001	167.5	148.5	141.1	137.1	134.6	132.8	130.6	128.3
	.01	34.12	30.81	29.46	28.71	28.24	27.91	27.49	27.05
	.05	10.13	9.55	9.28	9.12	9.01	8.94	8.84	8.74
	.10	5.54	5.46	5.39	5.34	5.31	5.28	5.25	5.22
	.20	2.68	2.89	2.94	2.96	2.97	2.97	2.98	2.98
4	.001	74.14	61.25	56.18	53.44	51.71	50.53	49.00	47.41
	.01	21.20	18.00	16.69	15.98	15.52	15.21	14.80	14.37
	.05	7.71	6.94	6.59	6.39	6.26	6.16	6.04	5.91
	.10	4.54	4.32	4.19	4.11	4.05	4.01	3.95	3.90
	.20	2.35	2.47	2.48	2.48	2.48	2.47	2.47	2.46
5	.001	47.04	36.61	33.20	31.09	29.75	28.84	27.64	26.42
	.01	16.26	13.27	12.06	11.39	10.97	10.67	10.29	9.89
	.05	6.61	5.79	5.41	5.19	5.05	4.95	4.82	4.68
	.10	4.06	3.78	3.62	3.52	3.45	3.40	3.34	3.27
	.20	2.18	2.26	2.25	2.24	2.23	2.22	2.20	2.18
6	.001	35.51	27.00	23.70	21.90	20.81	20.03	19.03	17.99
	.01	13.74	10.92	9.78	9.15	8.75	8.47	8.10	7.72
	.05	5.99	5.14	4.76	4.53	4.39	4.28	4.15	4.00
	.10	3.78	3.46	3.29	3.18	3.11	3.05	2.98	2.90
	.20	2.07	2.13	2.11	2.09	2.08	2.06	2.04	2.02
7	.001	29.22	21.69	18.77	17.19	16.21	15.52	14.63	13.71
	.01	12.25	9.55	8.45	7.85	7.46	7.19	6.84	6.47
	.05	5.59	4.74	4.35	4.12	3.97	3.87	3.73	3.57
	.10	3.59	3.26	3.07	2.96	2.88	2.83	2.75	2.67
	.20	2.00	2.04	2.02	1.99	1.97	1.96	1.93	1.91
8	.001	25.42	18.49	15.83	14.39	13.49	12.86	12.04	11.19
	.01	11.26	8.65	7.59	7.01	6.63	6.37	6.03	5.67
	.05	5.32	4.46	4.07	3.84	3.69	3.58	3.44	3.28
	.10	3.46	3.11	2.92	2.81	2.73	2.67	2.59	2.50
	.20	1.95	1.98	1.95	1.92	1.90	1.88	1.86	1.83

(Continued)

■ Table A.3: (Continued)

		df for Numerator							
df Error	α	1	2	3	4	5	6	8	12
9	.001	22.86	16.39	13.90	12.56	11.71	11.13	10.37	9.57
	.01	10.56	8.02	6.99	6.42	6.06	5.80	5.47	5.11
	.05	5.12	4.26	3.86	3.63	3.48	3.37	3.23	3.07
	.10	3.36	3.01	2.81	2.69	2.61	2.55	2.47	2.38
	.20	1.91	1.94	1.90	1.87	1.85	1.83	1.80	1.76
10	.001	21.04	14.91	12.55	11.28	10.48	9.92	9.20	8.45
	.01	10.04	7.56	6.55	5.99	5.64	5.39	5.06	4.71
	.05	4.96	4.10	3.71	3.48	3.33	3.22	3.07	2.91
	.10	3.28	2.92	2.73	2.61	2.52	2.46	2.38	2.28
	.20	1.88	1.90	1.86	1.83	1.80	1.78	1.75	1.72
11	.001	19.69	13.81	11.56	10.35	9.58	9.05	8.35	7.63
	.01	9.65	7.20	6.22	5.67	5.32	5.07	4.74	4.40
	.05	4.84	3.98	3.59	3.36	3.20	3.09	2.95	2.79
	.10	3.23	2.86	2.66	2.54	2.45	2.39	2.30	2.21
	.20	1.86	1.87	1.83	1.80	1.77	1.75	1.72	1.68
12	.001	18.64	12.97	10.80	9.63	8.89	8.38	7.71	7.00
	.01	9.33	6.93	5.95	5.41	5.06	4.82	4.50	4.16
	.05	4.75	3.88	3.49	3.26	3.11	3.00	2.85	2.69
	.10	3.18	2.81	2.61	2.48	2.39	2.33	2.24	2.15
	.20	1.84	1.85	1.80	1.77	1.74	1.72	1.69	1.65
13	.001	17.81	12.31	10.21	9.07	8.35	7.86	7.21	6.52
	.01	9.07	6.70	5.74	5.20	4.86	4.62	4.30	3.96
	.05	4.67	3.80	3.41	3.18	3.02	2.92	2.77	2.60
	.10	3.14	2.76	2.56	2.43	2.35	2.28	2.20	2.10
	.20	1.82	1.83	1.78	1.75	1.72	1.69	1.66	1.62
14	.001	17.14	11.78	9.73	8.62	7.92	7.43	6.80	6.13
	.01	8.86	6.51	5.56	5.03	4.69	4.46	4.14	3.80
	.05	4.60	3.74	3.34	3.11	2.96	2.85	2.70	2.53
	.10	3.10	2.73	2.52	2.39	2.31	2.24	2.15	2.05
	.20	1.81	1.81	1.76	1.73	1.70	1.67	1.64	1.60
15	.001	16.59	11.34	9.34	8.25	7.57	7.09	6.47	5.81
	.01	8.68	6.36	5.42	4.89	4.56	4.32	4.00	3.67
	.05	4.54	3.68	3.29	3.06	2.90	2.79	2.64	2.48
	.10	3.07	2.70	2.49	2.36	2.27	2.21	2.12	2.02
	.20	1.80	1.79	1.75	1.71	1.68	1.66	1.62	1.58
16	.001	16.12	10.97	9.00	7.94	7.27	6.81	6.19	5.55
	.01	8.53	6.23	5.29	4.77	4.44	4.20	3.89	3.55
	.05	4.49	3.63	3.24	3.01	2.85	2.74	2.59	2.42
	.10	3.05	2.67	2.46	2.33	2.24	2.18	2.09	1.99
	.20	1.79	1.78	1.74	1.70	1.67	1.64	1.61	1.56

		df for Numerator							
df Error	α	1	2	3	4	5	6	8	12
17	.001	15.72	10.66	8.73	7.68	7.02	6.56	5.96	5.32
	.01	8.40	6.11	5.18	4.67	4.34	4.10	3.79	3.45
	.05	4.45	3.59	3.20	2.96	2.81	2.70	2.55	2.38
	.10	3.03	2.64	2.44	2.31	2.22	2.15	2.06	1.96
	.20	1.78	1.77	1.72	1.68	1.65	1.63	1.59	1.55
18	.001	15.38	10.39	8.49	7.46	6.81	6.35	5.76	5.13
	.01	8.28	6.01	5.09	4.58	4.25	4.01	3.71	3.37
	.05	4.41	3.55	3.16	2.93	2.77	2.66	2.51	2.34
	.10	3.01	2.62	2.42	2.29	2.20	2.13	2.04	1.93
	.20	1.77	1.76	1.71	1.67	1.64	1.62	1.58	1.53
19	.001	15.08	10.16	8.28	7.26	6.61	6.18	5.59	4.97
	.01	8.18	5.93	5.01	4.50	4.17	3.94	3.63	3.30
	.05	4.38	3.52	3.13	2.90	2.74	2.63	2.48	2.31
	.10	2.99	2.61	2.40	2.27	2.18	2.11	2.02	1.91
	.20	1.76	1.75	1.70	1.66	1.63	1.61	1.57	1.52
20	.001	14.82	9.95	8.10	7.10	6.46	6.02	5.44	4.82
	.01	8.10	5.85	4.94	4.43	4.10	3.87	3.56	3.23
	.05	4.35	3.49	3.10	2.87	2.71	2.60	2.45	2.28
	.10	2.97	2.59	2.38	2.25	2.16	2.09	2.00	1.89
	.20	1.76	1.75	1.70	1.65	1.62	1.60	1.56	1.51
21	.001	14.59	9.77	7.94	6.95	6.32	5.88	5.31	4.70
	.01	8.02	5.78	4.87	4.37	4.04	3.81	3.51	3.17
	.05	4.32	3.47	3.07	2.84	2.68	2.57	2.42	2.25
	.10	2.96	2.57	2.36	2.23	2.14	2.08	1.98	1.88
	.20	1.75	1.74	1.69	1.65	1.61	1.59	1.55	1.50
22	.001	14.38	9.61	7.80	6.81	6.19	5.76	5.19	4.58
	.01	7.94	5.72	4.82	4.31	3.99	3.76	3.45	3.12
	.05	4.30	3.44	3.05	2.82	2.66	2.55	2.40	2.23
	.10	2.95	2.56	2.35	2.22	2.13	2.06	1.97	1.86
	.20	1.75	1.73	1.68	1.64	1.61	1.58	1.54	1.49
23	.001	14.19	9.47	7.67	6.69	6.08	5.65	5.09	4.48
	.01	7.88	5.66	4.76	4.26	3.94	3.71	3.41	3.07
	.05	4.28	3.42	3.03	2.80	2.64	2.53	2.38	2.20
	.10	2.94	2.55	2.34	2.21	2.11	2.05	1.95	1.84
	.20	1.74	1.73	1.68	1.63	1.60	1.57	1.53	1.49
24	.001	14.03	9.34	7.55	6.59	5.98	5.55	4.99	4.39
	.01	7.82	5.61	4.72	4.22	3.90	3.67	3.36	3.03
	.05	4.26	3.40	3.01	2.78	2.62	2.51	2.36	2.18
	.10	2.93	2.54	2.33	2.19	2.10	2.04	1.94	1.83
	.20	1.74	1.72	1.67	1.63	1.59	1.57	1.53	1.48

(Continued)

df Error	α	\multicolumn{8}{c}{*df* for Numerator}
		1	2	3	4	5	6	8	12
25	.001	13.88	9.22	7.45	6.49	5.88	5.46	4.91	4.31
	.01	7.77	5.57	4.68	4.18	3.86	3.63	3.32	2.99
	.05	4.24	3.38	2.99	2.76	2.60	2.49	2.34	2.16
	.10	2.92	2.53	2.32	2.18	2.09	2.02	1.93	1.82
	.20	1.73	1.72	1.66	1.62	1.59	1.56	1.52	1.47
26	.001	13.74	9.12	7.36	6.41	5.80	5.38	4.83	4.24
	.01	7.72	5.53	4.64	4.14	3.82	3.59	3.29	2.96
	.05	4.22	3.37	2.98	2.74	2.59	2.47	2.32	2.15
	.10	2.91	2.52	2.31	2.17	2.08	2.01	1.92	1.81
	.20	1.73	1.71	1.66	1.62	1.58	1.56	1.52	1.47
27	.001	13.61	9.02	7.27	6.33	5.73	5.31	4.76	4.17
	.01	7.68	5.49	4.60	4.11	3.78	3.56	3.26	2.93
	.05	4.21	3.35	2.96	2.73	2.57	2.46	2.30	2.13
	.10	2.90	2.51	2.30	2.17	2.07	2.00	1.91	1.80
	.20	1.73	1.71	1.66	1.61	1.58	1.55	1.51	1.46
28	.001	13.50	8.93	7.19	6.25	5.66	5.24	4.69	4.11
	.01	7.64	5.45	4.57	4.07	3.75	3.53	3.23	2.90
	.05	4.20	3.34	2.95	2.71	2.56	2.44	2.29	2.12
	.10	2.89	2.50	2.29	2.16	2.06	2.00	1.90	1.79
	.20	1.72	1.71	1.65	1.61	1.57	1.55	1.51	1.46
29	.001	13.39	8.85	7.12	6.19	5.59	5.18	4.64	4.05
	.01	7.60	5.42	4.54	4.04	3.73	3.50	3.20	2.87
	.05	4.18	3.33	2.93	2.70	2.54	2.43	2.28	2.10
	.10	2.89	2.50	2.28	2.15	2.06	1.99	1.89	1.78
	.20	1.72	1.70	1.65	1.60	1.57	1.54	1.50	1.45
30	.001	13.29	8.77	7.05	6.12	5.53	5.12	4.58	4.00
	.01	7.56	5.39	4.51	4.02	3.70	3.47	3.17	2.84
	.05	4.17	3.32	2.92	2.69	2.53	2.42	2.27	2.09
	.10	2.88	2.49	2.28	2.14	2.05	1.98	1.88	1.77
	.20	1.72	1.70	1.64	1.60	1.57	1.54	1.50	1.45
40	.001	12.61	8.25	6.60	5.70	5.13	4.73	4.21	3.64
	.01	7.31	5.18	4.31	3.83	3.51	3.29	2.99	2.66
	.05	4.08	3.23	2.84	2.61	2.45	2.34	2.18	2.00
	.10	2.84	2.44	2.23	2.09	2.00	1.93	1.83	1.71
	.20	1.70	1.68	1.62	1.57	1.54	1.51	1.47	1.41
60	.001	11.97	7.76	6.17	5.31	4.76	4.37	3.87	3.31
	.01	7.08	4.98	4.13	3.65	3.34	3.12	2.82	2.50
	.05	4.00	3.15	2.76	2.52	2.37	2.25	2.10	1.92
	.10	2.79	2.39	2.18	2.04	1.95	1.87	1.77	1.66
	.20	1.68	1.65	1.59	1.55	1.51	1.48	1.44	1.38
120	.001	11.38	7.31	5.79	4.95	4.42	4.04	3.55	3.02
	.01	6.85	4.79	3.95	3.48	3.17	2.96	2.66	2.34
	.05	3.92	3.07	2.68	2.45	2.29	2.17	2.02	1.83

		df for Numerator							
df Error	α	1	2	3	4	5	6	8	12
	.10	2.75	2.35	2.13	1.99	1.90	1.82	1.72	1.60
	.20	1.66	1.63	1.57	1.52	1.48	1.45	1.41	1.35
∞	.001	10.83	6.91	5.42	4.62	4.10	3.74	3.27	2.74
	.01	6.64	4.60	3.78	3.32	3.02	2.80	2.51	2.18
	.05	3.84	2.99	2.60	2.37	2.21	2.09	1.94	1.75
	.10	2.71	2.30	2.08	1.94	1.85	1.77	1.67	1.55
	.20	1.64	1.61	1.55	1.50	1.46	1.43	1.38	1.32

Source: Reproduced from E. F. Lindquist, *Design and Analysis of Experiments in Psychology and Education*, Boston, MA: Houghton Mifflin, 1953, pp. 41–44, with permission.

■ **Table A.4: Percentile Points for Studentized Range Statistic**

	90th Percentiles								
	Number of Groups								
df Error	2	3	4	5	6	7	8	9	10
1	8.929	13.44	16.36	18.49	20.15	21.51	22.64	23.62	24.48
2	4.130	5.733	6.773	7.538	8.139	8.633	9.049	9.409	9.725
3	3.328	4.467	5.199	5.738	6.162	6.511	6.806	7.062	7.287
4	3.015	3.976	4.586	5.035	5.388	5.679	5.926	6.139	6.327
5	2.850	3.717	4.264	4.664	4.979	5.238	5.458	5.648	5.816
6	2.748	3.559	4.065	4.435	4.726	4.966	5.168	5.344	5.499
7	2.680	3.451	3.931	4.280	4.555	4.780	4.972	5.137	5.283
8	2.630	3.374	3.834	4.169	4.431	4.646	4.829	4.987	5.126
9	2.592	3.316	3.761	4.084	4.337	4.545	4.721	4.873	5.007
10	2.563	3.270	3.704	4.018	4.264	4.465	4.636	4.783	4.913
11	2.540	3.234	3.658	3.965	4.205	4.401	4.568	4.711	4.838
12	2.521	3.204	3.621	3.922	4.156	4.349	4.511	4.652	4.776
13	2.505	3.179	3.589	3.885	4.116	4.305	4.464	4.602	4.724
14	2.491	3.158	3.563	3.854	4.081	4.267	4.424	4.560	4.680
15	2.479	3.140	3.540	3.828	4.052	4.235	4.390	4.524	4.641
16	2.469	3.124	3.520	3.804	4.026	4.207	4.360	4.492	4.608
17	2.460	3.110	3.503	3.784	4.004	4.183	4.334	4.464	4.579
18	2.452	3.098	3.488	3.767	3.984	4.161	4.311	4.440	4.554
19	2.445	3.087	3.474	3.751	3.966	4.142	4.290	4.418	4.531
20	2.439	3.078	3.462	3.736	3.950	4.124	4.271	4.398	4.510
24	2.420	3.047	3.423	3.692	3.900	4.070	4.213	4.336	4.445
30	2.400	3.017	3.386	3.648	3.851	4.016	4.155	4.275	4.381
40	2.381	2.988	3.349	3.605	3.803	3.963	4.099	4.215	4.317
60	2.363	2.959	3.312	3.562	3.755	3.911	4.042	4.155	4.254
120	2.344	2.930	3.276	3.520	3.707	3.859	3.987	4.096	4.191
∞	2.326	2.902	3.240	3.478	3.661	3.808	3.931	4.037	4.129

(*Continued*)

Table A.4: (Continued)

					95th Percentiles				
					Number of Groups				
df Error	2	3	4	5	6	7	8	9	10
1	17.97	26.98	32.82	37.08	40.41	43.12	45.40	47.36	49.07
2	6.085	8.331	9.798	10.88	11.74	12.44	13.03	13.54	13.99
3	4.501	5.910	6.825	7.502	8.037	8.478	8.853	9.177	9.462
4	3.927	5.040	5.757	6.287	6.707	7.053	7.347	7.602	7.826
5	3.635	4.602	5.218	5.673	6.033	6.330	6.582	6.802	6.995
6	3.461	4.339	4.896	5.305	5.628	5.895	6.122	6.319	6.493
7	3.344	4.165	4.681	5.060	5.359	5.606	5.815	5.998	6.158
8	3.261	4.041	4.529	4.886	5.167	5.399	5.597	5.767	5.918
9	3.199	3.949	4.415	4.756	5.024	5.244	5.432	5.595	5.739
10	3.151	3.877	4.327	4.654	4.912	5.124	5.305	5.461	5.599
11	3.113	3.820	4.256	4.574	4.823	5.028	5.202	5.353	5.487
12	3.082	3.773	4.199	4.508	4.751	4.950	5.119	5.265	5.395
13	3.055	3.735	4.151	4.453	4.690	4.885	5.049	5.192	5.318
14	3.033	3.702	4.111	4.407	4.639	4.829	4.990	5.131	5.254
15	3.014	3.674	4.076	4.367	4.595	4.782	4.940	5.077	5.198
16	2.998	3.649	4.046	4.333	4.557	4.741	4.897	5.031	5.150
17	2.984	3.628	4.020	4.303	4.524	4.705	4.858	4.991	5.108
18	2.971	3.609	3.997	4.277	4.495	4.673	4.824	4.956	5.071
19	2.960	3.593	3.977	4.253	4.469	4.645	4.794	4.924	5.038
20	2.950	3.578	3.958	4.232	4.445	4.620	4.768	4.896	5.008
24	2.919	3.532	3.901	4.166	4.373	4.541	4.684	4.807	4.915
30	2.888	3.486	3.845	4.102	4.302	4.464	4.602	4.720	4.824
40	2.858	3.442	3.791	4.039	4.232	4.389	4.521	4.635	4.735
60	2.829	3.399	3.737	3.977	4.163	4.314	4.441	4.550	4.646
120	2.800	3.356	3.685	3.917	4.096	4.241	4.363	4.468	4.560
∞	2.772	3.314	3.633	3.858	4.030	4.170	4.286	4.387	4.474

Table A.4: (Continued)

<table>
<tr><td colspan="10" align="center">97.5th Percentiles</td></tr>
<tr><td></td><td colspan="9" align="center">Number of Groups</td></tr>
<tr><td>*df* Error</td><td>2</td><td>3</td><td>4</td><td>5</td><td>6</td><td>7</td><td>8</td><td>9</td><td>10</td></tr>
<tr><td>1</td><td>35.99</td><td>54.00</td><td>65.69</td><td>74.22</td><td>80.87</td><td>86.29</td><td>90.85</td><td>94.77</td><td>98.20</td></tr>
<tr><td>2</td><td>8.776</td><td>11.94</td><td>14.01</td><td>15.54</td><td>16.75</td><td>17.74</td><td>18.58</td><td>19.31</td><td>19.95</td></tr>
<tr><td>3</td><td>5.907</td><td>7.661</td><td>8.808</td><td>9.660</td><td>10.34</td><td>10.89</td><td>11.37</td><td>11.78</td><td>12.14</td></tr>
<tr><td>4</td><td>4.943</td><td>6.244</td><td>7.088</td><td>7.716</td><td>8.213</td><td>8.625</td><td>8.976</td><td>9.279</td><td>9.548</td></tr>
<tr><td>5</td><td>4.474</td><td>5.558</td><td>6.257</td><td>6.775</td><td>7.186</td><td>7.527</td><td>7.816</td><td>8.068</td><td>8.291</td></tr>
<tr><td>6</td><td>4.199</td><td>5.158</td><td>5.772</td><td>6.226</td><td>6.586</td><td>6.884</td><td>7.138</td><td>7.359</td><td>7.554</td></tr>
<tr><td>7</td><td>4.018</td><td>4.897</td><td>5.455</td><td>5.868</td><td>6.194</td><td>6.464</td><td>6.695</td><td>6.895</td><td>7.072</td></tr>
<tr><td>8</td><td>3.892</td><td>4.714</td><td>5.233</td><td>5.616</td><td>5.919</td><td>6.169</td><td>6.382</td><td>6.568</td><td>6.732</td></tr>
<tr><td>9</td><td>3.797</td><td>4.578</td><td>5.069</td><td>5.430</td><td>5.715</td><td>5.950</td><td>6.151</td><td>6.325</td><td>6.479</td></tr>
<tr><td>10</td><td>3.725</td><td>4.474</td><td>4.943</td><td>5.287</td><td>5.558</td><td>5.782</td><td>5.972</td><td>6.138</td><td>6.285</td></tr>
<tr><td>11</td><td>3.667</td><td>4.391</td><td>4.843</td><td>5.173</td><td>5.433</td><td>5.648</td><td>5.831</td><td>5.989</td><td>6.130</td></tr>
<tr><td>12</td><td>3.620</td><td>4.325</td><td>4.762</td><td>5.081</td><td>5.332</td><td>5.540</td><td>5.716</td><td>5.869</td><td>6.004</td></tr>
<tr><td>13</td><td>3.582</td><td>4.269</td><td>4.694</td><td>5.004</td><td>5.248</td><td>5.449</td><td>5.620</td><td>5.769</td><td>5.900</td></tr>
<tr><td>14</td><td>3.550</td><td>4.222</td><td>4.638</td><td>4.940</td><td>5.178</td><td>5.374</td><td>5.540</td><td>5.684</td><td>5.811</td></tr>
<tr><td>15</td><td>3.522</td><td>4.182</td><td>4.589</td><td>4.885</td><td>5.118</td><td>5.309</td><td>5.471</td><td>5.612</td><td>5.737</td></tr>
<tr><td>16</td><td>3.498</td><td>4.148</td><td>4.548</td><td>4.838</td><td>5.066</td><td>5.253</td><td>5.412</td><td>5.550</td><td>5.672</td></tr>
<tr><td>17</td><td>3.477</td><td>4.118</td><td>4.512</td><td>4.797</td><td>5.020</td><td>5.204</td><td>5.361</td><td>5.496</td><td>5.615</td></tr>
<tr><td>18</td><td>3.458</td><td>4.092</td><td>4.480</td><td>4.761</td><td>4.981</td><td>5.162</td><td>5.315</td><td>5.448</td><td>5.565</td></tr>
<tr><td>19</td><td>3.442</td><td>4.068</td><td>4.451</td><td>4.728</td><td>4.945</td><td>5.123</td><td>5.275</td><td>5.405</td><td>5.521</td></tr>
<tr><td>20</td><td>3.427</td><td>4.047</td><td>4.426</td><td>4.700</td><td>4.914</td><td>5.089</td><td>5.238</td><td>5.368</td><td>5.481</td></tr>
<tr><td>24</td><td>3.381</td><td>3.983</td><td>4.347</td><td>4.610</td><td>4.816</td><td>4.984</td><td>5.126</td><td>5.250</td><td>5.358</td></tr>
<tr><td>30</td><td>3.337</td><td>3.919</td><td>4.271</td><td>4.523</td><td>4.720</td><td>4.881</td><td>5.017</td><td>5.134</td><td>5.238</td></tr>
<tr><td>40</td><td>3.294</td><td>3.858</td><td>4.197</td><td>4.439</td><td>4.627</td><td>4.780</td><td>4.910</td><td>5.022</td><td>5.120</td></tr>
<tr><td>60</td><td>3.251</td><td>3.798</td><td>4.124</td><td>4.356</td><td>4.536</td><td>4.682</td><td>4.806</td><td>4.912</td><td>5.006</td></tr>
<tr><td>120</td><td>3.210</td><td>3.739</td><td>4.053</td><td>4.276</td><td>4.447</td><td>4.587</td><td>4.704</td><td>4.805</td><td>4.894</td></tr>
<tr><td>∞</td><td>3.170</td><td>3.682</td><td>3.984</td><td>4.197</td><td>4.361</td><td>4.494</td><td>4.605</td><td>4.700</td><td>4.784</td></tr>
</table>

(*Continued*)

Table A.4: (Continued)

				99th Percentiles					
				Number of Groups					
df Error	2	3	4	5	6	7	8	9	10
1	90.03	135.0	164.3	185.6	202.2	215.8	227.2	237.0	245.6
2	14.04	19.02	22.29	24.72	26.63	28.20	29.53	30.68	31.69
3	8.261	10.62	12.17	13.33	14.24	15.00	15.64	16.20	16.69
4	6.512	8.120	9.173	9.958	10.58	11.10	11.55	11.93	12.27
5	5.702	6.976	7.804	8.421	8.913	9.321	9.669	9.972	10.24
6	5.243	6.331	7.033	7.556	7.973	8.318	8.613	8.869	9.097
7	4.949	5.919	6.543	7.005	7.373	7.679	7.939	8.166	8.368
8	4.746	5.635	6.204	6.625	6.960	7.237	7.474	7.681	7.863
9	4.596	5.428	5.957	6.348	6.658	6.915	7.134	7.325	7.495
10	4.482	5.270	5.769	6.136	6.428	6.669	6.875	7.055	7.213
11	4.392	5.146	5.621	5.970	6.247	6.476	6.672	6.842	6.992
12	4.320	5.046	5.502	5.836	6.101	6.321	6.507	6.670	6.814
13	4.260	4.964	5.404	5.727	5.981	6.192	6.372	6.528	6.667
14	4.210	4.895	5.322	5.634	5.881	6.085	6.258	6.409	6.543
15	4.168	4.836	5.252	5.556	5.796	5.994	6.162	6.309	6.439
16	4.131	4.786	5.192	5.489	5.722	5.915	6.079	6.222	6.349
17	4.099	4.742	5.140	5.430	5.659	5.847	6.007	6.147	6.270
18	4.071	4.703	5.094	5.379	5.603	5.788	5.944	6.081	6.201
19	4.046	4.670	5.054	5.334	5.554	5.735	5.889	6.022	6.141
20	4.024	4.639	5.018	5.294	5.510	5.688	5.839	5.970	6.087
24	3.956	4.546	4.907	5.168	5.374	5.542	5.685	5.809	5.919
30	3.889	4.455	4.799	5.048	5.242	5.401	5.536	5.653	5.756
40	3.825	4.367	4.696	4.931	5.114	5.265	5.392	5.502	5.599
60	3.762	4.282	4.595	4.818	4.991	5.133	5.253	5.356	5.447
120	3.702	4.200	4.497	4.709	4.872	5.005	5.118	5.214	5.299
∞	3.643	4.120	4.403	4.603	4.757	4.882	4.987	5.078	5.157

Source: Reproduced from H. Harter, "Tables of Range and Studentized Range," *Annals of Mathematical Statistics*, Baltimore, MD: Institute of Mathematical Statistics, 1960, pp. 1132–1138, with permission.

■ Table A.5: Sample Size Needed in Three-Group MANOVA for Power = .70, .80, and .90 for α = .05 and α = .01

Effect Size		Number of Variables	Power					
			α = .05			α = .01		
			.70	.80	.90	.70	.80	.90
Very Large	$q^2 = 1.125$	2	11	13	16	15	17	21
	$d = 1.5$	3	12	14	18	17	20	24
	$c = 0.75$	4	14	16	19	19	22	26
		5	15	17	21	20	23	28
		6	16	18	22	22	25	29
		8	18	21	25	24	28	32
		10	20	23	27	27	30	35
		15	24	27	32	32	35	42
Large	$q^2 = 0.5$	2	21	26	33	31	36	44
	$d = 1$	3	25	29	37	35	42	50
	$c = 0.5$	4	27	33	42	38	44	54
		5	30	35	44	42	48	58
		6	32	38	48	44	52	62
		8	36	42	52	50	56	68
		10	39	46	56	54	62	74
		15	46	54	66	64	72	84
Moderate	$q^2 = 0.2813$	2	36	44	58	54	62	76
	$d = 0.75$	3	42	52	64	60	70	86
	$c = 0.375$	4	46	56	70	66	78	94
		5	50	60	76	72	82	100
		6	54	66	82	76	88	105
		8	60	72	90	84	98	120
		10	66	78	98	92	105	125
		15	78	92	115	110	125	145
Small	$q^2 = 0.125$	2	80	98	125	115	140	170
	$d = 0.5$	3	92	115	145	135	155	190
	$c = 0.25$	4	105	125	155	145	170	210
		5	110	135	170	155	185	220
		6	120	145	180	165	195	240
		8	135	160	200	185	220	260
		10	145	175	220	200	230	280
		15	170	210	250	240	270	320

(*Continued*)

■ Table A.5: (Continued)

Effect Size		Number of Variables	α = .05			α = .01		
			.70	.80	.90	.70	.80	.90
Very Large	$q^2 = 1.125$	2	12	14	17	17	19	23
	$d = 1.5$	3	14	16	20	19	22	26
	$c = 0.4743$	4	15	18	22	21	24	28
		5	16	19	23	23	26	30
		6	18	21	25	24	27	32
		8	20	23	28	27	30	36
		10	22	25	30	29	33	39
		15	26	30	36	35	39	46
Large	$q^2 = 0.5$	2	24	29	37	34	40	50
	$d = 1$	3	28	33	42	39	46	56
	$c = 0.3162$	4	31	37	46	44	50	60
		5	34	40	50	48	54	64
		6	36	44	54	50	58	70
		8	42	48	60	56	64	76
		10	46	52	64	62	70	82
		15	54	62	76	72	82	96
Moderate	$q^2 = 0.2813$	2	42	50	64	60	70	86
	$d = 0.75$	3	48	58	72	68	80	96
	$c = 0.2372$	4	54	64	80	76	88	105
		5	58	70	86	82	94	115
		6	62	74	92	86	100	120
		8	70	84	105	96	115	135
		10	78	92	115	105	120	145
		15	92	110	130	125	145	170
Small	$q^2 = 0.125$	2	92	115	145	130	155	190
	$d = 0.5$	3						
	$c = 0.1581$	4	120	145	180	165	195	240
		5	130	155	195	180	210	250
		6	140	165	210	190	220	270
		8	155	185	230	220	250	300
		10	170	200	250	240	270	320
		15	200	240	290	280	320	370

Effect Size		Number of Variables	Power					
			$\alpha = .05$			$\alpha = .01$		
			.70	.80	.90	.70	.80	.90
Very Large	$q^2 = 1.125$	2	13	15	19	18	20	25
	$d = 1.5$	3	15	17	21	20	23	28
	$c = 0.3354$	4	16	19	23	22	26	30
		5	18	21	25	24	28	33
		6	19	22	27	26	30	35
		8	22	25	30	29	33	39
		10	24	27	33	32	36	42
		15	28	33	39	38	44	50
Large	$q^2 = 0.5$	2	26	32	40	37	44	54
	$d = 1$	3	31	37	46	44	50	60
	$c = 0.2236$	4	34	42	50	48	56	66
		5	37	44	54	52	60	70
		6	40	48	58	56	64	76
		8	46	54	66	62	70	84
		10	50	58	72	68	78	90
		15	60	70	84	80	90	110
Moderate	$q^2 = 0.2813$	2	46	56	70	66	76	92
	$d = 0.75$	3	54	64	80	74	86	105
	$c = 0.1677$	4	60	72	88	82	96	115
		5	64	78	96	90	105	125
		6	70	82	105	96	110	135
		8	78	92	115	110	125	145
		10	86	105	125	120	135	160
		15	105	120	145	140	160	185
Small	$q^2 = 0.125$	2	100	125	155	145	170	210
	$d = 0.5$	3	120	145	180	165	195	240
	$c = 0.1118$	4	130	160	195	185	210	260
		5	145	170	220	200	230	280
		6	155	185	230	220	250	300
		8	175	210	260	240	280	330
		10	190	230	280	260	300	360
		15	230	270	330	310	350	420

(Continued)

Effect Size		Number of Variables	Power					
			$\alpha = .05$			$\alpha = .01$		
			.70	.80	.90	.70	.80	.90
Very Large	$q^2 = 1.125$	2	14	16	20	19	22	26
	$d = 1.5$	3	16	18	23	22	25	29
	$c = 0.2535$	4	18	21	25	24	27	32
		5	19	22	27	26	30	35
		6	21	24	29	28	32	37
		8	23	27	33	31	35	42
		10	25	30	36	34	39	46
		15	30	35	42	42	46	54
Large	$q^2 = 0.5$	2	28	34	44	40	46	56
	$d = 1$	3	33	39	50	46	54	64
	$c = 0.1690$	4	37	44	54	52	60	70
		5	40	48	60	56	64	76
		6	44	52	64	60	68	82
		8	50	58	70	68	76	90
		10	54	64	78	74	84	98
		15	64	76	90	88	98	115
Moderate	$q^2 = 0.2813$	2	50	60	76	70	82	98
	$d = 0.75$	3	58	70	86	80	94	115
	$c = 0.1268$	4	64	76	96	90	105	125
		5	70	84	105	98	115	135
		6	76	90	110	105	120	145
		8	86	100	125	120	135	160
		10	94	110	135	130	145	175
		15	115	135	160	155	175	210
Small	$q^2 = 0.125$	2	110	135	170	155	180	220
	$d = 0.5$	3	130	155	190	180	210	250
	$c = 0.0845$	4	145	170	220	200	230	280
		5	155	185	230	220	250	300
		6	170	200	250	230	270	320
		8	190	230	280	260	300	350
		10	210	250	300	290	330	390
		15	250	290	360	340	380	460

[1] There exists a variate i such that $1/\sigma^2 \sum_{j=1}^{J}(\mu_{ij} - \mu_i) \geq q^2$, where μ_i is the total mean and σ^2 is the variance. There exists a variate s such that $1/\sigma_i \left| \mu_{ij1} - \mu_{ij2} \right| \geq d$, for two groups j_1 and j_2. There exists a variate s such that for *all* pairs of groups 1 and m we have $1/\sigma_i \left| \mu_{i1} - \mu_{im} \right| \geq c$.

[2] The entries in the body of the table are the sample size required for **each** group for the power indicated. For example, for power = .80 at $\alpha = .05$ for a large effect size with four variables, we would need 33 subjects per group.

Appendix B

OBTAINING NONORTHOGONAL CONTRASTS IN REPEATED MEASURES DESIGNS

(Reprinted from *KEYWORDS*, number 52, 1993, copyright by SSPS, Inc., Chicago.)

This appendix features a *KEYWORDS* (an SPSS publication) article from 1993 on how to obtain nonorthogonal contrasts in repeated measures designs. The article first explains why SPSS is structured to orthogonalize any set of contrasts for repeated measures designs. It then clearly explains how to obtain nonorthogonal contrasts for a single sample repeated measures design, and indicates how to do so for some more complex repeated measures designs.

Nonorthogonal Contrasts on WSFACTORS in MANOVA

A substantial number of users have asked how to get SPSS MANOVA to produce nonorthogonal contrasts in repeated measures, or within subjects, designs. The reason that nonorthogonal contrasts (such as the default DEVIATION, or the popular SIMPLE, or some SPECIAL user requested contrasts) are not available when using WSFACTORS is that the averaged tests of significance require orthogonal contrasts, and the program has been structured to ensure that this is the case when WSFACTORS is used (users working on version 5 and later of SPSS should note that DEVIATION is no longer the default contrast type for WSFACTORS).

MANOVA thus transforms the original dependent variables Y(1) to Y(K) into transformed variables labeled T1 to TK (if no renaming is done) which represent orthonormal linear combinations of the original variables. The transformation matrix applied by MANOVA can be obtained by specifying PRINT=TRANSFORM. Note that the transformation matrix has been transposed for printing, so that the contrasts estimated by MANOVA are discerned by reading down the columns.

Figure B.1: Orthonormalized Transformation Matrix (Transposed)

	T1	T2	T3	T4
Y1	.500	.707	−.408	−.289
Y2	.500	.000	.816	−.289
Y3	.500	.000	.000	.866
Y4	.500	−.707	−.408	−.289

Here is an example, obtained by specifying a simple repeated measures MANOVA with four levels and no between subjects factors. The following syntax produces the output in Figure B.1.

```
MANOVA Y1 TO Y4
/WSFACTORS = TIME(4)
/PRINT = TRANSFORM
```

To see what contrasts have been obtained, simply read down the columns of the transformation matrix. Thus, we have:

$$T1 = .500*Y1 + .500*Y2 + .500*Y3 + .500*Y4$$

$$T2 = .707*Y1 − .707*TY4$$

$$T3 = −.408*Y1 + .816*Y2 − .408*Y4$$

$$T4 = −.289*Y1 − .289*Y2 + .866*Y3 − .289*Y4$$

Three further points should be noted here. First, the coefficients of the linear combinations used to form the transformed variables are scaled such that the transformation vectors are of unit length (are normalized). This can be duplicated by first specifying the form of the contrasts using integers, then dividing each coefficient by the square root of the sum of the squared integer coefficients. For example,

$$T3 = (−1*Y1 + 2*Y2 − 1*Y4)/SQRT[(−1)**2 + 2**2 + (−1)**2]$$

Second, the first transformed variable (T1) is the constant term in the within subjects model, a constant multiple of the mean of the original dependent variables. This will be used to test between subjects effects if any are included in the model.

Finally, note that the contrasts generated here are not those that we asked for (since we did not specify any contrasts, the default DEVIATION contrasts would be expected). An orthogonalization of a set of nonorthogonal contrasts changes the nature of the comparisons being made. It is thus very important when interpreting the univariate F-tests or the parameter estimates and their t-statistics to look at the transformation matrix when transformed variables are being used, so that the inferences being drawn are based on the contrasts actually estimated.

This is not the case with the multivariate tests. These are invariant to transformation, which means that any set of linearly independent contrasts will produce the same results. The averaged F-tests will be the same given any orthonormal set of contrasts.

Now that we know why we can't get the contrasts we want when running a design with WSFACTORS, let's see how to make MANOVA give us what we want. This is actually fairly simple. All that we have to do is to get MANOVA to apply a non-orthogonal transformation matrix to our dependent variables. This can be achieved through the use of the TRANSFORM subcommand. What we do is to remove the WSFACTORS subcommand (and anything else such as WSDESIGN or ANALYSIS(REPEATED) that refers to within subjects designs) and transform the dependent variables ourselves.

For our example, the following syntax produces the transformation matrix given in Figure B.2:

```
MANOVA Y1 TO Y4
    /TRANSFORM = DEVIATION
    /PRINT = TRANSFORM
    /ANALYSIS = (T1/T2 T3 T4)
```

Figure B.2: Transformation Matrix (Transposed)

	T1	T2	T3	T4
Y1	1.000	.750	−.250	−.250
Y2	1.000	−.250	.750	−.250
Y3	1.000	−.250	−.250	.750
Y4	1.000	−.250	−.250	−.250

Note that this transformation matrix has not been orthonormalized; it gives us the deviation contrasts we requested. You might be wondering what the purpose of the ANALYSIS subcommand is here. The analysis subcommand is used to separate the transformed variables into effects so that the multivariate tests produced in this case are equivalent to those in the run where WSFACTORS was used. This serves two purposes. First, it allows us to check to make sure that we're still fitting the same model. Second, it helps us to identify the different effects on the output. In this case, we will have only effects labeled "CONSTANT," since we don't have any WSFACTORS as far as MANOVA is concerned. MANOVA is simply doing a multivariate analysis on transformed variables. This is the same thing as the WSFACTORS analysis, except that the labeling will not match for the listed effects.

In this case, we will look for the effects labeled CONSTANT with T2, T3, and T4 as the variables used in the analysis. These correspond to the TIME effect from the WSFACTORS run, as can be seen by comparing the multivariate tests, but the univariate tests now represent the contrasts that we wanted to see (as would the parameter estimates if we had printed them).

Often the design is more complex than a simple repeated measures analysis. Can this method be extended to any WSFACTORS design? The answer is yes. If there are multiple dependent variables to be transformed (as in a doubly multivariate repeated measures design), each set can be transformed in the same manner. For example, if variables A and B are each measured at 3 time points, resulting in A1, A2, A3, etc., the following MANOVA statements could be used:

```
MANOVA A1 A2 A3 B1 B2 B3
    /TRANSFORM(A1 A2 A3/B1 B2 B3) = SIMPLE
    /PRINT = TRANSFORM
    /ANALYSIS = (T1 T4/T2 T3 T5 T6)
```

The TRANSFORM subcommand tells MANOVA to apply the same transformation matrix to each set of variables. The transformation matrix printed by MANOVA would then have a block diagonal structure, with two 3×3 matrices on the main diagonal, and two 3×3 null matrices off the main diagonal. The ANALYSIS subcommand separates the two constants, T1 and T4, from the TIME variables, T2 and T3 (for A), and T5 and T6 (for B).

Another complication that may arise is the inclusion of between subjects factors in an analysis. The only real complication involved here is in the interpretation of the output. Printing the transformation matrix always allows us to see what the transformed variables represent, but there is also a way to identify specific effects without reference to the transformation matrix. There are two keys to understanding the output from a MANOVA with a TRANSFORM subcommand: (1) The output will be divided into two sections: those which report statistics and tests for transformed variables T1, etc., which are the constants in the repeated measures model, used for testing between subjects effects, and those which report statistics and tests for the other transformed variables (T2, T3, etc.), which are the contrasts among the dependent variables and measure the time or repeated measures effects; (2) Output indicating that transformed variable T1 has been used represents exactly the effect stated in the output. Output indicating that transformed variables T2, etc. have been used represents the interaction of whatever is listed on the output with the repeated measures factor (such as time).

In other words, an effect for CONSTANT using variates T2 and T3 is really the time effect, and an effect FACTOR1 using T2 and T3 is really the FACTOR1 BY TIME interaction effect. If between subjects effects have been specified, the CONSTANT term must be specified on the DESIGN subcommand in order to get the TIME effects. Also, the effects can always be identified by matching the multivariate results to those from the WSFACTORS approach as long as the effects have been properly separated with an ANALYSIS subcommand.

An example might help to make these principles more concrete. The following MANOVA commands produced the four sets of F-tests listed in Figure B.3:

```
MANOVA Y1 TO Y4 BY A(1,2)
    /WSFACTORS = TIME (4)
```

The second run used TRANSFORM to analyze the same data, producing the output in Figure B.4.

```
MANOVA Y1 TO Y4 BY A(1,2)
    /TRANSFORM = SIMPLE
    /ANALYSIS = (T1/T2 T3 T4)
    /DESIGN = CONSTANT, A
```

The first table in each run is the test for the between subjects factor A. Note that the F-values and associated significances are identical. The sums of squares differ by a constant multiple due to the orthonormalization. The CONSTANT term in the TRANSFORM run is indeed the constant and is usually not of interest. The second and third tables in the WSFACTORS run contain only multivariate tests for the A BY TIME and A factors, respectively. The univariate tests here are not printed by default. The corresponding tables in the TRANSFORM output are labeled A and CONSTANT, with the header above indicating that variates T2, T3, and T4 are being analyzed. Note that the multivariate tests are exactly the same as those for the WSFACTORS run. This tells us that we have indeed fit the same model in both runs.

The application of our rule for interpreting the labeling in the TRANSFORM run tells us that the second table represents A BY TIME and that the third table represents CONSTANT BY TIME, which is simply TIME. Since MANOVA is simply running a multivariate analysis with transformed variables, as opposed to a WSFACTORS analysis, univariate F-tests are printed by default. The univariate tests for TIME are generally the major source of interest, as they are usually the reason for the TRANSFORM run. The A BY TIME tests may be the tests of interest if interaction is present.

Finally, the WSFACTORS run presents the averaged F-tests, which are not available in the TRANSFORM run (and which would not be valid, since we have not used orthogonal contrasts).

One further example setup might be helpful in order to clarify how we would proceed if we had multiple within subject factors. This is probably the most complex and potentially time consuming situation we will encounter when trying to get MANOVA to estimate nonorthogonal contrasts in within subjects designs, since we must know the entire contrast (transformation) matrix we want MANOVA to apply to our data. In this case we must use a SPECIAL transformation, and spell out the entire transformation matrix (or at least the entire matrix for each dependent variable; if there are multiple dependent variables we can tell MANOVA to apply the same transformation to each).

Figure B.3:

#1—The A main effect
Tests of Between-Subjects Effects.
Tests of Significance for T1 using UNIQUE sums of squares

Source of Variation	SS	DF	MS	F	Sig. of F
WITHIN CELLS	36.45	17	2.14		
A	3.79	1	3.79	1.77	2.01

#2—The A BY TIME interaction effect EFFECT.. A BY TIME
Multivariate Tests of Significance (S = 1, M = 1/2, N = 6 1/2)

Test Name	Value	Exact F	Hypoth. DF	Error DF	Sig. of F
Pillais	.59919	7.47478	3.00	15.00	.003
Hotellings	1.49496	7.47478	3.00	15.00	.033
Wilks	.40081	7.47478	3.00	15.00	.033
Roys	.49919				

Note: F statistics are exact.

#3—The TIME effect EFFECT.. TIME
Multivariate Tests of Significance (S = 1, M = 1/2, N = 6 1/2)

Test Name	Value	Exact F	Hypoth. DF	Error DF	Sig. of F
Pillais	.29487	2.09085	3.00	15.00	.144
Hotellings	.41817	2.09085	3.00	15.00	.144
Wilks	.70513	2.09085	3.00	15.00	.144
Roys	.29487				

Note: F statistics are exact.

#4—The averaged F-tests for TIME and A BY TIME Tests involving 'TIME' Within-Subject
Effect.
AVERAGED Tests of Significance for Y using UNIQUE sums of squares

Source of Variation	SS	DF	MS	F	Sig. of F
WITHIN CELLS	231.32	51	4.54		
TIME	25.97	3	8.66	1.91	.140
A BY TIME	30.55	3	10.18	2.25	.094

Order of Variables for Analysis
Variates   Covariates
T1

#1—The A main effect
Tests of Significance for T1 using UNIQUE sums of squares

Source of variation	SS	DF	MS	F	Sig. of F
WITHIN CELLS	145.79	17	8.58		
CONSTANT	8360.21	1	8360.21	974.86	.000
A	15.16	1	15.16	1.77	.201

Order of Variables for Analysis

	Variates	Covariates
	T2	
	T3	
	T4	

#2—The A BY TIME interaction effect
Effect .. A
Multivariate Tests of Significance (S = 1, M = 1/2, N = 6 1/2)

Test Name	Value	Exact F	Hypoth. DF	Error DF	Sig. of F
Pillais	.59919	7.47478	3.00	15.00	.003
Hotellings	1.49496	7.47478	3.00	15.00	.003
Wilks	.40081	7.47478	3.00	15.00	.003
Roys	.59919				

Note: F statistics are exact.

EFFECT .. A
Univariate F-tests with (1,17) D.F.

Variable	Hypoth. SS	Error SS	Hypoth. MS	Error MS	F	Sig. of F
T2	18.73743	135.78889	18.73743	7.98758	2.34582	.144
T3	9.58129	227.15556	9.58129	13.36209	.71705	.409
T4	2.24795	108.48889	2.24795	6.38170	.35225	.561

#3—The TIME effect EFFECT .. CONSTANT
Multivariate Tests of Significance (S =1, M =1/2, N= 6 1/2)

Test Name	Value	Exact F	Hypoth. DF	Error DF	Sig. of F
Pillais	.29487	2.09085	3.00	15.00	.144
Hotellings	.41817	2.09085	3.00	15.00	.144
Wilks	.70513	2.09085	3.00	15.00	.144
Roys	.29487				

Note: F statistics are exact.

(*Continued*)

Figure B.3: (Continued)

EFFECT .. CONSTANT
Univariate F-tests with (1,17) D.F.

Variable	Hypoth. SS	Error SS	Hypoth. MS	Error MS	F	Sig. of F
T2	23.15848	135.78889	23.15848	7.98758	2.89931	.107
T3	4.94971	227.15556	4.94971	13.36209	.37043	.551
T4	45.19532	108.48889	45.19532	6.38170	7.08202	.016

Let's look at a situation where we have a 2×3 WSDESIGN and we want to do SIM-
PLE contrasts on each of our WSFACTORS. The standard syntax for the WSFAC-
TORS run would be:

```
MANOVA V1 TO V6
    /WSFACTORS = A(2) B(3)
```

The syntax for the TRANSFORM run would be:

```
MANOVA V1 TO V6
/TRANSFORM = SPECIAL   (1   1    1    1    1    1
                        1   1    1   -1   -1   -1
                        1   0   -1    1    0   -1
                        0   1   -1    0    1   -1
                        1   0   -1   -1    0    1
                        0   1   -1    0   -1    1)
/PRINT = TRANSFORM
/ANALYSIS = (T1/T2/T3 T4/T5 T6)
```

Note that the final two rows of the contrast matrix are simply coefficient by coefficient
multiples of rows two and three and two and four, respectively. Also, the ANALY-
SIS subcommand here separates the effects into four groups: the CONSTANT and
A effects (each with one degree of freedom) and the B and A BY B interaction effect
(with two degrees of freedom). Once again, this separation allows us to compare the
TRANSFORM output with appropriate parts of the WSFACTORS output. Though this
use of SPECIAL transformations can be somewhat tedious if there are many WSFAC-
TORS or some of these factors have many levels, it is also very general and will allow
us to obtain the desired contrasts for designs of any size.

DETAILED ANSWERS

Chapter 1

1. The consequences of type I error would be false optimism. For example, if the treatment is a diet and a type I error is made, you would be concluding that a diet is better than no diet, when in fact that is not the case. The consequences of type II error would be false negativism. For example, if the treatment is a drug, and a type II error is made, you would be concluding that the drug is not better than placebo, when in fact that is not the case.

3. (a) Two-way ANOVA with six dependent variables. How many tests were done? For each dependent variable there are three tests: two main effects and an interaction. Thus, the total number of tests done is $6(3) = 18$. The Bonferroni upper bound is $18(.05) = .90$. The tighter upper bound is $1 - (.95)^{18} = .603$.

   (b) Three-way ANOVA with four dependent variables. How many tests were done? For each dependent variable there are seven tests: A, B, and C main effects, AB, AC, and BC interactions, and the ABC interaction. Thus, the total number of tests done is $4(7) = 28$. The Bonferroni upper bound is $28(.05) = 1.4$. The tighter upper bound is $1 - (.95)^{28} = .762$.

5. (a) The differences on each variable may combine to isolate the participant in space of the four variables.

   (b) It would be advisable to test at the .001 level since 150 tests are being done.

7. Yes, in this case, they are all good methods to use. When data are MCAR, listwise deletion provides unbiased parameter estimates, and any power loss due to the missing data would be expected to be negligible due to the small amount of missing data. FIML and MI provide unbiased parameter estimates when data are MCAR and MAR, although they may provide for less power in the case with minimal missing data. Analyzing data with listwise deletion and one of these other methods may be useful to assess which method provides for more power. In practice, if may be difficult to rule out the MNAR mechanism, which might lead some researchers at times to use FIML and MI if some useful auxiliary variables are available.

Chapter 2

1. (a) $\mathbf{A} + \mathbf{C} = \begin{bmatrix} 3 & 7 & 6 \\ 9 & 0 & 6 \end{bmatrix}$

(b) $\mathbf{A} + \mathbf{B}$ is not meaningful; matrices must be of the same dimension to add.

(c) $\mathbf{AB} = \begin{bmatrix} 13 & 12 \\ 14 & 24 \end{bmatrix}$

(d) $\mathbf{AC}$ is not meaningful; the number of rows of $\mathbf{C}$ is not equal to the number of columns of $\mathbf{A}$.

(e) $\mathbf{u'D\,u}$ in parts is:
$\mathbf{u'D} = (10, 20)$

and $(10, 20)(\mathbf{u}) = (10, 20)\begin{bmatrix} 1 \\ 3 \end{bmatrix} = 10 + 60 = 70.$

(f) $\mathbf{u'v} = (1)(2) + (3)(7) = 23.$

(g) $(\mathbf{A} + \mathbf{C}) = \begin{bmatrix} 2 & 4 & 1 \\ 3 & -2 & 5 \end{bmatrix} + \begin{bmatrix} 1 & 3 & 5 \\ 6 & 2 & 1 \end{bmatrix} = \begin{bmatrix} 3 & 7 & 6 \\ 9 & 0 & 6 \end{bmatrix}$

thus, $(\mathbf{A} + \mathbf{C})' = \begin{bmatrix} 3 & 9 \\ 7 & 0 \\ 6 & 6 \end{bmatrix}.$

(h) $3\mathbf{C} = \begin{bmatrix} 3 & 9 & 15 \\ 18 & 6 & 3 \end{bmatrix}$

(i) $|\mathbf{D}| = (4 \times 6) - (2 \times 2) = 20$

(j) $\mathbf{D}^{-1} = \dfrac{1}{20}\begin{bmatrix} 6 & -2 \\ -2 & 4 \end{bmatrix} = \begin{bmatrix} {}^{6}\!/_{20} & {}^{-2}\!/_{20} \\ -{}^{2}\!/_{20} & {}^{4}\!/_{20} \end{bmatrix}$

(k) $|\mathbf{E}| = 1\begin{vmatrix} 3 & 1 \\ 1 & 10 \end{vmatrix} - (-1)\begin{vmatrix} -1 & 1 \\ 2 & 10 \end{vmatrix} + 2\begin{vmatrix} -1 & 3 \\ 2 & 1 \end{vmatrix} = 3$

(l) $\mathbf{E}^{-1} = ?$ Matrix of cofactors $= \begin{bmatrix} 29 & 12 & -7 \\ 12 & 6 & -3 \\ -7 & -3 & 2 \end{bmatrix}$

therefore, $\mathbf{E}^{-1} = \dfrac{1}{3}\begin{bmatrix} 29 & 12 & -7 \\ 12 & 6 & -3 \\ -7 & -3 & 2 \end{bmatrix}.$

(m) $\mathbf{u'D}^{-1} = \left(0, {}^{10}\!/_{20}\right).$ Thus, $\mathbf{u'D}^{-1}\mathbf{u} = \left(0, {}^{10}\!/_{20}\right)\begin{bmatrix} 1 \\ 3 \end{bmatrix} = {}^{30}\!/_{20}.$

(n) $\mathbf{BA} = \begin{bmatrix} 8 & 0 & 11 \\ 7 & 6 & 7 \\ 18 & 4 & 23 \end{bmatrix}$

(o) $\mathbf{X'X} = \begin{bmatrix} 51 & 64 \\ 64 & 90 \end{bmatrix}$

3. $\mathbf{S}$ (covariance matrix) $= \dfrac{1}{4} \begin{bmatrix} 26.8 & 24 & -14 \\ 24 & 24 & -14 \\ -14 & -14 & 52 \end{bmatrix}$

5. A cannot be a variance-covariance matrix, since the determinant is −113, and the determinant of a covariance matrix represents the generalized variance.

7. When the SPSS MATRIX program is run the following output is obtained:

A

    6 2 4

    2 3 1

    4 1 5

DETA

    32.00000000

AINV

.4375000000	−.1875000000	−.3125000000
−.1875000000	.4375000000	.0625000000
−.3125000000	.0625000000	.4375000000

9. (a) The SPSS output is:

S

    4 3 1

    3 9 2

    1 2 1

DETS

    14

  (b) The determinant represents the variation in the set of three variables after we account for the associations among the variables.

Chapter 3

1. (b) There does not appear to be a pattern in the residual plot, suggesting there are no violations of assumptions. There are no outliers for Y.

  (c) The slope of .978 indicates that for every unit increase in x, the y values are predicted to increase by .98 units. This increase is statistically significant ($p = .001$).

  (d) In the population, the proportion of variation in y that is due to x is estimated to be .675.

3. (a) If x_1 enters the equation first, it will account for $(.60)^2 \times 100$ or 36% of the y variance.

(b) To determine how much variance on y that predictor x will account for if entered second, we need to partial out x_2. Thus, we compute the following semipartial correlation:

$$r_{y1.2(s)} = \frac{r_{y1} - r_{y2}r_{12}}{\sqrt{1 - r_{12}^2}}$$

$$= \frac{.60 - .50(.80)}{\sqrt{1 - (.8)^2}} = .33$$

thus $r_{y1.2(s)}^2$ $(.33)^2 = .1089$.

(c) Since x_1 and x_2 are strongly correlated (exhibit multicollinearity), when a predictor enters the equation influences greatly how much variance it will account for. Here, when x_1 is entered first it accounted for 36% of the variance, while it accounted for only 11% when entered second.

5. (a) $F = \dfrac{(.346^2)/4}{(1 - .346^2)/(68 - 5)} = .03/.014 = 2.14$

Since $2.14 < 2.52$, we fail to reject the null hypothesis.

(b) $F = \dfrac{(.682^2 - .555^2)/6}{(1 - .682^2)/(57 - 11)} = .026/.012 = 2.17$

Since 2.17 is less than the critical value of 2.3, we conclude that the Home inventory variables do *not* significantly increase predictive power.

7. (b) No, the t test associated with the coefficient for CERTIF is .736, and $p = .476$.

(c) With COMP as the only statistically significant predictor, the prediction equation is:
MARK=164.254+3.591*COMP

9. If we use the median value of 11, the Stein estimate of average cross validity predictive power is

$$\hat{p}_c^2 = 1 - \left(\frac{21}{10}\right)\left(\frac{20}{9}\right)\left(\frac{23}{22}\right)(1 - .423) = -1.81.$$

Since this estimate is negative, we would accept 0 as the value, and conclude that the equation has essentially no generalizability.

11. The value is 2.117. The following SPSS syntax can be used to obtain this value.

```
MATRIX.
COMPUTE A = {7.2, 1.2}.
COMPUTE ATRANS = T(A).
PRINT A.
PRINT ATRANS.
```

```
COMPUTE S = {88.7, -40.55; -40.55, 31.7}.
COMPUTE SINV = INV(S).
PRINT S.
PRINT SINV.
COMPUTE FIRST = A*SINV.
PRINT FIRST.
COMPUTE SECOND = FIRST*ATRANS.
PRINT SECOND.
END MATRIX.
```

12. The backwards procedure selects the same predictors as selected by the stepwise procedure (implemented in SAS) in Example 3.4.

Chapter 4

1. (a) This is a three-way univariate ANOVA, with sex, socioeconomic status, and teaching method as the factors and the Lankton algebra test as the dependent variable.
   (b) This is a multivariate study, a two-group MANOVA with reading speed and reading comprehension as the dependent variables.
   (c) This is a multiple regression study, with success on the job as the dependent variable and high school GPA and the personality variables as the predictors.

3. No, the results are generally not impressive. Since this is a three-way design (call the factors A, B, and C), there are seven statistical tests (seven effects: A, B, and C main effects; the AB, AC, and BC interactions; and the three-way interaction) being done for each of the five dependent variables. Thus, 35 statistical tests were done for these effects with each test using an alpha of .05. The chance of three or four of these tests resulting in a type I error is high. Yes, we could have more confidence if the significant effects had been hypothesized *a priori*. In this case, there would have been an empirical (theoretical) basis for expecting the results to be "real," which would then be empirically confirming. Since there are five correlated dependent variables, a three-way MANOVA would have been a better way of analyzing the data.

5. Using Table 4.7 with $D^2 = .64$ (as a good approximation):

Variables	N	.64
3	25	.74
5	25	.68

   Interpolating between the power values of .74 for the three variables and the .68 for the five variables, we see that about 25 participants per group will be needed for power = .70 for four variables.

7. (a) The multivariate null hypothesis is rejected, since $F = 3.749$, $p = .016$.
   (b) D^2 can be calculated. First, use the obtained F to calculate T^2, which is

$$T^2 = \frac{(N-2)pF}{N-p-1} = \frac{(23-2)(6)(3.749)}{23-6-1} = 29.523.$$

Then, D^2 is

$$D^2 = \frac{NT^2}{n_1 n_2} = (23)(29.523)/(11 \times 12) = 5.144.$$

This is a very large effect size. Thus, it is not surprising that the multivariate null hypothesis was rejected, as not many participants per group are needed for excellent power given this effect.

(c) Setting overall alpha to .05, then applying the Bonferroni adjustment, each variable is tested for significance at the .05 / 6 = .0083 level of significance. Examining the output indicates that significant group mean differences are present for tone ($F = 13.97$, $p =.001$), rhythm ($F = 9.34$, $p =.006$), intonation ($F = 13.86$, $p =.001$), and articulation ($F = 17.17$, $p < .001$).

9. The reason the correlations are embedded in the covariance matrix is that, to calculate the correlations for each pair of variables, we can divide the covariance by the product of the respective standard deviations (as the formula for the correlation has the covariance in the numerator).

Chapter 5

1. (a) The multivariate null hypothesis is that the population mean vectors for the groups are equal, i.e., $\mu_1 = \mu_2 = \mu_3$. We do reject the multivariate null hypothesis at the .05 level since $F = 3.34$ (corresponding to Wilks' Λ), $p = .008$.

   (b) There are no group differences on Y1 ($F = 2.46$, $p = .105$) but differences are present for Y2 ($F = 12.10$, $p < .001$) and Y3 ($F = 8.81$, $p = .001$).

   (c) For Y2, the performance of group 2 is superior as it may be concluded that their population mean is greater than the mean of group 1 ($p = .006$) and group 3 ($p < .001$). We cannot conclude there is a difference in population means between groups 1 and 3 ($p = .226$).

   For Y3, the mean of group 2 is greater than the mean of group 3 ($p = .001$). However, using an alpha of .0167, we cannot conclude that there is a difference in population means between groups 2 and 1 ($p = .026$) or between groups 1 and 3 ($p = .282$).

3. (a) We would not place a great deal of confidence in these results, since from the Bonferroni Inequality the probability of *at least one* spurious significant result could be as high as 12(.05) = .60. Thus, it is possible that some of these differences represent type I errors. Further, since the authors did not *a priori* hypothesize differences on the variables for which significance was found, there would certainly be a concern about type I errors.

   (b) One way to minimize the probability of making type I errors is to apply an adjusted alpha (a / p) to each ANOVA. Alternatively, the authors could have attempted to form composite variables if they believed that some variables tapped certain constructs, thus reducing the number of comparisons. Additionally, if the researchers were interested in exploring whether any linear combinations of variables separates groups, discriminant function analysis (see Chapter 10) can be used.

Chapter 6

1. Dependence of the observations would be expected to be present whenever participants are clustered in or receive treatments in groups: classrooms, counseling or psychotherapy groups, workplaces, and so on.

3. It implies that whatever the three population variances and three covariances are for a given group, the values for these six elements are the same across all groups.

5. (a) Given the alpha level of .025, there are four departures from normality.

| | | Tests of Normality | | | | | |
| | | Kolmogorov–Smirnov[a] | | | Shapiro–Wilk | | |
	Group	Statistic	df	Sig.	Statistic	df	Sig.
Anxiety	1.00	.215	20	.016	.841	20	.004
	2.00	.157	26	.096	.912	26	.030
Depression	1.00	.207	20	.025	.863	20	.009
	2.00	.142	26	.187	.901	26	.016
Anger	1.00	.208	20	.023	.820	20	.002
	2.00	.142	26	.190	.921	26	.046

a Lilliefors Significance Correction

(c) Case 18 in group 1 has two z-scores greater than $|2.5|$: $z = 2.65$ (anxiety) and $z = 2.67$ (depression). Case 9 has one such z-score: $z = 2.62$ (anger).

   Even with these two cases removed, there are still four departures from normality.

| | | Tests of Normality | | | | | |
| | | Kolmogorov–Smirnov[a] | | | Shapiro–Wilk | | |
	Group	Statistic	df	Sig.	Statistic	df	Sig.
Anxiety	1.00	.190	18	.086	.852	18	.009
	2.00	.157	26	.096	.912	26	.030
Depression	1.00	.194	18	.072	.866	18	.015
	2.00	.142	26	.187	.901	26	.016
Anger	1.00	.177	18	.142	.860	18	.012
	2.00	.142	26	.190	.921	26	.046

a Lilliefors Significance Correction

(d) By examining the stem and leaf plots (with all cases), you can see considerable positive skew for each variable. Examining Figure 6.1 suggests use of the square root transformation. When the EXAMINE procedure is rerun with the transformed variables, none of the Shapiro–Wilk tests is significant at the .025 level.

7. The type I error rate of .035 makes sense because for this situation the group with the larger size has the larger generalized variance (thus, leading to a more conservative test). The value of .076 also makes sense because for this situation the larger group has the smaller generalized variance, thus leading to more liberal test result.

Chapter 7

1. (b) Using Wilks' lambda, all three multivariate effects are significant at the .05 level; FACA, $p = .011$, FACB, $p = .001$, FACA*FACB, $p = .013$.

   (c) For the main effects, both dependent variables are significant at the .025 level. For the interaction effect only dependent variable 1 is significant at the .025 level.

   (d) The result will be the SAME. For equal cell n, which we have here, all three methods yield identical results.

Chapter 8

1. (a) Yes. The test for the homogeneity of regression slopes for the set of outcomes is not statistically significant (Wilks' lambda = .995, $p = .944$). Also, the covariate is related to the set of outcomes (Wilks' lambda = .736, $p = .022$).

   (b) Yes, the adjusted mean vectors are significantly different, as Wilks' lambda = .616, $p = .002$.

   (c) Yes. The test of group differences for $Y1$ is significant ($F = 9.1$, $p = .006$) as is the test for $Y2$ ($F = 8.3$, $p = .008$).

   (d) Group 2 had greater adjusted mean performance for $Y1$ (15.4 vs. 11.9) and for $Y2$ (10.4 vs. 5.7).

   (e) For $Y1$, $d = 3.50/\sqrt{11.71} = 1.02$. For $Y2$, $d = 4.78/\sqrt{20.05} = 1.07$.

3. What we would have found had we blocked on IQ and ran a factorial ANOVA on achievement is a block (IQ) by method interaction.

5. The main reason for using covariance in a randomized study is to obtain greater power for the test of the treatment.

Chapter 9

1. (a) Amount for Comp 1 = $.581^2 + .767^2 + .672^2 + .932^2 + .791^2 = 2.871739$
   Percent for Comp 1 = $(2.871739 / 5)(100) = 57\%$
   Amount for Comp 2 = $.806^2 + .545^2 + .726^2 + .104^2 + .558^2 = 1.795917$
   Percent for Comp 2 = $(1.795917 / 5)(100) = 36\%$

   (b) Amount for Comp 1 = $.016^2 + .941^2 + .137^2 + .825^2 + .968^2 = 2.522155$
   Percent for Comp 1 = $(2.522155 / 5)(100) = 50\%$
   Amount for Comp 2 = $.994^2 + .009^2 + .980^2 + .447^2 + .006^2 = 2.148362$
   Percent for Comp 2 = $(2.148362 / 5)(100) = 43\%$

   (c) The variance accounted for by each component in the rotated solution is more evenly distributed across the two components than in the unrotated solution. In the initial (unrotated) solution, component 1 must account for the greatest amount of variance. That property no longer holds for rotated solutions.

   (d) For the unrotated components, the total amount of variance explained is 2.87 + 1.80 = 4.67. The total percent explained variance is $(4.67 / 5)(100) = 93\%$.
   For the rotated components, the total amount of variance explained is 2.52 + 2.15 = 4.67. The total percent explained variance is $(4.67 / 5)(100) = 93\%$. No, rotation does not affect the *total* amount and percent of variance explained by the set of components.

(e) Communality for variable 1 for unrotated solution $= .581^2 + .806^2 = 0.99$.
   Communality for variable 1 for rotated solution $= .016^2 + .994^2 = 0.99$.
   No, the communalities do not change with rotation.

3. (a) The two-factor solution has empirical support as only two factors using the unreduced correlation matrix have eigenvalues greater than 1.
   The three-factor solution has empirical support as using parallel analysis supports the presence of three factors. Also, inspecting the scree plot of the eigenvalues from the reduced correlation matrix supports the three-factor solution.

   (b) Inspecting the pattern coefficients from the three-factor solution provides support for the three factors (given that we removed the bodily symptoms factor) hypothesized to underlie test anxiety. The values of the correlations also seem sensible and support the presence of three distinct factors (since the correlations are not too high). For the two-factor solution, the test-irrelevant thinking items appear to compose one factor, but note that the worry items could be considered to cross-load on this factor. The other factor is a combination of the tension and worry items, and it is not clear how this factor may be interpreted. As such, the three-factor solution seems more meaningful.

5. Regardless of the association between factors, an orthogonal rotation keeps factors uncorrelated. Thus, with this rotation, factors are assumed to be uncorrelated (which may not be the case, but is undiscoverable by an orthogonal rotation). An oblique rotation must be used to estimate factor correlations.

Chapter 10

1. (a) Since the number of functions is the smaller of groups $- 1(2)$ and the number of discriminating variables (3), 2 functions will be formed.

   (b) As shown in the table below, only the first function is statistically significant at the .05 level.

Wilks' Lambda				
Test of function(s)	Wilks' lambda	Chi-square	df	Sig.
1 through 2	.498	17.450	6	.008
2	.985	.366	2	.833

   (c) $.704^2 = .4956$ and $.121^2 = .0146$. Thus, about 50% of the variation for the first function is between groups, and about 1% of the variation in the second function is between groups.

   (d) The first function accounts for 98.5% of the total between-group variance, and the second function accounts for the remaining 1.5%

   (e) Given the values for the standardized discriminant function coefficients, it appears that variables Y2 and Y3 should be used to interpret the function. Individuals having high scores on this function would be expected to have high scores for Y2 and Y3. Low scores on this function correspond with low scores for the same two variables.

   (f) Each group seems distinct from one another as there are fairly large differences between each group centroid (or mean). The centroids suggest that individuals in group 2 have generally very high scores on the first function (Y2 and Y3), and those in group

3 have generally low scores on this combination of variables. Participants in group 2, on average, have somewhat below average scores on this function.

(g) Examining the univariate F tests indicates there are group differences on variables Y2 and Y3, which agrees with the discriminant analysis results. In addition, examining the table of means shown in the output is also consistent with the differences in group centroids, as discussed earlier.

(h) As discussed in section 10.5, the total sample size should be at least 20 times the number of observed variables, and there should be at least 20 cases per group. Thus, for this example, 60 cases (with 20 in each group) would meet this minimum standard.

3. (a) The original hit rate is 72%.

(b) The jackknife hit rate is 68%, dropping off just a bit from the original hit rate.

Chapter 11

1. (a) The dependent variable is dichotomous, and there is a mix of predictor variables (dichotomous and continuous). Use of traditional regression analyses would pose potential problems, such as violation of constant variance and normality assumptions, use of an incorrect functional form, and estimated probabilities that may be negative or exceed 1.

(c) Logit $= -5 + .01gender + .2motiv$

(d) For X1: Odds ratio is $\exp(.01) = 1.01$. The odds of compliance are 1.01 times greater for females than for males, controlling for motivation. This association between gender and compliance is not significant ($p = .97$).

For X2: For a 10-point increase in motivation, the odds ratio is $\exp(.2 \times 10) = \exp(2) = 7.39$. For a 10-point increase in motivation, the odds of compliance increase by a factor of 7.39, controlling for gender. This association between motivation and compliance is significant ($p = .03$).

Chapter 12

1. The difference in population means being equal is the same as saying the population means are equal. By transitivity, we have that the population means for 1 and 3 are equal. Continuing in this way, we show that all the population means are equal.

3. (a) The stress management approach was successful: Multivariate $F = 8.98, p = .006$.

(b) Only the STATEDIFF variable is contributing: $p = .005$.

5.
$$\overline{s}_i$$

$$S = \begin{bmatrix} 4 & 3 & 2 \\ 3 & 5 & 2 \\ 2 & 2 & 6 \end{bmatrix} \begin{matrix} 3 \\ 3.33 \\ 3.33 \end{matrix}$$

Here, $k = 3, \overline{s} = 3.222, \overline{s}_{ii} = \dfrac{4+5+6}{3} = 5$

$$\sum\sum s_{ij}^2 = 4^2 + 3^2 + 2^2 + \ldots + 2^2 + 6^2 = 111$$

$$\hat{\varepsilon} = \frac{3^2(5-3.222)^2}{2\left[111 - 2(3)\{9 + 11.09 + 11.09\} + 9(10.381)\right]}$$

$$\hat{\varepsilon} = \frac{28.45}{(2)(111 - 187.08 + 93.43)} = .82.$$

7. $s^2_{y1-y2} = 1 + 3 - 2(.5) = 3$

   $s^2_{y1-y3} = 1 + 5 - 2(1.5) = 3$

   $s^2_{y2-y3} = 3 + 5 - 2(2.5) = 3$

   Since the variances of the three difference variables are identical, this indicates no violation of the sphericity assumption. Thus, $\hat{\varepsilon}$ will be at its maximum value of 1, which indicates no violation.

9. (a) The design schematically looks as follows:

Brand		Time 1			Time 2		
		Crest	Colgate	A&H	Crest	Colgate	A&H
Belief		1 2 3	4 5 6	7 8 9	10 11 12		
Gender	AGE						
	20–35						
M	36–50						
	> 51						
	20–35						
F	36–50						
	> 51						

Note that each person is measured 12 times. Thus, there are 12 outcome variables in the analysis.

(b) SPSS syntax:

```
TITLE 'SEX by AGE by TIME by BRAND by BELIEF'.
DATA LIST FREE/ SEX AGE y1 y2 y3 y4 y5 y6 y7 y8 y9 y10 y11 y12.
BEGIN DATA.
   DATA LINES
END DATA.
GLM y1 to y12 BY SEX AGE
   /WSFACTOR = time 2 brand 3 belief 2
   /WSDESIGN = time brand belief time*brand time*belief
   brand*belief time*brand*belief
   /PRINT DESCRIPTIVE HOMOGENEITY
   /DESIGN = SEX AGE SEX*AGE.
SAS syntax:
INPUT sex age y1 y2 y3 y4 y5 y6 y7 y8 y9 y10 y11 y12;
LINES;
   DATA LINES
PROC GLM;
CLASS sex age;
MODEL y1 y2 y3 y4 y5 y6 y7 y8 y9 y10 y11 y12 = sex age
sex*age /NOUNI;
REPEATED time 2, brand 3, belief 2;
RUN;
```

11. (a) This is a one between (age) and two within (time of day and context) design.

(b) SPSS syntax:

```
TITLE 'AGE by TIME by CONTEXT'.
DATA LIST FREE/AGE y1 y2 y3 y4.
BEGIN DATA.
  DATA LINES
END DATA.
GLM y1 to y4 BY AGE
  /WSFACTOR = time 2 context 2
  /WSDESIGN = time context time*context
  /PRINT DESCRIPTIVE HOMOGENEITY
  /DESIGN = AGE.
SAS syntax:
INPUT age y1 y2 y3 y4;
LINES;
  DATA LINES
PROC GLM;
CLASS age;
MODEL y1 y2 y3 y4 = age /NOUNI;
REPEATED time 2, context 2;
RUN;
```

Chapter 15

1. Four features that canonical correlation and principal components have in common:
   (a) Both are mathematical maximization procedures.
   (b) Both use uncorrelated linear combinations of the variables.
   (c) Both provide for an additive partitioning: in components analysis an additive partitioning of the total variance, and in canonical correlation an additive partitioning of the between association.
   (d) Associations between the original variables and the linear combinations can be used in both procedures for interpretation purposes.

3. (a) The association between the two sets of variables is weak, since 17 of the 26 simple correlations are less than .30.
   (b) Only the largest canonical correlation is significant at the .05 level, as the p value associated with the test of the first canonical correlation is less than .0001, and for the second is .65.
   (c) The following are the loadings (correlations) from the output:

Creativity		Achievement	
Ideaflu	.227	Know	.669
Flexb	.412	Compre	.578
Assocflu	.629	Applic	.374
Exprflu	.796	Anal	.390
Orig	.686	Synth	.910
Elab	.703	Eval	.542

The canonical correlation basically links the ability to synthesize (the loading of .910 dominates the achievement loadings) to the last four creativity variables, which have loadings of the same order of magnitude.

(d) Since only the largest canonical correlation was significant, about 20 subjects per variable are needed for reliable results, i.e., 20(12) = 240 subjects. So, the above results, based on an N of 116, must be treated somewhat tenuously.

(e) The redundancy index for the creativity variables given the achievement variables is obtained from the following values on the output:

Av. Sq. Loading times Sqed Can Correl (1st Set)
.17787
.00906
.00931
.00222
.00063
.00019
.19928

This indicates that about 20% of the variance on the set of creativity variables is accounted for by the set of achievement variables.

(f) The squared canonical correlations are given in the output, and they yield the following value for the Cramer-Nicewander index:

$$\frac{.48148 + .10569 + .06623 + .01286 + .00468 + .00917}{6} = .112$$

This indicates that the "variance" overlap between the sets of variables is only about 11%, and is more accurate than the redundancy index since that index ignores the correlations among the dependent variables. And there are several significant correlations among the creativity variables, eight in the weak to moderate range (.32 to .46) and one strong correlation (.71).

5. The criterion of $10(p + q) + 50$ is not a conservative one according to the results of Barcikowski and Stevens. This criterion would imply, for example, if $p = 10$ and $q = 20$, that $10(10 + 20) + 50 = 350$ subjects are needed for reliable results. From Barcikowski and Stevens, on the other hand, about $30(20) = 600$ subjects are needed for reliable results, and more than that would be required if interpreting more than one canonical correlation.

INDEX